INTERNATIONAL FINANCIAL MARKETS

A N D

THE FIRM

Piet Sercu

K.U. Leuven,
Department Toegepaste
Economische,
Wetenschappen

Raman Uppal

Faculty of Commerce
and Business Administration,
The University of British Columbia

SOUTH-WESTERN College Publishing

An International Thomson Publishing Company

CHAPMAN & HALL
University and Professional Division

ISBN: 0-538-84023-4

Printed in the United States of America

 2 3 4 5 6 MT 9 8 7 6 5

Commissioning Editor: Diane Van Bakel
Acquisitions Editor: Christopher Will
Production Editor: Robin Schuster
Production House: Shepherd, Inc.
Cover Design: Graphica

I(T)P
International Thomson Publishing
South-Western is an ITP Company. The ITP trademark is used under license.

Library of Congress Cataloging-in-Publication Data
Sercu, Piet
        International financial markets and the firm / Piet Sercu, Raman
    Uppal.
            p.   cm. — (Current issues in finance)
        Includes bibliographical references and index.
        ISBN 0-538-84023-4
            1. International finance. 2. Foreign exchange. 3. Money market.
    4. Banks and banking, International. 5. Investments, Foreign.
    6. Arbitrage. 7. Corporations—Finance. I. Uppal, Raman.
    II. Title. III. Series.
    HG3821.S47 1995
    332.1—dc20
                                                                        94-40599
                                                                            CIP

ABOUT THE AUTHORS

Piet Sercu

Professor Piet Sercu (born 1951) holds the degrees of Commercial Engineer, Master of Business Administration, and Doctor in Applied Economics at the Katholieke Universiteit Leuven. He taught at the Flemish Business School in Brussels (1980–1986), and afterwards at K.U. Leuven, where he currently teaches *Advanced International Business Finance* and *International Capital Budgeting* in the M.B.A. Program, and the Dutch-language equivalents in the undergraduate program. He also had one-semester Visiting Professor appointments at New York University, Cornell University, and the University of British Columbia, and is currently teaching *International Financial Management* at the London Business School.

He taught shorter finance courses in Helsinki, Bandung (Indonesia), Leningrad, and India (as UNDP expert and, in 1994, as a fellow of the European Indian Cooperation and Exchange Program), and regularly teaches doctoral courses in the European Doctoral Education Network. In Europe he also participated in training programs for Chinese managers (Philips; Lovanium International; China-Europe Management Center), and for Hungarian and Polish managers (Lovanium International).

Piet Sercu is part of the Finance faculty of the European Institute for Advanced Studies in Management, and is the Research Director/Doctoral Program Coordinator of his department. He was the 1994 Vice President and 1995 President of the European Finance Association.

Raman Uppal

Raman Uppal (born 1961) received his bachelor's degree in Economics (Honors) from St. Stephen's College, Delhi University, and his M.A., M.B.A., and Ph.D. degrees from the Wharton School of the University of Pennsylvania. He is the B.I. Ghert Family Foundation Junior Professor of Finance in the Faculty of Commerce and Business Administration, University of British Columbia, where he currently teaches the graduate and undergraduate courses on *International Financial Markets and Institutions* and *Multinational Financial Management*.

Professor Uppal's research focuses on understanding how market imperfections affect the welfare of investors, their optimal portfolios and hedging strategies, aggregate trade and capital flows, and the exchange rate and other asset prices. His research in the area of international finance examines the effects of commodity market imperfections in general equilibrium models of international economies. His work shows that the results on capital flows, international portfolios, and exchange rates can be very different in general equilibrium models compared to their partial equilibrium counterparts. His research in the area of option pricing examines how investors adjust their optimal hedging strategies in response to frictions, such as transactions costs and short-sales constraints, and the effect of this on the value of options.

Professor Uppal has been nominated for and has received several awards for excellence in teaching at Wharton and at the University of British Columbia.

THE CURRENT ISSUES IN FINANCE SERIES

The first book in the series, *Futures and Options* by Stoll and Whaley, provides an integrated treatment of futures and options, a field that has undergone dramatic developments in theory and in practice. This book, *International Financial Markets and the Firm* by Piet Sercu and Raman Uppal, deals with an equally dynamic area of finance—international financial markets. The book is rigorous and thorough, while at the same time treating practical issues facing investment managers, importers and exporters, and international companies. The authors provide excellent coverage of the workings of the foreign exchange market, of the forces affecting exchange rates, and of corporate financial management in an international economy. Sercu, who teaches in Belgium, and Uppal, who teaches in Canada, are ideally suited to provide a truly global perspective on a global topic. Like their book, they span the globe.

The publication of this book is itself an international effort, as it is co-published by South-Western College Publishing and Chapman & Hall, American and British subsidiaries of International Thomson Publishing. I salute them for their support of the series and thank Chris Will, in particular, for his efforts on behalf of the series. Students of finance can look forward to additional volumes in the Current Issues in Finance Series that will treat other important finance topics.

Hans R. Stoll
Consulting Editor, Current Issues in Finance Series

The Sercu-Uppal textbook is the first systematically to apply to International Corporate Finance the principles that normally serve as guidelines for financial investments. This line of reasoning gives it a degree of internal consistency unparalleled in other textbooks in this field.

Bernard Dumas
Hautes Etudes Commerciales (HEC), France

PREFACE

The last decade has witnessed a spectacular growth in the foreign exchange markets, euromarkets, and international bond markets. For example, the daily volume of trading on the exchange market and its satellites—futures, options, and swaps—is estimated to be more than USD 1,000 billion, which is approximately ten times the daily volume of international trade in goods and services. This growth in financial markets has been accompanied by an increase in international activity by multinational firms: firms continue to invest in foreign countries (for example, investment by Japanese firms in the US, Europe, and Southeast Asia), and also tend to raise capital in international markets (evidenced by the growth of euromarkets). This, along with the greater exchange rate volatility relative to that during the Bretton-Woods years, implies that issues of international finance are of increasing importance for corporate managers. The principal objective of this book is to provide a rigorous, comprehensive, consistent, and integrated treatment of both the working of currency markets and the financial management of multinational firms.

1 ORIENTATION OF THIS BOOK AND TARGET AUDIENCE

The focus of this book is on the international aspects of modern financial theory. We believe that a truly international viewpoint is vital for financial management in today's integrated world. For instance, it is important to qualify the idea of the "nationality" of a firm if its shares are held all over the world or if its cash flows depend on exchange rates. Thus, the focus of the book is on issues such as whether firms face exchange rate risk, how to measure the exposure of firms to this risk, and how to use exchange-contingent claims to hedge this risk.

The audience we address is also international. Partly because of this international orientation, the emphasis is not so much on institutional details, but rather on the concepts and on the links between them. Institutional details vary from country to country, and it would be impossible to describe the various institutional settings in one book. Thus, rather than discussing, for instance, the international tax rules for only one given "home" country, we try to provide an understanding of generic international taxation systems. For the same reason, we work with different base currencies throughout this textbook instead of using a single reference currency.

Our target audience is MBA students and third- and fourth-year undergraduate students majoring in finance. This book can also serve as background reading for Ph.D. and master's students in Economics, Finance, and International Business, and can be used by professionals in the business world. While we assume that the reader is familiar with basic concepts from an introductory course in corporate finance or economics, the book is to a large extent self-contained, and most background material that the reader may require is contained in appendices to the relevant chapters.

2   ISSUES IN INTERNATIONAL FINANCIAL MANAGEMENT

This book is a text on international *finance*. Thus, it does not address issues of multinational corporate strategy, and the discussion of international macroeconomics is kept to a minimum. Within the finance discipline, it addresses only the problems caused by the existence of many countries. The existence of nation-states matters first and foremost because most of them issue their own currencies, and because the relative market values of these currencies in the future are uncertain. The resulting exchange risk is the prime issue in this text. Other problems that may be caused by the existence of separate countries are segmented capital markets, different tax systems across countries, and political risk.

One way to describe this material is to think about the tasks assigned to an international financial manager. These tasks include asset valuation, international funding, the hedging of exchange risk, and management of other risks. We hasten to add that these functions cannot be viewed in isolation, as will become clear as we proceed.

2.1   Valuation

One task of a corporate manager is the valuation of projects with cash flows that are risk free in terms of the foreign currency. For example, the manager may need to evaluate a large export order with a price fixed in foreign currency and payable at a (known) future date. The future cash flow is risky in terms of the domestic currency because the future exchange rate is uncertain. Similar to the evaluation of a domestic project with cash flows that are risky in terms of the domestic currency, this export project will be subject to a Net Present Value (NPV) analysis. Thus, the manager needs to know how to compute present values when the source of risk is the uncertainty about the future exchange rate. Valuation becomes even more complicated in the case of foreign direct investment (FDI), where the cash flows are random even in terms of the foreign currency. The issues to be dealt with now are how to discount cash flows subject to both business risk and exchange risk, how to deal with tax complications inherent in FDI, and how to determine the cost of capital depending on whether or not the home and foreign capital markets are segmented.

2.2   Funding

A second task is, of course, funding the project. A standard financing problem is whether the firm should issue equity, debt, or equity-linked debt (like convertible bonds). If bonds are issued or a loan is taken out, the question is what the optimal maturity is, and whether the terms offered by a bank or a group of banks are attractive or not. In an international setting, the additional issue to be considered is whether the bond or loan should be denominated in home currency, or in another currency.

2.3   Hedging

Another of the financial manager's tasks may be to reduce risks, like exchange risk, that arise from corporate decisions. For example, a manager who has accepted a large order from a customer, with a price fixed in foreign currency and payable at some (known) future point in time, may need to find a way to hedge the resulting exposure to exchange rates.

In many instances, the problems of project evaluation and hedging are linked. For instance, a firm may be unwilling to accept a positive-NPV export contract unless the currency risk can be hedged. Also, the funding issue cannot be viewed in isolation from the hedging issue. For example, a Finnish corporation that considers borrowing in Yen, should not make that decision without pondering how this loan would affect the firm's total risk. That is, the decision to borrow Yen may be unacceptable unless a suitable hedge is available. In another example, a German firm that has large and steady dollar revenues from exports might prefer to borrow USD because such a loan provides not just funding, but also risk reduction. In short, project evaluation, funding, and hedging have to be considered together.

2.4 Management of Other Risks

Thus far, when discussing the uncertainties that an international manager needs to deal with, we focused on exchange risk. There are, however, many other sources of uncertainty that gain an extra dimension in the context of multinational operations. For example, credit risk gets an extra dimension when the defaulting debtor is subject to a different legal and judicial system than the creditor. The costs and delays of legal redress are much higher for international disputes. Accordingly, there are various instruments that have been specially designed to insure credit risk in international trade.

Closely related to the issue of credit risk is political risk in international trade. Even if the foreign debtor is willing to pay, he or she might be prevented from paying because, hard currency being scarce, the central bank of the debtor's country does not let him or her buy the necessary foreign exchange. This, of course, is a risk that is nonexistent when buyer and seller live in the same country. Fortunately, there are specific ways to insure against this "international" risk.

Again, credit risk and political risk cannot be viewed in isolation from the other issues. For instance, the evaluation of an export project should obviously take into account the default risk. Similarly, NPV computations for FDI projects should account for the risk that foreign cash flows may be blocked or that the foreign business may be expropriated.

3 STRUCTURE OF THIS BOOK

In the preceding section, we discussed the key issues in international finance on the basis of managerial functions. However, this is not a convenient way to arrange the text because the functions are all interlinked. Instead, we proceed as follows. We begin with an introductory chapter on the history of the international monetary system. The main textbook is divided into four parts: (I) International financial markets; (II) Exchange rate determination and forecasting; (III) Risk management; and (IV) International capital budgeting. Thus, while in Parts I and II the emphasis is on financial markets and equilibrium in the exchange markets, in Parts III and IV the focus is on corporate financial issues, such as risk management and capital budgeting. We briefly describe the contents of each part below.

3.1 Part I: International Financial Markets

Part I of the book describes the international financial market in its widest sense, that is, the exchange market plus its satellites, and the international money and capital markets. In Chapter 1, we describe spot markets. Forward markets, where price and quantity are contracted now but delivery and payment take place at a known future moment, are introduced in Chapter 2. Chapter 3 shows how to value a forward contract, and how the forward rate can be used for valuation, reporting, and for making corporate finance decisions. In Chapter 4, we describe how imperfections such as default risk and transactions costs affect operations in the forward market. Currency futures, which are closely related to forward transactions, are discussed in Chapter 5. Chapter 6 introduces currency options and explains how these options can be used to hedge against (or alternatively, speculate on) foreign exchange risk. How one can price currency options is explained in Chapter 7 (using the binomial model) and in Chapter 8 (using the Black-Scholes model).

In Chapter 9, we discuss international money and capital markets, and in Chapter 10, the swap market, which is related to the market for medium- and long-term fixed-income contracts.

At any instant, the market value of a forward, futures, or options contract depends on the prevailing spot rate (and, if the contract is not yet at the end of its life, also on the domestic and foreign interest rates). This dependence on the future spot rate means that these instruments can be used to hedge the exchange rate risk to which the firm is exposed. The dependence of these contracts on the future spot rate also means that their current market values can be expressed, by relatively simple arbitrage arguments, as functions of the current spot rate and of the domestic and foreign interest rate. Throughout this part of the text, a unified approach based on arbitrage-free pricing is used to value these assets whose payoffs are dependent on the exchange rate.

3.2   Part II: Exchange Rate Determination

The value of the financial instruments discussed in Part I can be determined without knowledge of why the spot rate was set at its current level—we use arbitrage arguments that take the spot rate as given. In Part II, then, we address the issue of what determines the spot rate. The traditional view, presented in Chapter 11, is Purchasing Power Parity: exchange rates are set so as to equate the values of goods across countries. We shall argue that, although Purchasing Power Parity is undeniably present in the long run, its short-run explanatory power is extremely low. As Keynes said, the exchange rate is not set in the commodity markets, but on the Exchange. That is, the supply and demand for currencies is related not just to commodity trade, but mainly to capital transactions. We discuss the Balance of Payments and the Keynesian view of exchange rates in Chapter 12.

Given the state of economic and financial theory at that time, Keynes did not model uncertainty, and provided no explicit asset pricing model. The first "asset"-type theory with a nice, explicit pricing formula is the Monetary Model, which relates the exchange-rate to the transactions demand for money. But this model attempts to price exchange rates in isolation, as if there were just one asset. The Portfolio Model, a more recent extension of the Monetary Model, points out that one cannot price an asset, like foreign exchange, in isolation from other assets. These asset pricing models of exchange rate determination are described in Chapter 13.

In Chapter 14, we examine the link between the forward rate and the future spot rate. We find that the forward rate is a poor predictor of the future spot rate. In Chapter 15, we study whether other variables, such as the lagged values of the spot rate or fundamental macroeconomic variables, are successful at predicting the change in the spot rate. The evidence we examine suggests that none of these variables is a very good predictor of the change in the spot rate.

The fact that there are significant and persistent deviations from Purchasing Power Parity implies that the exchange rate affects the contractual and operational cash flows of the firm. Given that the change in the spot rate cannot be forecast leads to the next set of issues: Should firms hedge against exchange risk and, if yes, how should they decide on the magnitude of the hedge?

3.3   Part III: International Risk Management

Part III considers risk management. The first type of risk we consider is exchange risk. From Part II, we know that it is difficult to predict exchange rates. The issue discussed in Chapter 16 is whether reducing this risk matters at all. We shall argue that financial decisions (including hedging policies) matter because financial and commodity markets are imperfect, and thus, the Miller-Modigliani theorem is not valid. Chapters 17, 18, and 19 then explain how to measure the impact of exchange rate changes on the value of contracts fixed in terms of foreign currency, on operational cash flows, and on consolidated financial statements, respectively. We also show how to hedge these exposures using the instruments described in Part I of the text.

While exchange risk, interest risk, and commodity price risk can be managed using financial instruments, there are some other types of risks that have to be managed by different means. Chapter 20 deals with credit risk/political risk management and financing techniques for international trade. We discuss the insurance and financing techniques used in standard open trade, and the countertrade techniques used in East-West trade.

3.4 Part IV: International Capital Budgeting

In Part IV of the text, we discuss how to make international investment decisions. In Chapter 21, we show how one needs to adapt the standard Adjusted NPV framework to evaluate such projects. Typically, one will evaluate such projects using present value computations based on the standard discounted cash-flow model, with the discount rate typically provided by the Capital Asset Pricing Model. To what extent the CAPM can be applied in an international context with exchange risk and/or segmentation of financial markets is analyzed in Chapter 22. The basic principles underlying international taxation systems and corporate tax planning are discussed in Chapter 23. Finally, in Chapter 24, we also discuss capital budgeting for joint-venture projects, where the issue of cost-benefit analysis is intertwined with the issues of profit-sharing and tax planning. In Chapter 25, we consider circumstances where exchange rate uncertainty is the sole source of risk in the future cash flows from an investment project. Using the insights from the chapters on currency options, we then explain how one can use the theory of financial option pricing to make real investment decisions in such cases.

4 HOW TO USE THIS BOOK

The material in this book is sufficient for two courses, each course about thirteen weeks long, with three hours of classroom time each week. We typically teach two courses on international finance, each of which is one semester long. The first course studies the markets and the determination of exchange rates, while the focus of the second course is on corporate issues. Thus, in the first course we cover the introductory chapter, Chapters 1–4, 6, 11–15 and either Chapter 5 or 9–10. In the second course, where we have students who have already taken the first course, we typically cover Chapters 7, 8, and 16–25. For a course that needs to cover just international financial markets, we recommend the introductory chapter, followed by Chapters 1–4, 6, 7 (Section 1), 11–15, and either Chapter 5 or 9–10. For a stand-alone course on multinational corporate finance, we recommend Chapters 1–3, 5, 6, 15–19, and 21–23. As a rule of thumb, each chapter is written so that it can be covered in three hours of class time. Thus, a thirteen-week course should aim to cover approximately thirteen chapters.

5 LEARNING FEATURES

Several pedagogical features have been included in the text so that it is possible to understand the material, to implement the new results introduced in the text, and to integrate new concepts with those already learned in an introductory corporate finance course and in other chapters of the text. These features include the following.

- *Numerical examples*: Almost all new concepts and analytical results are accompanied by numerical examples that illustrate how these results can be applied. Often, more than one numerical example is given, with the first one being a simple example and the second a more extensive one.

- *End-of-chapter summaries*: All chapters conclude with summaries that highlight the main points made in the chapter. Many of the summaries are a list of points of which a corporate treasurer or a firm manager should be aware.
- *End-of-chapter problems*: Numerous exercises to test one's knowledge are provided at the end of each chapter. These problems are at three levels: Quiz Questions, which test the basic understanding of the material in the chapter; Exercises, which test whether one can apply the concepts learned in the chapter to solve problems; and Mind-Expanding Exercises, which allow one to extend the results derived in the chapter. Solutions to all of these problems are available in the *Instructor's Manual*.
- *Appendices*: Background material and mathematical details of results described in the chapter are included in appendices at the end of relevant chapters.
- *Suggested readings*: At the end of the text, we have collected a list of selected readings related to topics covered in each chapter.
- *Instructor's manual*: An Instructor's manual, written with Marian Kane, can be received by instructors from the publisher. This manual contains chapter overviews/summaries highlighting the main issues covered in each chapter, answers to end-of-chapter exercises, and master transparencies (for selected chapters) that one can use in the classroom.

6 ACKNOWLEDGMENTS

There are many individuals who played an important role in the production of this book. First and foremost, we would like to thank the people from whom we learned much of what we know about international finance—Michael Adler, Paul De Grauwe, Bernard Dumas, Orlin Grabbe, Maurice Levi, Richard Marston, Alessandro Penati, and Sylvain Plasschaert. Bernard Dumas, in particular, has been very generous with his time and advice, and large parts of Chapters 17 and 18 are based on the material that he has published with Michael Adler. Tom Berglund and Francisco Delgado also provided several suggestions that improved the presentation of the material in the text.

We have benefited from the suggestions of several reviewers. These include: Raj Aggarwal, Arnoud W.A. Boot, Adrian Buckley, Joseph Finnerty, Coleman S. Kendall, A. Qayyum Khan, Yong H. Kim, V. Sivarama Krishnan, Nalin Kulatilaka, Richard M. Levich, Dileep Mehta, Trish Nealon, Charles Schell, and Jorge Urritia.

We are also grateful to the students in our classes and our teaching assistants who used earlier drafts of the book and suggested several improvements. We are particularly thankful to Louisa Choy, Chris Club, Kathy Dehoperé, Kristinn Geirsson, Marie R.M. Routledge, and Sigrid Vandemaele. The extensive and detailed comments of Marian Kane, Lisa Kramer, and Khang Min Lee led to a substantial improvement in the text.

Last, but not least, we are grateful to Chris Will at South-Western Publishing and Susan Brehm at Shepherd, Inc. for their continuing support during the writing of this book, and to Hans Stoll, the editor of the Current Issues in Finance Series, for his encouragement to work on this project.

We are responsible for any remaining errors in the book. We would appreciate any comments or suggestions that you may have about the book. You can either write to us or send email to *zen@finance.commerce.ubc.ca*.

We dedicate this book to our parents, Thérèse and Jan Sercu, and Anita and Iqbal Uppal, and to the women who have patiently supported us during the time it has taken to complete this project, Rita Mosselmans Sercu and Michelle Lee.

Piet Sercu
Raman Uppal

CONTENTS

AN INTRODUCTION TO INTERNATIONAL FINANCIAL MARKETS

Before we can learn about topics such as currency futures and options, currency swaps, the behavior of the exchange rate, the measurement of exchange risk, and valuation of real and financial assets in the presence of this risk, we need to understand a much more fundamental issue: namely, money. All of us are aware that money exists and that it is quite useful. Still, a review of why it exists and how it is created is crucial to understanding some of the finer points of international finance, such as how the ownership of money is transferred across countries, how a central bank's balance sheet is maintained, how money from one country can be exchanged for money from another, and so on. The price at which this buying and selling of currencies occurs is the *exchange rate*. Government policy, with respect to the exchange rate, is also an important institutional aspect.

This chapter is structured as follows. First, we explain how money gradually evolved from a commodity, with an intrinsic value, to fiduciary money whose value is based on trust, and how the role of banks has changed accordingly. In the second section, we consider international banking transactions. This then leads to our discussion, in the third section, about offshore banking (eurobanking). The emergence of the eurobond market is also explained in that section. Finally, the fourth section describes exchange-rate regimes—that is, government policy with respect to the exchange rate.

I.1   MONEY AND BANKING: A BRIEF REVIEW

In this section, we first review the role of money. We then look back a few millennia and explain how money has evolved over time from a bulky, commodity-type physical object into its current form, a record in a bank's computer.

I.1.1   The Roles of Money

Money has to do with buying and selling. The need for money arises in any economy in which economic units (for example, households, tribes, or fiefdoms) start to trade with each other. Pure, moneyless barter is inconvenient. A hungry blacksmith does not like to wander around until he meets a farmer whose horse has lost a shoe to make a deal. The blacksmith would rather compensate the farmer for the food by giving him something called *money*. The advantage of paying in money rather than in horseshoes is that the farmer can then spend the money on other things if and when the need arises, and on any goods he chooses. Thus, trade and exchange with money are much easier, and the costs of searching for someone who needs exactly what you are selling at a particular point in time are greatly reduced.

Three conditions are needed for money to be a successful least-cost medium of exchange. First, it must be storable; the farmer would not like the unspent money to evaporate or rot. Second, it must have a stable purchasing power; the farmer would not like to discover that his hoard of money can buy a far smaller amount of goods than he had anticipated. This, in turn, requires that the stock of outstanding money must not rise substantially faster than the volume of transactions. Third, money must be easy to handle. Once these conditions are met, money can fulfill its role as the *least-cost medium of exchange*. When prices are expressed in units of money, money also acts as a unit of account, or *numeraire*. Finally, money can also be lent and borrowed, which allows one to transfer purchasing power over time in a low-risk fashion.

I.1.2   How Money Is Created
In this part of Section I.1, we trace the development of money from commodities and metal coins in early economies to privately issued money and, more recently, to official currency notes issued by the central bank of a country.

Official Metal Coins
In relatively primitive economies, standard commodities played the role of money. In prehistoric Europe, domestic animals were used as money. For example, the Latin word for money, *pecunia*, simply derives from *pecus*, cattle. Also the ancient Greek silver *talanton* (weight) betrays its links to the old practice of using domestic animals as money: the original *talent* had the shape of a sheepskin, and it was about as heavy as a good-sized lamb—one slave could carry just one *talanton*.

Unless you are a cowboy, you would probably not think of herds of cattle as being easy to handle. The ascent as a medium of exchange of one particular class of commodities, namely precious metals, occurred because for a given amount of purchasing power, precious metals are far less bulky and easier to transport than cattle. Second, precious metals do not rust. And third, production was and is sufficiently costly to ensure that the stock of rare metal does not grow much faster than the economy as a whole, thus ruling out sudden inflation due to a rapidly expanding money stock.

Early gold and silver money was defined by its weight. For example, almost all medieval European states had a *pound* or a *libra* or a *lira* coin, referring to about half a kilo of gold or silver. What is striking is that the current value of the British or Irish or Maltese pound, not to mention the Italian or Turkish lira, is not near the value of half a kilo of silver. This debasing of the currency started quite early. One problem was that people reduced the true precious-metal content by melting down their coins, adding some cheap metal, and reminting the alloy.[1] To stop this practice, the local lord, or *Seigneur,* of the fiefdom installed an official mint to which people could bring precious metals for minting. The *Seigneur* then imprinted his quality stamp on the coins in return for a commission or tax, the *seignorage.* This was one way that governments earned money. Later, governments made the issuing of coins their sole monopoly. This allowed them to become poachers themselves and reduce the gold or silver value of their own coins.[2] The official minting monopoly meant that the rulers could pro-

---

[1] A related problem with precious metal coins was coin clipping: people scratched off part of the gold or silver around the edge, which reduced the intrinsic value of the coin but may have passed unnoticed. The ribs or other decorations that you still see on the sides of modern coins were originally meant to make coin clipping easier to detect.

[2] For instance, France's King Philippe Le Bel (Philip the Beautiful) was known in Flanders as, among other things, *Flup de Munteschroder* (Flup the Coin Debaser).

duce a coin at a cost below its purchasing power and make a substantial profit. This profit is still called *seignorage* in a broader sense.

This debasing threatened the stability of the money's purchasing power.[3] Fluctuations in purchasing power also arose when the gold and silver mines were exhausted or when Spain imported huge amounts of gold and silver into Europe from its colonies.

Privately Issued Paper Money

Another drawback of precious-metal money was that carrying huge amounts of gold from Italy to Scotland, for example, was rather cumbersome and risky. Traders therefore deposited money with international bankers and used bills of exchange and promissory notes to pay each other.[4] The bills were convertible into the underlying coins *at sight* (that is, whenever presented to the bank), and were as good as gold as long as the issuer was creditworthy.[5] Note that a merchant who pays with a promissory note that remains in circulation for years before being cashed in obtains an interest-free loan. By rolling over the notes, the merchant earns quite an advantage. This is seignorage (income from creating money) under a new guise.

Banks themselves then started issuing bills on a regular basis. Early bank notes were rather similar to the modern traveler's check—they were printed and issued by a private bank, in standard denominations, and were convertible at sight into the underlying, official coins. But bankers knew that, on average, only a small fraction of the circulating notes was actually cashed in; most of them remained in circulation for quite some time. This meant that, on the basis of one coin, a bank could issue notes of a much larger total value. Let us see how such an issuing bank's balance sheet is built up and how it creates money. Once you understand the following example, it becomes easier to understand how modern central banks work.

Example   I.1

Consider a bank that issues its own notes. On the bank's opening day, the following five transactions take place:

- A merchant, A, deposits 100 golden crown coins in exchange for notes. The notes become the bank's liabilities, since they are essentially promissory notes that can be cashed in for true money (gold coins). The merchant's coins go into the bank's vault and are part of its assets.
- Another merchant, B, asks for a loan of 200 crowns. The bank issues bank notes (a liability, since the borrower can cash in the notes for coins), and accepts a promissory note (or any similar claim) signed by B as the offsetting asset.
- The government, G, asks for a 150-crown loan. The bank hands over bank notes (that are, again, part of the bank's liabilities), and accepts a Treasury bill (T-bill) or a government bond as the corresponding asset.
- A foreign trader, F, wants to borrow 70 crowns. The bank issues notes, and it accepts a claim on the foreign trader as the corresponding asset.

---

[3] In the late 1200s, for example, there was so much inflation in England that the local pound was virtually abandoned. People simply preferred to use the currency of the Easterlings or Esterlings (the German Hansa merchants) and called their money the Pound (E)sterling. So "sterling-quality silver" originally meant "German-quality silver."

[4] A bill of exchange is a summary of the invoice; it is written (drawn) by the seller and presented to the customer who is asked to accept the bill (that is, acknowledge the existence of the debt by countersigning it) and to return it to the drawer. A promissory note, in contrast, is an "I owe you" note rather than a "you owe me" note; that is, it is written by the customer rather than by the seller. Bills and promissory notes can be sold to investors, or can be used to pay off other debts.

[5] This practice started about 1,000 years ago in Italy and went on until the nineteenth century. You can still find references to this practice in Thomas Mann's novel, *Buddenbrooks,* which is set in nineteenth-century northern Germany.

- A local exporter, *X*, converts dollar bank notes into crown bank notes worth 100 crowns. The bank issues crown bank notes (a liability), and it uses the dollar notes to buy foreign T-bills.

At the end of the day, the bank's balance sheet looks like Figure I.1.

Figure I.1 shows how bank notes are created, and how an issuing bank's balance sheet is constructed. The issuing bank's own bank notes are the liability side of its balance sheet. On the asset side we find the following:

- International reserves (gold and silver, plus claims on residents or governments of foreign countries).
- Claims on the domestic private sector.
- Claims on the domestic government.

Since the production cost of bank notes was quite low, private banks earned a large seignorage. The risk, of course, was that holders of the notes would lose confidence in the issuer, in which case there would be a *run on the bank,* with many people simultaneously trying to convert their notes into coins. In the US, for instance, there were widespread runs on banks in 1907. J.P. Morgan, a New York banker, helped solve the crisis by shipping in USD 100 million (100m) worth of gold from Europe.

Official Paper Money and the Central Bank

To avert such confidence crises (and probably also to regain the seignorage), most governments then assigned the production of bank notes to a government institution, the central bank.[6]

Initially, the official bank notes were still convertible at sight into *true money*—that is, into the coins issued by the Mint or the Treasury. For instance, until the mid-1900s, most bank notes still said that the note was "payable on sight" (although the 1910 Reichsmark note ominously added that you had to see the Berlin head office for that purpose). Indian Rupee bank notes still show a payable-at-sight phrase: "I [the Governor of the central bank] promise to pay to the bearer the sum of *x* Rupees." Still, for all practical purposes, the central bank's notes have become as good as (or even better than) the Treasury's coins, and have become the true underlying money in the eyes of the population. In many countries, coins are no longer *legal tender* above certain amounts. For instance, the seller of a

FIGURE I.1 Balance Sheet of a Bank

ASSETS		LIABILITIES	
Gold (*A*'s deposit)	100	Notes issued	100
Domestic credit (loan to *B*)	200		200
Credit to the government (loan to *G*)	150		150
Foreign credit			
(Loan to *F*)	70		70
(Dollar T-bills)	100		100
Total assets	620	Total notes issued	620

---

[6] There are exceptions: in Hong Kong, for instance, notes are still issued by two private banks. But even there, these banks are closely supervised by the government.

house cannot be forced to accept payment of the full amount in coins. Thus, money has become a fiduciary instrument. Unlike cattle or gold, modern money has no intrinsic worth of its own, nor is the value of modern money based on a right to convert bank notes into gold. Rather, the value of money is based on the trust of the people, who believe that money will have a reasonably stable purchasing power.[7]

One difference between a modern central bank and the private issuing banks of old is that the modern bank notes are no longer convertible into gold. If many central banks still hold gold, the reason is that they think of it as a good investment. Other differences between a modern central bank and a private *issuing* bank include the following.

- A central bank no longer deals directly with the public. Its customers are commercial banks, foreign central banks, and the government. Commercial banks, in fact, act as liaisons between the public and the central bank. For instance, commercial banks can borrow from the central bank by rediscounting commercial paper (by passing to the central bank, loans they extended to private companies), or by selling to the central bank the foreign currency they bought from the private sector.

- When a central bank buys a domestic or foreign asset from a commercial bank, it no longer pays entirely in the form of bank notes. Commercial banks demand notes only to the extent that their own customers demand actual currency; most of the payment for the asset the commercial bank sold is credited to its account with the central bank. One result is that the central bank's liabilities consist not only of bank notes, but also of commercial banks' deposits on their account with the central bank. This liability side is called the country's *monetary base* or M_0. The monetary base is still the basis for money creation by commercial banks.

Privately Issued Electronic Money

The official monopoly on the printing of bank notes did not mean that private banks lost all seignorage. Any private bank knows from experience that its borrowers rarely take up the full amount of its loans in notes or coins. Rather, customers tend to leave most of their borrowed funds in a checking account (also called a sight account, in Europe), and make payments by check (or, in Europe, mostly by giro or bank transfer). Therefore, loans make deposits. This means that private banks can (and do) extend loans for a much larger volume than the amount of notes, etc., that they keep in their vaults or with the central bank. Today, commercial banks create electronic money (loans recorded in the bank's computer) rather than physical money (bank notes). The ratio between the total amount of money (monetary base plus checking account money—M_1) and the monetary base (M_0) is the *money multiplier.*

This mechanism again creates the possibility of runs on commercial banks if deposit-holders want to convert all of their sight deposits into notes and coins. A recent example was the minor run on Hong Kong banks after the 1987 stock market crash. To avert runs and enhance credibility, private banks in many countries must meet **reserve requirements**: they must keep a minimum fraction of the customers' deposits in coins or bank notes, or more conveniently, in a non-interest-bearing account with the central bank. The central bank also agrees to act as *lender of last resort* and provide liquidity to private banks in case of a run.

---

[7] Israel's experience in the 1970s illustrates this point: when inflation came close to 1000 percent per year, people started expressing prices in USD rather than in Israeli pounds. The pound was no longer a trustworthy currency, nor was it a convenient numeraire because prices expressed in pounds had to be changed every day. Similar breakdowns occurred in Germany after World War II, when Lucky Strike cigarettes and chocolate bars became the effective currency.

This whole section is neatly summarized in the following formula:

$$M_1 = \text{Money supply} = mM_0 = m(D + G + \text{RFX}),$$ [1]

where m = the money multiplier.

    M_0 = the money base (notes and commercial banks' deposits with the central bank).

    D = credit to the domestic private sector.

    G = credit to the government.

  RFX = reserves of foreign exchange (including gold).

    M_0 = $D + G + \text{RFX}$, by virtue of the equality of the central bank's assets and liabilities.

Equation [1] says that the total money supply depends on the money multiplier and the monetary base, which, in turn, consists of domestic credit, credit to the government, and foreign reserves. The equation is also useful in explaining how monetary policy works, which is the topic of the next section.

Monetary Policy

Even though central banks generously leave most of the money creation to commercial banks, they still control the process. This control is exerted by the central bank's power over the monetary base and over the money multiplier.

• *Intervention in the foreign exchange markets*

Central banks can influence the monetary base by buying or selling foreign exchange (changing RFX in Equation [1]). This expansion of the central bank's asset side is accompanied by an expansion of the liability side (domestic money supply): the central bank pays in notes (or it credits the commercial banks' accounts with the central bank) for the foreign exchange it buys from the commercial banks. Thus, any change in RFX leads to an identical change in M_0, which then affects the amount of money that private banks can create on the basis of M_0.

• *Open market policy*

Likewise, central banks can influence the monetary base by restricting or expanding the amount of credit they give to the government or the private sector (that is, change D and G in Equation [1]). Open market policy works in the same way as interventions in the foreign exchange market: the central bank pays in notes (or it credits the commercial banks' accounts with the central bank) for the T-bills or commercial paper it buys from the goverment or from the private banks.

• *Reserve requirements*

Alternatively, the central bank can curb money creation by commercial banks by changing the reserve requirements (changing the upper bound on the multiplier m in Equation [1]). If banks have to hold more base money per unit of electronic money, the total amount of loans they can extend with a given amount of base money becomes smaller. Around 1990, for instance, India stepped up the reserve requirements to a staggering 50 percent in order to bring inflation back to single-digit levels. A 50 percent reserve requirement means that the money multiplier can be at most 2.

• *Credit controls*

The most direct way to control M_1 is to impose limits on the amounts that private banks can lend.

Having examined what money is and how it is created, we now turn to its more international aspects.

I.2   THE INTERNATIONAL PAYMENT MECHANISM

In this section, we explain how transactions involving the exchange of foreign currency are made, while discussing the effect these transactions have on the money supply.

I.2.1   Some Basic Principles

Recall that money has to do with the buying and selling of goods, services, or assets. A special problem arises if the buyer and the seller live in countries that have different currencies: then at least one of the parties has to handle a foreign currency. As long as currencies are defined by their weight in gold or silver and are freely minted, this creates no special problem. An ounce of gold is an ounce of gold everywhere, and currencies minted in various countries freely circulated elsewhere, traded on the basis of their intrinsic value.[8] Today, things are not that easy. If the invoice is in the exporter's currency, the importer often has to buy the currency of the exporter, or the exporter can agree to be paid in foreign currency, and then exchange the foreign money for domestic currency. If payment is in bank notes, the notes can simply be handed over, but most international payments are by check or bank transfer. The following example shows how such payments take place.

Example   I.2

Assume that a US importer, USM, pays by check in his own currency, USD 1 million (1m), to a UK exporter, UKX. Writing the check, of course, means that the US importer has a checking account with a US bank (USB). By definition, money on that account is convertible into dollar notes and coins. One possible scenario is that the UK exporter also has a checking account with a US bank. We shall assume that this is the same bank as the US importer's bank, USB. (If this is not the case, think of USB as the consolidation of all US banks.) UKX deposits the check into her account with USB, and can cash in that amount at any time. Clearly, the US money supply is not affected; there is only a transfer of ownership of electronic money from the US importer to the UK exporter. Figure I.2 illustrates how the relevant bank accounts are changed by the transaction.

---

[8] Traces of this old practice survived in the UK until the currency reform in the late 1960s. Next to the pound, subdivided into 20 shilling each worth 12 pence, there were also half-crowns (worth two shillings and sixpence) and guineas (one pound and one shilling). Originally, the crown and the guinea were different currencies.

FIGURE I.2 Balance Sheet of an Importer, an Exporter, and a Bank

USM'S BALANCE SHEET

	Before	After		Before	After
Deposit with USB	USD 5m	4m	(Liabilities)	USD 5m + X	4m + X + 1m
(Other assets)	USD X	X + 1 m			

USB'S BALANCE SHEET

	Before	After		Before	After
(Assets)	USD 7m + Y	7m + Y	USM's deposit	USD 5m	USD 4m
			UKX's deposit	USD 2m	USD 3m
			(Other)	USD Y	USD Y

UKX'S BALANCE SHEET

	Before	After		Before	After
Deposit with USB	USD 2m	USD 3m	(Liabilities)	USD 2m + Z	2m + Z
(Other assets)	USD Z	USD Z – 1m			

A US importer (USM) and a UK exporter (UKX) have initial deposits on their checking accounts with a US bank (USB) worth USD 5m and 2m, respectively. USM sends a check of USD 1m to UKX to settle an invoice, and UKX deposits the check with USB. After USB has processed this transaction, it shows up in their bank balances with USB (and in their other assets and liabilities, since the invoice is settled). The roman-font figures give the balance before the payment, and the italic-font figures give the balance after the payment.

In the modified example below, we see what happens if the UK exporter does not have an account in the US, but as in the previous example, decides not to sell the USD yet.

Example I.3

The UK exporter deposits the check into a USD checking account he or she holds with the London bank. The UK bank, UKB, records in its books that it owes the exporter USD 1m (a liability), and that it has received a check. UKB will then deposit the check into its account with USB, because this is where the money can be cashed in; thus, the UK bank's asset is a USD 1m claim on USB. The difference from the previous example is that, after this transaction, the UK exporter has a USD claim not on a US bank, but on a UK bank which, in turn, holds a claim on a US bank. The UK bank acts as a front between the owner of the funds (UKX) and the bank where the money is ultimately held (USB). Figure I.3 summarizes these transactions.

The fact that the UK exporter now has a USD claim not on a US bank but on a UK bank (which, in turn, holds a claim on a US bank) makes a difference. The London bank is not a US bank: that is,

FIGURE I.3   Balance Sheet of an Importer, an Exporter, and a Bank

USM'S BALANCE SHEET

	Before	After		Before	After
Deposit with USB	USD 5m	*4m*	(Liabilities)	USD 5m + X	*4m + X + 1m*
(Other assets)	USD X	*X + 1m*			

USB'S BALANCE SHEET

	Before	After		Before	After
(Assets)	USD 7m + Y	*7m + Y*	USM's deposit	USD 5m	USD *4m*
			UKB's deposit	USD 2m	USD *3m*
			(Other)	USD Y	USD *Y*

UKB'S BALANCE SHEET

	Before	After		Before	After
Deposit with USB	USD 2m	*3m*	UKX's deposit	USD 2m	*3m*
(Other)			(Other)		

UKX'S BALANCE SHEET

	Before	After		Before	After
Deposit with UKB	USD 2m	*3m*	(Liabilities)	USD 2m + Z	*2m + Z*
(Other assets)	USD Z	*Z − 1m*			

A US importer (USM) has deposits with a US bank (USB) worth USD 5m, and a UK exporter (UKX) has deposits with a UK bank (UKB) worth USD 2m, respectively. USM sends a check of USD 1m to UKX to settle an invoice. UKX adds this to her account with UKB, which adds this to its account with USB. The roman-font figures give the balances before the payment, and the italic-font figures give the balances after the payment.

it has no USD reserves deposited with the US central bank (the Federal Reserve or Fed), nor can it call on the Fed as a lender of last resort. This UK bank will, understandably, not give the exporter the right to convert the USD deposit into USD notes and coins at sight (that is, without prior notice and without costs). In that sense, the London USD checking account is not a sight account in the strict sense. If the exporter asks for dollar notes, the London bank could possibly cash in USD 1m from its US account and have the notes flown over, which would be expensive, or the London bank could buy USD dollar notes from somebody else in the UK, if that is cheaper. The implication is that USD held on a non-US bank account will generally have a different price (or exchange rate) than USD notes.

There is also seignorage associated with having a currency that is used internationally. Recall how local merchants, when paying with promissory notes that were not immediately cashed in, effectively obtained interest-free loans. The same still happens internationally: a small country, whose cur-

rency is not used anywhere else, has to pay for its imports by exporting goods, or by selling assets.[9]
In contrast, a large country like the US, which has a widely accepted currency, can pay in its own
money and still expect that this money will remain in circulation among international traders for many
years before it is cashed in for goods or for assets. This becomes an interest-free loan, with an unstated
time to maturity, from the rest of the world to the US.

I.3 EUROMARKETS

In the previous section, we mentioned that one can deposit a USD check into a sight account with a bank
located outside the US, but one can also make a time deposit by depositing the USD with a UK bank
for, say, three months. In return for interest income, the owner of these funds then transfers the right to
use the money during that period to the UK bank. This is an example of a eurodollar transaction. We
will first give an overview of euromarkets, and then discuss their effect on the money creation mechanism.

I.3.1 What Are Euromarkets?

Eurocurrency markets are offshore money and capital markets in the sense that the currency of denomination is not the official currency of the country where the transaction takes place.

Example I.4

A Norwegian investor may deposit USD with a bank located outside the US, perhaps in Oslo or in
London. This deposit is then considered a eurodeposit. (USD deposits with an international banking
facility, a US banking institution that is considered outside the US as far as banking regulations are
concerned, are also considered eurodeposits.) In contrast, if the USD deposit is made with a regular
US bank, the transaction is a domestic deposit, not a eurotransaction.

Such off-shore markets have long antecedents. In many European trading centers, bankers have
been accepting deposits and trading commercial paper denominated in many different currencies since
the Middle Ages.[10] The prefix *euro-* was first used for USD deposits and loans made in Paris and
London after World War II when the USD replaced the GBP as the leading international currency. The
term *eurodollar market* was later generalized to eurocurrency when off-shore markets for other currencies emerged. There are many reasons why some investors prefer to make their USD deposits outside the US, as well as why there is so much USD borrowing outside the US. One of these reasons is
that the euromarkets are less regulated than the US market: the absence of reserve requirements,

---

[9] The country can also borrow, but when the loan matures, it still has to pay with money earned from exports or from the
sale of assets. The interest on the loan is the price it pays for postponing the real payment.

[10] In Brugge, the main trading center in the low countries (Benelux) until the late 1400s, this took place on a little square
in front of two pubs, *Ter Beurse* and *De Oude Beurs,* after the purse (*Beurs*) shown in their coats of arms—hence the continental words *Boerse, Beurs, Bourse, Bolsa, Borsa,* and so on, for organized capital markets. The first organized exchange in
the West, with fixed opening hours, rules, members, and such, was the *Beurs* of Antwerp in 1531; commercial paper and T-bills
were traded in the afternoon while commodity forwards and options were traded in the morning. One of the *Beurs'* members
was Lord Gresham—*the* Gresham—who soon convinced Elizabeth I to build a similar *Bursa* in London. Amsterdam followed
a few years later, and added the anonymous joint-stock company to the list of financial instruments.

deposit insurance, transaction taxes, withholding taxes, etc., makes eurotransactions cheaper than similar transactions in the US domestic money market. Also, it is comparatively easy to evade income taxes on income from eurodeposits, which further increases the attractiveness of this market. These factors have allowed the emergence of a market for large, wholesale deals, at interest spreads that are narrower than the spreads that typically prevail in domestic markets. A detailed discussion of these and other explanations for the success of eurocurrency markets is provided in Chapter 9.

The term *eurocurrency markets* is potentially misleading for at least two reasons. First, eurocurrency markets are not currency markets where foreign exchange is traded; rather, they are money markets for short-term deposits and loans. Second, the prefix *euro-* is no longer accurate because there are important off-shore markets in the Middle East and especially in the Far East (Tokyo, Singapore, Hong Kong). An alternative prefix, *xeno-* (Greek for foreign) somehow never caught on; instead, one often speaks of Asia dollars. Thus, when we refer to any offshore transaction as *euro*—including for instance, GBP deposits in Singapore—we in fact mean *xeno*.

Banks accept deposits in order to relend them: deposits must also be accompanied by euroloans. The development of euromoney and euroloan markets was followed by the opening of markets for eurosecurities, the first of which was the *eurobond* market. A more recent phenomenon is the *euro-commercial paper* (ECP) market; a *euroequity* market is also emerging. We shall discuss these markets in Chapter 9.

I.3.2 Eurodeposits and Money Supply

There is some confusion about the effect of eurotransactions on the money supply. Many people have the ill-founded notion that electronic money can actually leave the country and thus reduce the money supply. Others claim that eurodeposits lead to near-infinite money creation. It is necessary to qualify both of these claims.

The claim that a eurodeposit decreases the domestic money supply overlooks the fact that eurobanks are just fronts between the nonresident owner of the funds and a bank in the currency's home country. For example, if a non-US company receives a USD check (drawn on a New York bank) from a US customer, it can deposit this money in a New York bank. In this case, the US money supply clearly is not affected; the only effect is that the ownership of those USD balances is transferred from a US resident to a nonresident. If the same non-US company deposits the check with a *London* bank for three months, the London bank will issue an *I owe you* (I.O.U.) in the form of a promissory note or a Certificate of Deposit to that investor and, in return, becomes the owner of the USD balances held with the New York bank. This again is just a change of ownership of the US funds, and does not affect the US money supply. If the London bank then extends a USD loan to yet another company, the right to use the New York-held dollars is transferred to that new company—again without affecting the US money supply. In short, not a single electronic USD ever leaves its home turf; thus, euromarkets certainly do not drain money from the US. It is true that ownership changes, but this is a result of international trade in goods and services or international lending and borrowing; it has nothing to do with euromarkets *per se*. It may also be true that USD owned by foreigners are, to a relatively larger extent, used to make international transactions rather than domestic (US) transactions. As a result, there is a decrease in the US money supply in the sense that the amount of USD effectively used within the US probably goes down. However, this again is a result of the change of ownership, which, in turn, reflects goods trade or financial transactions—not a result of the existence of euromarkets. If there were no euro-dollar markets, international traders would still earn USD from exports or from the sale of securities.

Presumably, they would then keep these US funds directly in a New York bank account, rather than via a bank in London or Paris, and still use most of the funds for international transactions.

A diametrically opposite view is that euromarkets actually *increase* the money supply of the currency in question because of the absence of reserve requirements. We already know that reserve requirements limit the amount of money that commercial banks can create. For instance, if the monetary base is USD 1,000 and the reserve requirements are 10 percent, banks can extend loans and accept deposits for, at most, USD 10,000. If there are no reserve requirements in euromarkets, the argument concludes, deposits would create infinite amounts of money. This conclusion is wrong for at least two reasons.

First, there are considerations other than reserve requirements, such as prudent self-imposed reserves and capital-requirement rules, that prevent banks from lending infinite amounts. For instance, in many domestic European money markets, the reserve requirements for commercial banks have been abolished for years without leading to an explosion of electronic money. This illustrates that self-imposed restraints on relending or capital-adequacy rules are sufficient to restrict the growth of the money supply.

The second argument against infinite money creation via euromarkets is that there is considerable leakage of funds from the system. Eurobanks are largely *thrifts* or *savings and loans* institutions, active in the time deposit/loan business; they are not commercial banks offering checking account services. We shall argue that such thrifts do not create money; rather, thrifts act as intermediaries in the money market, and leave money creation to commercial banks. To see this, start from an exogenous increase of the monetary base by USD 100, and assume that it is placed as a time deposit with a eurothrift. If the reserve requirements are zero, all of the USD 100 can conceivably be relent to another party.

- This other party may be another bank. These interbank loans do not add to the money supply, as they merely pass on the right to use the New York-held dollar balances to another party. The chain of interbank deposits cannot go on indefinitely, however, so ultimately, the funds will be lent to a corporation or an individual.
- If the borrower is a firm or a private individual, the loan is typically not used to make another time deposit. Rather, the borrower typically uses the funds to pay a debt or to buy goods. It is equally unlikely that, on average, the subsequent holder of the funds will immediately redeposit the money into the thrift circuit. Thus, there is substantial leakage from the no-reserve-requirement thrift circuit to the standard commercial bank circuit. Put differently, while commercial banks create money, thrift institutions like the eurobanks are essentially intermediaries in this process, and hardly add to money creation. Money creation is based on the "loans make deposits" principle; but *term loans* hardly make any *term deposits*.

I.4   EXCHANGE RATE REGIMES

We have seen how money is created and how it is transferred from one owner to another owner in a different country. In the examples we considered, money was transferred as a payment for goods. However, money can also be transferred as a payment for the money of another country. The price that one pays for one unit of the foreign currency is the *exchange rate*. This rate depends on the supply and demand for the foreign currency. Very often governments instruct their central banks to influence the supply and demand for a currency. The various policies with respect to the exchange rate that a goverment may adopt are discussed below, while exchange markets themselves are described in greater detail in Chapter 1.

Government *intervention* in the exchange markets occurs through the buying and selling of foreign currency by a country's central bank. In Section I.1.2, we noted that such intervention affects the country's monetary base and, hence, its money supply. Yet influencing the money supply is not the primary purpose of intervention in the foreign exchange market. Instead, the main purpose of intervention is to control or at least influence the exchange rate. Thus, the central bank buys foreign exchange when the exchange rate (the market price of foreign currency) is too low, and it sells foreign exchange when the exchange rate is too high. Most central banks intervene on the basis of policy objectives and rules formulated by the government. Loosely, a country's *exchange rate regime* can be defined as the set of rules that its central bank follows when buying and selling in the interbank market. These rules can vary greatly. We shall discuss them briefly in reviewing the postwar international monetary history.

I.4.1 Fixed Exchange Rates Relative to Gold

Before World War I, most countries had an official gold parity; that is, they fixed the price of gold in terms of their own currency. (This, in fact, refers to the old principle that gold was the true currency.) In the post-World War II era, only the USD had a fixed gold parity, officially USD 35 per ounce of fine gold with intervention points at 34.8 and 35.2.

"You shall not crucify mankind upon a cross of gold," was how the 1896 US Democratic presidential candidate, William Jennings Bryan, expressed his sentiments about the gold standard. As the dollar was convertible into gold, the ratio of outstanding dollars to gold reserves needed to remain credible in order to prevent runs on the gold stock. For example, an individual feels confident that he or she will be able to effectively exchange USD notes into gold when the number of USD notes exceeds their gold backing by only 2 to 1. If, however, the number of dollars exceeds their gold backing by 100 to 1, it is obvious that if, in a period of uncertainty, a small fraction of USD notes is converted into gold, then the remaining USD notes will have no gold backing left. If the USD-to-gold ratio is high, the slightest scare is then sufficient to send people flying to the bank, trying to be ahead of the others. Such a stampede usually achieves the very event the investors are afraid of: the bank runs out of gold. Thus, to avert panic, the US central bank (the Federal Reserve, or Fed) has to make sure that the money stock does not grow faster than the stock of gold. However, there is also a limit to the value of transactions that can take place in, for example, one month, with a given amount of dollars in circulation. For this reason, a limit on the stock of dollars also imposes a limit on the value of transactions made in dollars; maintaining a credible gold backing ultimately creates the risk of slowing down economic activity in the US and international trade, two domains where USD are used as the medium of exchange. The necessity of choosing between economic growth and credibility is often called the *Triffin Dilemma*, after Professor Triffin from Yale University, who again pointed out the problem in the early 1960s.

The US did not restrict the supply of dollars after World War II. Internally, this was no problem, because US residents were not allowed to convert dollars (or any other currency) into gold. Externally, there was a problem, though: the Vietnam War and the Great Society Program were financed by large-scale sales of dollars to foreigners. Unlike US residents, these non-US investors and central banks could always buy or sell gold in the London gold pool, where the Federal Reserve stabilized the USD gold price using the pooled gold stocks of the central banks of most western nations. Decreased credibility led to minor runs on gold, which further decreased credibility, which led to more runs on the gold stock. The US Federal Reserve Board (the Fed), which held about two-thirds of the world's gold stock in the late 1940s, soon saw its reserves dwindle. In the mid-1960s, the official gold market had to be closed to all private investors, while central banks were expected to avoid buying gold from the

Fed—France, notably, did not oblige. In 1971, the official gold price was raised from USD/oz. 35 to 38, but that did not avert the ultimate collapse of the system. In 1972, the US government gave up all pretense that the USD was convertible into gold at a fixed rate. The gold price soared, and has been in the range of USD 300–600 ever since.

Besides the Triffin Dilemma, the gold standard suffered from the fact that gold has industrial uses and is expensive to mine. From that perspective, the use of gold as the basis for a financial system is a waste of scarce resources. Finally, some politicians objected to allowing major gold producers like South Africa and the USSR cheap access to USD, while others resented the crucial role and seignorage gains this system granted to the US.

I.4.2   Fixed Exchange Rates vis-à-vis a Single Currency

Under a *fixed exchange rate regime,* the government wants to guarantee a virtually constant price for a particular foreign currency, and instructs the central bank to buy or sell as soon as the exchange rate deviates by x percent from that constant rate. The target exchange rate is called the country's *official parity*.

This system was strongly recommended under the Bretton Woods Agreement, signed in 1945 by the major western nations. For instance, between 1949 and 1967, the UK set the central parity with respect to the USD at USD/GBP 2.8, and instructed the Bank of England to *intervene* whenever the pound's value rose to 2.821 or dropped to 2.779. Thus, the *intervention points* were set by the government at 0.75 percent on each side of the official parity. As long as the Bank of England did not run out of USD, it would sell USD when the dollar became too expensive. If the dollar became too cheap, the Bank of England would buy. Likewise, Germany set the central parity at DEM/USD 4, and the Bundesbank would always make sure that the USD stayed in the range DEM/USD 3.97–4.03.

Note that the US did not declare an official parity with respect to any other currency; the Fed was never under any obligation to intervene in the exchange markets. Note also that there was no official parity (and hence no intervention) for non-USD rates either, for example DEM/GBP. There are, of course, implicit, indirect bounds on what the DEM/GBP rate can be. If there are limits on how expensive the USD can be in terms of DEM, and limits on how expensive the GBP can be in terms of USD, there is obviously an implied limit on how expensive the GBP can become in terms of DEM.

Fixed exchange rates work satisfactorily only as long as the countries maintain their competitiveness, but this requires similar economic policies. To see this, note that the UK could not possibly have 100 percent inflation and still maintain the exchange rate if its trading partners have near-zero inflation: with a stable exchange rate, the UK's exporters would have to quit foreign markets, and British firms selling in the UK would likewise be wiped out by foreign producers. In short, fixed rates require similar inflation rates across countries, which, in turn, require coordination of economic policy. There was very little policy coordination in the period following World War II, however, and this ultimately led to the demise of the fixed-rate system. As of the early 1960s, the comparatively high inflation rate in the UK meant that the GBP became manifestly overvalued (UK producers could no longer compete at USD/GBP 2.8), while the DEM was undervalued (German producers could undercut anyone anywhere, at DEM/USD 4). Also, international trade and exchange, heavily restricted immediately after the war, were gradually liberalized. With everyone free to buy and sell foreign exchange, and with a rapidly growing volume of international transactions, the Bank of England had to buy more and more GBP (that is, sell USD) if it wanted to support the value of the GBP. Likewise, the Bundesbank had to buy more and more USD to support the price of the USD and to keep down the price of the DEM. As a result, the Bank of England frequently ran out of USD while supporting the GBP, and the Bundesbank accumulated too many USD.

Often, the Bundesbank lent USD to the Bank of England (under a swap arrangement—for more details, see Chapter 10), or the UK borrowed USD from the International Monetary Fund, but these were only temporary solutions.[11] The idea, under the Bretton Woods Agreement, was that *structural* misalignments should be corrected by changes in the official parities (*re-* or *devaluations*). But this did not work very well. For one thing, the difference between a structural problem and a temporary problem was never defined. Moreover, devaluations were perceived by politicians as a sign of defeat, while revaluations were also unpopular because they hurt exporters. Nor did the IMF have the supranational power to impose parity adjustments on member countries. The result was that parity adjustments were postponed too long. As we have argued in the preceding section, the USD gold parity had also become unrealistic by that time. The combined effect of disequilibrium exchange rates and gold prices led to the collapse of the system of fixed parities in 1972. Since that year, the currencies of the major OECD countries have floated with respect to the USD.

Some countries still maintain fixed exchange rates, with narrow intervention bands, relative to one currency. In Table I.1, we see that, in Dec. 1992, twenty-four countries had a fixed rate with respect to the USD, fourteen against the FRF (*Communauté Financière Africaine,* which has its CFA-franc pegged at CFA-franc 20 per FRF) and twelve more countries had fixed rates relative to other currencies. In addition, four Gulf countries now have a loose link with the USD. The major OECD countries, however, have adopted different exchange rate regimes. In the following sections, we discuss fixed rates as they relate to a basket, multilateral intervention points (for example, the European Monetary System), and dirty floating.

I.4.3   Fixed Exchange Rates Relative to a Basket

After 1972, some countries unilaterally defined a target parity for a portfolio or *basket* of currencies with intervention points around that target. Table I.1 mentions five countries that have pegged their currency to the Special Drawing Right (SDR).[12] At one time, Sweden, Norway, and Finland pegged their currency to another existing basket, the ECU, which is described in Section I.4.4. In Table I.1, the countries mentioned under the heading "Other composite" have selected a basket of their own rather than taking an existing combination like the SDR. At one time, this group contained Australia, Sweden, Norway, and Finland. Before explaining how a basket regime works, we must consider how a basket is constructed.

---

[11] The International Monetary Fund (IMF) was created as part of the Bretton Woods Agreement with the responsibility of providing short-term financing to the central banks. It is funded by the participating countries.

[12] Special Drawing Rights are internationally created funds. They were invented at the end of the Bretton Woods period, in an attempt to create an alternative international currency next to the beleaguered USD, with the seignorage going to the IMF member states rather than to the US. The original SDR was at par with the USD. One difference with the USD is that the original SDR was issued by the IMF rather than by the Fed. Another difference is that the SDR is a purely electronic currency; an SDR deposit cannot be cashed in for SDR bank notes or coins. Central banks can make payments to each other in SDR, or convert SDRs into other currencies and *vice versa* at the going market value of the SDR. When in the 1970s the USD plunged relative to the DEM and JPY, the SDR was redefined as a basket of sixteen currencies. This definition was rather cumbersome, so after some time the basket was again redefined, this time in terms of just five currencies: USD 0.54, DEM 0.46, JPY 34, FRF 0.74, and GBP 0.071. These changes in the SDR composition, plus the fact that the interest earned on SDR was quite low, meant that the SDR was never very popular among central bankers.

TABLE I.1 Exchange Rate Systems Adopted by Various Countries

Exchange Rate Arrangements

(As of December 31, 1992)

Currency pegged to						Flexibility Limited in terms of a Single Currency or Group of Currencies		Adjusted according to a set of indicators[5]	More Flexible	
US Dollar	French Franc	Russian ruble	Other currency	SDR	Other composite[2]	Single currency[3]	Cooperative arrangements[4]		Other managed floating	Independently floating
Angola	Benin	Armenia	Bhutan (Indian Rupee)	Iran, I.R. of	Algeria	Bahrain	Belgium	Chile	China, P.R.	Afghanistan
Antigua & Barbuda	Burkina Faso	Azerbaijan	Estonia (deutsche mark)	Libya	Austria	Qatar	Denmark	Colombia	Ecuador	Albania
Argentina	Cameroon	Belarus		Myanmar	Bangladesh	Saudi Arabia	France	Madgascar	Egypt	Australia
Bahamas, The	C.African Rep.	Georgia		Rwanda	Botswana	United Arab Emirates	Germany		Greece	Bolivia
Barbados	Chad	Kyrgyzstan		Seychelles	Burundi		Ireland		Guinea	Brazil
Belize	Comoros	Moldova	Kiribati (Australian dollar)		Cape Verde		Luxembourg		Guinea-Bissau	Bulgaria
Djibouti	Congo				Cyprus		Netherlands		India	Canada
Dominica	Côte d'Ivoire				Czechoslovakia		Portugal		Indonesia	Costa Rica
Ethiopia	Equatorial Guinea		Lesotho (South African Rand)		Fiji		Spain		Israel	Dominican Rep.
Grenada	Gabon				Hungary				Korea	El Salvador
Hong Kong										
Iraq					Iceland				Lao P.D Rep.	
Liberia	Mali		Namibia (South African Rand)		Jordan				Maldives	Finland
Marshall Islands	Niger				Kenya				Mexico	Gambia, The
Mongolia	Senegal				Kuwait				Pakistan	Ghana
Nicaragua	Togo				Malawi				Poland	Guatemala
										Guyana

Oman
Panama
St. Kitts & Nevis
St. Lucia
St. Vincent and the
   Grenadines

Suriname
Syrian Arab Rep.
Trinidad and
   Tobago
Yemen, Republic of

Swaziland
  (South
  African
  Rand)

Malaysia
Malta
Mauritania
Mauritius
Morocco

Nepal
Papua New
  Guinea
Solomon Islands
Tanzania
Thailand

Tonga
Vanuatu
Western Samoa
Zimbabwe

Sao Tome &
  Principe
Singapore
Somalia
Sri Lanka
Tunisia

Turkey
Uruguay
Viet Nam

Haiti
Honduras
Italy
Jamaica
Japan

Latvia
Lebanon
Lithuania
Mozambique
New Zealand

Nigeria
Norway
Paraguay
Peru
Philippines

Romania
Russia
Sierra Leone
South Africa
Sudan

Sweden
Switzerland
Uganda
Ukraine
United
  Kingdom

United States
Venezuela
Zaïre
Zambia

TABLE I.1   Concluded

Classification Status[1]	1986	1987	1988	1989	End of Period 1990			1991				1992			
					QII	QIII	QIV	QI	QII	QIII	QIV	QI	QII	QIII	QIV
Currency pegged to															
US Dollar	32	38	36	32	28	25	25	27	26	25	24	23	24	26	24
French Franc	14	14	14	14	14	14	14	14	14	14	14	14	14	14	14
Russian ruble	—	—	—	—	—	—	—	—	—	—	—	—	—	5	6
Other currency	5	5	5	5	5	5	5	5	5	5	4	4	5	6	6
SDR	10	8	8	7	7	7	6	6	6	6	6	6	5	5	5
Other currency composite	30	27	31	35	35	35	35	35	35	34	33	32	32	31	29
Flexibility limited vis-a-vis a															
single currency	5	4	4	4	4	4	4	4	4	4	4	4	4	4	4
Cooperative arrangements	8	8	8	9	9	9	10	10	10	10	10	10	11	9	9
Adjusted according to a															
set of indicators	6	5	5	5	4	4	3	5	5	5	5	5	4	4	3
Managed floating	21	23	22	21	21	23	23	22	22	23	27	25	23	22	23
Independently floating[6]	19	18	17	20	23	26	25	27	28	29	29	33	36	41	44
Total[6]	150	150	150	152	150	152	150	156	155	155	156	156	158	167	167

[1]For members with dual or multiple exchange markets, the arrangement shown is that in the major market.

[2]Comprises currencies which are pegged to various "baskets" of currencies of the members' own choice, as distinct from the SDR basket.

[3]Exchange rates of all currencies have shown limited flexibility in terms of the US dollar.

[4]Refers to the cooperative arrangement maintained under the European Monetary System.

[5]Includes exchange arrangements under which the exchange rate is adjusted at relatively frequent intervals, on the basis of indicators determined by the respective member countries.

[6]Excluding the following seven countries which have not yet formally notified the Fund of their exchange rate arrangements: Cambodia, Croatia, Kazakhstan, San Marino, Slovenia, Turkmenistan, and Uzbekistan.

From *International Financial Statistics*, March 1993. Reprinted by permission of International Monetary Fund.

Example I.5

Suppose that since the election of President Groucho Marx the composition of Freedonia's trade has been fairly stable: about 60 percent of trade is with Germany, and 40 percent with the US. Thus, Freedonia can create a basket with these approximate weights for, respectively, the DEM and the USD, and tie its crown (the FRK) to that basket. Suppose the rates are currently FRK/DEM 3 and FRK/USD 5, and that the government finds these rates acceptable. To define the basket, it would have to find a number (n_M) of DEM and a number (n_D) of USD such that the DEM has a weight of 60 percent:

$$\frac{3n_M}{3n_M + 5n_D} = 0.6.$$

Arbitrarily setting $n_D = 1$, we find $n_M = 2.5$. Thus, President Marx defines the basket as containing USD 1 and DEM 2.5. To verify that the weight of the DEM is 60 percent, first compute the basket's current value. At the going exchange rates, FRK/DEM 3 and FRK/USD 5, one unit of the basket is worth:

$$(\text{DEM } 2.5)(\text{FRK/DEM } 3) + (\text{USD } 1)(\text{FRK/USD } 5) = \text{FRK } 12.5,$$

such that the DEM's weight is, indeed,

$$\frac{(\text{DEM } 2.5)\ (\text{FRK/DEM } 3)}{\text{FRK } 12.5} = 0.6.$$

Now that we understand how a basket is constructed, let us see how it is used in the central bank's intervention policy. The idea is that the basket should always be worth roughly its target level, FRK 12.5, and not deviate by more than 5 percent, for example. This implies intervention points of 11.875–13.125. At any given moment, the central bank can compute the spot value of the basket. If the basket hits or approaches an intervention point, the central bank intervenes: if the basket is too expensive, the central bank will sell USD and/or DEM and buy crowns, and *vice versa*.

Example I.6

If, for instance, the DEM is trading at FRK/DEM 3.2 and the USD at FRK/USD 4.9, the basket is worth:

$$(\text{DEM } 2.5)\ (\text{FRK/DEM } 3.2) + (\text{USD } 1)\ (\text{FRK/USD } 4.9) = \text{FRK } 12.9.$$

This is well within the admissible band (11.875–13.125). If the USD then appreciates to FRK/USD 5.10, the basket's value increases to:

$$(\text{DEM } 2.5)\ (\text{FRK/DEM } 3.2) + (\text{USD } 1)\ (\text{FRK/USD } 5.1) = \text{FRK } 13.1.$$

This is dangerously close to the upper bound, and the Freedonian central bank will probably already be in the market to support the crown.[13]

I.4.4 The 1979–1993 European Monetary System (EMS)

The purpose of the EMS is to restrict the fluctuations of the currencies of the EU member states relative to each other without, however, restricting the fluctuations of these currencies relative to outside currencies like the USD and the JPY.[14] For this reason, a similar, earlier system was called "the snake." (Picture the member currencies as contained within the skin of a snake, which, as a whole, floats relative to other currencies like the USD and the JPY.) Greece was never part of the EMS; the UK joined the system as late as 1991 and, along with Italy, dropped out in 1992.

The Official ECU

The EMS is built around a basket of all EU currencies, called the European Currency Unit or ECU.[15] Still, the role of the ECU is different from the role a basket plays in the system described in Section I.4.3, as we shall see. At the time of writing, the ECU had the composition given by the column n_j in Table I.2; the ECU consists of DEM 0.6242, GBP 0.08784, FRF 1.332, and so on. The table also shows the exchange rates S_j (in BEF per unit of foreign currency) on December 19, 1990, and the weights of each currency at that date. The composition of the basket has changed in the past, but is now irrevocably fixed.

As under a pure basket system, each member state selects a target value of the basket in terms of its own currency. In the EMS, this target value is called the *central parity*. And each central bank also continuously computes the value of the basket in terms of its own currency. The deviation between the actual value and the central parity is called the *divergence,* defined as:

$$\frac{\text{actual value} - \text{central parity}}{\text{central parity}}.$$

We see that a weak currency has a positive divergence. In a traditional basket system as described in Section I.4.3, the divergence would provide the signal for intervention. This, however, is not how the EMS works: intervention is based on the cross rates, which are the bilateral exchange rates among EMS member countries. First, the set of central rates of each currency with respect to the ECU are converted into a matrix of central cross rates between each pair of currencies. The EMS rule, then, is that the actual cross rate should not be allowed to deviate by more than about 2.25 percent from the cen-

---

[13] Note in passing that in this second example the weight of the DEM is

$$\frac{(\text{DEM } 2.5)\,(\text{FRK/DEM } 3.5)}{\text{FRK } 13.1} = 0.62,$$

which is no longer the initial weight (60 percent). Weights change whenever the exchange rates change.

[14] The European Union consists of Belgium, Denmark, France, Germany, Great Britain, Greece, Ireland, Italy, Luxembourg, the Netherlands, Portugal, and Spain. The earliest antecedent of the EU was the European Community for Coal and Steel (ECCS), which started off as a six-country group in 1954. In 1958, these countries signed the Euratom Treaty and the Treaty of Rome. The Rome Treaty founded the European Economic Community (EEC), which was a customs union with, additionally, a common agricultural policy and free movement of capital and labor. The ECCS, Euratom, and the EEC were soon merged into the European Community (EC). The UK, Ireland, and Denmark joined the EC in 1973, Greece in 1983, and Portugal and Spain in 1986. In 1993, the EC became the European Union (EU), by adding plans for a monetary union and a common foreign policy.

[15] Note incidentally, that ecu is also the name of an ancient French gold coin.

TABLE I.2   The European Currency Unit (ECU)

	S_j Exchange rates BEF/FC on 19/12/90	n_j Number of units FC per ECU	$S_j \times n_j$	w_j Relative weights in %
DEM	20.6925	0.6242	12.92	30.57
GBP	59.27	0.08784	5.21	12.33
FRF	6.0765	1.332	8.09	19.14
ITL	0.027401	151.8	4.16	9.84
NLG	18.3385	0.2198	4.03	9.54
BEF	1	3.301	3.30	7.81
LUF	1	0.13	0.13	0.31
DKK	5.35	0.1976	1.06	2.51
ILP	54.945	0.008552	0.47	1.11
GRD	0.197275	1.44	0.28	0.66
PTE	0.2326	1.393	0.32	0.76
ESP	0.3237	6.885	2.29	5.42

Value ECU = 42.26 BEF

$$w_j = \frac{S_j \times n_j}{\sum (S_j \times n_j)}; \text{ FC = foreign currency}$$

tral cross rate.[16] Thus, intervention is based on the bilateral exchange rates, and not on the divergence of a particular currency from its central ECU parity.

Example   I.7

Consider a simplified EMS with just three member states, Germany, France, and the UK. The simplified ECU consists of DEM 1, GBP 0.25, and FRF 2.5 (see column n_j, on page 22). The central parities (CP) selected by each country are DEM/ECU 3, GBP/ECU 1, and FRF/ECU 10 (column $CP_{j/ECU}$, in the table that follows). We compute the bilateral central parities as follows:

$$\text{FRF/DEM} = \frac{\text{FRF/ECU}}{\text{DEM/ECU}} = \frac{10}{3} = 3.333; \ \text{FRF/GBP} = \frac{\text{FRF/ECU}}{\text{GBP/ECU}} = \frac{10}{1} = 10$$

$$\text{GBP/DEM} = \frac{\text{GBP/ECU}}{\text{DEM/ECU}} = \frac{1}{3} = 0.333.$$

---

[16] The divergence limit is 6 percent for the weaker currencies (the UK, Italy, Spain, and Portugal, at one time). In 1991, the Benelux countries unilaterally and explicitly decided to keep their currencies within 1 percent of the DEM central cross rate. Before that date, the NLG/BEF rate was already kept within a 1 percent band around the central rate; this was the "worm within the snake."

This leads to the bilateral grid below, which also shows inverse rates (DEM/FRF, etc.).

Currency	n_j	$CP_{j/ECU}$	Bilateral grid: CP of		
			FRF	DEM	GBP
FRF	2.50	10	1.0	3.333	10
DEM	1.50	3	0.3	1.000	3
GBP	0.25	1	0.1	0.333	1

The fact that intervention is not based on the ECU divergence, but on the bilateral deviations from the bilateral central parities, does not mean that the divergence plays no role at all. To see whether the divergence is large, a *divergence indicator* is computed every day. This shows the actual divergence as a percentage of the maximum divergence, that is, the divergence if all foreign currencies would be simultaneously at the lower bound.

Example I.8

Suppose, for simplicity, that the DEM has a 50 percent weight in the ECU. If all other currencies trade at 2.25 percent below their central DEM parity, the ECU trades at only 1.125 percent below its central DEM parity, simply because half of the ECU is DEM, which obviously always trades at DEM/DEM 1. Still, the divergence indicator equals –100 percent: the ECU is at its lowest possible level relative to the DEM.

If the divergence exceeds ±75 percent of the maximum divergence allowed, the national government has to take appropriate economic policy measures to affect the exchange rates. In practice, this most often means that the central bank raises or lowers the domestic interest rate in order to make its currency more or less attractive.

How the Original EMS Worked

As we saw, all member states select a central parity with respect to the ECU and, therefore, a set of implied bilateral central parities. As soon as an actual cross rate deviates by more than about 2.25 percent from the central cross rate, there is intervention. This sounds rather like a Bretton Woods fixed-rate system. However, the EMS tries to improve on the Bretton Woods fixed-rate system in three respects.

- Intervention is done by both banks. That is, if the ITL/DEM rate hits an intervention point, both the Bundesbank and the Bank of Italy have to intervene. In contrast, the US never intervened under the Bretton Woods system.

Example I.9

Suppose that the FRF is at its lowest admissible value relative to the DEM. FRF will be bought and DEM sold, not just by the Banque de France but also by the Bundesbank, which acts as an agent for the Banque de France. Since the Bundesbank can produce unlimited amounts of DEM, intervention can go on forever—in principle. The only limit is that the DEM spent by the Bundesbank are assumed to be lent to the Banque de France, which has to repay them. Thus, the French government may still decide to abandon intervention if the Banque de France's DEM debts are running up too high.

- Each EMS state defends a rate with respect to each of the other currencies in the system. In contrast, under the Bretton Woods fixed-rate system, only the USD rate had to be defended.
- The EMS does not ignore the role of economic policy coordination. We have already mentioned the multilateral side of the system: each central bank has to watch, and potentially intervene in, each pairwise exchange market. The idea is that this would force all countries to cooperate, instead of forcing the weak countries to adjust their policies to Germany's. We have also mentioned the divergence indicator, which triggers adjustment of economic policy as soon as one country deviates (positively or negatively) from the average. Furthermore, realignments are discussed jointly by the governments of all member states, with emphasis on economic policy. Finally, central bankers meet regularly to coordinate money supplies and interest rates.

Despite these improvements over the Bretton Woods system, the EMS is not without problems, as the events in 1992 and 1993 proved.

The 1993 Suspension of the EMS
The early EMS had fairly frequent realignments. However, by 1990–91, the system seemed very stable, with converging inflation rates across member states. When, in 1990, even Margaret Thatcher admitted that it was not inconceivable that the GBP would be replaced by some form of common currency, optimism peaked. The euphoria was premature, though. In September 1992, Finland, which had unilaterally pegged the FIM to the ECU, gave in to continued pressure and abandoned its link with the ECU. Speculation then turned to the SEK, which soon gave up its link to the ECU as well, and then to the weaker EMS currencies like GBP, ITL, ESP, FRF, DKK, and IEP. In late September 1992, the ESP devalued, the ITL and GBP dropped out of the EMS, and Spain, Portugal, and Ireland reimposed capital controls. The Banque de France and the Bundesbank were able to successfully defend the FRF/DEM rate, and quiet returned to the markets until the summer of 1993.

The cause of the summer 1993 currency turmoil was a disagreement about economic policy. The Bundesbank wanted to stamp out inflation (caused by German unification) with a strict monetary policy and high interest rates. Many other countries, including France, preferred to lower interest rates in order to get their economies out of recession. This led to speculation that France might devalue, so as to be able to lower its interest rates.[17] Enormous interventions followed. In the end, the EMS intervention band was widened from 2.25 percent to 15 percent, which meant a virtual suspension of the EMS. By early 1994, most currencies had returned to rates within or close to the old 2.25 percent band. Still, the message of the 1992–93 turmoil is that the credibility of the system is vital for its survival, and that the only 100 percent credible system is one with just a single currency.

The Private ECU
To compound your confusion, there is also something called a *private* ECU. This was originally a purely banking product, although it had (and has) the moral support of the EU Commission. Lenders and borrowers can carry out money-market operations in ECU. Originally, an ECU deposit was just a portfolio of deposits in ten different currencies, and the bank's accounts showed an ECU deposit as ten small deposits of real currencies. For accounting purposes, an ECU transaction is currently treated as a single transaction in a category of its own (as if the ECU were an actual currency)—not as a bundle of ten or twelve transactions in separate currencies. In some countries, corporations can keep their accounts in ECU. Today, there are even private ECU forward and futures contracts, ECU bonds, and ECU options.

---

[17] A currency typically weakens when its interest rate is lowered, because the currency becomes less attractive to investors. We shall have a more in-depth discussion about this and related issues in Chapter 3.

Puzzlingly to some, the value of the private ECU often deviates from that of the official ECU by more than what transaction costs would justify. The reason is that there is no official intervention in the private ECU market: there is no window where an investor can convert a private ECU into the basket of currencies, and *vice versa*, nor is there any central bank that guarantees a minimum or maximum market price for the private ECU. Arbitrage takes place only to satisfy accounting rules and prudence regulations: commercial banks that have an unbalanced ECU book can still buy or sell the basket to obtain a position that is balanced in the eyes of their overseers. Banks dislike the cost of buying and selling often tiny amounts of twelve different currencies, though, and have formed an ECU pool where excess ECU positions can be passed on to banks with ECU shortfalls; even private banks rarely buy and sell ECU against the basket.

Stated differently, no one knows definitely what the private ECU really is. It is surely *not* a basket of currencies, and its price could potentially deviate from the price of the basket. There is a general feeling that it should be worth roughly as much as the official ECU, but this feeling is subject to waves of optimism or pessimism. For instance, after the 1992 Danish referendum and before the 1993 French referendum on the Maastricht Treaty (which contained specific plans for the common currency), the private ECU depreciated, and the interest rates that borrowers had to offer on ECU instruments substantially exceeded the interest rate on the basket of loans. All of this indicated the growing uncertainty regarding the future of the private ECU.

I.4.5   Other Exchange Rate Systems

Some countries have an unofficial target rate, and unofficial intervention points, with respect to a single currency or a basket. For example, the Swiss franc and the Austrian schilling are kept fairly stable with respect to the DEM. The intervention rates are never explicitly announced—and obviously change over time.

The Group of Five (G5), and currently, the Group of Seven, meet twice a year to discuss exchange-rate targets for the three main currency blocks (USD, JPY, and EMS).[18] Central banks often intervene in the USD/DEM and USD/JPY market on a unilateral or coordinated basis; the floating system prevailing in these major markets is to some extent an unofficial target system. This is known as *dirty floating*.

Other countries, including many Latin American countries, have experimented with a *crawling peg system,* where the official parity is revised fairly frequently. This sometimes happens semi-automatically, on the basis of a formula involving, for instance, inflation and balance-of-payments data. In Table I.1, three countries officially follow this system (see column "Adjusted according to a set of indicators").

The choice of the exchange rate mechanism has an important effect on how macro-economic equilibrium is achieved, and on how governments conduct economic policy. A related issue is how the equilibrium value of a floating exchange rate is determined in the market. We shall discuss this in Part II of this text. We can, however, obtain a surprising number of results without having to consider the equilibrium mechanism that determines exchange rates. Specifically, taking the current exchange rate as given, we can analyze forwards, futures, options, and swaps using simple arbitrage arguments. This is the objective of the next ten chapters.

---

[18] G5 consisted of the US, Japan, Germany, France, and the UK. Later, Canada and Italy joined the club as well (G7). A notable meeting was the G5 1985 "Plaza Agreement," where the G5 publicly agreed that the USD should decrease in value. This is often viewed as having provided an important impetus to the drop in the USD after its unprecedented rise in the early 1980s.

PART

In this part of the textbook, Part I, we describe the exchange market and its related instruments. Most readers will be more or less familiar with the market for "spot" foreign exchange, where foreign currencies are bought and sold for immediate or quasi-immediate delivery. Throughout Part I, we treat the spot exchange rate (and the closely related interest rates in the domestic and foreign money markets) as exogenously given. We investigate how other exchange-rate-related instruments can be analyzed and priced as functions of the spot rate and the interest rates using arbitrage arguments; that is, by arguing that two contracts (or combinations of contracts) with identical future cash flows should have the same price, no matter how uncertain these cash flows may be.

Chapter 1 starts with the mechanics of spot exchange markets. Besides providing a description of how this market operates, in this chapter we also introduce arbitrage arguments when we discuss cross-rates. We shall also illustrate how the simple arbitrage results obtained in a frictionless market provide only upper and lower bounds when transaction costs are introduced.

The next seven chapters (2–8) are devoted to contracts that "depend" on spot and money markets, not in a causal sense but in the sense that, once the spot rate and the interest rates are known, we can price the related contracts. The oldest such "derivative" contract is the forward sale or purchase, which is described in Chapter 2. In the forward market, foreign exchange is bought and sold for delivery and payment at a known future date rather than for immediate delivery. Chapter 3 is devoted to understanding the role and nature of forward exchange rates, providing crucial insights for day-to-day financial management; it is of vital importance for all later chapters.

Transaction costs, which are a logical concern for the treasurer who looks for optimal hedging or financing alternatives, are introduced into our discussion of forward rates in Chapter 4. Also, default risk is quite important in the way forward contracts are handled. This aspect has provided the motivation for a competing variant, the futures contract, discussed in Chapter 5. Currency options are a third exchange-related instrument. Unlike forward or futures contracts, options give the holder the right (rather than the unconditional obligation) to exchange known amounts of currencies at an initially agreed-upon exchange rate. Chapter 6 covers the general properties and applications of options. In Chapter 7, we use the binomial model to price option contracts. The continuous-time model, based on the work of Black, Scholes, Merton, and others, is presented in Chapter 8. It can be viewed as a special limit case of the binomial model.

The last two chapters of Part I of the book discuss long-term counterparts of money-market instruments and forward contracts. Chapter 9 describes international bank loans and eurobonds. An instrument that is very much related to bank loans and bonds is the swap contract; we discuss this in Chapter 10.

1

INTERNATIONAL FINANCIAL MARKETS

1 SPOT EXCHANGE MARKETS

In this chapter, we study the mechanics of the spot exchange market. The first section explains the various ways in which exchange rates can be quoted. The second section briefly describes the exchange markets themselves. In the third section, we consider exchange transactions in greater detail, focusing on bid and ask rates (that is, the rates at which a bank buys and sells). This also gives us an opportunity to learn about arbitrage. Specifically, in the third section, we shall apply arbitrage arguments to the simplest possible problem, the relation between rates quoted by different banks for the same currency. Understanding this simple application now will make it easier to digest more complicated versions of similar arguments later. One such application occurs in the fourth section, where we use arbitrage arguments to explain how exchange rates quoted, for example, by German banks (in DEM) relate to rates offered by New Zealand banks (in NZD).

1.1 EXCHANGE RATES

As we begin exploring exchange rates, we first provide a definition. We then describe the convention that is used to quote exchange rates throughout this book, as well as other conventions used in the exchange market. Finally, we explain how exchange rates are quoted in the presence of bid-ask spreads.

1.1.1 Definition of Exchange Rates

An **exchange rate** is the amount of a currency that one needs in order to buy one unit of another currency, or it is the amount of a currency that one receives when selling one unit of another currency. An example of an exchange rate quote is USD/CAD 0.8. This means that you can exchange CAD 1 for USD 0.80. One way to think of this is that you can buy a CAD by paying USD 0.80.

It is very important that you understand how exchange rates are calculated and quoted. While you are familiar with the idea of buying goods and services, you may be less used to buying money with money. With exchange transactions, you need to discover which money is being bought or sold. For example, if you deliver CAD and obtain USD, you may be buying USD and paying in CAD or you may be selling CAD and being paid in USD. There would be no ambiguity if one of the currencies were your home currency. A purchase then means that you obtained foreign currency and paid in home currency. A sale means that you delivered foreign currency and received home currency. If neither currency is your home currency, then you need to establish which of the two acts as the reference currency, that is, stands in for the home currency.

Example   1.1

Suppose that CAD 1.25m are delivered to a US investor and in exchange USD 1m are received by a Canadian investor. The US investor and the Canadian investor would view this transaction differently.

- The US investor would view this as a purchase of CAD 1.25m against a total payment of USD 1m, implying a unit price of

$$\frac{\text{USD 1m}}{\text{CAD 1.25m}} = \text{USD/CAD 0.80.}$$

- The Canadian would think of this transaction as a purchase of USD 1m for CAD 1.25m, implying a unit price of

$$\frac{\text{CAD 1.25m}}{\text{USD 1m}} = \text{CAD/USD 1.25.}$$

1.1.2   Our Convention: Home Currency per Unit of Foreign Currency

Once we decide which country is the home or reference country, we can quote exchange rates as the price in units of home currency (HC), per unit of foreign currency (FC). That is, we quote the rate as HC/FC. This is the convention adopted in this text. Under our convention, we say that one unit of foreign currency costs N home currency units (HC/FC), rather than stating that, with one unit of home currency, we can buy $m = 1/N$ units of foreign currency (FC/HC). In short, in this text, the foreign currency is always in the denominator. As we shall see, some countries do it differently.

Example   1.2

1. The quote USD/DEM is an American's natural quote for the DEM; it is the USD price an American gets or pays per DEM. Under our convention, Germans would quote DEM/USD.
2. The quote USD/CAD is an American's natural quote for the CAD, since the CAD is the currency in the denominator.

We adopt this convention because it is the most natural one: it is the convention we use when buying goods. For example, we say "the price is 5 dollars per umbrella" (HC/umbrella) not, "with one dollar you can buy one-fifth of an umbrella" (umbrellas per unit of home currency).[1]

---

[1] Home can be interpreted, of course, as the place where you live. Somewhat more general, "home currency" refers to the currency used in the place where the transaction occurs.

Our convention is standard in continental Europe, and is called the **direct quote**, or the "right" quote.

1.1.3   Other Quoting Conventions

The UK, as well as some former British Commonwealth countries (for instance, Australia, New Zealand, Ireland, and South Africa), use the **reverse quote**, the number of foreign units that can be bought with one unit of home currency, or **FC/HC**. This is called the *foreign currency equivalent of the home currency,* or the **indirect quote**, or "left" quote.

Recall from the previous chapter that until 1972, countries declared an official parity in relation to the USD, and based their intervention policies on this rate. For this reason, US professionals traditionally use the exchange-rate convention as quoted in the other country—for instance, DEM/USD—except in the case of the former British Commonwealth countries where one quotes USD/GBP, for example. *The Wall Street Journal* therefore shows *both* quotes, that is, DEM/USD *and* USD/DEM. Take a minute to look at Figure 1.1 and see if you understand the exchange rates as quoted.

> Q1. What is the dollar equivalent to the German mark based on the quotes in *The Wall Street Journal*?
>
> A1. If your answer is 0.6298 of a USD or 62.98 cents, you are correct.

FIGURE 1.1   Sample Spot Exchange Rate Quotes

Country	US $ equiv	Currency per US $
Australia (Dollar)	.7192	1.3904
Britain (Pound)	1.5420	.6485
France (Franc)	.18524	5.3985
Germany (Mark)	.6298	1.5980
Japan (Yen)	.008997	111.15

Excerpt: *The Wall Street Journal*. April 20, 1993.

	Day's spread	Close
US	1.3750–1.4045	1.3840–1.3850
Canada	1.9354–1.9614	1.9354–1.9388
W. Germany	3.3550–3.4325	3.3900–3.4000
France	10.360–10.505	10.1075–10.1175
Japan	278.25–282.00	279.00–280.00

Excerpt: *Financial Times*. January 22, 1986.

The Wall Street Journal first shows the price of the foreign currency in USD (under the heading "US$ equivalent"— the natural way to quote a price), and then the price of the USD in units of foreign currency ("Currency per US $"— the quote used by professionals). The *Financial Times* shows the number of foreign currency units per pound—the way an American or a Canadian, etc. would naturally quote the value of the GBP. The "Close" column in the *Times* shows two rates, one for selling and one for buying (see Section 1.1.4) at the end of the trading day and also the daily high and low ("Day's spread").

Q2. Determine the amount of Japanese yen per USD.

A2. If you answered 111.15 yen per USD, you are right.

1.1.4   Bid and Ask Rates

When you deal with foreign currency, you will discover that you pay a higher price at the time of purchase than when you sell one currency for another. For example, if you wish to *sell* USD for CAD you will be quoted one rate, say, CAD/USD 1.20, which means that for every USD you sell you will receive CAD 1.20. However, if you wish to *buy* USD, you will be asked to pay more than CAD 1.20—say, CAD 1.21. The rate at which the bank will buy a currency from you is called the **bid rate,** and the rate at which the bank will sell a currency to you is the **ask rate.** Stated differently, you buy at the ask rate, and you sell at the bid rate.

If exchange rates are being quoted with the currency of interest—the currency you are buying or selling—in the denominator, then the ask rate will be higher than the bid rate. The bid rate can be no higher than the ask rate; otherwise, you could make large, risk-free profits by buying at a low ask and immediately reselling at a high bid. No bank will allow you to buy low and then immediately resell at a profit without taking any risk, because your sure gains would obviously mean sure losses for the bank. While a situation "bid rate = ask rate" leaves no room for such arbitrage opportunities, the real-world situation is invariably "bid rate < ask rate." This is how the banks make money from foreign currency transactions. Another way to think of this difference between the ask and the bid rate is that the difference is the bank's commission for exchanging currencies. The difference between the buying and selling rates is called the **spread**, and you can think of the bank's implicit commission as being equal to half the spread. The following example explains why the commission is half of the spread rather than the spread itself.

Example   1.3

Suppose that you can buy CAD at FRF/CAD 4.22, and sell at FRF/CAD 4.18. With these rates, you can think of a purchase as occurring at the midpoint rate (FRF/CAD 4.20), grossed up with a commission of 0.02. Likewise, a sale can be thought of as a sale at the midpoint, 4.20, from which the bank withholds a commission of 0.02. Thus, the commission is the difference between the bid (or ask) and the midpoint rate.

To get an idea of whether your house bank charges a low commission, you can ask for a two-way quote to see if the spread is small. If this is the case, you probably do not have to check with other banks. However for large transactions, you should also compare the spot quotes given by different banks. (This will be examined further in Sections 1.3 and 1.4.) Historically, the lower the volume in a particular market, the higher the spread. In the retail end of the market, the spread increases for smaller transactions.

1.1.5   Inverting Exchange Rates in the Presence of Spreads

The next point is how a pair of quotes for one currency can be translated into a pair of quotes for a different currency. The rule is that the inverse of a bid quote is an ask quote, and *vice versa*. To conceptualize this, consider the following illustration.

Example   1.4

A German investor wants to buy FRF against CAD and contacts his house bank. Being neither French nor Canadian, the bank has no natural preference for either currency and might quote the exchange rate as either CAD/FRF or FRF/CAD.

    The German bank would make sure that its potential quotes are perfectly compatible. If it quotes from a Canadian viewpoint, the bank gives a CAD/FRF quote (which says how many CAD the investor must pay for one FRF—for instance, CAD/FRF$_{ask}$ 2). If it uses the French perspective, the bank gives a FRF/CAD$_{bid}$ quote, which says how many FRF the investor gets for one CAD.[2] The bank's alternative ways of quoting will be fully compatible if:

$$S[CAD/FRF]_{ask,t} = \frac{1}{S[FRF/CAD]_{bid,t}} \qquad [1a]$$

$$S[CAD/FRF]_{bid,t} = \frac{1}{S[FRF/CAD]_{ask,t}} \qquad [1b]$$

    To fully understand this, recall that the ask is the higher of the two quotes. But, if you invert two numbers, the inverse of the larger number will, of course, be smaller than the inverse of the smaller number. Because the inverse of a larger number is a smaller number, the inverse ask must become the bid, and *vice versa*.

Example   1.5

Suppose that you read the following quote in the newspaper: USD/DEM 0.4565–0.4580.

Q1. What is the bank's buying and selling rate for DEM?
A1. The bank's buying rate for DEM is USD 0.4565 and its selling rate is USD 0.4580; or you buy DEM at USD 0.4580 and sell at 0.4565.

Q2. What, therefore, are the bank's buying and selling rates for USD?
A2. The bank's buying rate for USD is 1/0.4580 = DEM/USD 2.1834 and the selling rate is 1/0.4565 = DEM/USD 2.1906; or you buy USD at DEM 2.1906 and sell at 2.1834.

    One corollary is that in countries like the UK, where the reverse or indirect quote is used, the rate relevant when you buy is the lower of the two, while the higher quote is the relevant rate when you sell. Thus, it is important to be aware of what the foreign currency is, and what convention is being used for quoting the exchange rate. Again, it is always easier and more convenient to have the foreign currency in the denominator. That way the usual logic will work: banks buy low and sell high.

---

[2] In this chapter, we will add the dimensions of the quote within square brackets. Later on, we will simply use S_t, without repeating the dimensions.

1.2   MAJOR MARKETS FOR FOREIGN EXCHANGE

In this section, we will describe the size and structure of the exchange market and the type of transactions one can make in this market.

1.2.1   How Exchange Markets Work

The foreign exchange market is not an organized exchange like many stock markets or futures markets, which have fixed opening hours, a centralized clearing mechanism, standardized contracts, and a specific location; rather, the exchange market consists of a **wholesale tier**, which is an informal network of about 500 banks and currency brokerages that deal with each other and with large corporations, and a **retail tier**, where you and I buy and sell foreign exchange. Most interbank dealing is still done over the telephone; most conversations are tape-recorded, and later confirmed by mail, telex, or fax. Reuters, which is already omnipresent with its information screens, is building a computer network which allows direct trading; bank consortia are making similar efforts. Thus, the location of the market is rather unimportant.

Many players in the wholesale market act as market makers. That is, any interested parties can ask market makers for a two-way quote (bid and ask quotes), without having to reveal whether they intend to buy or sell. Such a quote is binding: market makers undertake to buy or sell at the price that was indicated. Of course there are limits to the market makers' commitments to their quotes. First, potential customers should decide almost immediately whether to buy (*mine*), or to sell (*yours*), or not to deal; they cannot invoke a quote made, say, three minutes ago. Second, if the intended transaction exceeds USD 10m, market makers can refuse. For larger transactions, the trader asking for a quote should reveal immediately what the size of the transaction will be.

Another way of dealing in foreign exchange markets is through currency brokers. A bank or corporation can contact a broker, offering to sell, say, DEM 10m at DEM/USD 1.65. The broker, who at any given moment may have open telephone lines with hundreds of banks, will then shop around and see if there are any takers at this price. Roughly half of the transaction volume in the exchange market occurs through brokers.

A typical transaction in USD is about 1m. (Traders often drop the "millions," and refer to "one dollar" or "five dollars.") At any point in time, exchange markets on at least one continent are active, so that the world-wide exchange market is open twenty-four hours a day.

1.2.2   Markets by Location and by Currency

In April 1992, the daily volume of trading on the exchange market and its satellites—futures, options, and swaps—was estimated by the Bank of International Settlements (BIS) at more than USD 1 trillion.[3] This is about five to ten times the daily volume of international trade in goods and services, sixty times the US's daily GDP, eighty times Japan's GDP, and two hundred times Germany's GDP. The exchange market's daily turnover is also equal to the combined reserves of all central banks of IMF member states. That is, if the central banks would want to absorb all exchange trans-

---

[3] The Bank for International Settlements (BIS) was set up after World War II as part of the European Payment Union (EPU), and served as a netting institute for payments among EPU members. By netting the payments, the gross payments were reduced, which alleviated the problems of dollar shortages in the first years after the war. Currently, the BIS acts as a club for central bankers and regulators. One of its missions is to gather data on exchange markets, euromarkets, new financial instruments, bank lending to sovereign borrowers, and so on. The BIS is also the forum where regulators coordinate the capital requirement rules that they impose on financial institutions.

actions, their reserves would be depleted in one day. The major markets were, in order of importance, London (more than USD 300 billion), New York (almost USD 200 billion), and Tokyo (USD 130 billion). Less important markets were Singapore, Zurich, Hong Kong, and Frankfurt (all between USD 60 and 75 billion).

The most important markets, per currency, are the USD/DEM and the USD/JPY markets; together they represent over half of the world trading volume.

1.2.3   Markets by Delivery Date

The exchange market consists of two core segments—the spot exchange market and the forward exchange market.

The **spot market** is the exchange market for payment (of home currency) and delivery (of foreign currency) *today*. For most of this text we shall denote this spot rate by S_t. In practice, today means today *only* when you buy or sell notes or coins. (This section of the market is marginal.) For electronic money (that is, money that will be at your disposal in some bank account), delivery is within two working days for most currencies, and one day between Canada and the US or between Mexico and the US. If you buy DEM 2m today, at BEF/DEM 21, the DEM 2m will be in your account two working days from now, and the BEF 42m will likewise be in the counterpart's account two days from now. The two-day delay is largely a tradition from the past, when accounts were kept by hand.

The **forward market** is the exchange market for payment and delivery of foreign currency at some *future* date, say, three months from now. For example, supposing today is January 3, you could ask your bank to quote you an exchange rate to sell dollars for pounds for a date in March, and the transaction would be settled on that date in March, at the rate agreed upon on January 3 (irrespective of the spot rate prevailing on March 3). The forward market, in fact, consists of as many subsegments as there are delivery dates, and each subsegment has its own price. We shall denote this forward rate by $F_{t,T}$, with T referring to the future delivery date. (Forward rates will be discussed in greater detail in Chapters 2 and 3.)

The most active forward markets are for 30, 90, 180, 270, and 360 days, but bankers today quote rates up to ten years forward. Note that months are indicated as thirty days. A 30-day contract is settled one month later than a spot contract, and a 180-day forward contract is settled six months later than a spot contract—each time including the two-day delay convention.[4]

Example   1.6

A 180-day contract signed on March 2 stipulates delivery and payment on the second working day after September 2, although the actual number of calendar days is 184. You can always obtain a price for nonstandard maturities, too (for instance, 97 days—three months and seven days—or for a specific date).

In London, spot transactions represent about 50 percent of the total foreign exchange market volume. The forward market, together with the closely related swap market (see Chapter 10), make up another 47 percent of the volume. The remaining 3 percent of total trade consists of currency-futures contracts (a variant of forward contracts traded in secondary markets—see Chapter 5) and currency options (see Chapters 6–8).

---

[4] The details of settlement rules are discussed in Grabbe (1992).

1.3   THE LAW OF ONE PRICE FOR SPOT EXCHANGE QUOTES

In frictionless markets, two securities that have identical cash flows must have the same price. This is called the *Law of One Price*. There are two arguments that enforce this law. The first one is called arbitrage and the second one can be called least cost dealing. We explain these two concepts below.

Suppose that two assets or portfolios with identical cash flows do not have the same price. Then, any holder of the overpriced asset could simultaneously sell this asset and buy the cheaper asset, thus netting the price difference without taking on any additional risk. If one does not hold the overpriced asset, one could still take advantage of this mispricing by short-selling the overpriced asset and covering this with the purchase of the cheaper security. Such transactions are called *arbitrage*. These arbitrage transactions will generate an excess supply of the overpriced asset and an excess demand for the underpriced asset, moving the prices of these two assets towards each other. In frictionless markets, this process stops only when the two prices are identical. In the presence of transactions costs, the buying and selling stops when the cost for buying the underpriced asset and selling the overpriced one exceeds the price difference. Note that apart from the arbitrage gain, an arbitrage transaction does not lead to a change in the net position of the arbitrageur; that is, it yields a sure profit without requiring any additional investment.

The second mechanism that enforces the *Law of One Price* is *least cost dealing*. Here, in contrast to arbitrage, investors intend to make particular changes in their portfolios. Least cost dealing implies that when choosing between different ways of making given investments, investors will choose the cheapest way of doing so. Therefore, when choosing between assets with identical cash flows, investors will buy the underpriced assets rather than the more expensive ones. Likewise, when choosing which assets to sell, investors will sell the overpriced ones rather than the ones that are relatively cheap. This demand for the underpriced assets and supply of the overpriced ones will again lead to a reduction in the difference between the prices of these two securities. Note that the difference between the prices of the underpriced and the overpriced asset is bounded by the difference in the transactions cost for trading these assets.[5]

Although the arbitrage and least cost dealing mechanisms both tend to enforce the *Law of One Price*, there are two differences between these mechanisms.

- First, an arbitrage transaction is a round-trip transaction. That is, you buy and sell, thus ending up with the same position with which you started. As arbitrage requires a two-way transaction, its influence stops as soon as the price difference is down to the sum of the transactions costs (buying and selling). In contrast, in least cost dealing one wishes to make a particular transaction, and the issue is which of the two assets is cheaper to trade.[6] As a result, the influence of least cost dealing can go on as long as the price difference exceeds the difference of the two transactions costs.
- Second, arbitrage is a strong force because it does not require any capital. In contrast, least cost dealing will be a price-equilibrating mechanism only if there are investors who wish to make that particular transaction.

---

[5] Denote by P_U and k_U the price and transaction cost when dealing in the underpriced asset, and denote by P_O and k_O the counterparts for the overpriced asset. The advantage of buying the cheap asset rather than the expensive one remains positive as long as $P_U + k_U < P_O + k_O$; that is, as along as $P_O - P_U > k_U - k_O$.

[6] Accordingly, Deardorff (1979) refers to arbitrage as *two-way arbitrage* and to least cost dealing as *one-way arbitrage*.

In this section, we apply these arguments to spot rates quoted for the same currencies by different market makers. In a perfect exchange market with zero spreads, arbitrage implies that the rate quoted by bank X must equal the rate quoted by bank Y: there can be only one price for a given currency—otherwise, there is an arbitrage opportunity.

Example   1.7

If Citibank quotes DEM/USD 1.65, while Chemical Bank quotes DEM/USD 1.6501:

- There is an arbitrage opportunity. You can buy cheap USD from Citibank and immediately sell to Chemical Bank, netting DEM 0.0001 per USD. You will, of course, make as many USD transactions as you can. So will everybody else. The effect of this massive trading is that either Citibank or Chemical Bank, or both, will have to change their quotes. That is, situations with arbitrage profits are inconsistent with equilibrium, and are eliminated very rapidly.
- There is also an opportunity for least cost dealing. All buyers of USD will buy from Citibank, and all sellers will deal with Chemical Bank.

The only way to avoid such trading imbalances is if both banks quote the same rate.[7]

What we want to figure out is how arbitrage works when there are bid-ask spreads. The point is that, because of arbitrage:

- The rates cannot be *systematically* different.
- If the quotes do differ temporarily, they cannot differ by too much.

1.3.1   Arbitrage

Suppose bank X quotes BEF/DEM 20.50–20.55 while bank Y quotes BEF/DEM 20.60–20.65. If you see such quotes, you can make money easily: just buy DEM from bank X at BEF 20.55, immediately resell it to bank Y at BEF 20.60, and pocket a profit worth BEF 0.05 for each DEM. Note two crucial ingredients: (1) you are not taking any risk, and (2) you are not investing any capital since the purchase is immediately reversed. The fact that you immediately reverse the transaction explains why this is called arbitrage. If such quotes are found in the exchange market (or elsewhere, for that matter), large trades by a few alert dealers would immediately force prices back into line. The original quotes would not be equilibrium quotes. In equilibrium, the arbitrage argument says that you cannot make money without investing capital and without taking risk. Graphically, this *no arbitrage condition* says that any two banks' quotes should overlap by at least one point, like the quotes X' and Y in Figure 1.2.

1.3.2   Least Cost Dealing

Least cost dealing implies that even quotes like the pair (X', Y) in Figure 1.2 will not persist for very long. To see this, suppose that bank X' quotes BEF/DEM 20.61–20.66, while bank Y quotes BEF/DEM 20.60–20.65. In such a situation, all buyers of DEM will, of course, prefer to deal with bank Y, which has the lower ask rate (20.65); while all sellers will now deal with bank X', which has the better bid

---

[7] This is often put as "by arbitrage, the quotes must be the same," or "arbitrage means that the quotes must be the same." Phrases like this actually mean that to rule out arbitrage opportunities, the quotes must be the same.

FIGURE 1.2   Bounds Imposed on Spot Rates by Arbitrage Transactions

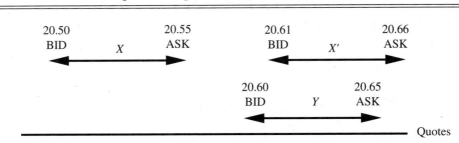

There is strong arbitrage opportunity between banks X and Y: you can buy cheap from X at its ask rate, and resell at a higher bid price to Y. In contrast, if the first bank's quote is X', you cannot profitably buy from either X' or Y and sell to the other.

rate (20.61). It is conceivable that these banks actually want this to happen—for instance if bank X' has a shortage of foreign currency, and bank Y wants to eliminate an excess position. But we would not expect this to be a long-run phenomenon. That is, if both banks want to be in the market for selling *and* buying, their quotes have to be equal.

In perfect markets without transactions costs, where ask equals bid, the implications of arbitrage and least cost dealing are, of course, the same: all quotes must be identical.

1.4   TRIANGULAR ARBITRAGE

Now that we know how exchange rates are quoted and what arbitrage means, let us look at the relationships that exist between spot rates quoted in various currencies. The forces that support these linkages are again arbitrage and least cost dealing.

- Someone engaging in **triangular arbitrage** tries to make money by sequentially buying and selling various currencies, ending with the original currency. For instance, you could convert FIM into USD, and then immediately convert the USD into DEM and the DEM back into FIM, with the hope of ending up with more FIM than you started out with. When there are transactions costs or commissions, the arbitrage condition says that, if you start with one currency and buy another and then immediately buy back the original, you should not make a profit. Actually, you are likely to end up with a loss. The potential loss is due to commissions, that is, the bid-ask spread. Thus, in this context, arbitrage implies that the exchange rates should be such that you cannot make any risk-free instantaneous profits after paying transactions costs.
- **Least cost dealing** is the search for the cheapest way to achieve a desired conversion. For instance, a Finnish investor who wants to buy PTE may buy directly, or may first convert FIM into USD and then convert these USD into PTE. Least cost dealing implies that the direct FIM/PTE market can survive only if its quotes are no worse than the implied rates from the indirect transaction.

In the case of perfect markets, the regular arbitrage and least cost dealing arguments lead to the same conclusion. We illustrate this in the following example.

Example   1.8

Suppose one USD is worth DEM 2, and one DEM is worth BEF 20; therefore, one USD must be worth BEF 40. With this BEF/USD rate:

- Nobody can make a free-lunch profit by any sequence of transactions.
- Everyone is indifferent between direct conversions between two currencies and indirect, triangular transactions.

Below, we see what the implications of arbitrage and least cost dealing are when there are bid-ask spreads. In order to simplify matters, we shall first show how to compute the implied rates from an indirect route. We shall call these implied rates the **synthetic rates**. Having identified these synthetic rates, we can then consider the mechanisms that enforce the *Law of One Price* used before to study the relationship between various quotes.

1.4.1   Computing Synthetic Cross-Rates

In general, a **synthetic** version of a **contract** is a combination of two or more other transactions that achieves the same objective as the original contract. That is, the combination of the two or more contracts *replicates* the outcome of the original contract. We shall use the notion of replication repeatedly in this textbook. For now, consider a simple spot transaction. A German investor wants to buy GBP.

- The investor can use the direct market and buy GBP against DEM. We will call this the original contract.
- Alternatively, the investor can first buy USD with DEM, and then immediately exchange the USD for GBP. This is a combination of two contracts. It replicates the original contract since, by combining the two transactions, the investor pays DEM, and ends up with GBP. Thus, this is a *synthetic* way of achieving the original transaction.

Note that the synthetic contract may be the more efficient way to deal, since the USD market has a lot of volume (or depth) in every country, and therefore has smaller spreads. Let us see how the synthetic DEM/GBP rates can be computed.

Example   1.9

Q. What are the synthetic bid and ask DEM/GBP rates if:

DEM/USD	2.4520–2.4530
USD/GBP	1.3840–1.3850?

A. The dimension of the rate we are looking for is DEM/GBP. Because the dimensions of the two quotes given to us are DEM/USD and USD/GBP, the way to obtain the synthetic rate is to multiply the rates, as follows:

$$\text{Synthetic } S[\text{DEM/GBP}] = S[\text{DEM/USD}] \times S[\text{USD/GBP}]. \qquad [2]$$

Note that on the right-hand side of the equation, the USD in the denominator of the first quote cancels out with the USD in the numerator of the second quote, leaving us with the desired DEM/GBP quote.

Let us now think about bid and ask synthetic quotes. To synthetically buy GBP against DEM, we first buy USD against DEM, that is, at the higher rate (ask); then we buy GBP against USD, again at the higher rate (ask).

$$\text{Synthetic } S[\text{DEM/GBP}]_{\text{ask}} = S[\text{DEM/USD}]_{\text{ask}} \times S[\text{USD/GBP}]_{\text{ask}} \qquad [3]$$
$$= 2.4530 \times 1.3850 = 3.397405.$$

Thus, we can synthetically buy GBP 1 at DEM 3.397405. By a similar argument, we can obtain the rate at which we can synthetically sell GBP against DEM.

$$\text{Synthetic } S[\text{DEM/GBP}]_{\text{bid}} = S[\text{DEM/USD}]_{\text{bid}} \times S[\text{USD/GBP}]_{\text{bid}}$$
$$= 2.4520 \times 1.3840 = 3.393568.$$

Thus, the synthetic rates are DEM/GBP 3.393568–3.397405.

This example is the first instance of the **Law of the Worst Possible Combination** or the **Rip-Off Rule**. You already know that for any single transaction, the bank gives you the worst rate from your point of view (this is how the bank makes money). It follows that if you make a sequence of transactions, you will inevitably get the worst possible cumulative outcome. This *Law of the Worst Possible Combination* is the first fundamental law of real-world capital markets. In our example, this law works as follows.

- For the purpose of selling GBP to the bank, an unfavorable rate is a low rate. Moreover, we are computing a product. The synthetic bid rate for the GBP (the lower rate, the one at which you sell) is the lowest possible product of the two exchange rates, which is obtained by multiplying the two low rates, the bid rates: $S[\text{DEM/USD}]_{\text{bid}} \times S[\text{USD/GBP}]_{\text{bid}}$.
- For the purpose of buying, an unfavorable rate is a high rate. Moreover, we are still computing a product. The synthetic ask (the higher rate, the one at which you buy) is the highest possible product of the two exchange rates, which is obtained by multiplying the two ask rates: $S[\text{DEM/USD}]_{\text{ask}} \times S[\text{USD/GBP}]_{\text{ask}}$.

Let us look at another example, which differs from the first one because it involves a quotient rather than a product. However, in this case, too, we end up with the worst possible outcome.

Example   1.10

Q. What are the DEM/GBP synthetic bid and ask rates, if the quotes are:

DEM/USD	2.3697–2.3725
GBP/USD	0.64371–0.64412?

A. From the dimensions of the quote we are looking for and the dimensions of the two quotes that are given to us, we need to divide DEM/USD by GBP/USD:

$$\text{Synthetic } S[\text{DEM/GBP}] = \frac{S[\text{DEM/USD}]}{S[\text{GBP/USD}]}.$$

To identify where to use the bid and where to use the ask rate, we could explicitly go through the two transactions. The simpler way is to ask the bank to convert the GBP/USD quote into USD/GBP: this transforms the problem into the problem we have already solved. The bank will gladly oblige, and quote:

$$S[\text{USD/GBP}]_{\text{bid}} = \frac{1}{S[\text{GBP/USD}]_{\text{ask}}}.$$

$$S[\text{USD/GBP}]_{\text{ask}} = \frac{1}{S[\text{GBP/USD}]_{\text{bid}}}.$$

We can then simply feed these formulas into the solutions of the previous example, and obtain:

$$\text{Synthetic } S[\text{DEM/GBP}]_{\text{ask}} = \frac{S[\text{DEM/USD}]_{\text{ask}}}{S[\text{GBP/USD}]_{\text{bid}}} = \frac{2.3725}{0.64371} = 3.6857. \qquad [4]$$

$$\text{Synthetic } S[\text{DEM/GBP}]_{\text{bid}} = \frac{S[\text{DEM/USD}]_{\text{bid}}}{S[\text{GBP/USD}]_{\text{ask}}} = \frac{2.3697}{0.64412} = 3.6790. \qquad [5]$$

In Example 1.10, to get the correct DEM/GBP quote, we need to divide the DEM/USD quote by the GBP/USD quote. Thus, to obtain the largest possible outcome (the synthetic DEM/GBP ask rate), we divide the larger number by the smaller; and to obtain the smallest possible outcome (the DEM/GBP bid rate), we divide the smaller number by the larger. This again illustrates the *Law of the Worst Possible Combination*.

1.4.2   Triangular Arbitrage with Transactions Costs

Now that we fully understand synthetic quotes, we can derive bounds imposed by arbitrage and least cost dealing on quotes in the wholesale market. Just think of the direct quotes as the quotes from bank X, and think of the synthetic quotes as the quotes from bank Y. Arbitrage then says that the two bid-ask quotes should overlap by at least one point; otherwise, you can buy cheap in the direct market and sell at a profit in the synthetic market or *vice versa*. Least cost dealing implies that if the direct market is to have customers, its ask should not exceed the synthetic ask, and its bid should not be lower than the synthetic bid. Thus, synthetic rates obtained from USD quotes, for instance, set fairly tight bounds on other cross rates. Figure 1.3 illustrates this reasoning.

The volume and depth of the wholesale market for dollars relative to almost any other currency is so large (and the spreads, therefore, so small) that a substantial part of the nondollar transactions are, in fact, executed by way of the dollar. In the retail markets, most customers have no direct access to cross rates. A French bank, for instance, would give quotes for FRF/DEM and FRF/GBP rates to its customers, but not for DEM/GBP. Should a customer sell DEM and buy GBP, the French bank would actually use the synthetic rates we just derived (as if the customer first went from DEM to FRF and then to GBP). Unless you have an account with a German or UK bank, or enough clout with your home bank, you would have little choice but to accept the large spread implied by the synthetic rates.

FIGURE 1.3   Bounds Imposed on Spot Quotes by Arbitrage and Least Cost Dealing

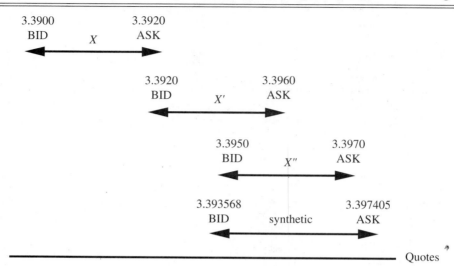

- There is an arbitrage opportunity between direct quote X and the synthetic quotes: you can buy low from bank X at its ask (3.3920), and resell at a higher synthetic bid price (3.393568).
- Compared to the synthetic quote, the direct quote X' attracts buyers only (at 3.3960, below the synthetic ask), while sellers sell at the synthetic rate (3.393568, above the direct bid).
- Compared to the synthetic quote, the direct quote X'' attracts both buyers (at 3.3970, below the synthetic ask) and sellers (at 3.3950, above the synthetic bid).

1.5   IMPLICATIONS FOR THE TREASURER

In this chapter, we have seen how spot markets work. From the treasurer's point of view, the immediately interesting aspect is the possibility for arbitrage and least cost dealing.

- Arbitrage consists of buying and immediately reselling (or *vice versa*), thus taking no risk and engaging no capital. One could try to do this across market makers (for one particular exchange rate) or in a triangular way. In practice, the likelihood of corporate treasurers finding such a riskless profit opportunity is tiny. Arbitrage by traders in the wholesale market eliminates this possibility almost as quickly as it arises. In addition, most firms deal in the retail market, where spreads are relatively wide.
- Least cost dealing consists of finding the best route for a particular transaction. In contrast to arbitrage, least cost dealing may work—not in the sense of creating large profits, but in the sense of saving on commissions. It is generally worth calling a few banks for the best rate when you need to make a large transaction. And it may pay to compute a triangular cross rate, especially through routes that involve heavily traded currencies like the USD or (within Europe) the DEM. Doing such a computation could enable corporate treasurers to find cheaper routes for undertaking transactions as compared to direct routes.

QUIZ QUESTIONS

1. Using the following vocabulary, complete the text: *forward; market maker or broker; least cost dealing; spot; arbitrage; retail; wholesale.*

   "When trading on the foreign exchange markets, the Bank of Brownsville deals with a (a) on the (b) tier, while an individual uses the (c) tier. If the bank must immediately deliver ITL 2 million to a customer, it purchases them on the (d) market. However, if a customer needs the ITL in three months, the bank buys them on the (e) market. In order to purchase the ITL as cheaply as possible, the bank will look at all quotes it is offered to see if there is an opportunity for (f). If the bank finds that the quotes of two market makers are completely incompatible, it can also make a risk-free profit using (g)."

2. From a Frenchman's point of view, which of each pair of quotes is the direct quote? Which is the indirect quote?

   (a) FRF/GBP 9; GBP/FRF 0.11
   (b) USD/FRF 0.17; FRF/USD 5.9
   (c) FRF/BEF 0.17; BEF/FRF 5.9

3. You are given the following spot quote: DEM/CAD 2.2035–2.2070.

   (a) The above quote is for which currency?
   (b) What is the bid price for DEM in terms of CAD?

4. You read in your newspaper that yesterday's spot quote was CAD/GBP 1.60–1.65.

   (a) This is a quote for which currency?
   (b) What is the ask rate for CAD?
   (c) What is the bid rate for GBP?

5. A bank quotes the following rates. Compute the DEM/JPY bid cross-rate (that is, the bank's rate for buying JPY).

	Bid	Ask
DEM/CAD	1.3	1.32
CAD/JPY	0.01	0.012

6. A bank quotes the following rates: CHF/USD 2.5110–2.5140 and JPY/USD 245–246. What is the minimum JPY/CHF bid and the maximum ask cross rate that the bank would quote?

7. A bank is currently quoting the spot rates of DEM/USD 3.2446–3.2456 and BEF/USD 65.30–65.40. What is the lower bound on the bank's bid rate for the BEF in terms of DEM?

8. Suppose that an umbrella costs USD 20 in Atlanta, and the USD/CAD exchange is 0.75. How many CAD do you need to buy the umbrella in Atlanta?

9. Given the bid-ask quotes for JPY/GBP 160–180, at what rate will:

   (a) Mr. Smith purchase GBP?
   (b) Mr. Brown sell GBP?
   (c) Mrs. Green purchase JPY?
   (d) Mrs. Jones sell JPY?

EXERCISES

1. You have just graduated from the University of Florida and are leaving on a whirlwind tour of Europe. You wish to spend USD 1,000 each in Germany, France, and Great Britain (USD 3,000 in total). Your bank offers you the following bid-ask quotes: USD/DEM 0.58–0.60, USD/FRF 0.16–0.18, and USD/GBP 1.48–1.51.

   (a) If you accept these quotes, how many DEM, FRF, and GBP do you have at departure?
   (b) If you return with DEM 300, FRF 1,000, and GBP 75, and the exchange rates are unchanged, how many USD do you have?
   (c) Suppose that instead of selling your remaining DEM 300 once you return home, you want to sell them in Paris. At the train station, you are offered FRF/DEM 3.33–3.55, while a bank three blocks from the station offers FRF/DEM 3.39–3.49. At what rate are you willing to sell your DEM 300? How many FRF will you receive?

2. Abitibi Bank quotes JPY/DEM 63.95–64.72, and Bathurst Bank quotes DEM/JPY 0.0152–0.0154.

   (a) Are these quotes identical?
   (b) If not, is there a possibility for least cost dealing or arbitrage?
   (c) If there is an arbitrage opportunity, how would you profit from it?

The following spot rates against the GBP are taken from the financial press of Wednesday, April 20, 1994. Use the quotes to answer the questions in Exercises 3 through 5.

	Closing midpoint	Change on day	Bid-offer spread
Austria ATS	17.7046	–0.0779	967–124
Belgium BEF	54.7634	–0.2764	230–037
Denmark DKK	9.8653	+0.047	603–702
Finland FIM	8.1350	+0.0134	257–443
France FRF	8.6213	–0.0333	178–248
Germany DEM	2.5144	–0.0144	133–154
Greece GDR	368.429	–1.877	972–886

Bid-ask spreads show only the last three decimal places.

3. What are the bid-ask quotes for:

   (a) ATS/GBP?
   (b) BEF/GBP?
   (c) DKK/GBP?
   (d) FIM/GBP?

4. What are the bid-ask quotes for:

   (a) GBP/ATS?
   (b) GBP/BEF?
   (c) GBP/DKK?
   (d) GBP/FIM?

5. What are the cross bid-ask rates for:
    (a) FRF/DEM?
    (b) FIM/GDR?
    (c) BEF/DKK?
    (d) ATS/DEM?

MIND-EXPANDING EXERCISES

1. When discussing triangular arbitrage and least cost dealing, we considered only the spot market.

    (a) Is it also possible to construct synthetic forward deals?
    (b) If so, what are the synthetic forward bid and ask rates?
    (c) How should the actual (direct) forward rates be related to the synthetic rates?

2. A spot transaction can always be thought of as paying an amount of currency A to the bank, and receiving an amount of currency B in return. Let us define the amount you pay to the bank as your input into the transaction, and the amount you receive in return as the output you get from the transaction. Let us further denote amounts of cash money of currency X by X_t. For example, define USD_t as an amount of immediately available dollars, GBP_t as an amount of immediately available pounds, and so on.

    Let us first familiarize ourselves with the concepts of input and output amounts:

    (a) If you sell an amount USD_t for a total proceeds of DEM_t, which is the input amount? Which is the output amount?
    (b) If you buy an amount USD_t for a total payment of DEM_t, which is the input amount? Which is the output amount?
    (c) If you sell an amount DEM_t for GBP_t, which is the input amount? Which is the output amount?

    We now have to discover which exchange rate, bid or ask, goes with each transaction:

    (d) Define a "factor" to be either S or $1/S$. If the spot rates quoted to you are $S[USD/DEM]_{bid}$ and $S[USD/DEM]_{ask}$, by what factor do you multiply the input amount to compute the corresponding output amount,
       • when you buy DEM with USD?
       • when you sell DEM for USD?
       (Specify whether you multiply by S or $1/S$, and whether you use bid or ask.)
    (e) If the spot rates quoted to you are $S[DEM/GBP]_{bid}$ and $S[DEM/GBP]_{ask}$, by what factor do you multiply the input amount to compute the corresponding output amount,
       • when you buy GBP with DEM?
       • when you sell GBP for DEM?
    (f) In your answer to the two previous questions, verify the *Law of the Worst Rate*:

       • Whenever the multiplication factor is S rather than $1/S$—that is, whenever you multiply an input amount by an exchange rate—you use the smaller exchange rate (the bid rate).
       • Whenever the factor is $1/S$ (that is, whenever you divide), you take the larger exchange rate (the ask rate).

    In short, the relevant rate is the one that produces the smaller output from a given input. Let us now consider triangular arbitrage and least cost dealing.

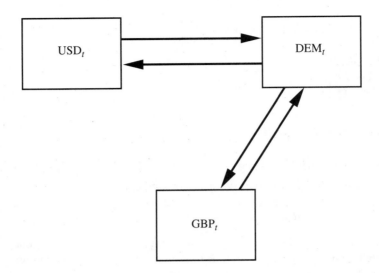

(g) Suppose that you convert an amount USD$_t$ into DEM$_t$, and then immediately convert this latter amount into pounds, what is the ultimate output (in pounds)?

(h) Suppose that you then convert the proceeds GBP$_t$, obtained in question (g), back into dollars. What are the proceeds in dollars?

(i) Use your answer in (h) to verify the *Law of the Worst Possible Combination.*

In the triangular diagram above, a spot transaction is represented by an arrow that starts from the input amount and ends in the output amount. For example, to represent a spot conversion of USD into DEM$_t$, we draw an arrow from the box USD$_t$ (your input) to the box DEM$_t$ (the output to you). The diagram helps you in fully understanding arbitrage and least cost dealing computations.

(j) Complete the diagram by adding, next to each arrow, the factors by which you multiply the input amount to compute the output amount. That is, if you divide an input by an exchange rate S, define the multiplication factor to be $1/S$, as in questions (d) and (e). The rates to be used are $S[\text{USD/DEM}]$, $S[\text{DEM/GBP}]$, or $S[\text{USD/GBP}]$, each time bid or ask.

(k) On the diagram, trace the sequences of transactions described in questions (g) and (h). For example, in question (g), the route followed is USD$_t$ → DEM$_t$ → GBP$_t$. Verify that the ultimate output amount is obtained by multiplying the original input amount by all factors shown next to the arrows you are following.

(l) On the diagram, point out the alternative routes that you consider when you do a least cost dealing computation for converting DEM into GBP.

(m) On the diagram, point out the route that you follow when you verify whether or not there is a triangular arbitrage opportunity when converting USD into DEM, DEM into GBP, and GBP back into USD.

(n) In the above arbitrage computations, what is the ultimate dollar output when you start with an initial dollar input of USD$_t$ = 1? (Hint: follow the arrows, and multiply by the factors next to each of them.) Then derive the no-arbitrage condition.

(o) In doing triangular arbitrage transactions like the one in question (n), does it matter what the starting point is?

(p) Suppose you do arbitrage and least cost dealing over four currencies rather than three. For example, suppose that you add the JPY to the diagram. Is there any additional insight obtained from a comparison of, say, the "quadrangular" sequence USD$_t$ → DEM$_t$→ JPY$_t$ → GBP$_t$ → USD$_t$ to the triangular sequence USD$_t$ → DEM$_t$ → GBP$_t$ → USD$_t$?

2 FORWARD CONTRACTS IN PERFECT MARKETS

In this chapter, we discuss forward contracts in perfect financial markets; that is, we assume that there are no transactions costs. We also assume that there are no taxes, or at least that capital gains (losses) and interest income (interest costs) are taxed in the same way. Finally, we ignore default risk. Some of the implications of these market imperfections will be discussed in later chapters.

In the first section, we describe the characteristics of a forward contract and how forward rates are quoted in the market. In the second section, we show, with a simple diagram, the relationship between the money markets, spot markets, and forward markets. Using the mechanisms that enforce the *Law of One Price*, in Section 2.3, we derive the *Interest Rate Parity Theorem*. In the fourth section, we show how to interpret the forward premium or *swap rate*. The fifth section concludes the chapter.

2.1 INTRODUCTION TO FORWARD CONTRACTS

Let us recall, from the first chapter, the definition of a forward contract. Like a spot transaction, a forward contract stipulates how many units of foreign currency are to be bought (or sold) and at what exchange rate. However, delivery and payment for a forward contract take place in the future (for example, one month from now) rather than quasi-immediately (one or two working days from now) as in a spot contract. The rate that is used for all contracts initiated at time t and maturing at some future moment T is called the time t forward rate for delivery date T. We denote it as $F_{t,T}$.

Like spot markets, forward markets are not organized exchanges, but over-the-counter (OTC) markets, where banks act as market makers or brokers look for counterparts. The most active forward markets are the markets for 30 and 90 days. Contracts for 180, 270, and 360 days are also quite common, and bankers today quote rates up to ten years forward. Recall that any multiple of thirty means that, relative to a spot contract, one extra calendar month has to be added to the delivery date.

Example   2.1

A 180-day contract signed on March 2 stipulates delivery and payment on the second working day after September 2.

You can always obtain a price for non-standard maturities, too; for instance, for ninety-seven days (three months and seven days—plus two working days) or for a specific date. In London, the forward market represents about half of the volume of the exchange markets.

Forward exchange rates can be quoted in two ways. The most natural and simple quote is to give the actual rate, sometimes called the **outright rate**. This convention is used in, for instance, *The Wall Street Journal,* the *Frankfurter Allgemeine,* and the Canadian *Globe and Mail.* The *Globe and Mail* is one of the few newspapers also quoting long-term rates as Figure 2.1 shows.

In Figure 2.1, the CAD/USD forward rate exceeds the spot rate for all maturities. Traders would say that the USD trades at a *premium.* Obviously, if the CAD/USD rate is at a premium, the USD/CAD forward rates must be below the USD/CAD spot rate; that is, the CAD must trade at a *discount.*

The second way of expressing a forward rate is to quote the difference between the outright forward rate and the spot rate—that is, the premium or discount. A forward rate quoted this way is called a **swap rate**. The Antwerp *Financieel-Economische Tijd,* or the London *Financial Times,* for example, follow this convention. Since both newspapers actually show bid and ask quotes, we will postpone actual excerpts from these newspapers until the next chapter where spreads are taken

---

FIGURE 2.1   Spot and Forward Quotes, Outright

Mid-market rates in Toronto at noon, Jan. 6.

	$1 U.S. in Cdn. $	$1 Cdn. in U.S. $
U.S. Canada spot	1.3211	0.7569
1 month forward	1.3218	0.7565
2 months forward	1.3224	0.7562
3 months forward	1.3229	0.7569
6 months forward	1.3246	0.7549
12 months forward	1.3266	0.7538
3 years forward	1.3316	0.7510
5 years forward	1.3579	0.7364
7 years forward	1.3921	0.7183
10 years forward	1.4546	0.6875

Excerpt: *Globe and Mail.* January 7, 1994.

into consideration. Figure 2.2 shows how *The Globe and Mail* quotes would have looked in swap-rate form. In Figure 2.2, the sign of the swap rate is indicated by a plus sign or a minus sign. The *Financial Times* denotes the sign as *pm* (premium) or *dis* (discount).

The origin of the term *swap rate* is the **swap contract**. In the context of the forward market, a swap contract is a spot contract immediately combined with a forward contract in the opposite direction.[1]

Example   2.2

To invest in the US stock market for a few months, a Portuguese investor buys USD 100,000 at PTE/USD 140. In order to reduce the exchange risk, she immediately sells forward USD 100,000 for ninety days, at PTE/USD 145. The combined spot and forward contract is a swap contract. The swap rate, PTE/USD 5, is the difference between the rate at which the investor buys and the rate at which she sells.

To emphasize the difference between a stand-alone forward contract and a swap contract, a stand-alone forward contract is sometimes called an **outright contract**. Thus, the two quoting conventions described above have their roots in the two types of contracts. Today, the outright rate and the swap rate are simply ways of quoting, used whether or not you combine the forward trade with a reverse spot trade.

In the following sections, we demonstrate that the sign of the swap rate is linked to the difference between the interest rates for the two currencies. To explain this relation, we first show how the spot market and the forward market are linked to each other by way of the money markets for each of the two currencies.

FIGURE 2.2   Forward Quotes in Swap Rate Form

Mid-market rates in Toronto at noon, Jan. 6.

		$1 U.S. in Cdn. $	$1 Cdn. in U.S. $
1	month forward	+0.07	−0.05
2	months forward	+0.13	−0.07
3	months forward	+0.18	−0.10
6	months forward	+0.35	−0.20
12	months forward	+0.55	−0.31
3	years forward	+1.05	−0.59
5	years forward	+3.68	−0.05
7	years forward	+7.10	−3.86
10	years forward	+13.36	−6.94

premium or discount, in cents.

---

[1] Confusingly, the terms *swap contract* and *swap rate* can have other meanings, as we shall explain in Chapter 10.

2.2   THE RELATIONSHIP BETWEEN EXCHANGE AND MONEY MARKETS

We have already seen how, using the spot market, one type of currency can be transformed into another at time t. For instance, you pay home currency to a bank and you receive foreign currency. To emphasize the fact that the amounts are delivered immediately, we add the t (= current time) subscript: you pay an amount HC_t in home currency and you receive an amount FC_t of foreign currency. If we similarly denote the future delivery date in a forward contract as T, we can say that the forward market allows you to convert a time-T-dated amount FC_T of foreign currency into a time-T-dated amount HC_T of home currency, and *vice versa*. For instance, at time T, you pay HC_T to a bank and you receive an amount of FC_T.

Intimately linked to the exchange markets are the money markets for the home and foreign country, that is, the markets for short-term deposits and loans. A home currency deposit means that you pay an amount of HC_t to the bank and the bank pays you an amount HC_T at time T; or, more compactly, you transform HC_t into HC_T. If you borrow, you receive an amount HC_t and you pay an amount HC_T to the bank; that is, you transform HC_T into HC_t. There is a foreign money market as well, with a similar function: it allows you to transform FC_t into FC_T, or *vice versa*.

Thus, in this section, we will consider four related markets—the spot market, the forward market, and the home and foreign money markets. One crucial insight we want to convey is that any transaction in one of these markets can be replicated by a combination of transactions in the other three. Let us look at the details.

2.2.1   Spot and Forward Markets

A spot exchange transaction has two sides (or "legs," as swap dealers like to put it). You give a financial institution an amount of one currency, and you receive some amount of another currency. Let us call the former your *input* into the transaction, and the latter your *output*.

Example   2.3

Suppose that you sell DEM 1m for BEF 21m. Your input to the transaction is an amount of DEM_t, that is, a million German marks, and the output from the transaction is the amount of BEF_t, which equals 21 million Belgian francs.

The ratio of the two amounts, or the proportionality factor that allows us to compute the amount of output from the amount of input, is an exchange rate. As we discussed in Chapter 1, it is necessary to agree upon a base currency. In the general discussion, we use the symbol S_t to be interpreted as a [home currency/foreign currency] rate and, for the examples in this and the next section, we use the BEF as the home currency and the DEM as the foreign currency. Thus, in these examples, S_t is the BEF/DEM rate. We need not distinguish between bid and ask because, for the time being, we assume perfect markets.

Let us derive two formulas that relate the output to the input and to the spot rate S_t. Our approach may at first seem slow. However, the merit of a careful and rigorous exposition will become clear when we discuss sequences of transactions and when we extend the analysis to encompass forward contracts on money-market operations. When you sell an amount FC_t (the input), the output amount HC_t can be computed as:

$$HC_t = FC_t \times S_t.$$

FIGURE 2.3   Diagram of Spot Market Transactions

To find the amount HC_t of home currency that is obtained if you convert an amount FC_t, you multiply FC_t by the factor next to the arrow from FC_t to HC_t; that is, $HC_t = FC_t \times S_t$. If you start with an amount HC_t, the resulting foreign currency amount FC_t is, likewise, $FC_t = HC_t \times 1/S_t$.

Likewise, when you deliver an amount HC_t (the input) for conversion into foreign currency, the output amount FC_t can be computed as:

$$FC_t = HC_t \times \frac{1}{S_t}.$$

In these equations, we have intentionally placed the output amount on the left and the input and the exchange rate on the right. Stated differently, we have discovered the proportionality factor (S_t, or $1/S_t$) by which we should *multiply* the input amount in order to find the output amount. This helps us to avoid confusion should we represent these equations (or transactions) in a diagram. We represent spot and forward transactions as going from an input (your initial position, or the amount of money you give to the bank) to an output (your end position, after the transaction; or the amount of money that the bank gives you). The direction of the transaction is shown by an arrow, and the proportionality factor (in this case, the exchange rate or its inverse) is shown next to the arrow. The diagram for spot transactions is shown in Figure 2.3.

Example   2.4

The spot rate S_t is BEF/DEM 21.[2]

1. You convert BEF 63m into DEM. That is, you are going from BEF to DEM. The input amount, BEF_t, is 63m. The output amount, DEM_t, is:

---

[2] In this example, the BEF is the home currency. If there is no obvious home currency—for instance, if you are dealing in two foreign currencies—you may have to check the dimensions of the input-output equation to figure out which rate is to be used where. For example, consider a London trader buying BEF and selling DEM. The input is DEM, and the output is BEF. To obtain the correct dimensions, the proportionality factor must be BEF/DEM: (output) BEF = (input) DEM × [BEF/DEM]. Of course, if the BEF is the home currency, the BEF/DEM is the Belgian investor's natural quote, S_t.

$$\text{DEM}_t = 63 \times \frac{1}{21} = 3\text{m}.$$

2. You sell DEM 2m. This is going from DEM to BEF. The input amount, DEM_t, is 2m. The output amount, BEF_t, then is:

$$\text{BEF}_t = 2\text{m} \times 21 = 42\text{m}.$$

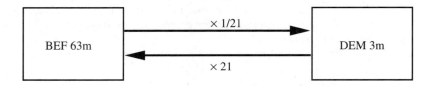

Forward markets can, of course, be represented in the same way. A forward sale of foreign currency means that, today (at time t), you promise to pay foreign currency at a future date, T, and in exchange, you receive future domestic currency at time T. Thus, the input is the amount FC_T; the output is the amount HC_T; and the proportionality factor by which the input has to be multiplied is the current forward rate for that maturity, $F_{t,T}$. Likewise, a forward purchase of foreign currency means that you promise to pay future home currency and, in exchange, you receive future foreign currency at time T. Thus, the input is the amount HC_T; the output is the amount of FC_T; and the proportionality factor by which the input has to be multiplied is the inverse of the current forward rate for that maturity T, $1/F_{t,T}$. Forward transactions are pictured in Figure 2.4.

FIGURE 2.4   Diagram of the Forward Market Transactions

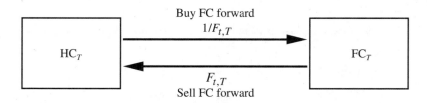

To find the amount HC_t of home currency that is obtained if you convert an amount FC_t, you multiply FC_t by the factor next to the arrow from FC_t to HC_t; that is, $\text{HC}_t = \text{FC}_t \times F_{t,T}$. If you start with an amount HC_t, the resulting foreign currency amount FC_t is likewise $\text{FC}_t = \text{HC}_t \times 1/F_{t,T}$.

2.2.2 Money Markets as Links between Spot and Forward Markets

In this section, we first explain our convention for quoting interest rates, and then move on to show how we convert a quoted interest rate into the effective rate of return. Finally we explain various money market operations, and conclude by showing how these money-market transactions can be combined with transactions in the exchange market to transfer money across time and across currencies.

Our Convention for Expressing Returns on Investments

Let us first agree on the terminology. We define the (effective) **market risk-free (rate of) return** as the simple percentage difference between the initial (time t) value and the maturity (time T) value of a nominally risk-free asset over a certain holding period.

Example   2.5

Suppose that you deposit BEF 100,000 for six months and that the deposit will be worth BEF 105,000 at maturity. The six-month **effective return** is:

$$\frac{105,000 - 100,000}{100,000} = 5\%.$$

You can also invest for nine months. Suppose that the value of this deposit after nine months is 107,200. Then the nine-month effective return is:

$$\frac{107,200 - 100,000}{100,000} = 7.2\%.$$

Of course, at any moment in time, the rate of return you can get depends on the time to maturity, which equals $T - t$ years. Thus, we will give the rate of return, r, two subscripts: $r_{t,T}$. In addition, we need to distinguish between the domestic and the foreign rate of return. We do this by denoting the domestic and the foreign return by $r_{t,T}$ and $r_{t,T}^{*}$, respectively.

It is important to understand that the above returns, 5 percent for six months and 7.2 percent for nine months, are not expressed on an annual basis. This is a deviation from actual practice: bankers always quote rates that are expressed on an annual basis. We shall call such a ***per annum (p.a.)* percentage** an **interest rate**. If the time to maturity of the investment or loan is less than one year, your banker will typically quote you a simple *p.a.* interest rate. Given the simple *p.a.* interest rate, you can then compute the effective return as:

$$r_{t,T} = [\text{time to maturity, in years}] \times [\text{simple } p.a. \text{ interest rate for that maturity}].$$

Example   2.6

Suppose that the *p.a.* simple interest rate for a three-month investment is 10 percent. The time to maturity, $T - t$, is 1/4 years. The effective return, then, is:

$$r_{t,T} = \frac{1}{4} \times 0.10 = 0.025.$$

The convention that we adopt in this text is to express all formulas in terms of effective returns, that is, simple percentage differences between end values and initial values. The alternative would be to express returns in terms of *per annum* interest rates, therefore, writing $(T-t)R_{t,T}$ (where capital R is the simple interest on a *p.a.* basis) instead of $r_{t,T}$. Unfortunately, then all formulas would look more complicated. More fundamentally, there are many ways of quoting an interest rate in *p.a.* terms, such as interest with annual, or monthly, or weekly, or even daily compounding; or banker's discount; or continuously compounded interest. To keep from having to present each formula in many versions (depending on whether you start from a simple rate, or a compound rate, etc.), we assume that you have already done your homework and have computed the effective return from your *p.a.* interest rate. The appendix shows how effective returns can be computed if the *p.a.* rate you start from is not a simple interest rate. The appendix also shows how returns should *not* be computed.

Money-Market Operations

Let us return to the main analysis. Investments and loans—the money market—are important because they form the link between the spot and forward exchanges. A **deposit** (or an investment in commercial paper or T-bills) is a transaction in which you invest money today and receive money in the future; that is, the input in a domestic investment transaction is an amount HC_t and the output is an amount HC_T. The proportionality factor by which the input amount, HC_t, is multiplied in order to find the output amount HC_T is $1+r_{t,T}$, where r is the domestic effective return at time t for expiration day T.

Likewise, a **loan** (or a sale of certificates of deposit, T-bills, or promissory notes) means that you receive money today (the output) and pay back the money in the future (your input into the banking system). For such a transaction, the proceeds of the loan can be computed from the input by multiplying the input amount, HC_T, by $1/(1+r_{t,T})$. For the foreign money market, a similar set of relationships holds, where the foreign return is denoted by $r^*_{t,T}$. Thus, the outputs can be computed from the inputs and the rates of return as follows:

$$\text{Investments}: \quad HC_T = HC_t \times (1+r_{t,T}), \text{ and } FC_T = FC_t \times (1+r^*_{t,T}).$$

$$\text{Loans}: \qquad HC_t = HC_T \times \frac{1}{1+r_{t,T}}, \text{ and } FC_t = FC_T \times \frac{1}{1+r^*_{t,T}}.$$

The diagrammatic version of these money market transactions is shown in Figure 2.5.

Money-Market and Exchange Operations

In Figure 2.6, we combine the four markets we have discussed so far—the spot, forward, and domestic and foreign money markets. This diagram is vital in understanding one-way and two-way arbitrage. Let us first explain how we can analyze a sequence of transactions using the diagram.

As an illustration of how to use the diagram when you make a sequence of transactions, consider a Belgian investor who buys an amount DEM_t, deposits them for six months, and sells forward the proceeds DEM_T in order to obtain a known amount of BEF at time T. Before using the diagram, let us compute the outcome if we start with BEF 1m. Let S_t = BEF/DEM 20, $r^*_{t,T}$ = 0.04 over six months, and $F_{t,T}$ = 20.8. The transactions are:

- Buy spot DEM: the input is BEF 1m, so the output of the spot transaction is:

$$DEM_t = 1m \times \frac{1}{20} = DEM\ 50,000.$$

FIGURE 2.5   Diagram of Domestic and Foreign Money Market Transactions

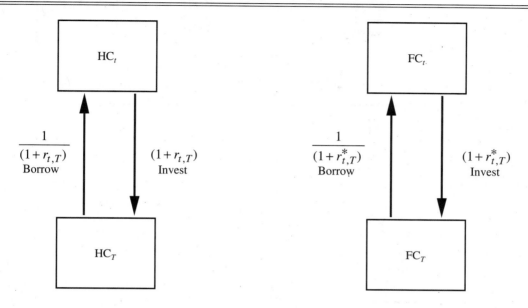

To find the amount HC_T of home currency that is obtained if you invest an amount HC_t, you multiply HC_t by the factor next to the arrow from HC_t to HC_T; that is, $HC_T = HC_t \times (1 + r_{t,T})$. If you start with an amount HC_T, the amount HC_t you can obtain by borrowing against the amount HC_T is:

$$HC_t = \frac{HC_T}{(1 + r_{t,T})}.$$

- Invest these DEM at 4 percent: the input for the money market operation is $DEM_t = 50,000$, so after six months you will receive an output equal to:

$$DEM_T = 50,000 \times 1.04 = DEM\ 52,000.$$

- This future DEM outcome is already sold forward at t; that is, you **cover** or **hedge** the DEM deposit in the forward market so as to make its time-T value risk free rather than depending on the time-T spot rate. The input for this transaction is $DEM_T = 52,000$, and the output in BEF at time T will be:

$$BEF_T = 52,000 \times 20.8 = BEF\ 1.0816m.$$

Using the diagram, let us now illustrate this equation—interpreting home currency as BEF and foreign currency as DEM. First, we identify the route. The input of the first transaction is $BEF_t = 1m$, while the output of the last transaction is $BEF_T = 1.0816m$. To obtain this ultimate

FIGURE 2.6   Diagram of Spot, Forward, and Money-Market Transactions

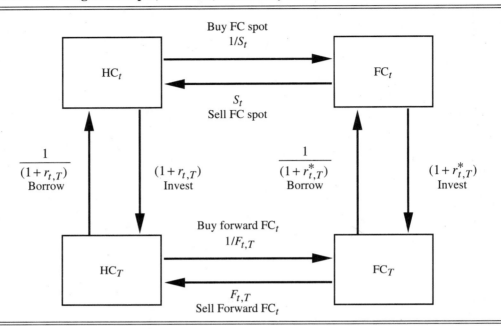

output, we have followed the arrows $\text{BEF}_t \rightarrow \text{DEM}_t$, then $\text{DEM}_t \rightarrow \text{DEM}_T$, and finally $\text{DEM}_T \rightarrow \text{BEF}_T$. To show this more clearly, Figure 2.7 reproduces only the arrows we actually use in this example. In order to quickly calculate the ultimate output (BEF_T) obtained from the first input (BEF_t), we multiply the latter by all of the proportionality factors found along the path that is being followed, and we immediately find the desired result:

$$\text{BEF}_T = 1\text{m} \times \frac{1}{20} \times 1.04 \times 20.8 = \text{BEF } 1.0816\text{m}.$$

The diagram is also a way of keeping track of the transactions in the various markets. Although it does not teach us anything new, once you understand and trust it, you can use it for doing such computations quickly.

Example   2.7

Suppose that a customer of yours will pay DEM 65,000 at time T, six months from now. You decide to sell forward, and take out a BEF loan with a time-T value that, including interest, exactly matches the proceeds of the forward sale. How much can you borrow on the basis of this invoice without taking any exchange risk? We again use $S_t = \text{BEF/DEM } 20$, $F_{t,T} = \text{BEF/DEM } 20.8$, and $r_{t,T} = 0.04$ for six months.

FIGURE 2.7   Spot, Forward, and Money-Market Transactions: A Covered Foreign Currency

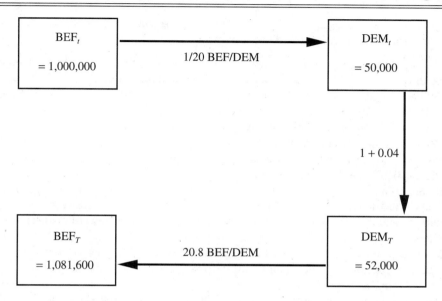

An amount BEF_t 1m is converted into DEM for investment. The proceeds of the DEM deposit are sold forward, at t, for a known amount of BEF at T.

The path chosen starts from $DEM_T = 65,000$. The forward sale brings us to BEF_T, while the loan then brings us to BEF_t. Following the diagram in Figure 2.6, the BEF loan that can be fully serviced using the DEM 65,000 income is:

$$BEF_t = 65,000 \times 20.8 \times \frac{1}{1.04} = BEF \ 13m.$$

To verify this, consider that when the loan matures, you will pay back (including 4 percent interest) BEF 13m × 1.04 = BEF 13.52m. This exactly equals the proceeds of the forward sale, 65,000 × 20.8 = BEF 13.52m.

The advantage of using the diagram will be even more marked when, in the next chapter, we add bid-ask spreads in all markets, and when we study forward forwards or forward rate agreements and their relationship to forward contracts.[3]

---

[3] Forward forwards and forward rate agreements (FRAs) are contracts that fix the interest rate for a deposit or loan that will be made (say) six months from now, for (say) three months. This can be viewed as a six-month forward deal on a three-month interest rate. See Chapter 9.

2.3   THE LAW OF ONE PRICE AND INTEREST RATE PARITY

The sequences of transactions that can be undertaken in the exchange and money markets, as summarized in Figure 2.6, can be classified into two groups.

- You could do a sequence of transactions that forms a **round-trip**. In terms of Figure 2.6, a round-trip means that you start in a particular box, and then make four transactions that bring you back to the starting point. For example, you may consider the sequence $BEF_T \rightarrow BEF_t \rightarrow DEM_t \rightarrow DEM_T \rightarrow BEF_T$. In terms of the underlying transactions, this means that you borrow BEF, convert the proceeds of the BEF loan into DEM, and invest these DEM; the proceeds of the investment are then immediately sold forward for BEF. The question that interests you is whether the BEF proceeds of the forward sale are more than enough to pay off the original BEF loan. If so, you have identified a way to make a sure profit without using any of your own capital. Thus, the idea behind a round-trip transaction is arbitrage, as defined in Chapter 1. The term *arbitrage* here implies that you first go into DEM (by way of the spot market), and then immediately reverse this transaction (in the forward market).
- Alternatively, you could consider a sequence of transactions where you end up in a box that is not the same as the box from which you start. The two sequences we considered in Section 2.2.2 are examples of such **non-round-trip** sequences. Trips like that have an economic rationale. In the first example, for instance, the investor wants to invest BEF for six months. The question here is whether the covered DEM investment ($BEF_t \rightarrow DEM_t \rightarrow DEM_T \rightarrow BEF_T$) yields more than a straightforward BEF investment ($BEF_t \rightarrow BEF_T$). If not, the investor will simply make a BEF deposit. Using the terminology of Chapter 1, this would be an example of *least cost dealing*—shopping around for the best alternative.

We have already seen in Chapter 2 that, in imperfect markets, the implications of arbitrage and least cost dealing are not the same. In particular, the bounds imposed on cross-rate bid-ask quotes by least cost dealing are tighter than the bounds imposed by arbitrage. In this chapter, we consider perfect markets. In such a framework, the inferences that can be made from arbitrage and least cost dealing are identical; still, it is useful to make a distinction already at this point.

2.3.1   Arbitrage and Interest Rate Parity

In this section, we use the arbitrage argument presented above to derive a relationship called the **Interest Rate Parity (IRP)** Theorem. Let us first review how arbitrage arguments work. Suppose that you find a round-trip sequence of transactions that generates a sure profit without requiring any capital. You will make as large a transaction as possible. So will everybody else! The effect of this massive trading is that at least one of the quotes will change rapidly. That is, situations with arbitrage profits are inconsistent with equilibrium, and are eliminated very quickly.

Let us set $T - t$, the maturity in Figure 2.6, equal to six months. We can then look at two alternative round-trip transactions.[4]

---

[4] There are other round-trip transactions, too. For instance, buying DEM_t and immediately selling them back for BEF_t is a round-trip, as is borrowing BEF six months, with reinvestment of the proceeds in BEF six months, etc. In our perfect markets, these transform $BEF_t = 1$ into $BEF_t = 1$, without gain or loss. The sequence of transactions we discuss in the text are the less obvious ones.

1. Borrow BEF for six months. Convert all of it into DEM_t. Invest this amount for six months, and immediately sell forward the amount of DEM_T you will receive six months from now. If that forward sale yields more BEF_T than what is needed to service (pay back) the loan, you have a money machine—which is inconsistent with equilibrium.

   This trip starts with a loan ($BEF_T \to BEF_t$) and goes full circle back to BEF_T. Suppose that you start with $BEF_T = 1$—that is, you start by writing a promissory note that will be worth BEF 1 six months from now. Thus $BEF_t = 1/(1 + r_{t,T})$. Converting this into DEM_t one gets:

$$DEM_t = \frac{1}{1 + r_{t,T}} \times \frac{1}{S_t}.$$

Investing this yields:

$$DEM_T = \frac{1}{1 + r_{t,T}} \times \frac{1}{S_t} \times (1 + r_{t,T}^*).$$

Finally, selling this DEM_T amount forward one gets:

$$\frac{1}{1 + r_{t,T}} \times \frac{1}{S_t} \times (1 + r_{t,T}^*) F_{t,T}.$$

The no-arbitrage condition says that, when starting with $BEF_T = 1$, the forward sale cannot yield more than $BEF_T = 1$:

$$\frac{1}{1 + r_{t,T}} \times \frac{1}{S_t} \times (1 + r_{t,T}^*) \times F_{t,T} \leq 1.$$

This implies that, in equilibrium, the forward rate must satisfy:

$$F_{t,T} \leq S_t \frac{1 + r_{t,T}}{1 + r_{t,T}^*}. \qquad [1]$$

A second bound is imposed on $F_{t,T}$ by the second trip in the opposite direction.

2. Borrow foreign currency (DEM) for six months. Convert the proceeds into domestic currency (BEF) and invest them for six months, and immediately sell forward the proceeds of the BEF deposit (that is, buy forward foreign currency). Again, the proceeds of the forward sale, DEM_T, should not exceed what is needed to service the initial DEM loan. Starting with $DEM_T = 1$, and following the arrows in Figure 2.6, this condition can be written as:

$$\frac{1}{1 + r_{t,T}^*} \times S_t \times (1 + r_{t,T}) \times \frac{1}{F_{t,T}} \leq 1.$$

Or, rearranging:

$$F_{t,T} \geq S_t \frac{1 + r_{t,T}}{1 + r_{t,T}^*}. \qquad [2]$$

By analyzing these two round-trips, we have derived a lower and an upper bound on the forward rate. Clearly there is only one way to reconcile both relations—constraints [1] and [2] imply:

$$F_{t,T} = S_t \frac{1 + r_{t,T}}{1 + r_{t,T}^*}. \qquad\qquad (\textit{Interest Rate Parity}) \quad [3]$$

Equation [3] says that, in equilibrium, the forward rate must be the spot rate adjusted for a factor that depends on the ratio of the domestic and foreign returns. Another way to write this is as follows:

$$1 + r_{t,T} = \frac{1}{S_t} \times (1 + r_{t,T}^*) \times F_{t,T}.$$

Using Figure 2.6, you can verify that the right-hand side computes the proceeds from a covered or hedged foreign currency investment, that is, the proceeds of a trip $\text{BEF}_t \to \text{DEM}_t \to \text{DEM}_T \to \text{BEF}_T$ that starts with $\text{BEF}_t = 1$. The equation itself then says that, when you finance this covered foreign deposit by a home currency loan, you just break even: the return on the covered investment (given by the right-hand side of the equation) exactly matches the cost of the loan (given on the left of the equation). For this reason, the Interest Rate Parity Theorem is often called **Covered Interest Parity**.

This type of arbitrage, and the corresponding relation between forward rates and interest rates, were known to Italian bankers as early as the Renaissance. As far as we know, however, the first published version of Interest Rate Parity is in Cournot's *Recherches sur les Principes Mathématiques de la Théorie des Richesses* (1838). In 1937, IRP was rediscovered by Paul Einzig, a *Financial Times* reporter, who picked it up from London bankers.

2.3.2   Least Cost Dealing

The diagram in Figure 2.6 also tells us that any non-round-trip sequence of transactions can be routed two ways. For instance, you can go directly from BEF_t to BEF_T, or you can go via DEM_t and DEM_T. The latter alternative corresponds to (1) converting your BEF_t capital into DEM_t, (2) investing these DEM_t, and (3) immediately selling forward the future proceeds of the DEM deposit, thus locking in a sure amount of BEF at time T—in short, a covered DEM deposit. Careful investors should compare the alternatives just as financial institutions do for any trip they consider. We now show that, in perfect markets where IRP holds, any two routes from position A to position B must produce the same output.

Example   2.8

Let us check the irrelevance of the route chosen for $\text{BEF}_t \to \text{BEF}_T$ (domestic lending versus covered foreign lending).

- Lend BEF. If we start with $\text{BEF}_t = 1$, we obtain a time T amount worth:

$$\text{BEF}_T = 1 + r_{t,T}.$$

- Alternatively, buy spot (that is, $\text{BEF}_t = 1 \to \text{DEM}_t = \frac{1}{S_t}$). Invest these

$$\text{DEM}_T = \frac{1}{S_t}(1 + r_{t,T}^*),$$

and sell forward the proceeds of the investment, to get:

$$\text{BEF}_T = \frac{1}{S_t}(1 + r^*_{t,T}) F_{t,T} .$$

The ultimate output, per unit of initial input, equals:

$$1 + r_{t,T} \text{ given that } F_{t,T} = S_t \frac{1 + r_{t,T}}{1 + r^*_{t,T}},$$

from the Interest Rate Parity Theorem in [3].

Thus, a covered foreign currency investment produces exactly the same return as an outright home currency investment. This closely resembles our earlier covered-interest arbitrage argument.

In the next two examples, we demonstrate the equivalence of the two ways of making an uncovered DEM investment and taking out a BEF loan, respectively.

Example 2.9

Consider the trip $\text{BEF}_t \rightarrow \text{DEM}_T$ (uncovered investment in foreign currency). The alternatives are:

- Buy foreign currency and invest. Starting with BEF 1, the proceeds (DEM_T) equal:

$$\text{DEM}_T = \frac{1}{S_t}(1 + r^*_{t,T}).$$

- "Replicate" the direct purchase of a foreign deposit by investing domestic currency and converting forward the final value into foreign currency. The proceeds equal:

$$\text{DEM}_T = \frac{1 + r_{t,T}}{F_{t,T}},$$

which equals $\frac{1}{S_t}(1 + r^*_{t,T})$ if Interest Rate Parity holds.

Example 2.10

Let us check the irrelevance of the route chosen for $\text{BEF}_T \rightarrow \text{BEF}_t$ (domestic borrowing versus covered foreign borrowing).

- Borrow BEF. Per unit of BEF_T, we obtain an amount:

$$BEF_t = \frac{1}{1 + r_{t,T}} \, .$$

- Buy forward DEM_T. If we promise the bank one unit of BEF_T, we shall obtain an amount of DEM_T equal to $1/F_{t,T}$. This can be used to service a DEM loan with current value:

$$DEM_t = \frac{1}{F_{t,T}} \frac{1}{1 + r_{t,T}^*} \, .$$

Selling these DEM in the spot market produces an amount:

$$BEF_t = \frac{1}{F_{t,T}} \frac{1}{1 + r_{t,T}^*} \times S_t \, ,$$

which equals $\dfrac{1}{1 + r_{t,T}}$ if $F_{t,T} = S_t \dfrac{1 + r_{t,T}}{1 + r_{t,T}^*}$, from Interest Rate Parity.

This concludes our discussion of least cost dealing.

2.3.3   Convergence

Convergence means that, as the interval $T - t$ decreases, the spot and forward rates tend to become closer to each other. This is common sense. The limit of $F_{t,T}$ for t approaching T, $F_{T,T}$, is an exchange rate for immediate delivery; therefore, $F_{T,T}$ must be equal to S_T. However, convergence also means that the difference between spot and forward—the swap rate—tends to decrease as time to maturity shortens. That is, it is not as if the swap rate could stay roughly constant until one day before expiration and then suddenly drop to zero. To see this, suppose that each day, starting on January 1, you ask your banker for a forward quote for delivery on December 31. There will be a different spot rate each day, and the *p.a.* interest rates change over time. Equation [3],

$$F_{t,T} = S_t \frac{1 + r_{t,T}}{1 + r_{t,T}^*} ,$$

then implies that changes in S_t will be reflected by similar movements in $F_{t,T}$. The equation also implies that, on average, the shorter the life of the contract, the closer the day's forward rate to the day's spot rate. This is because the effective returns, $r_{t,T}$ and $r_{t,T}^*$ tend to become smaller the shorter the interval $(T - t)$. If interest rates were constant over time and equal across all maturities, the swap rate would converge smoothly to zero. In practice, changes in interest rates will make convergence less smooth.

2.3.4   Interest Rate Parity and Causality

As we have seen, in perfect markets the forward rate is linked to the spot rate by pure arbitrage. Such an arbitrage argument, however, does not imply any causality. IRP is merely an application of the *Law of*

One Price, and the statement that two perfect substitutes should have the same price does not tell us where that "one price" comes from. Stated differently, showing $F_{t,T}$ as the left-hand-side variable (as we did in Equation [3]), does not imply that the forward rate is a "dependent" variable, determined by the spot rate and the two interest rates. Rather, what Interest Rate Parity says is that the four variables (the spot rate, the forward rate, and the two interest rates) are determined jointly, and that the equilibrium outcome should satisfy Equation [3]. The fact that, in London, the spot market represents only 50 percent of the total turnover likewise suggests that the forward market is not just an appendage to the spot market. Thus, it is impossible to say, either in theory or in practice, which is the tail and which is the dog.

Although IRP itself does not say which term causes which, many economists and practitioners have theories about one or more terms that appear in the Interest Rate Parity Theorem. One such theory is the Fisher equation, which says that interest rates reflect expected inflation and the real return that investors require. Another theory suggests that the forward rate reflects the market's expectation about the (unknown) future spot rate, $\tilde{S}_T$.[5] We shall argue in the next chapter that the latter theory is true in a risk-adjusted sense and, we shall return to the Fisher equation in Chapter 14. First, we will discuss alternative ways of quoting forward rates.

2.4   INTERPRETING THE FORWARD PREMIUM OR DISCOUNT

In this section, we use the Interest Rate Parity Theorem, Equation [3], to interpret the premium or discount, and we discuss the merits and the flaws of simplifications that are sometimes used to compute or evaluate swap or forward rates. First, we look at the swap rate, that is, the premium or discount expressed in units of home currency. We then consider the premium as a percentage of the spot rate.

2.4.1   The Swap Rate

When the forward rate exceeds the spot rate, the foreign currency is said to be *at a premium.* Otherwise, the currency is *at a discount* ($F_{t,T} < S_t$), or *at par* ($F_{t,T} = S_t$). In this text, we often use the word *premium* irrespective of its sign; that is, we treat the discount as a negative premium. From [4], the sign of the premium uniquely depends on the sign of $r_{t,T} - r^*_{t,T}$:

$$F_{t,T} - S_t = S_t \left[\frac{1 + r_{t,T}}{1 + r^*_{t,T}} - 1 \right] = S_t \, \frac{r_{t,T} - r^*_{t,T}}{1 + r^*_{t,T}}. \tag{4}$$

Thus, a higher domestic return means that the forward rate is at a premium, and *vice versa.*

As noted in our introduction to forward contracts, the forward premium or swap rate, $F_{t,T} - S_t$, is one way of quoting a forward rate. Market makers sometimes prefer to quote the forward rate as a swap rate rather than as an outright rate because, in the short run, changes in the theoretical swap rate are minimal. Within a day, for instance, interest rates are rather stable, which means that the fraction on the right-hand side of Equation [4] is constant for hours. Moreover, within a time span of a few hours, the movements of the spot rate stay within a limited range. As a result, the swap rate does not vary very much within short time spans. If you see the spot rate move up by five points (0.05 cents), you will probably also see that the forward rate moves up by about five points. In the

---

[5] We use a *tilde* (~) above a symbol to indicate that the variable is random or uncertain.

following example, we compute the swap rate in the correct way for two spot rates that are close to each other, and see how the correctly computed swap rate varies with spot rate.

Example   2.11

Let S_t = FRF/DEM 3, and let the 180-day FRF and DEM simple interest rates be 0.16 and 0.10 *p.a.*, respectively, implying $r_{t,T} = 0.16/2 = 0.08$ and $r^*_{t,T} = 0.10/2 = 0.05$. Then, after rounding, $F_{t,T} = 3 \times 1.08/1.05 = 3.0857$ is the outright quote. The swap rate, $F_{t,T} - S_{t,T}$, is 0.0857, quoted as +0.0857 (or 0.0857pm).

Suppose that a few hours later, the spot rate has changed from 3 to 3.02, but the interest rates are still the same. The new theoretical forward rate is $3.02 \times 1.08/1.05 = 3.1063$, implying a premium of 0.0863. This differs insignificantly from the swap rate at $S_t = 3$, which was 0.08657. Conversely, the error in setting the forward rate as the (new) spot rate, 3.02, plus the (old) swap rate, 0.08657, would have been insignificant.

Thus, working with a constant swap rate, while not fully correct, is a reasonably good approximation. In practice, the small deviations between the correct value and the approximate quote will not trigger arbitrage opportunities because the approximation will be dominated by bid-ask spreads.

2.4.2   The Percentage Premium or Discount

The second way to express the premium or discount is to quote it as a percentage, or even as an annualized percentage. Annualization is linear. For example, a three-month forward premium is annualized by multiplying it by four (or by dividing it by one-fourth, the contract's remaining life in years).

Example   2.12

Let S_t = FRF/DEM 3, $T - t = 0.5$ years, and $F_{t,T} = 3.0857$. The swap rate is 0.0857, and the percentage *p.a.* premium is therefore:

$$\frac{1}{T-t} \frac{F_{t,T} - S_t}{S_t} = \frac{1}{0.5} \frac{0.0857}{3} = 5.713\%.$$

If maturities are short and *p.a.* interest rates low, the annualized percentage premium is roughly equal to the difference in the simple interest rates. To understand this, note that Equation [4] can be written as:

$$\frac{1}{T-t} \frac{F_{t,T} - S_t}{S_t} = \frac{\left[\dfrac{r_{t,T} - r^*_{t,T}}{T-t}\right]}{1 + r^*_{t,T}}. \qquad [5]$$

The left-hand side is the linearly annualized forward premium, while the expression between the square brackets on the right is the difference between the linearly annualized returns—the simple *p.a.* interest rate differential. Historically, forward contracts tended to be made for short periods (usually one or three months), and interest rates were low.[6] Under these circumstances, the division by $(1 + r^*_{t,T})$ in Equation [5] would matter very little. Thus, busy traders, without pocket calculators or desk computers, ignored this division as a second-order refinement, and instead compared the *p.a.* percentage forward premium to the interest differential. Today, longer maturities are quite common and, by previous standards, interest rates are often high. Under these circumstances, the old rule of thumb can be rather misleading, as the following example shows.

Example   2.13

We start with a scenario characterized by a short time to maturity and low interest rates. Let $S_t = 10$, and $T - t = 1/12$ years (one month). The foreign and domestic simple interest rates are 5 percent and 4 percent *p.a.*, respectively. From Equation [5], the theoretical annualized percentage forward premium is:

$$\frac{4\% - 5\%}{1 + \dfrac{1}{12}(0.05)} = -0.996\%,$$

which is approximately the same as the *p.a.* interest differential, $4\% - 5\% = -1\%$. Now consider an example with double-digit interest rates and a longer maturity: let $S_t = 10$, and $T - t = 0.75$ years (nine months), with foreign and domestic simple interest rates of 14 percent and 10 percent, respectively. The theoretical forward premium, in percent per year, is:

$$\frac{10\% - 14\%}{1 + \dfrac{9}{12}(0.14)} = -3.62\%,$$

which now differs significantly from the *p.a.* interest differential, $10\% - 14\% = -4\%$.

This finishes our discussion of the uses and abuses of swap rates and forward premia quoted in percentage *p.a.* terms.

2.5   CONCLUDING REMARKS

In this chapter, we have analyzed forward contracts in a perfect market. We have discovered that forward contracts are essentially packaged deals, that is, transactions that are equivalent to a combination of a loan in one currency, a spot transaction, and a deposit in the other currency. In this sense, the forward contract is a distant forerunner of financial engineering. Finally, we have seen how exchange

---

[6] During the Napoleonic Wars, for instance, the UK issued perpetual (!) debt (the consolidated war debt, or *consol*) with an interest rate of 3.25 percent. Toward the end of the nineteenth century, Belgium issued perpetual debt with a 2.75 percent coupon. Barring episodes of hyperinflation, interest rates in the West stayed far below 10 percent until the 1970s.

markets and money markets are interlinked and can be used for arbitrage transactions and for finding the least cost way to make a particular transaction.

In perfect markets, it does not matter whether one uses forward contracts as opposed to their money-market replications. For instance, a German firm will not win or lose if it replaces a DEM deposit by a covered USD deposit since, from Interest Rate Parity, the two are equivalent. Note in passing that the DEM deposit is being compared to a *covered* USD deposit. It does matter, even in perfect markets, whether the firm invests its funds in DEM or (uncovered) USD. In terms of the diagram in Figure 2.6, it matters what particular end point is chosen, but not how that particular end point is reached.

We shall argue, in Chapter 4, that market imperfections weaken the above conclusions. As soon as there are bid-ask spreads, the way one chooses to go from a given starting point to a particular end point does matter (although one should not expect to make huge extra returns). However, as we shall show in Chapter 3, a surprising number of interesting conclusions and insights can be obtained even before introducing market imperfections.

QUIZ QUESTIONS

1. Suppose that the CAD/GBP rate is 2, and the 360-day interest rates are 10 percent for the CAD, and 21 percent for the GBP.
   (a) What is the forward rate for 360 days?
   (b) What is the swap rate?
   (c) What is the (percentage) forward premium?
   (d) What is the annualized forward premium?
   (e) How well does the simple interest differential (–11 percent) perform as a yardstick for evaluating the forward premium quoted by a bank?

2. Suppose that the JPY/USD rate is 200, and the 90-day interest rates are 8 percent *p.a.* for the JPY, and 10 percent *p.a.* for the USD.
   (a) What is the forward rate for 90 days?
   (b) What is the swap rate?
   (c) What is the (percentage) forward premium?
   (d) What is the annualized forward premium?
   (e) How well does the simple interest differential (–2 percent) perform as a yardstick for evaluating the forward premium quoted by a bank?

3. When quoting a swap rate, some veteran traders do not even bother to mention whether they have a discount or a premium in mind. How can you tell whether you should add the swap rate or subtract it from the spot rate to obtain the outright forward quote?

4. Which of the following statements are true?
   (a) Interest Rate Parity implies that the forward exchange rate converges to the spot exchange rate as the delivery date for the forward contract approaches.
   (b) Because the volume of trading on the spot market is greater than on the forward, the spot market "drives" the forward market.
   (c) Interest Rate Parity means that the foreign and domestic interest rates must be equal.
   (d) The causality implied by Interest Rate Parity means that the forward rate can be predicted from the spot exchange rate and the foreign and domestic interest rates.

5. From the perspective of a German company, which of the following are examples of covered or hedged transactions that do not involve any foreign exchange risk?
   (a) A USD 1 million accounts receivable.
   (b) A forward purchase of JPY 1 billion to be used for accounts payable due in three months.
   (c) A DEM investment.
   (d) A FRF 10 million investment that will expire in six months along with a FRF 5 million accounts payable due in six months.

EXERCISES

1. You are given the following data: the spot exchange rate is BEF/DEM 21; the *p.a.* simple interest rate on a three-month deposit is 8 percent in Belgium and 6 percent in Germany.

Compute:

(a) The time-T DEM value of a DEM$_t$ 1 investment.
(b) The time-t BEF value of a BEF$_T$ 1 loan.
(c) The forward rate for a three-month forward contract.
(d) The time-T BEF proceeds from a DEM$_T$ 1 forward sale, given the forward rate computed in (c).
(e) The present value of the proceeds in question (d).
(f) The time-t BEF value of a DEM$_t$ 1 spot sale.
(g) The value, in BEF$_t$, of the proceeds of a DEM$_T$ 1 loan.

2. You are given the following data: the spot exchange rate is CAD/DEM 0.75; the $p.a.$ simple interest rate on a six-month deposit is 4 percent in Canada and 6 percent in Germany. Compute:

(a) The forward rate for a three-month forward contract.
(b) The time-T CAD value of a CAD$_t$ 1 investment.
(c) The time-t DEM value of a DEM$_T$ 1 loan.
(d) The time-T DEM value of a CAD$_T$ 1 forward sale, given the forward rate computed in (c).
(e) The time-t DEM value of a CAD$_t$ 1 spot sale.

3. A Japanese manufacturer has an accounts receivable of USD 1 million due in 90 days. The spot and forward exchange rates are JPY/USD 110 and 109.8, respectively, and the simple interest rate for a three-month deposit is 2 percent $p.a.$ in Japan and 3 percent $p.a.$ in the US.

(a) If the manufacturer sells the USD 1 million forward for 90 days, how many JPY will she receive at time T?
(b) How could she replicate a forward sale in the spot and money markets?
(c) Is the manufacturer indifferent between (a) and (b)?
(d) If the manufacturer has a preference, is this an example of least cost dealing or arbitrage?

4. Given the following data, are there any arbitrage opportunities? If so, how would you make a risk-free profit?

	Spot rate, S_t	Forward rate, $F_{t,T}$	$r_{t,T}$	$r^*_{t,T}$
(a) BEF/DEM	20.5	20.60	3.5%	2.5%
(b) JPY/NLG	57.5	57.10	1.25%	3.0%
(c) ITL/FRF	283.0	285.73	4.5%	3.5%
(d) CHF/GBP	2.2	2.18	2.0%	3.0%

5. In the years between the two World Wars, UK investment bankers and brokers attracted USD deposits by offering the GBP interest rate plus the (annualized) percentage (%) forward premium. Would the resulting USD rate be too high or too low? Check how well the formula works when:

(a) The deposit has a thirty-day life, and UK and US rates are 3 percent and 2.5 percent (annualized), respectively;
(b) The deposit has a 360-day life, and UK and US rates are 12 percent and 8 percent (annualized), respectively.

MIND-EXPANDING EXERCISE

1. You have a long open position; that is, you are expecting a future foreign currency inflow. Under what conditions would you be indifferent between hedging this position via a forward transaction and hedging it via the money markets if the position is:

   (a) A foreign currency inflow that you would like to hedge.

   (b) A foreign currency accounts receivable that you would like to finance; that is, you would like to borrow now against the expected proceeds of the accounts receivable inflow (sell forward and borrow against proceeds in domestic currency, versus borrow foreign currency and sell the proceeds in the spot market, etc.).

INTEREST RATES, RETURNS, AND BOND YIELDS

2A.1 Links between Interest Rates and Effective Returns

We have defined the effective (rate of) return as the percentage difference between the initial (time t) value and the maturity (time T) value of a nominally risk-free asset over a certain holding period. For instance, suppose you deposit BEF 100,000 for six months, and the deposit is worth BEF 105,000 at maturity. The six-month effective return is:

$$\frac{105,000 - 100,000}{100,000} = 5\%.$$

In reality, bankers never quote effective rates of returns; they quote interest rates. An interest rate is an annualized return, that is, a return extrapolated to a twelve-month horizon. In the text, we emphasize this by adding an explicit *per annum* (or *p.a.*) qualification whenever we mention an interest rate. However, annualization can be done in many ways. It is also true that, for any system, there is a corresponding way to de-annualize the interest rate into the effective return—the number you need.

- Annualization can be *simple* (or linear): 5 percent for six months is extrapolated linearly, to 10 percent *per annum* (*p.a.*). A simple interest rate is the standard method for term deposits and straight loans when the time to maturity is less than one year. Conversely, the effective return is computed from the quoted simple interest rate as

$$1 + r_{t,T} = 1 + \{(T - t) \times [\text{simple interest rate}]\}.$$

Example 2A.1

Let $(T - t) = 1/2$ year, and the simple interest rate 10 percent *p.a.* Then:

$$1 + r_{t,T} = 1 + \left\{ \frac{1}{2} \times 0.10 \right\} = 1.05.$$

- Annualization can also be *compounded*, with a hypothetical reinvestment of the interest. Using this convention, an increase from 100 to 105 in six months would lead to an extrapolated growth of $105 \times 1.05 = 110.25$ after another six months. Thus, under this convention, 5 percent over six months corresponds to 10.25 percent *p.a.* Conversely, the return is computed from the quoted compound interest rate as:

$$1 + r_{t,T} = (1 + [\text{compound interest rate}])^{(T - t)}.$$

Example 2A.2

Let $(T - t) = 1/2$, and the compound interest rate 10.25 percent *p.a.* Then:

$$1 + r_{t,T} = (1 + 0.1025)^{1/2} = 1.05.$$

Compound interest is the standard method for loans and investments (without interim interest payments) exceeding one year.

- Banks can also compound the interest every quarter, every month, or even every day. The result is an odd mixture of linear and exponential methods. If the interest rate for a six-month investment is i *p.a.*, compounded m times per year, the bank gives you i/m per subperiod of $1/m$ year. For instance, the *p.a.* interest note may be $i = 12$ percent, compounded four times per year. This means you get $12/4 = 3$ percent per quarter. Your investment has a maturity of six months, which corresponds to two capitalization periods (of one quarter each). After compounding over these two quarters, an initial investment of 100 grows to $100 \times (1.03)^2 = 106.09$, implying an effective rate of return of 6.09 percent. Conversely, the effective return is computed from the quoted interest rate as:

$$1 + r_{t,T} = \left(1 + \frac{[\text{interest rate}]}{m}\right)^{(T-t) \times m}.$$

Example 2A.3

Let $(T - t) = 1/2$, and the quoted interest rate $= 9.878$ percent *p.a.* to be compounded every quarter (that is, $m = 4$). Then:

$$1 + r_{t,T} = \left(1 + \frac{0.09878}{4}\right)^{1/2 \times 4} = 1.05.$$

- In the theoretical literature, the frequency of compounding is often carried to the limit ("continuous compounding," $m \to \infty$). From your basic math course, you probably remember that:

$$\lim_{m \to \infty} \left(1 + \frac{[\text{interest rate}]}{m}\right)^m = e^{[\text{interest rate}]},$$

where $e = 2.7182818$ is the base of the natural (Neperian) logarithm. Conversely, the return is computed from the quoted interest rate as:

$$1 + r_{t,T} = e^{[\text{interest rate}] \times (T-t)}.$$

Example   2A.4

Let $(T - t) = 1/2$, and assume the continuously compounded interest rate equals 9.75803 percent. Then:

$$1 + r_{t,T} = e^{0.0975803 \times 1/2} = 1.05.$$

- Bankers' discount is yet another way of annualizing a return. This is often used when the present value is to be computed for T-bills, promissory notes, and so on—instruments where the time-T value (or **face value**) is known. Suppose the time-T value is 100, the time to maturity is 0.5 years, and the *p.a.* discount rate is 14 percent. The present value will then be computed as $100 \times (1 - 1/2 \times 0.14) = 93$. In other words, the discount, $100 - 93 = 7$, is just the face value (100), multiplied by $1/2 \times$ [bankers' discount rate] = 7 percent. Conversely, the return is found from the quoted bankers' discount rate as:

$$1 + r_{t,T} = \frac{\text{face value}}{\text{face value} \times \{1 - (T - t) \times [\text{discount rate}]\}}$$

$$= \frac{1}{1 - (T - t) \times [\text{discount rate}]}.$$

Example   2A.5

Let $(T - t) = 1/2$ and the *p.a.* bankers' discount rate = 9.5238 percent. Then:

$$1 + r_{t,T} = \frac{1}{1 - 1/2 \times 0.095238} = 1.05.$$

In summary, there are many ways in which a bank can tell its customer that the effective return is, for instance, 5 percent. It should be obvious that what matters is the effective return, not the stated *p.a.* interest rate or the method used to annualize the effective return. For this reason, in most of this text, we use effective returns. This allows us to write simply $1 + r_{t,T}$. If we had used annualized interest rates, all formulas would look somewhat more complicated, and would consist of many versions, one for each possible way of quoting a rate.

2A.2   Common Pitfalls in Computing Effective Returns

In conclusion, we describe the most common mistakes when computing effective returns. The first is forgetting to de-annualize the return. Always convert the bank's quoted interest rate into the effective return over the period $(T - t)$.

Example   2A.6

Let $T - t = 0.5$ years. What are the effective rates of return when a banker quotes a 12 percent *p.a.* rate, to be understood as (1) simple interest, (2) standard compound interest, (3) interest compounded quarterly, (4) interest compounded monthly, (5) interest compounded daily, (6) interest compounded continuously, and (7) bankers' discount rate?

Bank's quote	$1 + r_{t,T}$	
12%, simple interest	$1 + 0.12 \times 0.5$	$= 1.06$
12%, compound	$(1 + 0.12)^{0.5}$	$= 1.05830$
12%, compounded quarterly	$(1 + 0.12/4)^2$	$= 1.06090$
12%, compounded monthly	$(1 + 0.12/12)^6$	$= 1.06152$
12%, compounded daily	$(1 + 0.12/360)^{180}$	$= 1.06183$
12%, continuously compounded	$e^{0.12 \times 0.5}$	$= 1.06184$
12%, bankers' discount	$\dfrac{1}{1 - 0.12 \times 0.5}$	$= 1.06383$

Second, it is important to remember that there is an interest rate (or a discount rate) for every maturity, $(T - t)$. For instance, if you make a twelve-month deposit, the *p.a.* rate offered is likely to differ from the *p.a.* rate on a six-month deposit. Students sometimes forget this, because basic finance courses occasionally assume, for expository purposes, that the *p.a.* compound interest rate is the same for all maturities. Thus, there is a second pitfall to be avoided—using the wrong rate for a given maturity.

The third pitfall is confusing an interest rate with an internal rate of return on a complex investment. Recall that the return is the simple percentage difference between the maturity value and the initial value. This assumes that there is only one future cash flow, though many investments and loans carry numerous future cash flows. We shall discuss interest rates on multiple-payment instruments in Chapter 9. For now, simply remember that the interest rate on, say, a five-year loan with annual interest payments should not be confused with the interest rate on a five-year instrument with no intermediate interest payments (zero-coupon bond).

3

THE VALUE OF A FORWARD CONTRACT AND ITS IMPLICATIONS

In this chapter, we continue our discussion of forward contracts in perfect financial markets. The focus is no longer on the mechanics of forward trading and pricing—how a forward rate is related to the spot rate and the interest rates, or how the *Law of One Price* works. Rather, we now concentrate on deriving the value of a forward contract at inception, during its life, and at expiration. From our discussion, it will emerge that the forward rate reflects the market's risk-adjusted expectations about the future spot rate. This insight has far-reaching implications for financial reporting and decision making, for the pricing of exports, and for the firm's invoicing and risk-management policies.

In the first section, we determine the value of an outstanding forward contract. In Section 3.2, we consider a forward contract at expiration and a contract at inception. We will see that the forward rate is the risk-adjusted expected value or certainty equivalent of the future spot rate—a crucial concept for understanding many corporate finance issues and asset-pricing theories. In the third section, we discuss the corollaries of the certainty-equivalent property for financial reporting. The final section highlights the implication of the certainty-equivalent property for pricing and hedging policies.

3.1 THE MARKET VALUE OF AN OUTSTANDING FORWARD CONTRACT

In this and the next section, we discuss the market value of a forward contract at its inception, during its life, and at expiration. As is the case for any asset or portfolio, the market value of a forward contract is the price at which it can be bought or sold in the market.[1] The focus, in this section, is on the value of a forward contract that was written in the past but that has not yet matured. For instance, three

---

[1] You should not confuse the pricing with the issue of how useful a forward contract is or can be. Air, for instance, is useful but we can get it for free.

months ago (at time t_0), we may have bought a six-month forward contract for USD at $F_{t_0,T} =$ BEF/USD 40. This means that we now have an outstanding three-month contract, initiated at the rate of BEF/USD 40. This outstanding contract differs from a newly signed three-month forward purchase because the latter is initiated at the now-prevailing three-month forward rate, say BEF/USD 42. The question then is, how should we value the outstanding forward contract? This value is relevant for a number of reasons. At the theoretical level, the market value of a forward contract plays an important role in the theory of options, as we shall see later on. In day-to-day business, the value of an outstanding contract can be relevant in the following circumstances:

- If we want to negotiate early settlement of the contract.
- If there is default and the injured party wants to file a claim.
- If a firm wishes to "mark to market" the book value of its foreign-exchange positions in its financial reports.

Let us agree that, unless otherwise specified, "a contract" refers to a forward purchase of one unit of foreign currency. Today, at time t, we are considering a contract that was signed in the past, at time t_0, for delivery of one unit of foreign currency to you at T, against payment of the initially agreed-upon forward rate, $F_{t_0,T}$. Note the convention that we have adopted for indicating time: the current date is always denoted by t, the past by t_0, and the future (maturity) date by T. We shall derive the current market value of this outstanding contract in two ways, by **replication** and by **hedging**. Understanding these approaches now will help you to understand option pricing models later.

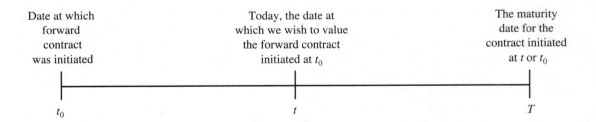

| Date at which forward contract was initiated | Today, the date at which we wish to value the forward contract initiated at t_0 | The maturity date for the contract initiated at t or t_0 |

t_0 t T

3.1.1   The Hedging Approach

Consider what happens if you close out the outstanding contract. That is, to the existing forward purchase contract you add a forward sales contract for the same expiration day (Figure 3.1). The new contract is, of course, at the current forward rate, $F_{t,T}$. At time T, you receive one unit of foreign currency, and you pay $F_{t_0,T}$ for it. (This is the cash flow from the old contract.) The new contract, initiated at time t, requires that you deliver one unit of foreign currency for which you get $F_{t,T}$. Therefore, the net remaining cash flow at time T becomes the *risk-free* amount $F_{t,T} - F_{t_0,T}$, and its present value is

$$\frac{F_{t,T} - F_{t_0,T}}{1 + r_{t,T}}.$$

Thus,

Value of a forward contract at time t that was initiated at t_0 at rate $F_{t_0,T} = \dfrac{F_{t,T} - F_{t_0,T}}{1 + r_{t,T}}.$ [1a]

FIGURE 3.1 Market Value of an Outstanding Forward Contract: The Hedging Approach

Cash flows at T from a forward purchase contract initiated at t_0 at the historic rate $F_{t_0,T}$	Cash flow at time T from hedging, that is, adding at time t, a forward sale at the rate $F_{t,T}$	Cash flow at time T from the original and the new forward
Leg 1: Inflow FC 1	Outflow FC 1	0
Leg 2: Outflow $F_{t_0,T}$	Inflow $F_{t,T}$	$F_{t,T} - F_{t_0,T}$
	Immediate outlay: 0	Present value: $\dfrac{F_{t,T} - F_{t_0,T}}{1 + r_{t,T}}$

FC = foreign currency

Example 3.1

If a trader buys a one-year forward contract for DEM 10m from bank A at BEF/DEM 21, and five minutes later sees the rate move up to 21.01, she will be happy. Her first contract is now a bargain. She could lock in her gain by selling DEM 10m at the new forward rate 21.01 to bank B. If she decides to do so, at expiration the net situation will be as depicted in Figure 3.2. That is, without any immediate outlay, she can transform the risky flows from her old contract into a sure BEF 100,000 cash flow. Thus, the present value cannot differ from 100,000 discounted at the BEF risk-free rate. If $r_{t,T} = 5$ percent $p.a.$, the contract has a value of BEF 95,238.

FIGURE 3.2 The Hedging Approach: A Numerical Example

Forward purchase contract: DEM 10m at $F_{t_0,T} =$ BEF/DEM 21	Hedging: Sell DEM 1m at $F_{t,T} =$ BEF/DEM 21.01	Combined cash flow at time T
Leg 1: In: DEM 10m	Out: DEM 10m	DEM 0
Leg 2: Out: BEF 210m	In: BEF 210.1m	BEF 100,000
	Immediate outlay: 0	Present value: $\dfrac{100,000}{1.05} =$ BEF 95,238

Given Equation [1a], an outstanding forward contract can have a negative value, especially when the historic forward rate exceeds the current forward rate for the same maturity. A negative value means that you are willing to pay in order to get out of the contract.

Example   3.2

Suppose that in the past you bought forward DEM 1m at $F_{t_0, T}$ = BEF/DEM 21, and suppose that now, at time t, the forward rate for the same maturity, T, is 20.70. For a new contract there is no up-front payment. However, your old contract costs you an extra $0.30 \times 1m$ = BEF 300,000 at time T, relative to the new contract. In present value terms, the extra cost is worth 300,000 discounted at $r_{t,T}$, say, 300,000/1.05 = BEF 285,714. This is the amount you would be willing to pay to get out of the old contract.

Our result with respect to the valuation of an existing forward contract has some important corollaries, which we discuss after describing how one can value a forward contract using the replication approach.

3.1.2   The Replication Approach

The first column of Figure 3.3 shows the two "legs" of a forward contract—the foreign currency inflow, and the home currency outflow. The second column demonstrates that the same flows can be replicated by:

- Buying and investing $1/(1 + r^*_{t,T})$ units of foreign currency, at a cost of $S_t \times 1/(1 + r^*_{t,T})$, in terms of the home currency.
- Borrowing $F_{t_0, T}/(1 + r_{t,T})$.

The combined net outlays, at time t, from the replicating strategy are given in the third column and are:

$$\frac{S_t}{1 + r^*_{t,T}} - \frac{F_{t_0, T}}{1 + r_{t,T}}.$$

Finally, the market value of the outstanding forward contract must equal the value of its replicating portfolio; otherwise, there is an arbitrage opportunity that should be eliminated immediately. This implies that the value at t of the forward contract initiated at t_0 must be equal to:

$$\frac{S_t}{1 + r^*_{t,T}} - \frac{F_{t_0, T}}{1 + r_{t,T}}.$$

In Equation [1b] below, we write this formally, in two versions:[2]

Value of a forward contract at time t that was initiated at t_0 at rate $F_{t_0, T}$ $= \dfrac{S_t}{1 + r^*_{t,T}} - \dfrac{F_{t_0, T}}{1 + r_{t,T}}$ [1b]

$$= \frac{F_{t,T} - F_{t_0, T}}{1 + r_{t,T}}.$$

---

[2] The second line is obtained by dividing and multiplying the term $\dfrac{S_t}{1 + r^*_{t,T}}$ by $(1 + r_{t,T})$ and using Interest Rate Parity.

FIGURE 3.3 Market Value of an Outstanding Forward Contract: The Replication Approach

Cash flow at T from a forward purchase contract initiated at t_0 at the rate $F_{t_0,T}$	Replication		
	Strategy at time t	Cash outlay at t, in HC terms	Cash flow at time T
Leg 1: Inflow FC 1	Buy and invest FC $\dfrac{1}{1+r^*_{t,T}}$	$S_t \dfrac{1}{1+r^*_{t,T}}$	Inflow FC 1
Leg 2: Outflow $F_{t_0,T}$	Borrow $\dfrac{F_{t_0,T}}{1+r_{t,T}}$	$-\dfrac{F_{t_0,T}}{1+r_{t,T}}$	Outflow $F_{t_0,T}$
		$\dfrac{S_t}{1+r^*_{t,T}} - \dfrac{F_{t_0,T}}{1+r_{t,T}}.$	

Replication of an outstanding forward contract using money market operations. HC denotes home currency, and FC denotes foreign currency.

3.2 IMPLICATIONS: THE VALUE AT EXPIRATION AND AT INCEPTION

We can use the result in Equation [1] to determine the value of a forward contract at its inception and at maturity. We also use Equation [1] to relate the forward rate to the risk-adjusted expected future spot rate.

3.2.1 Corollary 1: The Value of a Forward Contract at Expiration

The market value of a purchase contract, at its expiration, equals the difference between the initially agreed-upon forward rate, $F_{t_0,T}$, and the spot rate that prevails at time T:

$$\text{Expiration value of a forward contract with rate } F_{t_0,T} = S_T - F_{t_0,T}. \qquad [2]$$

Equation [2] can be derived formally from Equation [1b], using the fact that the effective return on a deposit or loan with zero time to maturity is zero (that is, $r_{T,T} = 0 = r^*_{T,T}$). The result is quite obvious, as the example shows.

Example 3.3

You bought forward, at time t_0, one USD at DEM/USD 2. At expiration, T, the USD spot rate S_T, is DEM/USD 2.1, so you receive a dollar now worth DEM 2.1, and you pay $F_{t_0,T}$ = DEM 2. The net value is DEM 0.1.

Equation [2] can be used to formally show how hedging works. Suppose that you have to pay one unit of foreign currency at some future time T. The foreign currency debt is risky because the cash outflow at time T, in home currency, will be equal to (minus) the future spot rate—and, at time t, this future spot rate is uncertain, a characteristic we stress by adding a *tilde* (~) over the variable. By adding a forward purchase, the combined cash flow becomes risk free, as seen in the following equation.

$$\text{Value of the debt at expiration:} \quad -\tilde{S}_T \qquad \qquad [3]$$

$$\text{Value of the forward contract at expiration:} \quad \tilde{S}_T - F_{t_0,T}$$

$$\text{Combined value at time } T: \quad -F_{t_0,T}$$

Putting this into words, we say that hedging the foreign-currency debt with a forward purchase transforms the risky debt into a risk-free debt, with a known outflow $-F_{t_0,T}$. We shall use this result again in Chapter 7, when we discuss option pricing, and in Chapters 17 to 19, where we discuss exchange rate exposure and hedging in greater detail. In a way, the type of hedging we just described is an extreme form of diversification.

3.2.2   Corollary 2: The Value of a Forward Contract at Inception

A contract signed at t_0 (the moment of valuation) stipulates future delivery at the time-t_0 price, $F_{t_0,T}$. Our claim is that the value of such a contract at t_0 is zero. You could have guessed this from the fact that there is no up-front payment when a forward contract is signed. To show the (initial) zero-value property formally, we use Equation [1] and consider the special case where $t_0 = t$, implying that $F_{t_0,T} = F_{t,T}$. (That is, the contract we are valuing is new.) Obviously,

$$\text{Value at } t_0 \text{ of a forward contract with rate } F_{t_0,T} = \frac{F_{t_0,T} - F_{t_0,T}}{1 + r_{t_0,T}} = 0. \qquad [4]$$

The value of a forward contract is zero at the moment it is signed because the contract can be replicated at zero cost. That is, if a bank tried to charge you money for a contract at the equilibrium (Interest Rate Parity) forward rate, you would refuse, and create a synthetic forward contract through the spot and money markets. Example 3.4 is basically the replication argument given in Section 3.1.2, with one minor modification: we consider $F_{t_0,T} = F_{t,T}$ (that is, we are replicating a contract at its inception date, rather than a contract signed in the past).

Example   3.4

Suppose $S_t = 10$, $r_{t,T} = 21$ percent, and $r^*_{t,T} = 10$ percent. Then, by arbitrage, $F_{t,T} = 11$. If a bank asks you to pay an up-front price for a forward purchase at $F = 11$, you would refuse. Instead, you would synthetically replicate the forward by borrowing $HC_t = 9.09091$ and converting it spot into $FC_t = 0.909091$, which is then invested at 10 percent. At T, you would cash in the foreign currency deposit, worth $0.909091 \times 1.1 = 1$; and you would pay off your home currency loan, at $9.09091 \times 1.21 = 11$. Thus, you can replicate a forward purchase contract, and it does not cost you anything.

A different way of looking at this zero-value property is as follows. If you buy forward DEM at, say, $F_{t,T} = BEF_T/DEM_T\ 21$ (which is a "normal" level at the time of writing), you may lose or win. You will lose if (and to the extent that) the future spot price turns out to be below 21, and you will win if (and to the extent that) the DEM turns out to be more expensive than 21. Now, if the forward price $F_{t_0,T}$ being quoted were ridiculously high (say, 40 rather than 21), the chances of winning would be slight, and the contract would have a negative value (you can only lose, so you insist on receiving an up-front payment to compensate you for the likely loss). Similarly, if the forward price $F_{t,T}$ were extremely low, say 10, this contract would give you an almost sure gain and therefore you would have to pay the seller the positive value that this contract must have. Thus, the market forward rate $F_{t,T}$ can be interpreted as the "in-between" price chosen such that, after adjustment for risk, the expected value of the possible losses exactly cancels out the expected value of the possible gains.

3.2.3   Corollary 3: The Forward Rate and the Risk-Adjusted Expected Future Spot Rate

The zero-value property of forward contracts discussed above has another extremely important interpretation. Suppose that the DEM/USD six-month forward rate equals two, implying that you can exchange one future USD for two future DEM and *vice versa* without any up-front cash flow. This must mean that the market perceives these amounts as being *equivalent* (that is, having the same value). If this were not so, there would have been an up-front compensation to make up for the difference in value.

Example   3.5

The market is unlikely to perceive one kilo of lead as being equivalent to one kilo of gold. If you wanted to exchange equal amounts of these metals, there would be an extra payment to compensate for the difference in value. Conversely, in an arm's-length transaction, if you are able to exchange one kilo of gold for 400 kilos of lead *without* any cash payment, the market value of 400 kilos of lead and one kilo of gold must be equal. Replace *one kilo of gold* with *one future USD,* and *400 kilos of lead* with *two future DEM*, and the same result holds.

Since any forward contract has a zero value, the present values of $USD_T\ 1$ and $DEM_T\ 2$ must be equal anywhere; that is, the equivalence of USD 1 and DEM 2 holds for any investor or hedger. However, the equivalence property takes on a special meaning if we pick the DEM (which is the currency in which our forward rate is expressed) as the home currency. In terms of DEM, we can write the equal-value property as:

$$PV_t(\tilde{S}_T) \;=\; PV_t(F_{t,T}), \qquad\qquad [5]$$

where $PV_t(.)$ is the *present-value* operator.

We can interpret Equation [5] in at least two ways. First, it can be read as a simple reflection of the zero-value property: $PV_t(\tilde{S}_T - F_{t,T}) = 0$. In words, the value at time t of the contract's maturity value (at T) in DEM is zero. We can lose or gain, but these prospects cancel out in present-value terms, from our standpoint at time t.

A second interpretation stems from the fact that in home currency, the forward price on the right-hand side of Equation [5] is a risk-free, known number whereas the future spot rate on the left is uncertain. That is, the forward rate $F_{t,T}$ is not just perceived at time t as being equivalent to one unit of foreign currency; this amount of future home currency is also a *certain*, risk-free amount. For this reason, we shall say that in home currency, the forward rate is the time-t **certainty equivalent** of the future spot rate, S_T.

Example   3.6

Suppose that the home currency is the DEM, and that the three-month DEM/USD forward rate is 2. Then $DEM_T 2$ is the certain amount of DEM that is equivalent to USD 1 three months from now. That is, in DEM the certainty equivalent of the future DEM/USD spot rate, three months from now, is DEM 2.

The notion of the certainty equivalent deserves some elaboration. Many introductory finance books discuss the concept of an investor's subjective certainty equivalent of a risky income. This is defined as the single known amount of income that is equivalent to the entire risky distribution.

Example   3.7

Suppose that you are indifferent between, on the one hand, a lottery ticket that pays out with equal probabilities either USD 1,000 or nothing, and on the other hand, a sure USD 450. Then, your personal certainty equivalent of the risky lottery is USD 450. You are indifferent between 450 for sure and the risky cash flow from the lottery. Another way of saying this is that, when valuing the lottery ticket, you have marked down its expected value, USD 500, by USD 50, because the lottery is risky. Thus, we can conclude that your personal certainty equivalent, USD 450, is the expected value of the lottery ticket *corrected for risk*.[3]

By analogy, a **market certainty equivalent** is defined as the single known amount that the market considers to be as valuable as the entire risky distribution. And market certainty equivalents are, of course, what matter if we want to price assets, or if we want to make managerial decisions that maximize the market value of the firm. We have just argued that the (DEM) market certainty equivalent of the future DEM/USD spot rate must be the current DEM/USD forward rate. In short, the market's

---

[3] Note, in passing, that correction for risk is not necessarily downward; most lottery tickets sell at prices *above* their expected value.

time-t expectation of the time-T DEM/USD spot rate, corrected for risk, is revealed in the DEM/USD forward rate, $F_{t,T}$. We shall express this formally as:

$$\mathrm{CEQ}_t(\tilde{S}_T) = F_{t,T}, \tag{6}$$

where $\mathrm{CEQ}_t(.)$ is the *certainty equivalent* operator.

A certainty equivalent operator is similar to an ordinary expectations operator, $E_t(.)$, except that it is a risk-adjusted expectation rather than an ordinary expected value. Like $E_t(.)$, it is also a *conditional* expectation, that is, the best possible forecast given the information available at time t. We use a t subscript to emphasize this link with the information available at time t.

The risk-adjusted expected value plays a crucial role in the theory of international finance. As we shall see in the remainder of this chapter and later in the book, the risk-adjusted expectation has many important implications for asset pricing as well as for corporate financial decisions.

3.2.4   Implications for the Valuation of Foreign Currency Assets or Liabilities

The certainty-equivalent interpretation of the forward rate implies that, for the purpose of corporate decision making, one can use the forward rate to translate foreign currency denominated claims or liabilities into one's domestic currency without having to worry about how to adjust for risk. This makes life much more simple. Rather than having to tackle a valuation problem involving a risky cash flow—the left-hand side of Equation [5]—we can simply work with the right-hand side where the cash flow is risk free. With risk-free cash flows, it suffices to use the observable domestic risk-free rate for discounting purposes.

Example   3.8

If the domestic BEF risk-free return is 10 percent *p.a.* and the 180-day forward rate is BEF/DEM 21, then the (risk-adjusted) economic value of a DEM 500,000 180-day invoice is:

$$\frac{\mathrm{DEM}_T\,500,000 \times \mathrm{BEF}_T/\mathrm{DEM}_T\,21}{1.05} = \mathrm{BEF}_t\,10\,\mathrm{m}.$$

As illustrated in the example, the expected spot rate is not needed in order to value this position, and discounting can be done at the risk-free rate of return. In contrast, if you had tried to value the position using the left-hand side of Equation [5], you would probably have had to discount the expected future spot rate at some risk-adjusted rate. Thus, the first problem would have been to estimate the expected future spot rate. Unlike the forward rate, this expectation is not provided in the newspaper or on the Reuters screens. Second, you would have had to use some asset-pricing theory like the international Capital Asset Pricing Model (CAPM) to calculate a risk-adjusted discount rate. In this second step, you would run into problems of estimating the model parameters and even of choosing the appropriate model. In short, the forward rate simplifies decision making considerably. We shall use this concept time and again throughout this text.

Let us formalize our discussion as follows. Equation [6] says that the forward rate is the risk-free amount at time T, which is as valuable as the uncertain future spot rate $\tilde{S}_T$. It follows that the present value of one unit of future foreign currency must equal the present value of the equivalent risk-free amount. In short, to value a foreign currency asset, we simply use the market's risk-adjusted expectation, as given by the forward rate, and discount it at the home currency risk-free rate:

$$PV_t(\tilde{S}_T) = \frac{CEQ_t(\tilde{S}_T)}{1+r_{t,T}} = \frac{F_{t,T}}{1+r_{t,T}} \tag{7}$$

$$= S_t \frac{1}{1+r^*_{t,T}}, \text{ from Interest Rate Parity.}$$

The last expression can be interpreted as follows. To value a foreign currency risk-free cash flow of one unit, first compute its present value in foreign currency. This is $1/(1+r^*_{t,T})$. In the second step, translate this current value from foreign currency units into home currency units, using the current spot rate, S_t. The resulting value is $S_t/(1+r^*_{t,T})$.

The certainty-equivalent property has a number of interesting implications for a firm's reporting, hedging, and financing decisions. We discuss these implications in Sections 3.3 and 3.4.

3.3   INSIGHTS FOR FINANCIAL REPORTING

3.3.1   Financial Reporting of Forward Contracts

The first practical application concerns the reporting of forward contracts in financial statements or, at least, in internal management reports. Equation [1a] shows us the value of a forward (purchase) contract: it equals the discounted difference between the historic and current forward rate. This is the way we should state forward positions in our annual reports (if we want them to be true and fair). Further, if this way of reporting is disallowed under the country's Generally Accepted Accounting Principles (GAAP), we should use it when we report the forward positions in our internal management reports—just like we should use replacement cost when reporting the value of inventory, or market value rather than historic costs for reporting the value of financial assets.

In contrast, *actual* standard accounting practice is to show forward positions in the notes or, in Europe, in the "order accounts," with the asset side and the liability side perfectly matched.

Example   3.9

Suppose that in the past you have bought forward DEM 1m at BEF/DEM 20.70, and sold USD 2m at BEF/USD 34.51. In the order accounts, this is reported as follows.

Forward Transactions

Forward purchase:		Payable	
DEM 1m at 20.70	BEF 20.70m	(forward purchase DEM)	BEF 20.70m
Receivable		Forward sale:	
(forward sale USD)	BEF 69.02m	USD 2m at 34.51	BEF 69.02m

The implied zero value of each such entry is correct the moment the contract is written (at its inception), but may be grossly misleading a few months later when the forward contracts no longer have a value of zero.

3.3.2   Using the Forward Rate to Value A/R or A/P

The present value of *accounts receivable* (*A/R*) or *accounts payable* (*A/P*) can be found by translating the foreign currency value at the forward rate, and then discounting at the domestic risk-free rate, as explained in Section 3.2.4. However, for A/R and A/P denominated in home currency, accountants rarely report the present values; they are content with the future values or face values. For consistency, then, A/R and A/P denominated in foreign currency should be reported in terms of their market value prior to discounting, that is, as the foreign currency face value translated at the forward rate for the appropriate maturity. In contrast, a standard accounting procedure for recording foreign currency denominated positions is to translate at the spot rate.[4]

Example   3.10

A Luxembourg firm sells three containers full of skateboards to International Leisure, Auckland, for NZD 100,000 payable six months from now. This invoice must be translated into LUF, since the exporter's books are kept in LUF. Standard procedure is to use today's spot rate, say LUF 25. The accounts receivable (A/R) entry would therefore be $25 \times 100,000 = $ LUF 2,500,000:

A/R	2,500,000	
Sales		2,500,000

It is not clear why the invoice is initially recorded at S_t. The likelihood of actually receiving LUF 2,500,000 on the (unhedged) claim is small. The current spot rate, S_t, is correct only for the recording of foreign currency payments that are received today—not for payments to be received at a future time T. To record a future inflow, the firm should have used the expected future spot rate, or even better, the risk-adjusted expected future spot rate—the forward rate. In the eyes of the market, the forward rate is as good as the uncertain future value $\tilde{S}_T$. Thus, the correct way to book this transaction, given a forward rate of LUF/NZD 23.5, would be:

A/R	2,350,000	
Sales		2,350,000

The motivation for using the forward rate is simply one of accurate valuation, or true and fair reporting. The way of recording does not affect the ultimate profit or loss because, when the account is settled, there will be a capital gain or loss that offsets the original accounting valuation.

---

[4] Sometimes the average spot rate over the last N days, or a "standard" exchange rate is used.

Example   3.11

Suppose that, when the account is settled, the spot rate is $S_T = $ LUF/NZD 24. If the original recording was at LUF/NZD 25, the entry at time T is:

Bank account	2,400,000	
Capital gains or losses	100,000	
A/R		2,500,000

If, on the other hand, the original recording was at LUF/NZD 23.5, the entry at time T would be:

Bank account	2,400,000	
Capital gains or losses		50,000
A/R		2,350,000

If one compares the two ways of recording the A/R, it becomes obvious that the difference in the original sales entries, 2,500,000 – 2,350,000 = LUF 150,000, is offset by the fact that a LUF 100,000 "loss" is converted into a LUF 50,000 "gain." Profits are not affected.

3.4   INSIGHTS FOR CORPORATE HEDGING AND INVESTMENT POLICIES

We conclude this chapter with a discussion of issues related to exchange risk and hedging. We start by arguing that the forward premium or discount is not the cost or profit from hedging. We then trace the implications for pricing and invoicing decisions and, lastly, raise the issue of the relevance of hedging against exchange risk.

3.4.1   The Forward Premium Is Not the Cost of Hedging

A common fallacy underlies the statement that hedging is expensive—a fallacy in the sense that the forward discount is viewed as the cost of hedging an A/R, and *vice versa*. That is, it is often argued that it is costly to hedge by selling forward because the forward rate is below the current spot rate. This view actually follows from the accounting convention of translating A/Rs at the spot rate.

Example   3.12

Suppose that the firm translates the A/R of NZD 100,000 at the spot rate and records an A/R of LUF 2.5m. When the firm hedges at a forward rate that is below the current spot, say LUF 23.5, the actual receipts will be 23.5 × 100,000 = LUF 2,350,000. As this payment settles the invoice shown at a book value of 2,500,000, the principles of accounting require that the difference be shown somewhere else, as a kind of capital gain or loss. However, here the loss is predictable, so it is called a "cost." Moreover, this cost is clearly not a production cost, so it is considered a financial cost. In short, this transaction will be recorded as:

Bank account	2,350,000	
Financial costs	150,000	
A/R		2,500,000

Thus, hedging A/Rs when the foreign currency is at a discount is viewed as being costly.[5] It is hard to reconcile this notion of cost with the fact that the forward contract is free. Clearly this financial result of hedging is created purely by the accounting rule of thumb of using the current spot rate for translating the NZD invoice. If the A/R entry had been translated using the appropriate forward rate, there would not have been any financial cost result of hedging.

Example   3.13

If the firm uses the forward rate to record the A/R, the initial accounting entries would be:

A/R	2,350,000	
Sales		2,350,000

and when the contract expires:

Bank account	2,350,000	
A/R		2,350,000

Thus, when the A/R is reported correctly, there is no cost, which is consistent with the fact that the initial value of the forward contract is zero.

3.4.2   Using the Forward Rate To Translate between Domestic Prices and Foreign Prices

The forward rate can also be used to make pricing decisions if there is trade credit, that is, if the customer is allowed to postpone payment. The rule is that, to translate a home currency price payable within N days into a foreign currency price that is payable within N days, one should use the forward rate.

Example   3.14

Your (Luxembourg) firm wants to charge LUF 100,000 cash on delivery (COD) to a French company, but it turns out that standard industry terms allow a ninety-day credit period. If the firm is rational and the domestic simple interest rate is 10 percent *p.a.* (that is, $r_{t,T} = 0.025$), it will charge LUF 102,500 for payment in LUF after ninety days. How should a FRF price be set? The spot rate is LUF/FRF 6, and the foreign rate of return is 3 percent.

- Assume that you charge FRF 102,500/6 = 17,083.333. If you draw a trade bill on the French customer and discount it, the net proceeds will be 17,803.333/1.03 = FRF 16,585.761, or after

---

[5] By a similar reasoning, hedging is sometimes said to be profitable when the forward rate is above the current spot. The signs denoting inflows and outflows are, of course, reversed when the item to be hedged is an A/P rather than an A/R.

conversion into LUF at the spot rate, $16,585.761 \times 6 = $ LUF $99,514.563$.[6] This is not the LUF 100,000 amount you wanted to obtain. Thus, you should not use the spot rate (LUF/FRF 6) to translate the LUF price into FRF.

- To get LUF 100,000, the net proceeds after discounting should be FRF $100,000/6 = 16,666.667$, which requires a FRF trade bill with face value (future value) FRF $16,666.667 \times 1.03 = 17,166.667$. The implicit rate to translate the LUF 102,500 terms into FRF 17,166.667 is 5.97087—the forward rate:

$$6 \times \frac{1.025}{1.03} = 5.9708738.$$

In short: for the purpose of converting a future LUF_T price into future FRF_T, we should use the forward rate for maturity T; the spot rate is correct only for converting immediate payments.

3.4.3   The "(Ir)relevance of Hedging" Controversy

One purpose of forward transactions is to hedge commercial contracts or investments expressed in foreign currency.

Example   3.15

Consider, as in Example 3.10, the Luxembourg exporter selling three containers of skateboards for NZD 100,000 payable three months from now. Because the value of NZD 100,000 at T depends on the spot rate at T, and therefore is uncertain, the firm sells forward the NZD 100,000 at today's forward rate $F_{t,T} = $ LUF/NZD 23.5. When the exporter receives the NZD, she delivers them to her bank and obtains LUF 2.35m, without any risk.

The issue we discuss here is whether such hedging is beneficial. The controversy can be summarized as follows:

- Some have claimed that forward hedging offers the firm a free lunch. Indeed, the hedger eliminates exchange risk at zero cost; and there may even be an expected gain for example, if, when hedging foreign receipts, the forward rate, $F_{t,T}$, exceeds the expected future spot rate, $E_t(\tilde{S}_T)$. This sounds like having your cake and eating it, too.
- The dissenters say that hedging is irrelevant. In their view, hedging is useful only if it increases the value of the firm. In perfect markets, a forward contract will not affect the value of the firm: the unhedged firm has a value V_U, and adding a zero-value forward contract will not affect this value. Thus, hedging is said to be irrelevant.

The free-lunch argument implicitly assumes that reducing the variance of the firm's cash flows or increasing their expected value leads to a higher current market value of the firm. This assumption has yet to be proven. For instance, replacing a risky cash flow by its certainty equivalent reduces risk

---

[6] Trade bills are defined in the introductory chapter.

and may increase the expected future value, but it should not affect the current value of the firm. Thus, the difference between the expected spot rate $E_t(\tilde{S}_T)$ and the forward rate is immaterial in terms of present value. The dissenting view, on the other hand, is irrefutable if markets are perfect, and if hedging does not affect the operating cash flows of the firm.[7] However, if markets are imperfect, hedging *will* affect the operating cash flows of the firm. For instance, if financial distress is costly, a firm may refuse a profitable export contract if it cannot hedge, but may accept it if hedging is possible. The value of the firm then increases, not because the forward contract in itself has a positive market value, but because it allows the firm to undertake a profitable export project while avoiding the expected cost of financial distress—that is, because of a change in the firm's operating cash flows. We shall pursue this discussion of when hedging can increase the value of a firm in Chapter 16.

3.4.4   The "Currency of Invoicing Dilemma"

There is also some controversy over whether or not the currency of invoicing matters. Does it matter whether prices are quoted in terms of the home currency or the foreign currency?

- The traditionalists state that someone must bear the exchange risk. Either you invoice in HC_T, in which case the foreign customer bears the exchange risk, or you invoice in FC_T, in which case you bear the exchange risk.
- The dissenters believe that, with the existence of a forward market, there is no problem. For instance, in Example 3.14, the Luxembourg exporter could charge FRF_T 17,166.667 and hedge to lock in LUF_T 102,500; or, she could charge LUF_T 102,500 and let the customer lock in FRF_T 17,166.167 by means of a forward hedge. The currency of invoicing, in the dissenters' view, merely shifts the hedging from seller to buyer, or *vice versa*. Finally, it does not matter which party hedges since, at a given point in time, each party can buy the foreign currency at the same rate.[8]

The opinion that the currency of invoicing does not matter is obviously valid if the buyer and the seller are effectively able to hedge at the same moment and at the same rates. Conversely, the invoicing currency may matter as soon as (1) there is a time lag between the moment a price is offered by the exporter and the moment the customer decides to actually buy the goods, or (2) the cost of hedging differs depending on who hedges. We illustrate these situations in the examples below.

Example   3.16

This example focuses on the delay between the price offer and the customer's decision. The currency of invoicing matters when you publish a list of prices that are valid for, say, six months. The problem here stems from the fact that there is a lag between the time that the FRF prices are announced and the time the customer purchases an item. Since you do not know the timing and volume of future sales, you cannot hedge perfectly if you list prices denominated in foreign currency.

---

[7] In the theory of corporate financial structure, this view corresponds to the Miller-Modigliani assumption that the firm's investment (and operations) policy is unaffected by the firm's financial and hedging policy.

[8] This even holds with bid-ask spreads: since the transaction is selling FFR against LUF, the firms would use the same effective rate if they trade at the same time.

Example   3.17

Now we'll look at a situation with differential cost of hedging. The Belgian sales branch of a Dutch stationery distributor instructs its customers to pay in NLG. Since the orders are frequent, and usually small, the Belgian customers pay substantial implicit commissions whenever they purchase NLG. It would be cheaper if the exporter let them pay in BEF and converted the total BEF sales revenue into NLG once a day or once a week.

In situations like this, one can still hedge approximately if sales are fairly steady and predictable. Johnson & Johnson's pharmaceutical division, Janssen Pharma, hedges all expected positions within a twelve-month horizon and adjusts its forward positions whenever sales forecasts are revised. However, in other cases, the time lag between the exporter's price offer and the importer's purchase decision may imply substantial sales uncertainty. In perfect markets, even this risk should be hedgeable at a low cost. In practice, the cost of hedging may very well depend on the currency in which prices are expressed.

Example   3.18

Here we consider an international tender, characterized by a time delay and a differential cost of hedging. Suppose that a Canadian hospital invites bids for a scanner.

- In an international tender, suppliers are usually invited to submit bids *in the buyer's currency* (CAD, in this case). A foreign contender's dilemma is whether or not to hedge, considering that:

  (1)   Forward hedging may leave the contender with an uncovered, risky forward position. Specifically, if the contract is not awarded to him, the bidding firm would then have to buy CAD_T just to fulfill its forward contract. The rate at which such a time T purchase will be made is uncertain.

  (2)   Not hedging at all means that, if the contender does make the winning bid, the CAD_T inflow is risky.

  Thus, whether or not the contender hedges, there is a potential risky cash flow in CAD. It is true that banks offer conditional hedges, that is, contracts that become standard forward contracts (or standard options) when the potential supplier wins the tender but are void otherwise. However, these products are very much tailored to specific situations. The bank must assess and monitor the probability that a particular contender makes the winning bid, which makes such a contract expensive in terms of commissions. Thus, hedging is costly when bids are to be expressed in the customer's currency.

- The alternative is that the buyer invites bids *in the suppliers' own currencies.* Indeed, the buyer can easily wait until all bids have been submitted, then translate them into CAD_T— using the prevailing forward rates—and, at the very same moment she notifies the lucky winner, lock in the best price by means of a standard forward contract. In this way, all risk and all unnecessary bid-ask spreads in hedging disappear. To illustrate this, suppose that the

Canadian hospital's procurement manager receives three bids in three different currencies, shown in column (a) below. She looks up the forward rates CAD_T/FC_T shown in column (b), and extracts the following CAD_T equivalent bid prices.

	(a) Offers	(b) Forward rates	CAD Equivalent = (a) × (b)
1	DEM_T 1,050,000	CAD_T/DEM_T 0.55	CAD_T 577,500
2	CHF_T 960,000	CAD_T/CHF_T 0.65	CAD_T 624,000
3	USD_T 500,000	CAD_T/USD_T 1.15	CAD_T 575,000

She accepts the US offer, and immediately buys forward USD. Thus, when prices are to be submitted in the customer's currency, a standard (and therefore cheap) forward hedge will suffice.

What this example shows, again, is that the currency of invoicing matters if the cost of hedging is not independent of the way prices are quoted. The Canadian hospital can use a cheap, standard contract if prices are submitted in the contending suppliers' home currencies. In contrast, with bids to be submitted in CAD, hedging is difficult and expensive for the bidders—because they are unsure about being awarded the contract. The solution in this case is to let the suppliers quote bids in their currency.

3.4.5   The Currency of Borrowing and the Interest Tax Shield

The zero-value property of a forward contract also has its implications for investment and financing decisions. For example, the firm needs to decide on the currency of borrowing; specifically, it has to decide whether to borrow in a high-interest currency or in a low-interest one. One potentially complicating factor is taxation. Interest expenses are tax-deductible, so the tax bill is likely to be affected by the currency of borrowing. But one should also think of capital gains or losses on the repayment of foreign currency loans, which affect profits and taxes. In this section we argue that, *ex ante* (that is, in terms of present values, at the time of making the borrowing decision), the currency of borrowing does not matter even in the presence of taxes, unless a different tax rate applies to interest expenses and capital gains.

Let us compare two loans with identical initial proceeds: one unit of foreign exchange versus S_t units of home currency. For simplicity, assume that the loans involve just one interest payment and one amortization payment, both at time T. At maturity, interest costs and amortization on the foreign currency loan amount to $\tilde{S}_T(1 + r^*_{t,T})$ units of home currency, while the total time-T outflow from borrowing S_t units of home currency is $S_t(1 + r_{t,T})$. Thus, the difference of the cash flows is:

$$\text{Cost difference} = [\text{cost of the foreign loan}] - [\text{cost of the domestic loan}] \qquad [8]$$

$$= \tilde{S}_T(1 + r^*_{t,T}) - S_t(1 + r_{t,T}) .$$

Ex post, these outflows will almost surely turn out to be different. But $\tilde{S}_T$ is not known at the time the decision is to be taken, and all we can do is base the decision on present values. Ignore taxes for the time being. We compute present values by computing risk-adjusted expected values and then discounting at the risk-free rate. The only term in Equation [8] that needs to be adjusted for risk is the term $\tilde{S}_T$. Thus:

$$\text{Present value of cost difference} = \frac{\text{CEQ}_t\,(\tilde{S}_T)(1+r_{t,T}^*)-S_t\,(1+r_{t,T})}{1+r_{t,T}} \tag{9}$$

$$= \frac{F_{t,T}\,(1+r_{t,T}^*)}{1+r_{t,T}} - S_t$$

$$= 0, \text{ from Interest Rate Parity.}$$

Thus, the cash flows from the domestic and foreign loans are *ex ante* equivalent. To see whether this conclusion is affected by taxes, we arrange the cost difference in [8] as follows:

$$\tilde{S}_T\,(1+r_{t,T}^*)-S_t\,(1+r_{t,T}) = [\tilde{S}_T r_{t,T}^* - S_t r_{t,T}] - [S_t - \tilde{S}_T]. \tag{10}$$

The first term, $[\tilde{S}_T\,r_{t,T}^* - S_t\,r_{t,T}]$, is the difference of the interest expenses, while $[S_t - \tilde{S}_T]$ is the capital gain on the repayment of the foreign loan. For example, suppose that the spot rate was 100 when we borrowed foreign currency, and it is down to 80 when we repay the loan; then there is a capital gain of 20. Of course, the present value of the right-hand side of [10] is still zero:

$$\text{PV}_t\,\{[\tilde{S}_T r_{t,T}^* - S_t\,r_{t,T}] - [S_t - \tilde{S}_T]\} = 0. \tag{11}$$

Assume that capital gains and interest are all taxed at the same corporate tax rate. Multiplying both terms in [11] by the corporate tax rate τ, we then obtain the following:

$$\text{PV}_t\,\{[\tilde{S}_T r_{t,T}^* - S_t\,r_{t,T}]\tau - [S_t - \tilde{S}_T]\tau\} = 0. \tag{12}$$

The term $[\tilde{S}_T\,r_{t,T}^* - S_t\,r_{t,T}]\tau$ is the difference in the interest tax shield when the firm borrows in foreign currency rather than in home currency. The second term, $[S_t - \tilde{S}_T]\tau$, is the tax on the capital gain on the foreign loan. Thus, Equation [12] says that, in terms of present values, the tax savings generated by higher interest expenses on the foreign loan are offset by the taxes on the capital gain. Thus, the currency of borrowing does not affect the present value of tax payments if the capital gains tax is the same as the tax on ordinary income. Note that this holds for any corporate tax rate τ. That is, the fact that firms from different countries pay different taxes is perfectly compatible with the zero-value property of forward contracts and the irrelevance of the currency of borrowing.

The above proof of the irrelevancy of the currency of borrowing assumes that taxes do not discriminate between capital gains and interest. Conversely, the currency of borrowing *is* relevant if capital gains (resulting from borrowing in a weak currency) are taxed at a lower rate than the standard tax rate. Likewise, the currency of lending may be relevant if capital gains resulting from investing in a strong currency are taxed at a lower rate than interest income.

Example   3.19

The UK used to have a rule that stated that exchange losses on long-term loans were deductible, but capital gains were tax-free. Given the risk-adjusted expectation that the AUD or NZD would depreciate relative to the GBP, a UK parent had an incentive to borrow in NZD or AUD. The expected capital gain would be tax-free, while the high interest payments would be fully tax-deductible.

The currency of borrowing may also be relevant if borrowing in a foreign currency serves to offset the exchange risk created by, for example, an export contract denominated in the same foreign currency that would have been unacceptably risky without a hedge. In such a case, borrowing in that particular foreign currency increases the value of the firm. Note, however, that the source of this gain is the export contract that is being hedged, not the foreign borrowing in itself; and the gain has nothing to do with tax shields.

QUIZ QUESTIONS

1. Which of the following statements are false? Why?
   (a) The forward rate $F_{t,T}$ is the certainty equivalent of the future spot rate. Therefore, the expected spot rate is equal to $F_{t,T}$.
   (b) Market makers set the forward rate $F_{t,T}$ so that it is equal to the future spot rate.
   (c) If you expect the spot rate to increase, it is more accurate to use the forward rate $F_{t,T}$ when recording an accounts receivable on the balance sheet at time t. Otherwise, use the spot rate. This rule ensures that your profits are maximized because your sales figures are maximized.
   (d) The forward rate $F_{t,T}$ is the risk-adjusted expected value of the future spot exchange rate.
   (e) It is expensive to record an accounts receivable on the balance sheet using a forward rate that is lower than the spot rate.
   (f) In perfect markets, the currency of invoicing is irrelevant, because both parties to a contract can immediately hedge in the forward market.
   (g) Bidders to an international tender should be asked to submit prices in their home currency.

2. Given the following data, compute the value today of an outstanding forward purchase contract initiated at t_0 for 1,000,000 units of foreign currency (where the exchange rate is HC/FC). Does the new value represent a gain or loss to the holder of the old contract? (Hint: first compute the new forward rate.)

	Spot rate S_t	Old forward rate, $F_{t_0,T}$	$r_{t,T}$	$r^*_{t,T}$
(a) BEF/DEM	20.5	22.0	3.5%	2.5%
(b) JPY/NLG	57.5	54.2	1.25%	3.0%
(c) ITL/FRF	283.0	289.4	4.5%	3.5%
(d) CHF/GBP	2.2	1.8	2.0%	3.0%

3. Repeat question 2 using the same data, but with an outstanding forward sale contract.

4. Lucky Lucas, a French chain of western-style restaurants, has received a shipment of Argentinian beef worth ARP 100,000 to be paid in 90 days. The invoice must be translated into FRF. The spot rate is FRF/ARP 4.2, and the forward rate is FRF/ARP 4.1.
   (a) Using the spot rate, how would you record the invoice at time t? What is the accounting entry at time T if the spot rate at T equals 4.25?
   (b) Using the forward rate, how would you record the invoice at time t? What is the accounting entry at time T if the spot rate equals 4.25?
   (c) Are the profits and cash flows affected by the way in which the recording is made?
   (d) Which method is economically correct, *ex ante*? Why?

EXERCISES

1. How do you evaluate the following claim: "The forward rate, if computed from Interest Rate Parity, entirely ignores the fact that the forward market is based on expectations. In reality, the market evaluates the currency's prospects, and takes into account not just the expected

value but also the risks. Any theory that would have us mechanically compute the forward rate from the current spot rate and the interest rates is totally crazy."

Before formulating your comments, think about the direction of causality (if any) implied by Interest Rate Parity.

2. Suppose that you sold forward (360 days) GBP 1m at the forward rate CAD/GBP 1.82 to hedge a payment from a British customer. Eleven months later the GBP trades at CAD/GBP 2.1, and (annualized) interest rates for 30 days are 12 percent for the CAD, 18 percent for the GBP. Unexpectedly, the customer pays one month early. Consider the following alternatives. You may:
   (a) Invest the GBP 1m for one month, and deliver them to the bank with which you signed the forward contract.
   (b) Sell the GBP 1m spot, and negotiate an early termination of the outstanding forward sale.
   (c) Sell the GBP 1m spot, and buy them forward 30 days so that you can deliver the required amount to your bank.
   Analyze each alternative. If the cash flows differ, trace the basis of the difference.

3. You, a Belgian importer, have made a large order for Dotty Dolls. You should receive the shipment in six months, just in time for pre-Christmas shopping. The sales contract demands immediate payment upon receipt of the shipment. The unit price for your bulk order of 50,000 dolls is HKD 10. The spot exchange rate BEF/HKD is 6, and the simple *p.a.* interest rates for a six-month investment in Belgium and Hong Kong are, respectively, 8 percent and 12 percent.
   (a) How would you hedge your payment for the dolls?
   (b) Suppose that three months after hedging the purchase, there is a fire in the doll factory. The dolls will not be delivered, but you still have an outstanding forward purchase contract for HKD 500,000. If the spot rate is now 6.1, and the simple *p.a.* interest rates for a three-month investment are 8 percent and 13 percent in Belgium and Hong Kong, respectively, what is the value of your forward contract? Have you made a gain or loss?

4. Graham Cage, the mayor of Atlantic Beach, in the US, has received bids from three dredging companies for a beach renewal project. The work is carried out in three stages, with partial payment to be made at the completion of each stage. The current FC/USD spot rates are DEM/USD 1.6, FRF/USD 5.5, and CAD/USD 1.3. The effective USD returns that correspond to the completion of each stage are the following: $r_{0,1} = 6.00$ percent, $r_{0,2} = 6.25$ percent and $r_{0,3} = 6.50$ percent. The companies' bids are shown below. Each forward rate corresponds to the expected completion date of each stage.

Company	Stage 1	Stage 2	Stage 3
Hamburg Dredging	DEM 1,700,000	DEM 1,800,000	DEM 1,900,000
forward rate DEM/USD	$F_{0,1} = 1.65$	$F_{0,2} = 1.70$	$F_{0,3} = 1.75$
Marseille Dredging	FRF 5,200,000	FRF 5,800,000	FRF 6,500,000
forward rate FRF/USD	$F_{0,1} = 5.50$	$F_{0,2} = 5.45$	$F_{0,3} = 5.35$
Vancouver Dredging	CAD 1,300,000	CAD 1,400,000	CAD 1,500,000
forward rate CAD/USD	$F_{0,1} = 1.35$	$F_{0,2} = 1.30$	$F_{0,3} = 1.25$

(a) Which offer should Mayor Cage accept?

(b) Was he wise to accept the bids in each company's own currency? Please explain.

5. Suppose you have a clause in a forward purchase contract that gives you a partial timing option: you can buy USD against DEM at a forward rate $F_{t_0,T}$, either at time T, or two months earlier. Right now you are at the intermediate decision date ($T - 2$ months). You must decide whether to buy now or at T.

(a) Assume that, at the beginning of this two-month period, the term structure of compound interest rates is flat for maturities up to one year, with a *p.a.* DEM interest rate of 10 percent and a USD interest rate of 6 percent. Would you decide to buy the USD now ($t = T - 2$ months), or would you rather wait? Make this decision in each of the following nine situations regarding the current spot rates S_t and contractual prices $F_{t_0,T}$:

contract price $F_{t_0,T}$:	1.5	2	2.5 (DEM/USD)
current spot rate			
1.5	...	...	...
2	...	...	...
2.5	...	...	...

(b) Repeat (a), but reverse the interest rates.

(c) How would your answers change if the clause is modified as follows: if you buy immediately, then the amount of DEM would be discounted (at the then prevailing DEM rate), while the amount of USD payable would be discounted (at the then prevailing USD interest rate). You should be able to do this without any computations.

MIND-EXPANDING EXERCISES

1. Suppose that you expect to receive FRF at a future date T. We can translate this FRF cash flow into home currency, LUF, and discount; or discount at a FRF cost of capital, and then translate. For simplicity, assume away uncertainty about the FRF cash flows. Which of the following alternatives are correct? Why? Under what assumptions?

(a) Translate FRF cash flows into home currency using the expected future spot rate, and discount at the home currency risk-free rate.

(b) Translate FRF cash flows into home currency using the forward rate for that maturity, and discount at the home currency risk-free rate.

(c) Discount at the FRF risk-free rate, and translate using the expected future spot rate.

(d) Discount at the FRF risk-free rate, and translate using the current spot rate.

(e) Translate FRF cash flows at the current spot rate, and discount at the home currency risk-free rate.

2. By "marking to market a forward contract" we mean "adjusting the forward rate fixed in an old contract to the currently prevailing forward rate" (see also Chapter 4). For instance, an

old DEM_{T_2} contract at $F_{t,T_2} = BEF/DEM$ 20.5 would be replaced, at time $T_1 < T_2$, by a new forward contract at the then prevailing rate $F_{T_1,T_2} = 20.6$.

Clearly the change in the terms of the contract will require some compensation from the loser to the winner. What payment should be made? Assume it is a purchase for DEM 10m, and that $r_{T_1,T_2} = 0.02$. Check if both parties are indifferent to marking to market.

3. A Future Rate Agreement (FRA) in principle fixes an interest rate for a deposit or loan starting at a future time $T_1 > t$ and expiring at $T_2 > T_1$. For instance, a six- to nine-month FRA at 10 percent (simple annualized interest) fixes the return on a three-month deposit, to be made six months from now, at $10\%/4 = 2.5\%$. Thus, this transaction has as its input BEF_{T_1}, and output $BEF_{T_2} = BEF_{T_1} \times (1 + r^{fwd}_{t,T_1,T_2})$.

   (a) Make a diagram showing all possible transactions; derive the no-arbitrage bounds; check that least cost dealing computations are unnecessary in the absence of spreads when the no-arbitrage conditions are met.

   (b) In practice, the deposit is notional, or theoretical. You do not have to effectively make a deposit; instead, at time T_1 there is a cash settlement of the difference between the contracted forward interest rate (r^{fwd}) and the time T_1 prevailing market rate. How do we compute the amount to be paid or received at T_1?

4. A friend, who works in the London City, claims that he has a bright idea for a new financial product: the Forward Operation On a Forward Exchange Liquidation (FOOFEL). A FOOFEL starts with a notional forward purchase contract signed at t and expiring at T_2; and it stipulates that, at a pre-specified time T_1 ($< T_2$), the loser will buy back this contract from the winner.

   (a) What payment should be made from the loser to the winner (as a function of S, F, r, and r^* observed at T_1)?

   (b) Explain the difference and similarity with a forward contract F_{t,T_2} having as an additional clause that it will be marked to market at T_1.

   (c) Is the FOOFEL aimed at hedgers, speculators, or both? If speculators use it, is this a bet on time-T_1 spot rates, or on interest rates, or what?

   (d) How should the initial contract price be set such that the FOOFEL has a zero initial value?

4 FORWARD CONTRACTS AND MARKET IMPERFECTIONS

In this chapter, we address some of the issues that arise when the forward market is imperfect. The first issue is **credit risk** (or **default risk**). Credit risk implies that bankers dislike long-term contracts unless a company's credit standing is excellent or it has put up substantial margin. Partly because of credit risk, there is no well-organized secondary market for forward contracts. We shall discuss how the problems arising from credit risk are addressed in the forward market. The second issue is the impact of transactions costs in exchange and money markets. We shall extend the diagram derived in Chapter 2, and show how our conclusions from the arbitrage and least cost dealing analyses have to be altered in the presence of transactions costs.

The structure of this chapter is as follows. In the first section, we explain the credit-risk issue, and describe various ways in which default risk can be reduced. In Section 4.2, we initiate an analysis of the impact of bid-ask spreads with a discussion of how forward rates are quoted in the presence of such spreads. In the third section, we identify the synthetic forward rates in the presence of spreads. The bounds on actual forward quotes imposed by arbitrage and least cost dealing then follow naturally, and are derived in Sections 4.4 and 4.5. Section 4.6 illustrates why, in the presence of spreads and discriminatory taxes, it is always worthwhile for the corporate treasurer to do the calculations necessary to determine the cheapest route for a given transaction.

4.1 CREDIT RISK IN FORWARD CONTRACTS

When asked for forward contracts, bankers worry about default by their customers. Although there are many ways to reduce credit risk, the traditional solutions are not perfect. As we shall see, the credit-risk problem also makes it difficult to organize a secondary market for standard forward contracts. This absence of a secondary market where investors can liquidate previously signed forward positions further limits the attractiveness of forward contracts. As we shall see in Chapter 5, the emergence of the futures markets is largely in response to the problems of credit risk and illiquidity of forward contracts.

4.1.1   Default Risk and Illiquidity of Forward Contracts

As we saw in Chapter 3, a forward contract has two "legs": on the maturity date of the contract, the bank promises to pay a known amount of one currency, and the customer promises to pay a known amount of another currency. Each of these legs can be replicated by a money-market position. However, it is important to understand that, from a bank's point of view, the credit risk present in a forward contract is of a different nature than the credit risk present in a loan. Specifically, the loan and the deposit are tied to each other by the **right of offset**. The right of offset allows the bank to withhold its promised payment without being in breach of contract, should the customer default.[1] That is, if the customer fails to deliver foreign currency (worth $\tilde{S}_T$), the bank can withhold its promised payment $F_{t_0,T}$. The net loss then is $\tilde{S}_T - F_{t_0,T}$, not $\tilde{S}_T$.

Banks usually cover each forward contract with an opposite forward contract, or with an offsetting spot and money-market transaction ("swap," in its classical meaning). If the counterpart to the original forward contract defaults, the bank is stuck with **reverse risk**. Because of the customer's default on the original contract, the bank's offsetting forward position has suddenly become an open, unhedged contract.

Example   4.1

Company C bought forward USD 1m against DEM. The bank, which has to deliver USD 1m, bought that amount in the interbank market to hedge its position. If Company C defaults, the bank has the right to withhold the delivery of the USD 1m. However, the bank still has to take delivery of (and pay for) the USD it had agreed to buy in the interbank market at a price X. Having received the (now unwanted) USD, the bank has no choice but to sell these USD in the spot market. Given default by C, the bank therefore has a risky cash flow of $(\tilde{S}_T - X)$.

The second problem with forward contracts is the lack of secondary markets. Suppose you wish to get rid of an outstanding forward contract. For instance, you have a customer who promised to pay you foreign currency three months from now and, accordingly, you sold forward the foreign currency revenue to hedge the A/R. Now you discover that your customer is bankrupt. In such a situation, you do not want to hold the outstanding hedge contract for another three months because you dislike the uncertainty of the contract's final value. Instead, you want to liquidate your forward position. (Likewise, a speculator would often like to cancel a previous engagement, either to cut losses or to lock in gains.) However, "selling" the original forward contract is difficult. First, there is no or-

---

[1] To obtain a security with the same credit risk in the case of a synthetic forward contract, the bank would have to insist that the customer hold the USD deposit part of its synthetic contract in an escrow account, to be released only after the customer's DEM loan is paid back. The forward contract is definitely the simpler way to achieve this security—which is one reason why an outright contract is cheaper than its synthetic version.

ganized market where you can auction off your contract. Second, each contract is tailor-made in terms of its maturity and contract amount, and not many people are likely to be interested in your specific contract. Third, your contract has guarantees for covering default risk (see below) and, without its consent, your bank may not want you to be replaced as a counterparty. Thus, the problem of illiquidity is partly explained by the credit-risk problem.

Example 4.2

Suppose a Spanish wine merchant received an order for ten casks of 1938 Amontillado, worth USD 1,234,567 and payable in 90 days, from a (then) rich American, Don Bump. The Spanish merchant hedged this transaction by selling the USD forward. However, after 35 days, Don Bump goes bankrupt and will obviously be unable to pay for the wine. The exporter would like to get out of the forward contract, but it is not easy to find someone else who also wants to sell forward exactly USD 1,234,567 for 55 days from the current date. In addition, the wine merchant would have to convince his banker that the new counterparty is at least as creditworthy as himself.

4.1.2 Standard Ways of Reducing Default Risk in the Forward Market

Banks have come up with various solutions that partially solve the problem of default risk.

- In the interbank market, the players deal only with counterparties that belong to "the club," that is, other banks and corporations that are well-known to one another and have excellent reputations. Even there, credit limits are set per bank to limit default risk.
- Likewise, corporations can buy or sell forward only if they are well-known by the bank, and even then, credit limits are set and/or margin has to be posted.

Example 4.3

Expecting a depreciation of the pound sterling, Berton Freedman wants to sell forward GBP 1m for six months. The 180-day forward rate is USD/GBP 1.5. The bank, worried about the contingency that the pound may actually go up, asks for 25 percent margin. This means that Mr. Freedman has to deposit 1m x USD/GBP $1.5 \times 0.25 =$ USD 375,000 with the bank, which remains with the bank until he has paid for the GBP. The interest earned on the deposit is Mr. Freedman's. This way, the bank is covered against the combined contingency of the GBP rising by up to 25 percent and Mr. Freedman defaulting on the contract.

For unknown or risky customers, the margin may be as high as 100 percent.

- Even within an agreed credit line, "speculative" forward positions are frowned upon—unless 100 percent margin is posted. Banks see forwards as hedging devices for their customers, not as speculative instruments.
- Maturities of forward contracts are short. Most contracts have maturities less than one year, and longer-term contracts are entered into only with customers who have excellent credit rat-

ings. To hedge long-term exposures one then needs to *roll over* short-term forward contracts. For example, the corporation can engage in three consecutive one-year contracts if a single three-year contract is not available.

Example   4.4

At time 0, an Austrian company wants to buy forward USD 1m for three years. Suppose that the bank gives it a three-year forward contract at $F_{0,3}$ = ATS/USD 10. Consider an example in which there are losses—which are banks' biggest concerns: the spot rate goes down to 9, 8, and 7 at times 1, 2, and 3, respectively. If, at time 3, the company defaults, the bank is stuck with USD 1m worth ATS 7m rather than the contracted value, 10m. Thus, the bank has a loss of $(S_3 - F_{0,3})$ = ATS 3m.[2]

Suppose instead that at $t = 0$, the bank gave a one-year contract at the rate $F_{0,1} = 10$. After one year, the customer pays ATS 10m for the currency, takes delivery of the USD 1m, and sells these (spot) at $S_1 = 9$. After verification of the company's current creditworthiness, the bank now gives it a new one-year contract at, say, $F_{1,2} = 8.8$. At time $t = 2$, the customer takes the second loss. If it is still creditworthy, the customer will get a third one-year forward contract at, say, $F_{2,3} = 7.9$. If there is default at time 3, the bank's loss on the third contract is just 900,000 rather than the 3m it would have lost with the single three-year contract.

From the bank's point of view, the main advantage of the alternative of rolling over short-term contracts is that losses do not accumulate. The uncertainty, at time 0, about the spot rate one year hence is far smaller than the uncertainty about the rate three years hence. Thus, the worst possible loss on a three-year contract exceeds the worst possible loss on a one-year contract. In addition, the probability of default increases with the size of the loss. Therefore, the bank's expected losses from default are larger the longer the maturity of the forward contract.

The example also demonstrates that rolling over is an imperfect substitute to a single three-year forward contract. First, the hedger does not know at what interest rates he or she will be able to finance the interim losses (or invest the interim gains). Second, the hedger does not know to what extent the forward rates will deviate from the spot rates at the roll-over dates: these future forward premia depend on the (unknown) future interest rates in both currencies. Third, the total cumulative cash flow, realized by the hedger over the three consecutive contracts, depends on the time path of the spot rates between time 1 and time 3—unless, as can be shown, the hedger adjusts the size of each intermediate contract.

From the above discussion, we see that the problem of credit risk is more or less solved by restricting access to the forward market, by requiring margins and pledges, and by limiting the maturities of forward contracts. The problem of illiquidity arising from the absence of secondary markets, however, is not addressed. One can negotiate an early (premature) settlement with the original counterparty of the forward contract. But this is a question of negotiation, not a built-in

---

[2] As mentioned, the bank will have covered its position in the forward market or in the spot market; the cost of the bank is likely to be very close to ATS 3m. In short, the loss of 3m is not just an opportunity cost, it is a real cash loss.

right for the holder of the contract. Also, one cannot rely on an immediately observable market price to determine the value of the outstanding contract. Rather, one has to compute the bounds on the fair value (using the *Law of the Worst Possible Combination*), and negotiate some price within these bounds.[3] Thus, the early settlement of forward contracts is rather inconvenient. As a result, and in contrast to futures contracts—as we shall see in Chapter 5—virtually all forward contracts remain outstanding until they expire, and actual delivery and payment is the rule rather than the exception.

4.1.3 Reducing Default Risk by Variable Collateral or Periodic Recontracting

As we saw in the previous section, one often needs to post margin when a forward contract is bought or sold. The margin may consist of an interest-earning term deposit, or of securities (like stock or bonds). It is important to understand that the margin is very different from a *payment* to the bank. A payment is made to pay back a debt, or to become the owner of a commodity or a financial asset. Whatever the reason for the payment, the bank that receives a payment becomes the owner of the money. In contrast, margin that is posted still belongs to the customer; the bank or broker merely has the right to seize the collateral if or when the customer defaults.

The required margin can be quite high because the bank is willing to take only a small chance that the contract's expiration value, if negative, is not covered by the margin. In about half of the cases, the collateral will turn out to have been unnecessary because there is roughly a 50 percent chance that $\tilde{S}_T - F_{t_0,T}$ will end up being positive. There are two ways to reduce the need for margin.

- *Variable collateral.* Under this system, the bank requests two kinds of margin. First, there is a small but permanent margin—say, the amount that almost surely covers the worst possible one-day drop in the market value of the forward contract.[4] If the market value of the contract becomes negative, the bank then asks for additional collateral in order to cover at least the current market value of the forward contract. If the customer fails to put up the additional margin, the bank seizes all margin put up in the past—including the initial safety margin—and closes out the outstanding contract in the forward market. Obviously, under such a system the amount of collateral that has to be put up is far smaller, on average, than what is required if a single,

---

[3] That is, the perfect-markets valuation formula $\dfrac{F_{t,T} - F_{t_0,T}}{1 + r_{t,T}}$ becomes:

$$\frac{F_{\text{bid},t,T} - F_{t_0,T}}{1 + r_{\text{ask},t,T}} \le \text{value purchase contract} \le \frac{F_{\text{ask},t,T} - F_{t_0,T}}{1 + r_{\text{bid},t,T}}$$

and

$$\frac{F_{t_0,T} - F_{\text{ask},t,T}}{1 + r_{\text{ask},t,T}} \le \text{value sales contract} \le \frac{F_{t_0,T} - F_{\text{bid},t,T}}{1 + r_{\text{bid},t,T}} .$$

For instance, the lower bound on the value of the purchase contract is obtained by considering the holder's option to close out and sell at the bid, assuming that the holder is in a borrowing position. The upper bound on the value of the purchase is what another person, who is looking for a forward purchase contract, would be willing to pay if in a lending position.

[4] In Chapter 3, we defined the market value of the contract as the *discounted* difference between the current forward rate and the historic forward rate.

FIGURE 4.1   Cash Flows When a Forward Contract Is Recontracted Periodically

	Cash flow at time t from recontracting	Value, at time 4, if cash flow is carried over to time 4
On day 1:	$\dfrac{F_{1,4} - F_{0,4}}{1 + r_{1,4}}$	$F_{1,4} - F_{0,4}$
On day 2:	$\dfrac{F_{2,4} - F_{1,4}}{1 + r_{2,4}}$	$F_{2,4} - F_{1,4}$
On day 3:	$\dfrac{F_{3,4} - F_{2,4}}{1 + r_{3,4}}$	$F_{3,4} - F_{2,4}$
On day 4:	(No recontracting)	$\underline{S_{4,4} - F_{3,4}}$ (Gain/loss on last contract)
		$S_4 - F_{0,4}$ (Total cash flows)

large initial margin has to be posted. The reason is that, under this system, collateral is called for only when needed, and only to the extent that it is needed at that time.

- *Daily recontracting.* Under this system, the new market value of yesterday's contract is computed every day. The party that ends up with a negative value then buys back the contract from the counterparty, and both sign a new contract at the day's new price. If the loser fails to settle the value of yesterday's contract, the bank seizes the initial margin, and closes out the contract in the forward market. Under this system, only a small amount of margin is needed, since the collateral has to cover only a one-day change in the market value.

It is useful to spell out the cash flows when there is periodic recontracting, because this will help in understanding what futures contracts are and why they differ from recontracted forwards. The interim cash flows (at times 1, 2, and 3) from recontracting a forward purchase contract are shown in the first column of Figure 4.1. In the second column, we show the time-T cash flow that arises if each interim cash inflow is invested until time T, and if all cash outflows are likewise financed by a loan expiring at T. For simplicity of notation, the time of initiating the first contract is set equal to 0, and the expiration time is $T = 4$. The crucial message is this: because recontracting triggers cash flows that are equal to the discounted change in the forward price, the total payment at time T is basically unaffected by the recontracting in the sense that, once one corrects for time value, the outflow is still equivalent to paying $F_{0,T}$ and receiving S_T at T. Or, stated differently, the investor can—without cost— "undo" the cash flows from recontracting by the simple expedient of investing all inflows until time T and financing all outflows by loans that expire at T.

Example   4.5

Suppose that, at time 0, investor B has bought forward GBP against ITL for delivery at time 3. In the tracting, respectively. We ignore the initial margin, since it is the same in both cases. All amounts are in ITL. The example assumes that the forward rate always goes down. This is the possibility about which bankers worry.

Forward price, $F_{t,3}$, in ITL/GBP	ITL return, $r_{t,3}$	Variable Collateral	Periodic Recontracting
At time 0: $F_{0,3} = 2500$	3%	B buys forward at $F_{0,3} = 2500$	B buys forward at $F_{0,3} = 2500$
At time 1: $F_{1,3} = 2400$	2%	Market value of contract is $\dfrac{2400 - 2500}{1.02} = -98.04.$ B puts up T-bills worth at least 98.04.	Market value of contract is $\dfrac{2400 - 2500}{1.02} = -98.04.$ B buys back the old contract for 98.04, and buys a new contract at $F_{1,3} = 2400.$
At time 2: $F_{2,3} = 2350$	1%	Market value of contract is $\dfrac{2500 - 2350}{1.01} = -148.5.$ B puts up additional T-bills so that market value of total collateral is at least 148.5.	Market value of contract is $\dfrac{2400 - 2350}{1.01} = -49.50.$ B buys back the old contract for 49.50, and buys a new contract at $F_{2,3} = 2350.$
At time 3: $S_3 = 2200$	0%	B's payments: time 3: 2500 All T-bills are returned to B.	B's total payments adjusted for time value: time 3: 2350 time 2: $49.50 \times 1.01 =$ 50 time 1: $98.04 \times 1.02 =$ 100 ———— 2500

• In the "Variable Collateral" column, investor B intially buys a contract at $F_{0,3} = 2500$; this contract remains outstanding until time $T = 3$. If its market value becomes negative, investor B has to make sure that the market value of the T-bills being put up as collateral covers at least the market value.

• In the "Periodic Recontracting" column, investor B signs a three-period contract, but after one period she buys it back and signs a (two-period) contract at the new two-period forward price; then, at time 2, this contract is bought back once more and replaced by a (one-period) contract at the new one-period forward price. Since at each day the market value is the discounted price change, the total payments are still equivalent to 2500 at time 3.

The system of variable collateral is used in some exchanges in continental Europe. Somewhat confusingly, these contracts are sometimes called futures contracts; in reality, they are collateralized forward contracts.

This finishes our discussion of credit risks in forward contracts. The second issue in this chapter is the impact of bid-ask spreads on Interest Rate Parity and on the relevance of least cost dealing. Let us first see how forward rates are quoted if there are bid-ask spreads.

4.2   HOW FORWARD RATES ARE QUOTED WITH BID-ASK SPREADS

With bid-ask spreads, a forward rate can still be quoted "outright" (that is, as an absolute number), or as a swap rate. The outright quote is like a spot quote; for instance, the rates may be CAD/USD (180 days) 1.187–1.190. Swap rates, on the other hand, show the numbers that are to be added to/subtracted from the spot bid and ask rates in order to obtain the forward quotes. One ought to be careful in interpreting such quotes, and make sure that the correct number is added to or subtracted from the spot bid or ask rate.

Example   4.6

The Antwerp *Financieel Ekonomische Tijd* of Wednesday, April 20, 1994 shows the following rates. Spot rates are quoted in units of BEF/FC. The swap rates are quoted in centimes per unit of foreign currency, that is, per one-hundredths of one franc.

	Spot	Previous day	1 month		2 month		3 month		6 month	
1 USD	35.2125	35.2425	+6.1	+6.3	+11.5	+12.0	+15.8	+16.5	+24.5	+26.0
1 ECU	39.8125	39.7850	−1.7	−1.0	−2.6	−1.6	−2.7	−1.3	−4.3	−1.5
1 GBP	51.4175	20.5855	+2.9	+3.5	+6.3	+7.4	+9.2	+10.9	+14.7	+17.7
1 FRF	6.0135	6.0160	−0.2	−0.0	−0.3	−0.1	−0.4	−0.1	−0.5	−0.1
1 NLG	18.3340	18.3410	+0.6	+0.8	+1.6	+2.0	+2.4	+2.9	+4.8	+5.8
100 JPY	34.0550	33.9450	+10.0	+10.4	+20.5	+21.3	+30.1	+31.2	+58.3	+60.6

To compute the outright forward rates from these quotes, one adds the first swap rate to the spot bid rate, and the second swap rate to the spot ask rate. The excerpt shows the midpoint spot rate rather than the bid-ask quotes. Suppose, however, that the bid and ask spot rates are 35.200–35.225 for the USD. Then the outright forward rates, one month, are computed as follows:

Bid: 35.2000 + 6.1/100 = BEF/USD 35.2610.
Ask: 35.2250 + 6.3/100 = BEF/USD 35.2880.

Similarly, if the bid and ask spot rates for the ECU are BEF 39.800–39.825, the forward rates are computed as:

Bid: 39.8000 − 1.7/100 = BEF/ECU 39.7830.
Ask: 39.8250 − 1.0/100 = BEF/ECU 39.8150.

Note from the example that in case of a premium we always add the smaller of the two swap rates to the spot bid rate, and the larger swap rate to the spot ask rate. As a result, the forward spread is wider than the spot spread. Likewise, in case of a discount, the number we subtract from the spot bid rate is larger, in absolute value, than the number we subtract from the spot ask rate; and this again produces a wider spread in the forward market than in the spot market. Finally, note that the difference between the swap rates becomes larger the longer the contract's time to maturity. This illustrates the **Second Law of Imperfect Exchange Markets**: the forward spread is always larger than the spot spread, and increases with the time to maturity. One explanation of this empirical regularity is that the longer the maturity, the lower the transaction volume; and in thin markets, spreads tend to be high. A second reason is that, the longer the maturity, the larger the chance that the customer's creditworthiness may have deteriorated by time T. This is especially relevant for contracts exceeding a few years. Thus, banks build in a default risk premium into their spreads, which, therefore, goes up with time to maturity. Later on we will see by how much the spreads can go up maximally with time to maturity.

The *Second Law* keeps you from getting irretrievably lost when confronted with bid-ask swap quotes, because the convention of quoting is by no means uniform internationally. Sometimes the swap rates are quoted, regardless of sign, as "small number–big number," followed by p (for premium) or d (for discount). That is, in the preceding example the USD and ECU quotes could have been shown as:

USD	1 month	6.1–6.3 p.
ECU	1 month	1.0–1.7 d.

Under this convention, the premia are shown in the same way as in the *Financieel Economische Tijd*, but the discounts are reversed: now the smallest discount is shown first, followed by the largest discount. The *Second Law* then tells us that, for the ECU, the rates must be:

	Spot	Swap	Forward
Bid:	39.8000	– 1.7/100	= BEF/ECU 39.7830
Ask:	39.8250	– 1.0/100	= BEF/ECU 39.8150
Spread	0.0250		BEF/ECU 0.0320

This way, the forward spread is larger than the spot spread. In contrast, if we had subtracted the first number from the bid spot rate and the second number from the ask spot rate, we would soon have found the error of our ways because the forward spread would be smaller than the spot spread:

	Spot	Swap	Forward
Bid:	39.8000	– 1.0/100	= BEF/ECU 39.7900
Ask:	39.8250	– 1.7/100	= BEF/ECU 39.8080
Spread	0.0250		BEF/ECU 0.0180

Let us now address weightier matters. One question to be answered is whether Interest Rate Parity still holds in the presence of spreads. A useful first step in this analysis is to determine the synthetic forward rates.

4.3 SYNTHETIC FORWARD RATES

The procedure we follow in determining the bounds on the forward rates is similar to what we did in the case of triangular arbitrage: first, we identify the synthetic forward rates implied by sequences of transactions that replicate an explicit forward contract, and then we derive the familiar arbitrage bounds. To determine the synthetic rates, we start by adjusting the exchange- and money-market-transactions diagram (Figure 2.6 of Chapter 2) for bid-ask spreads.

In the adjusted diagram of Figure 4.2, we use the same symbols (HC, FC, S, F, r, r^*) as before, but now they are complemented by the subscripts "bid" or "ask." As always, bid and ask correspond

FIGURE 4.2   Spot, Forward, and Money-Market Transactions in the Presence of Bid-Ask Spreads

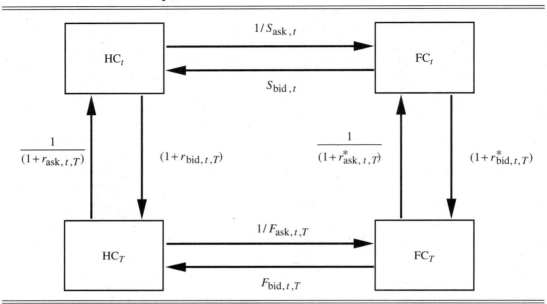

to low and high, respectively. That is, you sell foreign exchange at the bid and buy at the ask. In the money markets, you lend (invest) at the bid rate, and you borrow at the ask rate.[5]

To lay the groundwork for the analysis of the arbitrage bounds, we first identify the synthetic bid and ask rates that are implied by replication of forward contracts.[6]

4.3.1   The Synthetic Forward Bid Rate

The **synthetic bid rate** is the rate that we obtain when selling foreign currency forward—that is, delivering FC_T as input to the banking system and receiving a known output, HC_T, in return. From Figure 4.2, the alternative to a direct forward sale is to borrow foreign currency ($FC_T \rightarrow FC_t$), convert the proceeds of the loan into home currency in the spot market ($FC_t \rightarrow HC_t$), and invest this amount in domestic currency ($HC_t \rightarrow HC_T$). By referring to Figure 4.2, we immediately recognize which rates are relevant for constructing the synthetic bid rate—the foreign ask rate for borrowing, the bid spot rate for the sale, and the domestic bid return for the home currency investment.[7] Recall that FC_T is an amount of future foreign currency promised to the bank; the ultimate HC_T that corresponds to this input is:

$$HC_T = \frac{FC_T}{1 + r^*_{\text{ask},t,T}} \times S_{\text{bid},t} \times (1 + r_{\text{bid},t,T}).$$

---

[5] In the UK, the ask (interest) rate is called the *offer rate*—for instance, London Interbank Offer Rate (LIBOR). This terminology has been adopted in many European money markets (for example, PIBOR in Paris, HIBOR in Helsinki, and so on). We use "ask."

[6] The notions of synthetic rates and replication are defined in Chapters 2 and 3.

[7] Note, in passing, that for each step we get the worse of the two rates.

The implied synthetic bid rate then is the number of future home currency units obtained per unit of FC_T.

$$\textit{Synthetic} \text{ forward bid rate } = \frac{HC_T}{FC_T} = S_{bid,t} \frac{1 + r_{bid,t,T}}{1 + r^*_{ask,t,T}}. \qquad [1]$$

This has the same fundamental form as the Interest Rate Parity expression obtained in perfect markets; and the subscripts (bid, ask) appended to the basic formula again fit in with the *Law of the Worst Possible Combination*. Recall that we are selling forward synthetically. The worst rate when selling is the lowest. We see that the entries into the formula indeed produce the lowest possible numerical value: the smaller numbers (S_{bid} and r_{bid}) are in the numerator, and the higher (r^*_{ask}) in the denominator.

Example 4.7

Suppose that we see the following data:

Exchange rates	Interest rates (simple, *p.a.*)	Effective 6-month returns
Spot DEM/USD 1.5–1.505	USD 6%–6.25%	USD 3%–3.125%
	DEM 8%–8.25%	DEM 4%–4.125%

A German company will receive USD 1.25m ($= FC_T$) from a customer six months from now. The company needs no cash now; rather, it simply wants to eliminate the uncertainty created by the open USD position. Using the path $(USD_T) = FC_T \rightarrow FC_t \rightarrow HC_t \rightarrow HC_T = (DEM_T)$ in Figure 4.2, we calculate the DEM_T proceeds from a synthetic forward sale of USD as follows.

$$DEM_T = \frac{1,250,000}{1.03125} \times 1.5 \times 1.04 = DEM\ 1,890,909m,$$

which implies a synthetic forward bid rate of:

$$\text{Synthetic forward bid rate} = \frac{DEM_T}{USD_T} = \frac{1,890,909}{1,250,000} = DEM/USD\ 1.51273.$$

4.3.2 The Synthetic Forward Ask Rate

Next, we identify the **synthetic forward ask rate**. This is the rate we pay when buying forward—that is, obtaining a known amount FC_T as output from the banking system in return for a known input HC_T. From the diagram, the alternative to a direct forward purchase is to borrow domestic currency ($HC_T \rightarrow HC_t$), convert the proceeds of the loan into foreign currency in the spot market ($HC_t \rightarrow FC_t$), and invest this amount in the foreign money market ($FC_t \rightarrow FC_T$). Referring to Figure 4.2, we immediately see which rates are relevant—the domestic ask rate for borrowing, the ask spot rate for the spot purchase, and the foreign bid return for the foreign currency investment. The ultimate output FC_T obtained from the first input HC_T is:

$$FC_T = \frac{HC_T}{1 + r_{ask,t,T}} \times \frac{1}{S_{ask,t}} \times (1 + r^*_{bid,t,T}).$$

As before, the implied synthetic rate is the number HC_T of home currency obtained per unit of FC_T.

$$\text{Synthetic forward ask rate} = \frac{HC_T}{FC_T} = S_{\text{ask},t} \frac{1 + r_{\text{ask},t,T}}{1 + r^*_{\text{bid},t,T}}. \qquad [2]$$

This time, the subscripts (bid, ask) appended to the basic formula $F = S(1 + r)/(1 + r^*)$ produce the highest possible numerical value: we have S_{ask} and r_{ask} in the numerator and r^*_{bid} in the denominator. The reason should be obvious: we are considering a forward purchase, and the higher the price to be paid to the bank, the worse off the buyer is. So this time the *Law of the Worst Possible Combination* predicts that the highest possible outcome is the relevant one.

Example 4.8

We use the same data as in Example 4.7. Suppose that a German company has to pay USD to a supplier six months from now. The company has no cash now; it just wants to eliminate the uncertainty created by the open USD position. From Figure 4.2, a unit input $DEM_T = 1$ produces an output USD_T equal to:

$$USD_T = \frac{1}{1.04125} \times \frac{1}{1.505} \times 1.03 = 0.6572728,$$

which implies a synthetic forward ask rate for USD of:

$$\text{Synthetic forward ask rate} = \frac{DEM_T}{USD_T} = \frac{1}{0.6572728} = DEM/USD\ 1.52144.$$

In summary, the synthetic bid and ask forward rates are, respectively, the lowest and highest possible form of the basic formula $F = S(1 + r)/(1 + r^*)$. It follows that, in the presence of spreads, the synthetic bid is always less than the synthetic ask. Stated differently, when there are transactions costs, the synthetic rates have a positive spread. Further, this spread is fairly wide, because each synthetic forward (bid and ask) involves three component deals (that is—borrowing, spot conversion, and lending) and, therefore, implicit commissions for three transactions. Finally, the spread widens with the time to maturity. The reason is that bid-ask spreads on interest rates are roughly constant *p.a.*, so that the bid-ask spreads on the effective returns increase with time to maturity.

Example 4.9

We use the same data as in Example 4.7 and add 360-day interest rates.

Exchange rates	Interest rates (simple, *p.a.*)		Effective returns	
Spot DEM/USD	180 days USD	6%–6.25%	USD	3%–3.125%
1.5–1.505	DEM	8%–8.25%	DEM	4%–4.125%
	360 days USD	7%–7.25%	USD	7%–7.25%
	DEM	8%–8.25%	DEM	8%–8.25%

The synthetic forward rates are easily computed as:

180 day   DEM/USD 1.51273–1.52144 implying a spread of 0.0087.

360 day   DEM/USD 1.51049–1.52258 implying a spread of 0.0121.

Thus, the spread between longer-dated synthetic rates increases because, even though the bid-ask spread in the *p.a.* interest rates is 0.25 percent for each maturity, the bid-ask spread between the effective returns increases.

4.4   THE ARBITRAGE BOUNDS ON THE FORWARD BID AND ASK RATES

In this section, we first examine how one can derive the arbitrage bounds on forward bid and ask rates, and then we provide some examples that show how one would search for arbitrage opportunities.

4.4.1   Determination of the Arbitrage Bounds

Having obtained the synthetic bid and ask rates, we now determine the bounds that the direct forward rates must satisfy to preclude arbitrage. These arbitrage bounds are obtained by arguments that are similar to the ones invoked in the case of triangular arbitrage (Chapter 1): it should not be possible to make risk-free profits by buying and selling simultaneously. That is:

- You cannot make money by synthetically buying (at the "ask") and then selling in the direct forward market (at the "bid").

$$F_{\text{bid},t,T} \leq \text{Synthetic forward ask rate} = S_{\text{ask},t} \frac{1 + r_{\text{ask},t,T}}{1 + r^*_{\text{bid},t,T}}. \qquad [3a]$$

- You cannot make money by buying in the direct market (at the "ask") and then selling in the synthetic forward market (at the "bid"):[8]

$$F_{\text{ask},t,T} \geq \text{Synthetic forward bid rate} = S_{\text{bid},t} \frac{1 + r_{\text{bid},t,T}}{1 + r^*_{\text{ask},t,T}}. \qquad [3b]$$

- A final requirement is that we cannot make risk-free instantaneous gains by buying and immediately selling back forward.

$$F_{\text{bid}} < F_{\text{ask}}. \qquad [3c]$$

---

[8] You can easily check that the bounds [3a] and [3b] are the result of arbitrage, the approach used in Chapter 1. That is, if you start with $HC_T = 1$ and go full circle through HC_t, FC_t, FC_T back to HC_T, the ultimate output cannot exceed the first input:

$$\frac{1}{1 + r_{\text{ask},t,T}} \times \frac{1}{S_{\text{ask},t}} (1 + r^*_{\text{bid},t,T}) \times F_{\text{bid},t,T} \leq 1.$$

This directly leads to bound [3a]. The other round-trip, $FC_T \rightarrow FC_t \rightarrow HC_t \rightarrow HC_T \rightarrow FC_T$, likewise leads to bound [3b].

The following illustration will make all of these relationships less abstract.

Example   4.10

Suppose that we observe the following quotes in the spot and money markets.

Spot exchange rates (LUF/AUD):   23.00–23.05
Domestic (LUF) interest rates, 180 days: 10.00–10.25% (simple, *p.a.* interest rate)
Foreign (AUD) interest rates, 180 days: 20.00–20.25% (simple, *p.a.* interest rate)

We can synthetically buy and sell AUD six months forward at:

$$\text{Synthetic forward ask rate} = 23.05 \ \frac{1+0.1025/2}{1+0.2000/2} = \text{LUF/AUD } 22.0285.$$

$$\text{Synthetic forward bid rate} = 23.00 \ \frac{1+0.1000/2}{1+0.2025/2} = \text{LUF/AUD } 21.9296.$$

Thus, we predict that the direct bid rate $F_{bid,t,T}$ will be no higher than the synthetic ask, 22.0285, and the direct ask rate $F_{ask,t,T}$ no lower than the synthetic bid, 21.9296. In addition, $F_{bid,t,T}$ must not exceed $F_{ask,t,T}$.

Now that we have identified the synthetic rates, we can proceed exactly as in Chapter 1 in the case of triangular arbitrage. Figure 4.3 is analogous to Figure 1.2: below the exchange rate axis are shown the synthetic rates, and above the axis are depicted some conceivable forward bid-ask quotes by market makers. These quotes are indicated as (i), (ii), . . . , (vi). Some of these conceivable bid-ask quotes can be ruled out as inconsistent with the absence of arbitrage opportunities:

- To rule out arbitrage, two quotes given by different bankers have to overlap by at least one point; otherwise, you can buy cheaply from one market maker (for instance, market maker [i] in Figure 4.3) and sell at a higher price to another (for example, market maker [iii]).
- To rule out arbitrage, the quotes given by any given banker have to overlap with the synthetic quotes by at least one point; otherwise, you can buy cheaply from one market maker (for example, from market maker [i] in Figure 4.3) and sell at a higher price at the synthetic forward bid; or, you can buy at the synthetic forward ask rate and immediately resell at a higher bid rate (for instance, to market maker [vi]).

Thus, given the synthetic rates, only the direct quotes in (ii), (iii), (iv), and (v) rule out arbitrage; quotes like (i) and (vi) allow for arbitrage, and therefore, are unlikely to be observed in the foreign exchange market.

4.4.2   Examples of Arbitrage Computations

In this section, we show how a treasurer should do arbitrage computations. In the examples, we use the following data.[9]

---

[9] The spreads are of the order of magnitude relevant for small investors.

FIGURE 4.3 **Direct Forward Quotes Relative to Synthetic Forward Quotes: Arbitrage and Least Cost Dealing**

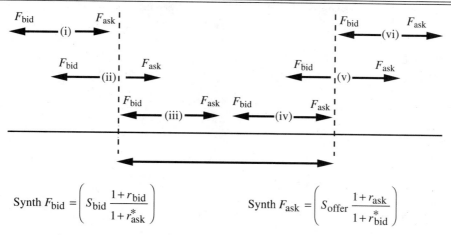

$$\text{Synth } F_{\text{bid}} = \left(S_{\text{bid}} \frac{1 + r_{\text{bid}}}{1 + r^*_{\text{ask}}} \right) \qquad \text{Synth } F_{\text{ask}} = \left(S_{\text{offer}} \frac{1 + r_{\text{ask}}}{1 + r^*_{\text{bid}}} \right)$$

Below the exchange-rate axis, we show the synthetic rates and above the axis we depict some conceivable forward bid-ask quotes by market makers (indicated as [i], [ii], ..., [vi]). Of these, quotes like (i) and (vi) are incompatible with the synthetic quotes because they allow arbitrage relative to the synthetic quotes. Quotes like (ii) and (v) can be predicted to be, at best, short-run phenomena on the basis of least cost dealing. With such quotes, market maker (ii) would have only buyers and (v), only sellers.

In the lower part of Figure 4.4, we have translated the annualized interest rates into returns. If you forget to translate, all subsequent work is pointless.

Clockwise Round-Trip
Analyzing a round-trip might reveal free lunches, that is, violations of the arbitrage bound. We start with LUF_T 1m and look first at the clockwise round-trip.

FIGURE 4.4 **Spot and Forward Quotes, Interest Rates, and Risk-Free Returns for Arbitrage and Least Cost Dealing Computations**

Exchange Rates	Bid	Ask
Spot	41.3950	41.5750
6-month forward	41.3150	41.5150
Interest Rates*		
LUF	10.0%	12.0%
ECU	8.0%	10.0%
Returns (6 months)		
LUF	5.0%	6.0%
ECU	4.0%	5.0%

* Simple interest rates

- Discount the LUF_T 1m promissory note.

$$LUF_t = \frac{1,000,000}{1.06} = LUF\ 943,396.$$

- Convert into spot ECU.

$$ECU_t = \frac{943,396}{41.575} = ECU\ 22,691.43.$$

- Then invest in an ECU deposit.

$$ECU_T = 22,691.43 \times 1.04 = ECU\ 23,599.09.$$

- Finally, sell forward the deposit's expiration value.

$$LUF_T = 23,599.09 \times 41.3150 = LUF\ 974,996.$$

The same final output can be obtained by following the arrows in Figure 4.2 from input LUF_t = 1m, and multiplying by all of the factors you meet along the path:

$$\text{Output } LUF_T = \frac{1,000,000}{1.06}\ \frac{1}{41.575} \times 1.04 \times 41.3150 = LUF\ 974,996.$$

Conclusion: the ultimate LUF_T-output is insufficient to cover the promissory note. Instead of making a profit, we would lose about 25,000 francs if we were to undertake this series of transactions.

Counter-Clockwise Transactions
The counter-clockwise round-trip works out as follows. Suppose that we start with LUF 1m in cash, which we invest and then combine with a covered loan. The steps are the following:

- Lend LUF.

$$LUF_T = 1m \times 1.05 = LUF\ 1.05m.$$

- Buy forward ECU with the proceeds of your deposit.

$$ECU_T = \frac{1.05m}{41.515} = ECU\ 25,292.063.$$

- Borrow ECU against this amount; you can borrow:

$$ECU_t = \frac{25,292.063}{1.05} = ECU\ 24,087.679.$$

- Convert the ECU into LUF using the spot rate.

$$LUF_t = 24{,}087.679 \times 41.3950 = LUF\ 997{,}109.479.$$

Again, the shortcut is to follow the arrows in Figure 4.2, starting from input $LUF_t = 1m$:

$$\text{Output } LUF_t = 1m \times 1.05 \times \frac{1}{41.515} \times \frac{1}{1.05} \times 41.3950 = LUF\ 997{,}109.479 < 1m.$$

Conclusion: Again, this round-trip produces a loss. We can expect results like these because arbitrage gains should not exist.

4.5   EMPIRICAL TESTS OF THE ARBITRAGE BOUNDS

The conclusion of the above arbitrage argument is that the "exact" Interest Rate Parity equality has been replaced by the bounds (given in relations [3a] and [3b]), which must hold to rule out arbitrage opportunities. Tests of these inequalities show that the bounds hold perfectly if one uses euro-interest rate data, that is, rates in offshore financial markets.[10] This result can be interpreted almost as a test of the quality of the data rather than as a test of market efficiency. Indeed, we know that all banks' computers continuously search for arbitrage gains; thus, free lunches exist, at best, for very short periods.

Not surprisingly, the bounds (given in relations [3a] and [3b]) are violated more often if one uses interest rates obtained from internal ("on-shore") money markets (like local T-bill markets, or bank deposit markets inside the currency's country of origin) rather than offshore money markets. There are a number of possible reasons why the bounds given in Equations [3a] and [3b] are sometimes not met when on-shore interest data are used.

- Purely domestic money markets are less perfectly integrated in terms of organization. For instance, trading times on US/UK T-bill markets do not coincide, the execution of an order on the T-bill market takes time, and so on. In contrast, doing a spot and a reverse forward deal in the interbank market takes only a few seconds, while the money-market deals can be made afterwards because interest rates are fairly stable.
- Access to purely domestic markets is sometimes limited or regulated—for instance, Belgium's T-bill market used to be reserved for Belgian-based banks or bank branches; Ireland had various controls over who was allowed to hold positions, etc.
- A "domestic" deposit in, say, GBP is under the control of the Bank of England, whereas a GBP deposit in Zurich is not.
    - This implies differences in "political risk." The Bank of England may have imposed currency controls by the time the London GBP deposit expires. In contrast, the Bank of England cannot control GBP deposits in Zurich, and the Swiss central bank does not care about pressure on the GBP—or at least not to the extent that it would consider enforcing currency controls on GBP in Switzerland.

---

[10] Euromarkets are defined in the introductory chapter.

- In "domestic" money markets, compulsory insurance (for instance, FDIC insurance in the US), reserve requirements, and such regulations, drive a wedge between effective and nominal interest rates. These factors are not present in the less unregulated euromarkets.
- In "domestic" deposit markets, time is often counted differently from the conventions in the forward market; thus, perceived returns may differ from effective returns.[11]

For the last two reasons, apparent arbitrage opportunities may not represent genuine free lunches—because of measurement errors, or because of barriers-to-entry into "on-shore" capital markets.

4.6   BOUNDS IMPOSED ON THE FORWARD RATE BY LEAST COST DEALING

The analysis thus far is very similar to our treatment of triangular arbitrage bounds on cross-rates. In Chapter 1, we discovered that, using least cost dealing arguments, we could rule out quotes that could not be ruled out simply on the basis of arbitrage. That is, in the presence of bid-ask spreads, the cost of doing a particular transaction in different ways will not be the same. Investors, by choosing the cheaper route, will affect prices. The same analysis can be applied here to obtain bounds on the forward rate, in addition to the bounds obtained by ruling out arbitrage opportunities.

4.6.1   Determining the Bounds Imposed by Least Cost Dealing

Deardorff (1979) was probably the first to point out that analyzing just the arbitrage bounds is insufficient. Indeed, he argues, even quotes like (ii) and (v) in Figure 4.3 cannot persist. The reason is that customers compare direct quotes with the synthetic rates. If one of the direct quotes is not within the spread of synthetic rates, this direct quote will never be used, implying that the market maker will soon end up with an unbalanced position.

- For example, with direct market quotes given by (ii) in the figure, all forward sellers would sell at the (higher) synthetic bid price. That is, in the (direct) forward market, there would be only purchases, no sales. As a result, market maker (ii) would soon run out of foreign currency, and would have to increase his or her quotes relative to the synthetic quotes. Moving up the quotes to level (iii) or higher would ensure that the market maker has both buyers and sellers.
- Similarly, with direct market quotes like (v) in the figure, all forward buyers would buy at the (lower) synthetic ask price, and the (direct) forward market would attract only sellers. As a result, market maker (v) would soon accumulate huge foreign currency balances, and would have to decrease his quotes relative to the synthetic quotes. Moving down the quotes to level (iv) or lower would ensure that the market maker has both buyers and sellers.

---

11 For eurobanking, the typical convention is 360 days/year, 30 days/month, as in the bond market or in the forward market. The purpose of this is to facilitate arbitrage calculations between synthetic and direct transactions. Some currencies—for example, the GBP and BEF—have a 365-day tradition. In "domestic" banking, a year is most often 365 days. In some on-shore (domestic) money markets, a year is 360 days with the number of days counted exactly; that is, if you borrow for a full year, you may end up paying 365/360 times the stated interest rate. If these little details are ignored, there may be illusory violations of the arbitrage bounds.

Deardorff argues that only quotes like (iii) or (iv), that is quotes that lie entirely within the pair of synthetic rates, are possible if market makers want a two-way market. In terms of the graph, the direct quotes should be entirely within the indirect quotes, rather than just sharing (at least) one point. Thus, the analysis of least cost dealing makes the following predictions.

- Typically, it is cheaper to buy in the direct market than in the synthetic market:

$$F_{\text{ask},t,T} < \text{Synthetic forward ask rate} = S_{\text{ask},t} \frac{1 + r_{\text{ask},t,T}}{1 + r^*_{\text{bid},t,T}}. \tag{4a}$$

- And, selling in the direct market dominates selling in the synthetic market:

$$F_{\text{bid},t,T} > \text{Synthetic forward bid rate} = S_{\text{bid},t} \frac{1 + r_{\text{bid},t,T}}{1 + r^*_{\text{ask},t,T}}. \tag{4b}$$

Notice we said that these inequalities should hold most of the time; indeed, market makers could *temporarily* set quotes like (ii) or (v) if they really want a one-way market—for instance, to clear an imbalance on their books. However, such quotes cannot be a long-term phenomenon; that is, Deardorff's bounds should not be violated systematically.

Of course, we also need $F_{\text{bid},t,T} < F_{\text{ask},t,T}$. In summary, the bounds imposed by least cost dealing, [4a] and [4b], combined with $F_{\text{bid},t,T} < F_{\text{ask},t,T}$, lead to the following set of inequalities:

$$S_{\text{bid},t} \frac{1 + r_{\text{bid},t,T}}{1 + r^*_{\text{ask},t,T}} \leq F_{\text{bid},t,T} < F_{\text{ask},t,T} \leq S_{\text{ask},t} \frac{1 + r_{\text{ask},t,T}}{1 + r^*_{\text{bid},t,T}}. \tag{4c}$$

4.6.2   Examples of Least Cost Dealing Computations

In this section, we show how to compute the least cost method for doing a particular transaction. In each of the applications, we do the following.

- First we decide what the starting point is: what is our position before we make any transactions? Note that this is the position we want to get rid of; that is, at some stage, we shall deliver this amount to the bank.
- Then figure out the end point: what kind of money do we ultimately want to receive from the bank?
- Compute the output amounts for a given, common input amount.
- Select the route with the highest output.

This method minimizes the chance of making an error. It is very simple to remember the rule that "more output is better." In contrast, any other rule creates confusion. For example, if one compares interest rates rather than outputs in units of money, one has to remember that the higher interest rate is "good" for a deposit, but "bad" for a loan—or, if a direct forward rate is compared to a synthetic rate, one has to keep in mind that for a forward sale the higher rate is the more attractive one, while for a purchase it is the other way around.

For simplicity, we always start with one unit of initial money when we look for the best route. Having found the best alternative, it is then easy to rescale the computations, such that either the starting point or the end point conforms to the desired amount. We shall not explicitly spell out each intermediate amount; we simply follow the relevant arrows from Figure 4.2, and state the final output amount. The data we use are the same as those used for the arbitrage computations. For your convenience, we reproduce the data below.

Exchange Rates	Bid	Ask
Spot	41.3950	41.5750
6-month forward	41.3150	41.5150
Interest Rates*		
LUF	10.0%	12.0%
ECU	8.0%	10.0%
Returns (6 months)		
LUF	5.0%	6.0%
ECU	4.0%	5.0%

* Simple interest rates

Domestic versus Covered Foreign Investment

The treasurer's problem is to find the best way to invest funds for six months—a $LUF_t \to LUF_T$ trip. The analysis proceeds as follows.

- If we invest LUF 1 directly, the total return (per franc of starting capital) is:

$$LUF_T = 1 + r_{bid,t,T} = LUF\ 1.05.$$

- The alternative is to convert LUF 1 into ECU, invest the proceeds and immediately sell forward the amount of ECU we shall receive at maturity. The total return per LUF starting capital will be:

$$LUF_T = \frac{1}{S_{ask,t}}(1+r^*_{bid,t,T})F_{bid,t,T} = \frac{1}{41.5750}(1.04)\ 41.3150 = LUF\ 1.0335.$$

Conclusion: The first alternative results in the highest output; that is, it is better to invest at home in LUF.

Domestic versus Covered Foreign Borrowing

This time, the treasurer is looking for the best way to borrow funds for six months. This is a $LUF_T \to LUF_t$ problem.

- Domestic borrowing, from a starting amount $LUF_T = 1$, produces:

$$LUF_t = \frac{1}{1+r_{ask,t,T}} = \frac{1}{1.06} = LUF\ 0.9434.$$

- The alternative is covered ECU borrowing. We convert $LUF_T = 1$ into ECU_T in the forward market, and find out how much we can borrow against this amount in the ECU money market. The proceeds are then converted into LUF in the spot market:

$$LUF_t = \frac{1}{F_{ask,t,T}} \times \frac{1}{1 + r^*_{ask,t,T}} S_{bid,t} = \frac{1}{41.5150} \times \frac{1}{1.05} \times 41.3950 = LUF\ 0.94963.$$

Conclusion: The latter strategy produces the higher output value per unit of LUF_T input; that is, the covered ECU loan is better than the LUF loan.[12]

Synthetic versus Direct Forward Sale

Suppose that you have a long open position in ECU, for instance, a six-month term deposit, a six-month Treasury Bill, or an invoice. You want to eliminate the exchange risk involved but you do not need any cash now. This is an $ECU_T \rightarrow LUF_T$ problem (since you want a risk-free amount of home currency in the future).

- The easiest way is to sell ECU forward; the proceeds per unit of ECU_T (the starting point) are:

$$LUF_T = 1 \times F_{bid,t,T} = LUF\ 41.315.$$

- Through the money markets and the spot market, we can make a synthetic forward sale of ECU. Borrow the present value of $ECU_T = 1$, convert these spot ECU into spot LUF, and invest the proceeds in the LUF money market, thus:

$$LUF_T = \frac{1}{1 + r^*_{ask,t,T}} S_{bid,t}(1 + r_{bid,t,T}) = \frac{1}{1.05} 41.3950 \times 1.05 = LUF\ 41.3950.$$

Conclusion: The second (synthetic) alternative results in the higher output. This is not a normal situation. Either the forward rate has to go up, or the spot has to go down.

Hedge and Finance a Long Open Position in ECU

In this example, we want to hedge and finance an ECU receivable, that is, transform a future ECU inflow into LUF cash today. Thus, the trip is $ECU_T \rightarrow LUF_t$.

- Borrow the present value of $ECU_T = 1$, then convert at the spot rate into LUF_t:

$$LUF_t = \frac{1}{1 + r^*_{ask,t,T}} \times S_{bid,t} = \frac{1}{1.05} \times 41.3950 = LUF\ 39.42381.$$

- Through the forward market, sell the ECU_T; then, borrow LUF, with the present value chosen so that the loan plus the interest fee can be exactly paid for from the LUF_T proceeds of the forward purchase:

---

[12] If these were interbank rates, such a situation would mean that the LUF interbank borrowing market has no customers. If that happens, the rates will have to adjust.

$$\text{LUF}_t = F_{\text{bid},t,T} \frac{1}{1 + r_{\text{ask},t,T}} = 41.3150 \frac{1}{1.06} = \text{LUF } 38.9764.$$

Conclusion: The first alternative (the ECU money market/spot market trip) is the better one.

Set Funds Aside for an ECU Liability

In this example, we have a debt in ECU and fear an appreciation of the ECU. We assume there is LUF cash, so there is no need to borrow LUF. Rather, the problem is to identify the best way to convert some of the available cash into future ECU without taking any risk. This is a $\text{LUF}_t \rightarrow \text{ECU}_T$ problem.

- You could buy ECU_t, and invest in the ECU money market. The result, per unit of LUF_t, is:

$$\text{ECU}_T = \frac{1}{S_{\text{ask},t}}(1 + r^*_{\text{bid},t,T}) = \frac{1}{41.5750}1.04 = 0.02502.$$

- You could also buy forward ECU, and immediately set aside LUF_t so that, including interest, the investment proceeds exactly meet our LUF_T liability under the forward contract. Per unit of LUF_t, this produces an ECU_T output equal to:

$$\text{ECU}_T = \frac{1}{F_{\text{ask},t,T}}(1 + r_{\text{bid},t,T}) = \frac{1}{41.5150}1.05 = 0.02529.$$

Conclusion: The second alternative dominates: it is better to hedge forward, and set aside LUF now.

Synthetic versus Direct Forward Purchase

As in the preceding problem, you want to hedge a future ECU outflow. However, you do not have any LUF available in cash. That is, the input will be future money rather than cash money. This is a $\text{LUF}_T \rightarrow \text{ECU}_T$ trip.

- Buying ECU forward produces:

$$\text{ECU}_T = \frac{1}{F_{\text{ask},t,T}} = \frac{1}{41.5150} = 0.02409.$$

- The longer trip involves borrowing LUF and buying spot ECU for investment, thus:

$$\text{ECU}_T = \frac{1}{1 + r_{\text{ask},t,T}} \frac{1}{S_{\text{ask},t}}(1 + r^*_{\text{bid},t,T}) = \frac{1}{1.06 \times 41.5750}1.04 = 0.02360.$$

Conclusion: The first alternative (forward hedging) dominates. This is what Deardorff would have predicted.

4.7 IMPLICATIONS OF SPREADS FOR THE FINANCIAL MANAGER

We conclude this chapter by discussing two consequences of bid-ask spreads. The first implication of bid-ask spreads is that any transaction or sequence of transactions ("trip") that is not a round-trip (not a pure arbitrage transaction) can be made through two different routes. In imperfect markets, it is a near certainty that one route will be cheaper than the other, and therefore, it generally pays to compare the two ways of implementing a "trip." The route chosen matters because:

- With spreads, it is impossible that for every single trip the two routes end up with exactly the same result, as we have seen in the previous section.[13]
- Even if the difference between the outcomes of the two routes is small in the wholesale market, that difference will be important in the retail market.
- Differential taxation of capital gains/losses and interest income/cost provides a third reason why two routes are likely to produce different outcomes. For most corporate transactions, however, taxes may not matter, since interest and short-term capital gains (like forward premia received or paid) typically receive the same tax treatment.

Example 4.11

A Swiss company wants to invest in CHF for one year, but is also considering a covered AUD investment. Suppose that the one-year CHF/AUD "ask" spot rate is 1, the "bid" forward rate is 0.85833, the one-year AUD "bid" interest rate is 20 percent, and the one-year CHF "bid" interest rate is 3 percent. First ignore taxes, and compare the CHF deposit to the covered AUD investment. A standard CHF deposit yields CHF_T 1.03. A covered AUD investment will yield $(1/1) \times 1.2 \times 0.85833 = 1.03$. Therefore, in this example, the company is indifferent between the two alternatives—before taxes. Now consider taxes. In both cases, the taxable income is 0.03—pure CHF interest income in the first case, and AUD interest income reduced by the capital loss (the forward discount) in the second case. Thus, in this example, taxes will be irrelevant if interest income and capital gains are taxed in the same way.

Under *personal* taxation rules, however, there may be tax discrimination between capital gains and interest or, in some countries, interest *paid* may sometimes not be tax-deductible while interest received *is* taxable. This means that taxes are no longer irrelevant. Likewise, multinational companies can borrow in a country with high taxes and invest in a tax haven or through a finance company or a re-invoicing center with a special tax status.[14] In such cases, there again might not be equal tax treatment of all elements in the round-trip or in the one-way trip. This possibility makes it worthwhile to compare the *after-tax* outcomes of the alternative routes.

---

[13] It cannot be ruled out that, for one particular trip, the two alternatives produce the same result, but then the irrelevance of the route can no longer hold for any other application.

[14] Examples of companies with a special tax status include the so-called *Dublin Dock Company* in Ireland and the *Coordination Center* in Belgium.

Example   4.12

A Belgian dentist pays (or should pay) a 10 percent income tax on declared interest income. If he buys a CHF T-bill and sells forward the proceeds, the interest component is taxable but, until 1992, the capital gain on the principal was tax-free. Suppose that $S_t = $ BEF/CHF 22, Interest Rate Parity holds before taxes, and the one-year BEF and CHF interest rates are 10 percent and 4 percent, respectively; then the forward rate is $22 \times 1.10/1.04 = $ BEF/CHF 23.2692. Now consider the after-tax results of each alternative:

- Investing BEF 22 at 10 percent yields, after the 10 percent interest income tax, $22 \times 1.09 = $ BEF 23.98.
- The investor's taxable income on a covered CHF investment would be 0.04 Swiss francs, realized at the forward rate, that is, $0.04 \times 23.2692 = $ BEF 0.9308 before tax, or BEF 0.8377 after the 10 percent tax. Together with the tax-free proceeds from selling forward the principal, this amounts to a total after tax output $0.8377 + 23.2692 = $ BEF 24.107.

Thus, the covered CHF investment partly replaces taxable BEF interest income by a tax-free capital gain. As a result, the two routes produce different outcomes after taxes even if, as in this example, there is no difference before taxes.

A second implication of bid-ask spreads relates to the cost of hedging. In Chapter 2, we argued that, in perfect markets, hedging has no impact on the value of the firm unless it affects the firm's operating decisions. However, we have just seen that, in the presence of bid-ask spreads, a forward hedge and a money-market hedge in general will not produce the same outcome; thus, there may already be a small cost associated with choosing the wrong hedge. Furthermore, if a firm keeps a net foreign exchange position open, it will have to pay transactions costs on the sale of these funds in the spot market when the position expires. If the firm does hedge, it will have to pay the cost in the forward market. Since spreads in the forward markets are higher, the extra cost represents the cost of the hedging operation. In Section 1.4 of Chapter 1, we argued that the cost of a single transaction can be approximated as half the difference between the bid-ask spread. Thus, the *extra* cost from hedging in the forward market instead of the spot is approximately given by half of the bid-ask spread in the forward market *minus* half the bid-ask spread in the spot market.

Example   4.13

The London *Financial Times* of January 12, 1993 gives the following CAD/USD spot and forward rates. We have added a column showing the bid-ask spreads for the spot and forward rates. We show

Maturity	Rates	Bid-ask spread	Half the forward spread minus half the spot spread	Extra cost, as a % of midpoint spot rate
Spot	1.2750–1.2760	0.0010	–	–
Forward 30 day	1.2705–1.2722	0.0017	0.00035	0.027%
Forward 90 day	1.2630–1.2655	0.0025	0.00075	0.059%

$$\text{* extra spread, as a } \% = \frac{\text{[half the difference of the spreads]}}{S_{\text{bid}} + S_{\text{ask}}}$$
$$2$$

the extra cost for hedging in the forward market relative to the spot market as an absolute amount, and the extra cost as a percentage of the midpoint of the spot bid-ask rates.

We see that the additional cost of hedging in the forward market instead of the spot is positive, but hardly staggering. To avoid confusion, we repeat that we measure this cost as half of the difference of the *spreads* in the forward market relative to the spreads in the spot market. Thus, this cost has nothing to do with the forward premium or discount. The latter difference, as we showed in Section 3.4.1, is a pure accounting *cost* construct without economic meaning.

QUIZ QUESTIONS

1. Which of the following are risks that arise when you hedge by buying a forward contract in financial markets that are imperfect?
    (a) Credit risk: the risk that the counterpart to a forward contract defaults.
    (b) Hedging risk: the risk that you are not able to find a counterpart for your forward contract if you want to close out early.
    (c) Reverse risk: the risk that results from a sudden unhedged position because the counterpart to your forward contract defaults.
    (d) Spot rate risk: the risk that the spot rate has changed once you have signed a forward contract.

2. Which of the following statements are true?
    (a) Margin is a payment to the bank to compensate it for taking on credit risk.
    (b) If you hold a forward purchase contract for JPY that you wish to reverse, and the JPY has increased in value, you owe the bank the discounted difference between the current forward rate and the historic forward rate, that is, the market value.
    (c) If the balance in your margin account is not sufficient to cover the losses on your forward contract and you fail to post additional margin, the bank must speculate in order to recover the losses.
    (d) Under the system of daily recontracting, the value of an outstanding forward contract is recomputed every day. If the forward rate for GBP/DEM drops each day for ten days until the forward contract expires, the purchaser of DEM forward must pay the forward seller of DEM the market value of the contract for each of those ten days. If the purchaser cannot pay, the bank seizes his or her margin.

3. Innovative Bicycle Makers must hedge an accounts payable of MAD 100,000 due in 90 days for bike tires purchased in Malaysia. Suppose that the GBP/MAD forward rates and the GBP effective returns are as follows:

Time	$t = 0$	$t = 1$	$t = 2$	$t = 3$
Forward rate	4	4.2	3.9	4
Effective return	12%	8.5%	4%	0%

    (a) What are IBM's cash flows given a variable-collateral margin account?
    (b) What are IBM's cash flows given periodic contracting?

4. Which of the following statements are correct?
    (a) A forward purchase contract can be replicated by: borrowing foreign currency, converting it to domestic currency, and investing the domestic currency.
    (b) A forward purchase contract can be replicated by: borrowing domestic currency, converting it to foreign currency, and investing the foreign currency.
    (c) A forward sale contract can be replicated by: borrowing foreign currency, converting it to domestic currency, and investing the domestic currency.
    (d) A forward sale contract can be replicated by: borrowing domestic currency, converting it to foreign currency, and investing the foreign currency.

5. The following spot and forward rates are in units of BEF/FC. The forward spread is quoted in centimes.

	Spot bid-ask	1 month		3 month		6 month		12 month	
1 NLG	18.20–18.30	+0.6	+0.8	+2.1	+2.7	+3.8	+4.9	+6.9	+9.1
1 FRF	5.95–6.01	−0.1	−0.2	−0.3	−0.1	−0.7	−0.3	−0.9	+0.1
1 CHF	24.08–24.24	+3.3	+3.7	+9.9	+10.8	+19.3	+21.1	+36.2	+39.7
100 JPY	33.38–33.52	+9.5	+9.9	+28.9	+30.0	+55.2	+57.5	+99.0	+105.0
1 ECU	39.56–39.79	−1.7	−1.0	−3.4	−1.8	−5.8	−2.9	−10.5	−5.2

6. Choose the correct answer.

   i. The one-month forward bid/ask quotes for CHF are:
      a. 27.387–27.942   b. 25.078–24.357   c. 24.113–24.277   d. 24.410–24.610

   ii. The three-month forward bid/ask quotes for ECU are:
      a. 39.526–39.772   b. 36.167–37.992   c. 39.641–40.158   d. 39.397–39.699

   iii. The six-month forward bid/ask quotes for JPY are:
      a. 38.902–39.273   b. 88.584–91.025   c. 33.686–33.827   d. 33.932–34.095

   iv. The twelve-month forward bid/ask quotes for NLG are:
      a. 18.731–19.352   b. 25.113–27.404   c. 17.305–17.716   d. 18.279–19.391

7. Suppose that you are quoted the following DEM/FC spot and forward rates:

	Spot bid-ask	3-mo. forward bid-ask	*p.a.* 3 month Euro-interest	6-mo. forward bid-ask	*p.a.* 6 month Euro-interest
DEM			5.65–5.90		5.47–5.82
USD	0.5791–0.5835	0.5821–0.5867	3.63–3.88	0.5839–0.5895	3.94–4.19
ECU	0.5120–0.5159	0.5103–0.5142	6.08–6.33	0.5101–0.5146	5.60–6.25
FRF	3.3890–3.4150	3.3350–3.4410	6.05–6.30	3.3720–3.4110	5.93–6.18
JPY*	0.5973–0.6033	0.5987–0.5025	1.71–1.96	0.5023–0.5099	2.47–2.75
GBP	0.3924–0.3954	0.3933–0.3989	5.09–5.34	0.3929–0.3001	5.10–5.35

*The exchange rate DEM/JPY is for 100 JPY.

   (a) What are the three-month synthetic-forward DEM/USD bid-ask rates?
   (b) What are the six-month synthetic-forward DEM/ECU bid-ask rates?
   (c) What are the six-month synthetic-forward DEM/FRF bid-ask rates?
   (d) What are the three-month synthetic-forward DEM/JPY bid-ask rates?
   (e) In a–d, are there any arbitrage opportunities? What about least cost dealing at the synthetic rate?

8. True or False: Occasionally arbitrage bounds are violated using domestic ("on-shore") interest rates because:

   (a) Offshore or euromarkets are perfect markets while "on-shore" markets are imperfect.

   (b) Offshore or euromarkets are efficient markets while "on-shore" markets are inefficient.

EXERCISES

1. Michael Milkem, an ambitious MBA student from Anchorage, Alaska, is looking for free lunches on the foreign exchange markets. Keeping his eyes glued to his Reuters screen until the wee hours, he spots the following quotes in Tokyo:

Exchange rates: Spot	DEM/USD	1.59–1.60	JPY/USD	100–101
	DEM/GBP	2.25–2.26	JPY/GBP	150–152
180-day Forward	DEM/USD	1.615–1.626	JPY/USD	97.96–98.42
	DEM/GBP	2.265–2.274	JPY/GBP	146.93–149.19

Interest rates (simple, *p.a.*)				
180 days	USD	5%–5.25%	JPY	3%–3.25%
	DEM	8%–8.25%	GBP	7%–7.25%

Given the above quotes, can Michael find any arbitrage opportunities?

2. Polyglot Industries will send its employee Jack Pundit to study French in an intensive training course at the Sorbonne. Jack will need FRF 10,000 at $t = 3$ months when classes begin, and FRF 6,000 at $t = 6$ months, $t = 9$ months, and $t = 12$ months to cover his tuition and living expenses. The exchange rates and *p.a.* interest rates are as follows:

FRF/USD	Exchange rate	*p.a.* interest rate USD	*p.a.* interest rate FRF
Spot	5.820–5.830		
90 days	5.765–5.770	3.82–4.07	8.09–8.35
180 days	5.713–5.720	3.94–4.19	8.00–8.26
270 days	5.660–5.680	4.13–4.38	7.99–8.24
360 days	5.640–5.670	4.50–4.75	7.83–8.09

Polyglot wants to lock in the FRF value of Jack's expenses. Is it indifferent between buying FRF forward and investing in FRF for each time period that he should receive his allowance?

3. Check that a money-market hedge replicates an outright forward transaction. Analyze, for instance, a forward sale of DKK 1 against DEM.

Exercises 4 through 6 use the following time-0 data for the fictitious currency, the Walloon Franc (WAF) and the Flemish Yen (FLY), on Jan. 1, 2000. The spot exchange rate is 1 WAF/FLY.

	Interest rates		Swap rate
	FLY	WAF	WAF/FLY
180 days	5%	10.125%	0.025
360 days	5%	10.250%	0.050

4. On June 1, 2000, the FLY has depreciated to WAF 0.90, but the six-month interest rates have not changed. In early 2001, the FLY is back at par. Compute the gain or loss (and the cumulative gain or loss) on two consecutive 180-day forward sales (the first one is signed on Jan. 1, 2000), when you start with a FLY 500,000 forward sale. First do the computations without increasing the size of the forward contract. Then verify how the results are affected if you do increase the contract size, at the roll-over date, by a factor $1 + r^*_{T_1,T_2}$—that is, from FLY 500,000 to FLY 512,500.

5. Repeat the previous exercise, except that after six months the exchange rate is at WAF/FLY 1, not 0.9.

6. Compare the analyses in Exercises 4 and 5 with a rolled-over money-market hedge. That is, what would have been the result if you had borrowed WAF for six months (with conversion and investment of FLY—the money-market replication of a six-month forward sale), and then rolled-over (that is, renewed) the WAF loan and the FLY deposit, principal plus interest?

5 CURRENCY FUTURES MARKETS

In the previous chapter, we studied the implications of transaction costs on forward rates and the Interest Rate Parity (or covered interest parity) theorem. We also pointed out that the usefulness of forward markets is restricted by other complications. Specifically, the standard ways of reducing default risk in forward contracts are imperfect. This implies that bankers dislike long-term contracts unless a company's credit standing is excellent or it has put up substantial margin. Second, there is no well-organized secondary market for forward contracts. We shall see how futures markets address and solve these problems.

In the first section below, we describe the institutional aspects of futures contracts. A crucial feature is that futures contracts address the problem of default risk by **daily marking to market**. This is very similar to daily recontracting of a forward contract, except that the *undiscounted* change in the market value of the contract is paid out in cash. In Section 5.2, we trace the implications of daily marking to market for futures prices. Especially, we shall show that the interim cash flows from marking to market create interest risk, which affects the futures prices. In Section 5.3, we address the question of how to hedge with futures contracts. We conclude, in the fourth section, by describing the advantages and disadvantages of using futures compared to forward contracts. Details of how to estimate the optimal hedge ratio and how uncertainty about interest rates affects futures prices are presented in the appendix.

5.1 CURRENCY FUTURES MARKETS

Futures contracts are designed to minimize the problems arising from default risk and to facilitate liquidity in secondary dealing. The best way to understand these contracts is to compare them with forward transactions. Like forward contracts, currency futures contracts are, in principle, contracts to deliver a given number of currency units on a given maturity date (T) and at a pre-specified price ($f_{0,T}$) to be paid "later on." (We shall explain below what we mean by this vague expression "later on.") Another similarity with forwards is that a futures contract has a zero *initial* market value: neither the buyer nor the seller has to pay anything when a contract is initiated at the going market rate. However, futures contracts differ from forward contracts in many other respects.

5.1.1   Organized Markets

As we saw, forward contracts are not really traded; they are simply initiated in the over-the-counter market (typically with the client's bank) and held until maturity. In the forward market, market makers quote prices but there is no organized way of centralizing demand and supply. The only mechanisms that tend to equalize the prices quoted by different market makers are arbitrage and least cost dealing; and, as traders are in permanent contact with only a few market makers, price equalization is imperfect. Nor is there any public information about when a transaction took place, and at what price.

In contrast, futures are traded on organized exchanges, with specific rules about the terms of the contracts, and with an active secondary market. Futures prices are the result of a centralized, organized matching of demand and supply. One method of organizing this matching of orders is the *open outcry* system, where floor members are physically present in a *trading pit* and auction off their orders by shouting them out. US exchanges work like this; so does the LIFFE in London, and likewise the MATIF in Paris.[1] Another method, used in some continental exchanges (including Germany's DTB and Belgium's Belfox) is to centralize the limit orders in a computerized Public Limit Order Book.[2] Brokers sit before their screens, and can add or delete their orders, or fill a limit order posted on the screen.

5.1.2   Standardized Contracts

All futures contracts are standardized by contract size (see Table 5.1) and expiration dates. This means that the futures market is not as fragmented—by too wide a variety of expiration dates and contract sizes—as the forward market. Although standardization in itself does not guarantee a high volume, it does facilitate the emergence of a deep, liquid market.

Expiration dates are typically the third Wednesdays of March, June, September, or December, or the first business day after such a Wednesday. Trading stops two business days before the expiration date, and actual delivery takes place on the second business day after the expiration date.

---

[1] LIFFE: London International Financial Futures Exchange (where also options are traded, since the merger with the London Traded Options Exchange). MATIF: Marché à Terme International de France (International Futures Market of France).

[2] DTB: Deutsche Termin Börse. Belfox: Belgian Futures and Options exchange. A **limit order** is an order to buy an indicated number of currency units at a price no higher than a given level, or to sell an indicated number of currency units at a price no lower than a given level. The limit orders submitted by an individual reveal the individual's supply and demand curve for the currency. By aggregating all limit orders across investors, the market supply and demand curves are obtained. The market opens with a **call**, that is, with a computer-determined price that equates demand and supply as closely as possible. Afterwards, the computer screens display the first few unfilled orders on each side (purchase orders, and sell orders).

TABLE 5.1   Examples of Currency Futures Contract Sizes

Exchange rate	Contract size at	Number	Other exchanges*
USD/GBP	IMM	62,500	PBOT, LIFFE, SIMEX, MACE
USD/DEM	IMM	125,000	LIFFE, PBOT, SIMEX, MACE
DEM/USD	OM-S	50,000	
USD/JPY	IMM	12,500,000	LIFFE, TIFFE, MACE, PBOT, SIMEX
USD/CAD	IMM	100,000	PBOT, MACE
USD/CHF	IMM	125,000	LIFFE, MACE, PBOT
USD/FRF	IMM	250,000	PBOT
USD/AUD	IMM	100,000	PBOT, SFX
USD/ECU	IMM	125,000	FINEX, PBOT
GBP/DEM	TCBOT	50,000	
NZD/USD	NZFE	50,000	
USD/NZD	NZFE	100,000	

IMM: International Money Market (CME, Chicago); OM-S: Optionsmarknad Stockholm; LIFFE:London International Financial Futures Exchange; TCBOT: Twin Cities Board of Trade, St. Paul/Minneapolis; NZFE: New Zealand Futures Exchange; PBOT: Philadelphia Board of Trade; SIMEX: Singapore International Monetary Exchange; MACE: Mid-American Commodity Exchange; TIFFE: Tokyo International Financial Futures Exchange; SFX: Sydney Futures Exchange; FINEX: Financial Instruments Exchange (New York Cotton Exchange).

* Non-exhaustive list. Contract size may differ from the size in the exchange first listed here.

Traditionally, only the three contracts nearest in maturity are traded. That is, until the end of March, the March, June, and September contracts are traded—and when the March contract expires, the exchange opens trading in the December contract, and so on. Thus, the maximum maturity contract that is available varies between six and nine months.[3]

5.1.3   The Clearing Corporation

Futures contracts are not initiated directly between individuals (or corporations) A and B. Rather, each party has a contract with the futures clearing corporation or clearing house. For instance, a sale from A to B is structured as a sale by A to the clearing house, and then a sale by the clearing house to B. Thus, even if B defaults, A is not concerned (unless the clearing house also goes bankrupt). The clearing corporation levies a small tax on all transactions, and thus has reserves that should cover losses from default.

The clearing house effectively "clears": if A buys from B and then some time later sells to C, the clearing house cancels out both of A's contracts, and only the contracts with B and C remain out-

---

[3] Today, interest rate futures and bond futures offer maturities of up to two or three years. This practice may spread to currency futures markets.

standing. Player A is effectively cleared of all responsibilities. In contrast, as we saw, a forward purchase by A from B and a forward sale by A to C remain separate contracts that are not cleared: if B fails to deliver to A, A has to suffer the loss and cannot invoke B's default to escape its (A's) obligations to C.

5.1.4   Marking to Market

As stated in the introduction to Section 5.1, the futures contract stipulates that the buyer pays the initially agreed-upon amount, $f_{0,T}$, "later on." With a forward contract, the meaning of "later on" is made quite clear: the price $F_{0,T}$ is paid entirely at time T. However, with futures contracts, the exact details of how much is paid at what time depend on the day-to-day movements of the futures price. This is because of marking to market. In order to explain marking to market in futures markets, we need to review the mechanism of daily recontracting of forward contracts. In Section 4.1.3, we explained that, when a forward contract is recontracted every day, the buyer receives a daily cash flow equal to the *discounted* change in the forward price. Thus, rising prices mean cash inflows for the buyer, and falling prices mean cash outflows. (The signs are reversed when the seller's point of view is taken.) Because the interim payments are based on the *discounted* forward price, the total amount paid is still equivalent to paying the initially contracted rate, $F_{t_0,T}$, at the contract's expiration date.

Futures contracts are often defined as forward contracts that are recontracted daily. This definition is misleading, although there is, in fact, an important analogy: with both types of contracts, adverse price movements are translated into daily cash outflows (payments), while advantageous price movements trigger daily cash inflows. Still, marking to market in futures markets differs from daily recontracting of forward contracts in that the daily cash flow is based on the *undiscounted* change in the price of the futures contract.

Example   5.1

The sequence of *ex post* daily cash flows in a three-day contract (dates 0, 1, 2, 3) to purchase foreign currency, is computed as follows:

Day	0	1	2	3
Futures price	100	98	96	97
Marking to market	–	pay 2	pay 2	receive 1
Final payment for delivery	–	–	–	pay 97

Thus, ignoring time value, the cumulative payments from the buyer are equal to $2 + 2 - 1 + 97 = 100$ units of home currency.

The cash flows to the seller are the reverse. In fact, what happens is that the buyer pays the seller if prices go down and receives money from the seller if prices go up. These daily payments from "winner" to "loser" occur through accounts the customers hold with their brokers, and they are transmitted from the loser to the winner through brokers, clearing members, and the clearing corporation. The **settlement price**, upon which the daily marking-to-market cash flows are based, is in principle equal to the day's closing price or **close**. However, futures exchanges want to make sure that the settlement price is not manipulated. One way to ensure this is to base the settlement price not on the actual closing price but on the average of the transaction prices in the last half hour of trading or, if there is no trading, the average of the market makers' quotes (LIFFE).

To generalize and to summarize: the home currency cash flows generated by a futures (purchase) contract are:

- As marking-to-market flows (positive or negative).
  - On day 1: $f_{1,T} - f_{0,T}$
  - On day 2: $f_{2,T} - f_{1,T}$
  - ...
  - On day T: $\underline{f_{T,T} - f_{T-1,T}}$

  Total: $f_{T,T} - f_{T-1,T}$ (ignoring the effects of time value)

- After the last marking to market, the buyer holds a futures contract that stipulates immediate payment of $f_{T,T}$—that is, there is a cash flow of *minus* $f_{T,T}$—against receipt of one unit of foreign currency. Obviously, then, $f_{T,T} = S_T$ (that is, there must be convergence).
- All in all, and ignoring the effects of time value, the cash flows are $(f_{T,T} - f_{0,T})$ over the life of the contract, and $-f_{T,T}$ at its expiration. In short, one pays $f_{0,T}$ over the entire life of the contract. However, unlike a forward contract, the exact timing of the payments in a futures contract is uncertain.

Thus far, we assumed that the buyer holds the futures contract until maturity. If, at some point in time τ before expiration, investor A sells his contract to B (through the clearing house, as we have seen), the day's marking-to-market cash flow $f_{t+1,T} - f_{t,T}$ is split. That is, if the transaction is at time τ (with $t < \tau < t + 1$), then investor A receives $f_{\tau,T} - f_{t,T}$, while B receives $f_{t+1,T} - f_{\tau,T}$. Investor B also takes over all responsibilities as of τ. The corollary of the last two points is that, when a buyer terminates at time τ a contract initiated at time t_0, the cumulative marking-to-market cash flows are $f_{\tau,T} - f_{t_0,T}$. This is the total gain or loss from holding the contract between times t_0 and τ apart from the effects of time value. The time value aspect will be discussed in Section 5.2.

Marking to market is the most crucial difference between forward and futures contracts. It means that if an investor defaults, the "gain" from defaulting is simply the avoidance of a one-day marking-to-market outflow: all previous losses have already been settled in cash. This implies the following:

- Compared to a forward contract, the incentive to default on a futures contract is smaller. By defaulting on the marking-to-market payment, one avoids only a payment equal to that day's price change. In contrast, in the case of a forward contract, defaulting means that the investor saves the amount lost over the entire life of the contract.

Example   5.2

Investor A bought DEM 1m at $f_{t_0,T}$ = USD/DEM 0.76. By the next to last day of trading, the futures price has drifted down to a level of USD/DEM 0.69. So investor A has already paid, cumulatively, 1m $\times$ (0.76 – 0.69) = USD 70,000 as marking-to-market cash flows. If, on the last day of trading, the price moves down by another ten points, then, by defaulting, investor A avoids only the additional payment of 1m $\times$ 0.001 = USD 1,000. In contrast, if this had been a forward contract, the savings from defaulting would have been the entire price drop between t_0 and T, that is, $1m \times (F_{t_0,T} - S_T) = 1m \times (0.76 - 0.689) = USD\ 71,000$.

- From the point of view of the clearing house, the counterpart of the above statement is that if an investor fails to make the required margin payment, the loss to the clearing house is simply the day's price change.[4]

In practice, the savings from defaulting on a futures contract (and the clearing house's loss if there is default) are even smaller than the above statement suggests because of a final characteristic of futures markets—the margin requirements.

5.1.5   Margin Requirements

There are two types of margin requirements when trading in futures markets. These are called **initial margin** and **maintenance margin**. The idea behind the margin requirements is that the margin should cover virtually all of the one-day risk. This, of course, further reduces both one's incentive to default as well as the loss to the clearing house if there is default.

If one takes a position in a futures market, an initial margin is required. As we have seen, in principle, every favorable price change triggers a cash inflow, while every adverse price movement leads to a cash outflow. In practice, the loser does not have to settle losses each day if the price movements are small. In order to avoid the cost and inconvenience of frequent but small payments, losses are allowed to accumulate to certain levels before a **margin call** (a request for payment) is issued. These small losses are simply deducted from the initial margin until a lower bound, the maintenance margin, is reached. At this stage, a margin call is issued, requesting the investor to bring the margin back up to the initial level.

Example   5.3

The initial margin on a GBP 62,500 contract may be USD 3,000, and the maintenance margin USD 2,400. The initial USD 3,000 margin is the initial equity in your account. The buyer's equity increases (decreases) when prices rise (fall). As long as the investor's losses do not exceed USD 600 (that is, as long as the investor's equity does not fall below the maintenance margin, USD 2,400), no margin call will be issued to her. If her equity, however, falls below USD 2,400, she must add variation margin that restores her equity to USD 3,000 by next morning.

5.1.6   How Futures Prices Are Reported

Figure 5.1 contains an excerpt from *The Wall Street Journal* of Friday, July 30, 1993, showing information on yen futures trading on Thursday, July 29 on the International Money Market (IMM) of the Chicago Mercantile Exchange (CME). Similar information is reported for futures on DEM, CAD, GBP, CHF, AUD (all at CME), and on a ten-currency basket (the USD Index or USDX contract traded at the New York Cotton Exchange).

---

[4] Failure to make the margin payment is interpreted as an order to liquidate the position. That is, if you bought and cannot pay, your contract will be added to the sales orders at the opening; if you were short, your contract will be closed out the next day by adding it to the purchase orders.

FIGURE 5.1   Financial Press Information on Futures Trading

FUTURES PRICES

[...]

CURRENCY

	Open	High	Low	Settle	Change	Lifetime High	Low	Open Interest
JAPAN YEN (CME)—12.5 million yen; $ per yen (.00)								
Sept	.9458	.9466	.9386	.9389	−.0046	.9540	.7945	73,221
Dec	.9425	.9470	.9393	.9396	−.0049	.9529	.7970	3,455
Mr94	....	....	....	.9417	−.0051	.9490	.8700	318

Est vol 28,844; vol Wed 36,595; open int 77,028, + 1.820

The head, JAPAN YEN, shows the size of the contract (12.5m yen) and states that the prices are stated in USD cents. The June 1993 contract had expired more than a month before, so the three contracts being traded on July 29, 1993, are the September and December 1993 contracts, and the March 1994 contracts. In each row, the first four prices relate to trading on Thursday, July 29—the price at the start of trading (open), the highest and lowest transaction price during the day, and the settlement price ("Settle"), which is representative of the transaction prices around the close.

The settlement price is the basis of marking to market. The column, "Change," contains the change of today's settlement price relative to yesterday. For instance, on Thursday, July 29, the settlement price of the September contract dropped by 0.0046 cents, implying that a holder of a purchase contract has lost 12.5m × (0.0046/100) = USD 575 per contract and that a seller has made USD 575 per contract. The next two columns show the highest and lowest prices that have been observed during the life of the contract. For the March contract, the "High-Low" range is more narrow than for the older contracts, since the March contract has been trading for little more than a month. "Open Interest" refers to the number of outstanding contracts. Notice how most of the trading is in the nearest-maturity contract. Open interest in the March '94 contract is minimal, and there has not even been any trading that day. (There are no open, high, and low data.) The settlement price for the March '94 contract has been set by the CME on the basis of bid-ask quotes.

The line below the price information gives an estimate of the volume traded that day and the previous day (Wednesday). Also shown are the total open interest across the three contracts, and the change in open interest relative to the day before.

5.2   EFFECT OF MARKING TO MARKET ON FUTURES PRICES

We now elaborate on our earlier claim that marking to market creates **interest rate risk**. If a corporation hedges a foreign currency inflow using a forward contract, there are no cash flows until the maturity date, T; and, at T, the money paid by the debtor is delivered to the bank in exchange for a known amount of home currency. In contrast, if hedging is done in the futures markets, there are daily cash flows. As we saw in Section 4.1.3, interim cash flows do not affect pricing if these cash flows are equal to the *discounted* price change, as is the case in a forward contract that is recontracted periodically. The reason is that, with daily recontracting, one can "undo" without cost the effects of recontracting by investing all inflows until time T and by financing all outflows by a loan expiring at T. The question we now address is whether the price will be affected if we drop the discounting of the price changes—that is, if we go from forward markets to futures markets. We will develop our argument in three steps, and illustrate each step using an example. For simplicity, we assume that next period there are only two possible futures prices and that investors are risk neutral. (A more general and rigorous proof is presented in Appendix 5B.)

Let there be three dates ($t = 0$, $t = 1$, and $T = 2$ = the maturity date), and let the initial forward rate be $F_{0,2}$ = USD 100. Let there be only two possible time-1 futures prices, either 105 or 95, and let these be equally probable.[5] We want to verify the conjecture that $f_{0,2} = F_{0,2}$ (= 100). The answer must be based on the difference of the cash flows between the two contracts:

- The buyer of the forward contract simply pays 100 at time 2. This is shown under the columns "Cash flows from forward," in Case 1 below.
- The buyer of the futures contract will pay 5 or receive 5, depending on the price change at time 1. The balance is then paid at time T (= 2). Thus, the buyer will receive/pay the cash flows shown under the columns "Cash flows from futures"—either −5 and −95, or +5 and −105.

The columns labeled "Difference in cash flows" show the cash flows for the futures contract relative to the cash flow of the forward contract.

5.2.1   Case 1: Zero Interest Rates

If interest rates are zero, a risk-neutral buyer of a futures contract does not mind paying 5 at time 1 if prices fall. A reason for the lack of concern is that this payment reduces the payment at time 2 by an equal amount, and there is no loss of time value given that the interest rate is zero. Nor does the investor see any advantage in the fact that, when prices rise, one receives 5 at time 1. There will be an

	Cash flows from forward		Cash flows from futures		Difference in cash flows: futures minus forward	
	time 1	time 2	time 1	time 2	time 1	time 2
If $f_1 =$ 95	0	−100	−5	−95	−5	+5
If $f_1 =$ 105	0	−100	+5	−105	+5	−5

---

[5] Given the time-1 prices 105 or 95, the only logical forward rate at $t = 0$ is 100. First note that, *at time* 1, futures prices and forward prices must be equal, since there is no more marking to market after time 1. Thus, 105 and 95 are also the two possible forward prices. Second, note that, in our example, the forward rate at $t = 0$ must be the expected next-period forward rate (that is, $F_{0,2} = (105 + 95)/2 = 100$). This absence of "expected return" in forward prices is explained by two facts. First, a forward contract requires no investment, so there is no pure time-value component in the expected change of the forward rate. Second, risk neutrality rules out a risk premium.

offsetting increase in what is payable next period. Stated somewhat differently, with zero interest rates, the investor can, without cost, undo the inflow or the outflow at time 1 by investing or borrowing at a zero rate of return. Thus, the buyer is perfectly indifferent between the cash flows from the futures and forward contract, and is willing to bid the same price for the two contracts. It follows that $F_{0,2} = f_{0,2}$.

5.2.2   Case 2: Positive but Constant Interest Rates

Now suppose that the risk-free return between time 1 and 2 is 10 percent.

- If the futures price rises, the buyer in the futures markets has an inflow of 5, which can be invested at 10 percent to yield 5.5 at time 2. The interest (0.5) is the net gain from marking to market when the price rises.
- But if the futures price falls, the buyer in the futures markets has an outflow of 5, which can be financed at 10 percent. The interest paid (0.5) is the net loss from marking to market if the price falls.

However, it is not known at time 0 whether prices will go up or down. That is, there is a 50 percent chance that there will be a time value gain of 0.5 from marking to market, and a 50 percent chance that there will be a time value loss of 0.5 from marking to market. Thus, a risk-neutral buyer sees no reason to prefer a forward contract over a futures, or *vice versa,* and will set identical prices for forwards and futures, as was conjectured in the example.

5.2.3   Case 3: Interest Rates Negatively Correlated with Price Changes

In reality, the future risk-free interest rate is not known in advance. It is well known that unexpectedly high interest rates are, on average, associated with unexpectedly low asset prices, because asset prices are discounted expected future values. Therefore, we can formulate a new question: what is the relationship between the forward price $F_{t,T}$ and the futures price $f_{t,T}$ if the interest rate is negatively related to the futures price?

Suppose that the risk-free return between time 1 and 2 is 8 percent when the futures price goes up, and 12 percent when the futures price goes down.

- If the futures price rises, the buyer in the futures market has an inflow of 5, which can be invested at 8 percent to yield 5.4 at time 2. The interest (0.4) is the net gain from marking to market when the price rises.
- If the futures price falls, the buyer in the futures market has an outflow of 5, which has to be financed at 12 percent. The interest paid (0.6) is the net loss from marking to market if the price falls.

Thus, at time 0 there is a 50 percent chance that there will be a time value gain of 0.4 from marking to market, and a 50 percent chance that there will be a time value loss of 0.6 from marking to market. The expected time value effect of $(0.4 - 0.6)/2 = -0.1$ makes a futures contract unattractive relative to the forward contract. It follows that we can no longer accept the conjecture that $f_{0,2} = 100 = F_{0,2}$. As a compensation for the expected loss in time value, the futures price at $t = 0$ will have to be below the forward price in order to reduce the total payment stream.

To sum up: if the interest rate is negatively related to the futures price, then the futures price is lower than the forward rate, and *vice versa.* The reason for this is that, if the futures price is negatively correlated with the interest rate, then gains on the (long) futures position tend to be made when the interest rate is unexpectedly low, and losses tend to be made when the interest rates are unexpectedly high. That is, money received from marking to market is typically reinvested at low rates, while intermediate losses are, on average, financed at high rates. Thus, the financing or reinvestment of intermediary cash flows is not an actuarially fair game. If futures and forward prices were identical, a buyer of a futures contract would, therefore, be worse off than a buyer of a forward contract. It follows that, to induce investors to hold futures contracts, futures prices must be lower than forward prices.

If the correlation were positive rather than negative, then marking to market would be an advantage to the buyer of a futures contract; as a result, the buyer would bid up the futures price above the forward price. Finally, if the correlation is zero, futures and forward prices will be the same. In practice, the empirical relationship between exchange rates and interest rates is not very strong. Moreover, simulations by, for example, French (1983) and Cornell and Reinganum (1981) have shown that even when the interest rate is negatively correlated with the futures price, the price difference between the forward and the theoretical futures price is very small—at least for short-term contracts on assets other than T-bills and bonds. Thus, for practical purposes, one can determine prices of futures contracts almost as if they were forward contracts.

5.3   HEDGING WITH FUTURES CONTRACTS

In this section, we see how one can use futures to hedge a given position. Because of its low cost, a hedger may prefer the currency futures market over the forward market. There are, however, problems that arise with hedging in the futures market.

- The contract size is fixed and is unlikely to exactly match the position to be hedged.
- The expiration dates of the futures contract rarely match those for the currency inflows/outflows that the contract is meant to hedge.
- The choice of underlying assets in the futures market is limited, and the currency one wishes to hedge may not have a futures contract.

That is, whereas in the forward market we can tailor the amount, the date, and the currency to a given exposed position, this is not always possible in the futures market. An imperfect hedge is called a **cross-hedge** when the currencies do not match, and is called a **delta-hedge** if the maturities do not match. When the mismatches arise simultaneously, we call this a **delta-cross-hedge**.

Example 5.4

Suppose that, on January 1, a US exporter wants to hedge a NLG 1m inflow due on March 1 (T_1). In the forward market, the exporter could simply sell that amount for March 1. In the futures market, hedging is less than perfect:

- There is no USD/NLG contract; the closest available hedge is the USD/DEM futures contract.
- The closest possible expiration date is, say, March 20 (T_2).
- The contract size is DEM 125,000. At the current central EMS parity of, say, NLG/DEM 1.1, this means NLG 137,500.

As we shall see, sometimes it is better to hedge with a portfolio of futures contracts written on different sources of risks rather than with only one type of futures contract. However, in order to simplify the exposition, we first consider the case where only one type of futures contract is being used to hedge a given position.

5.3.1   The Optimal Number of Contracts When One Type of Futures Contract Is Used

The problems of currency mismatch and maturity mismatch mean that, at best, only an approximate hedge can be constructed when hedging with futures. The standard rule is to look for a futures position that minimizes the variance of the hedged cash flow. Initially, we shall assume the following:

- There is one unit of foreign currency j to be received at time T_1—for instance, one guilder.
- A futures contract is available for a "related" currency i—for instance, the DEM—with an expiration date T_2 ($\geq T_1$).
- The size of the futures contract is one unit of foreign currency i (for instance, one DEM).
- Contracts are infinitely divisible; that is, one can buy any fraction of the unit contract.

Denote the number of contracts sold by β. The total cash flow generated by the futures contracts between times t and T_1 is then given by the size of the position, $-\beta$, times the change in the futures price between times t and T_1: $-\beta(\tilde{f}_{i,T_1,T_2} - f_{i,t,T_2})$.[6] Thus, the value of the *hedged* cash flow is:

$$\text{Cash flow at time } T_1 = \tilde{S}_{j,T_1} - \beta(\tilde{f}_{i,T_1,T_2} - f_{i,t,T_2}). \tag{1}$$

This general setup covers a number of interesting special cases, which we will examine in turn:

- The perfect match: the futures contract expires on the same date as the cash flow that is to be hedged (that is, $T_1 = T_2$), and the futures contract is written on the same currency as the one you are exposed to (that is, $j = i$).
- The cross-hedge: the futures contract expires on the same date as the cash flow that is to be hedged (that is, $T_1 = T_2$), but the futures contract is written on a different currency than the one that you are exposed to (that is, $j \neq i$).
- The delta-hedge: the futures contract is written on the same currency as the one to which you are exposed (that is, $j = i$), but it matures at a later date than the foreign currency cash flow that is to be hedged ($T_2 > T_1$).
- The combined case: the futures contract is of a different maturity ($T_2 > T_1$) and on a different currency ($i \neq j$) than the cash flow you wish to hedge.

Case 1: The Perfect Match

As the futures contract expires at $T_1 (T_2 = T_1)$, the convergence property means that $\tilde{f}_{i,T_1,T_2} = \tilde{S}_{i,T_1}$. Moreover, the currencies are assumed to match, that is, $i = j$. Thus, in the case of a perfect match, the cash flow in Equation [1] is:

$$\text{Cash flow at time } T_1 = \tilde{S}_{i,T_1} - \beta(\tilde{S}_{i,T_1} - f_{i,t,T_1}). \tag{2}$$

By setting $\beta = 1$, all risk can be eliminated, and the hedged cash flow becomes the risk-free amount f_{i,t,T_1}. Apart from the small uncertainty created by marking to market (which is ignored in Equation [1]), a perfectly matching futures contract works like a forward contract, and eliminates all risk.

---

[6] This, of course, ignores time value, but we will not be too particular because the hedge is imperfect anyway. The negative sign pre-multiplying β indicates that we sold, rather than bought, the futures contracts.

Case 2: The Currency-Mismatch Hedge or Cross-Hedge

We now consider a case where the futures contract matches the maturity of the foreign-currency inflow but not the currency ($j \neq i$). For instance, the US exporter's NLG inflow is hedged using a DEM future. We can still invoke the convergence property: at time T_1 when the NLG asset matures, the USD/DEM futures price will equal the USD/DEM spot price. Thus, when dates match but currencies do not, the cash flow in Equation [1] becomes:

$$\text{Cash flow at time } T_1 = \tilde{S}_{j,T_1} - \beta(\tilde{S}_{i,T_1} - f_{i,t,T_1}). \qquad [3]$$

The usual rule is to choose β such that the variance of this cash flow is minimized; but, at time t (when the futures contract is initiated), f_{i,t,T_1} is known. Thus, the only sources of variance are the two spot rates at time T_1. The problem can then be formulated as:

$$\text{Choose } \beta \text{ so as to minimize}$$

$$\text{var}(\tilde{S}_{j,T_1} - \beta \tilde{S}_{i,T_1}) = \text{var}(\tilde{S}_{j,T_1}) - 2\beta \, \text{cov}(\tilde{S}_{j,T_1}, \tilde{S}_{i,T_1}) + \beta^2 \, \text{var}(\tilde{S}_{i,T_1}).$$

The optimal number of contracts, β, is found by setting the derivative with respect to β equal to zero:

$$-2 \, \text{cov}(\tilde{S}_{j,T_1}, \tilde{S}_{i,T_1}) + 2\beta \, \text{var}(\tilde{S}_{i,T_1}) = 0 .$$

This implies that the number of contracts to be sold in order to hedge one unit of currency j, using a futures contract for one unit of currency i, is given by:[7]

$$\beta = \frac{\text{cov}(\tilde{S}_{j,T_1}, \tilde{S}_{i,T_1})}{\text{var}(\tilde{S}_{i,T_1})}. \qquad [4]$$

The ratio on the right-hand side is the slope coefficient in the regression of the time-T_1 spot rate $\tilde{S}_{j,T_1}$ (the one you are exposed to, the NLG) on $\tilde{S}_{i,T_1}$ (the one you use as a hedge, the DEM):

$$\tilde{S}_{j,T_1} = \alpha + \beta \, \tilde{S}_{i,T_1} + \tilde{e}. \qquad [5]$$

Note that this regression is forward-looking. What we are asked to do, in principle, is to formulate the joint distribution of the two spot rates at time T_1, using all relevant information that is available at the current time, t. In this sense, we should think of regression [5] as a cross-sectional regression, run across all conceivable future states of the world at time T_1. Conversely, it is wrong to think of regression [5] as a time-series regression on past data. First, the past may be a poor guide to the future.

---

[7] Note that in the perfect-match case (that is, $i = j$), the regression coefficient β equals 1, which brings us back to the solution identified for Case 1.

Second, even if the past were our only source of information about the future, the estimates obtained from a time series regression of the form [5] would be statistically unreliable. For technical reasons explained in Appendix 5A, time-series estimations of [5] must be based on changes in the spot and futures rates—for example, weekly or biweekly changes.[8]

In Section 5.3.2 we shall give an example where the regression coefficient is estimated from past data. In this and the following sections, we illustrate the technique using only forward-looking information—an approach that simultaneously helps us in understanding the nature and limitations of the hedge ratio or β. Consider regression [5]. This equation relates the USD/NLG spot rate at time T_1 to the USD/DEM spot rate at the same moment. We can, however, make a direct link between these spot rates by using the following triangular relationship:

$$\tilde{S}_{[USD/NLG],T_1} = \tilde{S}_{[DEM/NLG],T_1} \times \tilde{S}_{[USD/DEM],T_1}.$$

The variable on the left of this expression is the left-hand-side variable in regression [5], while the second variable on the right is the right-hand-side variable in regression [5]. Thus, the triangular relationship contains some useful information about the slope β in regression [5]. We know that the Dutch central bank keeps the guilder within a 1 percent band from its central EMS parity relative to the DEM, which is about DEM/NLG 0.9. Suppose that we feel very confident that that this will remain the case until at least time T_1. If we ignore uncertainty about the cross rate, the link between the USD/NLG rate and the USD/DEM rate can be specified as follows:

$$\tilde{S}_{[USD/NLG],T_1} = 0.9 \times \tilde{S}_{[USD/DEM],T_1}.$$

Comparing with regression [5], we see that if the DEM/NLG rate remains at the level 0.9, the regression coefficient β must be 0.9.

Example   5.5

The DEM trades initially at USD/DEM 1.6, and appreciates by 5 percent to 1.68—that is, by 8 cents. If the NLG starts off at USD/NLG $1.6 \times 0.9 = 1.44$, a 5 percent appreciation of the DEM takes the

---

[8] This does not affect the value of the true regression coefficient. Suppose that we want to estimate the regression

$$\tilde{S}_{j,T} = \alpha + \beta \, \tilde{S}_{i,T} + e_T,$$

and suppose that we decide to use only past data. We can then write the equation for times t_1 and t_2. Subtracting the former from the latter, we obtain:

$$\left[S_{j,t_2} - S_{j,t_1} \right] = (\alpha - \alpha) + \beta \left[S_{j,t_2} - S_{j,t_1} \right] + \left[e_{t_2} - e_{t_1} \right].$$

This equation has the same "true" slope coefficient as the original regression. However, as argued in the appendix, the time series of *changes* in exchange rates has better statistical properties than the time series of *levels* of exchange rates.

guilder to $1.68 \times 0.9 = 1.512$. This represents an increase of only 7.2 cents, nine-tenths of the change in the USD/DEM rate. Thus, to hedge a one-guilder asset, a futures contract on 0.90 DEM will suffice.

In practice, there is some uncertainty about the DEM/NLG spot rate at time T_1. This has two implications. First, uncertainty about the future DEM/NLG spot rate may mean that the optimal hedge ratio or β should differ from the expected value of the cross rate (0.9, in our example)—unless the uncertainty about the cross rate is uncorrelated with the USD/DEM spot rate. This follows from a rearrangement of the triangular relationship:

$$\tilde{S}_{[\text{USD/NLG}],T_1} = \tilde{S}_{[\text{DEM/NLG}],T_1} \times \tilde{S}_{[\text{USD/DEM}],T_1}$$

$$= 0.9 \times \tilde{S}_{[\text{USD/DEM}],T_1} + (\tilde{S}_{[\text{DEM/NLG}],T_1} - 0.9) \times \tilde{S}_{[\text{USD/DEM}],T_1}.$$

If $(\tilde{S}_{[\text{USD/DEM}],T_1} - 0.9)$ is independent of $\tilde{S}_{[\text{USD/DEM}],T_1}$, the conditional expectation of the entire term $(\tilde{S}_{[\text{DEM/NLG}],T_1} - 0.9) \times \tilde{S}_{[\text{USD/DEM}],T_1}$ is still zero, which means that this term satisfies the standard regression assumptions. Thus, if movements in the cross rate are independent of the value of the DEM relative to the USD, the true regression coefficient is still equal to 0.9, the expected cross rate. However, if the deviation of the cross rate from its expected value is correlated with the USD/DEM rate, a small adjustment in β may be necessary.

The second implication of the uncertainty about the cross rate is that, when a NLG inflow is hedged using a DEM futures contract, the hedge can never be perfect. Even if the conditional expectation of $(\tilde{S}_{[\text{DEM/NLG}],T_1} - 0.9) \times \tilde{S}_{[\text{USD/DEM}],T_1}$ is zero, its variance will be positive. Thus, the hedged cash flow will not be risk free.

Case 3: The Maturity-Mismatch Hedge or Delta-Hedge

We now consider the pure maturity-mismatch case. The futures contract is written on the same currency as the one that you are exposed to (that is, $j = i$—for instance, the guilder), but it matures at a later date than the foreign currency cash flow that is to be hedged ($T_2 > T_1$). In this case, the hedged cash flow (Equation [1]) can be specified as:

$$\text{Cash flow at time } T_1 = \tilde{S}_{j,T_1} - \beta(\tilde{f}_{j,T_1,T_2} - f_{j,t,T_2}). \tag{6}$$

The risk-minimization problem is the same as in Case 2, except that we now have $\tilde{f}_{j,T_1,T_2}$ instead of $\tilde{S}_{i,T_1}$. It follows that this time, the optimal number of contracts β is obtained from the regression of the guilder spot rate on the guilder futures price:

$$\tilde{S}_{j,T_1} = a + \beta \tilde{f}_{j,T_1,T_2} + \tilde{e}. \tag{7}$$

This is a forward-looking regression, as defined in the previous section. To interpret this, use our previous result that a futures price is almost indistinguishable from a forward price. Interest Rate Parity then says that:

$$\tilde{f}_{j,T_1,T_2} = \tilde{S}_{j,T_1} \times \frac{1+\tilde{r}_{T_1,T_2}}{1+\tilde{r}^*_{T_1,T_2}}. \qquad [8]$$

We have added *tildes* over the rates of return to stress the fact that, at time t (when the hedge is set up), we do not know what the interest rates will be at time T_1. The standard way of putting this is to say that there is **basis risk**. The **basis** is defined as the difference between the futures price and the spot price, and is conceptually and numerically close to the swap rate. Although the basis is to some extent unpredictable, it is nevertheless illuminating to consider the hypothetical case of known time-T_1 interest rates. Suppose, for instance, that it is perfectly predictable that, at time T_1, the interest rate factor $(1 + \tilde{r}_{T_1,T_2})/(1 + \tilde{r}^*_{T_1,T_2})$ will be equal to 1.03. Then we know that β should be equal to $1/1.03$:

$$\beta = \frac{\mathrm{cov}(\tilde{S}_{j,T_1}, \tilde{f}_{j,T_1,T_2})}{\mathrm{var}(\tilde{f}_{j,T_1,T_2})} = \frac{\mathrm{cov}(\tilde{S}_{j,T_1}, \tilde{S}_{j,T_1} \times 1.03)}{\mathrm{var}(\tilde{S}_{j,T_1} \times 1.03)} \qquad [9]$$

$$= \frac{\mathrm{cov}(\tilde{S}_{j,T_1}, \tilde{S}_{j,T_1}) \times 1.03}{\mathrm{var}(\tilde{S}_{j,T_1}) \times 1.03^2}$$

$$= \frac{1}{1.03}$$

Thus, assuming that we know that the time-T_1 USD/NLG forward premium will be 3 percent, Equation [9] implies that the fluctuations in the NLG futures rate will be 1.03 times the fluctuation in the NLG spot rate. Thus, if β were set equal to unity, the fluctuations in the hedge instrument would be larger than the fluctuations in the value of the cash flow that is being hedged. Thus, one needs to buy fewer contracts, which is what setting $\beta = 1/1.03$ achieves.[9]

Since in reality the time-T_1 forward premium is not known, the determination of β is not as easy as Equation [9] suggests. One element in our calculations would surely be our expectations about the time-T_1 forward premium. Another source of information can be past experience. We can look back to see how the NLG spot rate and the NLG forward rate with a maturity of $T_2 - T_1$ years have co-varied in the past. Appendix 5A discusses how such regressions should be run and why you should analyze *changes* in exchange rates rather than the exchange rates themselves. Another implication of interest risk is that the hedge is not perfect. This is because the item to be hedged is subject to exchange risk only, while the hedge instrument fluctuates because of exchange risk *and* interest risk.

---

[9]Another way to note this is that if:

$$\tilde{f}_{j,T_1,T_2} = 1.03\,\tilde{S}_{j,T_1}, \text{then } \tilde{S}_{j,T_1} = [1/1.03]\,\tilde{f}_{j,T_1,T_2}.$$

Comparing this last expression to the regression (Equation [7]), we see that β must be equal to $1/1.03$.

Because of this interest risk, the movements in the hedge instrument will not perfectly offset the movements in the cash flow that is being hedged.

Case 4:   The Delta-Cross-Hedge

It is now easy to solve the case where the two mismatch problems arise simultaneously: the futures contract is written on a different currency than the one you are exposed to *and* the futures contract matures at a later date than the foreign currency cash flow that is to be hedged. In this case, the hedged cash flow is:

$$\text{Cash flow at time } T_1 = \tilde{S}_{j,T_1} - \beta(\tilde{f}_{i,T_1,T_2} - f_{i,t,T_2}).$$

Compared to Equation [3], we now have $\tilde{f}_{i,T_1,T_2}$ instead of $\tilde{S}_{i,T_1}$. It follows that the optimal number of contracts β is obtained from the forward-looking regression of the USD/NLG spot rate (the source of risk in the cash flow) on the USD/DEM futures price (the hedge instrument), both at time T_1:

$$\tilde{S}_{j,T_1} = a + \beta \tilde{f}_{i,T_1,T_2} + \tilde{e}. \qquad [10]$$

This time, the right-hand-side variable, $\tilde{f}_{i,T_1,T_2}$, has two sources of uncertainty that are not present in the left-hand-side variable—the NLG/DEM spot rate, and the USD/DEM basis:

$$\tilde{f}_{[\text{USD/DEM}],T_1,T_2} = \tilde{S}_{[\text{USD/NLG}],T_1} \times \tilde{S}_{[\text{NLG/DEM}],T_1} \times \frac{1+\tilde{r}_{T_1,T_2}}{1+\tilde{r}^{\text{DEM}}_{T_1,T_2}}. \qquad [11]$$

If it were known with certainty that the interest rate factor would be equal to 1.03 and the DEM/NLG rate would be equal to 1/0.9, the fluctuations in the DEM futures price would exceed the fluctuations in the NLG spot rate by a factor 1.03/0.9 = 1.144. To offset this excess sensitivity in the futures price, it would suffice to buy 1/1.144 = 0.874 USD/DEM futures contracts.

Again, in reality the time-T_1 USD/DEM forward premium is not known, nor is the time-T_1 DEM/NLG spot rate. This implies that estimation from past data is probably useful in complementing our expectations. That is, we can look back and see how the USD/NLG spot rate and the USD/DEM forward rate with a maturity of $T_2 - T_1$ years have covaried in the past. A second implication is that, because of interest risk and cross-rate risk, the movements in the hedge instrument will not perfectly offset the movements in the cash flow being hedged.

Interpreting the Regression Output

Almost invariably, one uses regression analysis of past exchange rate data as one ingredient in the determination of β. The regression output also helps to answer a number of questions that are related to the quality of the hedge. First, in light of the cross-rate and interest risk that are present in the futures price, one might wonder how well an imperfect hedge can be expected to work. The coefficient of determination (R^2) of the regression sheds some light on this: R^2 estimates the percentage reduction in the variance of the cash flow that is being hedged.

Example 5.6

Suppose that, in your sample, the regression R^2 is 0.75. This means that hedging reduces the variance of the cash flow by an estimated 75 percent. Stated differently, after adding the futures hedge, the estimate is that only one-quarter of the original variance is left.

A second (and related) question is whether one can be confident that the hedge instrument is actually correlated with the exchange rate to which one is exposed. The problem is that variables that are fundamentally unrelated may still turn out to be correlated in a sample.[10] To sort out correlations that are probably genuine from nonsense correlation, one can consider the t-statistic. The higher this statistic, the lower the probability that the correlation is just a chance occurrence. Most statisticians would be sufficiently confident about the existence of a true correlation if the t-statistic exceeds 2. Note, however, that the reverse is not true. When the t-statistic is on the low side, say 1.4, we cannot simply conclude that the correlation is nonsense. All we can say is that perhaps the sample correlation is nonsense, and perhaps it reflects something genuine.

Adjusting for the Sizes of the Spot Exposure and the Futures Contract

Thus far, we have assumed that the exposure was one unit of currency j, and that the size of one futures contract is one unit of foreign currency i. If the exposure is a larger number, say n_{Sj}, then the number of contracts one needs to sell obviously goes up proportionally, while if the size of the futures contract is n_{fi} rather than unity, the number of futures contracts goes down proportionally. Thus, the generalized result is as follows: the number of contracts to be sold in order to hedge n_{Sj} units of currency j using a futures contract with size n_{fi} units of currency i is given by:

$$\beta = \frac{n_{Sj}}{n_{fi}} \frac{\mathrm{cov}(\tilde{f}_{i,T_1,T_2}, \tilde{S}_{j,T_1})}{\mathrm{var}(\tilde{f}_{i,T_1,T_2})}.$$

Example   5.7

Suppose that you consider hedging a NLG 2m inflow using DEM futures with a contract size of DEM 125,000. A regression based on 52 points of weekly data produces the following output:

$$\Delta S_{[USD/NLG]} = 0.003 + 0.89\, \Delta f_{[USD/DEM]}$$

with an R^2 of 0.83 and a t-statistic of 15.62. Then:

- In light of the high t-statistic, we are sure that there actually is a correlation between the USD/NLG spot rate and the USD/DEM futures price.

---

[10] An often-quoted example is the nonsense correlation between the growth rates in the economy and the length of skirts. The mini-skirted sixties happened to be high-growth years, while the maxi-skirted seventies were recession years.

- Hedging reduces the total uncertainty about the position being hedged by an estimated 83 percent.
- The optimal number of contracts to be sold is estimated as

$$\frac{2\,m}{125,000} \times 0.89 = 14.24$$

or, after rounding, 14 contracts.

5.3.2   Hedging with Futures Using Contracts on More than One Currency

So far, we have considered a hedge that contains one (type of) futures contract. Often, the hedger may want to hedge her position using contracts for two or more underlying assets.

Example   5.8

Suppose that the cash flow to be hedged is an ecu deposit. A perfect hedge would be possible only if the private ECU always traded at par with the official ECU, if there were futures contracts for each of the ecu's component currencies, and if the deposit expired on the same date as the futures contract. In reality, we must work with only USD/DEM, USD/FRF, and USD/GBP futures contracts. It is likely that a portfolio of these three futures contracts will be better at hedging the USD value of the ECU deposit than a futures position in only one of the three currencies.

Consider another example.

Example   5.9

As we saw in Case 3, if we delta-hedge a DEM inflow maturing at T_1 using a DEM futures maturing at T_2, the hedge is imperfect because the futures price at time T_1 depends not only on the USD/DEM spot rate but also on the DEM and USD interest rates at time T_1. Thus, by adding futures contracts on interest rates one can, to some extent, counterbalance the effects of interest rate fluctuations.[11]

The optimal numbers of the contracts in the hedge portfolio are estimated by conducting a multivariate regression of the relevant spot rate on all chosen futures prices.

Example   5.10

A US importer would like to hedge an ECU 2m outflow by buying DEM, CHF, and GBP contracts. The contract sizes are DEM 125,000, CHF 125,000, and GBP 62,500, respectively. The solution is to

---

[11] Interest rates futures are described in Chapter 9.

regress the ECU spot rate on USD/GBP, USD/DEM, and USD/CHF futures prices, following the procedure described in Appendix 5A, in order to identify the optimal contract sizes. Suppose that the regression output is as follows, with t-statistics shown in parentheses, and $R^2 = 0.74$.

$$\Delta S_{[USD/ECU]} = a + 0.91 \times \Delta f_{[USD/DEM]} + 1.59 \times \Delta f_{[USD/CHF]} + 0.14 \times \Delta f_{[USD/GBP]}$$
$$(12.3) \qquad\qquad (3.36) \qquad\qquad (1.45)$$

We conclude, in view of the high t-statistics, that the DEM and CHF futures prices are definitely correlated with the ECU spot rate. The low t-statistic for the GBP means that the positive estimate may be a result of chance: on the basis of our data there is no way of telling with sufficient confidence whether the GBP contract really improves the hedge or not. Finally, the R^2 implies that, including the GBP, the hedge will reduce the total variance of the ECU position by an estimated 74 percent. The contract sizes will be:

- DEM: $\dfrac{2\,m}{125,000} \times 0.91 = 14.56$ contracts (15, in practice)
- CHF: $\dfrac{2\,m}{125,000} \times 1.59 = 25.44$ contracts (25, in practice)
- GBP: $\dfrac{2\,m}{62,500} \times 0.14 = 4.48$ contracts (4, in practice).

This finishes our discussion of how to adjust the size of the hedge position for maturity and currency mismatches.

5.4   CONCLUSION: PROS AND CONS OF FUTURES CONTRACTS RELATIVE TO FORWARD CONTRACTS

Now that we understand the differences between futures and forwards, let us compare the advantages and disadvantages of using futures rather than forwards. The advantages of using futures include:

- Because of the institutional arrangements in futures markets, the default risk of futures contracts is low. As a consequence, relatively unknown players without an established reputation or without the ability to put up substantial margin can trade in futures markets. This is especially relevant for speculators who are not interested in actual delivery at maturity.[12]
- Because of standardization, futures markets have low transaction costs; commissions in futures markets tend to be lower than in forward markets.
- Given the liquidity of the secondary market for futures, futures positions can be closed out early with greater ease than forward contracts.

---

[12] This term should not be interpreted as pejorative. Speculators are people who insist on their right to "vote" on a price even if they don't need the underlying asset. In a properly functioning market, prices will be more efficient the more people involved in the supply-demand process.

Clearly, there are also drawbacks to futures contracts—otherwise, forward markets would have disappeared entirely.

- One drawback is the *standardization* of the futures contract. A creditworthy hedger has to choose between an imperfect but cheap hedge in the futures markets and a more expensive but exact hedge in the forward market. The standardization of the futures contracts means that often one will not be able to find a contract of exactly the right size or the exact same maturity as that of the underlying position to be hedged.
- Also, marking to market may create **ruin risk** for a hedger. A firm that expects to receive DEM 100m nine months from now faces no inflows or outflows when it hedges in the forward market. In contrast, the daily marking to market of a futures contract can create severe short-term cash flow problems. It is not obvious that interim cash outflows can always be financed easily.
- Assuming that financing of the interim cash flows is easy, marking to market still creates **interest rate risk**. The daily cash flows must be financed/deposited in the money markets at interest rates that are not known when the hedge is set up. This risk is not present in forward hedging. The correlation between futures prices and interest rates is fortunately rather low, implying that the interest rate risk is small.
- Futures contracts exist only for a few high-turnover exchange rates. This is because futures markets cannot survive without large trading volumes. Thus, for most exchange rates, a hedger has to choose between (1) forward contracts or money-market hedges, or (2) a cross-hedge in the futures markets. A cross-hedge is less effective because the relationship between the currency one is exposed to and the currency used as a hedge instrument is obscured by cross rate risk.
- Finally, futures markets are available only for short maturities. Maturities rarely exceed eleven months, and the markets are often thin for maturities exceeding six months. In contrast, forward contracts are readily available for maturities of up to one year, and today the quotes for forward contracts extend up to ten years.

We see that the competing instruments, forwards and futures, appear to cater to two different clienteles. As a general rule, forward markets are used primarily by corporate hedgers, while futures markets tend to be preferred by speculators.

QUIZ QUESTIONS

1. For each pair shown below, which of the two describes a forward contract? Which describes a futures contract?

   (a) standardized/made to order
   (b) interest rate risk/no interest rate risk
   (c) ruin risk/no ruin risk
   (d) short maturities/even shorter maturities
   (e) no secondary market/liquid secondary market

   (f) for hedgers/speculators
   (g) more expensive/less expensive
   (h) no credit risk/credit risk
   (i) organized market/no organized market

2. Match the vocabulary below with the following statements.

   (a) organized market
   (b) standardized contract
   (c) standardized expiration
   (d) clearing corporation
   (e) daily recontracting
   (f) marking to market
   (g) convergence
   (h) settlement price
   (i) default risk of a futures
   (j) initial margin

   (k) maintenance margin
   (l) margin call
   (m) variation margin
   (n) open interest
   (o) interest rate risk
   (p) cross-hedge
   (q) delta-hedge
   (r) delta-cross-hedge
   (s) ruin risk

   1. Daily payment of the change in a forward or futures price.
   2. The collateral deposited as a guarantee when a futures position is opened.
   3. Daily payment of the discounted change in a forward price.
   4. The minimum level of collateral on deposit as a guarantee for a futures position.
   5. A hedge on a currency for which no futures contracts exist and for an expiration other than what the buyer or seller of the contract desires.
   6. An additional deposit of collateral for a margin account that has fallen below its maintenance level.
   7. A contract for a standardized number of units of a good to be delivered at a standardized date.
   8. A hedge on foreign currency accounts receivable or accounts payable that is due on a day other than the third Wednesday of March, June, September, or December.
   9. The number of outstanding contracts for a given type of futures.
   10. The one-day futures price change.
   11. A proxy for the closing price that is used to ensure that a futures price is not manipulated.
   12. Generally, the last Wednesday of March, June, September, or December.
   13. Organization that acts as a "go-between" for buyers and sellers of futures contracts.
   14. The risk that the interim cash flows must be invested or borrowed at an unfavorable interest rate.
   15. A hedge on a currency for which no futures contract exists.
   16. The risk that the price of a futures contract drops (rises) so far that the purchaser (seller) has severe short-term cash flow problems due to marking to market.
   17. The property whereby the futures equals the spot price at expiration.
   18. Centralized market (either an exchange or a computer system) where supply and demand are matched.

The table below is an excerpt of futures prices from *The Wall Street Journal* of Tuesday, March 22, 1994. Use this table to answer Questions 3 through 6.

| | | | | | | Lifetime | | Open |
	Open	High	Low	Settle	Change	High	Low	Interest
JAPAN YEN (CME) — 12.5 million yen; $ per yen (.00)								
June	.9432	.9460	.9427	.9459	+.0007	.9945	.8540	48,189
Sept	.9482	.9513	.9482	.9510	+.0007	.9900	.8942	1,782
Dec	.9550	.9610	.9547	.9566	+.0008	.9810	.9525	384
Est vol 13,640; vol Fri 15,017; open int 50,355, + 414								
DEUTSCHEMARK (CME) — 125,000 marks; $ per marks								
June	.5855	.5893	.5847	.5888	+.0018	.6162	.5607	87,662
Sept	.5840	.5874	.5830	.5871	+.0018	.6130	.5600	2,645
Dec	.5830	.5860	.5830	.5864	+.0018	.5910	.5590	114
Est vol 40,488; vol Fri 43,717; open int 90,421, −1,231								
CANADIAN DOLLAR (CME) — 100,000 dlrs.; $ per Can $								
Jun	.7296	.7329	.7296	.7313	+.0021	.7805	.7290	43,132
Sept	.7293	.7310	.7290	.7297	+.0018	.7740	.7276	962
Dec	.7294	.7295	.7285	.7282	+.0016	.7670	.7270	640
Mar95	.7263	.7263	.7263	.7267	+.0015	.7605	.7260	152
Est vol 5,389; vol Fri 4,248; open int 44,905, −1,331								

3. What is the CME contract size for:

   (a) Japanese yen?
   (b) German mark?
   (c) Canadian dollar?

4. What is the open interest for the September contract for:

   (a) Japanese yen?
   (b) German mark?
   (c) Canadian dollar?

5. What are the daily high, low, and settlement prices for the December contract for:

   (a) Japanese yen?
   (b) German mark?
   (c) Canadian dollar?

6. What is the day's cash flow from marking to market for the holder of a:

   (a) JPY June contract?
   (b) DEM June contract?
   (c) CAD June contract?

EXERCISES

1. On the morning of Monday, August 21, you purchased a futures contract for 1 unit of CHF at a rate of USD/CHF 0.7. The subsequent settlement prices are shown in the table below.
    (a) What are the daily cash flows from marking to market?
    (b) What is the cumulative total cash flow from marking to market (ignoring discounting)?
    (c) Is the total cash flow greater than, less than, or equal to the difference between the price of your original futures contract and the price of the same futures contract on August 30?

August	21	22	23	24	25	28	29	30
Futures rate	0.71	0.70	0.72	0.71	0.69	0.68	0.66	0.63

2. On November 15, you sold ten futures contracts for 100,000 CAD each at a rate of USD/CAD 0.75. The subsequent settlement prices are shown in the table below.
    (a) What are the daily cash flows from marking to market?
    (b) What is the total cash flow from marking to market (ignoring discounting)?
    (c) If you deposit USD 75,000 into your margin account, and your broker requires USD 50,000 as maintenance margin, when will you receive a margin call and how much will you have to deposit?

November	16	17	18	19	20	23	24	25
Futures rate	0.74	0.73	0.74	0.76	0.77	0.78	0.79	0.81

3. On the morning of December 6, you purchased a futures contract for one USD at a rate of BEF/USD 55. The following table gives the subsequent settlement prices and the *p.a.* bid-ask interest rates on a BEF investment made until December 10.

December	6	7	8	9	10
Futures price	56	57	54	52	55
Bid-ask interest rates on BEF in percent	12.00–12.25	11.50–11.75	13.00–13.25	13.50–13.75	NA

    (a) What are the daily cash flows from marking to market?
    (b) What is the total cash flow from marking to market (ignoring discounting)?
    (c) If you must finance your losses and invest your gains from marking to market, what is the value of the total cash flows on December 10?

4. You want to hedge the DEM value of a CAD 1m inflow using futures contracts. On Germany's exchange, there is a futures contract for USD 100,000 at DEM/USD 1.5.

   (a) Your assistant runs a bunch of regressions:
      (1) ΔS [DEM/CAD] $= \alpha_1 + \beta_1 \Delta f$ [USD/DEM]
      (2) ΔS [DEM/CAD] $= \alpha_2 + \beta_2 \Delta f$ [DEM/USD]
      (3) ΔS [CAD/DEM] $= \alpha_3 + \beta_3 \Delta f$ [DEM/USD]
      (4) ΔS [CAD/DEM] $= \alpha_4 + \beta_4 \Delta f$ [USD/DEM]

      Which regression is relevant to you?

   (b) If the relevant β were 0.83, how many contracts do you buy? sell?

5. In the previous question, we assumed that there was a USD futures contract in Germany, with a fixed number of USD (100,000 units) and a variable DEM/USD price. What if there is no German futures exchange? Then you would have to go to a US exchange, where the number of DEM per contract is fixed (at, say, 125,000), rather than the number of USD. How many USD/DEM contracts will you buy?

6. A German exporter wants to hedge an outflow of NZD 1m. She decides to hedge the risk with a DEM/USD contract and a DEM/AUD contract. The regression output is, with t-statistics in parentheses, and $R^2 = 0.59$:

$$\Delta S_{[DEM/NZD]} = a + 0.15 \, \Delta f_{[DEM/USD]} + 0.7 \, \Delta f_{[DEM/AUD]}.$$
$$(1.57) \qquad\qquad (17.2)$$

   (a) How will you hedge if you use both contracts, and if a USD contract is for USD 50,000 and the AUD contract for AUD 75,000?

   (b) Should you use the USD contract, in view of the low t-statistic? Or should we only use the AUD contract?

MIND-EXPANDING EXERCISES

1. Consider the two possible following sequences of interest rates and futures prices (GBP/IEP) time 2:

	1/1/2000	7/1/2000	1/1/2001
Futures price			
Path A:		0.92 ————	1
	1.05		
Path B:		1.02 ————	1
p.a. simple interest rates	360 days	180 days	
GBP (HC)	0.050	0.060	n.a.
IEP (FC)	0.025	0.035	n.a.

Assume that you have a short futures position for IEP 50,000 and that there is marking to market twice a year. Check that by increasing the futures position on July 1, 2000, the hedge becomes path-independent.

The following question is based on rolled-over forward contracts. Suppose that you have a long-term open position that you want to hedge, but there is no corresponding long-term forward contract. Thus, you must roll over short-term contracts. For example, rather than taking out a single five-year contract, you take out five consecutive one-year contracts. When hedging a position, you increase the size of the new forward hedge at each roll-over date by a factor of $(1 + r^*_{t,t+1})$ (not by the factor $(1 + r_{t,t+1})$ used in Appendix 5B).

2. Consider the following possible paths of spot rates:

	1/1/2000	7/1/2000	1/1/2001
Spot rate			
Path A:	1.00	1.00	1.20
Path B:		1.20	1.20
p.a. simple interest rates	360 days	180 days	
HC	0.21	0.21	n.a.
FC	0.10	0.10	n.a.
1-year forward			
Path A:		1.10	n.a.
Path B:		1.32	n.a.

Show that, when initially selling forward 1,000 units of foreign exchange for six months and adjusting the size of the new six-month hedge on July 1:

(a) The price path does not matter.

(b) The results are the same as for a sequence of two six-month money-market hedges.

COMPUTING THE HEDGE REGRESSION COEFFICIENT

In the appendix, we discuss how to determine the β in a cross-hedge or delta-hedge. Suppose that we want to figure out the regression relationship between the time-T_1 spot price for currency j and a time-T_1 futures price for currency i. In principle, we should use a "forward-looking" estimate: we should come up with our perception of the joint distribution of the time-T_1 spot rate for currency j on the time-T_1 futures prices for currency i. As this is tricky, one usually estimates the relationship using past data. There are several technical problems in implementing such a regression.

- How should one correct for nonstationarity in the data?
- What is the optimal observation frequency—monthly, weekly, daily, or even hourly data?
- How should one cope with changes in the contract's life?

5A.1 Correcting for Nonstationarity

In estimating a cross-hedge or delta-hedge beta, one should regress *changes* in currency j's spot rate on *changes* in currency i's futures price. The argument starts from the observation that exchange rates, like many other economic time series (GNP, money supply, prices, and so on) have properties that are similar to the following process:

$$\tilde{Z}_{t+1} = Z_t + a_t + \tilde{\varepsilon}_{t+1}, \qquad [A1]$$

with $\tilde{\varepsilon}$ an unpredictable error term. It is clear that, for such a process, we can make a one-period forecast conditional on the current level. The best prediction of $\tilde{Z}_{t+1}$, conditional on Z_t is

$$E(\tilde{Z}_{t+1} | Z_t) = Z_t + a_t.$$

However, there is no unconditional expected value, in the sense of a long-run mean to which the time series is attracted. A variable without a well-defined unconditional expected value is called **nonstationary**.

Example   5A.1

It does not make sense to ask the question, "What is the central value towards which, in the long run, GNP/capita tends to revert." We do not expect GNP/capita to revert to some long-run historical mean.

If the mean of a time-series variable does not exist in the usual sense, the variance cannot be defined because the variance is defined as the expected squared deviation from the mean. Nonetheless, regression coefficients rely very much on the assumption that variances (and covariances) exist. How, then, should we detect relationships between nonstationary variables?

If a nonstationary variable has no well-defined mean and variance, one can use changes in the level of the variable ("first differencing"). Suppose S behaves like [A1]. Then the process:

$$\tilde{S}_{t+1} = S_t + a_t + \tilde{\varepsilon}_t$$

implies that:

$$\tilde{S}_{t+1} - S_t = a_t + \tilde{\varepsilon}_t.$$

That is, the *changes* in the exchange rate have a well-defined mean (which equals a_t) and a well-defined variance that equals $\mathrm{var}(\tilde{\varepsilon}_{t+1})$.[13] Suppose, then, that we want to estimate a regression $S_{t+1} = a + b f_{t+1} + e_{t+1}$ where S and f do not have a well-defined mean and variance. By first-differencing, we get $(S_{t+1} - S_t) = b (f_{t+1} - f_t) + (e_{t+1} - e_t)$. The regressand $(S_{t+1} - S_t)$ now has a well-defined mean and variance, and so has the regressor $(f_{t+1} - f_t)$. If the residual $(e_{t+1} - e_t)$ has the standard statistical properties, we can then use standard regression. One should therefore regress time-series data of *changes* in currency j's spot rate on *changes* in currency i's futures price.

5A.2   Optimal Observation Frequency

In the regression, one could use monthly, weekly, two-day, daily, or hourly observations. There is a trade-off, though, between the number of observations one uses and the measurement errors in the data. The shorter the observation interval, the more data points we have. Everything else held constant, this improves the precision of the estimates. The shorter the observation interval, though, the larger the effect of measurement errors in the data. This is because, with short holding periods, the price changes become very small, while the measurement errors do *not* shrink towards zero. The measurement problems include the following:

- Spot and futures price data may not be fully synchronized. That is, the data may not be observed at exactly the same point in time, for instance, due to a (randomly changing) reporting lag in futures prices.
- There may be small, temporary fluctuations in the spot and/or futures price around the "true" (efficient markets) value, for instance, because of central bank intervention.
- If transactions data are used rather than midpoint quotes for futures, one does not generally know whether the transaction was a purchase (at the ask) or a sale (at the bid); that

---

[13] If the variance of the noise is proportional to the current level, one could also consider *percentage* changes in the variable or, almost equivalently, changes in the log of the variable. These would again have a well-defined variance. This, incidentally, is one reason why all empirical studies on stock markets or exchange markets work with returns (percentage changes) rather than with prices.

is, the "bid-ask bounce" also introduces measurement errors in the futures price, the regressor.[14]

Thus, with short observation intervals, the variance of the errors becomes large relative to the variance of the signal, the true return. Such noise in the left-hand-side variable (the change in the spot rate) adversely affects the precision of the estimates. If there is noise in the regressor too, the regression coefficient is, in addition, biased towards zero.[15] Stoll and Whaley (1992) provide examples of how to select the optimal observation frequency, weighing bias against precision of the estimates. For example, in the case of S&P-500 futures, they select weekly observations.

One could, of course, try to have it both ways—use weekly rather than daily or intra-day observations in order to reduce the relative impact of noise, and then extend the number of observations by going back far into the past. The trouble with this suggestion is that economic relationships change over time. Recall that we are trying to estimate a future relationship (between $\tilde{S}_{j,T_1}$, and $\tilde{f}_{i,T_1,T_2}$) on the basis of past data. The older the data, the less relevant they may be for the future. This is especially true for exchange rates, where government policy plays an important role.

5A.3   Purging Spurious Changes from the Futures Price Data

Finally, we need to be careful about what type of futures prices we use in the regressions. We want to figure out the relationship between the time-T_1 spot price for currency j and a time-T_1 futures price for currency i, and we know that this futures contract's remaining time to maturity will equal $T_2 - T_1$. Yet, in a database of futures prices, the contract's time to maturity changes every day. Worse, databases often "chain" data from different contracts. For example, for October through December, the database has prices for the December contract. After the expiration day of this December contract, there would be three months of data of the March contract, and so on. Thus, there are spurious changes in the futures price data, due to the gradual decrease of the time to maturity in data on one contract. In addition, there are spurious jumps on the date when the database links data of a new three-month contract to data of an expiring contract. Yet, changes in the basis, $f_{t,T} - S_t$, due to changes in the contract's life, are irrelevant for our purpose. Thus, we should purge all spurious changes in the future premium from the data.

In our case, such a correction is easily done. We know that futures prices are close to forward prices. Time series of forward prices with a constant time to maturity are easily available if the time to maturity $T_2 - T_1$ is a standard one, like thirty days or sixty days. Even if you need data for a nonstandard time to maturity $T_2 - T_1$, it is relatively simple to compute from Interest Rate Parity what a time series of forward prices should be. You then have a very good idea of how a series of futures prices with a constant remaining life would look.

---

[14] Using midpoint quotes has the drawback that one does not know whether anybody was actually interested in this price. The price may have been out of equilibrium.

[15] Suppose that $Y = a + b X + e$, and that X is measured with error. We can observe only $X' = X + v$, with v uncorrelated with X or Y. The expectation of the regression coefficient of Y on X' then equals

$$\frac{\text{cov}(Y, X')}{\text{var}(X')} = \frac{\text{cov}(X,Y) + \text{cov}(v,Y)}{\text{var}(X) + 2\text{cov}(X,v) + \text{var}(v)} = \frac{\text{cov}(X,Y)}{\text{var}(X) + \text{var}(v)}.$$

In contrast, the expected regression coefficient of Y on the true X equals $\text{cov}(X,Y)/\text{var}(X)$. Thus, the denominator of the estimated slope is systematically too large.

THE EFFECT OF INTEREST RATES ON FUTURES PRICES: A FORMAL DISCUSSION

In this appendix, we discuss the role of interest rate uncertainty on the futures price. We shall first show that, as long as future domestic interest rates are perfectly predictable, marking to market cannot have any effect on the futures price. Under this condition, the uncertainty about the time path of the futures prices can be "undone" by the investor, so that interest rate uncertainty does not affect the pricing. We then argue that randomness in future domestic interest rates is likely to lead to futures prices that are somewhat below forward prices.

Suppose that we have a problem with a three-period horizon (four points in time), with the contract initiated at time 0, and marked to market at times 1, 2, and 3 ($= T$). The major difference, from a theoretical point of view, between futures and forward contracts is marking to market. Therefore, one way to understand its effect on pricing is to "move" all interim cash flows to the expiration date, T. This can be done by investing the intermediate inflows and by financing the outflows using loans.

Inspired by what we did in our analysis of recontracted forward contracts in Chapter 4, we could try the following rule: invest the time-1 inflow ($\tilde{f}_{1,3} - f_{0,3}$) immediately until time 3 ($= T$), at the multiperiod rate $\tilde{r}_{1,3}$, and do similarly for the later inflows. The time-3 value of all the marking-to-market cash flows will then be:

$$(\tilde{f}_{1,3} - f_{0,3})(1 + \tilde{r}_{1,3}) + (\tilde{f}_{2,3} - \tilde{f}_{1,3})(1 + \tilde{r}_{2,3}) + (\tilde{f}_{3,3} - \tilde{f}_{2,3}). \qquad [B1]$$

Equation [B1] shows that, when the same tactic as that used for recontracted forward is adopted, the time-3 cash flow from a futures contract depends on the interest rates. In addition, Equation [B1] shows that the time-3 value also depends on the interim futures prices. This is called **path-dependency**. We now show that path-dependency disappears when we move the cash flows towards time T by rolling over one-period money-market transactions.

5B.1 Claim 1: Uncertainty about Intermediate Futures Prices Can Be "Undone"

In this section, we show that the dependence of the time-T cash flow from a futures contract on the path of futures prices can be eliminated by a relatively simple adjustment. Specifically, if we increase the size of the contract every day by the factor $(1 + \tilde{r}_{t,t+1})$, and if we deposit the inflows (or finance the outflows) for only one day rather than all the way to time T ($= 3$), then the time path followed by the futures price is still immaterial. To demonstrate our claim, we analyze the cash flows at every point in time.

At time 0, we buy a futures contract of size $(1 + r_{0,1})$.[16] Taking this position does not involve any cash flows.

---

[16] This initial size is arbitrary. If we had started out with only one contract, we would have had to divide all later contract sizes by $1 + r_{0,1}$, too. This would not have affected the conclusion.

At time 1, there will be a cash flow from the futures contract equal to:

Cash flow from marking to market the current contract [B2]

$$= [\text{Change in the futures price}] \times [\text{Size of current contract}]$$

$$= (\tilde{f}_{1,3} - f_{0,3})(1 + r_{0,1}).$$

To shift this cash flow into the future, we now invest the gain (or borrow the amount lost) for *one* period. At time 1, we also change the size of the futures contract from $(1 + r_{0,1})$ units to $(1 + r_{0,1})$ $(1 + r_{1,2})$ units. This, in itself, does not involve any immediate payment.

At time 2, the futures contracts, now of size $(1 + r_{0,1})(1 + r_{1,2})$, generate a cash flow

Cash flow from marking to market the current contract [B3]

$$= [\text{Change in the futures price}] \times [\text{Size of current contract}]$$

$$= (\tilde{f}_{2,3} - f_{1,3})[(1 + r_{0,1})(1 + r_{1,2})].$$

In addition, the one-day deposit or loan taken out yesterday will expire, and trigger an additional cash flow equal to expression [B2] grossed up with interest between time 1 and time 2:

Effect of yesterday's marking to market [B4]

$$= [(f_{1,3} - f_{0,3})(1 + r_{0,1})](1 + r_{1,2}).$$

Adding [B3] and [B4], we conclude that:

Total time-2 cash flow $= (\tilde{f}_{2,3} - f_{0,3})(1 + r_{0,1})(1 + r_{1,2}).$ [B5]

Note the absence of the intermediate futures price $f_{1,3}$ from our computation of the total cash flow; that risk is eliminated. If interest rates were zero, $f_{1,3}$ would have canceled out automatically because, in a zero-interest world, we can simply add yesterday's cash flow, $f_{1,3} - f_{0,3}$, to today's, $\tilde{f}_{2,3} - f_{1,3}$. The same happens here, except that we have to slightly increase our position in order to capture the interest on $\tilde{f}_{1,3}$.

We again carry this net result, [B5], over to time 3 using a one-day loan or deposit. In addition, we increase the futures position, this time from $(1 + r_{0,1})(1 + r_{1,2})$ to $(1 + r_{0,1})(1 + r_{1,2})(1 + r_{2,3})$ contracts.

At time 3, the futures position of size $(1 + r_{0,1})(1 + r_{1,2})(1 + r_{2,3})$ yields a marking-to-market flow:

Cash flow from marking to market the current contract [B6]

$$= [\text{Change in the futures price}] \times [\text{Size of current contract}]$$

$$= (\tilde{S}_3 - f_{2,3})\big[(1 + r_{0,1})(1 + r_{1,2})(1 + r_{2,3})\big].$$

In addition, yesterday's loan or deposit, reflecting the net cumulative result of past marking to market, will expire. This leads to a second time-3 cash flow, expression [B5] grossed up with interest between time 2 and 3:

Effect of past marking to market

$$= \big[(\tilde{f}_{2,3} - f_{0,3})(1 + r_{0,1})(1 + r_{1,2})\big](1 + r_{2,3}). \tag{B7}$$

Summing [B6] and [B7], we conclude that:

Total cash flow, at time 3, from holding the futures contract since inception [B8]

$$= (\tilde{S}_3 - f_{0,3})(1 + r_{0,1})(1 + r_{1,2})(1 + r_{2,3}),$$

which is independent of the intermediate futures prices.

We have just shown that the risk related to the *time path of futures prices* can easily be eliminated. This means that it cannot affect the pricing of futures. Equally important, we have shown that a futures contract can be interpreted as a forward contract with the total contract size indexed to a rolled-over domestic deposit. To see this, note that the cash flow in [B8] consists of a first term, $(\tilde{S}_3 - f_{0,3})$, which is the payoff from a forward contract with initial contract price $f_{0,3}$. The remainder of [B8], the term $(1 + r_{0,1})(1 + r_{1,2})(1 + r_{2,3})$, can then be interpreted as a contract size. The amount $(1 + r_{0,1})(1 + r_{1,2})(1 + r_{2,3})$ is what one would obtain by investing one unit of home currency, day after day, at the one-day interest rate. But the size of the final position is not known in advance, because it depends on the intermediate interest rates $r_{1,2}$ and $r_{2,3}$. We are now ready to prove a new claim.

5B.2   Claim 2: If Future Interest Rates Are Known, Futures Prices Equal Forward Prices

Let us consider how the futures price, $f_{0,3}$, should be set at time 0. The cash flows from holding the contract are $(\tilde{f}_{1,3} - f_{0,3})$, $(\tilde{f}_{2,3} - \tilde{f}_{1,3})$, and $(\tilde{S}_3 - \tilde{f}_{2,3})$ at times 1, 2, and 3, respectively. The price $f_{0,3}$ should be set such that the futures contract has zero initial value. In short, the problem is to find a pricing rule such that:

$$PV_0(\tilde{f}_{1,3} - f_{0,3}) + PV_0(\tilde{f}_{2,3} - \tilde{f}_{1,3}) + PV_0(\tilde{S}_3 - \tilde{f}_{2,3}) = 0. \tag{B9}$$

where PV_0 is the present-value operator. If we state the problem as in [B9], the pricing rule is hard to identify because the interim prices show up in [B9], too. However, we have just shown that, using the overnight market, the investor can—without cost—eliminate the effect of the intermediate futures prices. This is a nice result, since it is easier to analyze just one (time-3) risky cash flow than three risky flows at different dates. In short, [B8] allows us to transform the complicated problem [B9] into a simpler problem:

$$\text{Find } f_{0,3} \text{ such that } PV_0\left[(\tilde{S}_3 - f_{0,3})\tilde{\Pi}\right] = 0, \qquad [\text{B}10]$$

where, for ease of notation, we have used $\tilde{\Pi}$ to denote $(1 + r_{0,1})(1 + \tilde{r}_{1,2})(1 + \tilde{r}_{2,3})$.

If the interest rates are perfectly known in advance, we can take the interest rate terms out of the PV operator. That is, if Π is risk free, then the present value of Π times a risky cash flow is just Π times the present value of the risky cash flow:

$$PV_0\left[(\tilde{S}_3 - f_{0,3})\Pi\right] = \Pi\,PV_0\left[(\tilde{S}_3 - f_{0,3})\right] = 0.$$

Thus, in the absence of interest uncertainty, we can divide by Π, which reduces our pricing problem to:

$$PV_0(\tilde{S}_3 - f_{0,3}) = 0. \qquad [\text{B}11]$$

But we already know how to solve this equation. We know, from Chapter 3, that the value of a forward contract at inception is zero, that is $PV_0(\tilde{S}_3 - F_{0,3}) = 0$. It follows that with fully predictable interest rates, $f_{0,3} = F_{0,3}$; that is, forward and futures prices are the same.

5B.3   Claim 3: If Interest Rates Are Stochastic and Negatively Correlated with Futures Prices, then Futures Prices Are below Forward Prices

If interest rates are random, then the valuation problem $PV_0[(\tilde{S}_3 - f_{0,3})\tilde{\Pi}] = 0$ can always be solved by taking risk-adjusted expectations and discounting at the risk-free, three-period rate of return:

$$PV_0\left[(\tilde{S}_3 - f_{0,3})\Pi\right] = \frac{CEQ_0\left[(\tilde{S}_3 - f_{0,3})\tilde{\Pi}\right]}{1 + r_{0,3}},$$

where CEQ ( ) is the certainty equivalent operator introduced in Chapter 3. We now have to set $f_{0,3}$ such that the present value is zero; and this condition is, of course, identical to the condition of a zero risk-adjusted expectation. We can therefore write the general problem as:

$$\text{Find } f_{0,3} \text{ such that } CEQ_0\left[(\tilde{S}_3 - f_{0,3})\tilde{\Pi}\right] = 0. \qquad [\text{B}12]$$

Risk-adjusted expectations obey the usual rules of standard expectations. This means that our problem can be expressed as:

$$\text{CEQ}_0\,(\tilde{S}_3 - f_{0,3})\,\text{CEQ}_0\,(\tilde{\Pi}) + \text{cov}(\tilde{S}_3 - f_{0,3}, \tilde{\Pi}) = 0. \qquad [\text{B13}]$$

The new term introduced by stochastic interest rates is the covariance term. If $\tilde{S}_3$ and $\tilde{\Pi}$ were independent, the covariance would be zero, and we would obtain the same result as before, $f_{0,3} = F_{0,3}$. However, independence between $\tilde{S}$ and $\tilde{\Pi}$ is not a very reasonable assumption. For instance, if the futures contract is written on a T-bill rather than on a currency, we would expect the covariance term to be negative. Indeed, unexpectedly high interest rates (a high $\tilde{\Pi}$) would be associated with unexpectedly low T-bill prices (a low $\tilde{S}$), and *vice versa*. If the futures contract refers to a stock, high interest rates still tend to correspond with low stock prices. Finally, unexpectedly high domestic rates tend to strengthen the home currency and weaken the foreign currency. In short, for financial assets, (cov $\tilde{S}_3$, $\tilde{\Pi}$) is typically negative. This means that the futures price $f_{0,3}$ must be set such that

$$\text{CEQ}_0\,(\tilde{S}_3 - f_{0,3}) = -\frac{\text{cov}(\tilde{S}_3 - f_{0,3}, \tilde{\Pi})}{\text{CEQ}_0\,(\tilde{\Pi})} > 0. \qquad (\text{B14})$$

To obtain an exact solution for $f_{0,3}$, we would need to know the value of the covariance. We would also need the risk-adjusted expected value (CEQ) of the term $\tilde{\Pi}$ (which depends, among other things, on the time-series properties of short-term interest rates). Finally, we would have to know the market's degree of risk aversion. In short, there is no general, simple formula that shows us how to set the futures price. But one conclusion should be obvious from Equation [B14]: $f_{0,3} < F_{0,3}$. To see this, rewrite the left-hand side of Equation [B14] as follows:

$$\text{CEQ}_0\,(\tilde{S}_3 - f_{0,3}) = \text{CEQ}_0\,(\tilde{S}_3) - f_{0,3} = F_{0,3} - f_{0,3}. \qquad [\text{B15}]$$

The right-hand side is positive because of the relation represented in [B14]. This proves our claim: if the correlation between $\tilde{\Pi}$ and $\tilde{S}$ is negative, the futures price is lower than the forward price.

6 CURRENCY OPTIONS

So far we have studied two contracts whose payoffs are contingent on the spot rate—foreign currency forward contracts and futures contracts. The payoffs from these instruments are linear in the future spot rate. That is, if you buy any of these instruments and the underlying exchange rate increases, you gain proportionally, and when the rate decreases, you lose money proportionally. In other words, the payoff of these instruments is symmetric: a unit drop in the exchange rate has the opposite effect on the contract's cash flow as a unit rise in the exchange rate. However, one would often rather not have this symmetric payoff. In many situations, one would like to make money when the price of the instrument goes up, but not lose money if the price goes down. **Options** are instruments that permit investors to achieve such asymmetric or nonlinear payoffs.

Options are somewhat harder to understand than forward contracts, and the pricing of options is also more complicated. On the other hand, a good understanding of these issues is valuable because options are instruments that are much more flexible for hedging or for speculating, compared to forwards or futures, and because option pricing theory has valuable applications in other fields, like investment analysis. We devote three chapters to the discussion of options. In this chapter, we describe the features of currency option contracts and their applications. In the next chapter, we show how one can price options in a discrete setting and, in Chapter 8, we derive the Black-Scholes formula for the valuation of options in a continuous setting.

This chapter is structured as follows. In the first section, we describe the features of call and put options on currency. In Section 6.2, we discuss how currency options are traded. In the third section, we introduce the concepts of time value and intrinsic value of options, and derive bounds on option prices. In Section 6.4, we study the payoff schedules of option positions. We also see how different options can be combined to obtain a desired payoff profile. This allows us to derive the relationship between call and put option prices—the Put Call Parity Theorem. In Section 6.5, we present some of the obvious and less obvious circumstances in which options can be used to hedge exchange risk or to speculate on the direction and volatility of the exchange rate. We conclude, in Section 6.6, with a discussion of the implications of options markets for financial management. The appendices describe options on futures, futures-style options, and futures-style options on futures, and discuss the effect of interest rates on the time value of options.

6.1   AN INTRODUCTION TO CURRENCY OPTIONS

In this section, we describe call and put options and explain the difference between European and American options. We also explain how one can interpret the decision to buy an option as a decision to buy insurance, and the price paid for the option as an insurance premium.

6.1.1   Call Options

A **call** (or call option) is a contract that gives the *holder* the right to buy a stated number of units of the "underlying" asset at a given price (which is called the **exercise price** or **strike price**) from the counterparty (called the *writer* of the option). In the case of a European option, this right can be exercised on a given maturity date T, while for an American option it can be exercised at any time until the terminal date T.[1]

Depending on the underlying asset on which the option is written, a call can be an option on a stock, a stock market index, a currency, a commodity, a bond, or an interest rate, or even a futures contract or a swap ("swaption").[2] In this chapter, we will mainly consider options on foreign currency. Appendix 6A discusses **options on futures**, and **futures-style options**.

Example   6.1

Suppose that you buy a call option on one DEM at USD/DEM 0.50 expiring on June 30. You, as the buyer or owner of the right, are the holder of the option. You are "**long the call**." The counterparty, who grants you this right, is the seller or writer of the call; he has an obligation to deliver one DEM to you at 50 cents if you want him to (that is, if you *exercise* the option). He is "**short the call**." The exercise price is USD/DEM 0.50. Thus, if the spot rate at time T turns out to be USD/DEM 0.55 or 0.60, you will exercise your right and buy DEM at USD/DEM 0.50 and save USD 0.05 or 0.10, respectively. Of course, if $\tilde{S}_T$ is less than 0.50, you will not exercise the option. There is no point buying DEM from the writer at USD/DEM 0.50 if you can obtain DEM for a lower price in the spot market.

If your option is a call on DEM 12,500 at USD/DEM 0.50, the writer may have to deliver DEM 12,500 to you at 50 cents each. For a contract size of DEM 12,500, this means that if and when you

---

[1] This terminology has to do with financial archaeology, not with the place where the option is written or traded. In the US, commodity options have traditionally been "American." In some European markets, option-like contracts, called "premium affairs," were part of the forward stock markets, and the decision whether or not to exercise was taken on the expiration day of all forward contracts—hence, the name "European" options. Most option contracts currently traded in Europe are American. There are some exceptions. For instance, Credit Suisse makes a market in European options, and the options implicit in over-the-counter "cylinder contracts" and currency option bonds (see below) are European.

[2] See Chapter 10 for a discussion of interest rate options and their links to options on T-bills or bonds.

decide to exercise your call option, you will pay USD 12,500 × 0.50 = USD 6,250 for the DEM 12,500—irrespective of the spot price at that moment. If the then prevailing spot price is 0.60, you will have saved USD 12,500 × (0.60 – 0.50) = USD 1,250.

To summarize: a call option allows you to obtain only the "nice" part of the forward purchase. Rather than paying X for the foreign currency (as in a forward purchase), you pay *no more than X,* and possibly less than X. Denoting the strike price or exercise price by X, we formally state this as follows. On the expiration day, a call option (on one unit of foreign currency) is worth:

- $\tilde{S}_T - X$ if the foreign currency is worth more than X.
- Otherwise zero.

More concisely, the value of a call option at maturity, denoted by $\tilde{C}_T$, is

$$\tilde{C}_T = \text{Max}(\tilde{S}_T - X, 0) \tag{1}$$

where "Max(x,y)" stands for "the larger of the two numbers x and y." Another popular concise notation is $(\tilde{S}_T - X)^+$ (where the "+" means "if positive; otherwise, zero").

For a European call option, the current market price is based solely on the final payoff $(\tilde{S}_T - X)^+$. In Chapters 7 and 8, we shall show that the current value of a European option is the risk-adjusted expected value of this final payoff, discounted back to the present. An American option, in contrast, can be exercised at any time τ prior to T. Thus, a writer is not sure what the American option's effective life is going to be, which makes its valuation more complicated. For early exercise to be rational, two conditions must be met.

- Obviously, the holder will *not* **exercise early** if the immediate payoff, $(S_\tau - X)$, is not positive.
- In addition, the (rational) holder will not exercise when the option's market value exceeds its immediate exercise value because, under these circumstances, it would be better to sell the option than to exercise it.

Example   6.2

Suppose that you have an American call option to buy 1 unit of DEM at X = USD/DEM 0.50. Currently, the DEM trades at 0.48. You will not exercise early. There is no point in paying USD 0.50 if a DEM can be bought spot for USD 0.48. (This does not mean that the option is worthless. Exercise may still become profitable later on.)

Suppose that, a few weeks later, the DEM has appreciated to 0.52. It might make sense to exercise early and earn 2 cents on the DEM. However, if the market price of the option at that moment is 3 cents, there is no point in exercising early. Exercising nets the holder only 2 cents, while selling the option yields 3 cents.

In short, early exercise of an American call is rational only if S_τ exceeds X *and* if the call's market price is no higher than $S_\tau - X$.

6.1.2   Put Options

As we saw, a European call option gives you the nice part of a forward purchase contract. Likewise, you might be interested in contracts that give you just the nice part of a forward *sale*—the right to sell at a pre-specified price when the currency trades below that price, without the obligation to sell at X when the currency is worth more. With such an option, you obtain *no less than X* per unit of foreign currency, and possibly more than X. In contrast, with a forward sale you always get X. A right to sell at X, without any obligation to do so, is called a **put option** or **put**.

Example   6.3 (Put)

You may buy the right to sell DEM 12,500 at a strike price of 0.60 (USD/DEM) on July 30. When exercised, this put will mean the delivery of DEM 12,500 at USD 0.60 per DEM (that is, USD 7,500 for the DEM 12,500). Of course, if at maturity S_T is more than 0.60, you will not exercise the option.

So the expiration value of a put is:

$$\tilde{P}_T = \text{Max}(X - \tilde{S}_T, 0) \tag{2}$$

which is sometimes denoted as $(X - \tilde{S}_T)^+$.

The holder of an American put may exercise also at any moment prior to T. By analogy to what holds for calls, the following two conditions must be met for early exercise of puts to be rational.

- The immediate exercise value of the put, $(X - S_\tau)$, must be positive.
- The put option's market value must be no higher than the value from immediate exercise, otherwise it would be better to sell the option than to exercise it.

6.1.3   Option Premiums and Option Writing

A firm that faces a future outflow of DEM might buy a call option on DEM with strike price X. The ensuing right to buy DEM at X means that this firm will pay no more then X per DEM. Thus, buying a call is like taking out an insurance contract against the risk of high exchange rates. Likewise, a firm that expects to receive future DEM might acquire a put option on DEM—the right to sell at X ensures that this firm gets no less than X for its DEM. Thus, buying a put is like taking out an insurance contract against low exchange rates. Like in any insurance contract, the insured party will pay an *insurance premium* to the insurer (the writer of the option). The price of an option is, not coincidentally, often called the **option premium** and acquiring an option contract is called *buying* an option. As with ordinary insurance contracts, the option premium is usually paid up front.

Insurance companies are willing to sell insurance policies because they receive a premium that covers the discounted expected costs and because they can diversify most of the risks. Likewise, option writers sell options because they receive a premium that covers the discounted expected exercise value of the claim and because they can diversify or hedge most of the risks. In the case of options, risk reduction is obtained not just by writing both puts and calls, but also by taking positions in forward contracts, or futures, or deposits and loans so as to offset most of the remaining risks. We shall explain how this is done in Chapters 7 and 8.

6.2 INSTITUTIONAL ASPECTS OF OPTIONS MARKETS

Whereas futures contracts are traded only on organized exchanges and forward contracts only over the counter, options are available both in over-the-counter markets and on organized exchanges (**traded options**).

6.2.1 Traded Options

An organized option exchange, like a futures market, has an organized secondary market, with a clearing house as a guarantor. If an investor bought an option some time ago and now sells it to someone else, his or her net obligation is zero. The clearing house wipes the slate clean. That is, the sale transfers all the rights to the new holder. Similarly, a writer who buys a traded option with the same terms as the one he or she originally wrote is effectively cleared from the potential obligation because the clearing house effectively clears.

Another idea that option exchanges have borrowed from futures markets is standardization. We illustrate this with the rules from the Philadelphia Options Exchange.

- Expiration dates: All options expire on the third Wednesday of March, June, September, or December, and only the contracts with the three nearest expiration dates are traded. Early exercise is possible until the last Saturday of the option's life.
- Contract sizes: One DEM option contract gives the right to buy or sell DEM 62,500, a yen contract JPY 6,250,000, and so on. One cannot trade fractions of contracts.
- Exercise prices: The strike prices must be multiples of one USD cent (for DEM, CHF, or CAD options), of 5 cents for GBP options, and multiples of 0.01 cent for JPY options.[3] With respect to the exercise prices being offered, options exchanges ensure that there are always contracts available with strike prices around the prevailing spot rate. Thus, as time elapses and the spot rate changes, options at different strike prices become available.

Traded options prices are shown daily in the financial press. Figure 6.1 gives you an example of a column from *The Wall Street Journal*.

The figures in the first column (148.57 for British pounds, 56.39 for Swiss francs) refer to the spot price for the currency itself, at the time the options exchange closed. By "Calls—Last," "Puts—Last" and the rather cryptic note, below the table, "Last is premium (purchase price)," *The Wall Street Journal* indicates that market prices refer to the last quote. Thus, at the close, you could buy a call (on GBP 12,500 per contract) that expires in September and with strike price of 140 (UScents/GBP), at 8.70 (UScents/GBP). If you buy one contract, you pay 12,500 × 0.0870 = USD 1,087.5. Similarly, a September put with strike price 140 (cents) is traded at 0.90 UScents/GBP, or at USD 1,125 per contract.

---

[3] Traders drop the word "cent"; that is, a DEM contract at 43 is an option with exercise price 43 cents per DEM, not 43 dollars per DEM. For the yen, a contract at 70 has an exercise price of 0.0070 USD/JPY.

FIGURE 6.1   Option Trading Data in the Newspaper

Option & Strike underlying price		Calls—Last			Puts—Last		
		Jul	Aug	Sep	Jul	Aug	Sep
12,500 British Pounds—cents per unit							
148.57	140	*r*	*s*	8.70	*r*	*s*	0.90
148.57	145	*r*	*r*	5.35	*r*	1.30	2.70
...							
62,500 Swiss Francs—cents per unit							
56.39	57	*r*	.074	1.10	*r*	*r*	*r*

r—not traded. *s*—no option offered. Last is premium (purchase price).

FIGURE 6.2   At-the-Money Option Premia from the Newspaper

Currency Options	**Call**	**Put**
USD	3	2
DEM	.5	.6
...		

At-the-money three-month options, expressed as a percentage of the face value.

6.2.2   Over-The-Counter Markets

Over-the-counter (OTC) options are written by financial institutions. These OTC options are more liquid than forward contracts. At any moment, the holder can sell them back to the original writer, who quotes two-way prices. Like forward contracts, OTC options are tailor made. In the OTC market, you can pick a particular expiration date, contract size, and strike price. As a consequence, the bid-ask spread in the OTC market is higher than in the traded-options market.

In OTC markets, most of the options are written at a strike price equal to the spot price of that moment ("**at-the-money options**"). Prices of at-the-money options are sometimes published as percentages of the underlying value. Figure 6.2 gives information on BEF OTC options on USD, DEM, . . . , as published in the Antwerp *Financieel Economische Tijd* (translated from Dutch).

In this example, an at-the-money call on one USD is trading at 3 percent of the face value. Thus, with a spot value of BEF/USD 34.105, this call costs 34.105 × 0.03 = BEF 1.02315. Therefore, an at-the-money call contract on USD 100,000 would cost 100,000 × 1.02315 = BEF 102,315. The percentage notation is convenient because when spot rates change, at-the-money option prices remain proportional to the spot rate if, at least, the interest rates and the degree of uncertainty about the future exchange rate evolution are unchanged.

6.3   BOUNDS ON OPTION VALUES

In this section, we define the popular notions of intrinsic value and time value of options. We then use these concepts to derive lower bounds on option prices. In Appendix 6B, we use these bounds to show under what conditions American options will not be exercised before maturity.

6.3.1   Intrinsic Value

An option is said to be *in the money* if immediate exercise generates a positive cash flow. If the spot rate equals the strike price, the option is said to be *at the money*. Otherwise, the option is *out of the money*. An option with a strike price that differs substantially from the current spot rate is called *deep in the money*, or *deep out of the money*. The term *around the money* is used to indicate that the strike price is close to the spot rate.

The **intrinsic value** is the option's value if you had to make the exercise decision right now. For options that are in the money, the intrinsic value is $(S_t - X)$ for calls, and $(X - S_t)$ for puts. For out-of-the-money options, the holder will not exercise immediately, and so the intrinsic value is zero.

Example   6.4 (Call)

For a *call* on DEM with strike price $X = $ UScents/DEM 43,

- The intrinsic value is 5 cents if the spot rate is 48 cents.
- The intrinsic value is 0 if the spot rate is UScents/DEM 40 (or any other rate equal to or below 43).

In short, the intrinsic value of a call at time t is $\text{Max}(S_t - X, 0)$ or $(S_t - X)^+$.

Example   6.5 (Put)

For a *put* option at $X = $ UScents/DEM 43, by analogy,

- The intrinsic value is 3 cents when the spot rate is 40.
- The intrinsic value is 0 when the spot rate is UScents/DEM 48 (or any other rate equal to or above 43).

In short, the intrinsic value of a put at time t is $\text{Max}(X - S_t, 0)$, or $(X - S_t)^+$.

6.3.2   Time Value

Even an out-of-the-money option should have a positive price, however small. This is because there is always a positive probability that the exchange rate changes in the favorable direction and the option moves back into the money before it expires. Clearly, *immediate* exercise of an out-of-the-money option cannot be the buyer's motivation, so such an option's market value is based entirely on the chance of profitable exercise at a later date. In options-speak, the option premium in this case is said to be pure **time value**.[4]

A similar reasoning applies to in-the-money options. When the DEM trades at 42.5, a put with strike price 43 has a positive immediate exercise value of 0.5. However, there may be a consensus in the market that the (uncertain) prospects of possible later exercise are worth even more than immediate exercise. The option would then trade above its intrinsic value of 0.5 cents, say at 0.55. The excess

---

[4] You should not confuse this concept with the other possible meaning of "time value," which is "the advantage of receiving a cash flow earlier rather than later"; the terminology is unfortunate, but has become standard.

of the premium over the intrinsic value—0.05 in the above example—is generally called the *time value* of the option. Thus, we can always decompose an observed market price of an option into the intrinsic value, and a residual time value:

$$\text{Option value} = \text{Intrinsic value} + \text{Time value}.$$

We have already stated, in Section 6.1.2, that an American option should not be exercised early when its market price exceeds the early exercise value. In our new terminology, we can rephrase this as follows: early exercise of an in-the-money option is not rational if the option has a positive time value. Early exercise means that you receive only the intrinsic value and lose the time value.

Perhaps you are wondering whether time value can be negative. To be able to answer this, we need to first discuss lower bounds on rational option prices.

6.3.3   Lower Bounds on Option Prices

A first bound relates the prices of American and European options. The American option must be worth no less than its European counterpart. An American option gives the holder all the rights of the European option *plus* the right of early exercise. Although this extra right might be perceived as worthless—notably when everybody agrees that early exercise will never happen—it can never have a negative value. Denoting European put and call prices by P and C, and the American counterparts by P^{am} and C^{am}, we therefore have the following result:

$$P_t^{am} \geq P_t, \ C_t^{am} \geq C_t \text{ for } t < T. \tag{3}$$

At the maturity date T, the above relations must be met as equalities (*if* the American option is still alive), that is, $P_T^{am} = P_T$ and $C_T^{am} = C_T$.

Let us now determine the bounds on the price of a European option. We know that, unlike a forward contract, an option will not be exercised when the strike price is less favorable than the spot price. This essential property has two crucial implications for the market value of any option.

- First—and again in contrast to a forward contract—it implies that an option can never have a negative market value prior to expiration. Nor can an option have a zero value—unless the probability of profitable exercise is exactly zero. Conversely, the option premium must be *strictly* positive as long as there is the slightest possibility of exercising and realizing a positive terminal value. In short,

$$P_t^{am} \geq P_t \geq 0, \ C_t^{am} \geq C_t \geq 0.$$

- The second corollary of the fact that an option gives a right instead of an unconditional obligation is that a European option should be worth at least the value of the comparable forward contract (a forward contract with an initial forward rate $F_{t_0, T}$ equal to the option's strike price and with the same maturity as the option). That is, a European call should be worth at least the value of the forward purchase contract with $F_{t_0, T} = X$, and a put should be worth at least as much as the comparable forward sales contract. Recalling from Chapter 3 the current market value of a forward contract initiated in the past at the rate X, we can determine the following bounds:

$$C_t \geq \frac{F_{t,T} - X}{1 + r_{t,T}} = \frac{S_t}{1 + r_{t,T}^*} - \frac{X}{1 + r_{t,T}};$$

$$P_t \geq \frac{X - F_{t,T}}{1 + r_{t,T}} = \frac{X}{1 + r_{t,T}} - \frac{S_t}{1 + r_{t,T}^*}.$$

We can summarize our results on the bounds on option prices as follows:

$$C_t^{am} \geq C_t \geq Max\left(\frac{S_t}{1 + r_{t,T}^*} - \frac{X}{1 + r_{t,T}}, 0 \right);$$ [4a]

$$P_t^{am} \geq P_t \geq Max\left(\frac{X}{1 + r_{t,T}} - \frac{S_t}{1 + r_{t,T}^*}, 0 \right).$$ [4b]

In the above relationships, the equalities hold in special cases:

- American and European options will have the same price if and only if the right of early exercise is perceived to be worthless, that is, when the market agrees that no rational holder will ever exercise early (the probability of early exercise is equal to zero).
- European options will be priced as forward contracts if and only if the probability of exercising the options is unity.[5]

6.4   A GRAPHICAL ANALYSIS OF EUROPEAN OPTIONS

In this section, we analyze the payoffs from different option strategies. Since the payoff to European options is generated only on a single date, these options are easier to analyze than their American counterparts. Thus, this section deals exclusively with European options. To introduce you to the payoff graphs, we shall first look at the graphical representation of contracts with which you are already familiar—forward contracts.

6.4.1   Graphical Analysis of Forward Contracts

We know that a forward purchase is a contract whose expiration value is $(\tilde{S}_T - F_{t,T})$, even if this is negative. This value can be shown as a straight-line function of S_T. For easy comparison with options, we shall denote the forward rate, $F_{t_0,T}$, at which the forward contract was initiated by X. Figure 6.3 shows the payoffs from a long and short forward position, respectively, using FP_T to denote the expiration value of a forward purchase, and FS_T to denote the expiration value of the forward sale. Figure 6.3

---

[5] If options are "deep in the money," their price will not be exactly equal to the value of the comparable forward contract, but they will still approach the price of the forward contract (from above). Note that this happens not when the option is cheap, but when both the option and its lower bound are high.

FIGURE 6.3   Expiration Value of a Forward Purchase or Sale

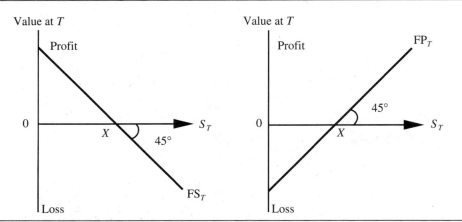

illustrates a well-known feature of forward contracts: a purchase ends in a gain (loss) when the spot rate is above (below) the agreed-upon price X, and *vice versa* for a forward sale.

The above schedules are the ones in which a speculator is interested. Let us also consider the point of view of a hedger. The forward purchase is used to hedge a risk-free foreign currency debt (FCD) and the forward sale for hedging a risk-free foreign currency asset (FCA). The expiration value schedules of foreign currency assets and debts are also linear functions of $\tilde{S}_T$. Figure 6.4 shows their schedules. The graph on the left reflects the fact that the time-T value of a unit foreign currency inflow increases one-for-one with the time-T spot rate. For the foreign currency outflow, on the right, a higher spot rate increases the outflow one-for-one (that is, the value to you becomes correspondingly more negative).

FIGURE 6.4   Expiration Value of a Foreign Currency Asset or Debt

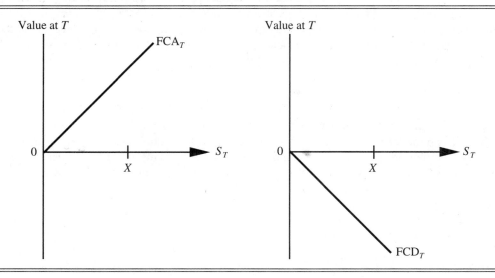

FIGURE 6.5   Hedging Foreign-Currency Assets and Liabilities with Forward Contracts

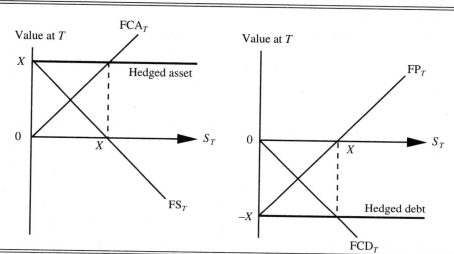

Let us now illustrate hedging using these graphs. At expiration, a portfolio consisting of a foreign currency asset and a forward sale is worth the sum of the two assets. Vertically summing the lines in Figures 6.3 and 6.4, with slopes -1 and $+1$ respectively, will yield a sum that is independent of $\tilde{S}_T$. To understand this, note that:

$$\text{Time-}T \text{ value of [asset } + \text{ forward sale]} = \tilde{S}_T + (X - \tilde{S}_T) = X$$

$$\text{Time-}T \text{ value of [debt } + \text{ forward purchase]} = -\tilde{S}_T + (\tilde{S}_T - X) = -X.$$

These sums provide the schedules, depicted as bold lines in Figure 6.5, for a foreign currency asset and a foreign currency debt, hedged with a forward sale and a forward purchase, respectively.[6]

This visually confirms something we knew all along: the value of a foreign-currency asset or liability, once hedged, becomes independent of the exchange rate. Let us now apply this graphical analysis to the payoffs from European options.

6.4.2   Exercise Value of a Call

Consider a call on DEM with strike price X = UScents/DEM 35. At expiration time T, the option's value, $\tilde{C}_T$, will relate to S_T as follows (with all amounts in UScents/DEM):

If $\tilde{S}_T =$	32	33	34	35	36	37	38
then $\tilde{C}_T =$	0	0	0	0	1	2	3

---

[6] In these and later graphs, payoffs for portfolios are shown as bold lines. Two parallel lines drawn very close to each other are to be interpreted as overlapping.

FIGURE 6.6   Expiration Value of a European Call

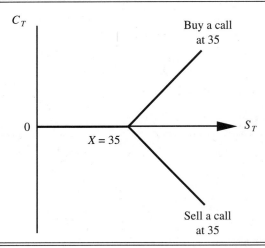

Graphically, this produces the piece-wise linear schedule shown in Figure 6.6.[7]

The value to a writer or seller is the negative of the value to the holder. For instance, if $\tilde{S}_T = 40$, the writer of the call has to buy DEM at 40 UScents, and deliver this to the holder of the call at $X = 35$ (or, when the writer already holds the DEM, he must forego a sale at 40). In short, the holder's 5-cent gain is the writer's 5-cent loss. Accordingly, we shall sometimes use the somewhat loose terminology *"minus a call"* when referring to a short position in the call. This is correct in the sense that:

- The payoff from a short (or written) call is minus the payoff from a long position in a call.
- The up-front cash flows also differ only by their sign. (The buyer pays the premium, the writer receives it.)

6.4.3   Exercise Value of a Put

Now consider a DEM put struck at $X = 35$ cents. At expiration day T, the put's value will depend on $\tilde{S}_T$ as follows (all prices in UScents/DEM):

If $\tilde{S}_T =$	32	33	34	35	36	37	38
then $\tilde{P}_T =$	3	2	1	0	0	0	0

Figure 6.7 shows this schedule.

---

[7] Note that we show the expiration value, not the profit or loss from a particular strategy. The profit or loss takes into account the initial outlay or inflow from buying or writing the option. There are a number of arguments against including the initial premium in the graphical analysis. First, combining money paid at the time of buying the option with cash flows at maturity, without correction for time value, is wrong. At the very least, one should gross up the premium with the interest accrued between the moment one paid the premium and the moment the option expired. Second, the expiration value is the same for all holders, while the premium depends on when one bought or sold the option. Furthermore, the premium is a sunk cost, but the expiration value is still to come and, therefore, is the relevant variable. Last, omitting the initial outlay makes it easier to explain strategies such as synthetic forwards, synthetic options, or synthetic bonds.

FIGURE 6.7   Expiration Value of a European Put

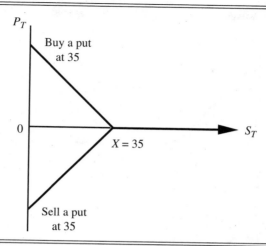

Let us now compare Figures 6.6 and 6.7 to the schedules for the forward contracts in Figure 6.3. We can see the following.

- Buying a call corresponds to the favorable part of a forward purchase since you (gladly) buy at X when $\tilde{S}_T > X$.
- Selling a call corresponds to the bad part of a forward sale since you are forced to sell at X when $\tilde{S}_T < X$, thus incurring a loss.
- Buying a put corresponds to the favorable part of a forward sale since you (gladly) sell at X when $\tilde{S}_T < X$.
- Selling a put corresponds to the bad part of a forward purchase since you are forced to buy at X when $\tilde{S}_T < X$, thus incurring a loss.

Options, therefore, allow you to buy or sell *parts* of forward contracts. An obvious corollary then is that you can reassemble forward contracts from option positions, as we shall now show.

6.4.4   Buy a Put and Sell a Call: A Synthetic Forward Sale

Consider a portfolio containing a put and "minus a call" (that is, a put plus a written call position), both struck at $X = 35$ cents. The payoff to this portfolio relates to $\tilde{S}_T$ as follows:

If	$\tilde{S}_T =$	32	33	34	35	36	37	38
then	$\tilde{P}_T =$	3	2	1	0	0	0	0
and	$-\tilde{C}_T =$	0	0	0	0	-1	-2	-3
Total:	$\tilde{P}_T - \tilde{C}_T =$	3	2	1	0	-1	-2	-3

FIGURE 6.8   Replicating the Final

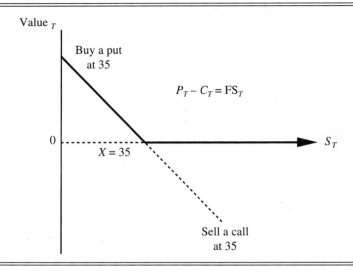

This is exactly the same payoff schedule associated with selling forward at 35 (with profit $35 - \tilde{S}_T$):

If	$\tilde{S}_T =$	32	33	34	35	36	37	38
then	$35 - \tilde{S}_T =$	3	2	1	0	−1	−2	−3

We can see that the net payoff of the put and the written call position, shown in Figure 6.8, reproduces the payoff of the forward sale (Figure 6.3).

6.4.5   The Put Call Parity Relationship for European Options

We have just argued that the payoff from a forward sale is identical to the payoff from a portfolio containing a put and a written call. Since the future payoffs are the same, by the *Law of One Price* the present values of the option portfolio and the forward sale must be the same also. Formally, we can state the equality of the time-T cash flows as follows:

$$\tilde{P}_T - \tilde{C}_T = \tilde{\mathrm{FS}}_T$$

$$\mathrm{Max}(X - \tilde{S}_T, 0) - \mathrm{Max}(\tilde{S}_T - X, 0) = X - \tilde{S}_T. \qquad [5]$$

From the equivalence at time T, it follows that in equilibrium, there must also be equivalence in terms of present values or current market values: the net investment in a portfolio of put minus call must be equal to the market value of the forward sale at a rate $F_{t_0, T} = X$ (see Chapter 3).

$$P_t - C_t = \frac{X}{1 + r_{t,T}} - \frac{S_t}{1 + r_{t,T}^*}$$

$$= \frac{X - F_{t,T}}{1 + r_{t,T}}. \qquad [6]$$

This relationship is called **Put Call Parity** (for European currency options). Equation [6] explains why, most of the time, at-the-money puts and calls do not have the same value. Consider the special case where $X = S_t$. Then Put Call Parity becomes

$$P_t - C_t = \frac{S_t - F_{t,T}}{1 + r_{t,T}} \text{ (at the money)}.$$

This expression says that $P_t > C_t$ if $S_t > F_{t,T}$. That is, a bet on a decrease of the spot rate (the at-the-money put) is worth more than a bet on an increase of the spot rate (the at-the-money call) if the forward rate is at a discount. When $F_{t,T}$ is below S_t, then in a risk-adjusted sense, the market expects the foreign currency to depreciate. This "expected" weakening of the foreign currency tends to make the put more valuable relative to the call.

Example   6.6

In Figure 6.2, the at-the-money put on USD against BEF is worth less than the at-the-money call, while for DEM options the relationship is reversed. What can we conclude about forward premiums?

 The put on USD is worth less than the call because the market expects the USD to appreciate (in risk-adjusted terms); that is, the USD must trade at a forward premium relative to the BEF. The put on the DEM is worth more than the call because the DEM trades at a forward discount relative to the BEF.

In Figure 6.2, the premiums are expressed as percentages of the spot rate. One advantage of this convention is that, in percentage terms, the difference between the two premiums is of a magnitude equal to the return differential. This can be seen by rewriting at-the-money Put Call Parity as follows:

$$\frac{P_t - C_t}{S_t} = \frac{r_{t,T}^* - r_{t,T}}{(1 + r_{t,T})(1 + r_{t,T}^*)} \text{ (at-the-money)}.$$

Thus, when premiums are expressed as percentages of the spot rate, time-pressed traders can quickly verify whether Put Call Parity holds approximately.

Example   6.7

In Figure 6.2, the difference between the percentage premiums on three-month USD call and put options against BEF equals 1 percent or 4 percent in *per annum* terms. If the *per annum* USD-BEF interest differential differs substantially from 1 percent × 4 = 4 percent, the trader can conclude that there is mispricing, and can initiate an arbitrage operation.

 A related insight that can be obtained from [6] is that puts and calls written *at the forward rate* will always command identical prices. The reason is that the forward rate represents the risk-adjusted expectation of the future spot rate. Almost by definition, then, the value of a bet that the future exchange rate $\tilde{S}_T$ will be higher than the risk-adjusted expectation, $\text{CEQ}_t(\tilde{S}_T)$, must be equal to the value of a bet that the exchange rate will be lower than the expectation. In practice, we see that options with the strike set at the forward rate—*at-the-forward options*—are gradually replacing the at-the-money options as the leading contracts.

6.4.6   Synthetic Assets and Arbitrage

Put Call Parity was derived here from an arbitrage argument based on the replication of a forward contract by means of options. However, a forward contract is itself a portfolio of domestic and foreign money-market instruments. In fact, in Equation [6], the term $X/(1 + r_{t,T})$ stands for the market value of a domestic T-bill expiring at T and having a face value equal to X, while $S_T/(1 + r^*_{t,T})$ represents the market value of a foreign currency T-bill with face value equal to one unit of foreign currency and maturity date T. Thus, Put Call Parity relates the prices of four assets: the put, the call, the domestic T-bill, and the foreign T-bill. By manipulating the Put Call Parity equation, it can be shown that, if you use three instruments from this set, you can create, synthetically, the payoff from the fourth instrument.

For instance, we can manipulate Equation [5],

$$\text{Max}(X - \tilde{S}_T, 0) - \text{Max}(\tilde{S}_T - X, 0) = X - \tilde{S}_T$$

to yield

$$\text{Max}(X - \tilde{S}_T, 0) - \text{Max}(\tilde{S}_T - X, 0) + \tilde{S}_T = X.$$

That is, you can create a synthetic risk-free home-currency inflow of X by buying a put, selling a call,[8] and buying a foreign currency T-bill that has a unit face value at time T. Let us illustrate this with the numerical examples used to explain the payoff graphs.

Suppose that we buy the foreign T-bill. We also buy a put; thus, at time T, we will sell spot currency at 35 if $\tilde{S}_T < 35$. In addition, we write a call; thus, at time T, we must sell the spot currency at 35 if $\tilde{S}_T > 35$. In short, we will sell at $X = 35$ whatever happens. Thus, the two options replicate a forward sale and transform the foreign T-bill into a domestic T-bill. This can be checked numerically:

If	$\tilde{S}_T =$	32	33	34	35	36	37	38
then	$\tilde{P}_T =$	3	2	1	0	0	0	0
and	$-\tilde{C}_T =$	0	0	0	0	−1	−2	−3
Total	$\tilde{S}_T + \tilde{P}_T - \tilde{C}_T =$	35	35	35	35	35	35	35

We obtain the same result graphically in Figure 6.9. The combined payoff from holding the foreign T-bill and the synthetic forward sale (that is, holding the put, writing the call) yields a risk-free payoff of 35. Thus, we have created a synthetic domestic currency bond from the three other assets (a foreign exchange position, a call, and a put). If the cost of this portfolio deviates from the market value of the domestic investment, $X/(1 + r_{t,T})$, arbitrageurs will step in and eliminate the difference.

---

[8] Buying the put and selling the call form a forward sale.

FIGURE 6.9   Replicating a Risk-Free Investment with a Put, a Call, and a Foreign Currency Asset

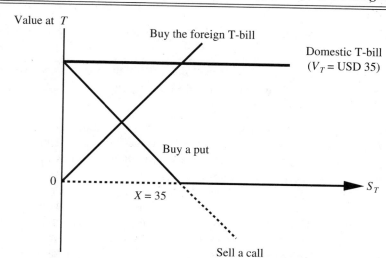

Example   6.8

Suppose that a put at $X = 35$ costs 3 cents, a call 4 cents, and a one-DEM T-bill 34 cents. Suppose that you buy a one-DEM T-bill at 34 and sell DEM 1 forward synthetically, by buying a put (at 3 cents) and writing a call (at 4 cents). Your net investment is $34 + 3 - 4 = 33$ cents. With a domestic risk-free return of, say 5 percent, the fair value of the portfolio would be $X/(1 + r) = 35/1.05 = 33.333$ cents. Thus, the portfolio is underpriced. You (and all others who discover the same inconsistency) will buy DEM T-bills and puts, write calls, and sell the domestic T-bill. Prices will adjust accordingly until the arbitrage opportunity disappears.

The example demonstrates just one possible alternative for expressing and using Equation [5]. A second way of manipulating the equation is as follows:

$$Max(X - \tilde{S}_T, 0) = X - \tilde{S}_T + Max(\tilde{S}_T - X, 0).$$

In words, the payoff of a put (on the left-hand side) is the same as the combined payoff of a forward sale plus a call. We leave the graphical analysis of this expression as an exercise. We can also rearrange Equation [5] as follows:

$$Max(\tilde{S}_T - X, 0) = \tilde{S}_T - X + Max(X - \tilde{S}_T, 0).$$

In words, the payoff of a call (on the left-hand side) is the same as the combined payoff of a forward sale and a put. These two relationships are used by traders to create synthetic European calls or puts and to arbitrage between the true options and their synthetic versions. Finally, we can rearrange Equation [5] as:

$$\tilde{S}_T = X - \text{Max}(X - \tilde{S}_T, 0) + \text{Max}(\tilde{S}_T - X, 0),$$

which says that you can replicate the payoff of the foreign T-bill by buying a domestic T-bill with face value X, and buying a call plus selling a put. (The last two form a forward purchase.)

Let us summarize our results in this section as follows.

- With a market for European puts and calls, we can synthetically create forward contracts. Conversely, combining forward contracts and calls, we can replicate puts; and, from forward contracts and puts, we can synthetically create calls. Of course, forward contracts themselves are simply positions in domestic and foreign T-bills.
- From a practical perspective, this means that brokers (who trade at very low costs) will arbitrage between the *direct* (market) prices of options or T-bills and the prices for *synthetic* European options or T-bills. This is similar to the arbitrage arguments used before, in Chapters 2 and 3. The result of this arbitrage is Put Call Parity, Equation [6].
- From a theoretical perspective, there is no need for two option pricing models—one for puts, and one for calls. Put Call Parity tells us that, if we have a call-pricing model, the put-pricing model is implied.

6.5   OPTIONS AS HEDGING OR SPECULATING DEVICES

In this section, we study various applications of options, and we discuss their potential advantages relative to forward or futures contracts. The key advantage of an option is that, to the holder, it provides only the favorable part of the payoff of a comparable forward contract. However, there are no free lunches. While the initial market value of a forward contract at $F_{t,T}$ is zero, an *at-the-forward* option has a positive price. More generally, the price of an option is always higher than the market value of the comparable forward contract, since the downside of the forward contract is eliminated in the case of options. A second advantage of options is they are more flexible instruments than forward contracts, whether they are used to hedge or to speculate on exchange rate changes.

6.5.1   Hedging the Risk of a Loss without Eliminating Possible Gains

Options can be used to hedge long and short positions in foreign currency. We provide a few examples using the point of view of a US corporation (USCo).

Example   6.9

Suppose that USCo has issued CHF Promissory Notes (thus, USCo is *short* foreign exchange). To hedge itself, the firm buys a call on CHF at X = USD/CHF 0.4 expiring at the same date, T, as the promissory notes. Then, the USD cost of paying back the CHF debt cannot be higher than USD/CHF 0.4, but it might be lower.

- If, at time T, the CHF trades above 0.4, USCo exercises its call option and buys CHF at 0.4.
- If $\tilde{S}_T < 0.4$, USCo simply buys its CHF in the spot market, and lets the call expire unexercised.

In contrast, if USCo had used a forward purchase at $F_{t,T} = $ USD/CHF 0.4, then it could not benefit from a possible lower value of the CHF. However, the forward purchase is free; the call is not.

So the downside risk on a foreign currency outflow can be hedged by a call. The put option, by analogy, hedges the downside risk of a foreign currency inflow.

Example   6.10

Suppose USCo holds DEM assets (USCo is *long* foreign exchange). To hedge itself, the firm buys a put on DEM at $X = $ USD/DEM 0.4 expiring at the same date, T, as the DEM asset. Then the USD proceeds from selling the DEM cannot be lower than USD/DEM 0.4, but they might be higher.

- If, at time T, the DEM trades below 0.4, USCo exercises its put option and sells DEM at 0.4.
- If $\tilde{S}_T > 0.4$, USCo simply sells its DEM in the spot market, and lets the put expire unexercised.

In contrast, if USCo had used a forward sale at $F_{t,T} = $ USD/DEM 0.4 then it could not benefit from a possible higher value of the DEM. However, the forward purchase is free; the put is not.

6.5.2   Hedging Positions with "Reverse" Risk

In the above examples, we used options to hedge a *risk-free* cash flow denominated in foreign currency. One can also use options to hedge foreign currency cash flows that are not certain, that is, foreign currency cash flows that are conditional on other events. Examples where inflows or outflows may be uncertain include the following.

- *International tenders.* The potential foreign exchange inflows may not materialize, notably when the firm contending for the contract loses the deal to another bidder. Thus, if this firm loses the contest but has already sold the potential foreign revenues forward, it is still obliged to fulfill the forward contract (*reverse exchange risk*).
- *Foreign exchange accounts receivable with substantial default risk.* If you hedge forward and the debtor does not pay, you again face reverse exchange risk.
- *International "deductible" reinsurance.* UAP, a French insurance company, may reinsure its fire risk for the year 1993 with a Lloyd's syndicate, in the sense that all damage above a threshold (or "deductible") of, say, FRF 100m will be covered by the London reinsurer. Clearly, the Lloyd's syndicate is exposed since it might have to pay out FRF if (and to the extent that) the insurance losses exceed FRF 100m. However, forward coverage is difficult. UAP's losses may not exceed FRF 100m; and, if they do, the extent by which the threshold is exceeded is uncertain.
- *Risky portfolio investment.* If a Finnish investor covers the exchange risk of a US stock portfolio position worth USD 100,000 by selling this amount forward, he or she may end up being over-insured (and short USD) if the US stock market declines and her portfolio is worth only USD 75,000.

In all of the above examples, options are more flexible hedging devices than forwards and futures in the sense that the holder cannot be forced to exercise. Note, however, that options do not hedge perfectly the cash flows described in the examples above! The option's value is contingent on the exchange rate, while the foreign cash flow is contingent on another event (like your winning the tender, or the customer defaulting). Since the exchange rate is independent of this other event, the hedge is not perfect. If an option is purchased to hedge such a contingent cash flow, the exchange rate still affects the total cash flows because the company will exercise an in-the-money option regardless of whether the other event was favorable or unfavorable.

Example   6.11

A Portuguese company submitted a CAD 1m bid in a tender to construct a hospital in Toronto. First, consider a hedge using a forward sale at $F_{t,T}$ = PTE/CAD 120. The firm's time-T cash flows, shown in the upper part of Table 6.1, are derived as follows: if the company wins the contract, it earns CAD 1m, which is worth PTE $\tilde{S}_T$, while its cash flow from the tender is zero if the contract is awarded to a competitor. The cash flows from the forward sale are $(120 - \tilde{S}_T)$, regardless of the outcome of the tender. Thus, the firm receives a combined cash flow of PTE 120 if it is awarded the contract, but has an unwanted open forward position if the contract goes to a competitor (reverse exchange risk). This unwanted position leads to losses in the event that $\tilde{S}_T > 120$.

Hedging with a put option, on the other hand, generates the cash flows shown in the lower part of the table. The cash flows from the put option are $Max(120 - \tilde{S}_T, 0)$ regardless of the outcome of the tender. We see that, even when an option is used to hedge the risk, the future spot rate still affects the cash flows because the company will exercise an in-the-money put even if it does not win the contract.

In Example 6.11, the put is a "good" hedge in the sense that it avoids having two bad events occur at the same time—not being awarded the contract *and* losing money on the forward sale (the upper-most cell in the column "Fail to win the contract"). However, it is not a perfect hedge. A "per-

TABLE 6.1   Option and Forward Contracts as Hedges of International Tenders

Strategy	$\tilde{S}_T$	Win the contract	Fail to win the contract
Hedge with forward sale	$\tilde{S}_T \geq 120$	$\tilde{S}_T + (120 - \tilde{S}_T) = 120$	$0 + (120 - \tilde{S}_T) \leq 0$
	$\tilde{S}_T < 120$	$\tilde{S}_T + (120 - \tilde{S}_T) = 120$	$0 + (120 - \tilde{S}_T) > 0$
Hedge with put	$\tilde{S}_T \geq 120$ (do not exercise put)	$\tilde{S}_T + (0) = \tilde{S}_T \geq 120$	0
	$\tilde{S}_T < 120$ (exercise put)	$\tilde{S}_T + (120 - \tilde{S}_T) = 120$	$(120 - \tilde{S}_T) > 0$

fect" hedge (in the sense of eliminating all uncertainty) would be a forward contract *conditional* on the other source of uncertainty. In Example 6.11, this would be a conditional forward contract that becomes void if you lose the tender contract. Some government export agencies and banks do provide such *tender-to-contract forward contracts* (and even tender-to-contract options).

6.5.3 Hedging Nonlinear Exposure

The expiration values of the foreign currency debts and claims considered in Section 6.5.1 were linear in the exchange rate; that is, they could be represented as straight lines on a diagram that plotted their home currency value against the future spot rate, $\tilde{S}_T$. However, the effect of unexpected exchange rate changes on your financial affairs may not be that simple. In some cases, the cash flow you wish to hedge may be a nonlinear function of the exchange rate. In this case, a linear instrument like a forward contract is not an appropriate hedging tool. Options are often better suited to hedge non-linear exposures because of their asymmetric payoff profiles.

Example   6.12

A French exporter of champagne expects to export 100,000 bottles to the US next year, at USD 10 per bottle, net of costs. Alternatively, she can sell this wine at home, at FRF 50 per bottle. Thus, if the dollar is trading below FRF/USD 5, she would chose not to export at all, but would sell her wares at home. Her problem is that she needs cash now. Borrowing FRF is risky because, with her existing financial commitments, she may go bankrupt if she does not earn some extra cash from exports.

Selling a call option on USD 1m with strike price FRF/USD 5 and market value FRF 0.4 per USD will solve two problems for the French exporter. First, it brings in immediate cash, FRF 0.4 per USD or 1m × 0.4 = FRF 400,000. Second, it makes the exporter's cash flows independent of the exchange rate. To understand why there is no exchange rate risk, we analyze how the sales revenue depends on the exchange rate.

- If the rate is below FRF/USD 5, each bottle is sold at home for a price of FRF 50; thus, the entire inventory is worth 100,000 × 50 = FRF 5m.
- For higher rates, a bottle is worth FRF 10 × $\tilde{S}$, since it would be exported and sold at USD 10 net; thus, with high exchange rates, the inventory is worth FRF 100,000 × 10 × $\tilde{S}_T$.

The payoff schedule is shown in Figure 6.10, on the left, as the kinked line labeled "Inventory." The alert reader has already noticed that this schedule is the same as the profile for a FRF 5m T-bill plus a call on USD 1m, struck at $X = 5$.[9] Thus, selling a call contract on USD 1m with the same strike price, $X =$ FRF/USD 5, offsets the exchange risk of inventory value exactly. The new profile, after writing the call option, is shown as the straight line labeled "Inventory + written call."

In contrast, suppose the exporter borrowed FRF 400,000 and hedged the expected sales revenue by selling forward USD 1m. Hedging with a forward sale would only have changed the payoff schedule from a "gain when $\tilde{S}_T$ is high" profile to a "gain if $\tilde{S}_T$ is low" picture, rather than eliminating the uncertainty created by exchange risk. That is, rather than being in trouble when there

---

[9] Or, equivalently, a USD 10 bond plus 10 puts on USD at $X = 0.5$. You can verify this graphically. You can also derive this from (or view it as an application of) Put Call Parity.

FIGURE 6.10   Hedging a Nonlinear Exposure: Options vs. Forwards

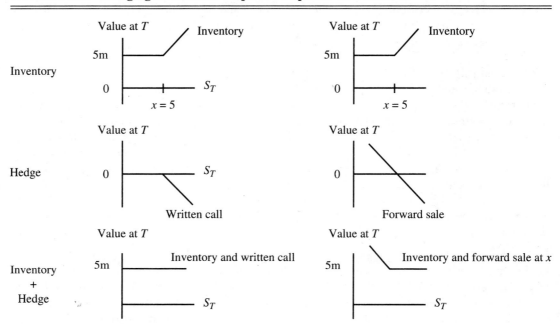

are no exports, the exporter would be in trouble when there *are* exports. This is shown on the right side of Figure 6.10.[10]

Thus, the firm's option to export is similar to a call; and writing a call against the potential export revenue means that we "sell" the uncertain future gains for immediate cash. By analogy, your customers' option to buy imported goods is like being the writer of a put, as is shown in the following example.

Example   6.13

A Danish wool trader faces potential competition from Australia. If there are no imports from Australia, the Danish price of wool will be DKK 100 per unit, and the trader's inventory will be worth DKK 100 per unit. Australian competitors sell at a roughly fixed net price of AUD 25 (including expenses like transportation costs and tariffs). The Australians will enter the Danish market as soon as the exchange rate drops below DKK/AUD 4, and then the Danish trader will have to lower prices in step with the competitors' translated DKK price, $25 \times S$. The Danish wool trader's position can be summarized as follows.

- For $\tilde{S} < 4$, one unit of wool will be worth $25 \times \tilde{S}$.
- For $\tilde{S} \geq 4$, the value of wool is DKK 100.

---

[10] The bold-line payoff scheme on the right appears to dominate the bold-line payoff scheme on the left. This is because the graphs do not show the income received at time t from selling the call.

TABLE 6.2 Hedging a Nonlinear Exposure with an Option

Position	Value if $\tilde{S}_T \geq 4$	Value if $\tilde{S}_T < 4$
Wool inventory (DKK)	100	$25 \times \tilde{S}_T$
25 Puts on AUD	0	$25 \times (4 - \tilde{S}_T)$
Total (hedged) position	100	100

If you plot this payoff as we did in the previous example, you will discover that one unit of wool is like a DKK 100 bond, minus a put on AUD 25 (that is, you implicitly wrote a put on AUD 25) with strike price $X = 4$. Thus, buying a similar put should eliminate the exposure. Table 6.2 shows the relevant figures in a table rather than in a graph. The bottom line shows that the portfolio of inventory and puts has a combined value that is independent of the future spot rate, $\tilde{S}_T$. That is, the exposure to the exchange rate is perfectly hedged.

From the above examples, we see that nonlinearities in the firm's future cash flow schedule may stem from competitive threats or price pressures that become active for only a certain range of exchange rates. In the next example, the source of the nonlinearity is a financial contract.

Example   6.14

A US company issued bonds giving the holder, at maturity T, the choice between USD 10,000 or DEM 20,000. If the holder is a US investor, he or she would most naturally view such a bond as a USD 10,000 bond plus a call on DEM 20,000 at $X = $ USD/DEM 0.5. That is, the investor gets paid USD 10,000, but has the right to exchange the USD 10,000 for DEM 20,000. The option (the right to choose) is clearly with the bondholder—thus, the issuing company has written the option. The company can hedge itself against potential losses by buying a call that offsets the implicit call it has written.

6.5.4 Speculating on Changes in Exchange Rates

In all of the applications considered so far, the objective has been to reduce the uncertainty arising from changes in the exchange rate. Options can also be used to speculate in exchange markets. Let us agree on the following definition: for someone to be called a speculator, (1) he or she must disagree with the market's perceived probability distribution function for an asset's future value, and (2) he or she must be willing to back up the dissident opinion with money (that is, buying the "underpriced" asset and selling, or shortselling, the "overpriced" asset).[11]

---

[11] Other possible definitions of speculation are possible. Probably the most common one is "taking high risks."

Buying puts (calls) is a convenient way of speculating on decreases (increases) in the exchange rate. Options require only a limited investment and imply, in the worst case, the loss of the premium paid up front.[12] It has to be added, in fairness, that the probability of losing the premium is quite high. In fact, for an at-the-money option, the probability of losing the entire investment is approximately 50 percent. In contrast, selling or buying forward has this drawback: it can lead to very large losses. In addition, as we saw in Chapter 4, a speculative uncovered forward transaction is likely to absorb substantial financial resources in the form of margin that must be posted.

Put writing can also be used to speculate on a rise in the exchange rate, and call writing is a way to speculate on a depreciation. In each case, the writer collects the premium up front and hopes that the option will expire unexercised. Misleadingly, such strategies are often said to "generate income," or "increase the return on the portfolio." In fact, writing options is a form of issuing risky debt—debt which, with about 50 percent probability, will trigger cash outflows at a later date, depending on what the exchange rate turns out to be at maturity.

6.5.5   Speculating on Changes in Volatility

In Section 6.5.4, the speculator essentially disagreed with the market's expectations about the currency's future value as reflected in the current spot and forward rate. It is, however, possible to agree about the expected value but disagree about the standard deviation (*volatility*) of the time-T exchange rate. That is, one might think that the market underestimates by how much the exchange rate may move—whether up or down. To capitalize on this belief, a strategy is needed that pays off when the exchange rate moves by a large amount—irrespective of whether the movement is up or down. The option strategy that allows one to speculate on the volatility of the exchange rate is to go long both the call and the put. This option strategy is called a **straddle** (if both options have the same strike price), or the **vertical combination** (if the call's strike price is different from the exercise price of the put).

The logic of the straddle is obvious from its payoff diagram in Figure 6.11. The holder makes large gains for any large change in S_T, whether it be positive or negative. Of course, the speculator

FIGURE 6.11   The Straddle as a Strategy to Separate on Volatility

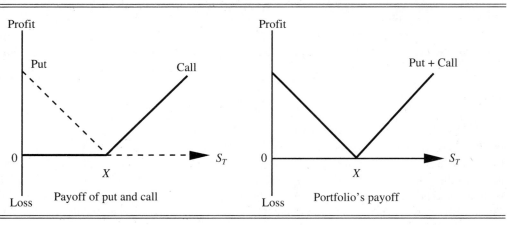

---

[12] A futures-style option, if closed out before it expires, is even less capital-intensive. Such options are discussed in the appendix.

has to pay the premiums for the put and for the call. However, since the market thinks that the movement of S_T is likely to be small, the price charged for the options is quite low, in the speculator's opinion. In short, the investor thinks that puts as well as calls are undervalued and, accordingly, buys both of them.

Example   6.15

Assume that the future exchange rate $\tilde{S}_T$ can take on only three possible values, the current level (10), or 9, or 11. These are shown below, together with the corresponding values of a put and a call at $X = 10$. We then specify two probability distributions—one as viewed by the market, and one which reflects your beliefs. The two distributions have the same mean, $E(\tilde{S}_T) = 10.00$, but yours has a higher variance.

If $\tilde{S}_T =$	9	10	11
then $\tilde{C}_T =$	0	0	1
and $\tilde{P}_T =$	1	0	0
Prob$_{market}$	0.2	0.6	0.2
Prob$_{you}$	0.3	0.4	0.3

The row labeled "Prob$_{market}$" shows the probabilities of each possible exchange rate as perceived by the market. Your perceived probabilities are shown in the row "Prob$_{you}$."

We compute the expected expiration value of each option over each set of probabilities by simply multiplying each possible (non-zero) payoff by its probability and summing. The market's expectation of the payoff from the call and the put are, respectively:

$$E_{market}(\tilde{C}_T) = 0 \times (0.2) + 0 \times (0.6) + 1 \times (0.2) = 1 \times 0.2 = 0.2.$$

$$E_{market}(\tilde{P}_T) = 1 \times (0.2) + 0 \times (0.6) + 0 \times (0.2) = 1 \times 0.2 = 0.2.$$

However, you expect higher payoffs for both options:

$$E_{you}(\tilde{C}_T) = 0 \times (0.3) + 0 \times (0.4) + 1 \times (0.3) = 1 \times 0.3 = 0.3.$$

$$E_{you}(\tilde{P}_T) = 1 \times (0.3) + 0 \times (0.4) + 0 \times (0.3) = 1 \times 0.3 = 0.3.$$

Your expectations of the expiration values are higher because you assign larger probabilities to extreme payoffs, and because extreme payoffs on the upward (downward) side add value to the call (put). Therefore, you believe that the market underprices both options. You buy both a put and a call option because you don't know about the *direction* of the price change. With a put and a call, you gain, whichever way the spot rate moves—as long as the change is sufficiently large.

By analogy, you short both the call and the put if you think that the market overestimates the volatility, and therefore, overprices all options. In that case, your strategy would be to write both options (the *short straddle* or the *short vertical combination*). Thus, options markets allow one to speculate on volatility, that is, on the likely absolute size of exchange rate movements, rather than just on the likely directions of changes. Speculation on volatility is not possible using forward contracts.

6.6   IMPLICATIONS FOR THE CORPORATE TREASURER

A currency option, being the right to buy or sell a known amount of foreign currency at an agreed-upon price, is a much more flexible instrument than a forward or futures contract. The payoffs of various "European" option positions (long or short the call, long or short the put) can be viewed as the favorable or unfavorable parts of the payoffs from forward positions. Specifically, option writers take on the negative-payoff part of a forward transaction, while the holders obtain the positive part of the payoff. Puts give the payoffs when the spot rate is below the strike price, while calls represent the payoffs when $\tilde{S}_T$ is above X. One implication of this is that forward contracts can always be used to convert a call into a put, and *vice versa*. This replication argument leads to the conclusion that the prices of both types of European options must be related (Put Call Parity).

Obviously, in order to convince the writer of an option to take over the unfavorable side of a forward contract, the holder has to pay the writer an up-front premium. Once an option has been bought, it can always be sold in the secondary market. Its market price can never drop below zero. Nor can the price drop below the value of a comparable forward contract. The holder of the option is prepared to pay the premium because the option acts as an insurance contract; that is, one can obtain insurance against the possible depreciation of a foreign currency by buying a put, while a call option offers insurance against a possible appreciation. Thus, when options are used to hedge linear exposures, they eliminate the possibility of a loss but not the potential gain, and when options are used as speculation devices, they limit the potential for losses. Options are also more appropriate when the exposure to be hedged is non-linear, or when the objective is to speculate on the absolute size of exchange rate changes. *American* options, lastly, can also be exercised before their expiration dates, which adds to the flexibility of the hedging or speculative strategy.

An issue that has not been discussed thus far is the pricing of options. This is the subject of the next two chapters.

QUIZ QUESTIONS

True-False Questions

1. The only difference between European and American options is that European options are traded only in Europe while American options are traded only in the US.
2. The buyer of an option has an obligation to purchase the underlying asset in the case of a call, or sell in the case of a put, while the seller of an option has the right to deliver in the case of a call, or take delivery in the case of a put.
3. A put offers the holder of an asset protection from drops in the underlying asset's value, while a call provides protection from an increase in the underlying asset's price.
4. The intrinsic value of a call is its risk-adjusted expected value.
5. The immediate exercise value of an option is its value alive.
6. If a call's strike price exceeds the spot rate, the call is in the money.
7. If an in-the-money put has positive value, its value is based purely on time value.
8. A European call will always be at least as valuable as a comparable American call.
9. An option is always at least as valuable as the comparable forward contract.
10. Put Call Parity implies that puts and calls written at the forward rate will have different values because, if the foreign interest rate exceeds the domestic rate, the forward rate is at a discount; therefore the exchange rate is expected to depreciate, making the put more valuable.
11. Speculators disagree with the market's probability distribution function for an asset's value; that is, they sell assets that the market perceives as overvalued and buy assets that the market perceives as undervalued.

Multiple-Choice Questions

The exercises below assume that the put and the call both have a strike price equal to X, a domestic T-bill has a face value equal to X, and both a foreign T-bill and forward contract pay off one unit of foreign currency at expiration. All instruments expire on the same date.

1. A forward sale can be replicated by:

   (a) selling a put and buying a call.
   (b) selling a foreign T-bill and buying a domestic T-bill.
   (c) buying a put and selling a call.
   (d) both b and c
   (e) all of the above

2. A put can be replicated by:

   (a) buying a call and selling foreign currency forward.
   (b) buying a foreign T-bill and selling a call.
   (c) buying a domestic T-bill, selling a foreign T-bill, and buying a call.
   (d) both a and c
   (e) all of the above

3. A call can be replicated by:

   (a) buying foreign currency forward and buying a put.
   (b) buying a foreign T-bill and selling a put.

(c) buying a put, selling a domestic T-bill, and buying a foreign T-bill.

(d) all of the above

(e) none of the above

Use the following table's data, excerpted from *The Wall Street Journal* of Tuesday, March 22, 1994, to answer the questions below.

Option & underlying	Strike price	Calls—Last			Puts—Last		
		Apr	May	Jun	Apr	May	Jun
31,250 British Pounds-cents per unit.							
148.61	147 1/2	r	r	r	0.95	1.80	r
148.61	150	0.60	r	1.85	r	r	r
148.61	155	0.07	r	0.57	r	r	r
148.61	157 1/2	0.03	r	r	r	r	r
62,500 German Marks-cents per unit.							
59.04	58	1.08	r	r	0.35	0.65	0.90
59.04	58 1/2	0.79	r	1.35	0.46	r	1.13
59.04	59	0.51	0.80	1.02	0.80	1.10	1.40
59.04	59 1/2	0.35	r	r	r	r	r
6,250,000 Japanese Yen-100ths of a cent per unit.							
94.18	93	r	r	r	r	r	1.29
94.18	93 1/2	r	r	r	0.72	r	r
94.18	94	r	r	r	r	1.41	1.68
94.18	94 1/2	0.81	r	r	1.12	r	r

r—not traded. s—no option offered. Last is premium (purchase price).

4. What is the last quote for an April call option on GBP with a strike price of 155?

5. What is the last quote for a May put option on DEM with a strike price of 58?

6. What is the last quote for a June put option on JPY with a strike price of 93 1/2?

7. For the options below, what is the intrinsic value? Is the intrinsic value greater than, less than, or equal to the option premium?

   (a) June call on GBP with a strike price of 150.
   (b) May put on GBP with a strike price of 147 1/2.
   (c) April call on DEM with a strike price of 59.
   (d) June put on DEM with a strike price of 59.
   (e) May call on JPY with a strike price of 93.
   (f) May put on JPY with a strike price of 94.

8. You hold a foreign exchange asset that you have hedged with a put. Show graphically how the put limits the potential losses created by low exchange rates, without eliminating the potential gains from high rates.

9. You have covered a foreign exchange debt using a call. Show graphically how the call limits the potential losses created by high exchange rates, without eliminating the potential gains from low rates.

10. Assume that the contracts discussed below are described with the GBP as the home currency and that the option's expiration date matches the expiration date of the cash flow to be hedged. Illustrate how the exchange rate affects the GBP value of:

    (a) a DEM 500,000 accounts receivable and a purchase of ten puts each worth DEM 50,000 with a strike price of GBP/DEM 0.42.
    (b) a JPY 10,000,000 accounts payable and a purchase of ten calls each worth JPY 1,000,000 with a strike price of GBP/JPY 0.0067.

EXERCISES

1. The Danish wool trader in Section 6.5.3 faces potential competition from Australian producers.

    (a) Graphically analyze the value of the trader's inventory as a function of the future spot price.
    (b) Explain why a put on AUD eliminates the dependence of the inventory's value on the exchange rate for DKK/AUD.

2. The UK firm, Egress Import-Export, Ltd, sells its goods at home for P_b when the value of the ITL is low. As the value of the ITL increases, it starts exporting its goods at the foreign price (net of costs) P_a, netting it $P_a \times \tilde{S}_T$.

    (a) Illustrate the value of Egress's goods as a function of the future spot price.
    (b) How can Egress eliminate its exposure to the ITL (that is, sell its potential ITL profits)?

3. The Luxembourg Plettery Steel Company has a debt of DEM 100,000, which is repayable in twelve months. Plettery's controller Jane Due is having trouble sleeping at night knowing that the debt is unhedged. The current LUF/DEM exchange rate is 20, and *p.a.* interest rates are 21 percent on LUF and 10 percent on DEM. Jane is considering a forward hedge (at $F_{t,T} = 20 \times 1.21/1.10 = 22$), but a friend tells her that he recently bought a call on DEM 100,000 with $X = 20$, and is willing to sell it to her at the historic cost, LUF 1 per DEM or LUF 100,000 for the total contract. What should she do?

4. Assume that the interest rates are 21 percent and 10 percent *p.a.* in Luxembourg and Switzerland, respectively. Consider a call and a put at $X = $ LUF/CHF 21.

    (a) What is the lower bound for European options with lives equal to $T - t = $ one year, six months, three months, one month, when $S_t = $ 18, 20, 22, 24, respectively?
    (b) If $S_t = 20$, $r_{t,T} = 0.21$, $r^*_{t,T} = 0.10$, a one-year call with $X = $ LUF/DEM 20 priced at 1 is undervalued. Show that, with this call price, we can buy a synthetic put at a negative price.

5. A charitable organization has issued a bond that gives the holder the option to cash in the principal as either USD 10,000 or DEM 20,000. This asset can be viewed as a USD 10,000 bond plus a call on DEM_T 20,000 at $X = 0.5$ USD/DEM.

    (a) Can the bond also be viewed as a DEM bond plus an option?
    (b) Explain how the two equivalent views are just an application of Put Call Parity.
    (c) The strike price, $X = $ USD/DEM, is the natural way of quoting a rate for a US investor. But buying DEM 20,000 at USD/DEM 0.5 is the same as selling USD 10,000 at $X' = $ DEM/USD 2. This way of expressing the transaction makes more sense to a German investor. Restate the conditions of the bonds using this DEM/USD strike price, and make the two possible interpretations of the option from a German investor's point of view.

6. The software giant, Kludge Systems, has issued a bond that gives the holder the choice between USD_T 10,000, DEM_T 20,000, and GBP 5,000. Can Kludge's bond be replicated using simple options?

7. You have purchased a zero-coupon FIM bond that gives you the choice between FIM 100,000 at $T_2 = 2$ or FIM 90,000 at $T_1 = 1$.

   (a) What options (put and/or call) are implicit in this bond? (Hint: there are two correct descriptions.)

   (b) Show that the two equivalent views of this instrument are an application of Put Call Parity.

8. The lower bound on a non-degenerate American put (that is, a put where there is still some uncertainty about whether $S_t > X$ or not) is:

$$P_t^{am} > P_t > \frac{X}{1+r_{t,T}} - \frac{S_t}{1+r^*_{t,T}}.$$

Assume that $S_t = 0$ and $r_{t,T} = 0$. Common sense says that you should exercise the put, since the exchange rate cannot fall any further. Yet the bound $P_t > X$ says that the put should trade above its intrinsic value. Where is the fallacy?

9. A *cylinder* option on the sale of foreign currency is a contract defined as follows:
   • If $\tilde{S}_T < X_1$, you sell foreign exchange at X_1, the floor
   • If $\tilde{S}_T > X_2$, where $X_2 > X_1$, you sell at X_2, the cap
   • If $X_1 \le \tilde{S}_T \le X_2$, you sell at $\tilde{S}_T$.

This contract restricts the uncertainty about the futures sales price to the range $X_1 \le \tilde{S}_T \le X_2$.

For instance, Barrel Imports has a sales contract to sell CAD against USD:
   • At X_1 = USD/CAD 0.80 if the CAD trades below 0.80.
   • At X_2 = USD/CAD 0.90 if the CAD trades above 0.90.
   • The spot rate if that rate is between 0.80 and 0.90.

   (a) Show the payoff of the contract graphically.
   (b) Show that it can be viewed as a combination of European options.
   (c) Illustrate the value of a foreign currency claim hedged with such a contract.

MIND-EXPANDING EXERCISES

1. Al Say holds an option that gives him the right to "sell" one unit of a DKK T-bill against X units of SEK T-bills, all bills maturing at the same time as the option. Will he exercise this put early?

2. Vera Vendible has an option that gives her the right to sell one DKK against SEK $X/(1 + r_{t,T})$ (that is, an option to exchange one DKK against X units of SEK T-bills). Will she exercise early?

3. What are the implications of Put Call Parity if the probability that $\tilde{S}_T$ exceeds X is zero? Unity?

4. You are the holder of a call, expiring at T, on a forward purchase contract with the same maturity. When you exercise, you will become the holder of an expiring forward contract with an "old" forward rate equal to X. That is, when you exercise, you must buy foreign exchange at the stated forward price X. Of course, you will only exercise when $\tilde{S}_T < X$. At expiration day, this option's value, therefore, is $(\tilde{S}_T - X)^+$, just like an ordinary foreign exchange cash option. So if the option is European, it will be priced like a standard option (on cash foreign exchange).

   Will options on the forward contract and on cash still be priced equally when the options are American? (In other words, can you prove that there will never be any early exercise?)

5. You have the option to buy, at time T, a forward purchase contract. The underlying contract matures at $T_2 > T$ (in this case, the forward contract is not yet expiring). If you exercise, you acquire an asset with a market value equal to $(F_{T,T_2} - X)/(1 + r_{T,T_2})$. Future interest rates are known.

   (a) How would you price the European option relative to a European cash foreign exchange option?

   (b) Is there any early exercise with American options? When? When not?

6. Suppose that your option is an option on a futures contract. Upon exercising the call at time T, you acquire a futures purchase contract maturing at $T_2 > T$ with value $(f_{T,T_2} - X)$. Future interest rates are known.

   (a) How do you price the European option relative to a European cash foreign exchange option?

   (b) Is there any problem with the early exercise of American options? When? When not?

7. Imagine an American call on one DEM against ATS, except that the payment is not ATS X (in cash), but an ATS T-bill with face value X maturing at time T. Equivalently, imagine a call on DEM where the payment is ATS X payable at the option's expiration time T, even if the option is exercised early. Will such an option be exercised early?

8. Do the same as in the previous question with an option to acquire a DEM T-bill with face value 1 maturing at time T, against the delivery of a LUF T-bill with face value X at T. Or, equivalently: will there be any early exercise if both the payment (ATS X) and the delivery (DEM 1) are at T, even if the decision to exercise is taken before t?

OPTIONS ON CURRENCY FUTURES, PREMIUM AFFAIRS, AND FUTURES-STYLE OPTIONS

In this appendix, we describe options on currency futures, premium affairs (or forward-style options), and futures-style options on currency or on currency futures. These more exotic instruments have been designed to facilitate both speculation and arbitrage across markets.

6A.1 Options on Currency Futures

A *call on a currency futures contract* with strike price X gives the holder the right to establish, without cost, a long position in a currency futures contract with futures price X, while the writer must take the short side of the futures contract. Like any other futures contract, this newly created futures contract is marked to market at the end of each day.

Example 6A.1

Consider a June DEM 62,500 futures contract with a current futures price 60 (cents/DEM). If you exercise a call with strike price 50 cents, you become the holder of a DEM 62,500 futures contract with a futures price of 50 cents (0.5 USD/DEM). This contract, like any outstanding futures contract, can be sold immediately. Such a sales transaction then triggers a marking-to-market cash flow of $62,500 \times (0.60 - 0.50) = \text{USD } 6,250$.

Thus, this option on a futures contract differs from an option on DEM itself ("on the cash") in the sense that it pays out the difference between the strike and the *futures* price that prevails at the time of exercise of the option. If an option on a futures is a European option that expires on the same day as the futures contract, then the option on futures and on spot will have the same value. This is because at maturity the future price and the spot are the same, $\tilde{f}_{T,T} = \tilde{S}_T$ (convergence property); thus, an option on the "cash" and an option on a maturing futures contract produce the same payoff. However, if the expiration times of the option and the futures contract do *not* coincide, the payoffs from a standard call, $\text{Max}(\tilde{S}_T - X, 0)$, and an option on the futures, $\text{Max}(\tilde{f}_{T,T_2} - X, 0)$, are no longer the same. The difference between the two payoffs is the basis, which is to some extent unpredictable. Therefore, when expiration times of the option and the futures contract differ, an option on the futures will be priced differently from an option on the cash.

Options on futures are attractive to professional option writers who often hedge their risks in the futures markets. Such a futures hedge absorbs less cash than a spot hedge. Thus, if one is hedging in the futures market, it is more convenient to create options on the same underlying instruments.

6A.2 Premium Affairs

Before the introduction of modern options in the eighties, **premium affairs** were traded in the Paris and Brussels forward stock markets. The only difference between a premium affair and a modern

(European) option is that the premium is paid at time T rather than at time t.[13] Thus, a premium affair is a **forward-style option**, that is, a forward contract on a modern (European) option. The buyer of such a forward-style option receives the option at T and, at that time, also pays the initially agreed-upon price. Immediately after receiving the option (and paying for it), the holder then decides whether or not to exercise the option.

Example   6A.2

You conclude a premium affair purchase on ten Petrofina stocks at $X = F_{t,T} =$ BEF 15,400 per share for a premium of BEF 380 per share. At time T, say two weeks later, you pay the option writer BEF $10 \times 380 =$ BEF 3,800, regardless of the stock's value. If, at T, the stock trades above 15,400, you also exercise the option and buy the ten stocks at 15,400.

Logically, then, the premium must be set equal to the price of a regular European option, grossed up with the normal time value, $r_{t,T}$.

Example   6A.3

Consider a standard modern six-month European call option on DEM at $X =$ USD/DEM 0.50, which trades at a price of USD 0.02. If the risk-free rate is 10 percent, $r_{t,T}$ equals 5 percent. Thus, the option's forward price is USD $0.02 \times 1.05 =$ USD 0.021. If the option is a forward-style option, the holder will pay USD 0.021 when the option expires, irrespective of what the option or the underlying asset is worth at that moment. After paying for the option, the new holder can then make the exercise decision. For instance, if the DEM trades at USD/DEM 0.48, the call holder does not exercise this option; however, if the DEM trades at USD/DEM 0.55, the call holder exercises and realizes the intrinsic value, $0.55 - 0.50 =$ USD 0.05 per DEM.

Type of Option	At time t	At time T (maturity)
Standard option	Sign the contract	Make the exercise decision:
	Pay $C_t =$ USD 0.20	$C_T = \text{Max}(\tilde{S}_T - X, 0)$
Forward-style option	Sign the contract	Pay $C_t \times 1.05 =$ USD 0.21.
		Make the exercise decision: $C_T = \text{Max}(\tilde{S}_T - X, 0)$

---

[13] In the forward stock market, no money changes hands and no shares are delivered until expiration day T (which, in Paris, is at the end of the current month). Because premium affairs were considered to be part of the forward market, payment of the agreed-upon premium was likewise deferred until time T, when the option expired.

6A.3   Futures-Style Options

Futures-style options were first introduced on the London International Financial Futures Exchange (LIFFE). They are basically futures contracts where the underlying asset is the option. Thus, they differ from premium affairs in the same way that futures contracts differ from forward transactions. As we saw, with a premium affair, the entire premium is paid at T. In contrast, the payment for a futures-style option is partly in the form of daily marking to market, and the balance is paid at T. That is, when buying a futures-style option, you simply pay an initial margin (in interest-earning cash or by posting securities). The agreed-upon price is paid later on, with a cash outflow each time the option price drops, and a cash inflow each time the option price rises. At maturity, the holder ends up with a marked-to-market futures contract on the option; that is, the holder buys the option at the prevailing spot price. The effect of marking to market is to reduce the risk of default relative to premium affairs.[14]

Example   6A.4

Suppose that you buy ten NOK 62,500 futures-style option contracts, with two days to go, at a premium of USD 0.021. Below, we show the cash flows that arise when, one day later, the futures price of the option is 0.030 and when, at maturity, the price is 0.035 (which must be the intrinsic value of the option, as the option matures on day two).

Day	Price of Option	Cash Flows	
0	0.021	–	
1	0.030	Marking to market: USD $10 \times 62{,}500 \times (0.030 - 0.021) =$	USD 5,625
2	0.035	Marking to market: USD $10 \times 62{,}500 \times (0.035 - 0.03)$ =	USD 3,125
		Buying the option: $(-)$ (USD $10 \times 62{,}500) \times 0.035$ =	(–)USD 21,875
		Total: USD $10 \times 62{,}500 \times 0.021$ =	(–)USD 13,125

Thus, as with an ordinary futures contract, the buyer of a futures-style option pays, all in all, the initial price (2.1 cents). Of course, this crude calculation, 2.1 cents per NOK, ignores time value.

A futures-style option is attractive to speculators. Consider an investor who thinks that calls are underpriced. He or she could buy a standard call (paying the premium) and hope to sell it later at a profit. However, the initial outlay required is even smaller if a futures-style option is bought. The hoped-for gain will then come in the form of inflows from marking to market until the time that the option position is reversed.

6A.4   Futures-Style Options on Futures

Another financial claim is the futures-style option on a futures contract. When exercised, the option creates a long position in a futures contract with price X (which will trigger an immediate marking-to-

---

[14] The forward contracts (and, therefore, also the premium affairs) in Paris have a life of one month at most. In Brussels, the maximum life is only two weeks. Thus, for these short-lived contracts, the variance of S_T is not very large, and the risk that the writer might default is rather small. In contrast, the contracts at LIFFE have maturities of up to nine months, which increases the variance and the default risk.

market cash flow), but the agreed-upon option premium is paid "later on," partly through marking to market and partly at T through the final purchase of the option. The *Deutsche Termin Börse* has futures-style options on futures contracts.

This option combines the advantages of options on futures and of futures-style options. Little capital is needed to open a position, and hedging the option in the futures market is easier when the instrument is written on the futures contract rather than on the cash. A futures-style option on futures, with futures and options expiring on the same date T, also facilitates arbitrage between European puts and calls, because no discounting is necessary. To understand this, start from the usual Put Call Parity for regular options "on cash" given in Equation [6]:

$$C_t - P_t = \frac{F_{t,T} - X}{1 + r_{t,T}}$$

and multiply each side by $(1 + r_{t,T})$:

$$C_t \times (1 + r_{t,T}) - P_t \times (1 + r_{t,T}) = F_{t,T} - X.$$

Recall that C_t and P_t are prices of standard options on "cash" foreign exchange. The futures price of an option is equal to the cash price of the option grossed up with interest over the interval (t,T). Thus, the terms $C_t \times (1 + r_{t,T})$ and $P_t \times (1 + r_{t,T})$ are the fair futures prices of the options. On the right-hand side, we see the forward price (which is virtually the same as the futures price) minus the strike price. In short, Put Call Parity for futures-style options on futures simplifies to the following no-arbitrage condition:

[Price of a futures-style call on futures]$_t$ – [Price of a futures-style put on futures]$_t$ = $f_{t,T} - X$.

Example   6A.5

Suppose that you observe $f_{t,T} = 35$, and a price of 3 for a futures-style call on a futures contract at $X = 33$. The futures-style put price on a futures contract at $X = 33$ must equal 1, in order to satisfy the no-arbitrage condition $3 - 1 = 35 - 33$. If the actual futures-style put price differs from unity, arbitrage will take place until the prices of calls, puts, and futures are back in line.

THE EFFECT OF THE FORWARD PREMIUM
ON THE PROBABILITY OF EARLY EXERCISE

In this appendix, we address two related issues: whether time value of currency options can be negative, and whether the prices of American options are close to those of European options. We start from the lower bound on option prices as derived in Section 6.3.3, Equation [4]:

$$C_t^{am} \geq C_t \geq \text{Max}\left(\frac{S_t}{1 + r_{t,T}^*} - \frac{X}{1 + r_{t,T}}, 0 \right);$$

[B1a]

$$P_t^{am} \geq P_t \geq \text{Max}\left(\frac{X}{1 + r_{t,T}} - \frac{S_t}{1 + r_{t,T}^*}, 0 \right).$$

[B1b]

6B.1   Time Value: American versus European Options

Can time value be negative? In other words, can an option trade below its intrinsic value? For an *American* option, such an event would immediately be eliminated by arbitrage. If an American call were trading at a price of 2 and if the payoff from immediate exercise were 4, anybody could buy at 2 and immediately exercise and get 4. In short, if the price of an American option were below its intrinsic value there would be a free lunch. Thus:

$$C_t^{am} \geq \text{Max}(S_t - X, 0);$$

[B2a]

$$P_t^{am} \geq \text{Max}(X - S_t, 0).$$

[B2b]

But for a *European* option, exercise is possible only at maturity, so for this type of option there is no free lunch if the premium is below the intrinsic value. Therefore, the only bounds for European options are provided by [B1a] and [B1b]—the "comparable forward contract" bounds. In light of this, European option premia will have a negative time value if two conditions are met simultaneously.

- First, the value of the option must be close to the value of the comparable forward contract— which, as will be argued, is the case when the option is very deep in the money.
- Second, the value of the comparable forward contract must be below the option's intrinsic value. This, we shall show, is the case when both interest rates are positive and equal, and *a fortiori* if the interest rate associated with the term being subtracted in [B1] tends towards zero (the domestic rate in [B1a], or the foreign rate in [B1b]).

In the next section, we shall then consider the opposite cases, where the value of the comparable forward contract always *exceeds* the intrinsic value. The insights from these twin cases will turn out to be vital for a good understanding of the value of the right of early exercise offered by an American option.

First consider a short-lived European call that is extremely deep in the money. Such an option will almost surely be exercised upon expiration because there is only a trivial chance that, by time *T*, the spot rate would have fallen below the exercise price. That is, a call that is very deep in the money is almost the same as a forward purchase contract. As a result, such an option will command a current price close to the current value of a comparable forward purchase contract. We conclude the following:

$$C_t \text{ approaches } \left[\frac{S_t}{1+r_{t,T}^*} - \frac{X}{1+r_{t,T}} \right] \text{ when } \frac{S_t}{X} \text{ approaches infinity.}$$

From the expression in square brackets we see that if both interest rates are positive and equal, the value of the comparable forward contract is below the option's intrinsic value. This effect of discounting is even stronger if the domestic rate of return is smaller than the foreign rate. Thus, if $r_{t,T}$ is smaller than or equal to $r_{t,T}^*$ while $r_{t,T}^*$ is positive, this call could easily trade below its intrinsic value.

Example   6B.1

Let $S_t = 100$, $X = 50$, and let $T - t$ be small, so that the remaining uncertainty is small. Under these conditions, a call is very deep in the money, and the chance that in a few weeks the price will have dropped from its current level of 100 to less than 50 is extremely small. That is, at time T the European call will almost surely be exercised. Thus, its current price is close to the value of a comparable forward purchase. With respect to the risk-free rates we consider two cases:

- $r_{t,T}^* = 0.005 = r_{t,T}$. Then:

$$C_t \text{ approaches } \left[\frac{100}{1.005} - \frac{50}{1.005} \right] = 49.75.$$

  This price is below 50, the option's intrinsic value.

- $r_{t,T}^* = 0.005$ and $r_{t,T} = 0.001$. Then the comparable forward purchase is worth even less:

$$C_t \text{ approaches } \left[\frac{100}{1.005} - \frac{50}{1.001} \right] = 49.55.$$

Thus, a deep in-the-money European call *can* legitimately trade below its intrinsic value if pure time value is important, and especially if the foreign interest rate exceeds the domestic rate.

The reasoning behind this result is as follows. The intrinsic value of a deep-in-the-money call is the value of immediate exercise. Relative to exercise at maturity, immediate exercise of a call has a cost and an advantage. The advantage is that one starts earning foreign interest immediately on the foreign exchange that is being bought, while the cost is that one forgoes domestic interest on the amount X that is being paid. When the foreign interest rate is high relative to the domestic rate, the advantage dominates: you would rather exercise early. Thus, the intrinsic value exceeds the value of later exercise.

An analogous argument can be made for put options. A deep-in-the-money European put will almost surely be exercised at time T. Therefore, the current value of such a put will approach the value of the comparable forward sale:

$$P_t \text{ approaches } \left[\frac{X}{1+r_{t,T}} - \frac{S_t}{1+r_{t,T}^*} \right] \text{ when } \frac{S_t}{X} \text{ approaches zero.}$$

From the expression in square brackets we see that if both interest rates are positive and equal, the value of the comparable forward sales contract is below the put option's intrinsic value. This effect of discounting is even stronger if the foreign rate of return is smaller than the domestic rate.

Example   6B.2

We assume that $S_t = 100$ and $X = 200$. The put is very deep-in-the-money, and will almost surely be exercised, because the probability of a price rise exceeding 100 percent in two weeks is trivially small. We conclude that the put will, therefore, trade at a price that is close to the value of the comparable forward sales contract. Consider the following scenarios with respect to the risk-free rates of return:

- $r_{t,T}^* = 0.005 = r_{t,T}$. Then:

$$P_t \text{ approaches } \left[\frac{200}{1.005} - \frac{100}{1.005} \right] = 99.50,$$

which is below the put's intrinsic value, 100. This effect of discounting is even stronger if the foreign rate is small:

- $r_{t,T}^* = 0.001$ and $r_{t,T} = 0.005$. Then:

$$P_t \text{ approaches } \left[\frac{200}{1.005} - \frac{100}{1.001} \right] = 99.10.$$

Thus, a deep in-the-money European put may trade below its intrinsic value if pure time value is important, and especially if the foreign interest rate is smaller than the domestic rate.

We conclude the following. First, for European options, one cannot invoke an immediate-exercise argument to rule out negative time values. Second, the potential for negative time values is especially relevant if the rate of return on the inflow side (foreign exchange for the call, domestic money for the put) is much higher than the rate of return on the option's outflow side. Third, the value of an option will be close to the value of the comparable forward contract (and, thus, potentially below the intrinsic value) when the option is very deep in the money.

6B.2   Option Premiums for American versus European Options

For American options, we have two lower bounds—the comparable forward contract (Equation [B1]), and the intrinsic value (Equation [B2]). We now show that, depending on which bound is tighter, American option prices may or may not be close to the corresponding European prices.

High Forward Premiums Make Early Exercise of American Calls Unlikely

Assume that the foreign interest rate is zero. Then the forward price of the foreign currency is at a premium. With $r_{t,T}^* = 0$, the lower bound (Equation [B1a]) becomes:

$$C_t^{am} \geq \text{Max} \left(S_t - \frac{X}{1 + r_{t,T}}, 0 \right).$$

This is a tighter bound than the intrinsic-value bound (Equation [B2a]) since:

$$S_t - \frac{X}{1+r_{t,T}} > S_t - X \text{ if } r_{t,T} > 0.$$

In other words, if $r^*_{t,T} = 0$ while $r_{t,T} > 0$, the call's market value is always above its intrinsic value. It follows that it would not be rational to exercise the call. It would be better to sell the option. If early exercise is irrational, this American option can be valued as if it were a European option.[15] A heuristic interpretation is that, with $r^*_{t,T} = 0$ and $r_{t,T} > 0$, the foreign currency is at a forward premium. That is, in a risk-adjusted sense, the currency is expected to appreciate—which makes postponing the exercise of the call the better decision.

Simulations by Geske and Johnson (1984) show that, in practice, the condition that $r^*_{t,T} = 0$ is not quite necessary. With (annualized) foreign interest rates at least 3 percent below domestic rates, the right of early exercise of a short-lived call is almost worthless, and we can ignore this right for pricing purposes.[16]

Large Forward Discounts Make American Puts Almost European

The treatment of put options is symmetric to that of American call options. Assume that the domestic interest rate is zero, implying that the forward rate is at a discount. When $r_{t,T} = 0$, the lower bound (Equation [B1b]) becomes:

$$P^{am}_t \geq \text{Max}\left(X - \frac{S_t}{1 + r^*_{t,T}}, 0 \right).$$

This is a tighter bound than the intrinsic-value bound (Equation [B2b]) since:

$$X - \frac{S_t}{(1 + r^*_{t,T})} X - S_t \text{ if } r^*_{t,T} > 0.$$

That is, if $r_{t,T} = 0$ while $r^*_{t,T} > 0$, the put's market value always exceeds its intrinsic value. Thus, the put will not be exercised early, and this American option can be valued as if it were European. The heuristic version of the argument is that, when $r_{t,T} = 0$ and $r^*_{t,T} > 0$, the foreign currency is at a forward discount. That is, in a risk-adjusted sense, the currency is expected to depreciate, which makes postponing the exercise of the put better than immediate exercise.

Simulations again show that, in practice, $r_{t,T} = 0$ is not quite necessary. With (annualized) foreign interest rates at least 3 percent above domestic rates, we can still ignore early exercise of a short-lived put for pricing purposes.

---

[15] Note that $r^*_{t,T} = 0$ corresponds to the case of non-dividend-paying stocks (NDPS); the no-early-exercise property for NDPS is well-known, and was first shown by Merton (1973).

[16] By "short-lived," we mean options with a time to maturity not exceeding nine months.

7 PRICING CURRENCY OPTIONS USING THE BINOMIAL MODEL

In Chapter 6, we described options and their possible applications. We know that the buyer of an option has to pay a premium, but we have not yet explained how this premium is set, or how one can judge whether or not a quoted price is fair. In the next two chapters, we address the issue of option valuation or option pricing. In this chapter, we describe a relatively simple approach, the binomial option pricing model as developed by Cox, Ross, and Rubinstein (1979). In the next chapter, we derive and discuss the model of Black and Scholes as it was applied to currency options by Garman and Kohlhagen (1983) and Grabbe (1983).

The binomial option pricing model assumes that, given the current level of the exchange rate, there are only two possible values for the exchange rate next period—"up" and "down." The exchange rate cannot stay constant. This binomial assumption may appear rather restrictive. However, the distribution of the total return (after many of these binomial price changes) becomes close to bell-shaped, and the binomial option pricing model converges to the celebrated Black-Scholes option pricing model. In this sense, the binomial model gives us an understanding of what goes on in the more complicated Black-Scholes model. This is why we start our analysis of currency option pricing with the simple binomial model.

The one-period binomial model, attributed to Sharpe (1978) and Rendleman and Bartter (1979), was later extended by Cox, Ross, and Rubinstein (1979) to a multiperiod setting capable of valuing options on dividend-paying stocks and American stock options. This approach is also used to value more complex derivative financial contracts, and even real (operating) options that arise in capital budgeting problems. The binomial model is especially helpful, because it is often difficult to apply the Black-Scholes approach when valuing complicated derivative securities. In short, the binomial model is useful not only as a way of understanding the Black-Scholes model, but also in itself, as a model for the pricing of complex options.

The structure of this chapter is as follows: In Section 7.1, we present, from various angles, the arbitrage arguments underlying the binomial approach in the context of valuing a call option one period before maturity. We also interpret the binomial approach as one based on risk-adjusted expected values. In Section 7.2, we introduce our notation and the assumptions underlying the multiperiod binomial model. In Section 7.3, we discuss the replication interpretation underlying the binomial model in greater detail. In Section 7.4, we extend the single-period-call pricing model to multiple periods, and in Section 7.5 we indicate how this approach ultimately leads to the Black-Scholes valuation formula. In Section 7.6, we explain how the binomial model can be used to value European contingent claims other than calls. A simple adjustment is needed to value American options; this is discussed in Section 7.7. In the appendix, we present the mathematical and statistical details of the binomial model and also show how it can be applied to value options on foreign currency T-bills and currency futures. Applications of the binomial valuation principles for capital budgeting purposes are discussed in Chapter 25.

7.1   THE LOGIC OF BINOMIAL OPTION PRICING

Binomial option pricing can be explained from two points of view, using either a replication approach or a hedging approach. Both the replication and the hedging can be done either in forward markets or in spot markets (using domestic and foreign money-market positions). Since you are familiar with forward contracts, we shall focus on replication and hedging in the forward market. We then conclude this section with an interpretation of option pricing in terms of risk-adjusted probabilities and certainty equivalents of the future spot exchange rate.

Both the hedging and the replication approaches are illustrated by the following numerical example. Consider a call on one DEM against Italian lira, the home currency, with strike price X = ITL/DEM 1,050. Assume the domestic (ITL) risk-free return is 5 percent per period and the DEM risk-free return is 3.9604 percent. The current (time-0) spot rate is S_0 = ITL/DEM 1,000. With the above data, the one-period forward rate will be ITL/DEM 1,010:

$$F_{0,1} = S_0 \frac{1 + r_{0,1}}{1 + r_{0,1}^*} = 1,000 \times \frac{1.05}{1.039604} = 1,010.$$

We assume that from the current spot rate, the exchange rate can "branch out" either to the up-level 1,100 or to the down-level 950 at time 1. Immediately after this change in the spot rate, the call expires. In Figure 7.1, we show the *binomial tree* for the spot price changes—a tree that, in a single-period model, has only two branches. We also include the expiration values of the call that correspond to each of the possible time-1 exchange rates.

FIGURE 7.1   Example of a One-Period Binomial Tree

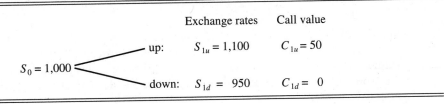

	Exchange rates	Call value
$S_0 = 1,000$ up:	$S_{1u} = 1,100$	$C_{1u} = 50$
down:	$S_{1d} = 950$	$C_{1d} = 0$

FIGURE 7.2   Exposure Line for a Call Option

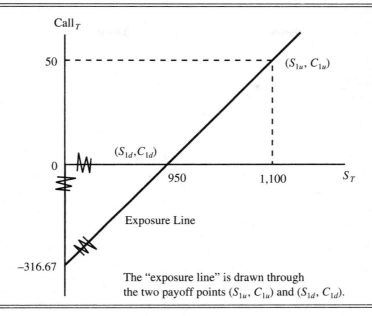

The "exposure line" is drawn through
the two payoff points (S_{1u}, C_{1u}) and (S_{1d}, C_{1d}).

Another useful way to show the possible pairs of exchange rates and call values is to plot the future call values against the corresponding future exchange rates (Figure 7.2). The graph shows the two possible outcomes as two points, through which we have drawn a straight line (labeled "Exposure Line"). The slope of this line, which we call the option's *exposure*, can be computed as:

$$\text{Exposure} = \frac{C_{1u} - C_{1d}}{S_{1u} - S_{1d}} = \frac{50 - 0}{1,100 - 950} = 1/3.$$

This number measures the relative sensitivity of the future call price with respect to the future exchange rate. In this sense, it is related to the notion of a (partial) derivative of C_1 with respect to S_1.[1]

7.1.1   The Replication Approach

In this section, we show how the payoff of an option can be replicated in the forward market. We then invoke the *Law of One Price*—two assets or portfolios with the same payoff must have the same price—to infer the price of the option from the value of the replicating portfolio.

From Figure 7.2, the payoff from the call [50 if S_1 = 1,100] and [0 if S_1 = 950] can be replicated by a forward purchase of 1/3 DEM and an ITL deposit whose value at T is 20. To verify this

---

[1] The derivative is partial in the sense that we are holding constant the time factor. That is, the call and asset values that are used in the computation of exposure are values at time 1.

numerically, simply compute the payoffs at time $T = 1$ from this portfolio in each of the two possible exchange rate "states":

- If $\tilde{S}_1 = 950$, the portfolio pays off $(1/3) \times (950 - 1,010) + 20 = 0$, and

- If $\tilde{S}_1 = 1,100$, the forward purchase pays off $(1/3) \times (1,100 - 1,010) + 20 = 50$,

which are identical to the payoffs of the call.[2] Since this portfolio replicates the payoffs of the call option, by arbitrage the call must command the same price as the portfolio. The market value of the forward contract at time 0 is zero. Thus, the price at time 0 of the portfolio is equal to the price of the deposit whose present value is ITL 20/1.05 = ITL 19.05. By the *Law of One Price*, then, we must have $C_0 = 19.05$.

7.1.2   The Forward Hedging Approach

In Section 7.1.1, we saw how the call, in a binomial world, has the same payoffs as a forward purchase of DEM 1/3 and an ITL deposit worth ITL 20 at time 1. It follows that we can hedge the call by selling forward 1/3 units of foreign currency. We verify this numerically:

- If $\tilde{S}_1 = 1,100$, the hedged call is worth $50 - 1/3\ [1,100 - 1,010] = $ ITL 20; and

- If $\tilde{S}_1 = 950$, the hedged call is worth $0 - 1/3\ [950 - 1,010] = $ ITL 20.

Thus, the call's payoff has become risk free. The hedging procedure is shown in Figure 7.3. The graph reproduces the call's exposure line with, as we know, a slope of 1/3. The forward sale of 1/3 of foreign currency is represented by its payoff line with slope −1/3, and zero expiration value if $S_1 = F_{0,1} = 1,010$.[3] Of course, the portfolio with the call and the forward hedge will be risk free, since the +1/3 and the −1/3 slopes offset each other.

Since the portfolio containing the call and the forward contract is risk free, in an arbitrage-free market this portfolio must be priced exactly like an ITL T-bill with future value 20, that is, at ITL 20/1.05 = ITL 19.05. Finally, the call must be worth the same as the hedged portfolio, because the current market value of the forward contract is zero. We conclude again that $C_0 = 19.05$.

It will have become obvious that the replication and hedging approaches are mirror images of each other. Whenever we can find a perfect hedge, we can also find a perfect replicating strategy, and the number of forward (purchase) contracts in the hedge is simply the negative of the number of forward (purchase) contracts in the replicating portfolio. Nor should it come as a surprise that replication or hedging can also be done in the spot market. In fact, the original derivations of the model by Black and Scholes (1973) and Cox, Ross, and Rubinstein (1979) relied on spot hedging and spot replication, respectively. The reason is that the original model is for the pricing of options on stocks

---

[2] We can also obtain this result by noting that the payoff of a forward purchase of *one* DEM at $X' = 950$ is $\tilde{S}_1 - 950$; so the payoff of a forward purchase of DEM 1/3 at $X' = 950$ is $(1/3)\ (\tilde{S}_1 - 950)$. This payoff is depicted as a line with slope 1/3 that crosses the S-axis at $S = 950$, which is the call's exposure line. Of course, if there were more than two possible future spot prices, the payoff of this forward purchase would not always be the same as the payoff of the call. The call's "true" payoff schedule is kinked at its strike price, $X = 1,050$, while the forward's payoff schedule is a straight line. However, by assumption of the binomial model, there are only these two possible values of S_T. Therefore, in this binomial world, the payoffs from the call and from the 1/3 forward purchase at 950 are always identical, whether the outcome is $S_1 = 1,100$ or 950.

[3] It does not matter that, in our binomial example, S_1 will never actually be 1,010. What matters is that the payoff is $-1/3 \times [1,100 - 1,010]$ if the spot exchange rate goes up, and $-1/3 \times [950 - 1,010]$ if the exchange rate goes down. A line with slope −1/3 that crosses the S_T-axis at $S_T = 1,050$ produces these payoffs.

FIGURE 7.3   Hedging the Call in the Forward Market

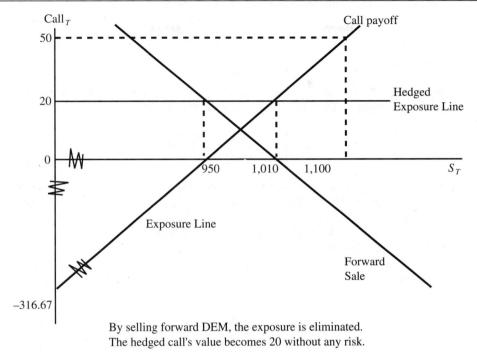

By selling forward DEM, the exposure is eliminated.
The hedged call's value becomes 20 without any risk.

$$F = 1,010$$

and, in stock markets, forward contracts are not available (at least not in the US). We shall leave the derivation of the spot replication and spot hedging models as exercises. After having worked your way through these exercises, you will appreciate the comparative simplicity that is obtained when forward contracts—rather than spot positions—are used.

7.1.3   The Risk-Adjusted Probability Interpretation

In this section, we interpret the binomial arbitrage approach as one that implicitly computes the call's risk-adjusted expected payoff (or certainty-equivalent). The call's current value is then obtained by discounting the certainty-equivalent payoff at the risk-free rate.

We know from Chapter 2 that the forward rate is a risk-adjusted expectation. In a binomial model, a regular expectation of the spot rate would be computed from the (true) probability p of the exchange rate moving up as follows:

$$E_0(\tilde{S}_1) = p \times 1,100 + (1-p) \times 950.$$

Since the only parameter in a binomial model is the probability of a price rise, the only way we can correct for risk is by correcting the probability p. That is, a risk-adjusted expected value must be based on a risk-adjusted probability of an "up." Let us denote the risk-adjusted probability by q. By definition, then, the certainty equivalent value of the future spot rate, $CEQ_0(\tilde{S}_1)$, is:

$$CEQ_0(\tilde{S}_1) = F_{0,1} = 1,010 = q \times 1,100 + (1-q) \times 950$$

$$= 950 + q \times (1,100 - 950).$$

Thus, once we observe the forward rate, we can infer the risk-adjusted probability q implicitly used by the market. In our example, the implied risk-adjusted probability is:

$$q = \frac{1,010 - 950}{1,100 - 950} = \frac{60}{150} = 0.4.$$

However, the risk-adjusted probability of observing $[S_1 = 1,100]$ is also the risk-adjusted probability that the call will be worth 50. This is because $[S_1 = 1,100]$ and $[C_1 = 50]$ are the same event, in the sense that C_1 equals 50 if and only if S_1 equals 1,100. Similarly, the down-state event $[S_1 = 950]$ is the same as the event $[C_1 = 0]$. In short, the risk-adjusted probabilities for the asset must also be valid for the call. So the risk-adjusted expected value of the call must be:

$$CEQ_0(\tilde{C}_1) = (0.4 \times 50) + (1 - 0.4) \times 0 = 20.$$

The present value is then obtained by discounting this risk-adjusted expected value at the risk-free rate:

$$C_0 = \frac{CEQ_0(\tilde{C}_1)}{1 + r_{0,1}} = \frac{20}{1.05} = 19.05.$$

We conclude that a one-period call option can be valued in three steps:

1. Extract the risk-adjusted distribution from the forward rate.
2. Compute the risk-adjusted expected value of the call, $CEQ_0(\tilde{C}_T)$.
3. Discount the risk-adjusted expected value at the risk-free rate.[4]

* * *

We now have some insight into the "arbitrage-free" logic underlying the binomial model, and we have also developed an interpretation of this model in terms of risk-adjusted probabilities. Before exploring this logic in greater detail and extending the model to a multiperiod setting, let us introduce our general notation and assumptions.

---

[4] This interpretation solves a riddle that may have puzzled some readers. In each of the arbitrage arguments, we were able to price the call without knowledge of the true probability "up." If we had known the true probability p, we could have computed the expected value of the call as $E_0(\tilde{C}_T) = p \times 50 + (1 - p) \times 0$. We could then have discounted this expectation at a rate that takes into account the risk, using an equilibrium model that tells us how to measure risk and how the required expected return changes with risk. However, in a binomial model, we do not need a separate equilibrium theory to adjust for risk. We can "observe," from the forward premium, the risk-adjusted probabilities implicitly used by the market.

7.2 NOTATION AND ASSUMPTIONS FOR THE MULTIPERIOD BINOMIAL MODEL

In a multiperiod extension of the binomial model, we shall use two additional assumptions, the first of which relates to the risk-free interest rates.

Assumption 1: The risk-free one-period rates of return on both currencies are constant.

For simplicity of notation, we therefore drop the cumbersome time subscripts used so far. That is, we shall simply write r and r^* rather than $r_{t,t+1}$ and $r^*_{t,t+1}$.

The next assumption has to do with the size of the up and down movements. The (multiplicative) up factor, u, will denote unity plus the percentage change upward; in our previous example, u was 1.1 (such that $S_{up} = 1{,}000 \times 1.1 = 1{,}100$). The (multiplicative) down factor, d, likewise denotes unity plus the return in the down state; in the example, d was 0.95 (such that the price $S_{down} = 1{,}000 \times 0.95 = 950$).

Assumption 2: The multiplicative factors u and d are constant over time.

It can be shown that the assumption of constant u and d corresponds to the Black-Scholes assumptions of (1) no sudden devaluations or revaluations or other discontinuities in the exchange rate process, and (2) a constant variance of the period-by-period percentage changes in the exchange rate. The assumption of constant interest rates is also present in the Black-Scholes model.

Assumption 3: The interest rates and the u and d factors satisfy:

$$d < \frac{1+r}{1+r^*} < u.$$

[1]

Assumption 3 is made to rule out free lunches (risk-free arbitrage profits). To understand this, multiply all terms by S_0, so that relation [1] becomes:

$$S_{down} < S_0 \frac{1+r}{1+r^*} = F_{0,1} < S_{up}.$$

Relation [1] says that the one-period forward rate must be somewhere between the two possible future spot rates; otherwise, you would have a money machine.

Example   7.1

Assume, as before, that $S_{down} = 950$ and $S_{up} = 1{,}100$; however, we now change the forward price to ITL/DEM 1,150 ($> S_{up} = 1{,}100$). With this forward rate, everybody can (and will) sell forward huge amounts of DEM, making a sure profit of ITL 50 (if $\tilde{S}$ is "up"), or more (if $\tilde{S}$ is "down"). However, these massive forward sales immediately drive the forward rate down to a level where there is always some chance of negative payoffs from a forward sale. That is, the proposed forward rate of ITL/DEM 1,150 cannot possibly be an equilibrium forward rate.

Example   7.2

We change the forward price to ITL/DEM 920 ($< S_{\text{down}} = 950$). Now everybody can (and will) buy forward huge amounts of DEM, making a sure profit of at least ITL 30. However, these massive forward purchases immediately drive the forward rate up to a level where there is always some chance of negative payoffs from a forward purchase.

Let us now introduce the notation for the exchange rate process. In this chapter, we give the exchange rate process, $\tilde{S}$, *two* subscripts. The first one is a time subscript and shows the number of periods (or price changes) since time 0, while the second one shows how many of these changes were "up."[5] A three-period process is shown in Figure 7.4. For example, to get to **node** (1,1)—every place where the tree is branching out is called a node—the exchange rate must increase. Thus $S_{1,1}$ is S_0 times the up factor. To reach node (2,2), the exchange rate has to rise again, so that its value at node (2,2) is $S_{1,1} \times u = (S_0 \times u) \times u = S_0 u^2$. Note also that an "up" followed by a "down" leads to the same value as a "down" followed by an "up." For example, if, starting from S_0, the exchange rate increases first (to $S_0 \times u$) and then falls (to $S_0 \times u \times d$), the time-2 level is the same as it would be if the exchange rate had first decreased (to $S_0 \times d$) and then increased (to $S_0 \times d \times u$).

One implication is that, since there are two ways to get to node (2,1), the probability of the outcome [$\tilde{S}_2 = S_{2,1}$] is higher than the probability that $\tilde{S}_2$ assumes one of the extreme values. More generally: the central values in the tree are always the more likely outcomes.

Example   7.3

To get to node (3,2) we need two up changes and one down. The exchange rate in node (3,2) accordingly is $S_{3,2} = S_0 u^2 d$. There are three ways to arrive at this node: the drop could come at time 1, or at time 2, or at time 3. In contrast, there is only one way to arrive at node (3,3): we need three consecutive rises.

Note that we have assumed that the price changes are multiplicative rather than additive. One reason for this is that it seems reasonable to assume a constant distribution of *percentage* price

FIGURE 7.4   Three-Period Binomial Tree

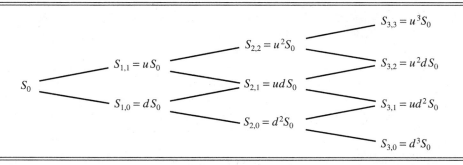

---

[5] When we occasionally drop the second subscript, we mean "for whatever the number of ups was"; then $\tilde{S}$ is an *ex ante* random variable. For instance, $\tilde{S}_1$ is random, and can take on two possible values, $S_{1,1}$ and $S_{1,0}$.

changes, rather than to postulate a constant distribution of price changes (in units of home currency, independently of the level of the exchange rate).

Example 7.4

With the multiplicative process, the changes are always either +10 percent or –5 percent, whatever the level of the exchange rate. In contrast, with an additive process, the changes would have been always either +100 or –50 whatever the level of the exchange rate—even if the exchange rate has already drifted down to 300, or drifted up to 2,000. Most people prefer the first view.

Another reason for preferring the multiplicative model over the additive model is that, with constant percentage return distributions, the exchange rate can never quite reach zero, even if it happens to go down all of the time. In contrast, with constant additive price changes, we may end up with negative exchange rates, and this defies common sense.

We already know that the central values in the binomial tree are the more likely outcomes. As a result of this, if you let the branching-out process go on for many periods, the resulting distribution for the time-n value of the exchange rate becomes reasonably bell-shaped for, say, fifteen steps. You can verify this by reviewing your statistics textbook, and examining how the probabilities evolve with an increasing number of steps. For example, if the probability of an "up" equals 0.5, the probabilities evolve as shown in Figure 7.5. With only five changes, a bell-shaped distribution is already emerging.

FIGURE 7.5   Probability Distributions of Future Exchange Rates

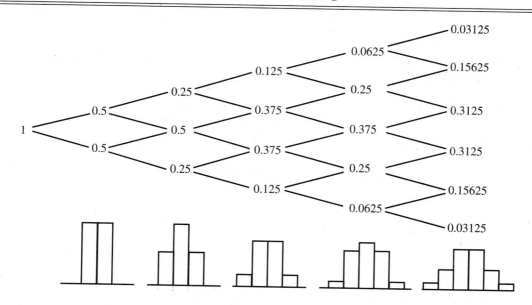

We consider a five-period binomial tree and show, instead of the spot rate, the probabilities of reaching each node as perceived at time 0. The longer the horizon, the more bell-shaped the distribution becomes.

Thus, the multiperiod binomial model quickly gets us very close to the bell-shaped distributions observed in practice. A practical issue is how to set the factors u and d, for a given number of periods, such that the distribution of the final spot rate is "reasonable" in terms of its mean and standard deviation. Since this is rather technical, we refer interested readers to Appendix 7A. We are now ready to take a closer look at the replication approach. We begin with the simplest possible problem, an option that expires next period.

7.3   THE ONE-PERIOD EUROPEAN CURRENCY CALL

The main objective of this section is to formalize the one-period call valuation model that we discussed in the first section. Specifically, we shall explicitly solve the replication problem, and formally link it to the notion of risk-adjusted expected values. In the next section, we will proceed to multiperiod valuation problems.

7.3.1   The Replication Approach

Using the replicating portfolio argument, we form a portfolio consisting of a domestic risk-free deposit B and b forward contracts. (Recall that, when the direction of the transaction is not specified, a contract refers to a purchase contract.) Each unit of home currency grows to $1 + r$ units without risk. In contrast, the time-1 home currency value of the forward contract is risky, as it depends on $\tilde{S}_1$. Next to our tree for the exchange rate in Figure 7.6, we compute the period-1 value of the replicating portfolio.

We want our portfolio to *replicate* the payoff from the call. That is, the value of the portfolio in the up state should equal the call's value in the up state; and the value of the portfolio in the down state should equal the call's value in the down state:

$$\text{up:} \quad B(1+r)+b[S_{1,1}-F_0]=C_{1,1} \tag{2a}$$

$$\text{down:} \quad B(1+r)+b[S_{1,0}-F_0]=C_{1,0} \tag{2b}$$

We now derive, in all its gory details, the solution for this system of two linear equations in two unknowns B and b.[6] To find b, we subtract Equation [2b] from Equation [2a], and obtain:

$$b = \frac{C_{1,1}-C_{1,0}}{S_{1,1}-S_{1,0}}. \tag{3}$$

FIGURE 7.6   The Value of a Portfolio as a Function of the Spot Rate

Exchange rate process	Value of the portfolio, $B(1+r)+b[\tilde{S}_1-F_0]$
$S_{1,1}=uS_0$	$B(1+r)+b[S_{1,1}-F_0]$
S_0	
$S_{1,0}=dS_0$	$B(1+r)+b[S_{1,0}-F_0]$

---

6 In Section 7.1 we graphically interpreted this problem as being equivalent to drawing an "exposure line" $C_1 = a + b\,S_1$ through the points $(C_{1,1}, S_{1,1})$ and $(C_{1,0}, S_{1,0})$. The interpretation of the line's intercept and slope are $a = B(1+r) - bF_0$ and $b =$ exposure.

Note that b equals the option's exposure as identified in Section 7.1.1. The domestic part of the replicating portfolio, B, can be found by substituting Equation [3] into Equation [2b]:

$$B(1+r)+(C_{1,1}-C_{1,0})\frac{S_{1,0}-F_0}{S_{1,1}-S_{1,0}}=C_{1,0}. \tag{4}$$

We now rewrite the fraction in Equation [4] as:

$$\frac{S_{1,0}-F_0}{S_{1,1}-S_{1,0}}=\frac{S_0 d-S_0\dfrac{1+r}{1+r^*}}{S_0 u-S_0 d}=\frac{d-\dfrac{1+r}{1+r^*}}{u-d}.$$

Then Equation [4] becomes:

$$B(1+r)+(C_{1,1}-C_{1,0})\frac{d-\dfrac{1+r}{1+r^*}}{u-d}=C_{1,0}.$$

Thus,

$$B=\frac{C_{1,1}\dfrac{\dfrac{1+r}{1+r^*}-d}{u-d}+C_{1,0}\left[1-\dfrac{\dfrac{1+r}{1+r^*}-d}{u-d}\right]}{1+r}. \tag{5}$$

Finally, we invoke the *Law of One Price*. Because the forward contract is free, the only investment in the replicating portfolio is the deposit. Thus,

$$C_0 = B, \tag{6}$$

where B is given in Equation [5].

Example   7.5

In Section 7.1, we considered the case where $C_{1,0}=0$, $C_{1,1}=50$, $r=0.05$, $(1+r)/(1+r^*)=1.01$, $u=1.1$, and $d=0.95$. From [5], the amount of ITL to be deposited then is:

$$B=\frac{50\dfrac{1.01-0.95}{1.1-0.95}+0}{1.05}$$

$$=\frac{50\times 0.4}{1.05}=19.05.$$

Thus, $C_0 = 19.05$.

We will also illustrate this formula (and other results in this chapter) using the tree shown in Figure 7.7. The exchange rate process starts at $S_0 = 100$, and has $u = 1.10$ and $d = 0.9$. We will further assume $1 + r = 1.05$, and in order to obtain a convenient forward rate of 102, we will set $1 + r^* = 1.0294118$.

Example 7.6

With the data in Figure 7.7, consider a one-period option with $X = 100$ expiring at time 1, so that $C_{1,1} = 10$ and $C_{1,0} = 0$. Then:

$$\text{The option's exposure } = b = \frac{10 - 0}{110 - 90} = 0.50,$$

$$C_0 = B = \frac{10\dfrac{1.02 - 0.90}{1.10 - 0.90} + 0}{1.05} = 5.714.$$

7.3.2   From Replication to Risk-Adjusted Expectations

Equations [5] and [6] can be written more compactly as:

$$C_0 = \frac{qC_{1,1} + (1 - q)C_{1,0}}{1 + r}, \text{ where } q = \frac{\dfrac{1 + r}{1 + r^*} - d}{u - d}. \qquad [7]$$

We argue that this option price can be interpreted as a risk-adjusted expected value, discounted at the risk-free rate. That is, in [7] we are basically computing C_0 as $\text{CEQ}_0(\tilde{C}_1)/(1 + r)$.

To see this, we note that Equation [7] looks like a risk-neutral valuation formula. First, in the numerator we compute $qC_{1,1} + (1 - q)C_{1,0}$. This is how we would compute the expected value of the

FIGURE 7.7   Two-Period Binomial Tree: A Numerical Example

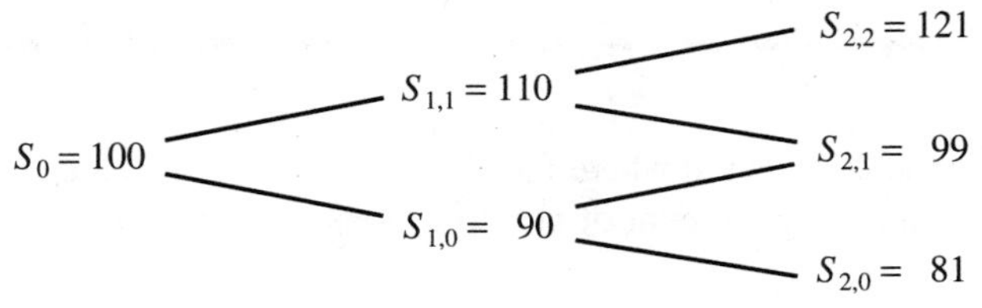

$u = 1.1; d = 0.9; 1 + r = 1.05; 1 + r^* = 1.0294118;$

forward factor $\dfrac{1 + r}{1 + r^*} = 1.02$

call if q were the probability of an up move. Second, note that $0 < q < 1$ (from Equation [1]); thus, in that sense, q is like a legitimate probability and the numerator is like an expected value. But Equation [7] also tells us that we should discount the numerator at the risk-free rate. This implies that the expected value must be a risk-adjusted expectation or certainty equivalent rather than the true expected value—otherwise, there would have to be a risk premium in the discount rate. In other words, q has the properties of a risk-adjusted probability rather than the characteristics of the true probability p. We conclude, therefore, that in Equation [7] the factor q is the risk-adjusted probability of an up move implicit in the forward rate, and that $q\,C_{1,1} + (1 - q)\,C_{1,0}$ is the certainty equivalent or risk-adjusted expectation. Thus, Equation [7] says that we can obtain the risk-adjusted probabilities from the forward rate, use these probabilities to compute the certainty equivalent, and then value the option as the discounted certainty equivalent.

We illustrate this by solving the preceding example using the risk-adjusted expectations version of the model.

Example   7.7

Assuming the exchange rate process given in Figure 7.7, we consider a one-period call with strike price 100, so that $C_{1,1} = 10$ and $C_{1,0} = 0$; then, from Equation [7], the risk-adjusted probability is:

$$q = \frac{\dfrac{1.05}{1.0294118} - 0.9}{1.1 - 0.9} = 0.6.$$

Therefore, in a risk-adjusted sense, the probability that the spot rate will go to the up state is 60 percent. It follows that:

$$\mathrm{CEQ}_0\,(\tilde{C}_1) = (0.6 \times 10) + (0.4 \times 0) = 6.$$

If the risk-adjusted expected value of the call at time 1 is 6, then the call's current value must be:

$$C_0 = \frac{6}{1.05} = 5.714.$$

Predictably, this is the same number that we computed in Example 7.6, when we did not explicitly use risk-adjusted probabilities.

7.4   THE N-PERIOD EUROPEAN CALL

The obvious drawback of the one-period model is that it assumes that the exchange rate can take one of only two possible values at expiration. This is a rather simplistic view and an undesirable feature of the single-period model. We would prefer a richer distribution, one that has many possible values at maturity and is close to bell-shaped.

In Section 7.2, we found that, if there are two changes, then there are already three possible exchange rates at the end, and that the middle outcome is more probable than the extreme outcomes. After thirty changes, there will be thirty-one possible exchange rates at the end, and the probabilities will be approximately bell-shaped. Thus, if we wanted to price a one-month option, we would be much closer to reality if, instead of modeling the time-T exchange rate as the result of a single, big change, we model it as the result of thirty small, daily changes. Of course, if we increase the number of sub-periods into which the one-month life of the option is divided, we must also shrink the factors u and d towards unity; otherwise, the variance of the exchange rate at expiration would no longer match reality. Likewise, the risk-free rate of return per subperiod must be rescaled—for instance, from a monthly rate to a daily rate.

In this section, we show how to extend the one-period binomial model to such a multiple-period setting. In the numerical examples, we omit the adjustments to the u, d, and r parameters that should be made if we divide a given option's life into more than one period. Working with familiar numbers is easier, and helps us focus on the logic of the pricing approach. The details of how one needs to adjust r, u, and d are given in Appendix 7A. The two-period examples we present below should be interpreted as going from a one-month valuation problem (with one single, big change in the exchange rate) to a two-month problem (with two consecutive, big changes in the exchange rate).

7.4.1   Dynamic Hedging or Replication

Let us consider a numerical example for a call, assuming that there are *two* price jumps before the option expires. We again use the tree in Figure 7.7, and consider a call with $X = 95$ that expires at the end of the second period. You can easily verify that, when plotting the three possible time-2 call values against the corresponding asset prices, the three points are no longer on one single line. That is, at time 0, we can no longer hedge or replicate the call using only one (two-period) forward contract. Therefore, we need to introduce a new assumption.

Assumption 4: At any discrete moment in the model, investors can trade and adjust their portfolios of home currency and foreign currency loans.

The above assumption corresponds to the Black-Scholes assumption that trading can be done continuously. As a result of Assumption 4, we can now use a dynamic hedge, that is, a series of one-period hedges that are revised every period. To see this, note that *at time* 1 the one-period valuation approach of Section 7.3 will still work. For instance, if at time 1 the exchange rate is 110, then there are only two possible values that the exchange rate can take at maturity—121 and 99. Thus, if at time 1 the rate is 110, then we can easily hedge or replicate—and, if we can hedge or replicate, we can use the numerically convenient risk-adjusted valuation formula [7] to value the call at node (1,1). For a European call, we use our result $q = 0.6$, and we immediately find the call price at node (1,1) using Equation [7]:

$$C_{1,1} = \frac{(26 \times 0.6) + (4 \times 0.4)}{1.05} = 16.38.$$

Likewise, if at time 1 the exchange rate has moved down to $S_{1,0} = 90$, then there are only two possible exchange rates at expiration, implying that a linear hedge or replication is possible; thus, we know the call will then be valued as:

$$C_{1,0} = \frac{(4 \times 0.6) + 0}{1.05} = 2.29.$$

We still have to find the value of the option at time 0. At time 0, there only two possible values for the exchange rate at time 1: $\tilde{S}_1$ is either 110 or 90, and we have just identified each of the corresponding call prices: $\tilde{C}_1 = 16.38$ if $\tilde{S}_1 = 110$, and $\tilde{C}_1 = 2.28$ if $\tilde{S}_1 = 90$. Thus, we now have to solve a one-period, two-outcome problem—and two points can be hedged (or replicated) linearly, implying a risk-adjusted expectation valuation relationship. Thus, the price at time 0 must be:

$$C_0 = \frac{(16.38 \times 0.6) + (2.29 \times 0.4)}{1.05} = 10.23.$$

In terms of the hedging model, this step-wise valuation implicitly uses a hedge that looks only one period ahead. That is, every period we select a hedge that offsets the uncertainty of the option's value one period ahead. The size of the required hedge, the option's **delta**, changes all of the time because it depends on the evolution of the exchange rate and time to maturity.

Example 7.8

Suppose that we want to hedge a call option that is implicit in a currency-option bond we hold. The bond and the implicit call option expire in two periods. To hedge the call, we determine its exposure, b, to the exchange rate one period ahead, and then take out a one-period forward contract of size b. At the end of the first period, we reassess the exposure, and take out a new forward contract.

For simplicity, we assume that the call has the same terms and conditions as the option we just analyzed. We can compute the deltas in our two-period problem as follows. The initial delta is:

$$b_0 = \frac{16.38 - 2.29}{110 - 90} = 0.705.$$

Therefore, at time 0, we sell forward 0.705 units of foreign currency, and lock in the certainty equivalent of the option, $C_0 (1 + r) = 10.23 \times 1.05 = 10.74$ without risk. The next hedge depends on which way the exchange rate has moved. If the rate goes down to node (1,0), then the option is fairly out of the money and becomes less sensitive to the exchange rate. Accordingly, in this case our forward sale is small:

$$b_{1,0} = \frac{4-0}{99-81} = 0.222.$$

In contrast, if the rate goes up to node $(1,1)$, the option moves deep into the money. Accordingly, to hedge the option we need to sell forward a greater amount:

$$b_{1,1} = \frac{26-4}{121-99} = 1.$$

Thus, we start the hedge at time 0 with 0.705 units sold forward. The time-1 hedge will be to sell forward either 1 or 0.222 units of foreign currency, depending on whether the exchange rate moves up or down.

In this section, we have solved a two-period valuation problem by breaking it up into a sequence of one-period problems, each of which can be solved using the one-period risk-adjusted expectations approach. You can already guess that any multiperiod problem can be solved using such a recursive approach. We could write a computer program that calculates the $n + 1$ possible time-n expiration values ("**boundary conditions**," in options-speak). From these expiration values, the program would then derive the n possible call prices, in each of the n nodes of time $n - 1$. Working backwards, we would then compute the $n - 1$ possible call prices in time $n - 2$, and so on, until we ultimately reach the (unique) price at time zero.

7.4.2   A Shortcut for European Options
For European options, it is not strictly necessary to value the call recursively by explicitly computing all of the call's future prices at each node. We can obtain a one-step valuation formula that leads straight from the nth-period payoffs to the time-0 price. To understand this, we shall first generalize the arguments used in Section 7.4.1.

Figure 7.8 shows a general two-period process for the exchange rate, and the corresponding call values ("boundary conditions") at maturity. Using the one-period results that we derived in Section

FIGURE 7.8   General Two-Period Binomial Tree

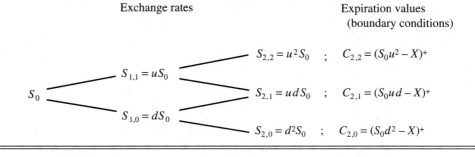

7.2, we can determine what the call value will be for each of the two possible states of time 1, that is, one period before maturity. The valuation is the same as in Equation [7]:

$$C_{1,1} = \frac{qC_{2,2} + (1-q)C_{2,1}}{1+r}. \qquad [8]$$

and

$$C_{1,0} = \frac{qC_{2,1} + (1-q)C_{2,0}}{1+r}. \qquad [9]$$

Since the two possible values of the option at time 1 are known, we can now apply the one-period approach again, to compute the value of the call at time 0:

$$C_0 = \frac{qC_{1,1} + (1-q)C_{1,0}}{1+r}. \qquad [10]$$

Obviously, we can immediately find C_0 in one step by plugging in the two possible time-1 values of Equations [8] and [9] into the time-0 formula, Equation [10]:

$$C_0 = \frac{q\left[qC_{2,2} + (1-q)C_{2,1}\right] + (1-q)\left[qC_{2,1} + (1-q)C_{2,0}\right]}{(1+r)^2} \qquad [11]$$

$$= \frac{q^2 C_{2,2} + 2q(1-q)C_{2,1} + (1-q)^2 C_{2,0}}{(1+r)^2}$$

or, using the expiration values,

$$C_0 = \frac{q^2 (S_0 u^2 - X)^+ + 2q(1-q)(S_0 ud - X)^+ + (1-q)^2 (S_0 d^2 - X)^+}{(1+r)^2}.$$

To make the math less abstract, let us review the numerical example from Section 7.4.1, reproduced in Figure 7.9 with an additional column labeled "Probability." This column lists the risk-adjusted probability of each of the three possible exchange rates at maturity.[7]

---

[7] The factor 2 in $2q(1-q)$ reflects the fact that there are two ways to get to that middle price, namely up-down and down-up, each with probability $q(1-q)$. This number, 2, is the binomial combination factor $[n!/(j!\,(n-j)!)]$ for the special case $n = 2, j = 1$. In general, the combination factor simply counts the number of (equally probable) ways to get to a particular endpoint.

FIGURE 7.9   The Two-Period Binomial Tree and the Risk-Adjusted Probabilities for $\tilde{S}_2$

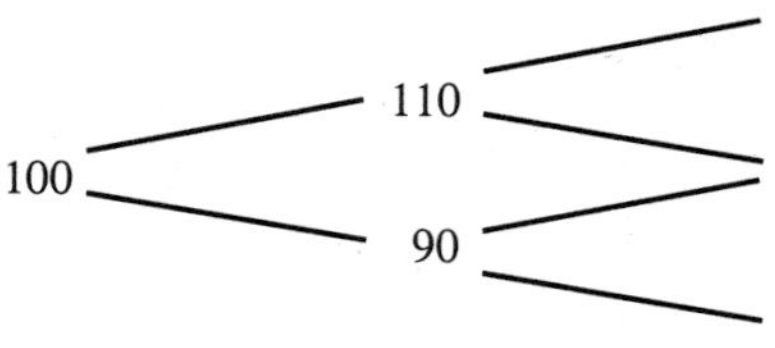

	Probability	Call payoff
121	0.36	26
99	0.48	4
81	0.16	0

Tree: $100 \to 110, 90$; $110 \to 121, 99$; $90 \to 99, 81$.

Probability of ending at node $(2,2) = q^2 = 0.6^2 = 0.36$.

Probability of ending at node $(2,1) = 2\,q\,(1 - q) = 2 \times 0.6 \times 0.4 = 0.48$.

Probability of ending at node $(2,0) = (1 - q)^2 = 0.4^2 = 0.16$.

According to the formula we just derived in Equation [11], we can find the value of a two-period call by simply computing the risk-adjusted expected value of the call,

$$\text{CEQ}_0\,(\tilde{C}_2) = (26 \times 0.36) + (4 \times 0.48) + (0 \times 0.16) = 11.28,$$

and then discounting, over two periods, at the risk-free rate. The resulting call price at time 0 is:

$$C_0 = \frac{11.28}{1.05^2} = 10.23.$$

That is, with our shortcut, we are doing exactly the same calculations as in Section 7.4.1, but more efficiently. The gains in terms of the number of computations saved are, of course, even more impressive when valuing options for more than two periods. This approach is easily generalized. With an n-period model, European options can be valued using only the expiration values and their risk-adjusted probabilities. In the limit, this leads toward the Black-Scholes formula, as we shall show in the next section.

7.5   TOWARD THE BLACK-SCHOLES FORMULA

Recall that the multiperiod model is used primarily to break down the life of a given option into a large number of subperiods, and model the exchange rate at maturity as the result of many small, random price changes. In this section, we show how the multiperiod European option pricing model with a large number of steps (n) approaches a Black-Scholes type solution involving standard normal probabilities. We first derive the general n-period binomial model. Then, we show how the model can be rewritten as an expression involving two binomial probabilities, and we indicate why these probabilities become standard-normal probabilities when the number of steps or subperiods is large. To close this section, we show the links between the final valuation expression, the exposure, and the **delta** or **hedge ratio**.

7.5.1   The General Formula

Figure 7.10 shows the binomial tree as well as the probabilities of each of the final values for three periods. For the valuation of the three-period call, we might again start from the time-1 call values (themselves derived from the two-period problem of Section 7.4.2), and do the final valuation at time 0. That is, we again value the call by recursively applying the certainty-equivalent approach, Equation [7]:

$$C_0 = \frac{qC_{1,1} + (1-q)C_{1,0}}{1+r}.$$

The inputs into this equation are the two time-1 call prices, each of which is the solution of a two-period valuation problem. Equation [11] solves a two-period valuation problem, except that in Equation [11], the two periods start from time 0 rather than from time 1. Thus, after making a trivial adjustment in the subscripts of Equation [11], we can use the following valuation formulas:

$$C_{1,1} = \frac{q^2 C_{3,3} + 2q(1-q)C_{3,2} + (1-q)^2 C_{3,1}}{(1+r)^2}.$$

$$C_{1,0} = \frac{q^2 C_{3,2} + 2q(1-q)C_{3,1} + (1-q)^2 C_{3,0}}{(1+r)^2}.$$

FIGURE 7.10   Three-Period Binomial Tree

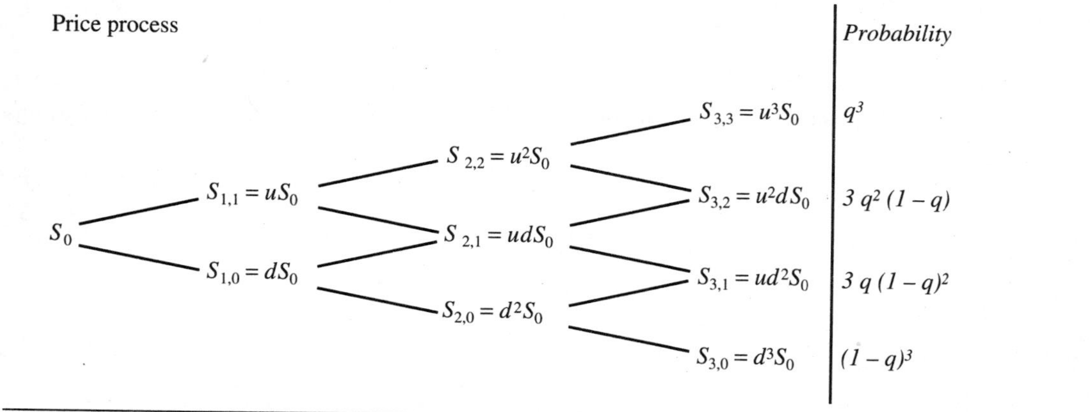

Price process	Probability
$S_{3,3} = u^3 S_0$	q^3
$S_{2,2} = u^2 S_0$	
$S_{1,1} = uS_0$	
$S_{3,2} = u^2 d S_0$	$3q^2(1-q)$
S_0	
$S_{2,1} = ud S_0$	
$S_{1,0} = dS_0$	
$S_{3,1} = ud^2 S_0$	$3q(1-q)^2$
$S_{2,0} = d^2 S_0$	
$S_{3,0} = d^3 S_0$	$(1-q)^3$

Therefore, the time-0 value of the call becomes:

$$C_0 = \frac{q\left[q^2 C_{3,3} + 2q(1-q)C_{3,2} + (1-q)^2 C_{3,1}\right] + (1-q)\left[q^2 C_{3,2} + 2q(1-q)C_{3,1} + (1-q)^2 C_{3,0}\right]}{(1+r)^3}$$

$$= \frac{q^3 C_{3,3} + 3q^2 (1-q)C_{3,2} + 3q(1-q)^2 C_{3,1} + (1-q)^3 C_{3,0}}{(1+r)^3}.$$

The next step is to use the boundary conditions for $\tilde{C}_3$, as follows:

$$C_0 = \frac{q^3 (S_0 u^3 - X)^+ + 3q^2 (1-q)(S_0 u^2 d - X)^+ + 3q(1-q)^2 (S_0 u d^2 - X)^+ + (1-q)^3 (S_0 d^3 - X)^+}{(1+r)^3}.$$

Notice that each term in the numerator contains one of the four possible end values for the call,

$$(S_0 u^j d^{3-j} - X)^+, j = 0, 1, 2, 3.$$

Each of these possible values is weighted by the corresponding probability:

$$q^3, 3q^2 (1-q), 3q (1-q)^2 \text{ or } (1-q)^3.$$

That is, the possible expiration values are weighted by the risk-corrected probabilities of getting 3, 2, 1, and 0 "ups" in three trials, respectively. This insight gives us the n-period generalization. We simply list all possible expiration values,

$$(S_0 u^j d^{n-j} - X)^+ \text{ for } j = 0, 1, \ldots, n$$

and weight each of them by the corresponding risk-adjusted probability (the chance of obtaining j ups in n trials),

$$\binom{n}{j} q^j (1-q)^{n-j},$$

where:

$$\binom{n}{j} = \frac{n!}{j!(n-j)!}$$

equals the number of ways one can combine j up movements and $n - j$ down movements, or the number of distinct paths in the tree that lead to outcome $S_{n,j}$. The sum of all of these probability-weighted possible outcomes gives us the risk-adjusted expected expiration value, $CEQ_0(\tilde{C}_n)$. Finally, to obtain the time-0 value of the call option, this time-0 certainty equivalent of the uncertain final call value is discounted at the risk-free rate of return over n periods:

$$C_0 = \frac{1}{(1+r)^n} \sum_{j=0}^{n} \binom{n}{j} q^j (1-q)^{n-j} (S_0 u^j d^{n-j} - X)^+. \qquad [12]$$

7.5.2   Probabilities under the Normal Distribution

We can simplify the above calculations even further. Many terms in the sum in Equation [12] will be zero, corresponding to out-of-the-money expiration values of the call option. Thus, we can reduce the number of terms by only considering outcomes where the call is in the money. Let a be the minimum number of up movements required for a non-zero expiration value. The following example shows how a is determined.

Example   7.9

Suppose that we model the possible exchange rate changes over the next sixty days by considering four 15-day subperiods, each with $u = 1.05$ and $d = 1/1.05$. The current exchange rate level is $S_0 = 100$, and we are considering call options with $X = 106$. We obtain the tree as shown in Figure 7.11.

- Consider a thirty-day option, that is, an option that expires after subperiod 2. If there are two appreciations, the exchange rate ends at $100\, u^2 = 110.25$, which is above the strike price $X = 106$. If there is one increase and one decrease, the period-2 price is $100\, ud = 100$, at which rate the call is out of the money. Two down movements would obviously make the option end even more out of the money. Thus, for a thirty-day option, we need at least $a = 2$ price increases to finish in the money.

FIGURE 7.11   Determining Minimum Number of Up Changes for the Call to End in-the-Money

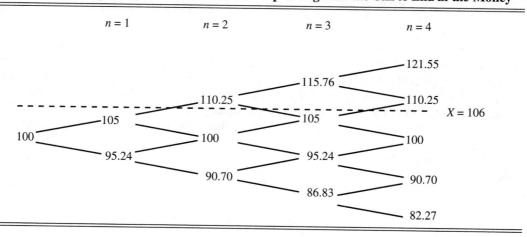

- Next consider a forty-five-day option that expires at $n = 3$. For this option, we need at least $a = 3$ up movements, because fewer than three "ups" result in an exchange rate below $X = 106$.
- For a sixty-day option that expires at $n = 4$, we need at least $a = 3$ increases since, with two "ups," the foreign currency would be worth only $100\, u^2 d^2 = 100$.

Thus, we have defined the number a such that all terms corresponding to $j < a$ are zero. Dropping all of these zero terms from the sum, we can write Equation [12] as follows:

$$C_0 = \frac{1}{(1+r)^n} \sum_{j=a}^{n} \binom{n}{j} q^j (1-q)^{n-j} (S_0 u^j d^{n-j} - X).$$ [13]

In order to facilitate later comparison with the Black-Scholes formula, we split the sum into two parts, one associated with the S_0 terms, and the other with the X terms:

$$C_0 = \frac{S_0}{(1+r)^n} \sum_{j=a}^{n} \binom{n}{j} q^j (1-q)^{n-j} u^j d^{n-j} - \frac{X}{(1+r)^n} \sum_{j=a}^{n} \binom{n}{j} q^j (1-q)^{n-j}.$$

In the expression with S_0, we rewrite the discounting term as follows:

$$\frac{1}{(1+r)^n} = \frac{1}{(1+r^*)^n} \times \left(\frac{1+r^*}{1+r}\right)^n = \frac{1}{(1+r^*)^n} \times \left(\frac{1+r^*}{1+r}\right)^j \times \left(\frac{1+r^*}{1+r}\right)^{n-j}.$$

The result is:

$$C_0 = \frac{S_0}{(1+r^*)^n} \sum_{j=a}^{n} \binom{n}{j} \left[qu\frac{1+r^*}{1+r}\right]^j \left[(1-q)d\frac{1+r^*}{1+r}\right]^{n-j} - \frac{X}{(1+r)^n} \sum_{j=a}^{n} \binom{n}{j} q^j (1-q)^{n-j}.$$ [14]

The expression by which the discounted strike price, $X/(1+r)^n$, is multiplied is a simple binomial probability, notably the (risk-adjusted) chance of observing at least a "ups" in n trials. However, the number a was defined such that, if the number of "ups" exceeds a, then the option ends in the money. Therefore, the probability next to the discounted strike price is simply the risk-adjusted chance of the call finishing in the money. We shall see that there is a similar probability in the Black-Scholes formula.

The summation associated with S_0 looks messier; however, we can again turn this sum into a kind of probability, if we define a new quantity π as follows:

$$\pi = q\left[u\frac{1+r^*}{1+r}\right].$$ [15]

This is the term that is raised to the jth power in the first sum on the right hand side of Equation [14]. The term next to it, with $n - j$ as its exponent, turns out to be simply $1 - \pi$. This can be verified as follows:

$$1 - \pi = 1 - q\left[u\frac{1+r^*}{1+r}\right] = 1 - \frac{\dfrac{1+r}{1+r^*} - d}{u-d}\left[u\frac{1+r^*}{1+r}\right] = 1 - \frac{u - ud\dfrac{1+r^*}{1+r}}{u-d}$$

$$= \frac{(u-d) - u + ud\dfrac{1+r^*}{1+r}}{u-d} = d\frac{u\dfrac{1+r^*}{1+r} - 1}{u-d} = \frac{u - \dfrac{1+r}{1+r^*}}{u-d}d\frac{1+r^*}{1+r}$$

$$= (1-q)d\frac{1+r^*}{1+r}.$$

This is the very factor that is raised to the power $(n - j)$ in expression [14]. Thus, Equation [14] simplifies to:

$$C_0 = \frac{S_0}{(1+r^*)^n} \sum_{j=a}^{n} \binom{n}{j} \pi^j (1-\pi)^{n-j} - \frac{X}{(1+r)^n} \sum_{j=a}^{n} \binom{n}{j} q^j (1-q)^{n-j}.$$

$$[16]$$

In Equation [16], the factor $S_0/(1 + r^*)^n$ is the home currency value of the foreign T-bill that matures together with the option. This factor is multiplied by the chance of obtaining at least a successes if the probability of a success in a single trial is π. Next, we see the discounted strike price, $X/(1 + r)^n$, which is the present value of a domestic T-bill with face value X. This term is multiplied by the chance of obtaining at least a successes if the probability of a success in one trial is q. These two asset prices, the foreign and domestic T-bill, each multiplied by a probability, will show up in the Black-Scholes formula described in the next chapter. A well-known result in statistics is that, if there are many drawings from a binomial distribution, the number of successes (up changes) will be approximately normally distributed. Thus, for large n, the probabilities in Equation [16] can be read from a standard normal table. In the next chapter, we shall show how to do this.

7.5.3   The Delta of an Option
Equation [16] tells us that the option has the same price as a portfolio containing the following two positions:

- $\Delta_0 = \dfrac{1}{(1+r^*)^n} \sum_{j=a}^{n} \binom{n}{j} \pi^j (1-\pi)^{n-j}$ units of foreign currency, each costing S_0 units of home currency; and

- A loan of $\dfrac{X}{(1+r)^n} \sum_{j=a}^{n} \binom{n}{j} q^j (1-q)^{n-j}$ units of domestic currency.

This is one of the many ways to define a replicating portfolio in an n-period model. The number of foreign currency units one needs in order to replicate the option is called the option's **delta** or **hedge ratio**. This last term reflects the familiar fact that hedging and replication are simply two sides of the same coin. If one can replicate an option by buying and investing Δ_0 units of foreign exchange (partly financed by a loan in home currency), then one can hedge the option by borrowing Δ_0 units of foreign exchange for one period—hence, the *hedge ratio* terminology.[8]

7.6   OTHER EUROPEAN-TYPE DERIVATIVE ASSETS

Thus far we have dealt only with the valuation of call options. However, the approach we followed for valuing calls, and more specifically the risk-adjusted probabilities, can be used to price any other derivative asset—such as puts, options on futures, options on forward contracts, and even real investment projects. To understand this, recall that by using the replicating approach, we merely used the risk-adjusted probabilities that are implicit in the forward rate. There is, of course, no reason why these risk-adjusted probabilities should work only for European calls. In fact, we could go through the whole derivation of the basic building block,

$$C_{t,j} = \frac{q\,C_{t+1,j+1} + (1-q)\,C_{t+1,j}}{1+r}, \qquad [17]$$

interpreting C as a general contingent claim rather than as a (European) call. The basic recursive relation would not be affected by this more general interpretation. The particular details about the claim—whether it is a call, a put, or some other contingent claim—are relevant only when the expiration values have to be computed to determine the terminal payoff. Once we have these boundary conditions, we proceed recursively as before.

To illustrate this relation, consider the valuation of a European put option. Our familiar exchange rate tree is reproduced in the left-hand part of Figure 7.12. On the right part of Figure 7.12, we value a European put with strike price $X = 100$. For now, you can ignore the numbers in parentheses. The fact that the claim to be valued is a put option is reflected in the expiration values in the column on the right of Figure 7.12. The boundary values are 0, 1, and 19 (for decreasing values of S_2), whereas they would have been 21, 0, and 0 for a European call option. Once the boundary values have been identified, we proceed as before. Specifically, if at time 1 the exchange rate is 110, we will value the put as the risk-adjusted and discounted expected value of the two possible values at time 2. For instance, if $q = 0.6$ and $r = 5\%$, the price of the option at node (1,1) is

$$P_{1,1} = \frac{(0.6 \times 0) + (0.4 \times 1)}{1.05} = 0.381. \qquad [18]$$

---

[8] An alternative to the spot hedge is a short-term forward hedge. To determine the required position in a long-term call option, we start from the spot hedge. Borrowing Δ_0 units of foreign currency will produce an outflow of $\Delta_0 (1 + r^*)$ units of foreign currency at the end of the subperiod. However, the same contractual outflow can be obtained by selling forward $\Delta_0 (1 + r^*)$ units of foreign exchange one period ahead. This was defined, in Section 7.1, as the option's exposure to exchange rate one period ahead, b. That is, the exposure to the next-period spot rate is $\Delta_0 (1 + r^*)$. As we have seen, this short-term exposure changes every period.

Another interesting alternative to the spot hedge is a long-term forward hedge (or a hedge in the futures markets) that matures at the same time as the option. To determine the required position in a long-term call option, we again start from the spot hedge. Borrowing Δ_0 units of foreign currency will produce an outflow of $\Delta_0 (1 + r^*)^n$ units of foreign currency at the end of the option's life. However, the same contractual outflow can be obtained by selling forward $\Delta_0 (1 + r^*)^n$ units of foreign exchange n period ahead. Thus, $\Delta_0 (1 + r^*)^n$ is the hedge ratio if the life of the forward contract or futures contract that is used as a hedge is the same as the life of the option. Although, with this hedging alternative, we chose a long-term instrument, our positions in this long-term instrument have to be revised every period depending on how deep in or out of the money the option is, and what the remaining life of the option is.

FIGURE 7.12   Valuing a Two-Period European Put Option

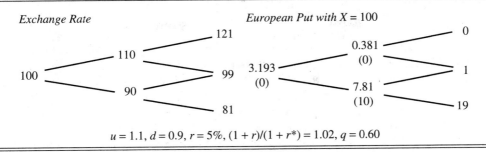

$u = 1.1, d = 0.9, r = 5\%, (1 + r)/(1 + r^*) = 1.02, q = 0.60$

Likewise, if at time 1 we are at node (1,0), we will value the put as

$$P_{1,0} = \frac{(0.6 \times 1) + (0.4 \times 19)}{1.05} = 7.810.$$ [19]

This implies that at time 0

$$P_0 = \frac{(0.6 \times 0.381) + (0.4 \times 7.810)}{1.05} = 3.193.$$ [20]

The above computation illustrates the procedure for the valuation of European puts. In Appendix 7B, we demonstrate that this approach for European options on spot foreign exchange is easily extended to options on foreign T-bills, or options on currency futures. The procedure remains the same.

Step 1. Start from the right-hand-side column, and derive the expiration values of the option.
Step 2. Derive the values in the preceding period as the discounted certainty equivalents.
Step 3. Return to Step 2, and repeat until the initial period is reached.

7.7   AMERICAN OPTIONS

In this section, we consider the valuation of American options. The main difference between American and European options is that, in the valuation of American options, one has to consider the possibility of early exercise. In contrast, European options can be exercised only at maturity. We shall show that when valuing American options, it suffices to add one extra step in the recursive valuation procedure we used for valuing European options. That is,

Step 1. Start from the right-hand-side column, and derive the expiration values of the option.
Step 2. Derive the values *alive* (that is, if the option is not exercised) in the preceding period as the discounted certainty equivalents.
Step 3. *If this value alive is less than the intrinsic value, set the value equal to the intrinsic value.*
Step 4. Return to Step 2, and repeat until the initial period is reached.

Relative to the valuation of European options, Step 3 is new. To demonstrate how the four steps are executed, we first review the valuation of the European put summarized in the right-hand side of

Figure 7.12. Each of the backward computations in Equations [18], [19], or [20] produces a value based on the risk-adjusted expected next-period value, assuming that the option will not be exercised before maturity. For a European option, the absence of early exercise is true by definition. Note that in this example the put has a negative time value at node (1,0); the European option is worth 7.81, while the intrinsic value is 10.[9] The low value of the European option simply reflects the low present value of the expected payoffs at the option's maturity.

With an American option, we can decide to exercise the option at any moment. It is rational to exercise early if the value obtained from immediate exercise is higher than the value of the option if it is kept alive (which is the value derived from the prospect of possible later exercise). Specifically, if we get to node (1,0), we have the following choice:

- If we exercise immediately, we receive the intrinsic value, which equals 10.
- If we decide not to exercise, the value of the option is based on the later payoffs (from possible exercise at time 2, in this example). The present value of later exercise is 7.81.

Thus, immediate exercise will be better than possible exercise at time 2. Since everybody agrees with this, nobody will be willing to sell the put for less than its immediate exercise value. Accordingly, the put's value at node (1,0) will be 10 (the intrinsic value or immediate exercise value), not 7.81 (the value alive).

This change in the put's value at node (1,0) has repercussions for the backward computations; after all, P_0 depends on $P_{1,0}$. Thus, if we compute the new value for P_0, using this revised value $P_{1,0}$, we find:

$$P_0^{am} \text{alive} = \frac{(0.6 \times 0.381) + (0.4 \times 10)}{1.05} = 4.03.$$

As a final check, we compare 4.03 to its intrinsic value in node 0; clearly, at time 0, later exercise (the value of the put if kept alive) is better than immediate exercise (the value "dead"), so we can indeed set $P_0 = 4.03$. We end up with the revised option value tree shown in Figure 7.13 (with the figures in parentheses again indicating the intrinsic values).

To reinforce our understanding of this process, we shall do one more example. In Figure 7.14, we have divided the remaining life of an option into three subperiods and drawn a three-period tree.

FIGURE 7.13   Valuing a Two-Period American Put Option

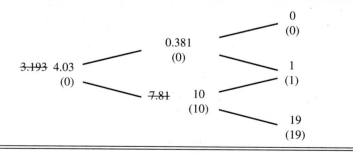

---

[9] In the right-hand side of Figure 7.12, the intrinsic values in each of the nodes are shown in parentheses below the European put values.

FIGURE 7.14   Valuing Three-Period European and American Put Options

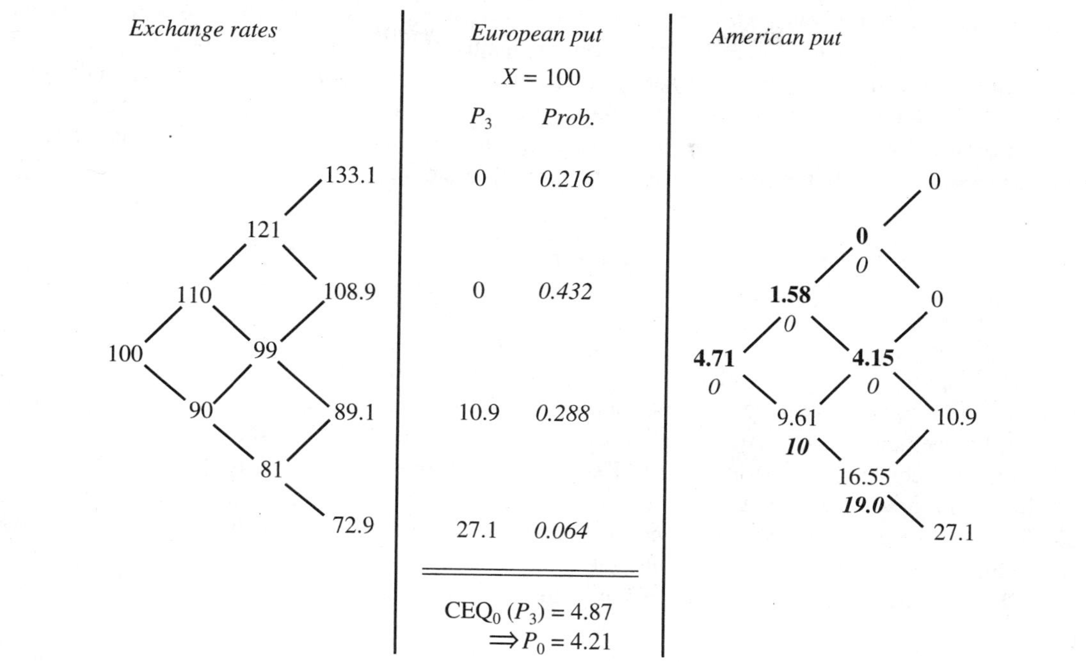

The first column in the middle part, labeled P_3, shows the expiration values for a put with strike price $X = 100$. We use these figures to value a European and an American put.

- The European put is analyzed in the middle part of the figure. Recall that the value of a European put is based solely on its exercise value at expiration, and that we can value such an option by computing the certainty equivalent $CEQ_0(P_3)$ of the time-3 expiration values at the three-period risk-free rate; that is, $P_0 = CEQ_0(P_3)/1.05^3$, where the risk-adjusted expectation can be computed on the basis of the outcomes (in column P_3 of Figure 7.14) and their probabilities (in the column next to P_3). The European put is worth 4.21.
- For the valuation of the American put, we start from the expiration values and compute the values alive one period before. These values alive are printed in the standard (non-italic) font. Next, we compare the value alive to the value dead, which is printed in italic font below the value alive. The larger of these two numbers, printed in boldface, is the one that is relevant for the next recursion. The value of the American put at time 0 is 4.71.

Thus, in this example, the present value of the right to exercise early is 0.50, which represents more than 10 percent of the value of the American option.

7.8   CONCLUSION

In this chapter, we have seen how to value currency options when the underlying asset, the exchange rate, is approximated by a binomial process. The valuation method we have studied is based on arbitrage arguments. One way to value options is to build a portfolio of domestic bonds and forward contracts that exactly *replicates* the short-run price evolution of the option; thus, the *Law of One Price* implies that the option must have the same value as the replicating portfolio. A closely related approach to option valuation is to *hedge* the option against short-term exchange rate changes. Since the resulting portfolio is risk-free, it is easily valued by discounting the known next-period value at the risk-free rate. Both approaches also have an appealing economic interpretation: option prices can be thought of as risk-adjusted expected future values discounted at the risk-free rate, where the information required to compute the risk-adjustment is implicit in the forward premium:

$$C_{t,j} = \frac{q\,C_{t+1,j+1} + (1-q)\,C_{t+1,j}}{(1+r)^{n-j}}, \text{ where } q = \frac{\dfrac{1+r}{1+r^*} - d}{u - d}.$$

Hedging or replication works only in the short run (one period ahead, in the binomial model). That is, with a linear instrument like the forward contract, we can replicate or hedge only the *short-run* price movements of the option. The reason is that, in the longer run, the sensitivity of the option's value to the exchange rate is not constant. Rather, the exposure of the option is changing, depending on how far in-the-money or out-of-the-money the option is, and the length of the option's remaining life. To track the option in the longer run, we need to adjust the forward positions dynamically. We described how one can compute the hedge ratios.

We have also seen that the formula for a European option can be written as:

$$C_0 = \frac{S_0}{(1+r^*)^n} \times [\text{term 1}] - \frac{X}{(1+r)^n} \times [\text{term 2}],$$

where terms 1 and 2 are probabilities that can be read from standard normal tables. These insights will turn up again in the next chapter, where we discuss the Black-Scholes formula for European options. Finally, we have described a simple numerical algorithm to value American options.

The applications of this binomial model stretch beyond the realm of financial assets. We shall use this binomial approach again in Chapter 25 to value investments that contain "operational" options, such as the option to close down a plant or the option to re-enter a market in light of the exchange rate prospects.

QUIZ QUESTIONS

True-False Questions

1. An option's exposure is the sensitivity of a change in the price of the underlying asset to a change in the option's price.
2. The binomial model uses the risk-adjusted probability q as the certainty equivalent for the unknown (true) probability p.
3. The factor u is the risk-adjusted probability of an upward change in the exchange rate.
4. Dynamic hedging assumes that at any discrete moment investors can readjust their portfolio holdings.
5. The delta or exposure of an option is constant.
6. The delta or hedge ratio is the number of calls one needs in order to replicate foreign currency.
7. The probability π is a cumulative probability while $(\sum_{j=a}^{n}) \binom{n}{j} q^j (1-q)^{n-j}$ is a probability for a single drawing.
8. The value of an American option should always be greater than or equal to its intrinsic value.

Multiple-Choice Questions

1. The replication approach to valuing a call option means:
   (a) that the payoffs of the call and its underlying asset are always identical.
   (b) buying forward a number of units of the underlying asset such that the payoffs of the option and the forward purchase are identical.
   (c) buying forward a number of units of the underlying asset such that the payoffs of the option and the forward purchase are identical up to a known amount, which is then replicated in the money market.
   (d) selling the call and buying forward a number of units of the underlying asset such that the payoffs are equal to zero.

2. The forward hedging approach to valuing a call option means:
   (a) buying the call and selling forward a number of units of the underlying asset such that the payoffs are equal to the value of a domestic T-bill.
   (b) buying forward a number of units of the underlying asset such that the payoffs of the option and the forward purchase are identical.
   (c) buying the call and selling forward a number of units of the underlying asset such that the payoffs are identical.
   (d) selling the call and buying forward a number of units of the underlying asset such that the payoffs are equal to zero.

3. To compute the certainty equivalent of the future payoff you need:
   (a) the true probability p.
   (b) the risk-adjusted probability q.
   (c) the expected probability $E(p)$.
   (d) the implied probability of p.

4. As the number of periods in the binomial model increases,

    (a) the resulting probability distribution of the future spot rate becomes bell-shaped.
    (b) the resulting probability distribution of the call price becomes bell-shaped.
    (c) the greater the likelihood that the exchange rate will become negative because price changes are additive.
    (d) the risk-adjusted expected probability q decreases.

Further Quiz Questions

1. If $S_0 = 100$ and the spot rate can increase by 6 percent or decrease by 3 percent, what is the spot rate at node:

    (a) (3,3)?
    (b) (3,2)?
    (c) (3,1)?
    (d) (3,0)?

2. Suppose that the current USD/DEM spot rate is 0.6, the effective risk-free rates of return are $r = 6$ percent and $r^* = 8$ percent, and the spot rate will either increase to 0.62 or decrease to 0.57 at time 1.

    (a) What is the risk-adjusted probability of a spot rate increase? Decrease?
    (b) What is the risk-adjusted expected value of the European call with a strike price of 0.59?
    (c) What is the time-0 value of the call?
    (d) What is the factor u (d) by which the spot rate increases? Decreases?
    (e) What is the option's exposure?
    (f) Would the option's value change if it were American?

3. Repeat the question above using a put with the same strike price, instead of a call.

EXERCISES

1. In the one-period example in Section 7.1.2, how could you make risk-free money if the call were valued at 10 rather than at 19.05?

2. In the same example, how would you change your answer if you discovered that the probability of "up" were 0.1, so that the exchange rate looked grossly overvalued?

3. For the two-period call example in Section 7.7:

    (a) Show the tree of European call values if $X = 90$.
    (b) Compare this with the call's intrinsic values at each node.
    (c) Check whether there is a chance of early exercise if the option were American.

4. Consider a one-period call option on the British pound. Suppose that the current exchange rate is USD/GBP 2, the exercise price is USD/GBP 1.9, the one-period risk-free rate on the USD is 5 percent, and the one-period risk-free rate on the GBP is 10 percent. Suppose that the spot rate can either go up by a factor of 1.1 (to USD/GBP 2.2) or down by 0.9 (to USD/GBP 1.8).

    (a) Write down the two equations that show how one can replicate the cash flow from the option by investing in the foreign currency and borrowing domestically. What is the value of the call option, using the replication approach?
    (b) Compute the risk-neutral probabilities and use these to value the above call option.

5. Suppose that the current spot rate is S_0 = USD/GBP 2 and the one-period interest rates today are r = 1.05 and r^* = 1.10. Also, you are given that in the next period the spot rate will either be USD/GBP 2.2 or USD/GBP 1.8.

   (a) What is the value today of a one-period put option on the GBP that has a strike price of USD/GBP 1.9?
   (b) Suppose that you already hold this put option. If you wish to hedge the payoff from the put, so that the net payoff of your portfolio is independent of the exchange rate, how many additional units of the spot should you buy/sell?

6. In this exercise, we numerically verify that the probabilities derived for European calls also work for other contracts by (i) valuing the contracts starting from the value of a call, and (ii) by checking whether a risk-adjusted probability evaluation provides the same answer.

   Consider the example used in Section 7.4. The data used were $u = 1.1$, $d = 0.9$, $(1 + r) = 1.05$, $(1 + r^*) = 1.0294118$, $S_0 = 100$; for our call, $X = 95$. The tree, including the (risk-adjusted) probabilities for time 2, is reproduced below; ignore the columns added to the right, initially.

DEM T-bill				*Prob.*	Call at 95	Put at 95	Forward at 95
			121	*0.36*	26	0	26
		110					
100			99	*0.48*	4	0	4
		90					
			81	*0.16*	0	14	-14

   (a) Compute the call value using the binomial model.
   (b) Compute the two-period forward rate directly (using Interest Rate Parity), and indirectly (using our risk-adjusted probabilities, that is, as $CEQ_0(\tilde{S}_2)$).
   (c) Compute the present value of an "old" forward purchase struck at $F_{t_0,2}$ = 95 directly (using the formula in Chapter 3), and indirectly (using q).
   (d) Value a European put with $X = 95$ directly (using Put Call Parity), and indirectly (using q).

7. Consider a four-month call option on the British pound. Suppose that the current exchange rate is USD/GBP 1.6, the exercise price is USD/GBP 1.6, the risk-free rate on the USD is 8 percent *p.a.*, the risk free rate on GBP is 11 percent *p.a.*, and the volatility of the spot rate (and the forward rate) is 10 percent. Using the results in Appendix 7A, translate the volatility into an up and down factor (u and d). Then solve the following problems:

   (a) What is the value that you would be willing to pay for this American call option if you used the one-period binomial approach to value it?
   (b) What would you be willing to pay for this option if the volatility were 14.1 percent?

8. Suppose that the spot rate is USD/CAD 0.75 and the volatility of this exchange rate is 4 percent *p.a.* The risk-free rate in the US is 7 percent *p.a.* and in Canada it is 9 percent *p.a.* Suppose that the exercise price is CAD 0.75 and the American put option matures in nine months.

(a) Find the value of this option using the one-period binomial approach.

(b) Find the value of this option using the two-period binomial approach.

9. A foreign currency put option is equivalent to a position in the foreign currency T-bill and a certain amount of borrowing/lending of the home currency. Is your replicating position in the foreign currency T-bill long or short? Why? Do you borrow or lend the home currency? Why?

10. Show that $CEQ_t(\tilde{F}_{T_1,T_2}) = F_{t,T_2}$.

11. What happens to the value of an option when both S_0 and X change by the same factor, holding u, d, r, and r^* constant?

MIND-EXPANDING EXERCISES

1. Below, we reproduce the formula for a European call on foreign exchange with, as its arguments, the characteristics (S_0, u, d) for the exchange rate process:

$$C_0 = \frac{S_0}{(1+r^*)^n} \sum_{j=a}^{n} \binom{n}{j} \left(qu\frac{1+r^*}{1+r} \right)^j \left[(1-q)d\frac{1+r^*}{1+r} \right]^{n-j} - \frac{X}{r_d^n} \sum_{j=a}^{n} \binom{n}{j} q^j (1-q)^{n-j}.$$

As argued in Appendix 7B, a European call on a foreign T-bill (maturing at the same time as the call itself) will have the same final payoff (and, therefore, also the same current value) as the standard currency option. Suppose, however, that you want to obtain a formula that has as its arguments the characteristics of the T-bill process $(V_0, u', d'$, as defined in Appendix 7B). How will the formula look?

2. Below, we reproduce the formula for a European call on foreign exchange with strike price X'', with as its arguments the characteristics (S_0, u, d) for the exchange rate process:

$$C_0 = \frac{S_0}{(1+r^*)^n} \sum_{j=a}^{n} \binom{n}{j} (qu\frac{1+r^*}{1+r})^j \left[(1-q)d\frac{1+r^*}{1+r} \right]^{n-j} - \frac{X''}{r_d^n} \sum_{j=a}^{n} \binom{n}{j} q^j (1-q)^{n-j}.$$

As argued in Appendix 7B, a European call on a futures contract with strike price X'' that matures at the same time as the call itself, will have the same final payoff and, therefore, also the same current value as the standard currency option. Suppose, however, that you want to obtain a formula that has as its arguments the characteristics of the futures process $(f_0, u''$, d'', as defined in Appendix 7B). How will the formula look?

3. Relate the European put formula, (where prob $(j < n; n, x) = \sum_{j=0}^{a-1} \binom{n}{j} x^j (1-x)^{n-j})$,

$$P_0 = \frac{X}{(1+r)^n} \text{Prob}(j < a; n, q) - \frac{S_0}{(1+r^*)^n} \text{Prob}(j < a; n, \pi)$$

to the European call formula and check for Put Call Parity. Recall that j is the (ex ante unknown) number of up changes, and a the minimum number of "ups" required to bring S_T above X.

CHOOSING THE PARAMETERS OF THE BINOMIAL MODEL

In this appendix, we first introduce **continuously compounded returns**, or changes of logs of prices, and compute their mean and variance. We then show how to set the u and d parameters in the geometric binomial model so as to obtain a desired mean and variance for the continuously compounded return on an asset between time 0 and time T (that is, at the end of the nth subperiod).

7A.1 Continuously Compounded Asset Returns

Consider a risky asset with price V_t. A familiar concept is the simple return on the risky asset between periods 0 and n:

$$R_{0,n} = \frac{V_n - V_0}{V_0}.$$

An alternative measure of return is the *continuously compounded* price change after n periods:

$$\rho_{0,n} = \ln \frac{V_n}{V_0} = \ln V_n - \ln V_0.$$

In general, the compounded return $\rho_{0,n}$ and the simple percentage return $R_{0,n}$ are related as follows:

$$\frac{V_n}{V_0} = 1 + R_{0,1} \Leftrightarrow \rho_{0,1} = \ln(1 + R_{0,1}).$$

This formula allows us to compare the two measures of return. You can verify that a simple percentage change is quite close to its continuously compounded counterpart as long as the changes in the price are small.[10]

Example 7A.1

Simple percentage return, $R_{0,n}$	Continuously compounded percentage return, $\rho_{0,n}$
0.001 (0.1%)	$\ln(1.001) = 0.0009995$ (0.09995%)
0.01	$\ln(1.01)\ = 0.009950$
0.05	$\ln(1.05)\ = 0.04879$
0.10	$\ln(1.10)\ = 0.09531$

---

[10] In the limit, they become identical. For example, standard calculus tells us that $\dfrac{dV}{V} = d \ln V$.

Continuously compounded returns are *additive over time*. For example,

$$\rho_{0,2} \equiv \ln\left(\frac{V_2}{V_0}\right) = \ln V_2 - \ln V_0$$

$$= (\ln V_2 - \ln V_1) + (\ln V_1 - \ln V_0) = \ln\left(\frac{V_2}{V_1}\right) + \ln\left(\frac{V_1}{V_0}\right) = \rho_{1,2} + \rho_{0,1}.$$

In other words, with continuously compounded returns, the two-period return is simply the sum of the two period-by-period returns. By analogy, the continuously compounded return over n periods is the sum of each of the n period-by-period continuously compounded returns.

We can now derive the following properties.

7A.2   Limiting Distribution: V_n Is Lognormal

If the period-by-period returns are mutually independent and identically distributed, then the total continuously compounded return over n periods converges to a normal distribution. This follows from the fact that the (continuously compounded) return over n periods is the sum of each of the period-by-period returns. From the **Central Limit Theorem**, a sum of independent and identically distributed random variables is close to normally distributed.[11]

Thus, conditional on V_0, the variable $\ln V_n = \ln V_0 + \rho_{0,n}$ is also normally distributed. If the log of a variable is normally distributed, then the variable itself is said to be lognormally distributed. With a large number of periods and independent returns, the final value V_n converges to a lognormal distribution.[12]

7A.3   Mean and Variance of the *N*-Period Return

In binomial option pricing, we assign values to the binomial parameters u and d so that the distribution has an expected value and variance that matches our empirical estimates. The first step is to identify the link between the parameters of the continuously compounded return and the binomial parameters u and d. The mean of the one-period return is easily found to be

$$E(\rho_{t,t+1}) = p\ln(u) + (1-p)\ln(d), \qquad\qquad\qquad [A1]$$

where p is the probability of an increase in V. The mean of the n-period return equals the mean of a sum of n returns, or the sum of the means. Each of the period-by-period means is given by Equation [A1]. Thus, the sum of these n means is simply n times the period-by-period mean:

$$E(\rho_{0,n}) = n\big[p\ln(u) + (1-p)\ln(d)\big]. \qquad\qquad\qquad [A2]$$

---

[11] We actually need a special version of the Central Limit Theorem. If we simply increase the number of steps and leave (u,d) unchanged, the variance of V_n increases without bound. Thus, any increase in n should be combined with a drop in the price changes so as to keep the variance of the distribution of $\rho_{0,n}$ constant.

[12] If we make the process additive rather than multiplicative, that is, $S_{t+1} = S_t + (u \text{ or } d)$, then the resulting distribution of S_n will be normal rather than lognormal.

The variance of the one-period return is:[13]

$$\text{var}(\rho_{t,t+1}) = \left[p\ln(u)^2 + (1-p)\ln(d)^2\right] - \left[p\ln(u) + (1-p)\ln(d)\right]^2$$

$$= p\ln(u)^2 + (1-p)\ln(d)^2 - p^2\ln(u)^2 - 2p(1-p)\ln(u)\ln(d) - (1-p)^2\ln(d)^2$$

$$= p(1-p)\ln(u)^2 + (1-p)[1-(1-p)]\ln(d)^2 - 2p(1-p)\ln(u)\ln(d)$$

$$= p(1-p)[\ln(u) - \ln(d)]^2.$$

[A3]

Therefore, the n-period variance, being the variance of a sum of n independent returns each having the above variance, is:

$$\text{var}(\rho_{0,n}) = np(1-p)[\ln(u) - \ln(d)]^2.$$

[A4]

7A.4   Choosing (u,d) and $(p, 1-p)$ To Achieve a Desired Distribution

We are now ready to set the parameters u and d such that, for a given number of subperiods, this choice produces a desired mean and variance for the time-T spot rate.

Let $T - t$ = length of the total period, in years. For example, $T - t = 0.5$ years.

Let $h = \dfrac{T-t}{n}$ = length of each of the n subperiods. For example, if $n = 180$, then $h = \dfrac{T-t}{180} = \dfrac{1}{360}$ years.

Then Equations [A2] and [A4] become:

$$E(\rho_{0,n}) = \frac{T-t}{h}[p\ln(u) + (1-p)\ln(d)], \text{ and}$$

[A5]

$$\text{var}(\rho_{0,n}) = \frac{T-t}{h}p(1-p)[\ln(u) - \ln(d)]^2.$$

[A6]

Clearly, if n, u, and d were chosen at random, we might end up with a very unreasonable distribution at time T (the nth subperiod). The issue therefore is how we can "fit" the parameters to get some desired annual mean and variance, μ and σ^2, of the change in the log exchange rate. The answer is to choose the change parameters and the probabilities as follows:

$$\ln(u) = \sigma\sqrt{h} \text{ and } \ln(d) = -\sigma\sqrt{h}.$$

[A7a]

(that is, set $u = 1/d = e^{\sigma\sqrt{h}}$),[14] and

$$p = \frac{1}{2} + \frac{\mu\sqrt{h}}{2\sigma}, \quad (1-p) = \frac{1}{2} - \frac{\mu\sqrt{h}}{2\sigma}.$$

[A7b]

---

[13] We use the result $E[(y - E(y))^2] = E[y^2 - 2\,y\,E(y) + (E(y))^2] = E(y^2) - 2\,E(y)\,E(y) + (E(y))^2 = E(y^2) - (E(y))^2$.

[14] There are two constraints (one on the mean, one on the variance), and three parameters: u, d, and p. Therefore, we have to impose a third constraint (or, alternatively, we have to eliminate one parameter). The additional constraint, $d = 1/u$, ensures that, after one up and one down, the price is back at its original level.

We verify that these solutions satisfy the prespecified mean and variance, as follows. If Equation [A7] holds, the one-period return has mean:

$$E(\rho_{t,t+1}) = p\ln(u) + (1-p)\ln(d)$$
$$= \sigma\sqrt{h}\,[\,p - (1-p)\,]$$
$$= \sigma\sqrt{h}\,(2p-1) = \sigma\sqrt{h}\left(1 + \frac{\mu\sqrt{h}}{\sigma} - 1\right)$$
$$= \mu h = \mu\frac{T-t}{n}.$$

Thus, the total return over n periods has mean:

$$E(\rho_{0,n}) = n \times \left(\mu\frac{T-t}{n}\right) = \mu(T-t),$$

where μ is the expected continuously compounded return *per annum,* and $(T-t)$ is the horizon (in years). Likewise, the one-period return's variance, under Equation [A7], becomes

$$\mathrm{var}(\rho_{t,t+1}) = p\ln(u)^2 + (1-p)\ln(d)^2 - \mu^2 h^2,$$

or, as $\ln(u)^2 = \ln(d)^2 = \sigma^2 h$,

$$= \sigma^2 h[\,p + (1-p)\,] - \mu^2 h^2 = (\sigma^2 - \mu^2 h)h = (\sigma^2 - \mu^2 h)\frac{T-t}{n}.$$

When h is sufficiently small, the variance of the total n-period return converges to $\sigma^2(T-t)$:[15]

---

15 This gives the mean and the variance as a function of the true probability, p. The risk-adjusted probability, q, is not quite the same, and will produce a slightly different variance. Replacing p by q means replacing the true expected percentage change, μ, by the forward premium: $(r-r^*)/(1+r^*)$. For short periods,

$$p = \frac{1}{2} + \mu\frac{\sqrt{h}}{2\sigma} \quad \text{and} \quad q = \frac{1}{2} + \frac{r-r^*}{1+r^*}\frac{\sqrt{h}}{2\sigma}$$

will be close to each other and to $1/2$. However, around a probability of $1/2$ the variance is virtually unaffected by a small change in the probability:

$$\frac{\partial\,\mathrm{var}(\rho_{0,n})}{\partial p} = \frac{\partial\{np(1-p)[\ln(u)-\ln(d)]^2\}}{\partial p} = n(1-2p)[\ln(u)-\ln(d)]^2 = 0$$

for $p = 1/2$. Thus, for small periods ($h \to 0$) the variance is hardly affected by the definition of the probability as either p or as q, because both p and q are extremely close to $1/2$.

$$\text{var}(\rho_{0,n}) = (\sigma^2 - \mu^2 h)(T - t) \to \sigma^2 (T - t), \ h \text{ small.}$$

Lastly, one needs to translate the *p.a.* risk-free interest rate into a risk-free return appropriate for a period of h years. To do this, we use the principles outlined in the appendix to Chapter 3. The standard approach is to take the interest rate for the option's maturity and translate this into a compound rate of return per subperiod (of length h).

Example   7A.2

Let $T - t = 0.5$, and let the 180-day simple interest rate be 10 percent *p.a.* That is, the effective risk-free return over 180 days is 5 percent. We divide the option's life into thirty subperiods of six days each. The problem then is to find a risk-free six-daily return r such that $(1 + r)^{30} = 1.05$. This yields

$$r = 1.05^{1/30} - 1 = \ 0.1627662\%.$$

OPTIONS ON FOREIGN CURRENCY T-BILLS AND ON CURRENCY FUTURES

We can extend our insights on the valuation of options on spot exchange to options on foreign T-bills and options on currency futures. The point that we want to make is that, for European options, these models differ from the option on the "cash" only in terms of notation and that, for both European and American options, the risk-adjusted probability is the same regardless of the underlying asset. If the risk-adjusted probabilities, as reported in standard articles or textbooks, seem to differ depending on whether the option is on the cash, or on a T-bill, or on a currency futures, this is because the notation in the literature cannot be carried over from one model to the other.

To understand that there must be a link between options on currency, options on foreign T-bills, and options on currency futures, we consider the following call options:

- A European call on one unit of foreign exchange, maturing at n and with strike price X. The payoff from this option after the nth subperiod is:

$$\tilde{C}_n = \text{Max}(\tilde{S}_n - X, 0). \tag{B1}$$

- A European call, maturing at n and with strike price X, on a unit foreign currency T-bill that also matures at n. The payoff from this option is also given by Equation [B1] because the bill is worth one unit of foreign exchange after the nth subperiod.
- A European call, maturing after the nth subperiod with strike price X, on a forward contract with the same time to maturity. Exercising the call means that you become the holder of a maturing forward purchase contract with initiation forward price X. Because, in period n, the "old" contract is worth $S_n - X$, and because exercising will occur only if the contract has a positive value, the option's payoff is the same as for the other type of options.

Clearly, all of these European options must have the same value since they have the same payoffs at the maturity date. Often, there is confusion about this because, in the literature, one often uses the same notation, u and d, to indicate the changes in the spot rate, the futures price, and the price of non-dividend-paying assets like the foreign currency T-bill. The result of this notational inconsistency is that the formula for the risk-adjusted probability looks different depending on whether one considers options on foreign exchange, on non-dividend-paying assets like the foreign T-bill, or on futures. To obtain a consistent treatment, we need only to realize that the jumps (u and d) for the three alternative underlying processes are related but different. Once one accounts for that aspect, the models become perfectly compatible.

7B.1 The Relationship between the Change Factors

Consider a foreign currency T-bill, which is like a non-dividend-paying stock in that its total return consists entirely of capital gains. The T-bill's price in units of home currency in the t-th subperiod, V_t, equals $S_t / (1+r^*)^{n-t}$. So its price change is

$$\frac{V_{t+1}}{V_t} = \frac{\dfrac{S_{t+1}}{(1+r^*)^{n-(t+1)}}}{\dfrac{S_t}{(1+r^*)^{n-t}}} = \frac{S_{t+1}}{S_t}(1+r^*).$$

The change in S could be either up or down, indicated by u or d; thus, the changes in the T-bill price are either $u\,(1+r^*)$ or $d\,(1+r^*)$. Let us denote these changes as u' and d'. Thus, the up and down factors for the foreign T-bill process are

$$u' = u(1+r^*) \text{ and } d' = d(1+r^*). \tag{B2}$$

The relationship is similar for forward rates or currency futures prices.[16] The futures price at time t for delivery in subperiod n is

$$f_t = S_t \left(\frac{1+r}{1+r^*} \right)^{n-t}.$$

Thus, the change in the futures price is

$$\frac{f_{t+1}}{f_t} = \frac{S_{t+1} \left(\dfrac{1+r}{1+r^*} \right)^{n-(t+1)}}{S_t \left(\dfrac{1+r}{1+r^*} \right)^{n-t}} = \frac{S_{t+1}}{S_t}\left(\frac{1+r^*}{1+r} \right).$$

Again, a change in S could be either u or d; therefore, the change in the futures price is either

$$u\frac{1+r^*}{1+r} \text{ or } d\frac{1+r^*}{1+r}.$$

Let us denote these changes as u'' and d''. We have found that the up and down factors for the futures price process are

$$u'' = u\frac{1+r^*}{1+r} \text{ and } d'' = d\frac{1+r^*}{1+r}. \tag{B3}$$

---

[16] In the logic of the binomial model, forward and futures prices are identical because interest rates are assumed to be known in advance. See Chapter 5 for a discussion of the link between forward and futures prices.

FIGURE 7B.1   Relationship between the Binomial Trees for Spot Exchange Rates, T-bill Prices, and Forward Exchange Rates

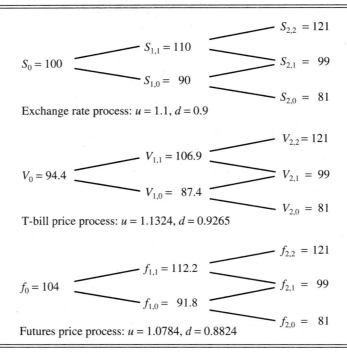

Exchange rate process: $u = 1.1$, $d = 0.9$

T-bill price process: $u = 1.1324$, $d = 0.9265$

Futures price process: $u = 1.0784$, $d = 0.8824$

In Example 7B.1, we illustrate the links between the trees for the three different processes we are considering, and between the corresponding sets of change parameters.

Example   7B.1

In the top part of Figure 7B.1, we reproduce our familiar exchange rate tree from Figure 7.7. Recall that $(1 + r) = 1.05$ and $(1 + r^*) = 1.0294118$. Below the process for the exchange rate, we reproduce the corresponding trees for T-bills and futures prices, by directly computing the prices in the following manner:

- For the T-bill price we use $V_0 = \dfrac{S_0}{(1+r^*)^2}$, $V_1 = \dfrac{S_1}{1+r^*}$, and $V_2 = S_2$.

- For the futures price we use $f_0 = S_0\left(\dfrac{1+r}{1+r^*}\right)^2$, $f_1 = S_1\dfrac{1+r}{1+r^*}$, and $f_2 = S_2$.

We can now illustrate the links between the up and down factors (up to the effects of price rounding):

- T-bill price:

$$u' = \frac{V_{1,1}}{V_0} = \frac{106.7}{94.4} = 1.13 \quad = u(1+r^*) = 1.1 \times 1.0294$$

$$d' = \frac{V_{1,1}}{V_0} = \frac{87.4}{94.4} = 0.93 \quad = d(1+r^*) = 0.9 \times 1.0294.$$

- Futures price:

$$u'' = \frac{f_{1,1}}{f_0} = \frac{112.2}{104} = 1.08 \quad = u\frac{1+r^*}{1+r} = 1.1 \times \frac{1.0294}{1.05}$$

$$d'' = \frac{f_{1,1}}{f_0} = \frac{91.8}{104} = 0.88 \quad = d\frac{1+r^*}{1+r} = 0.9 \times \frac{1.0294}{1.05}.$$

7B.2   The Adjusted Expressions for q

Now that we have discovered the relationship between the processes for the exchange rate, the T-bill, and the futures price, we can derive q in terms of any set of parameters (u and d, or u' and d', or u'' and d''). First, consider the foreign T-bill. It is important to understand that the probabilities of the T-bill going up and of S going up must be the same, because any jump in S is reflected in V. So we can write q in terms of u' and d' as:

$$q \equiv \frac{\frac{1+r}{1+r^*} - d}{u - d} = \frac{(1+r) - d(1+r^*)}{u(1+r^*) - d(1+r^*)} = \frac{(1+r) - d'}{u' - d'}.$$

This is the formula typically derived for non-dividend-paying assets, like a non-dividend-paying stock or a foreign T-bill—except that most articles or textbooks denote the up and down factors for the non-dividend-paying asset by u and d instead of by u' and d'. Conversely, as soon as one realizes that the u and d for the non-dividend-paying asset are not the same as the u and d for the exchange rate, there no longer is a contradiction between the two versions of the formula for q.

Now consider the futures price as the underlying process. Since uncertainty about the futures price is due to uncertainty about S, the probabilities of the futures price going up and of S going up must be the same. So we can write q in terms of u'' and d'' as:

$$q = \frac{\frac{1+r}{1+r^*} - d}{u - d} = \frac{1 - d\frac{1+r^*}{1+r}}{u\frac{1+r^*}{1+r} - d\frac{1+r^*}{1+r}} = \frac{1 - d''}{u'' - d''}$$

which is the formula typically derived for options on futures—except that most articles or textbooks denote the up and down factors for the futures price by u and d instead of by u'' and d''. In short, it does not matter what formula we use to compute q, as long as we are consistent. For instance, we should not use the T-bill formula, $q = [(1 + r) - d']/(u' - d')$, if the jump sizes used are those from the spot exchange rate process, u and d.

The fact that there is only one risk-adjusted probability for the processes of the spot exchange rate, the foreign T-bill, and the futures price implies that European options on each of these processes have the same value. For American options, the option on foreign currency, futures, and T-bills will all have different values. This difference in values is *not* due to a different probability of an up-movement; rather, the difference arises because the *early* exercise values are not the same for the three options. For instance, if you exercise a call option at time t, the payoffs are as follows:

- $S_t - X$ for the currency call,

- $f_t - X = S_t \left(\dfrac{1+r}{1+r^*} \right)^{T-t} - X$ for the call on the futures, and

- $V_t - X = \dfrac{S_t}{(1+r^*)^{T-t}} - X$ for the T-bill.

8

PRICING EUROPEAN OPTIONS: THE LOGNORMAL MODEL

In the binomial option pricing model discussed in the preceding chapter, the exchange rate process was modeled as a sequence of discrete changes that occur at discrete points in time. In contrast, the mathematical context in which Black and Scholes (1973) and Merton (1973) developed their seminal option pricing model is one where time changes *continuously,* and the exchange rate (or, in the original version, the stock price), S, follows a *continuous* path. However, the logic underlying the Black-Scholes-Merton option pricing model and its adapted versions for valuing foreign currency options is similar to the logic underlying the binomial model.[1]

In the first section of this chapter, we compare the assumptions of the continuous-time model with those of the binomial model. In Section 8.2, we outline an option pricing model in a setting where time is discrete but where the exchange rate at the option's expiration date has the same continuous ("lognormal") distribution as in the Black-Scholes-Merton model. The model that we describe—developed by Samuelson (1967), Rubinstein (1976), and Brennan (1979)—does not require the special mathematics of the original derivation. In Section 8.3, we apply the model to value and hedge a European call option. The pricing of other options is described in the fourth section. The final section presents the conclusions. In Appendix 8A, we derive some useful properties of the lognormal distribution. Finally, we present the theoretical underpinnings for the continuous-time model in Appendix 8B.

---

[1] The currency option pricing models were developed by Garman and Kohlhagen (1983) and Grabbe (1983).

8.1   ASSUMPTIONS OF THE CONTINUOUS-TIME OPTION PRICING MODEL

The hedging approach used to value options in the preceding chapter was based on the assumption that investors can hedge the option's value by adding $(-)\Delta$ units of the underlying asset to their portfolios.[2] The value of the option can then be deduced by valuing the risk-free hedged portfolio and subtracting the cost of the hedge. The binomial version of this approach was first published by Rendleman and Bartter (1979), Sharpe (1978), and Cox, Ross, and Rubinstein (1979). However, the technique of forming a risk-free portfolio by combining call options with the asset that underlies the option was discovered by Black and Scholes (1972, 1973) and Merton (1973). The Black-Scholes-Merton assumption that time and the underlying asset price are continuous rather than discrete affects the precise details of the hedging strategy. For example, in a continuous setting the delta of the call is a partial derivative $(\partial C/\partial S)$ rather than the slope of a line drawn through two discrete points, and the hedged call is risk free only for infinitesimally short periods because all variables change each instant. However, the fundamental no-arbitrage logic is the same as in a discrete model: a hedged portfolio, being risk free over a short interval of time, should earn the risk-free rate of return over that interval. Black and Scholes wrote this condition down as a partial differential equation, which they then solved. (See Appendix 8B for the technical details.) The assumptions of the Black-Scholes-Merton model are given below:

1. *The process for the exchange rate is continuous.* There are no sudden changes in the exchange rate (or, in the original model, the stock price). In graphical terms, this means that you can draw the time path of the spot rate without lifting your pen from the paper.
2. *The value of the option is a continuous and twice differentiable function of the underlying process S.* Assumptions 1 and 2 are necessary in order for the hedging (or replication) approach to work. Hedging works only if one can predict how a small change in the spot rate affects the value of the call option. Assumption 1 ensures that, over a short time interval, the changes in the exchange rate will be small. Assumption 2 implies that the effect of a small change in the spot rate on the call price (the call's exposure) is always well-defined.
3. *Trading is continuous,* so that the size of the hedge can be adjusted continuously to changes in the exposure (caused by changes in S and in the option's life). For instance, you could not invoke the Black-Scholes-Merton logic for the valuation of options on non-traded assets, or on exchange rates that are traded through monthly auctions. The assumption of continuous trading corresponds to the assumption in the binomial model that you can rebalance your hedge in every subperiod.
4. *The distribution of the percentage changes in the exchange is lognormal*—or, the continuously compounded change in the spot rate is normally distributed. Interested students can read about the properties of this distribution in Appendix 8A. This assumption corresponds to the binomial model's assumption that changes are multiplicative rather than additive.[3]

---

2 Recall, from Chapter 7, that the delta (Δ) represents the number of foreign currency units that have to be borrowed in order to hedge the option. The link between the delta and the exposure is explained in footnote 8 to Section 7.5.3.

3 In the empirical literature, there is no consensus as to whether or not distributions of security prices satisfy the assumption of normality. Most studies find that empirical distributions over, say, ten years of data, are too peaked in the center and too fat-tailed to be distributed normally. However, it is not clear to what extent this phenomenon is due to changing variances rather than to period-by-period non-normality. If you mix normal distributions having different standard deviations, you are bound to find a fat-tailed, peaked overall distribution.

5. *The risk-free rate(s) and the variance of the ("continuously compounded") percentage changes in the spot rate are constant over the option's life.* This corresponds to the assumption in the binomial model that u, d, r, and r^* are constant over time. Neither approach handles stochastic changes in the *volatility* of $\tilde{S}$.[4]

8.2 A DISCRETE-TIME DERIVATION OF THE CONTINUOUS-TIME MODEL

The original Black-Scholes-Merton approach to option pricing requires a special type of calculus to deal with the fact that the changes in the underlying asset price are not only continuous but also random. Thus, we prefer to discuss this method in an appendix (Appendix 8B). An alternative, and simpler, approach to deriving the Black-Scholes-Merton result is based on early work by Samuelson (1967) and Rubinstein (1976), which was later generalized by Brennan (1979). The Samuelson-Rubinstein-Brennan model is set in discrete time but, like the Black-Scholes-Merton model, it assumes that the spot rate at time T is lognormal. This approach can be summarized in three steps (which are similar to the three steps in the preceding chapter):

1. Compute the expected value of the option at maturity, $E_t(\tilde{C}_T)$.
2. Correct this expected value for risk. That is, compute the risk-adjusted expectation $CEQ_t(\tilde{C}_T)$ from $E_t(\tilde{C}_T)$, by replacing $E_t(\tilde{S}_T)$ with its certainty-equivalent value, $CEQ_t(\tilde{S}_T) = F_{t,T}$.
3. Discount the risk-adjusted expected future value at the risk-free rate to determine the call's value at time t, C_t. That is,

$$C_t = \frac{CEQ_t(\tilde{C}_T)}{1 + r_{t,T}}.$$ [1]

This approach to option pricing, often called the risk-neutral or risk-adjusted approach, is mathematically less complicated and is closer to the classical valuation models.[5] After describing the details of this model we shall explain how the model can be used to hedge an option.

8.2.1 Step 1: Computing the Expected Value of a Call Option

To illustrate the approach, we initially consider an example where the distribution of the exchange rate at time T is discrete. We then show how to go from this discrete setting to the case where the exchange rate has a continuous distribution.

---

[4] If the interest rates and the jumps (u, d) change but are known in advance, we can determine what q will be at each node, and still use the risk-adjusted backward valuation approach to value options. In the continuous case, the same holds, as Merton (1973) showed. Merton (1973) and Grabbe (1983) derived option pricing models where the *interest rates* can vary stochastically. Hull and White (1987) derive a model with stochastic changes in volatility.

[5] In standard capital budgeting, Steps 2 and 3 are usually combined into one by discounting at a risk-adjusted cost of capital. Early option pricing models (see, for example, Smith (1976) for a review) also attempted such a two-step approach, but failed to come up with the correct risk-adjusted discount rate. The problem is that, even if a stock has a constant risk (measured by, for example, its beta), an option's risk changes all of the time. A deep out-of-the-money option, for instance, hardly moves when the stock price changes, while there is an almost one-to-one relationship between call and stock-price changes for deep in-the-money calls. Thus, if the option's risk changes continuously and unpredictably, we cannot come up with *the* appropriate discount rate. The three-step approach overcomes this problem.

An Example with Discrete Spot Rates

Consider the example in Figure 8.1 for a call on DEM with strike price $X = 43$ (all exchange rates are to be interpreted as UScents/DEM). We first list the possible exchange rates at expiration and the probability of each outcome (that is, we specify the distribution function).[6] We then determine the corresponding expiration values for the call. Note that the event "$\tilde{C}_T = 3$" is the same as the event "$\tilde{S}_T = 46$"; that is, $\tilde{C}_T = 3$ if and only if $\tilde{S}_T = 46$. Thus, the probability of $\tilde{C}_T = 3$ is the same as the probability of $\tilde{S}_T = 46$. We can make analogous statements for each of the other pairs $(\tilde{S}_T, \tilde{C}_T)$. Therefore, we can easily find the distribution function of $\tilde{C}_T$. This distribution is shown in the lower half of Figure 8.1. From the distribution of $\tilde{C}_T$, we then compute $E_t(\tilde{C}_T)$ by adding all possible option values, $\tilde{C}_T = \text{Max}(\tilde{S}_T - X, 0)$, after weighting them with the corresponding probability:

$$E_t(\tilde{C}_T) = 0 + 0 + \ldots + (1 \times 0.15) + (2 \times 0.1) + (3 \times 0.05) + (4 \times 0) = 0.5. \qquad [2]$$

Clearly, we do not have to look at the possible expiration values corresponding to $\tilde{S}_T < X$, because these expiration values are zero. Thus, we are basically summing all possible products $(\tilde{S}_T - X) \times \text{prob}_{t,T}(\tilde{S}_T)$ over the range $\tilde{S}_T \geq 43$ (where 43 is the strike price).[7] The next step is to split the sum into two parts. These parts arise naturally if we go back to the initial cash flows and explicitly write down how the call's expiration values were computed. For example, the call's expiration value when $\tilde{S}_T = 44$ was computed as $44 - 43$ (where 43 is the strike price), the expiration value $\tilde{C}_T = 2$ when $\tilde{S}_T = 45$ was computed as $45 - 43$, and so on. Thus, the expected value can be written as:

$$E_t(\tilde{C}_T) = (43 - 43) \times 0.20 + (44 - 43) \times 0.15 + (45 - 43) \times 0.1 + (46 - 43) \times 0.05. \qquad [3]$$

We now group all terms involving the exchange rate values (43, 44, . . .) together into one term, and all terms that involve the strike price (43) into a second term:

$$E_t(\tilde{C}_T) = [(43 \times 0.20) + (44 \times 0.15) + (45 \times 0.1) + (46 \times 0.05)]$$
$$-43 \times [0.20 + 0.15 + 0.1 + 0.05]. \qquad [4]$$

FIGURE 8.1   Deriving the Probability Distribution of $\tilde{C}_T$ from That of $\tilde{S}_T$

$\tilde{S}_T$ may be	38	39	40	41	42	43	44	45	46	47
with $\text{prob}_{t,T}$	0	0.05	0.10	0.15	0.20	0.20	0.15	0.10	0.05	0
then $\tilde{C}_T = (\tilde{S}_T - X)^+ = 0$	0	0	0	0	0	0	1	2	3	4
with $\text{prob}_{t,T}$	0	0.05	0.10	0.15	0.20	0.20	0.15	0.10	0.05	0

---

[6] Any such distribution function is conditional on time t information and depends on the horizon (the time to maturity of the option). We would use a more dispersed distribution for more distant horizons T; and if the current spot value moves (or another relevant piece of information changes), we would revise the distribution downwards or upwards and, in general, also change the probabilities.

[7] In our simple *discrete* distribution example, we could have dropped the case of $S_T = 43$ too; but, with *continuous* distributions, we do have to start as of 43, since the first profitable S_T is infinitesimally close to 43. Therefore, we consider all cases starting from $S_T = 43$.

In symbols, the above computation can be summarized as follows:

$$E_t(\tilde{C}_T) = \sum_{S_T=X}^{\infty} S_T \times \text{Prob}_{t,T}(S_T) - X \times \sum_{S_T=X}^{\infty} \text{Prob}_{t,T}(S_T) \qquad [5]$$

$$= [\text{Sum } A] - X \times [\text{Sum } B]. \qquad [6]$$

The first term, labeled "Sum A," can be called a **partial mean**. It is an expected value where only part of the range of possible outcomes has been used. The partial mean, in our example, is 22.[8] "Sum B" is the probability that the exchange rate will be at least 43. This probability, in our example, is exactly 50 percent. The expected value of the call, then, is $22 - (43 \times 0.50) = 0.5$.

The Expected Call Value When the Spot Rate Is Distributed Lognormally

The procedure for computing the expected value of a call with a continuous distribution for the exchange rate is analogous. Instead of summing, we integrate; and, instead of using discrete probabilities, we use $f(S_T)\,dS_T$, where $f(S_T)$ is the density function. We assume that S_T is distributed lognormally, that is, the natural logarithm of $\tilde{S}_T$ is normally distributed. The mean of $\ln\tilde{S}_T$ is denoted by $\mu_{t,T}$, and the standard deviation of $\ln\tilde{S}_T$ is denoted by $\sigma_{t,T}$.[9]

$$E_t(\tilde{C}_T) = \int_X^{\infty} S_T f(\tilde{S}_T; \mu_{t,T}, \sigma_{t,T})\,dS_T - X\int_X^{\infty} f(S_T; \mu_{t,T}, \sigma_{t,T})\,dS_T \qquad [7]$$

$$= [\text{Integral } A] - X \times [\text{Integral } B].$$

Since the details that follow are somewhat technical, we refer the mathematically interested reader to Appendix 8A for the details of the solution of Equation [7]. This solution is:

$$E_t(\tilde{C}_T) = E_t(\tilde{S}_T)N(d_1') - XN(d_2') \qquad [8]$$

where $N(d_i')$ denotes the cumulative standard normal probability, that is, the probability that a standard normal variate z is below or equal to d_i', and:

$$d_1' = \frac{\ln\dfrac{E_t(\tilde{S}_T)}{X} + \dfrac{1}{2}\sigma_{t,T}^2}{\sigma_{t,T}}, \qquad [9a]$$

---

[8] The fact that this partial mean is not at all of the order of magnitude of 43 to 46 illustrates that the partial mean is not the conditional expected value (the best forecast you can make, if you know that $S_T \geq 43$). The conditional expectation of S_T is

$$E_t(S_T|S_T \geq 43) = \frac{\text{partial mean}}{\text{Prob}(S_T \geq 43)} = 44.$$

[9] The conditional standard deviation for horizon T has to be interpreted as the standard deviation of the continuously compounded return. Indeed, conditional on time-t information,

$$\text{var}_t\left(\ln\frac{S_T}{S_t}\right) = \text{var}_t(\ln S_T) - \text{var}_t(\ln S_t) = \text{var}_t(\ln S_T)$$

because S_t is known at time t.

$$d_2' = \frac{\ln \dfrac{E_t(\tilde{S}_T)}{X} - \dfrac{1}{2}\sigma_{t,T}^2}{\sigma_{t,T}} = d_1' - \sigma_{t,T}.$$
[9b]

The interpretation of solution [8] is analogous to the interpretation of its discrete counterpart, Equation [6]. That is, Integral B is the probability that the call will expire in the money, and Integral A is the partial mean of $\tilde{S}_T$, the expected value where only the range $\tilde{S}_T \geq X$ is used rather than all possible values of $\tilde{S}_T$. We see that, in order to compute the expected value of the call option at expiration, we have to know $E_t(\tilde{S}_T)$. However, the market's expectation of the future spot rate is not observable. Fortunately, the risk-correction procedure in the second step of our calculations solves this problem.

8.2.2   Step 2: Correcting the Call's Expected Expiration Value for Risk

We have just expressed $E_t(\tilde{C}_T)$ as a function of two parameters of the distribution, $E_t(\tilde{S}_T)$ (which itself depends on $\mu_{t,T}$ and $\sigma_{t,T}$, the mean and standard deviation of the log of $\tilde{S}_T$), and $\sigma_{t,T}$. It can be shown that, under some conditions, the appropriate risk adjustment is done by replacing $E_t(\tilde{S}_T)$ by $F_{t,T} =$ $CEQ_t(\tilde{S}_T)$, the risk-adjusted mean or certainty equivalent of the future spot rate.[10,11] The risk-adjusted expectation of the call's expiration value, therefore, is:

$$CEQ_t(\tilde{C}_T) = F_{t,T}N(d_1) - XN(d_2)$$
[10]

with

$$d_1 = \frac{\ln \dfrac{F_{t,T}}{X} + \dfrac{1}{2}\sigma_{t,T}^2}{\sigma_{t,T}},$$
[11a]

$$d_2 = d_1 - \sigma_{t,T}.$$
[11b]

8.2.3   Step 3: Discounting the Risk-Adjusted Expiration Value of the Call

We obtain the present value of the call option by discounting the risk-adjusted expected terminal value of the call at the risk-free rate. That is, we divide $CEQ_t(\tilde{C}_T)$ by $(1 + r_{t,T})$,

$$C_t = \frac{CEQ_t(\tilde{C}_T)}{1 + r_{t,T}}$$

$$= \frac{F_{t,T}}{1 + r_{t,T}} N(d_1) - \frac{X}{1 + r_{t,T}} N(d_2).$$
[12]

---

[10] For the curious readers, the conditions are: either we can form a perfect hedge (like in the Black-Scholes or binomial world), or $\tilde{S}_T$ is a joint lognormal with the market return and investors have "Constant Proportional Risk Aversion" (COPRA) utility functions. Loosely, **COPRA** implies that the fraction of the investor's wealth invested in risky assets is independent of the level of her wealth.

[11] Note that we are *not assuming* that $E_t(\tilde{S}_T) = F_{t,T}$. Rather, we are replacing the true mean, $E_t(\tilde{S}_T)$, by the risk-adjusted mean, $F_{t,T}$, in order to correct for risk. This is analogous to replacing the true binomial probability p (in $E(\tilde{S}) = p\,S_u + (1 - p)\,S_d$) by the risk-adjusted probability q (in $CEQ(\tilde{S}) = q\,S_u + (1 - q)\,S_d$).

Finally, we use the Interest Rate Parity formula for the forward rate and obtain the following expression:

$$C_t = \frac{S_t}{1 + r_{t,T}^*} N(d_1) - \frac{X}{1 + r_{t,T}} N(d_2).$$ [13]

There is a strong similarity between Equation [13] and the n-subperiod binomial model discussed in 7.5.1–7.5.2. We recognize the price of the unit foreign discount bill or foreign T-bill, $S_t / (1 + r_{t,T}^*)$, followed by a probability, and the price of a domestic T-bill with face value X, $X/(1 + r_{t,T})$, also followed by a probability.[12] It is true that we now have standard normal probabilities instead of binomial probabilities; however, it is known that a binomial probability approaches a normal distribution in the limit, as the number of trials (or subperiods) approaches infinity.

8.2.4   Standard Notation for the Continuous-Time Call Pricing Model

Thus far, we expressed the model in terms of effective rates of return (not annualized in any way); also, the mean and variance of $\ln \tilde{S}_T$ were the effective numbers, without any annualization. The convention in the literature and among practitioners, however, is to quote all data on an annualized basis.

- The variance of the log exchange rate is assumed to be constant over time, and the *p.a.* variance is typically denoted by the (non-subscripted) symbol σ^2. To obtain the effective variance for the time to maturity $(T - t)$, one has to deannualize this *p.a.* figure:

$$\sigma_{t,T}^2 = \sigma^2 (T - t),$$

  where σ^2, non-subscripted, is the variance *per annum*.

Example   8.1

Let the *p.a.* variance be $\sigma^2 = 0.02$. (That is, the *p.a.* standard deviation or *volatility* is $\sqrt{0.02} = 0.1414 = 14.14\%$.) For an option with 201 days to go, the time to maturity in years is $201/365 = 0.55$ years. Therefore, the effective variance is computed as[13]

$$\sigma_{t,T}^2 = 0.55 \times 0.02 = 0.011.$$

- The risk-free rate is typically a continuously compounded, *p.a.* interest rate, which is assumed to be constant over time. This rate is most often denoted by the (non-subscripted)

---

[12] There is a notational difference: in this chapter, $r_{t,T}$ stands for the effective rate of return over the option's entire life; in the preceding chapter, r stands for the effective return per subperiod (with length $(T - t)/n$ years). Thus, the link is that $(1 + r)^n = 1 + r_{t,T}$.

[13] Since the yearly continuously compounded return is the sum of 365 daily continuously compounded returns with, by assumption, a constant daily variance, the annualized variance is 365 times the daily variance. The variance over a 201-day horizon therefore is $201/365 = 0.55$ times the variance of the annual return.

symbol r. To obtain the effective return, we have to de-annualize this rate, using the convention described in the appendix to Chapter 3:

$$(1 + r_{t,T}) = e^{r(T-t)}.$$

Likewise,

$$(1 + r^*_{t,T}) = e^{r^*(T-t)}$$

where r and r^*, non-subscripted, are the *p.a.* continuously compounded interest rates.

Example   8.2

Let the *p.a.* continuously compounded risk-free interest rate be 9.7347 percent *p.a.* in home currency, and 5.9031 percent in foreign currency. We compute the effective returns as:

$$1 + r_{t,T} = e^{0.097347 \times 0.55} = 1.055$$
$$1 + r^*_{t,T} = e^{0.059031 \times 0.55} = 1.033.$$

We can now show how the pricing formula, Equation [13], looks when we use the conventional way of denoting the risk-free rate and the volatility. In the standard version of the equation, we replace the effective risk-free returns by the exponential expressions, as shown above, and we replace the effective variance by the *p.a.* variance times time to maturity. The forward rate (inside d_1 and d_2) is typically denoted indirectly, by means of the spot rate and the two continuously compounded *p.a.* interest rates:

$$F_{t,T} = S_t \frac{1 + r_{t,T}}{1 + r^*_{t,T}} = S_t e^{(r-r^*)(T-t)}$$

which implies that, in the d_i expressions, we can replace $\ln(F_{t,T})/X$ by $\ln(S_t)/X + (r - r^*)(T - t)$. After all of these notational changes, we obtain the standard way of presenting the valuation equation:

$$C_t = S_t e^{-r^*(T-t)} N(d_1) - X e^{-r(T-t)} N(d_2), \qquad [14]$$

where

$$d_1 = \frac{\ln(S_t/X) + (r - r^*)(T - t) + \frac{1}{2}\sigma^2(T - t)}{\sigma\sqrt{(T-t)}}$$
$$d_2 = d_1 - \sigma\sqrt{(T-t)}.$$

This is known as the Garman-Kohlhagen option pricing model.

8.3   HOW TO USE THE CONTINUOUS-TIME OPTION VALUATION FORMULA

We start our discussion of how to use the option pricing model with a numerical example. We then describe how the valuation model can be used to implement a delta-hedging strategy.

8.3.1   How To Value a Call Option

Let us show how to use model [14] by valuing a call option on DEM. The data are as follows:

- The current spot rate is S_t = USD/DEM 0.45, or 45 cents, and the strike price is X = USD/DEM 0.43, or 43 cents. We shall use exchange rates expressed in cents, and keep in mind that the Black-Scholes-Merton formula then yields an option premium that is expressed in cents. (If all exchange rates are expressed in dollars, the resulting option premium is a number of dollars.)
- The option expires in 201 days. Thus, $(T - t)$ = 201/365 = 0.55 years.
- The volatility is 14.14 percent. This is a *per annum* figure, so the effective variance equals $\sigma^2(T - t)$ = 0.55 × $(0.1414)^2$ = 0.011, and the effective standard deviation is $\sigma\sqrt{(T-t)}$ = $0.1414\sqrt{0.55}$ = 0.10487.
- The *p.a.* risk-free interest rates are 9.7347 percent on USD, and 5.9031 percent on DEM. Thus, $e^{r\,(T-t)}$ = 1 + $r_{t,T}$ = 1.055, and $e^{r^*(T-t)}$ = 1 + $r^*_{t,T}$ = 1.033.[14]

This information allows us to compute the forward rate:

$$F_{t,T} = S_t e^{(r-r^*)(T-t)} = S_t \frac{1+r_{t,T}}{1+r^*_{t,T}} = 45\frac{1.055}{1.033} = 45.958 \text{ (cents)}.$$

Therefore, $\ln(F/X)$ = $\ln(45.958/43)$ = $\ln(1.0688)$ = 0.066536 (that is, the forward rate or risk-adjusted expected spot rate is 6.65 percent in the money). From this we can then compute:

$$d_1 = \frac{0.066536 + \frac{1}{2}0.011}{0.10487} = 0.686908$$

$$d_2 = d_1 - 0.10487 = 0.582038.$$

From a standard normal table or, more conveniently, from one of the more recent spreadsheet programs, we can find out that this implies the following normal probabilities:

$$N(d_1) = 0.753930 \text{ and } N(d_2) = 0.719729.$$

---

[14] This assumes that you obtain a continuously compounded interest rate. If the *p.a.* interest rate is a simple rate, say 10 percent on USD, we compute $r_{t,T}$ as 0.10 × 0.55 = 0.055.

The last two items to be computed are the value of the DEM T-bill, and the price of a domestic T-bill with face value $X = 45$ cents. The price of the DEM T-bill is:

$$S_t e^{-r^*(T-t)} = \frac{S_t}{1 + r^*_{t,T}} = \frac{45}{1.033} = 43.5624 \text{ (cents)}.$$

and the present value of the strike price (or the value of a USD T-bill with face value 43) is:

$$X e^{-r(T-t)} = \frac{X}{1 + r_{t,T}} = \frac{43}{1.055} = 40.7583 \text{ (cents)}.$$

Assembling the T-bill prices and their associated $N(d_i)$ terms, we ultimately obtain the value of the call:

$$C_t = (43.5624 \times 0.753930) - (40.7583 \times 0.719729) = 3.50807 \text{ (cents)}.$$

8.3.2   How To Use the Formula for Delta-Hedging

We saw in Chapter 7 how replication or hedging arguments can be used to value the option. Equally important, replication or hedging can be used by investors to limit their risks. For example, an institutional investor who writes options is probably interested in a replication strategy, because option writing is quite risky. Replication is useful for the writer because the fluctuations in the value of the replicating portfolio offset the fluctuations of the market price of the option the investor wrote. The holder of an option, on the other hand, may be interested in a hedge, which is simply the negative of replication. In this section, we explain how the Black-Scholes-Merton model can be used to identify the replicating portfolio and, by implication, the hedge.

To obtain this information, let us review the above numerical example. When valuing the call, we have in fact computed the value of a portfolio containing a certain amount of DEM and USD T-bills.

- The first term in Equation [13] says that one buys $N(d_1) = 0.7539$ DEM T-bills. Since each DEM T-bill costs DEM $1/1.033$, the amount of DEM required in order to buy these T-bills is:

$$\frac{N(d_1)}{1 + r^*_{t,T}} = \frac{0.7539}{1.033} = \text{DEM } 0.73.$$

- The second term in the solution of C_t corresponds to a purchase of $-N(d_2) = -0.7197$ USD T-bills, each with a face value of 43 cents. Thus, the amount invested in domestic T-bills is:

$$-43 \times \frac{N(d_2)}{1 + r_{t,T}} = -43 \times \frac{0.7197}{1.055} = -29.33 \text{ UScents,}$$

that is, one takes out a loan of 29.33 UScents.

Holding time constant, if the DEM appreciates by 1 cent, then the value of this portfolio will increase by 0.73 cents, because the portfolio contains DEM 0.73. It can be shown that, as in the binomial approach, the return on this portfolio of DEM and USD T-bills exactly mimics the return on the call over a short interval. This implies that 0.73 is also the number of DEM we have to buy and invest in order to replicate the change in the call's price following a change in the exchange rate; in short, 0.73 is the delta or hedge ratio if we hedge in the spot market. Looking back at how we identified the number 0.73, we can conclude that we can use the following spot position to replicate the call:

$$\Delta_{spot} = \frac{N(d_1)}{1+r_{t,T}^*} = \text{ number of foreign currency units to be bought } \textit{spot} \text{ and invested.}$$

Alternatively, we can rewrite the first term in the option pricing formula in a way that shows what the position should be if we replicate in the market for currency forwards or futures. We consider contracts that expire at the same time as the option. To bring out the forward price, it suffices to reverse the transformation from Equation [12] to Equation [13]:

$$S_t \frac{N(d_1)}{1+r_{t,T}^*} = S_t \frac{1+r_{t,T}}{1+r_{t,T}^*} \frac{N(d_1)}{1+r_{t,T}} = F_{t,T} \frac{N(d_1)}{1+r_{t,T}}. \tag{15}$$

This expression says that, if the forward rate or the futures price (for delivery at T) changes by one cent, then the price of the option will change by $N(d_1)/(1 + r_{t,T})$ cents.

Thus, to replicate the call in the futures market, we need the following position:

$$\Delta_{forward} = \frac{N(d_1)}{1+r_{t,T}} = \text{ number of currency units to be bought } \textit{forward} \text{ (for delivery at } T\text{).}$$

8.4   RELATED OPTION PRICING MODELS

In this section, we describe how the currency call pricing model given in Equation [13] or Equation [14] is related to other option valuation models in the finance literature.

8.4.1   The Value of European Put Options

We can find the value of a *European put* by starting from the Put Call Parity Theorem and substituting the valuation formula for the call:

$$P_t = \frac{X}{1+r_{t,T}} - \frac{S_t}{1+r_{t,T}^*} + C_t$$

$$= \frac{X}{1+r_{t,T}} - \frac{S_t}{1+r_{t,T}^*} + \left[\frac{S_t}{1+r_{t,T}^*}(N(d_1)) - \frac{X}{1+r_{t,T}}(N(d_2)) \right]. \tag{16}$$

Combining the terms with X and S_t, and noting that $1 - N(d) = N(-d)$,[15] we obtain:

$$P_t = \frac{X}{1+r_{t,T}}(1 - N(d_2)) - \frac{S_t}{1+r_{t,T}^*}(1 - N(d_1))$$

$$= \frac{X}{1+r_{t,T}}N(-d_2) - \frac{S_t}{1+r_{t,T}^*}N(-d_1).$$

---

[15] $N(d_1)$ is the area to the left of d_1, so $1 - N(d_1)$ is the area to the right of d_1, which equals the area to the left of $-d_1$, given that the standard normal distribution is symmetrical about zero.

Setting $e_1 = -d_2$, and $e_2 = -d_1$, we obtain:

$$P_t = \frac{X}{1 + r_{t,T}} N(e_1) - \frac{S_t}{1 + r_{t,T}^*} N(e_2)$$

$$= Xe^{-r(T-t)} N(e_1) - S_t e^{-r^*(T-t)} N(e_2).$$

Example 8.3

We value a put option on DEM. The data are the same as in the example used in Section 8.3.1:

- S = USD/DEM 0.45, and the strike price is X = USD/DEM 0.43.
- The option expires in 201 days. Thus, $(T - t) = 201/365 = 0.55$ years.
- The volatility is 14.14 percent, implying $\sigma^2(T - t) = 0.011$ and $\sigma\sqrt{T - t} = 0.10487$.
- $e^r (T - t) = 1 + r_{t,T} = 1.055$, and $e^{r^*(T - t)} = 1 + r_{t,T}^* = 1.033$. Thus, the forward rate is $S_t e^{(r - r^*)(T - t)} = 0.45958$, the DEM T-bill is worth

$$Se^{-r^*(T-t)} = \frac{0.45}{1.033} = 0.435624,$$

and the USD 0.45 T-bill is worth $Xe^{-r (T - t)} = 0.407583$.

As before, $\ln(F/X) = \ln(45.958/43) = \ln(1.0688) = 0.066536$. From this (see Equation [11]) we derive:

$$e_2 = -d_1 = -\frac{0.066536 + \frac{1}{2}0.011}{0.10488} = -0.686908, \text{ implying } N(e_2) = 0.246070$$

$$e_1 = -d_2 = -d_1 + 0.10487 = -0.583098, \text{ implying } N(e_1) = 0.279914.$$

Thus, the put is worth $0.279914 \times 0.407583 - 0.246070 \times 0.435624 = 0.007040$, or 0.70 cents.

8.4.2   The Value of European Options on a Futures Contract

A European *call on a futures contract* on foreign exchange (or on any other asset) can also be priced using our basic formula. In Chapter 5, we explained that when interest rates are known—which is assumed to be the case in the Black-Scholes model—forward and futures prices are identical, and even when interest rates are uncertain, we can ignore the difference between the two prices since it is very small. Thus, we set $f_{t,T} = F_{t,T}$. In the problem section, you are asked to prove that the price of a call option on futures is simply our interim result of Equation [12], reproduced below:

$$\text{Value at time } t \text{ of a European call on a futures contract} = \frac{f_{t,T}}{1 + r_{t,T}} N(d_1) - \frac{X}{1 + r_{t,T}} N(d_2), \qquad [17]$$

where d_1 and d_2 are as defined in Equation [11].

8.4.3 The Value of European Currency Options with Stochastic Interest Rates

Note that, in the valuation formula [13], the strike price always appears together with the discount factor; that is, we always see

$$\frac{X}{(1+r_{t,T})},$$

even within d_1 and d_2. Merton writes this as $X B(t,T)$, where $B(t,T) = 1/(1 + r_{t,T})$ is the time-t price of a domestic unit-discount bond maturing at T. He then shows that the model still holds when $B(t,T)$ is stochastic (that is, when interest rates and bond prices are not fully predictable) as long as the bond's variance is known in advance.[16] Using this result, Grabbe (1983) derived a currency option pricing model similar to Merton's, featuring the forward rate, and allowing interest risk in both currencies:

$$C = S_t\, B^*(t,T)\, N(d_1) - X\, B(t,T)\, N(d_2) \qquad [18]$$

where $B^*(t,T)$ = foreign unit T-bill price (in its own currency)
  $B(t,T)$ = domestic unit T-bill price (in its own currency)

$$d_i \quad = \frac{\ln F_{t,T}/X \pm \dfrac{1}{2}\sigma_{t,T}^2}{\sigma_{t,T}} = \frac{\ln F_{t,T}/X \pm \dfrac{1}{2}\sigma^2\,(T-t)}{\sigma\sqrt{T-t}}$$

σ^2 = annualized *average* variance of $d\ln F$

$F_{t,T}$ $= S\dfrac{B^*(t,T)}{B(t,T)} = $ the forward rate.

Thus, when interest rates are stochastic, a small adjustment to the Black-Scholes-Merton model suffices: we should use the average variance of the forward rate (for delivery at T), rather than the variance of the spot rate, to value currency options. The variance of the forward rate is typically higher than the variance of the spot rate because domestic and foreign interest rates are uncertain and imperfectly correlated. Grabbe's model therefore prices options higher than the Garman-Kohlhagen model.

8.5 CONCLUSIONS

In this chapter, we have shown how the logic of the discrete binomial option pricing model extends to the case where both time and the distribution of exchange rates are continuous. The intuition underlying the discrete-time, binomial model and the continuous-time model is the same: delta-hedging allows the call writer to hedge the option against fluctuations in the call's value caused by fluctuations of exchange rates. By arbitrage, then, such a risk-free portfolio should earn the risk-free rate of return. The value of such a risk-free portfolio is easy to compute and, after subtracting the cost of hedging,

---

[16] Clearly the zero-coupon bond's volatility cannot be constant. One instant before expiration, for instance, its standard deviation is zero. Usually one assumes that the volatility is proportional to the bond's life or duration.

one obtains the value of the option. In this setting, one assumes that interest rates and volatilities are constant, trading is continuous, and the exchange rate is lognormal.

For mathematical simplicity, our derivation of the Black-Scholes-Merton equation was based on a somewhat different logic, which assumes lognormal distributions in discrete time. In this approach, one corrects the expected terminal payoff of the option for risk and discounts at the risk-free rate. As soon as the call is priced, Put Call Parity allows us also to value a European put option. The model can also be modified to value European options on futures contracts, or to value options when the interest rates are changing stochastically over time.

Option valuation is closely related to the hedging or replication of options. The size of the position one should take when covering the risk of an option depends on whether hedging is in the spot market or in the market for forwards or futures expiring at T. We should however remember that the option's delta gives us a perfect hedge against fluctuations in the call's value only under the assumptions stated in Section 8.1.

1. The model assumes continuous rebalancing. The reason is that, when exchange rates and time change continuously, the delta changes, too. However, in practice, rebalancing occurs far less frequently. The consequence is that the linear hedge will not mimic the call price as perfectly as one would like.[17]

2. Sudden jumps in the exchange rate, and changes in its volatility, are not taken into account by the model. Thus, delta hedging will not protect us against jumps in the exchange rate, or changes in volatility. For instance, after the Plaza Agreement (discussed in the introductory chapter), uncertainty in the market rose substantially. This change in the variance led to unexpected increases in all option prices—to the dismay of option writers who thought they were well-hedged.[18]

3. Another warning is that it may be inappropriate to assume that the variance of the log exchange rate, $\sigma_{t,T}^2$, is proportional to the horizon $T - t$, especially in the long run. In Chapter 12, we shall argue that exchange rates are (weakly) attracted to a theoretical equilibrium rate that depends on relative inflation.[19]

4. The continuous-time model assumes that interest rates are constant. This is manifestly untrue and, worse, exchange rate changes seem to be strongly related to changes in interest rates. The currency option pricing model by Grabbe (1983), discussed in Section 8.4.3, suggests a simple and elegant solution to this problem.

5. Exchange rate changes have distributions that are fat-tailed; that is, the probability of extreme events is somewhat higher than the lognormal model predicts. As a result, options should probably be priced higher than what the lognormal model predicts, because option prices increase with volatility.

---

[17] In specialized books on options, for instance Hull (1993) or Stoll and Whaley (1992), one can find discussions on **gamma-hedging**, a refinement that improves the performance of delta hedging when rebalancing is infrequent.

[18] In the final section of Chapter 6 we showed, using a numerical example, that options are worth more if the variance increases. You can also illustrate this by experimenting with larger "up" and "down" factors in the binomial model. Option pricing models that include jumps in the underlying asset price are discussed in Ahn (1990), Bates (1988), Jones (1984), Merton (1973, 1976), and Naik and Lee (1990).

[19] Option pricing models that include a stochastically changing variance are Wiggins (1987) and Hull and White (1987).

QUIZ QUESTIONS

Matching Questions
Match each phrase or set of symbols with the statement(s) to which it corresponds most.

(a) Continuous trading

(b) Continuous exchange rate process

(c) Lognormality

(d) σ^2

(e) constant σ^2

(f) $N(d_i)$

(g) $N(d_1)$

(h) $N(d_2')$

(i) $\Delta_{spot} = N(d_1)/(1 + r_{t,T}^*)$

(j) volatility

(k) $F_{t,T} N(d_1)$

(l) $E_T(\tilde{S}_t) N(d_1')$

(m) $CEQ_t(\tilde{C}_T)$

(n) $N(d_1)/(1 + r_{t,T})$

1. Risk-adjusted partial mean of $\tilde{S}_T$.
2. The assumption that corresponds to the assumption in the binomial model of multiplicative changes in the spot exchange rate.
3. An option's exposure to the futures rate $f_{t,T}$.
4. Cumulative standard normal probability.
5. The assumption that ensures that changes in the exchange rate are small over short intervals.
6. The probability of exercising.
7. The partial mean $\tilde{S}_T$.
8. The assumption that makes it possible to continuously rebalance the portfolio based on the option's ever-changing exposure.
9. The risk-adjusted expectation of the call value at time T.
10. The number of currency units needed to replicate an option.
11. The *p.a.* variance of the log exchange rate.
12. The condition that says that the continuously compounded changes in the exchange rate are normally distributed.
13. The assumption that corresponds to the assumption in the binomial model of the multiplicativity of the changes in the spot exchange rate.
14. *P.a.* standard deviation (of an exchange rate).
15. Cumulative probability of a call ending in the money.

Further Quiz Questions
1. Are the following comments true or false? Please explain your answers.

   (a) A major flaw of the Black-Scholes model is that it assumes risk neutrality.

   (b) The Black-Scholes model cannot be adjusted for interest rate risk.

2. Suppose that, everything else held constant, S and X change by the same factor. How does this affect:

   (a) the risk-adjusted probability of exercising?

   (b) the partial mean of $\tilde{S}_T$ (above X)?

   (c) the value of a call?

   (d) the value of a put?

3. Consider the Garman-Kohlhagen call pricing formula:

$$C_t = S_t e^{-r*(T-t)} N(d_1) - X e^{-r(T-t)} N(d_2).$$

(a) $N(d_2)$ refers to which area under the normal curve?
(b) $N(d_2)$ refers to the (risk-adjusted) probability of what?
(c) The size of the domestic deposit held in the replicating portfolio is given by?
(d) The analogous (*foreign*) interest-earning currency held in the replicating portfolio is given by?
(e) The home currency value of the foreign deposit in the replicating portfolio is given by?
(f) The hedge ratio is given by?

4. Consider the Garman-Kohlhagen put pricing formula:

$$P_t = X e^{-r*(T-t)} N(e_1) - S_t e^{-r'(T-t)} N(e_2).$$

(a) $N(e_1)$ refers to which area under the normal curve?
(b) $N(e_1)$ refers to the (risk-adjusted) probability of what?
(c) The size of the domestic deposit held in the replicating portfolio is given by?
(d) The analogous (*foreign*) interest-earning currency held in the replicating portfolio is given by?
(e) The home currency value of the foreign deposit in the replicating portfolio is given by?
(f) The hedge ratio is given by?

EXERCISES

1. Suppose that the current spot rate for the Timbuktu Dirham is USD/TID 50. Use the Garman-Kohlhagen formula to calculate the price of a European call option on TID, if the strike price is USD/TID 45, the time to maturity of the call is 91 days, the annual variance of the spot exchange is 20 percent and the *p.a.* USD interest rate is 6 percent, while the TID interest rate is 0 percent.

(a) What is the option's price?
(b) What is the delta of this call option?
(c) What would the price of this option be if it were an American option?

2. Suppose that the USD/CAD spot rate is 0.75 and the volatility of this exchange rate is 4 percent *p.a.* The risk-free rate is 7 percent *p.a.* on USD and 10 percent *p.a.* on CAD. Suppose that the exercise price is USD/CAD 0.75 and the European put option matures in 274 days.

(a) Find the value of this option using the Garman-Kohlhagen approach.
(b) What is the put option's exposure?
(c) What would the price of this option be if it were an American option?

3. In the call formula, we see

$$\frac{\ln(S_t/X)}{\sigma_{t,T}}$$

inside $N(\bullet)$. This expresses the continuously compounded percentage difference between S_t and X relative to the standard deviation and is a good measure of in-the-moneyness.

(a) Verify that the call price converges to zero when

$$\frac{\ln(S_t/X)}{\sigma_{t,T}}$$

approaches zero (deep out-of-the-money).

(b) Verify that the call price converges to the forward purchase contract's value when

$$\frac{\ln(S_t/X)}{\sigma_{t,T}}$$

approaches plus infinity (deep-in-the-money).

4. Consider a five-year currency option bond that gives the holder the option to cash in the principal either as USD 10,000, or as CHF 20,000. The bond carries a 6 percent USD coupon paid once a year (that is, each annual coupon is USD 600). Assume a flat 9 percent *p.a.* term structure for USD bonds, and a flat 3 percent *p.a.* term structure for CHF bonds. The current exchange rate is $S_t = 0.5$ USD/CHF, and the volatility is 0.15 (that is, the standard deviation of a yearly continuously compounded exchange rate change is 15 percent). Find the fair price of the bond, if you know that the prices of one-, two-, . . . , five-year calls are 4.36, 6.81, 8.82, 10.54 and 12.01 cents, respectively.[20]

5. Redo Exercise 4, but assume that the option also includes the coupons; the holder can cash in either USD 600 or CHF 1,200, at any coupon date.

6. Redo Exercise 5, but treat the bond as a CHF 20,000 bond plus five calls on USD at X' = CHF/USD 2. If you sit back and think for two or three minutes, you may be able to find the (CHF) value analytically rather than going through the computations as in the previous question.

7. Compute for each of the two preceding exercises how much of the bond's total value is due to the option and how much is due to the straight bond. Explain intuitively why the option component has a much higher relative importance from the USD point of view than from the CHF point of view.

8. Suppose that, for the option bond described in Exercise 5, we want to lower the USD coupon such that the issue price is at par. Without any calculations, should this crucial coupon rate be

(a) above 9 percent (the USD rate)?
(b) above 6 percent (the bond's coupon)?
(c) between 6 percent and 3 percent?
(d) below 3 percent (the CHF rate)?

Why?

---

[20] Hint: as shown in the appendix to Chapter 10, with a flat 9 percent term structure, you can price a straight USD bond as V_0 = USD 10,000 + (600 – 900) × $a(R,n)$ where $a(R,n) = (1 – (1 + R)^{-n})/R = 3.8896512$ is the annuity factor for $R = 0.09$, n = 5, and where USD 900 represents the coupon that would be "normal" under the current circumstances. You compute the bond's discount as the discounted shortfall in the coupon relative to the normal rate.

9. How should we set the bond's coupon rate if we want a bond issue price equal to the par value when:

   (a) the option bears on the principal only?

   (b) the option also bears on each of the coupons?

MIND-EXPANDING EXERCISES

1. (Ito's Lemma, Appendix 8B.) Assume that the price level x follows the process:

$$\frac{dx}{x} = a\,dt + s\,dz.$$

   Show, from Ito's Lemma, how the mean percentage change in the purchasing power $\Pi = x^{-1}$ is always less, in absolute value, than the mean inflation rate,[21] but that the random components in the inflation rate and in the percentage change of the purchasing power are the same, up to the sign.

2. Derive the value of a call, expiring at T_1 and with a strike price X, on a futures contract expiring at T_2. Ignore interest risk.

3. A call on *one* DEM at $X = 0.5$ USD/DEM each is a put on *one-half* USD at $X' = 2$ DEM/USD. Or more generally, a call on DEM 1 at a strike price of X is a put on USD X at a strike price of $X' = 1/X$. Verify this using the continuous-time formula [14]. (Hint: since we are changing the reference currency, it is advisable not to use an r, r^* notation. You will be less confused if you use a notation like $r_\$$ [for USD] and r_M [for DEM].)

---

[21] Interpret x as the consumption price level, that is, the price of a standard basket of goods. The purchasing power Π of one unit of currency is defined as the number of consumption baskets you can buy with one unit, that is, $\Pi = 1/x$. If there is 10 percent inflation, x goes up from 100 to 110. The purchasing power decreases, but by less than 10 percent: Π goes from 0.01 to 0.0090909, which represents a drop of 9.0909 percent. If the inflation rate is smaller, the change in the purchasing power becomes closer to the inflation rate (up to the sign), but it always remains smaller in absolute terms.

DERIVATION OF THE EXPECTED EXPIRATION VALUE OF THE CALL OPTION

In this appendix and in Appendix 8B, the expression "x is normal" is used as shorthand for "x is a normally distributed random variable," and the expression "y is lognormal" means that y is a lognormally distributed random variable, that is, ln y is a normal.

In this appendix, we solve the following equation:

$$E_t(\tilde{C}_T) = \int_X^\infty S_T f(S_T; \mu_{t,T}, \sigma_{t,T}) dS_T - X \int_X^\infty f(S_T; \mu_{t,T}, \sigma_{t,T}) dS_T \qquad [A1]$$

$$= [\text{Integral } A] - X \times [\text{Integral } B].$$

We start with Integral B, which represents the probability of exercising the European option.

8A.1 The Probability of Exercising

The probability that $\tilde{S}_T \geq X$ can be read from the standard normal tables. To obtain the standard normal, we first take logs—after all, it is the *log* of the spot rate that is assumed to be normal, not the spot rate itself—and then we standardize by subtracting the expected value and dividing by the standard deviation:

$$(\tilde{S}_T \geq X) \Leftrightarrow (\ln \tilde{S}_T \geq \ln X) \Leftrightarrow \left(\frac{\ln \tilde{S}_T - \mu_{t,T}}{\sigma_{t,T}} \geq \frac{\ln X - \mu_{t,T}}{\sigma_{t,T}} \right). \qquad [A2]$$

The term, $(\ln \tilde{S}_T - \mu_{t,T})/\sigma_{t,T}$, is a standard normal variate. Therefore, the probability that the call ends in the money, $\text{Prob}(\tilde{S}_T \geq X)$, can be computed as the probability that a random drawing from a standard normal distribution is at least $(\ln X - \mu_{t,T})/\sigma_{t,T}$. For example, if $(\ln X - \mu_{t,T})/\sigma_{t,T} = 1.28$, the chance of ending up in the money is 20 percent; if $(\ln X - \mu_{t,T})/\sigma_{t,T} = 1.645$, the probability of ending up in the money equals 10 percent, and so on. Thus,

$$\text{Prob}(\tilde{S}_T \geq X) = \text{chance that a standard normal variate exceeds } \frac{\ln X - \mu_{t,T}}{\sigma_{t,T}}.$$

This standard normal probability can be visualized as the area under the standard normal curve to the right of the cutoff point. The convention in option pricing theory, however, is to use areas to the left of some cutoff point. Such a translation is easy, since the standard normal distribution is symmetric around zero. The chance that a drawing from a standard normal distribution produces a number exceeding 1.65 is equal to the chance that a standard normal number turns out to be below –1.65. Or, more generally, the area under the curve to the right of a cutoff point Z is the same as the area to the left of the cutoff point $-Z$. Thus,

$$\text{Prob}(\tilde{S}_T \geq X) = \text{chance that a standard normal is below } -\frac{\ln X - \mu_{t,T}}{\sigma_{t,T}} = \frac{\mu_{t,T} - \ln X}{\sigma_{t,T}},$$

or, more formally:

$$\text{Prob}_t \, (\tilde{S}_T \geq X) = \text{Prob} \, (\tilde{z} \leq d_2') \equiv N(d_2'), \qquad \text{[A3]}$$

where $\tilde{z}$ = a standard normal; $N(d_2')$ denotes the cumulative standard normal probability, that is, the probability that a standard normal z is below or equal to d_2', and

$$d_2' = \frac{\mu_{t,T} - \ln X}{\sigma_{t,T}}. \qquad \text{[A4]}$$

In short, we have evaluated Integral B in Equation [A1] as follows:

$$\int_X^\infty f(S_T ; \mu_{t,T}, \sigma_{t,T}) dS_T = \text{Prob}_t \, (\tilde{S}_T \geq X) = N(d_2'). \qquad \text{[A5]}$$

8A.2   The Partial Mean of $\tilde{S}_T$

In this section, we derive Integral A in Equation [A1]. In the first step, we work out the integrand $S_T f(S_T; \mu_{t,T}, \sigma_{t,T})$. The math property we use is the perfect square, $(a + b)^2 = a^2 + 2ab + b^2$. We then derive three corollaries—the partial mean, the expected value, and the link between the expected value and the cumulative normal arguments, d_1' or d_2'. We drop subscripts for ease of notation.

Lemma: Assume $\tilde{S}$ is lognormal. Then $Sf(S;\mu,\sigma) = \exp\left\{\mu + \frac{1}{2}\sigma^2\right\} f(S; \mu + \sigma^2, \sigma)$.

Proof: The density for a lognormal variate $\tilde{S}$ is

$$f(S;\mu,\sigma) = k \exp\left\{-\frac{1}{2}\left[\frac{\ln S - \mu}{\sigma}\right]^2\right\}$$

where

$$k = \frac{1}{\sigma\sqrt{2\pi}}.$$

We substitute this density function into the integrand in Integral A of Equation [A1], and we write S as $\exp\{\ln S\}$. Thus, the integrand can be written as

$$S f(S;\mu,\sigma) = \exp\{\ln S\} k \exp\left\{-\frac{1}{2}\left[\frac{\ln S - \mu}{\sigma}\right]^2\right\}$$

$$= k \exp\left\{\ln S - \frac{1}{2}\left[\frac{\ln S - \mu}{\sigma}\right]^2\right\}.$$

[A6]

Consider the argument of the exponential, and rearrange it as follows:

$$\ln S - \frac{1}{2}\frac{(\ln S - \mu)^2}{\sigma^2} = -\frac{1}{2}\frac{-2(\ln S)\,\sigma^2 + \left[(\ln S)^2 - 2\mu\ln S + \mu^2\right]}{\sigma^2} \qquad [A7]$$

$$= -\frac{1}{2}\frac{-2(\ln S)(\mu + \sigma^2) + (\ln S)^2 + \mu^2}{\sigma^2}.$$

We now bring out a perfect square $[\ln S - (\mu + \sigma^2)]^2 = (\ln S)^2 - 2(\ln S)(\mu + \sigma^2) + (\mu + \sigma^2)^2$. The part $(\ln S)^2 - 2(\ln S)(\mu + \sigma^2)$ of this perfect square is already present in [A7]. Thus, to complete the square, we add and subtract $2\mu\sigma^2 + \sigma^4$:

$$\ln S - \frac{1}{2}\left(\frac{\ln S - \mu}{\sigma^2}\right)^2 = -\frac{1}{2}\frac{-2(\ln S)(\mu + \sigma^2) + (\ln S)^2 + \mu^2 + 2\mu\sigma^2 + \sigma^4 - 2\mu\sigma^2 - \sigma^4}{\sigma^2}$$

$$= -\frac{1}{2}\frac{(\ln S)^2 - 2(\ln S)(\mu + \sigma^2) + (\mu^2 + 2\mu\sigma^2 + \sigma^4) - 2\mu\sigma^2 - \sigma^4}{\sigma^2}$$

$$= -\frac{1}{2}\frac{\left[\ln S - (\mu + \sigma^2)\right]^2 - 2\mu\sigma^2 - \sigma^4}{\sigma^2}$$

$$= -\frac{1}{2}\left[\frac{\ln S - (\mu + \sigma^2)}{\sigma}\right]^2 + \mu + \frac{1}{2}\sigma^2. \qquad [A8]$$

Equation [A8] is a transformation of the argument of the exponential function in the second line of Equation [A6]. Thus, substituting Equation [A8] into Equation [A6], we obtain:

$$S f(S; \mu, \sigma) = \exp\left\{\mu + \frac{1}{2}\sigma^2\right\} k \exp\left\{-\frac{1}{2}\left[\frac{\ln S - (\mu + \sigma^2)}{\sigma}\right]^2\right\} \qquad [A9]$$

$$= \exp\left\{\mu + \frac{1}{2}\sigma^2\right\} f(S; \mu + \sigma^2, \sigma)$$

where $f(S; \mu + \sigma^2, \sigma)$ is the density of a lognormally distributed variable with a shifted mean—μ has been replaced by $\mu + \sigma^2$.

Equation [A9] will be used to relate the partial mean of S to the general mean of S. First, we identify this general mean.

Corollary 1: The expected value of a lognormal variate $\tilde{S}$ is

$$E(\tilde{S}) = \exp\left\{\mu + \frac{1}{2}\sigma^2\right\}$$

where $\mu = E(\ln \tilde{S})$ and $\sigma^2 = \mathrm{var}(\ln \tilde{S})$.

Proof:

$$E(\tilde{S}) \equiv \int_0^\infty S f(S;\mu,\sigma)\,dS \qquad\qquad [A10]$$

$$= \exp\left\{\mu + \frac{1}{2}\sigma^2\right\} \int_0^\infty f(S;\mu+\sigma^2,\sigma)\,dS$$

$$= \exp\left\{\mu + \frac{1}{2}\sigma^2\right\}.$$

We have used the Lemma, and the fact that the integral, measuring the entire area under a lognormal probability distribution function, equals unity.

Thus, we have an interpretation of the term we factored out in Equation [A9]. This allows us to write the partial mean as follows:

Corollary 2: The partial mean of $\tilde{S}$, from $S = X$ to $S = \infty$, is given by $E_t(\tilde{S}_T)N(d_1')$, where

$$d_1' = \frac{(\mu + \sigma^2) - \ln X}{\sigma}.$$

Proof: We apply the Lemma, and then Corollary 1.

$$\int_X^\infty S f(S;\mu,\sigma)\,dS = \exp\left\{\mu + \frac{1}{2}\sigma^2\right\} \int_X^\infty f(S;\mu+\sigma^2,\sigma)\,dS \qquad [A11]$$

$$= E(\tilde{S}) \int_X^\infty f(S;\mu+\sigma^2,\sigma)\,dS.$$

In words: for the purpose of computing the partial mean of a lognormal, we multiply the expected value, $E(\tilde{S})$, by a probability that $\tilde{S}$ is above X computed as if the mean of $\ln \tilde{S}$ were $\mu + \sigma^2$. To rewrite this probability as a standard normal probability, we follow the same steps that led to equations [A2] and [A3], except that μ is replaced by $\mu + \sigma^2$. Thus, in Equation [7]:

$$\text{Integral } A = E_t(\tilde{S}_T)N(d_1'), \qquad\qquad [A12]$$

where

$$d_1' = \frac{(\mu + \sigma^2) - \ln X}{\sigma} = d_2' + \sigma. \qquad\qquad [A13]$$

8A.3   The Link between the Probabilities and the Expected Spot Rate

Combining our results of Sections 8A.1 and 8A.2, we obtain Equation [8] in the text:

$$E_t(\tilde{C}_T) = E_t(\tilde{S}_T)N(d_1') - XN(d_2').$$
[A14]

Using the first Corollary of Section 8A.2, we can write the d_1' and d_2' factors as explicit functions of $E_t(\tilde{S}_T)$:

$$d_1' = \frac{\mu + \sigma^2 - \ln X}{\sigma} = \frac{\mu + \frac{1}{2}\sigma^2 + \frac{1}{2}\sigma^2 - \ln X}{\sigma} = \frac{\ln(E(\tilde{S})) + \frac{1}{2}\sigma^2 - \ln X}{\sigma}$$

$$= \frac{\ln\frac{E(\tilde{S})}{X} + \frac{1}{2}\sigma^2}{\sigma}.$$
[A15]

$$d_2' = d_1' - \sigma = \frac{\ln\frac{E(\tilde{S})}{X} - \frac{1}{2}\sigma^2}{\sigma}.$$
[A16]

STOCHASTIC CALCULUS AND THE BLACK-SCHOLES EQUATION

In this appendix, we provide an introduction to continuous-time stochastic calculus and its application to the option pricing problem. In the first section, we briefly describe the type of processes that Black and Scholes (1973) and Merton (1973) assumed for the stock price in their option pricing models. We assume that the spot rate, $\tilde{S}$, follows such a process. In the second section, we consider Ito's Lemma, which tells us the relationship between the change in a dependent variable (like the price of a call on foreign exchange) and the change in the independent variable (the change in the spot price). Finally, the third section presents the Black-Scholes-Merton differential equation that the value of the call must satisfy, and interprets this differential equation as justifying the discrete-time lognormal model described in this chapter.

8B.1   Ito Processes

Consider an additive, normal, random walk in continuous time. We first discuss the links between consecutive observations of this continuous process made at regular discrete intervals (say, once a year or once a quarter), and then take the limit when the observations become continuous.

If we measure the level once a year, we will observe a normally distributed change relative to the level observed one year before. The change between now and next year can always be written as the sum of a deterministic component (the expected change) and a random component (the unexpected change). The random component is written as a standard normal multiplied by the annual standard deviation:

$$\tilde{x}_{t+1} = x_t + a + \phi\,\tilde{\varepsilon}_{t,t+1}$$

where x = the level of the random variable at time t
a = the annual growth or "drift" in x, or the expected change
$\phi\,\varepsilon_{t,t+1}$ = the unexpected change
ϕ = the standard deviation of the annual change, and
$\varepsilon_{t,t+1}$ = a standard normal (that is, a normally distributed variable with mean zero and standard deviation one).

(We use a and ϕ to denote the drift and the standard deviation of the changes in x because we wish to reserve the symbols μ and σ as notations for the mean and standard deviation of the changes in the *log* of a process, to be consistent with the notation in Appendix 8A.) By iterating the above equation, we can link the level after N years to the initial level (x_t), the *drift* (a), and the random changes ($\phi\,\varepsilon_{t,t+1}$) in each year:

$$\tilde{x}_{t+N} = x_t + aN + \phi(\tilde{\varepsilon}_{t,t+1} + \tilde{\varepsilon}_{t+1,t+2} + \ldots + \tilde{\varepsilon}_{t+(N-1),t+N}).$$

The sum of these N standard normal variables is also normal. Its mean is zero, its total variance equals N, and its total standard deviation therefore equals $\sqrt{N}$. Thus, we can write the total change between times t and $t + N$ as

$$\tilde{x}_{t+N} - x_t = aN + \phi \sqrt{N} \, \frac{\tilde{\varepsilon}_{t,t+1} + \tilde{\varepsilon}_{t+1,t+2} + \ldots + \tilde{\varepsilon}_{t+(N-1),t+N}}{\sqrt{N}} = aN + \phi \sqrt{N} \tilde{\varepsilon}_{t,t+N}$$

where

$$\tilde{\varepsilon}_{t,t+N} = \frac{\tilde{\varepsilon}_{t,t+1} + \tilde{\varepsilon}_{t+1,t+2} + \ldots + \tilde{\varepsilon}_{t+(N-1),t+N}}{\sqrt{N}}$$

is still a standard normal, and a and ϕ are still the mean and standard deviation of the *p.a.* change in x.

As $\tilde{x}$ is a continuous process, we can also measure $\tilde{x}$ at any moment between t and $t + 1$. We claim that the expression $\tilde{x}_{t+N} - x_t = aN + \phi \sqrt{N} \tilde{\varepsilon}$ is true for $N < 1$. For example, if we observe x at times t and $t + 0.25$—that is, if we set $N = \frac{1}{4}$—the formula suggests that

$$\tilde{x}_{t+\frac{1}{4}} - x_t = \frac{1}{4} a + \sqrt{\frac{1}{4}} \, \phi \, \tilde{\varepsilon}_{t,t+\frac{1}{4}},$$

implying a mean of $\frac{1}{4} a$, and a variance of $\frac{1}{4} \phi^2$, for the quarterly change. We claim that this still describes the process for $\tilde{x}$. To understand this, note that if we sum four of these quarterly changes, we again obtain an annual change. Thus, if the above expression is correct, the sum of four quarterly changes should have mean a and variance ϕ^2. This is easily verified to be true. If the quarterly mean indeed equals $\frac{1}{4} a$, the mean of the sum of four quarterly changes will be $4 \times \frac{1}{4} a = a$, the annual expected change, as it should be. Further, if the quarterly variance indeed equals $\frac{1}{4} \phi^2$, the variance of the sum of four independent quarterly changes will be equal to $4 \times [\frac{1}{4} \phi^2] = \phi^2$, the annual variance, as it should be. In summary, the formula $\tilde{x}_{t+N} - x_t = aN + \phi \sqrt{N} \tilde{\varepsilon}_{t,t+N}$ still works for $N < 1$. Now we let N become arbitrarily small; that is, we consider the limit as $N \to dt$. Then,

$$dx = a \, dt + \phi \sqrt{dt} \, \tilde{\varepsilon}, \tilde{\varepsilon} \text{ a standard normal}$$

$$= a \, dt + \phi \, dz,$$

[B1]

where dz can be viewed as shorthand for $\sqrt{dt} \, \tilde{\varepsilon}$. (Following the conventional notation in continuous time math, when writing changes like dz or dS, we shall drop the *tildes* that have hitherto indicated that a variable is random.) In this expression, a and ϕ still are the mean and standard deviation of the annual change. The term $dz = \sqrt{dt} \, \tilde{\varepsilon}$ is called the *standard* **Wiener Process**, and x is an example of a *generalized* process in the sense that its mean is a (rather than 0, as in the Wiener Process), and its variance equals ϕ^2 (rather than one, as in the Wiener Process).

Example   8B.1

To understand the term dz, think of dt as one day, that is, $1/365$ year. The disturbance $\tilde{\varepsilon}$ has a mean of zero and a standard deviation of one. The daily change dz then has a mean of zero and a standard deviation of $\sqrt{dz} = \sqrt{1/365} = 0.0523$. This standard deviation was chosen such that, if every day we drew a random variable with this standard deviation, the sum of 365 such drawings is a standard normal: $\text{var}(\sum_{i=1}^{365} dz_{t+i/365}) = 365 \times \text{var}(dz) = 365 \times (1/365) = 1$. That is, dz accumulated over a full year produces a standard normal.

We can further generalize the process for x by assuming that the *instantaneous mean, a dt,* and the *instantaneous variance, $\phi^2 dt$,* change continuously rather than staying constant.

Example   8B.2

A popular assumption for a stock price S is that the *percentage* price changes, rather than the dollar price changes, have a constant mean and variance or, conversely, that the mean and standard deviation of the instantaneous change in S, dS, at each instant are proportional to the price level S itself. Thus, we set $a = S\alpha$, and $\phi = S\sigma$, with α and σ constant numbers. Then the process describing the change in the stock price S is

$$dS = S \, \alpha \, dt + S \, \sigma \, dz$$

or

$$\frac{dS}{S} = \alpha \, dt + \sigma \, dz.$$

We shall show that, if S follows the above process (known as the **geometric Brownian motion** or **geometric Ito process**), then the log of S will follow a random walk with an annual continuously compounded return volatility of σ. This **log random walk** was assumed by Black and Scholes in their option pricing model. To discover the precise link between $(dS)/S$ and $d\ln S$ when there is randomness, and also to derive the Black-Scholes-Merton model, we need **Ito's Lemma**.

8B.2   Ito's Lemma

Ito's Lemma explains how functions of Ito processes change over time. For instance, if f is a well-behaved function of x and y, and if x and y are Ito processes, then Ito's Lemma gives us an expression for df, the instantaneous change in $f(x,y)$.

In standard calculus, where dx and dy are deterministic rather than random, the total change in f is given by

$$df = \frac{\partial f}{\partial x} \, dx + \frac{\partial f}{\partial y} \, dy.$$

However, in our context, dx and dy are random. This randomness generally invalidates standard calculus. To show why and how standard calculus has to be adjusted, we first consider a function of a single Ito process.

Ito's Lemma Applied to a Function of One Ito Process

To see the effect of randomness in x on the link between df and dx, consider a univariate function $f = f(x)$. The differential df is the result of a Taylor series expansion,

$$f(x_1) - f(x_0) = f_x(x_1 - x_0) + \frac{1}{2} f_{xx}(x_1 - x_0)^2 + \frac{1}{6} f_{xxx}(x_1 - x_0)^3 + \dots$$

where, f_x, f_{xx}, and f_{xxx} denote the first, second, and third derivative, with all derivatives being evaluated in the starting point $x = x_0$. Thus, the change in f, Δf, is

$$\Delta f = f_x \Delta x + \frac{1}{2} f_{xx} (\Delta x)^2 + \frac{1}{6} f_{xxx} (\Delta x)^3 + \ldots$$

In deterministic math, we set Δx equal to an infinitesimally small number dx:

$$df = f_x dx + \frac{1}{2} f_{xx} (dx)^2 + \frac{1}{6} f_{xxx} (dx)^3 + \ldots$$

If dx is infinitesimally small, then $(dx)^2$, $(dx)^3$, etc. are small enough to be negligible relative to dx itself. Thus the formula obtained from standard calculus, $df = f_x dx$, holds. However, the argument that $(dx)^2$ is negligible is no longer generally correct if dx is an Ito process. If:

$$dx = a\, dt + \phi\, dz$$

then

$$\begin{aligned}
(dx)^2 &= (a\, dt + \phi\, dz)(a\, dt + \phi\, dz) \\
&= a^2 (dt)^2 + 2(a\, dt)(\phi\, dz) + (\phi\, dz)^2 \\
&= a^2 (dt)^2 + 2(a\, dt)(\phi\, \tilde{\varepsilon} \sqrt{dt}) + (\phi\, \tilde{\varepsilon} \sqrt{dt})^2 \\
&= a^2 (dt)^2 + 2a\, \phi\, \tilde{\varepsilon}(dt)^{3/2} + \phi^2 \tilde{\varepsilon}^2 dt.
\end{aligned}$$

Time is deterministic. Therefore, the usual logic for deterministic variables applies to dt. If dt is infinitesimally small, then any power larger than unity of dt can be ignored. This means that the first term in the above expression, containing $(dt)^2$, can be dropped as being of very small (second) order. Likewise, the second term can be dropped because it contains $(dt)^{3/2}$. However, the last term remains, because it equals $\phi^2 \tilde{\varepsilon}^2\ dt$, which is of order dt. In short, we now have:

$$(dx)^2 = \phi^2 \tilde{\varepsilon}^2\ dt,$$

rather than the deterministic result $(dx)^2 = 0$, which requires $\phi = 0$. It is easily checked that $(dx)^3$ and all other higher-order terms are negligible, because all of these terms contain powers of dt greater than unity. Thus, given the random process for x, the Taylor expansion for small changes becomes:

$$\begin{aligned}
df &= f_x dx + \frac{1}{2} f_{xx} (dx)^2 \quad\quad\quad\quad\quad\text{[B2]} \\
&= f_x dx + \frac{1}{2} f_{xx} \phi^2 \tilde{\varepsilon}^2 dt.
\end{aligned}$$

Thus, the change in f has two components. The first term contains the (total) change in x, dx, and the second term contains $\phi^2 \tilde{\varepsilon}^2\ dt$, the square of the random part of dx. The second term is new, relative to standard calculus. It emerges whenever there is randomness in dx (that is $\phi > 0$) *and* the link between f and x is non-linear (that is $f_{xx} \neq 0$). Let us consider the mean and variance of the term $\phi^2\, \tilde{\varepsilon}^2\ dt$. The mean of $\phi^2 \tilde{\varepsilon}^2\ dt$ equals $\phi^2\, dt$ because $E(\tilde{\varepsilon}^2) = 1$, $\tilde{\varepsilon}$ being a standard normal. The varance of $\phi^2\, \tilde{\varepsilon}\ dt$ equals var$(\tilde{\varepsilon}^2)$ $\phi^4\, (dt)^2$, but this is negligible because it contains the term $(dt)^2$. In words, the mean of the new term,

$$\frac{1}{2} f_{xx} \phi^2 \tilde{\varepsilon}^2 dt,$$

is nontrivial as soon as there is randomness and nonlinearity, but deviations of $\phi^2 \tilde{\varepsilon}^2 \, dt$ from its mean are negligible.[22]

This last result allows a further simplification of Equation [B2]. Because deviations from the mean are negligible, we can simply set $\phi^2 \tilde{\varepsilon}^2 \, dt$ equal to its mean, $\phi^2 \, dt$, and write Equation [B2] as:

$$df = f_x \, dx + \frac{1}{2} f_{xx} \phi^2 \, dt, \qquad \text{[B3]}$$

which is Ito's Lemma. An application of Ito's Lemma to the case of geometric processes follows.

Example   8B.3

Suppose that

$$\frac{dx}{x} = \alpha \, dt + \sigma \, dz \text{ or } dx = x(\alpha \, dt + \sigma \, dz).$$

That is, assume that the *percentage* changes have a constant mean (denoted by α) and a constant standard deviation (denoted by σ). Then, the total change in $f(x)$ is given by:

$$\begin{aligned} df &= f_x \, dx + \frac{1}{2} f_{xx} \phi^2 \, dt \\ &= f_x x (\alpha \, dt + \sigma \, dz) + \frac{1}{2} f_{xx} x^2 \sigma^2 \, dt. \end{aligned} \qquad \text{[B4]}$$

We already mentioned that if the process for x is given by

$$\frac{dx}{x} = \alpha \, dt + \sigma \, dz.$$

then x will be lognormal (that is, $\ln(x)$ will be normal). We are now ready to demonstrate this.

Example   8B.4

Let $f(x) = \ln(x)$, and

$$\frac{dx}{x} = \alpha \, dt + \sigma \, dz.$$

The first and second derivatives of $f(x)$ are

---

[22] To understand the non-randomness in the second order term, it is helpful to go back to the origins of this type of process. Processes like dz were originally derived from a binomial process (by a French economist, Bachelier, who worked out the math in his dissertation "*La théorie de la speculation*," 1900, to model stock prices). Consider a binomial process for $\ln(V)$, which can go up to $\ln(V) + a$ or down to $\ln(V) - a$ with probability 0.5. The expectation of the change is zero. The squared change, a^2, is also equal to its expectation, $E(\Delta\ln(V)^2) = \frac{1}{2} a^2 + \frac{1}{2} a^2 = a^2$. Thus, there is no distinction between the squared change and its expectation. The same result holds here: $\phi^2 \varepsilon^2 \, dt = E(\phi^2 \varepsilon^2 \, dt) = \phi^2 \, dt$.

$$f_x = \frac{1}{x} \text{ and } f_{xx} = -\frac{1}{x^2},$$

so that

$$d\ln(x) = f_x dx + \frac{1}{2} f_{xx} \phi^2 dt$$

$$= f_x x(\alpha\, dt + \sigma\, dz) + \frac{1}{2} f_{xx}\, x^2 \sigma^2\, dt$$

$$= \left[\frac{1}{x}\right] x(\alpha\, dt + \sigma\, dz) - \frac{1}{2}\left[\frac{1}{x^2}\right] x^2 \sigma^2 dt$$

$$= \left(\alpha - \frac{1}{2}\sigma^2\right) dt + \sigma\, dz.$$

Thus,

- The *p.a.* mean $\mu = \alpha - \frac{1}{2}\sigma^2$ of the continuously compounded return (the change in $\ln(x)$) is systematically lower than the mean of the *p.a.* simple return, α. This reflects (and quantifies) a fact that we already know from Appendix 7A: continuously compounded returns are systematically below the corresponding simple returns (see Example 7A.1).
- Over short intervals dt, the random component of the continuously compounded return is indistinguishable from the random component in the simple return.
- Over any small interval dt, $d\ln(x)$ is normal. Thus, over any finite interval Δt, $\Delta\ln(x)$ will be normal, because it is the "sum" of many normal instantaneous changes. Thus, x itself is lognormal.

Ito's Lemma Applied to a Function of Two Lognormal Processes

So far, we have discussed cases where f is a function of only one random process x. Many variables are a function of more than one random process. For instance, f could be the price, in home currency, of a foreign stock; if V denotes the value of the stock in foreign currency and S denotes the exchange rate, then $f(V, S) = V \times S$. Or f may be the value of a portfolio, which depends on the prices of the assets in the portfolio. We now relate the change in f to the changes in two Ito processes x and y, each with its own instantaneous mean and variance:

$$dx = a_x\, dt + \phi_x\, dz_x \text{ and } dy = a_y\, dt + \phi_y\, dz_y.$$

The second-order Taylor expansion of $f(x,y)$ now is

$$df = f_x dx + f_y dy + \frac{1}{2}\left\{ f_{xx}(dx)^2 + 2 f_{xy} dx\, dy + f_{yy}(dy)^2 \right\}. \tag{B5}$$

Invoking our results from the previous section, we can set $(dx)^2 = \phi_x^2\, dt$ and $(dy)^2 = \phi_y^2\, dt$, the instantaneous variances of dx and dy. We now show an analogous result—$(dx)(dy)$ equals the instantaneous covariance between the random parts in dx and dy. To understand this, note that after the elimination of terms containing $(dt)^{3/2}$ and $(dt)^2$, the product $(dx)(dy)$ yields,

$$dx\,dy = (a_x\,dt + \phi_x\,dz_x)(a_y\,dt + \phi_y\,dz_y)$$
$$= (\phi_x\,dz_x)(\phi_y\,dz_y)$$
$$= (\phi_x\,\tilde{\varepsilon}_x\,\sqrt{dt})(\phi_y\,\tilde{\varepsilon}_y\,\sqrt{dt})$$
$$= \phi_x\,\phi_y\tilde{\varepsilon}_x\tilde{\varepsilon}_y\,dt.$$

This expression is of order of magnitude dt. That is, unlike the standard total differential in deterministic math, the term $(dx)(dy)$ is not of second order, and hence it does not vanish. However, just like in the case of $(dx)^2$, we need only to include the expected value of $(dx)(dy)$; the variance of $(dx)(dy)$ around its mean is of second order. We show this as follows:

- The expectation of $(dx)(dy)$ contains $E(\tilde{\varepsilon}_x\,\tilde{\varepsilon}_y)$, which is the covariance of the standardized random parts in dx and dy. However, the covariance of two standardized variables is, by definition, the correlation between the two variables, which we denote by $E(\tilde{\varepsilon}_x\,\tilde{\varepsilon}_y) = \rho$. Thus, the expectation of $dx\,dy$ equals $\phi_x\,\phi_y\,\rho\,dt$, the instantaneous covariance between dx and dy. This is of the order dt, and cannot be ignored.
- Obviously, the variance of $\phi_x\,\phi_y\,\tilde{\varepsilon}_x\,\tilde{\varepsilon}_y\,dt$ around its mean will again be of order $(dt)^2$, implying that we can set $\phi_x\,\phi_y\,\tilde{\varepsilon}_x\,\tilde{\varepsilon}_y\,dt$ equal to its mean, $\phi_x\,\phi_y\,\rho\,dt$.

To summarize: in Equation [B5], we can set $(dx)^2 = \phi_x^2\,dt$, and $(dy)^2 = \phi_y^2\,dt$, and $(dx)(dy) = \phi_x\,\phi_y\,\rho\,dt$; then:

$$df = f_x\,dx + f_y\,dy + \frac{1}{2}\Big\{ f_{xx}\phi_x^2 + 2f_{xy}\rho\,\phi_x\phi_y + f_{yy}\phi_y^2 \Big\}dt. \qquad \text{[B6]}$$

As before, the addition of

$$\frac{1}{2}\Big\{ f_{xx}\phi_x^2 + 2f_{xy}\rho\phi_x\phi_y + f_{yy}\phi_y^2 \Big\}dt$$

to the standard (deterministic) total differential, $df = f_x\,dx + f_y\,dy$, becomes important whenever x and y are random and f is nonlinear.

Example   8B.5

In this example, we describe the application of Ito's Lemma to the lognormal case. When $a_x = x\,\alpha_x$, $a_y = y\,\alpha_y$, $\phi_x = x\,\sigma_x$ and $\phi_y = y\,\sigma_y$ with α_x, α_y, σ_x, σ_y constants, then x and y are lognormals. When expressed in terms of the constants α_x, α_y, σ_x, σ_y, and ρ, the formula [B6] takes the following form:

$$df = f_x\,x(\alpha_x + \sigma_x\,dz_x) + f_y\,y(\alpha_y + \sigma_y\,dz_y) \qquad \text{[B7]}$$
$$+ \frac{1}{2}\Big\{ f_{xx}x^2\sigma_x^2 + 2f_{xy}\,xy\rho\sigma_x\sigma_x + f_{yy}y^2\sigma_y^2 \Big\}dt.$$

Example   8B.6

We will now look at stock returns in domestic and foreign currency. Consider the price process $f = VS$, where V is a foreign-currency stock price and S is the exchange rate, and where both V and S are log random walks:

$$\frac{dV}{V} = \alpha_V \, dt + \sigma_V \, dz_V \text{ and } \frac{dS}{S} = \alpha_S \, dt + \sigma_S \, dz_S.$$

Thus, $f = VS$ is the home currency price of the stock, and $(d\,VS)/(VS)$ equals the return on the foreign stock, measured in terms of domestic currency. Let us first link this return to the foreign currency return dV/V and the exchange rate change dS/S, using Ito's Lemma. Given that $(fV, S) = VS$, the derivatives are $f_V = S, f_S = V, f_{SS} = 0, f_{SV} = 1, f_{VV} = 0$. Ito's Lemma given in Equation [B7] implies that

$$d(VS) = S \, dV + V \, dS + \frac{1}{2}\left\{0 + 2\,VS\,\rho_{SV}\,\sigma_V\,\sigma_S + 0\right\}dt, \qquad \text{[B8]}$$

which, in turn, implies that

$$\frac{d\,VS}{VS} = \frac{dV}{V} + \frac{dS}{S} + \rho_{SV}\,\sigma_V\,\sigma_S \, dt.$$

Example 8B.6 shows that the cross term, $\rho_{SV}\,\sigma_V\,\sigma_S$, is important when the foreign currency return and the exchange rate change are correlated. In contrast, there is no cross term when the asset's foreign-currency return is risk free, for example, when the asset is a foreign T-bill, because a deterministic variable cannot be instantaneously correlated with another variable. We shall use this insight within Section 8B.3 and in Chapter 22.

Example   8B.7

We shall now discuss returns on a portfolio. Consider the function $f = n_s S + n_v V$, where V is the price of one asset, S is the price of another asset, and n_v and n_s are the number of shares of each asset held. Thus, f is the value of a portfolio. Since f is a linear function of V and S, the second-order derivatives are zero:

$$f_S = n_s, f_V = n_v, f_{SS} = 0, f_{VV} = 0, f_{SV} = 0.$$

Thus, applying Ito's Lemma:

$$df = n_s \, dS + n_v \, dV$$

$$= n_s S \frac{dS}{S} + n_v V \frac{dV}{V}$$

and dividing through by f:

$$\frac{df}{f} = \frac{n_S S}{f}\frac{dS}{S} + \frac{n_V V}{f}\frac{dV}{V}.$$

That is, the portfolio return is the value-weighted average return of the asset returns,

$$\frac{dS}{S} \text{ and } \frac{dV}{V},$$

with weights

$$\frac{n_S S}{n_S S + n_V V} \text{ and } \frac{n_V V}{n_S S + n_V V},$$

respectively.

We shall use this relationship in Chapters 13 and 22 when we discuss portfolio theory. The interim result $df = n_s\,dS + n_v\,dV$ will be used in the next section.

Ito's Lemma Applied to a Function of an Ito Process and Time

Having discussed the functions $f = f(x)$ and $f = f(x,y)$ we now consider $f = f(S,t)$, where t is calendar time. For example, f may be the price of a European option, which depends on time (because time to maturity matters) and on the stock price S. Assume that all other potential variables, like variance and interest rates, are constant (or at least deterministic). We can determine df as in Equation [B6]. However, time is non-stochastic, so it has no variance or covariance with dS. Thus, the change in f can be specified as:

$$df = f_t\,dt + f_S dS + \frac{1}{2}f_{SS}\phi_S^2 dt. \qquad [B9]$$

Example   8B.8

If $dS = S\,(\alpha\,dt + \sigma\,dz)$, then the change in $f = f(s,t)$ equals

$$df = f_t\,dt + f_S S(\alpha\,dt + \sigma\,dz) + \frac{1}{2}f_{SS}\,S^2\sigma_S^2 dt. \qquad [B10]$$

We are now ready to determine the Black-Scholes-Merton differential equation and indicate how it relates to the call pricing formula described in this chapter.

8B.3   The Black-Scholes-Merton Option Pricing Differential Equation

Derivation of the Differential Equation

Assume that the price of a contingent claim (like a call, a put, or any other derivative asset) is a continuous and twice differentiable function of the exchange rate, S, and of time, t; that is, $C = C(S,t)$.

Next assume that S is a log random walk: $dS = S\,\alpha\,dt + S\,\sigma\,dz$. Ito's Lemma, Equation [B10], then says that the change of the price of the contingent claim is related to the exchange rate change and the passage of time as follows:

$$dC = C_t\,dt + C_S\,dS + \frac{1}{2}C_{SS}\,S^2\sigma_S^2 dt. \qquad [\text{B10}]$$

Now consider buying *one* unit of foreign exchange, and investing this unit at the instantaneous foreign risk-free return $(dV)/V = r^*dt$. You can think of V as the value, in foreign currency, of a foreign deposit with an initial value of one unit of foreign currency. After one instant, the *home* currency value of this investment will have increased by the capital gain, dS, and the foreign return, r^*dt, on the initial investment S. This can be seen by setting, in Equation [B8], $\sigma_v = 0$ (so that the cross-term drops) and $V = 1$ (so that $VdS = dS$):

$$d\,VS = S\,r^*\,dt + dS.$$

We now use the insights obtained in Example B7. If we combine $n_s = -C_S$ units of foreign currency (invested at the foreign risk-free rate) and $n_c = 1$ contingent claims into a portfolio, this portfolio's initial value will be $p = C + (-C_S)\,S$. After an instant dt, the portfolio's value will change by the change in the call price and the total return on the foreign deposit:

$$dp = dC + (-C_S)\,d\,VS$$
$$= dC - C_S\,(dS + Sr^*\,dt)$$

or, using Equation [B10],

$$dp = [C_t\,dt + C_S\,dS + 1/2\,C_{SS}\,S^2\,\sigma_S^2 dt] - C_S\,(dS + S\,r^*\,dt)$$

and, after canceling out $C_S\,dS$ and $-C_S\,dS$,

$$dp = \left[C_t - C_S\,S\,r^* + \frac{1}{2}C_{SS}\,S^2\sigma_S^2\right]dt. \qquad [\text{B11}]$$

The crucial result is that the change in the value of the portfolio, dp, no longer contains the risky term dS: the uncertainty in the value of the contingent claim arising from the randomness in the exchange rate is perfectly hedged by an offsetting position in the foreign money market. Thus, dp is risk free every instant. To preclude arbitrage, the return on this risk-free portfolio, $(dp)/p$, should equal the instantaneous domestic risk-free return $r\,dt$:

$$\frac{dp}{p} = r\,dt \text{ or } dp = p\,r\,dt. \qquad [\text{B12}]$$

Since the portfolio consists of one contingent claim (worth C), and $-C_S$ units of foreign exchange (worth S each), the portfolio's initial value is $p = C - C_S\,S$. Substituting this into Equation [B12] and equating the result with Equation [B11], we obtain the differential equation that the value of the option must satisfy:

$$\left[C_t - C_S Sr^* + \frac{1}{2}C_{SS}S^2\sigma_S^2\right]dt = [C - C_S S]r\,dt,$$

or:

$$C\,r = C_t + C_S\,S(r - r^*) + \frac{1}{2}C_{SS}\,S^2\,\sigma_S^2. \tag{B13}$$

Black and Scholes (1973) derived the differential equation ([B13]) for the case $r^* = 0$ (that is, S is the price of a non-dividend-paying stock). If r^* is interpreted as the *p.a.* dividend yield, Equation [B13] is the Merton (1973) equation for a stock that pays out a continuous dividend strem $S\,r^*\,dt$.

Interpretation as a Risk-Adjusted Version of the Expected Capital Gain on the Option

It is useful to interpret the partial differential equation in terms of risk-adjusted expectations, as follows. Go back to Equation [B10] to obtain the change of the call price:

$$dC = C_t\,dt + C_S\,dS + \frac{1}{2}C_{SS}\,S^2\sigma_S^2 dt,$$

and rewrite this as:

$$= C_t\,dt + C_S\,S\,\frac{dS}{S} + \frac{1}{2}C_{SS}\,S^2\sigma_S^2 dt.$$

Next, take expectations. The exchange rate S is assumed to be a geometric process with instantaneous drift

$$E\left(\frac{dS}{S}\right) = \alpha_S dt.$$

Therefore, the expected capital gain on the option is:

$$E(dC) = C_t\,dt + C_S\,S\,\alpha_S\,dt + \frac{1}{2}C_{SS}\,S^2\,\sigma_S^2\,dt. \tag{B14}$$

If we denote the expected instantaneous rate of return on the call, $E(dC)/C$ by $\alpha_C\,dt$, and divide both sides by dt, we obtain:

$$C\,\alpha_C = C_t + C_S\,S\,\alpha_S + \frac{1}{2}C_{SS}\,S^2\,\sigma_S^2. \tag{B15}$$

Now, compare Equation [B15], term by term, with the differential Equation [B13].

- We see that, in the Black-Scholes-Merton Equation, [B13], $(r^* - r)$ replaces the true drift of S, α_S, in Equation [B15]. In the context of the discrete-time model in the main text of this chapter, this corresponds to the change from the true mean $E_t(\tilde{S}_T)$ to the risk-adjusted mean, $\mathrm{CEQ}_t(\tilde{S}_T) = F_{t,T}$. This is also analogous to the substitution of q for p in the binomial model.
- We also see that, in the Black-Scholes-Merton Equation [B13], the domestic risk-free rate replaces the true expected return on the contingent claim (α_C in Equation [B15]). This corresponds to discounting the risk-adjusted expected terminal value at the risk-free rate, as we did in the main text of this chapter and in the binomial model of the previous chapter.

In short, the Black-Scholes-Merton equation is one way of justifying the risk adjustment (by replacing $E(\tilde{S}_T)$ with $F_{t,T}$) and the subsequent discounting at the risk-free rate.

Solving the Partial Differential Equation

To obtain a solution for the partial differential equation in Equation [B13], we have to solve it subject to its boundary conditions. For a European call, for instance, the boundary condition is that, at $t = T$, $\tilde{C}_T = \text{Max}(\tilde{S}_T - X, 0)$. This is a well-known problem in physics, with the Black-Scholes-Merton formula (Equation [14]) as its solution. Alternatively, we can obtain the same result by computing the true expectation, replacing $E_t(\tilde{S}_T)$ by $F_{t,T}$, and discounting at the risk-free rate, as we did in this chapter.

9 INTERNATIONAL BOND AND MONEY MARKETS

In Chapters 1 to 8, we focused on exchange markets and the markets for forwards, futures, and options —contracts whose values are contingent on the exchange rate. In this chapter, we examine international money and bond markets. We do so because these markets provide short-term and long-term funding for large corporations and because they are linked to the exchange markets. From our study of Chapters 2 through 4, we are already familiar with the links between money markets and spot/forward markets. As we shall see, there are similar links between long-term capital markets and markets for currency swaps. Swaps are the topic of the next chapter.

We defined euromarkets in the introductory chapter of this text as offshore capital markets, in the sense that the currency of denomination is not the official currency of the country where the transaction takes place. For example, a Norwegian investor may deposit USD not in the US but with a bank located outside the US, for example, in Oslo or in London. We have also emphasized that eurocurrency markets are money markets, that is, markets for short-term deposits and loans, and not currency markets where foreign exchange is traded. For simplicity, when we say *euro-* we also include other offshore markets in the Middle East and especially in the Far East (Tokyo, Singapore, Hong Kong).

The earliest activity in the eurofinancial markets was in the deposit and loan segments, the segments where banks act as intermediaries between investors and borrowers. The emergence and growth of the eurobanking business was mainly the result of low costs, which enable a more narrow bid-ask spread. The success of this unregulated, wholesale banking market was soon imitated in the bond section and in the short-term securities part of the capital market (eurobonds and eurocommercial paper, respectively).

One can make a distinction between *foreign* and *offshore* transactions:[1]

- A *foreign* transaction differs from a purely domestic transaction only because the user of the funds is foreign. That is, a deal is set up where a corporation, a government, or an international institution:

    (1) Borrows in a country that is not its own.
    (2) Uses banks or securities houses from that foreign country.
    (3) Denominates the loans or bonds in that country's currency.

    Sometimes a whole series of parallel foreign bonds is issued. For example, financial institutions like the World Bank or the European Investment Bank may simultaneously issue LUF bonds in Luxembourg, FRF bonds in France, and so on. Each of the issues is, however, denominated in the target market's currency and placed with the help of intermediaries from the target country. In these respects, such a parallel issue is not an offshore transaction.

- In offshore transactions, in contrast,

    (1) Many national markets are tapped simultaneously.
    (2) There is help from *one* international consortium of banks.
    (3) The loans or bonds are denominated in *one* currency.

    For example, the European Investment Bank may issue ECU bonds in all EC countries simultaneously, with the help of one syndicate.

We have organized this chapter in the following way: In the first section, we describe the eurobanking world: eurocurrency markets for short-term international deposits, eurobank loans, credit lines, and forward contracts on eurointerest rates (the Forward Forward [FF] and the Forward Rate Agreement [FRA]). We discuss the counterparts of these banking products in the securities markets, namely, the eurobond and eurocommercial paper (ECP) markets in the second section. In Section 9.3, we discuss eurocurrency futures, an instrument that is similar to a forward contract on eurocurrency interest rates. We conclude in Section 9.4. The appendix reviews some basics about fixed-income transactions. The focus is on the no-arbitrage links between interest rates on zero-coupon instruments (like the money-market positions we discussed in Chapters 2 to 4), the rates on bonds and long-term loans, and the "forward" interest rates used in an FF or an FRA.

9.1   EUROBANKING PRODUCTS

The eurobanking segment is the oldest segment of the offshore markets. Even before World War II, there was a small market for USD deposits and loans in London, the world financial center. However, the market took off only in the sixties. We start by explaining the reasons for its rapid growth since then.

9.1.1   Why Eurocurrency Markets Exist

We distinguish between circumstances that facilitated the emergence of the market and reasons for its long-term success.

---

[1] There is no uniform terminology in the literature. Sometimes the labels are *international* versus *offshore* bank loans or bond issues, sometimes *foreign* versus *international*. The terminology is, of course, less crucial than the concepts.

Historic, Proximate Causes

There are a number of historical explanations for the development of euromoney markets:

- *Liberalization of trade and exchange*

The eurodollar markets began to expand in the fifties and sixties, after the lifting of the widespread exchange controls. These controls had been imposed after World War II because of the scarcity of USD (the only internationally accepted currency at the time). Note, however, that while liberalization of the exchange market is a *necessary condition* for the emergence of euromoney markets, it is not an *explanation* of that emergence.

- *The US trade deficit*

The liberalization of the European exchange markets was possible only because the shortage of USD did not last long. Immediately after the war, the US launched an international aid program (the Marshall Plan), which pumped dollars into the world economy. In addition, the US imported more goods and services than it exported—and could do so because unlike most other countries, it could pay in USD. (Non-US firms and individuals were willing to hold USD to make international payments.) In addition, US corporations were important international investors, buying companies or building plants and paying for them in dollars. Thus, the deficit on the *trade balance* and the *capital balance* meant that more and more USD ended up in the hands of foreign investors and foreign central banks.[2] Note, again, that this is not a true explanation for the rise of euromoney markets. The fact that there were foreign-held USD does not explain why part of these USD balances were held with European banks rather than directly with US banks. The next three arguments relate to positive incentives for *eurodollar* transactions.

- *Political risks*

Since the fifties, the cold war created political risks for communist countries that wished to hold USD deposits. The US government could seize Soviet deposits held in New York. For that reason, the Soviet Union and China shifted their dollar balances to London and Paris, out of reach of the US government.

- *UK capital controls and restrictions*

Since the nineteenth century, London has been the world's center for offshore financing. After World War II, however, the GBP was chronically overvalued, and the UK had serious balance-of-payments problems.[3] Thus, the British government limited foreign borrowing in GBP. As a result, UK banks borrowed USD (that is, accepted USD deposits), which were then used to extend USD loans instead of GBP loans.

- *US capital controls and restrictions*

In the US, the balance-of-payments disequilibrium and the growing overvaluation of the USD led to increased US interest rates. President Kennedy tried to alleviate the problem by imposing the *Interest*

---

[2] We shall have a closer look at the trade balance and the capital balance in Chapter 11. At this stage, all you need to know is that a **deficit** means that the value of the outflows from a country exceed the value of the inflows.

[3] Until 1949, the GBP maintained the gold parity that was originally fixed in 1752 by Isaac Newton. In view of the increase in money supply after World War I and, especially, World War II, this had become a very unrealistic rate. The pound devalued by 40 percent in 1949, and by 16 percent in 1967.

Equalization Tax (1963–74) on foreign borrowing in the US. This tax allowed internal US interest rates to remain below USD interest rates offered in Europe. President Kennedy and later, President Johnson, also imposed *foreign credit restraints* (1965, 1968–74) that hindered borrowing by foreigners in the US market. Simultaneously, *Regulation Q* (enacted in 1966, relaxed in 1974, and abolished in 1986) imposed interest ceilings on domestic USD deposits with US commercial banks. The combined effect of all of this was that US corporations and investors preferred to hold USD deposits in Europe (where they obtained better rates), and these dollars were then re-lent to non-US borrowers who were not allowed to borrow USD in the US. Finally, Nixon's voluntary (and later, mandatory) *curbs on capital exports* had the unexpected result of US multinationals avoiding depositing their funds in the US, fearing that the funds would be blocked there. The funds were deposited, instead, in euromarkets.

Comparative Advantages in the Long Run

The eurodollar markets did not collapse after all of the regulations described above were abolished. Nor can the above factors explain the more recent emergence of offshore markets for other currencies, like the DEM, the JPY, or the ECU, and—to a lesser extent—the CHF, FRF, NLG, etc. The long-term explanation of the success of these offshore markets is their lower bid-offer spread (that is, the difference between interest rates on loans and interest rates on deposits), which in turn reflects the lower costs of offshore banking as compared to domestic banking. There are many reasons for the low operating costs.

• *A lean and mean machine*

The offshore market is essentially a wholesale market, where large volumes of transactions allow narrow spreads. Eurobanks, unlike many domestic commercial banks, do not offer politically or socially inspired subsidized loans. Nor do they need an expensive retail network.

• *Low legal costs*

Most euroborrowers are sovereign states or high-grade corporations. This means that there are hardly any costs of credit evaluation, bonding, and monitoring.

• *Fewer regulations*

There is no compulsory deposit insurance, which means that there are no insurance costs. Nor are there any reserve requirements (which are, in fact, similar to taxes on deposits),[4] and local monetary authorities tend to be far more lenient as far as credit restraints are concerned when borrowing does not involve their home currency.[5]

• *Lower Taxes*

Eurobanks are often located in tax havens or are part of a financial network involving tax havens. Also in mainstream OECD countries, offshore transactions often receive beneficial tax treatment when

---

[4] A 5 percent reserve requirement would mean that a bank, when receiving a deposit for 100, has to deposit 5 in a non-interest-earning account with the central bank. Thus, only 95 can be re-lent. This increases the effective cost of accepting the deposit.

[5] It is true that eurobanks are subject, like any other banks, to the so-called Bank of International Settlements (BIS) rules. However, these are not reserve requirements. Rather, the BIS rules set the minimum amount of equity a bank should have, in light of its balance-sheet and off-balance-sheet positions.

compared with domestic businesses (for example, a waiver of stamp duties or withholding taxes; in this respect, many OECD countries have followed the lead of tax-haven countries).[6] Furthermore, many investors with undeclared income—the "Swiss dentist" or the "Belgian dentist," as *The Economist* and *Euromoney* fondly call them—appreciate the opportunities for tax avoidance or tax evasion available in euromoney markets. Foreign deposits are often fiscally anonymous (that is, the bank cannot be forced to reveal their identity to a foreign tax authority), or are often in the form of bearer securities.[7]

In the following sections, we describe the products offered by eurobanks. The first product we discuss is the deposit.

9.1.2   Eurodeposits
Forms of Deposits
Initially, eurodeposits were typically *time deposits* or *term deposits,* that is, non-negotiable, registered instruments with a fixed life. A *certificate of deposit* (CD) is the tradable security version of the traditional term deposit: it is negotiable (that is, can be sold to another investor at any time) and is often a bearer security (that is, the owner is not registered as such with the issuing company or institution; holding the piece of paper is assumed to be proof of ownership).

Fixed versus Floating Interest
The bulk of the deposits have a very short duration—for instance, overnight, one or two weeks, or one, three, or six months. These short-term deposits or CDs pay no interim interest; there is a single payment, principal and interest, at expiration. For long-term CDs or long-term deposits (up to seven years), there is a fixed coupon or floating-rate coupon. For CDs with floating rate coupons, the life of the CD is subdivided into subperiods of usually six months. The interest to be earned over each such period is fixed at the beginning of the period, called the *reset date,* and this interest rate is based on the then-prevailing market interest rate. This market rate is usually the London Interbank Offer Rate (LIBOR) or the Interbank Offer Rate in the currency's domestic financial center.[8] It may also be the US T-bill rate, or the US prime rate.

Example   9.1

An investor buys a FRF 100,000 floating-rate CD with a life of two years, at PIBOR (the Paris Interbank Offer Rate) reset every six months. The initial interest rate is 10 percent *p.a.,* which implies that after six months the investor receives $100,000 \times 10\%/2 = $ FRF 5,000. The reset date is two days before this amount is paid out, and the six-month PIBOR on this reset date may turn out to be, say, 7 percent *p.a.*

---

[6] A **stamp duty** is a tax on transactions in securities. A **withholding tax** is a tax levied on interest or dividends, withheld when the interest or dividend is paid out (rather than collected afterwards, on the basis of a tax return). See Chapter 23.

[7] A bearer security is a piece of paper that is issued to investors without recording or registering their names, and that can subsequently be resold without notifying the issuing company. The holder of the bearer securities simply clips off an expiring coupon—in fact, the word *coupon* derives from the French verb *couper,* that is, to clip—and cashes in the corresponding interest payments or dividends through a bank. In contrast, ownership of a registered security can be transferred only by recording the new owner in the company's registers, and the company pays interest or dividends by mailing checks to the owners of the bonds or stocks. Many investors dislike the idea that tax authorities can verify the register of bondholders or shareholders to find out who earned how much.

[8] Like PIBOR (Paris, for the FRF), AIBOR (Amsterdam, for the NLG), and so on.

This means that the second interest payment will be only $100,000 \times 7\%/2 = $ FRF 3,500. There will be two more of these reset dates. At the end of the last period, the principal is also paid back.

You can view such a floating-rate CD as a series of short-term CDs that are automatically rolled over without reinvestment of the interest earned each period. Sometimes a floating-rate CD has a *cap* or a *floor*—that is, the interest rate that the investor actually receives has an upper or lower bound. We shall discuss caps and floors in the next section, which describes euroloans.

9.1.3   Eurocredits and Euroloans

Eurobanks offer essentially the same products as domestic banks—namely, loans and credit lines. One difference is that euroloans tend to be of the floating-rate type, whereas many domestic loans have an interest rate that is fixed over the entire life of the loan. Another difference is that euroloans tend to be extended by a group of banks (a consortium) rather than by a single institution. A *consortium* (or *syndicate*) that extends a loan consists of many banks that play different roles.

- The *lead bank* (or *lead manager*) negotiates with the borrower for tentative terms and conditions, obtains a mandate, and looks for other banks that provide the money or undertake to provide the money.
- The banks that provide the actual funding are called *participating banks.*
- Because the funding is not yet arranged at the time of the negotiations, the lead manager often contacts a smaller number of *managing banks* to underwrite the loan, that is, guarantee to make up for the shortage of funds if there is a shortage.
- The *paying agent,* finally, is the bank that receives the service payments from the borrower and distributes them to the participating banks.

Any given bank can play multiple roles. For instance, the lead bank is almost invariably also the largest underwriter (hence, the name "lead manager") and often provides funding as well. The main objective of syndication is to spread the risks, but it also eliminates the moral hazard of the borrower paying off the larger banks and ignoring the small debt holders. Because of the paying agent system, the borrower either defaults toward all banks, or toward none.

As in domestic banking, the borrower often signs *promissory notes* (that is, *I owe you* [IOU] documents), one for each payment. The advantage of receiving promissory notes is that they are negotiable. That is, if the lending bank needs funds, it can pass on the promissory note to another financial institution as security for a new loan, or it can sell the promissory note.

Figure 9.1 shows a typical "tombstone"—that is, a severe-looking advertisement—reporting a straight bank loan. The borrower is Endesa Chile Overseas Co., a subsidiary of Empresa Nacional de Electricidad. The parent guarantees the subsidiary's loan—a common practice. "Term loan" refers to a loan with a fixed amount and life (in contrast to a credit line, where the borrower withdraws money or pays back in light of the circumstances). The lead bank and payment agent is Credit Suisse First Boston. See below for examples where more information on the syndicate is given.

Revolving or Floating-Rate Loans

Because eurodeposits have short maturities (mostly one, three, and six months), eurobankers have a natural desire to match these with short-term loans. If there were a maturity mismatch, banks would face the risk that, after having lent long-term at a fixed rate, they may have to refinance short-term at unexpectedly high interest rates.

FIGURE 9.1   Tombstone Reporting a Straight Bank Loan

This announcement appears as a matter of record only.   DECEMBER, 1993

U.S. $85,000,000

Endesa Chile Overseas Co.

Term Loan

Guaranteed by

Empresa Nacional de Electricidad S.A.

Arranger and Facility Agent

Credit Suisse First Boston Limited

Example   9.2

A bank accepts a three-month, DKK 100m deposit at 5 percent *p.a.* and extends a loan for six months at 6 percent *p.a.* For simplicity, assume that this deposit and this loan represent the bank's entire balance sheet. After the deposit has expired, the bank must pay DKK 100m $\times (1 + 5\%/4) =$ DKK 101.25m to the original lender. Since there are no cash inflows from the loan, the bank must borrow this amount (that is, accept a new three-month deposit). If, at that time, the three-month rate has increased to 10 percent *p.a.*, then after another three months the bank has to pay $101.25 \times (1 + 10\%/4) =$ DKK 103.78125m though it receives only 100m × (1 + 6%/2) = DKK 103m from the original six-month borrower. Thus, the bank lost DKK 781,250 because of the increase in the short-term interest rate.

In the above example, the maturity mismatch is not large because the loan is assumed to be for only six months. However, borrowers often have long-term capital needs, and rolling over short-term loans (at interest rates revised at each roll-over date) is awkward for the borrower; the bank can always refuse to extend a new loan or drastically increase the spread over LIBOR. The need to reconcile the banker's desire for a safe interest margin with the borrower's preference for long-term guaranteed funding gave rise to the **revolving loan** or **floating-rate loan**. This is a medium-term or long-term loan where the interest rate is reset every period on the basis of the then-prevailing money market rate plus a spread. For example, if interest is payable every six months, then at the beginning of every such period, the interest rate for the next half-year is set equal to the then-prevailing six-month LIBOR rate, increased with a spread of, say, 1/2 percent *p.a.* Thus, the bank is protected against interest risk, and the borrower's funding is guaranteed for an agreed-upon period at a preset spread over the base rate. The basis of the interest rate in rolled-over loans is typically the LIBOR or a similar interbank rate. Occasionally, the US prime rate or the US T-bill rate is chosen.

Revolving Loans with Caps or Floors

Sometimes there is a **cap** and/or a **floor** to the effective interest rate. For instance, the contract may say that the interest rate will never exceed 10 percent *p.a.* (cap), or fall below 7 percent *p.a.* (floor). These caps or floors are like European-type options on T-bills or on eurodeposits or euroloans.

Example   9.3

Suppose that you have a one-year, NZD 1m loan, with half-yearly interest payments capped at 10 percent *p.a.*—that is, 5 percent per half-year. The interest rate for the period that starts immediately is already known—say, 8 percent *p.a.* The 5 percent cap on the next six-month effective return means that, after six months, you have the right to borrow NZD 100m at 5 percent for another six-month period. That is, you have the right to place six-month promissory notes with expiration value NZD 1.05m at a price of NZD 1m—a right that is valuable to you if at the reset date the six-month rate is above 10 percent *p.a.* Thus, you have the right to sell (that is, you hold a *put* option on) a NZD 1.05m note at a strike price X = NZD 1m.

Suppose that you have a one-year, NZD 1m loan, with half-yearly interest payments with a floor at 7 percent *p.a.*—that is, 3.5 percent per half-year. The interest rate for the period that starts immediately is already known; for instance, it may be 8 percent *p.a.* or 4 percent effective. The 7 percent floor means that, after six months, your bank can insist that you write a six-month promissory note with a face value NZD 1.035m, and can buy it from you at a price of NZD 1m. This right is valuable to the bank if at the reset date the six-month rate is below 7 percent *p.a.* Thus, the bank has the right to buy (that is, holds a *call* option on) a NZD 1.035m note at a strike price X = NZD 1m.

In short, the floor is a call option on a promissory note, and the option is held by the lender and written by the borrower. The cap is a put option on a promissory note, and the option is held by the borrower and written by the lender.

Costs of a Euroloan

There are various costs associated with a euroloan. These include:

- An up-front **management fee** and **participation fee**, usually on the order of 0.5 to 1 percent. The *up-front* feature means that this amount is deducted from the principal. That is, the borrower receives only 99 percent to 99.5 percent of the nominal value of the loan.
- A (small) paying agent's fee to cover the administrative expenses.
- The risk spread above the risk-free rate (that is, above LIBOR in the case of a floating-rate loan, or above the long-term fixed rate paid by a government of excellent credit standing). This spread depends on the quality of the borrower, the political risk of his or her country,[9] the maturity and grace period, and the up-front fee. Also, the market situation affects the spread.

In principle, the fees are compensation for the services of the intermediaries, while the spread is a compensation for default risk. However, one can trade a higher up-front fee for a lower spread, and *vice versa*. For instance, borrowers often accept a high up-front fee in return for a lower spread because the spread is sometimes seen as a quality rating. One corollary of the trading of up-front fees for risk spreads is that the spread that country X pays may be a poor indicator of the creditworthiness of country X. Another corollary is that reliable comparisons between offers from competing banks can be made only if there is a *single* measure of cost. Thus, when comparing offers from competing syndicates, one should convert the up-front fees into equivalent spreads, or the spreads and paying-agent fees into equivalent up-front costs.

Example   9.4

Suppose that an up-front fee of USD 3,700 is asked on a five-year loan of USD 100,000 with an annual interest payment of 10 percent (including spreads) and one single amortization at the loan's maturity date. The effective proceeds of the loan are, therefore, USD $100,000 - 3,700 =$ USD 96,300. The effective interest rate can be estimated by computing the internal rate of return or *yield,* denoted by y, on the transaction:

$$\text{Find } y \text{ such that } \frac{10,000}{1+y} + \frac{10,000}{(1+y)^2} + \frac{10,000}{(1+y)^3} + \frac{10,000}{(1+y)^4} + \frac{110,000}{(1+y)^5} = 96,300.$$

This equation can be solved on a spreadsheet or on a calculator. The solution is, approximately, $y = 11$ percent, which is 1 percent above the stated rate. Conversely, the up-front fee is equivalent to adding 1 percent *p.a.* to the stated rate.

In the above example, the future payments are known because the loan had a fixed interest rate. If the loan has a floating rate, one can no longer compute the yield because the future cash flows are unknown. However, the up-front fee can still be translated into an equivalent annual payment or **equivalent annuity**, using the interest rate on a fixed-rate loan with the same life and the same default risk.

---

[9] In our context, political risk is the risk that the borrower's government may block payments of interest or principal to foreign debtors if the country is short of foreign currency.

The equivalent annuity can then be converted into an equivalent percentage spread by dividing the annuity by the loan's nominal value.

Example 9.5

We use the same data as in Example 9.4, except that the loan has a floating rate. If the normal market rate on a fixed-rate loan with the same life and default risk as the floating-rate loan is 11 percent, the equivalent annuity (EqAn) of USD 3,700 up-front is determined as follows:

$$\text{Find EqAn such that } \frac{\text{EqAn}}{1.11} + \frac{\text{EqAn}}{(1.11)^2} + \frac{\text{EqAn}}{(1.11)^3} + \frac{\text{EqAn}}{(1.11)^4} + \frac{\text{EqAn}}{(1.11)^5} = 3,700.$$

This can be rewritten as:

$$3,700 = \text{EqAn} \times \left\{ \frac{1}{1.11} + \frac{1}{(1.11)^2} + \frac{1}{(1.11)^3} + \frac{1}{(1.11)^4} + \frac{1}{(1.11)^5} \right\}$$

$$= \text{EqAn} \times 3.6959.$$

It follows that

$$\text{EqAn} = \frac{3,700}{3.6959} = \text{USD } 1001.$$

Thus, the up-front fee is equivalent to a spread of 1,001/100,000, that is, about 1 percent *p.a.*

Credit Lines

In addition to outright loans, eurobanks also offer standby credits. These come in two forms:

- A standard line of credit (**credit line**) of, say, GBP 10m gives the beneficiary the right to borrow up to GBP 10m, at the prevailing interest rate plus a preset spread. The difference between a credit line and a loan is that with a credit line the company is not forced to actually borrow the money. Interest (in the strict sense) is payable only on the portion actually used, while on the unused funds only a **commitment fee** of 0.25 to 1 percent *p.a.* needs to be paid. A credit line is, in principle, a short-term commitment. In practice, a credit line tends to get extended, but this is not an automatic right to the creditor. Unless stated otherwise, the credit line can be revoked by the bank if there are substantial changes in the creditor's credit standing.
- Under a **revolving commitment**, the creditor has the irrevocable right to borrow up to a stated limit, at the then-prevailing rate plus a preset spread during an agreed-upon period of (usually) several years. For instance, a borrower may have the right to issue six-month

promissory notes worth up to GBP 50m at interest of six-month LIBOR plus 1.5 percent *p.a.* This is similar to a credit line, except that it cannot be revoked during its life.

A credit line is like an option on the preset spread, and the revolving commitment is like a series of such options (one expiring every six months, for instance). These contracts are options, and not forward contracts, because the beneficiary can always borrow elsewhere if the market-required spread drops. The credit line and the revolving commitment differ from caps in the sense that the contract imposes a ceiling on the spread, not on the interest.

Figure 9.2 contains a tombstone reporting a credit line. This credit line replaces ("consolidates") one or more earlier financing facilities, and is to be used only for pre-export financing. As mentioned

FIGURE 9.2   Tombstone Reporting a Credit Line

This announcement appears as a matter of record only.

MEXICO DESARROLLO INDUSTRIAL MINERO, S.A. DE C.V.
Industrial Minera México, S.A. de C.V.
Mexicana de Cobre, S.A. de C.V.

$400,000,000
Consolidating Facility
Medium Term Pre-Export Financing

Agent
ING BANK

Co-Agents
BANQUE PARIBAS   **CHEMICAL BANK**

Co-Leads

BANCO MEXICANO, S.A.	BANCOMER, S.A.
BANQUE FRANCAISE DU COMMERCE EXTERIEUR	DEUTSCHE BANK AG
SOCIETE GENERALE	BANQUE INDOSUEZ
BANQUE NATIONALE DE PARIS	GENERALE BANK

Funds provided by

ING BANK	BANQUE PARIBAS
CHEMICAL BANK	BANCO MEXICANO, S.A.
BANCOMER, S.A.	BANQUE FRANCAISE DU COMMERCE EXTERIEUR
DEUTSCHE BANK AG	SOCIETE GENERALE
ASLK-CGER BANK NV-SA	BANCO LATINOAMERICANO DE EXPORTACIONES, S.A.
BANQUE INDOSUEZ	BANQUE NATIONALE DE PARIS
CREDIT SUISSE	GENERALE BANK
MULTIBANCO COMERMEX, S.A.	BANQUE WORMS
THE FIRST NATIONAL BANK OF MARYLAND	

Structured and arranged by
ING BANK

ING 🦁 BANK   Internationale
Nederlanden
Bank

April 1993

Courtesy of ING Capitol

at the bottom of the tombstone, the lead bank is ING Bank. ING also acts as agent, but has delegated some of its functions to Paribus and Chemical. The eight co-leads are the underwriters. Seventeen banks (including the lead and co-leads) provide the actual funding.

Example   9.6

A company has the right to borrow at 1 percent above LIBOR. If the company's credit rating deteriorates, or if average spreads in the market increase, the 1 percent spread has become a bargain relative to what would have to be paid on new borrowing, and the credit will be effectively used. If, on the other hand, the company's rating improves, or if average spreads in the market fall, the 1 percent spread may be very high. If the company uses the credit line, it still has to pay the agreed-upon 1 percent spread. However, the company can also borrow elsewhere, at a spread that reflects its better standing or the lower average spreads. Thus, the company has a cap option on the 1 percent spread.

9.1.4   The Forward Forward and the Forward Rate Agreement
Forward Contracts on Interest Rates

We have seen that loans often contain options on interest rates (caps and floors).[10] Besides interest rate options, there are also *forward* contracts on interest rates. Such forward contracts come under two guises—the **Forward Forward contract (FF)**, or the **Forward Rate Agreement (FRA)**.

A Forward Forward contract fixes an interest rate today (t) for a deposit or loan starting at a future time T_1 ($> t$) and expiring at T_2 ($> T_1$).

Example   9.7

Consider a six-to-nine-month Forward Forward contract for 10m Finnish marks at 10 percent *p.a.* (simple interest). This contract guarantees that the return on a three-month deposit of FIM 10m, to be made six months from now, will be $10\%/4 = 2.5\%$. At time T_1 (six months from now), the FIM 10m will be deposited, and the principal plus the agreed-upon interest of 2.5 percent will be received at time T_2 (nine months from now).

A more recent, and more popular, variant is the Forward Rate Agreement. Under an FRA, the deposit is *notional*—that is, the contract is about a hypothetical deposit rather than an actual deposit. Instead of effectively making the deposit, the holder of the contract will settle the gain or loss in cash, and pay or receive the present value of the difference between the contracted forward interest rate and market rate that is actually prevailing at time T_1.

---

[10] These options can also be bought separately rather than as part of a loan or bond package.

Example 9.8

Consider a nine-to-twelve-month FIM 5m notional deposit at a forward interest rate of 12 percent *p.a.* (that is, a forward return of 3 percent). If the Helsinki Interbank Offer Rate (HIBOR) after nine months (T_1) turns out to be 10 percent *p.a.* (implying a return of 2.5 percent), the FRA has a positive value equal to the difference between the promised interest (3 percent on FIM 5m) and the interest in the absence of the FRA, 2.5 percent on FIM 5m. Thus, the investor will receive the present value of this contract, which amounts to:

$$\text{FIM 5m} \times \frac{0.03 - 0.025}{1.025} = \text{FIM } 24,390.2.$$

In practice, the reference interest rate on which the cash settlement is based is computed as an average of many banks' quotes, two days before T_1. The contract stipulates how many banks will be called, from what list, and how the averaging is done. In the early eighties, FRAs were quoted for short-term maturities only. Currently, quotes extend up to ten years.

Why FRAs Exist

Like any forward contract, an FRA can be used either for hedging or for speculation purposes. Hedging may be desirable in order to facilitate budget projections in an enterprise or to reduce uncertainty and the associated costs of financial distress. Banks, for example, use FRAs, along with T-bill futures and bond futures, to reduce maturity mismatches between their assets and liabilities. For instance, a bank with *average* duration of three months on the liability side and twelve months on the asset side, can use a three-to-twelve month FRA to eliminate most of the interest risk.[11] An FRA can, of course, serve as a speculative instrument too.

FRAs have some advantages over T-bill futures and bond futures; these advantages are similar to those of forward exchange contracts over currency futures contracts, as discussed in Chapter 5. First, FFs or FRAs are pure forward contracts, which means that there is no marking to market. It follows that, by using FFs or FRAs, one avoids the additional interest risk that arises from marking to market. Second, in the absence of marking to market, there is no ruin risk. The firm need not worry about potential cash outflows that may lead to liquidity problems and insolvency. Third, in the absence of marking to market, there is an exact arbitrage relationship between spot rates and forward rates; hence these contracts are easy to value. In contrast, the pricing of a futures-style contract is more difficult because of interest risk. Finally, FRAs are tailor-made, over-the-counter instruments and are, therefore, more flexible than (standardized) futures contracts. For these reasons, FFs and FRAs are better suited for arbitrage or hedging than are futures.

As we shall show in the next paragraph, FRAs can be replicated from term deposits and loans. For financial institutions, and even for other firms, FRAs (and interest futures) are also superior to such synthetic FRAs in the sense that they do not inflate the balance sheet.

---

[11] The hedge will never be perfect if we bridge the difference between *average* durations, though.

Example   9.9

Suppose that you need a three-to-six month FF for ITL 1b. Replication would mean that you borrow (somewhat less than) ITL 1b for three months and invest the proceeds for six months. Thus, your balance sheet would have increased by ITL 1b, without any increase in profits or cash flows compared to the case where you used an FF or an FRA.

The drawback of using an FF or FRA is that there is no organized secondary market. However, as in the case of forward contracts on foreign currency, long-term FRA contracts are often collateralized or periodically recontracted. This reduces credit risk. Thus, a fairly active over-the-counter market for FRAs is emerging.

The Valuation of FFs (or FRAs)

We now discuss the pricing of FFs (or FRAs—both have the same value): How should one value an outstanding contract, and how should the market set the normal forward interest rate at a given point in time? In this section, we adopt the following notation:

t_0 : the date on which the contract was initiated

$t\ (\geq t_0)$: the moment the contract is valued

T_1 : the expiration date of the forward contract (that is, the date that the gains or losses on the FRA are settled, and the date at which the notional deposit starts)

$T_2\ (>T_1)$: the expiration date of the notional deposit

$r_{t_0,T_1,T_2}^{\text{forw}}$: the effective return between T_1 and T_2, without annualization, promised on the notional deposit at the date the FRA was signed, t_0

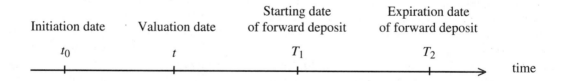

First consider the valuation of a T_1-to-T_2 forward forward deposit for ITL 1 that has been outstanding since time t_0, and promises a return of $r_{t_0,T_1,T_2}^{\text{forw}}$. Like a currency forward, this contract has two legs, each of which can be replicated in the money markets—the outflow by a loan, and the inflow by a deposit—except that now the loan and deposit differ by maturity rather than by currency. By matching the cash flows of each money-market operation with the corresponding leg of the FF, the entire FF can be replicated and hence also valued. Figure 9.3 summarizes the replication of the FF, as follows:

- In the first column, we show the cash flows from the FF: there will be an outflow of one unit of currency at time T_1, and an inflow of $1 + r_{t_0,T_1,T_2}^{\text{forw}}$ at time T_2.
- In the second column, we list the actions to be taken at time $t\ (\geq t_0)$ in order to replicate each of the cash flows from the FF.
- Column three (labeled "Cash flows in future") shows the cash flows arising from the replication strategy. The loan, at time t, of $1/1 + r_{t,T_1}$ units, will create an outflow of one unit at time T_1—exactly as in the first leg of the FF. The deposit, made at time t, of

$$\frac{1+r^{\text{forw}}_{t_0,T_1,T_2}}{1+r_{t,T_2}},$$

will lead to an inflow of $(1+r^{\text{forw}}_{t_0,T_1,T_2})$ at time T_2 again exactly as in the second leg of the FF. Thus, column three demonstrates that the proposed replication strategy achieves its purpose.

- Column four, lastly, shows the cost of the replicating strategy, that is, the money one needs at time t to form the portfolio. One does not need any cash, at time t, to get a loan; actually, at time t the loan *generates* cash rather than absorbing cash—hence the minus sign before the amount of the loan. The deposit, in contrast, requires cash at time t. Thus, the net amount of cash needed at time t to form the replicating portfolio equals the size of the deposit,

$$\frac{1+r^{\text{forw}}_{t_0,T_1,T_2}}{1+r_{t,T_2}},$$

minus the proceeds of the loan,

$$\frac{1}{1+r_{t,T_1}}.$$

Or, more briefly, the net cost is the difference of the present values of the cash flows.

FIGURE 9.3   An Example of How to Value an FF

| Cash flows from outstanding FF deposit | Replication strategy | | |
	Action today (t)	Cash flows in future	Cash outlays today
Time T_1: -1	Borrow $\dfrac{1}{1+r_{t,T_1}}$ maturing at T_1	-1 at T_1	$-\dfrac{1}{1+r_{t,T_1}}$ (Inflow of cash)
Time T_2: $+(1+r^{\text{forw}}_{t_0,T_1,T_2})$	Deposit $\dfrac{1+r^{\text{forw}}_{t_0,T_1,T_2}}{1+r_{t,T_2}}$ maturing at T_2	$+(1+r^{\text{forw}}_{t_0,T_1,T_2})$ at T_2	$\dfrac{1+r^{\text{forw}}_{t_0,T_1,T_2}}{1+r_{t,T_2}}$ (Outflow)
Total: T_1-to-T_2 FF at $r^{\text{forw}}_{t_0,T_1,T_2}$			$\dfrac{1+r^{\text{forw}}_{t_0,T_1,T_2}}{1+r_{t,T_2}} - \dfrac{1}{1+r_{t,T_1}}$

To rule out arbitrage opportunities, the market value of the FF must be equal to the cost of the replicating portfolio. Thus, we conclude the following:

$$\text{Market value at time } t \text{ of a } T_1\text{-to-}T_2 \text{ FF initiated at } r^{\text{forw}}_{t_0,T_1,T_2} = \frac{1+r^{\text{forw}}_{t_0,T_1,T_2}}{1+r_{t,T_2}} - \frac{1}{1+r_{t,T_1}}. \qquad [1]$$

Example   9.10

The cash flows from an outstanding three-to-six month FIM 10m FF at 10 percent *p.a.* are FIM (–)10m three months from now, and FIM (+)10.25m six months from now. These cash flows are replicated by a portfolio that contains the following items:

- A three-month loan with expiration value 10m at time T_1 (implying an outflow of FIM 10m three months from now).
- A six-month deposit with expiration value 10.25m at T_2 (implying an inflow of FIM 10.25m six months from now).

Suppose that the current three- and six-months interest rates are 9 percent and 9.125 percent *p.a.* Then the replicating portfolio is worth:

$$\text{Market Value of FF} = PV(\text{inflows}) - PV(\text{outflows})$$

$$= \frac{\text{FIM } 10.25\text{m}}{1+(6/12)\times 0.09125} - \frac{\text{FIM } 10\text{m}}{1+(3/12)\times 0.09} = \text{FIM } 22{,}798.$$

This valuation is useful for reporting purposes or when there is premature termination of a contract. Another application is that it allows us to identify the equilibrium forward rate of return at time t. This follows from the zero-value property of a forward contract at inception, that is, at time $t = t_0$. Thus, we have to find the rate $r^{\text{forw}}_{t,T_1,T_2}$ such that the market value of a (new) T_1-to-T_2 FF at $r^{\text{forw}}_{t,T_1,T_2}$ is equal to zero. From Equation [1], this means that the forward return has to satisfy:

$$\frac{1+r^{\text{forw}}_{t,T_1,T_2}}{1+r_{t,T_2}} - \frac{1}{1+r_{t,T_1}} = 0. \qquad [2]$$

This immediately implies the following relationship between forward interest rates and spot interest rates:

$$1+r^{\text{forw}}_{t,T_1,T_2} = \frac{1+r_{t,T_2}}{1+r_{t,T_1}}. \qquad [3]$$

Equation [3] implies that

$$(1+r_{t,T_2}) = (1+r_{t,T_1})(1+r^{\text{forw}}_{t,T_1,T_2}).$$

To interpret the right-hand side, note that this represents the proceeds of a standard time deposit expiring at time T_1, where the deposit is contractually rolled-over to time T_2 at the initial forward rate $r^{\text{forw}}_{t,T_1,T_2}$. Thus, Equation [3] says that the proceeds of a (direct) time deposit expiring at time T_2, $1+r_{t,T_2}$, are the same as the proceeds of a (synthetic) time deposit consisting of a shorter-lived deposit prolonged by a Forward Forward. Similarly, a t-to-T_2 loan will cost the same as a t-to-T_1 loan rolled over at the forward interest rate. In short, in the absence of spreads, there are no least-cost dealing opportunities if the no-arbitrage condition [3] is satisfied.

As in the case of currency forwards, no causality is implied by our way of expressing Equation [3]. The three rates are set jointly and have to satisfy Equation [3]. As in Chapter 2, one could argue that causality, if any, may run from the forward interest rate towards the spot rate because the forward rate reflects the risk-adjusted expectations about the future interest rate. We shall use Equation [3] when we discuss eurocurrency futures.

This finishes our discussion of eurobanking products. We now describe the counterparts in the eurosecurities markets.

9.2 EUROSECURITY MARKETS

Almost simultaneously with the emergence of euromoney markets, firms and governments started issuing USD bonds outside the US, and sold the bonds to non-US residents. Such a bond issue is called a **euro-dollar bond** issue. As of the sixties, and particularly in the seventies, eurobonds were denominated in currencies other than the USD. Also in the seventies, corporations and governments started issuing short-term paper, although this short-term **eurocommercial paper** market did not take off until the late eighties.

The markets to be discussed in this section are the tradable-security versions of the banking products, which we discussed in the preceding section. Figure 9.4 matches the eurobanking products with the closest equivalent in the eurosecurities markets. You may check these correspondences as we proceed.

9.2.1 Eurobonds
Why Eurobond Markets Exist
The explanations for the long-term success of offshore securities markets are largely similar to the ones cited for eurocurrency markets:

• *Fewer regulations for offshore public issues*

A bond issue aimed at the general public of one particular country is subject to many rules and regulations (although less so now than in the fifties and sixties). There are usually all kinds of publication

FIGURE 9.4   Relationships between Eurobanking Products and Eurosecurities

Eurobanking Products	Eurosecurities Counterpart
Short-Term	
Eurocurrency Market	**Eurocommercial Paper Market**
Short-term loan	ECP issue
Short-term credit line	ECP program
Rolled-over credit line	Note-issuing facility
Revolving commitment	Revolving underwritten facility
Medium and Long-Term	
Euroloans	**Eurobonds**
Fixed-rate loan	Fixed-coupon bond
Revolving loan	Floating-rate note
Revolving loan with cap	HIBO (higher-bound) bond
Revolving loan with floor	LOBO (lower-bound) bond

requirements, and the issue has to be examined and approved by one or more regulatory agencies. In many countries, there are also issuing calendars (and, hence, queues) because the local government does not want foreigners to affect the country's reserves, money supply, or exchange rate; nor does the government want foreigners to "crowd out" local borrowers—especially the government itself. In contrast, "offshore" transactions tend to be less regulated. For one thing, monetary authorities and capital market regulators are less concerned with issues that do not involve their own currencies and are not (or not primarily) targeted at local investors. This is especially true for tax-haven states that are often used as launching pads for international issues.

- *Swift and efficient private placement*

By traditional US standards, publication requirements in Europe were never very stringent, and no rating is required for euro-issues.[12] Even these comparatively lax requirements can be largely or entirely avoided if the issue is private rather than public. For loans privately placed with a limited number of professional investors, there is no queuing, and there are no (or almost no) disclosure requirements.

- *Simple contracts*

As borrowers are generally of good credit standing, eurobonds tend to be unsecured; thus, legal costs, as well as the expenses of bonding and monitoring, are avoided.

- *Tax games*

Eurobonds, being anonymous bearer bonds, make it easier to evade income taxes. Withholding taxes can be avoided by issuing the bonds in tax havens, and most OECD countries have recently waived withholding taxes for nonresidents.

- *Large issues*

Issues below USD 100m are rare. The relatively large size of these issues allows for low issuing costs.

- *Disintermediation*

Since the mid-seventies, impetus for the growth of the eurosecurities market has come from the general disintermediation movement. **Disintermediation** means "cutting out the intermediary"; that is, corporations borrow directly from investors. This evolution was the result of two forces. First, many banks lost their first-rate creditworthiness when parts of their loan portfolios turned sour (due to the international debt crisis and the collapse of the real estate markets). As a result, these banks were no longer able to fund at the AAA rate, which meant that top borrowers could borrow at a lower cost than banks could—by tapping the market directly. Second, as a response to the lower profits from lending and borrowing and to the stricter capital adequacy rules, banks preferred to earn fee income from bond placements or commercial paper issues. Unlike operations involving deposits and loans, this commission business creates immediate income (rather than income from bid-offer spreads, received later on) and does not inflate the balance sheet.

---

[12] A bond rating is an explicit classification of the issue into one of the existing classes of creditworthiness. The best-known US rating agencies are Standard and Poor's and Moody's. The rating agency investigates the prospects of the firm at the time of issuing, but this takes time and costs money. The agency also keeps track of the issuer's standing later on, and can downgrade or up-grade a bond issue. "AAA" (pronounced "triple A") is S&P's best rating, and has become standard language to indicate prime quality.

Institutional Aspects

We briefly describe some institutional aspects of the eurobond market.

• *Bearer securities*

Eurobonds are bearer bonds, that is, actual pieces of paper, with *coupons* that can be clipped off and cashed in by the holder. The principal of the bond is represented by the *mantle,* which is the main part of the paper (after the coupons have been clipped off). In many countries, an investor can cash in coupons and principal paid out by **bearer securities** without having to reveal his or her identity to the bank that acts as paying agent. In contrast, if the security had been a **registered security**, the issuer would know the identity of the current holder of each bond, and pay interest by mailing a check.

• *Interest payments*

Eurobonds originally carried (and to a large extent still carry) fixed coupons. **Floating-rate notes (FRN)** are a more recently introduced instrument. Periodically (most often, every six or twelve months), the interest rate is reset on the basis of the then-prevailing six- or twelve-month LIBOR plus a preset spread. Sometimes, the FRN has a cap or floor on the floating interest rate. Capped FRNs are sometimes called **HIBO bonds** (higher-bound bonds), and floored FRNs **LOBO bonds**. Perpetual FRNs were briefly fashionable in the mid-eighties.

• *Amortization*

Amortization of the bond's principal amount typically occurs at maturity. Such bonds are known as **bullet bonds**. Alternatively, the borrower may undertake to buy back predetermined amounts of bonds in the open market every year. This is called a **purchase-fund provision** or a **sinking-fund provision**. Under a variant provision, the borrower does not have to buy back the bonds if market prices are above par. Instead, the borrower has a right to call a predetermined part of the issue every year.

• *Currency of denomination*

The currency of denomination of the bonds is most often a single currency (especially the USD, DEM, JPY, and CHF). In addition, the private ECU is becoming increasingly popular as the currency of denomination. Other currency baskets, such as the SDR or the European Unit of Account, have never really caught on. Some bonds have **currency options** attached to them. Such currency options bonds are discussed in Chapter 6. Occasionally, you also see a **dual currency bond**, which pays out its coupons in one currency and the principal in another currency.

Example   9.11

Suppose that the holder of a five-year bond receives an annual coupon of USD 1,000 and can choose to receive at maturity either USD 10,000 or DEM 20,000. This is equivalent to a regular 10 percent USD 10,000 bond, plus a five-year European-type call option on DEM 20,000 at X = USD/DEM 0.5. Alternatively, this is equivalent to a dual-currency bond (paying USD 1,000 in annual interest and a principal of DEM 20,000), plus a put option on DEM 20,000 at X = USD/DEM 0.5.

• *Stripped bonds*

Bond stripping essentially means that the coupons and the principal components of the bond are sold separately. If bonds are actual pieces of paper made out to bearer, you can strip bonds at home with a pair of scissors: just clip off all of the remaining coupons, and sell them separately from the *mantle,* the piece that stands for the principal. On a larger scale, and especially when bonds are registered rather than bearer securities, stripping is done by buying coupon bonds, placing them into an incorporated mutual fund or a trust, and issuing separate claims against this portfolio, representing either the coupons or the principal.

The main consequence of stripping is that the principal can be sold separately, as a zero-coupon bond. The motivation for stripping is that zero-coupon bonds, offering capital gains rather than interest, get favorable tax treatment in many countries. In some countries, including Japan and Italy, capital gains are entirely exempt from personal taxation. Thus, the principal is sold to Japanese or Italian investors, and the (taxable) coupons are sold to low-tax investors.

- *Issuing procedures*

Placement of eurobonds is most often through a syndicate of banks or security houses. The *lead bank* or lead manager negotiates with the borrower, brings the syndicate together, makes a market (at least initially), and supports the price during and immediately after the selling period. There are often, but not always, *managing banks* that underwrite the issue and often buy part of the bonds for their own account.[13] The *placing agents* call their clients (institutional investors or individuals) and sell the bonds on a commission basis. The *fiscal agent* takes care of withholding taxes, while the *trustee* bank monitors the bond contract (if any such contract exists; most bonds are unsecured and do not have bonding clauses).

Prospective customers can find information about the issuing company and about the terms and conditions of the bond in a *prospectus.* Often, an unofficial version of the prospectus is already circulating before the actual prospectus is officially approved. This preliminary prospectus is called the *red herring.* On the basis of the red herring, investors can already buy forward the bonds for a few weeks before the actual issuing period starts. This period of unofficial trading is called the *gray-market period.*

- *Secondary market*

The secondary market for eurobonds is not always very active. Many bonds are listed on the Luxembourg Bourse, but this is largely a matter of formality. A few hundred issues trade more or less actively on London's International Stock Exchange Automated Quotation (SEAQ International) computer system. Through SEAQ International, market makers post bid-and-ask prices for non-UK blue-chip stocks and for eurobonds. There is also an over-the-counter market, where (bored) bond dealers keep buying and selling to each other. Multilateral *clearing* institutions like Euroclear in Brussels and Cedel in Luxembourg reduce the costs of physical delivery of the bond certificates themselves.

Eurobonds represent the long end of the eurosecurities market. We now turn to markets for securities with shorter times to maturity.

9.2.2   Eurocommercial Paper

Commercial paper refers to short-term securities (from seven days to a few years) issued by private companies. Just as eurobonds are the disintermediated version of long-term eurobank loans, euro-

---

[13] The US alternative of a "bought deal" was not uncommon in the late eighties, but has now largely disappeared. Under such a deal, the lead bank does not wait to form a syndicate, but immediately buys the whole issue.

commercial paper **(ECP)** forms the disintermediated counterpart of short-term bank loans. ECP markets have existed in an embryonic form ever since banks drew promissory notes on their borrowers as a way to confirm loan agreements. However, the market became important only in the eighties when, as part of the general disintermediation movement, large corporations with excellent credit standing started issuing short- and medium-term paper, which is placed directly with institutional investors. The volume of the market remains low relative to the bond and bank-loan market.

The market consists of notes, promissory notes, and CDs. *Notes* are medium-term paper with maturities from one to seven years, usually paying out coupons; many Europeans would simply call them bonds. *Promissory notes* have shorter lives (sometimes as short as seven days), and are issued on a discount basis, that is, without interim interest payments. Notes and promissory notes issued by banks are called *certificates of deposit* (CDs).

Although an ECP issue can be a one-time affair, many issuers have an **ECP-program contract** with a syndicate. A bare-bones ECP program simply eliminates the bother of getting a syndicate together each time commercial paper needs to be placed, but many programs also offer some form of underwriting commitment (for issues up to a given amount and within a given period). Such a commitment can stipulate the following terms:

- *A fixed spread* (for example, 0.5 percent above LIBOR)

This is called a **Note Issuing Facility (NIF)**. This preset spread may become too high later on, notably if the borrower's rating goes up or if the average spread in the market goes down. In such cases, the borrower loses—he pays too much, in view of the changed circumstances—and the placing agent gains because he or she can place the paper above the initially anticipated price. In contrast, if the preset spread becomes too low, the borrower wins; the cost is then born by the underwriter, who has to buy the issue at a price that exceeds the fair market value.

- *A capped spread*

This is called a **Revolving Underwritten Facility (RUF)**. As we just noted, the issuer's equilibrium spread may decrease if the company's creditworthiness improves or if market spreads go down. Under a RUF, the borrower would then be allowed to issue at this lower spread. The equilibrium spread may also increase; however, under a RUF, the cap protects him against adverse changes. The underwriter suffers from such unfavorable changes. The placing agent will no longer gain from favorable changes; this gain is, in fact, passed on to the borrower.

The difference between a NIF and a RUF is less important than what it may seem at first. Even a NIF is an option on a spread, not a forward contract on a spread, because the borrower is under no obligation to use the facility. That is, if spreads go down in the market, the borrower can simply forget about the NIF and issue paper through a new syndicate or under a new agreement. Under such circumstances, the advantage of the RUF to the borrower is that it avoids the cost and complications of setting up a new issuing program. Figure 9.5 shows two tombstones for a program.

The last segment of the eurosecurities market to be discussed is the international equity markets.

9.2.3 International Equity Markets

Relative to the *fixed-income* side of the international capital market—bonds and commercial paper—the international equity markets are somewhat underdeveloped. Perhaps the biggest obstacle to international portfolio investment is the fact that valuing stocks requires more information than is required for high-quality bonds. Since investors are wary of buying stocks about which they know nothing, only a few hundred big companies are actually traded internationally. Besides, even

FIGURE 9.5   Euro-Commercial Paper Tombstones

This announcement appears as a matter of record only.

Dufour
Dufour International Holdings Limited

U.S. 30,000,000
Euro-commercial Paper
Revolving Facility

Arranged by

Credit Investment Bank Limited

• **Credit Bank**

This announcement appears as a matter of record only.

Alpina S.P.R.L.

U.S. $60,000,000
Euro-commercial Paper
Revolving Facility

Arranged by Credit Investment
Bank Limited

for this subset of stocks, international dealing is made complicated by the substantial differences in the ways trading and price-setting are organized across the world, the direct and indirect costs of getting a listing, and differences between registered and bearer-share markets. We discuss these issues in turn.

Stock markets across the world can have quite different operating systems.

• *Quote-driven markets*

Some markets work with market makers, that is, financial institutions that post prices at which they are prepared to buy and sell. Examples include the London Stock Exchange, London's SEAQ International, and America's NASDAQ.[14] The last two are really over-the-counter markets, that is, fairly informal networks rather than formal exchanges with fixed opening hours, membership rules, strict listing requirements, and so on.

• *Order-driven markets*

In Canada, and in many European countries, investors enter their limit orders into a computer, which automatically clears them as well as possible and displays the unexecuted orders on a Public Limit Order Book.

• *Mixed markets*

NYSE and AMEX,[15] for instance, have market makers, but also specialists who keep a limit order book.

---

[14] SEAQ: Stock Exchange Automated Quotation; NASDAQ: National Association of Security Dealers Automated Quotation.

[15] NYSE: New York Stock Exchange. AMEX; American Exchange (located close to the NYSE).

Given these different operating principles, it is not easy to set up a world market for stocks. European proposals to set up "umbrella" systems that link various exchanges have come to naught (at least at the time of writing). This means that companies interested in world-wide share ownership have to obtain a listing on many separate exchanges. This is costly. For instance, the costs of maintaining a listing, including translation expenses, by a foreign company on the Tokyo Stock Exchange runs from USD 100,000 to 500,000 per year. Quite apart from the listing fees, multiple listings create extra costs since each exchange tends to have its own information requirements. That is, corporations may have to prepare different financial statements, with different frequencies, for various individual exchanges. The relative stringency of the US information requirements and the cost of a listing have held back many non-US firms from seeking a listing on the NYSE or AMEX. A third obstacle to internationalization is the fact that some countries have a tradition of bearer shares (anonymous pieces of paper), whereas in other countries the stockholders are registered in the company's Register of Shareholders. Investors familiar with bearer shares often do not cherish the idea of giving up their anonymity.

Some of these problems can be reduced, at a cost, by the use of intermediaries. For one thing, investors discouraged by a lack of information about foreign stocks are nevertheless willing to buy indirectly into less well-known foreign companies through mutual funds (called "unit trusts" in the UK). The managers of these funds are, presumably, better informed about the stocks they pick. Second, companies avoid the cost of an official listing by having their shares traded, indirectly, in over-the-counter markets. To that end, financial institutions in the US create American Depository Receipts (ADRs), which are claims issued by financial institutions against the foreign shares themselves (see Figure 9.6). Finally, intermediaries also convert registered stocks into bearer stocks. Financial institutions buy shares (registering themselves as shareholders), and then issue bearer securities as claims against these shares. These certificates are listed on one or more exchanges, or are traded over the counter.

The most important international stock market is London's SEAQ International. The turnover of non-British stocks on SEAQ is comparable to London's turnover of local stocks, and SEAQ claims that about half of the world's cross-border stock trades are routed through it.[16] One reason for SEAQ's success is the low commissions charged, at least for large trades. This is partly due to the absence of transaction taxes (called *stamp duties,* in the UK) on international security transactions.

We conclude this chapter with a description of eurocurrency futures, the traded counterpart of the FFs or FRAs offered by banks.

9.3   EUROCURRENCY FUTURES CONTRACTS

Eurocurrency futures contracts can be used to hedge (or to speculate on) *interest risk,* in contrast to currency futures (discussed in Chapter 5) that allow one to hedge exchange risk. That is, eurocurrency futures are the futures-style counterparts of Forward Forward contracts and Forward Rate Agreements, in the same way as futures contracts on currencies relate to currency forward contracts. The oldest eurocurrency futures contract was the eurodollar contract traded at the International Money Market on the Chicago Mercantile Exchange (CME). Eurodollar futures have also been

---

[16] It is very difficult, though, to compare trading volumes across differently organized exchanges. If investor *A* sells 1,000 worth of stock to investor *B* through a public limit order book, this is recorded as a volume of 1,000. On SEAQ, in contrast, *A* sells to a market maker, who sells to *B*'s market maker, who then sells to *B*. This would create a volume of 3,000 (or even 4,000, if the two market makers trade with each other through an inter-broker dealer). In addition, any trade by a SEAQ member is reported as a London trade, even if the trade was actually executed in Paris or Frankfurt.

FIGURE 9.6   Tombstone of a Global Issue of Shares and ADRs

All of these securities having been sold, this announcement appears as a matter of record only.

REPSOL

Repsol, S.A.

Global Offering
of
40,000,000 Shares of Capital Stock

Global Coordinator	Co-Global Coordinator
Goldman, Sachs & Co.	Banco Bilbao Vizcaya, S.A.

16,857,724 American Depositary Shares

This portion of the offering has been sold in the United States by the undersigned.

Goldman, Sachs & Co.

Lehman Brothers

Merrill Lynch & Co.

Morgan Stanley & Co.
Incorporated

Arnhold and S. Bleichroeder, Inc.	Bear, Stearns & Co. Inc.	Deutsche Bank Capital Corporation	Dillon, Read & Co. Inc.	Donaldson, Lufkin & Jenrette Securities Corporation
Howard, Weil, Labouisse, Friedrichs Incorporated	Kidder, Peabody & Co. Incorporated	McDonald & Company Securities, Inc.	J.P. Morgan Securities Inc.
PaineWebber Incorporated	Salomon Brothers Inc	Smith Barney, Harris Upham & Co. Incorporated	S.G. Warburg & Co. Inc.

23,142,276 Shares of Capital Stock

This portion of the offering has been sold outside the United States by the undersigned.

Spain

Banco Central Hispano

Argentaria Bolsa, Sociedad de Valores y Bolsa		Banco Bilbao Vizcaya, S.A.

Banco Santander de Negocios, S.A.

AB Asesores, S.V.B.	BANESTO	Banco Popular Español, S.A.
Beta Capital S.V.B., S.A.	Bilbao Bizkaia Kutxa – NORBOLSA, S.V.B., S.A.
Caja de Ahorros y Pensiones de Barcelona "La Caixa"	Caja de Madrid

Confederación Española de Cajas de Ahorros (CECA)

FG Inversiones Bursátiles, S.A., S.V.B.

Continental Europe

Paribas Capital Markets	Credit Suisse First Boston Limited
Banco Bilbao Vizcaya, S.A.	Goldman Sachs International Limited	UBS Limited
ABN AMRO Bank N.V.	Banque Indosuez	Credit Lyonnais Securities
Deutsche Bank Aktiengesellschaft	Swiss Bank Corporation	Banco Exterior (Suiza) SA
BHF-BANK		Caisse des Depôts et Consignations
Creditanstalt-Bankverein		Dresdner Bank Aktiengesellschaft
Enskilda Securities Skandinaviska Enskilda Limited	Mediobanca – Banca di Credito Finanziario S.p.A.
Pictet International Ltd		Société Générale

Rest of World

Morgan Stanley International

Baring Brothers & Co., Limited		Daiwa Europe Limited
Goldman Sachs International Limited	S.G. Warburg Securities	Wood Gundy Inc.
The Development Bank of Singapore Ltd		Jardine Fleming
J.P. Morgan Securities Ltd.		Nomura International

Ord Minnett Securities Limited

United Kingdom

S.G. Warburg Securities	Banco Santander de Negocios, S.A.
Goldman Sachs International Limited	Kleinwort Benson Limited
Barclays de Zoete Wedd Limited	James Capel & Co.
Cazenove & Co.	N M Rothschild & Sons Limited
	Smith New Court Securities Limited

J. Henry Schroder Wagg & Co. Limited

Advisors to Instituto Nacional de Hidrocarburos

| Lazard Brothers & Co., Limited | Lazard Frères & Co. Limited | Lazard Frères et Cie |

March, 1993

introduced in the London International Financial Futures Exchange (LIFFE) and the Singapore Monetary Exchange (SIMEX). Currently, most financial centers of countries with a well-developed capital market have a contract written on the local interbank interest rate—for instance, the FRF PIBOR contract that is traded on the *Marché à Terme International de France* (MATIF) in Paris, and the BEF BIBOR contract traded on Belfox in Brussels. As can be seen from Figure 9.7, many exchanges also trade a few foreign contracts—for instance, DEM in LIFFE and MATIF, JPY in SIMEX. Many of the European futures contracts are in effect **collateralized forward contracts**, where the investor puts up more collateral (securities, or interest-bearing deposits) if the price evolution is unfavorable, rather than making a true payment. As was explained in Chapter 5, a collateralized forward contract is not subject to interest risk.

FIGURE 9.7   Description of Some Interest Rate Futures Contracts

	Underlying	Exchange	Contract size*	Longest**
AUD	90-day accepted bills	SFX	500,000	3y
BEF	3-month BIBOR	BELFOX	25,000,000	9m
CAD	Canadian B/A	ME	1,000,000	2y
DEM	3-month LIBOR	LIFFE, MATIF, DTB	1,000,000	9m
EIP	3-month DIBOR	IFOX	100,000	9m
BRA	Domestic CD	BM&F	10,000	11m
GBP	3-month eurosterling	LIFFE	500,000	9m
JPY	3-month LIBOR	TIFFE, SIMEX	1,000,000	9m
FRF	3-month PIBOR	MATIF	5,000,000	9m
NZD	90-day accepted bills	NZFE	500,000	2y
USD	3-month LIBOR	CME, SIMEX, LIFFE, TIFFE	1,000,000	2y
USD	1-month LIBOR	CME, CBOT	3,000,000	2y
USD	30-day Federal Funds	CBOT	5,000,000	2y

* At first exchange listed; contract size at other exchanges may differ.
** Life of longest contract at first exchange listed; m = month, y = year.
SFX: Sidney Futures Exchange; BELFOX: Belgian Futures and Options Exchange; ME: Montreal Exchange; LIFFE: London International Financial Futures Exchange; MATIF: Marché à Terme International de France; DTB: Deutsche TerminBörse; IFOX: Irish Futures and Options Exchange; BM&F: Bolsa y Mercantil y de Futuros (São Paulo); TIFFE: Tokyo International Financial Futures Exchange; SIMEX: Singapore Monetary Exchange; NZFE: New Zealand Futures Exchange; CME: Chicago Mercantile Exchange (includes IMM); CBOT: Chicago Board of Trade.

Let us now see how a eurocurrency futures contract works. A useful first analogy is to think of such a contract as similar to a futures contract on a CD, where the expiration day, T_1, of the futures contract precedes the maturity date, T_2, of the CD by, typically, three months. Thus, such a futures contract serves to lock in a three-month interest rate at time T_1.

Example   9.12

Suppose that in January you agree to buy, in mid-March, a CD that expires in mid-June. The maturity value of the CD is 100, and the price you agree to pay is 98. This means that the return you will realize on the CD during the last three months of its life is $(100 - 98)/98 = 2.0408$ percent, or 8.1632 percent on a yearly basis. Thus, this forward contract is analogous to signing an FRA at 8.1632 percent for three months, starting mid-March.

In the example, we described the futures contract as if it were a forward contract. If there is marking to market, the interest risk stemming from the uncertain marking-to-market cash flows will affect the pricing. Another complication with futures is that the quoted price is often different from the effective price, as we discuss below. Still, it helps to have Example 912 in mind to keep from getting lost in the institutional details. We first derive how *forward* prices on T-bills or CDs are set, and how they are linked to the forward interest rate. We then discuss the practical problems with such a system of quotation, and explain how this has led to a futures *quote*, which differs substantially from the forward price on a T-bill or CD.

9.3.1   The Forward Price on a CD

The forward price on a CD is just the face value (1, most often quoted as 100 percent) discounted at the forward rate of return $r_{t,T_1,T_2}^{\text{fwd}}$. To understand this property, suppose that the forward contract expires at T_1, and its underlying asset is a euro-CD maturing at T_2 ($> T_1$). Since the euro-CD has no coupons, its current price is:

$$V_t = \frac{1}{1 + r_{t,T_2}} \qquad [4]$$

where, as always in this textbook, r_{t,T_2} denotes an *effective* return, not a *p.a.* interest rate. The CD's forward price at t, for delivery at T_1, is this spot value grossed up with the effective interest between t and T_1:

$$\text{Forward price}_{t,T_1,T_2} \text{ on a CD} = V_t (1 + r_{t,T_1})$$

$$= \frac{1 + r_{t,T_1}}{1 + r_{t,T_2}},$$

and, from Equation [3],

$$= \frac{1}{1 + r_{t,T_1,T_2}^{\text{fwd}}}. \qquad [5]$$

Example   9.13

Consider a six-month forward on a nine-month bill with face value USD 1. Let the *p.a.* interest rates be 10 percent for nine months, and 9.5 percent for six months. Then $r_{t,T_2} = (9/12) \times 10\% = 0.075$, so that the spot price (quoted as a percentage) is equal to:

$$V_t = \frac{1}{1.075} = 93.02326\%.$$

Also, $r_{t,T_1} = (6/12) \times 9.5\% = 0.0475$; thus, the forward price today is:

$$F_{t,T_1} = 0.9302326 \times 1.0475 = 97.44186\%.$$

Alternatively, we can compute the six-month forward price on a nine-month T-bill using Equation [5]. We first compute the forward interest rate,

$$1 + r_{t,T_1,T_2}^{\text{fwd}} = \frac{1.075}{1.0475} = 1.026253.$$

Then the forward price is:

$$\frac{1}{1.026253} = 97.44186\%.$$

For some time, interest rate futures markets in Sydney were based on this system of forward prices for CDs. Although the system is perfectly logical, traders and investors are not fond of quoting prices in this way. One reason is that traders and dealers are more familiar with *p.a.* interest rates than with forward prices for deposits or CDs. The process of translating the forward interest rate into a forward price is somewhat laborious: Equation [5] tells us that the unfortunate trader has to divide the *per annum* forward rate by four, add unity, and take the inverse to compute the normal forward price as the basis for trading. A second problem is that real-world interest rates are typically rounded to one basis point (0.01 percent). Thus, unless forward prices are also rounded, marking to market will result in odd amounts. These very practical considerations lead to a more user-friendly manner of quoting prices for futures on CDs.

9.3.2   Eurodollar Futures

To make life easier for the traders, rather than quoting a true futures price, most exchanges quote three-month eurodollar futures contract prices as:

$$\text{Quote} \; = \; 100 - [\textit{per annum} \text{ forward interest rate}] \qquad\qquad [6]$$

and base the marking to market on *one-fourth* of the change in the quote.

Before we explain the marking-to-market rule, let us first consider the quotation rule given in Equation [6]. This quote decreases when the forward interest rate increases—just as a true forward price on a T-bill—and the long side of the contract is still defined as the one that wins when the quote goes up, the normal convention in futures or forward markets. However, one major advantage of this price-quoting convention is that a trader or investor can make instant decisions on the basis of available forward interest quotes, without any additional computations.[17]

Example   9.14

Let the *p.a.* forward interest rate be 12 percent for a three-month deposit starting at *T*. The true forward price would have been computed as

$$\frac{1}{1 + \dfrac{1}{4}(0.12)} = 97.087\%.$$

In contrast, the eurodollar forward quote can be found immediately as 100 percent − 12 percent = 88 percent.[18]

---

[17] The NZD contract at NZFE is even quoted as the forward interest rate itself, in percentage.

[18] A similar practice prevails in most T-bill futures markets. Among professionals, interest on T-bills is quoted on a *bankers' discount* or *discount yield* basis, that is, the annualized discount as a fraction of the face value or expiration value. T-bill futures are therefore quoted as 100 − [percentage *p.a.* forward discount rate]. For example, the discount in our "normal" forward price is (100 − 97.44186) percent = 2.55814 percent for three months, or 2.55814 × 4 = 10.23256 percent *p.a.* The T-bill futures quote would therefore be 100 − 10.23256 percent = 89.77 percent.

The second advantage of the "100 minus interest" way of quoting is that such quotes are, automatically, multiples of one basis point because interest rates are multiples of one basis point. With a standard contract size of USD 1m, one tick (equal to 1/100 of a percent) in the interest rate leads to a tick of $1m \times 0.0001 = $ USD 100 dollars in the underlying quote (no odd amounts here). Note that, since marking to market is based on one-fourth of the change in the quote, a one-tick change in the interest rate leads to a USD 25 change in the required margin.

To understand why marking to market is based on one-fourth of the change of the quote, go back to the correct forward price, Equation [5]. The idea is to undo the fact that the change in the quote (Equation [6]) is about four times the change in the correct forward price (Equation [5]). To understand this, note that $T_2 - T_1$ coresponds to three months (¼ year). Thus, as a first-order approximation,

$$\frac{1}{1+r^{\text{fwd}}_{t,T_1,T_2}} \approx 1 - r^{\text{fwd}}_{t,T_1,T_2} = 1 - \frac{1}{4}\left(4 r^{\text{fwd}}_{t,T_1,T_2}\right) = 1 - \frac{1}{4}\left[p.a. \text{ forward interest rate}\right]. \qquad [7]$$

Thus, the *change in* the true forward price is about one-fourth of the *change in* the futures quote.[19] To bring marking to market more or less in line with normal (price-based) contracts, the changes in the quote (or in the *p.a.* forward interest rate) must be divided by four. If this were not done, a USD 1m contract would, in fact, hedge a deposit of roughly USD 4m, which would have been *very* confusing for the buyers and sellers.

Example   9.15

Suppose that you hold a five-month, USD 1m CD and you want to hedge this position against interest rate risk two months from now. If, two months from now, the three-month interest rate drops from 10 percent to 9.5 percent, the market value of your deposit increases from $1m/(1 + (1/4) 0.10) = 975,610$ to $1m/(1 + (1/4) 0.095) = 976,801$, a gain of USD 1,191. The price quoted for a futures contract would change by 0.5 percent or, on a USD 1m contract, by USD 5,000. Marking to market, however, is one-fourth of that, or USD 1,250. So the marking-to-market cash flows on the eurodollar futures contract would reasonably match the change in the deposit's market value.

The pros and cons of interest futures, as compared to FRAs, are the same as for any other futures contract. The main advantage is an active secondary market where the contract can be liquidated at any

---

[19] We can show this more rigorously using derivatives. Define $x = 4 r^{\text{fwd}}_{t,T_1,T_2} = $ the *p.a.* interest rate; then the quote is $1 - x$ while the true forward price is $1/(1 + (1/4)x)$. Thus,

$$\frac{\partial \frac{1}{1+(1/4)x}}{\partial(1-x)} = \frac{1/4}{(1+(1/4)x)^2} \approx 1/4.$$

That is, a unit change in the quote is accompanied by a change in the true forward price of about one-fourth.

moment. Speculators especially like this. Among the drawbacks, the interest-risk problem created by marking to market is fairly important here, since overnight rates are, of course, strongly related to changes in the quotes themselves. Another drawback for hedgers with small exposures is the standardization of the size and maturity of the contract at USD 1m per contract. If three-month futures are used to hedge against a change in the four-month or nine-month interest rate, the hedge is, at best, imperfect. In Chapter 5, we saw how to adjust the hedge to limit the effects of a mismatch of maturity and size.

9.4 CONCLUSIONS

The main differences between euro- and domestic transactions are that the eurotransactions are off-shore, and the market is a liquid and unregulated wholesale market. As a result, spreads and costs are quite low, and the euromarkets have become an increasingly important source of funding for medium-size or large corporations. Apart from this, the transactions one can make in euromarkets are not fundamentally different from the transactions in standard domestic markets: there are time deposits and term loans, credit lines, and markets for bonds and short-term paper. A more recent instrument is the forward or futures contract on interest rates.

We have also seen that interest rates (spot and forward interest rates, and yields at par—discussed in the appendix) are all linked by arbitrage. Forward interest rates in various currencies are likewise linked through the forward markets. In the next chapter, we discuss the swap market, which links the yields-at-par across currencies.

QUIZ QUESTIONS

True-False Questions

1. The abolition of the Interest Equalization Tax, Regulation M, the cold war, and the US and UK foreign exchange controls have taken away most of the reasons why euromarkets exist. As a result, we can expect these markets to decline in the near future.
2. Without the US trade deficit, the euromarkets would have developed more slowly.
3. With a floating-rate loan, the bank is free to adjust the interest rate at every reset date in light of the customer's creditworthiness.
4. One of the tasks of the lead bank under a syndicated bank loan is to make a market, at least initially.
5. The purpose of using a paying agent is to reduce exchange risk.
6. Caps and floors are options on interest rates. Because interest rates are not prices of assets, one cannot price caps and floors using an option pricing model that is based on asset prices.
7. Because euroloans are unsecured, the spread over the risk-free rate is a very reliable indicator of the borrower's general creditworthiness.
8. FRAs are not really a good hedge against future interest rates because one does not actually make the deposit or take up the loan.
9. A note-issuing facility forces the borrowing company to borrow at a constant spread, while a revolving underwritten facility gives the borrower the benefit of decreasing spreads without the risk of increasing spreads.
10. The fact that eurobonds are bearer securities makes them less attractive to most investors.
11. Bond stripping is always done with a pair of scissors: you just clip off the coupons.
12. Disintermediation is the cause of the lower creditworthiness of banks, and has lead to capital adequacy rules.
13. Ignoring the small effects of marking to market, the standard quote for a eurocurrency futures price is basically a forward price on a CD.

Multiple-Choice Questions

1. Eurocurrency and euroloan markets are attractive because:
   (a) the spread between the buy and ask exchange rates is lower than in the interbank exchange market.
   (b) the bid-ask spread between the lending and borrowing interest rates is lower.
   (c) eurobanks are not subject to reserve requirements.
   (d) eurobanks are not subject to capital adequacy rules (the so-called BIS rules).

2. Eurobanks borrow for short maturities and lend for longer maturities. They can reduce the interest risk by:
   (a) extending fixed-rate loans.
   (b) extending floating-rate loans.
   (c) extending revolving loans.
   (d) going short in forward forwards (that is, getting a forward contract on a loan, not on a deposit).
   (e) going short in FRAs.

    (f) going long in eurocurrency futures.

    (g) buying forward the currency in question.

3. A cap on a floating-rate euroloan:

    (a) protects the borrower against high short-term interest rates.

    (b) protects the lender against high short-term interest rates on the funding side.

    (c) is similar to a call option on short-term paper with the cap rate, as nominal rate; and the borrower is the holder of the call option.

    (d) is similar to a put option on short-term paper with the cap rate, as nominal rate; and the borrower is the holder of the put option.

    (e) is similar to a put option on short-term paper with the cap rate, as nominal rate; and the lender is the holder of the put option.

4. Which of each pair best describes eurobanking?

    (a) retail/wholesale

    (b) individual lender/bank consortium

    (c) reserve requirements/limited or no reserve requirements

    (d) unsecured/secured

    (e) fixed-rate lending/floating-rate lending

    (f) foreign exchange markets/money markets

    (g) open to all companies/open to the better companies only

5. **Matching Questions**: Choose from the following list of terms to complete the sentences below: *paying agent, managing banks, trustee bank, placing agents, market, lead bank (or lead manager), participating banks, prospectus, gray market, fiscal agent, buy forward, underwrite, lead manager, red herring.*

      A consortium (or *syndicate*) that extends a euroloan consists of many banks that could play different functions. In a euroloan, the _____ negotiates with the borrower for tentative terms and conditions, obtains a mandate, and looks for banks to provide the money or undertake to provide the money if there is any shortfall in funds. The banks that provide the actual funding are called _____. Because at the time of the negotiations the funding is not yet arranged, the _____ often contacts a smaller number of _____ banks who _____ the loan, that is, guarantee to make up for the shortage of funds if there is any such shortfall. The _____, finally, is the bank that receives the service payments from the borrower and distributes them to the participating banks.

      Placement of eurobonds is most often via a syndicate of banks or security houses. The lead bank or _____ negotiates with the borrower, brings the syndicate together, makes a _____ (at least initially), and supports the price during and immediately after the selling period. There are often, but not always, _____ that underwrite the issue and often buy part of the bonds for their own account. The _____ call their clients (institutional investors or individuals) and sell the bonds on a commission basis. The _____ takes care of withholding taxes, while the _____ monitors the bond contract. Prospective customers can find information about the issuing company and about the terms and conditions of the bond in a _____. Often an unofficial version of the prospectus is already circulating

before the actual prospectus is officially approved; this preliminary prospectus is called the
_____. On the basis of this document, investors can already
_____ the bonds for a few weeks before the actual issuing period starts.
This period of unofficial trading is called the _____ period.

EXERCISES

1. You are an A-quality borrower, and you pay 10 percent on a five-year loan with one final
   amortization at the end. This is 1 percent above the spread paid by an AAA borrower. What
   will be the up-front fee for which your bank should be willing to lower the rate by 1 percent?

2. A bank offers you the following rates: 10 percent fixed, or (when you borrow floating-rate)
   LIBOR + 2 percent. You prefer to borrow floating-rate, as you expect a drop in interest rates.
   Another bank offers you LIBOR + 1.5 percent, but asks a substantial up-front fee. How can
   you compute which bank offers the better terms?

3. On January 2, you sign a six-to-nine month FRA for FRF 10m at 10 percent $p.a.$ Six months
   later the three-month LIBOR rate turns out to be 8 percent $p.a.$
   (a) What is the cash settlement on July 2?
   (b) What are the cash flows that arise from a similar Forward Forward?
   (c) Which of the two (the FRA or the FF) has the higher present value (on July 2)?

4. On January 2, the six- and nine-month interest rates are 5 and 5.5 percent $p.a.$, respectively.
   What is the six-to-nine-month forward rate? Ignore bid-ask spreads in interest rates.

5. On January 2, you signed a six-to-nine FRA for LUF 100m at 10 percent $p.a.$ Three months
   later the LIBOR rates for three, six, and nine months are at 8.75 percent, 8.9 percent, and 9.5,
   respectively. What is the market value of the outstanding FRA?

6. You bought an option that limits the interest rate on a future six-month loan to, at most, 10
   percent $p.a.$
   (a) If, at the beginning of the six-month period, the interest rate is 11 percent, what is the
       expiration value of this option?
   (b) What is the option's expiration value if the interest rate turns out to be 8 percent?

7. You bought an option that limits the interest rate on a future six-month deposit to at least 10
   percent $p.a.$
   (a) If, at the beginning of the six-month period, the interest rate is 11 percent, what is the
       market value of this option?
   (b) What is the option's value if the interest rate turns out to be 8 percent?

8. The six- and nine-month interest rates are 10 percent and 11 percent $p.a.$, respectively.
   (a) What is the current six-to-nine forward interest rate?
   (b) What is the forward price of a six-month (= T_1) forward contract on a nine-month
       (= T_2) CD?
   (c) What is the futures quote (ignoring effects of marking to market)?
   (d) If the underlying CD has a face value of USD 10,000, what is the marking-to-market cash
       flow when the six- and nine-month interest rates both increase by 0.5 percent?

MIND-EXPANDING EXERCISES

1. On January 2, the six- and nine-month interest rates are 5–5.125 and 5.5–5.6125 percent *p.a.*, respectively.

   (a) Use the *Law of the Worst Possible Combination,* discussed in Chapters 1 and 4, to derive the synthetic forward bid interest rate, *p.a.*; what loans or deposits are used to construct a synthetic forward deposit?

   (b) Do the same for the synthetic ask rate.

2. Prove the following claims:

   (a) The cash flows, from a floating-rate deposit with semiannual coupons, are identical to the cash flows from a series of independent six-month deposits where the principal is reinvested at each expiry date.

   (b) Assuming a constant default risk, a FRN always trades at par (or very close to par) around the reset date.

   (c) A HIBO-bond, in contrast, could trade below par and a LOBO-bond above par around the reset date.

3. In Section 9.1.4, we valued an FF via replication. Value the same contract using a hedging argument—that is, an investor can lock in gain (or stop loss), by closing the outstanding FF with a reverse FF at the current market conditions.

4. Assume that the one-year forward rates for starting dates 0, 1, 2, 3, and 4 are 10, 10.25, 10.50, 10.55, and 10.60 percent. Compute the term structure of spot interest rates for maturities of one to five years.

5. Using the same data, compute the term structure of yields at par for loans with a single amortization at the end.

6. Using the same data, compute the term structure of yields at par for loans with constant annuities.

7. With the same data, verify how well (or how badly) the value of an *n*-year annuity ($n = 1, \ldots, 5$) is approximated when one uses the five-year yield at par with a bullet bond rather than the complete term structure of spot returns.

TERM STRUCTURES, BOND YIELDS, AND INTEREST RATES

In this appendix, we review some basics about fixed-income transactions like loans and bonds. The focus is on the no-arbitrage links between interest rates on zero-coupon instruments (like the money-market positions we discussed in Chapters 2 to 4), the rates on bonds and long-term loans, and the forward interest rates used in an FF or an FRA.

The rates of return we have used in Chapters 1 through 8 are *zero-coupon* rates of return, that is, rates of return on zero-coupon type instruments. For instance, when we set up the spot/forward diagram in Chapter 2, the deposits or loans taken out at t were fully paid back, including principal as well as interest, at expiration time T without there being any interim interest payments before T. In contrast, bonds with a maturity exceeding one year traditionally have annual (or, in North America, semi-annual) interest payments (*coupons*). Medium or long-term bank loans likewise have quarterly, semi-annual, or annual interest payments. The interest rate paid on such a loan (or offered on a bond issued at par—the *yield at par*) is likely to be what one first thinks of when asked for the definition of a long-term interest rate. We shall, however, show that zero-coupon interest rates are a much neater, and much better-defined concept than rates on bonds or loans. We shall then argue that forward interest rates are even more fundamental than zero-coupon rates.

We present these arguments from two perspectives. First, we start from the term structure of forward interest rates, move towards the resulting term structure of zero-coupon rates, and then see how these zero-coupon rates determine bond yields at par or interest rates on loans with periodic interest payments. Next we reverse the order, and show how financial analysts and swap dealers first extract the term structure of zero-coupon interest rates from the data on yields at par, and then extract the term structure of forward rates from data on zero-coupon rates. In our discussion, one should keep in mind that all rates used in this text are effective simple rates of return over the period $(T - t)$—not annualized interest rates. The link between such a simple return and a *per annum* interest rate is explained in the appendix to Chapter 2.

9A.1 Future Short-Term Rates and Current Long-Term Zero-Coupon Rates: The Certainty Case

Suppose, initially, that there is no uncertainty: all investors know what the future one-period interest rate will be. We shall assume that we are at time 0, and consider the payment dates 1, 2, and 3. The current one-period rate is denoted as $r_{0,1}$, and the (known) future one-period rates of return interest rates are denoted as $r_{1,2}$ and $r_{2,3}$, respectively. We claim that these future short-term interest rates determine the whole current term structure, that is, the set of current long-term effective returns ($r_{0,2}$ and $r_{0,3}$). This can be shown using arbitrage arguments.

In the absence of interest risk, you can create a synthetic two-period zero-coupon bond by investing money between time 0 and 1 (at $r_{0,1}$), and then reinvesting principal plus interest for another period (at $r_{1,2}$). After two periods, one unit of initial investment will have grown into $(1 + r_{0,1})(1 + r_{1,2})$ units. Since this synthetic two-period zero-coupon bond is a perfect substitute for an outright two-period zero-coupon bond, the total proceeds, if one immediately invests for two periods, must be the same as the proceeds from the rolled-over deposit. That is, to rule out arbitrage opportunities, we must have:

$$(1 + r_{0,1})(1 + r_{1,2}) = (1 + r_{0,2}), \qquad [A1]$$

where $r_{0,2}$ is the effective simple return between times 0 and 2—not an annualized interest rate. Similarly, one can replicate an outright three-period investment by rolling over a one-period deposit three times. The no-arbitrage condition then states the following:[20]

$$(1 + r_{0,1})(1 + r_{1,2})(1 + r_{2,3}) = (1 + r_{0,3}).$$ [A2]

Example   9A.1

Suppose that the one-period rates of return are 10 percent, 11 percent, and 11.5 percent for times 0 to 1, 1 to 2, and 2 to 3, respectively.

- Investing 100 at time 0 for one period yields 110 at time 1, which can be reinvested at 11 percent to yield 122.1 at time 2. That is, you realize a total effective return of 22.1 percent. The alternative to the rolled-over investment is a single investment for two periods. If the return on such a two-period investment deviates from 22.1 percent, there is an arbitrage opportunity. Thus, $r_{0,2}$ must equal 22.1 percent.
- Investing 100 at time 0 for one period yields 110 at time 1, which can be reinvested at 11 percent to yield 122.1 at time 2; the 122.1 can then be reinvested once more, at 11.5 percent, to yield 136.1415 at time 3. That is, you realize a total effective return of 36.1415 percent. The alternative to the rolled-over investment is a single investment for three periods. If the return on such a three-period investment deviates from 36.1415 percent, there is an arbitrage opportunity.

The long-term zero-coupon rates of return can be annualized using any of the techniques described in the appendix of Chapter 2. When the maturity exceeds one year, one typically uses compound interest. Thus, if one period corresponds to one year, the two- and three-year rates of return can be translated into $(1.221)^{1/2} - 1 = 10.4989$ percent compound *p.a.*, and $(1.361415)^{1/3} - 1 = 10.833$ percent compound *p.a.*, respectively.

9A.2   From Forward Rates to Long-Term Zero-Coupon Rates

We have just shown that, in the absence of interest risk, the term structure of (known) future one-period rates of return fully determines the current term structure of zero-coupon returns. However, interest risk is very much a fact of real life. We can, nevertheless, still do transactions that are similar to the ones that we just described—by using forward forward contracts.[21] The effect of such contracts is, of course, that one can roll over a short-term deposit without taking on any interest risk. We could, therefore, go through an exercise similar to the one in Section 9A.1, and use the forward rates (which

---

[20] One could, of course, also obtain a synthetic three-period bond by immediately investing for two periods, and then rolling over at the rate of return for investing at time 2 until time 3. This must also yield the same outcome as an outright three-period investment: $(1 + r_{0,2})(1 + r_{2,3}) = (1 + r_{0,3})$. From Equation [A1], this will be perfectly compatible with Equation [A2].

[21] Recall from Section 9.1.4 that such a contract fixes at time t the interest rate on a deposit that will be made at a future point in time. The rate of return set for a deposit starting at T_1 and ending at T_2 is called the T_1-to-T_2 forward rate of return.

are, of course, known at time t) rather than the future spot rates (which, in reality, are not known at time t). Let us denote the forward rate of return as $r_{t,T_1,T_2}^{\text{fwd}}$.[22] Using forward contracts on interest rates, we can repeat our preceding analysis, and show that the following relationship must hold to rule out arbitrage opportunities:

$$(1 + r_{0,1})(1 + r_{0,1,2}^{\text{fwd}}) = (1 + r_{0,2}). \qquad \text{[A3]}$$

$$(1 + r_{0,2})(1 + r_{0,2,3}^{\text{fwd}}) = (1 + r_{0,3}). \qquad \text{[A4]}$$

Thus, the general conclusion is that once the term structure of *forward* interest rates is known, one can roll out the entire term structure of *spot* zero-coupon rates of return in this fashion. The interpretation of the forward rate of return should sound familiar: if there is interest risk, the market will use some kind of risk-adjusted expectation, revealed in the forward rate of return, and set the spot rate on the basis of today's risk-adjusted expectation. This general principle can then be made more specific in various ways. For instance, the classical expectations hypothesis says that the forward rate equals the expected future spot rate. Hicks then added that there might very well be a risk premium to compensate the holder of a multiperiod bond for the uncertainty about the market price of the bond before expiration. However, independently of how the market formed its expectations and corrected for risk, the market's risk-adjusted expected spot interest rate is revealed in the forward interest rate.[23]

9A.3   From Zero-Coupon Rates to Yields

Thus far, we have discussed only zero-coupon returns, although many types of investments or loans involve intermediate cash flows. We can, however, use zero-coupon bonds to replicate any bond with multiple cash flows. For instance, consider a three-year bond that pays out USD 1,000 in interest every year, plus the principal, USD 10,000, at the (final) maturity date. Buying this bond is like buying a portfolio of "basic" (zero-coupon) bonds. You can obtain the same cash flows by buying:

- A one-year zero-coupon bond with face value USD 1,000.
- A two-year zero-coupon bond with face value USD 1,000.
- A three-year zero-coupon bond with face value USD 11,000.

Suppose that the *p.a. compound interest rate* for investments maturing 1, 2, and 3 years from now are 7 percent, 7.1 percent, and 7.15 percent, respectively—that is, assume that:

---

[22] As elsewhere in this text, this percentage is not annualized in any way. In practice, bankers typically use linearly annualized figures. Thus, we assume that you have already de-annualized them into the effective return, the figure that matters.

[23] The fact that the risk-adjusted expectation is *revealed* in the forward rate does not mean that the risk-adjusted expectation *equals* the forward rate. Risk-adjusted expectations have to do with prices, and the interest rate is not a price. Thus, the forward *price* of a CD is the risk-adjusted expected value of the CD's future price:

$$1/(1 + r_{0,1,2}^{\text{frw}}) = \text{CEQ}_0\,(1/(1 + \tilde{r}_{1,2})).$$

$$1 + r_{0,1} = 1.07, \ 1 + r_{0,2} = (1.071)^2 = 1.147041, \text{ and } 1 + r_{0,3} = (1.0715)^3 = 1.2302.$$

The total cost of buying the portfolio of zero-bonds is, by definition, the sum of the values of the zero bonds, with each zero bond priced as its face value discounted at the interest rate for its own time to maturity:

$$\text{Cost of the replicating portfolio } = \frac{1,000}{1.07} + \frac{1,000}{(1.071)^2} + \frac{11,000}{(1.0715)^3} = 10,748.$$

This portfolio is, as we argued, just a synthetic version of the three-year coupon bond. Thus, by arbitrage, the value of the bond with coupons must also be 10,748.

Note that we price the coupon bond by discounting each payment at a different interest rate. This practice may be new to some of you. When pricing a bond, one often uses a single discount rate to discount all cash flows regardless of their timing. Let us see from where this method comes, and under what circumstances it is reliable.

9A.4   When and How to Use the Yields to Maturity

We start by noting that once we have the bond's value, we can always compute, by an intelligent trial-and-error method, the yield to maturity or internal rate of return. This yield is defined as the (single) discount rate that makes the sum of n discounted cash flows equal to the bond's observed market price:

$$\text{Find } y \text{ such that } \sum_{i=1}^{n} \frac{CF_{T_i}}{(1+y)^{T_i - t}} = \text{ observed time } t \text{ market price,} \qquad [A5]$$

where CF_{T_i} is the cash flow paid out at time T_i. Any spreadsheet, and many pocket calculators, can solve this problem for you. For example, you can verify that the yield to maturity or internal rate of return of the three-year 10 percent bond equals 7.14233 percent if its price is 10,748:

$$\frac{1,000}{1.0714233} + \frac{1,000}{(1.0714233)^2} + \frac{11,000}{(1.0714233)^3} = 10,748.$$

This internal rate of return is neither the one-year interest rate, nor the two-year interest rate, nor the three-year interest rate. In fact, it is a complex average of all three. In the above example, the bond's yield (7.14233 percent) is close to the three-year zero-bond interest rate (7.15 percent), because the bond's largest payment is at year three. Yet the effect of the two smaller interim coupon payments already produces a difference of 0.01 percent (1 basis point) between the yield and the true three-year interest rate. Thus, you should not confuse a yield to maturity with a proper interest rate. A proper interest rate relates to a zero-coupon type of transaction. A yield, on the other hand, is a complex average of various zero-coupon rates.

Once you have found the yield to maturity of a correctly priced bond, you can also price approximately, similar bonds using the same yield. The approximation error becomes important when the coupons or times-to-maturity of the two bonds deviate substantially, or when the zero-coupon interest rates for various times to maturity are very different.

Example   9A.2

Suppose that the one-, two-, and three-year compound interest rates are still 7 percent, 7.10, and 7.15 percent *p.a.*, respectively. You want to price a three-year, 12 percent coupon bond with face value 10,000. As we saw in Section 9A.3, the correct way to do this is to discount each payment at the appropriate interest rate for its maturity:

$$\text{Value of the 12 percent coupon bond } = \frac{1,200}{1.07} + \frac{1,200}{(1.071)^2} + \frac{11,200}{(1.0715)^3} = 11,271.9.$$

Using the yield to maturity obtained from the 10 percent bond, we find a reasonable approximate value:

$$\frac{1,200}{1.0714233} + \frac{1,200}{(1.0714233)^2} + \frac{11,200}{(1.0714233)^3} = 11,271.5.$$

Thus, by discounting using the yield of a very similar bond, we come very close to the correct value. The approximation is close because the 10 percent bond and the 12 percent bond have a very similar pattern of payments—two small payments at times 1 and 2, and one big payment at time 3. We conclude that the yield to maturity gives a reasonable approximation of the bond's true value if this yield is used only for bonds with very similar cash flows. We shall use this technique, for the sake of simplicity, in Chapter 10.

The main advantage of yields is the ease of computation. Rather than having to discount each cash flow separately at its own interest rate (as one does under the correct procedure), the method of single discount rates relies on results of geometric series to simplify the calculations. Some examples of simplified computations include:

- Value of an *n*-year unit annuity discounted at the rate *y*:

$$a(n,y) \equiv \sum_{t=1}^{n} \frac{1}{(1+y)^t} = \frac{1-(1+y)^{-n}}{y}. \tag{A6}$$

- Value of a unit bond with *n* annual coupons *c* discounted at the rate *y*:

$$\sum_{t=1}^{n} \frac{c}{(1+y)^t} + \frac{1}{(1+y)^n} = 1+(c-y)\,a(n,y). \tag{A7}$$

9A.5   The Yield at Par and the Swap Rate

The *yield at par* is defined as the coupon that one should assign to a bond in order to obtain a par market value (100 percent). With the term structure of 7 percent, 7.1 percent, and 7.15 percent for maturities 1, 2, and 3 years, respectively, the problem of identifying the yield at par can be formulated as follows:

Find the coupon c such that $\dfrac{c}{1.07} + \dfrac{c}{(1.071)^2} + \dfrac{1+c}{(1.0715)^3} = 1.$

This can be solved as:

$$c = \frac{1 - \dfrac{1}{(1.0715)^3}}{\dfrac{1}{1.07} + \dfrac{1}{(1.071)^2} + \dfrac{1}{(1.0715)^3}} = \frac{0.1871255}{2.6192623} = 7.1442\%.$$

Swap dealers follow this procedure when they compute interest rates on swaps as a function of zero-coupon interest rates. This is called the *yield at par* because this coupon is also the bond's yield to maturity:

$$\frac{7.1442\%}{1.071442} + \frac{7.1442\%}{(1.071442)^2} + \frac{107.1442\%}{1.071442^3} = 100\%.$$

To sum up our results thus far: the fundamental information on the market's risk-adjusted expectations about future interest rates is contained in the term structure of forward interest rates. From this, one can infer the term structure of zero-coupon rates. This term structure then implies a price for any bond, and a term structure of yields at par—the figures that the average investor thinks of as the most obvious definition of the term structure. To complete our analysis of interest rates, we will now go through the procedure in reverse order, and figure out the term structures of zero-coupon rates and forward rates implicit in a given term structure of yields at par. This is what swap dealers do when they want to set their rates on the basis of spot interest rates.

9A.6   From Bond Yields back to Zero-Coupon Rates

Suppose that you observe the following yields at par:

Time to maturity	1	2	3
Coupon yield	10%	10.25%	10.5%

Identifying the zero-coupon yield for a one-year security is easy. Because the one-year bond has no interim coupons, it is a zero-coupon bond with face value 110 payable at time 1. Thus, 10 percent is the zero-coupon yield. To verify this, note that:

$$100 = \frac{110}{1 + r_{0,1}} \Rightarrow r_{0,1} = 0.10.$$

The two-year yield at par is 10.25 percent. That is, one can issue a bond with cash flows (10.25, 110.25) at par. If the equilibrium price is 100, it must be that:

$$100 = \frac{10.25}{1 + r_{0,1}} + \frac{110.25}{1 + r_{0,2}}.$$

However, we already know that $r_{0,1}$ equals 10 percent. So we can find $r_{0,2}$:

$$1 + r_{0,2} = \frac{110.25}{100 - \dfrac{10.25}{1 + r_{0,1}}} = \frac{110.25}{90.6818} = 1.21579.$$

That is, $r_{0,2} = 21.579$ percent or 10.263 percent *p.a.*, compounded annually. The three-year rate can be identified the same way. The three-year yield at par is 10.5 percent, which means that a three-year bond with a 10.5 percent coupon would trade at par. The implicit three-year interest rate can be inferred from:

$$100 = \frac{10.5}{1 + r_{0,1}} + \frac{10.5}{1 + r_{0,2}} + \frac{110.5}{1 + r_{0,3}} = \frac{10.5}{1.10} + \frac{10.5}{1.21579} + \frac{110.5}{1 + r_{0,3}},$$

implying $r_{0,3} = 35.056$ percent (or 10.536 percent *p.a.*, compounded annually).

We have just shown how one can extract zero-coupon yields from a given term structure of yields at par. One could, of course, also extract them from data on bonds not trading at par. The entire secondary bond market is, in fact, the prime source of information for implicit zero-coupon interest rates. Since the payments dates of bonds do not coincide in the neat, simple way assumed in the above example, some interpolation must be used, but the basic principle is the same as the one used in this section.

10 CURRENCY AND INTEREST RATE SWAPS

From our analysis in Chapters 2 to 4 we know that a firm can hedge a *single* risk-free cash flow, denominated in foreign currency, by a forward sale or purchase. For example, if the firm had a zero-coupon type loan in foreign currency, it could transform this into a home currency loan by a forward purchase of the foreign currency. To hedge a *series* of cash flows with many different maturities, one could use a portfolio of different forward contracts, one for each cash flow. Alternatively, one could use a *currency swap*. Currency swaps allow a firm to take out a coupon loan in one currency, and then essentially change the effective currency of denomination of the entire loan—principal *and* interest payments—using just one contract.

This chapter is structured as follows. In the first section, we consider some predecessors to the modern currency swap: the classical short-term swap, the parallel loan and the back-to-back loan, and the currency swap between IBM and the World Bank negotiated in 1981. We then show, in Section 10.2, how the modern currency swap works, and why such deals exist. A somewhat more recent variant of currency swap is the interest rate swap or fixed-for-floating rate swap, which we discuss in Section 10.3. In Section 10.4, we consider a combination of the currency swap and the interest swap, called the fixed-for-floating currency swap or circus swap. Cocktail swaps, described in the fifth section, involve more than two types of loans and can be viewed as grouping various swaps into one comprehensive deal. Section 10.6 concludes this chapter.

10.1 EARLIER SWAP-LIKE CONTRACTS

To initiate our study of the modern swap, we shall first discuss the traditional short-term swap, that is, a contract associated with a single future cash flow. Studying this contract is useful in itself, and it also helps us to understand the modern, long-term swap where many future cash flows are exchanged. We then discuss two more contracts that are similar to currency swaps, namely the back-to-back loan and the parallel loan. We finish this section with a description of an early swap contract negotiated between IBM and the World Bank.

10.1.1   The Short-Term Currency Swap

Our explanation of the short-term currency swap starts with an example, which will then be used to interpret the nature and purpose of these contracts.

An Illustration of a Traditional Short-Term Currency Swap

During the Bretton Woods period (1945–1972), central banks often extended loans to each other. For example, to support the GBP exchange rate, the Bank of England would buy GBP and sell USD. On occasion it would run out of USD. Hoping that the pressure on the GBP (and the corresponding scarcity of USD reserves) was temporary, the Bank of England would borrow USD from, say, the Bundesbank, the central bank of Germany. The Bundesbank would ask for some form of security for such a loan. In a classical short-term swap deal, the guarantee was in the form of an *equivalent* amount of GBP to be deposited with the Bundesbank by the Bank of England. Barring default, on the expiration day, the USD and the GBP would each be returned, with interest, to the respective owners.[1]

Example   10.1

Assume, for simplicity, a spot rate of USD/GBP 2.5. The Bank of England receives USD 100m from the Bundesbank for six months, and deposits GBP 100m/2.5 = GBP 40m into an escrow account with the Bundesbank. The translation at the initial spot rate achieves the (initial) equivalence of the amounts exchanged; GBP 40m is worth USD 100m. If the initial six-month return were 3 percent on USD and 5 percent on GBP, the Bundesbank would return, after six months, GBP 40m $\times$ 1.05 = 42m, and the Bank of England would return USD 100m $\times$ 1.03 = USD 103m.

We have described the deal as a loan plus a deposit that serves as collateral. There are at least two ways in which such a contract can be interpreted.

Two Ways to View the Traditional Short-Time Swap Contract

First, a swap could be structured as two mutual loan contracts, one for USD 100m to the Bank of England, and the other for GBP 40m to the Bundesbank, with a **right-of-offset clause** linking the two loans. Such a clause says that if one party fails to fulfill its obligations, the other party is exonerated from its normal obligations and can sue the defaulting party for any losses. The clause, of course, reflects the fact that the GBP 40m actually serve as collateral for the USD loan, and *vice versa*. The mutually promised time-t and time-T cash flows are shown in the first and second column of Figure 10.1.

As shown in the last column of Figure 10.1, the mutual loan contract with right of offset can also be described as a spot sale by the Bundesbank of USD for GBP combined with a six-month forward purchase of USD. To understand this, look at the cash flows in Figure 10.1 not column by column (GBP loan versus USD loan), but row by row (time t versus time T). At the moment the contract is initiated, the Bundesbank delivers USD 100m and receives GBP 40m—exactly as if the Bundesbank had bought spot GBP at S_t = USD/GBP 2.5. The flows at time T are, in effect, USD 103 against GBP 42, which corresponds to an exchange transaction at an implicit forward rate of 103/42 = 2.45238.

---

[1] If the Bank of England failed to pay back the USD loan, the Bundesbank could seize the GBP posted as security.

FIGURE 10.1   The Short-Term Currency Swap

	USD loan [BB→BE]	GBP loan [BB→BE]	
At time t:	BB transfers USD 100m to BE	BE transfers GBP 40m to BB	Spot sale of USD 100m to BE at S_t = USD/GDP 2.5
At time T:	BE transfers USD 103m to BB	BB transfers GBP 42m to BE	Forward purchase of USD 103m from BE at $F_{t,T}$ = 2.45238
			Total: Swap contract

BB = Bundesbank, BE = Bank of England

This implicit forward rate is also the normal forward rate. Using the data from the above example, the forward rate is, indeed, USD/GBP $2.5 \times 1.03/1.05 = 2.45238$. As we have seen in Chapter 2, the combined spot and forward contract is called a *swap contract*.

Structuring the contract as a spot-forward transaction is simpler than the double loan contract described earlier, in the sense that the right of offset is automatic in a forward contract. Like any bank, the Bundesbank would simply not deliver the GBP if the Bank of England did not pay the agreed amount of forward USD (and *vice versa*). Further, if the contract involved a private firm rather than two central banks, the firm's shareholders or bondholders would be automatically informed about the implicit right-of-offset clause, because the forward contracts would have been listed separately in the notes to the balance sheets rather than among the ordinary assets and liabilities. In contrast, if there had been two loans, the financial statements would have had to contain explicit warnings about the right-of-offset clause since this clause means that the firm's claim becomes void if the firm defaults on its loan. In some countries, the clause must be officially registered. All of these complications are avoided if a spot-and-forward contract structure is chosen.[2]

Why Short-Term Swaps Exist

As we have seen, one reason why two firms may set up a swap contract is to secure a loan (or simultaneously secure two reciprocal loans). The safety offered by this type of contract becomes obvious if there is credit risk.

Example   10.2

The central bank of the former Soviet Union often used gold as security for hard-currency loans obtained from western banks, but repeatedly failed to pay back the loans. For the western counterparty, the risk was limited to the face value of the loan minus the market value of the gold. The Soviet Union always made good this loss.

---

[2] As an aside, we have glossed over a technical detail. In the usual sense of the word, a traditional short-term swap actually consists of a spot deal and a reverse deal *for the same amounts*—USD 100m and GBP 40. Thus, in the above example, there would be a six-month swap of USD 100m against GBP 40m, with an extra clause specifying that the interest be paid separately (USD 3m and GBP 2m).

Example   10.3

In a **repurchase order** (*repo*), an investor in need of short-term financing sells low-risk assets (like T-bills) to a lender, and buys them back under a short-term forward contract. This is another example of a swap contract (a spot sale reversed in the forward market). In terms of cash flows, this is equivalent to taking out a secured loan. Because of the virtual absence of risk, the interest rate implicit between the spot and forward price is lower than an ordinary offer rate and differs from the lending rate by a very small spread, called the "**haircut**."

There are other possible motivations for swaps. Transaction costs can be reduced if an investor intends to reverse the transaction made today at a future date.

Example   10.4

A French investor is optimistic about the likely returns on US stocks, but is less sanguine about the FRF/USD exchange itself. She can enter into a swap contract—buy spot USD to invest in US stocks, and sell USD forward to hedge the exchange risk. If the two transactions are undertaken simultaneously, with one package contract, the overall transaction costs would be smaller.

Finally, tax avoidance may be an objective for engaging in a swap contract. In countries where capital gains are exempt from personal taxes, a sale-and-buy-back arrangement transforms interest income into a capital gain.[3]

Example   10.5

A Luxembourg investor buys 10 kilos of gold from a bank at the spot price $S_t = $ LUF 5m and sells it back (forward) at $F_{t,T} = S_t (1 + r_{t,T}) = 5.25$m.[4] The cash flows are as follows.

- At time t, the customer pays LUF 5m for ten kilos of gold.
- At time T, the customer receives LUF 5.25m from the forward sale of the gold.

This is, of course, a disguised deposit of LUF 5m at a 5 percent return. However, the investor has earned a risk-free capital gain of LUF 250,000, which may be tax-free, whereas interest income would have been taxable.

---

[3] The rationale for transforming interest into capital gains may even be religious in origin. In the Middle Ages, for instance, the Catholic Church prohibited the payment of interest; swap-like contracts were used to disguise loans. Eldridge and Maltby (1991) describe a three-year forward sale for wool, signed in 1276 between the Cistercian Abbey of St. Mary of the Fountains and a Florentine merchant. The "margin" deposited by the merchant was, in fact, a disguised loan to the Abbey, serviced by the deliveries of wool later on. Swaps have been put to even more illegitimate uses. Banks that hold, say, convertible debt (for which the capital adequacy ratio is high) have occasionally swapped them for standard debt around the reporting date, so that no convertible debt shows up in its balance sheet. In other cases, firms have sold and bought back shares at rigged prices in order to avoid reporting capital losses on their investments.

[4] Think of gold as a currency that pays no interest. Thus, we can set $r^* = 0$ in the familiar Interest Rate Parity formula, and obtain $F_{t,T} = S_t (1 + r_{t,T})$ as the no-arbitrage relationship between spot and forward prices for assets without interest or dividends.

10.1.2   Back-to-Back and Parallel Loans

The right of offset, a crucial ingredient in modern (long-term) swaps, is also used in back-to-back and parallel loans.

Back-to-back loans were first inspired by the **investment dollar premium** that existed in the UK from the late sixties to the mid-seventies. In those years, the UK had a *two-tier* exchange rate. *Commercial* USDs (for payments on current account, like international trade and insurance fees) were available without constraints, but *financial* USDs (for investment) were rationed and auctioned off at premiums above the commercial rate. These premiums, of course, varied over time and thus were an additional source of risk to investors. In addition, the law said that when repatriating USD investments, a UK investor had to sell 25 percent of his financial USD in the commercial market; the premium lost was an additional tax on foreign investment. In summary, there was quite a cost attached to foreign investment by UK investors.

Back-to-back loans, promoted and arranged by UK merchant banks, were a way to avoid the investment dollar premium. Such a deal involved a foreign company (denoted USCo) that wanted to extend a loan to its UK subsidiary. The USCo, rather than lending to its UK subsidiary, lent USD to the UK institutional investor (UKII). Thus, the UKII borrowed USD and paid them back later, which meant that it did not have to buy USD initially and that there was no subsequent sale of USD. In short, the investment dollar premium was avoided. The second leg of the contract was that UKII lent GBP to the USCo's subsidiary, so that the USCo's needs were also satisfied. The expected gains from avoiding the implicit tax could then be divided among the parties. The flow of the principal amounts of the reciprocal loans is shown in Figure 10.2.

As it stands, the design of the back-to-back loan would be perfect if there were no default risk. Suppose, however, that the USCo's subsidiary defaults on its GBP loan from the UKII. If no precautions had been taken, UKII would still have to service the USD loan from the USCo, even though USCo's subsidiary did not pay back its loans. Writing a right-of-offset clause into each of the separate loan contracts solves this problem. If USCo's subsidiary defaults, then UKII can suspend its payments to USCo, and sue for its remaining losses (if any). Thus, the right of offset in the back-to-back loan is one element that makes this contract similar to the swap discussed in the preceding section. The similarity becomes even stronger if you consolidate the USCo with its subsidiary and view them as a single entity. Then, there clearly is a reciprocal loan between USCo and UKII, with a right of offset. Therefore, the only remaining difference with the short-term swap is that, in the back-to-back loan, there are interim interest payments whereas the classical short-term swap involves just a single payment.

A variant of the back-to-back loan is the **parallel loan**. If the USCo also faced capital export controls (for example, Nixon's "voluntary" and, later, mandatory controls on foreign direct investment), there would be no way to export USD to the UK counterpart. Suppose that there also was a UK

FIGURE 10.2   Flow of Initial Principals under a Back-to-Back Loan

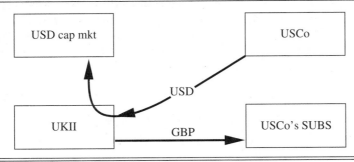

FIGURE 10.3   The Initial Flows of Principal under a Parallel Loan

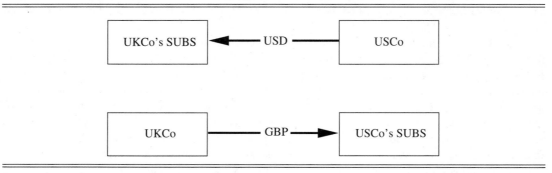

multinational that wanted to lend money to its US subsidiary, if it were not for the cost of the investment dollar premium. The parallel loan solves these companies' joint problem, as shown in Figure 10.3. (The diagram shows the direction of the initial principal amounts.) USCo lends to UKCo's subsidiary in the US (and, therefore, is not exporting any capital), while UKCo lends to USCo's subsidiary in the UK (and, therefore, is making no foreign investment either).

Thus, no money crosses borders, but each firm has achieved its goal. The UKCo's subsidiary has obtained USD, and the USCo's subsidiary has obtained GBP, and the parents have financed the capital injections. This parallel loan replicates the reciprocal loan inherent in the short-term swap when we consolidate the parents with their subsidiaries. In addition, the parallel loan has a right-of-offset clause that limits the potential losses if one of the parties defaults on its obligations.

As mentioned in the preceding section, there are many legal complexities associated with writing two loan contracts with mutual right-of-offset clauses.[5] The swap contract eliminates many of the legal complexities because it is a single contract with a right-of-offset clause built in rather than two separate contracts with cross references and cross conditions.

10.1.3   The IBM/World Bank Currency Swap

The 1981 IBM/WB swap was a deal negotiated directly between the two companies and tailored to suit a very specific situation. Still, the publicity surrounding the transaction helped to popularize the idea of swapping currencies on a long-term basis, and marked the beginning of the market for modern, long-term currency swaps.

In 1981, IBM wanted to get rid of its outstanding DEM- and CHF-denominated callable debt because the USD had appreciated considerably and the DEM and CHF interest rates had also gone up. As a result of these two changes, the market value of IBM's foreign debt, expressed in terms of DEM and CHF, was below its face value, and the gap between market value and book value was even wider in terms of USD. IBM wanted to lock in this capital gain by replacing the DEM and CHF debt by new USD debt. However, in order to do this, IBM would have incurred many costs:

---

[5] To maintain the security at 100 percent, there could also be a "topping-up" clause that indexes the GBP loan to the value of the USD. However, such a clause creates even more legal problems than a right-of-offset clause written into two separate loan contracts.

- IBM would have had to buy DEM and CHF currency, thus incurring transaction costs in the spot market.
- In addition, the loans were callable at a price above par; that is, IBM would have had to pay more than the DEM and CHF face value.
- Lastly, IBM would have had to issue new USD bonds to finance the redemption of its CHF and DEM debt. A bond issue costs at least a few percentages of the nominal value.

The World Bank (WB), on the other hand, wanted to borrow DEM and CHF to lend to its customers.[6] However, issuing new CHF and DEM bonds would have entailed issuing costs.

Note that IBM wants to withdraw CHF and DEM bonds (at a rather high cost) while WB wants to issue CHF and DEM bonds (also at a cost). To avoid all of these costs, IBM and WB agreed that WB would take over IBM's foreign debt. Specifically,

- The WB would not borrow CHF and DEM, but would borrow USD instead. With the proceeds, it would buy spot CHF and DEM needed to make loans to its customers.
- The WB undertook to service IBM's old DEM and CHF loans, while IBM promised to service the WB's (new) USD loan.

Thus, IBM has effectively traded its DEM and CHF obligations for USD obligations. The WB, on the other hand, took on DEM and CHF obligations to match the inflows from the loans it extended to its customers. In short, each party achieved its objective. One obvious joint saving of the swap was the cost of issuing new WB bonds in DEM and CHF, and redeeming the old IBM loans in DEM and CHF.

Of course, the amounts to be exchanged must be acceptable to both parties. The present value of IBM's (USD) payments to the WB should, therefore, be equal to the present value of the (DEM and CHF) inflows received from the WB.

Example   10.6

Assume, for simplicity, that IBM has an outstanding DEM debt with a face value of DEM 10m and a book value of USD 6m (based on the historic USD/DEM rate of 0.6), maturing after five years and carrying a 5 percent annual coupon. Assume the current five-year DEM interest rate is 10 percent and the DEM now trades at USD/DEM 0.4. In DEM, IBM's existing debt would have a present value of:[7]

$$\text{DEM } 10\text{m} \times [1 + (0.05 - 0.1) \times a(10\%, 5 \text{ years})] = \text{DEM } 8.105\text{m}. \tag{1}$$

At the current spot rate of USD/DEM 0.4, WB's undertaking to service this debt is worth 8.105×0.4 = USD 3.242m. The equal-value principle requires that IBM's undertaking have the same present value. Thus, the USD loan (issued at the then-prevailing rate for five years) must have a present value of USD 3.242m.

---

[6] Like any bank, the World Bank has a statutory obligation to match the currency of lending and borrowing.

[7] The bond pricing formula, $[1 + (c - y) \, a(n,y)]$, where c is the coupon, y is the normal current yield on the bond, and $a(n,y)$ is the n-year annuity factor, is explained in the appendix to Chapter 9.

As we have argued, one purpose of the entire IBM/WB deal was to avoid transaction costs. A nice by-product, in terms of taxes, was that IBM locked in its capital gain on its foreign currency debt without immediately *realizing* the profit. If IBM had called its DEM debt at 102 percent of its DEM par value, the cost of withdrawing the debt would have been $10m \times 1.02 \times$ USD/DEM $0.4 =$ USD 4.08, thus realizing a taxable capital gain of USD $6m - 4.08 =$ USD 1.92m. In contrast, under the swap, the DEM debt remains in IBM's books for another five years. That is, in accounting terms, the capital gain will be realized only when, five years later, IBM pays the swap principal (USD 3.242m) to the WB and receives DEM 10m to redeem its DEM debt. In short, the swap allowed IBM to defer its capital gains taxes.

10.2   THE FIXED-FOR-FIXED CURRENCY SWAPS

Let us review the example of the swap between the Bundesbank and the Bank of England, and then see in what way the modern currency swap is related to the short-term currency swap. Recall that, in Example 10.1, the Bundesbank lent USD 100m at a 3 percent effective return for six months, while the Bank of England lent GBP 50m at a 4 percent effective return for six months. One crucial characteristic to be remembered is that the contract has zero initial value. In one interpretation, the swap consists of a forward contract and a spot-exchange transaction. The spot contract has zero value because the amounts are exchanged at the current spot rate. The forward contract has zero value because the amounts to be exchanged at T are equivalent in the sense that their discounted values, after conversion at the spot rate S_t, are the same.

Example   10.7

The present value (PV) of the amounts exchanged by the Bundesbank and the Bank of England in Example 10.1 are:

$$PV_{USD} = \frac{USD\ 103}{1.03} = USD\ 100; \text{ and}$$

$$PV_{GBP} = \frac{GBP\ 42}{1.05} = GBP\ 40,$$

which, after translation into USD, amounts to $40 \times$ USD/GBP $2.5 =$ USD 100.

A second characteristic of the short-term swap worth repeating is that the rates used for setting the forward rate or, equivalently, for discounting the promised payments are the (near-riskless) short-term interbank rates. When doing a short-term swap, banks are willing to use these rates because the default risk is limited by the forward contract's right-of-offset clause, and because any remaining risks are largely eliminated by careful screening of the customers, and by requiring margins or other pledges.

Now consider a similar contract with a much longer maturity. For loans of, say, five years, the banks would traditionally insist that the borrowers periodically pay interest on the principal amounts. For instance, if the interest rates were 10 percent *p.a.* on GBP and 6 percent *p.a.* on USD, payable semiannually, then every six months the Bundesbank would pay GBP 2m, and the Bank of England would pay USD 3m. The principals would still be paid back together with the last interest payments. The contract would then become a **fixed-for-fixed currency swap**—the swap where the interest payments are fixed in advance.

   Other swap techniques, discussed in later sections, are directly related to the fixed-for-fixed currency swap. One of the loans could be of the revolving (floating-rate) type.[8] This would be a **fixed-for-floating currency swap**, or, if both loans are at floating rates, a **floating-for-floating currency swap**. As we shall see, the fixed-for-floating swap might even refer to loans in the same currency and this is called a **(fixed-for-floating) interest rate swap**. In this section, we focus on the fixed-for-fixed currency swap. We discuss its characteristics, its uses and, finally, the procedure to value an outstanding currency swap.

10.2.1   Characteristics of the Modern Currency Swap

In many ways, the modern fixed-for-fixed currency swap is simply a long-term version of the classical swap. A fixed-for-fixed currency swap can be defined as a transaction where two parties exchange, at the time of the contract's initiation, two principals denominated in different currencies but with the same market value,[9] and return these principals to each other when the contract expires. In addition, they pay interest periodically to each other on the amounts borrowed. The deal is structured as a single contract, with a right of offset. The features of a fixed-for-fixed currency swap are described below.

- *Swap rates*
  In a fixed-for-fixed currency swap, the interest payments for each currency are based on the currency's "swap (interest) rate" for the swap's maturity. These swap rates are simply yields at par for riskless bonds with the same maturity as the swap.[10] In practice, the swap rates are close to the long-term eurorates on high-quality **sovereign loans**, that is, loans by governments. For the following reasons, it is appropriate to use risk-free rates to compute the interest on the amounts swapped.

  - The bank's risks in case of default are limited because of the right-of-offset clause. In some cases, the contract parties also have to post margin.
  - The probability of default is small. This is because the customers are screened; small or low-grade companies get no chance. In addition, many swap contracts have a "credit trigger" clause, stating that, if the customer's credit rating is revised downward, the financial institution can terminate the swap, and settle for the swap's market value at

---

   [8] We have discussed these loans in Chapter 9. Recall that under such a loan agreement, the interest payable every N months is reset every time on the basis of the N-month risk-free rate that prevails at the beginning of each period.

   [9] The initial exchange of principals is sometimes omitted, and then the swap only contains an exchange of interest payments.

   [10] The N-year yield at par is the coupon that has to be assigned to an N-year bond in order to give it a market value equal to the par value (the principal). If the parties want a cash flow pattern that differs from the single-amortization loan, the swap dealer is usually willing to design a contract that deviates from the standard form. A fairly common cash flow pattern is the **constant-annuity swap**. Under this type of swap, the two loans have an amortization schedule such that the sum of the periodic amortizations and the interest payments on the outstanding balance is a constant amount. The swap rates for any nonstandard swap are different from the rates that apply to single-amortization swaps. The reason for this is that the present value of a series of cash flows is computed on the basis of the set of *spot* interest rates for the time to maturity of each single cash flow. The stated swap rate of the loan is the **yield to maturity** of the loan. Thus, an annuity loan will generally have a different yield to maturity than a bullet loan, even though the present values of these loans are computed using the same set of spot rates. You can find more details about the relationship between spot interest rates and yields in the appendix to Chapter 9.

that moment. Thus, the bank has an opportunity to terminate the contract before default actually occurs.

- Finally, because of the right of offset, the uncertainty about the bank's inflows is the same as the uncertainty about the bank's outflows. The fact that the uncertainties are the same implies that the corrections for risk virtually cancel out. That is, it hardly matters whether or not one adds a similar (and small) default risk premium to the risk-free rates when one discounts the two cash flow streams. The effect of adding a small risk premium when valuing one "leg" of the swap will essentially cancel out against the effect of adding a similar risk premium in the valuation of the other leg.

- *Zero initial value*

  The swap contract has zero value at inception. First, notice that the initial exchange of principals is a zero-value transaction because the amounts are initially equivalent. Second, the swap deal is constructed so that the future interest payments and amortization have equal present values.

Example   10.8

Suppose that you want to swap a DEM 18m loan for seven years into USD. The spot rate is DEM/USD 1.8, and the seven-year swap rates are 8 percent on DEM and 7 percent on USD, payable annually. We describe the payments and verify that the exchanged future payments are equivalent.

The USD principal amount that is equivalent to DEM 18m equals 18m/1.8 = USD 10m. If desired, there is an initial exchange of principals (you deliver DEM 18m, and obtain USD 10m). The swap implies that every year you pay USD 10m × 7% = USD 700,000, and you receive DEM 18m × 8% = DEM 1.44m. In addition, on the last coupon date, the principals are returned: you pay USD 10m and receive DEM 18m. In the table below, we summarize the payments, and use the < . . . > signs to denote the outflows.

	Leg 1 DEM 18m at 8% (lent)	Leg 2 USD 10m at 7% (borrowed)
Initial exchange of principals	<DEM 18.0m>	USD 10.0m
Annual interest payments (for 7 years)	DEM 1.44m	<USD 0.7m>
Payment of principal at the end of 7 years	DEM 18.0m	<USD 10.0m>

You can check that the present values of the inflows and outflows match:

$$PV_{USD} = \left[\sum_{t=1}^{7} \frac{0.7\,m}{1.07^t} \right] + \frac{10\,m}{1.07^7}$$

$$= 10\,m[1 + (0.07 - 0.07)\ a(7\%,\ 7\ years)] = USD\ 10m,$$

[2]

where $a(y\%, n$ years) is the annuity factor, $\sum_{t=1}^{n} \frac{1}{(1+y)^t}$. The DEM side is valued as follows:

$$PV_{DEM} = \left[\sum_{t=1}^{7} \frac{1.44\,m}{1.08^t} \right] + \frac{18\,m}{1.08^7}$$

[3]

$$= 18\,m[1 + (0.08 - 0.08)\, a(8\%,\ 7\ \text{years})] = \text{DEM } 18m,$$

which implies that the PV in terms of USD is 18m/1.8 = USD 10m.

- *Costs*
  The swapping bank charges a small commission of, say, USD 500 on a USD 1m swap, for each payment to be made. Most often this fee is built into the interest rates, which would raise or lower the quoted rate by a few basis points.

Example   10.9

Suppose that the seven-year yields at par are 7.17 percent on USD and 9.9 percent on DEM. The swap dealer quotes:

USD 7.13%–7.21%

DEM 9.85%–9.95%

If your swap contract is one where you "borrow" DEM and "lend" USD, you would then pay 9.95 percent on the DEM, and receive 7.13 percent on the USD.

Alternatively, the series of future commissions, one per payment, might be replaced by a single up-front fee with a comparable present value.

Example   10.10

For a ten-year USD 1m swap at 10 percent annually that has a USD 400 commission per payment, the equivalent up-front commission would be about $400 \times a(10\%,\ 10\ \text{years}) = 400 \times 6.15 = $ USD 2,460, or 0.246 percent of the face value.

Thus, although the swap remains a zero-value contract, the customer has to pay a small commission. (You can tell the difference between a price and a commission because the commission is always paid, whether one goes long or short; in contrast, the price is paid if one buys, and is received if one sells.) The commissions in the swap are small because of the low default risk (the costs of bonding and monitoring of a loan contract are avoided), and because of the large size of the transactions. A typical interbank swap transaction is for a few million USD; for corporations, swaps below USD 1m are rare.

10.2.2 Motivations for Fixed-for-Fixed Currency Swaps

A swap is a zero-value contract. At inception, the promised inflows and outflows have the same market value. This raises the question of why banks and firms undertake swaps. We argue that the advantage offered by swaps invariably reflects some form of market imperfection. Let us give a few examples of such market imperfections that make a swap valuable to a company:

1. *A comparative informational advantage in the home market*

It is usually cheaper to borrow from banks or lenders that know the company very well. In practice, this often means that the loan with the best spread is a home currency loan from the house bank. For example, Belgium's leading brewery, Interbrew, is well known in its home market and can obtain attractive loans denominated in BEF, that is, loans with a small spread over and above the risk-free rate. However, if Interbrew wanted to seek a loan in CAD, the risk premium required by Canadian banks may be much higher than the spread required by Belgian banks since Canadian banks are less familiar with Interbrew. By swapping a BEF loan into CAD, Interbrew would pay the CAD risk-free rate (the CAD swap rate) plus the spread it pays at home.

Example 10.11

Let the five-year swap rate be 13 percent for FRF and 7 percent for USD, and let the spot rate be FRF/USD 5. Suppose a French company, Générale des Eaux, can get a five-year FRF loan at 14 percent, which implies a spread of 1 percent above the FRF swap rate. However, the firm would actually like to borrow USD—for instance, to hedge USD inflows from USD sales revenue or from US investments. After shopping around, Générale finds that a USD loan could be obtained at 9 percent. This is 2 percent above the USD swap rate. Paying a 2 percent risk spread above the USD risk-free rate, rather than the 1 percent spread in a FRF loan, is a nontrivial cost associated with the USD loan.

By borrowing FRF at 14 percent, and swapping at FRF 13 percent/USD 7 percent, Générale can have the USD cash outflows it desires, without having to pay the costly risk spread on a direct USD loan. The table below summarizes the cash flows from the FRF loan and the swap. The first set of cash flows, in column (a), correspond to the FRF loan taken out by Générale (FRF 100m, at a 14 percent interest rate), and consists of the inflow of FRF 100m initially, followed by annual interest payments of FRF 14m, and the final amortization. The cash flows from the swap contract are analogous to the cash flows from two loans. In this instance, the swap can be thought of as a FRF 100m loan from Générale to the swap dealer at 13 percent (column [b_1]) and a USD 20m loan from the swap dealer to Générale at 7 percent (column [b_2]). Note that these swap loans are at the respective swap rates, independent of what Générale pays on its FRF loan or of what Générale would have paid on a USD loan. In the last column, we sum the cash flows horizontally, to see what the net payments are at each of the relevant dates.

Type of payment	(a) FRF loan FRF 100m, 14%	Swap contract		Total
		(b_1) Leg 1 FRF 100m, 13% (lent)	(b_2) Leg 2 USD 20m, 7% (borrowed)	(a) + (b_1) + (b_2) (loan + swap)
Initial principals	FRF 100m	<FRF 100m>	USD 20.0m	USD 20.0m
Annual interest	<FRF 14m>	FRF 13m	<USD 1.4m>	<USD 1.4m>
				<FRF 1.0m>
Principal at T	<FRF 100m>	FRF 100m	<USD 20.0m>	<USD 20.0m>

The last column shows that the company effectively borrows USD 20m at 7 percent plus a FRF spread of 1 percent on FRF 100m rather than a USD spread of 2 percent on USD 20m.[11]

The reason for the lower spread is that the default risk on the FRF loan is borne by the company's home bank (which extends a genuine loan, with credit risk on the entire principal), while the swapping bank bears only a small "reverse" risk and exchanges the risk-free FRF rate for the USD risk-free rate. Thus, it is logical that the risk spread asked by the home bank (in FRF) is the only cost in excess of the risk-free rate.

2. Subsidized loan

Many governments subsidize loans to stimulate investments or exports, but these subsidized loans are often available only in domestic currency and only to domestic companies. The subsidy means that the company has a comparative advantage when it borrows in home currency, but the home currency is not necessarily the company's preferred currency for a loan. The swap allows the company to keep the subsidy and to effectively borrow in the currency it wishes to.

Example   10.12

We continue with the same data as in the previous example, except that the French company can now get a five-year subsidized FRF loan at 8 percent, 5 percent below the FRF swap rate, to finance an export contract. Générale can borrow in the currency of its choice (the USD) without losing the subsidy, by first borrowing FRF at 8 percent and then swapping this loan into USD at FRF 13 percent/USD 7 percent. The combined cash flows of these transactions are summarized below.

Type of payment	(a) FRF loan FRF 100m, 8%	Swap contract		Total
		(b₁) Leg 1 FRF 100m, 13% (lent)	(b₂) Leg 2 USD 20m, 7% (borrowed)	(a) + (b₁) + (b₂) (loan + swap)
Initial principals	FRF 100m	<FRF 100m>	USD 20.0m	USD 20.0m
Annual interest	<FRF 8m>	FRF 13m	<USD 1.4m>	<USD 1.4m>
				FRF 5.0m
Principal at T	<FRF 100m>	FRF 100m	<USD 20.0m>	<USD 20.0m>

Thus, rather than having to pay the extra USD 2 percent spread that would have been due if the company had directly borrowed USD, Générale can effectively borrow at the USD swap rate (7 percent on USD 20m) without having to give up the interest subsidy of 13% − 8% = 5% *p.a.* on FRF 100m.

---

[11] This does not mean that the saving is 1 percent *p.a.*, because a future FRF amount cannot be compared to a future USD amount when future exchange rates are uncertain. To get a more reliable (but still imperfect) idea about the savings, one can compare the PVs of the risk spreads: present value of the 1 percent FRF risk spread on FRF 100m = a(13%, 5 years) × 1 = FRF 3.517m; and present value of the 2 percent FRF risk spread on USD 20m = a(7%, 5 years) × 0.4 = USD 1.640m, or FRF 8.2m.

3. *No access or limited access to "national" capital markets*

Sometimes the company cannot obtain a loan in its preferred currency because the market is closed to foreign borrowers. For example, the yen capital market was closed to foreign borrowers until the early eighties. Swaps can be used to overcome such restrictions. Renault, for instance, swapped a USD loan with Yamaichi Securities for JPY. This example is discussed in Section 10.4.

4. *Avoiding transaction costs*

In the IBM/World Bank swap discussed in Section 10.1.3, the main rationale was to avoid transaction costs. One can always replicate the swap using transactions in the markets for foreign exchange and bonds, but the cost of such a synthetic swap is likely to be higher than the cost of a swap.

Example   10.13

A British firm wants to hedge a series of NZD receivables. It can either buy a swap that transforms the NZD stream into a GBP stream, or, it can borrow NZD, convert them into GBP at the spot rate, and invest the proceeds in the GBP capital market. Such a synthetic swap, which involves three transactions, will be more expensive in terms of spreads and commissions than an outright swap (which requires only one transaction).

---

5. *Possible advantages of off-balance-sheet reporting*

Because of their initial zero-value characteristic and their right-of-offset clause, swaps are reported off balance sheet (just like forward contracts) rather than on balance sheet.[12] In some countries, this may make it possible for a firm or financial institution to circumvent or reduce regulatory constraints on its asset and liability structure. For example, a bank needs less long-term capital when it undertakes a swap contract than when it extends a loan for the same amount. The Bank for International Settlements' (BIS) regulations arbitrarily fix capital ratios as follows.[13]

Maturity	Pure currency swap	Pure interest swap	Fixed-for-floating currency swap
Less than 1 year	1%	0%	1%
More than 1 year	5%	0.5%	5%

---

[12] This accounting rule is not unreasonable. There is indeed a difference between a swap and two separate contracts (one claim and one liability). In the case of the swap, default on the liability wipes out the claim. For that reason, accountants think it would be misleading to show the swap contract as if it consisted of a standard separate claim and liability.

[13] The Bank for International Settlements of Basel, Switzerland, has no power to impose rules on banks anywhere. However, the BIS deserves credit for bringing together the regulatory bodies from most OECD countries in a committee called the BIS Committee, or the Basel Committee, or the Cooke Committee (after the committee's chairman), to create a common set of rules. The objective of establishing a common set of rules was to level the field for fair competition. The general capital requirement is 8 percent, meaning that the bank's long-term capital has to be at least 8 percent of its assets. For some assets and for off-balance-sheet positions, the risk is deemed to be less than the risk of a standard loan to a company, and the capital ratio is lowered correspondingly. For instance, a loan to the government is assumed to have zero credit risk, and does not require any additional capital. With many risk classes (denoted by j) the rule is as follows: long-term capital $\geq \Sigma_j$ [position in the risk class j] $\times$ [capital ratio for risk class j]. For example, if a bank has loans to companies (with capital ratio 8 percent) worth DEM 100m, loans to the government (with capital ratio 0 percent) worth 50m, and long-term currency swaps (with capital ratio 5 percent) worth 20m, the capital requirement for the bank is (100m × 8%) + (50m × 0%) + (20m × 5%) = 9m.

6. *Favorable tax treatment*

As we saw in the IBM/World Bank example, when the capital gain on a foreign currency loan or investment is locked in by retiring the debt or selling the asset, it is a (taxable) realized gain. When swapped, the gain remains unrealized until the swap expires, implying a tax deferral.

10.2.3   Valuing an Outstanding Fixed-for-Fixed Currency Swap

The last issue that we discuss in the section on fixed-for-fixed currency swaps is the valuation of such a swap after its inception. An assessment of the market value of a swap is required for the purpose of true and fair reporting to shareholders and overseeing authorities, or when the contract is terminated prematurely (by negotiation, or by default, or by the credit trigger clause).

Just as a forward contract, the fixed-for-fixed currency swap acquires a non-zero value as soon as the interest rates change, or as the spot rate changes. Since a swap is like a portfolio of (a) a loan and (b) an investment in long-term deposits (or in bonds), we can always value a swap as the difference between the market value of the loan and the market value of the investment.

Example   10.14

Two years ago, a company swapped a loan (asset) of GBP 50m into USD 100m for seven years, at the swap rates of 10 percent on the USD leg and 12 percent on the GBP leg. This reflected the long-term interest rates and the spot rate of USD/GBP 2 prevailing when the contract was signed. Now the five-year USD swap rate is 8 percent, the GBP swap rate is 14 percent, and the spot rate is USD/GBP 1.7. The procedure suggested by the International Swap Dealers Association is to value the swap by applying the traditional bond valuation formula to each of the swap's legs.[14] Thus, the company's USD outflows are valued as:

$$PV_{USD} = 100m \times [1 + (0.10 - 0.08) \times a(8\%, 5 \text{ years})] = USD\ 107.985m, \qquad [4]$$

while its GBP inflows are worth:

$$PV_{GBP} = 50m \times [1 + (0.12 - 0.14) \times a(14\%, 5 \text{ years})] = GBP\ 46.567m. \qquad [5]$$

At the spot rate of USD/GBP 1.7, these GBP inflows are worth USD 79.164m. The value of the contract therefore is USD 79.164 − 107.985 = (−)USD 28.821m.

This finishes our discussion of the fixed-for-fixed currency swap. We now turn to other types of swaps, the most important of which is the **interest rate swap** or **coupon swap**.

---

[14] The formula is [nominal value] $\times [1 + (c - y)\ a(n,y)]$ where c is the (coupon) interest rate stated in the contract, y is the current yield to maturity in the market for loans with the same maturity and amortization schedule, and

$$a(n,y) = \sum_{t=1}^{n} \frac{1}{(1+y)^t}$$

is the annuity factor. In this application, c is the historic swap rate and y is the current swap rate for the contract's remaining life. We discussed this valuation procedure, and its link to the more modern approach to bond valuation, in the appendix to Chapter 9.

10.3 INTEREST RATE SWAPS

In an interest rate swap, there is still an exchange of the service payments on two distinct loans. However, the two loans involved now differ not by currency, but by the method used to determine the interest payment (for instance, floating rate versus fixed rate). Because both underlying loans are in the same currency, there is no initial exchange of principals and no final amortization. In that sense, the two loans are *notional* (fictitious, or theoretical). The only cash flows that are swapped are the interest streams on each of the notional loans. In short, parties A and B simply agree to pay/receive the difference between two interest streams on the notional loan amounts.

The standard interest swap is the fixed-for-floating swap or coupon swap. The base swap is rarer. We discuss each of them in turn.

10.3.1 Coupon Swaps (Fixed-for-Floating)

We now describe the characteristics of a fixed-for-floating swap and how one can value such a financial contract.

Characteristics of the Fixed-for-Floating Swap

In our discussion of the fixed-for-fixed currency swap, we saw that, in terms of the risk spread above the risk-free rate, a firm often has a comparative advantage in one currency but may prefer to borrow in another currency. The firm can retain its favorable risk spread and still change the loan's currency of denomination by borrowing in the most favorable market and swapping the loan into the preferred currency. The same holds for the fixed-for-floating swap except that, instead of a preferred currency, the firm now has a preferred type of interest payment. For instance, the firm may have a preference for financing at a fixed rate, but the risk spread in the floating-rate market may be lower. To retain its advantage of a lower spread in the floating-rate market, the firm can borrow at a floating rate, and swap the loan into a fixed-rate loan using a fixed-for-floating swap.

Because the swap contract is almost risk free, the interest rates used in the swap contract are (near) risk-free rates. For the floating-rate leg of the swap, the rate is usually based on LIBOR or a similar money market rate, while the relevant interest rate for the fixed-rate leg is the same N-year swap rate as used in fixed-for-fixed currency swaps.

Example 10.15

An AA Irish company wants to borrow NZD to finance (and partially hedge) its direct investment in New Zealand. Because the company is better known in London than in Auckland, it decides to tap the euro-NZD market rather than the loan market in New Zealand. As NZD interest rates are rather volatile, the company prefers fixed-rate loans. But eurobanks, which are funded on a very short-term basis, dislike fixed-rate loans. The company's alternatives are the following:

- A euro-NZD fixed-rate bond issue would be possible only at 19 percent, which represents a hefty 3 percent spread above the NZD swap rate of 16 percent.
- From a London bank, the Irish company can get a NZD floating-rate bank loan at LIBOR + 1 percent.[15]

---

[15] This lower risk premium relative to the bond rate arises because the bond market has less information about the company than the bank does. Many firms are willing to privately divulge to a bank information that they would never consider publishing in a prospectus. Note also that, since the two loans are now in the same currency, we can unambiguously say that the savings is 2 percent *p.a.* This is not possible in the currency swap, as we argued in Section 10.2.2 (footnote 11).

The company can keep the lower spread required in the floating-rate market and still pay a fixed rate, by borrowing NZD at the NZD LIBOR + 1 percent, and swapping this into a fixed-rate NZD loan at the 16 percent swap rate. The payment streams, per NZD, are summarized below. To help you see the link between the payments under the swap contract and the underlying notional loans, we have added the theoretical principals at initiation and at maturity. In practice, the principals will not be exchanged.

Type of payment	(a) NZD loan NZD 1 at NZD LIBOR + 1%	Swap contract		Total
		(b₁) Leg 1 NZD 1 at LIBOR (lent)	(b₂) Leg 2 NZD 1 at 16% (borrowed)	(a) + (b₁) + (b₂) (loan + swap)
Initial principals	1	<1>	1	1
Annual interest	<LIBOR + 1%>	LIBOR	<16%>	<16% + 1%>
Principal at T	<1>	1	<1>	<1>

Thus, in a sense, this company borrows foreign currency at the NZD risk-free fixed rate (16 percent) plus the spread of 1 percent it can obtain in the "best" market (the floating-rate eurobank-loan market). Therefore, the company pays 17 percent fixed rather than the 19 percent that would have been required in the bond market.

From the above discussion, it is obvious that the potential advantages of the coupon swap are similar to the ones mentioned in the case of the fixed-for-fixed currency swap. What remains to be discussed is how to determine the value of the fixed-for-floating swap.

Valuing a Fixed-for-Floating Swap

We have seen that in a fixed-for-floating swap without default risk, the incoming stream is the service schedule of a risk-free floating-rate loan, and the outgoing stream is the service schedule of a traditional risk-free fixed-rate loan (and *vice versa* for the other contract party). The fixed-rate payment stream is easily valued by discounting the known cash flows using the prevailing swap rate for the remaining time to maturity. The question now is how should one value the floating-rate part for which the future payments are not known in advance.

Let us study the value of a series of floating-rate cash inflows. This series of (as yet unknown) inflows must have the same market value as a short-term deposit where the principal amount is reinvested periodically. The reason for this equivalence is that the cash flows are the same, as the example will show. To buy such a series of deposits we need to buy only the currently outstanding deposit. No extra money is needed to redeposit the maturing principals later on.

Example   10.16

Suppose that you want to replicate a risk-free USD 10,000 floating-rate bond with semiannual interest payments equal to LIBOR, the first of which is due within three months. At the last reset date, the six-month LIBOR was 10 percent *p.a.;* thus, the next interest payment equals $10,000 \times (1/2) \times 10\% = $ USD 500. The current three-month rate of return is 3 percent (or 12 percent *p.a.,* simple interest).

The above floating-rate bond can be replicated by "buying" USD 10,500 due three months from now at a present value cost of

$$\text{USD } \frac{10,500}{1.03} = \text{USD } 10,194.$$

After three months, you withdraw USD 500 to replicate the bond's first coupon, and you redeposit the remaining 10,000 at the then-prevailing, six-month return. When this investment expires, you again withdraw the interest and redeposit the 10,000 at the then-prevailing rate, and you continue to do so until the bond expires. Notice that the future payoffs of the rolled-over deposit are identical to the payoffs of the floating rate bond. The cost to you was only the initial USD 10,194. Then, by arbitrage, the floating rate bond is also worth 10,194.

To obtain a general expression for the value of a floating-rate bond, we adopt the following notation, which is also explained in Figure 10.4:

t_0 is the last reset date.
T_1 is the next reset date.
t is the present date (the valuation date, with $t_0 < t < T_1$).
r_{t_0,T_1} is the coupon effectively payable at T_1.
r_{t,T_1} is the effective current return until time T_1.

In this notation, the value of the currently outstanding deposit—or the value of the floating rate part of the swap—is given by

$$\text{Value of a risk-free floating-rate bond} = \text{Face value} \times \frac{1 + r_{t_0,T_1}}{1 + r_{t,T_1}}. \qquad [6]$$

The current market value of a coupon swap then equals the difference between the market value of the loan that underlies the incoming stream and the market value of the loan that underlies the outgoing stream.

FIGURE 10.4   Time Conventions When Valuing a Floating-Rate Bond

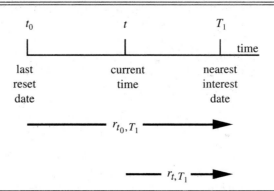

Example   10.17

Some time ago, a French company speculated on a drop in fixed-rate interest rates, and swapped FRF 10m floating rate (at the six-month FRF LIBOR) into fixed rate (at 13 percent, semiannual). That is, the contract stipulates that, every six months, the firm pays the six-month FRF LIBOR rate (divided by two) on a notional FRF 10m, and receives 13 percent/2 on the same notional amount. Suppose that FRF medium-term interest rates have fallen substantially below 13 percent. The company reckons it has made a nice profit on its swap contract, and wants to lock in the gain by selling the swap. Current conditions are as follows:

- The swap has five years and two months left until maturity.
- The current five-year FRF swap rate (for semiannual payments) is 9 percent *p.a.,* or 4.5 percent every six months.
- The FRF LIBOR rate, set four months ago for the current six-month period, is 6 percent *p.a.*
- The current two-month FRF LIBOR is 5.5 percent *p.a.*

To value the (incoming) FRF cash flows, note that there are eleven remaining interest payments at 6.5 percent each, the first of which is due two months from now. Discounted at 9/2 = 4.5 percent per half-year, the value is:[16]

$$PV_{\text{fixed FRF}} = 10m \times [1 + (0.065 - 0.045) \times a(4.5\%, 11)]1.045^{(2/3)} \tag{7}$$
$$= FRF\ 12,054,374.$$

The value of the FRF outflows is determined as in Equation [6]:

$$PV_{\text{floating FRF}} = 10\,m \times \frac{1 + 1/2 \times 0.06}{1 + 2/12 \times 0.055} = FRF\ 10,206,441. \tag{8}$$

The value of the fixed-rate leg exceeds the value of the floating-rate leg by

$$FRF\ 12,054,374 - 10,206,441 = FRF\ 1,847,933. \tag{9}$$

Thus, the company should receive this amount when it sells its swap contract.

---

[16] The valuation formula is derived as follows. Define a period as the time between two consecutive coupons; for instance, one period may be six months, as in our example. Suppose the effective coupon is c percent per period, the effective discount rate is y percent per period, there are n coupons to go, and the last coupon was paid $\tau = (<1)$ periods ago. For instance, in our example, we have $c = 6.5$ percent, $y = 4.5$ percent, and $\tau = (4\ \text{months})/(6\ \text{months}) = 2/3$ periods. This means the remaining coupons will be paid at "times" $j = 1 - \tau, 2 - \tau, \ldots, n - \tau$. Thus, the value of the cash flows is

$$PV = \sum_{j=1}^{n} \frac{c}{(1+y)^{j-\tau}} + \frac{1}{(1+y)^{n-\tau}} = \frac{1}{(1+y)^{-\tau}} \left[\sum_{j=1}^{n} \frac{c}{(1+y)^{j}} + \frac{1}{(1+y)^{n}} \right] = (1+y)^{\tau}[1 - (c-y)a(n,y)].$$

The expression $[1 - (c - y)\, a(n,y)]$ computes the value as if the first coupon were due six months (one period) from now. This term is to be increased by a factor $(1 + y)^{\tau}$ because all payments are actually τ periods closer than was assumed in the expression $[1 - (c - y)\, a(n,y)]$.

10.3.2   Base Swaps

Under a **base swap**, the parties swap two streams of floating-rate interest payments where each stream is determined by a different base rate. For example, a LIBOR-based revolving loan can be swapped for a US T-bill-based revolving loan. The spread between these two money-market rates is called the **TED spread (treasury-eurodollar spread)**. The TED spread is non-zero because T-bills and euro-CDs are not perfect substitutes in terms of political risk and default risk. TED swaps can be used either to speculate on changes in the TED spread, or to hedge a swap book containing contracts with different base rates.

Example   10.18

The US office of a major bank has signed a fixed-for-floating swap based on the USD T-bill rate, while the London office has signed a floating-for-fixed swap based on USD LIBOR. This bank now has the USD T-bill rate as an income stream, and the USD LIBOR rate as an outgoing stream. To cover the TED-spread risk, it can swap its T-bill income stream for a LIBOR income stream using a base swap. The counterparty to this swap may be a speculator or simply another swap dealer who faces the opposite problem.

10.4   CROSS-CURRENCY SWAPS

The **cross-currency swap**, or **circus swap**, is a currency swap combined with an interest rate swap (floating versus fixed rate), in the sense that the loans on which the service schedules are based differ by currency *and* type of interest payment. An early example is the Renault-Yamaichi swap already mentioned in Section 10.2.2. The historic background for the swap is as follows:

- Renault, a French car producer, wanted to get rid of its USD floating rate debt, and wanted to borrow fixed-rate JPY instead. However, because of Japanese regulations at the time, Renault was not permitted to borrow in the Japanese market.
- Simultaneously, Yamaichi Securities was being encouraged by Japan's Ministry of Finance to buy USD assets. It could have bought, for instance, Renault's USD floating rate notes but was unwilling to take the exchange risk.

With the help of Bankers Trust, an investment bank, Renault convinced Yamaichi to borrow fixed-rate JPY and to buy floating-rate USD notes of similar rating and conditions as Renault's notes. As illustrated in Figure 10.5, Yamaichi was to hand over the USD service income from the USD investment to Renault, who would use the floating-rate USD interest stream to service its own floating-rate notes. As compensation, Renault undertook to service Yamaichi's equivalent fixed-rate yen loan, and pay a spread to both Bankers Trust and to Yamaichi.

The advantages of the swap to each party were:

- Renault was able to access the JPY capital market and get rid of its USD liability. (A more obvious solution would have been to borrow JPY and retire the USD floating-rate notes with the proceeds. However, the first part of this transaction was not legally possible and the second part would have been expensive in terms of transaction costs or call premiums.)
- Yamaichi earned a commission. In addition, it now held USD assets (which was politically desirable) but these assets were fully hedged against exchange risk by the swap.
- Banker's Trust earned a commission on all of the payments that passed through its hands, plus a fee for arranging the deal.

FIGURE 10.5   Example of the Service Flows under a Circus Swap: Renault/Yamaichi

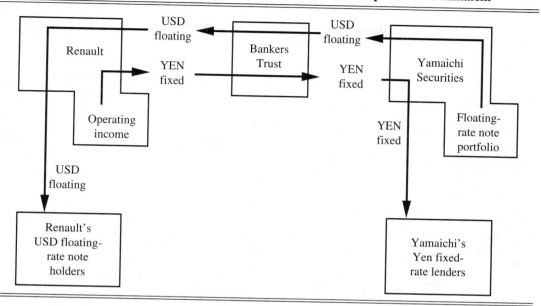

10.5   COCKTAIL SWAPS

Banks try to balance their exposures to various exchange rates and interest rates by offsetting the inflows and outflows of various swap contracts. The **cocktail swap**, then, is a combination of currency and interest rate swaps, often involving lots of parties, currencies, and interest rates, which leaves the bank unexposed—as long as there is no default, or as long as no contract is otherwise terminated prematurely. We shall present the simplest possible example, although it might not strike you as being *really* simple.

Example   10.19

- A medium-grade European company, *A,* wants to borrow USD. It has a comparative advantage in the market for eurodollar floating-rate bank loans. It would prefer to borrow fixed-rate USD but is discouraged from doing so because of the high risk premium in eurobond markets.[17] Therefore, the company borrows in the market for eurodollar floating-rate bank loans and then swaps its loan into fixed-rate USD.
- A US company, *C,* has a comparative advantage in the market for USD fixed-rate bank loans, but wants to borrow fixed-rate CHF (perhaps to hedge a Swiss investment, or because the

---

[17] As we saw in Chapter 9, the eurodollar bank loan market is essentially one with floating rates, since eurobank's funding has a very short duration (mostly three- and six-month deposits). Therefore the only source for fixed-rate euroloans is the eurobond market. A medium-grade company, loath to divulge sensitive information in a prospectus, would have to pay a larger risk premium in the bond market than in the market for bank loans.

CHF interest rate seems attractive). Therefore, this company borrows in the market for USD fixed-rate bank loans and then swaps its loan into fixed-rate CHF.

- A Swiss company, *D,* has an advantage in the CHF fixed-rate market but prefers to borrow floating-rate USD. Thus, this company borrows in the CHF fixed-rate market, and then swaps this loan into floating-rate USD.

Bank *B* acts as intermediary and takes all swaps onto its book. If the amounts borrowed all match, the bank is fully hedged (barring default). The payment streams are summarized in Figure 10.6.

Thus, although each swap taken separately exposes the bank to currency and/or interest risk, the combination of the three swaps reduces the risk to the "reverse" risk in case of default. Note that this set of transactions is a cocktail only from the financial intermediary's point of view. Each swap customer has a standard swap with a financial intermediary, and does not know (or care) that its contract is part of a more complicated scheme set up by the financial intermediary in order to balance its books.

FIGURE 10.6   Example of the Service Flows in a Cocktail Swap

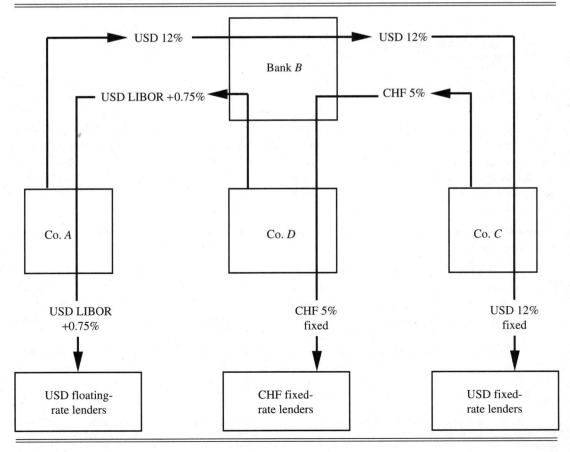

10.6   CONCLUSIONS

The interest paid on any loan can be decomposed into the risk-free rate plus a spread that reflects the credit risk of the borrower. Swaps allow a company to borrow in the market where it can obtain the lowest spread, and then exchange the risk-free component of the loan's service payments for the risk-free component of another loan that is preferred in terms of its currency of denomination or the way the periodic interest payments are determined (fixed or floating), as shown in Figure 10.7.

The difference between the spreads asked in different market segments usually reflects an information asymmetry—for instance, the firm's house bank often offers the best spreads—but may also reflect an interest subsidy. Another advantage is that the swap contract is a single contract, and is therefore likely to be cheaper than its replicating portfolio (borrowing in one market, converting the proceeds into another currency, and investing the resulting amount in another market). Other potential advantages include tax savings, or access to otherwise unavailable loans, or advantages of off-balance-sheet reporting.

Depending on the combination of the preferred type of loan and the cheapest available loan, one could use a fixed-for-fixed swap, a fixed-for-floating swap, or a circus swap. Each of these swaps can also be used to speculate on changes in interest rates or exchange rates. Likewise, basis swaps are used to hedge against, or to speculate on, changes in the TED spread. These four swaps are just the most common types; in fact, many more exotic swap-like contracts are offered. Thus, swaps have become increasingly popular with financial institutions and large corporations. All of these swaps are based on the principle of initial equivalence of the two legs of the contract. Thus, like forward contracts on exchange rates or currencies, the initial value of a swap is zero. To compute the market value of such a contract after inception, we just value each leg in light of the prevailing exchange rates and interest rates.

FIGURE 10.7   Swaps—An Overview

Preferred loan		Original loan with the lowest spread	
		Fixed-rate	Floating-rate
Fixed-rate:	in the same currency:	(Do not swap)	Use an Interest rate swap
	in another currency:	Use a Fixed-for-fixed Currency swap	Use a Circus swap
Floating-rate:	in the same currency:	Use an Interest rate swap	(Do not swap)
	in another currency:	Use a Circus swap	Use a Floating-for-floating Currency swap

QUIZ QUESTIONS

1. How does a fixed-for-fixed currency swap differ from a spot contract combined with a forward contract in the opposite direction?

2. Describe some predecessors to the currency swap, and discuss the differences with the modern swap contract.

3. What are the reasons why swaps may be useful for companies who want to borrow?

4. How are swaps valued in general? How does one value the floating-rate leg (if any), and why?

EXERCISES

1. The traditional short-term swap is:
   (a) a spot transaction and a reverse forward transaction.
   (b) a foreign-currency loan covered in the forward market.
   (c) a loan converted into another currency by a spot transaction (for the time-t proceeds) and forward transaction (for the time-T service payment).
   (d) a loan in one currency combined with a loan in another currency.
   (e) a loan in one currency combined with a loan in another currency and a right of offset between the two.
   (f) a loan in one currency combined with a loan in another currency for the same time-T value.

2. A repurchase order is:
   (a) a spot transaction of a low-risk asset combined with a short-term reverse forward transaction.
   (b) a loan covered against default risk by using a low-risk asset as security.
   (c) a fixed-for-floating currency swap.

3. A back-to-back loan provides:
   (a) a way to avoid the cost of forward transactions.
   (b) a way to obtain secured loans without openly acknowledging them on the balance sheet.
   (c) a way to avoid the investment dollar premium.

4. The modern long-term currency swap can be viewed as:
   (a) a spot sale and a forward purchase.
   (b) a combination of forward contracts, each of them having zero initial market value.
   (c) a combination of forward contracts, each of them having, generally, a non-zero initial market value but with a zero initial market value for all of them taken together.
   (d) a spot transaction and a combination of forward contracts, each of them having, generally, a non-zero initial market value but with a zero initial market value for all of them taken together.

5. The swap rate for a long-term swap is:

   (a) the risk-free rate plus the spread usually paid by the borrower.
   (b) the risk-free rate plus a spread that depends on the security offered on the loan.
   (c) close to the risk-free rate, because the risk to the financial institution is very low.
   (d) the average difference between the spot rate and forward rates for each of the maturities.

6. The general effect of a swap is:

   (a) to replace the entire service payment schedule on a given loan by a new service payment schedule on an initially equivalent loan of another type (for instance, another currency, or another type of interest).
   (b) to replace the risk-free component of the service payment schedule on a given loan by a risk-free component of the service payment schedule on an initially equivalent loan of another type (for instance, another currency, or another type of interest).
   (c) to change the currency of a loan.
   (d) to obtain a spot conversion at an attractive exchange rate.

7. You borrow USD 1m for six months, and you lend DEM 1.5m—an initially equivalent amount— for six months, at *p.a.* rates of 6 percent and 8 percent, respectively, with a right of offset. What is the equivalent spot and forward transaction?

8. Your firm has USD debt outstanding with a nominal value of USD 1m and a coupon of 9 percent, payable annually. The first interest payment is due three months from now, and there are five more interest payments afterwards.

   (a) If the yield at par on bonds with similar risk and time to maturity is 8 percent, what is the market value of this bond in USD? In Yen (at $S_t = \text{YEN/USD } 100$)?
   (b) Suppose that you want to exchange the service payments on this USD bond for the service payments of a 5.25-year JPY loan at the going yield, for this risk class, of 4 percent. What should be the terms of the JPY loan?

9. You borrow FIM 100m at 10 percent for seven years, and you swap the loan into DEM at a spot rate of FIM/DEM 4 and the seven-year swap rates of 7 percent (DEM) and 8 percent (FIM). What are the payments on the loan, on the swap, and on the combination of them? Is there a gain if you could have borrowed DEM at 9 percent?

10. Use the same data as in the previous exercise, except that you now swap the loan into floating rate (at FIBOR). What are the payments on the loan, on the swap, and on the combination of them? Is there a gain if you could have borrowed DEM at FIBOR + 1 percent?

11. You can borrow CAD at 8 percent, which is 2 percent above the swap rate, or at CAD LIBOR + 1 percent. If you want to borrow at a fixed-rate, what is the best way: direct, or synthetic (that is, using a floating-rate loan and a swap)?

12. You have an outstanding fixed-for-fixed FIM/DEM swap for FIM 100m, based on a historic spot rate of FIM/DEM 4 and initial seven-year swap rates of 7 percent (DEM) and 8 percent (FIM). The swap now has three years to go, and the current rates at FIM/DEM 4.5, 6 percent (DEM three years), and 5 percent (FIM three years). What is the market value of the swap contract?

13. Use the same data as in the previous exercise, except that now the DEM leg is a floating rate. The rate has just been reset. What is the market value of the swap?

MIND-EXPANDING EXERCISE

1. Sometimes a fixed-for-fixed currency swap is described as a combination of independent forward contracts. Show that, to replicate a fixed-for-fixed currency swap by a series of independent contracts, one needs identical term structures across the two currencies.

    Hint: Denote the foreign swap rate by s^*, and the domestic swap rate by s. Consider a swap where the foreign leg has a nominal value of one unit of foreign currency, and the home currency leg has a value of S_t units of home currency. The foreign currency cash flows from a swap are s^* units of foreign currency at every interim date, and $1 + s^*$ at the end, and the home currency cash flows from a swap are $S_t \times s$ units of home currency at every interim date, and $S_T \times (1 + s)$ at the end. What home currency cash flows does one receive or pay if each of the foreign currency cash flows is converted separately into home currency by a forward contract of that specific maturity, rather than exchanging the entire series for a series of home currency cash flows by one single swap contract? Under what conditions on the term structure of returns are the resulting home currency cash flows of the form ($S_t \times s$ at the interim dates, and $S_T \times (1 + s)$ at the end)?

PART

In this part of the book, Part II, we look at different theories of exchange rate determination. Recall that the spot rate is simply the price of a unit of foreign currency. Thus, it is not surprising that the various theories that we examine agree that the spot rate is determined by the demand and supply for foreign currency. The main disagreement between these theories is what drives the supply, and especially, the demand for the foreign currency. It is probably fair to say that no single theory is fully correct; so our aim is to help you to judge which theory is most applicable under a particular set of circumstances.

The theories of exchange rate determination that we will examine are the following: In Chapter 11, we study the Purchasing Power Parity (PPP) approach to exchange rate determination. According to this theory, the demand for the foreign currency is derived from the demand for foreign goods. In Chapter 12, we study the Balance of Payments (BOP) approach to exchange rate determination. This theory extends the PPP approach—the demand for the foreign currency is now assumed to arise from the elements in the Balance of Payments: demand for goods and services and also demand for foreign investment. The third theory that we consider is the Monetary approach to exchange rate determination. This theory combines the PPP approach and the Quantity Theory of Money to determine how changes in money supply affect the exchange rate. This theory is discussed in Chapter 13, along with the last theory of exchange rate determination that we will consider: the Portfolio approach. The Portfolio theory extends the Monetary theory by considering not only the demand for money but also the demand for other financial assets in determining the equilibrium exchange rate.

Having studied several theories of exchange rate determination, the next question is whether we can use any of these theories to predict the future spot exchange rate. In Chapter 14, we analyze whether it is possible to predict the change in the spot rate using the forward rate. In Chapter 15, we examine other variables to see if they can be used to predict the exchange rate, or explain its current value. The evidence that we study in these two chapters suggests that the relationship between the forward and the spot rate is weak, and that it is difficult to predict the future spot rate or explain its current value using either macroeconomic variables or past exchange rates.

2

EXCHANGE RATE DETERMINATION

11 PURCHASING POWER PARITY

In Part I of this book, we discussed financial securities such as currency forwards, futures, and options whose payoffs depend on the exchange rate. In determining the value of these securities, we assumed that the spot rate was given exogenously. In Part II of the text, we examine various theories of how the exchange rate is determined. In this chapter, we consider one of the early theories of exchange rate determination, the Purchasing Power Parity (PPP) theory. This theory is based on the concept that the demand for a country's currency is derived from the demand for the goods that this country produces. Thus, the exchange rate for a certain country's currency depends on the demand for the goods produced in that country. If prices of goods are low relative to those in other countries, then this exchange rate will be high.

The PPP relationship is important because it tells us whether changes in the nominal exchange rate have an impact on real variables such as the value of a firm or the return on a portfolio of assets. That is, if changes in the spot rate were exactly offset by changes in prices at home and abroad, then there would be no effect of changes in the spot rate on the real value of variables. On the other hand, if changes in the spot rate are not offset by changes in the price level at home relative to that abroad, then there is real exchange rate risk. The objective of this chapter is to understand what the PPP relationship implies and to examine whether or not this relationship is valid in the real world.

This chapter is organized as follows. In the first section, we examine the relationship between the price of a particular traded good at home and abroad, and the exchange rate. This relationship, on the level of individual goods, is called Commodity Price Parity (CPP). In Section 11.2, we extend this relationship to the level of baskets of commodities, where the relationship is called the absolute version of Purchasing Power Parity (PPP). In the third section, we examine the relative version of the PPP relationship that links changes in the price of a representative bundle of securities at home and abroad to changes in the exchange rate between these two countries. In Section 11.4, we report the results of empirical tests of CPP and PPP. The verdict is that the PPP relationship is weak, especially in the short run. In Section 11.5, we evaluate the PPP as a theory of how exchange rates are determined. We conclude, in the sixth section, with a discussion of the implications, for corporate managers, of the results of empirical tests of PPP.

11.1   COMMODITY PRICE PARITY

In this section, we assume that commodity markets are perfect, that is, that there are no costs for exporting goods from one country to another. We then show that, in such a setting there exists a no-arbitrage relationship between exchange rates and the prices of individual goods at home and abroad. In the second part of this section, we study the implications of this relationship for the consumption decision of economic agents.

11.1.1   The Concept of Commodity Price Parity (CPP)

Arbitrage in perfect goods markets implies that a particular good must have the same price across different countries, after translation into a common currency. That is, if the price of the same commodity were not the same across countries (after translation at a given exchange rate), then one could make money by buying the commodity in the country where it is cheap and selling it where it is more expensive. Such transactions will continue until the prices at home and abroad are equal. For example, if Big Macs (hamburgers) can be instantaneously transported from Amsterdam to New York at no cost, then the New York price of USD 2 for a Big Mac is consistent with an exchange rate of NLG/USD 2 only if the Amsterdam price is NLG 4.

More generally, denoting the domestic price of good j at time t by P_{jt} and the foreign price as P_{jt}^*, in a world with frictionless commodity markets there exists an arbitrage relation of the following form:

$$P_{jt} = S_t P_{jt}^*. \qquad [1]$$

This arbitrage relationship between the exchange rate and prices at home and abroad is called **Commodity Price Parity (CPP)**. Note that *no causality* is implied in an arbitrage condition like Equation [1]. That is, this equation neither states that the foreign price determines the price of the domestic good nor that the domestic price determines the foreign price and the exchange rate. Prices and exchange rates are set simultaneously in the world markets for goods and currencies, and are jointly determined by factors such as production costs, competitive conditions, money supplies, and inflation rates.

11.1.2   The Implications of CPP

One implication of CPP is that a consumer's nationality or place of residence does not affect his or her consumption opportunity set. If CPP holds, then a consumer's money buys the same amount of goods independent of the country where he or she spends it.

Example   11.1

Let the cost of a Big Mac hamburger be USD 2 in the US and NLG 4 in the Netherlands, and let the exchange rate be NLG/USD 2. Then, with a monthly salary of USD 600, an American can buy 300

Big Macs per month in either country. That is, if CPP holds, it implies that this American has no incentive to move to the Netherlands because the number of Big Macs he can buy in the Netherlands is the same as the number he can buy in the United States.

In other words, in perfect goods markets, there is no real exchange risk, in the sense that consumption in the home country is the same as consumption abroad.

Similarly, from a firm's point of view, there is no real exchange risk when CPP holds. That is, in perfect markets it makes no difference whether McDonald's exports Big Macs for sale in a foreign country or sells them domestically. It should be emphasized that if all real operating risk is to be eliminated, CPP must hold for all goods that one uses as inputs and competes against. For example, if one manufactures abroad, CPP must hold not only for the output that one produces but also for the inputs that one uses, including wages, and for the prices of complementary and substitute goods. If not, exchange rates will still matter, in the sense that the profits at home may differ from the profits abroad.

Of course, one may argue correctly that CPP is seldom valid throughout the world. While CPP is likely to hold for easily traded and homogenous commodities such as gold and silver, it is unlikely to hold for other commodities such as cars or houses, which are difficult to trade across countries. Indeed, the concept of CPP and its implications are discussed here not because they are empirically valid, but because the principle is so often used in international economics and international finance that it is important to understand it.

11.1.3   Why CPP May Not Hold

In Section 11.1.1, we saw that the derivation of CPP used arbitrage arguments: if the price of a given good is not the same across countries (after translation at a given exchange rate), then it is argued that one can make money by buying the commodity in the country where it is cheap and selling it where it is more expensive. In the real world, however, it may not be possible to arbitrage away differences between domestic and foreign prices because of imperfections in the goods market. These imperfections are discussed below.

• *Transaction costs*

Tariffs, transportation costs, insurance fees, and other such costs, mean that—even in the presence of price differences across countries—it may not be possible to make arbitrage profits. That is, there must be a sufficiently large deviation from CPP before the gross profits from trade are large enough to offset these costs. Thus, with such costs, commodity arbitrage only restricts the deviations from CPP to within a *band* defined by transaction costs, and that band can be quite wide.

Example   11.2

Let the price of good j (say, this book) in the US be $P_{jt} = $ USD 40 and the spot exchange rate be S_t = USD/GBP 2.0. Now, the CPP relationship that $P_{jt} = S_t\, P^*_{jt}$ predicts that the price of this book in the UK should be $P^*_{jt} = $ GBP 20. Suppose, however, that the book is selling in the UK for GBP 19. Then, in perfect markets, you could make USD 2 in (before-cost) arbitrage profits by buying the book in the UK and selling it in the US. However, if the shipping and insurance costs for exporting the book from one country to another are USD 4, then you have no incentive to import the book from the UK. Thus, in this case, the price of the book in the UK could be as low as GBP 18, or as high as GBP 22, before you would consider an arbitrage transaction.

• *Nontraded goods*

Many goods are essentially nontradable. For example, the price of goods such as housing or services (theater tickets, haircuts, or lawyer's fees) can differ enormously across countries because it is very difficult, almost impossible, to trade these goods. Thus, CPP will not hold for such goods, since differences in their prices across countries cannot be arbitraged away.

• *Quantitative restrictions*

In the presence of quotas, "voluntary" export restrictions, and other such barriers to trade, it is impossible to import more units once the import ceiling has been reached. Thus, if demand at home increases, the domestic price can be substantially higher than the world price.

• *Imperfect competition*

Imperfect competition in commodity markets is another factor that may prevent prices from being equalized across countries. For example, exclusive dealerships lead to segmented markets across which one cannot arbitrage. Similarly, manufacturers make parallel imports difficult so that they can profit from price discrimination. Entry costs also hinder arbitrage. Moreover, prices of some goods may be sticky in a market because exporters do not change their foreign list prices each time the exchange rate changes, either because they are reluctant to start price wars or because they are reluctant to lose market share and see their investments in distribution and brand awareness perish.

Example   11.3

In the late 1980s, when the USD depreciated against the Japanese yen, CPP would have suggested that Japanese firms increase the USD prices of their goods. Given that many of the Japanese firms compete against only a small number of American firms (in the automobile and computer industry, for instance), instead of increasing their prices in the US and thus losing market share, the Japanese firms decided to maintain their USD prices and suffer a reduction in profits.

11.2   ABSOLUTE PURCHASING POWER PARITY

In this section, we continue to assume that commodity markets are perfect and extend the CPP relationship to the level of representative consumption bundles, which are comprised of many goods. We then analyze the implications of this relationship for firms and for consumers. We conclude this section by examining the factors that may prevent this relationship from holding in the real world.

11.2.1   The Absolute Purchasing Power Parity Hypothesis

In a single-good setting, the number of goods you can buy is your *purchasing power*. In an economy with many goods, however, purchasing power is defined in terms of a representative bundle of goods. One PPP condition, called Absolute PPP, relates the absolute price levels in two countries to the level of the exchange rate between them. If, at a particular time *t*, the cost of a foreign country's representative bundle translated into domestic terms equals the cost of the domestic representative bundle, we say that **Absolute Purchasing Power Parity (PPP)** holds.

We denote the prices of the representative bundles at home and abroad by P_t and P_t^*, respectively—that is, without the j subscripts that refer to the individual goods. Then, Absolute PPP holds when $P_t = S_t\, P_t^*$, that is, when:

$$S_t = \frac{P_t}{P_t^*}.$$ *(Absolute PPP)*   [2]

As a theory of exchange rate determination, Absolute PPP states that the exchange rate must adjust so that the foreign price level translated at the spot rate is the same as the domestic price level.

11.2.2   The Real Exchange Rate and the Effective Real Exchange Rate

The PPP relationship that we have expressed above is in terms of S_t, the **nominal exchange rate**. This is the nominal exchange rate because it is in terms of money rather than in units of a "real" consumption bundle. We can redefine the Absolute PPP relationship in terms of another exchange rate, the **real exchange rate** R_t, which is adjusted for prices in the two countries. That is, the real exchange rate is the nominal spot rate deflated by the ratio of domestic to foreign prices:

$$R_t = \frac{S_t}{P_t / P_t^*} = \frac{S_t P_t^*}{P_t}.$$ [3]

Thus, the real exchange rate allows us to compare foreign prices, translated into domestic terms, with domestic prices. If Absolute PPP holds, then the real exchange rate will equal unity. If foreign prices translated into the home currency are higher than domestic prices, then the real exchange rate is greater than unity.

Example   11.4

Suppose that Canada's nominal exchange rate is CAD/USD 1.265, and the ratio of the Canadian price level to the US price level, P_t/P_t^*, is 1.15. Then, we can compute Canada's real exchange rate with the US as:

$$R_t = \frac{S_t}{P_t / P_t^*} = 1.265 / 1.15 = 1.1.$$

Thus, we can conclude that the US is less competitive than Canada since its prices are higher than Canadian prices, after taking into account the nominal exchange rate between the two countries.

The real exchange rate, however, allows us to compare the competitiveness of a country only against a single country. If we wish to compare the competitiveness of a country with respect to *all* of its trading partners, we need to compute the average real exchange rate, which is called the **effective real exchange rate**. If a country trades with M other countries, then its effective real exchange rate at time t is the weighted average of the real exchange rates $(R_{t,1} \ldots R_{t,M})$, where the weights $(w_{t,1} \ldots w_{t,M})$ are assigned according to the amount of trade of each foreign country with the home country as a proportion of total trade of the home country. That is:

$$R_t^{\text{Eff}} = w_{t,1} R_{t,1} + w_{t,2} R_{t,2} + \ldots + w_{t,M} R_{t,M}. \qquad [4]$$

The effective real exchange rate measures the price of the *average* foreign bundle relative to the domestic bundle. Thus, its interpretation is analogous to that of the real exchange rate: an increase in R_t^{Eff} signifies a gain in *average* competitiveness against one's trade partners.

Example   11.5

Suppose that Canada's real exchange rates, at time t, with the US, UK, and Belgium are 1.1, 0.8, and 0.7, respectively. Canada's trade with the US is 50 percent of its total trade, with the UK 30 percent, and with Belgium 20 percent. Then, Canada's real effective exchange rate is:

$$R_t^{\text{Eff}} = 1.1(0.50) + 0.8(0.30) + 0.7(0.20) = 0.93.$$

Given the current nominal exchange rates, Canada is slightly less competitive than its average trading partner.

11.2.3   Link between Absolute PPP and CPP

Let us now trace the link between Absolute PPP and CPP. It is probably obvious that, if CPP holds for every good in the representative consumption basket, and consumers in both countries choose the same consumption bundle, then Absolute PPP holds. To understand this, denote the quantity of good j consumed in the home country by n_{jt}, and denote its foreign counterpart by n_{jt}^*. Also, denote the total number of goods by N. Then, the domestic and foreign price levels can be defined as:

$$P_t = \sum_{j=1}^{N} n_{jt} \, P_{jt} \text{ and } P_t^* = \sum_{j=1}^{N} n_{jt}^* \, P_{jt}^*.$$

The assumption that CPP holds for each good implies that $P_{jt} = S_t \, P_{jt}^*$ for all j, while the assumption that consumers choose the same consumption bundles implies that $n_{jt} = n_{jt}^*$. This implies that $n_{jt} \times P_{jt} = n_{jt}^* \times S_t \, P_{jt}^*$. Summing this expression over j, we get Equation [2], which indicates that Absolute PPP holds.

Example   11.6

Consider a world with only two goods—milk and wine. Let both French and Canadian residents consume two liters of milk and a liter of wine per unit of time. Then the common representative consumption bundle is one liter of wine and two liters of milk. In the table that follows, we use a spot rate of FRF/CAD 5. You can easily verify that CPP holds for each good separately, and we show that Absolute PPP also holds.

Country	P_{milk}/liter	P_{wine}/liter	Price of the consumption bundle
France	FRF 5	FRF 15	$(2 \times FRF\ 5) + (1 \times FRF\ 15) = FRF\ 25$
Canada	CAD 1	CAD 3	$(2 \times CAD\ 1) + (1 \times CAD\ 3) = CAD\ 5$

To see that CPP holds for milk, note that the ratio of the price of milk in France and Canada, FRF/CAD 5, is equal to the exchange rate. The same is true for the relative prices of wine. Finally, to see that Absolute PPP holds, note that the relative price of the consumption bundle in France to that in Canada, FRF 25/CAD 5, is also equal to the spot exchange rate.

However, residents of different countries may not consume the same bundle of goods. This may be either because relative prices differ across countries, or because the consumers' preferences are different. It is not clear how one should compare purchasing powers across countries when consumption bundles differ.

Example   11.7

Consider, as in the previous example, a world with only two goods—milk and wine—and where the typical consumption bundle in Canada is, as before, two liters of milk and a liter of wine. However, the typical French resident consumes two liters of wine and only one liter of milk. The problem is how to define a consumption bundle for French consumers that is comparable to this Canadian bundle.

To find a consumption bundle of the typical French investor that can be compared to the representative Canadian consumption bundle, should one choose a bundle which, like the Canadian bundle, contains three liters, but in "French proportions" (two liters of wine, and one liter of milk)? Or a bundle that corresponds to the same number of calories? Any such criterion is flawed: if the French consumer really cared only about the number of liters, or the number of calories, he or she would not choose to consume the current consumption bundle—two liters of wine and one of milk. For example, if the French consumer cared only about the volume, then he or she would consume only one of the two goods—the good which is cheapest per liter. This is manifestly not what the French consumer does.

We conclude that the concept of Absolute PPP is problematic as soon as consumption bundles differ across countries. That is, it is important to note that, while in perfect markets the CPP relationship must be satisfied exactly to rule out arbitrage opportunities, the Absolute PPP relationship is a simplification. When applying this simplification to the real world, we face a number of measurement problems: which consumption bundle is the relevant one, and how large are the differences between the bundles across countries?

There are two solutions to the problem of differences in consumption baskets across countries. First, one could abandon the idea of comparing the true purchasing powers. It would still be interesting to see if there are *systematic* deviations from CPP, or conversely, whether good-by-good deviations from CPP tend to cancel out if we average across a wide bundle of goods. To that end, one could compute the price of some bundle of goods (which is not the true bundle of either country's consumers;

for instance, one could pick some average bundle). We shall see such comparisons in Section 11.5, where we review the empirical evidence on PPP. Second, we could consider a different concept of PPP, one that compares relative changes in prices across countries. This is discussed in Section 11.3.

11.2.4   The Implications of Absolute PPP

According to the Absolute PPP view of exchange rate determination, exchange rates must be such that there is equality between the domestic and foreign price levels. For a firm, Absolute PPP gives information about the competitive position of a country. That is, if prices at home deviate from those predicted by the PPP relationship, then this affects the competitive position of domestic firms. At the level of the economy, large deviations from PPP will cause an imbalance between exports and imports of goods and services and this will eventually affect relative prices in, and the exchange rate between, the two countries. Note that the PPP hypothesis focuses on the role of trade flows as determinants of the exchange rates but says little about other items such as direct and portfolio investment abroad.

Example   11.8

If prices in the UK are too high relative to those of its trading partners, British exporters will have trouble selling their goods abroad, and British consumers will prefer imported goods, which are relatively cheaper. Thus, until prices and the exchange rate adjust, the UK will be relatively less competitive. Of course, the trade imbalance will eventually exert downward pressure on prices in the UK because of the drop in domestic and foreign demand for British goods. The drop in demand for British goods will also lead to a decrease in the demand for the GBP, because fewer foreigners will buy GBP in order to purchase British goods. These changes will push translated British prices closer toward world prices and will also tend to depreciate the GBP.

11.2.5   Why Absolute PPP May Not Hold

In this section, we examine reasons why the Absolute PPP hypothesis may not be true in the real world.

Violations of CPP

As we have already seen, Absolute PPP is unlikely to hold if the prices of individual goods comprising the consumption bundle are not the same across two countries. That is, if the individual goods in the representative consumption basket do not satisfy CPP, then Absolute PPP is likely to be violated. We have already seen, in Section 11.1.3, that there are several reasons why CPP may not hold for some goods.

The next question, therefore, is whether it is possible that the deviations from CPP cancel out across goods in such a way that Absolute PPP holds even when CPP does not. We know that CPP deviations across several goods will *not* average out if they are predominantly in the same direction. Apparently, there often are common factors at work that cause most price differences to have the same sign. For instance, we are all aware that prices in big cities are, on average, higher than in small towns; the same may happen internationally.

International Differences in Consumption Bundles

Even if CPP holds for each good in the representative consumption basket, if the composition of the baskets themselves differs across countries, then Absolute PPP will not hold. This is to be expected, for the price level is an average of the prices in the consumption bundle and, if these averages are constructed differently across the two countries, then they need not be equal.

Example   11.9

Consider again a world with only two goods—milk and wine. Let the typical consumption of a Canadian resident be two liters of milk and a liter of wine per unit time while that of a French consumer is two liters of wine and one of milk. Assuming a spot rate of FRF/CAD 5, we find that CPP holds for each individual commodity (the ratio of commodity prices in France to Canada is equal to the spot rate of FRF/CAD 5). However, because the composition of the consumption bundles is different, the ratio of the price level in France (FRF 35) to the price level in Canada (CAD 5) is not equal to the spot rate, FRF/CAD 5, as shown below.

Country	P_{milk}/liter	P_{wine}/liter	Price of the consumption bundle
France	FRF 5	FRF 15	$(1 \times FRF\ 5) + (2 \times FRF\ 15) = FRF\ 35$
Canada	CAD 1	CAD 3	$(2 \times CAD\ 1) + (1 \times CAD\ 3) = CAD\ 5$

11.3   RELATIVE PURCHASING POWER PARITY

We now look at the dynamic version of the Absolute PPP relationship. The Absolute PPP hypothesis relates the price level in two countries to the nominal exchange rate between these countries at a given point in time. We now study the Relative PPP relationship that allows one to compare the change in the exchange rate to the change in price levels at home and abroad over time.

11.3.1   The Relative Purchasing Power Parity Hypothesis

The **Relative PPP hypothesis** states that the percentage change in the exchange rate reflects the difference between the inflation rate at home and abroad. We can derive this condition from Absolute PPP as follows:

$$S_t = \frac{P_t}{P_t^*}. \qquad\qquad \textit{(Absolute PPP at time t)} \quad [5]$$

$$S_T = \frac{P_T}{P_T^*}. \qquad\qquad \textit{(Absolute PPP at time T)} \quad [6]$$

Dividing the second equation by the first, we get:

$$\frac{S_T}{S_t} = \frac{P_T/P_T^*}{P_t/P_t^*}. \qquad\qquad\qquad\qquad\qquad [7]$$

To express the change in the spot rate in simple percentage terms, we subtract 1 from both sides of the equation:

$$\frac{S_T}{S_t} - 1 = \frac{P_T/P_T^*}{P_t/P_t^*} - 1 \qquad\qquad\qquad\qquad [8]$$

or, defining $s_{t,T}$ as the percentage change in the exchange rate between time t and T, $I_{t,T}$ as the domestic inflation rate between moments t and T, where $I_{t,T} = P_T/P_t - 1$, and denoting foreign inflation by $I_{t,T}^* = P_T^*/P_t^* - 1$, we get:

$$s_{t,T} = \frac{1 + I_{t,T}}{1 + I_{t,T}^*} - 1$$

$$= \frac{I_{t,T} - I_{t,T}^*}{1 + I_{t,T}^*}. \qquad \text{(Relative PPP)} \quad [9]$$

With this version of PPP, one often ignores the denominator on the right-hand side of Equation [9], which is a reasonable approximation if the foreign inflation rate is close to zero. This, then, leads to the approximation:

$$s_{t,T} = I_{t,T} - I_{t,T}^*. \quad \text{(Relative PPP, approximate form)} \quad [10]$$

Alternately, instead of using simple returns, one can define the changes in the variables in terms of logs, that is, as continuously compounded percentages. To do this, we take logs on both sides of [7]:

$$\ln \frac{S_T}{S_t} = \ln \frac{P_T}{P_t} - \ln \frac{P_T^*}{P_t^*}. \qquad \text{(Relative PPP)} \quad [11]$$

This says that the (continuously compounded) percentage change in the exchange rate is equal to the difference of the (continuously compounded) inflation rates. So, in contrast to Absolute PPP, *Relative* PPP tells us about the relation between the exchange rate changes and the percentage changes in the prices at home and abroad, rather than absolute price levels. As a theory of exchange rates, Relative PPP implicitly takes the inflation rates as determined by some outside factors (like the money supply and the level of economic activity). The theory then says that the exchange rate between two countries must change to reflect differences in inflation rates between these countries. That is, if PPP is to be maintained, then 5 percent inflation at home and 0 percent inflation abroad requires a 5 percent depreciation of the home currency.

Example   11.10

Let the time-t representative consumption bundle in the UK cost GBP 2,000, and let the same bundle cost DEM 20,000 in Germany. The equilibrium DEM/GBP exchange rate, according to Absolute PPP, is:

$$S_t = \frac{20,000}{2,000} = \text{DEM/GBP } 10.$$

By time T, say twenty years later, German prices have tripled (that is, inflation has been 200 percent), but British prices have risen tenfold (that is, inflation has been 900 percent). The new equilibrium exchange rate at time T, according to Absolute PPP, is:

$$S_T = \frac{60,000}{20,000} = \text{DEM/GBP } 3.$$

In contrast to Absolute PPP, which states what the *level* of the exchange rate should be given the level of prices at home and abroad, Relative PPP tells us how the exchange rate should *change* given the change in prices (inflation) at home and in the foreign country. From Equation [9], Relative PPP predicts that the equilibrium change in the spot rate over the twenty years, $s_{t,T}$, should be:

$$s_{t,T} = \frac{1+200\%}{1+900\%} - 1 = -70\%.$$

11.3.2 The Link between Relative PPP, Absolute PPP, and CPP

Let us now discuss the relationship of Relative PPP with Absolute PPP, the real exchange rate, and with CPP. From the example above, we already know that Absolute PPP is a sufficient condition for Relative PPP: if Absolute PPP holds, then so will Relative PPP. But the reverse is not true; that is, even if Absolute PPP does not hold, Relative PPP may still be true. For instance, Relative PPP may hold if there are *persistent* deviations in the average absolute price levels across countries, as shown in Example 11.11.

Example   11.11

We choose BEF as the home currency. If prices in London are persistently 80 percent higher than in Brussels, Relative PPP holds. That is, suppose that the price in London, translated in BEF is not equal to that in Brussels: $S_t\, P_{\text{London},t} \neq P_{\text{Brussels},t}$. Instead, suppose that the price level in London is 1.8 times that in Brussels: $S_t\, P_{\text{London},t} = P_{\text{Brussels},t} \times 1.8$. If, at time T, prices in London are still 1.8 times those in Brussels, then even though Absolute PPP continues to be violated, Relative PPP holds.

	At time 0	At time 1	% change
S_t	BEF/GBP 60	BEF/GBP 50	−0.1667
P_{Brussels}	BEF 100	BEF 110	0.10
P_{London}	GBP 3	GBP 3.96	0.32
$R = \dfrac{S\, P_{\text{London}}}{P_{\text{Brussels}}}$	$\dfrac{60 \times 3}{100} = 1.8$	$\dfrac{50 \times 3.96}{110} = 1.8$	0.0

In the table on the previous page, translated London prices are 80 percent higher than prices in Brussels at both points in time, and therefore the real exchange rate is 1.8, both at time 0 and time 1. We see that the change in the exchange rate, $(50 - 60)/60$, perfectly matches the Relative PPP prediction. That is, we can confirm the Relative PPP relation given in Equation [9]:

$$\frac{50 - 60}{60} = \frac{0.10 - 0.32}{1.32} = -0.1667.$$

From this example, we also see that if Relative PPP holds, then the change in the real exchange rate, R_t, is zero between time 0 and time 1.

Thus, Relative PPP is a weaker relation than Absolute PPP in the sense that the former may hold when the latter does not. In addition, Relative PPP is more general than its absolute counterpart in the sense that Relative PPP (or at least the deviation from Relative PPP) can always be evaluated, even in cases where the consumption bundles differ across countries. This is because even if one cannot compare different consumption bundles directly, it is still possible to compare *changes* in the prices of these baskets of goods. We show this in Example 11.12.

Example   11.12

Consider Example 11.9 where the consumption bundles of the Canadian and French consumer are different—that is, where the typical consumption bundle in Canada is two liters of milk and a liter of wine, and the typical French resident consumes two liters of wine and only one liter of milk. We consider two dates, time 0 and time 1, and assume that the exchange rate at time 0 is FRF/CAD 5, and at time 1 is FRF/CAD 4. The data on commodity prices and exchange rates are given in the following table.

Note, first, that in this example, CPP holds within each period; that is, the ratio of the price of milk in France to the price in Canada is equal to the exchange rate in that period.

Time 0: S_0 = FRF/CAD 5

	P_{milk}	P_{wine}	Price of the consumption bundle
France	FRF 5	FRF 15	$(1 \times FRF\ 5) + (2 \times FRF\ 15) = FRF\ 35$
Canada	CAD 1	CAD 3	$(2 \times CAD\ 1) + (1 \times CAD\ 3) = CAD\ 5$
$\dfrac{P_{j,\ France}}{P_{j,\ Canada}}$	$\dfrac{5}{1} = 5 = S_t$	$\dfrac{15}{3} = 5 = S_t$	

Time 1: S_1 = FRF/CAD 4

	P_{milk}	P_{wine}	Price of the consumption bundle
France	FRF 5	FRF 16	$(1 \times FRF\ 5) + (2 \times FRF\ 16) = FRF\ 37$
Canada	CAD 1.25	CAD 4	$(2 \times CAD\ 1.25) + (1 \times CAD\ 4) = CAD\ 6.5$
$\dfrac{P_{j,\ France}}{P_{j,\ Canada}}$	$\dfrac{5}{1.25} = 4$	$\dfrac{16}{4} = 4$	

We find that the French inflation rate is $I_{0,1} = (37 - 35)/35 = 0.05714$, and the Canadian inflation rate is $I^*_{0,1} = (6.5 - 5)/5 = 0.30$.

Note that even though the consumption bundles of the French and the Canadian consumer are different, we can still compute the inflation rates in the two countries. Of course, given that the consumption bundles are different, Relative PPP may not hold.

The exchange rate change in the above example is $s_{0,1} = (4 - 5)/5 = 0.20$. For Relative PPP to hold, the exchange rate should have changed by only $(0.05714 - 0.30)/1.30 = 0.1868$. Thus, there was a small deviation from Relative PPP in this example.

Example 11.12 also illustrates the link between Relative PPP and CPP: even when CPP holds for every single good, Relative PPP may not (generally) hold if the consumption bundles differ across countries.[1]

11.3.3   The Implications of Relative PPP

Relative PPP, in contrast to Absolute PPP, gives information about the change in the competitive position of a country and the change in the relative purchasing power of a given amount of money across countries. Relative PPP also tells us how the real return on an investment differs for investors from different countries. We discuss these issues below.

Firm managers are concerned about their competitiveness in the world market. Relative PPP (or the change in the real exchange rate, see below) indicates that if the exchange rate does not adjust for the differences in inflation rates (that is, PPP is violated), then the firm may be becoming less competitive relative to the rest of the world. For instance, suppose that domestic inflation is 5 percent while foreign inflation is zero. Under Relative PPP, the foreign exchange rate should appreciate by 5 percent. If this is the case, the relative prices at home versus abroad will remain constant. If, however, the foreign currency appreciates by less than 5 percent, the implication is that domestic producers are now less competitive than before. According to the PPP theory, when price levels abroad and at home are not the same, the quantities of exports and imports will change so as to correct the difference between the prices in the two countries. Thus, deviations from Relative PPP give indications about *changes* in relative competitiveness.

Deviations from Relative PPP also tell us how the purchasing power of a given amount of money has changed across countries, that is, whether a domestic consumer's purchasing power has increased, or decreased, relative to a foreign consumer's purchasing power.

Example   11.13

Based on the table in Example 11.12, we can draw the following conclusions:

- The purchasing power of a French consumer with an income of FRF 3,500 decreased from FRF 3,500/FRF 35 = 100 (units of the French consumption bundle) to FRF 3,500/FRF 37 = 94.6, that is, by 5.4 percent. Thus, at time 1, the income of the French consumer buys only 94.6 units of the representative consumption basket rather than the 100 units it could buy at time 0.

---

[1] However, in the above example, there are only a very small number of goods (two), and the weights differ a lot across countries. In the real world, with many different goods, it is possible that Relative PPP may hold reasonably well if the differences in the consumption bundles across countries average out.

- For a Canadian consumer whose income is equal to FRF 3,500, the CAD value of the same FRF 3,500 changed from

$$\frac{\text{FRF } 3,500}{\text{FRF/CAD } 5} = \text{CAD } 700 \text{ to } \frac{\text{FRF } 3,500}{\text{FRF/CAD } 4} = \text{CAD } 875.$$

At the same time, the purchasing power of FRF 3,500 decreases from CAD 700/CAD 5 = 140 units of the Canadian consumption bundle to CAD 875/CAD 6.5 = 135 units, that is, a 3.57 percent decrease.

Thus, the Canadian consumer has fared somewhat better in relative terms (although we still cannot say who has the highest *absolute* purchasing power). The reason is the deviation from Relative PPP: the CAD dropped by 20 percent but in order to maintain relative purchasing power, it should have dropped by only 18.7 percent. The effect is that FRF 3,500 is worth more CAD, at time 1, than it should have been worth according to Relative PPP.

The example suggests that deviations from Relative PPP also affect the real returns on an investment. That is, if a French investor and a Canadian investor both hold the same asset portfolio, and if the value of this portfolio remains unchanged in FRF, then the Canadian's real return is less negative than the French investor's real return on the same investment. Thus, Relative PPP indicates how the real return from holding a given portfolio differs across investors from different countries.

Recall that if Commodity Price Parity holds for every good, then consumption is independent of the place of residence or nationality, and the profits of a firm are independent of the market and currency in which the goods are sold. Analogously, if Relative PPP holds, the return in real terms from a portfolio investment in a given asset is also independent of the nationality of an investor, thus making exchange risk irrelevant for portfolio investment purposes. That is, if changes in prices are offset by changes in the spot exchange rate, then the exchange rate does not affect real returns. However, when PPP is violated, investors from different countries use different deflators to evaluate the real returns from a given portfolio; thus, the real return from the same investment may differ for investors from different countries.

Example   11.14

In the table below, we show the time-t and time-T exchange rates for HKD/DEM, as well as the HKD and DEM prices of Apple common stock (or any stock from any country). The nominal return on the Apple stock in Hong Kong is computed by calculating the difference in the share price in terms of HKD.

	Time t	Time T	% change
Spot exchange rate, HKD/DEM	4.00	4.25	6.25%
Nominal price of Apple stock, in HKD	500.00	595.00	19.00%
Nominal price of Apple stock, in DEM	125.00	140.00	12.00%

Thus, the return in Hong Kong is (595 − 500)/500 = 19 percent. The return in DEM, on the other hand, is (140 − 125)/125 = 12 percent. Thus, we see that because the exchange rate has changed between t and T, the nominal return on Apple stock in HKD differs from the return in DEM.

However, investors care about *real* returns and not nominal ones because investors care about returns in terms of their consumption bundle. To compute real returns, we first consider the case where Relative PPP holds. Assume, for simplicity, that there is no inflation in Germany while the inflation in Hong Kong is 6.25 percent. In this case, the Relative PPP relationship given in Equation [7] holds. To compute the real returns in HKD and the DEM, we need to deflate the returns with their respective inflation rates. Thus, the real return in DEM is 12 percent, since the inflation rate in Germany is zero. The real return to a Hong Kong investor is

$$\frac{0.19 - 0.0625}{1.0625} = 12\%.$$

Thus, in the case that Relative PPP holds, changes in the spot rate are exactly offset by the inflation rates in the two countries, and the real return from holding an asset is the same across countries.

We now study the real returns for the case where Relative PPP is violated. Assume, in this case, that the inflation rate in Germany is 3 percent rather than zero. Obviously, there is a deviation from Relative PPP since the exchange rate change of 6.25 percent is larger than that warranted by the inflation rates in Hong Kong and Germany. Computing the real returns, we find that in terms of DEM the real return is only

$$\frac{0.12 - 0.03}{1.03} = 8.74\%.$$

Thus, we see that when Relative PPP does not hold, the real return from a given portfolio is different for investors in different countries.

One implication of violations of Relative PPP is that because the real returns on any given asset differ, investors from different countries may choose very different portfolios. Further details of international portfolio choice are given in Chapter 13.

11.4   EMPIRICAL TESTS OF THE PRICE PARITY RELATIONS

We have described the theoretical relationships between the exchange rate and international prices for individual goods (CPP), the exchange rate and international price levels (Absolute PPP), and changes in the exchange rate and international inflation rates (Relative PPP). While describing these relationships, we have also discussed why they may not hold in the real world. In this section, we examine the data to see if exchange rates reflect the differences in international prices as predicted by CPP and PPP. We find that the data overwhelmingly reject the PPP hypothesis. In the following two sections, Sections 11.5 and 11.6, we examine the implications of this rejection.

11.4.1   Empirical Tests of CPP
If you have traveled to foreign countries, you probably know that the price of the same good can differ vastly across countries. Even a globally marketed product like the Big Mac hamburger is not priced the same across countries, as CPP would predict. This is clear from the survey (of prices of the Big Mac in different countries) that *The Economist* reports every three months (see Figure 11.1). In Figure 11.1, US prices are standardized to be 100. Comparing the prices of the Big Mac across countries, we

FIGURE 11.1   Price Level & Price of Big Mac per Country, 1990

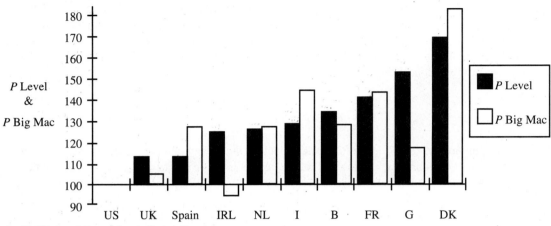

(Big Mac prices from *The Economist*, October 1990;
IRL = Ireland, NL = Netherlands, I = Italy, B = Belgium, FR = France, G = Germany, DK = Denmark)

see that the difference can be enormous. For example, compared to the price in the US, the 1990 price of the Big Mac was 80 percent higher in Denmark and about 40 percent higher in Italy and France.

Another example of a violation of CPP can be seen by comparing the list price for the *The Economist* in different countries (which is given on the front cover of the magazine) with the exchange rates (reported on the last page of the magazine).

Isard (1977), in an article with the telltale title, "How Far Can We Push the Law of One Price," concludes that "there are persistent and large deviations even for narrowly defined goods." Richardson (1978) compared prices in Canada and the US for specific commodities and found that CPP did not hold very well. In general, CPP holds only for easily traded, homogenous commodities such as oil, gold, and silver. The issue, therefore, is whether these deviations from CPP tend to disappear when we look at a bundle of representative goods rather than at a single commodity.

11.4.2   Empirical Tests of Absolute PPP

Computations of the price of the "average" consumption bundle in the European Union, translated into a common currency, show that the price level of this typical basket varies widely across countries. This can be seen from the shaded bars in Figure 11.1. Note that the US price level has been standardized to 100. From the figure, we can see that there are large differences in the price levels between countries. For example, the 1990 price level in UK was about 10 percent higher than that in the US, while the price level in Denmark was approximately 70 percent higher.

When we plot the price levels against GDP per capita of various countries (Figure 11.2), we find that there is a strong positive correlation between price levels and per capita GDP. This strong relationship suggests that the observed deviations from absolute PPP are not purely due to chance. In fact, the pattern suggests that highly developed countries with high GNP per capita tend to be more expensive than other economies. One implication of this result is that per capita GDP is a poor guide to real purchasing power. That is, a higher per capita GDP does not necessarily suggest a better real standard of living. For example, in 1990, Danish prices were twice as high as Portuguese prices. Thus, only if

FIGURE 11.2   GDP/Capita and Price Level, 1990

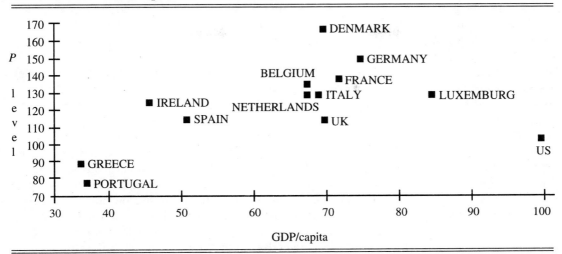

GDP/capita

the per capita income of Denmark were more than twice that of Portugal could we say that the standard of living was better in Denmark than in Portugal.

There have also been some formal regression tests of the Absolute PPP hypothesis (which appears in Equation [2]). To test whether $S_t = P_t/P_t^*$, one runs the following regression:

$$S_t = a + b\ (P_t/P_t^*) + e_t,$$

where the joint null hypothesis is that the slope coefficient, b, is equal to unity and the intercept, a, is zero. There are several technical problems with this regression test, including for instance, the nonstationarity of the exchange rate and the prices; that is, the mean and variance of the distribution of exchange rates and prices are not well defined. The econometric problems encountered in such regressions are discussed in Appendix A of Chapter 5. Therefore, instead of examining the regression tests of Absolute PPP, we focus on tests of Relative PPP.

11.4.3   Empirical Tests of Relative PPP

From our discussion in Section 11.3, we know that Relative PPP is a weaker condition than Absolute PPP; that is, Relative PPP may hold even when Absolute PPP is violated. This is because, even if the price levels are different across countries (after translation into a common currency), as long as this difference is constant over time, Relative PPP will hold. This implies that, even when there are violations of CPP, or there are differences in the composition of the consumption bundles across countries, it is possible that Relative PPP will hold. This is one reason why one prefers testing the Relative PPP hypothesis to Absolute PPP.

To test the Relative PPP hypothesis, the typical regression equation that is used in the literature is of the following (continuously compounded) form based on Equation [11]:

$$\ln \frac{S_{t+1}}{S_t} = a + b \left[\ln \frac{P_{t+1}}{P_t} - \ln \frac{P_{t+1}^*}{P_t^*} \right] + e_t, \qquad [12]$$

where on the left-hand side we have the percentage change in the exchange rate between time t and T, and where the term within the square brackets on the right-hand side is the difference between the domestic and foreign inflation rates over this period. The null hypothesis is that, if Relative PPP holds, the slope coefficient, b, should be equal to unity and the intercept, a, should equal zero.

A frequently cited study of Relative PPP is the one by Cumby and Obstfeld (1984) where they test an equation that is similar to Equation [12]. In their sample, they reject the Relative PPP hypothesis for all five countries (against the US). This test was extended to the case of eleven countries by Huang (1987), and PPP was rejected for most of these countries as well.

Other empirical tests of PPP have also found that the Relative PPP relationship is quite weak. In the late seventies and early eighties, pessimism about Relative PPP peaked. Some authors tested (and often could not reject) the hypothesis that deviations from Relative PPP accumulated randomly over time (Roll [1977], Adler and Lehman [1983]). That is, it seemed that, even in the long run, Relative PPP would fail. However, these discouraging results appear partly due to the low power of the tests that were conducted. Abuaf and Jorion (1990), using a different methodology, show that cumulative deviations from Relative PPP tend to halve after three years—that is, cumulative deviations from Relative PPP have some tendency to correct themselves in the long run. Stated differently, the variance of PPP deviations does not increase proportionally with time.

One would expect the tendency of the exchange rate to revert back to the value predicted by PPP to be somewhat stronger among well-integrated economies. In Figure 11.3, we show the results of an event study of realignments of the exchange rate within the European Monetary System. The study tests whether a devaluation of a currency relative to the DEM is preceded by higher inflation in that country relative to inflation in Germany. The study also examines to what extent (and how fast) a typical devaluation is undone by subsequent inflation in the devaluing country. Similar to a standard stock market *event study,* this test groups all data on the basis of time relative to the date of realignment. That is, across about thirty exchange rate changes, the study computes the average deviation from Relative PPP in the month of the devaluation itself (time 0 relative to the event, that is, in the same month as the event). Similar computations are made for the month just before the devaluation (time − 1 relative to the event), two months before, and so on, going back as far as twenty-four months before the realignment. Finally, average Relative PPP deviations are also computed for each of the twenty-four months following the devaluation. These forty-nine-month averages give us an idea about the average

FIGURE 11.3   Event Study of EMS Devaluations: Cumulative Deviations from Relative PPP

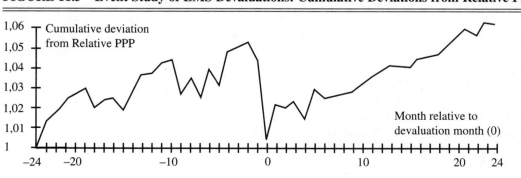

Month (time 0 is the devaluation month)

deviation from Relative PPP for each month (relative to the realignment month). The reference currency is the DEM, which did not devalue relative to any other EU currency.

Since a deviation from Relative PPP is the percentage change in the real exchange rate, we can detect the typical pattern of the real exchange rate by cumulating the percentages over time. The cumulated percentages are shown in Figure 11.3. The graph indicates that two years before a devaluation, there typically is a gradual appreciation of the real exchange rate by about 4.5–5 percent. Foreign goods become more and more expensive relative to German goods. The devaluation then brings the average real exchange rate back to its level from two years before. Apparently, however, inflation differences persist, with the result that the devaluation is "undone" by higher inflation within two years of the devaluation.

These results are consistent with those of other tests. Many researchers (for example, Huizinga [1990], Huang [1990] and Abuaf and Jorion [1990]), using a wide range of techniques, have found some support for the hypothesis that exchange rates tend to revert back to their PPP values over the long run.[2] That is, there is statistically significant evidence of Relative PPP over the long run, although the relationship remains very weak.

Thus, we conclude that the Relative PPP relationship may have some power in the medium to long run (several years rather than several months). Relative PPP may also hold rather well in the short run when inflation is high. Under conditions of high inflation, economic agents are very sensitive to prices and thus prices adjust rapidly. This was the case in Germany around 1930 and after World War II, and in Brazil in the 1970s. For an empirical study of Relative PPP in high inflation countries, see McNown and Wallace (1989), who study the PPP relationship in Brazil, Chile, Israel, and Argentina (where prices increased by 250,000 times between 1976–86). Even in these studies, however, there are substantial period-by-period deviations from Relative PPP. For example, Figure 11.4 shows a time series of monthly percentage inflation rates in Serbia from mid-1992

FIGURE 11.4   Monthly Serbian Inflation and Monthly Depreciation of the Dinar, 10/92–9/93

---

[2] For additional references see Betton, Levi, and Uppal (1991) or Apte, Sercu, and Kane (1992). For theoretical models that explain how one can have deviations from PPP that persist even in the long run, see Dumas (1992) and Sercu, Uppal, and Van Hulle (1994).

to mid-1993, along with monthly percentage appreciation in the DEM. At first sight, we see a rather good fit between the two series. However, upon closer inspection, there are deviations as high as 800 percent per month. Also De Grauwe, Janssens, and Leliaert (1985) find that there are large deviations from PPP when there is hyperinflation. Thus, the exchange rate and the difference in inflation levels across countries usually do not fully and perfectly offset each other.

Based on the empirical tests of PPP, we can safely conclude that, at least in the short run, there definitely is real exchange risk. Moreover, the conventional claim that "PPP holds in the long run" ought to be taken with a lot of skepticism. In fact, common sense says that if there is real exchange risk in the short run, there definitely is real exchange risk in the long run. The uncertainty about PPP deviations can hardly become smaller the longer the time horizon. Rather, all we can observe is that the variance of PPP deviations increases less than proportionally with time—which is far from saying that the relationship becomes near-perfect in the long run.

11.5   PPP AS A THEORY OF EXCHANGE RATE DETERMINATION

To interpret PPP as a theory of exchange rate determination, one needs to assume that the direction of causality is such that the exchange rate is determined by the price levels at home and abroad. That is, one needs to assume that the money supply and output determine prices, which in turn determine the exchange rate. According to the PPP theory of exchange rate determination, if domestic prices were lower than foreign prices (after translation into domestic terms), then the demand for domestic exports would increase while that for imports from abroad would fall. This would lead to a change in relative prices at home and abroad, and also to a decrease in the desired demand for the foreign currency, leading to its depreciation. This process would continue until the exchange rate was such that the foreign price level, translated at this exchange rate, was equal to the domestic price level.

As we have seen in the previous section, there is little empirical support for the PPP theory: deviations from PPP are frequent, large, and persistent. If the PPP theory were an accurate description of the world, then we should expect the exchange rate to change *slowly* over time, because price levels change slowly and real trade flows react even more slowly to prices.[3] However, in the real world, we observe *frequent* changes in the exchange rate. Thus, it is unlikely that changes in the exchange rate are determined by relative inflation rates at home and abroad. Rather, in the short run, exchange rates move because of factors other than inflation rates, and there is not enough variability in inflation rates to offset the frequent changes in exchange rate. Moreover, the commodity arbitrage argument that underpins PPP applies only to traded goods, and these are a small percentage of the total output for a developed economy (for example, non-traded goods such as services represent 60 to 80 percent of GNP in the OECD). In addition, even for traded goods the markets are so imperfect that substantial price deviations are possible. Thus, it is safe to conclude that, at best, PPP is a theory that deals with the *long-run* behavior of the exchange rate.

---

[3] For example, when the price of coconuts falls in Hawaii, relative to the price of wine, one does not see a sudden shift away from the consumption of coconuts. It might take a year for consumption patterns to adjust.

From the above discussion of the PPP theory of exchange rates one can make the following observations:

- The PPP approach, with its exclusive focus on trade as a determinant of the supply and demand of foreign exchange, ignores financial transactions. Thus, in Chapter 12 we will study how other items in the Balance of Payments, such as portfolio investment abroad, influence the exchange rate.
- Given the large variation in the nominal spot rate relative to the variation in inflation rates, it is unlikely that, in the short run, exchange rates can be explained by international inflation differentials. It is more likely that the short-term variation in exchange rates is caused by interest rate changes, or news about the relative state of the domestic and foreign economies, or even changes in the prices of other assets. We shall explore this notion further in Chapter 13, where we view foreign exchange as a financial asset and we use a portfolio-choice model to determine the equilibrium value of the exchange rate.
- The empirical finding that inflation rates hardly react to exchange rate changes in the short run implies that changes in the real exchange rate, $R_t = (S_t P_t^*)/P_t$, are primarily a result of changes in the nominal exchange rate. That is, deviations from Relative PPP are almost the same as nominal exchange rate changes. This implies that the assumption that inflation is nonrandom is a good approximation to reality. We make use of this assumption in Chapter 13 to derive the demand for foreign currency, and in Chapter 22 to derive the cost of capital that is used for making international capital budgeting decisions.

11.6   IMPLICATIONS FOR MANAGERS OF THE EVIDENCE ON PPP

We conclude this chapter with a discussion of the implications for corporate risk management of the empirical findings of tests of the PPP relationship.

The first important result, from Section 11.4, is that CPP and Absolute PPP rarely hold. The empirical evidence also shows that violations of Relative PPP are frequent and persistent. That is, in the short run, the exchange rate does not compensate for the differences in the inflation rates at home and abroad, implying that there is substantial *real exchange risk* in the short run. There is some evidence that deviations from Relative PPP tend to partially correct themselves in the long run (over many years). This evidence of reversion of exchange rates towards their PPP value may be comforting to theorists. However, corporate treasurers and portfolio managers typically have horizons that are much shorter, and thus, they must take real exchange rate risk into account when making financial decisions.

The existence of real exchange risk affects the decision to sell or invest abroad rather than at home. That is, profits from exporting and from direct investment abroad will be affected by exchange rate movements. Similarly, production costs in different countries can diverge at any point in time, and will fluctuate substantially over time. The existence of exchange risk also affects asset prices. Real returns on any given asset will differ depending on where the investor lives and how the exchange rate moves. This, as we will see in Chapter 13, has important implications for portfolio choice.

The good news is the empirical finding that, apart from hyperinflation episodes, changes in the real exchange rate, $R_t = (S_t P_t^*)/P_t$, are mostly a result of changes in the nominal exchange rate. This implies that one can use contracts whose payoff depends on the *nominal* spot rate, such as futures and options, to hedge exposure to the *real* exchange risk.

QUIZ QUESTIONS

True-False Questions

1. CPP says that you can make a risk-free profit by buying and selling goods across countries.
2. CPP implies causality. It states that foreign prices are determined by domestic prices and other factors such as production costs, competitive conditions, money supplies, and inflation rates.
3. In order for a firm not to be affected by real exchange risk, CPP must hold not only for the goods a firm produces but also for all production inputs, and for the prices of complementary and substitute goods.
4. The equilibrium exchange rate suggested by the Absolute Purchasing Power Parity hypothesis depends on the relative relationship between the prices of a representative consumption bundle in the currencies of two countries.
5. Your purchasing power is the number of representative consumption bundles that you can buy.
6. The real effective exchange rate is the price of an average foreign consumption bundle in units of domestic currency.
7. Relative PPP shows how a consumer's purchasing power changes over time.
8. Absolute PPP may hold even when Relative PPP does not because absolute PPP looks at levels at a specific point in time, and levels are always comparable regardless of the composition of the consumption bundle.
9. Given the empirical evidence on the correlation between the nominal and real exchange rate, it is possible to use the nominal financial instruments to hedge real exchange risk.
10. Purchasing Power Parity is based on the idea that the demand for a country's currency is derived from the demand for that country's goods as well as the currency itself.

Multiple-Choice Questions

Choose the correct answer(s).

1. CPP may not hold because:

   (a) the prices for individual goods are sticky.
   (b) transaction costs increase the bounds on deviations from CPP, making it more difficult to arbitrage away price differences.
   (c) quotas and voluntary export restraints limit the ability to arbitrage across goods markets.
   (d) parallel imports lead to two different prices for the same good.
   (e) the prices of tradable goods fluctuate too much, which makes it difficult to take advantage of arbitrage opportunities.

2. Absolute Purchasing Power Parity may not hold when:

   (a) the prices of individual goods in the consumption bundle consistently deviate from CPP across two countries.
   (b) the consumption bundles of different countries are not the same.
   (c) the prices for individual goods are sticky.
   (d) there are tariffs, quotas, and voluntary export restraints.
   (e) competition is perfect.

3. Relative Purchasing Power Parity is relevant because:

(a) empirical tests have shown that Absolute PPP is always violated, while Relative PPP is a good predictor of short-term exchange rate exposure.

(b) consumption bundles are not always comparable across countries.

(c) price levels are not stationary over time.

(d) investors care about the real return on their international portfolio investments.

(e) investors care about the nominal return on their international portfolio investments.

Additional Quiz Questions

1. Empirical evidence suggests that PPP holds in the long run. Does this mean that hedging foreign exchange risk is irrelevant in the long run? Give at least two reasons to support your answer.

2. If the prices of goods are fairly sticky, does this mean that the nominal and real exchange rates are uncorrelated? Please explain.

EXERCISES

1. During a shopping spree in Hong Kong, C. Dundee has bought a Sony CD boom box (with woofers and tweeters) for HKD 2,000, jade jewelry for HKD 4,000, and four custom-made suits for HKD 25,000. The spot exchange rate is HKD/AUD 5.

(a) If CPP held, what should the same boom box, jewelry, and suits cost in Australia?

(b) Suppose Mr. Dundee is (unexpectedly) stopped at customs as he arrives in Melbourne, and must pay import duties of 20 percent. If the same boom box, knicknacks, and suits cost AUD 450, AUD 1,500, and AUD 8,000 in Australia, respectively, was his shopping spree worth at least the HKD 10,000 paid for airfare and hotels during his trip?

2. We live in a four-country world where people only grow and eat coconuts. We have the following data:

	Brazil	Mexico	Argentina	United States
Price of one coconut:	BRC 2000	MEP 5	ARP 1.5	USD 1.4
Exchange rate (in BRC):		BRC/MEP 400	BRC/APR 1200	BRC/USD 1,400

(a) Does Absolute Purchasing Power Parity hold for the BRC with respect to the MEP, ARP, and the USD?

(b) What is the real exchange rate for the BRC with respect to the MEP, ARP, and the USD?

(c) If Brazil trades equally with each country, what is the real effective exchange rate for the BRC?

(d) Is the cost of living in Brazil lower or higher than in Mexico, Argentina, and the US?

(e) Expected annual inflation is 100 percent in Brazil, 12 percent in Mexico, 25 percent in Argentina, and 6 percent in the US. According to Relative PPP, what are the expected spot rates (in BRC) one year from now?

3. Suppose that we live in a three-nut, four-country world. The table below lists prices (denoted as Xi) in each country at times t and $t + 1$, as well as the daily consumptions at time t for each country's representative consumer. Country A's relative trade with Country B is 35 percent, with Country C 50 percent, and with Country D 15 percent.

(a) Does CPP hold at time t between Country A and Country B? Between Country A and Country C? Between Country A and Country D?

(b) The consumption quantities in Country A and Country C are the same, so we can make meaningful Absolute PPP computations. Can we also make meaningful Absolute PPP computations between Country A and Country B? Between Country A and Country D? (Hint: Compare the consumption of Country A and Country B consumers, and identify a common underlying bundle. Then notice that no such common pattern exists between Country D and the three other countries.)

(c) Consider the first three countries. Take, as the underlying bundle, one coconut, four Brazil nuts, and four pine nuts, and calculate in which country the purchasing power of XA 11,000 is the highest at time t.

(d) Consider the first three countries. Take the same underlying bundle as before, and calculate where the purchasing power of XB 44 is the highest at time t.

(e) Does CPP still hold at time $t + 1$ between Country A and Country B? Between Country A and Country C? Between Country A and Country D?

(f) Does Absolute PPP hold at times t and $t + 1$ between the three Latin-American countries? (Assume, for simplicity, that the change in the relative prices across goods and across countries has not affected the composition of the basic consumption bundle.)

	Country A	Country B	Country C	Country D
	Cost per nut at t			
	Cost per nut at $t + 1$			
	Number of nuts in the average consumption bundle			
Coconut	1,500 XA	3 XB	6 XC	1 XD
	2,000 XA	4 XB	2.5 XC	1.75 XD
	5 nuts	3 nuts	5 nuts	10 nuts
Brazil nut	750 XA	1.5 XB	3 XC	0.75 XD
	1,000 XA	2 XB	2 XC	1.25 XD
	20 nuts	12 nuts	20 nuts	50 nuts
Pine nut	250 XA	0.5 XB	1 XC	0.25 XD
	325 XA	1.5 XB	0.75 XC	0.50 XD
	20 nuts	18 nuts	20 nuts	120 nuts
Spot exchange rate at t		500	250	1,500
Spot exchange rate at $t + 1$		600	300	1,300

(g) Compute the inflation rates in the usual fashion (that is, ignoring the changes in the consumption pattern that should accompany the change in the relative prices), and verify whether Relative PPP holds between times t and $t + 1$.

(h) Compare the forecasts from Absolute and Relative PPP for XA/XB and XA/XC. Explain the similarities or differences.

4. Suppose that, during the seventies, the consumer price indices in Antarctica and Greenland went up by 80 percent and 70 percent, respectively, while the indices of production costs went up by 65 percent and 60 percent, respectively. Greenland's exchange rate appreciated by 10 percent. Antarctica's trade unions claim that this means that the export sector is hugely profitable, implying that wages should rise. Do you agree?

5. In Antarctica and Greenland, the production technologies for an agricultural commodity differ because of soil quality and different capital/labor costs. The following are data on unit costs:

	Antarctica			Greenland		
	Input	Price at t	Price at T	Input	Price at t	Price at T
Land (rent)	10m²	100	120	8m²	1,100	1,500
Machines (rent)	3 units	300	400	2 units	4,000	5,100
Labor (wages)	8 units	100	110	10 units	600	700

(a) Which country is the cheaper location at time t and at time T, if the exchange rate is a constant 7 units of Greenland Crown per unit of Antarctica Dollar?

(b) Is the relative advantage constant?

(c) Make a comparison between the above production-cost calculations and the concepts of Absolute PPP versus Relative PPP.

(d) We said that Absolute PPP calculations do not make any sense if commodity preferences differ. What difference is there between comparing production costs in different countries (even if they have different production technologies) and comparing consumption price levels of different countries when preferences differ?

MIND-EXPANDING EXERCISE

1. Suppose that French wheat can be imported without cost into Canada. However, a customs duty is levied when Canadian wheat is imported into France.

(a) In what direction could deviations from CPP occur? (Hint: We can rule out any deviation that would lead to arbitrage gains by wheat traders.)

(b) Show that the relative version of CPP holds between times t and $t + 1$ if Canada is systematically the exporter or if France is systematically the importer. Explain why, in other cases, relative CPP is likely to fail.

12

THE BALANCE OF PAYMENTS

In Chapter 11, we examined the PPP hypothesis, which maintains that the exchange rate between two countries is determined by the relative prices in the two countries. The logic underlying PPP is as follows: if prices in the home country, translated at a given exchange rate, are high relative to prices in the foreign country, there will be a drop in demand for the goods produced by the home country and an increase in demand for the goods of the foreign country. This change in demand for the exports of the two countries will lead to a decrease in demand for the home currency and a corresponding increase in demand for the foreign currency. The shift in demand for the currencies will cause the exchange rate to depreciate so that the difference between the prices in the two countries is reduced. However, we find that there is little empirical support for the PPP hypothesis; the empirical evidence shows that there are large and persistent deviations from purchasing power parity.

The PPP approach to determining the exchange rate is based on the traditional view that the demand for currencies is derived from the demand for goods. Since this approach is not very successful in explaining how the exchange rate is determined, it needs to be extended. In this chapter, we examine the view that the exchange rate is determined by all items in the Balance of Payments (BOP) accounts. That is, according to the BOP theory, it is not just the demand for goods and services, but also international capital transactions that affect the exchange rate. For example, if the demand for investing in a foreign country increases, then according to the BOP theory, the foreign currency should appreciate. Since investment abroad is influenced by the relative interest rates at home and abroad, the BOP theory suggests that it is not only the prices of goods that influence the exchange rate but also the interest rates in the two countries.

In order to understand the sources of the demand for and the supply of foreign currency, we examine, in Section 12.1, the various accounts included in the Balance of Payments. In the second section, we study how the BOP is related to another set of accounts, the Net International Investments (NII) accounts. In Section 12.3, we describe the BOP approach to exchange rate determination and compare how an economy adjusts to imbalances in the current and capital account, under fixed exchange rates and under flexible rates. We conclude, in the fourth section, by critically evaluating the BOP approach to determining exchange rates. The relationship between the current account, saving and investment, and the government's fiscal policy is described in the appendix to this chapter.

12.1   WHAT IS THE BALANCE OF PAYMENTS?

In this section, we explain the Balance of Payments accounts and its subaccounts, along with the accounting convention used to record transactions in these accounts.

12.1.1   Definition of the Balance of Payments

The **Balance of Payments (BOP)** account is a statistical record of the flow of all of the payments between the residents of one country and the rest of the world over a given period of time (usually one year). In standard accounting terms, the BOP is like a country's statement of sources and uses of (international) funds. Thus, to record any international transaction, we need to know only the source and the use of the international funds. For instance, if foreign currency flows in, the BOP will tell us:

- (Source) Why did we receive foreign currency? Was it a payment received from abroad for goods that we exported? Or did a foreign investor buy assets from a domestic resident?
- (Use) What did we do with the foreign currency? Did we keep it in a foreign bank account? Did we buy foreign assets with it? Or did we sell the money to our central bank?

The above definition of the BOP has the following implications. First, note from the definition that the balance of payments is a record of the *flow* of payments over a period of time. It does not describe the country's *stock* of foreign assets and liabilities; in that sense, it is not at all like a company's balance sheet. Rather, just like a corporation's sources-and-uses statement, the BOP analyzes and explains changes in consecutive assets-and-liabilities statements. Second, every "source" must be "used" somewhere, which means that every entry must have a counterpart—or, stated differently, the BOP uses the double-entry system of bookkeeping. Thus, by definition, the overall BOP must balance. Conversely, if you hear or read that a certain country has a balance of payments deficit, it must be referring to some *subtotal* in the BOP, some subgroup of accounts rather than the whole BOP account. Thus, when you hear about a deficit, you should always ask yourself to which subaccount of the BOP the reference is being made. Third, note that the BOP is intimately related to the exchange market. That is, all transactions that affect the inflow (sources) or outflow (uses) of foreign currency are recorded in the BOP.

Let us first look at a framework of the BOP and discuss the main subaccounts in the BOP. We will also study the accounting conventions for recording debits and credits in the various subaccounts.

The BOP account is shown on the next page in Figure 12.1 the way an economist would present it. The BOP in this exhibit is split into three parts—the current account, the capital account, and settling transactions. For each account, there are three columns. The first column lists items that are sources of foreign exchange; the second column lists transactions that use foreign exchange; and the third column gives the net sources of foreign exchange, that is, sources *less* uses. We now discuss different sub-accounts of the BOP.

FIGURE 12.1   Balance of Payments

SOURCES	USES	BALANCE ACCOUNT (Sources *minus* Uses)
1. Current Transactions		
• Exports of goods	• Imports of goods	• Trade balance
• Exports of services	• Imports of services	• "Invisibles" balance
• Inward unilateral transfers	• Outward unilateral transfers	• Net inward transfers
• Private	• Private	
• Public	• Public	
		CA = Current account balance = Net inflow from current transactions
2. Capital transactions		
• Classified as private versus government		
• *or* Classified by type of transaction:		
• Inward portfolio investment	• Outward portfolio investment	• Net inward investment
• short term	• short term	
• long term	• long term	
• Inward direct investment	• Outward direct investment	• Net inward investment
		KA = Capital account balance = Net inflow from capital transactions
3. Settling Items		
3A. Central bank transactions		
• *De*creases in foreign reserves	• *In*creases in foreign reserves	• Net *de*creases in foreign reserves, $(-)\Delta$RFX
3B. Errors and Omissions		
• Unrecorded inflows	• Unrecorded outflows	• Errors, omissions (E&O)
	Grand total of BOP	$0 = \text{CA} + \text{KA} - \Delta\text{RFX} + \text{E\&O}$

12.1.2   Current Account (CA) Balance

The **current account (CA)** of the BOP is a record of the trade in goods and services, and of unilateral transfers between a country and the rest of the world.

- The CA includes the merchandise account, a record of the trade in *goods* between a country and the rest of the world. Recorded in this account, for example, are the export of wheat, lumber, and oil—and the import of cars and computers. The balance in this account, the excess of exports over imports, is called the **Balance of Trade (BOT)**.
- The CA also includes trade in *services,* or "invisibles"—for example, exports or imports of labor services like consulting, insurance, travel, and banking. This subaccount also includes dividends and interest income, which are the return (service flow) on the risk-free or risk-bearing capital that has been exported or imported.
- Finally, the CA includes **unilateral transfers**. Unilateral transfers are payments made abroad, or received from abroad, for which there is no corresponding international flow of goods or services. Transfers include items such as development aid, gifts, and wages repatriated by foreign workers. No goods or services are received in return for such transfers. You can think of an outward unilateral transfer as buying "goodwill" rather than goods or services.

Let us look at how a positive or a negative sign is assigned to transactions in the current account. It is natural to assign a positive sign to a "source" of international funds and a negative sign to a "use" of international funds. Thus, when recording transactions in the current account that generate a net inflow of foreign currency, such as an export of goods, we assign a positive sign. Items that require an outflow of funds, such as an import of services, on the other hand, are assigned a negative sign. Below, we examine three transactions to see how they are recorded in the current account of Canada. Recall that each transaction is recorded in two parts, that is, every entry in the BOP must have a counterpart.

Example   12.1

1. If StarDucks Canada, a Canadian firm, imports CAD 100m worth of coffee from Brazil, there will be a negative accounting entry in the current account for this side of the transaction in order to reflect the outflow of funds to pay for the imports. There must also be a corresponding accounting entry for the source of foreign exchange that is used to pay for the imports. For instance, StarDucks may have earned the funds by exporting coffee mugs to Brazil; this transaction would be reflected as a positive entry in the current account.[1]
2. If a freight charge of CAD 50,000 is paid to a US shipping line by StarDucks, this import of services will be recorded with a negative sign in the current account in order to reflect the outflow of funds to the US firm. Again, we need a corresponding transaction that generates the foreign exchange needed to pay for the import of US services. Let us assume that the source of foreign exchange is the export of some coffee to the US by StarDucks.
3. If CanMed, a Canadian producer of medicinal drugs, exports CAD 5m worth of medicine to Somalia, this is recorded as a positive entry in the current account because it represents a

---

[1] StarDucks could also have borrowed or sold some assets to pay for its imports. This would be a capital account transaction. Capital account transactions are discussed in the next section.

source transaction. The use side of the transaction could be imports, if CanMed uses the funds to buy chemical compounds from abroad.

Alternatively, if the Canadian government donates CAD 5m worth of CanMed medicines to Somalia, there will again be a positive entry in the current account (to reflect the export of medicine). The second part of this transaction will be a negative entry in the transfers account (also a part of the current account) to reflect the "import of goodwill," rather than chemical compounds.

12.1.3   Capital Account (KA) Balance

The **capital account (KA)** is a record of the inward and outward investment and amortization flows between a country and the rest of the world. The capital transactions recorded include those that result from the purchase or sale of real or financial assets.

Capital account transactions can be classified in one of two ways. The first way is to classify them as private or public transactions, that is, transactions made by private investors or by the government. The second way is to divide capital account transactions into **direct investment** or **portfolio investment**. Direct investment is a transaction in which the investor has a controlling share or participates in the management of the firm. Portfolio investment, on the other hand, is a transaction in which securities are held purely as a financial investment. It is often difficult to distinguish between direct investment and portfolio investment and, typically, the classification depends on the proportion of the firm held by the investor. The cut-off level of ownership beyond which an investment is classified as direct investment varies across countries but is usually around 10 percent.

The accounting rule for recording capital transactions is based on the same logic as that used to record transactions in the current account. The sale of assets to foreigners and the borrowing of funds abroad are transactions that are recorded with a positive sign because these transactions result in an inflow of international funds. Thus, a surplus in the capital account implies a *decrease* in the net holding of foreign assets by domestic residents. Analogously, the purchase of foreign assets is recorded with a negative sign.[2]

Example   12.2

1. Suppose that StarDucks Canada pays for the import of CAD 100m worth of coffee from Brazil by giving the Brazilian firm a 25 percent share of StarDucks. This transaction will be recorded as follows: a negative entry in the current account (corresponding to the import of coffee) and a positive entry in the long-term capital account (to reflect the inward direct investment by the Brazilian firm in Canadian securities).

2. Suppose that payment to the US company for the freight charges of CAD 50,000 (incurred by StarDucks firm on the import of coffee) is made with a CAD check drawn on a Canadian bank. This payment will be recorded as a positive entry in the Canadian capital account,

---

[2] This may be confusing because, in common language, the word *positive* is often associated with the idea of "good," and *negative* is associated with "bad"—and many people do tend to think of an export surplus in the current account as good and foreign borrowing as bad. Such confusion will be avoided if one remembers the rule that transactions that are a *source* of funds are recorded with a positive sign in the BOP accounts, while transactions that are a *use* of funds are recorded with a negative sign.

which reflects inward portfolio investment (CAD deposit) by the US firm in Canadian assets. This positive entry matches the negative accounting record made in the current account (for import of services).

3. Suppose that the US shipping company uses the CAD deposit to buy Canadian government bonds. From the Canadian point of view, the sale of long-term government bonds to a foreign investor is a *source* transaction, which is recorded as a positive entry in the long-term investment account. The counterpart to this entry is the decrease in short-term inward investment: Canada has *used* the funds from the sale of the long-term assets to pay off a short-term liability (the CAD deposit originally held by the US shipping company). Thus, the overall capital account is not affected by this portfolio rebalancing.

12.1.4   Changes in Official Reserves

The *official reserves* of a country include gold, government holdings of foreign currencies (mostly in the form of commercial paper, T-bills, and bonds), money deposited at the IMF, and Special Drawing Rights (SDRs) with the IMF.[3] Changes in the official reserves mirror or offset the imbalance between private inflows and outflows in the current and capital accounts, as explained below.

Note that the total value of the transactions in the current and capital accounts is the overall deficit or surplus for the entire economy (excluding the central bank). However, the total BOP must balance. Thus, if the private sector has been a net *user* of international funds, the shortfall must have been provided by the central bank—or, if the private sector as a whole was a net provider of foreign exchange, the surplus must have gone to the central bank. In short, the foreign exchange transactions in the current account and those in the capital account equal the change in reserves. Denote the current account balance by CA, the capital account balance by KA, and the change in official reserves by ΔRFX. Then, assuming that there is no error in measuring the transactions in these accounts, we have the following result:

$$CA + KA - \Delta RFX = 0$$

or, rewriting the above equation with the change in official reserves on the left-hand side:

$$\Delta RFX = CA + KA. \tag{1}$$

We shall examine this identity in greater detail in Section 12.3. To conclude our discussion of the change in official reserves account, we examine the accounting rule for recording transactions in this account.

The accounting rule for recording changes in official reserves is the same as that for the capital account: an increase in foreign assets held by the central bank is recorded with a negative sign. This is because an increase in assets held by the central bank is a *use* of foreign currency—in exactly the same way as an increase of foreign assets held by private investors is a use of foreign currency. Conversely, a decrease in the central bank's stock of foreign assets is a *source* of foreign currency for the country, like when a domestic company sells assets abroad to raise funds. Thus, the net

---

[3] Special Drawing Rights are internationally created funds. (See the introductory chapter.)

inflow in the third subtotal of Figure 12.1 shows the *decrease* in foreign reserves, $(-)\Delta RFX$, as a net source of funds.

12.1.5   Statistical Discrepancy/Errors and Omissions

The last item in the BOP is the **Statistical Discrepancy**. Since any sources-and-uses statement must balance by definition, the foreign exchange transactions in the current account and those in the capital account should equal the change in reserves. That is,

$$\Delta RFX = CA + KA. \qquad [1]$$

In practice, there is a problem with measuring all transactions accurately. The left-hand side of Equation [1] is measured by the government's records of its official reserves and, therefore, it is reasonable to assume that, in most countries, there is little error. However, the measurement of the right-hand side of Equation [1] can be quite difficult and errors can occur easily. Difficulties arise because of the differences in the *timing* between the date on which a transaction takes place and the date on which it is recorded. Furthermore, errors arise because of problems in estimating items such as expenditure on travel, and because of illegal or unreported transactions. It is generally believed that the errors on the KA are larger than those on the CA. Thus, in terms of statistically recorded transactions, Equation [1] generally does not hold with an equality. For this reason the item **Errors and Omissions (E&O)** is added to the right-hand side to get an equality relationship:

$$\Delta RFX = CA_{estimate} + KA_{estimate} + E\&O. \qquad [2]$$

The E&O term can be surprisingly large, sometimes of the same magnitude as the CA or KA. Thus, one needs to be very careful when reading these accounts and very cautious in interpreting the data from the BOP.

Throughout the rest of our discussion of the BOP, we shall think in terms of the more relevant true exports of goods, services, and assets rather than the recorded figures; thus, we will ignore these errors and omissions and assume that Equation [1] holds with equality. Equation [1] is used to analyze the relationship between a country's fiscal policy and its BOP accounts in the appendix to this chapter.

12.2   THE NET INTERNATIONAL INVESTMENT ACCOUNT

As described above, the BOP is an account that keeps track of the *flow* of foreign exchange into and out of the country. To measure the result of these cumulative inflows and outflows, we have the Net International Investment account, or the net external assets account. The **Net International Investment (NII) account** measures the *net* ownership of foreign assets. That is, the NII is designed to measure a country's *stock* of international assets and liabilities—somewhat like a company's statement of assets and liabilities.

Example   12.3

Here we compare the BOP and the NII. Suppose that you keep two accounts. The first account keeps track of your income and expenditures during the year. This account informs you about the inflow (sources) and outflow (uses) of funds and is analogous to a nation's BOP account. The second account shows you how much money you have at the bank and your net asset position. In itself, this account represents your solvency at a given point in time. This second account is analogous to the NII account. The NII account is what we should look at in order to judge the solvency of a country. Thus, while the BOP tells us whether a country's economy is getting better or worse, the NII tells us how good or how bad things actually are at a given point in time.

We now consider an example at the level of a country, rather than an individual.

Example   12.4

We must look at stock versus flow information from the BOP and the NII. Suppose that a country has been running a current account deficit of USD 20 billion for each of the last three years, but its NII has a positive balance of USD 1,000 billion. Then, even though the current account balance in the BOP accounts reflects a deficit, given the large positive balance in the NII, this current account deficit is not a problem—at least, not at this time.

Let us look at another example.

Example   12.5

The official estimate of the balance of NII of the UK at the end of 1990 was GBP 27b. This was a decrease from the 1986 peak of over 100b, and this decline mirrored four years of CA deficits.

There is obviously a link between the BOP and the NII; increases in the amount of foreign assets owned add to the NII. That is, the balance on the current and capital account leads to a change in the net asset position of the country. This change is reflected in the NII. Recall, however, that transactions in the current account and capital account are not recorded perfectly. For example, unrepatriated earnings are not recorded in the current account, nor are changes in the market values of foreign assets (arising from either a change in the local value of these assets or a change in the exchange rate). Thus, the true NII may change in a way not fully explained by the official BOP statistics.

Example   12.6

There may be large differences between the estimated net asset position of a country and the NII computed from the BOP. In 1992, the NII balance for the UK was reported as GBP 60 billion. However, the true mid-1992 net asset figure was estimated by one source as somewhere between GBP 80 and 100 billion.

12.3   THE BOP APPROACH TO EXCHANGE RATE DETERMINATION

In this section, we describe the factors that determine the exchange rate according to the BOP theory. We then examine the adjustment to imbalances in the current or capital account in two extreme economies—one where the exchange rate is fixed, and one where the exchange rate is perfectly flexible.

From your understanding of basic economics, you may recall that an imbalance in any market is corrected by an adjustment in price and/or quantity. Imbalances in the current and capital accounts are resolved similarly. If the demand for foreign exchange exceeds its supply, then either the price of foreign exchange, the spot rate, will increase and/or there will be an increase in the inflow of foreign exchange. If the price of the foreign currency is fixed, then the imbalance is offset by a change in the quantity of official reserves. In contrast, if the exchange rate is perfectly flexible, then the adjustment comes through a change in the exchange rate. Since exchange rates are rarely perfectly flexible, an imbalance in the current and capital accounts will typically come through an adjustment in both the exchange rate and the quantity of official reserves.

12.3.1   Factors Affecting Exchange Rates According to the BOP Theory

The price for foreign exchange, the spot rate, is determined by supply and demand for foreign exchange. In Chapter 11, we examined the view that the demand for a particular currency was derived from the demand for the goods produced by that country. The PPP theory suggests that, if prices of goods abroad are high relative to prices at home, then the demand for foreign goods is low, implying that demand for the foreign currency is low and, thus, we expect the foreign currency to depreciate. The empirical evidence, however, suggests that exchange rates often do not behave as predicted by the PPP theory. Thus, in this section, we extend the PPP approach. Now the demand for foreign currency depends not only on the demand for foreign goods but also on the desire of investors to invest abroad. That is, demand for foreign exchange is derived from transactions in the current account *and* those in the capital account. This approach to determining the exchange rate is called the BOP theory.

The objective of the BOP theory of exchange rates is to explain (a) why exchange rates and prices are not as predicted by the PPP theory and (b) why we see continuous capital flows between countries. The explanation offered for these two observations is based on a Keynesian view of the world that prices of goods are sticky (not flexible) in the short run. Thus, the PPP theory cannot explain the determination of the exchange rate in the short run. Moreover, given that prices adjust slowly to a change in economic circumstances, economies are in a state of persistent disequilibrium leading to the flow of capital between countries.

The BOP theory of exchange rate is a Keynesian *flow* approach to the determination of the exchange rate. This approach treats a currency like any other commodity and determines its price from its supply and demand. According to the BOP theory of exchange rates, the supply and demand for a currency arises from the elements of the BOP—trade in goods and services, portfolio investment, and direct investment. We divide the elements that determine the flow of foreign currency into two categories—the current account and the capital account.

The current account (which reflects the demand for goods and services) is determined by prices of goods at home (P) and prices of goods abroad, translated into domestic terms using the spot rate (SP^*). The functional relation between the current account balance and the relative prices abroad and at home, $(SP^*)/P$, is assumed to be positive; that is, an increase in $(SP^*)/P$ leads to an increase in the current account balance.

The current account is also assumed to be influenced by national income at home (Y) and foreign national incomes (Y^*). The effect of domestic income on the current account is assumed to be through imports: an increase in income leads to an increase in consumption. Since imports are a component of total consumption, imports increase with income, leading to a decrease in the current account. For the same reason, the relationship between foreign income, Y^*, and the domestic current account balance is positive. An increase in foreign income leads to an increase in imports by foreigners (increase of domestic exports), which increases the current account balance. One can summarize the effect of these various variables on the current account by stating that the CA is a function of $(SP^*)/P$, Y and Y^*.

$$CA = CA\left(\frac{SP^*}{P}, Y, Y^* \right).$$

[3]

The second category of transactions, those in the capital account, are assumed to depend on the relative interest rates at home and abroad. The functional relation between the domestic interest rate and the capital account balance is assumed to be positive; that is, an increase in the interest rate at home attracts foreign investment and leads to an inflow of international funds. Analogously, the relationship between the capital account balance and the foreign interest rate, r^*, is negative because an increase in interest rates abroad, all else being equal, leads to an outflow of investment funds. Finally, the capital account also depends on the current exchange rate, S, because the value of S will determine the value of the foreign return in terms of domestic units. Thus, in contrast to the PPP theory of exchange rates, the BOP theory acknowledges that the demand for a currency may also arise from investors' direct and portfolio investment decisions. The effect of interest rates on the capital account can be expressed as:

$$KA = KA\left(r, r^*, S \right).$$

[4]

Given the information in Equations [3] and [4], we first consider adjustment of the imbalances in the current or capital account in a world where the exchange rate is fixed, and then in one where the exchange rate is perfectly flexible.

12.3.2   Adjustment under Fixed Exchange Rates

Under a fixed-rate regime, the private sector can buy or sell any amount of goods or assets at a constant exchange rate. If, at this fixed rate, the plans of the private sector lead to a net demand for foreign exchange, then the central bank makes up for the shortfall—otherwise, the excess demand for foreign exchange would lead to an appreciation of the foreign currency, which is not allowed under a fixed-rate regime. Likewise, if there is a surplus of foreign exchange, the central bank buys up the net inflow of foreign exchange and adds it to its reserves in order to avoid an unwanted depreciation of the foreign currency. Thus, there is no price adjustment in the exchange market, and the central bank's interventions are the quantity adjustments that make it possible to keep the price of foreign currency fixed.

By expressing the current account and capital account balances as in Equations [3] and [4], we can describe the adjustment process under fixed exchange rates using the result in Equation [1]. The fixed exchange rate is one of the determinants of the current account, $CA = CA\ (SP^*/P, Y, Y^*)$, and the capital account, $KA(r,\ r^*,\ S)$.

Note, however, that in the short run we do not expect domestic or foreign income to change very much. Moreover, in the Keynesian world, prices are sticky. Thus, if we assume S to be constant, one way an imbalance in the current and capital accounts can be corrected is through a change in official reserves. That is, the fixed exchange rate, S, determines $CA\ (SP^*/P, Y, Y^*)$ and $KA(r,\ r^*,\ S)$, which determines ΔRFX by means of Equation [1].

$$\Delta RFX = CA\left(\frac{SP^*}{P}, Y, Y^* \right) + KA\left(r, r^*, S \right).$$

Thus, one possible cause of a country's central bank losing reserves is a CA deficit. This point should be rather obvious: if a country imports more than it exports, but does not sell any securities or real assets to foreigners (meaning that the other accounts are in balance), then the only way to pay for the excess imports, under fixed exchange rates, is by decreasing its official reserves of foreign assets.

Example   12.7

Assume that exchange rates are fixed and that all of the accounts in the BOP are balanced, except for the trade balance, where imports by the US exceed exports by USD 100 billion. Then, the official reserves of the US will decrease by USD 100 billion. That is, the country will pay for its excess spending (the use) by selling some of the central bank's reserves (the source).

The second way a central bank can deal with an imbalance is to change the domestic interest rate relative to the foreign interest rate. Suppose, for instance, that there is a deficit on the current account, and the central bank does not want to lose reserves. Then the central bank can obtain equilibrium by increasing the capital account, which, in the short run, requires an increase of r relative to $r*$. The higher return on domestic deposits induces investors to finance the current account deficit, and no official reserves have to be used.

12.3.3   Adjustment under Flexible Exchange Rates

In contrast to the case where exchange rates are fixed, when exchange rates are flexible there is no intervention by the central bank and no change in the holdings of official reserves. Instead, the adjustment to an imbalance in the demand for foreign exchange comes about through a change in the price of foreign exchange, S, and its effect on the current and capital accounts.

Suppose that the exchange rate is such that the private sector has an excess demand for foreign exchange. Obviously, if the central bank does not intervene, people will not be able to carry out their plans at the prevailing exchange rate, because there are not enough source transactions to finance all of the intended use transactions. Competition for scarce foreign funds then leads to a *price* adjustment, an appreciation of the foreign currency, which induces the private sector to alter its current account and capital account transactions until equilibrium is reached. Thus, a floating exchange rate regime is one in which the exchange rate is such that:

$$0 = \Delta \text{RFX} = \text{CA}\left(\frac{SP*}{P}, Y, Y*\right) + \text{KA}(r, r*, S).$$

In the following two examples, we show how imbalances in the current and capital accounts affect the exchange rate.

Example   12.8

Suppose that the US has a current account deficit of USD 100m, but the central bank does not intervene in the foreign exchange markets to settle this deficit. There must be a KA surplus to finance this: USD 100m worth of assets must be transferred from US residents to foreigners. For instance, the US may pay in dollars, which means that USD 100m is transferred to bank accounts held by foreigners. If exchange rates are not fixed, then in the conventional BOP view the price of USD must drop in order to convince foreign investors to hold these additional USD 100m.

Example   12.9

In 1997, control of Hong Kong will pass from the British to the Chinese. As a result of the political uncertainty arising from this event, investors from Hong Kong are investing large sums of money in Canada. Thus, there is a positive net portfolio investment in Canada, leading to a surplus in the capital account of the Canadian BOP. Under fixed exchange rates, the effect of this inflow would be an increase in the official reserves. Under flexible exchange rates, the excess demand for Canadian assets would lead to an appreciation of the CAD.

Below, we summarize how—according to the BOP theory of exchange rates—a change in prices, income, and interest rates affects the exchange rate.

All else being equal,

- An increase in domestic prices, P, leads to a decrease in exports and, thus, to a decrease in the demand for the domestic currency, implying a depreciation of home currency.
- An increase in domestic income leads to a depreciation of the home currency through an increase in demand for foreign currency driven by the increase in demand for imports.
- An increase in the domestic interest rate, r, leads to an increase in the demand for domestic assets, a decrease in the demand for foreign assets, and therefore an appreciation of the home currency.

From our discussion in Chapter 1, we know that, until the collapse of the Bretton-Woods system in the early seventies, exchange rates in most countries were fixed. Since then, however, many exchange rates have become flexible, though the central bank periodically intervenes in the exchange markets to revise the spot rate. This system of floating exchange rates with occasional intervention by the central bank is called *managed float* or *dirty float*. Three examples of this are the early European Monetary System (EMS), the meetings of the central bankers of the G7 countries who (try to) decide the value of each currency, and the joint interventions of two or more central banks. Obviously, under the managed float system, *both* the official reserves and the nominal and real exchange rates will change in response to imbalances in the capital and current accounts.

12.4   CONCLUSIONS

In this chapter, we have described the BOP accounts of a country and we have seen how transactions are recorded in the various subaccounts of the BOP. We established the relationship between imbalances in the current and capital account and changes in official reserves and the exchange rate reserves. That is, under fixed exchange rates, a shortfall in the current and capital account must be offset by an outflow of official reserves; under perfectly flexible exchange rates, an excess demand for the foreign currency will lead to its appreciation. We then explained the BOP approach to exchange rate determination, according to which the demand for foreign exchange is derived from both current and capital account transactions. Thus, the BOP approach extends the PPP theory (which maintains that the demand for foreign exchange is derived from the demand for goods) to include the effect of foreign investment.

The BOP theory of exchange rate determination is an improvement over the PPP theory because it allows the exchange rate to be influenced by a change in the demand for foreign assets. However, the analysis of the relationship between the exchange rate and portfolio investment is based on fairly restrictive assumptions. In particular, the assumption that the capital account is affected by only the riskless rates of return in the domestic and foreign country is not a very realistic view of the world. The BOP theory fails to consider the effect on portfolio decisions of the rates of return on other assets. Nor does it analyze the role of expectations and uncertainty—the key ingredients of modern financial theory. In the next chapter, we examine more recent theories of exchange rate determination, theories that treat the issue of asset demands in a more sophisticated way.

QUIZ QUESTIONS

True-False Questions

1. If a country has a BOP deficit, the total of all BOP subaccounts is negative.
2. The current account is a record of all trade in goods and services, while the capital account is a record of direct and portfolio investment and unilateral transfers.
3. When the US private sector purchases more goods or makes more investments abroad than foreigners purchase or invest in the US during a year, the Federal Reserve (the US central bank) must make up for the shortfall.
4. All errors and omissions in the BOP are a result of black market transactions.
5. When a corporation purchases a company abroad, and the value of the firm appreciates over time, the NII and the capital account of the BOP is updated to reflect this change.
6. According to the Keynesian approach to exchange rate determination, sticky prices are compensated for by the continuous flow of capital.
7. The BOP theory of exchange rate determination says that most changes in the exchange rate are due to the arrival of new information about the future.
8. Under a fixed exchange rate regime, if a country's private sector sells abroad more than it purchases, the central bank must sell foreign exchange.
9. BOP theory is flawed is because it assumes that investors only invest in risk-free domestic and foreign assets.

Multiple-Choice Questions

For the following three multiple-choice questions, assume that Antarctica is the home country, and its currency is the Antarctica dollar (AAD), and Greenland is the foreign country and its currency is the crown (GRC). Choose the correct answer.

1. All else being equal, an increase in income in Greenland leads to:
   - (a) an increase in consumption in Antarctica, and therefore an increase in imports, resulting in an appreciation of the AAD.
   - (b) a decrease in consumption in Antarctica, and therefore an increase in exports, resulting in a depreciation of the AAD.
   - (c) an increase in consumption in Greenland, and therefore an increase in imports, resulting in an appreciation of the AAD.
   - (d) an increase in consumption in Greenland, and therefore an increase in imports, resulting in a depreciation of the AAD.

2. All else being equal, a decrease in the interest rate r^* in Greenland leads to:
   - (a) decreased demand for assets in Greenland, and therefore a depreciation of the GRC.
   - (b) decreased demand for assets in Greenland, and therefore a depreciation of the AAD.
   - (c) an increase in consumption in Greenland, and therefore an increase in imports, resulting in an appreciation of the GRC.
   - (d) an increase in consumption in Antarctica, and therefore an increase in exports, resulting in a depreciation of the AAD.

3. All else being equal, a decrease in prices in Greenland leads to:
   - (a) an increase in exports to Antarctica, and therefore an appreciation of the AAD.
   - (b) an increase in exports to Antarctica, and therefore a depreciation of the AAD.

(c) an increase in consumption in Greenland, and therefore an increase in imports, resulting in an appreciation of the AAD.

(d) a decrease in consumption in Greenland, and therefore a decrease in imports, resulting in a depreciation of the AAD.

Additional Quiz Questions

1. The German subsidiary of a Canadian firm (that is, the subsidiary is owned by the Canadian firm) is sold to a German firm. The Canadian firm invests the funds obtained from the sale in Frankfurt. How is the transaction recorded in the Canadian BOP?

2. The BOP of Timbuktu showed the following entries for 1988: a capital account surplus of 50, a deficit in the services account of 15, and a trade deficit of 45. The change in the official reserves was zero. What was the balance of unilateral transfers for Timbuktu?

3. If the central bank sets an exchange rate that undervalues the foreign currency, then—other things being the same—what will be the impact on the following:

(a) RFX (increase/decrease)

(b) BOP (surplus/deficit).

4. If the current account balance has a surplus of USD 2 billion and the official settlements balance (RFX) has a deficit of USD 5 billion, what is the balance of the capital account?

5. A British importer purchases goods from a French company and obtains a trade credit for the full value of the shipment (equal to GBP 100). How should this transaction be recorded in the BOP of the UK?

6. Timbuktu, a country on the Atlantis continent, has a government deficit of 40 billion while private investment exceeds private savings by 10 billion. What is Timbuktu's current account balance if its exchange rate is fixed?

EXERCISES

1. Antarctica uses a system of fixed exchange rates, its current account deficit is 6 billion, and its capital account balance is USD 4 billion.

Based on this information, answer the following questions.

(a) What is the change in the official foreign exchange reserves of Antarctica?

(b) What is the gap between the income of Antarctica and its expenditure on domestic output?

(c) If there is only one other country in the world, Greenland, can you estimate the current account balance of Greenland?

2. The data below is taken from the BOP of Switzerland. Based on this data, decide whether the following statement is true or false and explain your answer.

"From 1979 to 1982, foreigners have been net issuers of SF-denominated bonds in the Swiss capital markets."

Capital account	1979	1980	1981	1982
Portfolio investment (in billions of dollars)	−11.8	−11.8	−11.9	−32.2

3. A company in Philadelphia purchases machinery from a Canadian company for USD 150 and receives one-year trade credit. The machinery is transported to Philadelphia by a Canadian trucking company that charges the US company USD 10. The US company insures the shipment with a US insurance company and pays a premium of USD 3. After delivering the machinery to Philadelphia, the Canadian truck continues its trip to Houston, where it picks up microcomputers sold by a Texan company to a Mexican company. This shipment, which is worth USD 170, is insured by a US insurance company for a premium of USD 4. No trade credit is given to the Mexican company. Compute the BOP for the US and assume that Canadian and Mexican companies maintain dollar deposits in New York.

4. Suppose that you are an analyst for the Central Bank of Zanzibar. Decide how the BOP accounts are affected by the following.

   (a) A budget deficit financed by foreign borrowing
   (b) An import quota for foreign cars
   (c) A purchase of a new embassy in Luxembourg
   (d) A grain embargo

5. The following data are taken from the balance of payments of Germany:

Capital account	1979	1980	1981	1982
Portfolio investment (in billions of dollars)	+2.9	−6.9	−5.4	−8.7

   Is the following statement consistent with the data shown above? *"After 1979, foreigners have issued DEM-denominated bonds in the German capital market in order to take advantage of the favorable interest rate differential with respect to the US capital market."*

6. The following passage is from an article that appeared in a newspaper: *"Last year, the US demand for capital to fund the federal deficit and to finance private investment in buildings and equipment exceeded net domestic savings by about USD 100 billion."* What can we infer about the magnitude of the US current account deficit?

7. The following passage is from an article that appeared in a newspaper. Which account of the German BOP is the article talking about?
   "FRANKFURT, West Germany—West Germany's balance of payments, which measures all flows of funds into and out of the country, was in surplus by the current equivalent of USD 210.3 million in February, up from the year-earlier surplus of USD 206.4 million, but sharply lower than January's surplus of USD 10.04 billion, the central bank said January's large surplus was caused in part by heavy central-bank intervention in support of the French franc prior to the realignment of the European Monetary System at mid-month."

8. The BOP of the US in 1982 and 1984 follows on page 389. Is it correct to state, as it has often been done, that the deterioration of the current account was primarily financed by sales of US Treasury securities to foreigners?

US BALANCE OF PAYMENTS
(billions of dollars)

	1982	1984
Trade Account	−36	−108
Service Account	35	17
Unilateral Transfers	−8	−11
CURRENT ACCOUNT	−9	−102
Changes in US assets abroad (private) of which:	−108	−16
Portfolio	−8	−5
Bank-reported	−111	−7
Direct investment	6	−6
Other	5	2
Changes in foreign assets in US (private) of which:	92	91
US Treasury Security	7	22
Other	85	69
PRIVATE CAPITAL	−16	75
OFFICIAL SETTLEMENTS	−8	−3
STATISTICAL DISCREPANCY	33	30

9. Venizio had a government surplus of 15 billion in the year 1988. In addition, private after-tax savings exceeded private investment spending by 10 billion. What was the current account balance of Venizio in 1988?

MIND-EXPANDING EXERCISE

1. You have been hired by the IMF to design a program to improve the current account balance. How should your program influence the following variables (increase/decrease):
   (a) Taxes
   (b) Government spending
   (c) Private savings

RELATIONSHIP BETWEEN THE BOP AND FISCAL POLICY

The relationship between the BOP accounts and a government's fiscal policy is quite simple once we recall the National Income Accounting identities. We use the following notation:

Y = GNP or value of all national output
Cexp = consumption expenditure
Iexp = investment expenditure
Gexp = government expenditure
A = "absorption" by domestic residents, $A \equiv C\text{exp} + I\text{exp} + G\text{exp}$
Sav^P = private savings
Tax = taxes, the government's income
netSav^P = *net* saving by private individuals = $(\text{Sav}^P - I\text{exp})$
netSav^G = *net* saving by the government = taxes – spending = $-[G\text{exp} - \text{Tax}]$
CA = current account balance = exports – imports

Now we are ready to derive the first result.

12A.1   Relationship between the Current Account and Domestic Absorption

In a **closed economy**, that is, an economy without exports or imports, the value of total output, Y, has to be equal to the value of spending on that output (total absorption, A). That is,

$$Y = A. \qquad\qquad [A1]$$

In an **open economy**, however, some domestic expenditures may be on imported goods, and some of the domestic production may be consumed abroad, that is, as exports. Therefore, to get the accounting identity for the open economy, we need to add exports and subtract imports from the right-hand side of the above equation. Of course, the difference between exports and imports is the current account balance, which allows us to rewrite Equation [A1] for an open economy as:

$$Y = A + \text{CA}.$$

or

$$Y - A = \text{CA}. \qquad\qquad [A2]$$

This equation has a number of interesting implications. Equation [A2] says that the CA *surplus* is equal to the excess of domestic income over domestic expenditure. This makes good sense: it is only that part of national output not consumed that is available for *net* exports. Thus, an improvement in the CA balance (right-hand side of Equation [A2]) can be achieved either through an increase in Y (production) or a decrease in A (domestic absorption).

- Any policy that attempts to improve the CA balance by means of a reduction in expenditures, A, is called an **expenditure-reducing policy**. Examples of such a policy include cutting government spending or implementing a general deflationary policy.
- An alternative policy to increase the CA is the use of an **expenditure-switching policy**. This is a policy that stimulates exports and selectively discourages imports (thus boosting output in the import-competing sectors). One frequently used policy instrument is the exchange rate. A devaluation of the exchange rate by the central bank makes imports expensive and exports cheaper relative to foreign goods and leads to an improvement in the CA balance. Other examples of expenditure-switching policies are import tariffs or export subsidies.

The question we wish to address is under what conditions an expenditure-switching policy will be successful in reducing the current account deficit. An expenditure-switching policy can be successful only when the economy is not already operating at its full-employment level. If the economy is already at the full-employment level, then Y cannot be further increased in the short run—and, from Equation [A2], if Y cannot increase, the only way to increase CA is to decrease A, that is, with an expenditure-reducing policy. Thus, to improve the CA balance when the economy is already at its full-employment level, the government must use an expenditure-reducing policy.

However, an expenditure-switching policy may fail even when the economy is not at its full-employment level. Consider one example of an expenditure-switching policy—a devaluation of the home currency. The devaluation, through a change in domestic prices relative to foreign prices, attempts to switch consumption towards domestic (nontraded) goods and away from importable and exportable goods, without affecting total absorption (A). However, even if the *quantity* of foreign goods consumed decreases, the total foreign currency *value* of expenditures on imports may not decrease and the foreign expenditure on exports may not increase. Thus, a devaluation of the home currency will have the desired effect on the current account only if consumers and producers at home and abroad are sufficiently price-sensitive.[4] Stated differently, the CA balance will improve only if a country reduces its absorption relative to its income. Thus, devaluations are not always successful in the management of the CA balance and, if they fail, an expenditure-reducing policy needs to be employed. The same argument holds for import tariffs or export subsidies: these policies are likely to affect the *quantities* of exports and imports in the desired direction, but not necessarily the *values* of exports and imports.

12A.2   The Relationship between Current Account and the Budget Deficit

Equation [A2] states that a country's current account surplus is equal to that part of its income that is not absorbed by its residents—the country's overall savings. Overall savings in a country can be divided into private saving and public saving:

$$CA = Y - A = netSav^P + netSav^G \qquad \text{[A3]}$$

---

[4] The condition under which a devaluation will lead to an improvement in the current account balance is called the **Marshall-Lerner condition**, after the two economists who first discussed this issue. This condition is that the sum of the demand (price) elasticity of exports and the demand (price) elasticity of imports is greater than one.

By definition, the CA balance equals the sum of net private saving and net government saving. Net private saving is the difference between private saving and investment, and its sign may vary over time and across countries. In contrast, there is very little variation in the sign of net government savings: virtually all governments actually *dissave*. To obtain an expression that uses the more familiar term *budget deficit,* we can rewrite Equation [A3] as follows:

$$CA = (Sav^P - Iexp) + netSav^G$$
$$= (Sav^P - Iexp) - (-netSav^G)$$
$$= (Sav^P - Iexp) - \text{Budget Deficit}. \qquad [A4]$$

Equation [A4] is useful for understanding the source of current account deficits.

Factors Giving Rise to a CA Deficit

Using Equation [A4], the origins of a CA deficit can be traced to one of the following factors:

- Too little private savings, Sav^P.
- Too much investment, $Iexp$, relative to Sav^P.
- A large government budget deficit.

Empirically, Sav^P is relatively stable in the short run. This means that changes in the CA deficit usually reflect changes in aggregate investment and in the government deficit. Note that a CA deficit that reflects an investment boom is not necessarily bad.

Example   12A.1

During the Reagan era, US Treasury officials argued that the increase in the CA deficit of the US and in its KA surplus (that is, US foreign borrowing) was due to a boom in investment rather than to a budget deficit. Many economists, however, argued that the CA deficit was due to the budget deficit. In the US, Sav^P is very stable (and rather low); thus, changes in the CA deficit essentially reflect changes in the budget deficit and changes in investment. Using the data given below and Equation [A4], we analyze whether the current account deficit in 1983–84 was the result of a large budget deficit or of an increase in investment.

(USD billions)

US	1980	1981	1982	1983	1984
CA	0	5	-11	-41	-100
Budget deficit	59	57	110	195	200
netSav^P	59	62	99	154	100

Comparing the data for 1982 with the data for 1984, it is obvious that almost the entire current account deficit was a result of an increase in the budget deficit. That is, the change in the current account between 1982–84 equals $-100 - (-11) = -\text{USD } 89$ billion, which matches almost exactly the increase in the budget deficit over this period, $200 - 110 = \text{USD } 90$ billion.

Financing Budget Deficits

By rewriting Equation [A4] and isolating the budget deficit on the left-hand side, we can establish the link between budget deficits and the capital account balance, KA.

First, we rearrange Equation [A4] into

$$\text{Budget Deficit} = (\text{Sav}^P - I\text{exp}) - \text{CA}. \qquad [A5]$$

Now, substituting the expression for the CA given in Equation [1] we get:

$$\text{Budget Deficit} = \text{netSav}^P + \text{KA} - \Delta\text{RFX}. \qquad [A6]$$

Thus, a budget deficit must be financed either (a) through private savings, (b) through the sale of private assets to foreigners, or (c) through a sale of official reserve assets. Under flexible rates and without any intervention in the exchange market by the central bank, there is no change in the official reserves and therefore choice (c) is not a feasible way of financing a budget deficit.

Examples from two specific countries should further clarify this discussion.

Example   12A.2

In reaction to the oil shocks in 1974 and 1980, West Germany averted a CA deficit (and a KA surplus, that is, foreign borrowing) by increasing netSav^G and by decreasing investment. More specifically, Germany reduced government spending and discouraged investment through a restrictive monetary policy. France, on the other hand, further increased its budget deficit, and followed a loose monetary policy, which decreased the interest rate and increased investment. These policies in France led to large CA deficits or KA surpluses (foreign borrowing), which ultimately forced France to revise its policies.

12A.3   Are Current Account Deficits Always Bad?

It should be clear from the discussion above that a CA surplus or deficit is neither good nor bad in and of itself; a CA deficit is good or bad relative to the circumstances that give rise to it.

If current foreign capital inflows are used to finance consumption rather than investment, then sooner or later, a country will have difficulty in repaying these loans. That is, international capital inflows that are used for investment purposes are quite different from those used for consumption. For example, if investment is more productive at home than abroad, that is, if the rate of return on investment is higher at home, then we should expect to see an inflow of foreign capital (KA > 0). Then, if ΔRFX = 0, it follows that a CA deficit will develop. However, this deficit is not necessarily bad if investments are made in "productive" projects such that money borrowed abroad can be repaid. Foreign capital is provided by thrifty countries like Japan or Germany that consume less than they earn and where, apparently, the returns on domestic investment are no longer high enough to absorb all savings locally.

Example   12A.3

Consider the changes in the CA and the changes in investment, as a proportion of GNP, for each of the following countries.

Country (1980s)	Change in CA / GNP	Change in Iexp / GNP
1. Norway	−6.6%	+5.5%
2. Belgium	−2.3%	+0.2%
3. Holland	+0.1%	−3.4%

We now consider the reason for the CA deficit in each country and examine whether the CA deficit is good or bad for the country. In Norway, the 5.5 percent figure indicates the large increase in investment as a percentage of GNP (in oil, most notably). Thus, the CA deficit in Norway is mainly due to this increase in investment and, therefore, the CA deficit is good news. In the case of Belgium, we see that the change in investments is quite small, and, therefore, the CA deficit is mainly due to an increase in government expenditures. Thus, in this case, the CA deficit is not good news. Finally, in the case of Holland, there is a sharp drop in the investment as a proportion of GNP. This drop in private investment can probably be explained by the fact that government expenditure increased to such an extent that it crowded out private investment. Given that the drop in private investment offset the increase in government expenditures, the net result on the CA is small.

13 PORTFOLIO THEORIES OF EXCHANGE RATE DETERMINATION

In Chapter 11, we examined the PPP hypothesis, which postulates that differences in inflation rates across two countries determine the exchange rate between them. We saw that the empirical support for this theory was quite weak. In Chapter 12, we considered the BOP theory of exchange rate determination. This theory extends the PPP model to include the effect of capital transactions on the exchange rate, but in a rather restrictive way. Specifically, the BOP theory assumes that portfolio decisions and capital flows depend only on the risk-free domestic and foreign interest rates. However, whether or not one buys foreign short-term bonds will depend not only on the foreign risk-free rate, but also on the expected capital gain or loss on the foreign currency, and on the extent that one can diversify the exchange risk. In addition, we know that portfolio decisions are also influenced by expected rates of return on assets other than the domestic and foreign risk-free bonds.

In this chapter, we extend the BOP analysis of the exchange rate to a more general asset demand framework. We examine the view that the exchange rate is determined by portfolio decisions of all investors. In such a setting, the equilibrium exchange rate is just one of the many prices that jointly determine the demand and supply for all assets in international financial markets. Thus, while the traditional theories of exchange rate determination focus on the demand for goods and services or short-term risk-free assets as the source from which demand for foreign exchange arises, under the portfolio theory, the demand for the exchange rate arises from the demand for all financial assets simultaneously.

This chapter is structured as follows. In the first section, we study the **monetary theory of exchange rate determination**, which is an early asset-pricing approach to exchange rate determination. According to this theory, the equilibrium exchange rate is one that equates the demand and supply of money in the domestic and foreign markets. We view this model as a useful way of summarizing the long-term determinants of exchange rates, or as a way to formulate long-run expected future spot rates. The limitation of this theory is that it attempts to price a single asset—foreign currency—in isolation from all other assets. However, portfolios of investors typically include assets other than money, and this has to be taken into account when determining the exchange rate. Thus, in the second section of this chapter, we introduce the assumptions of the mean-variance portfolio model and the mathematics required to calculate the expected return and variance of a portfolio of risky assets. In the third section, we derive the optimal portfolio weights and the equilibrium exchange rate in a simple portfolio choice model where investors can hold risky assets in addition to the home- and foreign-currency-denominated bonds. Our conclusions are presented in Section 13.4. A review of the calculation of the mean and variance of the return on a portfolio of risky assets with one risk-free asset is provided in the appendix.

13.1   MONETARY THEORY OF EXCHANGE RATE DETERMINATION

The asset approach—also called the monetary approach, since the asset we focus on is money—predicts that the spot rate behaves like any other speculative asset price: the value of the spot rate changes whenever relevant information is released. Because the arrival of new information is much more frequent than changes in relative goods prices, the asset approach can potentially explain the frequent changes in the exchange rate that one observes. In that respect, the asset approach overcomes a major limitation of the PPP approach. The monetary approach is also different from the (Keynesian) BOP approach because it does not assume that prices are sticky or that an economy is in a state of constant disequilibrium. That is, the monetary approach describes an economy that is in full-employment equilibrium, while the Keynesian approach may be a more accurate description of an economy with less than full employment of resources.

This section is divided into three parts. We present the monetary model of exchange rates in the first part, describe its implications in the second part, and outline the merits and shortcomings of this theory in the third part.

13.1.1   The Monetary Model

The monetary approach is based on the building blocks of the **Quantity Theory of Money (QTM)** and Purchasing Power Parity (PPP). The PPP relationship is explained in Chapter 11. We explain the QTM below.

The QTM is usually written as a money-demand equation. For the home country, for instance, the QTM states that the money supply must be equal to the money demand. The money demand, according to this theory, depends on the nominal transactions volume and the velocity of money (the number of times the money supply is turned over in a given period). We use the following notation to denote the variables relevant for the home country: P is the price level, Y the real output, L_d the money demand, L_s the money supply, and v is the velocity of the money. Then, we can write the condition for equilibrium in the money market; that is, money demand is equal to the supply of money, as:

$$L_s = L_d.$$

[1]

From the QTM, we also know that money demand, L_d, is proportional to the price level and income and inversely proportional to the velocity of money.[1] This can be expressed as:

$$L_d = \frac{PY}{v}.$$ [2]

We can combine Equations [1] and [2] and turn the result into a theory of the price level. To do this, we substitute Equation [2] in Equation [1], and rewrite the resulting equation with the price level on the right-hand side:

$$P = \frac{vL_s}{Y}.$$ [3]

One can derive a similar equation for a foreign country where the variables for the foreign country are denoted with an asterisk (*):

$$P* = \frac{v*L_s^*}{Y*}.$$ [4]

Finally, we can link the price equations for the two countries, in Equations [3] and [4], with the exchange rate, by way of the long-run equilibrium relation of PPP. Recall, from Chapter 11, the (Absolute) PPP relation:

$$S = \frac{P}{P*}.$$ [5]

Substituting Equations [3] and [4] for the prices into Equation [5], we find:

$$S = \frac{vL_s}{Y} \times \frac{Y*}{v*L_s^*} = \frac{v}{v*} \times \frac{Y*}{Y} \times \frac{L_s}{L_s^*}.$$ [6]

This equation describes the monetary model of exchange rates. Next, we discuss some of the implications of the monetary model and contrast them with the Keynesian view of exchange rate determination.

---

[1] Note that the velocity of money should be a *positive* function of the interest rate. That is, when the opportunity cost of holding money (rather than deposits or bonds) is high, more transactions are done with a given stock of money, or a given stock of money turns over faster. A key monetarist assumption is that, apart from interest rates, the velocity of money is primarily determined by the available technology. So, apart from interest-rate effects, the velocity of money is assumed to change slowly over time.

13.1.2 Implications of the Monetary Model

We now examine the implications of the monetary exchange rate model in Equation [6].

Relationship between the Exchange Rate and the Money Supply

Looking at Equation [6] for the exchange rate, we see that, holding all other variables fixed, the value of the foreign currency is positively related to the money supply in the home country and inversely related to the money supply in the foreign country. That is, from Equation [6], an increase in domestic money supply, L_S, leads to an increase in S, which is equivalent to an increase in the value of the foreign currency or, equivalently, a depreciation of the home currency. This should not come as a surprise. An increase in the supply of an asset should lead to a drop in its value.

The mechanism works as follows. An increase in the domestic money supply, L_S, leads to higher prices (see Equation [3]), and hence to an increase in S, that is, to a depreciation of the home currency. Equation [6] immediately shows the direct effect: increasing L_S means S must rise accordingly. There is also an indirect link: in the long run, more money leads to expected inflation, which increases interest rates and, hence, the velocity of money and the exchange rate, S.

In contrast to the monetarist view, Keynesians assume that commodity prices are constant (or sticky) and claim that an increase in the money supply stimulates *real* economic activity, Y, through its effect on overall spending and a decrease in the domestic interest rate, r. Thus, the result of a monetary expansion, according to the Keynesian BOP approach, would still be an increase in S, but through a different channel (as explained in Chapter 12). According to the Keynesian view, an increase in Y would lead to an increase in imports, while the decrease in the domestic interest rate would lead to capital outflows. Thus, the demand for the foreign currency would increase, implying that the home currency depreciates.

Relationship between the Exchange Rate and Real Activity

According to the monetary theory, an increase in expected real activity at home, Y, leads to a *decrease* in S, that is, an appreciation of the home currency. Thus, an increase in Y leads to an increase in the demand for real money; and, for a given nominal money stock and velocity, equilibrium in the money market can be achieved only by lowering prices of goods, which strengthens the home currency (a decrease in S).

This result is in direct contrast to the prediction of the Keynesian BOP approach, where an increase in Y is supposed to lead to an increase in imports and, therefore, a depreciation of the home currency. Monetarists argue that this Keynesian prediction (1) focuses on the current account and on interest rates and ignores the role of long-run expectations, and (2) assumes that the prices of goods are constant (which, at best, is true only in the short run).

Relationship between the Exchange Rate and Budget Deficits

Analyzing the effect of deficit spending on the exchange rate, monetarists claim that real activity is largely independent of monetary policy, especially in the long run. Thus, according to the monetarists, a budget deficit will not affect the long-run output, Y. Rather, it leads to either an increase in the interest rate (which increases velocity) or to money creation, both of which weaken the home currency (increase in S).

The Keynesians, on the other hand, view deficit spending as an economic stimulant. Thus, according to the Keynesian view, deficit spending would lead to an increase in Y and, therefore, an increase in imports, leading to a depreciation of the home currency (increase in S). Again, the effect of deficit spending is the same in the Keynesian and monetarist world, but the channels through which the exchange rate is affected are different.

13.1.3 Evaluation of the Monetary Theory of Exchange Rates

Evaluating the monetary theory of exchange rates, it is probably obvious that the exchange rate model described by Equation [6] holds, at best, only in the long run. There are at least a couple of reasons for the failure of the monetary theory in the short run. One, changes in the money supply are not incorporated into commodity prices instantly. That is, there is a lag between an increase in the money supply and the consequent increase in prices. Two, the PPP relationship, a relationship that is used to derive the exchange rate model in Equation [6], holds only in the long run, if at all.

Given the weak relationship between money supply and prices, and between prices and the exchange rate, the monetary model should be viewed as a theory that relates the long-term views on relative money supplies, economic activity, and the exchange rate. That is, Equation [6] tries to capture the important determinants of today's *long-run expectations* of the future exchange rate by expressing the long-term expected spot rate as a function of long-run expectations of money stocks, real activity, and velocity (which depends on interest rates). For instance, a change in today's money supply will not affect future exchange rates if the change is perceived to be completely transitory. More generally and more positively, Equation [6] says that in determining the exchange rate, we should take into account all information about long-run expected economic activity, the velocity of money, and money supply. Any new relevant information becomes quickly incorporated in expected exchange rates and changes current levels.

The major weakness of the monetary approach to exchange rate determination is precisely this last step—the details of the link between the expected future exchange rate and the current exchange rate. Many models assume certainty, which makes it possible to specify this link using only the risk-free interest rates. In a world of uncertainty, however, one cannot simply discount at the risk-free rate. Moreover, the required expected return on an investment in foreign currency depends on the expected returns and risks on all assets simultaneously and on the supplies of these assets. A related weakness of the monetary theory is that the demand for money is modeled as if cash were the only asset. In reality, the demand for money also depends on the expected returns on other assets. We now extend the monetary model to a setting where the equilibrium exchange rate is determined in the context of a portfolio problem where an investor has to choose among multiple assets. The model we use is the mean-variance model, where assets are analyzed as components of an optimally selected portfolio.

13.2 AN ASSET'S CONTRIBUTION TO PORTFOLIO MEAN AND VARIANCE

In this section, we introduce the assumptions of the mean-variance model and derive some basic results on the expected return and variance of the return of a portfolio of assets. If you are familiar with this material, you may want to skip to Section 13.3.

13.2.1 Assumptions of the Mean-Variance Model

The assumptions that we make to derive the optimal portfolios of investors are the following:

- In choosing their portfolio, investors care only about the expected real return and the variance of the real return of their portfolios.
- There is no inflation.
- Markets are perfect: there are no information costs or transaction costs, and taxes do not discriminate between capital gains and dividend or interest income.

13.2.2   The Expected Return on a Portfolio

To keep the analysis simple, we will assume that the investor has to choose between only three assets: a risk-free asset (denoted asset 0—for instance, a one-period bond) and two risky assets. The first risky asset, asset 1, is a stock (shares in a representative firm). The second risky asset, asset 2, is a foreign one-period bond, offering a return that is risk-free in terms of the foreign currency. The foreign bond is issued at par (that is, the issue price of the foreign bond is one unit of the foreign currency).[2] To the domestic investor, the return on this foreign bond is risky because the payoff depends on the exchange rate at the end of the period, which is uncertain. In home currency terms, the (rate of) return on the risk-free asset is denoted by r_0, and the returns on the risky assets by $\tilde{r}_1$ and $\tilde{r}_2$. Note that the tilde (~) is used to denote that a return is risky.

Let x_j denote the portfolio weight of asset j, that is, the proportion of an investor's total wealth invested in asset j. Then the (rate of) return on a portfolio consisting of assets 0, 1 and 2, denoted $\tilde{r}_p$, is given by:

$$\tilde{r}_p = x_0 r_0 + x_1 \tilde{r}_1 + x_2 \tilde{r}_2. \tag{7}$$

Given that this return on the portfolio is risky, we can calculate its expected value, the expected return:

$$E(\tilde{r}_p) = E(x_0 r_0 + x_1 \tilde{r}_1 + x_2 \tilde{r}_2)$$
$$= x_0 r_0 + x_1 E(\tilde{r}_1) + x_2 E(\tilde{r}_2). \tag{8}$$

The last line uses the property that the expectation of a sum is the sum of the expectations. Also, we have used the fact that, since the initial weights are known (not random), they can be taken out of the expectations operator. Equation [8] then says that the expected portfolio return is the weighted average of the component assets' expected returns. In this sense, the contribution of an asset, per unit of weight x_j, to the portfolio's expected return is simply the asset's own expected return.

We can also introduce the concept of expected *excess* return of an asset j over and above the risk-free rate. This excess return is given by $E(\tilde{r}_j - r_0)$. To rewrite Equation [8] in terms of the expected excess returns, note that the portfolio weights sum to one; that is, $x_0 + x_1 + x_2 = 1$. This implies that we can substitute $x_0 = 1 - x_1 - x_2$ in Equation [8]. Making this substitution, we can rewrite Equation [8] as follows:

$$E(\tilde{r}_p) = (1 - x_1 - x_2) r_0 + x_1 E(\tilde{r}_1) + x_2 E(\tilde{r}_2)$$
$$= r_0 + x_1 E(\tilde{r}_1 - r_0) + x_2 E(\tilde{r}_2 - r_0).$$

Subtracting r_0 from both sides of the equation, we obtain:

$$E(\tilde{r}_p) - r_0 = x_1 E(\tilde{r}_1 - r_0) + x_2 E(\tilde{r}_2 - r_0). \tag{9}$$

---

[2] The domestic risk-free asset and the foreign bonds that we consider are "outside" bonds; that is, they do not arise as a result of lending and borrowing between investors. A typical example of outside bonds are the bonds issued by governments.

Thus, the expected *excess* return on the portfolio equals the weighted average of the risky assets' expected excess returns.[3] In that sense, the contribution of each risky asset to the portfolio's expected excess return is the asset's own expected excess return.

Example 13.1

Suppose that we are given the following information about the one-period asset returns. The excess return on asset 1 is 0.150 *p.a.* and on asset 2 is 0.045 *p.a.* If the portfolio weights are given by x_1 = 0.70, x_2 = 0.20, and the investment in the risk-free asset is $1 - x_1 - x_2 = 1 - 0.70 - 0.20 = 0.10$, the expected excess return on this portfolio is:

$$E(\tilde{r}_p) - r_0 = (0.70 \times 0.150) + (0.20 \times 0.045)$$

$$= 0.114.$$

13.2.3   The Variance of the Return on a Portfolio

The risk of a portfolio is given by the standard deviation of the return of the portfolio. (The standard deviation is simply the square root of the variance.) We will show that the contribution of each asset in the portfolio to the variance of the total portfolio is the covariance of the return on this asset with the return on the portfolio. To demonstrate this, we rewrite the variance of the portfolio as follows:

$$\text{var}(\tilde{r}_p) = \text{cov}(\tilde{r}_p, \tilde{r}_p)$$

$$= \text{cov}(x_0 r_0 + x_1 \tilde{r}_1 + x_2 \tilde{r}_2, \tilde{r}_p)$$

$$= x_0 \, \text{cov}(r_0, \tilde{r}_p) + x_1 \, \text{cov}(\tilde{r}_1, \tilde{r}_p) + x_2 \, \text{cov}(\tilde{r}_2, \tilde{r}_p)$$

$$= x_1 \, \text{cov}(\tilde{r}_1, \tilde{r}_p) + x_2 \, \text{cov}(\tilde{r}_2, \tilde{r}_p). \qquad [10]$$

The first line says that the variance of a return is the covariance of this return with itself. The second line is obtained by simply filling in the definition of $\tilde{r}_p$ from Equation [7]. The third line is obtained by applying the property that the covariance between $\tilde{r}_p$ and a sum, $x_0 r_0 + x_1 \tilde{r}_1 + x_2 \tilde{r}_2$, is equal to the sum of the covariances of $\tilde{r}_p$ with each term in the sum. We also use the fact that the initial weights are known to take them outside the covariance operator. The last line follows from the fact that the covariance between the risk-free return and $\tilde{r}_p$ is zero. In words, the result in Equation [10] states that the portfolio variance is the weighted average of the component (risky)

---

[3] The above transformation relied on the fact that the sum of the portfolio weights is unity (the so-called "portfolio constraint"). The advantage of this transformation is that since this constraint is already incorporated into Equation [9], we do not have to consider it again when finding the optimal portfolio weights.

assets' covariances with the portfolio return. In this sense, the contribution of an asset, per unit of weight x_j, to the portfolio's risk is reflected in the asset's covariance with the portfolio return.[4]

We now show how one can compute the covariance of an individual asset's return with the return of a portfolio explicitly in terms of the portfolio weights:

$$\text{cov}(\tilde{r}_1, \tilde{r}_p) = \text{cov}(\tilde{r}_1, x_0 r_0 + x_1 \tilde{r}_1 + x_2 \tilde{r}_2)$$

$$= \text{cov}(\tilde{r}_1, x_1 \tilde{r}_1) + \text{cov}(\tilde{r}_1, x_2 \tilde{r}_2)$$

$$= x_1 \text{var}(\tilde{r}_1) + x_2 \text{cov}(\tilde{r}_1, \tilde{r}_2). \qquad [11]$$

Similarly,

$$\text{cov}(\tilde{r}_2, \tilde{r}_p) = x_2 \text{var}(\tilde{r}_2) + x_1 \text{cov}(\tilde{r}_1, \tilde{r}_2). \qquad [12]$$

Example 13.2

Suppose that the variance of asset 1 is 0.04 and that of asset 2 is 0.01, while the covariance between these two assets is 0.01. If the portfolio weights are given by $x_1 = 0.70$ and $x_2 = 0.20$, then find $\text{cov}(\tilde{r}_1, \tilde{r}_p)$, $\text{cov}(\tilde{r}_2, \tilde{r}_p)$, and the risk of the portfolio, which is measured by the standard deviation (*sd*) of the return of the portfolio.

For asset 1,

$$\text{cov}(\tilde{r}_1, \tilde{r}_p) = x_1 \text{var}(\tilde{r}_1) + x_2 \text{cov}(\tilde{r}_1, \tilde{r}_2)$$

$$= (0.70 \times 0.04) + (0.20 \times 0.01)$$

$$= 0.030.$$

Similarly,

$$\text{cov}(\tilde{r}_2, \tilde{r}_p) = 0.009.$$

Finally,

$$\text{var}(\tilde{r}_p) = x_1 \text{cov}(\tilde{r}_1, \tilde{r}_p) + x_2 \text{cov}(\tilde{r}_2, \tilde{r}_p)$$

$$= (0.70 \times 0.030) + (0.20 \times 0.009)$$

$$= 0.0228.$$

---

[4] One can show, by differentiating the expression in Equation [8], that $\partial E(\tilde{r}_p)/\partial x_j = E(\tilde{r}_j)$. It can also be shown that $\partial \text{var}(\tilde{r}_p)/\partial x_j = 2 \text{cov}(\tilde{r}_j, \tilde{r}_p)$. To show this, one needs to differentiate Equation [10] and keep in mind the definition of $\tilde{r}_p$ in Equation [7].

Thus,

$$\text{Risk of the portfolio} = sd(\tilde{r}_p)$$

$$= \sqrt{\text{var}(\tilde{r}_p)}$$

$$= 0.1510.$$

13.3   MEAN-VARIANCE PORTFOLIO CHOICE

In this section, we show how an investor's optimal portfolio is determined, as the investor trades off the return from an asset against its risk. Using graphs, we explain the choice of the optimal portfolio. Then we show how one can obtain the exact portfolio weights analytically. We conclude this section with a numerical example and a discussion of the implications of the portfolio theory of exchange rates. Note that to keep the exposition easy, we have assumed for now that there are no deviations from PPP and that international capital markets are not segmented.[5] The implications of real exchange risk and the imperfect integration of capital markets are discussed in Chapter 22.

13.3.1   Descriptive Explanation of Equilibrium in World Capital Markets

In Figure 13.1, we plot the expected returns of the two risky assets as a function of their risk, which is measured by the standard deviation of each return. The curve going through the points E_1 and E_2, shows the risk-return combinations that one can attain by holding different combinations of just the two risky assets. This curve is known as the *efficiency frontier*, for it shows the portfolios that have the maximum return for a given level of risk (standard deviation). Note that any portfolio that lies *below* the curve connecting the points E_1 and E_2 is inefficient: for the same level of risk, such a portfolio offers a lower return than that offered by portfolios *on* the curve. Portfolios *above* (to the left of) the efficiency curve, however, cannot be attained given the menu of risky assets that is available.

In drawing this graph, we assume that the two assets are not perfectly correlated. It can be shown that this implies that the graph connecting the two assets is curved. This curvature is often interpreted as the diversification gains from holding both risky assets.

While the efficiency frontier shows the risk-return combinations that one can attain by holding different combinations of just the two risky assets, we can also derive the weights of assets 1 and 2 in any given efficient portfolio. For example, in Figure 13.1, the risk-return combination given by the point E_1 corresponds to a 100 percent investment in asset 1 and zero in asset 2. Similarly, the risk-return combination implied by E_2 corresponds to a portfolio with 100 percent investment in asset 2 and none in asset 1. Finally, the point E_3 corresponds to a 50 percent investment in asset 1 and a 50 percent investment in asset 2. Note that as we move along the curve, away from E_1 and towards E_2, the investment in asset 1 declines and that in asset 2 increases. In Figure 13.1, we illustrate the determination of the portfolio composition by showing an additional axis, labeled x_1, which is parallel to the expected return axis. To see what the composition of a particular efficient portfolio is, we simply go from the portfolio's expected

---

[5] Capital markets are said to be segmented, either when there are capital controls that prevent domestic residents from holding foreign assets, or when there are restrictions on the amount of domestic assets that can be held by foreign investors.

FIGURE 13.1   **Risk and Return of a Portfolio of Two Risky Assets**

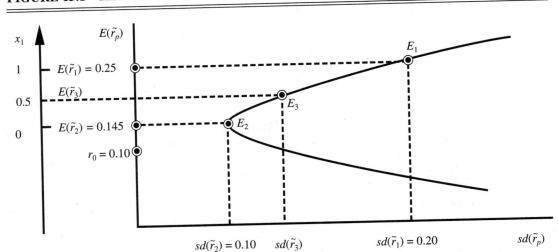

By changing the selected portfolio expected return, the investor also changes the portfolio's standard deviation. The relationship is nonlinear. The weight of asset one, x_1, can be read off from the x-axis drawn parallel to the $E(\tilde{r}_p)$-axis. For instance, to obtain the combination $[sd(\tilde{r}_3), E(\tilde{r}_3)]$, x_1 has to be set at 0.50.

return to the x_1-axis, and read off how we should select x_1 in order to achieve the selected risk/return combination.

Now we wish to find the best (most efficient) risk-return combinations that are available to an investor when the investor can hold the risk-free asset in addition to the two risky assets. This is shown in Figure 13.2. A familiar result in portfolio theory is that the expected returns and risks of portfolios consisting of the risk-free asset with return r_0, and of a selected risky portfolio, E, are found on a line originating from r_0 and going through E. If you are not familiar with this result, you should read the appendix to this chapter.

By changing our choice of the point E, the line of attainable risk-return profiles rotates upwards or downwards. Of course, a risk-averse investor would always prefer a line that slopes upwards as much as possible since portfolios on this line provide the highest possible return for a given level of risk. The best combinations of risk and return available to any investor are given by the straight line r_0T that originates from r_0 and is tangential to the curve E_1E_2. The portfolios on the line tangential to the curve E_1E_2 are optimal because: (1) we cannot attain portfolios on a steeper line (these are not feasible given the menu of assets available), and (2) any portfolio on a line that is flatter than the tangency line would be dominated by the portfolios on the line of tangency (portfolios on the tangency line would have a higher expected return for the same degree of risk).

When an investor can choose between risk-free and risky assets, the optimal portfolio must lie on the tangency line through r_0 and T. That is, any efficient portfolio can be designed by simply holding different proportions of the risk-free asset and the tangency portfolio T. This also means that the risky component of any investor's portfolio is the tangency portfolio T. Note that just as we inferred the composition of the risky portfolios corresponding to the points E_1 and E_2, we can similarly infer the composition of the tangency portfolio x_T.

FIGURE 13.2   Portfolios of Two Risky Assets and Risk-Free Assets

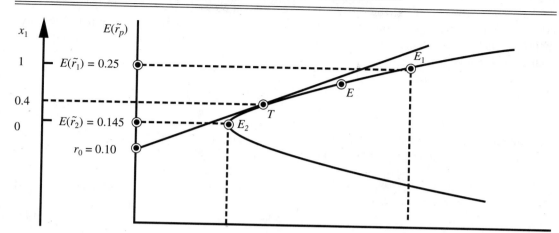

If the investor combines the risky portfolio E with risk-free assets, all attainable risk-return combinations are on the line $r_0 E$. The "best" risky portfolio is T: it offers the risk-return combinations on the line $r_0 T$. The weight of the first asset, x_1, in T can be read off from the x_1-axis drawn parallel to the $E(\tilde{r}_p)$-axis. In this figure, T consists of $x_1 = 0.40$ invested in the first risky asset, and $1 - x_1 = 0.60$ invested in the second risky asset.

Summarizing the above discussion, we note the following:

- If an investor has to choose a portfolio consisting only of risky assets, then the (minimum variance) frontier will be a hyperbola, as shown in Figure 13.1. The efficient frontier in this case is the top half of the hyperbola, as given by $E_1 E_2$.
- If the investor can invest in a risk-free asset in addition to the risky assets, then the efficient frontier for this investor is a straight line. The intercept of this straight line, r_0, as shown in Figure 13.2, is the risk-free rate, and this line is tangential to the frontier $E_1 E_2$.
- Given that in the presence of the risk-free asset the efficient frontier is a straight line, any portfolio on this straight line can be obtained by holding just two assets. In particular, any portfolio on this efficient frontier can be obtained by holding just the risk-free asset and the tangency portfolio.

13.3.2   Analytical Derivation of Optimal Portfolio Weights

We now derive the optimal portfolio weights, the equilibrium asset prices, and the equilibrium exchange rate analytically. The reasoning underlying this derivation is the same as that provided in the graphical description in the previous section.

As shown in Equations [9] and [10], each asset contributes its own expected excess return to the portfolio's expected excess return (we consider the return a "good"), and its own portfolio covariance risk to the total variance of the portfolio (we consider the covariance a "bad").

The problem of optimal portfolio choice is similar to a problem of choosing optimal consumption in microeconomics. In a budget-allocation problem, each additional unit of a commodity has its good side (marginal utility) and its bad side (the price you have to pay); and an allocation is optimal if the ratio of marginal utility to price is the same across all goods.[6] In our portfolio problem, the "good" is the asset's contribution to the expected excess portfolio return, and the "bad" is the asset's contribution to the portfolio variance. Thus, in an optimal portfolio, the ratio of marginal "good" and marginal "bad" must be equal across all assets. Let us denote the common ratio by θ; then the optimality condition is:

$$\frac{E(\tilde{r}_1 - r_0)}{\text{cov}(\tilde{r}_1, \tilde{r}_p)} = \frac{E(\tilde{r}_2 - r_0)}{\text{cov}(\tilde{r}_2, \tilde{r}_p)} = \theta. \qquad [13]$$

The common return/risk ratio, θ, reflects the investor's attitude towards risk, and is called the investor's measure of *relative risk aversion*. We can rewrite Equation [13] as:

$$E(\tilde{r}_1 - r_0) = \theta \, \text{cov}(\tilde{r}_1, \tilde{r}_p). \qquad [14a]$$

$$E(\tilde{r}_2 - r_0) = \theta \, \text{cov}(\tilde{r}_2, \tilde{r}_p). \qquad [14b]$$

For any portfolio to be optimal, the portfolio weights must satisfy Equations [14a] and [14b]. If, for instance, the ratio (expected excess return)/(covariance risk) for asset 1 were higher than that for asset 2, then asset 1 would be relatively more attractive to the investor; that is, asset 1 provides more marginal "good" per unit of marginal "bad" than asset 2. The investor would therefore increase asset 1's weight in the portfolio. However, this change in the weights would affect the asset's contribution to the portfolio's total risk. Thus, equilibrium is reached once the investor stops changing the portfolio weights, which happens only when the marginal return/risk ratio is the same for all assets and equals θ. The condition of Equation [14], in fact, is equivalent to the requirement that the optimal portfolio lie on the line through r_0 and T, which is tangential to the efficiency frontier.

Now that we have the optimality condition in Equation [14], we only need to know how to use this condition to infer the optimal portfolio weights and the exchange rate. Note that in Equation [14] we have two equations—one for asset 1 and another for asset 2. The optimal weights, x_1 and x_2, can be obtained by simultaneously solving these two linear equations. To solve these equations, we need to express $\text{cov}(\tilde{r}_1, \tilde{r}_p)$ and $\text{cov}(\tilde{r}_2, \tilde{r}_p)$ explicitly in terms of the portfolio weights x_1 and x_2, as done in

---

[6] Consider the problem of choosing the optimal consumption of goods x and y, given a budget B. Then the consumer's problem is to $\text{Max}_{x,y} \, U(x,y)$ subject to the budget constraint that $x \, p_x + y \, p_y = B$. By substituting for y from the budget constraint $y = (B - x \, p_x)/p_y$ we can avoid having to explicitly consider the budget constraint, just as we did in the portfolio problem. Thus, the problem now is to choose x to maximize $U(x, (B - x \, p_x)/p_y)$. The first order condition for this optimization problem is to set

$$0 = \frac{dU}{dx}, \text{ where } \frac{dU}{dx} = \frac{\partial U}{\partial x} + \frac{\partial U}{\partial y} \frac{dy}{dx} = \frac{\partial U}{\partial x} + \frac{\partial U}{\partial y} \left(-\frac{p_x}{p_y} \right).$$

This reduces to the condition that

$$\frac{\partial U / \partial x}{p_x} = \frac{\partial U / \partial y}{p_y}.$$

In words: the ratio of marginal "good" over marginal "bad" is the same across all commodities.

Equations [11] and [12]. Substituting Equations [11] and [12] into Equation [14], we get the following two equations in terms of the optimal portfolio weights, x_1 and x_2:

$$E(\tilde{r}_1 - r_0) = \theta\left[x_1 \text{ var}(\tilde{r}_1) + x_2 \text{ cov}(\tilde{r}_1, \tilde{r}_2)\right], \qquad [15a]$$

$$E(\tilde{r}_2 - r_0) = \theta\left[x_2 \text{ var}(\tilde{r}_2) + x_1 \text{ cov}(\tilde{r}_1, \tilde{r}_2)\right]. \qquad [15b]$$

Solving Equations [15a] and [15b], we get the solution for the optimal portfolio weights, x_1 and x_2.[7] We now look at a numerical example to see how one can compute the optimal portfolio of an investor.

Example 13.2

Suppose that we are given the following information about the one-period asset returns: the expected excess return on asset 1 is 0.150 *p.a.* and on asset 2 is 0.045 *p.a.* The variance of asset 1 is 0.04 and that of asset 2 is 0.01, while the covariance between these two assets is 0.01. The degree of our risk aversion is 5. To find the optimal portfolio with a risk aversion θ equal to 5, we plug the information that we have into Equations [15a] and [15b]:

$$0.150 = 5\left[(0.04)\, x_1 + 0.01\, x_2\right]$$

$$0.045 = 5\left[(0.01)\, x_2 + 0.01\, x_1\right].$$

Solving the above equations for x_1 and x_2, we get $x_1 = 0.70$, $x_2 = 0.20$, and the investment in the risk-free asset is $1 - x_1 - x_2 = 1 - 0.70 - 0.20 = 0.10$. Thus, the composition of the portfolio T that contains only risky assets can be obtained by computing the relative weights of asset 1 and asset 2: the weight of asset 1 in portfolio T is $0.7/(0.7 + 0.2) = 0.78$, and that of asset 1 in portfolio T is $0.2/(0.7 + 0.2) = 0.22$.

13.3.3 Equilibrium in the World Capital Markets

We have seen how the optimal portfolio *weights* for a particular investor are derived. To obtain the *amount* of each asset demanded by the investor, we multiply the optimal portfolio weight by the investor's wealth.

Example 13.3

In Example 13.2, the portfolio weight for asset 1 is 70 percent. If the investor's wealth is USD 10m, then this investor will demand $0.70 \times$ USD 10m = USD 7m of this asset. Similarly, the demand for asset 0 is $0.10 \times$ USD 10m = USD 1m, and the demand for asset 2 is 20 percent of USD 10m, or USD 2m.

---

[7] The analytical solution to these equations is the following:

$$x_1 = \frac{(E[\tilde{r}_1] - r_0)\,\text{var}(\tilde{r}_2) - (E[\tilde{r}_2] - r_0)\,\text{cov}(\tilde{r}_1, \tilde{r}_2)}{\theta\left[\text{var}(\tilde{r}_1)\text{var}(\tilde{r}_2) - (\text{cov}(\tilde{r}_1, \tilde{r}_2))^2\right]} \quad \text{and} \quad x_2 = \frac{(E[\tilde{r}_2] - r_0)\,\text{var}(\tilde{r}_1) - (E[\tilde{r}_1] - r_0)\,\text{cov}(\tilde{r}_1, \tilde{r}_2)}{\theta\left[\text{var}(\tilde{r}_1)\text{var}(\tilde{r}_2) - (\text{cov}(\tilde{r}_1, \tilde{r}_2))^2\right]}.$$

To find the equilibrium prices and the exchange rate that prevail in the economy, we proceed in two steps. First, we find the asset demands for each investor. Second, to obtain the *aggregate* demand for a particular asset, we sum the individual demands for that particular asset across all investors. The equilibrium price of each asset is the price that makes the aggregate demand for the asset equal to its total supply.

Let us make the simplifying assumptions that all investors worldwide are identical and, hence, that all investors would like to hold the same portfolio. Also assume that the total wealth worldwide is W. Then, just as in the example above, we know that the amount invested in asset 0 is $(x_0 \times W)$, in asset 1 is $(x_1 \times W)$, and in asset 2 is $(x_2 \times W)$. Recall that the second risky asset, asset 2, is a foreign unit bond issued at par. Suppose that the number of foreign unit bonds is B^*. Then, the equilibrium exchange rate is one that makes the demand for this bond equal to its supply: $x_2 \times W = S \times B^*$, which implies that the equal exchange rate is one for which $S = (x_2 \times W)/B^*$.

Example 13.4

We continue with the example considered above, where we calculated the optimal portfolio: 10 percent of wealth is invested in asset 0, 70 percent in asset 1, and 20 percent in asset 2. We also assume that all investors are identical and that the total portfolio wealth across all investors, W, is USD 100 billion. Assume that the supply of the domestic risk-free asset is 2 billion units, while the supply of stock is 1 billion shares and the number of foreign unit bonds outstanding is 4 billion.

The amount of wealth invested in the domestic bond (asset 0) is $0.10 \times$ USD 100b = USD 10b, so that the price of each unit of the domestic risk-free asset must be USD 10b/2b = USD 5. Similarly, the amount invested in equity is $0.70 \times$ USD 100b = USD 70b; thus, the share price must be USD 70b/1b = USD 70. Finally, the amount invested in the foreign country is $0.20 \times$ USD 100b = USD 20b; thus, the exchange rate is USD 20b/4b = USD 5 per unit of foreign currency.

13.3.4 Applying the Portfolio Theory of Exchange Rates

From the discussion in the previous section, it is clear that if the supply of one of the assets changes, all of the equilibrium prices will change. For instance, if more stock in the domestic firm is issued, the portfolio weights (and the expected returns and risks that determine these weights) have to change. A change in the portfolio weights will lead to a change in the demand for the foreign bond and will, therefore, affect the exchange rate. For instance, if the additional supply of shares leads to a decrease in the demand for the foreign asset, there will be a depreciation in the foreign currency. We now consider a few examples of how portfolio adjustments that follow shocks will affect equilibrium prices.

Example 13.5

Assume that there is an expansion in the number of domestic bonds (asset 0). For simplicity, assume that the supply of these bonds doubles. Then, at the prices prevailing before this bond issue, the amount of bonds in the typical investor's portfolio is too large, while the quantity of other assets held, the foreign bond and the risky equity, is too low. In the process of rebalancing their portfolios, investors will wish to get rid of the excess domestic bonds, and increase their holdings of the risky equity and the foreign bond. This implies that the domestic bond prices must fall while the price of the foreign bond must increase. A drop in the domestic bond prices implies an increase in the domestic interest rate. An increase in the price of foreign bonds implies that the exchange rate must appreciate and/or the foreign interest rate must drop.

Now let us consider the effect of an increase in the supply of foreign bonds.

Example 13.6

Assume that to finance the German reunification, there is an increase in the supply of foreign (German) bonds. Now investors hold too many foreign assets. In an attempt to rebalance their portfolios by selling foreign bonds, investors will depress the value of the DEM and possibly also bond prices in DEM.

Lastly, we consider an increase in the value of domestic equity.

Example 13.7

Assume that there is an increase in the value of Dutch (domestic) equity due to an exogenous event (say, the discovery of natural gas in Groningen). The average Dutch investor is better off because this discovery leads to an increase in wealth. However, the investor now holds too many domestic assets. The resulting partial substitution of foreign assets for Dutch assets weakens the spot value of the NLG, increases Dutch interest rates, and may also decrease foreign interest rates.

From the portfolio theory of exchange rates, we see that the adjustment to a change in the supply or demand of any asset affects the whole portfolio, and results in a change in both the domestic and foreign interest rates and the spot exchange rate.

13.3.5 Comparing the Portfolio Theory with the Monetary Theory of Exchange Rates

Now that we have specified the **portfolio theory of exchange rates**, note the differences between this model and the other approaches to exchange rate determination.

- In contrast to the more primitive *Keynesian and monetary model*, demand for foreign assets now depends not only on r and r^*, but also on the expected change in the exchange rate, $E_t(\tilde{S}_T)/S_t$, since this affects the risk and return from holding foreign assets.
- Again in contrast to the *monetary model*, the current account plays a direct role in this model. The link is as follows. A current account surplus means that the investors in the country with the surplus accumulate foreign assets. This implies that the wealth, W, of these investors has increased, and that these investors own a larger share of foreign assets. As we have seen, these changes affect the spot exchange rate and the interest rates.

- In contrast to the *PPP model*, which emphasizes the role of the current account items in the BOP, the focus of the portfolio model is on transactions in the capital account—adjustments in holdings of the relative amounts of domestic and foreign assets.

13.4 CONCLUSION

In this chapter, we have seen how portfolio decisions of investors determine the exchange rate. In our discussion of this model, we assumed that PPP holds and that international capital markets are not segmented. It can be shown that the exchange rate is determined in a similar fashion even when there are deviations from PPP or when markets are, to some extent, segmented.

The portfolio theory of exchange rates extends the monetary approach to include domestic and foreign bonds that investors may wish to hold in their portfolios. In contrast to the monetary model, where it is assumed that the exchange rate can be priced without reference to assets other than money, the portfolio theory explicitly analyzes the effect of the portfolio decisions that individuals make in choosing to hold domestic and foreign interest-bearing claims.

The portfolio approach also shows that the equilibrium exchange rate depends on the expected return and risk from holding financial assets. Thus, any news about the returns of financial assets will lead to a rebalancing of investors' portfolios and, therefore, will affect the exchange rate. Since information about assets returns arrives frequently, this theory predicts that the spot rate will also change often, as observed empirically.

An important insight from the above discussion of the portfolio theory is the role of expectations in determining the exchange rate. We saw that, in the mean-variance portfolio model, expectations about future returns affect the optimal portfolio of an investor and, hence, the exchange rate. In the next chapter, we will study how expectations of the future spot rate are related to the forward exchange rate and to the current exchange rate.

QUIZ QUESTIONS

Read each phrase below and decide whether it corresponds with *Balance of Payments Theory*, *Monetary Theory*, or *Portfolio Theory*.

1. The long-run equilibrium exchange rate follows from the equilibrium in the markets for the demand and supply of domestic money and foreign money and the PPP model.
2. All else being equal, any real economic activity in the home country results in an appreciation of the home currency.
3. The spot rate is affected by the release of new information.
4. To determine the equilibrium exchange rate, it suffices to know the supply and demand for domestic and foreign goods.
5. All else being equal, an increase in the expected return on a risk-free foreign asset leads to a depreciation of the home currency.
6. A monetary expansion weakens the value of the home currency, but has little or no effect on real activity.
7. All else being equal, an increase in real economic activity in the home country results in a depreciation of the home currency.
8. The equilibrium exchange rate is the one that equates the demand and supply of domestic and foreign risk-free and risky assets.
9. If there is a domestic capital account surplus, foreign investors are purchasing more of the country's assets. This leads to a depreciation of the domestic currency.
10. Excessive government spending financed by a monetary expansion stimulates an economy, resulting in greater real output and a depreciation of the home currency.

True-False Questions

1. The risk of a portfolio is measured by the standard deviation of its return.
2. The risk of an asset is measured by the standard deviation of its return.
3. Each asset's contribution to the total risk of a portfolio is measured by the asset's contribution to the total return on the portfolio.
4. A risk-averse investor always prefers the highest possible return for a given level of risk or the lowest risk for a given level of expected return.
5. The means and standard deviations of all optimal portfolios selected from a risk-free asset and a set of risky assets are found on the line that originates at r_0 and is tangent to the efficient portfolio of risky assets.
6. Relative risk aversion shows the price in currency units of a given amount of risk.
7. Relative risk aversion varies from asset to asset because some assets are riskier than others.
8. Portfolio theory assumes that all investors are equally risk averse.

Multiple-Choice Questions

1. According to Monetary Theory, which of the following events lead to an appreciation of the foreign currency?

   (a) An increase in the velocity of domestic money.
   (b) An increase in real foreign economic output.
   (c) An increase in the foreign money supply.
   (d) An increase in real domestic economic output.
   (e) An increase in the velocity of foreign money.

2. When using portfolio theory, we must make a number of assumptions. Which of the following assumptions are made? Which are not?

(a) The rates of inflation at home and abroad are equal.

(b) There are no information or transactions costs.

(c) There are no taxes.

(d) Investors want to know the distribution of wealth at the end of the period.

(e) Investors care about the future expected return on their portfolio and the variability of this return.

EXERCISES

1. In Country X, the money supply equals 1 million, real economic output equals 1 million units, and the velocity of money equals 5. In Country Y, the money supply equals 5 million, real economic output equals 10 million units, and the velocity of money equals 3. According to monetary theory, if X is the home country, what is the long-run equilibrium spot exchange rate?

2. The Country Prince Rupert's Land (PRL) has two companies, Hudson Bay Company (HBC) and Boston Tea Traders (BTT). In equilibrium, the returns of these two companies have the following distributions:

	Expected excess return	Covariances HBC	BTT
HBC	0.11	0.04	0.01
BTT	0.08	0.01	0.02

(a) Vary the weight of HBC from 0 to 1 by increments of 0.1, and compute how the portfolio covariance risks of HBC and BTT change as a function of the weights x_{HBC} and $x_{BTT} = 1 - x_{HBC}$.

(b) Find the optimal weights of x_{HBC} and $x_{BTT} = 1 - x_{HBC}$ and the average risk aversion.

(c) If the total value of the PRL stock market portfolio is 1,000, what is the value of HBC and BTT?

3. Consider the following covariance matrix and expected return vector for assets 1, 2, and 3:

$$V = \begin{vmatrix} 0.0100 & 0.0020 & 0.0010 \\ 0.0020 & 0.0025 & 0.0030 \\ 0.0010 & 0.0030 & 0.0100 \end{vmatrix} \qquad E(R_j) = \begin{vmatrix} 0.0330 \\ 0.0195 \\ 0.0250 \end{vmatrix}$$

(a) Compute the expected return on a portfolio with weights for assets $j = 0, \ldots, 3$ equal to [0.2, 0.4, 0.2, 0.2], when the T-bill (asset 0) yields a return of 1 percent. Do so directly, and then via the excess returns.

(b) Compute the variance of the same portfolio.

(c) Compute the covariance of the return on each asset with the total portfolio return, and verify that it is a weighted covariance.

(d) Is the above portfolio efficient?

(e) Are the following portfolios efficient?
   • weights $(0.7, 0.1, 0.1, 0.1)$ for assets $j = 0, \ldots, 3$
   • weights $(0.6, 0.2, 0.1, 0.1)$ for assets $j = 0, \ldots, 3$

(f) What is the portfolio held by an investor with risk-aversion measure $\theta = 2.5$?

(g) Assume that there are no "outside" bills, that is, all risk-free lending and borrowing is among investors. Therefore the average investor holds only risky assets. What is the portfolio composition? What is the average investor's risk-aversion measure θ?

RETURN AND RISK OF A PORTFOLIO CONTAINING RISK-FREE ASSETS

A typical portfolio contains both risky and risk-free assets. Such a portfolio can always be viewed as a combination of (1) the risk-free asset and (2) a sub-portfolio of only risky assets.

Example 13A.1

Let an investor divide her wealth, 100 USD, as follows: 10 is invested in the domestic risk-free asset, 70 is invested in the stock (asset 1), and 20 in the foreign currency bond (asset 2). Thus, the asset weights are $x_0 = 0.1$, $x_1 = 0.7$, and $x_2 = 0.2$. The sub-portfolio of risky assets is worth 90 USD of which 70/90 = 78 percent is invested in stocks (asset 1), and 20/90 = 22 percent is invested in foreign currency bonds. Thus, 10 percent of the total portfolio is invested in the risk-free asset, and 90 percent is invested in the sub-portfolio of risky assets.

In this section, we demonstrate the relationship between risk and return for a portfolio decomposed this way into a risk-free component and a sub-portfolio of only risky assets. Specifically, we show that, if one varies the weight of the risky sub-portfolio in the overall asset holdings, there is a linear trade-off between the expected return and the standard deviation of the overall portfolio. To show this, we will denote the *entire* portfolio of the risk-free and risky assets as portfolio p. The overall portfolio p consists of a fraction x_0 invested in the risk-free asset with return r_0, and a fraction $1 - x_0$ invested in some sub-portfolio of risky assets T, with return $\tilde{r}_T$. For instance, in Example 13A.1, the proportion invested in the risk-free asset, x_0, is 0.1. We now wish to determine the return, the variance, and the standard deviation of this portfolio p.

13A.1 Expected Return on a Portfolio with Risky and Risk-Free Assets

The return on the portfolio, $\tilde{r}_p$, is the weighted return of the two components, just as in Equation [7]:

$$\tilde{r}_p = x_0 r_0 + (1 - x_0)\tilde{r}_T.$$

Thus, the expected excess return on portfolio p can be calculated, as in Equation [9]:

$$E(\tilde{r}_p - r_0) = (1 - x_0)\left[E(\tilde{r}_T) - r_0\right]. \tag{A1}$$

13A.2 Risk of a Portfolio with Risky and Risk-Free Assets

The variance of the return on this portfolio is:

$$\text{var}(\tilde{r}_p) = \text{cov}(\tilde{r}_p, \tilde{r}_p)$$

$$= \text{cov}\left[x_0 r_0 + (1 - x_0)\tilde{r}_T, x_0 r_0 + (1 - x_0)\tilde{r}_T\right]$$

$$= (1 - x_0)^2 \text{var}(\tilde{r}_T).$$

In the above derivation, the first equation follows from the definition that the variance of a return is simply the covariance of the return with itself. The second step results from substituting in the definition of $\tilde{r}_p$, and the final step uses the fact that the covariance of a return with the risk-free return is zero.

Finally, assuming that $1 - x_0$ is positive, the risk or the standard deviation (sd) of the return on this portfolio is:

$$sd(\tilde{r}_p) = \sqrt{\text{var}(\tilde{r}_p)}$$

$$= \sqrt{(1 - x_0)^2 \, \text{var}(\tilde{r}_T)} \qquad \text{[A2]}$$

$$= (1 - x_0)sd(\tilde{r}_T).$$

Equation [A2] implies that the proportion invested in the risky asset can be expressed as a ratio of the risk of the entire portfolio relative to the risk of the sub-portfolio containing only the risky assets.

$$(1 - x_0) = \frac{sd(\tilde{r}_p)}{sd(\tilde{r}_T)}. \qquad \text{[A3]}$$

13A.3   The Linear Relationship between Risk and Return

We are now ready to prove the linear trade-off between the risk and return of the portfolio p that we mentioned earlier. Suppose that the investor selects a particular level of risk (standard deviation) for his portfolio. Equation [A2] shows how to set the weight on the sub-portfolio of risky assets, $(1 - x_0)$, to achieve this level of risk for the portfolio as a whole.

To determine which expected excess return corresponds with a selected level of risk, we use Equation [A1]. We now need to show that the relation between the risk of this portfolio and its expected excess return is linear. To do this, we substitute the expression for $(1 - x_0)$ from Equation [A3] into Equation [A1], and we get the following:

$$E(\tilde{r}_p) - r_0 = sd(\tilde{r}_p)\frac{E(\tilde{r}_T) - r_0}{sd(\tilde{r}_T)}. \qquad \text{[A4]}$$

From Equation [A4], we can see that the expected excess return on portfolio p is linearly related to the risk of portfolio p, $sd(\tilde{r}_p)$. That is, for every unit increase in the $sd(\tilde{r}_p)$, the expected excess return of portfolio p increases by $[E(\tilde{r}_T) - r_0]/sd(\tilde{r}_T)$.

In Figure 13A.1, this linear relationship is shown by the line originating from point r_0, and going through point T. For instance, one feasible strategy is to invest everything in the risk-free asset; then, we clearly are at point r_0. Another strategy is to invest everything in the risky sub-portfolio, which would put us at point T. Equation [A4] then tells us that if we want a standard deviation that is two-thirds of the risky asset's standard deviation, we will also have an excess return that is two-thirds of the risky asset's expected excess return. Likewise, if we want a standard deviation that is one-fourth of the risky asset's standard deviation, we will also have an excess return that is one-fourth of the risky asset's expected excess return. Thus, each point on the line shows the expected return and risk of one particular combination of risk-free assets and the risky portfolio T.

FIGURE 13A.1 Portfolios of Risk-Free Assets and the Risky Asset T

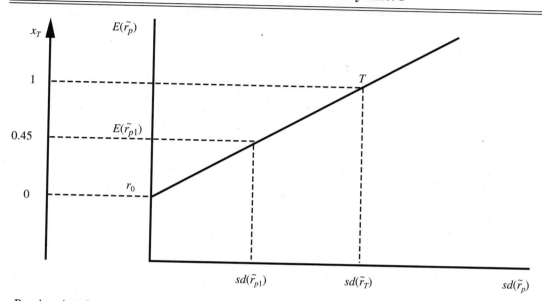

By changing the selected portfolio expected return, the investor also changes the portfolio's standard deviation. The relationship is linear. The weight of the risky component T, x_T, can be read off from the x-axis drawn parallel to the $E(\tilde{r}_p)$-axis. For instance, to obtain the combination $[sd(\tilde{r}_{p1}), E(\tilde{r}_{p1})]$, x_T has to be set at $x_T = 0.45$.

14 RISK AND RETURN IN FORWARD MARKETS

This chapter continues our study of the relationship between the spot exchange rate and other prices. In Chapter 11, on Purchasing Power Parity, we studied the relationship between commodity prices and the current spot rate and, in Chapters 12 and 13, we studied the relationship between various asset prices and the current spot rate. In this chapter, our focus is on the relationship between the price of a particular asset, a forward contract, and the *future* spot exchange rate. Our main objective is to see if the current forward rate contains information about the future spot rate; that is, can the current forward rate help predict the future spot rate. In the next chapter, Chapter 15, we examine other variables to see if they can be used to predict the exchange rate, or explain its current value. The evidence that we examine in this chapter and in the next leads us to conclude that the relationship between the forward and the spot rate is weak, and that it is difficult to predict the future spot rate or explain its current value using either macroeconomic variables or past exchange rates.

Recall, from Chapter 13, that foreign exchange can be viewed as just another financial asset. Thus, like other assets, the price of a foreign currency is affected by its expected return and its covariance with the return on the optimal portfolio that an investor chooses to hold. In this chapter, we examine the claim that the forward rate reflects the market's expectations of the future spot rate. In this view, a positive forward premium is said to correspond to an expected appreciation (that is, a "strong" currency), and a discount with an expected depreciation. We show, under certainty, that this is true by definition. However, in a world with uncertainty, the future spot rate is typically not equal to today's forward rate even if investors are risk-neutral or if all exchange risk is diversifiable.

This chapter is organized as follows. In the first section, we discuss the relationship between the forward rate and the expected future spot rate. In the second section, using regression analysis, we test the hypothesis that the expected future spot rate is equal to the current forward rate. The empirical evidence strongly rejects this hypothesis; that is, the forward rate is a biased predictor of the future spot rate. The rest of the chapter is devoted to understanding this rejection. In the third section, we examine whether or not the presence of risk premiums can explain the deviation between the forward rate and the future spot rate. In the fourth section, we examine whether or not the way in which investors form expectations about the future spot rate could explain why the expected future spot rate is not equal to the current forward rate. The test in the second section, of the relationship between the forward rate and the future spot rate, is in nominal terms. In the fifth section, we show the implications of formulating this test in real terms and we examine whether or not this real model can explain the forward bias. We conclude, in the sixth section, with a discussion of the implications of the forward bias for financial management.

14.1   THE UNBIASED EXPECTATIONS HYPOTHESIS (UEH)

In this section, we study the relationship between the current forward rate and the future spot rate. For simplicity, we begin by discussing this relationship when the future rate is certain. We then examine what this relationship should be when the future spot rate is uncertain. We conclude this section by studying the implications—of the hypothesized relation between the forward rate and the future spot rate—for the determination of the current spot rate.

14.1.1   The Certainty Case

Common sense dictates that, *under certainty*, $F_{t,t+1}$ must equal the future spot rate S_{t+1}. For example, if it is certain that the DEM will be worth BEF/DEM 22 six months from now, nobody will sell DEM forward for less than that, and nobody will buy forward for more than this amount.[1] In short,

$$F_{t,t+1} = S_{t+1},$$ [1]

in the absence of risk. There is a corollary to this relationship. From Interest Rate Parity (this relationship is discussed in Chapter 2), we know that

$$F_{t,t+1} = S_t \frac{(1+r_{t,t+1})}{(1+r^*_{t,t+1})}.$$ [2]

Substituting the Interest Rate Parity relationship in Equation [1], we get

$$S_t \frac{(1+r_{t,t+1})}{(1+r^*_{t,t+1})} = S_{t+1}.$$

Multiplying both sides by $(1 + r^*_{t,t+1})$ and dividing by S_t, we obtain

$$1 + r_{t,t+1} = (1+r^*_{t,t+1}) \frac{S_{t+1}}{S_t}.$$ [3]

---

[1] We sidestep the philosophical issue as to why there would be a forward market at all under certainty.

The left-hand side of Equation [3] gives us the (gross) return from investing one unit of the home currency in a risk-free bond. The right-hand side of Equation [3] is the total return if one invested this unit of home currency in a foreign risk-free asset instead.[2] Thus, Equation [3] says that, under certainty, the total return on the foreign T-bill is equal to the domestic risk-free return. This is, of course, the equilibrium condition that one expects in a world of certainty.

Very often, the total return from investing abroad is decomposed into the foreign return $r*$ and the capital gain expressed as a percentage, as follows:

$$1 \; + \; \text{total return on the foreign T-bill} = (1 + r^*_{t,\,t+1})\frac{S_{t+1}}{S_t}$$

$$= (1 + r^*_{t,\,t+1})(1 + s_{t,\,t+1})$$

where $s_{t,\,t+1} = (S_{t+1} - S_t)/S_t$ is the capital gain expressed as percentage. After computing the product we get

$$1 \; + \; \text{total return on the foreign T-bill} = 1 + [r^*_{t,\,t+1} + \; s_{t,\,t+1} + \; r^*_{t,\,t+1} \times s_{t,\,t+1}].$$

Thus, the total return is not just the foreign return $r^*_{t,\,t+1}$ plus the capital gain $s_{t,\,t+1}$; there is a cross product term, reflecting the fact that the capital gain is not only on the principal (one unit of foreign exchange), but also on the foreign interest earned. The cross product is often small and is, therefore, often ignored. Still, when one talks about foreign interest *plus* capital gain, this loose statement should be interpreted as including the cross term. Thus, Equation [3] says that the domestic return equals the foreign return "*plus*" the capital gain:

$$1 + r_{t,\,t+1} = 1 + [r^*_{t,\,t+1} + s_{t,\,t+1} + r^*_{t,\,t+1} \times s_{t,\,t+1}].$$

The corollary to Equation [3] is that currencies that are known to appreciate ($s_{t,\,t+1} > 0$) can afford to pay low interest rates ($r^*_{t,\,t+1} < r_{t,\,t+1}$); the anticipated (certain) appreciation of the foreign currency makes up for the relatively low interest rate it pays. Likewise, currencies that are "weak" ($s_{t,\,t+1} < 0$) have to pay high interest rates ($r^*_{t,\,t+1} > r_{t,\,t+1}$) to compensate the investors for an anticipated (certain) depreciation. This insight is qualitatively consistent with what we observe. European currencies like the DEM, CHF, or NLG that are historically considered to be "strong" have typically had lower interest rates, while historically weak currencies like the FRF or ITL have had to offer higher interest rates. Of course, *under uncertainty*, a currency that offers a high interest rate might depreciate by more or less than the interest differential warranted. Therefore, if there is uncertainty, the naive rule, if it works at all, can work only "on average." We shall examine this issue in detail when we discuss the empirical evidence on the relationship between the forward and spot rates.

---

[2] To understand this, note that with one unit of home currency you can buy $1/S_t$ units of foreign currency. By the end of the period, this investment has grown into $(1 + r^*_{t,\,t+1})/S_t$ units, and the home currency value of this total amount, at the exchange rate S_{t+1}, is the expression on the right-hand side of Equation [3].

14.1.2   UEH under Uncertainty

The relationship in Equation [1] is trivially true under certainty. It is often assumed that this relationship will be true even under uncertainty, in terms of expected values. That is, today's forward rate for a given maturity is assumed to be equal to the expected value of the future (random) spot rate. The fact that the future rate is uncertain is indicated by adding a tilde (~) over S. This conjecture that the expected future spot rate is equal to the current forward rate is commonly called the **Unbiased Expectations Hypothesis (UEH)**:[3]

$$E_t(\tilde{S}_{t+1}) \overset{?}{=} F_{t,t+1}. \qquad [4]$$

Note that we add a question mark over the equality sign in order to emphasize that this is an *ad hoc* hypothesis, not a result derived from a rigorous analysis. There are, in fact, a number of problems with this hypothesis. For one thing, it clearly assumes either that investors are risk-neutral, or that all exchange risk is diversifiable—that is, investors are indifferent between the certain forward rate and the expected value of the (random) future spot rate. Second, even if agents are risk-neutral, risk neutrality should be defined in real terms, not in nominal terms as in Equation [4]. In other words, the hypothesis assumes that there is no inflation or at least no uncertainty about inflation. Third, even if Equation [4] holds in one currency, it cannot hold in the other; that is:

$$\text{If } E_t(\tilde{S}_{t+1}) = F_{t,t+1}, \text{ then } E_t\left(\frac{1}{\tilde{S}_{t+1}}\right) > \frac{1}{F_{t,t+1}}. \qquad [5]$$

Example   14.1

If S_T, expressed in CAD/USD, takes on a value of either 1.1 or 0.9 with equal probability, the expectation is $E_t(\tilde{S}_{t+1}) = 1$; thus, according to UEH, from the Canadian point of view one would want to set $F_{t,t+1} = $ CAD/USD 1. In the US, where exchange rates are quoted in terms of USD/CAD, $E_t(1/\tilde{S}_{t+1})$ would equal

$$\frac{1/1.1 + 1/0.9}{2} = 1.0101,$$

so foreign investors would want to set their forward rate at USD/CAD 1.0101, or, inverting the quote, at CAD/USD 1/1.0101 = 0.99. Thus, we see that the two unbiased forward rates, one from the Canadian point of view and the other from the American point of view, are incompatible.

The result in Equation [5] is called the **Siegel Paradox**. Sometimes this paradox is dismissed as being empirically insignificant in the short run. However over long horizons, where there is greater

---

[3] We use the notation $E_t(\tilde{S}_{t+1})$ to denote the expectation at time t of the time $t+1$ spot rate, conditional on all information available at time t.

uncertainty, the Siegel Paradox may be important. Moreover, the paradox indicates that even in the short run UEH is, at best, an approximation.

14.1.3 The Implications of UEH for Exchange Rate Determination

With these caveats in mind, UEH can be developed into an approximate theory about how the current exchange rate is determined, given risk-free interest rates and investors' expectations about the future spot rate. UEH suggests that $F_{t,t+1} \overset{?}{=} E_t(\tilde{S}_{t+1})$. Substituting this condition for $F_{t,t+1}$ in the Interest Rate Parity condition in Equation [2], we get

$$E_t(\tilde{S}_{t+1}) \overset{?}{=} S_t \frac{(1+r_{t,t+1})}{(1+r^*_{t,t+1})}. \tag{6}$$

To turn this into a statement about the spot rate, we put the "dependent" variable on the left-hand side of the equality. IRP and UEH then imply the following:

$$S_t \overset{?}{=} E_t(\tilde{S}_{t+1}) \frac{1+r^*_{t,t+1}}{1+r_{t,t+1}}. \tag{7}$$

Equation [7] says that, under risk neutrality and the other conditions discussed above, the market discounts the expected spot rate at the interest differential. Thus, given the domestic and foreign risk-free interest rates, this equation says that if the expected value of the future spot rate increases, the current spot rate will also increase. Similarly, all else being the same, an increase in the foreign interest rate leads to an increase in the current spot rate.[4] In the next section, we test the UEH relationship to see if it is supported by the data. However, before we do that, we describe how Equation [7] can be used to explain the link between interest rates and the *current* spot rate.

14.1.4 The Relation between the Current Exchange Rate and Interest Rates

Equation [7] can be used to explain how central bankers try to influence the exchange rate by changing the interest rate. It is generally accepted that an increase in interest rates often strengthens a currency relative to foreign currencies. How does this mechanism work? And how can a rise in, say, the foreign interest rate *strengthen* the exchange rate if, as we argued in Section 14.1.1, high interest rates are a sign of *weak* currencies? The answer lies in understanding the role that expectations play in the determination of exchange rates. Let us look at an example.

Example 14.2

Assume, for simplicity, that UEH holds and that the FRF (home currency) and the USD interest rates, r and r^*, are both equal to 10 percent *p.a.* Then, in the UEH view given in Equation [7], initially no

---

[4] Unlike the price of a non-dividend-paying stock, the current spot rate can easily exceed its expected future value if the foreign interest rate is high enough. Recall that the high foreign interest rate is the inducement offered to investors to convince them to hold the currency despite its expected capital loss.

change in S is expected. Now assume that bad news about the US (foreign) economy suddenly leads to a downward revision of the expected next year spot rate from say FRF/USD 7 to 6.9. From Equation [7], if interest rates remain unchanged, the current spot rate would immediately react by dropping from 7 to 6.9, too. Exchange rates, like any other financial price, anticipate the future.

Now if the Fed (the US central bank) does not like this drop in the value of the USD, it can prop up the current exchange rate by increasing the US interest rate. To do this, the US interest rate will need to be increased from 10 percent to 11.59 percent, so that S_t = FRF/USD 7 even though $E_t(\tilde{S}_{t+1}) = 6.9$.

Thus, the higher US interest rate does strengthen the current USD spot rate, all else being equal. This still means that the currency is weak, in the sense that the USD is expected to drop towards $E_t(\tilde{S}_{t+1}) = 6.9$ in the future. That is, there is no contradiction, since "strengthening" has to do with the immediate spot rate (which perks up as soon as the US interest rate is raised), while "weakening" refers to the expected movements in the future.

However, this partial analysis may be incomplete, because a change in interest rates may also affect expectations. For instance, if the market believes that an increase in the foreign interest rate also heralds a stricter monetary policy, this would increase the expected future spot rate, and reinforce the effect of the higher foreign interest rate. Of course, if expectations change in the opposite direction, the current spot rate may decrease even when the foreign interest rate is increased.

Example   14.3

Suppose that the current interest rates are equal to 5 percent *p.a.* in both Canada (the home country) and the UK, and the current and expected exchange rate are CAD/GBP 2. The Bank of England now increases its interest rate to 5.025 percent *p.a.* in an attempt to increase the current value of its exchange rate. It is quite possible that this increase in interest rates is interpreted by the market as a negative signal about the future state of the UK economy; for example, the market revises expectations about the CAD/GBP exchange rate from 2 to 1.95. Thus, the change in the interest rate is insufficient to match the drop in the expected exchange rate. Instead of appreciating, the current exchange rate drops to CAD/GBP 1.95046.

In 1991 and 1992, the Japanese central bank increased the yen interest rate several times but each time the JPY depreciated. One interpretation of this experience is that investors revised their expectations about the future exchange rate downwards with each increase in the interest rate.

14.2   REGRESSION TESTS OF UEH

UEH states that the expected future spot rate is equal to the current forward rate. In this section, we will test this hypothesis to see how well it describes the observed behavior of spot and forward rates. We will show that the empirical evidence rejects UEH overwhelmingly. In Sections 14.3 and 14.4, we examine possible explanations for the rejection of the UEH.

The unbiasedness hypothesis—the expected future spot rate is equal to the forward rate—is given in Equation [4]. There are two problems in using regression analysis to test UEH as it is expressed in Equation [4]. The first problem is that Equation [4] is written in terms of expectations, which are unobservable. All that one can observe is the *realized* value of the spot rate at time $t+1$, S_{t+1}; one cannot observe its *expectation* today, $E_t(\tilde{S}_{t+1})$. However, this problem can be solved by noting that in an informationally efficient market, the deviation between the market's forecast and the actual outcome must be totally unpredictable. This allows us to rewrite Equation [4] in terms of observed spot rate, $\tilde{S}_{t+1}$, and its forecast error, $\tilde{\varepsilon}_{t,t+1}$. That is, if $E_t(\tilde{S}_{t+1}) = F_{t,t+1}$, then:

$$\tilde{S}_{t+1} = F_{t,t+1} + \tilde{\varepsilon}_{t,t+1}.$$
[8]

One could test the expression given in Equation [8] using regression analysis. However, there is a second problem in testing UEH as expressed in Equation [8]—the problem of nonstationarity of spot and forward exchange rates. As explained in the appendix to Chapter 5, nonstationary time series do not have a well-defined unconditional expected value (in the sense of a long-run mean to which the series is attracted) and they do not have well-defined variances. Thus, the coefficients obtained from such a regression do not have good statistical properties.

One way to convert the nonstationary variables in Equation [8] into stationary variables is to consider changes or percentage changes in the exchange rate rather than the levels of the spot and forward rates. That is, we subtract S_t from both sides of Equation [8] and divide by S_t to get the following test equation. If $E_t(\tilde{S}_{t+1}) = F_{t,t+1}$, then

$$\frac{\tilde{S}_{t+1} - S_t}{S_t} = \frac{F_{t,t+1} - S_t}{S_t} + \tilde{e}_{t,t+1}$$

where $\tilde{e}_{t,t+1}$ is the percentage forecast error. We can write this in terms of the following regression test equation:

$$\left(\frac{\tilde{S}_{t+1} - S_t}{S_t} \right) = \alpha + \beta \left(\frac{F_{t,t+1} - S_t}{S_t} \right) + \tilde{e}_{t,t+1}.$$
[9]

Finally, for notational ease, we define the percentage change in the spot rate as $\tilde{s}_{t,t+1}$, and the percentage difference between the forward and spot rates as the forward premium $FP_{t,t+1}$

$$\tilde{s}_{t,t+1} \equiv \frac{\tilde{S}_{t+1} - S_t}{S_t} \text{ and } FP_{t,t+1} \equiv \frac{F_{t,t+1} - S_t}{S_t},$$
[10]

which allows us to rewrite Equation [9] as follows:

$$\tilde{s}_{t,t+1} = \alpha + \beta\, FP_{t,t+1} + \tilde{e}_{t,t+1}.$$
[11]

Under UEH, $\tilde{s}_{t,t+1} = FP_{t,t+1} + \tilde{e}_{t,t+1}$; thus, the null hypothesis is that $\alpha = 0$ and $\beta = 1$. Cumby and Obstfeld (1984)—and many other economists—have run regressions similar to that in Equation [11]. While UEH would lead us to expect a value of β that is statistically close to 1, according to Froot and Thaler (1990), the average slope coefficient (obtained from seventy-five empirical studies) is, in fact, −0.88. While some studies find a slope coefficient that is positive, not a single study finds a slope that is equal to or greater than unity.

Note that since β is typically not equal to zero in the regression tests of UEH, the forward premium does have some power to predict the future spot rate—although the sign of the relationship is often opposite to what we would expect under UEH. However in practice, the unpredictable component $(\tilde{e}_{t,\,t+1})$ is very large in comparison to the predictable component $\beta \times FP_{t,\,t+1}$, and, thus, the exchange rate remains difficult to forecast.

Based on the overwhelming evidence from many empirical studies, we can safely conclude that β is significantly below unity. That is, the forward rate is a biased predictor of the future spot rate. There are two possible interpretations of the result that the slope coefficient is significantly less than unity. The first interpretation is that investors are not risk neutral and that the bias in the forward rate's prediction of the spot rate reflects a risk premium. We examine this hypothesis in the next section. The second interpretation is that investors make errors in forming expectations. This issue is discussed in Section 14.4.

14.3   CAN RISK PREMIUMS EXPLAIN VIOLATIONS OF UEH?

The argument underlying UEH is a naive generalization of the result under certainty that the forward rate is equal to the future spot rate. However, as noted above, there are a number of problems with this hypothesis. In particular, UEH assumes that investors are risk neutral or that exchange risk can be ignored for the determination of the future spot rate. Note that UEH given in Equation [4] compares a risky payoff, $E_t(\tilde{S}_{t+1})$ with a safe one, $F_{t,\,t+1}$. Thus, rejection of UEH on the basis of the data may simply imply that investors are risk averse and wish to be compensated for risk. In this section, we examine whether the existence of a risk premium in the currency markets can explain the rejection of UEH.

The risk premium of a given security or portfolio is defined as the return on this security or portfolio, over and above the risk-free return. Suppose that one invests S_t units of the home currency in the domestic risk-free bond and also buys a forward contract. The investment in the domestic bond yields $S_t(1 + r_{t,\,t+1})$. The expected payoff on the forward contract is given by $E_t(\tilde{S}_{t+1}) - F_{t,\,t+1}$. Note that this payoff is risky since it depends on the future spot rate. Thus, the total expected return on this portfolio of the domestic bond and the forward contract is:

$$\frac{E_t(\tilde{S}_{t+1} - F_{t,\,t+1}) + S_t(1 + r_{t,\,t+1})}{S_t} - 1,$$

and the expected *excess* return is:

$$\frac{E_t(\tilde{S}_{t+1} - F_{t,\,t+1}) + S_t(1 + r_{t,\,t+1})}{S_t} - 1 - r_{t,\,t+1}.$$

Simplifing the above expression, we find that the expected excess return on this risky portfolio is given by

$$\frac{E_t(\tilde{S}_{t+1}) - F_{t,\,t+1}}{S_t}.$$

We define this quantity, which is the expected relative profit on a forward contract, as the risk premium at time t, $RP_{t, t+1}$:

$$\frac{E_t(\tilde{S}_{t+1}) - F_{t, t+1}}{S_t} \equiv RP_{t, t+1}. \qquad [12]$$

The possible existence of a risk premium implies that UEH has to be amended, as follows. Adding and subtracting S_t in the numerator on the left-hand side of the above expression, we obtain:

$$\left(\frac{E_t(\tilde{S}_{t+1}) - S_t}{S_t}\right) - \left(\frac{F_{t, t+1} - S_t}{S_t}\right) = RP_{t, t+1}. \qquad [13]$$

Rewriting Equation [13] in terms of $\tilde{s}_{t, t+1}$ and $FP_{t, t+1}$, as defined in Equation [10], we get

$$E_t(\tilde{s}_{t, t+1}) - FP_{t, t+1} = RP_{t, t+1}. \qquad [14]$$

Thus, the difference between the expected percentage appreciation and the forward premium now equals the risk premium rather than zero. As we noted in Section 14.2, Equation [14] is written in terms of expectations that are unobservable to a researcher. Rewriting the equation in terms of observable variables leads to the following test equation:

$$\tilde{s}_{t, t+1} - FP_{t, t+1} = RP_{t, t+1} + \tilde{e}_{t, t+1}, \qquad [15]$$

where $\tilde{e}_{t, t+1}$, the percentage forecast error, should be totally unpredictable given the available information.

However, when testing Equation [15], there is an additional problem of which one needs to be aware. While the forward premium is fully observable, the risk premium, $RP_{t, t+1}$, is not. We can observe only the sum of the risk premium and the noise, $RP_{t, t+1} + \tilde{e}_{t, t+1}$. That is, we cannot observe which part of the realized *prediction error*,[5] $\tilde{s}_{t, t+1} - FP_{t, t+1}$, is a result of the unexpected arrival of new information and which part is an anticipated risk premium. The only information we have is that in an efficient market, the expected value of $\tilde{e}_{t, t+1}$ should be zero; that is, $\tilde{e}_{t, t+1}$ is uncorrelated with any past information. This implies that $\tilde{e}_{t, t+1}$ should be unrelated to $FP_{t, t+1}$ and $RP_{t, t+1}$. The fact that we cannot distinguish between the risk premiums and the error term points to a fundamental ambiguity in all tests of risk premiums used to explain the rejection of UEH. Since inefficiency cannot be ruled out *a priori*, we cannot distinguish between a true risk premium on the one hand and predictability of the error (market inefficiency) on the other hand. That is, in testing Equation [15], we are jointly testing UEH and market efficiency.

We now describe the results of tests that attempt to characterize the risk premiums in the currency markets.

---

[5] This term is misleading unless, like in the primitive unbiasedness hypothesis, one postulates that the risk premium is zero. With a non-zero risk premium, part of the "prediction error" is predictable. However, the terminology has somehow become standard.

14.3.1   Regression Tests of Risk Premiums

In the time-series regression test given in Equation [11], the slope coefficient is:

$$\beta = \frac{\text{cov}(\tilde{s}, \text{FP})}{\text{var}(\text{FP})}. \tag{16}$$

However, from Equation [15], we know that

$$\tilde{s}_{t,t+1} = \text{FP}_{t,t+1} + \text{RP}_{t,t+1} + \tilde{e}_{t,t+1}. \tag{17}$$

Fama (1984) combines these two results to characterize the risk premium. Substituting the expression in Equation [17] for $\tilde{s}_{t,t+1}$ into Equation [16], we can rewrite β as

$$\beta = \frac{\text{cov}(\text{FP} + \text{RP} + \tilde{e}, \text{FP})}{\text{var}(\text{FP})}$$

$$= \frac{\text{cov}(\text{FP}, \text{FP}) + \text{cov}(\text{RP}, \text{FP}) + \text{cov}(\tilde{e}, \text{RP})}{\text{var}(\text{FP})}. \tag{18}$$

Assuming efficiency, the term $\text{cov}(\tilde{e}, \text{RP})$ is zero since in an efficient market the risk premium contains no information about $\tilde{e}_{t,t+1}$. Also, $\text{cov}(\text{FP}, \text{FP}) = \text{var}(\text{FP})$. So, we can rewrite Equation [18] as

$$\beta = 1 + \frac{\text{cov}(\text{RP}, \text{FP})}{\text{var}(\text{FP})}. \tag{19}$$

From Equation [19], we see that the deviation of the slope coefficient, β, from 1 gives us information about variation in the risk premium. The regression coefficient can equal unity only if $\text{RP}_{t,t+1}$ is uncorrelated with, $\text{FP}_{t,t+1}$. Conversely, in an efficient market, a coefficient β that is different from unity suggests the existence of a risk premium that is correlated with $\text{FP}_{t,t+1}$. If $\beta < 1$, as is empirically the case, the implication is that $\text{cov}(\text{RP}, \text{FP}) < 0$. Assuming efficiency, Fama finds that variation of the risk premium over time must be greater than the variation of the expected change in the spot rate and the variation of the forward premium. These results imply that a change in the forward premium is typically associated with an even larger change in the risk premium, and the change in the risk premium is opposite in direction to the change in the forward premium.

The above results suggest that, in order to explain why the forward rate is a biased predictor of the future spot rate, the risk premium needs to be *large* in magnitude, and strongly *negatively correlated with the forward premium*. It is hard to come up with a reasonable explanation for this behavior of the risk premium. Thus, it is unlikely that the presence of a risk premium completely explains the relationship between the forward rate and the future spot rate.

14.3.2   Other Tests of the Risk Premium

Besides regression tests that try to determine the risk premium in exchange markets, there are several other tests that study the properties of the risk premium. Researchers have analyzed the time series of the realized *prediction error*, $\tilde{s}_{t,t+1} - \text{FP}_{t,t+1}$, which is defined in Equation [15]. These empirical tests have searched for the presence of risk premiums and/or inefficiencies (that is, predictability in the error term). The questions typically asked are:

- What is the mean of the forecast error over long periods and over subperiods? Is this mean significantly different from zero?
- How often is the sign of $FP_{t, t+1}$ the same as the sign of $\tilde{s}_{t, t+1}$; that is, how often does the forward premium correctly predict the direction of change in the spot rate?
- Is the forecast error predictable on the basis of past realized forecast errors, using either linear regression analysis, sophisticated time-series methods, or trading rules?
- Is the forecast error predictable on the basis of other available information, like interest differentials or forward premiums?

We briefly describe some of these tests and their findings.

Tests of Average Prediction Errors
Using time-series data over long periods of time, the means of variables such as the prediction error $(\tilde{s}_{t, t+1} - FP_{t, t+1})$ tend to be statistically indistinguishable from zero. This suggests that, over long time periods, the average risk premium may be zero (or close to zero). Cornell (1977) has found that the means of the prediction error are significantly different from zero when tested over subperiods, but the sign of the average error is unstable. Given the definition of the prediction error in Equation [15], Cornell's results suggest that either the risk premiums fluctuate over time, or that the market is inefficient—implying that $\tilde{e}_{t+1}$ is partly predictable.

Autocorrelation Tests
Fama (1984) and Cornell (1977), among others, have found significant autocorrelation in the forecast errors. A positive error, for instance, is more often than not followed by another positive error (although typically a smaller one). In an efficient market this must mean that there is a risk premium that changes over time, and that depends on the previous risk premium or on the previous unexpected exchange rate change.

Sign Tests
If the forward premium predicts to some extent the exchange rate change, then a positive forward premium should be followed by appreciations in more than 50 percent of the cases, while negative forward premiums should be followed by depreciations in more than 50 percent of the cases. Thus, one common test consists of counting how many times the forward premium accurately anticipates the sign of the subsequent exchange rate change.

Goodman (1982, 1983) counts the number of times that a forward premium is actually followed by an appreciation and/or the number of times a negative premium is followed by a depreciation. He finds that, over the limited time period of the study, the forward premium is "no better than a toss of a coin" as a predictor of the subsequent exchange rate change—except for the case of the CHF (which appreciated systematically over the period of their study, and had the lowest interest rates in the world). Based on this test, it seems that the forward premium is not an impressive predictor of the future spot rate.

14.3.3   Trading Rules Based on the Forward Bias
You may be wondering whether it is possible to use the predictability of the future spot rate to make abnormal returns by systematically investing in currencies with high interest rates (or high discounts in the forward or futures market) and financing the investments by borrowing low interest rate cur-

rencies. Tests of trading rules can be used to see if such a strategy is successful. We describe such tests below.

Robinson and Warburton (1980), and later Bell and Kettle (1983), have tested UEH using the interest differential rather than the forward premium. For example, one can rewrite the test equation in [11] by substituting the interest rate differential for $FP_{t,t+1}$:

$$\tilde{s}_{t,t+1} = \alpha + \beta \ (r_{t,t+1} - r^*_{t,t+1}) + \tilde{e}_{t,t+1}. \qquad [20]$$

UEH (Equation [20]) suggests that the capital gain on the exchange rate should be equal to the interest rate differential. This is equivalent to saying that the total return on a foreign risk-free investment (the sum of capital gains and interest income) should be equal to the return from the domestic bond, as discussed in Section 14.1. *Ex post*, we would expect some deviations from the equality between returns from the domestic bond and returns from the foreign bond. However, in the absence of a risk premium, these deviations should be random, that is, totally unsystematic and unpredictable on the basis of available information. To verify this conclusion, four alternative investment strategies are tested. These strategies require the following actions at the beginning of every month:

1. Invest in the currency with the highest nominal interest rate.
2. Invest in the currency with the highest real interest rate, based on recent inflation as measured by the consumer price index.
3. Invest in the currency with the highest real interest rate, based on recent inflation as measured by the wholesale price index.
4. Invest in the currency with the highest real interest rate corrected for "competitiveness" as measured by the International Monetary Fund's unit production cost index.

For each of these strategies, the average return over the sample period is computed. The results are that the average total returns (including foreign interest) differ significantly across strategies, and that these strategies tend to do better than the passive strategy of buying one currency and holding it until the end of the period (buy-and-hold). More precisely, interest rate differentials tend to *overcompensate* for expected depreciations—in the sense that high-interest currencies typically provide the highest total returns.[6]

Similarly, Thomas (1986) finds that trading using futures contracts instead of forwards and investing in currencies with high interest rates yields positive returns. Taylor (1992) also finds that simple trading rules, based on moving averages of futures prices, can generate positive returns.

It is important to understand, however, that evidence of positive returns in the exchange market does not necessarily imply that there are *abnormal* returns to be made. Remember that investing in the high-interest-rate foreign currency is not risk free. Thus, the return that one earns from such an investment may simply be the compensation for the risk that this investment involves. Also, regression tests such as Equation [11] indicate that the forward premium has very little power to predict the exchange rate. This implies that (the strategy of) investing in a high-interest-rate currency has high variance.

---

[6] This is, incidentally, also a commonly held belief among traders and bankers.

Example   14.4

Froot and Thaler (1990) show that while investing in a high-interest-rate currency may be profitable on average, the risk of this strategy is also quite large. Thus, this strategy may not be very attractive.

Froot and Thaler consider the regression equation stated in [11] or [20] and, on the basis of over seventy-five studies, assume that the value of the estimated slope coefficient, β, is approximately $(-)1$, and the average standard error is equal to 36 percent *p.a.* Thus, estimation based on Equation [20] implies that, by borrowing in the low-interest-rate currency and investing in a currency with an interest rate that is 1 percent higher, the total expected return is 2 percent *p.a.* (The interest rate differential is 1 percent, and the fact that β is assumed to be -1 implies that a 1 percent forward premium yields an expected capital gain of another 1 percent.) Thus, the predicted return on $500, invested for one year, is equal to $500 \times 0.02 = \$10$. However, the standard error of this expected return is $500 \times 0.36 = \$180$ *p.a.* This implies that an investor would make, on average, $10 *p.a.* but, allowing for the returns to vary two standard deviations, the investor could reasonably expect a return as high as $370 or as low as $(-)\$350$. This much variability in the return is not attractive for the investor, given that the expected return is only $10, and when the investor allows for transactions costs, such an investment is even less attractive.

In the next section, we examine another possible explanation for the bias in the forward rate's prediction of the future spot rate, that is, the possibility of errors in forming expectations.

14.4   OTHER EXPLANATIONS FOR VIOLATIONS OF UEH

In the previous section, we raised questions about the hypothesis that the presence of a risk premium explains the forward rate bias. In this section, we examine other hypotheses that have been advanced as potential explanations of the forward bias.

14.4.1   Errors in Forming Expectations

One explanation for the forward bias is that it is the result of investors making errors in forming expectations. According to this view, there is either *no* risk premium, or the premium does not change over time; instead, very often the exchange rate increases when investors had expected the currency to depreciate and accordingly had set the forward rate below par. Likewise, when the investors expect the currency to appreciate and set a positive forward premium, then on average the exchange rate decreases. We need to explain how such errors in expectations can arise in efficient markets.

The hypothesis that investors make errors in forming expectations relies on the assumption that it takes time for investors to learn about market conditions. Thus, the effect of changes in monetary policy or in the exchange rate policy may not be immediately reflected in market prices. Lewis (1989) finds that slow learning by market participants about changes in the US monetary policy could potentially explain about half of the forward rate bias. The problem with this explanation is that one needs to explain why this bias persists, that is, why investors do not eventually learn about how such events affect exchange rates.

14.4.2   The "Peso Problem"

Another explanation that has been advanced to explain the forward bias is that of the "peso problem."[7] According to this view, for long periods of time investors may assign a small but positive probability to certain relatively infrequent events (such as a devaluation, a change of monetary policy, a change of exchange rate regime, a war, or some other major event) which may never materialize in a limited sample period. The expectation of such an extreme event will be reflected in today's forward exchange rate. However, because of the infrequent occurrence of such an event, the econometrician may never get a chance to actually observe such an event. That is, even though the likelihood of such an event is reflected in prices, it will not be present in the sample of data collected by a researcher studying the forward-bias phenomenon.

The problem with this explanation is that, in order to explain the degree of the bias that we observe, either the probability of the extreme event needs to be rather large, or the effect of the event on the exchange rate must be truly enormous. The first explanation implies that the event is not in fact rare, since it occurs with a high probability, violating the underlying assumption of the "peso-problem" hypothesis. The second explanation is also flawed, at least for freely traded floating currencies. Over the past twenty years, there have been large exchange rate changes, but never of the order of magnitude that could explain, say, a 2 percent bias if the probability of the event is less than 1 percent.

Thus, we conclude that it is unlikely that the two explanations considered in this section—errors in forming expectations, and the "peso problem"—can completely explain the difference between the forward rate and the realized value of the future spot rate.

14.5   TESTING UEH IN REAL TERMS

The tests of UEH that we have considered above, in Sections 14.3 and 14.4, are specified in nominal rather than real terms. In this section, we examine an explanation of the forward rate bias where the test takes into account the inflation rates at home and abroad. To test for the forward bias in real terms, in the first part of this section, we show how inflation rates are related to spot and forward rates, and in the second part, we report the results of the test.

14.5.1   Relationship between Real and Nominal Returns

In Chapter 2, we derived Interest Rate Parity (IRP), which relates the forward premium to the interest differential. In this chapter, we have discussed the Unbiased Expectations Hypothesis (UEH), which links the forward premium to the expected change in the spot rate. Purchasing Power Parity (PPP), finally, links the expected exchange rate change to the inflation differential. Together, these three imply that there must be a fourth relationship that links the interest differential to the inflation differential (see Figure 14.1). This link is called the **Fisher Open Relationship**, the international version of Fisher's statement about nominal interest rates and inflation. We show below how one can derive the Fisher Open Relationship.

---

[7] The origin of this term is based on the behavior of the Mexican peso, which traded at a large discount for a long period of time, but was not devalued for years. Then, one day, its value dropped significantly.

FIGURE 14.1   The Four International Parity Relations Under Certainty

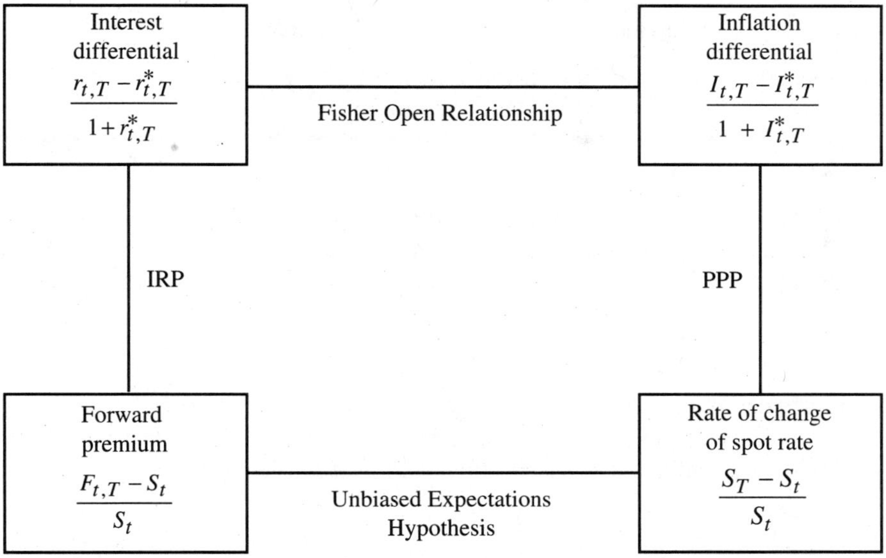

The Fisher Relationship

In this section, we first explain the standard Fisher Relationship for a single country, and then we extend this to an open economy so that we can show how the real risk-free rate of return in one country is related to that in another country.

Let ρ denote the real return to a domestic investor on the domestic risk-free asset and P the domestic price level. Also, define the inflation rate as $I_{t,T} = P_T/P_t - 1$. The realized real return is simply the realized percentage change in the real price of the local T-bill;[8] that is,

$$1 + \rho_{t,T} = \frac{1 + r_{t,T}}{1 + I_{t,T}}.$$

Thus,

$$\rho_{t,T} = \frac{1 + r_{t,T}}{1 + I_{t,T}} - 1$$

$$= \frac{r_{t,T} - I_{t,T}}{1 + I_{t,T}}. \qquad [21]$$

---

[8] If V is the domestic-currency price of a risk-free investment, then

$$1 + \rho_{t,T} = \frac{V_T/P_T}{V_t/P_t} = \frac{V_T}{V_t} \frac{P_t}{P_T} = \frac{1 + r_{t,T}}{1 + I_{t,T}}.$$

This equation is often approximated by

$$\rho_{t,T} \cong r_{t,T} - I_{t,T},$$ [22]

but this simplification is misleading if inflation is high.

Example   14.5

If inflation is 100 percent, and the nominal risk-free rate 130 percent, the real return on a deposit is $(1 + 1.3)/(1 + 1.0) - 1 = 15$ percent. Note that the real return is *not* 130% − 100% = 30%. The first-order approximation used in Equation [22], $\rho_{t,T} \cong r_{t,T} - I_{t,T}$, works only when inflation is low.

Fisher turned definition [21] into a theory by adding an assumption. It is postulated that investors care only about the expected *real* return. Thus, given the expected real return required under equilibrium, investors set the nominal rate as a function of expected inflation. That is,[9]

$$(1 + r_{t,T}) = [1 + E_t(\tilde{\rho}_{t,T})] \, [1 + E_t(\tilde{I}_{t,T})].$$ [23]

This is the *Fisher Equation*. Inverting our earlier example, we can calculate that if the desired real return is 15 percent and inflation is expected to be 100 percent, the market will require a nominal return of 130 percent. If expected inflation is low, the Fisher Equation can be approximated by

$$r_{t,T} \cong E_t(\tilde{\rho}_{t,T}) + E_t(\tilde{I}_{t,T}).$$ [24]

A similar equation will hold abroad:

$$(1 + r_{t,T}^*) = [1 + E_t(\tilde{\rho}_{t,T}^*)] \, [1 + E_t(\tilde{I}_{t,T}^*)]$$ [25]

and this equation can be approximated as

$$r_{t,T}^* \cong E_t(\tilde{\rho}_{t,T}^*) + E_t(\tilde{I}_{t,T}^*).$$ [26]

From Equations [24] and [26] we conclude that nominal interest rates, r and r^* (each denominated in its own currency), may differ across countries for two reasons. First, there may be differences in the inflation expected at home and abroad; so high inflation countries should (and do) have higher interest rates. Second, nominal rates may differ across countries if the (expected) real rates, ρ and ρ^*, are different across countries.

---

[9] There is an approximation implicit in Equation [23]. Taking expectations of Equation [21], you can see that we should have written $1/E_t[1/(1 + I_{t,T})]$ instead of $E_t(1 + I_{t,T})$. If the uncertainty about inflation is small, the approximation works well. See our discussion of the Siegel paradox in Section 14.1, where a similar problem arises.

One can derive the Fisher Open Relationship, which gives us the relation between the *real* rates of return in each country, as follows. We start by subtracting Equation [24] from Equation [26], and move the real rates of return to the left-hand side of the equation:

$$E_t(\tilde{\rho}^*_{t,T}) - E_t(\tilde{\rho}_{t,T}) \cong [r^*_{t,T} - E_t(\tilde{I}^*_{t,T})] - [r_{t,T} - E_t(\tilde{I}_{t,T})]. \qquad [27]$$

If, on the right-hand side of the above equation, we add and subtract the expected exchange rate change and rearrange, we obtain

$$E_t(\tilde{\rho}^*_{t,T}) - E_t(\tilde{\rho}_{t,T}) \cong \{E_t(\tilde{s}_{t,t+1}) - (r_{t,T} - r^*_{t,T})\} - \{E_t(\tilde{s}_{t,t+1}) - [E_t(\tilde{I}_{t,T}) - E_t(\tilde{I}^*_{t,T})]\}. \qquad [28]$$

Equation [28] is the Fisher Open Relationship. It gives us the difference in the real rates of return at home and abroad. Note that the first term in curly brackets on the right-hand side is the forward bias, or the risk premium in the forward rate (that is, the approximate form of the risk premium defined in Equation [12]). The second term is the expected deviation from Relative PPP. Thus, the expected real rates of return will be the same at home and abroad *only* if there is no forward bias *and* PPP holds. Given UEH and PPP, conversely, $E_t(\rho_{t,T}) = E_t(\rho^*_{t,T})$. Equation [27] then implies that interest differentials reflect expected inflation differentials.

A General Evaluation of the Above Relations

In Figure 14.1, expectations operators are conspicuously absent, and Relative PPP is presented as an exact relationship. In short, one has assumed certainty and perfect markets in order to get these relationships. Let us, therefore, return to the real world and see which of the four relationships in Figure 14.1 is supported empirically.

- The Interest Rate Parity relationship, which connects the forward rate to the spot rate and interest rates at home and abroad, holds very well for two reasons. First, since the forward rate, $F_{t,T}$, is known today, it is independent of whether investors are risk averse or not and whether the future is uncertain or not; thus, this relationship is not affected by risk. Second, Interest Rate Parity links purely financial prices, and arbitrage works quite well in financial markets. Thus, arbitrage ensures that the forward premium is what Interest Rate Parity predicts it should be. None of the other relationships are as strong as Interest Rate Parity.
- PPP gives the relationship between the exchange rate and the relative prices at home and abroad. However, for PPP to hold, one needs the ability to arbitrage across commodity markets. But commodity markets are imperfect; and for nontraded goods, we cannot even speak of an international market. Thus, PPP is an empirically weak force, as explained in Chapter 11.
- As explained in the first part of this chapter, UEH—which suggests that the future spot rate should be equal to the current forward rate—is not supported empirically. This is because of the uncertainty in exchange markets. First, the risk premium in exchange markets drives a wedge between the forward rate and the expected future spot rate. Second, even if there were no risk premium, uncertainty means that the realized spot rate can be very different from what investors had expected. Thus, the forward rate is a poor predictor of the future spot rate.
- The Fisher Open Relationship (Equation [28]) is weak. The expected difference between the real rate at home and the real rate abroad is zero only if there is no bias in the forward rate

prediction about the future spot rate and PPP holds. We know, however, that there is a significant forward bias and that PPP is violated frequently. In addition, as soon as we consider realized values rather than expectations, noise will further obscure this relationship. Thus, the interest differential is a poor predictor of the inflation differential.

14.5.2   A Test of UEH in Terms of Real Returns

In this section, we consider a test of UEH by Korajczyk (1985)—one that is formulated in real terms. Korajczyk suggests that since investors care about real returns rather than nominal ones, the risk premium should be defined in real terms and tests of UEH must be formulated in real terms.

The real version of the test equation is derived as follows. Start from the familiar (nominal) Equation [15]:

$$\tilde{s}_{t,t+1} = FP_{t,t+1} + RP_{t,t+1} + \tilde{e}_{t,t+1}. \tag{29}$$

Substitute the linear approximation, $FP_{t,t+1} = r_{t,t+1} - r^*_{t,t+1}$, into the above equation:

$$\tilde{s}_{t,t+1} = (r_{t,t+1} - r^*_{t,t+1}) + RP_{t,t+1} + \tilde{e}_{t,t+1}.$$

Next, subtract the inflation differential, $I_{t,t+1} - I^*_{t,t+1}$, on both sides. The result is

$$\tilde{s}_{t,t+1} - (I_{t,t+1} - I^*_{t,t+1}) = [r_{t,t+1} - I_{t,t+1}] - [r^*_{t,t+1} - I^*_{t,t+1}] + RP_{t,t+1} + \tilde{e}_{t,t+1}. \tag{30}$$

The expressions in square brackets on the right-hand side are the standard empirical approximations for the domestic and foreign *realized* real returns, that is, the risk-free rate of return in each country in excess of that country's realized inflation rate. By analogy, the expression on the left-hand side is often called the (change in) *real exchange rate* (as explained in Chapter 11). Taking expectations of Equation [30], we obtain a statement that equates the expected change in the real exchange rate to the expected difference in the real rates, plus the risk premium:

$$E_t[\tilde{s}_{t,t+1} - (I_{t,t+1} - I^*_{t,t+1})] = E_t[\rho_{t,t+1}] - E_t[\rho^*_{t,t+1}] + RP_{t,t+1}. \tag{31}$$

This is the real version of the usual regression equation we considered in Section 14.2, and no new assumptions have been made to derive this equation. The critical assumption that Korajczyk adds to this analysis is that of expected Relative PPP being true; thus, the *expected* change in the real exchange rate is assumed to be zero, although *ex post* deviations may be non-zero. Thus, setting the expected change in the real exchange rate equal to zero in Equation [31], one gets

$$E_t(\rho^*_{t,t+1}) - E_t(\rho_{t,t+1}) = RP_{t,t+1}. \tag{32}$$

In short, if we are willing to accept that Relative PPP holds in expectation, we can obtain an estimate of the risk premium using the real rates of return. Expected real interest rates are not perfectly observable, but there are many articles that explain how to estimate them (see, for example, Fama [1976], Nelson and Schwert [1977], and references in Korajczyk [1985]). Korajczyk includes such a proxy for the risk-premium in the regression equation. The result is that the proxy (1) is statistically significant, (2) gives a coefficient β of FP in the regression equation based on Equation [29] that is statistically close to 1, and (3) eliminates some of the auto-correlation in the residuals. This is what one would expect if the *actual* risk premium had been included into the regressions. Conversely, the fact that the proxy has these effects on the regression results also suggests that the risk premium does exist, and that it is related to the difference in the real rates of return in the manner assumed by Korajczyk. A more recent analysis by Hollifield and Uppal (1994) likewise suggests that changes in the real interest rates could potentially explain a part of the forward bias.

14.6   IMPLICATIONS FOR FINANCIAL DECISION MAKING

We shall briefly summarize the evidence on the relationship between the current forward rate and the future spot rate, and discuss the implications of the various relationships that we have considered in this chapter and in the other chapters in Part II of this text.

1. The forward premium is a poor and biased predictor of the change in the spot rate. A forward discount is (weakly) associated with later appreciations, and *vice versa*.
2. There is evidence of a risk premium in the exchange market, which is small (on average), but unstable, autocorrelated, and negatively related to the forward premium. It also seems to be related to the real interest rate differential, as it should be.
3. The bias in the forward rate does not necessarily imply that the forward rate contains no useful information. The forward rate is still the certainty equivalent future spot rate (the *risk-adjusted* expectation). Thus, the forward rate can be used to find the risk-adjusted value of future cash flows whose value depends on the spot rate. The present value of such cash flows can then be computed by discounting this risk-adjusted value at the risk-free rate. This valuation procedure—introduced in Chapter 3 and discussed in detail in Chapters 21, 22, and 25—is more convenient than discounting risky home-currency cash flows at a risk-adjusted discount rate.

Next, consider the four relationships shown in Figure 14.1. Although some of these relationships are weak, a few basic qualitative insights should be remembered.

First, we should never consider exchange rates in isolation; we should also consider the inflation differential. For instance, be wary of statements such as: "If it were not for its technological strength and its reputation for quality and excellent service, Germany would be pricing itself out of Europe's markets by its revaluations." If the inflation rate in Germany is lower than in the rest of Europe, its competitive position may remain unharmed or may even improve if revaluations do not entirely make up for inflation differentials.

Second, we should never compare interest rates in isolation—we should also be aware of the expected evolution of the spot rate and of the associated risk. Do not believe someone who says that "the NZD is a good investment because it offers a 20 percent interest rate." The NZD may be a weak currency, and an expected capital loss may more than offset the high interest rate. Further, even if the expected return is higher in one currency than in another, this may simply be the normal reward for the difference in the riskiness of the two currencies. In reasonably well-functioning markets, you should be very suspicious of so-called "bargain" interest rates.

Third, it is sometimes argued that if the unbiased expectations hypothesis holds, hedging does not matter "in the long run." That is, it is said that since the expected spot rate is equal to the forward rate on average, hedging is irrelevant. We should consider this statement with caution. For one thing, UEH does *not* work. Second, the above statement is about the *expected future value* of the firm and ignores risk. Modern financial theory takes the *current* value of the firm as the yardstick for the relevance of hedging. We argued in Chapter 3 that hedging may affect the value of a firm through its effect on the production and investment decisions of the firm. That is, given that financial and commodity markets are not perfect, financing (hedging) decisions and investment decisions will not be independent. We discuss the relevance of hedging in much greater detail in Chapter 16.

We conclude by noting that the forward rate is not a very good predictor of the future spot rate. In the next chapter, we examine other variables that may be used to forecast exchange rates.

QUIZ QUESTIONS

True-False Questions

1. UEH assumes that investors demand a premium for interest rate risk.
2. When computing the return from investing abroad, the capital gain earned on the foreign interest (that is, the cross product) is negligible when interest rates are high and exchange rate changes are small.
3. When the percentage change in the spot rate is regressed on the forward premium, UEH predicts $\beta = -1$, because a positive forward premium must make up for the depreciation in the spot rate in the future, while a negative forward premium must make up for the appreciation in the spot rate in the future.
4. Tests of UEH are ambiguous because it is difficult to distinguish between a true risk premium and inefficiency (predictability in the forecast error).
5. By using a trading rule, you can systematically make risk-free money by investing in currencies with high interest rates while financing the investment by borrowing in low interest rate currencies.
6. Tests using trading rules suggest that interest rate differentials tend to overcompensate for expected depreciations.
7. High-interest currencies offer the highest returns for the lowest level of risk.
8. The Fisher Open Relationship explains international differences in interest rates by international differences in inflation.
9. In a PPP framework, the Fisher Open Relationship explains international differences in interest rates by international differences in inflation.
10. According to the Fisher Equation, the expected real rate of return is a function of expected inflation and an exogenous nominal interest rate.
11. Because the forward rate is a biased predictor of the future spot rate, it is not useful for evaluating projects whose payoffs depend on an uncertain future spot rate.

Multiple-Choice Questions

Choose the correct answer(s).

1. The forward rate is an unbiased predictor of the future spot rate

   (a) under uncertainty.
   (b) when the inflation rates in the domestic and foreign countries are low.
   (c) when there is little central bank intervention.
   (d) under certainty.
   (e) when investors are risk-neutral and inflation rates are known in advance.

2. The Siegel Paradox

   (a) assumes that inflation is constant.
   (b) assumes that investors are risk-neutral and all exchange risk is diversifiable.
   (c) says that when an investor sets the forward rate equal to his or her expectations for the future spot rate, the resulting forward rate differs according to how the investor quotes the exchange rate. For example, for the GBP there is no problem because both foreign and UK investors quote the rate as foreign currency units per GBP.
   (d) says that when an investor sets the forward rate equal to expectations for the future spot rate, the result depends on what the investor's home currency is.

(e) says that the forward rate is a biased predictor of the spot rate only when there is great exchange rate uncertainty and the time to maturity of the forward contract is long.

(f) disappears when inflation is certain.

3. Empirical tests have shown that

(a) over long periods, the average risk premium in the forward rate may be close to zero.

(b) a positive forward premium will be followed by an appreciation in the spot exchange rate in significantly more than 50 percent of all cases.

(c) markets are inefficient because the risk premium is positive over time.

(d) investors clearly overestimate the probability of a single major event affecting the value of a currency.

4. Conceivable explanations of violations of UEH include the following:

(a) Investors want to be compensated for risk.

(b) Foreign exchange markets are inefficient.

(c) A currency's value fluctuates erratically whenever there is central bank intervention.

(d) A currency's riskiness changes erratically whenever there is central bank intervention.

(e) Investors incorrectly form expectations about the value of a currency.

(f) Latin American currencies like the peso are infrequently but positively affected by important events like a devaluation.

5. The domestic and foreign real rates of return on a given asset are the same

(a) when domestic and foreign investors demand the same risk premiums for each currency.

(b) when PPP holds.

(c) Both (a) and (b).

(d) None of the above. Because PPP never holds, so UEH will never hold.

EXERCISES

1. Suppose that there is no uncertainty. Inflation is 10 percent at home, and 5 percent abroad. Solve the following questions in the exact form, not with linear approximations.

(a) What is the change in the exchange rate if PPP holds?

(b) What are the nominal rates in the two countries if the real rate is 2 percent (on all assets—recall that we have certainty and PPP holds)?

(c) What is the forward premium?

(d) Is the forward premium equal to the change in the spot rate?

2. Suppose that there is no uncertainty and PPP holds. The domestic and foreign *p.a.* interest rates are 5 percent and 10 percent, respectively. The real *p.a.* interest rate is 2 percent. Solve the following questions in the exact form, not with linear approximations.

(a) What is the inflation differential across countries?

(b) Is the inflation differential equal to the change in the spot rate that is implicit in the forward premium?

3. A friend suggests to you that an investment in Turkish lira provides an excellent return because the real interest rate is very high. Specifically, inflation has been at a reliable 70–80

percent *p.a.*, and interest rates on lira T-bills are 100 percent *p.a.* If expected inflation is 75 percent, the expected real return is 100% − 75% = 25%, your friend argues.

(a) We know that the linear approximation, as used by your friend, does not work very well when inflation is high. How would you obtain a correct estimate of the real return if there were no inflation uncertainty?

(b) Is this still a perfect (unbiased) estimate of the expected return when future inflation is uncertain? Why (not)?

(c) Assuming that the correctly estimated real interest rate on lira T-bills is about 14 percent, and the expected real return on your home currency T-bill is 4 percent, is your friend's argument necessarily compelling? Why (not)? (Hint: your answer should be based on whether or not PPP holds and investors are risk-averse.)

MIND-EXPANDING EXERCISE

1. Imagine a world with perfect goods markets and perfect foresight. Then PPP and UEH would hold as identities. Show that, in the Fisher Relationship, both countries' real rates would become identical. Do not use linear approximation.

15 FORECASTING EXCHANGE RATES

In Chapter 11, we saw that there are significant and persistent deviations from Purchasing Power Parity. That is, domestic and foreign prices do not change in such a way as to fully compensate for the frequent changes in the spot exchange rate. Thus, there is real exchange rate risk. In Chapter 14, we concluded that the forward rate's performance as a predictor of the future spot rate is not very impressive. We now investigate whether we fare any better if we use other models to predict the exchange rate. The forecasting models that we consider are based on the Balance of Payments Theory of exchange rates that is described in Chapter 12 and the Portfolio Theory of exchange rates that is explained in Chapter 13. We also examine other forecasting methods based on the time-series properties of the exchange rate and on mechanical trading rules. In our survey of this vast area of research, we do not attempt to be complete; instead, we look at some representative studies and broadly summarize the results of a class of empirical tests.

One way to classify the various forecasting models is to divide them into *technical* forecasting models and *fundamental* forecasting models. Technical models analyze the past behavior of the exchange rate in an attempt to forecast the future changes in that rate. Examples of such tests include filtering models and models based on the moving average of the exchange rate. Fundamental forecasting models, on the other hand, try to predict future changes in the spot rate based on the fundamental variables in the economy. These fundamentals may include inflation rates, money supply, and information about industrial production. The forecasts based on these fundamentals may be made on the basis of an econometric model, or on a judgmental basis.

Although market efficiency and unpredictability of exchange rates are different concepts, we can also categorize the various studies on exchange rate forecasting using the Market Efficiency terminology introduced by Harry Roberts (1960). According to this classification, there are three types of tests—*weak-form* tests, *semi-strong form* tests, and *strong-form* tests. Weak form tests are those that attempt to forecast the future exchange rate on the basis of the past exchange rate; thus, they correspond to the technical models. Semi-strong form tests are those that predict the exchange rate on the basis of other available information, information besides realized exchange rates; thus, these correspond to fundamental models. Finally, forecasts made by agents such as central bankers, who may have more information than that available to the typical forecaster, would be classified as strong form tests.

The forecasting techniques described in this chapter are organized according to the second classification method, that is, on the basis of technical (weak-form), fundamental (semi-strong form), and strong-form models. In the first section, we review technical models that investigate whether or not future exchange rate changes can be predicted by using information about past exchange rates. In Section 15.2, we examine fundamental models and ask if exchange rates can be partially predicted on the basis of other currently available information, besides the information on past exchange rates. These tests include the use of the forward rate and the inflation rate as a basis for forecasting the future spot rate. Since this was already discussed in Chapter 14, the analysis will be restricted to a few regression studies. Strong-form tests, discussed in Section 15.3, refer to predictions made by specialists who might have inside information, or superior insight—like sophisticated econometric models. We shall look at the record of professional forecasting services and central banks. We conclude in the fourth section, where we summarize the implications of the various forecasting models for corporate treasurers. The overall evidence indicates that it is quite difficult to accurately predict future exchange rates. That is, economic theory may be useful for explaining the past and making broad predictions about the long-run effects of government policy, but it is not very successful in making precise predictions about the exchange rate in the short run.

15.1   TECHNICAL ANALYSIS

In this section, we look for ways of predicting the size or direction of future exchange rate changes on the basis of past observations of the spot rate. There are a number of possible techniques. We discuss autocorrelation models, runs tests, filter rules, and other chartist techniques.

15.1.1   Autocorrelation Models

As in Chapter 14, we define $s_{t-1,\ t}$ as the continuously compounded change of the spot rate, $\ln S_t - \ln S_{t-1}$, or as the (empirically close) simple percentage change, $S_t/S_{t-1} - 1$. Autocorrelation models are very similar to regressions of s_t on lagged observations of the same variable. The objective of autocorrelation tests is to see if one can predict the future exchange rate change based on the lagged exchange rate change. For example, can one predict how the exchange rate will change over the next week, given information on how it changed last week? The autocorrelation for lag L can be thought of as the coefficient of a time-series regression of the exchange rate change on its lagged value:

$$s_{t-1,\ t} = \alpha + \beta_L s_{t-L-1,\ t-L} + e_{t-1,\ t}.$$ [1]

Of course, one could include more lagged variables on the right-hand side and obtain the multivariate autocorrelation coefficients. For example, one could use both the change in the exchange rate last week and the change the week before in an attempt to predict the change in the exchange rate over the next week.

An interesting and popular test statistic is the first-order autocorrelation coefficient β_1 in Equation [1]. If β_1 is positive, an above-average increase in $s_{t-1,\ t}$ will typically be followed by another above-average increase, while an unusually large drop in the exchange rate will, on average, be followed by another above-average drop.

- Positive autocorrelation, if observed, could be consistent with many explanations:

  (1) The bandwagon theory: When an increase in the spot rates is observed, following an exogenous event, investors think that more increases will follow. Thus, they buy the foreign currency, which reinforces the initial increase, and so on.

  (2) Slow dissemination of information: At first, only well-informed players trade on good (or bad) news, and force a price change; then other groups gradually obtain the same information, trade on it, and induce more price changes in the same direction, and so on.

  (3) Positive autocorrelation could result from slow changes in risk or in the degree of risk aversion in the market. Waves of higher risk or higher risk aversion could lead to higher expected returns for fairly long periods, which means that above-average returns would tend to be followed by more above-average returns.

- Negative autocorrelation (increases tend to be followed by drops, and *vice versa*) could be explained by a possible tendency for the market to overreact to new information. A change would then generally be corrected afterwards. This view is implicit in the term *technical correction*, popularly used by the press: a price drop makes the asset more attractive, so demand increases, which forces the price back up.

Autocorrelation tests on the exchange market (see, for example, Fama [1976] and the references therein) generally reveal small, and typically significantly positive autocorrelations; also, autocorrelation coefficients are frequently larger than for common stocks. Still, the informative content of past exchange rates is low: the R^2 statistics from such tests rarely exceed 5 percent; thus, the predictability of the change in the exchange rate, based on past changes, is not economically significant.

15.1.2   Runs Tests

In runs tests, one represents the series of observed changes in the exchange rate by their signs, positive or negative. One then tests whether the observed series could possibly be drawn from a model that randomly generates pluses and minuses from a constant distribution.

Such tests reveal that there is some tendency for increases to be followed by more increases, and drops in the exchange rate to be followed by further drops. Again, the deviations from a random pattern are not very impressive, but the results confirm the (weak) persistence in exchange rate movements found in autocorrelation tests.

15.1.3   Filter Rules and Chartism

The trading rule frequently used in forecasting exchange rate is the **Alexander filter**. Alexander (1961) tested whether stock market movements tend to persist through time. If increases tend to be followed by increases, then a policy of buying after observing an x percent rise from a low would, on average, generate profits; and if price drops tend to be followed by more decreases, then selling after observing an x percent fall from a "high" would again pay, on average, as shown in Figure 15.1. The percentage x used to decide when to buy or sell is called the size of the filter. The filter is meant to detect significant changes as opposed to meaningless changes generated by temporary fluctuations in supply and demand. One could, of course, have a different filter size for buy decisions than that for sell decisions.

Sweeney (1988) finds statistically significant returns, before transaction costs, from using the Alexander filter in the exchange market. This confirms the weak persistence of movements found in runs tests and autocorrelation tests. Gernaey (1990) tests 584 different trading rules and finds that not even 10 percent of the rules produced profits that are significant at the 10 percent level before transaction

FIGURE 15.1   The Alexander Filter

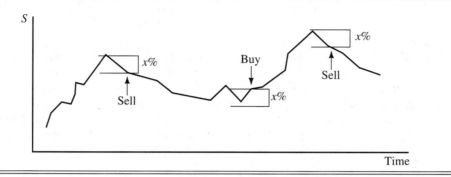

costs, and that only 0.3 percent of the rules are profitable after accounting for transaction costs. Curcio and Goodhart (1991) test whether decision makers' performance improved depending on whether they did or did not use a popular chartist package marketed by a London firm. They conclude that the software does not make any difference. Taylor (1992) concludes that technical trading rules do help.

15.1.4   An Evaluation: Does a Positive Autocorrelation Imply Market Inefficiency?

A market is (informationally) efficient or rational if all relevant information is immediately and correctly reflected in prices. If, in equilibrium, the return distribution perceived by the market is constant over time, then autocorrelation tests and runs tests should find no patterns at all. However, the asset's risk, or the market premium per unit of risk, may change slowly over time. This means that expected returns may change slowly over time. If this happens, then there would be a tendency for above-average returns to be followed by more above-average returns and, thus, the runs tests and autocorrelation tests may just be picking up the slow changes of expected returns over time rather than inertia or persistence in unexpected returns.

There are, in fact, a number of models that predict variation in the expected exchange rate change. For instance, the expected Relative Purchasing Power Parity hypothesis formulated by Roll (1979) (and explained in Chapter 14) suggests that the period-by-period expected degree of appreciation should equal the expected inflation differential for that period:

$$E_t(\tilde{s}_{t,t+1}) = E_t(\tilde{I}_{t,T}) - E_t(\tilde{I}^*_{t,T}).$$

The right-hand side is clearly predictable, as it changes slowly over time. Therefore, if Roll's model is correct, the slow change in the expected inflation differential could induce autocorrelation in the exchange rate change. Since this autocorrelation has nothing to do with *unexpected* returns, it has nothing to do with (in)efficiency. In short, we should not jump to conclusions and claim that exchange markets are somewhat inefficient if they are somewhat autocorrelated. Moreover, from a practical point of view, transaction costs may wipe out any profits from the so-called predictability of exchange rates (see, for example, Levich [1978]).

To conclude, the tests described above seem to suggest that it is not possible to predict very well future changes in exchange rates based only on past information about exchange rates. This also implies that the exchange market is close to being weak-form efficient. We now examine whether variables other than the spot rate are useful in predicting exchange rate changes.

15.2   FUNDAMENTAL MODELS OF EXCHANGE RATE FORECASTING

Fundamental models of exchange rate forecasting typically use macroeconomic variables to see if these variables can predict exchange rate changes. The information contained in these fundamental variables, such as interest rates and inflation, is used to make predictions about the future change in the exchange rate, either with the use of a formal economic model or based on judgment. In this section, we will examine the performance of the econometric models used to predict future exchange rates. Following the approach of Meese (1990), we first compare the statistical properties of the exchange rate to the properties of some of the fundamental variables that are used to predict the exchange rate in econometric models. We then describe the econometric models typically used to forecast the exchange rate. The performance of forecasting agencies is evaluated in the next section.

15.2.1   Properties of the Exchange Rate and the Fundamentals

To understand the performance of the fundamental econometric model of exchange rate forecasting, it is best to start with a comparison of the statistical properties of the variable that we are trying to predict and the properties of the variables that we are using to make this prediction.

The descriptive statistics that we examine, as in Meese (1990), are standard deviations of the changes in the exchange rate and the fundamentals, and the correlation between these variables. We study data on two exchange rates—the USD/JPY and USD/DEM—and the following fundamentals: differences in inflation rates, in money supply, and in industrial production between the US and Japan and between the US and Germany.

In Table 15.1, we report the standard deviation of the *level* of the exchange rates and the fundamental variables, and the standard deviation of the *changes*. From this table, we observe that the vari-

TABLE 15.1   Standard Deviation of Exchange Rates and Fundamental Variables

Variable	Standard deviation (of level)	Standard deviation × 100 (of first difference)
Log of spot USD/JPY	0.262	3.340
Log of spot USD/DEM	0.178	4.181
US-Japanese interest differential	0.026	0.801
US-German interest differential	0.016	0.785
Log of US-Japanese CPI	0.127	0.671
Log of US-German CPI	0.126	0.329
Log of US-Japanese M1	0.110	4.289
Log of US-German M1	0.085	2.2029
Log of US-Japanese industrial production	0.064	1.479
Log of US-German industrial production	0.072	2.056

The above statistics are computed using IMF monthly data from January 1975 to December 1989. The total number of observations is 174.

ation (standard deviation) in exchange rates changes is much larger than that in the fundamentals (except for the variation in the US-Japanese money supply growth rates).

In Table 15.2, we report the correlations between the variables listed in Table 15.1; each variable name is given in *abbreviated* form in Table 15.2. Inspecting the correlations between the exchange rate changes and changes (first differences) in the fundamentals in Table 15.2, we find that these correlations are very low, between 0.001 and 0.11, and none of these are statistically significant. Moreover, many of these correlations have signs that are difficult to explain. For example, the correlation between the exchange rate changes and inflation differentials in the US and Japan is negative. However, PPP would predict this to be positive (that is, countries with higher inflation should see their currencies depreciate—as explained in Chapter 11).

The challenge for any econometric model is to show how the relatively small variation in the fundamentals can lead to significantly larger volatility in exchange rates.

15.2.2   Econometric Models of the Exchange Rate

In this section, we discuss the performance of econometric models of exchange rate forecasting based on fundamental variables. The main conclusion is that these models do extremely poorly in forecasting the exchange rate. Even when the forecasts of these models are based on the *actual realized* value of

TABLE 15.2   Correlations between Exchange Rates and Fundamental Variables

Corr. of First Diff	USD JPY	USD DEM	JPY Interest	DEM Interest	JPY Price	DEM Price	JPY M1	DEM M1	JPY IndProd	DEM IndProd
USD/JPY	1.00									
USD/DEM	0.61	1.00								
JPY Interest	−0.07	−0.11	1.00							
DEM Interest	0.001	−0.05	0.084	1.00						
JPY Price	−0.05	−0.09	0.012	0.04	1.00					
DEM Price	0.07	−0.09	0.09	0.02	0.24	1.00				
JPY M1	−0.05	−0.02	−0.10	−0.09	−0.07	−0.001	1.00			
DEM M1	0.08	−0.09	−0.05	−0.01	−0.06	−0.002	−0.01	1.00		
JPY IndProd	0.006	−0.04	0.31	−0.25	0.01	0.10	−0.16	0.04	1.00	
DEM IndProd	−0.02	−0.02	0.15	0.16	0.18	0.04	0.04	−0.04	0.13	1.00

The above statistics are the correlations between the first differences of the variables given in Table 15.1. Variable names in Table 15.2 are abbreviations of the variables listed in the first column of Table 15.1. The correlations are computed using IMF monthly data from January 1975 to December 1989. The total number of observations is 174.

future explanatory variables (rather than their expected future value), these models can explain only a very small proportion of the total variation in the exchange rate; the R^2 is typically about 2 percent.

One example of an econometric test of whether the economic fundamentals can explain the exchange rate is given in Meese and Rogoff (1983):

$$\ln S_T = \alpha + \beta_1 (r_{t,T} - r_{t,T}^*) + \beta_2 (P_T - P_T^*) + \beta_3 (\ln L_T - \ln L_T^*)$$
$$+ \beta_4 (\ln Y_T - \ln Y_T^*) + \beta_5 (TB_{t,T} - TB_{t,T}^*) + e_T, \qquad [2]$$

where * refers to the variable for the foreign country, and S is the exchange rate (USD/foreign currency), r is the short-term interest rate, P is the domestic inflation rate, L is the domestic money supply, Y is the domestic industrial production, and TB is the cumulative trade balance at home. The test equation in [2] can be considered a reduced form equation of several structural models, including the purchasing power model that was discussed in Chapter 11 and the monetary model discussed in Chapter 13.

Meese and Rogoff (1983) compare the predictions for a one-, three-, six-, and twelve-month horizon from the above model to those from a random walk model. A random walk model is one where the change in the (log) spot rate is random, and this change is distributed normally. A random walk model that has no drift is given in Equation [3], and a more detailed discussion of the random walk model is given in the appendix to Chapter 7 and 8:

$$\ln S_{t+1} = \ln S_t + \varepsilon_{t,t+1}, \qquad [3]$$

where $\varepsilon_{t,t+1}$ is distributed normally with mean zero and standard deviation 1 per unit time.

Meese and Rogoff use the root mean square error (RMSE) criterion to compare the predictions of the econometric model to those from the random walk model. If we define the forecast for horizon k at time t as $\hat{S}(t+k)$, and the actual outcome as $S(t+k)$, the RMSE can be defined as:

$$RMSE = \left(\frac{\sum_{t}^{N} [\ln \hat{S}(t+k) - \ln S(t+k)]^2}{N} \right)^{0.5}.$$

The main conclusion of Meese and Rogoff is that the RMSE obtained from models such as the one in Equation [2] is rarely lower than the RMSE from the random walk model. That is, the gain in predictive power from using the fundamental variables in the economy is insignificant, since a naive and memoryless statistical model, such as the random walk, does almost as well. The random walk also does better than the forward rate at forecasting the future spot rate. This is consistent with the evidence from the empirical tests of UEH that are described in Chapter 14.

A statistically more reliable way of testing whether the fundamental variables can explain the variation in the spot exchange rate is through regression tests on *changes* of the variables. We test the following equation to see if the interest rate differential $(r_{t,T} - r_{t,T}^*)$, the inflation rate differential $(I_{t,T} - I_{t,T}^*)$, the differences in the growth rate in money supplies $(l_{t,T} - l_{t,T}^*)$, and the differences in the growth rates in industrial production can explain the change in the exchange rate, $s_{t,T}$:

$$s_{t,T} = \alpha + \beta_1 (r_{t,T} - r^*_{t,T}) + \beta_2 (I_{t,T} - I^*_{t,T})$$
$$+ \beta_3 (l_{t,T} - l^*_{t,T}) + \beta_4 (y_{t,T} - y^*_{t,T}) + e_{t,T}.$$

[4]

Using IMF monthly data from January 1975 to December 1989, we find that, for the case of the US versus Japan, the R^2 statistic is 0.0098 and, for the case of US versus Germany, the R^2 is 0.0118. None of the slope coefficients in either regression is significant even at the 10 percent level.

Besides Meese and Rogoff (1983), other studies have used fundamental variables to try to predict the exchange rate. Rogalski and Vinso (1977) test the relationship between the current account balance and the exchange rate. Recall, from Chapter 12, that the BOP model predicts slow changes in exchange rates, because the trade flows change slowly over time. Rogalski and Vinso find that all information in the current account balance is already present in the current spot rate and, therefore, this information is not very useful in predicting the future spot rate. Roll (1977) regresses the exchange rate plus the inflation differential on the lagged spot rate and tests whether adding past deviations from PPP improves the forecast. The results are negative.

15.2.3   Possible Explanations for the Failure of Fundamental Models

Several explanations have been offered to explain the poor record of fundamental models in explaining future changes in the interest rate. Meese (1990) classifies these explanations into two categories. The first class of explanations is that the model that is being used is the correct one but that there are estimation problems, such as simultaneity and the "peso problem" (discussed in Chapter 14) that affect the results. The second class of explanations is that the models themselves are mis-specified, that is, the actual model may not be linear, or it may have an omitted variables bias. For example, if the relationship between the exchange rate and the fundamental variables is nonlinear, then we should not be surprised at the poor predictive power of linear models. Similarly, if there is persistence in the conditional variance of exchange rates, we need a model that takes this conditional autoregressive heteroskedasticity into account (using ARCH or GARCH models). However, models that attempt to include the effect of such nonlinearities are still not able to improve upon the forecasting ability of the random walk model.

A second possible explanation of the failure of the models may be that, when including changes in fundamental variables as explanatory variables, these models implicitly assume that all of these changes were "news"—that is, deviations from what was previously expected. Yet, a drop in, say, industrial production may have been entirely anticipated by the market—in which case there would not be any reaction in the exchange market when the figure gets published. In fact, the drop may even have been smaller than what was forecasted, so that this drop may actually be good news rather than bad news. Thus, a second weakness of the models that we discussed is their failure to distinguish between anticipated and unanticipated changes. Only unanticipated changes can affect the exchange rate.

We conclude our discussion of fundamental models of exchange rate forecasting by noting that these models are unsuccessful at explaining changes in the spot rate. In particular, the naive random walk model outperforms both the regression-based models and the forward rate at forecasting the change in the exchange rate.

15.3   EVALUATING THE PERFORMANCE OF FORECASTERS

In the previous section, we discussed the performance of various economic models that try to predict the exchange rate based on information about the fundamentals in the economy. In this section, we evaluate the record of professional forecasters in predicting the future spot rate. We also look at the evidence to see if central banks, which have information about monetary policy that is not available to private investors, are successful at foreseeing the spot rate.

15.3.1   Evaluating the Performance of Forecasting Services

Goodman surveys the predictions made by forecasting services. He makes a distinction between econometric services, which use economic models such as the ones described in the above section to predict exchange rates, and services using technical (chartist) models to predict the spot rate. Goodman concludes that, while the first group is not very good at predicting the spot rate, the technical forecasters do somewhat better. The conclusions of reviews published by *Euromoney* in 1981–84 are similar.[1] Also, even the technical predictors' records appear to deteriorate over time.

   Levich (1979), in a comprehensive survey, concludes that forecasting services (econometric and judgmental) do poorly when the Mean Square Error (MSE) is used as the criterion for testing the accuracy of forecasts relative to the MSE for the forward rate.[2] However, he finds that they may have some ability to predict whether the future spot rate will be greater than or smaller than the current forward rate—the information needed to make the correct hedging decision and to undertake the correct speculative strategy, as explained below.

Example   15.1

To see why the *direction* of forecast (relative to the forward rate) may be at least as important as the absolute or squared error, suppose that the current three-month forward rate is USD/DEM 0.4205 and the forecast for the future spot is USD/DEM 0.4215.

   If you wish to speculate, based on this forecast, you would buy DEM forward. Now, suppose that the DEM does appreciate to USD/DEM 0.4245. Then the (absolute) size of the forecast error in this case is 0.4245 − 0.4215 = USD/DEM 0.0030. However, you will not be upset about this error, because you make a profit of 0.4245 − 0.4205 = USD/DEM 0.0040 by having bought forward.

   On the other hand, suppose that the realized spot rate was USD/DEM 0.4200. In this case, because the *direction* of the forecast (relative to the forward rate) was wrong, and the DEM depreciated, you would have lost 0.4200 − 0.4205 = (−)USD/DEM 0.0005. In this case, the *size* of the forecast error is only 0.4215 − 0.4200 = USD/DEM 0.0015, half of the forecast error in the previous scenario. Thus, the speculator would prefer to get a forecast that is correct in direction, and would not care about the absolute magnitude of the error.

   The difference between being *accurate* (in terms of predicting the direction of change) and being *close* (in terms of the absolute magnitude of the forecast error) is demonstrated in Figure 15.2, where we compare two situations. In the first situation, the forecast was that the future spot rate would be below the current forward rate. The actual spot rate turned out to be above the forward rate, and thus, one would have lost money if one had acted on the forecast. In the second situation, the realized spot rate was below the forward rate, as forecasted, and thus a speculative strategy based on the forecast would have generated a profit.

---

[1] Note that the databases of these studies strongly overlap, so that the repeated positive results for technical analysis are not independent.

[2] The MSE (and its root) were discussed in Section 15.2.2.

FIGURE 15.2 "Accuracy" versus "Closeness" as a Measure of Predictive Performance

In both situations below, the forward rate is "closer" to the outcome than is the forecast. Still, the forecast can be "accurate."

Situation 1:

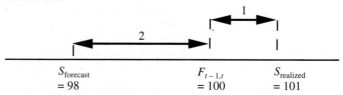

S_{forecast} $F_{t-1,t}$ S_{realized}
$= 98$ $= 100$ $= 101$

If you acted on the forecast and sold forward, you expected a gain of 2. However, you realized a loss of 1. The forecast was "inaccurate."

Situation 2:

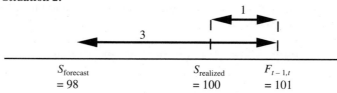

S_{forecast} S_{realized} $F_{t-1,t}$
$= 98$ $= 100$ $= 101$

If you acted on the forecast and sold forward, you expected a gain of 3. The gain turned out to be only 1, but was still positive. The prediction was "accurate."

To test how well forecasters can predict the direction that the spot will change (relative to the forward), Levich (1980) tests the number of times a profit is made from taking an open forward position on the basis of the forecast. Levich concludes that the relative number of correct signals for some forecasting services exceeds 50 percent significantly. Thus, it seems that some forecasters have some skill in predicting the direction of change in the spot. Levich's significance tests, however, ignore the dependence between the test results. If a US forecaster is lucky predicting the DEM, he or she almost surely will be lucky forecasting the related currencies, such as the CHF, NLG, and FRF. Thus, the evidence is hard to interpret. Moreover, when Levich (1982, 1983) did the same study a few years later, he found that the forecasting services that performed well in the first study were not the same as those that did well in the updated survey. Thus, it seems that no service can *consistently* predict the future spot rate relative to the forward.

To summarize the literature evaluating the performance of forecasters in predicting the future spot rate, the evidence suggests that predictions based on fundamental variables do not seem to be accurate. Technical forecasts, at least for short-term forecasts, seem to do better, though their record is not impressive.

15.3.2 Evaluating the Performance of Central Banks

Central banks claim that they intervene in currency markets to maintain an orderly market and to smooth out excessive swings in exchange rates; they also claim that they do not try to move the exchange rate away from its fundamental value. If this is true, central banks must be quite good at predicting exchange rates. The bank buys if it knows that the current low price of foreign currency is a temporary aberration that will soon be reversed, and it sells to speed up the drop of the currency that it knows is imminent anyway.

Milton Friedman once remarked that, if central bankers were really successful in distinguishing excessive swings from fundamental trends, they should be hugely profitable. Indeed, they would start buying when the exchange rate is below its equilibrium value, and they would start selling when the exchange rate is above its equilibrium value. However, when Taylor (1982) measured profits from intervention, he found that seven central banks out of eight actually made substantial losses from currency trading. In three cases, these losses could not even remotely be ascribed to chance. In short, the results from Taylor's study seem to suggest that either central banks are bad at outguessing the market, or they actually go against the market (at the taxpayers' expense). However, some of these results were sensitive to the time period of the study. For example, if Taylor's study is extended by two years, the central banks actually make a modest profit from their currency trading.

We now examine evidence from two studies conducted by the central banks themselves. De Nederlandsche Bank applied Taylor's methodology to its interventions in the currency markets and found that it made money on its spot market interventions, but lost money when it intervened in the forward market. The Bank of Canada studied its profitability and effectiveness over the period 1975–1988. They concluded that the government's trading in the currency market has been profitable and that this trading has tended to be stabilizing in the sense that the actions of the central bank helped move the exchange rate closer to its long-run equilibrium value and helped reduce its short-term volatility. However, despite this record of profitability over the 1975–88 period, the Bank of Canada incurred substantial losses during other periods. Thus, the evidence is mixed and one cannot conclude that central banks can predict the future spot rate, even though they have access to information about monetary and exchange rate policy—information that is not available to the typical investor.

15.4   IMPLICATIONS FOR TREASURY MANAGEMENT

In this chapter, we have evaluated two types of forecasting models—technical models that attempt to forecast the future exchange rate based on past values of the exchange rate, and fundamental models that use macroeconomic variables to predict the exchange rate.

The evidence suggests that the fundamental models are unsuccessful at predicting exchange rates in the short run. This result is consistent with the evidence on purchasing power parity that we discussed in Chapter 11. Inflation differentials between two countries cannot explain the changes in the exchange rate. The failure of fundamental models is also consistent with the results of tests of Unbiased Expectations Hypothesis that we examined in Chapter 14. The forward rate is a biased and poor predictor of future exchange rates. What is more remarkable is that the random-walk model of exchange rates outperforms sophisticated econometric models based on economic fundamentals in predicting the future change in the exchange rate.

At least in the short run, technical models seem to do better than fundamental models at predicting future exchange rates. However, it is not clear whether one can make abnormal returns (over and above the return for the risk taken) using technical analysis.

With this chapter, we come to the end of Part II of the book. In this part, we have examined whether prices in countries adjust in response to the exchange rate. We found that, at least in the short run, there are substantial deviations from Purchasing Power Parity, implying that firms and investors are exposed to real exchange rate risk. Given the presence of this risk, we would like to forecast changes in the future exchange rate. In Chapters 12 and 13, we described several exchange rate models, such as the balance of payments model, the monetary model, and the portfolio model of exchange rates, and in Chapter 14, we discussed the Unbiased Expectations Hypothesis, which suggests that the future spot rate is equal to the forward rate. We found that none of these models is successful at predicting the exchange rate. In the next chapter, we ask the question: Given that firms cannot forecast exchange rates, *should* they hedge exchange rate exposure? That is, can hedging increase the value of a firm?

QUIZ QUESTIONS

True-False Questions

1. Technical forecasting models analyze microeconomic variables in an attempt to forecast future changes in the exchange rate.
2. Fundamental analysis models analyze macroeconomic variables in an attempt to forecast future changes in the exchange rate.
3. By a "technical correction," one means that investors underreact to bad news so that the exchange rate does not drop as low as it should. This means that demand must fall further, in order to correctly value a foreign currency in terms of the home currency.
4. If the exchange rate bottoms out (that is, it hits a low point but begins to rise again), and then increases again by x percent, we can make substantial (and low-risk) profits by buying foreign currency—even when paying "retail" bid-ask spreads.
5. Because we cannot make significant profits from predicting the exchange rate based on past information, the exchange markets are weak-form efficient.
6. Runs tests have confirmed that positive changes in the exchange rate tend to be followed by positive changes, and negative changes by negative changes. This is consistent with the conclusions from autocorrelation tests.
7. The results from runs tests and autocorrelation tests provide unambiguous evidence that the foreign exchange market is inefficient.
8. Central bankers are able to forecast the future spot rate because they have inside information.
9. Central bankers are manifestly able to forecast the future spot rate because they have inside information, but they cannot forecast the current forward rate because they cannot know the future risk-free rates of return.

Multiple-Choice Questions

Choose the correct answer(s).

1. Technical analysis:

   (a) has been proven to be utterly useless as a way of predicting exchange rates.
   (b) relies on statistical and econometric models rather than on trading rules.
   (c) is solely based on a forecaster's sentiments about the exchange rate markets.
   (d) can only work when there is weak-form market efficiency.
   (e) provides evidence of semi-strong-form inefficiency (when technical analysis works, that is).

2. Fundamental analysis:

   (a) has been proven to be of little value as a way of predicting exchange rates.
   (b) relies on macroeconomic variables like inflation, interest rates, and real economic output.
   (c) may rely on a forecaster's sentiments about the exchange rate markets rather than solely on a formal, quantitative model.
   (d) can only work when there is weak-form market efficiency.
   (e) provides evidence of semi-strong-form inefficiency (when fundamental analysis works, that is).

PART

In Part II of the text, we considered various theories of exchange rate determination. In Chapter 14, we concluded that the forward rate's performance as a predictor of the future spot rate is rather dismal, and in Chapter 15, we saw that it is not easy to predict the future spot rate even when using macroeconomic variables or technical analysis. Also, from Chapter 11, we know that Purchasing Power Parity is a very weak force in the short run. That is, most exchange rate changes are "real" exchange changes rather than movements that offset inflation differentials, implying that prices of goods and production factors differ substantially across countries even after conversion into one common currency. Moreover, this variation in real exchange rates seems to persist for long periods of time. Thus, one conclusion that can be drawn from the material presented in Part II is that there is substantial variation in real exchange rates giving rise to exchange risk, and that it is difficult to predict the future exchange rate.

In this section of the text, Part III, we first ask whether firms should hedge against exchange rate risk. That is, can firms increase their value by hedging against currency risk? In Chapter 16, we argue that the presence of market imperfections gives rise to costs of financial distress. Hedging, by permitting firms to reduce the likelihood of incurring these costs, can lead to an increase in their value.

Given the arguments in favor of hedging, Chapters 17, 18, and 19 explain how one can measure the exposure of a firm to exchange rate risk, and how the various currency markets described in Part I of the text can be used to hedge against this risk. In Chapter 17, we describe how to measure and hedge the exposure of a firm's existing contracts to exchange rate risk. In Chapter 18, we describe how to measure the exposure of a firm's future cash flows to the exchange rate, and how to hedge this exposure using forward contracts and options. In Chapter 19, we study how to measure the accounting exposure of a firm, that is, the exposure that arises from the fact that a foreign subsidiary's accounts need to be translated into the currency of the parent for reporting purposes.

Exchange risk is not the only source of risk that a firm faces when engaged in international trade. Credit risks get an extra dimension when transactions are between parties located in different countries. And political risk—the risk that the foreign customer is not allowed to buy foreign exchange and make the promised payment—also arises in the context of international trade. In Chapter 20, we examine various international payments mechanisms designed to deal with these risks. We shall argue that these arrangements are rational solutions to the related issues of (a) how to obtain swift and efficient financing and (b) how to shift risks towards parties that are better placed to bear them.

3

INTERNATIONAL RISK MANAGEMENT

THE RELEVANCE OF HEDGING

At this stage of the text, we hope that you are convinced that (1) deviations from purchasing power parity are sufficiently large and persistent so as to expose firms to real exchange rate risk (Chapter 11), and that (2) it is difficult to predict exchange rates (Chapter 15). We have discussed, in Part I, how various financial instruments can be used to reduce or even eliminate the effect of unexpected exchange rate changes on the firm's cash flows. We have not yet discussed the *relevance* of hedging. The central question that we address in this chapter is: Do firms need to hedge foreign exchange risk?

In the first section of this chapter, we describe the conditions under which a firm's hedging policy does not affect its value. In Section 16.2, we argue that these conditions are seldom satisfied in the real world, and thus we conclude that a firm should hedge its exposure to the exchange rate. In Section 16.3, we examine some of the reasons offered against hedging exchange rate risk. Our conclusions are presented in Section 16.4.

16.1 CONDITIONS FOR IRRELEVANCE OF A FIRM'S HEDGING DECISION

If financial policy is based on the objective of maximizing shareholders' wealth, then hedging a particular risk faced by a firm makes sense only if this leads to an increase in the (current) value of the firm.[1] From basic finance, we know that the value of a firm is the sum of all of its future expected cash flows, discounted at the appropriate interest rate. Thus, hedging can increase the value of a firm either by increasing the expected cash flows or by decreasing the rate at which these cash flows are discounted.

---

[1] Hedging obviously changes the *future* value of the firm.

The Modigliani-Miller (1958) theorem gives us a set of sufficient conditions under which, for a given investment and operating policy, the firm's value is unaffected by its financial policy. These conditions are:

1. There are no taxes.
2. There are no costs of financial distress. If the firm as a whole has a positive value but cannot pay its bondholders the promised amounts, then the bondholders take over control from the shareholders, and continue the firm's operations (or sell the firm to others who continue the firm's operations). In short, when the firm defaults on its obligations, the value of the firm as a whole is not affected.
3. There are no transactions costs when firms issue securities or hedge their exposures. Nor do shareholders incur costs when they trade assets or enter into forward contracts.
4. Investors and the firm have equal access to financial markets, so that individuals can make the same transactions that firms can make, and at the same prices.
5. Investors and the firm have the same information about the firm's operations.

The logic underlying the Modigliani-Miller result is that the managers of a firm cannot increase its value by undertaking financial transactions that the shareholders can make themselves. This insight was originally applied to the case of a firm's capital structure decision: a firm's value cannot be increased by changing the proportion of debt to equity used to finance the firm. That is, if shareholders can borrow and lend on their own account, and at the same rate as the firm, then the firm's decision on how much to borrow should not affect its value. The logic underlying this argument is that if the firm does not borrow enough, then shareholders can increase their leverage by borrowing on their own account. Similarly, if the firm borrows more than what shareholders consider appropriate, then they can lend on their own account, thus undoing the actions of the firm.

In our context, the financial policy that we wish to evaluate is the firm's decision to hedge its exposure to exchange rates. Thus, applying the Modigliani-Miller result to the firm's hedging decision, we see that the firm's decision to hedge its exposure to exchange rates will not affect its value if shareholders could have achieved the same risk reduction through a transaction in the exchange market. Specifically, if spot and forward markets are perfect, then investors can undo at no cost the foreign currency positions that the firm managers take on. For instance, a corporate decision not to hedge a particular exposure that the shareholders would like to hedge will merely shift the hedging from the corporate level to the personal level, at no cost ("home-made" hedging). Thus, in an ideal world, whether or not a firm hedges its exposure to the exchange rates should not have any effect on its value.

The world that we live in, however, is not a perfect one, and the conditions under which the Modigliani-Miller result is true are rarely satisfied. In the next section, we examine how a firm's hedging decision may affect its value when these conditions are violated.

16.2   ARGUMENTS IN FAVOR OF HEDGING EXCHANGE RISK

In this section, we examine various market imperfections under which hedging a firm's exposure to exchange rates can increase its value. From the discussion above, we know that a financial policy will increase the value of a firm only if that policy leads to an increase in the expected after-tax cash flows of the firm or to a decrease in the rate at which these cash flows are discounted. Thus, in our discussion below, we will study the impact of hedging on the firm's cash flows, its taxes, its investment policy, and its cost of capital.

16.2.1   Corporate Hedging Reduces Costs of Bankruptcy and Financial Distress

A firm is said to be in financial distress when its income is not sufficient to cover its fixed expenses. The state of financial distress can lead to bankruptcy, which of course involves liquidation costs and other direct costs. Large, uncovered exposures, combined with adverse exchange rate movements, may send a firm into insolvency and bankruptcy, or may at least contribute to such an outcome.

Example   16.1

In 1992, Slite, a Swedish shipping company that ran a ferry line between Sweden and Finland, should have taken delivery of a ship that had been ordered some years before from a German shipbuilding company. However, at the time of signing the purchase contract, Slite had decided not to hedge the DEM outflow because the SEK was tied to a basket in which the DEM had a large weight, and because the DEM was at a substantial forward premium relative to the SEK. However, by September 1992, Sweden had been forced to abandon the link between the SEK and the DEM, which had appreciated by 30 percent against the SEK by the end of 1992. As a consequence of the appreciation of the DEM, Slite could no longer afford the ship, and the vessel was ultimately leased by a competitor, the Finnish-Swedish company, Silja. In the spring of 1993, Slite went bankrupt.

Outright bankruptcy is costly because of the costs associated with liquidation. In the absence of these costs, Slite's shareholders would simply have lost control of the firm to the bondholders, who would carry on the business as before (possibly after selling their ownership rights to others). That is, in the absence of bankruptcy costs, the event of insolvency would not have affected the value of the firm as a whole. In reality, of course, bankruptcy *is* costly; and the cost includes not only the fees paid to liquidators, lawyers, assessors, and courts, but also the potential end of operations, and loss of clientele and reputation.

Even before a firm actually goes bankrupt, financial distress can affect the operations and the value of the firm significantly. Thus, if hedging can reduce the volatility of the firm's cash flows, and hence the likelihood of the firm being in financial distress, hedging will increase the firm's current value. Let us consider three specific links between the financial state of a firm and its real operations.

- *The Product Market and Reorganization Costs*

Many firms sell products for which after-sales service is needed. The firms typically offer product warranties. A buyer's decision to purchase such products will depend on his or her confidence in the firm's after-sales service. These firms will sell more and will, therefore, be worth more the lower the probability of their going out of business. Hedging, by reducing the volatility of cash flows, decreases the probability of (coming uncomfortably close to) bankruptcy.

Example   16.2

When the US computer manufacturer Wang got into financial problems, one of Wang's customers noted that, "Before the really bad news, we were looking at Wang fairly seriously [but] their present financial condition means that I'd have a hard time convincing the vice president in charge of purchasing. . . . At some point we'd have to ask *How do we know that in three years you won't be in Chapter 11 [bankruptcy]?*" (Rawls and Smithson, 1990, p. 11).

Note that this argument depends on a capital market imperfection, that is, reorganization costs. In the absence of reorganization costs, a loss due to an adverse movement in exchange rates would not affect sales of the firm's product: the firm's new owners would carry on the business as before.

- *The Labor Market and Wage Costs*

Risk-averse employees are likely to demand higher wages if their future job prospects are very uncertain. In the event of bankruptcy, a forced change of job will generally entail monetary and/or non-monetary losses to employees. Thus, the employees will want to protect themselves by requiring higher wages when working for a firm that is more likely to be in financial distress.

Note that this source of wage risk premium seems to hinge on imperfections in the labor market. However, ultimately, the validity of this rationale for corporate hedging can still be traced to imperfections in the market for risks. If uncertainty of personal income were fully diversifiable or hedgeable, there would not be a risk premium in wages,

- *The Capital Market and Refinancing Costs*

Loan covenants can trigger repayment if the firm's income falls below a stated level. To the extent that refinancing is difficult or costly, it is useful for the firm to reduce income volatility by hedging. Costs associated with refinancing include transaction costs, and especially, the indirect or agency costs of refinancing when a firm is in financial distress. Of course, these costs again represent a "friction" in the capital market.

We conclude that, in the presence of financial distress costs, there is a unique optimal hedging policy: the firm should minimize the variance of its cash flows. This is, in fact, the criterion we already applied in Chapter 5 when we discussed how the firm should select its optimal position when hedging in the futures markets: the number of contracts, β, is chosen so as to minimize the variance of the firm's cash flows. The generalization of this result is that a firm, which has assets and liabilities denominated in many currencies, should minimize the probability of bankruptcy by a hedging policy that minimizes the variance of its overall cash flows.[2]

16.2.2   "Home-Made" Hedging Is Not an Efficient Substitute for Corporate Hedging

The Modigliani-Miller proposition that hedging is irrelevant assumes that financing decisions by shareholders on their personal account are perfect substitutes for the corporate financing decisions that the shareholders would have preferred. The term *perfect substitutes* should be read in a double sense: the "home-made" financial contracts are assumed to have the same effect, and are concluded at the same prices, as the corporate financial decisions they replace. In practice, "home-made" financing decisions fail to meet both criteria.

As we develop this point, note that there is a preferred hedging policy: when financial distress is costly, the firm should minimize the variance of its cash flows. (The agency cost arguments below lead to the same conclusion.) Suppose that, for some reason, the firm does not follow this optimal policy. Then, "home-made" hedging by the firm's shareholders may not be a good substitute for the following reasons.

- One reason is that, in the real world, shareholders have far less information than the managers about the firm's exposure. If shareholders have very imprecise knowledge of the firm's exposure, "home-made" hedging will be far less effective than corporate hedging.
- The existence of financial distress costs (or agency costs—see below) is a second reason why "home-made" hedging is an imperfect substitute for corporate hedging. In reality, no individual shareholder can buy a contract that perfectly hedges against the costs of financial distress.

---

2 In fact, there is no reason to restrict hedging to exchange rate risk. All risks arising from operations, and for which a (cross) hedge is available, should be included in the variance minimization.

Thus, no "home-made" hedging decision produces the same time-T payoffs as the corporate hedging decisions. If a perfect substitute for corporate hedging is impossible, the Modigliani-Miller argument is no longer applicable.

One could argue that shareholders can always make an *approximate* substitute for corporate hedging. For instance, if they know that the firm is likely to get into trouble if a particular exchange rate moves in a particular direction and if business conditions are adverse, the shareholders can select portfolios that tend to have higher payoffs under these circumstances. However, such "home-made" hedging would fail the second criterion for a perfect substitute: that corporations and individuals have the same access to hedging instruments.

- Because of economies of scale, firms can obtain better terms for forward or money-market hedging than the individual shareholder. Thus, shareholders may value financial transactions undertaken for them by the firm.
- Short-selling constraints can provide an additional reason why hedging is better undertaken by the firm rather than left to individual shareholders. In idealized markets, investors can easily borrow (or sell forward) any currency that they choose. However, in financial markets, personal borrowing in foreign currencies is not easy, and forward positions require substantial margin or else are discouraged by banks. It is true that going short is easy in futures markets; but the size of the futures contracts may be prohibitive for many shareholders. Moreover, for many currencies, there simply are no futures markets.[3]

Thus, corporations have better hedging opportunities than individual shareholders, which again means that "home-made" financial decisions are an imperfect substitute for corporate decisions.

16.2.3   Hedging Reduces Agency Costs

Financial distress costs are not the only link between hedging and the firm's operations. Following Jensen (1986), one could argue that agency costs also create such a link. Agency costs are the costs that arise from the conflict of interest between shareholders, bondholders, and the managers of the firm. These agency costs can affect the firm's wage bill, its choice of investment projects, and its borrowing costs. Hedging, by reducing the volatility of a firm's cash flows, can reduce the conflict of interests between different claimants to the firm's cash flows and can increase the firm's debt capacity and reduce its cost of capital.

One conflict is that between the managers of the firm and the shareholders. The source of the problem is that, through their wages and bonus plans, the wealth of the managers depends to a large extent on the performance of the firm. Since managers cannot sell forward part of their lifetime future wages in order to diversify, the only way that they can reduce the risk to their human wealth is to hedge the exposure by creating negatively correlated cash flows through positions in the foreign exchange, commodity futures, and interest futures markets. As argued above, "home-made" hedging (by the managers) is not a good substitute for corporate hedging because personal hedging is expensive and difficult. In addition, there is likely to be a maturity mismatch between the hedge and the exposed human wealth, which creates a ruin-risk problem similar to the one mentioned in connection with marking to market in futures markets (see Chapter 5). The reason for the mismatch is that affordable forward contracts are likely to have short maturities, while the wages that are exposed will be realized in the longer

---

[3] Note, in passing, that incomplete information and differential hedging opportunities are valid arguments in favor of corporate hedging only when an optimal corporate hedging policy exists. If there is no well-defined objective desirable to all shareholders, the fact that the firm can trade at better spreads is not very helpful, nor is the fact that the firm faces less stringent short-selling constraints. For example, if some shareholders want the firm to have an FRF exposure while others prefer it to swap its FRF into USD, one of these groups may have to undo, at relatively great costs, the transaction that the firm undertook at low costs.

run. The maturity mismatch between the short-term hedge and the long-term exposure becomes a problem when the value of human wealth goes *up*. Then, the short-term hedge triggers immediate cash outflows, while the benefits in terms of wages will not be realized until much later. That is, the personal hedge creates liquidity problems and, in the limit, may lead to personal insolvency.

For the above reasons, managers dislike hedging on a personal basis, and want the firm to hedge instead. If the firm does not hedge, managers can react in two ways. First, they are likely to insist on higher wages, as a premium for the extra risk they have to bear. Second, if the firm has investment opportunities that are very risky, the managers may refuse to undertake such projects even if they have a positive net present value. As the shareholders have imperfect information about the firm's investment opportunities, there is little they can do about these actions of the managers. Thus, the shareholders are better off if the firm hedges its exposures. This policy will simultaneously hedge the managers' exposures, and thus reduce wage bills, and will lead to the managers adopting the optimal investment policy.

Another example of agency costs is the conflict that arises between shareholders and bondholders in the choice of investment projects. This conflict arises because bondholders get (at most) a fixed return on their investment, while shareholders receive the cash left over after bondholders have been paid off. That is, the shareholders have a call option on the value of the firm, with the face value of the firm's debt as the option's strike price. We know, from Chapter 6, that the value of an option increases when the volatility of the underlying asset increases. Thus, in the case of a levered firm that is close to financial distress, shareholders may have an incentive to undertake very risky projects even if the project's net present value is negative. This is because the value of equity (the option on the future value of the firm as a whole) increases even though the current value of the firm as a whole goes down. Obviously, if this happens, the bondholders are worse off. Similarly, when a firm is close to bankruptcy, shareholders may have an incentive not to take on risk-reducing projects, even if these projects have a positive net present value. This is because, although the current value of the firm goes up when the project is undertaken, the value of the option (the equity) goes down. Bondholders, of course, recognize and anticipate these potential conflicts of interest and, therefore, adjust the terms of their loan appropriately. Thus, by hedging and reducing the variability of the firm's cash flows, one can reduce the potential for conflicts of interest associated with financial distress, and one can thereby reduce the cost of borrowing.

16.2.4   Hedging Reduces Expected Taxes

Hedging reduces expected cash flows if taxes are convex rather than linear functions of income. One example of a convex tax function is a progressive tax schedule, where the tax rate increases with income. In this case, smoothing the income stream will imply a lower average tax burden.

Example   16.3

Suppose that if income is USD 100, you pay USD 45 in taxes, while if income is USD 50, you pay only USD 20 in taxes. The expected tax when the earnings are USD 50 without risk then equals USD 20, while the expected tax is USD 22.5 when earnings are, with equal probability, either USD 100 or 0.

It may be argued that most countries' corporate tax rate schedules are, for all practical applications, flat. However, a more subtle type of convexity is created by the fact that, when profits are negative, taxes are usually not proportionally negative. In some countries, there *are* negative corporate taxes, but the amount refunded is limited to the taxes paid in the recent past. Such a rule is called *carry-back*: this year's losses are deducted from profits made in preceding years, implying that the taxes paid on these past profits are recuperated. Still, carry-back is limited to the profits made in only a few recent years, which means that negative taxes on losses are limited, too. In other countries, there is no carry-back at all. All one can do is deduct this year's losses from potential future profits *(carry-forward)*, which at best postpones the negative tax on this year's losses.

Example   16.4

In Belgium, firms are not allowed to carry back losses. If a particular Belgian firm's profits are either BEF 35m or BEF 15m with equal probability, the expected profit is BEF 25m and the expected tax (at 40 percent) is BEF 10m. In contrast, if its profits are either BEF 100m or –BEF 50m with equal probability, the expected profit is still BEF 25m but now the expected tax is (BEF 100m $\times$ 0.4 + BEF 0)/2 = BEF 20m. It is true that the potential BEF 50m loss can be carried forward and deducted from subsequent profits, but these later tax savings are uncertain, and even if they were certain, there would still be the loss of time value.

Now consider a case where a firm is allowed to carry back its losses. Even in this case, excessive variability of income can affect the tax liability if the current losses are larger than the profits against which they can be set off. In the US, for instance, there is a three-year carry-back provision. Suppose that a particular firm's profits in the last three years amounted to USD 30m. If, for the next year, its profits are either USD 35m or USD 15m with equal probability, the expected profit is USD 25m and the expected tax (at 40 percent) is USD 10m. In contrast, if its profits are either USD 100m or –USD 50m with equal probability, the expected profit is still USD 25m but the potential loss now exceeds the profits made in the past three years. This means that in case of losses, the firm can recuperate the taxes paid on the USD 30m recent profits (that is, there is a negative tax of USD 30m $\times$ 40% = USD 12m), and the remaining USD 20m "unused" losses can be carried forward. Thus, the expected tax is [(USD 100m $\times$ 0.4) + (–USD 30m $\times$ 0.4)]/2 = USD 14m rather than USD 10m. It is true that the unused losses of USD 20m can be deducted from subsequent profits, but these later tax savings are uncertain, and even if they were certain, there would still be a loss of time value.

16.2.5   Hedging May Also Provide Better Information for Internal Decision Making

Multidivisional multinationals need to know the operational profitability of their divisions. By having each division hedge its cash flows, a multinational knows each division's operating profitability without the noise introduced by unexpected exchange rate changes. This may lead to better decision making and may, thus, lead to an increase in expected cash flows.

Of course, the same information can be obtained in different ways, and the alternatives may be cheaper. The firm could request that all divisions keep track of their exposure at every moment, and could afterwards compute how profitable each division would have been if it had actually hedged. Another alternative, similar in spirit, is to shift all exchange risk towards a reinvoicing center. Under such an arrangement, a Canadian production unit sells its output to a reinvoicing center on a CAD invoice, while a Portuguese marketing subsidiary buys these products on a PTE invoice. In terms of information per subsidiary, this achieves the same objective as the subsidiary-by-subsidiary hedging policy. The corporation may then decide, on other grounds, whether or not the reinvoicing center should hedge the corporation's overall exposure.[4]

---

[4] If the reinvoicing center is instructed to hedge its exposure, this is likely to be cheaper than a policy where each subsidiary hedges its own exposures. First, the reinvoicing center can economize on hedging costs because it can "net" (clear) offsetting exposures. Second, there are likely to be benefits from specialization and scale economies. Third, the reinvoicing center is often located in a tax haven and simultaneously serves to reduce (or at least postpone) taxation on part of the group's profits.

Actual hedging entails a (small) cost, but as-if-hedged financial reporting is not costless either, and the corporation's operations may be too small to justify the fixed costs of a reinvoicing center. Thus, the bottom line is that the choice between actual hedging and as-if-hedged financial reporting or reinvoicing will depend on the circumstances.

16.3   IRRELEVANT ARGUMENTS

In this section we discuss how three additional arguments sometimes advanced with respect to the relevance of hedging turn out to be invalid. We have, in fact, already briefly dismissed these arguments in Chapter 3.

16.3.1   The Forward Premium Indicates Whether Hedging Is Costly

A not-infrequent (but misleading) practice is to compare the forward rate to the current spot rate to determine the cost or benefit of hedging. That is, hedging a foreign currency inflow by selling it forward at a premium (discount) is said to be profitable (costly), and hedging a foreign currency outflow by buying it forward at a premium (discount) is said to be disadvantageous (advantageous). In Chapter 3, we dismissed the forward premium or discount as being an irrelevant accounting construct. In Chapter 4, we concluded that the appropriate cost of hedging is the transaction cost for forward transactions compared to those for spot transactions. Specifically, a useful first approximation of the cost of any transaction is one-half of the bid-ask spread. However, in our case, the forward deal replaces a spot transaction. This means that we should measure the cost of hedging as the increase in the implicit commission incurred by dealing at the forward rate rather than the spot rate. This can be measured as approximately half of the difference between the bid-ask spreads in the forward market and in the spot market. As was illustrated in Chapter 4, this cost is low indeed. We repeat the computations.

Example   16.5

The London *Financial Times* of January 12, 1993, gives the following CAD/USD spot and forward rates. We have added columns showing the spread. For the forward quotes, we also show the increase in the spread relative to the spot market, and the extra cost (half of the difference of the spreads, as a percentage of the midpoint spot rate).

Maturity	Rates	Bid-ask spread	Half the forward spread minus half the spot spread	Extra cost, as a % of midpoint spot rate
Spot	1.2750–1.2760	0.0010	–	–
Forward 30 day	1.2705–1.2722	0.0017	0.00035	0.027%
Forward 90 day	1.2630–1.2655	0.0025	0.00075	0.059%

$$*\text{extra spread, as a } \% = \frac{[\text{half the difference of the spreads}]}{\dfrac{S_{\text{bid}} + S_{\text{ask}}}{2}}$$

16.3.2 A Zero-Value Contract Cannot Change the Firm's Value

In Chapter 3, we showed that a forward contract has a zero market value at its inception. This fact is often used to argue that adding a forward contract to the firm's existing operations will not change the value of the firm. The argument can be generalized to other hedge instruments. For instance, an option is not a zero-value contract, nor is it a foreign currency deposit or loan. Yet, buying an option or a foreign currency deposit does not affect the current value of the firm because the firm pays the fair price for the contract it buys; and borrowing foreign currency does not affect the firm's value because the firm obtains a fair price for the securities it issues.

The problem with this argument is, of course, that it implicitly assumes that the firm's other cash flows are not affected by the hedge. In Section 16.2, we argued that such an assumption is untenable. In the presence of financial distress, agency costs, convex tax schedules, and other market imperfections, the decision to hedge (or not to hedge) will affect the firm's operations, and many of these effects are driven by the variability of the firm's cash flows

This link between expected cash flows and variability also refutes a special version of the zero-value fallacy that is based on the Capital Asset Pricing Model. The **Capital Asset Pricing Model (CAPM)** suggests that only systematic risk matters. Thus, if exchange risk is unsystematic, it does not matter, for it will be diversified away in investors' portfolios. If, on the other hand, exchange risk is systematic and markets are perfect, then one will earn the appropriate return for bearing this risk. Using forward contracts to hedge this risk will only move the firm along the security market line. That is, the reduction in risk is accompanied by an appropriate drop in expected return so that there is no effect on the firm's value. This argument is misleading because it looks at the firm as if it were a portfolio of stocks and bonds. Adding a new item to a portfolio of securities does not affect the payoffs from any of the stocks and bonds in the portfolio; and the absence of interactions between the components of a portfolio, in effect, means that covariance is the only risk that matters. In contrast, when there are financial distress or agency costs, convex taxes, and so on, adding a hedge to the firm's operation *is* likely to affect the firm's cash flows from operations; these interactions or nonlinearities mean that the variance of the firm's cash flows can also affect its value.

16.3.3 Hedging Affects the Interest Tax Shield

The last fallacy to be discussed is that hedging matters because it affects the interest tax shields. The issue is most often raised when the hedging alternative being considered is a money market hedge rather than a forward transaction. Suppose, for instance, that a Spanish company has accounts receivable denominated in the Swiss franc, and that the firm needs to borrow in order to finance its operations. CHF interest rates are much lower than ESP interest rates—say 6 percent as compared to 20 percent. If it borrows in ESP, the firm has a tax shield of 20 percent, and can reduce its taxes correspondingly. If it borrows in CHF, the loan also acts as a hedge, but the tax shield is a mere 6 percent. Thus, the argument concludes, the currency of borrowing affects the tax shields and, ultimately, the value of the firm.

As pointed out in Chapter 3, the logical error in this argument is that it overlooks the fact that the taxes are affected not only by the interest paid, but (in the case of foreign currency borrowing) also by the capital gain or loss when the foreign currency depreciates or appreciates between time t (when borrowing starts) and time T (when the loan matures). Once this capital gain or loss is also taken into consideration, it is easily proven that the currency of borrowing does not affect the current value of the firm even when there are taxes, as long as the tax on capital gains equals the tax on interest.

16.4   CONCLUSION

In Part II, we have argued that there are deviations from PPP. These deviations can be very large at any given point in time, and they also tend to persist over time. It typically takes three years before the distance between the actual spot rate and the PPP prediction is reduced by half. Moreover, it is difficult to predict exchange rates. All of this implies that firms that sell goods abroad, or import goods, or firms that compete with foreign firms or may have to compete with foreign producers in the future are exposed to real exchange rate risk. In this chapter, we have argued that it is important that firms hedge this risk.

The Modigliani-Miller (1958) result states that financial policies, such as a firm's hedging strategy, cannot increase the value of a firm. However, this result is true only in perfect markets. Given the presence of convex tax schedules, costs of financial distress, and agency costs, hedging exchange risk can increase the value of a firm through its affect on future expected cash flows and the firm's borrowing costs. From this perspective, the decision *not* to hedge is really a decision to speculate. However, a firm's expertise is likely to be in its own business, not in speculating on foreign exchange. Thus, it is best for corporations to hedge their exposure to the exchange risk so that the adverse effect of volatility of exchange rates on their operations is minimized and they can focus their efforts on maximizing the present value of cash flows from operations.

QUIZ QUESTIONS

True-False Questions

1. In perfect markets, a manager's decision to hedge a firm's cash flows is irrelevant because there is no exchange rate risk.
2. In perfect markets, a manager's decision to hedge a firm's cash flows is irrelevant because the shareholders can hedge exchange risk themselves.
3. If a large firm keeps track of the exposure of each of its divisions, the firm has better information about each division, and is therefore better able to make decisions.
4. If a firm does not have a hedging policy, the managers may insist on higher wages to compensate them for the risk they bear because part of their lifetime future wealth is exposed to exchange rate risk.
5. If the firm does not have a hedging policy, the managers may refuse to undertake risky projects even when they have a positive net present.
6. The risk-adjusted expected future tax savings from borrowing in your local currency always equals the present value of the expected tax savings from borrowing in a foreign currency.
7. The cost of hedging is roughly half of the difference between the forward premium and the spot exchange rate.
8. A reinvoicing center assumes the exchange rate risk of the various subsidiaries of a multinational corporation if it allows each subsidiary to purchase or sell in its "home" currency.

Valid-Invalid Questions

Determine which statements below are valid reasons for the manager of a firm to hedge exchange rate risk and which are not.

1. The manager should use hedging in order to minimize the volatility of the cash flows and therefore the probability of bankruptcy even though the expected return on the firm's stock will also be reduced.
2. Firms may benefit from economies of scale when hedging in forward or money markets, while individual shareholders may not.
3. The chance of financial distress is greater when a firm's cash flows are highly variable, and financial distress is costly in imperfect markets.
4. Shareholders do not have sufficient information about a firm's exposure.
5. Risk-averse employees demand a risk premium when the volatility of a firm's cash flows is high.
6. Short selling is often difficult or impossible for the individual shareholders.
7. Hedging a foreign currency inflow is beneficial when the forward rate is at a premium, because it is profitable and therefore desirable. In contrast, such hedging is not desirable when the forward rate is at a discount.
8. Since a forward contract always has a zero value, it never affects the value of the firm—but it is desirable because it reduces the variability of the cash flows.
9. Hedging reduces agency costs by reducing the variability of the firm's cash flows. Hedging means that the manager bears less personal income risk, making the manager more likely to accept risky projects with a positive net present value.
10. Hedging is desirable for firms that operate in a flat-tax-rate environment because income smoothing means that they can expect to pay less taxes.
11. Managers have an incentive to hedge in order to reduce the variability of the firm's cash flows because even though a firm may be able to carry forward losses, there is the loss of time value.

Multiple-Choice Questions
Choose the correct answer(s).

1. The Modigliani-Miller theorem, as applied to the firm's hedging decision, states that

   (a) in perfect markets and for given cash flows from operations, hedging is irrelevant because by making private transactions in the money and foreign exchange markets, the shareholders can eliminate the risk of the cash flows.

   (b) bankruptcy is not costly when capital markets are perfect.

   (c) a firm's value cannot be increased by changing the proportion of debt to equity used to finance the firm. Thus, the value of the tax shield from borrowing in home currency exactly equals the risk-adjusted expected tax shield from borrowing in foreign currency.

   (d) if the shareholders are equally as able to reduce the risk from exchange rate exposure as the firm, then hedging will not add to the value of the firm.

   (e) markets are perfect so hedging by the manager of the firm and the shareholders is irrelevant.

2. Hedging may reduce agency costs because

   (a) some of the uncertainty of a manager's lifetime income has been diversified away.

   (b) the shareholders will always prefer volatile projects while the debtholders will prefer non-volatile ones.

   (c) risk-averse employees will demand a risk premium from a firm that is more likely to be in financial distress.

   (d) customers will think twice about purchasing goods from a company that may not be able to offer long-term customer service.

   (e) a reduction in the variability of the firm's cash flows may reduce the likelihood for conflicts between the debtholders and the shareholders.

3. Which of the following statements represent capital market imperfections?

   (a) Agency costs.

   (b) The difference between half of the bid-ask spread between the spot and forward markets.

   (c) The potential costs from renegotiating a loan that has gone into default.

   (d) The time value lost from having to carry forward losses into a future tax year.

   (e) Fees for liquidators, lawyers, and courts in the event of bankruptcy.

EXERCISES

1. Using the following data, compute the cost of hedging for each forward contract in terms of implicit commission and in terms of the extra spread as a percent of the midpoint spot rate.

Maturity	Rates	Bid-ask spread	Cost of hedging	Extra spread as a % of midpoint spot rate
Spot	49.858–49.898	0.040		
Fwd 30 days	49.909–49.965	0.056		
Fwd 60 days	49.972–50.043	0.071		
Fwd 90 days	50.061–50.157	0.096		
Fwd 180 days	50.156–50.292	0.136		

2. In the wake of the North American Free Trade Agreement, the firm All-American Exports, Inc. has begun exporting baseball caps and gloves to Mexico. Suppose that All-American is subject to a tax of 30 percent when it earns profits less than or equal to USD 10 million and 40 percent on the part of profits that exceeds USD 10 million. The table below shows the company's profits in USD under three exchange rate scenarios, when the firm has hedged its income and when it has left its income unhedged. The probability of each level of the exchange rate is also given.

	Profits		Probability
	Hedged	Unhedged	
S_{high}	15m	20m	25%
$S_{\text{unchanged}}$	10m	10m	50%
S_{low}	5m	0	25%

(a) Compute the taxes that All-American must pay under each scenario.

(b) What are All-American's expected taxes when it hedges its income?

(c) What are All-American's expected taxes when it does not hedge its income?

3. In order to hedge its Mexican peso earnings, All-American is considering borrowing MEP 25 million, but is concerned about losing its USD interest tax shield. The exchange rate is USD/MEP 0.4, $r_{t,T} = 8\%$, and $r_{t,T}^{*} = 6\%$. The tax rate is 35 percent.

(a) What is All-American's tax shield from borrowing in USD?

(b) What is All-American's tax shield from borrowing in MEP?

(c) What is the risk-adjusted expected tax shield from borrowing in MEP?

17 MEASURING AND MANAGING CONTRACTUAL EXPOSURE TO THE EXCHANGE RATE

We have established three important facts about the effect of exchange rate volatility on a firm's value. Firstly, changes in the nominal exchange rate are not offset by corresponding changes in prices at home and abroad (Chapter 11). That is, there are persistent and significant deviations from purchasing power parity, implying that there is real exchange rate risk. Secondly, the forward rate is not successful in forecasting the exchange rate (Chapter 14) nor are other fundamental variables (Chapter 15). Thirdly, given the market imperfections in the real world, hedging exchange rate risk can lead to an increase in the value of the firm (Chapter 16). We may conclude, therefore, that a firm should hedge its exposure to the exchange rate.

The objectives of this chapter are to introduce the concept of exchange rate exposure, and to define the various types of exposure that a firm faces—contractual exposure, operating exposure, and accounting exposure. We then show how a firm can measure and manage the contractual exposure that it faces. Operating exposure and accounting exposure are described in Chapters 18 and 19.

In the first section of this chapter, we distinguish between *exchange rate risk* and *exposure to the exchange rate*. We then explain how one can classify the effects of exchange rate changes into two categories. First, exchange rate changes may have an impact on accounting values (known as **accounting exposure** or **translation exposure**). Second, the exchange rate may affect the firm's cash flows and market value (called **economic exposure**), either through its effect on existing contracts (defined as **contractual** or **transaction exposure**) or through its impact on the future operating cash flows of the firm (known as **operating exposure**). We devote the rest of this chapter to contractual exposure. In Section 17.2, we study how one can measure and hedge the contractual exposure arising from a single contract or from a series of contracts maturing on the same date. In Section 17.3, we see how one can devise a single measure of the exposure arising from a number of transactions with different maturities but denominated in the same currency. We also explain the various ways that one can hedge this exposure in an efficient way. We conclude, in the fourth section by explaining that even if a firm hedges all of its contractual exposure, it is still exposed to operating exposure.

17.1   THE CONCEPTS OF RISK AND EXPOSURE

We need to distinguish between the terms **exchange risk** and **exchange exposure**. We interpret exchange risk as synonymous with uncertainty about the future spot rate. One measure of exchange risk is the standard deviation (or the variance) of the future spot rate change. A firm is said to be *exposed to* exchange risk if its financial position is affected by unexpected exchange rate changes. A large exposure means that a given exchange rate change has a large impact on the firm. That is, exposure measures how the value of a firm is affected by changes in the exchange rate.

17.1.1   Definition of Exposure
More specifically, following Adler and Dumas (1983), we define exposure to the time-T exchange rate as an *amount*, in *foreign currency*, such that

$$\text{Exposure} = \frac{\text{Total unexpected effect on financial position of firm at time } T, \text{ measured in home currency}}{\text{Unexpected change in } S_T}.$$

Thus, exposure can be thought of as the sensitivity of the firm's financial situation to the exchange rate, that is, the impact in home currency on the firm's financial affairs, per unit change in the exchange rate. Financial position here includes both the financial statements and the cash flows of the firm.

Example   17.1

Assume that the USD is your home currency. At time t, you buy a DEM T-bill maturing at time T, with face value DEM 100,000, and a USD T-bill with face value at maturity (time T) equal to USD 50,000. You clearly are exposed (that is, there is exposure) because your wealth at time T, measured in terms of USD, depends on the future value of the DEM, which is uncertain today. Your exposure amounts to DEM 100,000, since the time-T USD value of your portfolio relates to the future spot rate as:

$$\tilde{V}_T = \text{USD } 50,000 + \text{DEM } 100,000 \times \tilde{S}_T.$$

And, the time-t expected value of your portfolio is:

$$E_t(\tilde{V}_T) = \text{USD } 50,000 + \text{DEM } 100,000 \times E_t(\tilde{S}_T).$$

This implies, in home currency (USD) terms, that there is an impact of USD 100,000 per unit *unexpected* change in the spot rate; that is:

$$\tilde{V}_T - E_t(\tilde{V}_T) = \text{DEM } 100,000 \times [\tilde{S}_T - E_t(\tilde{S}_T)].$$

Note how, in the above example, 100,000 is the derivative of $\tilde{V}_T$ with respect to $\tilde{S}_T$. It would also be the value of the regression coefficient if you regressed future values of $\tilde{V}_T$ on the corresponding possible values of $\tilde{S}_T$. Thus, while exchange rate uncertainty can be thought of as a variance, exposure is a partial derivative or a regression coefficient. Recall, from Chapter 7, that we can also compute the exposure of an option. This is shown below.[1]

Example   17.2

Consider, at time 0, a call option on DEM with strike price ITL 1,050, maturing at time $T = 1$. The two possible spot rates at time 1 are ITL/DEM 1,100 and ITL/DEM 950, implying that the payoff to the call is either ITL 50 or 0. Thus:

$$\text{The call's exposure at time } 0 = \frac{C_{1,\text{up}} - C_{1,\text{down}}}{S_{1,\text{up}} - S_{1,\text{down}}} = \frac{50 - 0}{1,100 - 950} = \text{DEM}\frac{1}{3}.$$

It should be clear that the exposure of a firm depends on the interval $(T - t)$ over which cash flows are considered, and that this exposure varies over time. For example, a firm's exposure to the exchange rate may increase over time as the proportion of its revenue from exports increases relative to the revenue from domestic sales. This is similar to the change in the exposure of a call option over time.

17.1.2   Exposure: A Taxonomy

Let us now describe how the exposure of a firm to the exchange rate can be classified. The finance literature usually distinguishes between two types of exposure—economic exposure and accounting exposure.

1. *Economic exposure*

Economic exposure examines the effect of an unexpected change in the exchange rate on the firm's *future cash flows*. Economic exposure is further divided into two categories—contractual exposure (also known as transaction exposure) and operating exposure.

- *Contractual exposure*

  Contractual exposure or transaction exposure arises if there are assets or liabilities (such as accounts receivables [A/R], accounts payables [A/P], foreign loans or foreign deposits) that are denominated in foreign currency and whose value in home currency, therefore, depends on future exchange rates. Contractual exposure reflects the exposure of *past* contractual undertakings that have *future* cash flow implications because the asset or liability is still outstanding.

- *Operating exposure*

  Operating exposure, in contrast to contractual exposure, refers to the effect of changes in the exchange rate on the future cash flows of the firm through the effect on *future* operational or

---

[1] The binomial option pricing model is discussed in Chapter 7.

strategic decisions. Changes in the exchange rate may affect the firm's competitive position through, perhaps, a change in prices, costs, or sales volume.

Thus, while contractual exposure looks at the effect of changes in the exchange rate on a firm's *current* portfolio of binding commitments denominated in foreign currency, operating exposure considers the effect on a firm's *future* cash flows from operations.

2. *Accounting exposure*

Accounting exposure (or translation exposure) refers to the effect of unexpected changes in spot rates on a firm's *consolidated* balance sheet and income statement. Consolidation here refers to the translation of the financial statements of the firm's foreign subsidiaries into the currency in which the parent firm reports its accounts.

In the rest of this chapter, we focus on contractual exposure. The measurement and management of operating exposure are considered in the next chapter, Chapter 18, and accounting exposure is discussed in Chapter 19.

17.2 CONTRACTUAL EXPOSURE FROM TRANSACTIONS FOR A PARTICULAR DATE AND CURRENCY

In this section, we consider contractual exposure from a particular transaction. We describe how to measure the exposure from a single transaction and how that transaction can be hedged. We also explain that one can add up the contractual exposure from different contracts if these contracts mature on the same date and are denominated in the same currency. Of course, a firm typically has many contracts denominated in a given foreign currency and these contracts may have different maturity dates. In such a case, it is inefficient to hedge individually the transactions for each particular date. In Section 17.3, we show how one can define an aggregate measure of the firm's exposure to foreign-currency-denominated contracts that have different maturity dates, and how one can hedge this exposure with a single transaction.

17.2.1 Measuring Exposure from Transactions on a Particular Date

The contractual exposure from a single transaction in a particular foreign currency is simply the value of the contract at maturity. That is, since a unit change in the exchange rate affects the cash flows of a firm by the amount of the contract, it follows that contractual exposure is given by the contract amount.

Example 17.3

Assume that your firm (located in the US) has an A/R next month of DEM 100,000. Then, for a unit change in the USD/DEM exchange rate, the USD value of the cash flows from this A/R change by USD 100,000. For example, if the future exchange rate changes from USD/DEM 0.5 to 0.6, then the USD value of the A/R changes from USD 50,000 to 60,000. Thus, the exposure of the firm is

$$\frac{60,000 - 50,000}{0.6 - 0.5} = \text{DEM } 100,000.$$

TABLE 17.1 Measurement of Contractual Exposure for a Given Currency and Date

Inflows (for a particular date and currency)	FC accounts receivable* FC long-term sales contracts FC deposits, bonds, notes Forward purchase of foreign currency
Outflows (for a particular date and currency)	FC accounts payable FC long-term purchase contracts FC loans, bonds, notes due Forward sales of foreign currency
Net Exposure by currency and date	= Total inflows – Total outflows

*FC is short for "denominated in foreign currency."

An ongoing firm is likely to have many contracts outstanding, with varying maturity dates and denominated in different foreign currencies. One can measure the exposure for each given future day by summing the outstanding contractual foreign currency cash flows *for a particular currency and date* as shown in Table 17.1.[2]

The net sum of all of the contractual inflows and outflows gives us the firm's net exposure—an amount of *net* foreign currency inflows or outflows for a particular date and currency, arising from contracts outstanding today.

Example   17.4

Suppose that a US firm, Wire and Cable, Inc., has the following DEM commitments (where DEM is the foreign currency):

1. A/R: DEM 100,000 next month and DEM 2,200,000 two months from now
2. Expiring deposits: DEM 3,000,000 next month
3. A/P: DEM 2,300,000 next month, and DEM 1,000,000 two months from now
4. Loan due: DEM 2,300,000 two months from now

We can measure the exposure to the DEM at the one- and two-month maturities as shown in the table on page 474.

---

[2] Note that we define exposure on an *enterprise* basis. In contrast, the US Financial Accounting Standards Board (FASB) guidelines FASB 52 inadvertently defined exposure on a single transaction basis. Under FASB 52, a DEM 100,000 receivable might already be matched by a DEM 100,000 payable; still, a forward sale designated to be a hedge of the first position would be treated, accounting-wise, as a *hedge* even though it actually increased the firm's risk.

	Transaction	One month from now	Two months from now
Inflows	A/R	100,000	2,200,000
	Deposit	3,000,000	
Outflows	A/P	(2,300,000)	(1,000,000)
	Loan		(2,300,000)
Net Exposure		800,000	–1,100,000

Thus, we see that the net exposure to the DEM one month from now is DEM 800,000 and two months from now is –DEM 1,100,000.

Note that from a contractual exposure point of view, the future exchange rate would not matter if the net future cash flows were zero, that is, if future foreign currency denominated inflows and outflows exactly canceled each other out. This, of course, is what traditional hedging is about, where one designs a hedge whose cash flows exactly offset those from the contract being hedged. Thus, if one could match every contractual foreign currency inflow with a corresponding outflow of the same maturity and amount, then the net contractual exposure would be zero. However, perfect matching of *commercial* contracts (sales and purchases, as reflected in A/R and A/P) is difficult. For example, exporters often have foreign sales that vastly exceed their imports. An alternative method for avoiding contractual exposure would be to denominate all contracts in one's domestic currency. However, factors such as the counterparty's preferences, their market power, and their company policy may limit a firm's ability to denominate foreign sales and purchases in its own home currency or in a desirable third currency. Given that a firm faces contractual exposure, one needs to find out how this exposure can be hedged. Fortunately, one can use *financial* contracts to hedge the net contractual exposure. This is the topic of the next section.

17.2.2   Hedging Contractual Exposure from Transactions on a Particular Date

If a firm does not wish to be exposed to exchange risk arising from contractual exposure (for the reasons discussed in Chapter 16), the firm could easily reduce this exposure using the financial instruments analyzed in Part I of the book. Perfect hedging means that one takes on a position that *exactly* offsets the existing exposure. This can be done by using forward contracts or foreign currency loans (Chapter 3). For instance, to hedge foreign exchange receipts, we can either create contractual future foreign currency outflows by *borrowing* foreign exchange, or we can *sell forward* foreign currency. Alternatively, we could hedge by using futures contracts (Chapter 5) or currency swaps (Chapter 10), which provide only near-perfect hedges since they have some interest rate risk.

Example   17.5

We have seen, in Example 17.1, that holding a DEM T-bill with a time-T face value of DEM 100,000 has an exposure of +DEM 100,000. Thus, to hedge this exposure, one can sell forward the amount DEM 100,000 for maturity T. Alternatively, one could short spot foreign exchange, that is, borrow the present value of DEM 100,000. At maturity, this loan would offset the cash flows from the DEM T-bill.

Let us consider another example of hedging.

Example   17.6

To hedge the net exposure of the firm Wire and Cable, Inc., computed in Example 17.4, one could hedge the one-month exposure with a thirty-day forward sale of DEM 800,000, and the two-month exposure by a sixty-day forward purchase of DEM 1,100,000.

Forward contracts allow one to hedge the exposure to exchange rates perfectly. Options are "imperfect" hedges in the sense that they do not entirely eliminate uncertainty about future cash flows; rather, as explained in Chapter 6, options remove the down-side risk of an unfavorable change in the exchange rate, while leaving open the possibility of gains from a favorable move in the exchange rates. If a firm's treasurer wishes to keep the possibility of making money in the event of a favorable change in exchange rates, then options are a more suitable hedging instrument than forwards.

Example   17.7

The firm Wire and Cable, Inc. could buy a thirty-day put option on DEM 800,000, and a sixty-day call option on DEM 1,100,000. Buying these options provides a lower bound on the firm's inflows of DEM 800,000, and an upper bound on its outflows of DEM 1,100,000.

If one were willing to accept imperfect hedging, then one could also cross-hedge contractual exposure by offsetting the exposure in one currency with exposure (in the opposite direction) in another currency that is highly correlated with the first. For example, a British firm that has an A/R of CAD 120,000 and an A/P of USD 100,000 may consider itself more or less hedged against contractual exposure given that movements in the USD and the CAD are highly correlated. Similarly, if an Indian firm exports goods to Holland, Belgium, and France, and imports machinery from Germany, there is some diversification across these currencies given that the movements in these currencies are highly correlated.

So far, we have limited our discussion to contractual exposure. However, there is also the possibility of default on these contracts, which gives rise to credit risk. This creates the following dilemma:

- If one leaves the foreign currency A/R unhedged (open) and the debtor does pay, we will be worse off if the exchange rate turns out to be unexpectedly *low*.
- On the other hand, if one hedges and the debtor defaults, one is still obliged to deliver foreign exchange to settle the forward contract. Thus in this case, one would have to buy foreign currency in the spot market, at the future (time-T) spot rate. In such a case, one is worse off if the exchange rate turns out to be unexpectedly *high*. This is called **reverse exchange risk**.[3]

---

[3] We discussed reverse exchange risk when we analyzed swaps (Chapter 10) and when we discussed the possible advantages of futures and options over forward contracts (Chapters 5 and 6).

If the default risk is substantial, one can eliminate it, at a cost,[4] by obtaining bank guarantees or by buying insurance from private or government credit-insurance companies. Foreign trade credit insurance instruments that allow one to hedge against credit risk are discussed in Chapter 20.

In this section, we have seen how one can aggregate the exposure from transactions that have the same maturity date and that are denominated in the same currency. Typically, however, a firm will have exposures with a great many different maturities. Measuring the contractual exposure for each day is rather inefficient, and hedging the exposure on each transaction date individually is likely to be costly. For example, if a firm has a planning horizon of one year, it could potentially have about 250 net exposures to hedge. In Section 17.3, we explain how one can meaningfully aggregate contractual exposure across dates, thus obtaining *one* pooled measure of exposure, and the various ways to hedge this aggregate exposure with a single money-market or forward contract.

17.3   AGGREGATE CONTRACTUAL EXPOSURE OVER SEVERAL TRANSACTIONS FOR A PARTICULAR CURRENCY

In this section, we see how one can add up the contractual exposures for different maturities into one aggregate quantity, and how one can hedge this pooled exposure. We will consider three cases—one, where the interest rates are zero; two, where the interest rates are positive but there is no uncertainty about future interest rates; and three, where interest rates are positive and their future values are uncertain.

17.3.1   Aggregate Exposure When Interest Rates Are Zero

If interest rates were zero, then it would be easy to aggregate exposures across different maturity dates. One would simply add up the net exposures across all dates to obtain the total net exposure at time 0. One could then hedge this position with a forward contract of any maturity since interest rates are zero.

Example   17.8

Recall Example 17.4, where the contractual exposure of the firm Wire and Cable, Inc. to $DEM_{1\text{-month}}$ is DEM 0.8m and exposure to $DEM_{2\text{-month}}$ amounted to –DEM 1.1m. If interest rates are zero, then one could carry over the exposure of the first month to the second month, and the aggregate exposure of this firm would be DEM 0.8m – DEM 1.1m = –DEM 0.3m. Thus, one could hedge this with a two-month forward purchase of DEM 0.3m.

17.3.2   Aggregate Exposure When Interest Rates Are Positive but Certain

Adding the exposures over time is correct only if the foreign interest rate is zero. However, since in the real world there is time value, mere aggregation can be grossly misleading, especially if the maturity dates of the various contracts differ substantially. Let us assume that interest rates are positive but known, that is, there is no uncertainty about future interest rates. In this case, we measure the aggre-

---

[4] The term *cost* may be misleading. The firm replaces an uncertain future payoff with a risk-free future payoff; that is, the firm forgoes the default-risk spread in a risky contract. There is no loss in risk-adjusted present value, unless the bank overcharges you for the insurance that it sells.

gate exposure *after* taking into account the time value of the cash flows. One can aggregate the net exposures across different maturities by computing their present value, or by computing their future value on a particular date. The aggregate contractual exposure can then be hedged with a single forward contract.

Example   17.9

Recall Example 17.4, where the contractual exposure of Wire and Cable, Inc. to $DEM_{1\text{-month}}$ is DEM 0.8m and exposure to $DEM_{2\text{-month}}$ is –DEM 1.1m. Suppose that it is known today that the one-month effective DEM return, one month from now, is 1 percent. Then, using a DEM 0.8m deposit that starts one month from now, the firm can transform its first cash flow into DEM 808,000 available two months from now. Combining this exposure with the contractual outflow of DEM 1,100,000 at $t = 2$ months, gives the firm with a net exposure of –DEM 292,000 for the maturity $t = 2$ months. Thus in this case, the firm can hedge its contractual exposure with the purchase of a single two-month forward contract for the amount DEM 292,000.

17.3.3   Aggregate Exposure When Interest Rates Are Uncertain

So far, we have assumed that there is no uncertainty about future interest rates. Of course, in the real world one does not know what the future interest rates are going to be. For instance, in the above example, we assumed that it is known that the interest rate one month from now, for a one-month deposit, is 1 percent. In reality, one would know only that between month 1 and month 2, the DEM 0.8m will earn interest; what this interest rate will be is not known *today*. If the maturity dates of the various contracts being aggregated are very different and distant, both the expected amount of interest and its variance will have a significant impact on the pooled exposure. Thus, when we pool the cash flows over various maturities, we have interest rate risk in addition to exchange rate risk. The hedging strategy that one designs must account for both interest rate risk and exchange rate risk. There are at least two ways that one can design such a strategy—by using Forward Rate Agreements (FRAs), and by designing the hedge so that both the present value of the hedge and its duration match that of the pooled contractual exposure to be hedged. We describe these two methods below.

Combining Future Rate Agreements with Currency Hedges

One simple way to pool flows with different future dates without incurring interest risk is to use forward interest rate agreements (FRAs), that is, by using contracts where the interest rate for a future deposit or loan is fixed today.[5] Since FRAs allow one to determine today at what rate future cash flows can be deposited or borrowed, using FRAs eliminates interest rate risk. Thus, to determine how to compute the pooled exposure, one needs to find the value, at one future date T, of all of the contractual exposures using these forward interest rates. To hedge this pooled exposure, one simply takes an offsetting position in a forward contract with the same present value as that of the pooled exposure.

---

[5] Forward deposits and loans are similar to forward contracts on currency. While forward exchange contracts allow one to determine today the rate at which one currency can be exchanged for another at a future date, Forward Rate Agreements set today the interest rate for a deposit or loan at a future date. Forward Rate Agreements are discussed in Chapter 9.

Example   17.10

Suppose that the effective forward return for deposits (the one-to-two-month forward interest rate) is 1.5 percent. Then, with a DEM 800,000 deposit that starts one month from now (but whose interest rate is determined today), Wire and Cable, Inc. can transform its first cash flow into DEM 812,000 available two months from now. Combined with the contractual outflow of DEM 1,100,000 that matures two months from now, this leaves the firm with a net exposure of –DEM 288,000 two months from now. This amount can be hedged with a two-month forward purchase of DEM 288,000.

Note that the firm still uses two contracts to hedge its contractual exposure—an FRA and a two-month forward purchase. That is, the firm has replaced the DEM 800,000 one-month forward sale with a DEM 800,000 FRA. However, FRAs tend to be cheaper than forward contracts because no foreign currency transaction is involved. Moreover, the firm has also reduced the forward purchase required to hedge the cash flow in the second period from DEM 1,100,000 to only DEM 288,000, which should allow it to reduce its transactions costs.

The following example involves forward loans rather than deposits, but uses the same principle as that in the previous example.

Example   17.11

Suppose that the firm HiTekCanada has net contractual flows of (–)DEM 1m one year from now, DEM 2m two years from now, and DEM 1m three years from now. Also suppose that the one-to-two-year forward interest rate is 12 percent *p.a.*, and the one-to-three-year interest rate is 12.26 percent. This means that one can transform, through a forward loan, the DEM 2m two years hence into the amount DEM 2/1.12 one year from now, and the DEM 1m three years hence into DEM $1/1.1226^2$ one year from now. Using these FRAs, the currency exposure is concentrated at year one, and the pooled exposure at time 1 is:

$$-\text{DEM } 1m + \text{DEM }\frac{2m}{1.12} + \text{DEM }\frac{1m}{1.1226^2} = \text{DEM } 1.58m.$$

This exposure can be hedged with the sale of a single forward contract for the amount DEM 1.58m and maturity one year. The two FRAs and the one (small) currency hedge are cheaper than three currency hedges.

In the example above, HiTekCanada has a portfolio of three DEM cash flows. Clearly, the exposure from these cash flows is perfectly hedged when one uses either three forward contracts (as discussed in Section 17.2) or two FRAs to pool the exposures at a single point in time and hedges these with a single forward contract. That is, in both of these hedging strategies, even if DEM interest rates change, the DEM market value of the hedge will change by exactly the same amount as the change in the value of the three cash flows, and the firm's value will be unaffected. Note, however, that both hedging strategies use three financial contracts—either three forward contracts or two FRAs combined with one forward contract. In the next section, we explain how one can hedge the DEM cash flows against interest-rate and exchange-rate risk using a single contract.

Matching Duration of Pooled Exposure with That of the Hedge

If forward money market contracts are not available or are too expensive, and if hedging the exposure for each maturity date with individual forward contracts is too expensive, then one needs to devise a hedging strategy that uses only a few financial contracts and hedges against both interest rate risk and exchange rate risk. In this section, we see how one measures the pooled exposure of a set of contracts to the exchange rate and the interest rate, and how one can develop a strategy to hedge against both of these exposures.

Note that by definition a firm is perfectly hedged if, at every point in time, the hedge position has the same (offsetting) value as that of the contracts being hedged. However, there are two sources of uncertainty—exchange rates and interest rates. Thus, the hedge position that one designs must match the changes in the value of the exposures from both the changes in the exchange rate and the interest rate. The pooled exposure to exchange rates can be measured by computing the present value of the firm's outstanding contracts using the current interest rates; and, the exposure to interest rates can be measured using the concept of duration.[6] Thus, changes in the value of the hedge will offset changes in value from contractual exposure if the hedge meets the following two conditions simultaneously: It has the same present value as the present value of the pooled exposure, and it has the same duration as that of the various contracts being hedged.[7]

Example   17.12

Suppose that the contractual exposure of HiTekCanada is (–)DEM 1m one year from now, DEM 2m two years hence, and DEM 1m three years hence. If the current interest rates for DEM are 10 percent *p.a.*, 11 percent *p.a.*, and 11.5 percent *p.a.* for one-, two-, and three-year maturities, the present value (PV) of these cash flows is:

$$PV = DEM \frac{-1m}{1.1} + \frac{2m}{1.11^2} + \frac{1m}{1.115^3} = DEM\,1,435,553.$$

---

[6] Duration measures the percentage decrease in the market value of a series of cash flows, for one percentage increase in the (continuously compounded) per annum yield-to-maturity. It can be shown that the duration of a series of cash flows C_t, is a weighted average of the times-to-maturity of the individual cash flows, with the weights being the present values of each cash flow expressed as a fraction of the portfolio's total present value. From the definition of duration we have that:

$$\text{Duration} = \frac{-\partial \text{ total NPV/total NPV}}{-\partial \ln(1+r)} = \frac{-\partial \text{ total PV/total PV}}{\partial(1+r)/(1+r)} = \left(\frac{1+r}{\text{total PV}}\right)\frac{-\partial \text{ total PV}}{\partial(1+r)}.$$

Rewriting the total PV explicitly,

$$\text{Duration} = \left(\frac{1+r}{\text{total PV}}\right)\frac{-\partial\left(\sum_{t=0}^{N} C_t/(1+r)^t\right)}{\partial(1+r)}.$$

Differentiating with respect to $(1 + r)$, we get that,

$$\text{Duration} = \left(\frac{1}{\text{total PV}}\right)\sum_{t=0}^{N}\frac{C_t \times t}{(1+r)^t} = \sum_{t=0}^{N}\left(\frac{PV_t}{\text{total PV}}\right)\times t.$$

[7] Portfolios with different compositions but identical duration will behave identically to exchange rate changes as long as their yields change by the same amount (that is, when the entire term structure of interest rates shifts upward or downward without changing shape) and if the changes in interest rates are small (as is typically the case in the short run).

Thus, to hedge these contracts against exchange rate changes, one needs a contract with a DEM outflow that has a present value of (−)DEM 1,435,553.

As explained in footnote 6, duration is a weighted average of the times-to-maturity of the individual cash flows, with the weights being the present value of the cash flows for a particular maturity t expressed as a fraction of the total present value, that is, $PV_t/$(total PV). If there are N dates on which cash flows occur between today (time 0) and maturity, we can write duration as:

$$\text{Duration} = \Sigma_{t=0}^{N}\left(\frac{PV_t}{\text{total PV}}\right)\times t.$$

In the example for the firm HiTekCanada that we are considering, we can calculate duration as in the table below.

Maturity	PV_t	$\dfrac{PV_t}{\text{Total PV}}$	$\left(\dfrac{PV_t}{\text{Total PV}}\right)\times t$
$t = 1$	$\dfrac{-1\text{m}}{1.1} = \text{DEM} -0.9091\text{m}$	$\dfrac{-0.9091}{1.435553} = -0.6333$	$-0.6333 \times 1 = -0.6333$
$t = 2$	$\dfrac{2\text{m}}{1.11^2} = \text{DEM } 1.6232\text{m}$	$\dfrac{1.6232}{1.435553} = 1.1308$	$1.1308 \times 2 = 2.2615$
$t = 3$	$\dfrac{1\text{m}}{1.115^3} = \text{DEM } 0.7214\text{m}$	$\dfrac{0.7214}{1.435553} = 0.5025$	$0.5025 \times 3 = 1.5075$
	Total PV = DEM 1.435553m	Total = 1.0	Duration = 3.14 years

To hedge against interest rate risk, we require that the forward contract used to hedge this contractual exposure have the same duration as the contractual cash flows. If a portfolio has just one cash flow, its duration is the time-to-maturity of that single cash flow. Thus, the forward contract that would match the duration of these three contractual cash flows is one that has a maturity of 3.14 years.

We conclude that in order to hedge the exposure from these three contractual cash flows, one needs to sell DEM forward. To hedge the exposure to interest rates, the maturity of the forward contract needs to be 3.14 years; to hedge the exposure to exchange rates the present value of DEM outflow in the forward contract needs to be DEM 1,435,553. Given that the three-year interest rate is 11.5 percent *p.a.*, the size (future value) of the forward contract must be about $1,435,553 (1.115)^{3.14}$ = DEM 2.01959m.

Note that the duration is a weighted average of the three maturities, with weights equal to the discounted values of each cash flow. In the above example, the weighted average exceeds the longest maturity, three years. This is because one of the shorter-lived cash flows is negative, which leverages up the portfolio's exposure to interest rate changes. If the amounts and times-to-maturity of the cash flows are rather similar, differences in the sign of the cash flows can have dramatic leverage effects on the average duration, as demonstrated in Example 17.13.

Example   17.13

Consider a set of outflows with present value –99 and average duration four years, and a second set of inflows with present value 100 and average duration five years. This produces an overall duration of $[(-99 \times 4) + (100 \times 5)]/[-99 + 100] = 104$. Clearly, the 104-year interest rate, if one were available, would probably behave very differently than a four- or five-year interest rate. Using a hedge that has a duration of 104 years is unlikely to be very good.

Thus, in cases where the contracts to be hedged consist of both inflows and outflows, it is typically better to combine all of the inflows and hedge them with one forward contract, and to pool all of the outflows and hedge them with a second forward contract. For the same reason, if cash flows with the same sign have very different maturities, it is better to form subportfolios of cash flows with similar maturities—say, less than one year, one to five years, and more than five years. One then computes the duration for each subportfolio, and creates a hedge for each portfolio separately.

Example   17.14

For the firm HiTekCanada considered in Example 17.13, one would hedge the outflow of DEM 1m with one forward contract and hedge the two inflows of DEM 2m and DEM 1m with another forward contract. The forward contract used to hedge the *outflow* of DEM 1m is one that matches the present value and duration of this cash flow—a one-year forward purchase of DEM 1m. The duration of the two *inflows* can be calculated as in the table below.

Maturity	PV_t	$\dfrac{PV_t}{\text{Total PV}}$	$\left(\dfrac{PV_t}{\text{Total PV}}\right) \times t$
$t = 2$	$\dfrac{\text{2m}}{1.11^2}$ = DEM 1.6232m	$\dfrac{1.6232}{2.344644\text{m}} = 0.6923$	$0.6923 \times 2 = 1.3846$
$t = 3$	$\dfrac{\text{1m}}{1.115^3}$ = DEM 0.7214m	$\dfrac{0.7214}{2.344644\text{m}} = 0.3077$	$0.3313 \times 3 = 0.9230$
	Total PV = DEM 2.344644m	Total = 1.0	Duration = 2.308 years

Thus, the single forward contract that will hedge the two inflows is a forward sale of maturity 2.308 years and future value of approximately 2,344,644 $(1.11)^{2.308}$ = DEM 2,983,200.

It is important to realize that when compared to FRAs as a tool to hedge interest rate risk, the duration method works only imperfectly. One reason is that it assumes that all shifts in the term structure of continuously compounded interest rates are parallel. Since this ignores changes in the shape of the term structure, any hedging strategy based on duration is bound to be approximate. Moreover, duration works only locally, that is, for very small changes in interest rates. Third, duration changes as time elapses and as interest rates change. Thus, after some time, the duration of the pooled hedge and the original cash flows will no longer match. Then one has to decide whether to accept the extra risk or to revise the hedge portfolio (and incur transaction costs) to bring the interest sensitivities back into line. Thus, while compared to hedging with FRAs, a hedging strategy based on duration requires fewer financial contracts, it provides only approximate hedging and may also need to be revised over time.

17.4   WHAT DOES MANAGEMENT OF CONTRACTUAL EXPOSURE ACHIEVE?

We conclude this chapter by arguing that it is not sufficient for a corporate treasurer to hedge only the firm's contractual exposure. We argue that even if a firm continuously hedges contractual exposure, its exposure to the exchange rate will not be completely eliminated. There will still be exposure to the exchange rate from two sources: (1) exposure to variations in the forward rate, and (2) operating exposure through the effect of the exchange rate on the volume of sales. We explain these issues below.

Consider an Italian firm, Viticola, which exports wine to the US. Viticola can choose between at least two invoicing policies: (a) invoice in USD at constant US prices, and hedge each invoice in the forward market; or (b) invoice in ITL at constant home currency prices. In both cases, Viticola has zero contractual exposure. Still, the exchange rate affects its profits. We argue that the first policy implies that Viticola is now exposed to variations in the forward exchange rate. Moreover, while this policy minimizes the variability of Viticola's export volume, it creates huge swings in the ITL value of Viticola's revenue from US sales. The second policy maintains roughly constant profit margins, but may lead to huge swings in sales volumes, thus affecting Viticola's total revenue.

First, consider the policy of invoicing at constant USD prices and hedging forward. Assume that the Italian firm maintains a constant USD sales price, and extends three months credit to its US customers. If the firm hedges its contractual exposure systematically every time a new invoice is sent, its ITL cash flows ninety days later will be proportional to the ninety-day forward rate prevailing at the invoicing date. If, on the other hand, Viticola does not hedge its contractual exposure, its cash flows will be proportional to the spot rate prevailing when the invoice matures. In the long run, both series will have a similar variability since the volatility of the spot rate is similar to that of the forward rate. Thus, even perfect hedging of contractual exposure does not reduce the long-run variability of cash flows; it merely facilitates three-month budget projections. These issues are illustrated in the example below.

Example   17.15

Suppose that Viticola sets the price of a bottle of wine at USD 10. If Viticola does not hedge its transaction exposure, the revenue in ITL from US sales is random, and depends on the ITL/USD spot rate prevailing in three months time: USD $10 \times \tilde{S}_{3 \text{ months}}$. If, on the other hand, Viticola hedges each contract, the ITL cash flows from the sale of each bottle is USD $10 \times F_{t,t+3 \text{ mo}}$. However, although the forward rate for three months from now is known today, the future forward rates are as uncertain as the future spot rates. Thus, the revenue from *future* sales is uncertain: USD $10 \times \tilde{F}_{n,n+3 \text{ mo}}$, where n is greater than t. Every decrease in the ITL/USD exchange rate is reflected in lower revenue for Viticola.

Next, let us look at the second policy: invoicing at constant ITL prices and letting the exchange rate determine the USD price. From a contractual exposure point of view, Viticola is perfectly hedged since the contract is denominated in its home currency. Clearly, however, a policy of holding constant the domestic currency price may create huge swings in the USD price of the product and, therefore, may result in huge changes in the volume of Viticola's sales and profits, as illustrated below.

Example   17.16

Suppose that Viticola decides to set the price of each bottle of wine it sells at ITL 16,000. At the current spot rate of ITL/USD 1,600, this implies a price of USD 10, a price at which Viticola can sell 10,000 bottles in the US, and its total revenue from US sales is ITL 160,000,000. Assume that next month the ITL appreciates to ITL/USD 1,500. Given that Viticola does not change its ITL price, the US price, translated at the new exchange rate, is now USD 10.67. At this new price, in the competitive wine market, Viticola can sell only 9,000 bottles. Thus, the revenue of Viticola now declines to $9,000 \times 16,000 = 144,000,000$. Clearly, the total revenue of Viticola is exposed to the exchange rate.

The alert reader may already have concluded that, in the long run, the *pricing* policy is actually more important than the invoicing decision. For instance, the exporter may invoice in ITL but adjust the ITL prices every month to compensate for changes in the exchange rate so as to keep the USD price roughly constant. In terms of contractual exposure, there is no risk (as invoicing is in ITL), but the variability of the profit margins remains. At the other extreme, the exporter may invoice in USD and hedge forward, but also adjust the USD price every month in order to maintain roughly constant ITL prices. Again, there is no contractual exposure, but the variability of the USD price and, hence, of the sales volumes remains. Whatever the policy, or whatever combination of policies a firm uses, *future profits will remain exposed to exchange rate changes*. Therefore, to hedge against changes in the exchange rate, one has to go beyond simply hedging contractual exposure. This is the topic of the next chapter, where we examine how the firm can hedge against the effect that the exchange rate has on its sales volume and profits from operations.

QUIZ QUESTIONS

True-False Questions

1. Exchange risk describes how volatile a firm's cash flows are with respect to a particular exchange rate.
2. Exchange exposure is a measure of the sensitivity of a firm's cash flows to a change in the spot exchange rate.
3. Hedging exposure means eliminating all risk from a net position in a foreign currency.
4. If you need to hedge a series of exposures with different maturities and you use duration hedging, it is best to hedge the negative exposures separately from the positive exposures.
5. Contractual exposure is the absolute change in the firm's cash flows for a unit change in the spot exchange rate.
6. Operating exposure is the exposure that results when the forward rate is at discount with respect to the spot rate at the moment you sign a sales or purchase contract.
7. Contractual exposure is additive for one maturity and one currency.
8. Options are undoubtedly the best choice for hedging foreign currency exposure because the possibility of profiting from a favorable change in the exchange rate remains open without the losses from an unfavorable change in the exchange rate.
9. Reverse exchange risk is the risk that arises when you receive a foreign currency A/R that you left unhedged, and the exchange rate at the time of receipt is unexpectedly low.
10. When interest rates are zero, we can aggregate exposures of a given currency across time.
11. If interest rates are positive but certain, we aggregate the exposure of one currency across time once we take time value into account.
12. By pooling the aggregate exposure of one currency across time, we can ignore time value, because we have arbitraged away interest rate risk. The only risk that remains is exchange rate risk.
13. Duration is the average life of a loan.

Matching Questions

Suppose that you are a manager at a British firm, and you are responsible for managing exchange rate exposure. Determine whether the following statements are related to accounting exposure, operating exposure, or contractual exposure.

1. Your German subsidiary has recently made new investments.
2. You bought a call option on ESP to hedge an ESP accounts payable.
3. You have just sold goods to an American customer. The customer has ninety days to pay in USD.
4. You have just developed an exciting new product. The success of this product depends on how it is priced in the local currencies of your export markets.
5. You have made a bid to deliver your exciting new product to schools in France during the next academic year. You will learn whether or not the bid has been accepted in three months.
6. You sell wool but face potential competition from Australia. If there are no imports, the price of your wool will be GBP 1. However, Australians enter your market once the exchange rate falls below GBP/AUD 2.

EXERCISES

1. The Dutch firm, Benelux Business Concepts, has a one-year BEF A/P totaling BEF 100,000 and a one-year LUF A/R totaling LUF 200,000. The BEF/LUF exchange rate is fixed at 1.

   (a) Can BBC offset its BEF A/P with its LUF A/R?

   (b) If so, how much exposure remains?

2. The Dutch manufacturer Cloghopper has the following JPY commitments:

   1) A/R of JPY 1,000,000 for thirty days.
   2) A/R of JPY 500,000 for ninety days.
   3) Sales contract (twelve months) of JPY 30,000,000.
   4) A forward sales contract of JPY 500,000 for ninety days.
   5) A deposit that at maturity, in three months, pays JPY 500,000.
   6) A loan for which Cloghopper will owe JPY 8,000,000 in six months.
   7) A/P of JPY 1,000,000 for thirty days.
   8) A forward sales contract for JPY 10,000,000 for twelve months.
   9) A/P of JPY 3,000,000 for six months.

   (a) What is Cloghopper's net exposure for each maturity?

   (b) How would Cloghopper hedge the exposure for each maturity on the forward market?

   (c) Assume that the interest rate is 5 percent (compound, *per annum*) for all maturities and that this rate will remain 5 percent with certainty for the next twelve months. Also, ignore bid-ask spreads in the money market. How would the company hedge its exposure on the spot market and the JPY money market? Describe all money-market transactions in detail.

   (d) If the interest rate is 5 percent (compound, *per annum*) for all maturities and will remain 5 percent with certainty for the next twelve months, how would the company hedge its exposure on the forward market if only one forward contract is used?

   (e) Assume that Cloghopper prefers to use traded options rather than forward contracts. The option contracts are not divisible, have a life of either 90, 180, 270, or 360 days, and for each maturity the face value of a contract is JPY 1,000,000. How could Cloghopper hedge its exposure? Do the options offer a perfect hedge for each maturity?

   (f) Drop the assumption of a flat and constant term structure. If Cloghopper wants to hedge its exchange rate exposure using one forward contract and its interest rate exposure using FRA contracts, how would the analysis of parts (c) and (d) be affected? A verbal discussion suffices.

   (g) The term structure is flat right now (at 5 percent *p.a.*, compound), but is uncertain in the future. Consider the spot hedge of part (c). If, instead of FRAs, duration is used to eliminate the interest risk, how should Cloghopper proceed?

MIND-EXPANDING EXERCISE

1. Masiello Manufacturing, an Italian clothing manufacturer, has a ten-year sales contract for the delivery of men's suits to the American retailer Moxies. Sales will equal USD 5

million each year. The interest rate in the US is 10 percent (assume that the interest rate curve is flat).

(a) How can Masiello hedge its exchange rate and interest exposure using a single (zero-coupon) USD loan?

(b) The alternative is to take out ten separate zero-coupon USD loans, each having a final value of USD 5m. However, zero-coupon loans with long lives are unusual, and Masiello's bank accordingly proposes a single loan, with regular interest payments. How should the amortization schedule of the loan be set so as to avoid the periodic rebalancing caused by duration?

(c) Compare the single loan of part (b) to the portfolio of ten separate zero-coupon loans, in terms of payments to the lender(s), and in terms of tax shields.

18 MEASURING AND MANAGING OPERATING EXPOSURE TO THE EXCHANGE RATE

In Chapter 17, we explained that the economic exposure of a firm can be divided into two parts—contractual exposure and operating exposure—and we discussed how a firm could measure and hedge contractual exposure. The objective of this chapter is to explain how one can measure operating exposure to the exchange rate and how one can hedge this exposure.

Note that while contractual exposure focuses on the effect of the exchange rate on future cash flows whose value in foreign currency terms is *contractually fixed in the past*, operating exposure analyzes the impact of future exchange rates on *noncontractual future* cash flows. That is, while contractual exposure studies the impact of the exchange rate on the home currency value of cash flows whose foreign currency value is *certain*, operating exposure examines the effect of the exchange rate on the operational cash flows of the firm, cash flows that may be *random* even in terms of the foreign currency. Thus, the complicating factor relative to contractual exposure is that the impact of exchange rate changes on future operating cash flows depends on (a) the economic environment that the firm competes in, and (b) how the firm reacts to changes in the exchange rate, given its competitive environment.

In Section 18.1, we define operating exposure and describe the sources of operating exposure. In Section 18.2, we explain how operating exposure may depend on economic environment that a firm faces. In Section 18.3, we explain the different ways one can measure operating exposure and how this can be hedged by using a variety of financial instruments. We conclude, in Section 18.4, by summarizing the major issues of which a firm treasurer needs to be aware when dealing with economic exposure.

18.1   INTRODUCTION TO OPERATING EXPOSURE

In this section, we define what we mean by operating exposure and we explain why the operations of firms that have neither export transactions nor import transactions may still be exposed to the exchange rate.

18.1.1   Definition of Operating Exposure

As discussed in Chapter 17, **operating exposure** measures the effect of changes in the exchange rate on the firm's future cash flows from operations. Thus, operating exposure measures how the exchange rate affects a firm's cash flows through its impact on the sales volume, the sale price, and the production costs of a firm. As in Adler and Dumas (1983), we can define operating exposure to the exchange rate at time T as an *amount*, in *foreign currency*, such that

$$\text{Operating Exposure} = \frac{\text{Total unexpected change in the time-}T\ operational\ \text{cash flows, measured in HC}}{\text{Unexpected change in } S_T}.$$

Thus, operating exposure is the sensitivity of a firm's operational cash flows to the exchange rate. Note that the above definition measures the change in the cash flows of the firm, per unit change in the exchange rate, and that the cash flows considered are those from operations and not those from the change in value of existing assets of liabilities of the firm.

18.1.2   The Sources of Operating Exposure

There are two misconceptions about the source of operating exposure. The first is that only those firms that have foreign operations are exposed to the exchange rate; that is, only those firms that buy or sell goods abroad or use imported inputs are exposed to the exchange rate, while firms that have only domestic operations are not exposed to the exchange rate. The second misconception, already discussed in the concluding section of Chapter 17, is that if a firm denominates all of its sales and purchases in terms of its own currency, it faces no exposure to the exchange rate. We discuss these two views below, and argue that firms with only domestic operations may still face exchange rate exposure, and that even if firms denominate all of their foreign transactions in terms of the home currency, they may still be exposed to the exchange rate.

　　Let us first examine the view that a firm with no foreign operations does not face any operating exposure. This view could be true only in a closed economy, that is, an economy where there is no competition from firms located abroad, and where consumers in the home country cannot import goods from abroad. However, in an open economy, there is competition from foreign firms and consumers always have the choice of spending their income on substitute goods produced abroad. Thus, in an open economy, a change in the exchange rate—through its effect on the cost of inputs, outputs, substitute goods, and complementary goods—influences the competitive position of domestic firms relative to foreign firms. This change in the competitive position is reflected in a change in the cash flows of the firm, as can be seen in the examples below.

Example   18.1

Consider a firm located in the US. Assume that the firm's production is based in the US, and that the firm uses only inputs that are produced in the US and that the firm's entire sales are in the US. The naive view would suggest that this firm's operations are not exposed to the exchange rate. This view is false if the firm faces competition from abroad. Every time the USD appreciates, the foreign competitors gain; they can lower their USD prices and still obtain the same amount of their own home currency. US firms that faced this type of situation include Caterpillar, Kodak, General Motors, and Chrysler. In the early 1980s, when the USD appreciated against the JPY, all of these firms lost market share to their Japanese competitors, Komatsu, Fuji, Honda, and Toyota respectively. This erosion of market share led to large decreases in profits for the US firms.

Let us now examine the view that a firm that denominates all transactions in terms of its home currency is not exposed to the exchange rate. It is true that if a firm denominates all of its transactions in its home currency, it is not exposed to *contractual* exposure. However, if prices of goods are fixed in terms of the home currency, when the exchange rate changes this is reflected in a change in the translated foreign price because the translation is now at the new exchange rate. This change in the foreign price will affect the sales volume. Thus, while there is no contractual exposure, changes in the exchange rate will lead to a change in the revenue of the firm. The amount of the change in the revenues, from a unit change in the exchange rate, depends on the degree of competition in the market in which the firm operates.

Example   18.2

Suppose that a French firm exports its entire output of mineral water to the US. This firm charges FRF 15 for every bottle of water that it sells. Assume that the current spot exchange rate is FRF/USD 7.5. The price of this bottle of mineral water, in the US, is therefore equal to USD 2. Every time this exchange rate decreases, it implies that the USD price of the exported good increases. For example, if the FRF/USD exchange rate changes to 5, the price of this bottle in the US increases to USD 3. If the market in the US is a competitive one, then unless this French firm decreases its FRF price, its sales will decrease. Thus, even though this firm denominates all of its sales in FRF, its revenue is exposed to the exchange rate.

To see the various factors that can affect the operating exposure of a firm, consider the following example, which illustrates that a firm's cash flows are affected by changes in the exchange rate, and that the extent of the effect depends on a firm's short- and long-run decisions.

Example   18.3

In the 1970s, Volkswagen's profits from exports to the US were severely affected by the fall of the USD from DEM/USD 4 to about DEM/USD 2. In the short run, Volkswagen had to decide to what extent it should change the USD price of its cars, trading off sales volume against profit margin. Volkswagen's long-run problem was to decide whether to continue competing in the US market and, if so, whether or not it should move production from Germany to the US or to Latin America.

From the above discussion, we conclude that if competing firms are located in different countries, a change in the exchange rate affects their relative competitive position and, therefore, the cash flows of the firms. The magnitude of the effect of a unit change in the exchange rate on the cash flows of a firm thus depends on the extent to which the exchange rate deviates from PPP, the market's response to prices (that is, the magnitude of the demand and supply elasticities and the degree of competition in the market), the proportion of the fixed versus the variable component in the cost of producing the product, the sourcing of inputs, and taxes.

18.2   THE IMPORTANCE OF THE ECONOMIC ENVIRONMENT IN WHICH THE FIRM OPERATES

Using the example of a Danish firm, Dansk AS, which is a subsidiary of the Canadian firm, Archyographik Systems (AS Canada), we explain the effect of economic environment on a firm's exposure to exchange rates. The analysis is divided into two parts. We first consider two extreme scenarios, one where the Danish economy is assumed to be closed to the rest of the world, and the second where the Danish economy is perfectly integrated internationally. After considering these two extreme cases, we consider three intermediate possibilities: (a) Dansk AS is the only producer of archyographic systems in Denmark and costs are fixed in the short run; (b) Dansk AS is one of many producers of archyographic equipment in Denmark, and the Danish firms dominate the market in Europe; and, (c) Dansk AS is one of many producers in the world and therefore must sell at the world price. In all of these cases, we will look at the change in the DKK value and the CAD value of Dansk AS in response to a 25 percent devaluation of the DKK.

In the example that we consider, assume that Dansk AS has the projected income statement that appears in Table 18.1. The figures in this table are not expected to change as long as the exchange rate maintains its current value of CAD/DKK 0.20.

TABLE 18.1   Exposure of the UK Subsidiary to the BEF/GBP Exchange Rate in a Binomial Model

Item	
Total sales (2m units at DKK 20)	DKK 40,000,000
Direct costs (2m units at DKK 12)	<24,000,000>
Cash overhead expenses	<5,100,000>
Depreciation	<900,000>
Profit before taxes	10,000,000
Taxes (50%)	<5,000,000>
Profit after taxes	DKK 5,000,000
Add back depreciation	900,000
Cash flow in DKK	DKK 5,900,000
Cash flow in CAD (at S = CAD/DKK 0.2)	CAD 1,180,000

Now suppose that there is an unexpected devaluation of the DKK with respect to the currencies of the rest of the world; the new exchange rate is CAD/DKK 0.15, which, when compared to the old rate (CAD/DKK 0.20), implies a 25 percent devaluation of the DKK.[1]

In order to evaluate the effects of this devaluation, we first describe two polar cases in terms of the openness of the Danish economy—perfectly closed (rather like Tibet) or perfectly open (like Monaco or Luxembourg).

18.2.1   Scenario 1: Perfectly Closed Economy

Imagine that Denmark is so isolated from the rest of the world that the whole country has no imports or exports. Thus, internal costs and prices are unaffected by exchange rate changes. Then one can make the following observations:

- Given that there are no exports or imports, the DKK cash flows are clearly unaffected by the devaluation of the DKK.
- Since there is no change in the value of the DKK cash flows, this implies that the DKK value of Dansk AS does not change following the devaluation.[2]
- Since the DKK value of Dansk AS has not changed, therefore, the CAD value of cash flows and of Dansk AS, following the 25 percent devaluation of the DKK, decreases by 25 percent.

Thus, in the case of a closed economy, the local (DKK) value of the subsidiary does not change at all, while the foreign (CAD) value changes by exactly the same proportion as the devaluation of the DKK. This implies that from the Danish point of view, the exposure of Dansk AS to the exchange rate is zero. On the other hand, from the Canadian point of view, the exposure of Dansk AS to the DKK/CAD exchange rate is the DKK value of Dansk AS.

18.2.2   Scenario 2: Perfectly Open Economy

Now we study the impact of the exposure of the firm under an alternative scenario, one where Denmark is assumed to be a perfectly open economy. That is, Denmark is assumed to be a small and open economy and is, therefore, an international price-taker: DKK prices for all goods and factors of production quickly adjust to world levels, translated at the current exchange rate. Commodity Price Parity (Chapter 11) holds. Under this scenario, the revaluation of the outside currencies by 33.33 percent in terms of DKK implies the following:

- All DKK prices and costs increase by 33.33 percent, and so do profits.
- Therefore, all future DKK cash flows increase by 33.33 percent, except for past contracts written in terms of DKK and items such as the depreciation tax shield.
- Since the DKK value of the cash flows increases almost exactly with the change in the exchange rate (except for contractual exposure effects), the CAD value of the cash flows is virtually unaffected.
- Since the CAD value of the cash flows is not affected, the CAD value of Dansk AS is essentially unaltered.

---

[1] Note, in passing, that from the DKK point of view, all currencies went up, not by 25 percent, but by 33.33 percent. The old DKK/CAD rate was 1/0.20 = 5, while the new DKK/CAD rate is 1/0.15 = 6.667. This asymmetry of devaluation and revaluation percentages is a constant source of bewilderment to the media.

[2] The current value of Dansk AS is the value of all of its future cash flows discounted at the appropriate risk-adjusted interest rate.

The second scenario demonstrates that because Commodity Price Parity holds, the Canadian parent, AS Canada, faces *no real exchange risk*. From AS Canada's point of view, as far as exchange risk is concerned, Dansk AS may as well be located in Canada. Nor does it matter if Dansk AS is exporting or selling only in Denmark: the CAD value of Dansk AS is independent of where Dansk AS sells its output.

The two cases considered above are so extreme that neither could be completely true. In reality, the situation is usually somewhere between these two extremes, in the sense that a country is partly open, and the firm is partially exposed to the exchange rate. The effect of the devaluation on the firm's cash flows then depends on the firm's reaction, which, in its turn, depends on the competitive position of the firm. We briefly discuss three possible intermediate situations. The corresponding *pro forma* income statements are shown in Table 18.2. In the table, we assume that, currently, half of the output of Dansk AS is exported, while the other half is sold in Denmark.

18.2.3   Scenario 3: Sticky Prices and Price Discrimination

In this scenario, we assume that Dansk AS faces little competition, either in Denmark or internationally. Thus, following the devaluation, the price of archyographic systems does not change in Denmark. Furthermore, we assume that the Danish government imposes a price and wage freeze following a devaluation because it realizes that a quick adjustment of internal prices to world levels will render the devaluation pointless.[3] We further assume that since Dansk AS is the only producer of archyographic systems in Denmark, it can maintain its export prices at the world level (CAD 4).[4] This is possible since Dansk AS has full control over its distribution network, so that the ensuing discrepancy of internal Danish prices (DKK 20) and export prices (CAD 4, or DKK 26.67 at the new exchange rate of CAD/DKK 0.15) does not lead to parallel trade. Finally, because of the price freeze the production costs of Dansk AS do not change following the devaluation.

Compared to the initial situation, under this scenario, the sales price does not change in either the Danish or the Canadian market. Thus, we expect little change in the domestic and foreign sales volumes. Moreover, the costs do not change. As shown in the Scenario 3 column in Table 18.2, the impact of the devaluation is that the (one-year) cash flow of Dansk AS rises dramatically, both in terms of DKK and CAD, when compared to the initial situation.[5] Under this scenario, and in contrast to the two polar cases considered above, Dansk AS has an exposure to the exchange rate in both CAD and DKK terms.

18.2.4   Scenario 4: Pass-Through Pricing

We now assume that Denmark is Europe's leading producer of archyographic equipment and that there are many producers inside Denmark, but little competition from producers located outside Denmark.

Given the above assumption about the degree of competition between the numerous Danish producers, following a devaluation of the DKK, some of the Danish producers will lower their

---

[3] That is, a devaluation or revaluation is pointless in a perfectly open (small) economy. This is the reason why mini-states like San Marino, Andorra, Monaco, Liechtenstein, the Vatican, and even Luxembourg don't bother to create their own currencies. They are not "feasible currency areas."

[4] Note, from Table 18.1, that before the devaluation of the DKK, the price of the output of Dansk AS is DKK 20. We assume that the export price is also the same; that is, at the exchange rate of CAD/DKK 0.20, the foreign price is CAD 4.

[5] Note that the principal source of this increase in cash flows is the increase in the revenue from export sales and the fact that costs do not change.

TABLE 18.2   The Impact of a Devaluation on Dansk's Cash Flow: Three Examples

Item	Before Devaluation	After Devaluation		
	Initial Situation From Table 18.1 (in 1,000)	Scenario 3 Sticky Prices and Price Discrimination (in 1,000)	Scenario 4 Pass-Through Pricing (in 1,000)	Scenario 5 International Price-Takership (in 1,000)
Sales				
In Denmark	1m × 20 = 20,000	1m × 20 = 20,000	1.5m × 20 = 30,000	1m × 26.67 = 26,667
Exports	1m × 20 = 20,000	1m × 26.67 = 26,667	1.5m × 20 = 30,000	1m × 26.67 = 26,667
Total sales	40,000	46,667	60,000	53,334
Costs				
Direct	2m × 12 = 24,000	2m × 12 = 24,000	3m × 13 = 39,000	2m × 12 = 24,000
Overhead	5,100	5,100	5,100	5,100
Depreciation	900	900	900	900
Total Cost	30,000	30,000	45,000	30,000
Income				
Before tax (sales – cost)	10,000	16,667	15,000	23,334
After tax (50%)	5,000	8,334	7,500	11,667
Cash Flow				
Add back depreciation	900	900	900	900
Change in working capital*	0	<667>	<2,000>	<1,333>
Net cash flow in DKK	5,900	8,567	6,400	11,234
Net cash flow in CAD	5,900 × 0.20 = 1,180	8,567 × 0.15 = 1,285	6,400 × 0.15 = 960	11,234 × 0.15 = 1,685
Change in cash flow (DKK)		8,567 – 5,900 = 2,667	6,400 – 5,900 = 500	11,234 – 5,900 = 5,334
Change in cash flow (CAD)		1,285 – 1,180 = 105	960 – 1,180 = –220	1,685 – 1,180 = 505

*10% of change in sales

(CAD) export prices in an attempt to increase their share of the Canadian market. Consequently, Dansk AS and its Danish competitors may end up maintaining their Danish *and* export prices at DKK 20 (equal to CAD 3 at the new exchange rate). On the other hand, foreign competitors, following the devaluation, face higher costs relative to those of the Danish competitors and, in the short run, continue to sell at the old CAD price of CAD 4 (that is, they now charge DKK 26.67). Because of the lower price relative to producers located outside Denmark, the entire sales volume of Dansk AS increases by 50 percent. The increase in production, however, requires overtime and the unit variable cost jumps to DKK 13.

The Scenario 4 column in Table 18.2 shows that the devaluation of the DKK leads to an increase in the cash flows of Dansk AS when measured in terms of DKK. This increase in cash flows is a consequence of the increase in sales volume. However, because the costs of production increase from DKK 12 to 13, and because Dansk AS has to sell at the lower price of CAD 3 rather than at CAD 4, the increase in cash flows is smaller than the increase under Scenario 3. In fact, from a CAD point of view, the increase in the DKK cash flows is not large enough to offset the 25 percent devaluation of the DKK. Thus, in terms of CAD, there is a *decrease* in the cash flows of Dansk AS compared to the CAD cash flows in the initial situation. In contrast to the case considered in Scenario 3, Dansk AS is now positively exposed to the exchange rate from the DKK point of view, while from the CAD point of view the effect of the devaluation is negative.

18.2.5   Scenario 5: International Price-Takership

In this last case, we assume that only foreign firms compete with Dansk AS in the Danish market. We also assume that, after the devaluation of the DKK, foreign competitors continue to sell at the CAD prices of CAD 4 (that is, DKK 26.67 at the new exchange rate of CAD/DKK 0.15). This implies that Dansk AS can increase its Danish price to DKK 26.67. Since archyographic equipment is sold mainly to industrial users, demand in Denmark is very inelastic, so that no change in sales volumes or costs is expected.

The cash flows of Dansk AS under this scenario are shown in Table 18.2, in the column titled Scenario 5. We see that under this scenario, there is a substantial increase in both the DKK value and the CAD of the cash flows, compared to the cash flows in the initial situation. The source of this increase is the increase in the DKK price of the output coupled with the fact that the production costs have not changed.

From the various scenarios considered in Table 18.2, we can draw the following conclusions:

- The effect of the devaluation on the firm's value depends on the openness of the economy, the openness of the firm's domestic market sector,[6] the competitive position of the firm abroad and at home, and the firm's strategy.
- Forecasting the effect of changes in the exchange rate on future cash flows requires assumptions about competitors' reactions, and other variables such as inflation.
- From the Danish point of view, the devaluation is a boon; that is, the DKK value of Dansk AS is positively related to the DKK value of the CAD under all three scenarios. This means that, from a Danish perspective, the economic exposure of Dansk AS is positive.
- From a Canadian point of view, the devaluation may be temporarily bad news (as in Scenario 4), or good news (as in Scenarios 3 and 5). More generally, depending on the environment, the CAD value of Dansk AS may be positively related to the value of the DKK (as in Scenarios 3 and 5), or negatively related to the value of the DKK (as in Scenario 4).[7]

In the next section, we explain how one can estimate the operating exposure of a firm to changes in the exchange rate and how one can devise a strategy to hedge this exposure.

---

6 The openness clearly differs across sectors, so the openness of one sector could be higher or lower than the openness of the economy as a whole. This variability, then, affects the relative price of the sector's output versus average prices within the country.

7 There is no contradiction between our two last observations. If the DKK value of Dansk AS rises by more than 33.33 percent, the devaluation is good news from the point of view of *both* currencies; if the DKK value rises by less than 33.33 percent, the devaluation is good news in DKK terms but bad news from the CAD point of view.

18.3   MEASURING AND HEDGING OPERATING EXPOSURE

We begin by explaining the general procedure for measuring operating exposure, and then illustrate how this procedure can be used when there are only two possible values for the future exchange rate and the value of the firm is known (exactly) for each particular value of the exchange rate. We then extend the situation to the case where the value of the firm is not known exactly, even though there are only two possible future values of the exchange rate. Finally, we show how one can measure exposure when the future exchange rate can take one of many possible values.

18.3.1   The General Linear Approach to Measuring and Hedging Operating Exposure

Note from the definition of operating exposure given in Section 18.1, that exposure measures how the cash flows of the firm change, for a unit change in the exchange rate. Adler and Dumas (1983) suggest the use of simulations to compute the economic exposure. The simulation requires that we come up with a number of possible future values for the spot exchange rate and compute the value, in home currency, of the cash flows for each possible future exchange rate value. The exposure of the firm to the exchange rate can then be computed by running a cross-sectional (as opposed to time-series) regression. This regression is shown below, where we have used i to index each possible future exchange rate value, and the corresponding value of the firm.

$$\tilde{V}_T(i) = a_{t,T} + b_{t,T}\tilde{S}_T(i) + \tilde{e}_T(i),$$
[1]

where $\tilde{V}_T(i)$ is the (home-currency) value of the cash flow of the firm if the exchange rate is $\tilde{S}_T(i)$, and $\tilde{S}_T(i)$ is one of the possible time-T exchange rates in terms of home currency per unit of foreign currency. The term $\tilde{e}_T(i)$ is the residual, and by definition this is uncorrelated with $\tilde{S}_T(i)$.[8]

From the above linear regression, we see that the regression coefficient, $b_{t,T}$, measures the change in the cash flow for a unit change in the exchange rate. Also, given that the dimension of the exchange rate is home currency per unit of foreign currency, it follows that the regression coefficient, $b_{t,T}$, is an amount of foreign currency. Thus, $b_{t,T}$ is the exposed amount of cash flows or the exposure. Also note that since $\tilde{V}_T(i)$ is expressed in terms of the domestic (reference) currency, the dimension of $a_{t,T}$ and of $\tilde{e}_T(i)$ is the home currency. The intercept, being a constant, is obviously independent of the future exchange rate; and, the regression slope is chosen to be such that the error term is uncorrelated with the future exchange rate. Thus, $a_{t,T} + \tilde{e}_T(i)$ is the portion of cash flows that is unexposed to variations in the exchange rate. Therefore, the regression in Equation [1] allows us to decompose the change in the value of the firm into two parts—a part that is linearly exposed to the exchange rate, which is given by $b_{t,T}$, and a part that is uncorrelated with the exchange rate, $a_{t,T} + \tilde{e}_T(i)$. Once the firm has identified its exposure, $b_{t,T}$, it can hedge this exposure using financial claims. For example, the firm could hedge this exposure in the forward market, by selling forward the amount $b_{t,T}$.

To see that the forward sale of the foreign currency amount, $b_{t,T}$, hedges the firm against the variation in exchange rates at time T, we can compute the value of the hedged firm. Recall, from Chapter 2, that the payoff from a forward purchase is given by the spot rate at maturity, less what one

---

[8] A similar regression equation is discussed in Chapter 5. In a cross-hedge using futures contracts one often uses *time-series* data to *estimate* the optimal hedge ratio, but the true hedge ratio is from a regression across scenarios.

has to pay for the foreign currency, that is: $\tilde{S}_T(i) - F_{t,T}$. Since we have *sold* the amount $b_{t,T}$ forward, the payoff from the forward contract is: $-b_{t,T}[\tilde{S}_T(i) - F_{t,T}]$. Thus, the value of the hedged firm, that is, the value of the firm *plus* the payoff from the forward contract is:

$$\tilde{V}_{T,\,\text{hedged}}(i) = \tilde{V}_t(i) - b_{t,T}[\tilde{S}_T(i) - F_{t,T}]. \qquad [2]$$

Substituting in the value of $\tilde{V}_T(i)$ from Equation [1]:

$$\tilde{V}_{T,\,\text{hedged}}(i) = [a_{t,T} + b_{t,T}\tilde{S}_T(i) + \tilde{e}_T(i)] - b_{t,T}[\tilde{S}_T(i) - F_{t,T}].$$

Canceling out the common terms, one gets:

$$\tilde{V}_{T,\,\text{hedged}}(i) = a_{t,T} + b_{t,T}F_{t,T} + \tilde{e}_T(i). \qquad [3]$$

That is, the hedged value is unexposed (is uncorrelated with $\tilde{S}_T(i)$). Comparing the value of the unhedged firm in Equation [1] with the value of the hedged firm in Equation [3], we find that, as a result of the hedge, the firm's value now depends on the known forward rate rather than the random future spot rate. Note, however, that the hedged value of the firm is not completely riskless—there is still some residual risk, $\tilde{e}_T(i)$. Since this risk is uncorrelated with the exchange rate, it cannot be hedged with linear exchange-contingent claims.

We illustrate, with a series of examples, the above-described general approach to measuring exposure.

18.3.2   Exposure Measurement with Two Possible Future Exchange Rates

In this section, we consider the case where one expects the future exchange rate to take on one of only two possible values. That is, one simulates the value of the firm for only two alternative exchange rates; in terms of our notation in Section 18.3.1, this corresponds to the case where $i = \{1, 2\}$. Moreover, we assume that there is no residual risk, that is, the value of the exposed item is fully known once the exchange rate is known. This implies that the possible outcomes for the value of the firm can be summarized by only two points in a plot of $\tilde{V}_T$ against $\tilde{S}_T$. This is similar to the situation considered in Chapter 7, when we considered the binomial option pricing model.

We study two examples—one in this section and the other in Section 18.3.3—and in each case we compute the operating exposure of the firm and the strategy to hedge this exposure given two possible values for the firm, with each value corresponding to a particular value of the exchange rate.

Consider a Belgian company that wishes to hedge its exposure to the exchange rate from its ownership of a marketing affiliate located in UK. Next year's cash flows from the subsidiary were expected to be GBP 1.7m. However, recently, the UK has experienced a sudden surge in inflation. In view of this, the Belgian firm considers two possible future outcomes for the future BEF/GBP exchange rate, and the corresponding value of its British subsidiary. These two outcomes are described below, and are depicted in Figure 18.1.

FIGURE 18.1   Exposure in a Binomial Model without Residual Risk

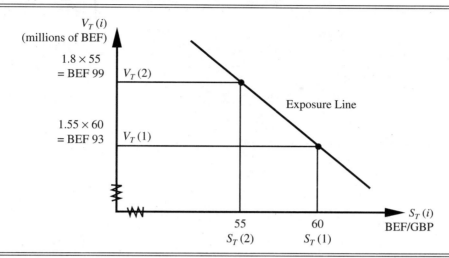

- Outcome #1: In the near future, the UK government may follow a strongly deflationary policy and stabilize the exchange rate at BEF/GBP 60. Such a deflationary policy is expected to depress sales and would decrease the cash flow of the marketing affiliate to GBP 1.55m. (This estimate of the cash flow would usually be arrived at on the basis of a detailed budget similar to the one shown in Table 18.1.)
- Outcome #2: Alternatively, the UK government may let the GBP depreciate and follow a moderately deflationary policy. In this case, the exchange rate would be BEF/GBP 55, and management expects a cash flow of GBP 1.8m.

Since we have just two possible outcomes, and the value of the firm depends only on the exchange rate, the regression (exposure) line fits these two points exactly.

We now need to decompose the value of the firm into two parts—one that is uncorrelated with the exchange rate (and is given by the intercept, $a_{t,T}$) and the other that depends on the exchange rate, $b_{t,T}$. The two possible outcomes are summarized in Table 18.3.

One can identify the slope, $b_{t,T}$, and the intercept, $a_{t,T}$, of the regression line using the following approach (similar to the approach adopted to value options using the binomial model in

TABLE 18.3   The Two Possible Outcomes To Be Hedged or Replicated

	Spot rate (i) at T	Value (i) at T in BEF (millions)
Outcome 1: $S(1) = 60$ BEF/GBP	$V(1) = $ GBP $1.55 \times 60 = $ BEF 93
Outcome 2: $S(2) = 55$ BEF/GBP	$V(2) = $ GBP $1.80 \times 55 = $ BEF 99

Chapter 7). We have two equations, Equations [4] and [5] below, and we need to solve for two quantities, $a_{t,T}$ and $b_{t,T}$:

$$a_{t,T} + b_{t,T} S_T(1) = V_T^{\text{BEF}}(1). \tag{4}$$

$$a_{t,T} + b_{t,T} S_T(2) = V_T^{\text{BEF}}(2). \tag{5}$$

Substituting in the values for $S(i)$ and $V(i)$ we get:

$$a_{t,T} + b_{t,T} 60 = \text{BEF } 93\text{m.} \tag{6}$$

$$a_{t,T} + b_{t,T} 55 = \text{BEF } 99\text{m.} \tag{7}$$

The slope is easily identified from Equations [6] and [7] as:

$$b_{t,T} = \frac{93\text{m} - 99\text{m}}{60 - 55} = -\text{GBP } 1.2\text{m.}$$

The intercept $a_{t,T}$ can be found from either Equation [6] or Equation [7]. Using Equation [6], we find that $a_{t,T}$ is:

$$a_{t,T} = \text{BEF } 93\text{m} - b_{t,T} 60 = \text{BEF } 93\text{m} - (-1.2 \times 60) = \text{BEF } 165.$$

Thus, from the point of view of the Belgian firm, the UK subsidiary is similar to a portfolio that contains a BEF riskless bond with time-T value BEF 165m (unexposed), and GBP debt with time-T value GBP 1.2m. We can verify this by computing the value of this portfolio for the two possible exchange rates and noting that the value of the portfolio for each exchange rate outcome is the same as that of the firm, as shown in Table 18.4.

TABLE 18.4   Replication of the Cash Flows from Domestic and Foreign Bonds

	Value in BEF	
	if $S_T = 60$	if $S_T = 55$
BEF assets	165m	165m
−GBP 1.2m	−72m	−66m
Total BEF value	BEF 93m	BEF 99m

TABLE 18.5   The Hedging Cash Flows

S_T BEF/GBP	Unhedged firm	Value at time T	
		Forward Contract $= -b[\tilde{S}_T - F_{t,T}]$	Hedged firm $=$ value of unhedged firm + value of forward
60	BEF 93m	$1.2 \times [60 - 58]$	BEF 95.4
55	BEF 99m	$1.2 \times [55 - 58]$	BEF 95.4

Given that the exposure we have computed is negative (–GBP 1.2m), we need to *buy* forward for maturity T the amount GBP 1.2m if we want to hedge this exposure. If the current forward rate is BEF/GBP 58, the hedged portfolio's future worth is BEF 95.4m, irrespective of the future value of the spot rate. That is, all exposure is eliminated. To verify this, in Table 18.5, we compute the two possible values of the hedged firm, using the fact that the value of the hedged firm is its unhedged value plus the payoff from the forward contract.

In this example, the fit of the regression is perfect (that is, there is no residual risk) because we consider just two exchange rate outcomes and, therefore, hedging the exposure eliminates *all* uncertainty. However, in practice, the value of the firm may depend on factors other than the exchange rate, and one may wish to consider more than two future possible exchange rates when simulating how the value of the firm changes with exchange rates. We consider these extensions in the next two sections.

18.3.3   Exposure Measurement in a Problem with Residual Risk

In a more realistic setting than the one considered in the example above, the value of the firm may depend on factors other than the exchange rate. In this case, the most one can do is to obtain a line of best fit, the regression or exposure line, which fits the value of the firm for the two exchange rates being simulated up to some residual. This residual is the quantity that is uncorrelated with the exchange rate and has a zero mean. The strategy to hedge the exchange rate in this case is the same as before: sell forward the amount $b_{t,T}$. Thus, the effect of residual risk is that the hedged value is, to some extent, still uncertain: by definition, residual risk is not hedgeable using a linear foreign exchange contract since this residual risk is uncorrelated with the future spot rate. We now provide an example of a situation where the value of the firm is computed for only two possible exchange rates and the value of the firm depends on factors other than the exchange rate.

Consider a UK firm that has set up a subsidiary in a fictitious country, Freedonia. Assume, for simplicity, that the subsidiary's cash flow, in terms of the Freedonian crown (FRK), can take on one of two (equally probable) values, FRK 150 or FRK 100, depending on whether the Freedonian economy is booming or in a recession. Let there also be two equally probable time-T spot rates, GBP/FRK

1.2 and 0.8. Thus, measured in terms of the home currency, the GBP, there are four possible outcomes for the future cash flows: $150 \times 1.2 = $ GBP 180, $150 \times 0.8 = $ GBP 120, $100 \times 1.2 = $ GBP 120, and $100 \times 0.8 = $ GBP 80. These possible cash flows are shown in Table 18.6. In each cell, we also show the *joint* probability of that particular combination of outcomes for the exchange rate and the state of the economy. If the health of the Freedonian economy were independent of the level of the spot rate, the probability of each cell would be $0.5 \times 0.5 = 0.25$. However, independence between these events is unlikely. When the FRK is expensive, a recession is more probable than a boom because an expensive currency means that Freedonia is not very competitive. The inverse happens when the crown is trading at a low level. Thus, we assume that the probability of the exchange rate being high *and* the economy booming is 0.15, and the cash flow in this event is FRK $150 \times$ GBP/FRK $1.2 = $ GBP 180. The cash flows and the probabilities for the other states of the world are shown in each of the four cells in Table 18.6.

To understand the impact of the exchange rate, one can compute the conditional expectations of the cash flow (in GBP) for each possible exchange rate. For instance, from the table, if the exchange rate is high (GBP/FRK 1.2), then chances of a boom are 3 to 7. That is, conditional on the high exchange rate, your best possible forecast of the cash flow in GBP is:

$$E_t(\tilde{V}_T \mid S_T = 1.2) = \frac{(180 \times 0.15) + (120 \times 0.35)}{0.5} = \text{GBP 138.} \qquad [8]$$

Similarly, conditional on the low exchange rate, the best forecast of the GBP cash flow is

$$E_t(\tilde{V}_T \mid S_T = 0.8) = \frac{(120 \times 0.35) + (80 \times 0.15)}{0.5} = \text{GBP 108.} \qquad [9]$$

The exposure to the UK parent from this subsidiary in Freedonia can be computed, as previously, by plotting each conditional expectation (GBP 138 or 108) against the corresponding

TABLE 18.6   Unhedged Cash Flows of the Subsidiary

Exchange rate	State of the economy		Expected cash flow conditional on S_T
	Boom: Cash flow FRK 150 Probability: 0.50	Recession: Cash flow FRK 100 Probability: 0.50	
S_T high: GBP/FRK 1.2 Probability: 0.50	Cash flow: GBP 180 Joint probability: 0.15	Cash flow: GBP 120 Joint probability: 0.35	138
S_T low: GBP/FRK 0.8 Probability: 0.50	Cash flow: GBP 120 Joint probability: 0.35	Cash flow: GBP 80 Joint probability: 0.15	108

TABLE 18.7   Hedged Cash Flows of the Subsidiary

Exchange rate	State of the economy		Expected cash flow conditional on S_T
	Boom: Cash flow FRK 150 Probability: 0.50	Recession: Cash flow FRK 100 Probability: 0.50	
S_T high: GBP/FRK 1.2 Probability: 0.50	Cash flow: GBP 180 – 18 = 162 Joint probability: 0.15	Cash flow: GBP 120 – 18 = 102 Joint probability: 0.35	120
S_T low: GBP/FRK 0.8 Probability: 0.50	Cash flow: GBP 120 + 12 = 132 Joint probability: 0.35	Cash flow: GBP 80 + 12 = 92 Joint probability: 0.15	120

spot rate (GBP/FRK 1.2 or 0.8), and drawing a line through these points.[9] The slope of this line, then, is:

$$b_{t,T} = \frac{138 - 108}{1.2 - 0.8} = \text{FRK } 75.$$

Thus, to hedge itself against exchange rate exposure, the UK parent should sell forward, for maturity T, the amount FRK 75. We can see that this strategy hedges the firm against exchange rate exposure by computing the cash flows of the hedged firm, that is, by adding to each cell in Table 18.6 the gain or loss from the forward hedge. The gain or loss on the forward hedge is, of course, $-b_{t,T}[\tilde{S}_T(i) - F_{t,T}]$. Suppose the forward rate is GBP/FRK 0.96.

- If the spot rate turns out to be high ($S_T = 1.2$), hedging produces a loss: $-75 \times [1.2 - 0.96]$ $= -\text{GBP } 18$, whether Freedonia's economy is booming or in a recession. So, in Table 18.7, we subtract GBP 18 from each of the cash flows in the first row of Table 18.6 (the cash flows corresponding to the high exchange rate of $S_T = 1.2$). Thus, hedging reduces the corresponding conditional expectation from GBP 138 to $138 - 18 = \text{GBP } 120$.
- If the exchange rate happens to be low, hedging leads to a gain of $-75 \times [0.80 - 0.96] = \text{GBP } 12$. In Table 18.7 this amount is added to each of the cash flows in the second line of Table 18.6. The gain increases the corresponding conditional expectation, from GBP 108 to GBP 120.

---

[9] To see that this is the slope coefficient, note that by definition the exposure $b_{t,T}$ picks up *all* covariance between the value of the firm, $\tilde{V}_T$, and the exchange rate, $\tilde{S}_T$. That is, we select $b_{t,T}$ such that $E_t(\tilde{e}_T | S_T) = 0$. Thus $\tilde{V}_T = a_{t,T} + b_{t,T} \tilde{S}_T + \tilde{e}_T$ means that $E_t(\tilde{V}_T | S_T) = a_{t,T} + b_{t,T} S_T$, which implies that the regression line runs through the conditional expectations. Alternatively, the regression coefficient can be computed using $b_{t,T} = \text{cov}(\tilde{V}_T, \tilde{S}_T)/\text{var}(\tilde{S}_T)$. The exchange rate variance is $E_t[\tilde{S}_T - E_t(\tilde{S}_T)]^2 = 0.5 [1.2 - 1.00]^2 + 0.5 [0.8 - 1.00]^2 = 0.04$. The covariance is $E_t[(\tilde{V}_T - E_t(\tilde{V}_T))(\tilde{S}_T - E_t(\tilde{S}_T))] = 0.15 (180 - 123)(1.2 - 1) + 0.35 (120 - 123)(1.2 - 1) + 0.35 (120 - 123)(0.8 - 1) + 0.15 (80 - 123)(0.8 - 1) = 3$. Thus, $b_{t,T} = 3/0.04 = 75$. Notice how a small covariance is not the same as a small exposure.

We see that the conditional expectations of the hedged GBP cash flows now no longer depend on the spot rate:

$$E_t(\tilde{V}_{T,\text{hedged}} \mid S_T = 1.2) = \frac{(162 \times 0.15) + (102 \times 0.35)}{0.5} = \text{GBP } 120,$$

$$E_t(\tilde{V}_{T,\text{hedged}} \mid S_T = 0.8) = \frac{(132 \times 0.35) + (92 \times 0.15)}{0.5} = \text{GBP } 120.$$

Thus, the forward contract hedges the value of the subsidiary against changes in the exchange rate. However, the hedged value of the firm is no longer constant across all possible outcomes; that is, the value of the subsidiary still depends on whether the economy is in a state of a "boom" or a "bust." This remaining uncertainty about the value of the firm has, by construction, nothing to do with exchange rate uncertainty.[10] If one wanted to hedge the remaining exposure to the state of the economy, too, then one would need to find a financial instrument whose payoff depends on the state of the economy.

18.3.4   Linear Exposure Measurement and Hedging in a Multi-State Problem

In Section 18.3.2, we explained how one could measure the exposure of a firm using *two* values for the exchange rate, simulating the cash flows corresponding to each exchange rate, and then estimating the exposure using regression analysis. In Section 18.3.3, we explained that, if the value of the firm depends on factors other than the exchange rate, then such a regression will not give an exact fit between the value of the firm and the exchange rate; that is, there will be residual risk. Typically, when one simulates the possible future exchange rate outcomes, one would like to consider more than just two possible exchange rates. In this section, we consider the more general case where one simulates the value of the firm for more than just two exchange rate values.

In this more general case, one can still use regression analysis to determine how the value of the firm depends on the future exchange rates. The first step in finding the exposure of a firm is to decide on a sufficiently wide "sample" of possible future exchange rates. The next step consists of thinking about the implication of each possible exchange rate scenario for the cash flows or for the market value of the firm. This analysis should lead to a table that shows, for each possible spot rate $S_T(i)$, the corresponding conditional expected cash flow or value. However, now that we are considering more than two possible exchange rate outcomes, we will generally not be able to fit a straight line through all of the combinations of firm values and exchange rates. What we can do, however, is obtain the line of best fit through these points, the regression line, which minimizes the residual risk. The slope of this line measures the exposure of the firm to the exchange rate. This exposure can be hedged, as before, with an offsetting forward contract. We illustrate this procedure with the following example.

Example   18.4

Consider a Belgian firm that exports 2,000 units of premium beer to the US. This beer, sold by the ounce, is priced at USD 1/ounce, and the Belgian exporter receives the BEF value of USD 1 depending on the prevailing spot rate. Some of the inputs used in producing this wonderful nectar are imported

---

[10] Stated differently, any linear hedge other than the forward sale of FRK 75 will produce even more residual variance, because the linear regression coefficient ($b_{t,T} = 75$) is designed to minimize the variance of the residuals.

and, therefore, when the BEF/USD exchange rate appreciates to more than BEF/USD 22, the cost of these inputs increases. The cash flows of this Belgian firm, simulated for different future values of the exchange rate, are given in Table 18.8, where we have assumed that the tax rate is 50 percent.

To estimate the exposure in this case, one runs the regression described in Equation [1], using the data on the BEF cash flows and the spot rate given in Table 18.8:

$$\tilde{V}_T(i) = a_{t,T} + b_{t,T}\tilde{S}_T(i) + \tilde{e}_T(i),$$ [10]

where $i = 1, 2, 3,$ or 4, depending on the simulation being considered, $\tilde{V}_T(i)$ is expressed in units of the home currency, BEF, and the spot rate is expressed in terms of BEF/USD. Running this regression, we find the following relationship between the cash flows of the firm and the BEF/USD spot rate:

Regression equation:

$$\tilde{V}_T = -1,828.57 + 471.43\ \tilde{S}_T$$

Standard errors:

$$(2,790.22)\,(117.80)$$

That is, the slope coefficient, $b_{t,T}$, is 471.43 and the constant, $a_{t,T}$, is $-1,828.57$. From the standard error of the slope coefficient, we can see that this coefficient is significantly different from zero. The regression output also shows that the R^2 is 0.89, implying that a substantial part of the variation in the cash flows of the firm is explained by changes in the exchange rate; that is, there is substantial exposure to the exchange rate. However, the relationship between the exchange rate and the cash flows of the firm is not exact. There is some residual risk, which is equal to $1 - R^2 = 11$ percent of the total

TABLE 18.8   Four Possible Exchange Rates and the Corresponding Cash Flows

Item	Simulation 1 S_T = BEF/USD 20 Probability = 1/4	Simulation 2 S_T = BEF/USD 22 Probability = 1/4	Simulation 3 S_T = BEF/USD 24 Probability = 1/4	Simulation 4 S_T = BEF/USD 28 Probability = 1/4
Sales (in BEF)				
Exports to US	$2,000 \times 20 = 40,000$	$2,000 \times 22 = 44,000$	$2,000 \times 24 = 48,000$	$2,000 \times 28 = 56,000$
Costs (in BEF)				
Cost of inputs	$2,000 \times 10 = 20,000$	$2,000 \times 10 = 20,000$	$2,000 \times 11 = 22,000$	$2,000 \times 14 = 28,000$
Other costs	6,000	6,000	6,000	6,000
Total costs	26,000	26,000	28,000	34,000
Cash Flow: in BEF				
Before tax: sales – costs	14,000	18,000	20,000	22,000
After tax (50%)	BEF 7,000	BEF 9,000	BEF 10,000	BEF 11,000

uncertainty. This residual risk can also be observed by comparing the cash flows given by the regression equation (the fitted cash flows) to the actual cash flows. The variance of the difference between the fitted values and the actual cash flows is the residual risk and is shown in Figure 18.2. This residual risk is uncorrelated with the exchange rate and, therefore, cannot be hedged using linear exchange-rate-dependent securities.

  To hedge itself against exchange rate exposure, the Belgian exporter could sell forward for maturity T the amount USD 471.43.

18.3.5 Managing Nonlinear Exposure to the Exchange Rate

So far, in Sections 18.3.1 to 18.3.4, we have considered only the possibility of a linear hedge. However, if one plots the conditional expectations of the firm's value against each possible spot rate, one may find that the true relationship is nonlinear. For example, this relationship may be convex (that is, a positive relationship that is increasing at an increasing rate, or a negative relationship that is decreasing at a decreasing rate). The reason for this nonlinear relationship may be the dynamic elements in operating exposure. Corporate decisions tend to limit the damage done by unfavorable exchange rate movements, thus mitigating their negative impact on a firm's cash flows. Corporate decisions also tend to exploit the new opportunities offered by favorable changes in spot rates, thus accentuating the positive effect of the exchange rate on the firm's cash flows.

Example 18.5

Consider the year 1970, and suppose that the exchange rate is DEM/USD 4 and that Volkswagen receives about USD 2,000 for every automobile (Beetle) sold in the US. Now when the exchange rate changes to DEM/USD 3 or DEM/USD 5, one of Volkswagen's *feasible* strategies is to be passive and

FIGURE 18.2 Linear Exposure in a Situation with Four Possible Spot Rates

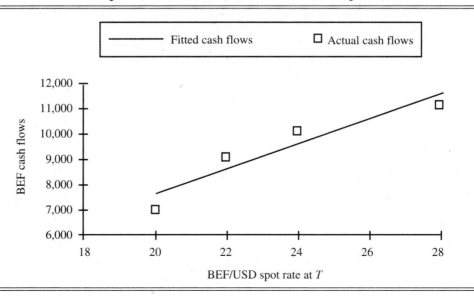

continue to ask for USD 2,000 per car at this new exchange rate. If Volkswagen adopts this strategy, its exposure to the exchange rate is likely to be linear. However, Volkswagen may have a strategy that is better than the passive strategy. For instance, an exchange rate of DEM/USD 5 implies that Volkswagen can reduce its USD price *and* still increase its (DEM) profit margin; and Volkswagen will adopt this strategy if it leads to more profits than the constant-USD-price strategy. Likewise, a falling dollar means that Volkswagen can increase its USD price in order to limit the reduction in its profit margin; and Volkswagen will again adopt this strategy if it means more profits (or smaller losses) than the constant-USD-price strategy. In short, whatever the direction of the change in the exchange rate, the active corporate strategy that responds to this change in the exchange rate will dominate the passive strategy. This argument implies that the exposure of Volkswagen's operations to the exchange rate is likely to be convex, as shown in Figure 18.3, rather than linear.

If the exposure for a firm to the exchange rate is nonlinear, then the firm can potentially do better by not using the linear approach to hedge exposure that is described above. The regression approach forces a straight line through a relationship which is essentially nonlinear. It is true that the residuals from the linear regression are uncorrelated with the exchange rate, but zero correlation is not the same as independence or unpredictability. When nonlinearity is important, at least within the range of possible time-T spot rates, there are two ways to measure exposure and devise a hedging strategy. One approach is to select a portfolio of options with a combined payoff that approximates the operational cash flows in a piece-wise linear way, and hold this portfolio of options to hedge the exchange rate exposure. An alternative approach is to divide the horizon, $T -$ t, into, say, fifteen subperiods, construct a binomial tree that matches the volatility of S_T, and hedge the exposure dynamically with a sequence of linear hedges revised every period. This

FIGURE 18.3   A Convex Exposure Schedule

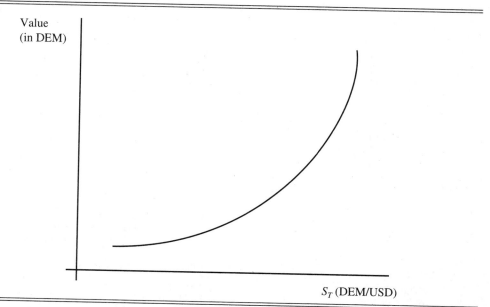

approach, of course, is the same as the one described in Chapter 7, where the cash flow being hedged was the payoff to an option. We illustrate this with a numerical example based on the case of Volkswagen described in Example 18.5.[11]

Example   18.6

Suppose that the current spot rate is DEM/USD 4. Volkswagen estimates the volatility of the spot rate to be such that the exchange rate in three months may either be DEM/USD 4.5 or DEM/USD 3.5 and, in six months, it may take on one of two possible values depending on the value after three months:[12] it may either be DEM/USD 4, DEM/USD 5, or DEM/USD 3. If the exchange rate at the end of six months is DEM/USD 4 or below, the cash flows that Volkswagen will receive at that time are equal to DEM 3m. However, if the exchange rate is above DEM/USD 4, Volkswagen can decrease its USD sales price and substantially increase its volume of sales in the US. In this case, the cash flows of Volkswagen from the US will be equal to $\tilde{S}_{6\text{-month}} \times$ DEM 1m, that is, if the spot rate is DEM/USD 5m, then the cash flows will be DEM 5m. The nonlinear exposure of the firm is illustrated in Figure 18.4.

Assume, for simplicity, that the US interest rate is 2.02 percent over three months, and the DEM interest rate is 1 percent over three months. Also, assume that these interest rates are constant over the next six months. The information about spot rates, interest rates, and the cash flows is summarized in Figure 18.5.

We now use the method explained in Chapter 7 (and similar to that used in Section 18.3.1) to replicate the above cash flows using forward contracts on the foreign currency (in this case the USD)

FIGURE 18.4   VW's Convex Exposure Schedule with Three Possible Spot Rates

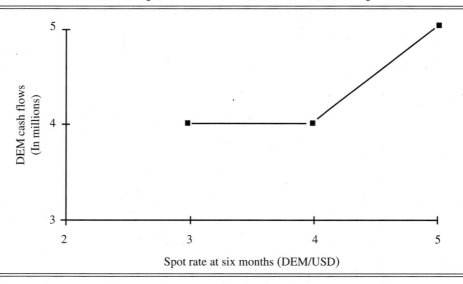

---

[11] For another example of hedging nonlinear exposure with options, see Chapter 6.

[12] For expositional ease, only three possible values are considered. As explained in Chapter 7, one could extend this analysis to consider a large number of possible exchange rates at maturity.

FIGURE 18.5   The BEF Value of UK Subsidiary When Its Exposure Is Hedged

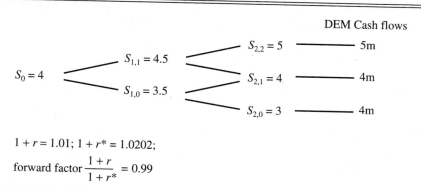

DEM Cash flows

$S_{2,2} = 5$ ———— 5m

$S_{1,1} = 4.5$

$S_0 = 4$

$S_{2,1} = 4$ ———— 4m

$S_{1,0} = 3.5$

$S_{2,0} = 3$ ———— 4m

$1 + r = 1.01$; $1 + r^* = 1.0202$;

forward factor $\dfrac{1+r}{1+r^*} = 0.99$

and DEM riskless bonds. Since the details of this method are given in Chapter 7, only the essential calculations are shown. Basically, one needs to find at time t and node j the amount to be invested in domestic bonds, $B_{t,j}$, and the number of forward contracts, $b_{t,j}$, that replicate the cash flows of the Volkswagen; that is, to find the solution of:

$$\text{up: } B_{t,j}(1+r) + b_{t,j}[S_{t+1,j+1} - F_{t,j}] = V_{t+1,j+1},\tag{11}$$

and

$$\text{down: } B_{t,j}(1+r) + b_{t,j}[S_{t+1,j} - F_{t,j}] = V_{t+1,j}.\tag{12}$$

We need to solve the above equations at time 1, for the two possible exchange rates, $S_{1,1}$ and $S_{1,0}$, and then we need to come back one period and solve the same problem at time 0. These calculations are as follows.

At time 1, if the spot rate is 4.5, then the forward rate is DEM/USD 4.455 and the problem is to choose the amount to be invested in domestic bonds, $B_{1,1}$, and the number of forward contracts to hold, $b_{1,1}$, so that the payoff from this position matches the cash flows of the firm in the next period. This implies that $B_{1,1}$ and $b_{1,1}$ need to satisfy the following two equations:

$$1.01\, B_{1,1} + b_{1,1}[5 - 4.455] = 5,$$

and

$$1.01\, B_{1,1} + b_{1,1}[4 - 4.455] = 4.$$

Solving these two equations, we find that $B_{1,1} = 4.4109$ and $b_{1,1} = 1$. This implies that the replicating portfolio contains 1 forward contract and the value of the replicating portfolio is DEM 4.4109.

If, at time 1, the exchange rate were 3.5, then the forward rate would be DEM/USD 3.465, and the two equations that one would have to solve to obtain $B_{1,0}$ and $b_{1,0}$ are the following:

$$1.01 \, B_{1,0} + b_{1,0} \, [4 - 3.465] = 4,$$

and

$$1.01 \, B_{1,0} + b_{1,0} \, [3 - 3.465] = 4.$$

Solving these two equations, we find that $B_{1,0} = 3.9604$ and $b_{1,0} = 0$. Thus, the replicating portfolio in this case contains no forward contracts, and the value of this replicating portfolio is DEM 3.9604.

At time 0, we need a portfolio that replicates the value of the cash flows at time 1 for the two exchange rate outcomes. This replicating portfolio can be obtained by solving the following two equations for B_0 and b_0:

$$1.01 \, B_0 + b_0 \, [4.5 - 3.96] = 4.4108,$$

and

$$1.01 \, B_0 + b_0 \, [3.5 - 3.96] = 3.9604.$$

Solving these two equations, we find that $B_0 = 4.1263$ and $b_0 = 0.4504$. Thus, the replicating portfolio in this case contains 0.4504 forward contracts, and the value of this replicating portfolio is DEM 4.1263.

To conclude, in this example, the *dynamic* hedging strategy is to start at time 0, by selling short 0.4504 forward contracts of three-month maturity. If, at time 1, the exchange rate is DEM/USD 4.5, one can hedge the exposure by selling one forward contract and, if the exchange rate is DEM/USD 3.5, then there is no exposure and no new forward contract is required.

18.4   CONCLUSIONS FOR TREASURY MANAGEMENT

Let us conclude this chapter by summarizing a few crucial results and integrating them with ideas mentioned in earlier chapters.

We can divide economic exposure into two categories—contractual (transaction) exposure and operating exposure. Managers typically focus on contractual exposure, which arises from accounts receivable, accounts payable, long-term sales or purchase contracts, or financial positions expressed in foreign currency. This is because if one's source of information is accounting data, as it typically is, then transaction exposure is very visible and easy to measure. In contrast, operating exposure is much harder to quantify than contractual exposure; it requires a good understanding of competitive forces and of the macroeconomic environment in which the firm operates. For many firms, however, operating exposure is more important than contractual exposure, and it is critical that firms make an attempt to identify and measure the exposure of operations to exchange rates.

Also, it is incorrect to assume that a firm with no foreign operations is not exposed to the exchange rate. For example, if a firm's competitors are located abroad, then changes in exchange rates will affect a firm's competitive position and its cash flows. Another common fallacy is the presumption that a policy of systematic hedging of all *transaction* exposure suffices to protect the firm against *all* exchange rate effects. As explained above, even if a firm perfectly hedges all contractual exposure, its operations are still exposed to the exchange rate.

Whether one considers transaction or operating exposure, one can use a forward contract (or the equivalent money-market hedge) to hedge the corresponding uncertainty in the firm's cash flow. Recall, however, that a forward or spot hedge is a double-edged sword. It is true that bad news about future operations is offset by gains on the forward hedge. However, you would likewise lose on the forward hedge if the exchange rate change improves the value of your operations. For example, in 1991, the Belgian group Acec Union Minière had hedged against a "further drop" of the USD. Instead, the USD rose, causing losses of no less than BEF 900m on the forward contracts. Four managers were fired. If you dislike this symmetry implicit in the payoff of a forward contract, you may consider hedging with options rather than forwards, to limit the downward risk without eliminating potential gains from exchange rate changes.

A second potential problem that a treasurer needs to be aware of, when using short-term forward contracts to hedge long-term exposure, is the possibility of ruin risk; that is, liquidity problems that arise when there is a mismatch between the maturity of the underlying position and the hedging instrument. These liquidity concerns are especially important when hedging with futures contracts that are marked to market.

Third, it is important to keep in mind that the estimate of exposure that one calculates changes over time, and may not be very precise at any given moment. However, this measure is useful—even if it gives us only an approximate indication of the sign and size of a firm's exposure—because it forces us to think about the way exchange rates affect the firm's operations.

Finally, hedging provides one with a financial gain that is intended to offset operating losses, but it does not reduce the operating losses themselves. Thus, one may wish to complement a policy of financial hedging with strategic changes in operations, for example, revising the marketing mix, reallocating production, choosing sourcing policies to reduce exposure, and so on. Similarly, when making scenario projections about the possible future exchange rates, we should also make contingency plans for various possible future exchange rates.[13] Note, however, that it is much cheaper and more efficient to hedge against exchange risk with financial claims than by changing operations. More importantly, it is much easier to undo financial hedges than to undo investment decisions. Thus, one should not make sub-optimal real investment decisions simply because they reduce exposure to exchange rates. Rather, one should choose the optimal real decisions and then use financial instruments to hedge these operations against exchange risk.

---

[13] The oil producer Royal Dutch/Shell is famous for this type of planning. When, in the mid-70s, oil prices rose to USD 30, most of the world merrily extrapolated prices towards USD 40 or even USD 60. So did Shell; but it also considered the case of oil prices around USD 20 and 15. When the unthinkable did indeed happen, Shell was not shocked or in disarray; it simply set in motion its "USD 15" contingency plan.

QUIZ QUESTIONS

True-False Questions

1. A firm that has no operations abroad does not face any operating exposure.
2. Only firms with exports, or firms that compete against foreign exporters, face operating exposure.
3. A firm that denominates all of its contracts in home currency, or hedges all of its foreign currency contracts, faces no operating exposure.
4. Almost every firm faces some operating exposure, although some firms are only exposed indirectly (through the country's general economic activity).
5. As large economies have a big impact on world economic activity, companies in such countries tend to be very exposed to exchange rates.
6. Small economies tend to fix their exchange rate relative to the currency of larger economies, or tend to create currency zones (like the EMS). Therefore, companies in small economies tend to be less exposed to exchange rates.
7. The smaller a country, the more open the economy. Therefore, exposure is relevant for most of the country's firms.
8. Everything else being the same, the larger the monopolistic power of a firm, the smaller its exposure because such a firm has more degrees of freedom in adjusting its marketing policy.
9. Consider an exporting firm that has substantial monopolistic power in its product market. Everything else being the same, the more elastic foreign demand is, the more an exporting firm will profit from a devaluation of its own currency. Similarly, the less elastic foreign demand is, the less an exporting firm will be hurt by an appreciation of its own currency.
10. Most information needed to measure operating exposure can be inferred from the firm's past export and import contracts.

Multiple-Choice Questions

Choose the correct answer(s).

1. In a small, completely open economy,

   (a) PPP holds relative to the surrounding countries.
   (b) A 10 percent devaluation of the host currency will be offset by a 10 percent rise in the host country prices.
   (c) The value of a foreign subsidiary, in units of the foreign parent's home currency, is unaffected by exchange rate changes.
   (d) The real value of a foreign subsidiary to an investor from the host country is unaffected by exchange rate changes.
   (e) In the absence of contracts with a value fixed in the host currency, the real value of a foreign subsidiary to an investor from the parent's home country is unaffected by exchange rate changes.
   (f) In the absence of contracts with a value that is fixed in foreign currency, the real value of a foreign subsidiary to an investor from the host country is unaffected by exchange rate changes.
   (g) There is little or no advantage to having one's own currency: exchange rate policy has virtually no effects.

2. In a completely closed economy,

   (a) PPP holds relative to the surrounding countries.

   (b) A 10 percent devaluation of the host currency will be offset by a 10 percent rise in the host country prices.

   (c) The value of a foreign subsidiary, in units of the foreign parent's home currency, is unaffected by exchange rate changes.

   (d) The real value of a foreign subsidiary to an investor from the host country is unaffected by exchange rate changes.

   (e) In the absence of contracts with a value fixed in host currency, the real value of a foreign subsidiary to an investor from the parent's home country is unaffected by exchange rate changes.

   (f) In the absence of contracts with a value that is fixed in foreign currency, the real value of a foreign subsidiary to an investor from the host country is unaffected by exchange rate changes.

   (g) There is little or no advantage to having one's own currency: exchange rate policy has virtually no effects.

3. In an economy that is neither perfectly open nor completely closed,

   (a) Consider a company that produces and sells in this economy. Apart from contractual exposure effects, its value in terms of its own (local) currency is positively exposed to the value of other currencies.

   (b) The value of an importing firm located in this economy could either go up or go down when the local currency devalues: the effect depends on such factors as the elasticity of local demand and foreign supply.

   (c) Consider a company that produces and sells in this economy. Apart from contractual exposure effects, its value in terms of a foreign currency is positively exposed to the value of its currency expressed in terms of other currencies.

4. Suppose that the value of the firm, expressed in terms of the owner's currency, is a linear function of the exchange rate up to random noise.

   (a) The firm's exposure is the constant $a_{t,T}$ in $V_T(i) = a_{t,T} + b_{t,T} S_T(i) + e_{t,T}(i)$.

   (b) The exposure is hedged by buying forward $b_{t,T}$ units of foreign currency.

   (c) Hedging means that all risk is eliminated.

5. Suppose that the value of the firm, expressed in terms of the owner's currency, is a nonlinear function of the exchange rate up to random noise. Suppose that you fit a linear regression through this relationship, and you hedge with a forward sale with size equal to the regression coefficient.

   (a) All risk will be eliminated.

   (b) There is remaining risk, but it is entirely independent of the realized value of the exchange rate.

   (c) There is remaining risk, but it is uncorrelated to the realized value of the exchange rate.

   (d) There is no way to further reduce the variance of the firm's hedged value.

   (e) There is no way to further reduce the variance of the firm's hedged value if only exchange rate hedges can be used.

   (f) There is no way to further reduce the variance of the firm's hedged value if only *linear* exchange rate hedges can be used.

EXERCISES

SynClear, of Seattle, Washington, produces equipment to clean polluted waters. It has a subsidiary in Canada that imports and markets its parent's products. The value of this subsidiary, in terms of CAD, has recently decreased to CAD 5m due to the depreciation of the CAD relative to the USD (from the traditional level of USD/CAD 0.85 to about 0.75). SynClear's analysts argue that the value of the CAD may very well return to its former level if, as seems reasonable, the uncertainty created by Canada's rising government deficit and Quebec's possible secession is resolved. If the CAD recovers, SynClear's products would be less expensive in terms of CAD, and the CAD value of the subsidiary would rise to about 6.5m.

1. From the parent's (USD) perspective, is the exposure of SynClear Canada to the USD/CAD exchange rate positive or negative? Explain the sign of the exposure.

2. Determine the exposure, and verify that the corresponding forward hedge eliminates this exposure. Use a forward rate of USD/CAD 0.80, and USD/CAD 0.75 and 0.85 as the possible future spot rates.

3. SynClear's chairman argues that, as the exposure is positive and the only possible exchange rate change is an appreciation of the CAD, the only possible change is an increase in the value of the subsidiary. Therefore, he continues, the firm should not hedge: why give away the chance of gain? How do you evaluate this argument?

   In the remainder of this series of exercises, SynClear Canada's cash flows and market values are assumed, more realistically, to depend on other factors than just the exchange rate. The Canadian economy can be in a recession, or booming, or somewhere in between, and the state of the economy is a second determinant of the demand for SynClear's products. The table below summarizes the value of the firm in each state and the joint probability of each state:

State of the economy	Boom	Medium	Recession
$S_T = 0.85$: Joint probability	0.075	0.175	0.25
Value$_T$ (USD)	5.25	4.75	4.50
$S_T = 0.75$: Joint probability	0.25	0.175	0.075
Value$_T$ (USD)	4.25	3.857	3.50

4. What are the expected cash flows conditional on each value of the exchange rate?

5. Compute the exposure, the optimal forward hedge, and the value of the hedged firm in each state. The forward rate is USD/CAD 0.80.

MIND-EXPANDING EXERCISES

We modify the SynClear Canada example: there are five possible exchange rates, and SynClear Canada's value, in USD is a nonlinear function of the exchange rate. For simplicity, we ignore risk caused by other factors than the exchange rate: from the text, or from Exercises 4 and 5, we already know how to handle other risks. The value V as a function of the exchange rate S is as follows:

S_T	0.750	0.775	0.80	0.825	0.850
Probability	0.10	0.20	0.40	0.20	0.10
$V_T(S_T)$ (in USD)	4.00	4.25	4.45	4.60	4.70

1. Suppose that SynClear USA wants to use a linear hedge. What is the linear regression of $V(S)$ on S? (Note that you have to take into account the fact that the outcomes are not equally probable. A correct but computationally simple way to do this is to compute a linear regression as if you had ten equally probable outcomes where the case "$S = 0.775$" occurs two times, the case "$S = 0.80$" four times, and the case "$S = 0.825$" two times.)

2. (a) If the forward rate is USD/CAD 0.80, what is the value of the firm after this linear hedge?
   (b) What is the expected value?
   (c) Is the deviation from the mean predictable on the basis of the exchange rate?

3. (a) What portfolio of options would eliminate all uncertainty?
   (b) What is the future value of the hedged subsidiary?
   (c) The hedge that you engineered in part (b) locks in a rather low value for the subsidiary. Does this mean that hedging using a portfolio of options lowers the value of the firm?

4. To value the subsidiary, you could construct a replicating portfolio. How would you construct this portfolio?

19 MEASURING AND MANAGING ACCOUNTING EXPOSURE

In Chapter 17, we explained that firms that have contracts denominated in foreign currency are exposed to the exchange rate, because a change in the exchange rate leads to a change in the value of such contracts. In Chapter 18, we explained that a firm's operations may also be exposed to the exchange rate: a change in the exchange rate affects the value of the firm through its effect on the firm's costs and sales volume. In this chapter, we discuss a third kind of exposure, accounting exposure. This is the exposure that a firm faces if it has subsidiaries located in foreign countries. **Accounting exposure** refers to the change in the value of the subsidiary, as given by its financial statements, when these statements are translated into the currency of the parent firm. This exposure is also called **translation exposure**.

In the opening section of this chapter, we discuss what we mean by accounting exposure and how this is different from economic exposure. In Section 19.2, we list some of the reasons why the financial statements of a subsidiary need to be translated into the currency of the parent firm. In Section 19.3, we describe the four main translation methods. We conclude, in Section 19.4, with a discussion of the relevance of translation exposure.

19.1 WHAT IS ACCOUNTING EXPOSURE?

In this section, we present the definition of accounting exposure and explain how the exposure that arises as a consequence of the translation of financial statements is different from economic exposure.

19.1.1 Definition of Accounting Exposure

Accounting exposure, also called translation exposure, is the effect of exchange rate changes on the translated value of a foreign subsidiary's financial statements. Recall that, in Chapter 17, we defined exposure to the time-T exchange rate as an amount, in foreign currency, such that

$$\text{Exposure} = \frac{\text{Total unexpected effect on financial position of firm, measured in home currency at time } T}{\text{Unexpected change in } S_T} \quad [1]$$

or, equivalently:

$$\text{Unexpected effect on financial position of firm} = \text{Exposure} \times \text{Unexpected change in } S_T. \quad [2]$$

If one interprets the words "financial position" in this definition as the accounting value Net Worth, given by the financial statements of a firm, then the above defines accounting exposure. In contrast, in Chapters 17 and 18, where we discussed economic exposure, we interpreted "financial position" to imply the firm's *future cash flows*. In other words, translation exposure measures the effect of exchange rates on the *accounting* value of a foreign subsidiary, while economic exposure measures the effect on the cash flows and the market value of a firm. The differences between accounting exposure and economic exposure, comprising contractual exposure and operating exposure, are discussed below.

19.1.2   Comparing Accounting Exposure to Economic Exposure

Accounting exposure differs fundamentally from economic exposure. Table 19.1 compares the two concepts. The conclusion, from Table 19.1, is that the impact of economic exposure on the value of a firm is likely to be much larger than that of accounting exposure because accounting exposure, typically, affects the value of a firm only through its effect on taxes, while economic exposure has an impact on the value of a firm both through its effect on the value of existing contracts that the firm has signed, and through its effect on the value of future operations. In light of this, should we worry about translation exposure at all and, if so, should we worry what the best translation method is? The question of why one needs to translate the financial statements of a subsidiary into the home currency of the parent is answered in the next section. The various methods that can be used to translate these financial statements are described in the sections that follow.

19.2   WHY FIRMS NEED TO TRANSLATE FINANCIAL STATEMENTS

If some of the subsidiaries of a firm are located abroad, their financial statements are typically maintained in terms of the local (foreign) currency. For example, consider the subsidiary of a US firm, and assume that the subsidiary is located in France. The accounts of the subsidiary will be maintained in terms of the French currency, FRF. There are a number of reasons why the financial statements of the subsidiary need to be translated into other currencies—most often, the parent company's home currency, as described below.

- Translation is often necessary for tax purposes, because the tax authorities of the parent's home country often have to review the subsidiaries' financial statements to establish the tax basis (as explained in Chapter 23). Taxes in the parent's home country, on income earned by the foreign subsidiary are, of course, payable in home currency. This means that the foreign income has to be translated into the home currency. Also, capital gains arising from exchange

TABLE 19.1   Economic Exposure vs. Accounting Exposure

Economic Exposure	Accounting Exposure
1. Economic exposure is concerned with cash flows (real money), not just accounting figures, and with the corresponding economic value or market value of the firm.	1. Accounting exposure focuses only on accounting values. In itself, a change in an accounting value due to translation does not affect the firm's cash situation and market value—except possibly through its effect on taxes.
2. Economic exposure is a forward-looking concept. It focuses on *future* cash flows, including contractually fixed cash flows and future operating cash flows.	2. Accounting exposure is a backward looking concept. It relates to past decisions as reflected in the subsidiary's financial statements.
3. Economic exposure considers all cash flows and sources of value, whether or not they are recorded in the financial statements.	3. Accounting exposure looks only at items on the balance sheet or income statement. It ignores off-balance-sheet contracts, and cash flows from future operations.
4. Economic exposure also exists for firms without foreign subsidiaries, such as exporting firms, import-competing firms, and even *potential* import-competing firms.	4. Accounting exposure arises only when a firm has foreign subsidiaries.
5. Economic exposure depends on economic facts—the firm's set of outstanding commitments denominated in the foreign currency (contractual exposure), and the economic environment in which the firm operates (operating exposure).	5. Accounting exposure depends on the accounting rules chosen. The subsidiary' internal rules (such as the inventory valuation or depreciation method) affect its accounting value, and translating its value into the parent's currency can also be done in different ways.

rate changes may be taxable; thus, to compute the capital gain, one needs to translate the value of the foreign subsidiary into home currency terms. Thus, translation exposure, even though it deals with accounting data, can have an impact on cash flows through its effect on the tax basis.

• Most countries require consolidation of the parent's and subsidiaries' financial statements for reporting purposes. Consolidation here refers to the integration of the financial statements of the firm's subsidiaries into the parent's asset and liabilities (A&L) and profit and loss (P&L) statements. Of course, one needs to first translate the financial statements of the subsidiary before they can be consolidated with those of the parent.

- The parent firm itself may feel the need to translate the financial statements of foreign subsidiaries. This is because one needs to consolidate data in order to make investment and financial decisions, and to evaluate the performance of the subsidiary. For example, to get some idea about the importance of the foreign business, one needs to determine its value in terms of a common currency. Of course, importance cannot be determined on the basis of a single figure or backward-looking accounting data. Still, translated accounting data give an approximate idea of the relative importance of the foreign activities.
- In order to make performance measures comparable, foreign data need to be translated into a common currency. For example, many firms have bonus plans that link their managers' compensation to their performance. Decisions to promote or fire managers are also based on performance. To make such decisions, one needs to translate the financial statements of the foreign subsidiaries into the currency of the parent.
- To value the entire firm (as an outside investor or financial analyst), one needs far more than just accounting data. Still, valuation is often partially based on accounting values; or, at the very least, the accounting value serves as a benchmark. For instance, if the discounted cash flow value of the entire firm turns out to be four times its book value, one would surely take a closer look at both types of information. Again, the book value of the firm as a whole cannot be computed unless assets and liabilities of foreign subsidiaries are first translated into a common currency.

In the next section we discuss the general objectives that any method used to translate the accounts of the subsidiary into the currency of the parent firm tries to accomplish, and the details of the various methods that are used for translation.

19.3   THE CHOICE OF DIFFERENT TRANSLATION METHODS

Accounting exposure arises because the outcome of translating a subsidiary's balance sheet from foreign currency to home currency depends on the exchange rate at the date of consolidation, an exchange rate that is uncertain. Firms may like to hedge this exposure to reduce or eliminate the swings in reported profits that arise simply due to these translation effects. This exposure, of course, depends on the rules used to translate the accounts of the subsidiary into the currency of the parent firm. There are a variety of approaches that one can adopt to translate the income statement and balance sheet items of the subsidiary into the currency of the parent firm.

Example   19.1

Suppose that a Canadian firm buys a firm in England for GBP 1m, when the exchange rate is CAD/GBP 2.0. A year later, the exchange rate is CAD/GBP 2.1. Thus, assuming that the subsidiary is still worth GBP 1m and translation is done at CAD/GBP 2.1, its translated value in terms of the currency of the parent is CAD 2.1m. One question is how to report this increase in the value of the British subsidiary in the accounts of the parent firm. For example, should the exchange rate effect be shown as part of the reporting period's income, or should it just be mentioned on the balance sheet, as an unrealized gain? A second question is whether one *should* translate the GBP value at the new rate. If this asset is translated at the *historical* exchange rate—the translation prevailing when the asset was purchased—then there is no translation exposure.

Example 19.1 illustrates what the controversy between accountants is all about. Accountants do not agree which assets should be translated at the historical exchange rate and which at the current exchange rate. There is also some disagreement about whether and when exchange rate gains or losses should be recognized as income. The main objective of accountants in devising the translations rules is that these rules be consistent with the rules for domestic accounting. However, from a firm's point of view, the principal requirement is that the rules be such that they provide accurate information about the performance of the subsidiary. Firms also wish that the rules be such that they do not lead to wide swings in the figures reported in the financial statements.

In the rest of this section, we describe four different translation methods and the philosophy underlying each method. Each method has a set of rules for translating items in the balance sheet and the income statement. The rules for translating items in the income statement are quite similar across the different methods; hence, we will focus on the rules for items reported in the balance sheet. To illustrate the differences between these methods, we shall consider the example of a Swedish subsidiary of a German firm. A simplified balance sheet of the Swedish subsidiary is shown in the second column (value in SEK) of Table 19.2. We shall explain the notion of accounting exposure by considering translation on December 31, 1993, at two different exchange rates, DEM/SEK 0.333 and DEM/SEK 0.300, and by seeing how the value of the subsidiary changes depending on the accounting method being used. Throughout this discussion, our focus will be to study what the different translation methods imply for the firm's accounting exposure.

19.3.1   The Current/Non-Current Method

The **Current/Non-Current Method** for translating the financial statements of foreign subsidiaries is one that was commonly used in the US until the mid-1970s. As its name suggests, the criterion underlying this method is maturity; that is, whether an item is translated at the current exchange rate or the historical rate depends on its maturity. Thus, according to this method, current assets and liabilities in the balance sheet are translated at the current exchange rate, while non-current items, such as long-term debt, are translated at the historical rate. The logic underlying this is that the value of short-term assets and liabilities is fixed in SEK terms and changes with the exchange rate. For example, the value of a SEK T-bill is fixed in SEK nominal terms; and, in the short-term, goods prices are sticky and therefore quasi-fixed in SEK terms, too. Long-term assets and liabilities, in contrast, will not be realized in the short run—and by the time they are realized, the current exchange rate change may very well turn out to have been undone by later, opposite changes in the spot rate. That is, the effect of a current exchange rate change on the realization value of long-term assets and liabilities is very uncertain. As accountants hesitate to recognize gains or losses that are very uncertain, the Current/Non-Current Method simply deems that the long-term assets and liabilities be unexposed.

Consider the example of the Swedish subsidiary, the data for which is given in Table 19.2. Accountants who favor the Current/Non-Current Method agree that long-term items should be recorded at the historical exchange rate; accounting conservatism would suggest that a decrease in the net long-term items following a devaluation not be recognized. Thus, for the purpose of translating long-term assets and debts, we should use the historic exchange rate. Accountants who favor this method also agree that the subsidiary's SEK-denominated short-term assets and liabilities and its inventories should be translated at the current exchange rate. From the above discussion, we see that,

TABLE 19.2 An Example of the Current/Non-Current Method

| | | Value in DEM on Dec. 31, 1993 | | Change |
	Value in SEK	if DEM/SEK 0.333	if DEM/SEK 0.300	in DEM value
Assets				
Cash, securities	1,000	333	300	
A/R	1,000	333	300	
Inventory	1,000	333	300	
Plant, equipment	5,000	*1,625*	*1,625*	
Total Assets (a)	8,000	2,624	2,525	−99
Debts				
A/P	500	166.5	150	
Short-term debt	2,000	666	600	
Long-term debt	2,400	*780*	*780*	
Total Debts (b)	4,900	1,612.5	1,530	−82.5
Net Worth = (a) − (b)	3,100	1,011.5	995	−16.5

Under the Current/Non-Current Method, the Net Worth accounts and Long-Term Assets and Liabilities keep their historical DEM value (given in italics), while short-term items are translated from SEK into DEM at the current exchange rate. The Equity Adjustment necessary to balance Assets and Liabilities is proportional to the subsidiary's Net Working Capital, SEK 1,000 + 1,000 + 1,000 − 500 − 2,000 = SEK 500.

under the Current/Non-Current Method, translation at the current rate is restricted to only the short-term assets and liabilities. Thus, exposure is given by the difference in short-term assets and liabilities, that is, Net Working Capital. This is illustrated in Example 19.2.

Example   19.2

In Table 19.2, we assume that long-term debt was issued and long-term assets (plant and equipment) were bought in early 1993, at which time the exchange rate was DEM/SEK 0.325. Thus, these items are recorded at their historical values (indicated as italicized text) and are not affected by the exchange rate. We could have predicted the effect on Net Worth, −DEM 16.5, from Equation [2]:

Effect of exchange rate change under the Current/Non-Current Method

$$= [\text{Exposure}] \times \Delta S$$

$$= [\text{Current Assets} - \text{Current Liabilities}] \times \Delta S$$

$$= [\text{Net Working Capital}] \times \Delta S$$

$$= \text{SEK } 500 \times \text{DEM/SEK } (0.300 - 0.333) = -\text{DEM } 16.5.$$

The Current/Non-Current Method suffers from several limitations. The assumption underlying this method seems to be that there is mean-reversion in exchange rates; that is, exchange rate fluctuations tend to be undone in the medium run, which (if true) means that they affect short-term assets only. However, as discussed in Chapter 11, there is little empirical support for this view (except for the small movements of exchange rates around a central parity): typically, changes in exchange rates are *not* undone in the medium run, and floating exchange rates behave like random walks. In addition, this method suffers from the weakness that the consolidated accounts are not compatible with the subsidiary's accounts. Also, the value of the long-term assets and liabilities seems to differ depending on whether the assets and liabilities are held by an independent Swedish company or by a foreign-owned entity.

To translate the subsidiary's income statement, the Current/Non-Current Rate Method uses an average exchange rate for the period, assuming that cash flows come evenly over the period—except for incomes or costs corresponding to non-recurrent items (like depreciation of assets). These are translated at the same rate as the corresponding balance sheet item. This creates another inconsistency between the SEK and DEM P&L figures, and between the translated P&L and A&L figures.

The rules for translating different items under the Current/Non-Current Method are summarized in the second column of Table 19.3. (The other columns summarize the translation methods to be described below.)

19.3.2   The Monetary/Non-Monetary Method

The **Monetary/Non-Monetary Method** translates monetary items in the balance sheet using the current exchange rate, and non-monetary items at the historical rate(s). That is, accountants who favor the Monetary/Non-Monetary Method agree that a SEK-denominated claim or liability loses its value by the same percentage as the drop in the value of the SEK. Thus, this loss in value should be recognized by recording the item at the current exchange rate. However, the value of goods and equipment is assumed to behave differently. It is argued that since, in the long run, inflation differentials should undo exchange rate changes (PPP), the real value of real assets will not be affected. Thus, according to this method, we should adjust only the *monetary* (not the real) assets and liabilities for changes in the exchange rate. It follows that only the net foreign-currency monetary position, financial assets minus debt, is exposed. This can be verified from the example given in Table 19.4.

Example   19.3

In Table 19.4, the Net Worth figures under each of the two possible year-end exchange rates differ by DEM 95.7. This effect of the exchange rate change could have been predicted, from Equation [2], by computing [Exposure] × ΔS:

Effect of exchange rate change under the Monetary/Non-Monetary Method

$$\begin{aligned}
&= [\text{Exposure}] \times \Delta S \\
&= [\text{Financial Assets} - \text{Debts}] \times \Delta S \\
&= \text{SEK}[2,000 - 4,900] \times \text{DEM/SEK}(0.300 - 0.333) = +\text{DEM } 95.7.
\end{aligned}$$

TABLE 19.3   The Translation Methods—An Overview

(US Classification)	Current/Non-Current	Temporal and Monetary/Non-Monetary (FASB 8)	Current Rate (FASB 52)
		Balance Sheet	
Assets			
Cash, securities	*C*	*C*	*C*
A/R	*C*	*C*	*C*
Inventory	*C*	*H**	*C*
Plant, equipment	*H*	*H*	*C*
Liabilities			
A/P	*C*	*C*	*C*
Short-term debt	*C*	*C*	*C*
Long-term debt	*H*	*C*	*C*
Net Worth	Mixed *H*	Mixed *H*	Mixed *H*
Exposure	Net working capital	Financial assets minus debt	Net worth
		Income Statement	
Dividends and interest	Average	Average	Actual
Royalties	Average	Average	Actual
Sales revenue	Average	Average	*C* or average
Costs	Average	*H*	*C* or average
Depreciation	*H*	*H*	*C* or average

H means translation at the historic rate (prevailing when the position is first created), *C* means translation at the current rate (prevailing on the date of consolidation). Mixed *H* refers to sums of terms added at various moments in time, at the then-prevailing rate. Average means an average of daily, or end-of-the-week, or end-of-the-month rates over the accounting year. * indicates that, under US FASB 8, inventory could be translated at the current exchange rate if domestic inventories were shown at market value on the balance sheet.

Oddly enough, the firm made translation gains under this method, whereas, under the other methods, there is a translation loss. In fact, this measure of exposure, financial assets minus debts, is likely to be negative for most firms. Thus, under the Monetary/Non-Monetary Method, a devaluation will typically lead to an accounting gain rather than to a loss. A second criticism is that the Purchasing Power Parity view of the world has received little empirical support. Third, under this method of translating the balance sheet items, there is an inconsistency between the Swedish accounts and the consolidated accounts. In fact, the German accountants are basically telling their Swedish colleagues that they make systematic errors in the valuation of the long-term real assets, and that the historic value in

TABLE 19.4   An Example of the Monetary/Non-Monetery Method

	Value in SEK	Value in DEM on Dec. 31, 1993		Change in DEM value
		if DEM/SEK 0.333	if DEM/SEK 0.300	
Assets				
Cash, securities	1,000	333	300	
A/R	1,000	333	300	
Inventory	1,000	_325_	_325_	
Plant, equipment	_5,000_	_1,625_	_1,625_	
Total Assets (a)	8,000	2,616	2,550	–66
Debts				
A/P	500	166.5	150	
Short-term debt	2,000	666	600	
Long-term debt	2,400	799.2	720.0	
Total Debts (b)	4,900	1,631.7	1,470.0	–161.7
Net Worth = (a) – (b)	3,100	984.3	1,080	+95.7

Under the Monetary/Non-Monetary Method, monetary items in the balance sheet are translated at the current exchange rate. Non-monetary items, on the other hand, are translated at the historical exchange rate, as indicated by italicized text. The financial assets – debts = (1,000 + 1,000) – (500 + 2,000 + 2,400) = –DEK 2,900.

DEM is more correct. This is debatable. Purchasing Power Parity theory says that the true DEM and the SEK values of a given asset should be the same, but this in itself does not mean that the true DEM value is independent of the exchange rate.

To translate the subsidiary's income statement, the Monetary/Non-Monetary Method uses an average exchange rate for the period, except for incomes or costs corresponding from non-monetary sources (like depreciation of assets). These are translated at the same rate as the corresponding balance sheet item. This again creates an inconsistency between the SEK and DEM P&L figures, and between the translated P&L and A&L figures.

The rules for translating different items under the Monetary/Non-Monetary Method are summarized in the third column of Table 19.3, given on page 522.

19.3.3   The Temporal Method

The **Temporal Method** of translating the financial statements of a foreign subsidiary is similar to the Monetary/Non-Monetary Method. The only difference between the two methods is that, under the monetary system, inventory is translated at the historical exchange rate, since it is a non-monetary asset. Under the Temporal Method, inventory may be translated at the current exchange rate if it is recorded in the balance sheet at current market prices. The US system that was used from 1976 to 1981, FASB 8, was based on the Temporal Method. The advantage of this approach is that it is consistent with the accounting rules used for the parent firm. The problem with this approach is that one is using many different exchange rates—the historical rate for some items, the current rate for other items, and the average rate for translating income. Thus, it is difficult to *interpret* the final number that one obtains. Another criticism of this method is that, by making translation effects part of reported income, it does not allow firms to maintain reserves for currency losses. Thus, translation gains and losses are reflected in the income statement of the firm and can lead to large swings in reported earnings. The Current Rate Method, known as FASB 52 in the US, is designed to overcome some of these problems.

19.3.4   The Current Rate Method

This is the simplest approach for translating financial statements. According to the **Current Rate Method**, all balance sheet items are translated at the current exchange rate. Typically, exchange gains are reported separately in a special equity account on the parent's balance sheet, thus avoiding large variations in reported earnings, and these unrealized exchange gains are not taxed. To translate the income statement, one translates all items at either the current exchange rate or the average exchange rate of the reporting period. The first method is chosen for consistency with the balance sheet translation. The second method is based on the argument that expenses that have been made gradually over the year should be translated at the average exchange rate. Profits, the argument goes, are realized gradually over the year, and should be translated at an average rate. This, of course, contradicts the translation of the balance sheet at a single exchange rate.

As all assets and debts are translated at the current rate, it is easy to figure out the exposure. If the final exchange rate rises by ΔS, the equity adjustment goes up by [Net Worth in SEK] $\times \Delta S$. Thus, the exposure to the parent is the subsidiary's Net Worth, as shown below.

Example   19.4

The Swedish subsidiary's simplified balance sheet is shown in Table 19.5. To compute the exposure of this firm, we first translate all assets and debts into DEM at one possible year-end exchange rate, DEM/SEK 0.333, and then at another possible year-end rate, DEM/SEK 0.300. The difference between the two Net Worths could have been predicted as follows:

Effect of exchange rate change under the Current Rate Method

$$= [\text{Exposure}] \times \Delta S$$

$$= [\text{Total Assets} - \text{Total Debts}] \times \Delta S$$

$$= [\text{Net Worth}] \times \Delta S$$

$$= \text{SEK } 3,100 \times \text{DEM/SEK}(0.300 - 0.333) = -\text{DEM } 102.3.$$

While the translation of all assets and liabilities at the same exchange rate, as proposed by the Current Rate Method, is an improvement over the other methods, this method is not without limitations. For example, the practice of translating the historical local-currency value of assets at the current exchange rate gives a quantity that has no economic interpretation. Of course, the accounting practice of valuing assets at the historical cost in host currency also biases the valuation.

TABLE 19.5   An Example of the Current Rate Method

		Value in DEM on Dec. 31, 1993		Change in
	Value in SEK	if DEM/SEK = 0.333	if DEM/SEK = 0.300	DEM value
Assets				
Cash, securities	1,000	333	300	
A/R	1,000	333	300	
Inventory	1,000	333	300	
Plant, equipment	5,000	1,665	1,500	
Total Assets (a)	8,000	2,664	2,400	−264
Debts				
A/P	500	166.5	150	
Short-term debt	2,000	666	600	
Long-term debt	2,400	799.2	720	
Total Debts (b)	4,900	1,631.7	1,470	−161.7
Net Worth = (a) − (b)	3,100	1,032.3	930	−102.3

Under the Current Rate Method, all assets and debts items are translated from SEK into DEM at the current rate.

The rules for translating different items under the Current Rate Method are summarized in the last column of Table 19.3, given on page 522.

19.4   CONCLUSIONS FOR MANAGERS

As we have seen, there are various methods to translate a subsidiary's balance sheet into the parent's currency. Many regulating bodies favor the Current Rate Method. For example, the US Financial Accounting Standards Board has essentially imposed this method (FASB #52, 1982), and similar rules were issued soon thereafter in the UK and Canada. The International Accounting Standards Committee has likewise come out in favor of the Current Rate Method (IASC #21, 1983—a text that, unlike FASB #52, is well-written, lucid, and short). However, the IASC can provide recommendations only; it has no statutory power to impose accounting rules anywhere. In continental Europe there is no consensus as to what method is to be followed. For example, in many countries (including, until the early nineties, Italy and Belgium), consolidation was not mandatory and, therefore, not regulated, while in other countries (including Germany), the obligation to consolidate was not extended to foreign subsidiaries. The EC 7th Directive, passed in 1983 and implemented in most member states by the early nineties, imposes consolidation but does not prescribe any particular translation method. The only requirement is that the notes to the accounts should disclose the method that was used.

Given the wide choice that is offered in many countries, one could question which method is best. And even where one particular method is imposed, one could wonder whether it is useful to adopt a different method for internal reporting purposes. Even more fundamentally, one could ask whether accounting exposure matters at all. These are the issues discussed in this concluding section.

19.4.1   Which Method Is Best?

From the discussion of the various translation methods, we see that the question of which translation method to choose is similar to the issue of whether the firm should use the method of last-in/first-out (LIFO), or first-in/first-out (FIFO), or some average cost, for the purpose of valuing its inventory. One could argue that the accounting method for inventory valuation does not matter, since a shift from, say, LIFO to FIFO does not change the firm's physical inventory or cash flows (except possibly through an effect on taxes). Moreover, one could argue that neither LIFO nor FIFO nor average cost is correct; only replacement value is theoretically sound. In the same vein, one could argue that the choice of the translation method does not affect reality—except possibly through its effect on taxable profit—so that the whole issue is, basically, a non-issue. Furthermore, while in the case of inventory valuation, one could argue that LIFO, being generally closer to replacement value, is the least of all evils, it is not obvious which of the translation methods generally corresponds best to economic value. The whole issue is, perhaps, best settled on the basis of practical arguments. Accounting data are already complicated enough, so that the Current Rate Method is probably a good choice, given its simplicity and internal consistency.

19.4.2   The Relevance of Accounting Exposure for Firms

Accounting exposure, as a measure of the firm's exposure to exchange rate changes, suffers from at least three major limitations. These limitations are described below.

First, accounting data, by their very nature, are not forward looking. Accounting data focus on financial and investment decisions that have been made in the past, but ignore decisions that have implications for future cash flows. For example, consider a Canadian firm that has bid on a project, at time t, to build a recreational park in Spain. The decision on the bid will be made one month from now. If the Canadian firm wins the bid, they will sign a contract at that time. Work on the project will begin in $t + 3$ month's time, an A/R is issued at $t + 6$, and payment will be received at the end of the project, one year after time t. This sequence of events is shown in Figure 19.1.

Even though this firm knows at $t + 1$ whether it will be receiving a foreign currency inflow at the end of the year, if it bases its hedging policy on accounting exposure, it will not initiate a hedge. In fact, it is quite likely that the above foreign currency inflow will not be reflected in the financial

FIGURE 19.1   Sequence of Events under a Tender

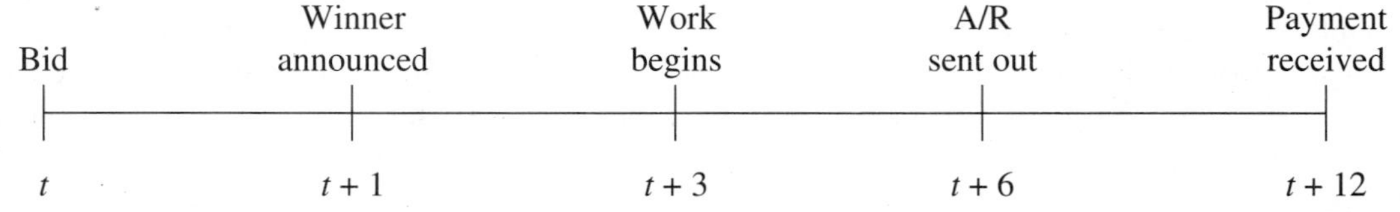

Bid	Winner announced	Work begins	A/R sent out	Payment received
t	$t + 1$	$t + 3$	$t + 6$	$t + 12$

statements of the firm until $t + 6$, even though the contract is signed at $t + 1$. Thus, accounting exposure is a poor measure of the risks that the firm faces.

Second, accounting exposure is an incomplete measure of the risks that a firm faces because accounting exposure ignores operating exposure. That is, there is no room in the financial statements of a firm to reflect the operating exposure that a firm faces.

Finally, accounting exposure is limited by the fact that assets are valued at historical cost. That is, no matter which method of translation one uses, the asset or liability value that is translated is the historical value. Thus, the accounting exposure does not reflect reality, even if the translation is done at current exchange rates.

Although accounting exposure suffers from the limitations described above, often accounting data are the only data that are readily available to a firm. Thus, it is important, that if firm treasurers use these data to make hedging decisions, they be aware of these limitations and adjust the accounting data, to the extent possible, for these limitations.

Having described the weaknesses of using accounting exposure to decide on a firm's hedging policy, we conclude by discussing the importance of accounting exposure for the value of a firm. Note, from the definition of accounting exposure, that accounting exposure has no cash flow implications—except possibly through its effect on taxes. Tax treatment differs from country to country. In Belgium, for instance, translation results are determined according to any of the methods discussed above, at the firm's discretion. However, accounting policy must be consistent; the parent cannot switch from method to method each year depending on the year's accounting input and desired financial statement output. The translation effect can be part of reported income (and, therefore, taxable/deductible) if the company records the translation gain or loss on the income statement; in case of a loss, its "durability" has to be proven to the tax authorities. The firm can also record the gains or losses from translation directly on the balance sheet, as unrealized gains/losses (deferral). Again, the only requirement is that the firm's accounting practice be consistent. In the US, translation gains or losses are currently computed, using the Current Rate Method described in Section 19.3.4, and are neither part of reported income nor taxable income. Thus, in many cases there are no tax repercussions, which implies that management should not attach undue importance to its accounting exposure. This does not mean that exposure is not important; however, what matters is *economic* exposure, not translation exposure.

QUIZ QUESTIONS

True-False Questions

1. As taxes on the subsidiary's income are invariably computed by the host country on the basis of the subsidiary's income statement, there is no need whatsoever to translate this income into the parent's home currency for tax purposes.
2. Taxes are always based on the parent's consolidated worldwide income (which, of course, requires translation).
3. The choice of the translation method is similar to the choice between LIFO, FIFO, or average cost—no accounting method can possibly affect the true value of the firm.
4. Accounting exposure is irrelevant if taxes are not affected. It follows that the firm need not worry about exchange rate changes at all.
5. The International Accounting Standards Committee has imposed the current rate method worldwide.
6. According to the Monetary/Non-Monetary Method, the true value of a real asset is the same in the two countries, and it is given by its foreign currency value translated at the current rate.

Matching Questions

Which exposure concept—*translation exposure* or *economic exposure*—matches best with the following statement?

This exposure:

1. Has to do with the firm's cash flows and market value.
2. Is forward-looking.
3. Ignores off-balance sheet items and future operations.
4. Only exists for firms with foreign subsidiaries.
5. Is relevant for all firms in a nonsheltered sector, including firms that could potentially become exporters or could potentially have to compete against foreign imports.
6. Depends on the accounting method used if and only if the accounting method affects taxes.
7. Depends on economic reality.

Which translation method(s), if any, match(es) best with the following statement? The translation methods are *Current Rate, Current/Non-Current, Monetary/Non-Monetary*.

1. Maximum consistency between the translated Asset and Liability statements and the originals (in host currency).
2. Imperfect consistency between the changes in the translated Asset and Liability statements and the translated Profit and Loss statement.
3. Short-term liabilities are exposed, but long-term liabilities are not.
4. Short-term real assets are exposed, but long-term real assets are not.
5. Short-term financial assets are exposed.
6. Exposure corresponds with net working capital.
7. Exchange rates are viewed as mean-reverting.
8. PPP holds.
9. Exposure corresponds to Net Worth.
10. Most firms have translation gains when the host currency appreciates.

11. For most firms, exposure to the exchange rate (units of the parent's home currency per unit of foreign currency) is negative. That is, there is a translation gain if the host currency depreciates.
12. PPP holds, so real assets are not exposed.

EXERCISES

1. Why does the need arise to translate the financial statements of subsidiaries into a reference currency?

2. You are given the following balance sheet information for the first two years of a Norwegian subsidiary's life, 19X3 and 19X4 (in millions of NOK, the subsidiary's currency).

Assets		
Cash		3
Inventory		4
Fixed assets		
Investments 19X3	4	
Investments 19X4	1	
		$\frac{5}{12}$
Liabilities		
Equity		
Equity 19X3	4	
New equity mid-19X4	1	
		5
Retained earnings 19X4		2
Long-term debt		
Issued 19X3	2	
Issued 19X4	1	
		3
Short-term debt		$\frac{2}{12}$

Notes: at the end of 19X3 and 19X4, the exchange rates were USD/NOK 0.30 and 0.15, respectively. The rate in mid-19X4, when the equity was increased, was 0.16. Fixed assets were bought in 19X3 and 19X4; the figures shown are net of all 19X3–5 depreciation.

Assume that the firm uses the Current Rate Method to translate its subsidiary's asset and liability statement.

(a) Compute the exposure of these 19X4 balance sheet items to the 19X5 exchange rate.
(b) Translate this balance sheet into USD—once assuming a rate of USD/NOK 0.20 at the end of 19X5, and once assuming a rate of USD/NOK 0.25. That is, compute the translated values of all items except equity adjustments, compute the total value of the assets,

and finally compute the equity adjustments as the item that balances the totals for assets and liabilities.

(c) Verify that the exposure, as computed in (a), multiplied by the difference in the two 19X5 rates (USD/NOK 0.05), produces the difference in the Net Worths computed in part (b); that is, verify that ΔNet Worth = Exposure $\times \Delta S$.

3. In the previous exercise, change the translation method to the Current/Non-Current Method.

4. In the previous exercise, change the translation method to the Monetary/Non-Monetary Method.

MIND-EXPANDING EXERCISE

1. In Exercises 2–4, we asked you to compute the exposure of the 19X4 balance sheet items to the 19X5 exchange rate—not the exposure of the 19X5 balance sheet items to the 19X5 exchange rate. Verify that the traditional definitions of exposure—net worth, net working capital, or the net monetary position—only work perfectly if we restrict attention to assets and liabilities that were in place one year before the translation.

20 MANAGING THE RISKS IN INTERNATIONAL TRADE

In Chapter 16, we argued that a firm could increase its value by reducing the variability of its cash flows and by hedging exchange rate risk. In Chapters 17 and 18, we described how firms could measure economic exposure to the exchange rate and how they could hedge this by using financial instruments. In Chapter 19, we explained how the exchange rate could affect the translated value of the financial statements of subsidiaries. In this chapter, our focus is on how one can hedge other risks that arise in international trade—risks that are not related to the exchange rate—and the related issue of how the exporter can obtain trade finance in an efficient manner.

Some of the risks that arise in international trade are the following:

- The exporter may not ship the goods (**default risk**).
- The goods shipped may not conform to the contract's specifications (**delivery risk**).
- The importer may not pay, or may pay too little or too late (**credit risk**).
- The importer's country may have run out of reserves by the time payment is due (**transfer risk**). In the case of transfer risk, the central bank or the trade ministry may not allow the importer to buy hard currency[1] and transfer these funds to the supplier of the goods.

The *financing* issue relates to the fact that the supplier usually has to buy the goods long before they are shipped. There is an interval between the time that the exporting trader (or producer) must

---

[1] The lack of hard currency is a problem because in the case of trade with countries that restrict the convertibility of their currency, the exporter typically requests payment in some hard (freely convertible) currency. In addition, a country with currency controls typically forbids payment in its own currency. The reason is that if payment in the importer's currency were allowed, the exporter would still have serious difficulties in converting this money into hard currency, and might therefore be willing to sell the blocked foreign currency balances to another nonresident at a discount. As this would lead to a parallel exchange market beyond the control of the monetary authorities, it is typically forbidden to pay in the importer's currency.

pay for labor and inputs and the time that the importer is obliged to pay for the goods, and this time interval must be bridged.

In this chapter, we describe various payment techniques that allow one to finance trade efficiently, reduce the buyer's incentive to default, and shift the risks (insofar as they are not already eliminated by the payment contract) toward parties that can better assess these risks or bear them at a lower cost. In Section 20.1, we discuss payment modes and contract structures not backed by bank guarantees. In Section 20.2, we consider payment structures involving bank guarantees. In Section 20.3, we look at other standard ways of coping with default risk—factoring and credit insurance. In Section 20.4, we examine linked import-export techniques for trade with developing countries and eastern European countries. In Section 20.5, we discuss countertrade and, in Section 20.6, we set forth our conclusions. The appendix contains additional institutional details of the payment mechanisms discussed in the text.

20.1   PAYMENT MODES WITHOUT BANK PARTICIPATION

Initially, we ignore the issue of how to finance international trade, and focus on how instruments are designed so as to limit default and transfer risks. We consider two extreme contract structures: (1) trading on an open account with payment upon or after delivery, and (2) payment before shipment. Then, we focus on the financing aspect of international trade, and present the case for the use of *trade bills*.

20.1.1   Cash Payment after Delivery

Within a country, a supplier usually sends goods on an **open account**, that is, on the basis of a simple invoice. The customer pays either upon delivery—in cash, by bank transfer, or by check—or at an agreed later date. The crucial characteristic of such a contract is that it allows the buyer to take possession of the goods and inspect them before payment is made.

The practice of shipping goods on open account is also wide-spread in international trade, especially when the importer and exporter have a long-standing, positive business relationship and when transfer risk is negligible. If the foreign customer is new, if his or her credit standing deteriorates, or if the customer's country is short of foreign exchange reserves, the exporter faces default risk and transfer risk. Specifically:

a.1. The customer might refuse to take possession of the goods.

a.2. The customer may be unable (or simply unwilling) to pay for the goods.

a.3. The importing firm may not be able to buy foreign currency because its central bank has a shortage of foreign exchange.

In Table 20.1, the pros and cons of various techniques are summarized: The entries in the column "Payment after delivery" corresponding to risks a.1 to a.3 are marked with a minus, indicating that from the *exporter's* point of view, payment after delivery is rated poorly with respect to these risks. (The second line for a.1, a.2, and a.3 is explained in Section 20.2, and the other columns of the exhibit are explained in Sections 20.2 and 20.3.)

It should be clear that apart from transfer risks, these problems are not fundamentally different from the problems encountered in domestic trade. However, they acquire a special importance in the case of international trade because the importer and the exporter operate under different legal and judicial systems and the costs of transportation are much greater. For instance, in case a.1, the exporter has not lost possession of the goods, but incurs ever-increasing warehousing costs. Thus, the exporter must choose to have the goods shipped back, or to auction them off abroad; and both solutions are costly.

TABLE 20.1   Risks to the Importer and Exporter under Alternative Payment Structures

	Payment after delivery	Payment before shipment	Documents against payment (D/P)	Documents against acceptance (D/A)	Irrevocable L/C	Irrevocable, confirmed L/C
a. Exporter's point of view						
a.1. Importer refuses goods	–	+	+	+	+	+
Importer refuses documents	n/a	n/a	0	0	+	+
a.2. Importer defaults	–	+	+	–	+	+
Issuing bank defaults	n/a	n/a	n/a	n/a	–	+
a.3. No license to import the goods	–	+	±	±	+	+
No license to remit payment	–	+	±	±	+	+
b. Importer's point of view						
b.1. Exporter does not send goods	+	–	+	+	+	+
b.2. Goods sent do not conform	+	–	+?	+?	+?	+?
b.3. No license to ship the goods	+	–	+	+	+	+

A (+) rating means that the exporter (in part **a** of the table) or the importer (in part **b**) is adequately covered against the risk described in the first column of the corresponding line. A (–) rating means that the risk is uncovered. The (±) rating for risk a.3 reflects the double consideration that, if the importer has no license, he or she may not pick up the documents (–), but once the documents are picked up, the exporter should not worry about the license (+). We added a question mark to the (+) ratings in line b.2 for all documentary techniques (see Section 20.2), because the documents never give an exhaustive description of the goods. A "0" indicates that the risk is small and "n/a" implies that this risk is not applicable.

20.1.2   Cash Payment before Shipping

If the exporter is in a very strong bargaining position relative to the importer, we might see the opposite situation: the supplier ships the goods only after receiving payment from the foreign customer. In contrast to the case where goods are shipped on open account, now the importer bears all of the risk because:

b.1. The supplier may not ship any goods at all.

b.2. The supplier may ship the goods too late, the goods may be substandard, or the quantities may not conform with the contract.

b.3. The supplier may not have obtained an export license, implying that the exporter is not allowed to ship the goods.

In Table 20.1, the corresponding entries in the column "Payment before shipment" are marked with a minus, indicating that from the *importer's* point of view this payment technique is poorly rated as far as risks b.1–b.3 are concerned. We also note that under "Payment before shipment," the exporter avoids the risks a.1–a.3. This is reflected by the plus marks: with respect to risks a.1–a.3, the exporter prefers payment before shipment. Likewise, the importer gives positive ratings to "Payment after delivery" as far as risks b.1–b.3 are concerned. Thus, the two payment modes discussed are the two extreme ways in which the risks can be shifted from the exporter to importer and *vice versa*. In the next section, Section 20.2, we shall see how compromise solutions can be found. Before that, we shall consider the financing issue, and explain why trade bills are often used to facilitate financing.

20.1.3 Trade Bills

The second practical issue in international trade is the financing of working capital. In international trade, there can be a rather long period of time between the moment the producer/exporter has to pay for inputs and the moment the importer receives payment from the final customer. The mode of payment determines which party has to provide which part of the financing. For example, when payment takes place before the goods are shipped, most or all of the financing of incremental working capital has to be provided by the buyer/importer, while the seller/exporter has to come up with most or all of the financing when payment is after delivery. Obviously, it is in the exporter and importer's joint interest to minimize the total financing cost. Unless one party can obtain financing at a cost below regular bank rates, the investment is usually financed through bank loans. Bank loans are easily obtained, and at attractive rates, if payment involves a *trade bill* (also known as a *draft* or a *bill of exchange*).

What Is a Trade Bill?

As the word suggests, in many ways a trade bill is like a summary of the invoice, it refers to an underlying commercial transaction, and it states the amount to be paid, the date on which the payment is due, and the place and manner of payment. The supplier (*the drawer*) *draws* the bill on the customer (*the drawee*). Like an invoice, a trade bill is a "You Owe Me" document. Unlike an invoice, a trade bill is specifically designed to be negotiable; it can be passed on to a financial institution in return for cash. However, a trade bill is not as reliable as an I.O.U. (I Owe You) document, such as a promissory note written and signed by the debtor. That is, the trade bill in itself contains no confirmation by the drawee that the debt actually exists. To give a trade bill the same credibility as a promissory note, the drawer typically sends it to the drawee with a request to *accept* it, that is, to add the drawee's signature and thus to acknowledge and confirm the existence of the underlying debt. A trade bill drawn on and accepted by the importer is called a **trade acceptance**; a bill drawn on and accepted by a bank is called a **banker's acceptance**.

In many ways, an acceptance payable *on sight* is similar to a check: it can be cashed in at any moment. Very often, however, the bill is payable some time after delivery on a date explicitly stated on the bill. In such a case, the exporter can still get immediate cash by borrowing against the discounted face value of the bill or acceptance, and giving the acceptance to the lender (who will collect the debt from the drawee). This is called discounting the bill. Discounting is done by commercial banks or by specialized institutions (such as a **discount houses**).

Advantages and Disadvantages of Trade Bills

Lending money by discounting a trade bill is comparatively safe from the bank's point of view—and therefore comparatively cheap for the exporter—for a number of reasons:

- Bills and acceptances are negotiable, that is, they can be sold and resold in the money market like any other form of commercial paper. For instance, a commercial bank that has discounted a bill can remobilize its funds by passing along the paper to another financial institution. This is known as rediscounting.[2]

---

[2] In many countries, the central bank or an affiliated official institution extends or contracts credit to the private sector by increasing or reducing its holdings of bills and acceptances bought from banks. This is especially true for the European countries conquered by Napoleon; Napoleon was a great promoter of trade bills. The *code civil*, which he introduced and which still forms the basis of most continental legal systems, contains detailed legislation of bills. Thus, trade bills are quite popular in these countries.

- In many countries, banks can rediscount *export* bills and acceptances at subsidized rates, by dealing with a government agency that promotes exports.
- Bills are self-financing. If a bank or discount house discounts a bill, the bank or discount house will receive the paper and collect the debt directly from the drawee. That is, no complicated provisions must be made to cover the risk of the exporter cashing in the accounts receivable and spending the money rather than paying back the bank loan.
- To increase the cost of defaulting on a bill, many countries officially publish lists of all protested bills, including the name of the person or firm that defaulted. Clearly, a company's name appearing on such a list would immediately ruin the company's credit standing throughout the country. Managers will, therefore, think twice about defaulting on a bill.
- The discounting bank (or any other third holder of the bill) has *recourse* on the preceding holder of the bill in case of default—unless discounting is done explicitly on a no-recourse basis, which is rare. That is, from the exporter's point of view, discounting is really like obtaining an advance against the bill; the drawer, as the first holder of the bill, backs[3] the bill and, therefore, still bears the default risk and the transfer risk. Conversely, from the point of view of the bank, there is at least one additional signature (the exporter's) backing the acceptance, which makes it safer than a promissory note.

For all of these reasons, banks favor bills—especially export bills—and are willing to discount them at attractive interest rates. However, from the point of view of credit risk and transfer risk, the instrument remains almost as risky as an invoice. For instance, the drawee might not even accept the bill, might default on it, or might not have a license to remit foreign exchange.

Although in a breach of contract (cases a.1–2, and b.1–2 on our checklist in Table 20.1), legal redress can be sought, it is impossible to underestimate the difficulties of legal procedures in a foreign environment.[4] The exporter's position is even more precarious if default is due to a decision made by the importing company's government. If the foreign government is also the *customer*, the exporter can ask a court to seize the foreign government's assets located abroad. Usually, however, a government has only a few marketable foreign assets, and there may be many claims on these assets. In contrast, if the problem is simply one of a shortage of hard currency, a foreign government that blocks the payment is not acting as a party to a commercial contract and, by international common law, a sovereign, acting as a sovereign rather than as a contract party, is beyond any court's power. In short, the exporter can achieve very little in court if his payment is blocked.

We conclude that legal redress in case of default by either the exporter or the importer is slow and costly; thus, compromise contracts are sought. How these compromise contracts work and how they can be combined with bank guarantees are discussed in the next section.

---

3 The term *backing* (or *endorsing*) actually stems from the fact that the holder, when (re)discounting a bill, signs it on the back (*dorsum*, in Latin).

4 First, the injured party might not speak the language, is unlikely to be familiar with the legal system and, in many countries, has the general disadvantage of being viewed as "the foreigner." Second, although the contract typically stipulates which court will deal with any disputes (possibly even an international arbitration court such as the Chamber of Commerce in Paris or Stockholm), the next problem is how to enforce the court's ruling outside of its jurisdiction. Third, litigation is often time-consuming and costly. Finally, even if a court's ruling is enforced, the judgment may come too late. For instance, the prospect of financial compensation in lieu of the goods, or belated delivery of the goods, are imperfect alternatives for an importer who needs the goods *now*. Likewise, the exporter may go bankrupt if swift payment is not made for the goods shipped.

20.2   DOCUMENTARY PAYMENT MODES WITH BANK PARTICIPATION

Given the inadequacy of legal redress, one often chooses a mode of payment in which the risks are shared (rather than borne entirely by either the exporter or the importer), and that reduces both the probability as well as the cost of default. As we shall see, such contracts usually involve at least one financial institution, which acts as a kind of trustee for the chief contractants. In addition, some of the risks of the transaction are often shifted to the intermediary. We shall argue that this is economically efficient if the intermediary is better placed to assess or bear these risks.

To get an idea of the generic solution, consider the following scenario. The exporter entrusts the goods to a middleperson who inspects them; likewise the importer sends payment to the same middleperson/trustee. If both the goods and the payment conform to the contract, the trustee forwards the goods and the money to the respective recipients; if not, the goods and/or the money is returned to the original owner. The role of banks is, as we shall see, similar to that of a trustee. However, no regular bank would view the running of a big warehouse as part of its corporate mission. Thus, the arrangement is that the bank receives a set of documents rather than the goods themselves. The exporter and the importer have to agree on what documents will be required. These documents may serve many purposes. For example, the documents must give reasonable evidence that the goods have been shipped and conform with the contract. The documents should also represent title to the goods, so that the holder of the documents can claim them from the customs warehouse or from the shipping company's premises. Finally, the importer and exporter may agree to also include documents that guarantee that the goods will be cleared through customs.[5] Thus, a very complete set of documents is (almost) as good as the goods. One task of the intermediary, then, is to check the documents. Any further responsibilities of the bank depend on the contract. The list of documents that are typically exchanged is given in Section 20A.1 of the appendix.

We now describe the simplest example of such a payment mechanism, "Documents against Payment."

20.2.1   Documents against Payment

Under **Documents against Payment (D/P)**, the bank checks whether all documents listed in the contract are present. If nothing is missing, the bank remits these documents to the importer against payment—that is, the importer receives the papers only if and when the agreed-upon price is paid. The importer, being in possession of the documents, can then claim the merchandise from the warehouse.[6]

In many instances, D/P is a reasonable solution to the problem of default risk. You are encouraged to verify this on the basis of our checklist of risks in Table 20.1. We explain our rating of the D/P, given in Table 20.1, as follows:

- Risk a.1 (importer refusing the goods) is resolved, but now another risk arises—that the importer may never bother to claim the documents, or may refuse to accept them. In Table 20.1, we give D/P a "plus" relative to the risk that the importer does not pick up the goods, but we immediately add a new line which rates D/P as "zero" with respect to the risk that the importer does not pick up the documents. The "zero" (instead of a minus) reflects the

---

[5] This is typical for "letter of credit" arrangements (to be discussed below), but customs documents are occasionally used in other techniques too.

[6] Of course, the *remitting* bank expects a small consideration, which is of the magnitude of 1/8 percent of the contract value with, depending on the country, a cap amounting to a few hundred USD.

fact that if the importer refuses to pick up the documents, the exporter is still in possession of the goods. Thus, the exporter's net risk is not quite as high as under "Payment after delivery."

- Assuming that the documents are accepted, the goods will be paid for, and there is obviously no default risk (hence the "plus" for risk a.2, that is, importer defaulting).
- Transfer risk is not covered by D/P: the importer's central bank can still refuse an exchange license.
- From the importer's point of view, the documents prove that the goods have been shipped, which explains the "plus" rating with respect to risks b.1 and b.3. That is, the importer has shipped the goods and has the license to ship them.
- While the documents can provide a lot of information about the quality of the goods, they can never guarantee 100 percent conformity—hence our qualified plus rating ("+?") with regard to risk b.2. If there is no inspection certificate, even the "+?" may be overly optimistic.

In Table 20.1, we see that the "D/P" column receives far more plus ratings than do either payment before or after shipment mechanisms, and that there are no unambiguously negative ratings left. Thus, this technique is an improvement over the two extreme solutions considered in Section 20.1. From the pure financing side, a drawback of D/P is that it precludes the use of bills (which, as we saw in Section 20.1.3, allows for cheap financing). For that reason, a variant called **Documents against Acceptance (D/A)** is also available. This is discussed below. We will also see in Section 20.2.3, how D/P or D/A, suitably combined with bank guarantees, address the problems of the importer refusing goods or documents, or defaulting on the payment.

20.2.2   Documents against Acceptance

Under a Documents against Acceptance (D/A) arrangement, the drawer obtains some degree of certainty about acceptance by stipulating the following:

1. As under a D/P, the documents will be sent to a *remitting* bank rather than directly to the customer. The set of documents now includes a bill drawn by the exporter on the importer.
2. If the set of documents is complete, the bank will remit the documents to the importer as soon as the latter has accepted (signed) the bill. The acceptance then goes back to the exporter, who may discount it.

The main difference between D/P and D/A is that under D/A, the importer has accepted the bill but has not paid for the goods. Thus, under D/P, the importer can default after taking possession of the goods. This is reflected by the "minus" for risk a.2 in Table 20.1. Still, exporters may be willing to bear this risk because of the swift and cheap financing provided by acceptances.[7]

20.2.3   Obtaining a Guarantee from the Importer's Bank: The Letter of Credit

There is an obvious and simple way to reduce (or at least shift) the default risk in a D/A or D/P arrangement. The exporter can insist that the importer have the payment or bill guaranteed by his or her bank, which also acts as remitting bank. Of course, the exporter will insist on evidence of such a commitment *before* sending any documents. The letter issued by the importer's bank (*issuing bank*),

---

[7] An Anglo-Saxon variant would require the importer to sign a **trust receipt**, too. This document states that the goods remain the exporter's property as long as the bill is not paid, and that the importer sells them in the role of the exporter's agent only.

ascertaining that such a guarantee exists, is called the **Letter of Credit (L/C).** If, as is usual, the bank's guarantee is conditional on receiving a set of conformable documents, the arrangement is called a **documentary credit.**[8] Note that, in contrast to D/P or D/A payments, the issuing bank is now responsible for the payment as soon as it accepts that the documents conform to the contract. Therefore, rather than simply checking whether all the documents are present (as in a D/P or D/A contract), the bank will now scrutinize the documents very carefully for conformity. There are a number of ways in which the issuing bank can guarantee the payments, and these are described in Section 20A.2 of the appendix.

The rules underlying L/Cs are standardized internationally, according to the Uniform Rules and Usances of the International Chamber of Commerce. An exporting firm can strengthen its legal position if the issuing bank actually *signs* a bill (as is the case with L/Cs that stipulate D/P); the bank's engagement then also falls under the local legislation on bills rather than just under the International Usances.

Let us analyze the L/C arrangement from an economic point of view and see what it accomplishes. The first two arguments suggest the L/C lowers the *cost* of default. The next two imply that the *probability* of default is also lowered by including the importer's bank as a party to the transaction.

- Default may be crippling to a small exporting firm, while to a bank with a large portfolio of L/Cs the same risk is largely diversifiable. The L/C shifts the default risk to a party that is better placed to bear it.
- The bank issuing the L/C is typically the importer's house bank. This implies that, in the case of default, the monetary and nonmonetary costs of legal proceedings are lower because the importer's house bank operates in the same legal environment as the defaulting party.
- Being specialized in evaluating credit risks, and having privileged information about the importer, the issuing bank is in a better position to assess the importer's default risk than is the exporter.
- The likelihood of default by the importer is reduced because from the importer's point of view, it is more tempting to neglect her obligations toward an exporter in a distant country than toward the house bank.

Although the above L/C arrangement reduces the probability and cost of default, the L/C arrangement is still far from perfect. Occasionally, letters of credit turn out to be counterfeited or issued by banks that from their name and logo, look like branches of major international banks but are, in fact, just minor local banks. Finally, even if the issuing bank is sound, transfer risk still exists. In managing all of these problems, the exporter's house bank can play a useful role, as described below.

20.2.4   Advised or Confirmed Letters of Credit

There are several way in which an exporter can further reduce the default risk, even after having obtained an L/C. First, the exporter can ask the issuing bank to send the L/C to a designated bank trusted by the exporter, called an *advisory* bank. The advisory bank receives the L/C from the issuing bank; its task is to check whether that bank exists and is in good financial standing, whether the signatures seem to be legitimate, and whether the bank manager who signed the L/C actually has the power to do so. The advisory bank then forwards the L/C to the exporter, but without adding any guar-

---

8 Like any credit arrangement, the L/C may be *revocable* under certain conditions, or even at the issuing bank's will; thus, from the exporter's point of view, it is best to insist on an *irrevocable* L/C.

antees. That is, the exporter still bears the risk that the issuing bank might go bankrupt, or might not be able to obtain a foreign exchange license.[9]

Second, the exporter can also ask the importer to have the L/C *confirmed* by a bank located in the exporter's country, or at least confirmed by a well-known bank trusted by the exporter. Under such an arrangement, the confirming bank will actually guarantee the payment; that is, it will pay the exporter if the original issuing bank defaults, or if the transfer is blocked. Thus, a **confirmed L/C** also offers insurance against default on behalf of the issuing bank, and against transfer risks. Moreover, the confirming bank is bound to pay out in cash (D/P), or to discount a Banker's Acceptance without recourse on the drawer (D/A), if its confirmation was requested by the bank that issued the original L/C.[10] In such a case, from the exporter's view, it is as if the L/C had been issued by the confirming bank.

Third, the exporter could have the bank-backed bill or the issuing bank's acceptance discounted *without recourse*. This again shifts the transfer risk and the risk of default to the issuing bank. This technique is called **forfeiting**, and is used by specialized forfeiter companies (mainly in the UK, Switzerland, and Austria).[11] For exports to eastern Europe, where bills are uncommon, forfeiters are sometimes willing to discount regular commercial invoices on a no-recourse basis.

Confirmation offers advantages above and beyond pure risk shifting. These benefits are similar to those obtained from an L/C, as described in Section 20.2.3. In the next section, we consider two other ways of shifting risks in the context of international trade—factoring and credit insurance.

20.3   OTHER STANDARD WAYS TO COPE WITH DEFAULT RISK

The letter of credit is not the only way in which to insure against credit risks. Exporters can also use factor companies, or they can buy insurance from specialized insurance companies. We describe these two alternative ways of shifting risk below.

20.3.1   Factoring

A factor company, whether domestic or international, can offer the following services:

• *Pure debt collection (with recourse to the seller)*

Under such an arrangement, the seller cedes any claims to the factor company and receives payment if and when the customer pays, after the deduction of a fee of 1/8 to 1/2 percent. The factor does not *guarantee* payment, though. For international debts, the "export factor" will cooperate with a correspondent "import factor" to collect the debts.

• *Credit insurance*

If the agreement also includes credit insurance, the factor guarantees the payment in case of default, sometimes up to 100 percent, for a fee of 0.5 to 2 percent. Note that credit insurance usually does not imply insurance against transfer risks.

---

[9] Very often, the advisory bank is also willing to give an advance to the exporter if the documents are remitted and found to conform with the terms of the agreement; and, if it does so, the advance is on a no-recourse basis. However, the advisory bank can always refuse to give such an advance if the issuing bank and/or its country seem too risky.

[10] The rule is that the issuing bank should ask for confirmation. In continental Europe, banks also confirm at the exporter's request, which irritates Anglo-Saxon issuing banks.

[11] Forfeiting can also be used without an L/C. Then, however, the exporter still bears the risk of nonacceptance and, likewise, is not sure that the bill will be guaranteed by the importer's bank. Forfeiters, as a rule, do not discount paper without a bank guarantee.

• *Accounts receivable financing*

The factor can also finance the invoices, for example, up to 85 percent for uninsured invoices, and up to 100 percent for insured invoices, after the deduction of interest (at the overdraft rate, the prime rate, or the rate on straight loans). Financing of insured invoices also eliminates exchange risks as of the date on which the exporter obtains the cash.

Factoring is similar to no-recourse discounting of bills, or forfeiting. A major difference, however, is that factoring cannot be used on a transaction-by-transaction basis. In order to avoid ending up with only those transactions that have a poor credit rating, a factor company usually insists on handling *all* sales, or at least all sales for a given market. Very often the factor also first evaluates the importer and may impose credit limits per importer and/or per country.

20.3.2   Credit Insurance

Virtually every country has a government agency that insures credit and/or transfer risks, like the Export-Import bank in the US, the Export Credit Guarantee Department in the UK, and Hermes in Germany. If the export contract is with a foreign government institution, credit risks and transfer risks are often not separate and one needs to insure both, while for contracts with private customers the exporter can usually insure either risk separately. Relative to private **credit insurance companies**, government agencies tend to insure large export contracts and trade with developing countries, and most of them seem to sell insurance at subsidized rates as part of the government's overall export promotion policy. Insurance can be bought on a transaction-by-transaction basis, or for all contracts for a given market. The coverage is typically less than 100 percent. One risk covered by government insurance agencies, and not by L/Cs, private insurers, or forfeiters, is the risk of the contract being canceled before the goods are finished and shipped.

20.4   EXPORT-BACKED FINANCING

Suppose that a country has a temporary shortage of hard currency. Then firms in this country may find it difficult to import goods. In such a case, banks (or a group of banks) may grant advances to the firm against the firm's future exports. This is called **export-backed financing**. To ensure that the loan is safe, the lending bank typically adds two clauses to the loan contract. The first clause stipulates that the exporting firm must sell its output forward, and the second clause is that the buyer of the output should pay the bank rather than the exporting firm.[12] When this payment is received, the bank withholds the amount required to service its loan, and pays out the balance to the exporting firm.

---

[12] The forward transaction may be a standard forward contract, with fixed quantity and price or, alternatively, a commitment by the customer to buy at the (as yet unknown) future market price for a fixed overall value (*topping up clause*: when prices are low the quantity is increased, and *vice versa*). The commitment by the buyer may also be a pure quantity commitment, that is, to buy a fixed quantity at the (as yet unknown) market price. With the first and second types of contracts, the exporting firm is sure of its hard-currency revenue if, at least, it can deliver enough of the goods. This delivery risk still means that the bank will never finance 100 percent of the (discounted) value of the contract. When there is only a quantity commitment without fixed price, there is greater uncertainty about the revenue, so the bank will finance only 60 or 80 percent of the estimated future value of the exported output.

Example   20.1[13]

In October 1990, Belgium's *Generale Bank* extended a loan to *Mexicana de Cananea*, a copper-mining company. As part of the contract, Cananea sold copper forward to a Belgian commodity trader, Sogem. Sogem's payments for its copper purchases were to be made not to Cananea but rather to the Generale Bank. The balance (after withholding whatever was needed to service the loan) was then paid by the Generale Bank to Cananea. From the point of view of Cananea and Generale Bank, the forward contract with Sogem eliminated the price risk—assuming, of course, that Cananea could deliver the copper—while the arrangement also ensured that the proceeds of the forward sale would first go to the Generale Bank. Thus, from the Generale Bank's point of view, the only risk was the risk of nondelivery of the copper, which was considered to be a minor risk as Cananea is an open stripmine.

Let us consider another example.

Example   20.2

In the spring of 1994, two companies in Ghana are facing problems in obtaining hard currency credit.[14] Ghana Petroleum needs USD 30m to pay for its upcoming imports from British Oil, and Ghana Cocoa urgently needs hard currency: USD 20m to build a new processing plant, and USD 10m to buy fertilizers and pesticides for the next planting season. Ghana's main source of export revenue is cocoa, but shipments will not start until October and will last only until January. In view of Ghana's balance of payment problems, unsecured loans from foreign banks would carry a hefty spread above LIBOR.

Ghana Cocoa turns to one of its standard customers, the British cocoa importer, BCI, which regularly buys 25 percent of Ghana Cocoa's output. Ghana Cocoa's next crop is estimated at 255,000 tons, or (at an expected price of USD/ton 1,600) about USD 408m. With the help of a syndicate led by its London bank, BCI assesses the risks and uncertainties: output variability, price volatility, compatibility with the export quota under the International Cocoa Agreement, availability of export licenses, and transportation contracts. BCI finally agrees to buy 64,000 tons of cocoa, about one-fourth of the expected crop, in four equal lots from October to January, at 2 percent below the spot price prevailing in each month. The syndicate agrees to finance 60 percent of BCI's estimated purchases, that is, $0.6 \times [\text{USD } 408\text{m}/4] \times 0.98 = \text{USD } 60\text{m}$. The proceeds of this loan are distributed as follows:

- USD 20m is made available directly to Ghana Cocoa to finance purchases of equipment from various local and western suppliers.
- USD 10m is paid to Ghana Cocoa's Irish supplier of fertilizers. Implicitly, this replaces another loan to Ghana Cocoa, the proceeds of which are immediately used to pay for the fertilizer imports.

---

[13] *De Standaard*, October 25, 1990, p 17.

[14] This draws on a similar example in Corluy (1990).

- USD 30m is paid to British Oil as payment for Ghana Petroleum's imports, while Ghana Petroleum pays the Ghanaian Pound equivalent to Ghana Cocoa. These transactions implicitly replace (1) a loan of USD 30m to Ghana Cocoa, (2) an immediate spot sale of these USD 30m from Ghana Cocoa to Ghana Petroleum, and (3) a payment for the same amount by Ghana Petroleum to British Oil.

All in all, Ghana Cocoa has implicitly borrowed USD 60m, secured by its expected sales to BCI. As we saw, part of this USD 60m was implicitly re-lent to Ghana Petroleum; but Ghana Cocoa, being the earner of hard currency, has been made responsible for the service payments of this loan. When shipments start, BCI pays the going market price of cocoa minus 2 percent to the banking syndicate.

Such a combination of export, import, and (secured) financing transactions resembles countertrade-type transactions which we describe and analyze in the next section.

20.5   COUNTERTRADE

Countertrade, in a generic sense, refers to barter-like techniques for international trade. Countertrade was the basis of intra-Comecon trade, and was often used, albeit in diluted forms, in East-West trade. Developing countries with limited reserves of hard currency frequently make use of countertrade, too.

We view countertrade as a form of financial engineering, that is, as a combination of selling, buying, and—since there invariably is a delay between delivery and receipt of payment— cleverly secured financing. We shall argue that most of the alleged advantages of countertrade are simply the advantages of the components of such a package, that is, the advantages of trading as such, of using intermediaries, of obtaining finance, and of risk-shifting through forward trade or subcontracting deals. Thus, to explain why countertrade exists, we need to explain the additional advantage that can be obtained when all of these standard contracts are combined into a single contract between only two parties.

In Section 20.5.1, we briefly summarize the techniques of countertrade. In Section 20.5.2, we characterize countertrade as a package of standard transactions (imports, forward exports, and secured financing, plus various standard risk-shifting devices). In Section 20.5.3, we describe the advantages of countertrade.

20.5.1   Countertrade Techniques
Countertrade can be conducted in a variety of ways, as described below.

Barter Trade
(Pure) **barter trade** consists of an exchange of goods simultaneously or within a short interval. For example, a Bulgarian firm ships 300,000 bottles of its best Cabernet Sauvignon 1985 wine to Canada, and the Canadian firm sends a combine harvester in return.

Pure barter is rarely as simple as it looks at first sight. First, it is unlikely that the Canadian firm would consume all 300,000 bottles of Cabernet Sauvignon (however excellent the wine may be), nor will the Canadian firm have a network for distributing wine. Thus, in actual practice, the wine would be delivered to a trader, who sells it and pays the Canadian firm. There is also the issue of trust and security. Bulgaria, which in our example delivers the goods first, needs a guarantee that the Canadian firm will actually ship the harvester. This guarantee can be achieved by requiring that the Canadian company post a *performance bond* (that is, deposits cash or securities into an escrow account with an intermediary), which will be released to the Canadian firm only after it has fulfilled its part of the contract. The Canadian company gives proof of its performance by sending a stated set of documents to the bank, which will forward them to Bulgaria if they seem to conform with the terms and conditions of the contract.

Compensation Trade

Loosely speaking, **compensation trade** is the type of barter where one of the flows is partly in goods and partly in cash (hard currency). For example, Bulgaria may send 200,000 bottles of wine and CAD 100,000, in return for a harvesting machine. Again, the wine is likely to be sold through a trader, and the Canadian firm may have to post a bond. An L/C may be used to insure the cash component of Bulgaria's payment.

Counterpurchase Trade

Counterpurchase trade is even closer to standard trade than is compensation trade. It consists of an *autonomous* contract—for example, the purchase of one combine harvester against cash—and a second contract which is *conditional* on the first—for example, the purchase of CAD 300,000 worth of Cabernet Sauvignon. That is, the Canadian firm guarantees that it will counterpurchase a sufficient amount of Bulgarian goods within a given time span. The guarantee of the Canadian firm's performance may occur through the utilization of a performance bond or it may be otherwise enforced through penalty provisions.

Buy-Back

Under a **buy-back** deal, the Canadian firm builds a turnkey plant (and often also provides training and management assistance) in, say, Bulgaria and is paid in stated amounts of the plant's output at stated intervals. One limitation of this arrangement is that problems may arise in ensuring the quality and availability of the output. Another drawback is the inflexibility of the deliveries. If the Canadian firm were running the plant itself, it could decide to reduce or even stop production if demand drops, but this is not an option under a buy-back deal (unless the deal is renegotiated).

Switch Trade

Switch trade is similar to a negotiable counterpurchase contract. For instance, the Canadian exporter delivers a harvester and obtains the right to buy CAD 300,000 worth of Bulgarian goods within a stated period. Suppose that it finds CAD 200,000 worth of goods that can be used in-house or sold at attractive terms to a trader, but has difficulty using the remaining balance, CAD 100,000, within the stated period. Under switch trade, this balance can be sold by the firm to another firm or to another trader—usually at a discount. For instance, the Canadian firm may get CAD 80,000 for the remaining balance of, nominally, CAD 100,000.

After this brief description of countertrade techniques, we are now ready to discuss the fundamental nature of countertrade.[15]

20.5.2   The Fundamental Nature of Countertrade

In a sense, all countertrade techniques can be replicated by standard trade and financing contracts. In order to clarify the argument, we shall look at a number of examples, with a developing country (country *A*) importing goods from a firm located in a developed country (country *B*) in exchange for the exports of country *A* which will be delivered at a later date. (In actual practice, the timing may occa-

---

[15] The following sections draw on Sercu (1990) and Neale and Sercu (1991).

sionally be reversed, but that will not affect the analysis.) We claim that countertrade deals are simply packages of standard deals; that is, countertrade can be replicated from standard contracts, as described below.

One can replicate a countertrade transaction with a package of standard contracts. Consider a *pure barter deal*. To replicate a pure barter contract, one would need an import contract whereby *A* buys from *B*, an import-financing contract (loan to *A*), and a forward export contract signed by *A*, where the proceeds from the forward sale by *A* are used to service the loan that financed the imports from *B*. That is, pure barter is close to export-backed financing (discussed in Section 20.4).

Similarly, a *buy-back deal* can be replicated by an import contract under which *A* buys plant and equipment from one firm in country *B*, a loan to finance the import contract, and a long-term subcontracting scheme whereby the buyer of the equipment sells forward part of the plant's output to a second firm in country *B*. The proceeds from this subcontracting deal are used to service the import loan. In this form of countertrade, the single forward deal (implicit in pure barter) is replaced by a long-term subcontracting arrangement, which is basically just a series of forward contracts.

A *compensation* or *counterpurchase agreement* is similar to a forward export contract with a delivery option to *B* (who can pick and choose from a list of available goods), plus a limited timing option, that is, an option to decide *when* to exercise its right to purchase. These options are also available in commodity futures or bond futures contracts.[16]

20.5.3   Arguments in Favor of Countertrade: A Critical Evaluation

We just argued that, essentially, all countertrade techniques are simply combinations of standard contracts (imports, import financing, and forward-type exports) with risk-shifting arrangements. In other words, countertrade is not really a way of trading without cash, but a deal where several transactions are combined into a single package. Thus, to explain the benefits of countertrade, we need to determine what the additional gain is from combining these transactions into a single package. Some of these advantages are described below.

Asymmetric Information and Transactions Costs

With asymmetric and proprietary information and bid-offer spreads for transactions, the drafting, monitoring, and implementation of one contract is probably cheaper and easier than that of three separate but interlinked contracts—the turnkey project, the loan agreement, and the long-term sales contract. Buy-back contracts are typically ones where information asymmetries are likely to be important. When a turnkey engineering contract is signed, asymmetric information about the technology and the value of the product may provide a good reason to link the turnkey project to a subcontracting deal and the financing arrangement. For instance, when the firm that provides plant and technology also has to buy forward a substantial part of the output and has to buy forward a substantial part of the output and has to bear the default risk on the loan, this firm has no incentive to overstate the value of the technology or the likely size of the market. Likewise, the firm will have a positive incentive to build a high-quality plant.

Camouflaging (Part of) the Deal

A single packaged contract allows one to hide the true revenues and costs of the component transactions. For example, discounted prices are not always made explicit, or they can be hidden by offsetting

---

[16] In the case of a commodity futures or bond futures contract, however, the seller of the contract (not the buyer) has the delivery option.

misrepresentations. If made explicit, discounts may set a precedent invoked by other customers, or violate anti-dumping laws, or start a price war. For example, OPEC countries frequently use barter in order to hide price discounts (relative to the posted cartel price). On occasion, OPEC countries also treat countertrade exports as not being part of normal trade and, therefore, exclude the amount of oil exported from their export quota.[17] In this instance, not only the price but even the very existence of trade is camouflaged. Alternatively, the purpose of disguising the price may simply be to avoid recognition of losses on property or inventory. We give an example of pure domestic barter (from *The Economist*, April 17, 1993).

Example   20.3

A TV station has excess advertising time but is unwilling to openly lower its rates. A customer wants to sell a building, with book value USD 6m, but is unwilling to openly accept the true market value of USD 4m. The TV station sells air time at a 50 percent discount to a barter merchant. The merchant buys the building for, nominally, USD 6m, in exchange for air time worth, when valued at the normal retail rate, USD 6m. Taken together, the TV station and the customer are willing to pay USD 1m to the merchant for disguising the true prices of the building and the air time.[18]

The Economist concludes that "In a typical barter deal, both the sellers of the air time [or hotel rooms, or airline seats] and the end buyer are normally keen to avoid publicity."

In other cases, countertrade allows countries to export products that are not competitive or that are of poor quality, without being required to openly accept a low price. Explicitly stating the true price may be politically unpopular or psychologically undesirable, and it may also create problems with anti-dumping regulations.

There are many other arguments given in favor of countertrade; however, most of these can be dismissed, as explained below.

• *Countertrade is the only way firms from developing countries can access western markets.*

This is not a very convincing argument. Since most western parties in a countertrade deal sell their barter goods through a trader, a developing country could do the same.

• *Countertrade is a way to overcome protectionist measures such as quotas and tariffs.*

It is argued that countertrade allows one to conceal the actual origin of the goods or avoid part of the import duties by undervaluing the goods. However, if quotas or tariffs apply when, say, Russia sells its vodka directly to a trader, the same quota or tariffs will still apply if PepsiCo imports the vodka. It is true that a multinational, through re-exporting, could change the origin of the goods, but the re-exporting country must add enough value (say, 50 percent) before the new origin is accepted for customs purposes. Even then, the basic issue is still why the countertrading country could not deal directly with a producer in the intermediary country to change the origin of its goods.

---

[17] Dossier SNE, *Compensation Tiers Monde 1*, June 1985, p. 26.

[18] The merchant sells the building at 4m, and has to pay only 3m to the TV station for the air time.

- *Countertrade changes the image of the goods, since they are marketed by a western firm.*

The same effect could be obtained by simply enlisting the help of any western intermediary, like a trader, an import agent, or a marketing firm; thus, it is not clear why one needs to use countertrade to achieve this.

- *Countertrade allows one firm to shift (part of) the marketing cost to the other firm without having to pay the normal price for these marketing services.*[19]

If the cost of marketing the bartered goods is shifted (or partially shifted), this is merely an indirect way of obtaining a higher price for the goods. We see no obvious reason why the same relative price effect could not have been obtained under normal negotiations.

- *Countertrade is simple since an export transaction is matched with an import transaction.*

Quite the contrary is true: linking every import transaction to an export transaction leads to lengthy negotiations and complicated deals. It is difficult to match the supply and demand sides. Also, because several contracts are combined into one, the list of contingencies becomes very long. Francis (1985) has drawn up a rather depressing three-page list of things that could go wrong and that have to be taken into consideration when writing a countertrade contract.[20] Countertrade transactions are also complicated in terms of valuation for tax purposes, and compatibility with GATT rules and antitrust laws.

- *Countertrade is a good way to shift risks to the importing firm.*

If the objective is to shift risks to the importing firm, this can be achieved with independent forward or subcontracting contracts and without having to go through the complications of countertrade.

- *Countertrade provides automatic balance-of-payments equilibrium.*

First, there is nothing wrong with a temporary overall deficit. International capital markets, like national capital markets, serve to smooth variations in consumption and to separate investment decisions from consumption decisions. Secondly, even if equilibrium in the trade balance is desired, this should be understood in a multilateral way. There is nothing wrong with Belgium importing oil from Saudi-Arabia, the US importing endives and chocolate from Belgium, and Saudi Arabia importing cars and wheat from the US. Although each bilateral balance would show a disequilibrium, the overall trade account may be balanced. Finally, economizing on hard currency that is scarce can be achieved in a market-oriented way without using countertrade. For example, one could allow the exporters to auction off their hard currency among candidate importers.

20.6   CONCLUSION

In this chapter, we have considered various payment mechanisms that may be used to reduce the default risk and transfer risk that is present in international trade. We first evaluated two extreme models of payment—cash payment before goods are shipped and payment after the goods are

---

[19] Such a belief is also implicit in texts by western authors when they mention trade creation as one advantage. See, for example, Francis (1985), p.11. Dossier SNE, *Compensation Tiers Monde 3*, October 85, p. 32.

[20] Francis (1985), pp. 56–58.

delivered. We saw that the first method of payment was extremely unfavorable from the importer's point of view and the second one from the exporter's point of view. We then discussed how banks can perform an important role by being intermediaries in trade transactions. One way the exporter can guarantee payment for goods shipped is to obtain a Letter of Credit from the importer's bank. We also discussed that an exporter could use a factor company to reduce default risk. Alternatively, an exporter can buy insurance against default risk and transfer risk. This insurance is usually sold by government agencies that have been set up to promote exports, often at subsidized rates. Finally, we explained countertrade and the circumstances under which this would be preferred to separate import and export contracts.

QUIZ QUESTIONS

True-False Questions

1. Trade on open account, with payment after or on delivery, is the standard way of doing business internationally among unrelated parties without an established business relationship because this method of payment has proven its value in domestic trade.
2. Under payment on or after delivery, most of the risks are borne by the exporter.
3. Under payment before shipment, the exporter bears only the risk of contract cancellation prior to shipment.
4. Suppose that, under payment upon delivery, the importer does not accept the goods. Then the exporter has no problem whatsoever, as he still is in possession of the goods.
5. In international trade, there often is a relatively large time gap between production outlays and payment by the final customer. However, it does not generally matter who provides this working capital. In addition, the issue of how to finance working capital is entirely separable from the issue of how the payment is structured.
6. Discounting a bill is similar to selling the bill for a price equal to the discounted value of the nominal (future) value.
7. Discounting a bill simply means giving an advance on the bill equal to the discounted value of the nominal (future) value. In addition, the discounter receives the bill as security for the payment.
8. Discounting a bill is like factoring with financing but without credit insurance, except that discounting of bills can be done transaction by transaction. Likewise, discounting without recourse is like factoring with financing and credit insurance.
9. Forfeiting, or discounting without recourse, is like factoring with financing and credit insurance, except that discounting of bills can be done transaction by transaction.
10. Under international law, a foreign government can never be judged by a court.
11. Under ordinary D/A and D/P (without L/C) the intervening bank still guarantees the payment, and will therefore reject any set of documents that is not perfectly conformable with the contract.
12. A trust receipt is often used to reduce the seller's risks in a D/P arrangement.
13. A Letter of Credit is a statement by a bank that promises to extend a loan to the exporter if certain conditions are met.
14. An irrevocable L/C offers the same security as an acceptance signed by the importer and insured with a government agency against credit risks.
15. An irrevocable, confirmed L/C offers the same security as an acceptance signed by the importer and insured with a government agency against political and credit risks.
16. Under an L/C, the bank agrees to inspect the goods, and to pay the exporter or accept the bill if the goods are fully conformable with the contract.

EXERCISES

1. What are the risks borne by the exporter and exporter, respectively, under payment before shipment and payment on delivery, respectively?
2. What characteristics of trade bills make these instruments well-suited to obtain low-cost financing?
3. Why is legal redress in international trade disputes more difficult than in domestic trade?

4. The writing and confirming of L/Cs must achieve more than just risk shifting without over-all gains, otherwise these techniques would not exist. What are the advantages?

5. Some of the documents used in D/A, D/P, and documentary credits represent title to the goods. What purpose do the other documents serve?

6. Fill in the correct word from the following list: *accept, the drawer, trade bill, promissory note, the drawee, You Owe Me, I Owe You, banker's acceptance, trade acceptance.*

   As the word suggests, in many ways a _____ is like a summary of the invoice. The supplier (_____) *draws* the bill on the customer (_____). That is, like an invoice, a trade bill is a _____ document. In itself, a trade bill is not as trustworthy as an _____ document, such as a _____, which is written and signed by the debtor. To give a trade bill the same credibility as a _____, the drawer typically sends it to the drawee with a request to _____ it, that is, to add the drawee's signature and thus to acknowledge and confirm the existence of the underlying debt. A trade bill drawn on and accepted by the importer is called a _____; a bill drawn on and accepted by a bank is called a _____.

7. Complete the following table, by adding "+," "–," or "0" in each cell. A "+" rating means that the exporter (in part **a** of the table), or the importer (in part **b**) is adequately covered against the risk described on the left-hand side of the corresponding line. A "–" rating reflects that the risk is uncovered. A "0" rating reflects a compromise.

	Payment after delivery	Payment before shipment	Documents against payment (D/P)	Documents against acceptance (D/A)	Irrevocable L/C	Irrevocable, confirmed L/C
a. Exporter's point of view						
1. Importer refuses goods Importer refuses documents						
2. Importer defaults Issuing bank defaults						
3. No license to import the goods No license to remit payment						
b. Importer's point of view						
1. Exporter does not send the goods						
2. Goods sent do not conform						
3. No license to ship the goods						

MIND-EXPANDING EXERCISE

1. The Johannesburg branch of Shanghai Chartered Bank (SCB) is considering a three-month loan to Botswana Coffee Plantations (BCP), to be backed by BCP's export receipts.[21] The expected harvest is about 100 tons, and the expected world coffee price is about 7,000 crowns/ton.

   (a) SCB must decide how much it can lend if it can use BCP's entire export revenue as security. What precautions could SCB take to make sure that the export revenue is actually used to pay back the loan?

   (b) One of SCB's analysts is asked to estimate the worst-case export revenue. Unfortunately, both BCP and the coffee market have changed quite a lot since the company's founding 20 years ago, so that the analyst cannot simply use the history of BCP's export revenue to assess the risk.

   The analyst assumes that the actual output ($\tilde{O}$) and the price ($\tilde{P}$) are lognormally distributed, because this distribution is more consistent with the non-negativity of outputs and prices than a normal distribution and because then the revenue, ($\tilde{O} \times \tilde{P}$), is also conveniently lognormal. On the basis of commodity option prices and output data from similar plantations, the analyst then estimates the parameters of output and prices separately. The plan is to compute the confidence intervals for the normally distributed variable $\ln(\tilde{O} \times \tilde{P}) = \ln(\tilde{O}) + \ln(\tilde{P})$, which has mean and variance equal to $[\mu_o + \mu_p]$ and $[\sigma_{\tilde{o}}^2 + 2 \text{cov}_{o,p} + \sigma_{\tilde{o}}^2]$, respectively. From the lower bound on $\ln(\tilde{O} \times \tilde{P})$ the analyst can then infer the lower bound on ($\tilde{O} \times \tilde{P}$).

   From traded commodity option prices, SCB's analyst infers that the standard deviation of the log price is 10 percent over three months (20 percent *p.a.*). From past data on planted acreage and output for similar plantations, the standard deviation of BCP's output is estimated to be 15 percent over three months. Using the output and price expectations given above, what are μ_o and μ_p—the expected values of $\ln(\tilde{O})$ and $\ln(\tilde{P})$, rather than $\tilde{O}$ and the price $\tilde{P}$?

   (c) The analyst argues that, since Botswana has only a small share in the coffee market, the variance of the export revenue can be computed as if the covariance between local output and the world price is zero. Is this a conservative assumption or not? (Hint: what would be the sign of the covariance between the world output of coffee and the world price, and between BCP's output and the world price?)

   (d) How would SCB compute a 90 percent confidence interval for BCP's entire export revenue?

   (e) It turns out that BCP needs far less than 500,000 crowns. BCP signs a contract with HEC Jouy-en-Josas, a well-known and solid French coffee trader, to deliver 40 tons at the forward price of 6,900 crowns/ton. When computing the maximum amount it can lend on the strength of this forward contract, should SCB take a similar safety margin relative to the expected revenue from this transaction as the one computed in part (e)?

   (f) Suppose instead that HEC agrees to buy 50 tons at the (as yet unknown) future spot price for coffee. How should the analyst assess the risk in this case?

---

[21] Unlike Freedonia and Prisionia, Botswana actually exists. It is a peaceful, democratic, and relatively prosperous country north of the Republic of South Africa.

SOME INSTITUTIONAL DETAILS OF DOCUMENTARY CREDITS

20A.1 List of Documents that the Chief Contractants May Exchange

Documents Needed for the Customs Administration(s):

- A regular invoice (an original and duplicates).
- A customs invoice—used to clear the goods through customs (for example, as a basis for customs duties and for statistical purposes).
- A consular invoice—an invoice certifying that there is an import license for the transaction at hand.
- A certificate of origin delivered by the exporter's local chamber of commerce—this is necessary if the import duty depends on the country of origin or if there are country-by-country import quotas.
- Phytosanitary certificates for verification of compliance with local agricultural regulations.

Documents Needed by the Importer:

- The commercial invoice.
- An inspection certificate, that is, a report on the state and properties of the goods delivered for shipment. (Such a certificate is delivered by a specialized firm, for example, Switzerland's *Société Générale de Surveillance*, a company that is so well-regarded that it has actually been put in charge of some countries' customs administrations.)
- An insurance policy for each individual transaction or, if the exporter's insurance policy covers many transactions, an insurance certificate. (Proof of insurance is essential for a *cost, insurance, freight* [CIF] contract.)
- A mate's receipt which confirms that the goods have been loaded on board a vessel (vital for a CIF or *free-on-board* (FOB) contract, and useful whenever evidence of shipping is needed).
- A shipping list, describing the parcels, crates, or containers.
- A document that represents title to the goods—for transport by sea, the *bill of loading* or *bill of lading* (B/L), which simultaneously serves as the contract between the exporter and the shipping company.[22]
- A separate transportation contract in the case of transportation by air, rail, or road.

20A.2 How the Issuing Bank Can Guarantee Payment by the Exporter

- Under a bank-guaranteed D/P arrangement, the issuing bank's L/C states that the latter will pay cash as soon as the documents arrive and are found to conform with the contract. This technique is standard on the European continent, and it is equivalent to cash payment after inspection of the documents.

---

[22] The first mate, who receives the goods, adds his or her remarks to the B/L if there is visible damage to the packaging or if the number or nature of containers does not comply with the description given in the contract. Any such remarks make the B/L "dirty" and will prompt the bank to return the documents to the exporter. If everything seems to be perfect, the first mate gives a "clean" bill.

- Under the D/A variant, the L/C states that if the documents conform with the terms and conditions stated in the contract, then the bank guarantees that the buyer will accept and pay on the bill's expiration date. This may involve the issuing bank undertaking to endorse a bill drawn on the importer; that is, the bank signs the back of the bill, and as such becomes co-responsible for the payment. Alternatively, the bank may undertake to accept a bill drawn on itself (that is, on the bank, rather than on the importer), in which case the bank is, again, fully responsible for the payment.

The numbered arrows in Figure 20A.1 indicate the sequence of events for a bank-guaranteed exchange. The exporter and importer first negotiate and agree on what documents are required (as shown by arrow 0). The importer then asks his or her bank to open a documentary credit stating which documents are required and what the mode of payment will be (arrow 1). The importer pays the required commission and has the L/C sent to the exporter (arrow 2), either directly or through one or more other banks. The exporter ships the goods (arrow 3a), and forwards the required documents through his bank to the importer's bank (arrow 3b). Upon arrival of the documents, the issuing bank checks them for conformity with the L/C, and then pays, or guarantees the bill drawn on the importer, or accepts and mails back a bill drawn on itself (arrow 4a). The documents themselves are sent to the importer (arrow 4b), who uses them to claim the goods from the customs warehouse (arrow 5).

FIGURE 20A.1   Flow of Goods and Documents under an L/C Arrangement

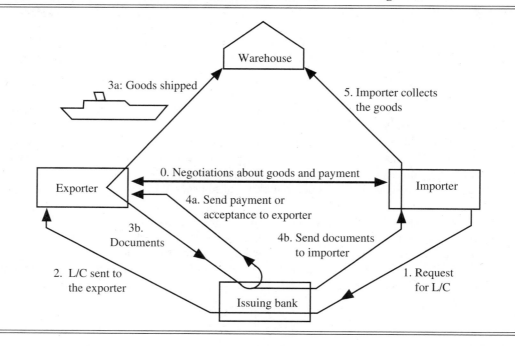

PART

In Part III of the text, we describe how firms can hedge against various risks that arise in the context of international trade and foreign investment. Part IV of the text is devoted to evaluating the decision to invest internationally.

When evaluating domestic investments, one typically uses a two-step approach. In the first stage, one evaluates the Net Present Value (NPV) of the cash flows of the firm from operations. In the second stage, one adjusts these cash flows for financing aspects. The present value computations are typically based on the standard discounted cash-flow model where the discount rate is provided by the Capital Asset Pricing Model (CAPM). The issue then is to what extent can the complexities of international investment analysis be handled within the traditional two-step adjusted NPV framework.

We start out, in Chapter 21, by describing how one needs to adjust the approach that is used for domestic projects when evaluating foreign projects. Essentially, one needs to add an intermediate stage, a stage where one accounts for the intricacies of intracompany financing. This chapter also explains how to adjust the value of the project for transfer and political risks. In Chapter 22, we analyze how to obtain the appropriate discount rate to value a stream of cash flows that are denominated in a foreign currency. This chapter includes a detailed discussion of how to extend the single-country CAPM to account for capital market segmentation and exchange risk when valuing cash flows denominated in a foreign currency. In order to do a proper NPV analysis, one also has to deal with taxes. With international investment projects, at least two tax authorities are involved. Chapter 23 provides an introduction to generic tax systems and describes how these systems deal with issues related to double taxation.

In the projects discussed in Chapter 21, it is assumed that the project is implemented as a branch of the investing firm, or at least in a wholly owned subsidiary. Yet many projects involve two or more parent companies who join forces to undertake a particular venture. The objective, in Chapter 24, is to develop a systematic approach for the valuation, profit sharing, and tax planning of such international join-venture projects.

In some circumstances, the cash flows from an investment project may depend mainly on future spot rates. In such a case, instead of using the adjusted NPV approach described in Chapter 21, one can use an option-like model to assess the project's present value. This approach, based on the option pricing theory described in Chapters 7 and 8, is simpler to implement than the NPV approach, and has the added advantage that it explicitly accounts for the flexibility the firm has in making decisions such as when to enter or exit a foreign market. This method of valuing investment projects is described in Chapter 25.

4

INTERNATIONAL INVESTMENT DECISIONS

INTERNATIONAL CAPITAL BUDGETING

In this and the next chapter, we describe the traditional approach to international **capital budgeting** or **investment analysis**, where one computes the **net present value (NPV)**, that is, the difference between the present value of the future cash flows and the initial outlay. The basic rule is to accept a project if the NPV is positive.

The structure of this chapter is as follows. In Section 21.1, we review the basics of standard (domestic) investment analysis. To understand some of the issues that arise when applying the NPV criterion internationally, we discuss, in Section 21.2, the various modes of foreign operations (exports, foreign marketing, foreign production, or cooperative schemes like licensing), as well as the legal forms that a company can choose from for its foreign operations (dependent agents, a branch, or an incorporated company). In Sections 21.3 through 21.7, we address the issues that arise when capital budgeting is applied to international investment projects. We conclude, in Section 21.8, with a checklist of issues one needs to keep in mind when preparing an investment analysis report. In the appendix, we briefly describe how one can estimate some of the cash flows.

21.1 DOMESTIC CAPITAL BUDGETING: A QUICK REVIEW

In this section, we review the concepts of NPV, Adjusted NPV, and Weighted Average Cost of Capital (WACC). We argue that it is easier and typically more accurate to use the NPV rule as opposed to the WACC criterion for making capital budgeting decisions.

21.1.1   Net Present Value (NPV)

The traditional approach to capital budgeting is to compute the net present value as the difference between the present value of the *expected* future cash flows (discounted at a constant cost of capital) and the initial outlay. The basic rule is to accept a project if its benefits exceed its cost, that is, if the NPV is positive. And if there are competing, mutually exclusive projects, one selects the alternative with the highest (positive) NPV. We shall briefly elaborate on the notions of cash flows and discounting, and then provide an example.

Discounted Cash Flows

As you should know, profits and cash flows differ with respect to timing. First, the initial outlay associated with an investment is generally up front, whereas the profit and loss (P&L) statements report these outlays over several years, in the form of annual depreciation charges. Second, the projected P&L statements assign revenues and production expenditures to the reporting period during which the final product was sold. However, the actual production expenditures generally occur long before the moment when a good is sold, and the customer often pays months or occasionally years after the moment of sale. Since we are interested in cash flows, not accounting profits, we should add back the depreciation charges to the projected profits, and recognize the investment outlays when they actually occur. Likewise, one has to correct for the leads in production outlays and lags in sales income (*investments in working capital*, in short) in order to correctly compute the present value of the cash flows.

We need to discount the expected cash flows to account for the fact that the cash flows are spread out over time. If the risk of these cash flows is fairly stable over time, we can take uncertainty into account by discounting the expected cash flows at a risk-adjusted **cost of capital**, that is, the risk-free rate plus a (usually positive) risk premium. According to the Capital Asset Pricing Model (CAPM), the relevant risk to be taken into account is not the total uncertainty of the investment in itself, but the project's contribution to the total risk of the firm's cash flows, and ultimately to the risk of the shareholders' wealth. The CAPM is discussed in Chapter 22. In this chapter, we take the cost of capital as given. In Chapter 25, we will discuss an alternative approach, where option pricing theory is used to make investment decisions.

Base Case NPV Computations: An Illustration

The following example illustrates the basic NPV procedure without any international ramifications. In Section 21.3, and in the next chapter, we shall discuss how our base NPV case must be adjusted to deal with the issues that arise when evaluating an international project.

Example   21.1

A Spanish company, Weltek, currently produces heavy-duty equipment for construction welding. The company is considering a proposal to set up a new business unit, which would produce and market electrodes for maintenance and repair welding in Spain. For simplicity, assume that the life of the project is five years. The initial investment consists of the following items (all figures are in millions of ESP):

- Land, worth ESP 100. This investment cannot be depreciated. The expected liquidation value after five years, reflecting expected inflation of 5 percent *p.a.*, is ESP 130.
- Plant and Equipment (P&E), worth ESP 350. This investment is depreciated linearly over five years, and has no scrap value at the end of the project's life.

- Entry costs: ESP 250, including training of the sales force, initial advertising, free samples, and so on. We assume that under local law, these expenditures are to be depreciated linearly over five years rather than deducted immediately from initial profits.[1]

Weltek is a 100 percent equity-financed firm and it has the funds that are necessary for a new investment. Estimates of sales, variable production costs, overhead, depreciation charges, and corporate taxes (35 percent) are shown in Table 21.1. All data take expected inflation (5 percent *p.a.*) into account. Negative taxes in year five correspond to the tax rebate the company gets from setting off the loss from this project against its other income. The figures for year six reflect the liquidation value of the land (130), and the tax bill in year six is calculated based on the accounting gain (liquidation value minus historic cost, or 130 – 100 = 30).

The sales revenue, variable costs, overhead, and taxes must be discounted back to time 0, taking into account investments in working capital. In the Appendix, we do this and obtain an NPV of –ESP 13m. The conclusion is that the cost exceeds the benefits and that, on the basis of the current data, the project should be rejected.

Incremental Cash Flows

The principle to be kept in mind is that since NPV measures the change in the shareholders' wealth, the cash flows to be used in the analysis are the **incremental cash flows**, that is, the change in the company's *overall* expected cash flows when the project is added to the company's existing activities.

TABLE 21.1   Present Value of the Cash Flows Generated in the Proposed New Business Unit

Year (*t*)	(a1) Sale of goods	(a2) Sale of land	(b) Variable costs	(c) Overhead	(d) Depreciation	(e) Taxable income	(f) Tax (35%)
1	650	—	260	105	120	165	58
2	1,000	—	400	110	120	370	130
3	1,100	—	440	116	120	424	148
4	600	—	240	122	120	118	41
5	300	—	120	128	120	–68	–24
6	—	130	—	—	—	30	11
PV	1991	40	872	312	—	—	198

Sales, variable costs, and overhead forecasts for the proposed new business unit are provided by the marketing and operations divisions. Depreciation of the investment outlays is described in the beginning of the example. For years 1 to 5, (*e*) = (*a*) – (*b*) – (*c*) – (*d*). For year 6, (*e*) = liquidation value of the land minus initial value; (*f*) = (*e*) × 0.35. Taxes and present values are rounded to the nearest integer.

---

[1] In many countries, these items may be deductible expenses in the year that they are actually made. We assume here that these are deemed to be investments that will generate income over many years.

In the above example, the determination of the cash flows started from the projected profit and loss (P&L) accounts of the proposed business unit. However, the incremental cash flow principle means that often one must also consider cash flows that are not accounted for by the P&L of the proposed new business unit. For example, sales made by the new business unit may partly replace existing sales made by another unit within that company or group. Likewise, the new unit often buys from (or sells to) the parent or other units in the group. If these effects on the overall cash flows are omitted, the NPV computations are misleading.

Example   21.2

Consider the project analyzed in Example 21.1. During a discussion of the investment proposal, a manager points out that the proposed unit will buy the coating for the electrodes from an existing business unit. Following a sound business principle, the *transfer price* used in the projected P&Ls is based on *arm's length* prices for similar coatings. Obviously this transfer price includes the profit of the supplying business unit. Although this profit is not included on the projected P&L statements for the proposed unit, it is nevertheless generated by the project and should be included in the evaluation of the new project.

Suppose that the intracompany transactions represent about one-fourth of the project's variable costs, and that each delivery valued at the arm's length price of one hundred pesetas increases the profits of the unit that acts as the supplier by fifty pesetas; that is, variable costs are half of the transfer price. The additional deliveries of coating material will not require any additional investment, nor will they affect the company's overhead. We leave the valuation of the profits the parent makes on its intracompany sales as an exercise. Assume that the result of valuing the incremental cash flows is ESP 71m. Let us now evaluate the project. The true NPV (using the incremental cash flows) equals:

- The NPV of the cash flows realized by the new business unit   −13m
- Plus the present value of the cash flows generated by the supplying unit   <u>71m</u>

    Total: ESP 58m

Thus, once one accounts for the cash flows generated outside the proposed business unit, the project is profitable.

Sensitivity Analysis

Anybody who has ever had to provide, or at least evaluate, the estimations and assumptions that accompany an NPV analysis will appreciate how tenuous many of the input data are. It is therefore important to experiment with variants of the assumptions after you have solved the base case. For instance, you should do a sensitivity analysis where you lower the sales figures by 10 percent, or 20 percent, or perhaps even 50 percent, and see how sensitive the NPV is to the sales estimates. A similar procedure can be followed with respect to production and overhead costs, and the discount rate. The estimate of the required return is imprecise because our estimates of the project's risk and the expected risk premium per unit of risk are not very exact. Even the initial investment itself deserves a closer look. In practice the projected outlays often are underestimated and, more often than not, the construction and start-up phase also lasts longer than initially projected. Finally, for international NPV problems, exchange rate forecasts may be necessary, and these forecasts should also be subject to a sensitivity analysis.

21.1.2   Adjusted Net Present Value (ANPV)

It has become standard practice to analyze new (domestic) investments in two steps. In the first stage, the analysis assumes that the whole investment is financed by equity, and that the money is readily available so that no new shares or bonds have to be issued. Accordingly, the cash flows do not take into account interest payments or loan amortizations; and the discount rate is based on the risk of the operating cash flows. In this stage of the valuation, the focus is on the inherent economic value of the project, not on the financing aspects. This is, in fact, what we did in Examples 21.1 and 21.2.

The financing aspects of undertaking the project are then considered in the second stage of the analysis, and lead to adjustments in the first-stage NPV calculations. This second stage results in an **adjusted net present value (ANPV)**. For instance, if new equity or bonds have to be issued, then the associated costs must be deducted from the NPV. Similarly, subsidies, in the form of capital grants or interest subsidies, are also taken into account in the second stage.

Example   21.3

Suppose that in order to implement the project we considered in Example 21.2, the company has to raise new equity at a cost of 15, and that it obtains a capital grant of 40 from the government because the investment is made in a rural area.[2] The ANPV is

$$\text{ANPV} = \text{NPV} - \text{issuing costs} + \text{subsidy} = \text{ESP } 58 - 15 + 40 = \text{ESP } 83. \qquad [1]$$

The NPV adjustments may also include tax savings created by corporate borrowing. This is discussed in the next section.

21.1.3   The Interest Tax Shield Controversy

Unlike dividends, interest payments are a tax-deductible expense for a corporation. Debt financing, therefore, typically reduces corporate taxes. The following example illustrates the potential advantage of the tax shield.

Example   21.4

Suppose that Ms. Taikoon is the sole owner of a Finnish company that makes a perpetual profit of FIM 50m before interest and taxes. She now extends a perpetual 10 percent loan of FIM 100m to the company, with the instruction to use the money to repurchase part of its stock. Apart from taxes, nothing has changed. Ms. Taikoon still is the sole recipient of all dividend and interest payouts, but the company's accounting profits decrease by FIM 100m × 10% = FIM 10m. Given a corporate tax rate of 40 percent, this implies annual corporate tax savings of 10m × 40% = FIM 4m.

If a company undertakes an investment project, the firm's gross present value increases, which means that its borrowing capacity also goes up. One of the adjustments in ANPV might therefore be

---

[2] All figures are still in millions of ESP.

the present value of taxes saved if the firm uses the new borrowing capacity. The savings would then be computed as follows, given the firm's long-run debt/assets ratio (δ), the corporate tax rate (τ), and the interest rate paid on the debt (R_{DEBT}, a *per annum* rate):

$$[\text{Additional borrowing capacity}]_t = \delta \times [\text{Gross Present Value of Project}]_t. \qquad [2]$$

$$[\text{Tax saving due to project}]_t = (R_{\text{DEBT}} \times \tau) \times (\delta \times [\text{Gross Present Value of Project}]_t). \qquad [3]$$

$$\text{PV of tax savings from project} = \sum_{t=1}^{T} \frac{R_{\text{DEBT}} \times \tau \times \delta \times [\text{Gross Present Value of Project}]_t}{(1 + R_{\text{DEBT}})^t}. \qquad [4]$$

However, this computation is likely to overestimate the tax savings. First, not all of the tax shields may effectively be used if the earnings before interest are not sufficiently large.

Example   21.5

Suppose that the profits of Ms. Taikoon's company are typically FIM 5m before interest and taxes, rather than FIM 50m. The FIM 10m in interest fees implies that annual profits will be systematically negative. Thus, the annual tax savings from interest payments are only 40 percent of the earnings before interest, that is, FIM 5m × 40% = FIM 2m, rather than the FIM 4m that we computed in Example 21.4.

Even if the company expects to be able to use its interest tax shield in most years, there is still a loss in time value whenever, for a particular year, the profits after interest payments are negative and part of the tax subsidy has to be carried forward into a future tax year.

Moreover, the above analysis of the tax shield generated by corporate borrowing is incomplete because it considers only corporate taxes. To determine whether paying out interest is more attractive than paying out dividends, we have to look at the *total* tax burden including, for instance, the shareholders' and bondholders' personal taxes. Differential taxation at the personal level may partially or wholly offset the discrimination at the corporate level, namely when, at the personal level, interest income is taxed more heavily than income from shares. For instance, in many countries, capital gains (which form a substantial part of the total remuneration of equity) remain untaxed, or are taxed at a rate below the standard rate. In some countries, individual investors can even obtain partial or full credit for *corporate* taxes when dividends are taxed at the personal level, in which case the tax advantage on debt at the corporate level is partially or fully undone at the personal level.[3]

---

[3] In Chapter 23, we discuss tax credit systems. The essence is that corporate taxes are treated as an advance personal tax. For example, if Ms. Taikoon receives a dividend of FIM 100, the tax man computes that the underlying before-tax corporate profit was 100/(1 − 0.4) = FIM 166.67. Under a credit system, Ms. Taikoon then has to declare a dividend income of 166.67 before taxes. If her tax rate is 40 percent, the total tax due is 166.67 × 40% = 66.67, but she obtains credit for the 66.67 paid by the corporation. Thus, the personal tax on dividends is zero if there is a credit system and if the personal and corporate tax rates are equal.

Example   21.6

Suppose that the company's profits are FIM 50m before interest and taxes. Ms. Taikoon pays no personal income taxes on dividends, but pays 40 percent tax on interest income. Then, the FIM 10m interest payments on the loan will still save FIM 4m in corporate taxes, but they will also lead to an additional FIM 4m personal income tax. Thus, on balance, there would be no tax gain from issuing debt in this case.

In view of the diversity of tax regulations with which your shareholders and bondholders may be confronted, it may be difficult to calculate the total tax subsidy, taking into account both corporate and personal taxes. For a firm whose shares and bonds are held internationally, this task is even more complicated—and, even if we could establish that there *is* a subsidy and if we had an approximate idea of its size, our problems would not be solved. It can be very difficult to figure out which part of the assumed interest tax subsidy accrues to the shareholders and which part to the bondholders. We would generally expect that the tax subsidy (if any) is somehow shared among shareholders and bondholders. The reason is that if borrowing is subsidized, the company's lenders will be able to raise the interest rate because of the increased demand for debt financing.

Example   21.7

Suppose that there are two hotels in town, the Equity Hotel and the Bond Hotel. Hotel expenses are initially assumed to not be tax-deductible, and both hotels charge USD 100 per night. A change in the legislation makes hotel bills from the Bond Hotel tax-deductible, while the expenses incurred at Equity Hotel remain part of the taxable profit. If the tax rate is 33.33 percent, one of the many possible new equilibria is that the Bond Hotel increases its prices to USD 150 per night. Then, the after-tax cost for a night at the Bond is $150 \times (1 - 33.33\%) = $ USD 100, which is equal to the cost of staying at the Equity. There is a subsidy of USD 50 in this case, and the subsidy is related to the tax deductibility—but it ends up in the pockets of the Bond Hotel rather than the company that deducts the Bond Hotel's bills from its profits.

Thus, the true beneficiary of a tax subsidy may be the supplier of the tax-deductible service (the Bond Hotel in the above example; or, in the interest tax shield case, the bondholder) rather than the user (the company and, ultimately, the firm's shareholders). We need detailed information about supply and demand in order to be able to say exactly who gets what part of the subsidy.[4] In summary, if we are not sure whether there is a tax subsidy, and how much of it accrues to shareholders, we surely have a good reason for keeping it separate from the main NPV calculations.

---

[4] Miller (1977), develops a theory which implies that *all* of the tax subsidy goes to the bondholders. Of course, Miller is rather selective in his assumptions, but his main point is that it is naive to believe that all of the subsidy (if any) accrues to the shareholders.

21.1.4   Why We Use ANPV Rather than the Weighted Average Cost of Capital

We conclude this section with a brief discussion of an alternative rule that is still occasionally used as a substitute for ANPV. In the **Weighted Average Cost of Capital (WACC)** approach, there is only one step: all cash flows are discounted at a rate that is the weighted average of the after-tax *p.a.* cost of debt, $R_{DEBT} (1 - \tau)$, and the cost of equity, $E(\tilde{R}_{EQUITY})$. This cost of equity is the *p.a.* rate of return expected by the shareholders. Thus, the WACC is computed as follows:

$$\text{WACC} = \frac{\text{Debt}}{\text{Equity} + \text{Debt}} \times R_{DEBT}(1 - \tau) + \frac{\text{Equity}}{\text{Equity} + \text{Debt}} \times E(\tilde{R}_{EQUITY}). \tag{5}$$

Relative to the ANPV approach, the WACC method has several disadvantages. First, it merges the first-stage NPV computation with the second-stage computation of the tax advantage from borrowing. In doing so, WACC assumes that the tax shield is always fully used, and the corporate tax savings are not offset by any fiscal discrimination at the personal level. Moreover, WACC attributes all of these savings to the shareholders. All this, as we have just argued, is questionable. Second, the WACC method only works for a one-period project or for a perpetuity; for any realistic set of cash flows, it yields, at best, an approximate value. (See, for instance, Brealey and Myers [1992] for a more detailed discussion of this issue.) In contrast, ANPV can handle any cash flow pattern. Third, the expected return on equity, used in the WACC formula, is typically measured using the risk of the firm's (levered) stock. This creates problems if the new project is in a different industry, or if the target Debt/Equity ratio for the new project differs from the target Debt/Equity ratio for the rest of the firm. For these reasons, we use the ANPV rather than the WACC method to make capital budgeting calculations.

21.2   FORMS OF FOREIGN ACTIVITY

In order to understand the problems that arise when the NPV criterion is applied to international investment projects, we need to understand the different ways in which a firm can generate and repatriate income from its foreign operations. This is relevant because the method of operations will affect the company's overall tax bills, as well as the transfer risk of its foreign cash flows. We first classify the forms of foreign involvement from a managerial or marketing point of view, and then from a legal point of view.

21.2.1   Modes of Operation: A Managerial Perspective

We restrict ourselves to a brief taxonomy; a complete discussion of the operational advantages and disadvantages of these various forms can be found in an international marketing or international management textbook.

1. **Pure exports** are one way to do business abroad. Under this mode of operations, the firm's skills are used at home in order to produce goods that are then sold abroad.
2. With **international product marketing**, the marketing of the firm's goods, and possibly also their production, is undertaken abroad. Most of the activities of multinational companies belong in this category.
3. In all of the above modes, the firm exploits its competitive advantage (in production, marketing, or general management) by marketing a product abroad. Alternately, the firm can

directly sell its skills to another company, without first using them to create a product. **Licensing** consists of the transfer of intellectual property (a production process, technical know-how, or a brand name), often for a limited period and for a restricted market. **Franchising** transfers the firm's marketing know-how, or a part of it. **Management contracts** transfer a general organizational or management skill. Under these forms of foreign involvement, the "seller" of the skill derives no revenue from product sales. Rather, for management contracts, a **management fee** is paid and, for the transfer of know-how, the firm is compensated in the form of a **royalty** (that is, a periodic payment proportional to the volume of sales, the value of sales, or the level of production) and often also an initial lump sum and/or a yearly lump-sum license fee.

Yet exports, international product marketing, international technology transfers, and cooperative agreements are not mutually exclusive. In practice, they are often used simultaneously. For instance, a firm may set up a wholly owned subsidiary for production and marketing abroad, implying that there is international product marketing. In addition, there may be a licensing contract and a management contract between the parent and the affiliate,[5] and there may also be exports of some products or components to its foreign business. One objective of such a mixed approach might be a reduction in the tax burden, by "unbundling" the cash transfers from subsidiary to parent—for example, paying out interest payments and royalties rather than just dividends. Another objective could be to reduce political risk. In the case of a joint venture, an additional consideration is that, by mixing the forms of foreign involvement, the risks and expected revenues can also be redistributed among the stakeholders. We shall return to these issues in Chapters 23 (on taxes) and 24 (on joint ventures).

21.2.2   Modes of Operation: A Legal Perspective

One alternative to the above classification is to classify foreign activities according to the legal form in which they are set up. In ascending order of foreign involvement, our list is as follows:

1. Exports may occur through **independent agents**. An independent agent is, by definition, an unrelated company or person who sells the firm's products abroad, so that there is no legal ownership link with the parent.
2. Exports may also occur through a **dependent agent** abroad. For instance, a French company may send one of its employees to Lima, Peru, to advertise its fine products. This employee is likely to rent an apartment there, and have a car, a phone, and a fax machine—all paid for by the French company. From the perspective of Peruvian law, however, the agent is just a private person living in Lima. Legally, the French exporter is not present in Peru.
3. A higher form of foreign presence is obtained by opening a **foreign branch**. By fulfilling some legal requirements, the French company can establish a legal presence in Lima. The formal opening of a branch implies that the phone or the car in Lima will be recognized as the French company's property, not the agent's, and that the contracts signed by the agent (if she or he has the power to do so) bind the French company, and not just the agent as an individual. Not being incorporated as a separate company, the branch remains essentially a part

---

[5] For instance, in 1990, intragroup royalty payments by US corporations amounted to USD 13 billion, while royalty payments to unrelated companies totaled only USD 4 billion (Hufbauer, 1992).

of the French company. It has no separate accounting system. All of its profits and losses are immediately and automatically part of the overall profits and losses of the company.[6]

A less common structure of foreign operations is the **joint branch**, which is an unincorporated operation jointly run by two or more owners. The profits and losses of the joint branch are split according to some previously agreed-upon rules, and each portion is automatically part of the corresponding owner's overall profits and losses. This structure is mainly used in temporary ventures, like foreign construction and engineering projects undertaken by a consortium of companies. The joint branch plays an important conceptual role in our analysis of joint ventures (Chapter 24).

4. Finally, one may set up an entity that is incorporated as a separate company. The separate foreign company may be a **wholly owned subsidiary** with one parent, or a **joint venture** where there are two or more parents. A separate company can, for instance, pay out dividends, royalties, or interest to its parent(s), lend money to its owner(s), obtain loans, or subscribe to the parent's stock, and so on. This is, by definition, not possible with a branch. For instance, one branch of the company cannot pay dividends to another branch or buy stock issued by another part of the same company.

* * *

We are now ready to look at the valuation issues in an international environment. In the remainder of this chapter, we assume that only one firm is involved in setting up the foreign business—just like in a typical "domestic" NPV problem. The joint venture case, where there is more than one shareholder, will be discussed in Chapter 24. The issues that arise in international capital budgeting include the following:

- *International taxation.* What are the tax implications of the subsidiary's remittance policy?
- *Incremental cash flows.* In international investment projects, there are often many interactions of the proposed business unit with the cash flows of the company's other units, and taxation issues make it more difficult to account for them. How should one compute the incremental cash flows?
- *Political risks.* Foreign-earned funds may be blocked abroad, because the host country has insufficient reserves of hard currency (*transfer risk*). Another political risk is *expropriation risk*. How should one account for such risks?
- *Exchange risk and capital market segmentation.* A major issue is how to account for exchange risk, and how to determine the cost of capital, when the foreign capital market is segmented from the capital markets in the parent's country. Segmentation arises when international capital flows are restricted or even prohibited. For instance, the government may forbid outward or inward portfolio investment, or limit foreign ownership of domestic shares to a given percentage of local companies' equity capital. Similarly, the company's bylaws may impose a ceiling on foreign ownership of its shares.

In this chapter, our discussion of the issues of taxation, exchange risk, and capital market segmentation will be brief; a more detailed discussion is provided in Chapters 22 and 23. Thus, Section 21.3 contains only an outline of the tax issues, and argues that because of the fiscal complications, one should adopt a three-stage Adjusted NPV procedure. Section 21.4 explains how to handle transfer risks. Section 21.5

---

[6] A branch is also taxable in the host country, like any other unincorporated "firm." (The inverse is not necessarily true. There may be host country taxation even if the foreign business is not legally established as a branch. See Chapter 23.)

discusses expropriation risk. In Section 21.6, we see how to take incremental cash flows into account. Section 21.7 introduces the issue of exchange risk and capital market segmentation.

21.3   TAXES AND THREE-STEP INTERNATIONAL CAPITAL BUDGETING

When valuing operations in a foreign country, we need to take into account the tax effects for the company as a whole. In an international context, taxation does not end with corporate taxes on the profits of the foreign subsidiary. The host country will tax not just the profits of the subsidiary, but also the parent when the subsidiary remits income to the parent. In addition, the parent's foreign income (dividends, interest income, royalties) is taxable in its home country, as are the parent's profits from sales to the foreign subsidiary. This interaction and potential proliferation of various taxes then gives rise to the following issues:

- How should one set the *transfer prices* for intragroup sales of goods and services so as to minimize taxes? That is, how should one allocate profits between the parent and the subsidiary? Or, if the foreign presence is in the legal form of a branch, how should one divide the company's total profits into a foreign-earned part and a domestic part?
- How should the foreign subsidiary remit its cash flows to the parent? That is, what is the optimal *remittance policy*? The subsidiary can remit cash to its parent through equity transactions, loans, dividends, interest payments, royalties, or management fees, and each method has different tax implications. The financial manager must make optimal use of the intricacies, shortcomings, and loopholes in tax rules or tax treaties that reduce double taxation on branch profits and on remittances from a subsidiary. In addition, the manager must make optimal decisions with respect to the timing and size of the dividend remittances.

In short, one issue in international capital budgeting is *tax planning*—but tax planning, we argue, is best separated from the valuation of the cash flows from operations. Recall that the first stage in a domestic-investment analysis problem focuses on the economics; the cash flows associated with financial decisions are considered later. In an international setting, we likewise start by focusing on the operational cash flows, and reserve the financing issues and their tax implications for a later stage. Note, however, that in international projects, the financing issues have an extra dimension. Like in a domestic project, one has to adjust the NPV of the operations for the costs and possible benefits associated with *external financing*, like borrowing from banks or unrelated bondholders, or issuing new shares. In addition, and unlike in a domestic project, one has to account for the costs and benefits associated with the *intragroup financial arrangements* between parent and subsidiary, like intragroup loans or license contracts. Thus, we recommend a three-step process for valuing international projects:

- In Step 1, the focus is on the cash flows from operations. Accordingly, we ignore all financial arrangements between the parent company and the foreign subsidiary, by assuming that the foreign venture is just an (unincorporated) *branch* of the parent rather than a legally separate company. We call this first step the **branch stage**.
- In Step 2, the foreign venture is incorporated as a separate company that can choose a remittance policy. We analyze the costs and benefits of the *intragroup* financial arrangement by which the foreign entity unbundles its remittances into license fees and royalties, interest payments, and dividends. We call this stage the **unbundling stage**.
- In Step 3, adjustments are made for the effects of **external financing**.

Comparing the valuation procedure of an international project to the procedure used for a domestic investment, we see that the only change is the addition of Step 2.

21.3.1   Step 1: The Branch Scenario or Bundled Approach

In the first stage, we assume that the project is implemented as a branch of the company, not a subsidiary. Unlike a subsidiary, a branch has no remittance policy, and the scope for tax planning is very limited. All cash flows are automatically and immediately owned by the parent. Thus, the focus at this stage is on the economics of the project—sales, costs, differences between cash flows realized by the project and overall incremental cash flows, exchange risks, political risks, and so on.

The practical implication is that if the projected P&L accounts contain interest payments to outside lenders or to other companies in the group, and royalties paid to a related company, you should immediately remove these items, and recalculate the taxes accordingly. This procedure not only keeps you from getting lost in tax details, but it also guarantees that you avoid two rather common pitfalls. One pitfall is to consider the royalties or interests on an intracompany loan as a "cost" to the subsidiary, while forgetting that these payments also represent an income to the parent. The other pitfall is to focus on the reduction of corporate taxes in the host country created by payments of royalties or interest, while forgetting that the parent is taxed on this royalty or interest income at home.

21.3.2   Step 2: The Unbundling Stage

The second step in the valuation process consists of analyzing the *intracompany* financial arrangements[7] that become possible as soon as we incorporate the branch into a wholly owned subsidiary. The second stage of the calculations is to some extent similar to the second stage in a standard (one-country) NPV problem, in the sense that the project's financing is examined. The reason why we separate the costs and benefits of intragroup financing (Step 2) from those of external financing (Step 3) is that the former can be estimated in a more reliable way than the latter. With intragroup contracts, we know exactly who the beneficiaries are and how they are currently taxed; and the benefits clearly accrue to the group as a whole. In contrast, it is hard to quantify the overall tax benefit generated by outside borrowing, and it is even harder to find out who is the actual beneficiary of the tax subsidy.

The reasons for separating the costs and benefits of intragroup financing (Step 2) from those of the pure economics of the project (Step 1) are the following. First, tax planning is complex and technical, and is best left to fiscal experts and tax consultants. This way, the managers can focus on the inherent merits of the project, without being unduly diverted by fiscal details. Second, when estimating the tax effects of incorporating a branch into a subsidiary, one needs to make tenuous assumptions about the size and timing of dividend payouts; and the hoped-for savings from fiscal planning may disappear when tax codes are changed. Thus, the safer procedure is to accept a project on the basis of its economic merits, and consider any additional gains from tax planning as a welcome but nonessential boon.

The following example illustrates how to adjust the branch NPV calculations for the effects of a royalty or intracompany loan contract.

---

[7] The term "intracompany" is a standard way to refer to transactions between related companies (for instance, between parent and subsidiary, or between subsidiary *A* and subsidiary *B* of the same parent). From a legal point of view, the term is somewhat imprecise, since there is more than one company.

Example   21.8

Let us give an international flavor to the investment project discussed in Table 21.1. The company that is considering setting up a company for the production and marketing of welding electrodes in Spain is now Weltek UK. The value of the operations in the form of a branch is assumed to be unaffected by this change of ownership; that is, the cash flows realized in Spain still have an NPV of −13m ESP, and the additional cash flows generated by profitable sales of inputs by Weltek UK to Weltek Spain increase the total NPV to ESP 58m. One of the managers points out that the corporate taxes paid by Weltek Spain will be substantially reduced if (1) Weltek Spain signs a license contract with Weltek UK and pays a royalty equal to 5 percent of its Spanish sales in compensation for the use of the parent's know-how; and (2) Weltek Spain borrows funds from a Spanish bank. The manager proposes a five-year loan of ESP 250m. The principal is amortized in five equal payments of ESP 50m and the yearly interest charged is 16 percent on the amount outstanding at the beginning of the year. The tax savings become obvious, the manager argues, if one compares the revised P&L projections in Table 21.2 with the projections in Table 21.1 (where there were no royalties or interest payments).

We evaluate this proposal as follows: first, it is not known what the total tax effect of the external loan actually is, nor is it known how much of the supposed benefit accrues to the shareholder, Weltek UK. Thus, we should leave this financing aspect to Step 3, if we wish to consider it at all. In contrast, the gain from paying out the royalty is easier to quantify.

In evaluating the benefit of the license contract, we should also consider the taxes that Weltek UK will pay on the royalty. Suppose that Weltek pays no taxes on dividends received from Weltek Spain (this is the "exclusion" rule; the actual UK rules are different), and that income from licensing is taxed in the UK at 30 percent, 5 percent below Spain's corporate tax rate. Thus, if the subsidiary pays out royalties worth ESP 100, there is a savings of ESP 35 in Spanish corporate taxes but an additional cost of ESP 30 in UK taxes, implying a net tax savings of 5 percent on the gross

TABLE 21.2   Projected P&L Statements Including Royalties and Interest

Reporting year	(a) Sales	(b) Variable costs	(c) Over-head	(d) Depreciation	(e) Royalty	(f) Interest	(g) Taxable income	(h) Tax (35%)
1	650	260	105	120	33	40	92	32
2	1,000	400	110	120	50	32	288	101
3	1,100	440	116	120	55	24	345	121
4	600	240	122	120	30	16	72	25
5	300	120	128	120	15	8	−91	−32

Sales and costs are the same as in Table 21.1. A royalty of 5 percent on annual sales is paid to Weltek UK. The interest payments relate to a 16 percent, five-year bank loan with an initial book value of ESP 250m, of which ESP 50m is amortized at the end of every year. Thus, the interest payments in column (*f*) start with 16 percent on ESP 250; the next year, ESP 50m has been paid back, so the interest is now 16 percent on ESP 200m, and similarly for years three to five. Column (*g*) = (*a*) − (*b*) − (*c*) − (*d*) − (*e*) − (*f*), and (*h*) = (*g*) × 35 percent. Figures are rounded to the nearest integer.

royalties. Weltek would, therefore, like to set the royalty as high as possible. Suppose that tax consultants tell Weltek that any royalty in excess of 6 percent would probably be rejected by the Spanish tax authorities as above normal.[8] In view of this information, Weltek UK decides to set the royalty at 6 percent rather than at 5 percent (as proposed in Table 21.2). The present value of the benefits (the 5 percent tax savings on the 6 percent royalty on sales) then is [9]

$$\text{PV tax saving} = 0.06 \times \Sigma_{t=1}^{5} \frac{\text{sales}_t}{1.18^{(t+0.5)}} \times 0.05 = 0.06 \times 2{,}190 \times 0.05 = \text{ESP } 6.6\,\text{m}.$$

The Step-2 adjusted NPV therefore is ESP 58m + 6.6m = ESP 64.6m.

We see that royalties can be one element in the company's tax-planning strategy. Tax planning is discussed in greater detail in Chapter 23.

21.3.3   Step 3: The Implications of External Financing

The third and final stage in the international capital budgeting process pertains to the aspects of *external* financing. If the group has to raise equity, or if the parent or subsidiary issues bonds or borrows from banks, there are likely to be costs. Likewise, there might be tax subsidies on borrowing. However, it is hard to know what extra present value is created by interest tax shields, and it is even harder to know who receives what part of the subsidy.

If you believe that there are fiscal subsidies on external borrowing, and feel you have a pretty good idea of how much of the tax benefits you will receive, all kinds of interesting issues arise in the third step. Who should borrow, the parent or the subsidiary? And should one borrow in a high-interest currency or in a low-interest currency? For answers to these questions, one might feel tempted to go back to the traditional (domestic) capital budgeting literature, where the well-known conclusion is that the present value of the corporate tax shield is a positive function of the corporate tax rate and of the interest rate. The message we want to get across is that these standard conclusions are not necessarily correct in an international setting.

Who Should Borrow?

One of the decisions to be made is whether the external loan should be taken out by the parent or by the subsidiary. On the basis of the standard (domestic) analysis one would conclude that it is optimal for the parent to borrow if the home country corporate tax is higher than the host country rate, and *vice versa.*

---

8 Tax laws of most countries have a rule saying that payments for goods and services bought from related foreign companies should be based on *arm's length* prices, that is, at prices that would be normal among independent parties. Thus, any part of an expense declared in Spain that exceeds the arm's length level will be rejected as a cost, and will be taxable in Spain as part of the subsidiary's profit. The UK taxes on the parent's income would still be based on the royalties as actually received, not on the arm's length royalty.

9 We assume that the royalties are paid every month on the basis of the sales (not on the basis of the actual payments from customers); that is, royalties are paid at times 1.5, 2.5, . . ., 5.5 on average. The present value of the tax saving is computed at a rate of 18 percent rather than the 20 percent cost of capital used for the entire cash flow because royalties are based on sales, which have a lower risk than the overall net cash flows. The reason is that net cash flows are like the payoffs from a portfolio of sales revenue (held long) and costs (held short). If the risk of costs is lower than the risk of sales revenue, the risk of the net cash flow will be higher than the risk of either the sales or the costs. The effect is similar to the effect of financial leverage.

Example   21.9

Suppose that the corporate tax rate is 16 percent in Hong Kong, while in Belgium it is 39 percent. If the Hong Kong subsidiary deducts HKD 100 as interest payments, this saves HKD 16 in Hong Kong taxes. If, on the other hand, the Belgian parent borrows, Belgian taxes worth HKD 39 are avoided. Thus, the impression is that borrowing should be done in Belgium.

However, the above analysis is incomplete, as it considers only the borrower's corporate taxes. One should also take into account that if the Hong Kong subsidiary does not borrow, its profits will be higher, which means that (sooner or later) its dividends will be higher than they would have been if there had actually been a loan in Hong Kong. These higher dividends will trigger additional Hong Kong taxes on dividend remittances, and also higher Belgian taxes on dividend income from the Hong Kong subsidiary. Thus, the decision cannot be made just on the basis of the corporate tax rates.

Example   21.10

Suppose that the corporate tax rate is 16 percent in Hong Kong, while in Belgium it is 39 percent. Suppose also that dividends paid out by a Hong Kong company are taxed at 5 percent in Hong Kong and at 39 percent in Belgium. To compute the total tax burden, start with HKD 100 earnings before taxes. This generates $100 \times (1 - 0.16)$ = HKD 84 after corporate tax, which can be paid out as a dividend. The Belgian shareholder receives, after Hong Kong tax on the dividend, $84 \times (1 - 0.05)$ = HKD 79.8, and, after Belgian corporate tax, $79.8 \times (1 - 0.39)$ = HKD 48.678. Thus, the total tax burden on Hong Kong profits is more than 50 percent. In contrast, the tax on Belgiam profits is only 39 percent. We conclude that an analysis of tax shields based purely on taxes on corporate profits (16 percent versus 39 percent) would have been misleading.

In Which Currency Should One Borrow?

The firm also needs to decide on the currency of borrowing; specifically, it has to decide whether borrowing should be in a high-interest currency or in a low-interest currency. On the basis of the standard (domestic) analysis, one may conclude that borrowing in high-interest currencies is beneficial in terms of tax subsidies. However, as we argued in Chapter 3, this rule of thumb, when used to compare loans in different currencies, is wrong because it ignores the capital gains or losses due to changes in exchange rates. In terms of risk-adjusted expectations, the capital gains or losses are exactly offset by the difference between the interest rates. It follows that, in terms of risk-adjusted expectations, the taxes on the capital gains or losses are exactly offset by the taxes on the difference between the interest rates, as long as taxes do not discriminate between interest and capital gains. Thus, the currency of borrowing does not matter, even in the presence of taxes, as long as the spot and forward markets are in equilibrium and the capital gains tax is the same as the tax on ordinary income.

21.4   TRANSFER RISKS

Beside issues arising from international taxation, one also must take into account transfer risks when valuing a foreign investment. *Transfer risk* refers to the possibility that when the reserves of hard currency in the host country are low, the cash generated abroad may be *blocked*. That is, the parent may not be able to repatriate the interest, dividends, or royalties it earned abroad, or the funds held in a foreign bank account opened by a branch office. As part of the valuation of an international project, we discuss three issues with respect to transfer risks. First, how can the risks be minimized proactively, that is, before the problem actually arises? Second, what can be done once the parent's funds are effectively blocked? Lastly, how can transfer risks be incorporated into the NPV analysis?

21.4.1   Proactive Management of Transfer Risk

We have seen in Step 2 of the capital budgeting process how unbundled intracompany payments, such as royalties and interest, can be used to reduce the total tax liability. In this section, we argue that unbundling can also be used to manage transfer risk. The reason is that countries with foreign currency reserve problems will not suddenly forbid *all* remittances. Some forms of remittances are more likely to be blocked than others.

- *Transactions on capital accounts*, such as equity transfers and loans granted to other companies in a group, are generally the first type of transactions to be blocked. If the subsidiary is regularly buying goods or services from other companies in the group, then the subsidiary can still make a disguised loan to its supplier by speeding up ("*leading*") the payments for the goods it bought. This way money can be taken out of the country without openly making a loan.

Example   21.11

Every month, a subsidiary buys USD 1m worth of goods from its parent, and pays sixty days later. Suppose that after the imposition of currency controls in July, the parent shortens the credit period to thirty days. As shown below, this means that the parent receives two payments in August—one for the deliveries made two months before and one for the deliveries of last month.

Old payment schedule		New payment schedule	
July	1m for order of May	July	1m for order of May
August	1m for order of June	August	1m for order of June
			1m for order of July
September	1m for order of July	September	1m for order of August
October	1m for order of August	October	1m for order of September

This is equivalent to keeping the credit period at sixty days *and* making an interest-free loan from the subsidiary to the parent for USD 1m without a stated expiration date.

The same effect is obtained by delaying ("*lagging*") payments from the parent to the subsidiary. If you want to be able to use *leading and lagging*, you have to proactively establish a tradition of intragroup transactions. However, you should not expect too much. Governments with besieged currencies often impose limits on credit terms for exports and imports.

- *Dividends* are usually next on the list of transfers that are blocked (or at least limited).[10] However, even dividends are not always entirely blocked. Rather, as a first measure, a government will *limit* dividend payments (to 5 percent of equity, for example). Strategies that increase the capital base may be used to reduce the effect of such a dividend ceiling. For instance, one could increase the capital base by cheaply taking over a local company with a huge nominal capital but a low market value, or bringing in equipment as equity-in-kind, at a rather generous valuation. Another useful proactive defense against the risk of blocked dividends is to include the parent's own government, a government agency, or the International Finance Corporation (IFC),[11] as a minority shareholder of the subsidiary. From the host government point of view, antagonizing the World Bank or a government is (somewhat) more embarrassing than blocking dividends due to a private foreign company.

- *Interest payments and license fees* are next on the list of payments to be blocked by a foreign government that is short of hard currency. Interest on intracompany loans and royalties paid to the parent are blocked less often than dividends. Moreover, interest payments made to a foreign bank are blocked less often than similar payments on an intracompany loan. Therefore, a not-uncommon strategy is to use a bank as a front. The parent lends funds to an international bank, which then re-lends these funds to the subsidiary. (The parent's deposit serves as a guarantee for the loan, so that the bank's risk is minimal.) Again, a host government will think twice before it blocks interest payments to an international bank. Finally, loans structured as bearer bond issues are even less subject to sovereign risks than bank loans. For example, during the international-debt-crisis years in the eighties, there was no instance of default or rescheduling of eurobonds.[12]

- Finally, *management fees* and *payments for intracompany trade and for technical assistance* are blocked only in extreme circumstances. These payments are not viewed as financial transfers, but as payments for imports of goods and services. Of course, it would look suspicious if the parent suddenly increased its transfer prices after the imposition of exchange controls. The correct proactive defense therefore is to start charging high transfer prices long before the exchange controls are imposed.[13] In the same vein, the parent may create a management contract, or may "sell" technical assistance on a more or less regular basis, rather than taking these funds out of the country as dividends. Note, however, that most countries reserve the right to reject transfer prices that are deemed to be above the arm's length value, that is, the normal market price paid between independent parties.

---

[10] If they have the choice, monetary authorities prefer to block dividends rather than interest or royalty payments because dividends are not contractually fixed.

[11] The IFC is a subsidiary of the World Bank, which takes equity participations. Apart from bringing in capital (and official World Bank support), the IFC can also help by offering its expertise about countries, markets, and such, and by helping with feasibility and profitability studies—for a fee.

[12] When bank debt is to be rescheduled, a government in distress knows which banks are involved; in contrast, renegotiating a bond issue is difficult if the securities are (or are said to be) held by many anonymous individual investors.

[13] Note that there may be various costs associated with intracompany trade at high transfer prices. First, import duties on the goods sold to the subsidiary will be higher. Second, if the corporate tax paid by the parent is higher than the rate paid by the subsidiary, high transfer prices *may* imply a higher tax burden for the group as a whole. Third, buying goods from the parent rather than producing them locally can be expensive in terms of direct production and transportation costs.

21.4.2   Management of Transfer Risk after the Imposition of Capital Controls

Once currency controls have been imposed, the firm can overcome these by leading the payments from subsidiary to parent and lagging the payments from parent to subsidiary. It can increase transfer prices and management fees or charge more for technical assistance. However, substantial changes in transfer pricing or credit terms will trigger reactions from the host country authorities. Thus, substantial amounts of money are likely to remain effectively blocked. Such blocked funds are not irrevocably lost.

- The parent may invest them in the local money or capital markets, new projects, or inventory. Internationally traded goods may be a comparatively good investment, since their value is less subject to devaluation risks. Still, there is likely to be some loss of value, since these "second-best" investments would otherwise not have been made.
- Alternatively, the parent may try to spend the funds as wisely as possible, perhaps by buying local goods or services that would otherwise have been bought elsewhere, by organizing executive meetings and conferences in the host country, or by buying airline tickets from the local carrier. Again, there will almost certainly be a loss of value, since these purchases would normally have been undertaken elsewhere, at lower prices (since the host country currency is likely to be overvalued, and import restrictions make host country prices artificially high).

21.4.3   How to Account for Transfer Risk in NPV Calculations

Three approaches can be used to quantify the impact of transfer risks on a project's value:

- First, we could add an extra risk premium (for transfer risk) to the project's discount rate. In general, this is not recommended because we have no idea how to determine this risk premium.[14]
- Second, if we have an idea about the probability of the funds being blocked and about how much value will be lost if the funds are actually blocked, we can take this into account when computing the expected cash flows. However, quantifying this information is not easy. Also, we do not know at what rate the (adjusted) expected cash flows are to be discounted.
- Fortunately, transfer risks can typically be insured by private insurance companies or government-run insurance agencies. This means that the present value of the (after-tax) insurance premiums can be used to estimate the risk-adjusted expected value of the transfer risks. This approach is probably the best. It uses readily available market information and is a strategy that is easy to implement.

Example   21.12

Let us return to Example 21.2. Our earlier NPV computation, ESP 58m, assumes that the funds generated in Spain are immediately and automatically available to the parent. This would be true if

---

[14] If the host country has internationally traded bonds outstanding that are denominated in hard currency, we can observe some kind of transfer risk premium by comparing the yield on these bonds to the yield on risk-free bonds in the same currency. However, the transfer risks of a project's cash flows are likely to be higher than the risks present in bearer bonds issued by the host country's government. Thus, the risk premium observed for eurobonds understates the risk premium required for other claims.

TABLE 21.3   Computation of Weltek's Insurance Premia against Transfer Risk

Reporting year	Book value of assets	Insurance premium
0	700	7.0
1	580	5.8
2	460	4.6
3	340	3.4
4	220	2.2
5	100	1.0

The initial book value of the assets consists of 100 for the land, and 600 for the other assets; the latter component is depreciated linearly over five years. The insurance premium is calculated as 1 percent of the book value of the assets.

Weltek UK does not incorporate its foreign business as a separate company, *and* if there is no risk that the funds will be blocked in Spain. Worried about the latter contingency, Weltek contacts the UK Export Credit Guarantee Department, and learns that it can buy insurance against transfer risks for dividends (up to 10 percent of the book value of equity) and for repatriation of the invested capital, at 1 percent *p.a.* of the book value of the foreign operations, payable at the beginning of each year. The cost of insurance is computed in Table 21.3. Weltek will pay this fee as long as the subsidiary is not bankrupt or otherwise liquidated; that is, the risk of the insurance payments is the same as the risk of default by its subsidiary. In view of the low risk, Weltek discounts these amounts at the rate the subsidiary would pay on a bank loan, which is 17 percent. Because this fee is tax-deductible, the true cost to Weltek is

$$PV = \left(7 + \frac{5.8}{1.17} + \frac{4.6}{1.17^2} + \frac{3.4}{1.17^3} + \frac{2.2}{1.17^4} + \frac{1}{1.17^5}\right) \times (1 - 0.35) = ESP\ 12.4.$$

We see that political risk reduces the NPV by ESP 12.4.

21.5   OTHER POLITICAL RISKS

Other political risks, besides transfer risk, include the possible *expropriation* of a company, the "distress" sale of equity following the imposition of minimal local ownership rules, or the *nationalization* of entire economic sectors.

Again, one can often buy insurance against these forms of expropriation. One way to incorporate the expected cost of expropriation, therefore, is to use insurance premiums as part of the cash flows. However, this approach does not work as well for expropriation risks as it does for transfer risks. This is because, first, compensation is typically based on accounting values, which can deviate substantially from true values, especially under inflationary circumstances. Second, it usually takes some time before the damage is recognized and assessed; so there is the loss of time value. Finally, expropriation can take place covertly. A government can slowly strangle a company, for example, by refusing it investment licenses or import licenses. In the end, such a company has no choice but to sell its operations to a local firm. In this case, there is no formal expropriation, and therefore no compensation from any insurance contract. Fortunately, expropriations and nationalizations are less fashionable and frequent than they used to be, so that when considering foreign investment, this risk is rather small for most host countries. Given the small risk, the imperfections in the insurance contract as a protection against expropriation risks are not a major concern in the NPV calculations.

21.6   INCREMENTAL CASH FLOWS

The incremental cash flow principle means that one should consider not only the cash flows that can be inferred from the subsidiary's projected P&L accounts, but also the change in the cash flows elsewhere in the company. In international projects, interactions with other activities are the rule rather than the exception because foreign production usually comes after exports (which would disappear if the foreign investment project were accepted) and because there tends to be a lot of intracompany trade. In addition, the probability of overlooking these interactions may be greater than in the case of a domestic investment proposal. One reason is that foreign investments are usually implemented by legally separate companies, each with its own separate accounting systems, rather than business units within a single company where there is just one, overall accounting system. Another reason is that the subsidiary's managers may be tempted to consider only their own company's profits if their bonus plans depend on the subsidiary's profits rather than on the subsidiary's contribution to the profits of the group as a whole.

21.7   EXCHANGE RISK AND MARKET SEGMENTATION

In the examples we have considered, Weltek UK computed the NPV of its foreign investment in units of the host currency, the peseta. This is natural in the sense that sales prices and production costs are normally first estimated in host currency. However, this procedure can be very inappropriate. When computing the NPV in host currency, we are, in fact, valuing the project in the way an investor from the host country would value it (apart from the fact that taxes may be different when the owner is foreign). However, the valuation of a project by a local investor may differ from the valuation by a foreign investor if the host and home capital markets are not well integrated. The reason is that if investors are not free to trade securities, the cost of capital will not be equalized internationally. We shall return to this important issue in the next chapter.

21.8   A CHECKLIST FOR NPV ANALYSIS

To conclude this chapter, we list the points one should consider when valuing international projects. We also take the opportunity to add a few minor points that have not been explicitly discussed above. The first three items in our checklist relate to the fact that the purpose of the valuation procedure is to determine the value of the project to the parent's shareholders. This has the following implications:

1. *Incremental Cash Flows*

One implication is that we should take into account cash flow effects outside the subsidiary. Most cash flow projections start from the subsidiary's projected P&Ls. However, the project may also affect cash flows of the parent, or of other companies in the group. On the positive side, there may be profits when a related company sells to the new subsidiary, or when it buys from the new subsidiary and then re-sells the goods to other customers. On the negative side, the new project may take away sales and profits from an existing business.

2. *Integrated or Segmented Markets*

The second implication relates to the discounting procedure. When the host and home capital markets are well integrated, the value of the project is the same to all investors in these countries. Thus, one can discount the expected cash flows denominated in host currency, and use the same discount rate as local investors would have done. In segmented markets, however, this procedure is invalid, and one of the methods discussed in the next chapter must be adopted instead.

3. *Taxes*

The third implication is that our analysis should include the host-country corporate taxes, withholding taxes, and the home-country corporate taxes. These taxes are not found in the subsidiary's projected P&L statements.

The remaining points relate to the general procedure for international capital budgeting.

4. *Separation of Operating and Financing Issues*

In order to separate the operating and financing issues, capital budgeting for international applications should be done in three steps. The first step assumes that the project is implemented in a *branch*, which ignores all gains that can be made by unbundling the payments. Thus, one should remove intragroup interest payments and royalties from the P&L statements, and recompute the taxes to reflect the branch scenario.

5. *Inflation*

The projected P&L statements often start from a constant-price scenario. When including the effects of inflation, one can often do better than postulating a uniform percent inflation to all items in the cash flow statement for all years. First, it is not necessary for the rate to be constant over time; if inflation is unusually high right now, one should expect it to be brought down to a lower, long-run level in the coming years, and *vice versa*. Second, the effect of inflation is not necessarily the same for all cash flow items. In the long run, raw materials prices tend to lag behind the prices of semi-finished goods, consumer goods, and services—in that order.

6. *Profits versus Cash Flows*

Costs are typically disbursed months before the time of selling, while revenues are received months afterwards, but this difference in timing is not reflected in the projected P&L statements. One simple way to handle these leads and lags is to build them into the discounting procedure. Alternatively, you can try to quantify investments in working capital, as explained in the appendix. If you use this alternative procedure, you should forecast accounts payable, inventory, and accounts receivable, count any change in working capital as a cash flow, and remember to cash in ("recover") the remaining working capital at the end of the evaluation horizon.

7. *Terminal Value*

In most cases, it is unreasonable to assume that all fixed assets are worthless at the end of the evaluation horizon. This means that a terminal value has to be assessed. Three procedures are popular.

- First, the terminal value could be set equal to the book value. This has the merit of simplicity, and it is also likely to be conservative, implying that a positive NPV based on this assumption is safe.
- Second, the company can be valued as a going concern, using a long-term average price/cash flow ratio for comparable firms.
- Third, an explicit forecast can be avoided by repeating the NPV computations for many different terminal values, until the critical liquidation value is found where the NPV switches from negative to positive. Often, one can tell whether this critical terminal value is above, below, or within the range of actual terminal values that can be reasonably expected.

8. *Sensitivity Analysis*

The sales, costs, and exchange rate forecasts are probably as debatable as the estimates of the terminal value. Therefore, you should also experiment with a number of (optimistic and) pessimistic scenarios and see whether, and to what extent, reasonable variations in these estimates affect the sign of the NPV. Another item of uncertainty is the discount rate, because the cost of capital estimate is never very precise. Finally, even the investment outlays themselves, and the effective start-up date of operations, deserve some experimentation.

9. *NPV as Just One Element*

Almost tautologically, NPV works only with quantifiable aspects—expected cash flows. However, analysts understandably hesitate to quantify aspects of the project that have very diffuse cash flow implications. For instance, a new project may lead to others that can be very profitable. In many cases, we have only very vague ideas about what type of extensions or spin-off businesses could result and what their cash flow implications would be. Even if we have an idea about the nature of possible later extensions, it is often anybody's guess whether the probability of such an extension is 30 percent, 20 percent, or 10 percent. Equally hard to quantify are elements like the repercussions on the company's image, or political risks. Yet non-quantifiability does not mean irrelevance. Therefore, you should at least think very hard about the qualitative considerations, and include these in your analysis along with the NPV computations.

QUIZ QUESTIONS

True-False Questions

1. Net Present Value analysis assumes that the risk of the project is constant.
2. ANPV and WACC are essentially substitutes; neither is superior to the other.
3. The sum of a project's profits, when accumulated over time without taking time value into account, is identical to the sum of the project's cash flows.
4. The sum of a project's investments and disinvestments in working capital, when accumulated over time without taking time value into account, is zero.
5. When the firm has the choice between either gradually depreciating an investment or charging the investment off entirely to the year's Profit and Loss account, the first choice is generally recommended. It does not affect the total amount paid in taxes (over the project's entire life), and it avoids unnecessary fluctuations in profits.
6. When applying NPV, you should take great care in reallocating the firm's general overhead, and charge a fair portion of this overhead to the new project—for instance, proportionally with sales or direct costs.
7. When valuing a project, you should not include in the cash flow estimates of the (arm's length) profits made by other business units on their sales to the new unit. That is, the project should be viable even when it must pay normal (arm's length) prices for the components it buys.
8. Adjusted NPV contains corrections for qualitative aspects that were ignored in the first-stage NPV calculations.
9. Since borrowing reduces corporate taxes, one should always compute the tax savings (borrowing capacity × interest rate × tax rate), and add their present value to the first-stage NPV.
10. The WACC correctly measures the gain to the shareholders from undertaking a project, if and only if (1) the project is either a perpetuity or a one-period venture; (2) the tax shield is always fully used; and (3) all gains accrue to the shareholders.
11. Exports occur through a dependent agent or through a branch, while operating through a subsidiary falls into the category of international marketing.
12. A firm that is very good at marketing will often become a franchisee; likewise, a firm that is very good at developing a new technology or that possesses a valuable brand name will typically become a licensee.
13. The licensor or franchiser typically receives a stated fraction of the project's profits.
14. Having a foreign branch is like having a dependent agent abroad, except that the foreign operations are incorporated as a separate company.
15. The incremental value principle says that since the gains from tax planning and "tax-treaty shopping" are unambiguously related to the project, these gains should be considered in the decision to accept or reject.
16. When conducting an NPV analysis, one should be as realistic as possible, and subtract, for example, the license fees, interest payments and amortization of intracompany loans, and management fees from the project's cash flows.
17. Since the money paid to bank(s) to service loan(s) does not accrue to the shareholders, one should subtract these payments from the operational cash flows before computing the NPV.
18. A sound rule of thumb is that the company should borrow in a weak currency for two reasons. First, the firm can expect a capital gain when the loan is paid back. Second, the high interest payments mean that there is a large interest tax shield.

19. To account for expropriation risk, one simply deducts the insurance premium (after taxes) because this premium is equal to the market's risk-adjusted expected cost of expropriation.
20. The best way to account for transfer risk is to add a risk premium to the discount rate. The next best way is to subtract the expected losses on blocked funds from the operating cash flows.
21. Leading and lagging are ways to speculate on changes in transfer prices.

Additional Quiz Questions

1. What are the reasons why the tax savings from corporate borrowing are often smaller than the present value of (borrowing capacity × borrowing rate × tax rate)?

2. Why does a firm often combine, for example, exports, foreign marketing, and licensing— rather than choosing only one of the above methods of operations?

3. What are the main differences between an independent agent and a dependent agent? A dependent agent and a branch? A branch and a subsidiary? A subsidiary and a joint venture?

4. Why is it better to separate the analysis of intracompany financial arrangements from the analysis of the operations and the analysis of the effects of external financing?

5. Describe how the proactive and reactive management of transfer risk differ.

6. What cash flows are not shown in the projected Profit-and-Loss accounts for the project, but should nevertheless be taken into account when doing an NPV analysis?

EXERCISES

1. Consider Example 21.2. Suppose that intracompany transactions represent one-fourth of the project's variable costs, and every delivery valued at the arm's-length price of 100 pesetas increases the profits of the supplying unit by 50 pesetas; that is, variable costs are half of the transfer price. Additional deliveries of coating material will not require any additional investment, nor will they affect the company's overhead. Evaluate the profits that the parent makes on its intracompany sales, and incorporate them into the NPV analysis.
   To take into account leads and lags (*investments in working capital*), assume that

   • The supplying unit ships the coating, on average, six months before the subsidiary sells its final product (that is, shipment occurs at times 1, 2, . . . , 5).
   • Production of the coating consists of grinding and mixing, and takes virtually no time; the supplying unit usually has about one month's worth of raw material in inventory, and pays its own suppliers thirty days after delivery. Workers are paid every week. Thus, the supplying unit's cash outflows also take place at times 1, 2, . . ., 5.
   • The new business unit pays sixty days after delivery; taking into account one month for the actual shipment, this means that the supplying unit is paid at times 1.25, 2.25, . . ., 5.25.

2. Again consider Example 21.2. We add a second interaction. Specifically, assume that Weltek UK is currently exporting to Spain, via an independent agent. If Weltek chooses to continue exporting instead of setting up production in Spain, unit variable costs will be higher (due to transportation cost, tariffs, etc.); and sales will be lower than expected because the agent is not as interested in promoting Weltek's goods as Weltek itself. On the other hand, no investments in fixed assets and marketing organization are required if exporting remains the mode

of operation, and exporting does not create any extra overhead. Weltek's profits from exporting, and the corresponding taxes, are presented below.

Year t	(a) Sales	(b) Variable costs	(c) Overhead	(d) Depreciation	(e) Taxable	(f) Tax (35%)
1	420	231	0	0	189	66
2	551	303	0	0	248	87
3	463	255	0	0	208	73
4	243	134	0	0	109	38
5	128	70	0	0	58	20
PV	1,169	673	0	n.a.	n.a.	153

$(e) = (a) - (b) - (c) - (d)$; $(f) = (e) \times 0.35$.

Due to shipping delays and the increased inventory levels needed in view of the distance, production for exports takes place six months before the moment of sale to the final Spanish customer (that is, at times 1, 2, . . . , 5). Production costs lead production by three months. Compute the PV of the export profits lost when the project is undertaken, and decide whether Weltek UK should still consider direct investment in Spain. Use a 20 percent cost of capital.

3. An Andorra company, Walden Inc., considers a proposal to produce and sell market inverters in Prisonia. The Prisonian dollar (PRD) is fully convertible into any OECD currency, and the country's capital market is unrestricted and well integrated with western markets. The life of the project is three years. The initial investment consists of land (PRD 1,000) with an expected liquidation value of PRD 1,100; plant, equipment, and entry costs equal PRD 6,000, and are to be depreciated at 66 percent in year 1, 33 percent in year 2, and 1 percent in year 3. Estimated figures for sales, variable costs, and overhead are as follows.

Book year	Sales	Variable costs	Overhead	Depreciation	Taxes
1	5,500	2,500	1,000	3,960	0
2	10,000	4,200	1,200	1,980	264
3	12,800	5,600	1,300	60	2,336
4	1,100*	—	—	—	40

* proceeds from the sale of the land

Sales occur, on average, in the middle of the year; variable costs are disbursed one month earlier, and customers pay three months later. Overhead and taxes are paid in the middle of the year. The investment occurs in the middle of year 0, and liquidation occurs in the middle of the fourth year. The discount rate is 15 percent for the operating cash flows, and 10 percent for the investment itself. (The initial loss can be carried forward, but this is already reflected in year-2 taxes.) Is this a viable proposal?

MIND-EXPANDING EXERCISES

1. Consider a firm with a healthy cash flow but very low profits—because, for example, of high depreciation allowances. Your boss argues that such a firm should probably borrow in a strong (low-interest) currency, because the high tax shield from weak-currency loans is more likely to be lost than the low tax shield from strong-currency loans. Is this analysis accurate?

2. Denote the initial investment by I_0, the operating cash flows by OC_t, the loan by D_0, and the service payments on this loan by $Serv_t$. The standard NPV is computed as

$$\sum_{t=T_1}^{t=T_N} \frac{OC_t}{(1+R)^t} - I_0.$$

   (a) Assume zero taxes and no uncertainty. One could, conceivably, compute an NPV from the shareholders' point of view by considering the cash flows after interest payments and the initial investment over and above the amount borrowed:

$$\sum_{t=T_1}^{t=T_N} \frac{(OC_t - Serv_t)}{(1+R)^t} - (I_0 - D_0).$$

   Explain why, with zero taxes and no uncertainty, this produces the same answer as a standard NPV analysis. (Hints: (1) How does one compute the PV of a sum (or difference) of two risk-free cash flows? (2) What is the link between the PV of the service payments and the amount borrowed, D_0?)

   (b) Does uncertainty affect this conclusion?
   (c) Does the introduction of taxes affect this conclusion?

ALTERNATIVE WAYS TO ACCOUNT FOR INVESTMENT IN WORKING CAPITAL

21A.1   Modeling Investments in Working Capital as a Cash Flow

One popular way to take into account the lead between outlays and accounting costs, and the lag between accounting revenue and actual inflows, is as follows:

- For every year, one estimates the total investment in net working capital (NWC, that is, cash + inventory + accounts receivable – accounts payable) by multiplying annual sales by a constant number:

$$[\text{Total net working capital}]_t = [\text{Annual sales}]_t \times \left[\text{Projected} \left(\frac{\text{NWC}}{\text{Annual sales}} \right) \right]. \qquad [\text{A1}]$$

If credit terms and inventory policy abroad and at home are the same, *and* current working capital at home is optimal, the projected ratio of NWC/Sales can be obtained from the firm's current balance sheet. Otherwise, a project-specific NWC/Sales ratio has to be used.

- Each year's additional investment in working capital—the number we wish to determine—is then computed as the change in the current year's total NWC relative to last year's NWC.
- At the end of the evaluation horizon ($t = T$), one "recovers" working capital, that is, one counts all remaining NWC as a cash inflow. This corresponds to selling all inventory at cost, paying all outstanding accounts payable, and cashing in all accounts receivable.

Example   21A.1

The projected sales for years one to six are as shown in the first line of the following table. The company's investments in working capital are typically 10 percent of its sales. This is reported in the second line. The third line, "Additions to NWC," shows changes in net working capital from the previous year. From the profits (20 percent of sales), depreciation (50 per year), and NWC we then compute cash flows:

Year	1	2	3	4	5	6
Sales	150	200	250	200	50	0
Net working capital	15	20	25	20	5	0
Additions to NWC	15	5	5	–5	–15	–5
Accounting profit	30	40	50	40	10	
Add back depreciation	50	50	50	50	50	
Correct for change in NWC	–15	–5	–5	5	15	5
Cash flow	65	85	95	95	75	5

Thus, in the first three years, additional investment in working capital is positive. The reason for this result is that increasing sales lead to more and more credit to customers and a larger inventory, while the increasing credit from suppliers is not sufficient to finance the increase in accounts receivable and inventory. In the last three years, credit to customers shrinks and inventory can be decreased, which means that the cash inflows exceed the accounting profits.

The second part of the table corrects the projected accounting profits by adding back depreciation allowances and subtracting additions to net working capital.

21A.2   Accounting for the Leads and Lags in the Discounting Procedure

The alternative way to account for the leads and lags in production costs and sales revenue is to build these leads and lags directly into the discounting procedure. This is the approach we adopt. The approach abandons the usual assumption that cash flows occur at the end of each year. Working on a continuous time line allows us to be more realistic about the timing of each cash flow item, and provides a simple way to take into account investments in working capital. For instance, assume the time frame in Example 21.1 is as follows:

- The investment outlay (ESP 700) is paid for, on average, 0.5 years from the decision date.
- Sales start one year from now, and are spread evenly over the year. That is, sales occur on average at times $1.5, 2.5, \ldots, 5.5$—but customers pay three months later; that is, cash actually comes in, on average, at times $1.75, 2.75, \ldots, 5.75$—and production costs are, on average, paid three months before the goods are sold; that is, on average, the costs are paid at times $1.25, 2.25, \ldots, 5.25$.
- Overhead is paid, on average, in the middle of the year (at times $1.5, 2.5, \ldots, 5.5$).
- Taxes are paid at the end of each year (at times $2, 3, \ldots, 6$ for the ordinary income tax, and time 7 for the liquidation tax)
- The liquidation value is realized at time 6.5.

Discounting of the (risky) operating cash flows is done at a compound rate of 20 percent *p.a.* Discounting of the initial investment itself is at the short-term risk-free rate of 12 percent *p.a.* because there is no risk associated with the investment itself. Taking into account the timing of the cash flow as outlined above, we discount the cash flows given in Table 21.1,[15] and compute the NPV as follows:

$$\text{NPV} = \sum_{t=1}^{5} \frac{\text{sales}_t}{1.2^{(t+0.75)}} - \sum_{t=1}^{5} \frac{\text{variable costs}_t}{1.2^{(t+0.25)}} - \sum_{t=1}^{5} \frac{\text{overhead}_t}{1.2^{(t+0.5)}} - \sum_{t=1}^{6} \frac{\text{taxes}_t}{1.2^{(t+1)}} - \frac{\text{investment}}{1.12^{(0.5)}} + \frac{\text{sale of land}}{1.2^{(6.5)}}$$

$$= 1991 - 872 - 312 - 198 - 661 + 40$$

$$= -\text{ESP } 13.$$

[1]

---

[15] Recall that depreciation is not a cash flow, and is included in the table only because it affects the taxes.

EXCHANGE RISK AND CAPITAL MARKET SEGMENTATION

With respect to our discussion of international capital budgeting in Chapter 21, two issues were left unanswered. First, we worked with expected cash flows denominated in foreign currency and we discounted them at the same rate as the one required by a foreign investor. This, we said, assumes capital market integration. We still need to explain this argument, and we also have to see how one should proceed when capital markets are not integrated, that is, when they are segmented.[1] A second question is how to determine the discount rate or cost of capital in integrated markets and in segmented markets.

This chapter addresses these issues in the following order. First we discuss the effect of capital market integration or segmentation on the capital budgeting procedure. In Section 22.1, we consider the case where cash flows are risk free in terms of foreign currency, and explain why capital budgeting can be done in terms of foreign currency when the home- and host-country capital markets are integrated, and how the procedure is to be modified when the home- and host-country capital markets are segmented from each other. In Section 22.2, we extend these results to the case where cash flows are risky in terms of foreign currency. The remainder of the chapter then relates to the determination of the cost of capital. In the third section, we present the traditional single-country Capital Asset Pricing Model (CAPM), starting from the efficient-portfolio problem discussed in Chapter 13. In Section 22.4, we explain how to modify this model when assets are priced in an international market. The case that we discuss is one where capital markets are integrated across many countries, but where

---

[1] Segmentation arises when international capital flows are restricted or even prohibited. For instance, the government may forbid outward or inward portfolio investment, or limit foreign ownership of domestic shares to a given percentage of local companies' equity capital. Similarly, a company's bylaws may impose a ceiling on foreign ownership of its shares. Many Swedish or Swiss companies have rules of this type, and issue two classes of stocks, restricted shares and unrestricted shares.

imperfections in the goods markets create real exchange risk. Section 22.5 concludes with a review of the implications of this chapter for capital budgeting.

22.1   PROCEDURES FOR VALUING RISK-FREE FOREIGN CASH FLOWS

To initiate our discussion of the effect of capital market integration or segmentation on the capital budgeting procedure, we first consider the case where cash flows are risk free in terms of foreign currency. We explain why capital budgeting can be done in terms of foreign currency when the home- and host-country capital markets are integrated, and how the procedure is to be modified when the home- and host-country capital markets are segmented from each other.

22.1.1   The Link between Capital Market Segmentation and Exchange Risk

In the examples of international NPV computations given in Chapter 21, we worked with expected cash flows denominated in foreign currency and we discounted these cash flows at the rate of return required by a foreign investor. The reason why one usually starts from cash flows denominated in foreign currency is related to the empirical fact, noted in Chapter 11, that prices in any given country are sticky and to a large extent independent of exchange rate changes. Therefore, when one prepares cash flow forecasts it is natural to start from currently prevailing prices and costs in foreign currency, and then predict future prices and costs in foreign currency on the basis of expectations about foreign inflation. However, the ultimate purpose of capital budgeting is to find out whether the project is valuable to the parent company's shareholders—and we usually think of these shareholders as measuring present values in their *home* currency and using the cost of capital that is relevant to them. In short, although the natural input data are cash flow forecasts expressed in foreign currency, at some point we have to make the transition from foreign currency to home currency.

In the examples of the last chapter, this transition from foreign currency (ESP) to home currency (GBP) was made at the last possible stage, and was not even carried out explicitly. Rather, in Chapter 21, we calculated the value as if the owner were a host-country investor, and we implicitly used the notion that the value in terms of GBP is equal to the value in terms of ESP, multiplied by the current exchange rate. This type of valuation in foreign currency, as if the owner were a host-country investor, is correct if the host- and home-country financial markets are *integrated*, that is, if there are no restrictions on cross-border portfolio investment between the two countries and if investors effectively hold many foreign assets.

The implication of market integration is that all investors, regardless of their place of residence, use the same cost of capital when they compute the price of any given asset (in some given reference currency) from the expected cash flows of this asset (expressed in the same reference currency). One way to explain this claim is by contradiction. If investors from countries *A* and *B* used a *different* cost of capital when computing the price of some given asset (in some given base currency) from the asset's expected cash flows (measured in the same base currency), then the price of the asset in country *A* would differ from the price of the same asset in country *B*. The resulting arbitrage opportunities would lead to international trading in the shares until the price difference disappeared. By equating prices across countries, international arbitrage also equates the costs of capital that various investors use when linking the asset's price to the expected cash flows paid out by the asset. Thus, in integrated markets, a home-country investor and a host-country investor fully agree about the project's value.

In *segmented* markets, in contrast, one cannot simply value a foreign cash flow as if it were owned by host-country investors. In the absence of free capital movements, there is no mechanism that equates prices and discount rates across the two markets. Thus, to the managers of the parent firm, the relevant question becomes: What price would *home*-country investors normally be prepared to pay for the project? The way to proceed is to identify cash flow patterns that have similar risks and that are already priced in the home-country capital market. Once we have identified a similar asset that is already priced in the home capital market, we can then use the same discount rate for the project that we want to value as that for the traded assets. To implement this procedure, we need a theory, like the Capital Asset Pricing Model, to tell us what types of risk are relevant, how these risks should be measured, and what return is expected in the home-country capital market in light of the project's risks. Since we use the home-country capital market as the yardstick, the discount rate is the required return *in home currency*— and if the cost of capital is expressed in home currency, we have to translate the expected cash flows and their risks from foreign currency into home currency before we discount. For such a translation, we need expected values for the future spot rates for various maturities. A related issue is whether, and under what conditions, we can avoid such exchange rate forecasts by using the risk-adjusted market expectations, which are reflected in the forward rates for these maturities.

To understand the three procedures that could potentially be followed, we first consider the simplest possible problem: the foreign cash flow to be valued is a single risk-free payment of one unit of foreign currency, to be received at time T. Then, in later sections, we shall generalize the approach to cash flows that are risky in terms of foreign currency.

22.1.2   The Valuation of Risk-Free Foreign-Currency Cash Flows

We first discuss three ways in which to value a one-unit foreign currency cash flow, and show that all three methods give the same home currency value in well-integrated markets. (Most of this discussion reviews arguments already used in Chapters 3 and 4 when we discussed forward contracts.) Next, we address the issue of which method (if any) must be used to compute the present value of the foreign cash flows when markets are segmented.

- The first way to value the project is to compute the present value of the foreign cash flow in the foreign market, and then translate this foreign-currency value into domestic units at the current spot rate. The foreign currency value of the project is $PV_t^*(1_T) = 1/(1 + r_{t,T}^*)$. Thus, the value of the project in terms of the domestic currency is computed as

$$S_t PV_t^*(1_T) = \frac{S_t}{1 + r_{t,T}^*}. \qquad [1]$$

- The second way to value the project is to start from the cash flow in foreign-currency terms, translate this into an expected cash flow in home-currency terms, and compute its present value using the standard capital-budgeting procedures. Since the cash flow equals one unit of foreign currency without risk, the expected cash flow in home currency is the expected value of the future spot rate, $E_t(\tilde{S}_T)$, which we then discount using the discount rate that the market normally expects in light of the riskiness of $\tilde{S}_T$. Let us denote the market's risk-adjusted discount rate by $E_t(\tilde{r}_{t,T})$. Then, the second procedure can be formally summarized as

$$PV_t(\tilde{S}_T) = \frac{E_t(\tilde{S}_T)}{1 + E_t(\tilde{r}_{t,T})}. \qquad [2]$$

- The third approach is to value the hedged cash flow. That is, one sells forward the one unit of foreign currency. Such a hedging operation replaces the risky home currency cash flow, $\tilde{S}_T$, by a riskless inflow $F_{t,T}$. Since the latter amount is risk free in terms of home currency, the project's present value can be computed by discounting $F_{t,T}$ at the home risk-free rate, $r_{t,T}$.

$$\text{PV}_t(F_{t,T}) = \frac{F_{t,T}}{1 + r_{t,T}}. \qquad [3]$$

Using the insights from Chapter 3, it is easy to prove that in integrated capital markets, all three approaches lead to the same valuation. To show the equivalence of Equation [3] with the first approach, Equation [1], note that, in unrestricted markets, Interest Rate Parity must hold. Substituting $F_{t,T} = S_t(1 + r_{t,T})/(1 + r_{t,T}^*)$ into the right-hand side of Equation [3] then leads to the conclusion that

$$\text{PV}_t(F_{t,T}) = \frac{F_{t,T}}{1 + r_{t,T}} = \frac{S_t \dfrac{1 + r_{t,T}}{1 + r_{t,T}^*}}{1 + r_{t,T}} = \frac{S_t}{1 + r_{t,T}^*} = S_t\,\text{PV}_t^*(1_T). \qquad [4a]$$

To show that Equation [2] also leads to the same value, we refer to our interpretation of the zero-value property of a (new) forward contract. Specifically, in Chapter 3 we argued that in free and unrestricted capital markets, the zero-value property says that the amounts to be exchanged in a forward contract are equivalent:

$$\frac{E_t(\tilde{S}_T)}{1 + E_t(\tilde{r}_{t,T})} = \frac{F_{t,T}}{1 + r_{t,T}}. \qquad [4b]$$

That is, because the forward rate reflects the market's risk-adjusted expectation of $\tilde{S}_T$, the two approaches must produce the same value. The difference between the two methods is merely formal. In Equation [2], we correct for risk in the denominator; in Equation [3], the risk correction is in the numerator. This difference should not matter as long as we make no mistakes in estimating the market's expectations and risk-adjusted required returns.

Another way of explaining the equivalence of Equations [2] and [3] is as follows. Equation [3] is based on the assumption that any investor can hedge. However, in free and unrestricted capital markets, a forward hedge has a zero market value, so it cannot alter the project's value. Thus, the valuation of the risky prospect, Equation [2], must be the same as the valuation of the hedged prospect, Equation [3]. In short, when markets are integrated and all investors are free to do any operation that they want in the spot, forward, and money markets, then procedures [1], [2], and [3] must lead to the same present value.

What if exchange and money markets are not integrated? Obviously, when investors are not free to invest wherever they please, the first method (Equation [1]) will generally fail to produce the correct value for the home-country investor. This is because, in the absence of free capital flows, there is no mechanism that equates the home value of an asset with its translated foreign value. The third method (Equation [3]) will also fail in segmented markets. When access to forward markets (or to foreign money markets) is rationed, there will generally be an unsatisfied demand for either forward sales or forward purchases. Therefore, a forward hedge will generally not have a zero market value. Thus, adding the hedge *will* affect the market value (if exchange and money markets are not free, that is). Or, arguing somewhat differently: when the market value of a forward contract is not zero, the exchanged amounts are no longer equivalent, implying that the forward rate is no longer the certainty equivalent of the future spot rate. We conclude that methods [1] and [3] are incorrect in segmented money and exchange markets. Thus, in segmented markets, there is only one way to value the project: make explicit exchange rate forecasts, and discount the translated cash flows at a rate that reflects the corresponding risk.

22.2 PROCEDURES FOR VALUING RISKY FOREIGN CASH FLOWS

In this section, we extend the preceding analysis to cash flows that are risky in foreign currency terms. Our notation is as follows:

$$\tilde{C}_T^* = \text{the (risky) foreign currency cash flow,}$$

$$\tilde{C}_T = \tilde{S}_T \tilde{C}_T^* = \text{ the (risky) cash flow, expressed in home currency.}$$

We now generalize each of the three methods above, and evaluate them. To keep the exposition simple, the examples still assume that there is just one future, foreign currency cash flow, $\tilde{C}_T^*$, to be received at time T. Each of the three methods will be illustrated using a numerical example introduced in Chapter 18. We summarize the example below.

Example 22.1

A British company is considering a project in Freedonia. Assume that the Freedonian crown (FRK) cash flow can take on either of two (equally probable) values, FRK 150 or FRK 100, depending on whether the Freedonian economy is booming or in a recession. Let there also be two, equally probable time-T spot rates, GBP/FRK 1.2 and 0.8. Thus, measured in GBP, there are four possible cash flows: $150 \times 1.2 = \text{GBP } 180$, $150 \times 0.8 = \text{GBP } 120$, $100 \times 1.2 = \text{GBP } 120$, and $100 \times 0.8 = \text{GBP } 80$. These numbers are shown in Table 22.1. In each cell, we also show the *joint* probability of each particular combination. When the FRK is expensive, a recession is more probable than a boom because an expensive currency means that Freedonia is not very competitive. The inverse happens when the crown is trading at a low level; then it is more likely that the economy will be booming. These effects are reflected in the probabilities shown in each of the four cells in Table 22.1.

TABLE 22.1 The Distribution of the Home-Currency Cash Flow

		State of the Economy	
		State: boom FRK cash flow: 150 Probability: 0.50	State: recession FRK cash flow: 100 Probability: 0.50
$\tilde{S}_T$	S_T high: GBP/FRK 1.2 Probability: 0.50	Cash flow: GBP 180 Joint probability: 0.15	Cash flow: GBP 120 Joint probability: 0.35
	S_T low: GBP/FRK 0.8 Probability: 0.50	Cash flow: GBP 120 Joint probability: 0.35	Cash flow: GBP 80 Joint probability: 0.15

We now generalize each of the three methods introduced in the preceding section to the case where the foreign currency cash flow is risky.

22.2.1   Discount First, then Translate Foreign-Currency Value into Home Currency

When the foreign cash flows are risky, the analog of [1] consists of first discounting the foreign currency cash flows at the foreign rate of return that local (host-country) investors would require for a similar investment, and then translating this foreign-currency present value at the current spot rate.

Example   22.2

When the Freedonian and British capital markets are integrated, the only cash flow figure we have to extract from Table 22.1 is the expected cash flow in FRK. Since each of the states of the Freedonian economy is assumed to be equally probable, the expected cash flow in FRK is

$$(0.50 \times 150) + (0.50 \times 100) = \text{FRK } 125.$$

Thus, the only remaining issue is to find the discount rate in FRK (the FRK risk-free rate plus an appropriate correction for risk). The Capital Asset Pricing Model, to be discussed in Sections 22.3 and 22.4, provides a way to estimate the appropriate risk premium.

Let us now examine the assumptions underlying this valuation approach. Recall that we are interested in the value of the project *to the parent company's shareholders*. Therefore, this first method assumes that capital markets for risky as well as risk-free assets are well integrated. Only then will the appropriately discounted and translated FRK value (to a Freedonian investor) be the same as the GBP value (to a non-Freedonian investor). That is, foreign risk-free rates must be set in a free and open market, and the markets for risky assets must also be well-integrated with world capital markets.

22.2.2   Translate into Home Currency Using Future Spot Rates, then Discount

When the foreign cash flow is risky, the analog of [2] is to translate the foreign cash flows into home currency using the distribution of the future spot rates. The resulting home currency flows are then valued as if they were generated by a project at home. Note that the translation part is, in general, more complicated than just multiplying the expected foreign-currency cash flow by the expected spot rate. If the foreign-currency cash flow depends, to some degree, on the exchange rate, the cross-term or covariance term will have to be taken into account:

$$E_t(\tilde{C}_T) = E_t(\tilde{C}_T^* \tilde{S}_T) = E_t(\tilde{C}_T^*) \times E_t(\tilde{S}_T) + \text{cov}_t(\tilde{C}_T^*, \tilde{S}_T). \tag{5}$$

The covariance term, $\text{cov}_t(\tilde{C}_T^*, \tilde{S}_T)$, is related to the project's exposure in foreign currency, and in home currency.

Example 22.3

We now need to compute the expected cash flow in GBP from the data in Table 22.1. One way to obtain this expected value is to consider each of the four possible cash flows in GBP, and weight them by the corresponding probabilities, as follows:

$$E_t(\tilde{C}_T) = (180 \times 0.15) + (120 \times 0.35) + (120 \times 0.35) + (80 \times 0.15) = \text{GBP } 123.$$

Note that the expected spot rate is GBP/FRK 1, and the expected cash flow in foreign currency is FRK 125. The expected GBP cash flow differs from $E_t(\tilde{C}_T^*) \times E_t(\tilde{S}_T) = 125 \times 1$ because of the relation between $\tilde{C}_T^*$ and $\tilde{S}_T$. In fact, our computations imply that the covariance must equal -2.

The expected GBP cash flow, GBP 123, is to be discounted at the appropriate *home* currency discount rate, that is, the GBP risk-free rate plus a risk premium that reflects the risk of the GBP cash flows to the British investor.[2] The Capital Asset Pricing Model, to be discussed in Sections 22.3 and 22.4, provides a way to estimate the appropriate discount rate.

Evaluating the assumptions underlying this method, we find that the second approach is very general. One problem with this method is how to get a reliable estimate of the market's required return, but this is an issue in any NPV computation. The second problem with this approach is that we need the covariance between the foreign cash flows and the exchange rate or, alternatively, the joint distribution of these two variables. Finally, we need exchange rate expectations, which, as we saw in Chapter 15, are difficult to determine. The problem of identifying the expected exchange rate is avoided if we can use the (observable) forward rate as a risk-adjusted expectation. This then brings us to the third method.

22.2.3 Translate into Home Currency Using Forward Rates, then Discount

By analogy to [3], the third way to value a risky foreign currency cash flow is by using the forward rate as the certainty equivalent of the future spot rate. The focus then is on the hedged cash flows (in GBP) and their associated risk. Their present value is computed as if the cash flows were generated by a project at home.

The third method requires one to decompose the asset's value (in GBP) using the *regression* approach outlined in Chapter 18:

$$\tilde{C}_T = a_{t,T} + b_{t,T} \tilde{S}_T + \tilde{e}_T. \tag{6}$$

The regression coefficient, $b_{t,T}$, is a number of units of foreign currency and measures the *exposure* of the GBP cash flows, while $a_{t,T} + \tilde{e}_T$ is the unexposed part. (Recall that, although $\tilde{e}_T$ is risky, it is

---

[2] Recall that if capital markets within, say, the OECD are well integrated, the UK value would also be correct for any other investor from any other OECD country.

uncorrelated with $\tilde{S}_T$.) To hedge this exposure, we sell forward $b_{t,T}$ units of foreign exchange. The hedged cash flows will be

$$\tilde{C}_{T,\text{hedged}} = a_{t,T} + b_{t,T}\,\tilde{S}_T - b_{t,T}\,(\tilde{S}_T - F_{t,T}) + \tilde{e}_T.$$

$$= a_{t,T} + b_{t,T}\,F_{t,T} + \tilde{e}_T. \qquad\qquad [7]$$

We see that the hedged cash flow is not perfectly risk free (as there is noise, $\tilde{e}_T$), but at least it has become uncorrelated with the exchange rate. Thus, we compute the hedged cash flows in the home currency, and discount at a domestic currency rate that takes into account the remaining risk.[3]

Example   22.4

In Chapter 18, we computed the exposure of the GBP cash flows shown in Table 22.1 as $b_{t,T} = \text{FRK}$ 75. The hedged cash flows are then computed by adding, to each cell, the gain or loss of the hedge. Suppose that the forward rate is GBP/FRK 0.96. If the spot rate turns out to be high ($\tilde{S}_T = 1.2$), hedging changes each cash flow by $-75 \times (1.2 - 0.96) = -\text{GBP } 18$, while if the rate happens to be low, hedging leads to a gain of $-75 \times (0.80 - 0.96) = \text{GBP } 12$. The hedged cash flows are shown in Table 22.2. We see that the conditional expectations of the hedged GBP cash flows no longer depend on the spot rate:

$$E_t\,(C_{T,\text{hedged}} \mid S_T = 1.2) = \frac{162 \times 0.15 + 102 \times 0.35}{0.5} = \text{GBP } 120.$$

Table 22.2   The Distribution of Hedged Cash Flows

		State of the Economy	
		State: boom FRK cash flow: 150 Probability: 0.50	State: recession FRK cash flow: 100 Probability: 0.50
$\tilde{S}_T$	S_T high: GBP/FRK 1.2 Probability: 0.50	Hedged cash flow: GBP 162 Joint probability: 0.15	Hedged cash flow: GBP 102 Joint probability: 0.35
	S_T low: GBP/FRK 0.8 Probability: 0.50	Hedged cash flow: GBP 132 Joint probability: 0.35	Hedged cash flow: GBP 92 Joint probability: 0.15

---

[3] There is a link with the option pricing theories in Chapters 7 and 8: we are replacing the true expected value of the future spot rate, $E_t(S_T)$, by its risk-adjusted expectation, $F_{t,T}$. To understand this, just compare the expected values of Equations [6] and [7].

$$E_t(C_{T,\text{hedged}} \mid S_t = 0.8) = \frac{132 \times 0.35 + 92 \times 0.15}{0.5} = \text{GBP } 120.$$

Thus, the unconditional expected value of the hedged cash flow must be GBP 120, too. This is the expected cash flow that must be discounted in the third approach.[4]

Let us now evaluate the assumptions underlying this method. When replacing the expected spot rate in Equation [6] by the forward rate (see Equation [7]), this method assumes that there is a forward market (or, equivalently, a spot market for risk-free foreign currency assets) which is unregulated and open to all shareholders.[5] Under this assumption, (1) any non-Freedonian shareholder of the project *can* effectively hedge the exposure, and (2) the forward hedge, having zero market value, will not change the project's value. The markets for risky assets, like stocks, need not be fully integrated internationally to apply this method.

We have seen how to obtain expected cash flows, but not how to obtain appropriate discount rates when cash flows are risky. This is the task in the remainder of this chapter. Section 22.3 reviews the single-country Capital Asset Pricing Model (CAPM). Section 22.4 extends the model to a multi-country setting.

22.3   THE SINGLE-COUNTRY CAPM

Our discussion of the traditional (single-country) CAPM starts from the asset demand theory that was used in Chapter 13 to explain the portfolio approach to exchange rate determination. The key assumption of this asset demand theory is that investors rank portfolios on the basis of (1) the expected nominal portfolio return and (2) the variance of the nominal portfolio return. Implicit in the use of nominal returns is an assumption that inflation is deterministic, or at least that inflation uncertainty has little impact on asset pricing. The theory of optimal portfolios, as developed by Markowitz (1952), can also be interpreted as a theory that tells us how expected returns are related to risk in an efficient portfolio. This relationship is due to Sharpe (1964), Lintner (1965), and Mossin (1965).

22.3.1   Efficient Portfolios: A Review

In Chapter 13, we saw how investors select **efficient portfolios**. A portfolio is efficient if it has the lowest variance among all conceivable portfolios with the same expected excess return.[6] For

---

[4] The discount rate to be used when discounting this hedged expected cash flow (GBP 120) is different from the discount rate to be used when discounting the unhedged expected cash flow (GBP), because the risk differs. We return to this issue in Section 22.5.

[5] Often, there are no long-term forward quotes; or, the market for a particular exchange rate may be so thin that even short-term forward quotes are not readily available. In the absence of direct forward quotes, we may use $S_t (1 + r_{t,T})/(1 + r^*_{t,T})$ as a stand-in for the forward rate. This is correct if the shareholders have free access to money markets or euromarkets in both currencies. If neither country's internal money market is well integrated into the world system, euro-interest rates are to be preferred over internal interest rates.

[6] The excess return on a risky asset is the return in excess of the risk-free rate of return.

a portfolio to be efficient, the ratio of any asset's marginal "good" (its contribution to the portfolio's expected excess return) to the asset's marginal "bad" (its contribution to the portfolio's variance of return) must be the same across all assets. In Chapter 13, we identified the asset's contribution to the portfolio's expected excess return as the asset's own expected excess return, while the asset's contribution to the portfolio variance can be thought of as the covariance between the asset's return and the portfolio return. Thus, the efficiency condition can be written as follows:

$$\frac{E(\tilde{r}_j - r)}{\text{cov}(\tilde{r}_j, \tilde{r}_p)} = \theta, \text{ for all risky assets } j = 1, \ 2, \ldots, N, \tag{8}$$

where r is the risk-free rate of return, and $\tilde{r}_j$ the uncertain return on asset j. The common return/risk ratio, θ, depends on the investor's attitude toward risk, and is called the investor's measure of **relative risk aversion**. A second result derived in Chapter 13 is that any efficient portfolio is a combination of (1) the risk-free asset, and (2) the tangency portfolio of risky assets.

Example   22.5

Let there be two risky assets ($j = 1, 2$), with the following expected excess returns and covariances of return:

	$E(\tilde{r}_j - r)$	(co)variances	
Asset 1	0.092	$\text{var}(\tilde{r}_1) = 0.04$	$\text{cov}(\tilde{r}_1, \tilde{r}_2) = 0.05$
Asset 2	0.148	$\text{cov}(\tilde{r}_2, \tilde{r}_1) = 0.05$	$\text{var}(\tilde{r}_2) = 0.09$

Given these data, a portfolio p with weights ($x_1 = 0.4$, $x_2 = 0.6$) is efficient. We can verify the efficiency of this portfolio in two steps:

- First we compute the contribution of each asset to the total risk of portfolio p *(covariance)*, as follows:

  Asset 1: $\text{cov}(\tilde{r}_1, \tilde{r}_p) = x_1 \, \text{cov}(\tilde{r}_1, \tilde{r}_1) + x_2 \, \text{cov}(\tilde{r}_1, \tilde{r}_2) = (0.4 \times 0.04) + (0.6 \times 0.05) = 0.046$.

  Asset 2: $\text{cov}(\tilde{r}_2, \tilde{r}_p) = x_1 \, \text{cov}(\tilde{r}_2, \tilde{r}_1) + x_2 \, \text{cov}(\tilde{r}_2, \tilde{r}_2) = (0.4 \times 0.05) + (0.6 \times 0.09) = 0.074$.

- Next we compute the excess return/risk ratio for each asset:

$$\frac{E(\tilde{r}_1 - r)}{\text{cov}(\tilde{r}_1, \tilde{r}_p)} = \frac{0.092}{0.046} = 2 \text{ and } \frac{E(\tilde{r}_2 - r)}{\text{cov}(\tilde{r}_2, \tilde{r}_p)} = \frac{0.148}{0.074} = 2.$$

The excess return/risk ratio is the same for the two assets, which implies that the portfolio is efficient. Moreover, this must be the tangency portfolio of risky assets. This is because (1) *any* efficient portfolio is a combination of the risk-free asset and the tangency portfolio of risky assets, and (2) *this* particular efficient portfolio contains no risk-free assets.

The portfolio in the example will be selected by an investor with relative risk aversion equal to $\theta = 2$. One way to detect differences in risk aversion among investors is to watch the proportions they invest in the risk-free asset. An investor with a higher relative risk aversion will allocate more of his or her wealth to the risk-free asset, and less to the tangency portfolio of risky assets.

Example   22.6

Suppose that an investor invests half of his or her wealth in the tangency portfolio identified in the previous example, and the remainder in the risk-free asset. That is, the weights in portfolio p' are $x_0 = 0.5$ for the risk-free asset, and ($x_1 = 0.2$, $x_2 = 0.3$) for the risky assets. We can easily verify that p' is still an efficient portfolio and that this investor has a relative risk aversion equal to 4:

- The risks of the assets in portfolio p' are computed as follows:[7]

$$\text{Asset 1: cov}(\tilde{r}_1, \tilde{r}_{p'}) = x_1 \text{cov}(\tilde{r}_1, \tilde{r}_1) + x_2 \text{cov}(\tilde{r}_1, \tilde{r}_2) = (0.2 \times 0.04) + (0.3 \times 0.05) = 0.023.$$
$$\text{Asset 1: cov}(\tilde{r}_2, \tilde{r}_{p'}) = x_1 \text{cov}(\tilde{r}_2, \tilde{r}_1) + x_2 \text{cov}(\tilde{r}_2, \tilde{r}_2) = (0.2 \times 0.05) + (0.3 \times 0.09) = 0.037.$$

- The excess return/risk ratio equals 4 for both risky assets:

$$\frac{E(\tilde{r}_1 - r)}{\text{cov}(\tilde{r}_1, \tilde{r}_{p'})} = \frac{0.092}{0.023} = 4 = \frac{E(\tilde{r}_2 - r)}{\text{cov}(\tilde{r}_2, \tilde{r}_{p'})} = \frac{0.148}{0.037}.$$

This illustrates how the investor's relative risk aversion can be deduced from his or her portfolio choice. Relative to the tangency portfolio chosen by an investor with $\theta = 2$, the more risk-averse investor with $\theta = 4$ simply reduces the proportion invested in the risky assets by half. This, as we saw, also reduces the (covariance) risks of each risky asset in the total portfolio by half.

22.3.2   The Market Portfolio as the Benchmark

Let us now go from an individual investor's portfolio to the **market portfolio**—defined as the aggregate asset holdings of all investors in a particular group. The group typically considered in the standard CAPM is composed of all investors in one country. This set of investors is assumed to have

---

[7] We use the fact that the return on the risk-free asset does not co-vary with any risky asset's return.

homogeneous opportunities, that is, equal access to the same list of assets, and *homogenous expecta-tions*, that is, equal perceptions about the return characteristics of the assets. The effect of these homo-geneity assumptions is that all of the investors agree about the composition of the tangency portfolio. If each investor holds the risk-free asset plus the same tangency portfolio, the aggregate portfolio must also be a combination of the risk-free asset plus that very same tangency portfolio. That is, the aggre-gate portfolio must have the same properties as any individual efficient portfolio. Therefore, for the market portfolio (denoted by subscript m), a relationship similar to Equation [8] must hold, with θ now defined as an *average* of the individuals' risk aversions:

$$\frac{E(\tilde{r}_j - r)}{\text{cov}(\tilde{r}_j, \tilde{r}_m)} = \theta, \text{ for all risky assets } j = 1, \ldots, N.$$

We can easily transform this relationship into a statement about expected excess returns:

$$E(\tilde{r}_j - r) = \theta \, \text{cov}(\tilde{r}_j, \tilde{r}_m) \text{ for all risky assets } j = 1, \ldots, N. \tag{9}$$

Although Equation [9] is not yet written in the standard CAPM form, this equation is a capital asset pricing model because it tells us what the expected excess return should be as a function of the asset's covariance risk in the market portfolio. To apply the model, we need to know the relative risk aversion for the average investor, as well as the asset's covariance risk relative to the market portfolio. In prac-tice, the covariance risk is usually estimated in *relative* form, that is, as a fraction of the portfolio's total risk, $\text{var}(\tilde{r}_m)$. Thus, Equation [9] can be rewritten as

$$E(\tilde{r}_j - r) = [\theta \, \text{var}(\tilde{r}_m)] \frac{\text{cov}(\tilde{r}_j, \tilde{r}_m)}{\text{var}(\tilde{r}_m)},$$

or

$$E(\tilde{r}_j - r) = [\theta \, \text{var}(\tilde{r}_m)] \beta_j \text{ for all risky assets } j = 1, \ldots, N. \tag{10}$$

In Equation [10], $\beta_j = \text{cov}(\tilde{r}_j, \tilde{r}_m)/\text{var}(\tilde{r}_m)$ is the asset's rescaled covariance risk, or the asset's *beta*. The advantage of rescaling the covariance risk is that β_j is also the slope coefficient from the so-called *mar-ket model*, the regression of the return from asset j, on the return from the market portfolio:

$$\tilde{r}_j = \alpha_j + \beta_j \tilde{r}_m + \tilde{\varepsilon}_j. \qquad (\textit{Market Model}) \quad [11]$$

Thus, the rescaled risk (the asset's relative risk, or market sensitivity) in Equation [10] can be esti-mated using time-series data of past stock returns and market returns. To be able to apply Equation [10] as a CAPM, we also need to identify θ, the relative risk aversion of the representative investor. The value of this parameter can be deduced by, for instance, looking at the market portfolio—the aver-age investor's portfolio. If, for every asset j, we multiply both sides of Equation [9] by j's market weight x_j, and then sum over all assets $j = 1, \ldots, N$, we obtain the following:

$$\sum_{j=1}^{N} x_j\, E(\tilde{r}_j - r) = \theta \sum_{j=1}^{N} x_j\, \mathrm{cov}(\tilde{r}_j, \tilde{r}_m)$$

$$= \theta\, \mathrm{cov}\left(\sum_{j=1}^{N} x_j \tilde{r}_j, \tilde{r}_m\right)$$

$$= \theta\, \mathrm{cov}(\tilde{r}_m, \tilde{r}_m).$$

This can be interpreted more concisely as follows:

$$E(\tilde{r}_m) - r = \theta\, \mathrm{var}(\tilde{r}_m). \tag{12}$$

It follows that

$$\theta = \frac{E(\tilde{r}_m - r)}{\mathrm{var}(\tilde{r}_m)}. \tag{13}$$

In words, the market's relative risk aversion θ is revealed by the excess return/risk ratio of the market as a whole.

Example 22.7

Assume the same data as in Example 22.6. Suppose that the market portfolio has weights ($x_0 = 0.5$, $x_1 = 0.2$, $x_2 = 0.3$). This portfolio has the same composition as portfolio p' in Example 22.6, which, as we already know, corresponds to a relative risk aversion of 4. Alternatively, we can discover the relative risk aversion as follows:[8]

$$\frac{E(\tilde{r}_m - r)}{\mathrm{var}(\tilde{r}_m)} = \frac{\displaystyle\sum_{j=1}^{N} x_j\, E(\tilde{r}_j - r)}{\displaystyle\sum_{j=1}^{N} x_j\, \mathrm{cov}(\tilde{r}_j, \tilde{r}_m)} = \frac{(0.2\times 0.092)+(0.3\times 0.148)}{(0.2\times 0.023)+(0.3\times 0.037)} = \frac{0.0628}{0.0157} = 4.$$

. Thus, the excess return/risk ratio of the market as a whole reveals the average investor's relative risk aversion, θ. Intuitively, if the expected excess return on the market for a given variance is high, it must be that the average investor has to be offered a lot of expected return before this investor is will-

---

[8] We can use the same covariance risks $\mathrm{cov}(\tilde{r}_j, \tilde{r}_{p'})$ as in Example 22.6. As shown in Chapter 13, the portfolio variance is a weighted average of the portfolio covariance risks of each component asset. We also use the fact that the return on the risk-free asset does not co-vary with any risky asset's return.

ing to take that risk. If the market portfolio is observable, we can estimate the average investor's relative risk aversion from a long series of past data, by computing the mean return and the variance of the return on the market portfolio.

Substituting Equation [13] into Equation [10], we get the traditional **CAPM** equation:

$$E(\tilde{r}_j) - r = \beta_j E(\tilde{r}_m - r),$$

[14]

with $\beta_j = \text{cov}(\tilde{r}_j, \tilde{r}_m)/\text{var}(\tilde{r}_m)$ denoting the asset's "beta" or market sensitivity. We can summarize this model as follows:

- The beta is a measure of the asset's *relative* risk—that is, the asset's market covariance risk $\text{cov}(\tilde{r}_j, \tilde{r}_m)$, rescaled by the portfolio's total risk, $\text{var}(\tilde{r}_m)$. Beta can be estimated from the market model regression (Equation [11]).
- A risky asset with beta equal to zero has an expected return that is equal to the risk-free rate, even if the asset's return is uncertain.
- If an asset's beta or relative risk is non-zero, the asset's expected return will contain a risk premium. The additional return that can be expected per unit of beta is the market's expected excess return above the risk-free rate.

22.3.3   A *Replication* Interpretation of the CAPM

A useful interpretation of the market model regression (Equation [11]) and the CAPM (Equation [14]) is as follows: Suppose that we want to hedge stock j, using the market portfolio as the hedge instrument. To hedge the stock, we form a hedge portfolio H containing an investment in the stock market portfolio (with weight x_m) and an investment in the risk-free asset (with weight $1 - x_m$). We choose the weight x_m such that the variance of $\tilde{r}_j - \tilde{r}_H$ is minimal, that is, such that the portfolio H produces the *best possible replication* of return $\tilde{r}_j$. The return on the hedge portfolio is

$$\tilde{r}_H = x_m \tilde{r}_m + (1 - x_m) r,$$

[15]

and the *best possible replication* objective can be written as

$$\underset{x_m}{\text{Minimize}} \ \text{var}[\tilde{r}_j - (x_m \tilde{r}_m + (1 - x_m) r)].$$

This is the same problem as the one we considered in Chapter 5, when we discussed hedging with futures.[9] We can therefore use the same solution: $x_m = \text{cov}(\tilde{r}_j, \tilde{r}_m)/\text{var}(\tilde{r}_m)$, which is simply the

---

[9] Except that now we want to minimize the variance of a (percentage) *return* rather than the variance of a market *value*, and we now are looking for an optimal portfolio weight rather than an optimal number of contracts.

stock's beta. Thus, the beta tells us how one can best replicate the return from stock j if the replicating instruments are the market portfolio and the risk-free asset.

Example   22.8

Suppose that $\beta_j = 0.75$. If we invest 75 percent in the market and 25 percent in the risk-free asset, we hold a portfolio that offers the best possible replication of asset j's return, among all portfolios that consist only of the market portfolio and the risk-free asset.

The CAPM then tells us that the expected return on stock j is equal to the expected return on its best replicating portfolio. To understand this, set $x_m = \beta_j$ in Equation [15], and take expectations:

$$E(\tilde{r}_H) = \beta_j\, E(\tilde{r}_m) + (1 - \beta_j)\, r$$

$$= r + \beta_j\, [\,E(\tilde{r}_m) - r\,]$$

$$= E(\tilde{r}_j),$$

where the last result follows from Equation [14]. Thus, the logic of the CAPM is to some extent similar to the logic of asset-pricing-by-replication, as used in Part I of this book, except that we now use the *best possible* replication rather than *exact replication*. Because the replication is not exact, we need the CAPM assumptions to justify why the expected return on an asset should be the same as the expected return on its best replicating portfolio, and why the market portfolio is the only replication instrument that is necessary.

22.3.4   When to Use the Single-Country CAPM

The CAPM as derived in Section 22.2.2 is routinely used in capital budgeting to determine the return that shareholders expect on investments with a given level of beta risk. For many countries, *beta-service companies* provide estimates of the expected excess market return and of betas for various industries. Yet, one ought to interpret these figures with some caution. The assumption that underlies many of these estimates is that the CAPM holds country-by-country, in the sense that the market portfolio is equated with the portfolio of all assets issued by firms from that country alone. For example, beta service companies in the US tend to compute the beta of, say, the US computer industry by regressing the returns from a portfolio of US computer firms on the Standard and Poor's index, which is an index of five hundred US stocks traded on the New York Stock Exchange. Likewise, in France, one would often estimate the risk of, say, the French steel industry by regressing the returns from a portfolio of steel companies on the index of French stocks. In the same vein, the expected excess return on the market would be estimated from past returns on the Standard and Poor's index or on the index of French stocks traded at the Paris *Bourse,* respectively.

Is the market portfolio of assets held by a country's investors the same as the portfolio of assets issued by the country's corporations? This is only true if investors have access to local shares only *and* if all local shares are held by residents of the country. That is, if one equates the market portfolio with the portfolio of locally issued shares, capital markets are assumed to be fully *segmented.* However, in most countries there are no rules against international share ownership; investors can easily diversify into foreign assets, and foreigners are allowed to buy domestic shares. Thus, the traditional interpretation that the market portfolio consists of the index of stocks issued by local companies is valid only in segmented markets.

Example   22.9

Until recently, the stock markets of India, South Korea, and Taiwan were almost perfectly segmented from the rest of the world in the sense that foreigners could buy only a small fraction of the local stocks, and local investors could not easily buy foreign assets. Thus, the Indian market portfolio was essentially the same as the portfolio of stocks issued by Indian firms, and similar for Korea and Taiwan.

In the presence of market segmentation, the cost of capital to be used by, say, a Canadian firm is likely to be different from the cost of capital to be used by an Indian firm, even when these companies are evaluating similarly investments. The question addressed in the next section is how, say, a Canadian firm should determine its cost of capital. There are no rules that prevent Canadian investors from buying US or European assets, nor are nonresidents barred from buying Canadian stocks. Thus, the index of stocks issued by Canadian firms may be a poor proxy for the portfolio held by the average Canadian investor. It follows that a Canadian firm cannot use the single-country CAPM to set the cost of capital for an investment project, whether the project is domestic or foreign.

22.4   THE INTERNATIONAL CAPM

As we just stated, there are no rules preventing Canadian investors from buying US or European assets; nor are there any regulations barring nonresidents from buying Canadian stocks. Still, this mere fact is not sufficient to lead to international diversification by investors. In Section 22.4.1, we argue that there are, in fact, strong incentives for investors to diversify internationally. Section 22.4.2 then explains the role of exchange risk for asset pricing in an internationally integrated capital market. In Section 22.4.3, we derive a two-country version of the International CAPM of Solnik (1973) and Sercu (1980, 1981a). The generalization to the case with many countries and stochastic inflation is discussed in Section 22.4.4. We conclude, in Section 22.4.5, with a review of empirical tests of the International CAPM.

22.4.1   International Diversification and Its Implications for the Single-Country CAPM

Diversification into foreign assets is helpful if the returns on the additional assets are imperfectly correlated with the return on another asset already held. In practice, returns on foreign assets *are* imperfectly correlated with returns on domestic assets.[10] Thus, it is always useful for an investor to include foreign assets in a portfolio. As an illustration, Figure 22.1 shows an estimated efficient set computed from only US assets, and a second efficient set derived from a menu of assets that includes all OECD and NIC (Newly Industrialized Countries) markets. The wider menu clearly improves the investment

---

[10] Even when one computes correlations among national stock indices, the coefficients are surprisingly low—typically no higher than 0.5, even when monthly returns are used to estimate correlations. For individual assets, where the firm-specific "noise" is much higher, the correlations are even lower. For daily or weekly returns, the correlations are likewise lower. Roll (1992) and Heston and Rouwenhorst (1994) discuss some reasons why correlations are low.

FIGURE 22.1   The Efficient Set without and with International Diversification

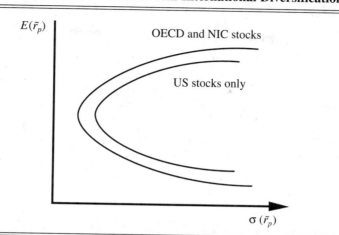

opportunity set; at any level of standard deviation, higher expected returns are available or, at any level of expected return, it is possible to reduce the risk relative to the portfolio with only US stocks.

Thus, international diversification is beneficial for the investor, and investors do use this added opportunity to reduce risks. Clearly, it is then no longer acceptable to use a CAPM equation with, as its benchmark portfolio, the local stock index (defined as the index of all securities issued by firms incorporated in the country). First, this benchmark omits foreign assets, which represent an important component of the local investor's asset holdings. Second, this benchmark ignores the fact that a substantial part of the stocks issued by local corporations are, in fact, held by nonresidents.[11] All of this means that, in internationally integrated markets, the true stock market portfolio for any country is unobservable—and, with an unobservable national stock market portfolio, the standard CAPM is of no practical use to managers who, for instance, want to assess the cost of capital or evaluate the performance of their investment advisers.

22.4.2   The Roles of Exchange Risk in International Asset Pricing

How can we get around this problem of an unobservable market portfolio? One could argue that, even if we do not know what shares are held by whom, we can still observe the *world* market portfolio, or at least the portfolio of assets from countries that allow free capital movements, which coincides roughly with the OECD.[12] As investors do hold assets from all over the OECD, and as the OECD market portfolio is observable, a very simple approach to international asset pricing would be to interpret the OECD as one huge country, and use the OECD market portfolio as the benchmark.

---

[11] The same problem arises when one includes into the market portfolio all stocks—domestic or foreign—that are *listed* on the national stock exchange(s). Investors can (and do) buy foreign assets in foreign stock exchanges, or can (and do) buy foreign assets through mutual funds that are traded over-the-counter; and all of these investments are missing from the menu of locally listed stocks.

[12] This OECD market portfolio is the sum of all securities issued by all firms in the OECD, and this portfolio can be obtained by constructing a value-weighted sum of all member countries' local stock indices. A well-known proxy for such an international stock market index is the Morgan Stanley Capital International (MSCI) index.

There is, however, one important reason why international asset pricing in integrated capital markets cannot simply be reduced to an as-if-one-country CAPM. Even though international capital transactions are unrestricted and have low costs, transactions in the commodity markets are still difficult and costly. These imperfections in the goods market, as we saw in Chapter 11, lead to substantial deviations from relative purchasing power parity and to *real exchange risk*. The (real) return on, say, IBM common stock as realized by a German investor differs from the (real) return realized by a Dutch investor on the same asset. As a result, the distributions of the real return from a given asset depend on the nationality of the investor. This then violates the *homogeneous expectations* assumption of the CAPM, which states that all investors agree on the probability distribution of the (real) asset returns. In a sense, the investors' perceptions about return distributions are segmented along country lines because goods prices differ across countries, implying that investors from various countries have different views on the distributions of real returns on any given asset or portfolio.

Example   22.10

An extreme example is the return on the T-bill. Suppose that there is no inflation. To a US investor, the CAD T-bill is one of the available *risky* assets. To a Canadian investor, the CAD T-bill is risk free. On the other hand, the USD T-bill is a risky asset to a Canadian investor, and it is risk free to a US investor. Thus, the perceived distribution of (real) returns depends on the nationality of the investor.

Thus, we need to derive a CAPM that takes into account the heterogeneous viewpoints of investors from various countries. In keeping with our discussion of the standard CAPM, we initially ignore inflation. To simplify the analysis, we shall assume there are just two countries, the US and Canada. Once you understand the two-country model, you can easily generalize to the case of many countries.

The problem is that the Canadian investor's portfolio choice is based on how each asset contributes to the variance and expected excess return on the portfolio *measured in CAD*, while the US investor's portfolio choice is based on the assets' contributions to a portfolio whose risk and return are *expressed in USD*. To make aggregation possible, we have to choose a common numeraire. Let us (arbitrarily) choose the CAD as the reference currency, and let us agree on the following notation: the asterisk refers to the foreign country (the US), p^*, refers to the portfolio held by the US investor, $\tilde{r}_{p}^{*}$ denotes the return, in USD, on p^*, and $\tilde{r}_{p*}$ denotes the return on p^* in terms of CAD. The relationship between returns measured in CAD and in USD then is as follows:

$$1 + \tilde{r}_{p*} = (1 + \tilde{r}_{p}^{*})(1 + \tilde{s}_{\text{CAD/USD}}).$$
[16]

Conversely,

$$1 + \tilde{r}_{p}^{*} = \frac{1 + \tilde{r}_{p*}}{1 + \tilde{s}_{\text{CAD/USD}}}.$$
[17]

Thus, although the US investor is really concerned about the distribution of $\tilde{r}^*_p$, we can also think of the investor as being concerned about the joint distribution of the portfolio return expressed in CAD, $\tilde{r}_{p*}$, and the exchange rate change $\tilde{s}_{CAD/USD}$.[13] The implication is that the average world investor, being a combination of Canadian and US investors, can be thought of as being concerned about the return in CAD and the CAD/USD exchange rate.

22.4.3   The Two-Country CAPM

We have seen that in a single-country model, the investors care about the distribution of one variable (the portfolio return). In a two-country model, the investors care about the joint distribution of two variables—the portfolio return measured in base currency (the CAD) and the exchange rate. This implies that, for the average investor, the mean and variance of the portfolio return are no longer sufficient to rank portfolios. We first discuss what moments are needed to rank portfolios,[14] and then we present the corresponding fundamental risk-return relationship.

Distribution Parameters Needed to Rank Portfolios

In a mean-and-(co)variance framework, the joint distribution of the portfolio return (in terms of CAD) and the CAD/USD exchange rate would be summarized by the *means and variances* of the portfolio return and of the exchange rate, plus the *covariance* between them: $E(\tilde{r}_p)$, $\text{var}(\tilde{r}_p)$, $\text{cov}(\tilde{r}_p, \tilde{s})$, $E(\tilde{s})$, and $\text{var}(\tilde{s})$. These are the moments on which portfolio choice of the average world investor is based. The first three of these moments depend on the portfolio composition, that is, on the asset weights x_j:

- Expected excess portfolio return:

$$E(\tilde{r}_p - r) = E(\sum_{j=1}^{N} x_j \tilde{r}_j - r) = \sum_{j=1}^{N} x_j E(\tilde{r}_j - r).$$ [18]

- Variance of the portfolio return:

$$\text{var}(\tilde{r}_p) = \text{cov}(\sum_{j=1}^{N} x_j \tilde{r}_j, \tilde{r}_p) = \sum_{j=1}^{N} x_j \text{cov}(\tilde{r}_j, \tilde{r}_p).$$ [19]

- Covariance of the portfolio return with the exchange rate:

$$\text{cov}(\tilde{r}_p, \tilde{s}) = \text{cov}(\sum_{j=1}^{N} x_j \tilde{r}_j, \tilde{s}) = \sum_{j=1}^{N} x_j \text{cov}(\tilde{r}_j, \tilde{s}),$$ [20]

where $\tilde{s}$ is the percentage change in the CAD/USD spot rate. The other relevant moments are $E(\tilde{s})$ and $\text{var}(\tilde{s})$. These are not affected by the portfolio weights x_j, and can be ignored in the portfolio

---

[13] For the technically interested reader: we can use Ito's Lemma (introduced in Appendix B of Chapter 8) to translate the USD portfolio return into CAD. If all returns are interpreted as annualized returns over short intervals, the relevant relationship is $\tilde{r}^*_{p*} = \tilde{r}_{p*} - \tilde{s} - \text{cov}(\tilde{r}_{p*}, \tilde{s}) + \text{var}(\tilde{s})$. (Recall that the covariance and variance term reflect the expected value of the largest cross-terms, plus the fact that, for short periods, the variability in these cross-terms is trivial.) If the US investor ranks portfolios on the basis of $E(\tilde{r}^*_{p*})$ and $\text{var}(\tilde{r}^*_{p*})$, he or she can also be viewed as ranking the portfolios on the basis of $E(\tilde{r}_{p*})$, $\text{var}(\tilde{r}_{p*})$, $E(\tilde{s})$, $\text{cov}(\tilde{r}_{p*}, \tilde{s})$, and $\text{var}(\tilde{s})$.

[14] In statistics, the moments of a joint distribution are the means, variances, covariances, skewness, kurtosis, and so on.

problem.[15] Thus, Equations [18]–[20] describe the relevant moments and their link to portfolio choice. Relative to the one-country model, there is a new risk dimension—the covariance of the portfolio return with the exchange rate. From Equation [20], we see that this covariance is determined by the portfolio weights and the individual assets' covariances with exchange rates. These covariances are discussed in the next section.

Exchange Rate Covariance Risk for Individual Assets

For a better understanding of the exchange rate covariance risk of individual assets, it is convenient to scale the covariance risk by the exchange rate variance. Consider the following regression equation:

$$\tilde{r}_j = \alpha_j + \gamma_j \, \tilde{s}_{CAD/USD} + \tilde{\varepsilon}_j. \tag{21}$$

The regression coefficient γ_j equals $cov(\tilde{r}_j, \tilde{s})/var(\tilde{s})$—the asset's exchange rate covariance risk, scaled by the variance of the exchange rate change. In this sense, γ_j measures the relative exchange risk of asset j, or the *relative exposure* of asset j to the exchange rate. We now consider the exchange rate exposure of three types of assets: a foreign risk-free asset, a foreign stock, and a domestic stock.

- The first asset we consider is the USD T-bill, asset 1. The return, measured in CAD, on the USD T-bill increases by one percent if the CAD/USD spot rate increases by one percent. This follows from[16]

$$\tilde{r}_{USD} \equiv \text{CAD return on the USD T-bill} = r^*_{USD} + \tilde{s}_{CAD/USD}. \tag{22}$$

  Clearly, if $\tilde{r}_{USD} = r^*_{USD} + \tilde{s}_{CAD/USD}$, then, in the relative exposure regression Equation [21], we must have $\gamma_{USD} = 1$ (and $\alpha_{USD} = r^*_{USD}$, $\tilde{\varepsilon}_{USD} = 0$). In this sense, the exposure regression (Equation [21]) for the foreign T-bill will reveal a very clear nationality for that asset. In CAD terms, the USD T-bill is exposed one-to-one to its "own" exchange rate, CAD/USD.

- Let us now consider a Canadian stock, asset 2. From Chapter 18, we know that typically an appreciation of the USD relative to the CAD is good news for the Canadian firm, because its competitive position has improved. Thus, for a Canadian firm, the relative exposure (γ_j) is usually positive, albeit less than unity.

- Finally, consider a share of a US corporation, asset 3. Holding constant the USD price of the stock, a one percent appreciation of the USD adds one percent to the return on that stock in

---

[15] To understand this, think of a standard microeconomics problem where firms have to decide on an optimal output. In this problem, fixed costs are relevant in the sense that they affect profits. However, fixed costs can be ignored for the production decision in the sense that fixed costs do not affect the output decision; two firms, identical in all respects except for their fixed costs, will arrive at exactly the same decision. Likewise, the mean and the variance of the exchange rate are relevant in the sense that they will affect expected utility, but they can be ignored in the portfolio problem because the portfolio weights do not affect $E(\tilde{s})$ and $var(\tilde{s})$ and *vice versa*.

[16] For the purists: the cross-term in Equation [16] is dropped because, for short intervals (see Appendix B to Chapter 8), the only relevant component in such a cross-term is the covariance; and r^*_{USD}, being nonstochastic, has a zero covariance with $\tilde{s}_{CAD/USD}$.

CAD. However, an appreciation of the USD simultaneously is bad news for this company, because its competitive position has deteriorated. Thus, the price of the stock measured in USD typically drops when the USD appreciates. This drop in the USD value of the stock weakens the effect of the exchange rate itself, and will lead to a relative exposure that is below unity.

Example   22.11

Suppose that, empirically, the stock price in USD of a US firm goes down by, on average, 0.25 percent for a 1 percent increase in the CAD/USD rate. This then implies that the return, in CAD, on the stock will go up by about 0.75 percent for a one percent rise in the CAD/USD rate. That is, the Canadian investor has to subtract the 0.25 percent capital loss in USD terms from the 1 percent gain on the USD.

We conclude that exchange rate covariance risks can be very different for different assets. The relative exposure of a foreign T-bill is unity, but the relative exposure of a *foreign* stock is likely to be less than unity. And the relative exposure of a *domestic* stock is likely to be positive. In terms of relative exposure, a Canadian firm could even be more *foreign* than a US firm; that is unlike T-bills, stocks have no clear-cut nationality.

The Relation between Risk and Return in the Asset Market

We argued that, in general, investors care about exchange rate covariance risk and we have explained that stocks can have complex correlation patterns with the exchange rate. Since investors care about this exchange risk, the assets' covariance with the exchange rate change will be associated with additional risk premiums per unit of exchange rate covariance risk. We end up with optimal aggregate portfolio conditions that are simple generalizations of Equation [9] for a one-country problem:

$$E(\tilde{r}_j - r) = \theta \operatorname{cov}(\tilde{r}_j, \tilde{r}_w) + \eta \operatorname{cov}(\tilde{r}_j, \tilde{s}), \qquad [23]$$

where the subscript w (within the first covariance term) refers to the world market portfolio, and where θ and η are prices of the corresponding covariance risks. In Sercu (1980), it is shown that θ is the aggregate relative risk aversion of the world market as a whole, and η depends on the risk aversion and wealth of the foreign country.

Equation [23] is basically a capital asset pricing model. The expected return required by the market, over and above the risk-free rate, is said to consist of two risk premiums for covariance risks. First, there is the covariance of the asset return with the return on total invested wealth, $\tilde{r}_w$; and second, there is covariance risk of the asset return with respect to changes in the exchange rate. The reason for the first risk premium is the same as in the single-country CAPM. Holding everything else constant, the investor dislikes variance of invested wealth, and is concerned about how much the stock adds to the variance of the total portfolio return. The premium for exchange covariance risk can be traced back to the fact that the average investor is also concerned about the covariance of CAD returns with the exchange rate. As a result, the average investor will consider how much an asset adds to the covariance of the portfolio return with the exchange rate.[17]

Interpreting the Risk Premiums θ *and* η

The International CAPM, as represented in Equation [23], is not yet operational because the risk premiums (θ and η) per unit of each covariance risk are not readily observable. In the one-country CAPM, we solved a similar problem by looking at the market portfolio's excess return/risk characteristics; and, as a by-product, we discovered a link with the market model regression of $\tilde{r}_j$ on the market return. This can be done here, too. To identify the two risk premiums, we now need *two* benchmarks. In view of the fact that the covariances are taken with respect to the world market portfolio and the exchange rate, we take the world market portfolio as one benchmark, and, as the second benchmark, we choose the pure exchange risk asset, the foreign (USD) T-bill. Thus, we have a system of two special versions of Equation [23]:

- For the world market portfolio, with expected return $E(\tilde{r}_w)$, we have

$$
\begin{aligned}
E(\tilde{r}_w) - r &= \theta \operatorname{cov}(\tilde{r}_w, \tilde{r}_w) + \eta \operatorname{cov}(\tilde{r}_w, \tilde{s}) \\
&= \theta \operatorname{var}(\tilde{r}_w) + \eta \operatorname{cov}(\tilde{r}_w, \tilde{s}).
\end{aligned}
\tag{24}
$$

- For the USD T-bill, with expected total return (in terms of CAD) equal to $E(\tilde{s}) + r^*$, we have

$$
\begin{aligned}
E(\tilde{s}) + r^* - r &= \theta \operatorname{cov}(\tilde{s}, \tilde{r}_w) + \eta \operatorname{cov}(\tilde{s}, \tilde{s}) \\
&= \theta \operatorname{cov}(\tilde{s}, \tilde{r}_w) + \eta \operatorname{var}(\tilde{s}).
\end{aligned}
\tag{25}
$$

Equations [24] and [25] allow us to identify θ and η as functions of the expected excess returns on the benchmarks and the covariance matrix of the benchmark returns. Let us consider an analytically simple case where the return on the world market portfolio is uncorrelated with the exchange rate. If $\operatorname{cov}(\tilde{r}_w, \tilde{s}) = 0$, we can easily solve Equation [24] for θ and Equation [25] for η. If $\operatorname{cov}(\tilde{r}_w, \tilde{s}) = 0$, then:

$$
\theta = \frac{E(\tilde{r}_w) - r}{\operatorname{var}(\tilde{r}_w)} \text{ and } \eta = \frac{E(\tilde{s}) + r^* - r}{\operatorname{var}(\tilde{s})}.
\tag{26}
$$

Substituting these results into Equation [23], we then obtain

$$
\begin{aligned}
E(\tilde{r}_j - r) &= \frac{E(\tilde{r}_w) - r}{\operatorname{var}(\tilde{r}_w)} \operatorname{cov}(\tilde{r}_j, \tilde{r}_w) + \frac{E(\tilde{s}) + r^* - r}{\operatorname{var}(\tilde{s})} \operatorname{cov}(\tilde{r}_j, \tilde{s}), \\
&= \frac{\operatorname{cov}(\tilde{r}_j, \tilde{r}_w)}{\operatorname{var}(\tilde{r}_w)} E(\tilde{r}_w - r) + \frac{\operatorname{cov}(\tilde{r}_j, \tilde{s})}{\operatorname{var}(\tilde{s})} E(\tilde{s} + r^* - r),
\end{aligned}
$$

---

[17] See section 22.4.2 for a discussion of why the average investor cares about covariance of CAD returns with the exchange rate.

or

$$E(\tilde{r}_j - r) = \beta_j E(\tilde{r}_w - r) + \gamma_j E(\tilde{s} + r^* - r),$$ [27]

where, if $\text{cov}(\tilde{r}_w, \tilde{s}) = 0$, $\beta_j = \text{cov}(\tilde{r}_j, \tilde{r}_w)/\text{var}(\tilde{r}_w)$ is the stock's market sensitivity from the market model regression (Equation [11]), and $\gamma_j = \text{cov}(\tilde{r}_j, \tilde{s})/\text{var}(\tilde{s})$ is the stock's relative exposure from the regression (Equation [21]). In the appendix, we show that, when $\text{cov}(\tilde{r}_w, \tilde{s}) \neq 0$, result [27] still holds with the proviso that β_j and γ_j can no longer be estimated from separate regressions. Rather, when $\text{cov}(\tilde{r}_w, \tilde{s}) \neq 0$, β_j and γ_j must be estimated *jointly*, using a single regression of the following form

$$\tilde{r}_j = \alpha + \beta_j \tilde{r}_w + \gamma_j \tilde{s} + \tilde{\varepsilon}_j.$$ [28]

When β_j and γ_j are defined as the regression coefficients from Equation [28], then Equation [27] becomes the CAPM that describes equilibrium expected returns in a world with two countries, real exchange risk, and an integrated capital market.[18] To interpret the regression (Equation [28]) and the International CAPM (Equation [27]), note that regression (Equation [28]) again identifies the *best possible replication* of asset j that one can achieve using the two benchmark portfolios, the world market portfolio, and the foreign T-bill, along with the risk-free asset.

Example   22.12

Suppose that, for a US stock, the coefficients in Equation [28] are estimated as $\beta_j = 1.2$ and $\gamma_j = 0.75$. Consider portfolios that consist of an investment in the world market portfolio (with weight x_w), an investment in the USD T-bill (with weight x_s), and weight $1 - x_w - x_s$ invested in the CAD risk-free asset. If $\beta_j = 1.2$ and $\gamma_j = 0.75$, we invest $x_w = 1.2$ in the world market portfolio, $x_s = 0.75$ in the USD T-bill, and $1 - 1.20 - 0.75 = -0.95$ in the domestic risk-free asset. This portfolio provides the best possible replication of the return from asset j using just the two benchmark portfolios as replicating instruments.

The International CAPM then says that the expected return on a stock j is the same as the expected return on the stock's best replication portfolio. This can be shown as follows. In the first line, we write the return on a general portfolio with weights x_w and x_s for the world market and the foreign T-bill, and in the second line we group terms in x_w and x_s:

$$E(\tilde{r}_H) = x_w E(\tilde{r}_w) + x_s [E(\tilde{s}) + r^*] + (1 - x_w - x_s)r$$
$$= r + x_w E(\tilde{r}_w - r) + x_s E(\tilde{s} + r^* - r).$$

---

[18] In the general case, the multivariate coefficients are no longer given by $\beta_j = \text{cov}(\tilde{r}_j, \tilde{r}_w)/\text{var}(\tilde{r}_w)$ and $\gamma_j = \text{cov}(\tilde{r}_j, \tilde{s})/\text{var}(\tilde{s})$.

For best replication, we have to set $x_w = \beta_j$ and $x_s = \gamma_j$. Thus,

$$E(\tilde{r}_H) = r + \beta_j E(\tilde{r}_w - r) + \gamma_j E(\tilde{s} + r^* - r)$$

$$= E(\tilde{r}_j),$$

from Equation [27].

22.4.4   Extensions of the Two-Country CAPM

We discuss two extensions to the CAPM described above. First, we show how the two-country integrated-market model can be generalized to cases where there are more than two countries in the unified capital market. Second, we discuss the adjustments for inflation risk.

The General No-Inflation International CAPM

Suppose that there are $L > 1$ foreign countries, that is, $L + 1$ countries including the base country. In such a setting, the world's average investor is concerned about variance of the return on invested wealth (the world market portfolio), and about the covariance of this portfolio return with each of the L exchange rates. That is, Equation [23] is generalized into

$$E(\tilde{r}_j - r) = \theta \, \text{cov}(\tilde{r}_j, \tilde{r}_w) + \eta_1 \, \text{cov}(\tilde{r}_j, \tilde{s}_1) + \eta_2 \, \text{cov}(\tilde{r}_j, \tilde{s}_2) + \ldots + \eta_L \, \text{cov}(\tilde{r}_j, \tilde{s}_L). \quad [29]$$

Thus, there will be L relevant exchange rate exposures, and a beta. These measures of risk are to be estimated jointly from the following generalization of the exposure/market model regression (Equation [28]):

$$\tilde{r}_j = \alpha_j + \beta_j \tilde{r}_w + \gamma_{j1} \tilde{s}_1 + \gamma_{j2} \tilde{s}_2 + \ldots + \gamma_{jL} \tilde{s}_L + \tilde{\varepsilon}_j. \quad [30]$$

The combination of Equations [29] and [30] produces a result analogous to Equation [27]:

$$E(\tilde{r}_j - r) = \beta_j E(\tilde{r}_w - r)$$
$$+ \gamma_{j1} E(\tilde{s}_1 + r_1^* - r) + \gamma_{j2} E(\tilde{s}_2 + r_2^* - r) + \ldots + \gamma_{jL} E(\tilde{s}_L + r_L^* - r). \quad [31]$$

The regression coefficients in Equation [30] still correspond to the portfolio weights that provide the best possible replication of the return on asset j. The International CAPM (Equation [31]) then tells us that the asset is entitled to the same expected excess return as its best replicating portfolio.

The International CAPM with Inflation Risk

As we described in Section 22.4.2, real exchange risk is a prime source of complication in international asset pricing. When there are deviations from relative purchasing power parity, the real return from a particular asset realized by a US investor differs from the real return realized by a Canadian investor. Thus far, we assumed no inflation and ignored the difference between nominal and real returns as well as between nominal and real exchange rate changes. However, when there is inflation, investors are concerned with *real* returns, and the source of differences between real returns to Canadians and real returns to US investors is the change in the *real* exchange rate (as discussed in Chapter 11).

With uncertain inflation, we should deflate all returns using the base currency's inflation rate, and we should replace the exchange rate changes by changes in real exchange rates. However, Adler and Dumas (1983) show, in a very elegant way, how Equation [31] has to be adjusted to account for inflation risk. Their empirical work also shows that this adjustment is not very important. Because of the low covariances between asset returns and inflation rates, covariances between real excess returns on different assets are almost indistinguishable from covariances between nominal excess returns on these assets.

22.4.5 Empirical Tests of the International CAPM

In this chapter, we are suggesting that you replace your familiar single-market CAPM equation by a more complicated version, Equation [31]. The first issue is whether one of the basic assumptions of the international model, the absence of controls on capital flows, is reasonable. Second, are the empirical data compatible with the International CAPM and, if so, can we also reject the single-country view of the world?

Let us first examine the effect of direct controls on foreign investment. The controls may either limit foreign investment into a country or restrict domestic residents from investing abroad. Restrictions on foreign investment into a country may be imposed in different ways—in the form of a limit on the fraction of equity that can be held by foreigners or a restriction on the types of industries in which foreigners can invest. Details on the type and magnitude of these restrictions can be found in Eun and Janakiramanan (1986, Table 1). There may also be domestic controls on how much a resident can invest abroad. For example, Japanese insurance companies may not invest more than 30 percent of their portfolio in foreign assets, and only 30 percent of Spanish pension funds may be invested abroad. Two questions need to be answered. One, if these restrictions exist, do they have a significant impact on the choice of the optimal portfolio and hence, potentially, on asset pricing? Two, how significant are these constraints today?

Bonser-Neal, Brauer, Neal and Wheatley (1990) examine whether the restrictions on investing abroad are binding. They look at closed-end country funds and find that these mutual funds trade at premiums relative to their net asset values, indicating that the French, Japanese, Korean, and Mexican markets are at least partially segmented from the US capital market. Hietala (1989) studies the effects of the Finnish law that prevented investors from investing in foreign securities and finds that there is a significant difference between the returns on domestic assets required by residents compared to foreigners. Gultekin, Gultekin, and Penati (1989) find strong evidence that the US and Japanese markets were segmented prior to 1980.[19] However, while there were substantial controls on capital flows before the 1980s, this is no longer true. Halliday (1989) reports that there are few constraints on investing in foreign stock markets. This is especially true for investing in the markets of developed countries. For example, there are no controls on investment by foreigners into Austria, Belgium, Denmark, Ireland, Italy, Japan, Netherlands, the UK, the US, and West Germany. The controls studied by Hietala (1989) and Gultekin, Gultekin, and Penati (1989) were removed in 1986 and 1980, respectively. Also,

---

[19] For other studies on capital market segmentation, see Errunza and Losq (1985), Jorion and Schwartz (1986), Cho, Eun, and Senbet (1986), and Wheatley (1988).

looking at restrictions that limit domestic residents from investing abroad, one sees that these constraints are often not binding. For example, Fairlamb (1989) reports that in 1988 only 8 percent of Spanish funds were actually invested in foreign assets, while the limit was 30 percent. Thus, while direct controls on foreign investment may have been important in the past, they are probably no longer an important determinant of portfolio choice and asset pricing in the main OECD countries.

Let us now discuss the more direct tests of international asset pricing models. Solnik (1973), who did the first theoretical and empirical work in international asset pricing, tests a special case of Equation [31], where the world market risk premium and exposure risk premiums could be merged into one single term.[20] He concludes that the data are consistent with his International CAPM, although he does not test his model against the single-country alternative.

A test that does compare an international asset pricing model against the single-country alternative was carried out by Stehle (1976). Specifically, Stehle tries to find out empirically whether US stocks are priced in a national market or in a world market. He, too, uses a restricted version of Equation [29], assuming that all risk premiums, η_i, are zero.[21] When $\eta_i = 0$, the only difference between the international model (Equation [29]) and the national model is the definition of the market portfolio. Specifically, in Equation [29], the benchmark portfolio is the world market portfolio, while in Equation [9], it is the national market portfolio. Stehle's tests are not able to empirically reject one in favor of the other, and Stehle concludes that asset pricing is done in a single-market context. Dumas (1976), however, argues that when the data do not allow one to distinguish between single-country asset pricing and international asset pricing, then one ought to retain the simplest view—that is, one should conclude that there is one international market instead of the many separate national markets.

As already mentioned, Gultekin, Gultekin, and Penati (1989) provide strong evidence that the US and Japanese markets were segmented prior to 1980. However, they also show that after the enactment of the Foreign Exchange and Foreign Trade Control law in 1980, there is no longer any significant evidence against the hypothesis that US and Japanese stocks are priced in an integrated market.

There have been many additional empirical investigations, with a large portion of them testing special restricted versions of Equation [29]. The conclusions tend to be ambiguous. A careful recent test is by Dumas and Solnik (1991). They test the Solnik-Sercu International CAPM (Equation [29]), allowing for changes in risks and risk premiums over time. Using data from major OECD countries, they reject Stehle's hypothesis that the exposure risk premiums, η_i, are zero, but they do not reject the full version (with non-zero risk premiums for exchange rate exposure). They also reject single-country asset pricing (with a purely local benchmark). All of this lends support to the International CAPM, at least for the major OECD countries that do not impose explicit restrictions on capital movement.

22.5   CONCLUSIONS FOR CAPITAL BUDGETING

In this section, we summarize our discussion on the determination of the cost of capital. International asset pricing is complicated by two issues—exchange risk, and segmentation of capital markets. If the

---

20 Solnik assumed that stocks *do* have clear-cut nationalities, in the sense that the slope coefficient γ_j in regression [21] is zero for a domestic (Canadian) stock and unity for a foreign (US) stock. This allows him to simplify the model.

21 Stehle selected a utility function that implies $\eta = 0$. Thus, in this special International CAPM, only the market risk is rewarded. But the one-benchmark model may be approximately correct even without this restriction on utility functions, as long as exchange risk premiums are small. In Chapter 14, we found that they are, in fact, small in the short run, and close to zero in the long run.

capital market of the home country and the host country are integrated, the cash flows of an investment project can be valued in any currency, including the host currency. This simplifies capital budgeting in the sense that no exchange rate forecasts are necessary for the translation. On the other hand, in integrated markets it becomes impossible to observe the portfolio of risky assets held by the average investor in any of the individual countries. Thus, the International CAPM has to be used, which means that exchange rate expectations still show up in the cost of capital.

Thus, the first issue is whether or not there is integration. Having selected either the single-country CAPM or the International CAPM, the next issue is to obtain estimates of the model parameters. We need the stock market sensitivity or beta and, in the International CAPM, the exchange rate exposures. We also need the expected return on the corresponding benchmark portfolios.

22.5.1   Determining the Relevant Model

If the capital market of the home country and the host country are segmented from each other, the investing firm should set the cost of capital equal to the return that is expected by its own shareholders. This means that a particular investment may be profitable for a foreign firm but not profitable for a local firm.

Example   22.13

The Indian stock market has been segmented from the rest of the world. If an Indian firm makes an investment in India, the firm will estimate the beta by regressing returns from a portfolio of stocks in the same industry on the Indian stock market index. Note that the returns from this investment are likely to be strongly correlated with the Indian market index because there are important common factors, like the business cycle or interest rates, that affect all Indian firms in similar ways. Thus, the investment is relatively risky for an Indian firm. But the same project may be low-risk from the point of view of, say, an Austrian firm. The reason is that, because the Indian economy has been strongly isolated from the rest of the world, the returns from the Indian project will be almost uncorrelated with the returns on the Austrian market portfolio (which is strongly diversified internationally).

Note that segmentation of the home-country and the host-country capital markets does not mean that each market is a single-country market. The shareholders of the Austrian firm are likely to live in many different countries, and they all have access to non-Austrian shares, too. Thus, it may be appropriate for the Austrian firm to set its cost of capital using an international model, that is, using the OECD market portfolio as a proxy for the true benchmark relevant to its shareholders.

22.5.2   Estimating the Risk of a Project

The market risk and the exchange risk exposures are defined as the slope coefficients in the following regression:

$$\tilde{r}_j = \alpha_j + \beta_j \tilde{r}_w + \gamma_{j1}\, \tilde{s}_1 + \gamma_{j2}\, \tilde{s}_2 + \ldots + \gamma_{jL}\, \tilde{s}_L + \tilde{\varepsilon}_j. \qquad [30]$$

Estimates obtained from time series of past data are subject to substantial estimation errors. A standard solution is to estimate the risks from returns on *industry portfolios* rather than from individual stock data. That is, one estimates returns on, typically, an equally weighted portfolio of all stocks in the same industry i:

$$\text{Return for the } i\text{-th industry portfolio} = \tilde{r}_i = \sum\nolimits_{j \in I_i} \frac{\tilde{r}_j}{N_i},$$

where the set I_i contains all of the firms that belong to industry i, and N_i is the number of firms in industry i. One then estimates the risks by using, in regression [30], the industry portfolio returns rather than individual stock returns. The underlying idea is that, as portfolio returns are more diversified, there is less residual noise in the regression, which improves the quality of the estimates.

Example   22.14

Suppose that Toyota considers building a new plant in the UK, which would sell its output in the entire European Union. Then Toyota could estimate the beta and gammas of the European car industry as a whole, rather than estimating the risks using just a simple stock.

Still, the portfolio approach assumes that all firms in the index have the same risks. In practice, one would often have serious difficulties in identifying a sufficiently large number of firms that have the same exposure as the project at hand.

Example   22.15

Suppose that Oerlikon, a Swiss firm, wants to build a plant for the production and sale of maintenance welding electrodes in India. There may be a number of Indian firms active in the welding industry, but not one of them is priced in the OECD capital market. Hence, Oerlikon cannot directly measure the risk of the Indian welding industry relative to the OECD market portfolio.[22] Thus, when valuing the project, Oerlikon would have to use an indirect, forward-looking approach to assess the risk. For instance, Oerlikon could argue that (1) the maintenance welding industry is not very cyclical, (2) the Indian business cycle is largely independent of economic cycles in the OECD, so that (3) the beta of this Indian project relative to the OECD market portfolio is bound to be low. In addition, Oerlikon could argue that the exposures to OECD exchange rates are small or zero because the Indian economy is relatively closed.

22.5.3   Estimating the Risk Premiums

Assuming that we have an approximate idea of the beta and gammas, we need estimates of the expected risk premiums per unit of risk. The expected excess return on the world market portfolio is rather hard to estimate. The sample averages of returns observed in the past differ substantially across

---

[22] A procedure that consists of translating rupee returns on Indian stocks into an OECD currency and then estimating the risks is flawed because the prices of these Indian companies in the Bombay stock market are different from what they would have been if the assets had been priced internationally.

sample periods, and it is also known that the expected return changes over time.[23] Still, we know that there is a positive risk premium on the world stock market, and variations over time in the expected excess return may not be overly important when the NPV evaluation horizon is, say, one decade.

Turning to the expected excess return on the various foreign T-bills, these risk premiums also change over time, as we have seen in Chapter 14—and, unlike for the world market risk premium, we are not even sure whether the long-run mean actually differs from zero. Since exchange risk premiums are small in the short run and close to zero in the long run, for practical applications one might have to be content with an approach that ignores these and use the following simplified version of Equation [31]:

$$E(\tilde{r}_j - r) \cong \beta_j E(\tilde{r}_w - r). \tag{32}$$

where the beta is still estimated from a multivariate regression (Equation [30]) rather than from a bivariate regression (Equation [11]).[24]

You should not be overly discouraged by these approximations. No model is perfect; and, as we described in Section 22.4.5, the International CAPM works better than competing models. Still, you should recall our recommendation from Chapter 21. The cost of capital is measured imperfectly, and NPV computations should be undertaken for a range of reasonable discount rates, to see to what extent the accept/reject recommendation is sensitive to the estimate of the cost of capital.

---

[23] The return is partially predictable on the basis of (1) the risk spread (the difference between low-grade bond yields and government bond yields), (2) the term spread (the difference between short-term and long-term bond yields), and (3) the dividend yield.

[24] The need to use a multivariate regression in model [32] follows from the fact that our basic model is Equation [29], not Equation [9]. Equation [29] simplifies to the univariate equation, [9], only if either the prices of exchange covariance risk, η_k, are all zero, or the covariances between asset returns and exchange rate changes themselves are zero. The first case requires very special utility functions, and the second case cannot possibly be true for all assets and reference currencies simultaneously. Thus, we do need the multivariate model. Moreover, although the risk premium for exchange risk can be small—see below— it is unlikely to be *exactly* zero. That is, we use the one-factor world model, [32], merely as an approximation. If we would, in addition, use a univariate beta, we would introduce another (unnecessary) error to the approximation.

Note, finally, that non-zero ηs and non-zero covariances with exchange rate changes can be perfectly compatible with a small risk premium on a foreign T-bill. In the two-country case, for instance, the foreign T-bill must satisfy

$$E(\tilde{s} + r^* - r) = \theta \, \text{cov}(\tilde{s}, r_w) + \eta \, \text{cov}(\tilde{s}, \tilde{s}).$$

In this expression, both covariances are likely to be positive. Moreover, it can be shown that, while θ is positive, η is likely to be negative. Thus, the risk premium on the foreign T-bill *can* be small even if η and $\text{cov}(\tilde{s}, \tilde{s})$ are both non-zero.

QUIZ QUESTIONS

True-False Questions

1. The entire NPV analysis can be conducted in terms of the host (foreign) currency if money markets and exchange markets are fully integrated with the home market.
2. The entire NPV analysis can be conducted in terms of the host currency if money markets, stock markets, and exchange markets are fully integrated with the home market.
3. Forward rates can be used as the risk-adjusted expected future spot rates to translate the host-currency cash flows into the home currency. The home-currency cash flows can then be discounted at the appropriate home-currency discount rate if money markets and exchange markets are fully integrated with the home market.
4. Regardless of the degree of market integration, the host-currency expected cash flows can always be translated into the home currency (by multiplying them by the expected spot rate), and then discounted at the home-currency discount rate.
5. Regardless of the degree of market integration, the host-currency expected cash flows can always be translated into expected cash flows expressed in home currency. The home-currency cash flows can then be discounted at the home-currency discount rate that takes into account all risks.
6. If you use the forward rate as the risk-adjusted expected spot rate, there is no need to worry about the dependence between the exchange rate and the host-currency cash flows.
7. If markets are integrated and you translate at the forward rate, the cost of capital need not include a risk premium for exchange rate exposure.
8. If markets are integrated and you translate at the forward rate, the cost of capital need not include a risk premium for exposure to any currency.
9. If you discount expected cash flows that are already expressed in home currency, the cost of capital should include a risk premium for exposure to the host-currency exchange rate.
10. If you discount expected cash flows that are already expressed in home currency, the cost of capital should include a risk premium for exposure to all relevant exchange rates.
11. If you translate at the forward rate, you can entirely omit exchange rate expectations from the NPV procedure.
12. Exchange rate risk premiums are sizeable. In fact, they are about as large as the (world) market risk premium.
13. A highly risk-averse investor will only accept variance risk if he or she is fully certain to be compensated for this risk.
14. A highly risk-averse investor will never select a high-variance portfolio.
15. A risk-averse investor will select a high-variance portfolio only if the expected excess return is sufficiently high.
16. A risk-averse investor will select a low-return portfolio only if the variance is sufficiently low.
17. A particularly risk-averse investor will always select a low-return portfolio. This is because low return means low risk, and because the investor does not want to bear a lot of risk.

For the next set of questions, assume that access to money markets and exchange markets is unrestricted and the host-currency cash flow is risk free. Are the following statements true or false?

18. You can translate at the expected spot rate and discount at a risk-adjusted home-currency cost of capital.
19. You can translate at the forward rate, and discount at a home-currency rate that takes into account exchange risk.

20. You can translate at the forward rate, and discount at the risk-free home-currency rate.
21. You can discount the host-currency cash flows at the foreign risk-free rate, and then translate the result at the current spot exchange rate.
22. You can discount the host-currency cash flows at the foreign risk-free rate, and then translate the result at the expected future spot exchange rate.
23. You can discount the host-currency cash flows at the foreign risk-free rate, and then translate the result at the forward exchange rate.
24. If access to forward markets or foreign and domestic money markets is restricted, then the true value is always overstated if the foreign currency cash flow is translated at the forward exchange rate and then discounted at the domestic risk-free rate.

Additional Quiz Questions

1. Suppose that you observe an efficient portfolio. There are two methods with which you can infer the degree of risk aversion of the investor that selects this particular portfolio. What are these two methods?

2. What's wrong with the following statement: "The CAPM says that the expected return on a given stock j is equal to the best possible replication that one can obtain using the risk-free assets and the set of all risky assets (other than stock j)."

3. Below, we reproduce some equations from the derivation of the CAPM. Equation [1] is the efficiency criterion. Equation [4] is the CAPM. Explain the equations.

$$\frac{E(\tilde{r}_j - r)}{\text{cov}(\tilde{r}_j, \tilde{r}_m)} = \theta, \text{ for all risky assets } j = 1, \ldots, N \tag{1}$$

$$E(\tilde{r}_j - r) = \theta \ \text{cov}(\tilde{r}_j, \tilde{r}_m) = [\theta \ \text{var}(\tilde{r}_m)]\frac{\text{cov}(\tilde{r}_j, \tilde{r}_m)}{\text{var}(\tilde{r}_m)} = [\theta \ \text{var}(\tilde{r}_m)]\beta_j \tag{2}$$

$$\sum_{j=1}^{N} x_j E(\tilde{r}_j - r) = \theta \sum_{j=1}^{N} x_j \ \text{cov}(\tilde{r}_j, \tilde{r}_m) = \theta \text{cov}(\sum_{j=1}^{N} x_j \tilde{r}_j, \tilde{r}_m) = \theta \text{cov}(\tilde{r}_m, \tilde{r}_m) \tag{3}$$

$$E(\tilde{r}_j) - r = \beta_j [E(\tilde{r}_m) - r]. \tag{4}$$

4. Suppose that investors from a country have access to a large set of foreign stocks, and that foreign investors can also buy stocks in that country. Which of the following statements is (are) correct?

   (a) The single-market CAPM, where the market portfolio is measured by the index of all stocks issued by local companies, does not hold.
   (b) The single-market CAPM, where the market portfolio is measured by the index of all stocks held by local investors, does not hold.
   (c) The single-market CAPM, where the market portfolio is measured by the index of all stocks held by local investors, is formally correct but not fit for practical use, because the correct index is not readily observable.
   (d) The single-market CAPM, where the market portfolio measured by the index of all stocks worldwide, is correct provided that there is a unified world market for all stocks.
   (e) The single-market CAPM, where the market portfolio is measured by the index of all stocks worldwide, is correct provided that there is no (real) exchange risk.

EXERCISES

1. Suppose that you have the following data:

$E(\tilde{r}_j - r)$	(co)variance risks	
0.03	$\mathrm{var}(\tilde{r}_1) = 0.04$	$\mathrm{cov}(\tilde{r}_1, \tilde{r}_2) = 0.02$
0.04	$\mathrm{cov}(\tilde{r}_2, \tilde{r}_1) = 0.02$	$\mathrm{var}(\tilde{r}_2) = 0.06$

Asset 0 is the (domestic) risk-free asset, and asset weights in a portfolio are denoted as x_j, where $j = 0, \ldots, 2$. Which of the following portfolios is efficient, and if the portfolio is efficient, what is the investor's degree of risk aversion?

(a) $x_0 = 0, x_1 = 0.4, x_2 = 0.6$
(b) $x_0 = 0, x_1 = 0.6, x_2 = 0.4$
(c) $x_0 = 0, x_1 = 0.5, x_2 = 0.5$
(d) $x_0 = 0.2, x_1 = 0.4, x_2 = 0.4$
(e) $x_0 = 0.5, x_1 = 0.25, x_2 = 0.25$
(f) $x_0 = -1, x_1 = 1, x_2 = 1$
(g) $x_0 = 1, x_1 = 0, x_2 = 0$
(h) $x_0 = 2, x_1 = -0.5, x_2 = -0.5$

2. Return to the example discussed in Chapter 21, of Weltek UK, which is considering an investment in Spain. Suppose that Spain has reverted to its pre-1970 policies, and does not allow its residents to buy foreign assets; nor are foreigners allowed to buy Spanish shares in the stock market. Moreover, Spanish interest rates are set by the government. Local industry is heavily protected, and trade with the rest of the OECD is minimal. Foreign direct investment is permitted but only after obtaining a license. From our discussion in this chapter, we determine that we must use Approach 2 (expected spot rates, etc.). We make one possible set of assumptions.

Assumption 1:
Expected Spot Rates. The ESP is deemed to be initially overvalued, which implies an expected devaluation of 12 percent either this or next year. On top of this, we expect a further depreciation by about 3 percent *p.a.* to reflect Spain's higher expected inflation rate relative to the UK.

Year	0	1	2	3	4	5	6
(a) Lagged adjustment	1	0.940	0.890	0.890	0.890	0.890	0.890
(b) Forecast	1	0.913	0.840	0.815	0.793	0.774	0.748

Line (a) models the expected 12 percent devaluation in years 1 or 2 by two consecutive 6 percent devaluations. The lagged adjustment would be the forecast if, as of year 0, Spain's inflation rate were equal to the UK's inflation rate. But Spain's future inflation rate is expected to be a 5 percent *p.a.*, versus only 2 percent in the UK. In line (b) we therefore add the effect of differences in the expected future inflations by multiplying each year's line-(a) number by $(1.02/1.05)^T$.

Assumption 2:
Covariance Risk of ESP Cash Flows with the Exchange Rate. Because of trade barriers, the exchange rate has no impact on the ESP cash flows. Thus, we can set the covariance between the ESP cash flows and the exchange rate equal to zero. The expected GBP cash flows are then equal to the ESP expected cash flow times the expected exchange rate.

Assumption 3:

Cost of Capital. The cost of capital is estimated at 17 percent, close to the risk-free rate. This is because the Spanish economy is (assumed to be) very isolated from the rest of the world, implying that neither the cash flows (in ESP) nor the GBP/ESP exchange rate is correlated with the OECD market portfolio.

Compute the NPV of Weltek UK's investment in Spain.

3. Suppose that the capital markets of the following three countries are well integrated: North America (with the dollar), Europe (with the ECU), and Japan (with the yen). Suppose that you choose the yen as the reference currency.

   (a) Why does the average investor care about the JPY/USD and JPY/ECU exchange rates (beside how it relates to how his or her wealth is measured in JPY)?

   (b) What moments are needed in a mean-and-(co)variance framework, to summarize the joint distribution of asset returns? Which of these are affected by the portfolio choice?

4. Suppose that your assistant has run a market-model regression for a company that produces sophisticated drilling machines, and finds the following results (*t*-statistic in parentheses):

$$r_j = \alpha + \beta\, r_m + \gamma\, s + e_j,$$

$$r_j = 0.002 + 0.56\, r_m + 4.25\, s + e_j.$$
$$\quad (0.52) \quad (1.25) \quad\quad (2.06)$$

   Your assistant remarks that, as the estimated beta is insignificant, the true beta is zero. The exposure, in contrast, is significant, and must be equal to the estimated coefficient. How do you react?

5. Suppose that the world beta for a German stock (in DEM) equals 1.5, and its exposures to the dollar, the yen, and the pound are 0.3, 0.2, and 0.1, respectively.

   (a) What is the best replicating portfolio if you can invest in a world-market index fund, as well as in dollars, yens, pounds, and marks?

   (b) What additional information is needed to identify the cost of capital?

6. Suppose that there are two countries, the US (which is the foreign country) and Canada. The exposure of the company XUS, in terms of USD, is estimated as follows:

$$\tilde{r}^{*}_{XUS} = 0.12 + 0.30\, \tilde{s}_{USD/CAD} + \tilde{\varepsilon}.$$

What is the company's exposure in terms of CAD?

MIND-EXPANDING EXERCISES

1. Critically discuss the following popular statements:

   (a) "If an investor buys foreign stocks, he or she is also investing, in a sense, in the corresponding foreign currency."

   (b) "If a German investor buys oil futures, he or she is also investing in USD because oil prices are quoted in USD."

(c) "If a German investor buys zinc or lead futures on FOX, London's (commodity) Futures and Options Exchange, the investor is also investing in GBP because the zinc or lead futures are quoted in GBP."

2. Suppose that there are just two countries. The CAD T-bill rate is 6 percent *p.a.*, and the USD rate 5 percent. In terms of CAD, the world market portfolio and the USD T-bill are expected to outperform the CAD T-bill rate by 8 percent and 1 percent *p.a.*, respectively. You run a regression on past data, which yields the following estimates:

$$\tilde{r}_{XUS} = 0.08 + 0.8\,\tilde{r}_w + 0.25\,\tilde{s}_{CAD/USD} + \tilde{\varepsilon}.$$

What is the expected return, in CAD, on XUS common stock (a) if you use the International CAPM, and (b) if you use the regression only? How do you explain the differences? Which is more reliable?

3. Suppose that there are three countries: the US, Canada (the reference country), and the European Union. From the US point of view, there are two exchange rates, USD/CAD and USD/ECU. The exposure of company XUS, in terms of USD, is estimated as follows:

$$\tilde{r}^*_{XUS} = 0.03 + 0.20\,\tilde{s}_{USD/CAD} + 0.15\,\tilde{s}_{USD/ECU} + \tilde{\varepsilon}^*.$$

What is the exposure in terms of CAD? That is, what are $\gamma_{XUS,CAD/USD}$ and $\gamma_{XUS,CAD/ECU}$ in

$$\tilde{r}_{XUS} = \alpha + \gamma_{XUS,CAD/USD}\,\tilde{s}_{CAD/USD} + \gamma_{XUS,CAD/ECU}\,\tilde{s}_{CAD/ECU} + \tilde{\varepsilon}?$$

(Hint: substitute $\tilde{s}_{CAD/USD} \cong -\tilde{s}_{USD/CAD}$ and $\tilde{s}_{USD/ECU} \cong \tilde{s}_{CAD/ECU} - \tilde{s}_{CAD/USD}$ into the original exposure regression, and then use $\tilde{r}^*_{XUS} \cong \tilde{r}_{XUS} + \tilde{s}_{CAD/USD}$. It can be shown that these linear approximations induce very little error in the implied CAD exposures, although they are more off the mark with regard to the implied CAD intercept.)[25]

---

[25] See Sercu (1981, Appendix) for a more formal derivation of the link between the two exposure regressions.

LINKING THE INTERNATIONAL CAPM TO MULTIVARIATE REGRESSIONS

In this appendix, we show how the International CAPM with multiple risk premiums can be linked to the regression

$$\tilde{r}_j = \alpha_j + \beta_j \, \tilde{r}_w + \gamma_j \, \tilde{s}_1 + \ldots + \gamma_{jL} \tilde{s}_L + \tilde{\varepsilon}_j,$$

where $\tilde{r}_j$ is the return on asset $j = 1, \ldots, N$
$\tilde{r}_w$ is the world market portfolio return
$\tilde{s}_k$ is the percentage change in the spot rate of country k's currency, $k = 1, \ldots, L$
L is the number of foreign countries (country 0 is the reference country)
$\tilde{\varepsilon}_j$ is the error term, with

$$\text{cov}(\tilde{\varepsilon}_j, \tilde{r}_w) = 0 = \text{cov}(\tilde{\varepsilon}_j, \tilde{s}_k), k = 1, \ldots, L. \qquad [A1]$$

We shall confine ourselves to the two-country case and, accordingly, drop the subscript k that identifies the foreign country. Thus, the only two countries the above regression reduces to:

$$\tilde{r}_j = \alpha_j + \beta_j \, \tilde{r}_w + \gamma_j \tilde{s} + \tilde{\varepsilon}_j. \qquad [A2]$$

First, we derive the regression coefficients. To do so, we compute the covariances of asset j's return with the world market portfolio return and with the exchange rate. To obtain these covariances, we simply substitute Equation [A1] into $\text{cov}(\tilde{r}_j, \tilde{r}_w)$ and $\text{cov}(\tilde{r}_j, \tilde{s})$, respectively, and we note that the covariance of a sum with a particular variable is the sum of the covariance with this variable. The result is

$$\text{cov}(\tilde{r}_j, \tilde{r}_w) = \beta_j \, \text{var}(\tilde{r}_w) + \gamma_j \, \text{cov}(\tilde{r}_w, \tilde{s}),$$

and

$$\text{cov}(\tilde{r}_j, \tilde{s}_s) = \beta_j \, \text{cov}(\tilde{r}_w, \tilde{s}) + \gamma_j \, \text{var}(\tilde{s}).$$

This is a linear system of two equations in two unknowns, β_j and γ_j:

$$\begin{bmatrix} \text{cov}(\tilde{r}_j, \tilde{r}_w) \\ \text{cov}(\tilde{r}_j, \tilde{s}) \end{bmatrix} = \begin{bmatrix} \text{var}(\tilde{r}_w) & \text{cov}(\tilde{r}_w, \tilde{s}) \\ \text{cov}(\tilde{r}_w, \tilde{s}) & \text{var}(\tilde{s}) \end{bmatrix} \begin{bmatrix} \beta_j \\ \gamma_j \end{bmatrix},$$

which allows us to immediately solve for the regression coefficients:

$$\begin{bmatrix} \beta_j \\ \gamma_j \end{bmatrix} = \begin{bmatrix} \mathrm{var}(\tilde{r}_w) & \mathrm{cov}(\tilde{r}_w, \tilde{s}) \\ \mathrm{cov}(\tilde{r}_w, \tilde{s}) & \mathrm{var}(\tilde{s}) \end{bmatrix}^{-1} \begin{bmatrix} \mathrm{cov}(\tilde{r}_j, \tilde{r}_w) \\ \mathrm{cov}(\tilde{r}_j, \tilde{s}) \end{bmatrix}. \qquad [A3]$$

The second step is to derive the risk premiums. Our basic CAPM states that for any risky asset,

$$E(\tilde{r}_j) - r = \theta \, \mathrm{cov}(\tilde{r}_j, \tilde{r}_w) + \eta \, \mathrm{cov}(\tilde{r}_j, \tilde{s}). \qquad [A4]$$

To identify the two unknowns (θ and η), we need two benchmark portfolios. Our first benchmark is the market portfolio itself, and our second is the foreign currency risk-free investment. For this pair, Equation [A4] looks like

$$E(\tilde{r}_w) - r = \theta \, \mathrm{var}(\tilde{r}_w) + \eta \, \mathrm{cov}(\tilde{r}_w, \tilde{s}),$$

and

$$E(\tilde{s}) + r^* - r = \theta \, \mathrm{cov}(\tilde{s}, \tilde{r}_w) + \eta \, \mathrm{var}(\tilde{s}),$$

or, more compactly,

$$\begin{bmatrix} E(\tilde{r}_w) - r \\ E(\tilde{s}) + r^* - r \end{bmatrix} = \begin{bmatrix} \mathrm{var}(\tilde{r}_w) & \mathrm{cov}(\tilde{r}_w, \tilde{s}) \\ \mathrm{cov}(\tilde{s}, \tilde{r}_w) & \mathrm{var}(\tilde{s}) \end{bmatrix} \begin{bmatrix} \theta \\ \eta \end{bmatrix}. \qquad [A5]$$

This immediately provides the solution, which in matrix notation is:

$$\begin{bmatrix} \theta \\ \eta \end{bmatrix} = \begin{bmatrix} \mathrm{var}(\tilde{r}_w) & \mathrm{cov}(\tilde{r}_w, \tilde{s}) \\ \mathrm{cov}(\tilde{s}, \tilde{r}_w) & \mathrm{var}(\tilde{s}) \end{bmatrix}^{-1} \begin{bmatrix} E(\tilde{r}_w) - r \\ E(\tilde{s}) + r^* - r \end{bmatrix}. \qquad [A6]$$

The last step is to link the regression coefficients with the risk premiums and the covariances. We substitute Equation [A6] into the CAPM Equation [A4] written in matrix notation:

$$E(\tilde{r}_j) - r = \begin{bmatrix} \mathrm{cov}(\tilde{r}_j, \tilde{r}_w) & \mathrm{cov}(\tilde{r}_j, \tilde{s}) \end{bmatrix} \begin{bmatrix} \theta \\ \eta \end{bmatrix}$$

$$= \begin{bmatrix} \mathrm{cov}(\tilde{r}_j, \tilde{r}_w) & \mathrm{cov}(\tilde{r}_j, \tilde{s}) \end{bmatrix} \begin{bmatrix} \mathrm{var}(\tilde{r}_w) & \mathrm{cov}(\tilde{r}_w, \tilde{s}) \\ \mathrm{cov}(\tilde{s}, \tilde{r}_w) & \mathrm{var}(\tilde{s}) \end{bmatrix}^{-1} \begin{bmatrix} E(\tilde{r}_w) - r \\ E(\tilde{s}) + r^* - r \end{bmatrix}. \qquad [A7]$$

The first product of matrices on the right-hand side of Equation [A7] is simply the transpose of the right-hand side of Equation [A3]; that is, rows have become columns, and *vice versa*:

$$\begin{bmatrix} \beta_j & \gamma_j \end{bmatrix} = \begin{bmatrix} \text{cov}(\tilde{r}_j, \tilde{r}_w) & \text{cov}(\tilde{r}_j, \tilde{s}) \end{bmatrix} \begin{bmatrix} \text{var}(\tilde{r}_w) & \text{cov}(\tilde{r}_w, \tilde{s}) \\ \text{cov}(\tilde{s}, \tilde{r}_w) & \text{var}(\tilde{s}) \end{bmatrix}^{-1}. \qquad [\text{A3}']$$

Thus, Equation [A7] becomes

$$\begin{aligned} E(\tilde{r}_j) - r &= \begin{bmatrix} \beta_j & \gamma_j \end{bmatrix} \begin{bmatrix} E(\tilde{r}_w) - r \\ E(\tilde{s}) + r^* - r \end{bmatrix} \\ &= \beta_j E(\tilde{r}_w - r) + \gamma_j E(\tilde{s} + r^* - r). \end{aligned} \qquad [\text{A8}]$$

In short, with two covariance risks, each having its own risk premium, the CAPM is now linked to the regression of the asset's return on the two relevant types of uncertainty. Each regression coefficient becomes the measure of risk or exposure to that type of uncertainty, and the expected excess return on the corresponding benchmark is the expected reward per unit of exposure.

23 INTERNATIONAL TAXATION

In Chapter 21, we described how to apply the net present value criterion to international investment projects. We recommended that the analysis be done in three steps. In the first step, we value the cash flows from operations as if the project were implemented in a foreign *branch*, that is, without incorporating the foreign business unit as a separate company. In the second step, we consider the effects of the intragroup financial arrangements that become possible when the foreign business unit is incorporated as a separate company, the *subsidiary*. In the third and last stage, we add the effects of outside financing. The main motivation for the branch valuation stage is that this approach postpones many of the complications that arise because of tax issues, and helps one to focus on the operational aspects of the project. The simplification in this first step arises from the fact that a branch cannot have a *remittance policy*; its profits are automatically part of the overall corporation's profits, and the funds held by the branch are really funds held by the overall company (albeit in a foreign bank account). In contrast, a subsidiary has to explicitly remit funds to its parent(s); and it can do so in various ways, each having its own tax implications.

In this chapter, we explain how to compute the taxes to be paid on profits, how taxes can be minimized by transfer pricing or unbundling the cash flows in a particular way. Rather than going into the details of tax charters of specific countries, we shall focus on the general principles of stylized, generic tax systems and tax treaties. The first issue, discussed in Section 23.1, is whether or not the host country (or, in fiscal jargon, the **source country**) has the right to tax the profits of this branch. We shall describe how and when this right to levy taxes can lead to double or triple taxation, and how legislators try to obtain a more neutral tax situation by reducing multiple taxation. The two main systems are the credit system, and the exclusion system. In Sections 23.2 and 23.3, we consider how each of these two (conflicting) tax systems are applied to a branch. Section 23.4, then, looks at the wholly owned subsidiary (WOS) or joint venture (JV) and describes the various ways such a subsidiary can remit funds to its shareholders. Sections 23.5 and 23.6 discuss taxation of a subsidiary under the credit system and the exclusion system. We summarize our discussion in Section 23.7.

23.1   MULTIPLE TAXATION VERSUS TAX NEUTRALITY

Fiscal laws all over the world claim the right to tax on two different principles:

- The *residence* principle: All *residents* of the country (that is, private persons living in the country, and incorporated companies established in the country) can be taxed on their *worldwide* income.
- The *source* principle: All income earned inside the country, whether by residents or nonresidents, is taxable in this country. Earning, in this context, means that some income-generating activity is carried on inside the country, or that dividends, interest income, or royalties have been received from a resident of the *source* country.

The two principles are in perfect agreement when the entire income of a resident is earned in the country of residence. In an international context, however, the two principles have different implications. Consider a German academic who works one semester as a visiting professor in the US. According to the source principle, he or she may have to pay taxes in the US on labor income earned in the US. According to the residence principle, the professor is also taxable at home, on worldwide income— including the US income. This implies that the US income can be taxed twice, unless some form of relief against double taxation is provided.

In Section 23.1.1, we describe the conditions under which the source principle can be invoked when a firm is active internationally, and how this can give rise to double or even triple taxation. We then explain, in Section 23.1.2, the alternative tax neutrality principles underlying the measures taken by governments to avoid multiple taxation. Sections 23.1.3 and 23.1.4 discuss each of the systems in greater detail, while Section 23.1.5 compares the two systems.

23.1.1   When Can Double or Triple Taxation Occur?

In our review of international taxation, we first consider two extreme modes of foreign operations— direct exports (without foreign representation), and the wholly owned subsidiary (WOS) or the joint venture company (JV). After this discussion, we cover the middle ground between these two extremes.

The Case of Direct Exports

Under *direct exports*, all business transactions are made at home. Not only does production take place in the exporter's home country, but the decision to accept or not to accept export orders is also taken in the domestic headquarters. Thus, a pure exporter is not a resident of the foreign country. Nor does the pure exporter "earn" anything abroad; there is no foreign activity, and the company does not receive any dividends, license income, or interest income from the foreign country. Therefore, the foreign country can invoke neither the residence principle nor the source principle. Conversely, the resulting export profits are domestic income, and are taxed in the firm's home country only. Thus, in this case, double taxation is not an issue.

The Case of a Foreign Subsidiary

At the other extreme, a WOS or a JV is legally a separate entity incorporated abroad. In this case, there is a proliferation of potential taxes:

- The WOS or JV is unambiguously a resident of the host country. Thus, the host country will invoke the residence principle and impose its normal corporate taxes on the profits of the WOS or JV.
- In principle, however, the parent is also subject to taxes on all income it receives from the subsidiary. Such additional taxes may be levied by both countries.
  - The host country will note that the parent earns some income in the country, and that the source principle therefore applies. That is, the host country may levy a tax on the dividends, interest fees, or royalties paid out to the parent. This tax is called a **withholding tax**.[1]
  - In addition, the parent's home country will, in principle, invoke the residence principle of taxation, and tax the parent on its worldwide incomes.

Example 23.1

A Belgian subsidiary of a French company makes a profit of BEF 170,000 before taxes. Belgian corporate taxes are BEF 70,000. The entire after-tax profit of BEF 100,000 is paid out as a dividend to the French parent company through Kredietbank, a Belgian bank. If the withholding tax is 25 percent, Kredietbank will withhold BEF 25,000 from the ("gross") dividend and transfer it to the Belgian tax administration. The balance, the "net" dividend of BEF 75,000, will be paid to the foreign shareholder. Finally, the French parent will have to declare its Belgian income of BEF 75,000 in its French tax return and potentially pay taxes on it.

In short, when the foreign business unit is incorporated as a separate company, there is potential for double or triple taxation. This is in marked contrast with the pure exports case, where income is taxed only once, at the corporate level at home.

Intermediate Cases: The Permanent Establishment

What about the intermediate cases—the dependent agent, or the branch? As we saw in Chapter 21, from a legal point of view, there is a foreign presence if the enterprise formally opens a branch. The definition of *presence* from the fiscal point of view is subtly different. The host country can invoke the source principle as soon as an activity is conducted in the country. The tax terminology for conducting an activity in a given country is "having a **permanent establishment**" there. Under the influential OECD Model Treaty for the reduction of double taxation, such a permanent establishment (PE) is said to exist when two conditions are met simultaneously:

- There is a permanent physical presence (like an office or a warehouse).
- Some vital entrepreneurial activity takes place in the host country; that is, the foreign office does more than just render services (like storing goods, advertising, or centralizing orders).

---

[1] In accordance with the source principle, this withholding tax is levied only on the income earned by the parent in that particular host country, not on the parent's worldwide income. The withholding tax is flat (not progressive), and in most cases the rate is lower than the regular income tax rate. The tax is withheld immediately when the dividend is received, rather than being levied afterwards on the basis of a tax return. The reason for withholding the tax at the source is that the foreign recipient of the dividend, not being a resident of the host country, cannot be forced by the host country to file a tax return or to pay taxes. Therefore, the host country collects its tax while the money is still in the host country, by withholding it from the dividend payment. In practice, the bank that pays out the dividend is instructed to withhold the tax and pay it to the tax authorities.

Example   23.2

If the agent of a US corporation in Peru simply faxes incoming orders to the company headquarters for acceptance or rejection, there is no PE and, therefore, no taxation in Peru. However, if the agent ultimately decides whether or not the order is to be accepted, or if there is local production, then there *is* a PE, and the profits made on the Peruvian sales are taxable in Peru.

The double taxation issue also arises for the PE. Not being incorporated as a separate company, the PE's profit is also part of the overall company's profit and will be subject to taxes in the parent's country under the residence principle. Note that, unlike the case of an incorporated foreign unit, the host country can tax only the PE's profits. There are no dividend payments, interest fees, or license payments between the branch and the main office, implying that there cannot be any withholding tax.

23.1.2   Tax Neutrality

Even tax authorities concur—reluctantly—that full double taxation is too much of a good thing, and thus they wish to provide relief against multiple taxation. In this section, we consider the alternative principles underlying such relief measures. Relief from double taxation can be provided by unilateral measures built into the host country's standard tax rules. It can also be provided by a bilateral tax treaty between two countries. If there is such an international treaty, it supersedes the national rules; that is, the national rules are the default options that hold if there is no tax treaty. Today, most tax treaties are based on the OECD Model Tax Treaty—even treaties signed with or between non-OECD countries. Such international tax agreements all have the same structure and use the same legal definitions. They may, however, differ from the model on the percentage of withholding taxes, or on the right to tax more or less special cases (like the wages of visiting professors). Thus, one should always check the bilateral treaty rather than assuming that it is identical to the OECD Model Tax Treaty.

An Example of Double Taxation

To understand the alternative principles underlying the measures that mitigate multiple taxation, let us consider a German company that establishes a business in Tunisia, under the form of a branch/permanent establishment. As we saw, the issue of double taxation arises because the tax authorities levy taxes on the basis of two principles. The *residence* criterion says that all residents of a country are taxable. Therefore, the German company, being a resident of Germany, is taxable in Germany, on the basis of its world income. The *source* principle says that the Tunisian branch, earning income in Tunisia, can be taxed in that country on its Tunisian income. In the absence of any relief for double taxation, the Tunisian income would therefore be taxed both in Germany and in Tunisia.

Example   23.3

Assume that the income of the Tunisian branch, after translation into DEM, is DEM 100, and suppose that the tax rate is 40 percent in Germany and 35 percent in Tunisia. In the "Double Taxation" column in Table 23.1, we show what happens when there is no relief against double taxation. The Tunisian

TABLE 23.1   International Taxation of a Branch: Double Taxation, the Exclusion Method, and the Credit Method

	Double Taxation	Exclusion Method	Credit Method
Tunisia			
Branch profit	100	100	100
<35% tax> (a)	<35>	<35>	<35>
Net profit	65	65	65
Germany			
Net Tunisian profit	65	65	65
Gross up	0	0	35
Taxable income	65	0	100
<40% tax>	26	0	40
Tax credit	0	0	<35>
Net tax due (b)	26	0	5
Total taxes (a) + (b)	61	35	40
Net income	39	65	60

Assume that the income of the Tunisian branch, after translation into DEM, is DEM 100, and suppose that the tax rate is 40 percent in Germany and 35 percent in Tunisia. In the "Double Taxation" column, the Tunisian income after Tunisian taxes, DEM 100 − 35 = 65, is added to the German income, and is taxed again at 40 percent in Germany. In the "Exclusion Method" column, the Tunisian income is simply excluded from the German taxable income and from German taxes. Under the column "Credit Method," the net income (DEM 65) is grossed up with the Tunisian tax (DEM 35) and the tax basis is DEM 65 + 35 = 100. On this grossed-up income, the total tax should be DEM 40, but the German head office obtains a credit for taxes paid abroad (DEM 35), and pays only the balance (DEM 5) in Germany.

income after Tunisian taxes, DEM 100 − 35 = 65, is added to the German income, and is taxed again at 40 percent in Germany.[2] Thus, the total tax is DEM 61.

In the above example, under the Double Taxation scheme, the total corporate tax burden is 61, of which 35 is paid in Tunisia and 26 in Germany. This is high relative to two possible benchmarks. If the same DEM 100 had been earned in Germany, taxes would have been only DEM 40 and, if the branch had been an independent Tunisian entity, taxes would have been only DEM 35. Whatever the benchmark chosen, taxes are not "neutral." That is, there is a fiscal penalty associated with the fact that ownership and operations straddle two countries.

Tax laws aim to reduce or possibly even eliminate the above discrimination between the foreign-owned branch and a purely German or purely Tunisian company. **Tax neutrality** (that is, the absence of

---

[2] The German parent is allowed to deduct the Tunisian taxes from its worldwide income, as part of its expenses. For simplicity, we also assume that both tax authorities agree on the allocation of profits to the Tunisian branch.

tax penalties associated with international ownership) can be achieved on the basis of either of two, generally conflicting approaches. One principle says that the Tunisian branch should be taxed the same way as a purely Tunisian entity (that is, at 35 percent). The alternative principle says that the total tax burden should be the same whether the German firm earns its income at home or in Tunisia (that is, at 40 percent).

Capital Import Neutrality and the Exclusion System

The first principle is based on the argument that there should be no penalty or advantage attached to the fact that the branch is foreign-owned. This is called the **Capital Import Neutrality** principle: a foreign-owned entity should be allowed to compete on an equal basis with a Tunisian-owned competitor. To achieve this, the German tax authorities would have to exempt foreign-source income from German taxes, that is, *exclude* foreign branch profits from taxable income. This is called the **exclusion method**.

Example   23.4

Assume that the income of the Tunisian branch, after translation into DEM, is still DEM 100, and suppose that the tax rate is 40 percent in Germany and 35 percent in Tunisia. In the "Exclusion Method" column of Table 23.1, we show the effect of the exclusion tax rule. The Tunisian income is simply excluded from the German taxable income, which of course means that there is no German tax on the Tunisian income. Thus, the overall tax is just the Tunisian tax (DEM 35).

Capital Export Neutrality and the Credit System

Under the alternative principle—which is called **Capital Export Neutrality**—the German tax authorities do not want to create a tax incentive for firms to export capital and employment to a relatively low-tax country like Tunisia. Thus, the principle is that the overall corporate tax should be the same as if the branch had been located in Germany. Under this system, the German tax authorities "gross up" the after-tax income with all foreign taxes, implying that they recompute the before-tax income; they then apply the home-country tax rules to that income, and give credit for foreign taxes already paid.

Example   23.5

Under capital export neutrality, the German tax authorities want the Tunisian branch's before-tax income, DEM 100, to be taxed at 40 percent. The figures are shown under the column "Credit Method" in Table 23.1. The procedure consists of "grossing up" the net income (DEM 65) with all taxes (DEM 35) that have been levied on that income. Thus, the tax basis in Germany is DEM 65 + 35 = 100. On this grossed-up income, the German tax authorities then apply the German tax rate of 40 percent, which is the German norm. Thus, the total tax should be DEM 40. As foreign taxes are less than DEM 40, the German company must pay some taxes in Germany to bring its total taxation up to the "normal" level. In other words, the total tax burden is 40, but the German main office obtains a credit for taxes paid abroad (DEM 35), and pays only the balance (DEM 5) in Germany.

Limitations to Tax Neutrality

Each of the alternative neutrality principles—capital import neutrality or capital export neutrality—reduces the overall tax burden to a level deemed to be "normal." However, the definition of what is normal differs depending on the principle adopted. Thus, there will generally be no universal neutrality, in the sense of simultaneous capital import *and* export neutrality. Universal neutrality requires that the two tax rates be the same. For instance, if the Tunisian tax rate were also 40 percent, a credit system would, in principle, be indistinguishable from an exclusion system, as is easily verified.

In practice, there are other reasons why taxes are seldom neutral. A credit system, as it is applied in practice, never completely achieves its professed objective of capital export neutrality, and an exclusion rule rarely achieves complete capital export neutrality. Some of the practical problems in applying either system are discussed in the following sections. First, we consider the case of a branch, and then a subsidiary.

23.2   INTERNATIONAL TAXATION OF A BRANCH: THE CREDIT SYSTEM

We shall first describe some of the practical problems that can arise when the credit method applies to the income of a foreign branch; next, we discuss the meaning of tax planning under these circumstances. The problems we discuss are (1) disagreement between the two tax authorities about what the taxable income is, and (2) the problem of excess tax credits.

23.2.1   Disagreement on the Tax Basis

One of the practical problems in applying either the credit system or the exclusion system to branch income is that the company's worldwide profits have to be divided into the portion earned by the branch (or each of the branches, if there are many), and the portion earned by the main office. Allocating sales over the different entities does not usually create problems; however, the computation of the cost of goods sold is somewhat trickier, and the allocation of overhead to the various offices can be even more troublesome. The reason is that the overhead or the indirect cost, by definition, cannot be allocated in any practical, logical way; this then implies that rules of thumb have to be used. If the national tax authorities have different cost allocation rules, taxes will not be neutral even if the tax rates in the two countries are equal. In fact, the company runs the risk that some of its indirect costs may not be tax-deductible anywhere.

Example   23.6

Assume that sales are DEM 1,200 in Germany, and DEM 400 in Tunisia, and the corresponding direct costs of goods sold are DEM 700 and 300, respectively. Total indirect (overhead) costs are DEM 300, and have to be allocated to Germany and Tunisia using some rule of thumb.

- Assume that the German tax authorities allocate this overhead in proportion to *direct cost*. As the head office accounts for 70 percent of the direct costs, 70 percent of the DEM 300 overhead (that is, DEM 210) is assigned to the main office for the purpose of German tax computations.
- On the other hand, the host-country tax agency allocates overhead in proportion to *sales*. The Tunisian branch has 25 percent of overall sales, so the Tunisian tax authorities assign one-fourth of the overhead, DEM 75, to the branch.

With DEM 210 deductible in Germany and DEM 75 in Tunisia, not all overhead (DEM 300) has been deducted worldwide. Stated differently, DEM 15 will be taxed twice, as shown in Table 23.2.

TABLE 23.2   Effect of Different Indirect Cost Allocation Rules on Taxable Incomes

	Germany	Tunisia	Total
	Management Accounting System		
Sales	1,200	400	1,600
<Direct cost>	<700>	<300>	<1,000>
Contribution	500	100	600
<Overhead>	—	—	<300>
Total gross income	—	—	300
	Tax Returns		
Sales	1,200	400	1,600
<Direct cost>	<700>	<300>	<1,000>
<Allocated overhead>	$\frac{700}{700+300}\, 300 = <210>$	$\frac{400}{1,200+400}\, 300 = <75>$	<285>
Taxable income	290	25	315

The indirect cost, 300, cannot be allocated to either the main office or the foreign branch in any objective and logical way, so any proper management accounting system will not allocate it. In this example, the rules used by the German and Tunisian tax authorities in allocating the indirect cost imply that only 285 of the total overhead (300) is tax-deductible. That is, 15 is taxed twice.

23.2.2   The Problem of Excess Tax Credits

Another problem in attaining capital export neutrality is that a credit system is seldom fully neutral if foreign taxes exceed the domestic norm. In such a case, there is rarely a full refund of the excess taxes paid abroad.

Example   23.7

If the Tunisian tax rate in Table 23.1 is 45 percent, the after-tax branch profit in Tunisia is DEM 55. For the purpose of German taxation, this after-tax income will be grossed up, under the credit system, from DEM 55 to DEM 100. The German norm requires a total tax bill of DEM 40. As the Tunisian taxes already exceed this norm, there is no additional German tax. Instead, there is an *unused tax credit* or *excess tax credit* of DEM 5.

Now this excess tax credit is not necessarily fully lost. Since foreign incomes from all countries are typically bundled together before the final tax computations are made, excess tax credits from one branch could be used to offset home-country taxes due on income from branches in low-tax countries.[3]

Example   23.8

In the Table 23.3, we examine the case where the Tunisian tax is 50 percent. We work out two simple cases where, in addition to the Tunisian income, the parent also has branch income from Hong Kong

TABLE 23.3   Taxation of a Branch: The Credit System—Taxes Assessed on Total Foreign Income

	Case 1		Case 2	
	Tunisia	Hong Kong	Tunisia	Hong Kong
Tax rate	50%	25%	50%	25%
Sales	220	200	220	100
<Costs>	<120>	<100>	<120>	<60>
Branch profit	100	100	100	40
<Taxes>	<50>	<25>	<50>	<10>
Net profit	50	75	50	30
Germany				
Net branch profit	50	75	50	30
Gross-up	50	25	50	10
Taxable	100	100	100	40
Total foreign taxable income	200		140	
Tax due (40%)	80		56	
<Credit>	50 + 25 = <75>		50 + 10 = <60>	
Net tax due	5		0	
Unused tax credit	0		4	
Total taxes paid	80 (40% of 200)		60 (43% of 140)	

In Case 1, the total foreign tax is less than the 40 percent due on the total foreign income, and the head office actually has to pay additional taxes to bring the overall tax burden up to DEM 80. In Case 2, the total tax is still above the 40 percent due on total foreign income. As a result, the German company still ends up with an unused tax credit (although less than if there had been no Hong Kong branch).

---

[3] In some countries (for instance, the UK), credits for foreign taxes can be used against domestic income taxes, though this can still leave the firm with excess tax credits.

(taxed at 25 percent). Note that the Tunisian tax exceeds the German norm, but the Hong Kong tax rate is below the 40 percent German tax rate. Depending on the size of the Hong Kong profits, there may or may not be excess tax credits left if German taxes are assessed on the basis of total foreign income rather than on a country-by-country basis.

We see that, in Case 1 (where low-taxed Hong Kong profits are a large part of foreign income), the total foreign tax (50 in Tunisia and 25 in Hong Kong) is less than the 40 percent due on the total foreign income, DEM $200 \times 0.40 = $ DEM 80. That is, the excess Tunisian tax is used to offset some of the taxes due on the Hong Kong profits, and the head office actually has to pay additional taxes to bring the overall tax burden up to 40 percent.

In Case 2, the Hong Kong sales and profits are so small that the total tax (50 in Tunisia and 10 in Hong Kong) is still above the 40 percent due on total foreign income, DEM $140 \times 0.40 = 56$. That is, the excess Tunisian taxes exceed the additional tax that is due on the Hong Kong profits. As a result, the German company still ends up with an unused tax credit (although less than if there had been no Hong Kong branch). The effective tax rate on the Tunisian income, in this case, decreases from 50 percent to 43 percent, but not all the way to 40 percent.

The net excess tax credit in Case 2 of Table 23.3, DEM 4, is not necessarily lost. The parent country's revenue service may use what is known as *carry-forward* or *carry-back rules*.

- **Carry-forward**: If, in the near future, we have to pay additional home-country taxes, we shall be allowed to use this year's excess foreign taxes as a credit. Thus, there is a kind of refund, but it is delayed (implying a loss of time value), and it is limited to home-country taxes that would be payable within the next few years—for instance, five years if there is a five-year carry-forward.
- **Carry-back**: If, in the recent past, we have paid more than DEM 4 in additional host-country taxes, we can now claim them back. Such a carry-back rule is a pure refund of excess tax credits, but the refund is limited to home-country taxes paid in the last few years—for instance, two years if there is a two-year carry-back.

If a carry-back rule exists, the parent would first carry back as much as possible; any credits not recuperated this way would then be carried forward up to the maximum allowed number of years.

Example   23.9

Suppose that there is a two-year carry-back and a three-year carry-forward rule in Germany, and that the German company paid German taxes on foreign income worth DEM 1 two years ago, and DEM 1.5 last year. The current (DEM 4) excess credit is treated as follows:

- DEM 1 will be carried back two years, resulting in a refund of DEM 1.
- DEM 1.5 will be carried back one year, resulting in an additional refund of DEM 1.5.
- The balance, $4 - 1 - 1.5 = $ DEM 1.5, will be carried forward, that is, it can be used within the next three years as a credit against possible German taxes on foreign income.

Carry-forward and carry-back rules imply that occasional excess tax credits can be recuperated (possibly with a delay). However, if a corporation *systematically* has excess tax credits, these excess taxes are lost forever, and thus, the credit system may not be fully capital-export neutral.

23.2.3   Tax Planning for a Branch under the Credit System

The general objective of corporate tax planning is to minimize taxes. The rule of the credit system is that taxes on foreign branch income are never lower than the foreign income times the standard home tax rate. One element of this rule is the determination of the foreign branch income. As we saw, there can be conflicts between the indirect cost allocation rules used by the company and the rules adopted by the tax authorities involved. Thus, a first implication is that it is important to know the rules used by tax authorities, and to minimize the risk that part of the expenses would be rejected for tax purposes in one of the countries involved.

The second element in the credit system says that, given the home country's assessment of the foreign branch income, the tax rate will never be less than the standard home tax rate. As we saw, the effective tax rate can be higher than this, notably when there are excess foreign tax credits and when these unused tax credits cannot be fully carried back or offset against other tax liabilities. Thus, given the assessment of foreign branch income, the implication is that one should minimize excess tax credits.

The only thing that can be done in this respect within the framework of a branch is the reallocation of profits from high-tax branches to low-tax branches, with the purpose of reducing total foreign taxes, and hence, also excess tax credits. One way to achieve this is to reallocate indirect expenses strategically. As we saw, the scope for indirect cost reallocation is limited. A second way to reallocate profits is to change the *transfer prices*, that is, the prices used to value goods and services sold between the branches (or subsidiaries) of one company or group of companies. There is some scope for using transfer pricing to reduce taxes because there is never an unambiguous way to determine the true cost of goods sold, and because the concept of a normal profit margin is equally ill-defined.

Example   23.10

In Table 23.4, we continue with Case 2 of Example 23.9 (Tunisian tax 50 percent, Hong Kong tax 25 percent, German tax 40 percent), with a DEM 4 excess foreign tax credit. The parent attempts to decrease the total foreign tax by increasing the transfer price for technical and management assistance rendered by the Hong Kong branch to the Tunisian branch by DEM 40. Thus, expenses in Tunisia increase by DEM 40, and income in Hong Kong rises by the same amount. Total before-tax income for the branches remains the same, but DEM 40 in income has been transferred from high-tax Tunisia to low-tax Hong Kong. The effect is that Tunisian income taxes decrease by DEM $40 \times 50\% =$ DEM 20, while Hong Kong income taxes increase by only DEM $40 \times 25\% =$ DEM 10. In short, total foreign taxes are lower by DEM 10, which eliminates the unused tax credit.

Two factors impose limits on what can be achieved by transfer pricing. First and foremost, the host-country tax authorities may reject part or all of the increased expenses, on the basis that these costs are above the *arm's length* level that would have been paid if the buyer and the seller had been unrelated. Such a rejection of part of the declared costs would result in some expenses not being deductible anywhere, so that taxes would be higher than before the cost reallocation. Second, if profits are reallocated through a change in the prices charged for the delivery of goods rather than services, one side effect is that import taxes levied on the traded goods will increase. The issue then is whether the (certain) additional cost in terms of import duties is smaller than the hoped-for gain in terms of income taxes.

TABLE 23.4   The Effect of Profit Reallocation on Foreign Taxes and Credits

	Before		After	
	Tunisia	Hong Kong	Tunisia	Hong Kong
Tax rate	50%	25%	50%	25%
Sales	220	100	220	140
<Costs>	<120>	<60>	<160>	<60>
Branch profit	100	40	60	80
<Taxes>	<50>	<10>	<30>	<20>
Net profit	50	30	30	60
Germany				
Net branch profit	50	30	30	60
Gross-up	50	10	30	20
Taxable Income	100	40	60	80
Total foreign taxable income	140		140	
Tax due (40%)	56		56	
<Credit>	<60>		<50>	
Net tax due	0		6	
Unused tax credit	5		0	
Total taxes paid	60 (43% of 140)		56 (40% of 140)	

The first part of the table reproduces Case 2 of Table 23.3, where there was an excess tax credit. In the right-hand side of the table, the parent reallocates profits worth DEM 40 from Tunisia to Hong Kong by charging DEM 40 for technical assistance rendered by the Hong Kong branch to the Tunisian branch amount. Thus, Tunisian income taxes decrease by DEM 20, while Hong Kong income taxes increase by DEM 10. Total foreign taxes are lower by DEM 10, which eliminates the excess tax credit .

23.3   INTERNATIONAL TAXATION OF A BRANCH: THE EXCLUSION SYSTEM

We now discuss the exclusion system of taxation. As we saw, unused tax credits and disagreements about the tax basis are some of the reasons why a credit system rarely is perfectly capital-export neutral. We explain below that the exclusion system, as it is applied in reality, rarely achieves its professed objective of capital-import neutrality. We first discuss the problems with this tax system, and then summarize its implications for tax planning.

23.3.1   Partial Exclusion and Progressive Taxes

In practice, an exclusion system is rarely capital-import neutral in the sense that exclusion is often incomplete.

- First, in their unilateral legislation, many countries limit the exclusion privilege to a certain percentage (for example, to 50 percent, 75 percent, or 90 percent of the foreign branch income) rather than granting full exemption. The justification given is that some of the expenses deducted by the main office from its domestic income are really associated with the management of the foreign branch. Since these expenses are hard to identify precisely, they are assumed to be a given percentage of the foreign profits. Thus, if the costs associated with running a foreign branch are deemed to be 10 percent of the profits of the branch, the exclusion privilege for these profits will be 90 percent.[4]
- Second, in bilateral tax treaties, many countries grant (near-) complete exclusion only if the foreign tax rate is rather similar to the home tax rate. Otherwise, they argue, there is too much of an incentive to shift profits toward low-tax foreign countries. This, of course, belies the stated objective of the system, capital-import neutrality.
- Third, if taxes are progressive, the tax authorities first compute what the normal average tax rate would be on the company's *worldwide* income, and then apply this average tax rate to its *taxable* income (that is, domestic profits plus non-excluded foreign income). If tax schedules are progressive, this procedure obviously increases the average tax rate. This rule is illustrated in Figure 23.1.

FIGURE 23.1   "Preservation of Progressiveness" Violates Import Neutrality

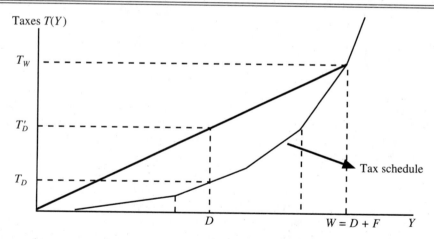

Worldwide income W is the sum of domestic income D and foreign income F. The tax authority first computes the total tax T_W that would have been due if the taxed income had been W, then computes the average tax rate T_W/W (which is the slope of the bold line through the origin), and applies this average tax rate to the taxable income D. The resulting tax is T_D'. In contrast, under a truly import-neutral system the tax would have been T_D.

---

[4] The home country's right to tax part of the foreign income is recognized in the EU *Parent-Subsidiary Directive* on the taxation of intracompany dividends, but the exclusion percentage cannot be lower than 95 percent (for dividends paid between EU member countries). The US has an 85 percent exclusion privilege for dividends received by US corporations from other US corporations. (For foreign dividends, the US applies the credit system.)

23.3.2   Disagreement on the Tax Basis

As under the credit system, the exclusion system requires that the company's worldwide profits be divided into the portion earned by the branch and the portion earned by the main office. Thus, conflicts can arise with respect to the allocation of indirect costs and with respect to transfer prices.

23.3.3   Tax Planning for a Branch under the Exclusion System

Under the exclusion system, tax planning consists of first identifying the country with the lowest *overall* tax burden, and then trying to allocate as much profit as possible to the corresponding branch. If the exclusion privilege is 100 percent (that is, if foreign profits are fully exempt from domestic taxes), we only have to compare the home and the foreign tax rate to identify the most tax-friendly country. If there is less than 100 percent exclusion, we have to take into account the home-country tax on the non-excluded part of the foreign income.

Example   23.11

An Italian company has a branch in France. We consider two scenarios:

- Suppose that the French tax on branch profits is 30 percent, and the Italian corporate tax is 35 percent, with a 100 percent exclusion privilege for profits of the foreign branch. A French branch profit of FRF 100 before taxes will lead to a profit of FRF 70 after French taxes, with no additional taxes in Italy, while a similar profit in the head office will generate only FRF 65 after (Italian) tax. If, through transfer pricing or reallocation of overhead, we can reduce Italian income by FRF 100 and increase French income by FRF 100, FRF 5 can be saved in taxes. Thus, the objective in this case is to increase French profits and decrease Italian profits.
- Suppose now that the (Italian) exclusion privilege for profits of the foreign branch is only 75 percent. A branch profit of FRF 100 will lead to a profit of FRF 70 after French taxes, but one-quarter of this, that is, FRF $70 \times 0.25 = 17.5$, will be taxable in Italy at 35 percent. The total tax is then FRF 30 (in France), plus $17.5 \times 0.35 =$ FRF 6.125 (in Italy), that is, FRF 36.125 altogether. In contrast, a similar profit in Italy will be subject to a tax of only FRF 35. Thus, in this case, the firm should try to shift profits from France to Italy.

The limitations of such profit shifting are similar to the limitations discussed in connection with the credit system: the tax collector in the high-tax country may reject a portion of the declared costs, and import duties may be affected by the transfer pricing policy. However, although the tax planning rules look similar under the credit system and the exclusion system, their effects are different in one important respect. Under a full exclusion system, a company gets to keep all tax savings below the domestic tax rate while, under a credit system, any such savings have to be paid at home as additional domestic taxes.

Example   23.12

Suppose that a German company has a total foreign income of DEM 140, and owes DEM 60 (that is, 42.86 percent) in foreign taxes. The German tax rate is 40 percent. Suppose that by transfer pricing between its foreign branches, the company lowers its total foreign tax by DEM 10, to DEM 50. If the credit system applies in Germany, an additional tax of DEM $(140 \times 40\%) - 50 =$ DEM 6 will be due, so that the net savings is only DEM 4. In contrast, if Germany has an exclusion system, no additional tax will be levied, and the net savings equal DEM 10.

In the remainder of this chapter, we see how the two generic systems for the reduction of multiple taxation are applied in the case of subsidiaries. We shall see that the approach is similar to the branch case.

23.4   REMITTANCES FROM A SUBSIDIARY: AN OVERVIEW

Our discussion so far has pertained to the simplest form of doing business abroad—the branch. Under this mode of operations, the firm is immediately and automatically the sole owner of all cash flows that arise from the foreign investment. Funds generated by one branch can be used to finance investments in another branch or in the main office, or they can be paid out by the company to its shareholders as dividends without any complication. In contrast, a foreign subsidiary must make explicit payments if ownership of the funds is to be transferred to the parent or to a related company. One may argue that, for a wholly owned subsidiary (WOS), the issue of who owns the cash—subsidiary or parent—is a legal concern without economic relevance. That is, it may seem that if the parent owns the subsidiary, it also owns its cash and can use this cash anywhere. The problem, however, is that if we want to transfer money from a subsidiary in one host country to the parent or to a subsidiary in another country, we have to respect the legal separation of the subsidiary from the rest of the group of companies. If the money is needed somewhere else, our WOS cannot just donate funds to the parent or to a sister company; it has to use an established, accepted way to transfer these funds—and such a transfer has tax repercussions. In this section, we review the various ways in which a subsidiary can transfer cash to other companies in the group. Sections 23.5 and 23.6 then discuss how dividends and other remittances are taxed under the credit and exclusion system, respectively.

23.4.1   Transactions "On Capital Account"
Capital transactions between parent and subsidiary can be on equity or on loan accounts. As far as equity transactions are concerned, the subsidiary may buy back some of its own shares from the parent, or it may buy stock issued by the parent or by sister companies. Alternatively, the subsidiary can lend funds to its parent or sister companies, or amortize outstanding loans prematurely, or agree to alter the credit periods on intracompany sales (which represents an implicit way to extend or reduce intracompany loans).

The advantage of capital transfers is that, in principle, they are not subject to immediate income taxes in either country.[5] Still, these transfers raise the issue of income taxes in later periods (when dividends or interest payments are received by the subsidiary). Also, regulatory agencies may dislike cross participation; or, the tax authorities of both countries may treat share repurchases or subscriptions to the parent company stock as disguised dividends, and tax them as such.

23.4.2   Dividends
Dividends are a simple way of transferring ownership of funds from a subsidiary to the parent company. There are some major differences between a WOS paying out dividends and a branch that transfers cash, which are discussed on the next page.

---

[5] There may be a registration tax on newly issued stock, though.

1. Unlike a branch, a subsidiary has a *timing option* as far as home-country taxation is concerned. A dividend can be declared more or less independently from the reporting period's income—and the parent, being a separate entity, cannot be taxed unless it actually receives dividends (or interest payments and royalties, for that matter). This *deferral principle* implies that, under a credit system as well as a partial exclusion system, home-country taxation of foreign profits can be postponed by deferring the payout of dividends from the subsidiary to the parent.[6]

Example   23.13

In the first seventy-five years of its existence, the Australian subsidiary of General Motors never paid out any dividend. Thus, as far as US taxes were concerned, the existence of the Australian subsidiary did not matter. In contrast, if GM's Australian activities had been under the form of a branch, there would have been US tax repercussions each year.

2. The amount that can be paid out as dividends by a subsidiary tends to be smaller than the subsidiary's total cash flow. The reason is that the dividends are paid out of profits, and profits are net of depreciation charges. Thus, a subsidiary can never transmit, as a dividend, the part of the cash flow that corresponds to depreciation allowances. In contrast, in the branch case, the entire cash flow—including depreciation—is (automatically) available to the main office.
3. The home *tax shield on losses made by the branch* is lost when the branch is incorporated. This is because losses by a branch are part of the parent's income and are therefore automatically and fully tax-deductible from the parent's home profits.[7] Losses of a subsidiary, in contrast, cannot be offset against the parent's profits since the subsidiary is a separate unit.[8]
4. As we have seen, the fact that the subsidiary's profits and the parent's dividends are incomes to different legal entities also leads to *withholding taxes*. The host-country tax authorities invoke the source principle and tax not only the subsidiary, but also the parent. In contrast, a branch does not pay any withholding taxes since it does not pay any dividends.[9]

The last two aspects in the above list show that there are tax disadvantages associated with a full-equity WOS. As we shall see in Sections 23.5 and 23.6, these disadvantages can be mitigated by unbundling the payout stream, that is, by remitting cash under forms other than just dividends.

---

[6] There are exceptions to this deferral principle. For instance, under Subpart F, the US levies a tax on the profits of wholly owned "base companies" as if these profits had been paid out as dividends. A **base company** is a kind of reinvoicing center and holding company which gathers profits from all over the world in a tax haven (within the leeway left by transfer pricing restrictions in the various host countries). Without the Subpart F rule, a US multinational could postpone US taxation (and redirect funds to other group companies) until the funds are actually needed within the US.

[7] Depending on the two tax laws, the loss could even be deductible twice—once when it is taken over by the head office for *home*-country tax purposes, and once when the branch carries forward or backward its losses to different income periods for *host*-country tax purposes.

[8] This is true unless the parent's local tax authority can be convinced that the losses justify a permanent reduction in the value of the participation. This is not easy.

[9] Again, there are exceptions. For example, until recently France levied a deferred withholding tax when the foreign *parent* paid out dividends. The withholding tax was based on the French branch's share in the foreign company's overall profits.

23.4.3   Other Forms of Remittances (Unbundling)

Thus far, we have considered only capital transfers and dividends as ways in which the WOS can transfer funds to the parent or to related companies. In addition to dividends, the subsidiary can also pay out royalties, interest, or management fees for services rendered (or claimed to be rendered)—items that are, by definition, impossible for a branch to pay to the parent. In addition, the subsidiary can lease equipment from its parent, and remit both the principal and the interest on the implicit loan under the form of lease payments.[10] These alternative payment forms are tax-deductible expenses to the subsidiary and, therefore, reduce the subsidiary's tax bill. However, to complete the picture, we also have to think of the recipient's taxes, both in the host country (withholding taxes) and in the company's home base (corporate income taxes, hopefully with some relief for the withholding tax).

23.4.4   Transfer Pricing

A subsidiary can remit funds to a related company by agreeing to pay more for its purchases of goods and services from the other company, or by charging less for sales to the other company. This, we saw, is also possible with a branch, except that in the case of a subsidiary, the transactions are regular purchases and sales, with invoices and actual payments, rather than accounting entries that allocate profits to different branches within the same company.

After this review of the various ways in which a company can transfer funds, we now consider the tax treatment of dividends, royalties, and interest payments in the home country. Again, we have to distinguish between the exclusion rule and the credit system.

23.5   INTERNATIONAL TAXATION OF A SUBSIDIARY: THE CREDIT SYSTEM

When a subsidiary remits dividends to its parent, or royalties or interest payments to a related company, the same principles apply as in the branch case. Under the credit system, each payment is grossed up with the foreign taxes that have been levied on the income, and these foreign taxes are used as a credit against the home-country tax that is normally payable on the recipient's total foreign income (or, in some countries, the recipient's worldwide income). The only complication that could arise is the tax credit that accompanies a dividend.

23.5.1   Direct and Indirect Tax Credits on Foreign Dividends

In a strict legal sense, the only tax paid by the *parent* on the dividend is the withholding tax (if any); the corporate tax on the subsidiary's profits is, legally speaking, paid by a separate entity. Economically, though, the parent and a WOS are one entity. Thus, if the parent received no credit for the corporate taxes paid by the subsidiary, there would be a substantial fiscal penalty attached to the incorporation of a branch into a subsidiary. For this reason, the credit system uses a kind of look-through rule. It goes back all the way to the subsidiary's before-tax income (out of which the dividend was paid), and grants

---

[10] Under a **capital lease contract**, a *leasing company* or *lessor* buys a piece of equipment and lends it to a user, the *lessee*, for the entire normal life of the equipment. At the end of the contract, the lessor has an option to buy the equipment at a price that corresponds to the initial estimate of the terminal value. The lessee's periodic *lease payments* compensate the lessor for the principal and the interest of the investment. Such a lease contract is very similar to the lessee buying the equipment with borrowed money and using the equipment as security for the loan. Note that, in some countries, the right to depreciate the equipment is with the legal owner (the lessor) while in other countries the depreciation is done by the user (the lessee). Thus, in the case of international leasing, a piece of equipment can sometimes be depreciated twice. OECD countries are taking measures against such double depreciation.

a credit for corporate taxes paid by the WOS. Thus, a dividend carries with it *two* tax credits—the *direct* tax credit for the withholding tax *paid* on the dividend, and the *indirect* tax credit for the corporate taxes *deemed paid* on the dividend. Apart from this, the logic is the same as in the branch case.

A 100-Percent-Equity WOS: The Full-Payout Case

Consider the following example of a fully equity-financed subsidiary, which is owned by the parent firm.

Example   23.14

In Table 23.5, we consider again a German-owned Tunisian operation with an income of DEM 100. The Tunisian corporate tax rate is 35 percent, and the withholding tax on dividends is 17 percent. The

TABLE 23.5   Comparison of a Branch with a Full-Equity WOS: Full vs. Partial Payout

	Branch	Full-equity WOS 100% payout	Full-equity WOS 50% payout
Tunisia			
Tunisian profit	100	100	100
<Income tax>	<35>	<35>	<35>
After-tax profit	65	65	65
Gross dividend	—	65	32.5
<Withholding tax>	—	<11>	<5.5>
Net dividend	—	54	27.0
Germany			
Net branch income or dividend	65	54	27.0
Gross-up: Direct credit	35	11	5.5
Indirect credit	—	35	17.5
Taxable foreign income	100	100	50.0
German tax due	40	40	20.0
Tax credit: <Direct credit>	<35>	<11>	<5.5>
<Indirect credit>	—	<35>	<17.5>
Net German tax due	5	0	0.0
Excess tax credit	0	6	3.0

The branch case is described in Table 23.1 (under column titled "Credit Method"). In the full-payout, full-equity WOS case, the withholding tax on the DEM 65 gross dividend is DEM $65 \times 0.17 =$ DEM 11. In Germany, the DEM 54 net dividend is grossed up with the direct credit for the withholding tax, DEM 11, and with the indirect credit for Tunisian corporate taxes, DEM 35, to obtain a taxable income of DEM $54 + 11 + 35 = 100$. If the German parent's tax rate is 40 percent, DEM 40 is due. As Tunisian taxes were already DEM $35 +$ DEM $11 =$ DEM 46, the parent will potentially be left with an excess tax credit of 6. In the 50 percent payout case, the withholding tax is of course proportionally lower, and the indirect tax credit is also halved: the indirect tax credit is $32.5/65 \times 35 = 17.5$. Thus, the German tax and the excess tax credit are reduced proportionally.

first column repeats the tax computations for a branch under the Credit Method that appeared in Table 23.1. The middle column considers a WOS with the same income, which is paid out entirely as a dividend. Ignore the third column for the time being. In the middle column, the Tunisian corporate tax of DEM 35 leaves DEM 65 as the after-tax profit, which is, by assumption, fully paid out. The withholding tax on this gross dividend is DEM $65 \times 0.17 = $ DEM 11. The net dividend, therefore, is DEM $65 - 11 = 54$. In Germany, this net dividend is grossed up with the *direct* credit for the withholding tax, DEM 11, and with the *indirect* credit for Tunisian corporate taxes, DEM 35. That is, one goes back to the before-tax Tunisian income, DEM $54 + 11 + 35 = $ DEM 100. If the German parent's tax rate is 40 percent, DEM 40 is due on this income, but Tunisian taxes were already DEM $35 + $ DEM $11 = $ DEM 46. Thus, the parent will potentially be left with an excess tax credit of 6.

The example illustrates how the credit system intends to avoid fiscal discrimination between the branch and a full-equity, full-payout WOS (which is, after all, very close to a branch). The only difference is the withholding tax, which in this example, potentially creates an excess tax credit. If this excess tax credit cannot be absorbed elsewhere or carried back or forward, it might be advantageous to defer the dividend (and its withholding tax) to a year in which excess tax credits can be used against other income taxes. This is the timing option implicit in the deferral system. Another solution might be to "unbundle" the payout. Before we discuss unbundling, however, we discuss the rules that apply when the payout is less than 100 percent or when the foreign company is not 100 percent owned by the recipient.

The General Case

In many countries, the *indirect* tax credit is obtained only if the recipient company has a controlling interest in the foreign company that pays out the dividend. In the US, for instance, the rule is that the recipient must own at least 25 percent of the foreign company, directly or indirectly. Thus, the indirect tax credit is lost when the participation is classified as a pure portfolio investment rather than as an active participation in the foreign company.

If the dividend is less than 100 percent of profits, then in principle, the indirect tax credit is computed as

$$\text{Indirect tax credit} = \frac{\text{Gross dividend (before withholding tax)}}{\text{Corporate profit after corporate taxes}} \times \text{Corporate taxes.} \qquad [1]$$

In the full payout case, the ratio in the first part of this formula equals unity. With a partial payout, the tax credit is reduced proportionally.

Example   23.15

The rule for indirect tax credits is illustrated in the last column of Table 23.5. Since the dividend is only 50 percent of the profits after Tunisian taxes, the indirect tax credit is reduced proportionally:

$$\text{Indirect tax credit} = \frac{32.5}{65} \times 35 = 17.5.$$

Together with the withholding tax, this still creates a 46 percent total foreign tax rate, which leaves the parent with a 6 percent (that is, DEM 3) potential excess tax credit.

We finish our discussion of tax credits on dividends with some technical notes on Equation [1]. First, as in the branch case, the subsidiary's before-tax income as computed by the parent's tax authorities may differ from the one in the subsidiary's tax return, since the parent's home tax collector may reallocate expenses and reassess the foreign income. Thus, the corporate profits after corporate taxes in Equation [1] are to be interpreted as the *reassessed* foreign profits minus the (effectively paid) foreign tax. The possibility of reassessments of foreign profits means that we cannot write Equation [1] as Indirect tax credit = (gross dividend) $\times \tau/(1 - \tau)$, where τ = the foreign corporate tax rate.[11]

Second, if the after-tax corporate profit in a given year is negative and there is a dividend, then Equation [1] would imply a negative credit. One solution is to set the credit equal to zero if the formula yields a negative number. However, this means that there is no tax shield when a subsidiary pays a dividend out of retained earnings in a year where its earnings are negative—even though the retained earnings were taxed in the past. A related problem is associated with the fact that the effective foreign tax rate fluctuates over time, for instance, because of tax breaks received abroad or because of reassessments of foreign profits by the parent's tax authorities. If the subsidiary pays out its retained earnings in a year where the effective foreign tax rate happens to be low, then there would be a low tax credit even though the effective taxes in the past were high. To reduce these problems, the US tax code bases the tax credits on the cumulative taxes and the cumulative after-tax profits since 1986 (the year of a major tax reform):

$$\text{Indirect tax credit} = \text{Max}\left(\text{Gross dividend} \times \frac{\text{Cumulative taxes since 1986}}{\text{Cumulative after-tax earnings since 1986}}, 0\right). \quad [2]$$

If the host and home tax authorities always agreed on the taxable income *and* if the foreign tax rate were a constant, denoted by τ, then the ratio in Equation [2] would be equal to $\tau/(1 - \tau)$. By cumulating the taxes and the net profits over time, this formula dampens the fluctuations in the indirect tax credit that could occur with formula [1] if, in a given year, the company receives a tax break or if there is a substantial upward reassessment of the subsidiary's profits.

23.5.2   Tax Planning through Unbundling of the Intragroup Transfers

We saw, in Table 23.5, that the compounding of host-country corporate taxes and withholding taxes increases the chance that the parent company ends up with excess foreign tax credits. In the branch case, the basic remedy against such unused foreign tax credits is to make sure that there is enough low-tax foreign income from elsewhere, so that the total foreign tax on the entire foreign income does not exceed the domestic norm. The same applies in the case of subsidiaries. The parent can combine dividends from high-tax host countries with dividends from low-tax host countries. In addition, the subsidiary from any given host country can **unbundle** the payments, and remit low-taxed royalties, interest, and management fees next to a (high-taxed) residual dividend.

---

[11] If the reassessed profits equal the profits declared and taxed in the host country, then host-country taxes in year t are equal to $\tau \times \text{Profits}_t$ and after-tax earnings for year t are equal to $(1 - \tau) \times \text{Profits}_t$. Thus, Equation [1] would equal

$$\text{Gross Dividend} \times \frac{\tau \, \text{Profits}_t}{(1 - \tau)\text{Profits}_t} = \text{Gross Dividend} \times \frac{\tau}{1 - \tau}.$$

Example   23.16

In Table 23.6, we modify the example presented in Table 23.5 as follows: part of the equity is converted into an intracompany loan carrying an interest payment of DEM 40 subject to a 20 percent withholding tax. This has the following effects:

- The Tunisian profit, corporate tax, net profit, dividend, and withholding tax are all lowered. So is the grossed-up dividend, which is now DEM 60 rather than DEM 100.

TABLE 23.6   The Effects of Unbundling the Payout

	Full Equity	DEM 40 paid to parent as interest	
Tunisia			
Tunisian profit before interest	100	100.0	
Interest paid to parent	–	<40.0>	
Taxable corporate income	100	60.0	
<Income tax>	<35>	<21.0>	
After-tax profit	65	39.0	
		dividend	interest
Gross amounts paid out	65	39.0	40
<Withholding tax>	<11> (17%)	<6.6> (17%)	<8> (20%)
Net amount paid out	54	32.4	32
Germany			
Net amount received	54	32.4	32
Gross-up: Direct credit	11	6.6	8
Indirect credit	35	21.0	–
Taxable foreign income	100	60.0	40
Total taxable foreign income		100.0	
German tax due	40	40.0	
<Tax credit>	35 + 11 = <46>	21 + 6.6 + 8 = <35.6>	
Net German tax due	0	4.4	
Excess tax credit	6	0	
Total taxes	46	40	

The full-equity case is from the column titled "Full Equity WOS" Table 23.5. In the right-hand-side column, the subsidiary's earnings before interest and taxes are partly paid out as a DEM 40 interest payment on a loan from the parent. This reduces the taxable profits and the host-country corporate tax, and, still assuming a full payout, also the dividend and the withholding tax on it. For home-country taxation purposes, each income (dividends and interest) is grossed up separately with the taxes levied on it. Since the total foreign tax rate on interest payments is lower than the total tax rate on profits and dividends, the excess foreign tax credit problem is reduced and, in the example, even entirely eliminated.

- The decrease in the dividend is amply compensated by the interest income. The net interest payment carries its own tax credit, and is grossed up to DEM 40.
- Total grossed-up foreign income, for the purpose of German taxation, is the sum of grossed-up dividend income and interest income. This amounts to DEM 100, exactly as before. However, total foreign taxes after unbundling (DEM $21 + 6.6 + 8 = 35.6$) are lower than before unbundling (DEM $35 + 11 = 46$). Thus, the original excess foreign tax credit is eliminated.

Let us analyze the origin of the tax savings in a different way:

- The group avoids Tunisian corporate taxes on the DEM 40 interest payment. This savings amounts to DEM $40 \times 35\% =$ DEM 14. In addition, dividend payout is lower by DEM $40 \times (1 - 35\%) = 26$, which leads to an additional savings in withholding taxes of DEM $26 \times 17\% = 4.42$. Thus, total Tunisian taxes on profits and dividends decrease by DEM $14 + 4.42 = 18.42$. As a percentage, the savings amounts to $18.42/40 = 46\%$, which is, of course, the total foreign tax rate on profits and dividends as computed in Table 23.5.
- Instead, the Tunisian tax on the interest payment is the 20 percent withholding tax.

Thus, total foreign taxes go down by DEM $40 \times (46\% - 20\%) = 10.4$. This is sufficient to eliminate the excess tax credits.

If foreign taxes can be used to offset taxes on *worldwide* income (including the parent's domestic income), it is less likely that the firm will be left with unused tax credits. However, some countries, including the US, separate the taxation of domestic income from the taxation of foreign income. The natural temptation of US corporations with excess foreign tax credits then is to transform domestic income into low-tax foreign income.

Example   23.17

Assume that a US firm has an excess tax credit, and that the firm holds domestic bonds. The strategy would be to sell these bonds, and buy foreign bonds—for instance, USD bonds issued by an offshore financing center of a big US multinational corporation. Economically, nothing has changed, but the tax effect is that the domestic interest income has been transformed into (low-taxed) "foreign" interest income. Excess foreign tax credits from foreign operations can then be used to avoid income taxes on the interest from the bonds.

To forestall such strategies, the US tax authority divides foreign income into different so-called *baskets*, for example, *active foreign income* from subsidiaries in which the parent has a substantial equity participation, and *passive foreign income* from other sources. The foreign bonds would surely be passive income, the dividends from the WOS would not. Overall taxes would then be computed per basket, not allowing any transfer of excess tax credits from one basket to the other.

Our last comment concerns foreign tax breaks and tax holidays. As we saw, with a credit system, there is no way to pay less than the home tax rate; tax planning can achieve no more than a reduction or elimination of what you pay above the domestic tax rate. However, this means that tax holidays or rebates granted by the host country are effectively undone by additional taxation in the home country.

Essentially, by their tax concessions, host-country tax authorities transfer money to the home-country tax authorities rather than to the investing company. This is especially offensive to developing countries, who see their tax incentives disappear into the treasuries of rich countries. Bilateral tax treaties signed with developing countries therefore sometimes contain *tax sparing* clauses which let the investing parent keep the tax benefit.

23.6   INTERNATIONAL TAXATION OF A SUBSIDIARY: EXCLUSION SYSTEM

We now study the exclusion system as applied to subsidiaries in foreign countries. A home country that adopts the exclusion system will typically apply the exclusion privilege only to dividends received from abroad. The reason is that for other forms of remittances from the subsidiary to the parent—like royalties, interest payments, and lease payments—the foreign tax (if any) is a withholding tax; and because this tax is much lower than a typical corporate tax, it would be unreasonable to also exempt nondividend income from home-country taxation. Therefore, a credit system rather than an exclusion system often applies to nondividend remittances, or the exclusion percentage is much lower than that for dividends.

Under such an exclusion system, tax planning is easy. Compute the overall tax burden per form of remittance (dividends paid out of profits, royalties, interest payments, and lease payments), and remit as much as possible under the lowest-tax form. The total tax on dividends and on the underlying profits then consists of host-country corporate taxes and withholding taxes, plus possibly some home-country tax if the exclusion privilege is not 100 percent. Taxes on other remittances include withholding taxes, and home taxation. The following example illustrates how one computes and compares the *total* tax burdens on each form of remittance.

Example   23.18

Suppose that 95 percent of the dividends received by a Belgian company from its foreign subsidiary are excluded from taxable income, while a standard credit system applies to nondividend income. Corporate taxes are 39 percent. Suppose that the foreign subsidiary is subject to a 25 percent tax on profits, a 5 percent withholding tax on dividends, and a 17 percent withholding tax on interest payments and royalties. In Table 23.7, we compare the after-tax proceeds if BEF 100 is paid out as a royalty, and if BEF 100 is treated as part of the subsidiary's profit and then paid out as a dividend. We conclude that, in this example, profits (paid out as dividends) are preferred over royalties.

An exclusion system offers one, large, potential loophole. As we know, a firm can remit most of the subsidiary's gross earnings as nondividend income to escape corporate taxes in the host country. A gain will already result if home-country taxes are lower than host-country taxes, but we can even avoid most or all of the home-country taxes if the deductible remittances enter the home country in the form of tax-exempt dividends. To achieve this, the subsidiary's remittances are paid not to the parent but to an offshore holding company fully owned by the parent and located in a tax haven. The holding company receives this income, pays a minimal tax on it, and then transfers the income as dividends to the parent. Under an exclusion system, this eliminates virtually all taxation.

TABLE 23.7   Computation of Total Taxes on Different Remittances

	Payout in the form of profits and dividends	Payout in the form of royalties, interest
Before-tax amount paid out by subsidiary	100.00	100
Corporate tax	<25.00>	—
After tax	75.00	100
Withholding tax	<3.75> (5%)	<17> (17%)
Net receipts of parent	71.25	83
Gross-up	–	17
Taxable income of parent	3.5625 (5% of 71.25)	100
Home tax (39%)	1.3894	39
Tax credit	–	17
Net home tax	1.3894	22
Total taxes	30.1394	39

Of the after-tax net dividend, only 5 percent (that is, $71.25 \times 5\% = 3.5625$) is taxed at the Belgian corporate tax rate of 39 percent, which implies that the only Belgian tax on profits and dividends is $3.5625 \times 39\% = 1.389375$ (rounded to 1.3894 in the table). Total taxes are the foreign corporate tax, the withholding tax, and the small Belgian tax. For royalties and interest, by assumption, the standard credit system applies. The net income is first grossed up, and then taxed at the 39 percent rate with a credit for the BEF 17 paid in foreign withholding tax.

Example   23.19

If a US subsidiary remits interest income to its Belgian parent, the taxes are (1) US withholding taxes, and (2) Belgian corporate taxes (with only partial credit for the US withholding tax). Alternatively, until a recent tax reform, the parent could create a 100-percent-owned holding company in the Netherlands, which then sets up a 100-percent-owned holding company in the Dutch Antilles that, in turn, owns the US subsidiary. Interest by the US subsidiary was paid out free of US withholding taxes to the Antilles holding company, which pays a minimal corporate tax (1.5 to 3 percent) on its interest income. The funds were then remitted as dividends (with zero withholding tax) to the Netherlands, where a minimal corporate tax applied, and then to Belgium, where an exclusion system applied.[12] Thus, the Belgian corporate tax on interest income was replaced by a minimal Antilles and Dutch tax, with no further Belgian tax on the dividends.

Another variant of this strategy caters to corporations that have portfolio investments. Rather than buying domestic bonds and paying taxes on the coupon income, the company (or a financial insti-

---

[12] The Dutch company was needed because, under Belgian law, a dividend from a tax haven like the Antilles does not benefit from the dividend exclusion privilege.

tution) can set up an incorporated mutual fund in, say, Luxembourg. The fund buys the bonds, escapes normal Luxembourg corporate taxation (since it is a mutual fund), and pays out the coupons under the form of tax-free dividends to its corporate investors. Again, taxable coupon income would be transformed into tax-free dividend income.

To close this loophole, countries often refuse to sign bilateral tax treaties with tax havens (or refuse to extend a treaty, if the special tax rule for offshore companies became effective after the original treaty was signed). In the absence of such a treaty, then, there would be a unilateral rule offering partial rather than full exclusion. Another countermeasure could be a look-through rule. The holding company is ignored because it is a construct with, as its sole purpose, the avoidance of taxes. Under such a rule, taxes are based on economic substance rather than on legal form; that is, the dividends would be taxed as the underlying royalties or interest fees. A third possible countermeasure is to refuse exclusion of dividends from low-tax countries, from foreign companies that enjoy a special low-tax status, or from incorporated mutual funds.

23.7   CONCLUSION

This chapter provides an introduction to the broad principles of international tax law. To reduce double taxation, countries apply either the exclusion principle or the credit system. In principle, under the exclusion system, the only tax is the foreign tax, so that a foreign-owned company can compete with a purely local company (*capital import neutrality*). In principle, a credit system ensures that the total tax on foreign income is the same as on domestic income, so that there is no fiscal incentive for foreign investment (*capital export neutrality*). However, the actual application of either system usually falls short of the system's stated aim since, in practice, taxes are never fully capital-import or capital-export neutral. In addition, tax rates differ across countries, so that the exclusion system and the credit system would lead to different results even if each system were implemented in a perfect way. These considerations make tax planning a worthwhile exercise for the corporate treasurer.

Tax planning consists of determining where to allocate costs and profits (within the leeway offered by arm's length rules), and how to remit the cash flows. Taxes depend on how much is remitted under the form of royalties, interest payments, lease payments, and management fees; taxes also depend on how indirect costs are allocated and on how transfer prices are set. Under a credit system, there is a preference for the form of remittance that attracts minimal foreign taxes. This rule minimizes the loss from unused tax credits but cannot reduce the total tax rate below the domestic rate. Under the exclusion system, the overall tax burden (home and foreign taxes) is computed for each type of remittance, and the lowest-tax form is preferred; total taxes can fall below the domestic rate. Next to actual financial remittances (such as dividends, royalties, and interest payments) and quasi-remittances (such as management fees, transfer pricing, and lease payments), one could also use equity transactions or intragroup loans to transfer funds from the subsidiary to the parent or to another related company.

Tax planning and "treaty shopping" are rather complex, and rules tend to change quickly in response to newly discovered loopholes. For these reasons, tax planning is better left to specialists, and no investment project should be accepted solely on the basis of hoped-for gains from tax planning. Stated differently, you should look at these gains as an extra sweetener, but not as a consideration that could actually tilt the balance in favor of adopting a project.

QUIZ QUESTIONS

True-False Questions

1. The term "permanent establishment" (PE) is just tax-speak for "branch." That is, every branch is a PE and vice versa.
2. As soon as there is a permanent physical presence abroad, there is a PE.
3. A PE has a separate accounting system, while a branch does not.
4. If a person lives or earns income in more than one country, there may be double taxation.
5. The source principle says that any person earning money in a particular country is taxable in that country on his or her worldwide income.
6. Withholding taxes are levied by the host country on the taxpayer's worldwide income.
7. The legal basis for withholding taxes on nonlabor income paid to foreigners is the residence principle.
8. The Capital Import Neutrality principle says that the foreign branch ought to be taxed as if it were a locally owned company.
9. The Capital Export Neutrality principle says that the foreign branch ought to be taxed as if it were a locally owned company.
10. The Capital Export Neutrality principle says that there should be no fiscal benefit or penalty associated with the fact that ownership and operations straddle two countries.
11. The deferral principle applies equally to the exclusion system and the credit system.
12. The disagreement on how to compute the income of a foreign branch arises only under the credit system.
13. The disagreement on how to compute the income of a foreign branch arises under both the credit system and the exclusion system.
14. The disagreement on how to compute the income of a foreign subsidiary arises only under the credit system.
15. The disagreement on how to compute the income of a foreign subsidiary arises under both the credit system and the exclusion system.

Below, a *marginal* tax rate is to be understood as the *additional* taxes you pay per cent or penny or öre of additional foreign income from one particular host country. The average tax rate is to be understood as the total tax paid on all foreign income as a percentage of the foreign income. For the questions that relate to the credit system, it is assumed that foreign income is taxed separately from domestic income. Verify whether the following statements are true or false.

16. Under a 100-percent-exclusion system, the marginal tax rate on foreign income is the foreign corporate tax rate (τ_c^*).
17. Under a 100-percent-exclusion system, the marginal tax rate on foreign income is the foreign corporate tax rate (τ_c^*) plus the foreign withholding tax (τ_w).
18. Under a 100-percent-exclusion system, the marginal tax rate on foreign income is given by

$$1 - (1 - \tau_c^*)(1 - \tau_w) = \tau_c^* + \tau_w - \tau_c^* \tau_w.$$

19. Under a credit system, the marginal tax rate on foreign income is the home-country corporate tax rate τ_c.

20. Under a credit system, the marginal tax rate on foreign income is the higher of either the home-country corporate tax rate τ_c or the marginal foreign tax.

21. Under a credit system, the marginal tax rate on foreign income is bounded from above and below by the home-country corporate tax rate τ_c and the marginal foreign tax.

22. Under a credit system, the average tax rate on foreign income is the home-country corporate tax rate τ_c.

23. Under a credit system, the average tax rate on foreign income is either the home-country corporate tax rate τ_c or the average foreign tax—whichever is higher.

24. Under a credit system, the average tax rate on foreign income is bounded from above and below by the home-country corporate tax rate τ_c and the average foreign tax.

Additional Quiz Questions

1. Suppose that foreign activity is conducted through a wholly owned subsidiary. Which assumptions are needed to achieve both Capital Import and Capital Export Neutrality?

   (a) The home and host corporate tax rates are the same.
   (b) There is no withholding tax on dividends.
   (c) The tax basis is computed in exactly the same way in both countries.
   (d) There is full payout.
   (e) There are no interest payments, no license payments, no lease payments, and no management fees between WOS and parent.
   (f) A credit system applies to nondividend remittances from WOS to parent.

2. What does one mean by the *residence principle* and the *source principle*? What do these principles imply for the taxation of income on

   (a) Pure (direct) exports?
   (b) Exports through a dependent agent?
   (c) Exports through a branch/PE?
   (d) Foreign activities through a subsidiary?

3. Explain, using a numerical example of your own, how differences between the host- and home-country rules for the allocation of overhead can impair the neutrality of a credit system or an exclusion system.

4. How do companies take advantage of the basic exclusion system for dividends? Which additional tax rules can be applied to prevent these unintended uses?

5. How can one reduce excess foreign tax credits by transforming domestic income into foreign income? Which additional tax rules can be applied to prevent such tactics?

6. Conventional wisdom says that tax planning means minimizing foreign taxes. Is this true under the exclusion system? Is it true under the credit system? If your answer was yes in both cases, is there no difference between these systems regarding the tax savings you make by tax planning?

7. The bartender at your favorite pub sneers that, by using transfer pricing, a company can always eliminate its excess foreign tax credits. Do you agree, or do you think that your friend is forgetting something? Why?

EXERCISES

1. A foreign-owned company earns 100,000 in its host country. The host-country corporate tax is 50 percent, the withholding tax 20 percent, and the home-country tax is 40 percent.

   (a) What is the total tax if there is no relief from double taxation?
   (b) Still assuming full double taxation, what tax could have been avoided if the business had been conducted through a branch/PE?
   (c) Go back to the case of a WOS. What is the total tax burden if there is full payout and if the exclusion principle applies in the home country?
   (d) What is the total tax burden if there is full payout and if the exclusion privilege is only 80 percent?
   (e) What is the total tax burden if there is full payout and the host country uses a credit system?
   (f) In question (e), does it matter whether the host country taxes foreign income separately from domestic income?

2. Suppose that the corporate tax schedule in Finland is as follows:

   - 25 percent tax on income below FIM 50,000.
   - 30 percent tax on income between FIM 50,000 and FIM 100,000.
   - 35 percent tax on all income exceeding FIM 100,000.

   (a) What is the tax if a Finnish corporation's income is FIM 200,000, whereof 100,000 are profits on domestic sales and 100,000 are profits on exports to Hong Kong (without PE in Hong Kong)?
   (b) Assume that Hong Kong levies a flat 15 percent corporate tax, and no withholding tax on dividends, and that Finland applies a pure exclusion system. Is there any incentive to set up a branch/PE in Hong Kong? If so, what is the worldwide tax?
   (c) Add to question (b) a rule under which Finland preserves the progressiveness of the tax schedule (see Figure 23.1). Is there still an incentive to set up a branch/PE in Hong Kong? If so, what is the worldwide tax?
   (d) Repeat question (c) and assume that Hong Kong's tax schedule is identical to Finland's, and that Hong Kong also preserves progressiveness. Is there still an incentive to set up a branch/PE in Hong Kong? If so, what is the worldwide tax?

3. The company Think Tankards has a stable foreign income, which is taxed at a low rate abroad. In each of the three preceding income years, it effectively paid USD 50m in additional US taxes on foreign income, and it expects to do the same for the years to come. For the current year, however, there is a USD 100m excess foreign tax credit. How is this excess credit treated under each of the following carry-forward/carry-back rules? What is the present value of the loss if future tax breaks are discounted at 15 percent?

   (a) No carry-back, one-year carry-forward.
   (b) No carry-back, two-year carry-forward.
   (c) One-year carry-back, two-year carry-forward.
   (d) Two-year carry-back, two-year carry-forward.

4. A Belgian bank holds BEF 10 billion worth of seven-year BEF government bonds, with a direct yield of 10 percent (that is, its annual interest income is BEF 1b).

(a) Until the tax reform in 1992, the bank could transform its interest income into dividend income, which enjoyed a 90 percent exclusion privilege. Specifically, the bank sold its bonds to a Dublin dock company (DDC), which was fully owned by an Irish holding company (IHC), which in turn was fully owned by the Belgian bank (BB). Interest income received by the DDC was taxed at 10 percent, and then paid out as a dividend to IHC, which did not pay any taxes (100 percent exclusion within Ireland). IHC then paid the dividend to its owner, BB.[13] Assume no withholding tax between Belgium and Ireland, and a 90 percent dividend exclusion and a 40 percent corporate tax rate in Belgium. What was the annual tax gain?

(b) A tax consultant suggested that BB would gain even more by swapping its seven-year, 10 percent BEF bonds into NZD, which at that time yielded 20 percent. Thus, the consultant argued, the gains would be doubled. What crucial feature is overlooked in this argument? (Hint: you need an insight from Chapter 4.)

(c) Although the argument of the tax consultant is full of holes, it is basically correct: there *is* a gain from swapping the BEF into NZD. What is the gain? (Hint: you again need an insight from Chapter 4.)

5. Your two foreign outposts, a branch in Germany and one in Singapore, each have sales of 100. The host-country tax rates are 40 percent and 20 percent, respectively.

(a) If your home country uses the credit system and has a 30 percent tax, how would you (try to) allocate total costs (120) over the two subsidiaries? Assuming an unlimited potential to shift costs, is there an incentive to allocate *all* costs to one branch?

(b) Assume that your country uses a credit system, and that you have very little leeway in reallocating costs over the two branches. So you consider increasing the transfer price charged by Singapore to Germany. Imports into the European Union are taxed at 25 percent. Would you increase or decrease the transfer price?

(c) In question (b), at what level of the import duty τ_m is the advantage wiped out?

(d) Same question as (a), except that your home country applies a 90 percent exclusion rule?

6. Your only source of foreign income is a marketing WOS in Hong Kong, where the tax rate is 20 percent. At home you pay 35 percent. There is no withholding tax.

(a) Under the 100 percent exclusion method, would you use a high transfer price or a low transfer price for sales to the subsidiary?

(b) Same question as (a), except that the credit method applies.

(c) Same question as (a), but there is a 10 percent import duty on sales to Hong Kong.

7. Suppose that the German parent has sales equaling 200, and the Tunisian branch, 100. Direct costs are 80 and 30, respectively. German tax authorities allocate overhead, which amounts to 120, on the basis of sales, while in Tunisia allocation is proportional to direct cost. German and Tunisian taxes are 40 percent. Are you vexed by or happy with this discrepancy between the rules? Consider both the credit system and the exclusion system.

---

[13] A nice additional detail was that BB held mostly preferred stock of IHC, redeemable after seven years, rather than common stock. Redeemable preferred stock issued by a financial company comes into the same BIS risk class as government bonds, while common stock would have absorbed more capital.

8. A US corporation has two foreign marketing branches, one in France and one in Hong Kong. The current situation is summarized as follows (all numbers in thousands of USD):

	Hong Kong	France	US (domestic income)
Sales	1,000	5,000	10,000*
Costs: purchases from parent	500	2,500	n/a
other expenses	100	500	6,000
depreciation	100	500	1,000
Profits	300	1,500	3,000
Corporate taxes	45 (15%)	600 (40%)	900 (30%)
Profits after taxes	255	900	2,100

*including sales to subsidiaries.

(a) The US tax rate is 30 percent, and taxation of foreign and domestic income is separated, with the foreign tax credit applied to the tax on foreign income only. Is there still a US tax due, or is there an unused tax credit?

(b) The parent is currently making a profit on its "sales" to the branches, but considers changing the profit allocation. The company thinks that it can increase or decrease the transfer price by up to 5 percent without creating any problems with the tax authorities, on the condition that the transfer price remains the same for both branches. Should the company increase the price or decrease it?

(c) Is your conclusion in (a) or (b) affected if domestic and foreign income is taxed together (that is, the tax is computed on worldwide income, and then the tax credit is applied)?

9. Sales and costs are 200 and 100, respectively, for the Tunisian, and 100 and 60 for the Hong Kong branch. The tax rates are 50 percent in Tunisia, and 25 percent in Hong Kong. The parent's home country, Germany, has a 40 percent tax rate and applies the credit system.

(a) Verify that there is an excess tax credit of 4.

(b) Verify that when the parent shifts costs worth 40 from Hong Kong to Tunisia, the original excess tax credit has been replaced by a foreign tax shortfall of 6.

(c) Suppose that the Tunisian tax authorities unexpectedly reject the additional costs (40), so that this part of the costs is not deductible anywhere. What is the total tax?

MIND-EXPANDING EXERCISE

1. A UK company wants to help a long-standing supplier in the US who is in need of cash. The alternatives considered are the following:

- The UK company can buy D worth of seven-year bonds, newly issued by the US company, at a $p.a.$ interest rate of R_B.
- Alternatively, the UK company can buy D worth of preferred stock, newly issued by the US company. The stock is redeemable after seven years and carries a $p.a.$ preferred dividend of R_P.

The rate on the loan, R_B, must be an arm's length rate; that is, R_B is given. In order for the preferred-stock alternative to be acceptable, the preferred dividend rate R_P should be set such that (1) the US company is not worse off with preferred stock, and (2) the UK company is not worse off either. We only investigate the tax aspects. Below, we demonstrate the well-known result that the US company is not worse off if $R_P \le R_D (1 - \tau_{US})$, where τ_{US} is the US corporate tax rate:

Residual cash flows for the US borrower

	With bonds	With preferred stock
Earnings before interest and taxes	X	X
<Interest paid>	$<R_B D>$	$<0>$
Taxable	$X - R_B D$	X
Earnings after taxes	$(X - R_B D)(1 - \tau_{US})$	$X(1 - \tau_{US})$
<Preferred dividend paid>	$<0>$	$<R_P D>$
Available for common shareholders	$(X - R_B D)(1 - \tau_{US})$	$X(1 - \tau_{US}) - R_P D$

From the last line, the US borrower will accept preferred stock if $R_P \le R_B(1 - \tau_{US})$.

Your task is to find the condition on R_P that must be met for the UK lender to be no worse off than with debt at R_B. The corporate tax rates are denoted by τ_{UK} and τ_{US}, respectively. The US withholding tax on dividends (including preferred dividends) is 5 percent, and the withholding tax on interest is 10 percent. The UK applies a credit system where foreign-paid taxes can be used as a credit for UK taxes due on worldwide income. You can assume, therefore, that there will be no unused tax credit.

In the table below, we already provide the analysis for the case where bonds are used. Make a similar analysis for the case where preferred stock is used, identify the condition on R_P under which the UK lender is no worse off than with bonds at R_B, and lastly, verify whether there is a solution that makes neither the lender nor the borrower worse off.

UK lender: After-tax cash flows

		With bonds	With preferred stock
Gross interest or dividend		$R_B D$	
<Withholding tax>		$<R_B D \times 0.10>$	
Net (cash) income		$R_B D \times 0.90$	
Gross-up:	direct	$R_B D \times 0.10$	
	indirect	none	
Tax basis		$R_B D$	
Tax due		$R_B D \, \tau_{UK}$	
<Credit:	direct>	$<R_B D \times 0.10>$	
	indirect>	<none>	
Net UK tax due		$R_B D \times (\tau_{UK} - 0.10)$	
Income after taxes		$= R_B D (1 - \tau_{UK})*$	

*from [Net cash income] – [Net UK tax due] = $R_D B [0.9 - (\tau_{UK} - 0.10)]$

24

VALUATION AND NEGOTIATION OF JOINT VENTURE PROJECTS

Our discussion in Chapter 21 of the Net Present Value (NPV) approach to capital budgeting assumes that a project is implemented as a branch of the investing firm or as a wholly owned subsidiary. Yet many projects involve two or more parent companies that join forces to undertake a particular venture. The purpose of this chapter is to present a coherent and practical approach for the valuation, determination of profit sharing rules, and tax planning of such international **joint-venture projects**.

NPV is an essential ingredient in the process of negotiating a joint venture in the sense that NPV allows any partner to verify whether the expected benefits of a proposed joint-venture contract exceed its costs. However, joint-venture negotiations are much more complicated than simple NPV calculations, because the prospective partners also have to determine the profit-sharing rules. From Chapter 21, we know that there are many ways to allocate cash flows between two companies:

- The profit-sharing contract could be a straightforward **pure-equity contract**, where the partners simply contribute their share in the initial investment, and then distribute the operating cash flows in proportion to their relative initial investments.
- There could also be a **license contract** between the joint venture and a partner (or even two or more partners). Under such a contract, a lump-sum fee and/or royalties is paid to the licensor. These license payments are subtracted from the operating income of the joint-venture company, and the residual cash flow then is shared among the shareholders in proportion to their initial investments. Thus, the distribution of the (total) operating cash flows is *nonproportional*.
- A third way to affect the distribution of the gains is to allow one partner to bring in an intangible asset at a negotiated value. The effect is that this partner's share in the equity and in the later cash flows exceeds his share in the initial cash investment. The same effect can be obtained by agreeing to overvalue a physical asset brought in by one of the partners.

The issue is how such a joint-venture contract should be negotiated, taking into account factors such as restrictions on foreign equity ownership in the host country, ceilings on royalty percentages, differences in taxes paid by the partners on their respective dividend incomes, differential tax treatment of dividends versus license income, and capital market segmentation (which implies that the partners may use different discount rates).

It is difficult to value and negotiate such joint-venture contracts without the help of a systematic framework. The purpose of this chapter is to offer such a framework. One crucial issue is how to distribute the **synergy gains**—that is, the present value of the cash flows over and above the value of the cash flows that the joint venture partners can obtain on their own. Elementary bargaining theory provides us with a simple rule for the division of the synergy gains: give every partner an equal share in the gains. The simplest way to implement an agreed-upon division of the gains is to set up a purely proportional joint venture. Likewise, any nonproportional contract can also be designed so that the expected synergy gains are still shared equally.

Thus, we suggest that the negotiation and valuation of a joint-venture contract start with the simplest possible contract, a simple pure-equity or proportional contract. In this first stage of the analysis, the focus is on the economics of the project rather than on tax planning and legal constraints, and the procedure is very similar to an NPV analysis for a wholly owned subsidiary. After this first-stage evaluation, two separate adjustments follow. The first adjustment to the pure-equity solution focuses on special intragroup arrangements (such as a license contract between one of the parents and the joint-venture company), while the second adjustment relates to extra-group financial arrangements (such as borrowing from third parties). The focus of this chapter is on the first stage (the proportional contract) and on the nonproportional elements in the joint-venture contract (the intragroup financial arrangements).

The chapter is structured as follows. In Section 24.1, we present the case for the three-step evaluation procedure of international projects in general, and for joint-venture proposals in particular. In Section 24.2, we state the basic principle of bargaining theory that we use in this chapter. In Section 24.3, we show how to apply this basic principle to the simplest possible case, the pure-equity joint branch with neutral taxes and integrated capital markets. In Section 24.4, we explain how to adjust the joint-branch solution for differences in the tax rate or the cost of capital. Section 24.5 introduces the most common deviation from the pure-equity framework—a license contract or management contract. Section 24.6 discusses various ways in which the results presented here can be generalized—for example, to account for transfer pricing or for a contribution of equity in kind.[1]

24.1   THE THREE-STEP APPROACH TO JOINT-VENTURE CAPITAL BUDGETING

The standard procedure for investment analysis is to evaluate the project in two steps. In the first stage, the project is assumed to be financed by equity, and the funds are assumed to be already available; accordingly, the focus is on the valuation of operating cash flows. In the second stage, this NPV is then adjusted for financing aspects. As we saw in Chapters 21, 22, and 23 valuing international projects

---

[1] An equity input *in kind* is an input which is not in the form of cash. Such a noncash input could be a tangible asset—like land or equipment, or an intangible asset—like a brand name, a distribution network, or production or marketing knowledge (*know-how*).

gives rise to many additional issues, including political risk, the effects of the project on the operating cash flows of the parent company or other related companies, the effect of exchange risk and capital market segmentation on the cost of capital, and the impact of international taxation on the remittance policy. The remittance policy is important because most foreign ventures are carried out under the form of a separate company (a subsidiary). Domestic projects, in contrast, are typically assumed to be in-house projects so that the investing firm is immediately and automatically the full owner of the project's cash flows. Refining a suggestion by Shapiro (1985), international capital budgeting can, therefore, be implemented in three steps:

(1) Step 1, the *bundled* valuation, where the project is assumed to be carried out in the form of a foreign branch and where the focus is on the economics of the project (for example, operational cash flows and exchange and political risks).
(2) Step 2, the *unbundling* stage, where the tax implications of various *intracompany* financial arrangements are considered.
(3) Step 3, the adjustments for the effects of *external* financing.

An additional complication in valuing international projects arises when the project takes the form of a joint venture. Joint ventures are useful when there is a complementarity between the partners' assets or competitive advantages, or when the partners want to share the uncertainty. For a joint venture, we can essentially follow the three-step approach outlined above for a wholly owned subsidiary. That is, we can first do the NPV exercise, assuming the foreign business is conducted as a joint branch. We define a joint branch as an unincorporated entity with proportional sharing of all cash flows (that is, not only profits or losses, but also financing of working capital, and depreciation).[2] The valuation of a joint-branch version of the project is intrinsically interesting for at least two reasons:

- First, it separates tax planning issues from economic issues. All cash flows held by the branch are automatically the property of the owners of the branch. It is true that by considering the joint-branch case, we ignore potential tax advantages of a clever remittance policy—but anticipated tax gains from non-equity contracts may disappear when loopholes are closed, and assumptions about dividend payout (and the corresponding advantage of tax deferral relative to a joint-branch structure) are inevitably shaky. For these reasons, it is helpful to know what part of the NPV is tax-related and what part is based on the intrinsic economic merits of the project.
- The joint branch may, in fact, be the best way to structure the contract. Relative to a pure-equity, incorporated joint-venture, the joint branch can avoid withholding taxes on dividends. Thus, by first valuing the branch mode of operating, the company can quantify the effects of incorporating the joint venture into a separate company, and estimate whether the cost in terms of withholding taxes is offset by fiscal advantages from royalties and other remittance techniques.

---

[2] In practice, the joint branch's working capital needs can be financed through bank loans. However, as each parent implicitly guarantees the loans of the joint branch, outside borrowing by the joint branch is essentially the same as outside borrowing by the parents. If there are no costs or tax issues, such borrowing would not affect the NPV; and if there are borrowing costs and tax benefits, these should be considered in Step 3. Likewise, the joint branch can invest free cash flows in the money market. However, in the absence of tax effects or transactions costs, this does not affect the NPV; and transactions costs or tax effects associated with outside lending should be analyzed in Step 3.

Once the joint-branch solution has been analyzed, it becomes relatively straightforward to adjust it for non-equity arrangements in the joint-venture contract (Step 2), as we shall show in a number of examples. The Step 3 adjustments for external financing can be done in the standard way outlined in Chapter 21, and will not be discussed in this chapter.

The three-step approach for joint ventures is similar to the approach recommended for wholly owned projects. However, there are complications in a joint-venture capital budgeting problem that do not arise in wholly owned projects. For one thing, NPV analysis is intertwined with the issue of profit sharing and is, therefore, hard to separate from the contract negotiations. To further complicate matters, the valuation of a project's cash flows by one partner may differ from the valuation by the other partner(s) because of different tax rules (Chapter 23), or because of different required returns reflecting capital market segmentation (Chapter 22). To come to grips with the issue of valuing and negotiating a complicated joint-venture project, we first introduce a simple rule for profit sharing.

24.2   A FRAMEWORK FOR PROFIT SHARING

We adopt the standard bargaining model of Nash (1950), Rubinstein (1982), and Sutton (1986) to integrate NPV analysis with the joint-venture negotiations between two companies. Let us denote these two companies by A and B. One element in the negotiations is the value of the partners' alternatives, that is, the value that each of the prospective partners can realize if the joint-venture negotiations fail. For example, in the absence of a joint-venture agreement, the best alternative of company A may be to pursue a similar investment on its own, to work together with a third party, to go on exporting as before (if this was the case), or to abandon the project altogether. The value of each player's best alternative can be identified by standard NPV analysis. We denote the net present values of the players' *best* alternatives as NPV_A and NPV_B, respectively, and we initially assume that all parties agree on these values and other relevant data.

Obviously, no party will accept a joint-venture contract that gives it less than what it can realize without the joint-venture. For this reason, the value of the best alternative is called the player's **threat point**. As each player wants at least the NPV it can get from its best alternative, positive synergy gains are almost a prerequisite for successful negotiations. Given the existence of positive synergy gains, the issue then is how to divide these gains. In practice, the usual rule of thumb is to split the difference equally. This equal-gains rule has received theoretical support on axiomatic grounds (Nash 1950), and has also been derived as the outcome of a potentially multi-stage, time-consuming, bargaining game among players with equal patience (Rubinstein [1982], Sutton [1986]).[3] Thus, we adopt the rule that A and B should make equal (and positive) gains:

$$A\text{'s gain} = B\text{'s gain} > 0, \tag{1}$$

where A's gain = [NPV of A's cash flow from the joint venture] – NPV_A,
       B's gain = [NPV of B's cash flow from the joint venture] – NPV_B.

---

[3] If the cost of delaying the implementation is higher to one partner than to the other partner, the synergy gain will not be split equally. In what follows, we assume that the cost of delaying the implementation is equal for both partners. It is straightforward, following Sutton's (1986) analysis, to identify a different distribution rule and adjust our procedure accordingly.

Example   24.1

Suppose that firm A can realize a net present value of $NPV_A = 100$ on its own, while B can realize $NPV_B = 200$. Negotiations about a joint venture can be successful only if A obtains at least 100, and B at least 200 from the joint operation. That is, the threat points are 100 and 200, respectively. Suppose that, with a joint venture, a total NPV of 500 can be obtained. The synergy gain then is $500 - (100 + 200) = 200$. If A gets 200 and B receives 300, the synergy gain is split equally: A's gain is $200 - 100 = 100$, and this gain equals B's gain, $300 - 200 = 100$.

Thus, we have to devise a joint-venture contract that splits the gains according to Equation [1]. We start with the simplest possible case, a purely proportional contract in a context where taxes are neutral and capital markets are integrated. We then consider the effects of different tax rates and discount rates. Finally, we analyze licensing contracts and management fees. Whatever the contract, our approach is to express the cash flows received by A and by B as functions of the contract parameters (like the equity share or the royalty percentage), and then to choose these parameters so that the gains to the partners are equal.

24.3   CASE I: A SIMPLE PRO-RATA JOINT BRANCH WITH NEUTRAL TAXES AND INTEGRATED CAPITAL MARKETS

Consider a joint-branch contract where both the initial investment and the later cash flows are shared on the basis of an initially agreed-upon percentage. We shall assume, for the time being, that the initial investment, I_0, brought in by A and B consists entirely of cash or physical assets with an easily ascertainable and verifiable market value. That is, we do not consider intangible assets (like know-how, brand name, or clientele), whose valuation is part of the negotiations. Similarly, for the time being, we ignore profits that A or B could make from sales to the subsidiary. Any such sales are assumed to be invoiced at cost. In this section, we also assume that the partners are subject to the same tax rules and use the same discount rate (that is, we assume integrated capital markets).[4] We use the following notation:

ϕ = A's share in the investment and the later cash flows

τ = A and B's effective tax rate on branch profits

Rev_t = the year t sales revenue of the joint branch on a cash basis (that is, the effective cash receipts from the customers, not the amount invoiced)

$Opex_t$ = year t operating expenses of the branch on a cash basis (that is, the effective disbursements, not the cost of goods sold as shown in the profit and loss statements)

$Sales_t$ = year t sales (the amount invoiced for the year as shown in the profit and loss statement)[5]

---

[4] In integrated capital markets, exchange rates are not an issue in the sense that cash flows expressed in A's currency, discounted at a currency-A cost of capital, must yield the same value as the cash flows expressed in B's currency, discounted at a currency-B cost of capital and converted at the spot rate into currency A. See Chapter 22 for details.

[5] The main difference between Sales and Rev is the change in Accounts Receivable.

$Cost_t$ = year t costs (the cost of goods sold as shown in the profit and loss statement)[6]

I_0 = value of cash and tangible assets invested in the joint venture at time 0

$$PV(CF) = \sum_{t=T_1}^{T_N} \frac{CF_t}{(1+R)^t}$$

       = the present value operator for a series of cash flows CF_t, $t = T_1, \ldots, T_N$, measured relative to the valuation date, $t = 0$. For instance, CF could be the series of revenues or taxes

R = a *per annum* compound discount rate that reflects the riskiness of the cash flow that is being discounted

With homogeneous tax rates and discount rates, the NPV of the entire joint-venture project, NPV_{JV}, is well-defined. In fact, this NPV is computed in exactly the same way as the net present value of a wholly owned project:

$$NPV_{JV} = PV(Rev - Opex - Taxes) - I_0 \tag{2}$$
$$= PV(Rev - Opex - (Sales - Cost)\,\tau\,) - I_0.$$

Shareholder A pays a fraction ϕ of the initial investment I_0 and receives a fraction ϕ of the subsequent cash flows $[Rev_t - Opex_t - (Sales_t - Cost_t)\,\tau]$. Likewise, B's share in the investment and the later cash flows is $1 - \phi$. Thus, A's part and B's part in the NPV of the joint project are as follows:

$$\text{NPV of } A\text{'s cash flows from the joint venture} = \phi\, NPV_{JV}, \tag{3}$$

$$\text{NPV of } B\text{'s cash flows from the joint venture} = (1 - \phi)\, NPV_{JV}. \tag{4}$$

We substitute these relationships into the equal-gains rule (Equation [1]):

$$A\text{'s gain} = B\text{'s gain}$$

where

A's gain = (NPV of A's cash flows from the joint venture, as shown in [3]) $- NPV_A$,

B's gain = (NPV of B's cash flows from the joint venture, as shown in [4]) $- NPV_B$.

Thus, in the present application we can write Equation [1] as follows:

$$\phi\, NPV_{JV} - NPV_A = (1 - \phi)\, NPV_{JV} - NPV_B. \tag{5}$$

---

[6] The main differences between Opex and Cost are the change in Accounts Payable and Inventory and the depreciation allowances.

This is readily solved for ϕ:

$$\phi = \frac{1}{2} + \frac{NPV_A - NPV_B}{2\,NPV_{JV}}. \qquad [6]$$

Thus, company A will obtain an equity share greater than 50 percent if its threat point, NPV_A, is higher than B's threat point, NPV_B—that is, if A's best alternative is more valuable than B's best alternative.

Example   24.2

Assume that Company A can proceed without B (that is, there is a positive NPV_A), but B cannot proceed without A's help. For instance, partner A is the foreign parent and possesses, say, proprietary know-how, while the local parent, company B, has a well-established brand name and distribution network but lacks the technical skills that are needed to produce the new product. The complementarities in the partners' strengths and weaknesses lead to synergy gains. Assume the following data:

$$NPV_{JV} = 493;\ NPV_A = 152;\ NPV_B = 0.$$

Then

$$\phi = \frac{1}{2} + \frac{152 - 0}{2 \times 493} = 65.4\%.$$

Thus, under the pure-equity solution with integrated markets and identical tax rules, A and B share the initial investment and all cash flows on a 65.4/34.6 basis. Partner A gets more of the equity because its alternative ($NPV_A = 152$) is of more value than B's ($NPV_B = 0$).

From a practical point of view, we note that, in the case discussed here, a joint-venture negotiation and evaluation requires three NPV computations—NPV_A, NPV_B, and NPV_{JV}. Each of them—even NPV_{JV}—is computed in exactly the same way as in a wholly owned project. For a joint-venture contract to be rational, the difference between NPV_{JV} and ($NPV_A + NPV_B$) must be positive. If the synergy gain is positive, the fair equity share for partner A is given by Equation [6]. This solution assumes neutral taxes and integrated markets. We now show how the pure-equity solution for ϕ needs to be adjusted when the tax rates or discount rates for the partners are different.

24.4   CASE II: VALUING A PRO-RATA JOINT BRANCH WHEN TAXES OR DISCOUNT RATES DIFFER

In the case discussed in the previous section, we could unambiguously define NPV_{JV} without knowing ϕ. This is no longer possible if A and B's tax rates or discount rates differ. For instance, if the foreign parent A is taxed more heavily than B,[7] the total value of the joint venture is higher the larger B's stake, since this reduces the overall tax burden. A similar problem arises in segmented capital markets if the two prospective parents use different discount rates. For example, if the host country has a closed capital market, a foreign firm like A is likely to require lower returns than B's shareholders because many risks that cannot be diversified away by B's local shareholders are diversifiable from the point of view of A's internationally oriented shareholders. In this case, the value of the joint venture is higher the greater the share that accrues to A.

24.4.1   Different Tax Rates

We first determine the optimal sharing rule in the presence of heterogeneous tax rates. We use the following notation:

τ_A = A's effective tax rate on branch profits—host-country taxes and possible home-country taxes,
τ_B = B's effective tax rate on branch profits.

Recall that we are still considering a joint branch where the two partners share all cash flows according to an agreed-upon percentage ϕ. The NPV realized by firm A is the present value of its share in the before-tax operating cash flows, ϕ ($Rev_t - Opex_t$), minus the present value of the taxes paid by A on its part of the joint-branch income, ϕ ($Sales_t - Cost_t$) τ_A, and minus A's share in the initial investment, $\phi\, I_0$:

$$\text{NPV of } A\text{'s cash flow} = PV[\phi\,(Rev - Opex)] - PV[\phi\,(Sales - Cost)\,\tau_A] - \phi\, I_0 \qquad [7]$$

$$= \phi\,[PV(Rev - Opex) - PV((Sales - Cost)\,\tau_A) - I_0]$$

$$= \phi\,NPV_{JV,\,A}$$

$$\text{where } NPV_{JV,\,A} \equiv PV[Rev - Opex] - PV[(Sales - Cost)\,\tau_A] - I_0.$$

The second line of Equation [7] says that A's share is just ϕ times the NPV of the joint venture computed as if the entire joint-branch cash flow would be paid to A (and, therefore, as if the tax rate applicable to the joint branch's entire income were τ_A). In Equation [7], we have denoted this figure by $NPV_{JV,\,A}$. By a similar argument, B gets ($1 - \phi$) times $NPV_{JV,\,B}$, where in $NPV_{JV,\,B}$ all taxes are computed using a tax rate τ_B, as if B would receive the entire cash flow. Finally, ϕ has to satisfy the equal-gains rule (Equation [1]):

$$A\text{'s gain} = B\text{'s gain},$$

where

$$A\text{'s gain} = (\text{NPV of } A\text{'s cash flows from the joint venture, as shown in [7]}) - NPV_A,$$

$$B\text{'s gain} = (\text{NPV of } B\text{'s cash flows from the joint venture, analogous to Equation [7]}) - NPV_B.$$

---

[7] Relief from international double taxation is provided either by giving credits for foreign taxes (as is the case in the UK and the US, for instance), or by applying an exclusion privilege to foreign dividends or branch profits (as is the case in some European countries). Under an exclusion system, a withholding tax levied by the host country on the income received by the foreign partner (A) results in A paying more taxes than the local partner (B) on the same income. Under a credit system, the effective tax rate for A will be higher than for B if there is a withholding tax combined with excess foreign tax credits for A, or if there is a higher home tax rate for A. See Chapter 23 for details.

Thus, the equal gains rule is now specified as

$$\phi \, \text{NPV}_{JV,\,A} - \text{NPV}_A = (1 - \phi) \, \text{NPV}_{JV,\,B} - \text{NPV}_B. \tag{8}$$

The solution for ϕ is

$$\phi = \frac{\text{NPV}_{JV,\,B}}{\text{NPV}_{JV,\,A} + \text{NPV}_{JV,\,B}} + \frac{\text{NPV}_A - \text{NPV}_B}{\text{NPV}_{JV,\,A} + \text{NPV}_{JV,\,B}}. \tag{9}$$

Let us compare this with Equation [6].

- We see that Equation [6] is a special case of Equation [9], because Equation [6] assumes equal taxes and, therefore, $\text{NPV}_{JV,\,A} = \text{NPV}_{JV,\,B}$. Thus, when $\text{NPV}_{JV,\,A} = \text{NPV}_{JV,\,B}$ the first term simplifies to 0.5, and the denominator of the second term simplifies to $2\,\text{NPV}_{JV}$, as in Equation [6].
- The second term in Equation [9] still implies that ϕ is a positive function of $\text{NPV}_A - \text{NPV}_B$: if A's best alternative is more valuable than B's, A should obtain a larger share of the before-tax cash flows of the joint venture.
- Equation [9] says also that if the partners' best alternatives are equally valuable, A's share will nevertheless exceed 0.5 if $\text{NPV}_{JV,\,B} > \text{NPV}_{JV,\,A}$. To understand this, note that the relationship $\text{NPV}_{JV,\,B} > \text{NPV}_{JV,\,A}$ means that B pays less in taxes than A. Thus, under the equal-gains rule, B has to give A a larger share in the joint-venture cash flows, as a compensation for the fact that A has to pay more taxes at home than B.[8]

Example   24.3

Assume the following:

$$\tau_A = 40\%; \qquad \tau_B = 35\%; \qquad \text{NPV}_A = 135; \qquad \text{NPV}_B = 0;$$

$$\text{NPV}_{JV,\,A} = 465 \text{ (using } A\text{'s 40\% tax rate, and a 20\% discount rate);}$$

$$\text{NPV}_{JV,\,B} = 493 \text{ (using } B\text{'s 35\% tax rate, and a 20\% discount rate).}$$

---

[8] To show this, we could write A's total tax rate, τ_A, as the sum of the tax paid by the branch, τ_{JV}, and the additional tax Δ_A that A pays at home: $\tau_A = \tau_{JV} + \Delta_A$. Then the right-hand side of Equation [7] can be written as $\phi \, \text{PV}[(\text{Rev} - \text{Opex}) - (\text{Sales} - \text{Cost}) \, \tau_{JV}] - \phi \, \text{PV}[(\text{Rev} - \text{Cost}) \, \Delta_A] - \phi \, I_0$. Likewise, the counterpart for B is $(1 - \phi) \, \text{PV}[(\text{Sales} - \text{Opex}) - (\text{Rev} - \text{Cost}) \, \tau_{JV}] - (1 - \phi) \, \text{PV}[(\text{Rev} - \text{Cost}) \, \Delta_B] - (1 - \phi) \, I_0$. Thus, A and B obtain the fractions ϕ and $(1 - \phi)$ of the cash flows after joint-venture taxes, and they subtract from this the additional taxes they pay on their respective shares in the profits. If these additional taxes differ, ϕ must be adjusted for the difference in the additional tax rates.

From these data we can derive the solution:

$$\phi = \frac{493}{493 + 465} + \frac{135 - 0}{493 + 465} = 65.6\%.$$

Let us compare this to the base case considered in Example 24.2, where ϕ was 65.4 percent. We see that the introduction of different taxes hardly affects the value of ϕ, at least with the data we used in this example. On the one hand, company A's position is weakened by its lowered NPV_A (which decreased from 152 in the previous example to 135, reflecting A's higher tax rate). On the other hand, A gets compensated from B for its higher tax burden. With the data in Example 24.3, the latter effect dominates marginally.

24.4.2   Different Discount Rates

Essentially the same approach can be adopted if the partners use different discount rates, or if the tax rates as well as the required returns for after-tax cash flows differ. Suppose that partner A requires a 20 percent return, and partner B requires 25 percent. Again, denote by $\text{NPV}_{JV, A}$ the NPV of the entire cash flow discounted at 20 percent—that is, the value of the joint venture if all of its cash flows would accrue to A. Likewise, denote by $\text{NPV}_{JV, B}$ the result if discounting is at B's required rate of return, 25 percent, as if B were to obtain the entire joint-venture cash flow. If company A gets a fraction ϕ of the cash flows in return for a fraction ϕ of the investment, it can compute the NPV of its share in the benefits and costs as $\phi \, \text{NPV}_{JV, A}$; likewise, B's share in the benefits and costs is $(1 - \phi)$, so that the NPV of its part equals $(1 - \phi) \, \text{NPV}_{JV, B}$. Thus, the preceding analysis and the resulting solution, (Equation [9]), can still be used when the two partners use different discount rates.

Finally, if both the tax rates and the discounts rates differ, we compute $\text{NPV}_{JV, A}$ as the value of the entire benefits using A's tax rate and A's cost of capital, and similarly $\text{NPV}_{JV, B}$, and we then use (Equation [9]) to find the solution. From a practical point of view, we note that when taxes or discount rates differ, a joint-venture negotiation and evaluation requires four NPV computations—NPV_A, NPV_B, $\text{NPV}_{JV, A}$ and $\text{NPV}_{JV, B}$. Each of them is computed in exactly the same way as in a wholly owned project, and the joint-venture cash flows are to be evaluated twice—once using A's tax rate and cost of capital, and once using B's rates. These four numbers then allow us to set the equity share in a fair way.

As we argued in Section 24.1, the pure-equity solution discussed thus far is interesting because it keeps us from getting lost in a maze of tax details from the onset. Also, such a purely proportional contract may make good sense because it avoids conflicts of interest that may arise with nonproportional sharing rules. However, the pure-equity solution may not be legally feasible (for instance, because the solution violates limits on foreign ownership), or it may not be optimal with respect to taxes. Then a license contract may be useful. This is the topic of the next section.

24.5   CASE III: AN UNBUNDLED JOINT VENTURE WITH A LICENSE CONTRACT OR A MANAGEMENT CONTRACT

Thus far, we have considered only those contracts where profits and other cash flows are shared in proportion to the investments. In Step 2 of the Adjusted NPV procedure discussed in Section 24.1, the joint operation becomes an incorporated business, and an "unbundled" remittance policy becomes possible. That is, in Step 2, we continue to analyze the effect of cash flows from the joint-venture company to the parents, but we focus on nonproportional ways of sharing the cash flows.

One popular ingredient in nonproportional contracts is a licensing deal or a management contract, stipulating some or all of the following payments: (1) a royalty tied to sales, (2) an up-front licensing fee, and (3) periodic fixed payments.[9] Another contract that deviates from the strictly proportional approach is the contract in which one of the parent companies brings in its know-how as equity *in kind*, or where one of the parents is allowed to overvalue a tangible asset contributed as equity *in kind*. In such a nonproportional contract, there are now many decision variables. For instance, there is the profit share, the royalty percentage and the lump-sum payments from the license contract or management contract, the up-front payment for the know-how or another intangible asset, or the accounting valuation of noncash inputs. Thus, we can choose some of these parameters on the basis of other considerations (like restrictions on foreign-equity ownership, political risks, tax advantages, fiscal restrictions on royalty percentages, and so on) and use the remaining parameters to achieve the desired division of the synergy gains.[10] In this section, we analyze a license contract. The analysis of a management contract is analogous. Contributions in kind are similar to an up-front payment, except for possible tax-related details, and are discussed in Section 24.6.

24.5.1   Possible Motivations for a License Contract

License contracts provide for the payment of a royalty, computed as a percentage p of the sales over an agreed-upon period. Typically, the licensing fees are contractually limited over time. Some countries also impose an upper bound on the life of a license contract. Besides royalties, often there are also periodic lump-sum fees L_t. The time-t subscript to L reflects possible variations over time; for instance, there may be a substantial up-front payment and smaller subsequent payments.

There are many motivations for combining licensing with equity participation.

- *Risk sharing* may be one motivation for a license contract. For instance, if the licensor is closer to financial distress than is the other partner, licensing provides income with a low variance.

- *Information asymmetries* with respect to the size of the market or the quality of the local partner's inputs may be a second reason. The willingness of the better-informed partner to accept a big share of the risk then acts as a signal for the project's quality, and the shareholder with the information disadvantage obtains a license income that is less risky and easier to assess.

- *Constraints on the equity that can be invested* can be a third reason for a license contract. Royalty payments are a way to share the synergy gains when one partner cannot invest the amount of cash that would be necessary in a pure-equity contract. For instance, one partner may be short of cash, and unwilling to borrow (because of the costs of financial distress) or

---

[9] The effect of the fixed payments is to increase the break-even output to the user of the know-how or the brand name (the *licensee*). This creates an incentive for the licensee to work harder. Another nonproportional sharing rule can be obtained by arranging loans between a parent and the joint venture. A loan at the normal market rate of interest is not a way to transfer NPV, though; and "abnormal" interest rates are likely to be treated, for tax purposes, as disguised dividends. So licensing contracts, or other ways to compensate for the know-how, are the prime instruments we analyze in Step 2. In addition, an incorporated joint venture can also borrow from outside sources, but this is considered in Step 3.

[10] Ideally, an optimization approach should be adopted—but tax considerations, combined with legal restrictions, always lead to *a priori* obvious corner solutions. Considerations like public relations or political risks may lead to interior solutions, but such aspects are hard to model in a formal, quantitative way. In practice, one has little choice but to experiment, and possibly iterate, until a reasonable-looking solution is found.

to issue equity (because of the loss of independence in a closely held corporation). Similarly, there may be legal restrictions on foreign-equity ownership imposed by the host country, public relations considerations (for instance, a desire for a local image), or political risks.

- *Tax considerations*, finally, may provide a powerful motivation for incorporating a licensing deal in a joint-venture contract. The license payments are tax-deductible expenses to the joint-venture company. If foreign dividends or branch profits are heavily taxed in the host country, the overall tax rate on branch profits or dividends is likely to exceed the effective tax rate on licensing income under any tax system.

Note that tax considerations do not always lead one to favor a license contract. For instance, suppose that A's home country grants an exclusion privilege for foreign dividends or foreign branch profits rather than a credit for foreign taxes. If the host-country company's corporate taxes are low, overall taxes on A's dividend income can then be lower than the taxation of A's licensing income. In such a case, taxes would penalize a license contract relative to dividends or branch profits.

Example   24.4

Assume that a Hong Kong subsidiary pays 16 percent in corporate taxes, and there is no withholding tax on dividends. If the foreign investor is not taxed on foreign dividends (because the investor's home country applies the exclusion system), total taxes on profits and dividends are only 16 percent. Royalty payments, in contrast, are not taxed in Hong Kong because they are tax-deductible expenses, but they are taxed in the parent's home country at the standard rate, say 35 percent. Thus, from a tax point of view, a license contract is expensive.

In themselves, tax considerations always lead to **corner solutions**.[11] Either the licensing income or the equity participation, ϕ, equals zero when taxes are the only criterion. Such corner solutions may be unacceptable or infeasible. For instance, a zero-equity solution would give control of the joint venture to company B, which may be unacceptable to firm A. In other situations, a tax-driven zero-equity solution may necessitate a royalty percentage and/or lump-sum annual fee which would be deemed not "at arm's length" by the tax authorities; that is, the required royalty payments may be so high that the host tax authorities would treat part of the license payments as disguised dividends. Similarly, a solution without licensing income may lead to an equity share ϕ that is incompatible with, for example, explicit legal restrictions on foreign ownership or a desired local image. In short, in many cases, *both* the equity fraction ϕ and the licensing income will be positive, reflecting non-tax considerations. For example, if there is a legal limit to ϕ and dividends are taxed at a lower rate than license income, one sets A's equity share equal to the legal limit and one then adds a license contract so as to give A enough of the synergy gains, and *vice versa*.

24.5.2   The Equal-Gains Principle with a License Contract
We use the following notation:

p = the royalty percentage (relative to sales) received by A
L_t = the lump sum amount received by A in year t

---

[11] Corner solutions are solutions where a decision variable is set equal to its upper or lower limit. Examples of corner solutions are $\phi = 0$, $\phi = 1$, $L_t = 0$, $p = 0$, and so on.

LP_t = total license payments received by A in year t; $LP_t = p\,\text{Sales}_t + L_t$

$\tau_{A,D}$ = A's effective total tax rate on dividends (including taxes on the underlying profits)

$\tau_{A,L}$ = A's effective total tax rate on licensing income

$\tau_{B,D}$ = by B's effective tax rate on dividends (including taxes on the underlying profits)

In the remainder of this chapter, "Cost_t" remains defined as in Sections 24.3 and 24.4, that is, as the cost of goods sold plus the depreciation of tangible assets, but not including license fees and so on.

Under a scheme with non-zero equity and non-zero royalties, B initially invests $(1 - \phi)$ of the required cash, while A invests ϕ of the cash needed. From the yearly operating cash flows, the annual lump-sum fee L_t plus a royalty of p percent on sales goes to A. The residual is then split between A (which gets the fraction ϕ) and B (which receives $1 - \phi$). We now have to choose a combination of L_t, p and ϕ such that company A still gets half of the synergy gains. Using a conservative approach, we shall assume full dividend payout.[12]

We first consider A's annual cash flows, where company A is defined as the parent that receives the royalty. A's cash flows consist of the after-tax royalty, plus A's share in the residual cash flows, minus taxes paid by A on its share in the profits. In Equation [10], we then rearrange the terms to determine the differences between this contract and the pure-equity case:

Cash flow from the joint venture accruing to A at time t [10]

$$= LP_t\,(1 - \tau_{A,L}) + \phi\,(\text{Rev}_t - \text{Opex}_t - LP_t) - \phi\,(\text{Sales}_t - \text{Cost}_t - LP_t)\,\tau_{A,D}$$

$$= LP_t\,[(1 - \tau_{A,L}) - \phi\,(1 - \tau_{A,D})] + \phi\,[\text{Rev}_t - \text{Opex}_t - (\text{Sales}_t - \text{Cost}_t)\,\tau_{A,D}].$$

The last term in the square brackets, $[\text{Rev}_t - \text{Opex}_t - (\text{Sales}_t - \text{Cost}_t)\,\tau_{A,D})]$, is a joint-venture cash flow as if A were the sole owner of an all-equity project. Bearing in mind that A also pays a fraction ϕ of the initial investment, it follows that A's share in the NPV of the joint venture can be written as

NPV of A's cash flow from the joint venture [11]

$$= PV_A(LP)\,[(1 - \tau_{A,L}) - \phi\,(1 - \tau_{A,D})] + \phi\,\{PV_A[\text{Rev} - \text{Opex} - (\text{Sales} - \text{Cost})\,\tau_{A,D}] - I_0\}$$

$$= PV_A(LP)\,[(1 - \tau_{A,L}) - \phi\,(1 - \tau_{A,D})] + \phi\,NPV_{JV,A},$$

where, $PV_A(LP)$ is equal to $p\,PV_A(\text{Sales}) + PV_A(L)$; $PV_A(\text{Sales})$ is the present value of the sales, discounted at a rate that reflects the riskiness of the sales from A's shareholders' point of view; and, $PV_A(L)$ is the present value of the before-tax lump-sum payments, discounted at a rate that reflects the risk of these lump-sum payments to A's shareholders.

The rate used to discount sales or the lump-sum payments L is probably lower than the rate used in $NPV_{JV,A}$, because sales and lump-sum payments are likely to be less risky than the entire (all-equity) cash flows in $NPV_{JV,A}$. One could use the JV's borrowing rate as a first approximation for the discount rate.

---

[12] This assumption ignores the possible tax advantage of deferring the payout, but the advantage is often small and can be quantified only after making arbitrary and tenuous assumptions about future payouts.

Equation [11] shows us how A's NPV in a pure-equity problem is to be adjusted for royalty payments. Analogously, we derive B's adjusted NPV by considering B's annual cash flows:

Cash flow$_t$ from the joint venture accruing to B [12]

$$= (1 - \phi) \, (\text{Rev}_t - \text{Opex}_t - \text{LP}_t - (\text{Sales}_t - \text{Cost}_t - \text{LP}_t) \, \tau_{B,D})$$

$$= (1 - \phi) \, [\text{Rev}_t - \text{Opex}_t - (\text{Sales}_t - \text{Cost}_t) \, \tau_{B,D})] - (1 - \phi) \, \text{LP}_t (1 - \tau_{B,D}).$$

This implies the following:

NPV of B's cash flow from the joint venture   [13]

$$= (1 - \phi) \, \text{NPV}_{JV,B} - (1 - \phi) \, \text{PV}_B \, (\text{LP}) \, (1 - \tau_{B,D}).$$

The equal-gains rule (Equation [1]) is implemented as before:

$$A\text{'s gain} = B\text{'s gain},$$

where

$$A\text{'s gain} = (\text{NPV of } A\text{'s cash flow from the joint venture, as in Equation [11]}) - \text{NPV}_A,$$

$$B\text{'s gain} = (\text{NPV of } B\text{'s cash flow from the joint venture, as in Equation [13]}) - \text{NPV}_B.$$

We consider two specific applications below.

24.5.3   Finding Fair Equity Share when Terms of License Contract Are Given

In one possible illustration, assume that tax considerations or other factors induce the joint-venture partners to fix p and L at an exogenous bound. For instance, if license income is taxed at a lower rate than profits and dividends, we set the license fees at the highest level that is still acceptable to the tax authorities. If, due to constraints on the terms of the contract, the license income fails to give partner A a sufficient share in the synergy gains, some equity is needed to do so. We can then solve as follows for the equity fraction, ϕ, that A requires:

$$\phi = \frac{[\text{NPV}_{JV,B} - (1 - \tau_{B,D})\text{PV}_B(\text{LP})] + (\text{NPV}_A - \text{NPV}_B) - (1 - \tau_{A,L})\text{PV}_A(\text{LP})}{[\text{NPV}_{JV,A} - (1 - \tau_{A,D})\text{PV}_A(\text{LP})] + [\text{NPV}_{JV,B} - (1 - \tau_{B,D})\text{PV}_B(\text{LP})]}.$$

For a discussion and interpretation of this expression, we break the above equation into two terms,

$$\phi = \frac{[\text{NPV}_{JV,B} - (1 - \tau_{B,D})\text{PV}_B(\text{LP})]}{[\text{NPV}_{JV,A} - (1 - \tau_{A,D})\text{PV}_A(\text{LP})] + [\text{NPV}_{JV,B} - (1 - \tau_{B,D})\text{PV}_B(\text{LP})]}$$

$$+ \frac{(\text{NPV}_A - \text{NPV}_B) - (1 - \tau_{A,L})\text{PV}_A(\text{LP})}{[\text{NPV}_{JV,A} - (1 - \tau_{A,D})\text{PV}_A(\text{LP})] + [\text{NPV}_{JV,B} - (1 - \tau_{B,D})\text{PV}_B(\text{LP})]}.$$

[14]

- Consider the first term. If markets are integrated and the tax rates on dividends are identical, we can drop the A or B subscripts in this expression. Each of the three terms in square brackets then measures the same thing—the NPV of the project net of the license payments. Thus, in a world with equal taxes and equal costs of capital, the first term simplifies to one-half, and the denominator of Equation [14] becomes twice the NPV of the project net of license payments. That is, if $R_{A,D} = R_{B,D}$, $\tau_{A,D} = \tau_{B,D}$ then Equation [14] simplifies to:

$$\phi = \frac{1}{2} + \frac{(\text{NPV}_A - \text{NPV}_B) - (1 - \tau_{A,L})\text{PV}(\text{LP})}{2[\text{NPV}_{JV} - (1 - \tau_D)\text{PV}(\text{LP})]}.$$

- If tax rates or discount rates differ, a lower tax rate for B or a lower discount rate for B will still increase the first term of Equation [14] above one-half. As in Section 24.4, the explanation is that this comparative advantage must be shared with A, by giving A a higher share in the cash flows of the joint branch.
- The second term in Equation [14] reflects the now-familiar effect of each players' alternatives. If A has better outside alternatives than B, A will obtain a larger fraction of the equity. However, the difference between the threat points is now reduced by A's license income after taxes, $(1 - \tau_{A,L}) \, \text{PV}_A(\text{LP})$. Thus, the license income can be viewed as a side payment that partly compensates for the difference in the value of the players' best alternatives. The imbalance between the threat points not yet compensated for by license payments is then reflected in the equity fraction ϕ.

Example   24.5

Return to our equal-tax, integrated-markets situation from Example 24.2, with

$$\text{NPV}_A = 152; \; \text{NPV}_B = 0; \; \text{NPV}_{JV, A} = \text{NPV}_{JV, B} = 493; \; \tau_{A,D} = \tau_{B,D} = 0.35; \; \tau_{A,L} = 0.30.$$

With these tax rates, there is a tax incentive to maximize the license income because royalty income is taxed at 30 percent while the tax on profits and dividends is 35 percent. Assume that, to satisfy legal or fiscal limits, p is set at 0.05 and that $L_t = 0$. If $\text{PV}_A(\text{Sales}) = \text{PV}_B(\text{Sales}) = 2{,}962$, the present value of after-tax license income is $0.70 \times 0.05 \times 2{,}962 = 103.67$. With these inputs, the fair equity percentage is to be set at

$$\phi = 0.5 + \frac{(152 - 0) - 103.67}{2 \times [493 - 103.67]} = 0.562.$$

This is lower than A's equity share in the absence of a license contract (65 percent) because the license payments greatly reduce the imbalance between the threat points. If the license payments had been worth 152 rather than 103.67, the outcome would have been a 50/50 equity share.

24.5.4   Finding the Fair Royalty for a Given Equity Share

In the preceding section, the royalty percentage p was set at an upper bound (5 percent), and we computed the equity share ϕ that is necessary to obtain a fair sharing of the synergy gains. In other situations, the contract parameter that is already determined may be ϕ, and the terms and conditions of the license contract are then to be set so as to satisfy the equal-gains principle. For instance, a desire for maximal control within government-set limits on foreign ownership may suggest that we set ϕ equal to the legal bound—or, higher taxes on dividend income may suggest that we set $\phi = 0$. For a given choice of ϕ, the remaining decision variables are L_t and p. Then, for any given value of L_t,

$$p = \frac{\left\{ \begin{array}{l} [(1-\phi)\text{NPV}_{JV,B} - \text{PV}_B(L)(1-\phi)(1-\tau_{B,D}) - \text{NPV}_B] \\ \quad -[\phi\text{NPV}_{JV,A} - \text{PV}_A(L)[(1-\tau_{A,L}) - \phi(1-\tau_{A,D})] - \text{NPV}_A] \end{array} \right\}}{\text{PV}_A(\text{Sales})[(1-\tau_{A,L}) - \phi(1-\tau_{A,D})] + \text{PV}_B(\text{Sales})(1-\phi)(1-\tau_{B,D})}. \quad [15]$$

Example   24.6

We consider Example 24.5, except that we remove the tax advantage for royalties:

$$\text{NPV}_A = 152; \ \text{NPV}_B = 0; \ \text{NPV}_{JV,A} = \text{NPV}_{JV,B} = 493; \ \tau_{A,D} = \tau_{A,L} = \tau_{B,D} = 0.35.$$

Company A prefers maximum control, subject to the legal limit $\phi \le 0.49$, so ϕ is set at 0.49. We set $L_t = 0$. The present value of sales is still 2,962. With these inputs, the royalty percentage should be

$$p = \frac{[0.51 \times 493 - 0 - 0] - [0.49 \times 493 - 0 - 152]}{2,962[0.65 - 0.49 \times 0.65] + 2,962[0.51 \times 0.65]} = 8.24\%.$$

An important message from this section is that license payments and equity shares are substitutes for each other, and should be analyzed simultaneously. For instance, Veugelers (1994) finds that 52 percent of the 221 international production joint ventures in her sample are 50/50 companies and that, in only 8 percent of the cases, one of the shareholders owns less than 25 percent of the shares. If one is not aware of the existence of side payments like license income, one would tend to infer that, in most cases, the players have comparable alternatives NPV_A and NPV_B. However, in light of our analysis, a more careful conclusion is that the partners tend to prefer balanced equity holdings, and then use side payments to settle most of the difference between their threat points.

24.6   CONCLUDING COMMENTS

Relative to the valuation of domestic investment projects, international capital budgeting is more complicated because there are often political risks, international taxation issues, and interactions with other parts of a firm's business. Analogously to our recommendation regarding WOS projects in Chapter 21, we propose to evaluate joint-venture projects in three steps. First, value the project assuming an all-equity branch mode of operating; then, value the tax effects of creating a subsidiary and unbundling the remittances; and, finally, add the effects of external financing. For joint-venture projects, the NPV analysis is intimately related to the issue of how the total NPV is to be shared between the partners. An additional problem is that with heterogeneous taxes or different discount rates, the project's total value depends on the profit-sharing rule. In this chapter, we show how, once there is agreement on sales and cost projections with and without the joint venture, the solution follows almost mechanically from the equal-gains principle.

The principle applied in our analysis allows one to tackle problems even when there are many departures from the simple, proportional contract. The approach is to start from each partner's after-tax cash flows under a proposed contract, compute present values, and insert these into the equal-gains equation. We have illustrated this approach by starting from a purely proportional joint-venture contract with equal tax rates and equal discount rates. Next, we have shown how differential tax rates and discount rates can be taken into account. As an interim result, we note that the step one (joint-branch) part of any joint-venture project can be analyzed by solving the problem as if the whole project were a wholly owned subsidiary. Partner A analyzes the problem using her own tax rate and discount rate on the entire cash flow, while B does the same, using his tax rate and cost of capital. If each of these NPVs is positive, we can then find the fair-sharing rule by combining the NPVs with the threat points. After this analysis of the proportional JV, we considered license payments or management fees.

The approach proposed in this chapter can be generalized in many ways. First, we have assumed symmetric information: A and B fully share all relevant data and agree on their implications. If the partners do not agree on the values, the above approach can still be used to formulate and evaluate proposals. Each negotiating team can use its own estimates of the relevant data and compute the implications for joint-venture proposals as a starting point in the bargaining. Second, we have assumed that there are only two partners. If there are three or more, the equal-gains rule still applies. For instance, when three partners with equal bargaining strengths are involved, each should get one-third of the synergy gains. Third, we have assumed that the synergy gains were shared equally. However, one could easily adjust the formulas for any other division of the incremental value among the partners. Fourth, we have assumed that all sales of goods and services between the joint venture and the parents are done at cost. This ensures that all benefits from the venture are included in the negotiations. In practice, transfer prices will usually include a profit margin: most tax authorities would not accept zero-profit sales to a related company. In addition, strategic transfer pricing may be used to shift profits and cash flows from high-tax to low-tax locations, or to obtain a fair sharing of the synergy gains that would otherwise be unattainable due to host-country regulations on equity ownership, dividend payments, license fees, and so on. From an NPV perspective, the extra flows transferred in this way to A or B are very similar to license payments because they are deductible expenses for the joint venture and taxable income for the supplier/parent. Thus, transfer-pricing profits can be added to the formulas in essentially the same way as royalties. Lastly, we have assumed that all equity contributions are in the form of cash or tangible assets with an objective market value. In practice, one partner often contributes an intangible asset, whose valuation is a matter of negotiation. Similarly, the partners may agree to overstate the value of a tangible asset brought in. Receiving equity rights on the basis of an intangible asset or through overvaluation of an intangible asset is very similar to receiving an up-front fee, L_0, as the following example shows.

Example   24.7

Assume that the project requires an initial cash investment of GBP 120, and that there are no taxes. Suppose also that the value of the best alternative decision for the foreign partner, A, is higher than B's threat point by GBP 80. In a purely proportional contract, this means that A's share, ϕ, must exceed 0.50. Suppose, however, that foreign investors are not allowed to own more than 50 percent of the equity of the joint venture. To agree to a contract that gives A only 50 percent of the future cash flows, A needs a side payment that compensates for the difference in the threat points. For instance, if despite the 50/50 rule for the sharing of the future cash flows, A and B agree that A contributes 20 in cash, and B contributes 100, then the difference between the threat points is compensated by the difference between the cash inputs. This can be achieved in two ways:

- To make the unequal cash inputs legally compatible with $\phi = 0.50$, A and B can agree that A is also contributing some intangible asset that is valued, for the purpose of the contract, at 80. Thus, A has an equity share of

$$\phi = \frac{\text{book value of } A\text{'s inputs}}{\text{book value of total inputs}} = \frac{20 + 80}{20 + 100 + 80} = 50\%,$$

  although the effective cash input of A is only 20 out of a total of 120.
- Alternatively, A may formally pay 100 in cash, and receive from the joint venture an up-front license payment $L_0 = $ GBP 80 in return for its know-how. A's share in the equity is still $100/200 = 50\%$, and its *effective* cash injection is still GBP $100 - 80 = 20$.

Thus, receiving an up-front license payment, which is then ploughed back as equity, is similar to receiving shares for an intangible asset.

There may be subtle tax differences between receiving license income and being allowed to contribute an intangible asset as equity. Apart from these tax complications, however, we can adopt the approach used in Section 24.5 to identify the value of L_0 that is compatible with some royalty percentage, p, some equity sharing rule, ϕ, and an equal sharing of the synergy gains. To conclude, our proposed approach can be applied to the very different circumstances that frequently arise in practice, and can help the financial manager in analyzing the profit-sharing problem rigorously and systematically.

QUIZ QUESTIONS

Suppose that company A can realize an NPV of 200 from doing the project on its own, while company B can realize 100. The NPV from joint operations is 400. There are no taxes.

True-False Questions

1. In a pure-equity contract, A will get two-thirds of the equity of the JV, while B will get one-third.

2. In a pure-equity contract, A will get two-thirds of the synergy gain from the JV, while B will earn one-third.

3. A's bargaining position is stronger than B's (because of its higher threat point), so A will get more than half of the synergy gain.

4. In a pure-equity contract, A will usually receive half of the synergy gain from the JV unless A's bargaining position is stronger or weaker than B's—that is, unless A is less impatient or more impatient than B.

5. In a nonproportional contract, A will not usually agree to receive only one-half of the synergy gain of the JV.

6. In order to agree to a 50/50 joint venture, A will expect an additional payment of 100 from B.

7. In order to agree to a 50/50 joint venture, A will need a side payment of 100 from the joint venture.

Additional Quiz Questions

1. Why does the investment analysis of a joint venture comprise more than just an NPV analysis?

2. What additional assumptions are needed to make the following statement true: "In a joint venture where neither partner can achieve anything without the other's help, the ownership should be divided 50/50."

3. In negotiating a license contract, one should consider the opportunity cost, that is, money that could have been earned by signing a license contract with another company. How is this accounted for in our approach?

4. Why might a company prefer licensing over direct investment?

5. Tax rules, in themselves, favor corner solutions where either equity or licensing income is not used. Still, we often observe that both are used. Give some reasons why a contract may include both equity and non-equity features.

EXERCISES

The exercises below focus on the logic used in this chapter rather than on number crunching. You should try to solve them without using any of the solutions from the text.

1. Suppose that company A's project has an NPV of 200 on its own, while company B can realize 100. The synergy gain is 200. There are no taxes, the financial markets are integrated, and A and B have equal bargaining strengths.

   (a) How much of the total NPV (500) should go to A, and how much to B?
   (b) To achieve this, what should the equity holdings be in a pure-equity JV?

(c) Suppose that A and B agree that A will receive licensing fees from the JV worth 80 (in present value).

    (1) How much of the total NPV (500) is left to be shared in proportion to the original cash inputs?

    (2) Write down the equal-gains principle, and solve for ϕ.

    (3) Verify whether the synergy gains are shared equally.

(d) Suppose, instead, that A and B agree on a 50/50 joint venture. What is the present value of the licensing income or management fees that A must receive in order to accept this equity structure?

2. Suppose that company A's project has an NPV of 200 on its own, while company B can realize 100. The synergy gain is 200. There are no taxes, and the financial markets are integrated. Assume, however, that B has a better bargaining position, and is able to obtain 45 percent of the equity in the first-pass negotiations (the pure-equity joint venture).

(a) What part of the synergy gains goes to A, what part to B?

(b) Suppose that, in the second-stage negotiations, A asks for a license contract worth 80 (in present-value terms). How should the equity shares be adjusted to preserve the division of the synergy gains (that is, to make both parties equally well-off as in the pure-equity solution)?

(c) Which licensing contract is compatible with a 50/50 joint venture and the bargaining strengths used in part (a) of this question?

3. In Freedonia and Prisonia there are no taxes, and the capital markets are well-integrated across the two countries. Two multinational utility firms, FreeCorp and PriCorp, have WOSs that compete in the Prisonian market for electric power. Right now, the aggregate annual revenue of both producers is 1,050m/year, without any growth prospects. The current market value of FreeCorp's wholly owned subsidiary is 200m, while PriCorp's WOS is worth 100m. Both companies are fully equity-financed. FreeCorp and PriCorp are negotiating a merger of their Prisonian subsidiaries. This would stop competition and would allow the producers to increase the price of electric power by 10 percent. Total sales would drop slightly, to 1,000m/year, but the higher profit margin would lead to a JV with a market value of 400m.

(a) Assume initially that the newly formed JV would be a fully equity-financed firm (no bonds, royalties, management fees, etc.). The merchant bank that acts as the adviser proposes that, as FreeCorp's assets are currently worth 200m and PriCorp's assets 100m, FreeCorp should get two-thirds of the shares.

    (1) Evaluate this proposal: who gets how much of the synergy gains?

    (2) Formulate a counterproposal if you disagree.

(b) The Prisonian Foreign Investment Act restricts the equity share of foreign owners to 50 percent at most.

    (1) How much of the synergy gain accrues to each parent if $\phi = 50$ percent and if there is no other contract (like a license contract, for instance)?

    (2) As a result of the above contract, what is the side payment that PriCorp must make to FreeCorp, one way or another, so that the gains are fairly shared?

(c) PriCorp proposes that FreeCorp receive an annual management fee of 0.5 percent of annual sales as payment for the accounting software contributed by FreeCorp. Given perpetual sales of 1,000m/year and a yield on perpetual bonds equal to 10 percent, the present value of this perpetual management fee is

$$\frac{0.5\% \times 1,000\,\text{m}}{10\%} = 50\,\text{m}.$$

However, the proposal is vague about whether the management fee is paid out by the JV or by PriCorp.

(1) From FreeCorp's point of view, does it make a difference whether the management fee is paid out by the JV or by PriCorp?

(2) If it makes a difference, evaluate the proposed management fee for each case, and formulate a counterproposal.

25 INTERNATIONAL CAPITAL BUDGETING USING OPTION PRICING THEORY

In Chapter 21, we showed how to use the adjusted net present value (NPV) approach to determine the value of international projects. An alternative method for valuing international investments is one that is based on the option pricing theory that was discussed in Chapters 7 and 8. Under certain conditions, the option pricing approach may be more appropriate than the adjusted NPV method, for example, when (1) the decision being valued involves an irreversible investment;[1] (2) the investment decision can be postponed, or production can be expanded, contracted, suspended, or shifted to another plant—in short, when the firm has some flexibility; and (3) uncertainty is resolved gradually over time. In such cases, the traditional NPV approach tends to undervalue projects because it ignores the firm's flexibility in all of these decisions. In fact, these decisions—whether and when to enter a new market, to expand or contract production, and so on—cannot be made on the basis of standard, static Adjusted NPV. For instance, the decision whether or not to suspend exports cannot be taken without considering the option to reenter the foreign market; and the value of the latter option should also reflect the firm's option to expand, contract, suspend, or quit operations altogether.

Projects with flexibility have some common characteristics. First, there usually is an initial expenditure, which is to some extent irreversible. Second, this initial investment can be delayed. Third, after the investment, the project's operations can be changed over time. These characteristics of an investment project make it like a compound American option. Making an investment means that, upon paying a known amount (the initial investment), one becomes the owner of the project's gross present

---

[1] An irreversible investment is one that cannot be recovered. For example, the cost of research and development (before the manufacturing of a certain good can begin) is irreversible. Even if one decides against producing this good, the research cost is gone and cannot be recovered.

value. This is similar to exercising a call option, which likewise requires that the holder pay a known amount (the strike price) to become the owner of the underlying asset. The firm's right to postpone the investment makes the option *American*, because exercising the option can be delayed. The firm's rights to expand, contract, and suspend production are like conversion options; and, in analogy with an option to convert a bond into a stock, the decision to change the project's characteristics may entail a known cost (like entry or exit costs, hiring and firing costs, additional investment outlays, and so on). Finally, the option to liquidate the project is like an American put, with the plant's net liquidation value as the put option's strike price. Thus, an investment project can be interpreted as a complicated real option, and its value can be determined in the same manner as that of a financial option. Just as it may not be optimal to exercise an American option as soon as it is in the money, there are conditions under which it may be optimal to postpone exercising a real option. In contrast, the naive, static NPV rule states that one should undertake a project as soon as its present value exceeds its cost; that is, exercise the option as soon as it is in the money.[2] Thus, if an investment, liquidation, or expansion decision has elements of irreversibility or can be postponed, the static NPV approach leads to an underestimation of the project's value. The size of the error, when using the static NPV criterion instead of the option pricing approach, will increase as the volatility of the cash flows from the project increases and as the discount rate decreases.

In the first section of this chapter, we review the major options that arise in real projects, and discuss when it is most appropriate to use the option pricing method rather than the NPV approach. In the second section, we show how the naive NPV rule typically underestimates the value of investment projects that have option features imbedded in them. We also show how the NPV approach can be adjusted, in some cases, to yield the same result as that of the option pricing method. We then show, in Section 25.3, how the same valuation problem can be solved conveniently using the option pricing approach developed in Chapter 7. In Section 25.4, we illustrate how to analyze multiple-option problems, by starting with a one-option project and then adding additional decisions. We conclude, in the fifth section, by describing the advantages and limitations of the option pricing technique.

25.1   SITUATIONS WHERE THE OPTION PRICING APPROACH IS SUITABLE

Recall, from Chapter 7, that we found the value of a currency option by replicating the cash flows from the option and then arguing that, to preclude arbitrage, the value of the replicating portfolio should be identical to that of the option. Similarly, to find the value of an investment project using option pricing methods, we need to find financial instruments to replicate the cash flows to the project. This is easy to do when the variation in the value of a project is primarily a result of changes in the exchange rate. In such a situation, the value of the project can be replicated with a portfolio of domestic and foreign bonds.

The importance of using option pricing techniques is greatest when the volatility of the future exchange rate is high, because it is then that the flexibility to change the operations of the firm is most valuable. Also, when the volatility of the future exchange rate is high, it is difficult to estimate the expected future revenues from a project and the appropriate discount rate. For example, the risk of the project is obviously changed whether one decides to effectively use the plant for production and

---

[2] A more sophisticated version would consider the "start now" and "start later" versions as two mutually exclusive projects, and select the one with the higher NPV. However, other real options are much more difficult to handle; and even if timing is the only option, standard NPV still gives no clue on how changes in risk ought to be handled.

exports, close it temporarily, or liquidate it entirely. Thus, the standard capital budgeting approach, with its assumption of constant risk and required return, is difficult to apply.

In practice, investment decisions may have many different option features. In fact, any decision that can be postponed that involves an irreversible investment can be valued as an option using techniques similar to those described above. Some of these option features are described below.

- Firms have the option to delay an investment decision. That is, based on market conditions and the current exchange rate, one could decide not to start a project today and instead postpone the decision to the future.
- Another option is the decision to keep a given plant in operation in any given period or to close it down for the time being, where the latter decision implies the payment of lay-off costs. Similarly, the decision to restart the plant where reentry entails a cost is also an option.
- At any moment the plant could be liquidated for its salvage value. The plant could also be put to another use. These decisions, too, have option features.
- The decision to enter a certain foreign market is also an option, if entry entails an irreversible cost, can be postponed, and is contingent on the exchange rate. Similarly, the decision to exit a market can be analyzed using option valuation techniques. Analysis based on option pricing methods has been used to explain why, for example, Japanese firms did not exit the US market when the Japanese yen appreciated in the 1980s.
- Firms may decide to invest sequentially rather than all at once. In such a situation, the decision to continue with the investment process, or to abandon it, can be analyzed using option pricing tools. Deciding when to expand production capacity can be analyzed similarly.
- Finally, several of these options may exist simultaneously, and there may be positive or negative interactions between them. For example, the decision to exercise one option may affect the exercise policy for other options. In this context, the incremental value of an additional option, when others have been accounted for already, is typically less than its value in isolation.

25.2   VALUATION USING THE NPV CRITERION

In this section, we value a single project that contains the option to delay the production decision for one period.[3] Using a numerical example, we show that the standard NPV approach ignores the option to postpone production and, therefore, leads one to underestimate the value of the project. We then show how one can obtain the correct value of the project; in fact, if timing is the only option, valuation can be done by applying NPV in a recursive fashion. In the next section, we show how the correct value of the same project can be obtained using option pricing techniques.

Suppose that a risk-neutral investor in the US is deciding whether or not to buy a certain plant that produces one unit of output *per annum*. This output is exported to the UK where its sale price is fixed at GBP 1. It takes one period to produce the single unit of output; thus, the dollar value of the revenue is uncertain and depends on the exchange rate prevailing in the next period. The current risk-free interest rate in the US, denoted r, and in the UK denoted r^*, are assumed to be 5 percent *p.a.* The spot exchange rate at $t = 0$, S_0, is USD/GBP 2 and in the next period, $t = 1$, the exchange rate may either increase by the factor $u = 1.1$ to USD/GBP 2.2, or decrease by the factor $d = 0.9$ to USD/GBP 1.8, with

---

[3] This problem was first analyzed by Tourinho (1979).

FIGURE 25.1   Cash Flows in a Project with a Timing Option

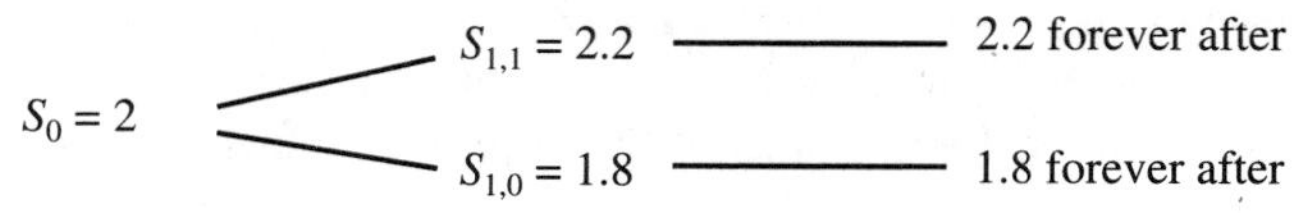

$$S_0 = 2$$

$S_{1,1} = 2.2$ ——————— 2.2 forever after

$S_{1,0} = 1.8$ ——————— 1.8 forever after

$$u = 1.1;\ d = 0.9;\ 1 + r = 1.05;\ 1 + r^* = 1.05;\ p = 0.5$$

equal probability, $p = 0.5$. For simplicity, the exchange rate is assumed to stay the same after $t = 1$. The initial (irreversible) investment that this project requires is USD 38. What is the value of this project to the US investor at $t = 0$?[4]

Figure 25.1 summarizes the exchange rate process and the interest rate data needed for the analysis. We first calculate the value of this project using the traditional *static* NPV criterion, ignoring the option to postpone the investment decision until $t = 1$. If the investor goes ahead with the project at $t = 0$, the expected cash flow from $t = 1$ onwards is USD 2 (that is, the average of USD 2.2 and USD 1.8). Thus, the static NPV rule suggests that the net present value of this perpetuity at $t = 0$, $\text{NPV}_0^{\text{static}}[S_0]$, is:

$$\text{NPV}_0^{\text{static}}[S_0 = 2] = -38.0 + \frac{2.0}{0.05} = \text{USD } 2.0. \tag{1}$$

Applying the static NPV criterion, we would conclude that since the NPV is positive, the investor should go ahead with the project at $t = 0$. However, couldn't the investor do better by delaying the production decision until $t = 1$? To answer this question, we adapt the standard NPV criterion and apply it recursively, as shown below. Applying the NPV rule in this fashion allows us to account for the flexibility of postponing the decision to undertake the project.

The correct value of the project, including the value of the option to postpone the investment decision, can be calculated using the *dynamic* NPV approach, as follows.

Step 1: We first calculate the NPV at time 1, in the two possible exchange rate states. The NPV of undertaking the project when the spot exchange moves up to USD/GBP 2.2, is:

$$\text{NPV}_1[S_1 = 2.2] = -38.0 + \frac{2.2}{0.05} = \text{USD } 6.0. \tag{2}$$

Since the NPV is positive, the decision at time 1 will be to go ahead with the project if $S_1 = 2.2$. This is similar to exercising the option. That is, when $S_1 = 2.2$, the option to invest expires in the money, and is worth the project's NPV:

$$V_1[S_1 = 2.2] = \text{Max}\{\text{NPV}_1[S_1 = 2.2], 0\} = \text{USD } 6.0. \tag{3}$$

---

[4] This example is similar to the numerical example in Pindyck (1991).

Similarly, the NPV of undertaking the project when the spot exchange moves down to USD/GBP 1.8, is:

$$\text{NPV}_1[S_1 = 1.8] = -38.0 + \frac{1.80}{0.05} = -\text{USD } 2.0. \qquad [4]$$

Thus, we see that in the event that the exchange rate at $t = 1$ turns out to be USD/GBP 1.8, it is better not to undertake the project. The strike price (USD 38) exceeds the market value of the project (1.80/0.05 = 36). That is, if $S_1 = 1.8$, the value of the option to invest is zero:

$$V_1[S_1 = 1.8] = \text{Max}\{\text{NPV}_1[S_1 = 1.8], 0\} = \text{USD } 0. \qquad [5]$$

Step 2: To compute the NPV to the (by assumption, risk-neutral) shareholder at $t = 0$, we consider the average of the two equally probable possible scenarios at $t = 1$ and discount back one period. We find that:

$$V_0^{\text{opt}}[S_0 = 2] = \frac{(0.5 \times 6.0) + (0.5 \times 0)}{1.05} = \text{USD } 2.86 \qquad [6]$$

Step 3: At this point, we are ready to decide whether to go ahead with the investment right now (at $t = 0$) or to postpone the decision until the next period. From the above calculations, the correct choice is obvious. If we wait until the next period, the value of the project is USD 2.86, which exceeds the value if we invest right away, USD 2.0. That is, we prefer to postpone the decision.

From the above example, we see that the static NPV criterion only considers the possibility of either accepting or rejecting the project at $t = 0$. It ignores the possibility of postponing this decision to the next period, $t = 1$. As long as there is some uncertainty about the future spot rate, the option to postpone the decision to invest is valuable and should be taken into account. In the example, the value of the option to postpone the production decision is given by the difference between the static and dynamic NPVs: 2.86 − 2.00 = USD 0.86. This option is valuable because uncertainty is reduced as time goes by; that is, the investor can take advantage of the additional knowledge at time 1 to decide whether or not to undertake the project.

In Table 25.1, we show how the value of this option varies with the volatility of the spot rate process for the numerical example considered above. The table lists, for various levels of the volatility, the static valuation, the dynamic (optimal) valuation, and the percentage difference between both values (that is, the value of the timing option, as a percentage of the true value). We see that, as the volatility of the spot exchange rate increases, the value of the option to postpone the investment decision, and therefore the total value of the project, increases. We also see, from the last column, that ignoring the value of this option can lead one to significantly underestimate the true value of the project, especially when volatility is high. For example, when the volatility of the exchange rate is 10 percent *p.a.*, 30 percent of the value of the project arises from the option component.

In the example considered above, we assumed that the investor is risk neutral. This allowed us to discount expectations of risky cash flows using the risk-free rate. We also assumed that the probability of an up move in the spot exchange rate was equal to the probability of a move in the downward direction. In practice, investors are risk averse, and it is difficult to estimate the probabilities of the different values that the exchange rate may take. The option pricing approach allows us to overcome these two problems. As shown in Chapter 7, and in the next section, risk aversion can be accounted for by replacing the true probabilities with risk-adjusted probabilities, and the latter can be inferred

TABLE 25.1   The Effect of Volatility on the Value of Real Options

Volatility	NPV of Project	True Value of Project	Value of Option
σ	$V_0^{\text{static}}[S_0]$	$V_0^{\text{opt}}[S_0]$	$\dfrac{\text{column 3} - \text{column 2}}{\text{column 3}}$
0.05	2.00	2.00	0.00
0.06	2.00	2.10	0.05
0.07	2.00	2.29	0.13
0.08	2.00	2.48	0.19
0.09	2.00	2.67	0.25
0.10	2.00	2.86	0.30
0.11	2.00	3.05	0.34
0.12	2.00	3.24	0.38
0.13	2.00	3.43	0.42
0.14	2.00	3.62	0.45
0.15	2.00	3.81	0.48

In Table 25.1, we compute the value of the project described in the numerical example for different levels of spot rate volatility using the standard static NPV approach (column 2), and using the dynamic NPV approach that includes the value of real options (column 3). The last column reports the proportion of the total value of the project arising from the option to postpone the investment decision.

from the prices of traded assets. When expectations are calculated with respect to these risk-adjusted probabilities, the expected cash flows can be discounted using the risk-free rate. We describe the option pricing approach below.

25.3   VALUATION USING OPTION PRICING METHODS

The project described in the previous section is very similar to an American call option. The investor has the right to exercise (undertake) the project by paying the strike price (the initial investment), and the payoff to the project depends on the future evolution of the exchange rate. That is, the irreversible investment of USD 38 represents the strike price, and the payoff to the option is USD 6 if the exchange rate is USD/GBP 2.2, and 0 if the exchange rate is USD/GBP 1.8. Thus, the value of the above project can be determined using the theory developed to price financial options.

We use the risk-adjusted expectations approach described in Chapter 7 to determine the value of the project. Essentially, the risk-adjusted expectations approach uses the risk-adjusted probabilities inferred from the prices of traded assets. In our context, we use the information contained in the forward rate to determine the risk-adjusted probabilities, as described in Chapter 7. Once the risk-adjusted probabilities have been determined, one can discount expected cash flows at the risk-free rate and, therefore, determine the value of the risky project.

Note that from Covered Interest Parity, the one-year forward rate is:

$$F_{0,1} = S_0 \frac{1+r}{1+r^*} = \text{USD/GBP } 2.$$ [7]

However, we also know that the forward rate is the risk-adjusted expectation or the certainty equivalent ($\text{CEQ}_t(S_T)$) of the future spot rate—and, in a binomial model, risk adjustment means that the true probabilities (p and $1 - p$) are replaced by risk-adjusted probabilities (q and $1 - q$). That is,

$$F_{0,1} = \text{CEQ}_0[S_1] = q\, S_{1u} + (1-q)S_{1d},$$ [8]

or, in the example at hand,

$$2 = q\ 2.2 + (1-q)1.8.$$

Solving for q, in our example the risk-adjusted probability is 0.5. To determine the value of the project, $V_0[S_0]$, we can use these probabilities and discount the expected value at the risk-free rate. That is,

$$V_0[S_0 = 2] = \frac{(0.5 \times 6) + (0.5 \times 0)}{1.05} = \text{USD } 2.86.$$ [9]

This is the same answer that we obtained in Section 25.2 using the dynamic NPV approach because, in our example, the risk-adjusted probability happens to be the same as the true probability, $p = 0.5$. Thus, we see that the option pricing approach applies quite naturally to value investments with embedded options.[5] In the appendix, we show analytically how the static NPV of a project will differ from the value calculated using option pricing methods.

25.4   VALUATION OF INTERDEPENDENT OPTIONS

In Sections 25.2 and 25.3 we have presented a very simple example to show how one can account for a real option embedded in an investment project. This model can be extended in various directions. One could easily include other aspects of the cash flow that are usually considered in standard NPV problems. For example, taxes, inflation and other predictable changes in costs and foreign prices, investment in working capital, and the dependency of foreign sales prices and unit variable costs at different levels of production can all be considered when calculating the cash flows from the project. A more interesting extension is to consider a project with several options. In this section, we start with a two-period problem, which, like the example considered in Section 25.2, includes the possibility of postponing production for one period. We then extend this example to the case where several other options are present simultaneously, and the exercise of one option affects the exercise of other options. We show how such a project can be valued using option pricing techniques.

---

[5] For a more detailed analysis of the equivalence between the dynamic programming approach and the option pricing method, see Pindyck (1991).

25.4.1   Valuing a Project with Only a Timing Option

We assume that the interest rates at home and abroad are still the same, and equal to 5 percent *per annum*. The exchange rate process is now characterized by $u = 1.2$ and $d = 0.8$. Thus, the risk-adjusted probability, q, is equal to 0.5, and the exchange rate can change to either USD/GBP 2.4 or USD/GBP 1.6 at time 1, and then, depending on the value at time 1, change once more to USD 2.88, USD 1.92, or USD 1.28 per GBP at time 2. This information is summarized in Figure 25.2.

Now consider an investment project with the following features:[6]

(a) We have to value a plant that is already operating, and is capable of producing only a single unit of additional output. After it produces this one unit, the value of the plant declines to zero.

(b) Production of the unit of output takes one period, and costs $K = $ USD 1.8, which is paid at the time that the production decision is made ($t = 0$ or $t = 1$). That is, if at time 0, we decide to produce, we immediately buy raw materials and hire labor for a total cost of USD 1.8, and start production. The product will then be ready by time 1, and fetches GBP 1. If the go-ahead decision is taken at time 1, everything is postponed by one period.

We can determine the value of this project just as we did for the example in the previous section. We first calculate the NPV of the decision to postpone the project for one period. This is done in two steps. First we find the value *at time 1* of the postponement decision, in each of the two possible exchange rate states. Second, we find the value *at time 0* of postponing the investment decision.

Step 1: If one decides to postpone the production decision for one period, then the NPV of undertaking the project at $t = 1$ in the case when the spot exchange is USD/GBP 2.4, equals:

$$\text{NPV}_1[S_1 = 2.4] = -1.8 + \frac{(0.5 \times 2.88) + (0.5 \times 1.92)}{1.05} = -1.8 + 2.29 = \text{USD } 0.49. \qquad [10]$$

Since this is positive, the option to produce is worth USD 0.49 if $S_1 = 2.4$. Similarly, the NPV of undertaking the project at $t = 1$ in the case if the spot rate is USD/GBP 1.6 is given by:

$$\text{NPV}_1[S_1 = 1.6] = -1.8 + \frac{(0.5 \times 1.92) + (0.5 \times 1.28)}{1.05} = -1.8 + 1.52 = -\text{USD } 0.28. \qquad [11]$$

FIGURE 25.2   A Two-Period Binomial Tree

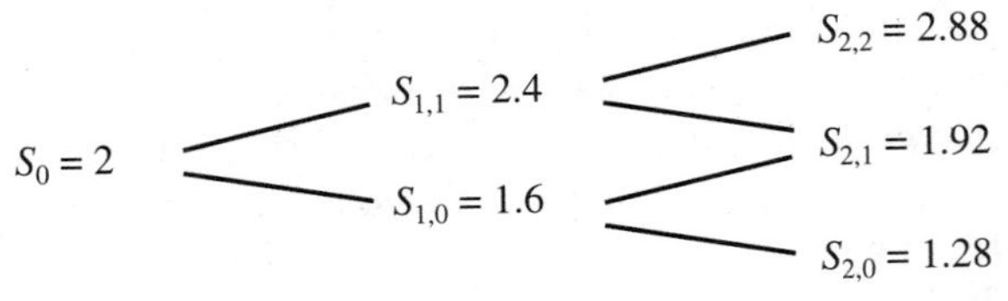

$u = 1.2; d = 0.8; 1 + r = 1.05; 1 + r^* = 1.05.$

---

[6] We have made several assumptions about the project to simplify the discussion. A more extensive example is presented as a mini-case at the end of this chapter; also, see Trigeorgis (1993). For closed form solutions when these options are present, see Sercu and Van Hulle (1992).

Thus, we see that in the event that the exchange rate at $t = 1$ turns out to be USD/GBP 1.6, it is better not to undertake the project. The option to produce is worthless because the strike price (USD 1.8) is below the market value. In this case, then, the value of the option to produce is simply 0. We summarize our results about the value of the project at time 1 as follows:

$$V_1[S_1 = 2.4] = \text{USD } 0.49.$$
$$V_1[S_1 = 1.6] = \text{USD } 0.00.$$

Step 2: We can now compute the NPV at $t = 0$ of the decision to postpone the project for one period by considering the risk-adjusted expectation of the values for each of two possible exchange rates at $t = 1$:

$$V_0[S_0 = 2 \mid \text{postpone for one period}] = \frac{(0.5 \times 0.49) + (0.5 \times 0)}{1.05} = \text{USD } 0.23.$$

Step 3: If, on the other hand, one decides to produce at $t = 0$, the value of the project would be:

$$V_0[S_0 = 2 \mid \text{produce at } t = 0] = -1.8 + \frac{(0.5 \times 2.4) + (0.5 \times 1.6)}{1.05} = \text{USD } 0.10.$$

To decide whether it is optimal to postpone or not, one needs to compare the following:

$$V_0^{\text{opt}}[S_0 = 2] = \max \begin{cases} V_0[S_0 = 2 \mid \text{postpone for one period}] = \text{USD } 0.23 \\ V_0[S_0 = 2 \mid \text{produce at } t = 0] = \text{USD } 0.10 \end{cases}$$
$$= \text{USD } 0.23.$$

From the above calculations, it is clear that, in this case, it is optimal to wait until next period to decide whether or not to undertake the project. This result should not be surprising because the value of the option to wait is quite large when the uncertainty about the exchange rate is as large as 20 percent (up or down) per period.

25.4.2   Valuing a Project with Other Options

Now consider the following changes and additional features of the plant that is to be valued.

(c) Note that, at time 0, the plant is already operating. While it is possible to exit the market temporarily by postponing the production decision by a period, the cost of suspending operations (like severance pay, and so on) is $X = \text{USD } 0.10$. Moreover, reentering the market entails advertising and promotion costs, and the hiring and training of sales people. This reentry cost is denoted by N, which we assume is equal to USD 0.10.

(d) The immediate ($t = 0$) liquidation value of the plant is $L_0 = \text{USD } 0.30$. If the plant is not liquidated right away, nor used to produce, its liquidation value at $t = 1$ is $L_1 = \text{USD } 0.20$, and at $t = 2$ is $L_2 = \text{USD } 0.00$. If the plant is used to produce, its liquidation value drops to zero immediately. Note also that, as the plant currently is in operation, liquidation means that the exit cost has to be paid.

We see that now this project contains several option features in addition to the option to postpone production for one period. At $t = 0$, one may choose to start production by incurring the cost K

TABLE 25.2 Possible Decisions and Their Immediate Cash Flow Implications

	Notation	Up-Front Cash Flow
At time 0:		
(1) Decision 1: Produce at $t = 0$ (output is received at time 1)	$D_{0,1}$	$-K \quad = -1.8$
(2) Decision 2: Liquidate at $t = 0$	$D_{0,2}$	$L_0 - X = 0.20$
(3) Decision 3: Postpone the decision for a period	$D_{0,3}$	$-X \quad = -0.10$
At time 1 (if Decision 3 was made at $t = 0$):		
(1) Decision 1: Produce at $t = 1$ (output is received at time 2)	$D_{1,1}$	$-K - N = -1.9$
(2) Decision 2: Liquidate at $t = 1$	$D_{1,2}$	$L_1 = 0.20$

$K = 1.8$ is the production cost. The liquidation value at $t = (0, 1, 2)$ is L_t. The entry and exit costs are N and X, respectively. The decision to produce also triggers a cash flow of $\tilde{S}_{t+1}$ in the subsequent period.

(immediate exercise of a call option), liquidate the plant right away (exercise of a put option), or wait for one period (postpone the exercising of these options). If one decides to wait one period, then at $t = 1$ there is another choice to be made—to reenter and produce or to liquidate the plant. Note that the options available at $t = 0$ are mutually exclusive: only one of the three options can be exercised. Also, these availability of the option at $t = 1$ depends on the decision made at $t = 0$. In Table 25.2, we list the possible decisions that can be made at times 1 and 2,[7] the notation that will be used when we refer to these decisions, and the up-front cash flows associated with each choice.

It would be quite difficult to calculate the value of this project, at $t = 0$, using the standard NPV approach. In particular, it would be very difficult to determine the expected cash flow. An additional problem with the traditional NPV approach is that its assumption of a constant cost of capital is inappropriate, given the changing risks of the payoffs being considered.

To value the above project using option pricing techniques, we need to determine which of the various possibilities enumerated above produces the highest value of the project. We again use the risk-adjusted probabilities approach to determine the value of each alternative course of action. All expectations below are taken with respect to the risk-adjusted probabilities, which allows us to discount the expected cash flows at the risk-free rate. We start by valuing the real option available at $t = 1$.

If at $t = 0$, one had postponed the production decision ($D_{0,3}$), then at $t = 1$ one has to decide between starting production or liquidating. Let $V_t[S_t \mid D_{tj}]$ denote the value of a cash flow at t, as a function of S_t, given the decision D_{tj}. If one decides to start production at $t = 1$, there is an entry cost $N = 0.1$ to be paid, as well as a production cost $K = 1.8$. With a (risk-adjusted) probability $q = 0.5$ and an interest rate $r = 0.05$, the value of the project at time 1 is computed as follows:

- If the exchange rate is $S_{1u} = $ USD/GBP 2.4:

$$V_1[S_{1u} \mid D_{1,1}] = -N - K + \frac{q2.88 + (1-q)1.92}{1+r} = \text{USD } 0.39. \qquad [12]$$

---

[7] At $t = 1$, it is never optimal to postpone the production decision for another period because the demand after $t = 2$ is zero.

- If the exchange rate is $S_{1d} = \text{USD/GBP } 1.6$:

$$V_1[S_{1d} \mid D_{1,1}] = -N - K + \frac{q1.92 + (1-q)1.28}{1+r} = -\text{USD } 0.38. \qquad [13]$$

The alternative is to liquidate. Then the value of the project is independent of the exchange rate and given by:

$$V_1[S_{1u} \mid D_{1,2}] = V_1[S_{1d} \mid D_{1,2}] = L_1 = \text{USD } 0.20. \qquad [14]$$

The optimal decision—if, at $t = 1$, the exchange rate is "up"— is found by comparing the value when producing (Equation [12]) to the value of the liquidation decision (Equation [14]). The best choice, when $S_1 = 2.4$, is to produce immediately:

$$V_1[S_{1u} \mid D_{0,3}] = \max \begin{cases} V_1[S_{1u} \mid D_{1,1}] = \text{USD } 0.39 \\ V_1[S_{1u} \mid D_{1,2}] = \text{USD } 0.20 \end{cases} \qquad [15]$$

$$= \text{USD } 0.39.$$

If, at time 1, the exchange rate is "down," we likewise compare Equation [13] to Equation [14], and decide to liquidate:

$$V_1[S_{1d} \mid D_{0,3}] = \max \begin{cases} V_1[S_{1d} \mid D_{1,1}] = -\text{USD } 0.38 \\ V_1[S_{1d} \mid D_{1,2}] = \text{USD } 0.20 \end{cases} \qquad [16]$$

$$= \text{USD } 0.20.$$

Thus, we conclude that if, at $t = 0$, we had decided to postpone production for one period, then the optimal decision at $t = 1$ would be to produce if the exchange rate was USD/GBP 2.4 and to liquidate if the exchange rate was USD/GBP 1.6. These two possible implications of the decision to postpone are, of course, crucial ingredients when, at time 0, this decision is compared to its alternatives.

We now move back one period and determine the optimal decision at $t = 0$. The value of the three possible decisions at $t = 0$ can be determined as follows:

If one decides to produce at $t = 0$, then the value of the project is given by:

$$V_0[S_0 \mid D_{0,1}] = -K + \frac{q2.4 + (1-q)1.6}{1+r} = \text{USD } 0.10. \qquad [17]$$

If one delays the production decision for one period, then the value of the project is the (exit) cost, plus the expected value of the optimal decision at $t = 1$. We have already calculated the value of the optimal decisions at $t = 1$ for the two possible exchange rates in Equations [15] and [16] above. Plugging in these values, we find that the value of postponing the decision for one period is:

$$
\begin{aligned}
V_0[S_0 \mid D_{0,3}] &= -X + \frac{qV_1[S_{1u} \mid D_{0,3}] + (1-q)V_1[S_{1d} \mid D_{0,3}]}{1+r} \\
&= -X + \frac{(0.5 \times 0.39) + (0.5 \times 0.20)}{1.05} \\
&= \text{USD } 0.18.
\end{aligned}
\tag{18}
$$

Comparing [18] to [17], it is still better to postpone the production decision for one period than to produce at $t = 0$, even though postponement entails an exit and possibly a reentry cost. This, however, does not necessarily mean that the firm should postpone its decision. The firm now also has to consider its option to liquidate at $t = 0$. If one decides to liquidate the plant at $t = 0$, then the value of the project is:

$$
V_0[S_0 \mid D_{0,2}] = L_0 - X = \text{USD } 0.20.
\tag{19}
$$

The value of the project at time 0 is given by the maximum value of the three possible decisions computed in Equations [17]–[19]. That is,

$$
V_0[S_0] = \max \begin{cases} V_0[S_0 \mid D_{0,1}] = \text{USD } 0.10 \\ V_0[S_0 \mid D_{0,2}] = \text{USD } 0.20 \\ V_0[S_0 \mid D_{0,3}] = \text{USD } 0.18 \end{cases}
\tag{20}
$$

$$
= \text{USD } 0.20.
$$

Thus, the optimal choice in this case is to liquidate at $t = 0$, and the plant's value, accordingly, is USD 0.20.

25.5   CONCLUDING REMARKS

Very often, the project being evaluated involves an irreversible expenditure, or one can postpone undertaking the project, or it is possible to make decisions later that change the project's characteristics. Such decisions include new investments, entry into new markets, expansion of existing facilities, temporary suspension of operations, or the abandonment of operations. In this chapter, we have shown that under these circumstances, using the naive NPV criterion to make international capital budgeting decisions is not appropriate. The traditional NPV approach is static in that it ignores the flexibility of a manager to affect future operations. Thus, the traditional NPV criterion, if naively applied, underestimates the value of real investments. The value of this flexibility can be quite large when the volatility of the future exchange rate is high, and when the firm's decisions have a large impact on the cash flows.

The option pricing technique, explained in Chapter 7, provides an alternative approach to valuing international investment projects. This method takes into account the option features contained in investment decisions, and is easy to apply when the primary source of risk for the project being considered is the exchange rate. Essentially, the option pricing method involves finding a set of risk-adjusted probabilities from the prices of traded securities. These probabilities can then be used to find the risk-adjusted expected value of the risky cash flows from the project, and its present value can be calculated using the risk-free discount rate.

We conclude with a discussion of some of the problems of implementing the option pricing technique to value real investments. The result of the option pricing approach can be very sensitive to the way the behavior of the underlying driving variable is modeled. In this chapter, the exchange rate is modeled as a random walk. Still, one can question the assumption of a constant volatility of exchange rates over long horizons because, in the long run, the purchasing power parity factor constrains the possible movements of the exchange rate. While this is not a problem when valuing financial options that are typically of short maturities, it may be a handicap when valuing projects that have cash flows occurring over several years.[8] A related caveat is that, for rather long horizons, the assumption of constant interest rates may be rather inappropriate.[9] In spite of these limitations, the last twenty years have seen major advances in the area of option pricing, and these powerful results can be used with great advantage to analyze capital budgeting decisions.

---

[8] To understand how the model can be adjusted to take into account stochastic volatility, see Hull and White (1987), Wiggins (1987), Melino and Turnbull (1990), and Naik (1992).

[9] For models that determine the value of real options in the presence of a stochastic term structure of interest rates, see Ingersoll and Ross (1992), and Naik and Lee (1993).

QUIZ QUESTION

Capital Budgeting can be compared to a compound American option. Decide which option contract type and exercise decision corresponds with each capital budgeting decision given below. For each option exercise decision choose from: the decision to exercise or to delay exercise of an American call, an American put, or an American conversion option.

	Capital Budgeting Decision	Option Exercise Decision
1.	Delay an investment	
2.	Keep a plant in operation	
3.	Close a plant down	
4.	Restart a plant	
5.	Liquidate a plant	
6.	Put a plant to another use	
7.	Postpone market entry	
8.	Exit market	
9.	Invest sequentially	

EXERCISES

1. Your employer, an Italian company, considers a proposal to use an existing plant to produce goods for export to India. To minimize computational problems, assume that the plant's output is either the full capacity level (100 units/period) or zero, and that the output, if positive, can be sold at a known Indian rupee price of INR 10. Thus, sales revenue equals

$$\text{Rev}\,(S_t) = \begin{cases} S_t \times 100 \times 10 \text{ if there is production.} \\ 0, \text{ otherwise} \end{cases}$$

At any time, the company can decide to produce, to sell the plant, or to mothball it (that is, to just maintain the plant, without any production). Production and distribution take time: to be able to sell in period n, the firm would have to start a production run at time $n - 1$, *before* the period-n exchange rate is known. The life of the equipment ends at time 2. Thus, at time 2, you will sell the plant. The various cash flows are summarized in the table below.

Previous decision:	Produce		Mothball	
New decision:				
Produce	No entry cost		Entry cost:	ITL 50 now
	Other costs:	ITL 800 next period	Other costs:	ITL 800 next period
	Revenue:	INR 1,000 next period	Revenue:	INR 1,000 next period
Mothball	Exit cost:	ITL 20 now	No exit cost	
	Fixed cost:	ITL 100 next period	Fixed cost:	ITL 100 next period
Liquidate	Exit cost:	ITL 20 now	No exit cost	
	Inflow:	ITL 200/172/155 now	Inflow:	ITL 200/172/155 now

Unit variable production cost is ITL 5. Maintaining a plant in mothballs costs ITL 100/period, while the fixed cost of the plant when it is producing is ITL 300/period. If production is suspended, an exit cost of 20 is incurred, and if the plant is started up again, the entry cost is 50. At any moment, the plant could also be liquidated (or put to another use), at a liquidation value of 200 (at time 0), 172 (at time 1), or 155 (at time 2).

The tree below shows the exchange rate process for the two periods. The risk-adjusted probability to be used for the valuation is $q = 0.7381$.

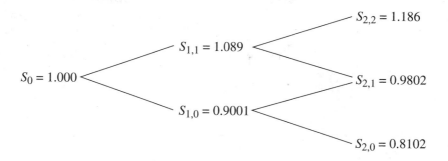

$S_0 = 1.000$

$S_{1,1} = 1.089$

$S_{1,0} = 0.9001$

$S_{2,2} = 1.186$

$S_{2,1} = 0.9802$

$S_{2,0} = 0.8102$

At time 0, the company could decide to pay the entry cost and start production. Before computing the value of this decision, you need to know what the time-1 decisions will be, conditional on this time-0 decision. The time-1 decisions depend on the exchange rate at time 1 and, of course, on the time-2 cash flow implications of each possible decision. These cash flows are computed below:

Time-2 cash flows from the project, if at time 1 you have decided to produce (decision P_1)

Node	S_{j2}	Liqvalue	Sales: $100 \times 10 \times S_{j2}$	Cost	Exit cost	Total
2	1.186	155	1,186	<800>	<20>	521
1	0.9802	155	980	<800>	<20>	315
0	0.8102	155	810	<800>	<20>	145

Time-2 cash flows from the project, if at time 1 you have decided to mothball (decision M_1)

Node	S_{j2}	Liqvalue	Sales	Cost	Exit cost	Total
2	1.186	155	0	<100>	0	55
1	0.9802	155	0	<100>	0	55
0	0.8102	155	0	<100>	0	55

In questions (a) and (b) we ask you to identify the best time-1 decisions, given that the time-0 decision was to start production. Question (c), then, relates to the value of the decision to produce at time 0.

(a) Consider the case where, at time 1, the exchange rate is $S_1 = 1.089$. If you had already paid the entry cost at time 0, what would you decide: to go on producing, mothball, or liquidate? Denote the value of each decision by $V(S_1 = 1.089 \mid X_1, P_0)$, where the current decision X_1 could be either P_1 (produce), M_1 (mothball), or L_1 (liquidate), and where P_0 refers to the time-0 decision (produce).

(b) Still assuming that, at time 0, you decided to start production, what would your decision be if the exchange rate moved down at time 1, rather than up? That is, compute $V(S_1 = 0.9001 \mid X_1, P_0)$ for each new decision X_1.

(c) In questions (a) and (b), you have computed the time-2 cash flow implications of starting up at time 0. What, then, is the value of the P_0 decision at time 0? This value consists of the present value of the operating cash flow realized at time 1, plus the value at time 1 of the (best) subsequent decisions—which you computed in (a) and (b).

The company's alternative at time 0 is to postpone the production decision—that is, pay no entry cost, and maintain the plant without producing. In questions (d) and (e), we ask you to identify the best time-1 decisions given that there was no production at time 0. Question (f), then, relates to the value of the decision to mothball the plant at time 0.

(d) Consider the case where, at time 1, the exchange rate is $S_1 = 1.089$. If you had decided to mothball the plant at time 0, what would you decide: to start producing, to continue waiting, or to liquidate? Denote the value of each decision by $V(S_1 = 1.089 \mid X_1, M_0)$, and refer to the last table for the time-2 cash flows.

(e) Still assuming that, at time 0, you decided to mothball the plant, what would your decision be if the exchange rate moved down at time 1, rather than up? That is, compute $V(S_1 = 0.9001 \mid X_1, M_0)$ for each new decision X_1.

(f) What is the value of the M_0 decision at time 0? This value consists of the present value of the maintenance cost paid at time 1, plus the value at time 1 of the (best) subsequent decisions—which you computed in (d) and (e).

We are now ready to make the time 0 decision:

(g) At time 0, will you decide P_0, M_0, or L_0?

(h) At time 0, what is the exposure of the plant to the time-1 exchange rate? How would you hedge this exposure?

MIND-EXPANDING EXERCISE

1. In the above exercise, mothballing was not really a relevant option. At time 0, we immediately went into production, and at time 1, it is *a priori* pointless to mothball: stopping production without immediate liquidation would mean a drop in the nominal liquidation value, a loss of time value, and the equally pointless payment of the fixed maintenance cost of 100. But all of this is due to the small number of periods.

Suppose that a similar exercise is solved with far more periods, say 10 or 15. Where in the exchange rate tree would you expect the mothballing decisions to occur? To answer this question, think of the following. Mothballing means keeping the plant as an option for either production or liquidation. First, would *production* decisions be taken when the INR is expensive (when we are in the higher branches of the tree), or when the INR is cheap (when we are in the lower branches of the tree)? Second, would *liquidation* decisions be taken in the lower end of the tree or in the higher end? Finally, is mothballing (keeping one's options open) more valuable when the remaining life of the plant is long or when the remaining life is short?

ANALYTIC SOLUTION: OPTIMAL TIMING PROBLEM IN CONTINUOUS TIME

In the text, we considered the simplest possible setting to show how one can derive the value of an exporting firm when the value includes the option to postpone the project. In Sections 25.2 and 25.3, we modeled uncertainty over a single period only, and therefore we had to consider the possibility of waiting only one period to undertake the project. More generally, uncertainty may be resolved continuously over time, and the decision on when to exercise may have to be made at each instant. The solution to this problem, when the value of the project depends on the exchange rate, is described below.[10] This also allows us to derive analytically the difference between the value of a project obtained using the traditional NPV criterion and that from the option pricing approach. An introduction to the continuous time mathematics used here is given in Appendix 8B.

Assume, as in the numerical examples in the text, that the foreign and domestic interest rates are equal and constant over time, and that the US plant can produce one unit of output that it can always sell in the UK at GBP 1. Thus, the revenue of the plant at any instant t, Rev_t, is given by the spot rate at that instant, S_t. We also assume that the evolution of the spot rate is given by a geometric random walk, with volatility σ and zero drift.[11]

$$dS_t = \sigma S_t dz_t. \qquad [A1]$$

We shall show that the value of the firm as a function of the current spot rate, $V_t^{\text{opt}}[S_t]$, is:

$$V_t^{\text{opt}}[S_t] = \begin{cases} \dfrac{S_t}{r} - K, & \text{if } S_t \geq S^{\text{opt}}, \\ AS_t^{\alpha}, & \text{if } S_t < S^{\text{opt}}. \end{cases} \qquad [A2]$$

In the above equation, S^{opt} is the critical level of the spot rate at which one is indifferent between undertaking and not undertaking the project; that is, when S exceeds S^{opt}, one should go ahead with the project. A is a positive constant that makes the two expressions in Equation [A2] equal to one another when

$$S = S^{\text{opt}}; \text{ and } \alpha = 0.5\left[1 + \sqrt{1 + 8r/\sigma^2}\right].$$

In sum, the valuation criterion in Equation [A2] suggests that the project should be undertaken only if the exchange rate is above a certain critical level, S^{opt}, in which case its value at that time is $S_t/r - K$. For exchange rates below this level, it is better to postpone undertaking the project and then the value of the project is given by AS_t^{α}.

---

[10] This analysis is based on Dixit (1992) and Sercu and Van Hulle (1992).

[11] The drift is zero in a risk-neutral world. This assumption is made so that we can focus on the effect of uncertainty rather than expected changes in the exchange rate. As shown in Dixit (1992), this assumption can be relaxed quite easily.

We now determine the constant A and the critical spot rate level, S^{opt}. The value of A needs to be such that at S^{opt} the two expressions on the right-hand side of Equation [A2] are equal. Thus,

$$A = \frac{S^{opt}/r - K}{(S^{opt})^{\alpha}}.$$

Finally, to determine S^{opt}, we use the "smooth pasting" condition.[12] This condition requires that the *derivative* of the two expressions in Equation [A2], evaluated at S^{opt}, be equal. Differentiating the two expressions in Equation [A2], setting them equal to each other, and solving for S^{opt}, we get:

$$S^{opt} = \frac{\alpha}{\alpha - 1} r K = \frac{\alpha}{\alpha - 1} S^{npv},$$

where $S^{npv} = r K$ is the critical value of the spot rate where the *static* NPV changes sign (from negative to positive). The factor $\alpha/(\alpha - 1)$ indicates the magnitude of the adjustment that has to be made to the static NPV criterion. We show, below, that

$$\alpha = 0.5 + 0.5\sqrt{1 + 8r/\sigma^2}.$$

Thus, as long as the discount rate is low or volatility is high, α is close to unity, and therefore, $\alpha/(\alpha - 1)$ is large. This implies that the option value is important, and that the naive NPV rule needs to be adjusted. In terms of the discount rate, the above valuation approach suggests that the project should be undertaken only if its NPV is positive at the adjusted discount rate

$$r^{opt} = \frac{\alpha}{\alpha - 1} r.$$

That is, the discount rate needs to be adjusted upwards to account for the option value of the project. In fact, what many surveys on capital budgeting have found is precisely this: managers adjust discount rates upwards subjectively.[13] Thus, our discussion formalizes the upward risk adjustment to discount rates that is often made on a judgmental basis while evaluating real investments.

The derivation of the result in Equation [A2] proceeds in exactly the same way as the valuation in Section 25.2, with the only difference being that here time and the process for the exchange rate are continuous rather than discrete. Consider a portfolio, $\Pi[S_t]$, which consists of a long position in the project being evaluated and a short position in the foreign bond. The amount of dollars invested (short)

---

12 For details of this boundary condition, see Merton (1973), Dixit (1991), and Dumas (1991).

13 See, for example, Oblak and Helm (1980), Jog and Srivastava (1991), and references therein.

in the foreign bond is xS. Then, the change in the value of this portfolio, $\Pi[S_t] = V[S_t] - xS_t$, using Ito's Lemma, is given by:

$$d\Pi(S_t) = \left\{ 0.5 S_t^2\, V_{SS}(S_t)\, dt + S_t V_S(S_t)\, \sigma\, dz_t \right\} - \left\{ x\, r^* S_t dt + x S_t \sigma\, dz_t \right\},$$

where r^* is the foreign interest rate, $xr^*S_t dt$ is the interest income, and $xS_t \sigma\, dz_t$ the (stochastic) capital gain on the foreign bonds. If we set $x = V_S(S_t)$, we see that this portfolio is riskless and, therefore, in the absence of arbitrage opportunities, it must earn the riskless rate of return. That is,

$$0.5 S_t^2\, V_{SS}(S_t) - V_S(S_t)\, r^*\, S_t = r\left\{ V(S_t) - V_S(S_t)\, S_t \right\}.$$

Given our assumption that $r = r^*$, this equation reduces to:

$$0.5\ S_t^2\ V_{SS}(S_t) - rV(S_t) = 0.$$

The solution to this differential equation is of the form $V(S_t) = S_t^a$, where

$$a = 0.5 \left[1 \pm \sqrt{1 + 8r/\sigma^2} \right],$$

and one root of a is positive while the other is negative. Denote the positive root by α and the negative root by β. Then the general solution is:

$$V[S_t] = AS_t^\alpha + BS_t^\beta,$$

where A and B are constants whose values are to be determined. Since the value of the firm must go to zero as S_t approaches zero, we must have $B = 0$—otherwise the factor S_t^β (with $\beta < 0$) will drive the project's value to (plus or minus) infinity when S_t approaches zero. Thus, the solution for our problem is $V(S_t) = AS_t^\alpha$, with $\alpha > 0$.

REFERENCES AND SUGGESTED READINGS

INTRODUCTION

Giddy, Ian, 1994. *Global Financial Markets*. Lexington, MA: D.C. Heath and Co.

Gros, Daniel, and Niels Thygesens, 1992. *European Monetary Integration*. London: Longman.

Houthakker, Hendrik, 1978. "The Breakdown of Bretton Woods." *Economic Advice and Executive Policy*. See Sichel.

Levi, Maurice, 1989. *International Finance: Financial Management and the International Economy*. 2nd ed. New York: McGraw-Hill.

Shapiro, Alan C., 1991. *Multinational Financial Management*. 4th ed. Needham Heights, MA: Allyn & Bacon.

Solnik, B., 1991. *International Investments*. 2nd ed. Reading, MA: Addison-Wesley.

Ungerer, Horst, Jouko J. Hauvonen, Augustos Lopez-Claros, and Thomas Mayer, 1990. "The European Monetary System: Developments and Perspectives." IMF Occasional Paper # 73.

CHAPTER 1

Coninx, K.A., 1986. *Foreign Exchange Dealer's Handbook*. Homewood, IL: Dow Jones-Irwin.

George, Abraham, and Ian Giddy, eds., 1983. *International Finance Handbook*. 2 vols. New York: John Wiley & Sons.

Grabbe, O., 1992. *International Financial Markets*. New York: Elsevier.

Walmsley, Julian, 1986. *The Foreign Exchange Handbook: A User's Guide*. New York: John Wiley & Sons.

CHAPTER 2

Aliber, Robert Z., 1973. "The Interest Rate Parity Theorem: A Reinterpretation." *Journal of Political Economy* (December), 1451–1459.

Cournot, A.-A., 1974. *Recherches Sur les Principes Mathématiques de la Théories des Richesses*. Henri Guitton, ed. Paris: Calmann-Levy.

Dooley, Michael P., and Peter Isard, 1980. "Capital Controls, Political Risks, and Deviations form Interest-Rate Parity." *Journal of Political Economy* (April), 370–384.

Einzig, Paul, 1937. *The Theory of Forward Exchange*. London: Macmillan.

CHAPTER 3

Callier, P., 1976. "One-way Arbitrage, Foreign Exchange and Secondary Markets: A Note." *Journal of Finance* 31 (September), 1067–83.

Dumas, Bernard, 1978. "Theory of the Trading Firm Revisited." *Journal of Finance*, 1019–29.

Giddy, Ian H., 1976. "Why It Doesn't Pay to Make a Habit of Forward Hedging." *Euromoney* (December), 96–100.

Kohlhagen, Steven W., 1978. "Reducing Foreign Exchange Risks." *Columbia Journal of World Business* (Spring), 33–38.

Levi, Maurice D., and Piet Sercu, 1991. "Erroneous and Valid Reasons for Hedging Foreign Exchange Rate Exposure." *Journal of Multinational Financial Management* 1(2), 25–37.

Madura, Jeff, and Wallace Reiff, 1985. "A Hedging Strategy for International Portfolios." *Journal of Portfolio Management* (Fall), 70–74.

Serfass, William D., Jr., "You Can't Outguess the Foreign Exchange Market." *Harvard Business Review* (March-April), 134–37.

Stulz, René, and Clifford W. Smith, 1985. "The Determinants of Firms' Hedging Policies." *Journal of Financial and Quantitative Analysis* (December), 391–405.

CHAPTER 4

Bahmani-Oskooee, Mohsen, and Satya P. Das, 1985. "Transactions Costs and the Interest Rate Parity Theorem." *Journal of Political Economy* 93 (August), 793–799.

Branson, William H., 1979. "The Minimum Covered Interest Differential Needed for International Arbitrage Activities." *Journal of Political Economy* (December), 1029–1034.

Clinton, K., 1988. "Transactions Costs and Covered Interest Arbitrage: Theory and Evidence." *Journal of Political Economy* (April), 358–70.

Cornell, Bradford, 1978. "Determinants of the Bid-Ask Spread on Forward Exchange Contracts Under Floating Exchange Rates." *Journal of International Business Studies* (Fall), 33–41.

Deardorff, Alan V., 1975. "One-Way Arbitrage and Its Implications for the Foreign Exchange Markets." *Journal of Political Economy* 87 (April), 351–364.

Frenkel, Jacob A., and Richard M. Levich, 1975. "Covered Interest Arbitrage: Unexploited Profits?" *Journal of Political Economy* 83 (April), 325–338.

Frenkel, Jacob A., and Richard M. Levich, 1977. "Transaction Costs and Interest Arbitrage: Tranquil Versus Turbulent Periods." *Journal of Political Economy* (December), 1209–1226.

Frenkel, Jacob A., and Richard Levich, 1979. "Covered-Interest Arbitrage and Unexploited Profits: A Reply." *Journal of Political Economy* (April), 418–422.

CHAPTER 5

Carlton, D.W., 1984. "Futures Markets: Their Purpose, Their History, Their Growth, Their Successes." *Journal of Financial Markets* (Fall), 237–271.

Chang, Carolyn W., and Jack S.K. Chang, 1990. "Forward and Futures Prices: Evidence from the Foreign Exchange Markets." *Journal of Finance* (September), 1333–1336.

Cornell, Bradford, and Marc R. Reinganum, 1991. "Forward and Futures Prices: Evidence from the Foreign Exchange Markets." *Journal of Finance* (December), 1035–1045.

Cox, J.C., J.E. Ingersoll, and S.A. Ross, 1981. "The Relation between Forward Prices and Futures Prices." *Journal of Financial Economics* (December), 321–346.

French, K., 1983. "A Comparison of Futures and Forward Prices." *Journal of Financial Economics* (November), 311–342.

Hull, John, 1993. *Options, Futures, and Other Derivative Securities*. 2nd ed. Englewood Cliffs, NJ: Prentice Hall, Inc.

Jarrow, R.A., and G.S. Oldfield, 1981. "Forward Contracts and Futures Contracts." *Journal of Financial Economics* (December), 373–382.

Park, H.Y., and A.H. Chen, 1985. "Differences between Futures and Forward Prices: A Further Investigation of Marking to Market Effects." *Journal of Futures Markets* (February), 77–88.

Stein, Jerome L., Mark Rzepczynski, and Robert Selvaggio, 1983. "A Theoretical Explanation of the Empirical Studies of Futures Markets in Foreign Exchange and Financial Instruments." *Financial Review* 18 (February), 1–32.

Telser, L., and H. Higginbotham, 1977. "Organized Futures Markets: Costs and Benefits." *Journal of Political Economy* (October), 969–1000.

CHAPTER 6

Black, Fischer, 1975. "Fact and Fantasy in the Use of Options." *Financial Analysts Journal* 31 (July-August), 36–41 and 61–72.

Geske, Robert, and H.E. Johnson, 1984. "The American Put Valued Analytically." *Journal of Finance* 39(5), 1511–1524.

Hull, John, 1993. *Options, Futures, and Other Derivative Securities.* 2nd ed. Englewood Cliffs, NJ: Prentice Hall, Inc.

Ross, Stephen A., 1976. "Options and Efficiency." *Quarterly Journal of Economics* 90 (February), 75–89.

Stoll, H.R., 1969. "The Relationship Between Put and Call Option Prices." *Journal of Finance*, 801–824.

Stoll, Hans R., and Robert E. Whaley, 1993. *Futures and Options: Theory and Applications.* Cincinnati, Ohio: South-Western Publishing Company.

CHAPTER 7

Black, Fischer, and Myron Scholes, 1973. "Pricing of Options and Corporate Liabilities." *Journal of Political Economy* (May), 637–654.

Brennan, M.J., 1979. "The Price of Contingent Claims in Discrete Time Models." *Journal of Finance* 34(1), 53–68.

Cox, John C., and Stephen Ross, 1976. "The Valuation of Options for Alternative Stochastic Processes." *Journal of Financial Economics* (March), 145–166.

Cox, John C., Stephen Ross, and Mark Rubenstein, 1979. "Option Pricing: A Simplified Approach." *Journal of Financial Economics* (July), 229–264.

Garman, Mark B., and Steven W. Kohlhagen, 1983. "Foreign Currency Options Values." *Journal of International Money and Finance* (December), 231–237.

Grabbe, J. Orlin, 1983. "The Pricing of Call and Put Options on Foreign Exchange." *Journal of International Money and Finance* 2 (December), 239–253.

Hull, John, 1993. *Options, Futures, and Other Derivative Securities.* 2nd ed. Englewood Cliffs, NJ: Prentice Hall, Inc.

Hull, John, and Alan White, 1987. "Hedging the Risks from Writing Foreign Currency Options." *Journal of International Money and Finance* (June), 131–152.

Rendleman, R., and B. Bartter, 1980. "The Pricing of Options on Debt Securities." *Journal of Financial and Quantitative Analysis* 15 (March), 11–24.

Sharpe, William F., 1978. *Investments.* Englewood Cliffs, NJ: Prentice-Hall International, Inc.

CHAPTER 8

Ahn, C.M., 1992. "Option Pricing When Jump Risk is Systematic." *Mathematical Finance* 2.4, 299–308.

Bachelier, L., 1964. "Théorie de la Spéculation." *Annales de l'Ecole Normale Supérieure* 3. Paris: Gauthier-Villars. English translation in Cootner ed., 1964.

Bates, David S., 1993. "Pricing Options Under Jump-Diffusion Processes." Rodney L. White Center Working Paper (October), 37–88.

Black, Fischer, and Myron Scholes, 1973. "Pricing of Options and Corporate Liabilities." *Journal of Political Economy* (May), 637–654.

Black, Fischer, and Myron Scholes, 1974. "From Theory to a New Financial Product." *Journal of Finance* 29(2), 399–412.

Bodurtha, J.N., and G.R. Courtadon, 1987. "Tests of an American Option Pricing Model on the Foreign Currency Options Market." *Journal of Financial and Quantitative Analysis* (June), 153–167.

Brennan, M.J., 1979. "The Price of Contingent Claims in Discrete Time Models." *Journal of Finance* 34(1), 53–68.

Brennan, Michael J., and Eduardo S. Schwartz, 1977. "The Valuation of American Put Options." *Journal of Finance* 32 (May), 449–462.

Cox, John C., Stephen Ross, and Mark Rubenstein, 1979. "Option Pricing: A Simplified Approach." *Journal of Financial Economics* (July), 229–264.

Garman, Mark B., and Steven W. Kohlhagen, 1983. "Foreign Currency Options Values." *Journal of International Money and Finance* (December), 231–237.

Geske, Robert, and H.E. Johnson, 1984. "The American Put Valued Analytically." *Journal of Finance* 39(5), 1511–1524.

Grabbe, J. Orlin, 1983. "The Pricing of Call and Put Options on Foreign Exchange." *Journal of International Money and Finance* 2 (December), 239–253.

Hull, John, 1993. *Options, Futures, and Other Derivative Securities.* 2nd ed. Englewood Cliffs, NJ: Prentice Hall, Inc.

Hull, John, and Alan White, 1987. "Hedging the Risks from Writing Foreign Currency Options." *Journal of International Money and Finance* (June), 131–152.

Hull, John, and Alan White, 1987. "The Pricing of Options on Assets with Stochastic Volatilities." *Journal of Finance* 42 (June), 281–300.

Jones, P., 1984. "Option Arbitrage and Strategy with Large Price Changes." *Journal of Financial Economics* 13, 91–113.

Margrabe, W., 1978. "The Value of an Option to Exchange One Asset for Another." *Journal of Finance* 33 (March), 177–86.

Merton, Robert C., 1973. "Theory of Rational Option Pricing." *Bell Journal of Economics and Management Science* 4 (Spring), 141–183.

Merton, Robert C., 1976. "Option Pricing When Underlying Stock Returns are Discontinuous." *Journal of Financial Economics* (January-March), 125–44.

Merton, Robert C., 1990. "On the Mathematics and Assumptions of Continuous Time Models." *Continuous Time Finance.* Cambridge, MA: Basil Blackwell, 57–93.

Naik, V., and M. Lee, 1990. "General Equilibrium Pricing of Options on the Market Portfolio with Discontinuous Returns." *Review of Financial Studies* 3.4, 493–521.

Rendleman, R., and B. Bartter, 1980. "The Pricing of Options on Debt Securities." *Journal of Financial and Quantitative Analysis* 15 (March), 11–24.

Rubinstein, Mark, 1976. "Valuation of Uncertain Income Streams and the Pricing of Options." *Bell Journal of Economics and Management Science*, 407–425.

Samuelson, Paul A., and R.C. Merton, 1969. "A Complete Model of Warrant Pricing that Maximizes Utility." *Industrial Management Review* (Winter).

Sharpe, William F., 1978. *Investments.* Englewood Cliffs, NJ: Prentice-Hall International, Inc.

Stoll, Hans R., and Robert E. Whaley, 1993. *Futures and Options: Theory and Applications.* Cincinnati, Ohio: South-Western Publishing Company.

Wiggins, J., 1987. "Option Values under Stochastic Volatility: Theory and Empirical Estimates." *Journal of Financial Economics* 19, 351–372.

CHAPTER 9

Dufey, Gunter, and Ian H. Giddy, 1978. *The International Money Market.* Englewood Cliffs, NJ: Prentice Hall, Inc.

Einsig, Paul, 1970. *The Euro-dollar System.* 4th ed. New York: Macmillan.

Fama, Eugene, and A. Farber, 1979. "Money, Bonds, and Foreign Exchange." *American Economic Review* 69 (September), 639–649.

Grabbe, J. Orlin, 1982. "Liquidity Creation and Maturity Transformation in the Eurodollar Market." *Journal of Monetary Economics* 9 (July), 39–72.

Guttentag, Jack M., and Richard J. Herring, 1985. "The Current Crisis in International Lending." *Studies in International Economics* (January).

Herring, R.J., and R.C. Marston, 1976. "The Forward Market and Interest Rates in the Eurocurrency and National Money Markets." In Stein et al., eds., *Eurocurrencies and the International Monetary System.* Washington: American Enterprise Institute.

Hudson, Nigel R.L., 1979. *Money and Exchange Rate Dealing in International Banking.* New York: John Wiley & Sons.

Kerr, Ian M., 1984. *A History of the Eurobond Market: The First 21 Years.* London: Euromoney Publications.

Riehl, Hienz, and Rita Rodriguez, *Foreign Exchange and Money Markets.* Prentice-Hall, Inc.

Stein, Carl H., John H. Makin, and Dennis E. Logue, eds., 1976. *Eurocurrencies and the International Monetary System.* Washington: American Enterprise Institute.

Stigum, Marcia, 1988. *The Money Markets.* Irwin, New York: Dow Jones.

CHAPTER 10

Antl, Boris, ed., 1983. *Swap Financing Techniques.* London: Euromoney Publications.

Bicksler, J., and A.H. Chen, 1986. "An Economic Analysis of Interest Rate Swaps." *Journal of Finance,* 645–655.

Fierman, Jaclyn, 1987. "Fast Bucks in Latin Loan Swaps." *Fortune* (August 3), 91–99.

Hull, J.C., 1988. "An Analysis of the Credit Risks in Interest Rate Swaps and Currency Swaps." *Recent Developments in International Banking and Finance* 3 (December). Lexington, MA: D.C. Heath.

International Swap Dealer's Association, 1986. *Code of Standard Working Assumptions and Provisions for Swaps.* New York.

Layard-Liesching, R., 1986. "Swap Fever." *Euromoney* (January), 108–113. Supplement.

Monroe, Ramon, 1987. "LDC Debt Swaps." *FRBSF Weekly Letter* (September 4). San Francisco: Federal Reserve Bank of San Francisco.

Salomon Brothers Inc., 1985. *The Interest Rate Swap Market: Yield Mathematics, Terminology, and Conventions.* (June).

Simons, Katerina, 1989. "Measuring Credit Risk in Interest Rate Swaps." *New England Economic Review* (November/December). Boston: Federal Reserve Bank of Boston.

Smith, C.W., C.W. Smithson, and L.M. Wakeman, 1986. "The Evolving Market for Swaps." *Midland Corporate Finance Journal* (Winter), 20–32.

Turnbull, S.M., 1987. "Swaps: A Zero Sum Game." *Financial Management* (Spring), 15–21.

CHAPTER 11

Abauf, Niso, and Phillippe Jorion, 1990. "Purchasing Power Parity in the Long Run." *Journal of Finance* 45, 157–174.

Adler, Michael, and Bruce Lehmann, 1983. "Deviations from Purchasing Power Parity in the Long Run." *Journal of Finance* (December), 1471–1487.

Apte, P., M. Kane, and P. Sercu, 1994. "Evidence of PPP in the Medium Run." *Journal of International Money and Finance* (4).

Betton, Sandra, Maurice Levi, and Raman Uppal, 1991. "Index-Induced Errors and Purchasing Power Parity: Bounding the Possible Bias." Working Paper, University of British Columbia.

Cumby, Robert E., and Maurice Obstfeld, 1981. "A Note on Exchange-Rate Expectations and Nominal Interest Differentials: A Test of the Fisher Hypothesis." *Journal of Finance* 36(3), 697–703.

De Grauwe, Paul, Marc Janssens, and Hilde Leliaert, 1985. "Real-Exchange-Rate Variability from 1920 to 1926 and 1973 to 1982." *Princeton Studies in International Finance* 56 (September), 50p.

Dumas, Bernard, 1992 "Dynamic Equilibrium and the Real Exchange Rate in a Spatially Separated World." *The Review of Financial Studies* 5(2), 153–180.

Huang, Roger D., 1987. "Expectations of Exchange Rates and Differential Inflation Rates: Further Evidence on Purchasing Power Parity in Efficient Markets." *Journal of Finance* 42(1), 69–79.

Huang, Roger D., 1990. "Risk and Parity in Purchasing Power." *Journal of Money, Credit, and Banking* 22(3) (August), 338–356.

Huizinga, J., 1987. "An Empirical Investigation of the Long-run Behavior of Real Exchange Rates." Carnegie-Rochester Series on Public Policy, 149–214.

Isard, P., 1977. "How Far Can We Push the Law of One Price?" *American Economic Review* 67 (December), 942–948.

Lucas, R., 1982. "Interest Rates and Currency Prices in Two-Country World." *Journal of Monetary Economics* (November), 149–214.

McNown, R., and M.S. Wallace, 1989. "National Price Levels, Purchasing Power Parity, and Cointegration: A Test of Four High Inflation Economics." *Journal of International Money and Finance* 8, 533–546.

Richardson, J., 1978. "Some Empirical Evidence on Commodity Arbitrage and the Law of One Price." *Journal of International Economics* 8, 341–351.

Roll, Richard, 1979. "Violations of Purchasing Power Parity and Their Implications for Efficient International Commodities Markets." *International Finance and Trade*. See Sarnat and Szego.

Sercu, P., R. Uppal, and C. Van Hulle, 1994. "The Exchange Rate in the Presence of Transactions Costs: Implications for Tests of Purchasing Power Parity." Working Paper Series, European Institute for Advanced Studies in Management.

CHAPTER 12

Anderson, Gerald H., Nicholas V. Karamouzis, and Peter D. Skaperdas, 1987. "A New Effective Exchange Rate Index for the Dollar and Its Implications for U.S. Merchandise Trade." *Economic Review* 2nd Quarter 1987. Cleveland: Federal Reserve Bank of Cleveland, 2–22.

Bame, Jack J., 1976. "Analyzing U.S. International Transactions." *Columbia Journal of World Business* (Fall), 72–84.

Bank for International Settlements, 1985. *Payment Systems in Eleven Developed Countries*. Bank Administration Institute (May).

Clark, Don, 1987. "Regulation of International Trade in the United States: Tokyo Round." *Journal of Business* (April), 297–306.

Craig, Gary A., 1981. "A Monetary Approach to the Balance of Trade." *American Economic Review* (June), 460–466

Frenkel, J.A., ed., 1983. *Exchange Rates and International Macroeconomics*. Chicago: University of Chicago Press.

Kravis, Irving B., and Robert Lipsey, 1978. "Price Behaviour in Light of Balance of Payment Theories." *Journal of International Economics* (May), 193–246.

LaCivita, Charles, 1987. "Currency, Trade, and Capital Flows in General Equilibrium." *Journal of Business* (January), 113–135.

Miles, Marc A., 1979. "The Effects of Devaluation in the Trade Balance and the Balance of Payments: Some New Results." *Journal of Political Economy* (June), 600–620.

Neumann, Manfred J.M., 1984. "Intervention in the Mark/Dollar Market: The Authorities Reaction Function." *Journal of International Money and Finance* 3 (August), 223–240.

Obstfeld, Maurice, 1984. "Balance-of-Payment Crises and Devaluation." *Journal of Money, Credit, and Banking* (May), 208–217.

Salop, Joanne, and Erich Spitaller, 1980. "Why does the Current Account Matter?" *International Monetary Staff Fund Papers* (March), 101–134.

Taylor, Dean, 1982. "Official Intervention in the Foreign Exchange Market, or Bet Against the Central Bank." *Journal of Political Economy* (April).

CHAPTER 13

Aliber, R.Z., 1974. "Attributes of National Monies and the Interdependence of National Monetary Policies." In R.Z. Aliber ed., *National Monetary Policies and the International Financial System*. Chicago: University of Chicago Press, 111–126.

Batten, Dallas S., and Daniel L. Thornton, 1984. "Discount Rate Changes and the Foreign Exchange Market." *Journal of International Money and Finance* (December), 279–92.

Bergstrand, Jeffrey H., 1983. "Selected Views of Exchange Rate Determination after a Decade of 'Floating.'" *New England Economic Review* (May-June). Boston: Federal Reserve Bank of Boston, 14–29.

Brittian, Bruce, 1977. "Tests of Theories of Exchange Rate Determination." *Journal of Finance* (May), 519–529.

Crockett, Andrew, 1981. "Determinants of Exchange Rate Movements: A Review." *Finance and Development* (March), 33–37.

Dornbusch, Rudiger, 1980. "Exchange Rate Economics: Where Do We Stand?" *Brookings Papers on Economic Activity I*, 143–185.

Frenkel, J.A., and H.G. Johnson, eds., 1978. *The Economics of Exchange Rates—Selected Studies*. Reading, MA: Addison-Wesley.

Friedman, Milton, and Robert V. Roosa, 1977. "Free versus Fixed Exchange Rates: A Debate." *Journal of Portfolio Management* (Spring), 68–73.

Marrinan, Jane, 1989. "Exchange Rate Determination: Sorting Out Theory and Evidence." *New England Economic Review* (November-December), 39–51.

CHAPTER 14

Almouti, K., 1980. "Spot Rates, Forward Rates, and the Expectations Hypothesis in the Foreign Exchange." Working Paper, London Business School.

Bell, Steven, and Brian Kettell, 1983. *Foreign Exchange Handbook*, Graham and Trotman.

Bilson, John F., 1982. "The Speculative Efficiency Hypothesis." *Journal of Business* (July), 435–431.

Chiang, Thomas C., 1986. "On the Predictors of the Future Spot Rates—A Multi-Currency Analysis." *The Financial Review* (February), 69–83.

Cornell, Bradford, 1976. "Spot Rates, Forward Rates and Exchange Market Efficiency." *Journal of Financial Economics* (December), 1161–1176.

Cornell, Bradford, 1977. "Spot Rates, Forward Rates and Market Dynamics." *Journal of Political Economy* 5(1), 55–65.

Cornell, Bradford, and J. Kimball Dietrich, 1978. "The Efficiency of the Market for Foreign Exchange Under Floating Exchange Rates." *Review of Economics and Statistics* (February), 111–120.

Cumby, Robert E., and Maurice Obstfeld, 1981. "A Note on Exchange-Rate Expectations and Nominal Interest Differentials: A Test of the Fisher Hypothesis." *Journal of Finance* 36(3), 697–703.

Cumby, Robert E., and Maurice Obstfeld, 1984. "International Interest Rate and Price Level Linkages under Flexible Exchange Rates: A Review of Recent Evidence." In J. Bilson and R. Marston, eds., *Exchange Rate Theory and Practice*. Chicago: University of Chicago Press, 121–151.

Dornbusch, Rudiger, 1976. "Expectations and Exchange Rate Dynamics." *Journal of Political Economy* (December), 1161–1176.

Fama, Eugene F., 1976. "Efficient Capital Markets: A Review of Theory and Empirical Work." *Journal of Financial Economics* 3(4), 361–377.

Fama, Eugene, 1984. "Forward and Spot Exchange Rates." *Journal of Monetary Economics* (November), 320–338.

Froot, Kenneth A., and Takatoshi Ito, 1989. "On the Consistency of Short-Run and Long-Run Exchange Rate Expectations." *Journal of International Money and Finance* 8(4) (December), 487–510.

Froot, K., and R. Thaler, 1990. "Anomalies: Foreign Exchange." *Journal of Economic Perspectives* 4, 179–192.

Geweke, J., and E. Feige, 1979. "Some Joint Tests of the Market Efficiency of Markets for Forward Foreign Exchange." *Review of Economics and Statistics* (October), 334–341.

Goodman, Stephen H., 1978. "No Better than the Toss of a Coin." *Euromoney* (December), 75–85.

Goodman, Stephen H., 1979. "Foreign Exchange Rate Forecasting Techniques: Implications for Business and Policy." *Journal of Finance* 34(2), 415–427.

Goodman, Stephen H., 1982. "Two Technical Analysts Are Even Better than One." *Euromoney* (August).

Goodman, Stephen, and Richard Jaycobs, 1983. "How the Current Forecasting Services Rate." *Euromoney* (August), 132–139.

Grossman, S., and J. Stiglitz, 1980. "On the Impossibility of Informationally Efficient Markets." *American Economic Review* 70 (June), 393–408.

Hansen, Lars Peter, and Robert Hodrick, 1980. "Forward Exchange Rates as Optimal Predictors of Future Spot Rates: An Econometric Analysis." *Journal of Political Economy* 88 (October), 829–853.

Huang, Roger D., 1984. "Some Alternative Tests of Forward Exchange Rates as Predictors of Future Spot Rates." *Journal of International Money and Finance* (August), 153–167.

Kane, Alex, Leonard Rosenthal, and Greta Ljung, 1983. "Tests of the Fisher Hypothesis with International Data: Theory and Evidence." *Journal of Finance* (May), 539–551.

Korajczyk, Robert A., 1985. "The Pricing of Forward Contracts for Foreign Exchange." *Journal of Political Economy* (April), 346–368.

Levich, Richard M., 1979. "Are Forward Exchange Rates Unbiased Predictors of Future Spot Rates?" *Columbia Journal of World Business* (Winter), 49–61.

Levich, Richard M., 1979. "On the Efficiency of Markets for Foreign Exchange." In R. Dornbusch and J.A. Frenkel, eds., *International Economic Policy: Theory and Evidence*. Baltimore, MD: Johns Hopkins University Press.

Lewis, K., 1985. "Changing Beliefs and Systematic Rational Forecast Errors with Evidence from Foreign Exchange." *American Economic Review* 79, 621–636.

Mishkin, Frederic S., 1984. "Are Real Interest Rates Equal across Countries? An Empirical Investigation of International Parity Conditions." *Journal of Finance* (December), 1345–1357.

Nelson, Charles R., and G. William Schwert, 1977. "Short-Term Interest Rates as Predictors of Inflation: On Testing the Hypothesis that the Real Rate of Interest is Constant." *American Economic Review* 65(3) (June), 478–486.

Robinson, Bill, and Peter Warburton, 1980. "Managing Currency Holdings: Lessons from the Floating Period." *London Business School Economic Outlook* (February), 18–27.

Taylor, S., 1992. "Tests of the Random Walk Hypothesis against a Price Trend Hypothesis." *Journal of Financial and Quantitative Analysis* 17, 37–61.

Thomas, Lee R., 1985-1986. "A Winning Strategy for Currency-Futures Speculation." *Journal of Portfolio Management* 12(1), 65–69.

Thomas, Lee R., 1986. "Random Walk Profits in Currency Futures Trading." *Journal of Futures Markets* 6(1), 109–126.

Wolff, Christian C.P., 1987. "Forward Foreign Exchange Rates, Expected Spot Rates, and Premia: A Signal Extraction Approach." *Journal of Finance* 42(2), 395–406.

CHAPTER 15

Alexander, Sidney S., 1961. "Price Movements in Speculative Markets: Trends or Random Walks." *Industrial Management Review* 2 (May), 7–26. Reprinted in Cootner (1964), 199–218.

Bilson, John F., 1982. "The Speculative Efficiency Hypothesis." *Journal of Business* (July), 435–431.

Chiang, Thomas C., 1986. "On the Predictors of the Future Spot Rates—A Multi-Currency Analysis." *The Financial Review* (February), 69–83.

Cornell, Bradford, and J. Kimball Dietrich, 1978. "The Efficiency of the Market for Foreign Exchange Under Floating Exchange Rates." *Review of Economics and Statistics* (February), 111–120.

Curcio, R., and C. Goodhart, 1991. "Chartism: A Controlled Experiment." LSE Financial Markets Group Discussion Paper no. 124 (October).

Fama, Eugene, 1984. "Forward and Spot Exchange Rates." *Journal of Monetary Economics* (November), 320–338.

Fama, Eugene, L. Fisher, M. Jensen, and R. Roll, 1969. "The Adjustment of Stock Prices to New Information." *International Economic Review* 10 (February), 1–21.

Finnerty, J.E., J. Owers, and F.J. Creran, 1987. "Foreign Exchange Forecasting and Leading Economic Indicators: The U.S.-Canadian Experience." *Management International Review* 2, 59–70.

Gernaey, Kurt, 1988. *Technische Trading Rules: Een Empirische Onderzoek op de Belgische Vrije Wisselmarkt voor de Periode 20/02/76 tot 20/08/87.* S.N. Leuven.

Goodman, Stephen H., 1978. "No Better than the Toss of a Coin." *Euromoney* (December), 75–85.

Goodman, Stephen H., 1979. "Foreign Exchange Rate Forecasting Techniques: Implications for Business and Policy." *Journal of Finance* 34(2), 415–427.

Goodman, Stephen H., 1982. "Two Technical Analysts Are Even Better than One." *Euromoney* (August).

Goodman, Stephen, and Richard Jaycobs, 1983. "How the Current Forecasting Services Rate." *Euromoney* (August), 132–139.

Jaycobs, Richard, 1984. "Getting It Right at the Right Time." *Euromoney* (August), 148–154.

Levich, Richard M., 1978. "Tests of Forecasting Models and Market Efficiency in the International Money Market." In Jacob A. Frenkel and Harry G. Johnson, eds., *The Economics of Exchange Rates: Selected Studies.* Reading, Mass: Addison-Wesley Publishing Company, Inc.

Levich, Richard M., 1980. "Analyzing the Accuracy of Forex Advisory Services: Theory and Evidence." In Levich and Wihlborg, eds., *Exchange Risk and Exposure.* Lexington, MA: D.C. Heath & Co., 99–128.

Levich, Richard M., 1982. "Evaluating the Performance of the Forecasters." In R. Ensor, ed., *The Management of Foreign Exchange Risk.* London: Euromoney Publications.

Levich, Richard M., 1983. "Currency Forecasters Lose Their Way." *Euromoney* (August), 140–148.

Meese, R., 1990. "Currency Fluctuations in the Post-Bretton Woods Era." *Journal of Economic Perspectives* 4.1, 117–134.

Meese, R., and K. Rogoff, 1981. "Empirical Exchange Rate Models of the Seventies: Are They Fit to Survive?" *International Finance Discussion Papers* 184, (June).

Meese, R., and K. Rogoff, 1983. "Empirical Exchange Rate Models of the Seventies: Do They Fit Out-of-Sample?" *Journal of International Economics* 14, 3–24.

Roberts, Harry, 1967. "Statistical Versus Clinical Prediction of the Stock Market." Paper presented at seminar on the Analysis of Security Prices, Univ. of Chicago, May.

Rogalski, R.J., and J.D. Vinso, 1977. "Stock Returns, Money Supply and the Direction of Causality." *Journal of Finance* 32(4), 1017–1030.

Roll, Richard, 1977. "Violations of PPP and Their Implications for Efficient International Commodity Markets." In Marshall Sarnat and Giorgio P. Szego, eds., *International Finance and Trade* 1. 133–176.

Sweeney, Richard J., 1986. "Beating the Forex Market." *Journal of Finance* 41(1) (March), 163–182.

Sweeney, Richard J., 1988. "Some New Filter Rule Tests: Methods and Results." *Journal of Financial and Quantitative Analysis* 23(3), 285–300.

Taylor, S., 1992. "Tests of the Random Walk Hypothesis against a Price Trend Hypothesis." *Journal of Financial and Quantitative Analysis* 17, 37–61.

Wolff, Christian C.P., 1987. "Forward Foreign Exchange Rates, Expected Spot Rates, and Premia: A Signal Extraction Approach." *Journal of Finance* 42(2), 395–406.

CHAPTER 16

Adler, M., and B. Dumas, 1983. "International Portfolio Choice and Corporation Finance: A Synthesis." *Journal of Finance* 38.3, 925–984.

Adler, Michael, and Bernard Dumas, 1984. "Exposure to Currency Risk: Definition and Measurement." *Financial Management* (Summer), 41–50.

Chiang, Thomas C., 1980. "Forward Exchange Rates as Optimal Predictors of Future Spot Rates: An Econometric Analysis." *Journal of Political Economy* 88.5 (October), 829–853.

Chiang, Thomas C., 1988. "The Forward Rate as a Predictor of the Future Spot Rate—A Stochastic Coefficient Approach." *Journal of Money, Credit, and Banking* 20.2 (May), 212–232.

Cornell, Bradford, and Alan C. Shapiro, 1983. "Managing Foreign Exchange Risks." *Midland Corporate Finance Journal* (Fall), 16–31.

Dufey, Gunter, and S.L. Srinivasulu, 1984. "The Case for Corporate Management of Foreign Exchange Risk." *Financial Management* (Summer), 54–62.

Edderington, L.H., 1979. "The Hedging Performance of the New Futures Market." *Journal of Finance* (March), 157–170.

Giddy, Ian H., 1976. "Why It Doesn't Pay to Make a Habit of Forward Hedging." *Euromoney* (December), 96–100.

Giddy, Ian H., 1983. "The Foreign Exchange Option as a Hedging Tool." *Midland Corporate Finance Journal* (Fall), 32–42.

Hansen, Lars P., and Robert J. Hodrick, 1983. "Risk Averse Speculation in the Forward Exchange Market: An Econometric Analysis of Linear Models." In Jacob A. Frenkel, ed., *Exchange Rates and International Macroeconomics.* Chicago: University of Chicago Press.

Hodrick, Robert J., and Sanjay Srivastava, 1984. "An Investigation of Risk and Return in Forward Foreign Exchange." *Journal of International Money and Finance* 3.1 (April), 5–29.

Hsieh, David A., "Tests of Rational Expectations and No Risk Premium in Forward Exchange Markets." *Journal of International Economies* 17, 173–184.

Jensen, Michael, 1986. "Agency Costs and Free Cashflow, Corporate Finance, and Takeover." *American Economic Review* (May), 323–329.

Koedijk, Kees G., and Mack Ott, 1987. "Risk Aversion Efficient Markets and the Forward Exchange Rate." *Review of the Federal Reserve Bank of St. Louis* (December), 5–13.

Korajczyk, Robert A., 1985. "The Pricing of Forward Contracts for Foreign Exchange." *Journal of Political Economy* (April), 346–368.

Lessard, Donald R., and John B. Lightstone, 1986. "Volatile Exchange Rates Can Put Operations at Risk." *Harvard Business Review* (July-August), 107–114.

Levi, Maurice D., and Piet Sercu, 1991. "Erroneous and Valid Reasons for Hedging Foreign Exchange Rate Exposure." *Journal of Multinational Financial Management* 1(2), 25–37.

Modigliani, F., and M.H. Miller, 1958. "The Cost of Capital, Corporation Finance and the Theory of Investment." *American Economic Review* 48 (June), 261–297, .

Rawls, S.W., and C. Smithson, 1990. "Strategic Risk Management." *Journal of Applied of Corporate Finance* 2(4), 6–18.

Shapiro, Alan C., 1984. "Currency Risk and Relative Price Risk." *Journal of Financial and Quantitative Analysis* (December), 365–373.

Smith, Clifford W., and Rene M. Stulz, 1985. "The Determinants of Firms' Hedging Policies." *Journal of Financial and Quantitative Analysis* (December), 391–405.

Stulz, R., 1984. "Optimal Hedging Policies." *Journal of Financial and Quantitative Analysis* (June), 127–140.

CHAPTER 17

Abdel-Malek, Talaat, 1976. "Some Aspects of Exchange Risk Policies Under Floating Rates." *Journal of International Business Studies* (Fall-Winter), 89–97.

Adler, Michael, and Bernard Dumas, 1984. "Exposure to Currency Risk: Definition and Measurement." *Financial Management* (Summer), 41–50.

Adler, Michael, and D. Simon, 1986. "Exchange Rate Surprises in International Portfolios." *Journal of Portfolio Management* (Winter).

Ankrom, Robert K., 1974. "Top Level Approach to the Foreign Exchange Problem." *Harvard Business Review* (July-August), 79–80.

Cornell, Bradford, and Alan C. Shapiro, 1983. "Managing Foreign Exchange Risks." *Midland Corporate Finance Journal* (Fall), 16–31.

Dufey, Gunter, 1978. "Corporate Finance and Exchange Rate Variations." *Financial Management* (Summer), 51–57.

Eaker, Mark R., 1981. "The Numeraire Problem and Foreign Exchange Risk." *Journal of Finance* (May), 419–426.

Garner, C. Kent, and Alan C. Shapiro, 1984. "A Practical Method of Assessing Foreign Exchange Risk." *Midland Corporate Finance Journal* (Fall), 6–17.

Giddy, Ian H., 1977. "Exchange Risk: Whose View?" *Financial Management* (Summer), 23–33.

Heckman, C.R., 1985. "A Financial Model of Foreign Exchange Exposure." *Journal of International Business Studies* (Summer).

Heckman, C.R., 1986. "Don't Blame Currency Values for Strategic Errors: Protecting Competitive Position by Correctly Assessing Foreign Exchange Exposure." *Midland Corporate Finance Journal* (Fall).

Lessard, Donald R., and John B. Lightstone, 1986. "Volatile Exchange Rates Can Put Operations at Risk." *Harvard Business Review* (July-August), 107–114.

Shapiro, Alan C., 1975. "Exchange Rate Changes, Inflation, and the Value of the Multinational Corporation." *Journal of Finance* (May), 485–502.

CHAPTER 18

Abdel-Malek, Talaat, 1976. "Some Aspects of Exchange Risk Policies Under Floating Rates." *Journal of International Business Studies* (Fall-Winter), 89–97.

Adler, Michael, and Bernard Dumas, 1984. "Exposure to Currency Risk: Definition and Measurement." *Financial Management* (Summer), 41–50.

Adler, Michael, and D. Simon, 1986. "Exchange Rate Surprises in International Portfolios." *Journal of Portfolio Management* (Winter).

Ankrom, Robert K., 1974. "Top Level Approach to the Foreign Exchange Problem." *Harvard Business Review* (July-August), 79–80.

Cornell, Bradford, and Alan C. Shapiro, 1983. "Managing Foreign Exchange Risks." *Midland Corporate Finance Journal* (Fall), 16–31.

Dufey, Gunter, 1978. "Corporate Finance and Exchange Rate Variations." *Financial Management* (Summer), 51–57.

Eaker, Mark R., 1981. "The Numeraire Problem and Foreign Exchange Risk." *Journal of Finance* (May), 419–426.

Garner, C. Kent, and Alan C. Shapiro, 1984. "A Practical Method of Assessing Foreign Exchange Risk." *Midland Corporate Finance Journal* (Fall), 6–17.

Giddy, Ian H., 1977. "Exchange Risk: Whose View?" *Financial Management* (Summer), 23–33.

Heckman, C.R., 1985. "A Financial Model of Foreign Exchange Exposure." *Journal of International Business Studies* (Summer).

Heckman, C.R., 1986. "Don't Blame Currency Values for Strategic Errors: Protecting Competitive Position by Correctly Assessing Foreign Exchange Exposure." *Midland Corporate Finance Journal* (Fall).

Lessard, Donald R., and John B. Lightstone, 1986. "Volatile Exchange Rates Can Put Operations at Risk." *Harvard Business Review* (July-August), 107–114.

Shapiro, Alan C., 1975. "Exchange Rate Changes, Inflation, and the Value of the Multinational Corporation." *Journal of Finance* (May), 485–502.

CHAPTER 19

Abdel-Malek, Talaat, 1976. "Some Aspects of Exchange Risk Policies Under Floating Rates." *Journal of International Business Studies* (Fall-Winter), 89–97.

Adler, Michael, and Bernard Dumas, 1984. "Exposure to Currency Risk: Definition and Measurement." *Financial Management* (Summer), 41–50.

Adler, Michael, and D. Simon, 1986. "Exchange Rate Surprises in International Portfolios." *Journal of Portfolio Management* (Winter).

Ankrom, Robert K., 1974. "Top Level Approach to the Foreign Exchange Problem." *Harvard Business Review* (July-August), 79–80.

Cornell, Bradford, and Alan C. Shapiro, 1983. "Managing Foreign Exchange Risks." *Midland Corporate Finance Journal* (Fall), 16–31.

Dufey, Gunter, 1978. "Corporate Finance and Exchange Rate Variations." *Financial Management* (Summer), 51–57.

Eaker, Mark R., 1981. "The Numeraire Problem and Foreign Exchange Risk." *Journal of Finance* (May), 419–426.

Garner, C. Kent, and Alan C. Shapiro, 1984. "A Practical Method of Assessing Foreign Exchange Risk." *Midland Corporate Finance Journal* (Fall), 6–17.

Giddy, Ian H., 1977. "Exchange Risk: Whose View?" *Financial Management* (Summer), 23–33.

Heckman, C.R., 1985. "A Financial Model of Foreign Exchange Exposure." *Journal of International Business Studies* (Summer).

Heckman, C.R., 1986. "Don't Blame Currency Values for Strategic Errors: Protecting Competitive Position by Correctly Assessing Foreign Exchange Exposure." *Midland Corporate Finance Journal* (Fall).

Lessard, Donald R., and John B. Lightstone, 1986. "Volatile Exchange Rates Can Put Operations at Risk." *Harvard Business Review* (July-August), 107–114.

Shapiro, Alan C., 1975. "Exchange Rate Changes, Inflation, and the Value of the Multinational Corporation." *Journal of Finance* (May), 485–502.

CHAPTER 20

Business International Corporation, *Financing Foreign Operations*, New York.

Corluy, Walter, 1990. *Financiering en Risicobeheer in de Internationale Handel*. Brussels: M.I.M.

Dossier SNE, Compensation Tiers Monde 1, Juin 85.

Dossier SNE, Compensation Tiers Monde 3, Octobre 85.

Francis, Dick, 1987. *The Countertrade Handbook*. Cambridge: Woodhead and Faulkner.

Healey, N., 1989. "Two Pigs for a Personal Computer." *Management Today* (October), 116–118.

Hennart, J.-F., 1986. "Some Empirical Dimensions of Countertrade." *Journal of International Business Studies* 7(2), 47–62.

Kokut, B., 1986. "On Designing Contracts to Guarantee Enforcibility: Theory and Evidence from East-West Trade." *Journal of International Business Studies* 7(2), 47–62.

Lecraw, D., 1989. "The Management of Countertrade: Factors Influencing Success." *Journal of International Business Studies* 20(1) (Spring), 41–59.

McVey, T.B., 1985. "Policy Issues in Countertrade." In B.S. Fisher and K.M. Harte, eds., *Countertrade in the World Economy*. Praeger, p. 268.

Menzler-Hokkanen, I., 1989. "Countertrade Arrangements in International Trade: A Tool for Creating Competitive Advantage?" *Scandinavian Journal of Management* 5(2), 105–122.

Mirus, R., and Yeung, B., 1986. "Economic Incentives for Countertrade." *Journal of International Business Studies* 27(3) (Fall), 27–39.

Neale, C.W., and Piet Sercu, 1992. "Accounting for Domestic Countertrade." In Kreinen, ed., *International Commercial Policy*. Francis Taylor.

Neale, C.W., and Piet Sercu, 1992. "Motives for and the Management of Countertrade in Domestic Markets." *Journal of Marketing Management* 8(4).

Neale, C.W., and Piet Sercu, 1992. "Why Firms Countertrade in Overseas and Domestic Markets." *International Trade Journal.*

Parsons, J., 1985. "A Theory of Countertrade Financing of International Business." MIT Sloan School of Management Working Paper No.1632–85.

Schneider, Gerhard W., 1974. *Export-Import Financing.* New York: The Ronald Press.

Sercu, Piet, 1990. "Pros and Cons of Countertrade: A Critical Note." *Tijdschrift voor Economie en Management.*

Shapiro, Alan C., 1991. *Foundations in Multinational Financial Management.* Needham Heights, MA: Allyn & Bacon.

Zurawicki, L., 1988. "Marketing Rationale for Countertrade." *European Management Journal* 6(3) (Autumn), 299–308.

CHAPTER 21

Adler, M., and B. Dumas, 1983. "International Portfolio Choice and Corporation Finance: A Synthesis." *Journal of Finance* 38.3, 925–984.

Brealey, Richard A., and Stewart C. Myers, 1991. *Principles of Corporate Finance.* 4th ed. New York: McGraw-Hill, Inc.

Grauer, F.L.A., R.H. Litzenberger, and R.E. Stehle, 1976. "Sharing Rules and Equilibrium in an International Capital Market Under Uncertainty." *Journal of Financial Economics* 3 (June), 233–256.

Hawkins, Robert G., Norman Mintz, and Michael Provissiero, 1976. "Government Takeovers of U.S. Foreign Affiliates." *Journal of International Business Studies* (Spring), 3–15.

Lessard, Donald R., 1974. "World, National, and Industry Factors in Equity Returns." *Journal of Finance* (May), 379–391.

Lessard, Donald R., 1979. "Evaluating Foreign Projects: An Adjusted Present Value Approach." In Donald R. Lessard, ed., *International Financial Management.* Boston: Warren, Gorham & Lamont.

Lessard, Donald R., and Alan Shapiro, 1982. "A Framework for Global Financing Choices." Working Paper, Sloan School of Management, MIT. (October), p. 17.

Miller, Merton H., 1977. "Debt and Taxes." *Journal of Finance* 32(2), 261–275.

Shapiro, Alan C., 1978. "Capital Budgeting for the Multinational Corporation." *Financial Management* (Spring), 7–16.

Shapiro, Alan C., 1980. "Managing Blocked Currency Funds." Working Paper, University of Southern California.

Shapiro, Alan C., 1981. "Managing Political Risk: A Policy Approach." *Columbia Journal of World Business* (Fall), 63–70.

Shapiro, Alan C., 1991. *Multinational Financial Management.* 4th ed. Needham Heights, MA: Allyn & Bacon.

Truitt, J. Frederick, 1970. "Expropriation of Private Foreign Investment: Summary of the Post-World War II Experience of American and British Investors in the Less Developed Countries." *Journal of International Business Studies* (Fall), 21–34.

CHAPTER 22

Adler, M., and B. Dumas, 1983. "International Portfolio Choice and Corporation Finance: A Synthesis." *Journal of Finance* 38.3, 925–984.

Bekaert, G., and C.R. Harvey, 1993. "Time-varying World Market Integration." Working Paper.

Black, F., 1974. "International Capital Market Equilibrium with Investment Barriers." *Journal of Financial Economics* (December).

Bonser-Neal, C., G. Brauer, R. Neal, and S. Wheatley, 1990. "International Investment Restrictions and Closed-End Country Fund Prices." *Journal of Finance* 45.2, 523–547

Cho, D. Chinhyung, Cheol S. Eun, and Lemma W. Senbet, 1986. "International Arbitrage Pricing Theory: An Empirical Investigation." *Journal of Finance* 41(2) (June), 313–329.

Cooper, I., and E. Kaplanis, 1986. "Costs to Crossborder Investment and International Equity Market Equilibrium." In J. Edwards et al., eds., *Recent Advances in Corporate Finance*. Cambridge: Cambridge University Press.

Cooper, I., and E. Kaplanis, 1991. "What Explains the Home Bias in Portfolio Investment?" *Review of Financial Studies*. Forthcoming 1995.

Dumas, Bernard, 1977. "Testing International Asset Pricing: A Discussion." *Journal of Finance* 32(2), 512–516.

Dumas, Bernard, 1992 "Dynamic Equilibrium and the Real Exchange Rate in a Spatially Separated World." *The Review of Financial Studies* 5(2), 153–180.

Dumas, B., and B. Solnik, 1991. "The World Price of Foreign Exchange Risk." Working Paper, Groupe HEC, 51p.

Elton, E., and M. Gruber, 1984. *Security Evaluation and Portfolio Analysis*. Englewood Cliffs, NJ: Prentice Hall, Inc.

Errunza, V.R., and E. Losq, 1985. "International Asset Pricing Under Mild Segmentation: Theory and Test." *Journal of Finance* 40(1) (March), 105–124.

Eun, C., and S. Janakiramanan, "A Model of International Asset Pricing with a Constraint on the Foreign Equity Ownership." *Journal of Finance* 41.4, 897–914.

Fairlamb, D., 1989. "The Elusive El Dorado of Spanish Pensions." *Institutional Investor* (April), 177–184.

French, K., and J. Porterba, 1991. "Investor Diversification and International Equity Markets." *American Economic Review* 81.2, 222–226.

Grauer, F.L.A., R.H. Litzenberger, and R.E. Stehle, 1976. "Sharing Rules and Equilibrium in an International Capital Market Under Uncertainty." *Journal of Financial Economics* 3 (June), 233–256.

Gultekin, M., B. Gultekin, and A. Penati, 1989. "Capital Controls and International Capital Market Segmentation: The Evidence from the Japanese and American Stock Markets." *Journal of Finance* 44.4, 849–869.

Halliday, L., 1989. "The International Stock Exchange Directory." *Institutional Investor* (March), 197–204.

Hodrick, R.J., 1981. "International Asset Pricing with Time Varying Risk Premium." *Journal of International Economics* (November).

Jorion, P., and E. Schwartz, 1986. "Integration vs. Segmentation in the Canadian Stock Market." *Journal of Finance* 41.3, 603–613.

Levy, H., and M. Sarnat, 1970. "International Diversification of Investment Portfolios." *American Economic Review* 60, 668–675.

Lintner, J., 1965. "The Value of Risky Assets and the Selection of Risky Investments in Stock Portfolios and Capital Budgets." *Review of Economics and Statistics* 1965(1), 13–37.

Markowitz, H., 1952. "Portfolio Selection." *Journal of Finance* 7(1), 77–91.

Mossin, J., 1965. "Equilibrium in a Capital Asset Market." *Econometrica* 1965(4), 768–783.

Roll, Richard, and B. Solnik, 1977. "A Pure Foreign Exchange Asset Pricing Model." *Journal of International Economics* (May).

Scott, James H., Jr., 1977. " An Empirical Test of the Alternative Hypothesis of National and International Pricing of Risky Assets: A Discussion." *Journal of Finance* 32(2), 516–518.

Sercu, P., 1980. "A Generalization of the International Asset Pricing Model." *Revue de l'Association Française de Finance* 1, 91–135.

Sercu, P., 1981. "Mean-Variance Asset Pricing with Deviations from Purchasing Power Parity." Doctoral Dissertation Series, DTEW, K.U. Leuven.

Sharpe, W., 1964. "Capital Asset Prices: A Theory of Market Equilibrium Under Conditions of Risk." *Journal of Finance* 19(3), 425–442.

Solnik, B., 1974a. "Why Not Diversify Internationally Rather Than Domestically?" *Financial Analysts Journal*, 48–53.

Solnik, B., 1974b. "An Equilibrium Model of the International Capital Market." *Journal of Economic Theory* 8, 500–524.

Solnik, B., 1974c. "The International Pricing of Risk: An Empirical Investigation of the World Capital Market Structure." *Journal of Finance* 29(2), 365–378.

Solnik, B., 1977. "Testing International Asset Pricing: Some Pessimistic Views." *Journal of Finance* 32(2), 503–512.

Stapleton, R.C., and M.G. Subrahmanyam, 1977. "Market Imperfections, Capital Asset Equilibrium, and Corporate Finance." *Journal of Finance* (May).

Stehle, R., 1977. "An Empirical Test of the Alternative Hypotheses of National and International Pricing of Risky Assets." *Journal of Finance* (May).

Stulz, R., 1981a. "A Model of International Asset Pricing." *Journal of Financial Economics* 9, 383–406.

Stulz, R., 1981b. "On the Effects of Barriers to International Investment." *Journal of Finance* 36.4, 923–934.

Stulz, R., 1983. "The Demand for Foreign Bonds." *Journal of International Economics* 15, 225–238.

Stulz, R., 1992. "International Portfolio Choice and Asset Pricing: An Integrative Survey." Working Paper WPS 92–31, Ohio State University.Stulz, R., 1984. "Optimal Hedging Policies." *Journal of Financial and Quantitative Analysis* (June), 127–140.

Uppal, R., 1992. "A General Equilibrium Model of International Portfolio Choice." *Journal of Finance* 48(2), 529–553.

Wheatley, S., 1988. "Some Tests of International Equity Integration." *Journal of Financial Economics* 21, 177–212.

CHAPTER 23

Bischel, Jon E., and Robert Feinschreiber, 1977. *Fundamentals of International Taxation*. New York: Practicing Law Institute.

Gifford, William C., and William P. Streng, 1979. *International Tax Planning*. 2nd ed. Washington, DC: Tax Management. Inc.

International Bureau for Fiscal Documentation. *Guides to European Taxation. Taxation of Patents, Royalties, Dividends, and Interest in Europe.*

Kyrouz, M.E., 1975. "Foreign Tax Rates and Tax Bases." *National Taxation Journal* (March), 61–80.

OECD, 1977. *Model Treaty for the Reduction of International Double Taxation on Income and Wealth*. Paris.

Price Waterhouse. *International Tax Review*. New York: Price Waterhouse.

CHAPTER 24

Adler, M., and B. Dumas, 1983. "International Portfolio Choice and Corporation Finance: A Synthesis." *Journal of Finance* 38.3, 925–984.

Brealey, Richard A., and Stewart C. Myers, 1991. *Principles of Corporate Finance*. 4th ed. New York: McGraw-Hill, Inc.

Contractor, J., 1981. *International Technology Licensing*. Lexington Books.

Lessard, D., 1985. "Evaluating Foreign Projects: An Adjusted Present Value Approach." In Donald R. Lessard, ed., *International Financial Management: Theory and Application*. New York: John Wiley & Sons.

Lessard, Donald R., and Alan Shapiro, 1982. "A Framework for Global Financing Choices." Working Paper, Sloan School of Management, MIT. (October), p. 17.

Miller, Merton H., 1977. "Debt and Taxes." *Journal of Finance* 32(2), 261–275.

Nash, J., 1950. "The Bargaining Problem." *Econometrica* 18(1), 155–62.

Rubinstein, A., 1982. "Perfect Equilibrium in a Bargaining Model." *Econometrica* 50(1), 97–109.

Shapiro, Alan C., 1978. "Capital Budgeting for the Multinational Corporation." *Financial Management* (Spring), 7–16.

Shapiro, Alan C., 1985. "International Capital Budgeting." In Donald R. Lessard, ed. *International Financial Management*, Theory and Application, Wiley.

Shapiro, Alan C., 1991. *Multinational Financial Management*. 4th ed. Needham Heights, MA: Allyn & Bacon.

Sutton, J., 1986. "Non-Cooperative Bargaining Theory: An Introduction." *Review of Economic Studies*, 709–724.

Truitt, J. Frederick, 1970. "Expropriation of Private Foreign Investment: Summary of the Post-World War II Experience of American and British Investors in the Less Developed Countries." *Journal of International Business Studies* (Fall), 21–34.

Veugelers, R., 1994. "Profiles of Joint Ventures in Europe." K.U. Leuven Research Report.

CHAPTER 25

Baldwin, Carliss Y., 1982. "Optimal Sequential Investment When Capital Is Not Readily Reversible." *Journal of Finance* 37(3) (June), 763–782.

Baldwin, Richard, 1988. "Hysteresis in Import Prices: The Beachhead Effect." *American Economic Review* 78(4) (September), 773–785.

Baldwin, Richard, and Paul Krugman, 1989. "Persistent Trade Effects of Large Exchange Rate Shocks." *Quarterly Journal of Economics* 104(4) (November), 634–654.

Bernanke, Ben S., 1983. "Irreversibility, Uncertainty and Cyclical Investment." *Quarterly Journal of Economics* 98 (February), 85–106.

Bertola, Giuseppe, 1989. "Irreversible Investment." Working Paper, Princeton University.

Breeden, D.T., and R. Litzenberger, 1978. "Prices of State-Contingent Claims Implicit in Option Prices." *Journal of Business* 51 (October), 621–51.

Brennan, Michael J., and Eduardo S. Schwartz, 1985. "Evaluating Natural Resource Investments." *Journal of Business* 58(2), 135–158.

Caballero, Ricardo J., 1991. "Competition and the Non-Robustness of the Investment-Uncertainty Relationship." *American Economic Review* 81(1) (March), 279–288.

Caballero, Ricardo J., and Vittorio Corbo, 1988. "Real Exchange Rate Uncertainty and Exports: Multi-Country Empirical Evidence." Columbia University Department of Economics Discussion Paper No. 414 (December).

Cox, J.C., and C. Huang, 1987. "Option Pricing Theory and Its Applications." In G. Constantinides and S. Bhattacharya, eds., *Frontiers of Financial Theory*. Totowa, New Jersey: Rowan and Littlefield.

Delgado, F., 1989. "Hysteresis, Menu Costs, International Pricing and Deviations from the Law of One Price." Working Paper, The Wharton School.

Dixit, Avinash, 1988. "A Heuristic Argument for the Smooth Pasting Condition." Princeton University (March).

Dixit, Avinash, 1989. "Entry and Exit Decisions under Uncertainty." *Journal of Political Economy* 97(3) (June), 620–638.

Dixit, Avinash, 1989. "Hysteresis, Import Penetration, and Exchange Rate Passthrough." *Quarterly Journal of Economics* 104 (May), 205–228.

Dixit, Avinash, 1989. "The Role of Investment in Entry Deterrence," *Economic Journal* 90 (March), 95–106.

Dixit, Avinash, 1991. "Irreversible Investment and Competition Under Uncertainty." Working Paper, Princeton University.

Dixit, Avinash, 1991. "Irreversible Investment with Price Ceilings." *Journal of Political Economy* 99 (June), 541–557.

Dixit, Avinash, 1992. "Investment and Hysteresis." *Journal of Economic Perspectives* 6(1) (Winter), 107–132.

Dumas, B., 1988. "Pricing Physical Assets Internationally." NBER Working Paper Series No. 2569. Forthcoming in the Review of Financial Studies.

Franke, G., 1992. "Exchange Rate Volatility and International Trade." *Journal of International Money and Finance*.

Harisson, J.M., 1984. *Brownian Motion and Stochastic Flow Systems*. New York: John Wiley & Sons.

He, Hua, and Robert S. Pindyck, 1989. "Investments in Flexible Production Capacity." MIT Sloan School of Management Working Paper No. 2102–89 (March).

Ingersoll, Jonathan E., and Stephen A. Ross, 1988. "Waiting to Invest: Investment and Uncertainty." Yale University (October).

Majd, Saman, and Robert S. Pindyck, 1987. "Time to Build, Option Value, and Investment Decisions." *Journal of Financial Economics* 18(1) (March), 7–27.

Majd, Saman, and Robert S. Pindyck, 1989. "The Learning Curve and Optimal Production under Uncertainty." *RAND Journal of Economics* 20(3) (Autumn), 331–343.

Mankiw, N. Gregory, 1985. "Small Menu Costs and Large Business Cycles: A Macroeconomic Model." *Quarterly Journal of Economics* 100 (May), 529–539.

Mason, Scott, and Robert C. Merton, 1985. "The Role of Contingent Claims Analysis in Corporate Finance." In Edward Altman and Marti G. Subrahmanyam, eds., *Recent Advances in Corporate Finance.* Richard D. Irwin, 7–54.

McDonald, Robert, and Daniel Siegel, 1985. "Investment and the Valuation of Firms When There Is an Option to Shut Down." *International Economic Review* 26 (June), 331–349.

McDonald, Robert, and Daniel Siegel, 1986. "The Value of Waiting to Invest." *Quarterly Journal of Economics* 101 (November), 07–727.

Meyers, Stewart C., and Saman Majd, 1985. "Calculating Abandonment Value Using Option Pricing Theory." MIT Sloan School of Management Working Paper No. 1462–83, (January).

Paddock, J., D. Siegel, and J. Smith, 1987. "Option Valuation of Claims on Real Assets: The Case of Offshore Petroleum Leases." *Quarterly Journal of Economics* 103 (August), 479–508.

Pindyck, Robert S., 1988. "Irreversible Investment, Capacity Choice, and the Value of the Firm." *American Economic Review* 78 (December), 969–985.

Pindyck, Robert S., 1990. "Irreversibility and the Explanation of Investment Behavior." In D. Lund and B. Øksendahl, eds., *Stochastic Models and Option Values.* Amsterdam: North Holland.

Pindyck, Robert S., 1991. "Irreversibility, Uncertainty and Investment." *Journal of Economic Literature* 26(3) (September), 1110–1148.

Sercu, P., 1992. "Exchange Rates, Volatility, and the Option to Trade." *Journal of International Money and Finance.*

Sercu, P., and C. Van Hulle, 1992. "Exchange Risk, Exposure, and the Value of the Exporting Firms." *Journal of Banking and Finance* (Spring).

INDEX

Citations referring to footnotes show the page number followed by the note number. For example, 32n.3 means page 32, note 3.